NELSON

MATHEMATICS 11

Authors

David Zimmer
Chris Kirkpatrick
Ralph Montesanto
Christine Suurtamm
Susanne Trew
Dan Charbonneau
Robert McLeish

NELSON
THOMSON LEARNING

Australia • Canada • Mexico • Singapore • Spain • United Kingdom • United States

NELSON

THOMSON LEARNING

Mathematics 11

David Zimmer, Chris Kirkpatrick, Ralph Montesanto, Christine Suurtamm, Susanne Trew, Dan Charbonneau, Rob McLeish

Director of Publishing
David Steele

Publisher, Mathematics
Cheryl Turner

Project Manager
Robert Templeton, First Folio Resource Group, Inc.

Senior Production Editor
Linh Vu

Content Editors
Don Rowsell, Jackie Lacoursiere

Copy Editor
Susan Marshall

Senior Designer
Suzanne Peden

Creative Director
Angela Cluer

Production Coordinator
Sharon Latta Paterson

Cover Design
Linda Neale

Composition
Nelson Gonzalez

Photographs and Permissions
Vicki Gould

Design
Suzanne Peden, FIZZZ Design Inc.

Creative Art/Technical Art
Irma Ikonen, David McKay, Deborah Crowle, Steven Corrigan Peter Papayanakis, Linda Neale

Printer
Transcontinental Printing Inc.

The authors wish to thank David Hamilton and Linda Nigro, of First Folio Resource Group Inc., and Matthew Calder, Jane Lee, Kristy McGowan, and Marianne Van den Hengel for their assistance in the development of this book.

Printed and bound in Canada.
1 2 3 4 5 6 7 8 9/XX/0 9 8 7 6 5 4 3 2 1

For more information, contact Nelson Thomson Learning, 1120 Birchmount Road, Scarborough, Ontario, M1K 5G4. Or you can visit our Internet site at http://www.nelson.com.

Canadian Cataloguing in Publication Data

Main entry under title:
Nelson mathematics 11
Includes index.
ISBN 0-17-615757-3

1. Mathematics. I. Zimmer, David. II. Title; Mathematics 11. III. Title: Nelson mathematics 11

QA39.2.N44 2001 510
C2001-930132-4

Assessment Consultant

Damian Cooper

Advisory Panel

Kaye Appleby
Retired
(formerly Thames Valley DSB)

Richard Clausi
Elmira DSS,
Waterloo DSB

Stewart Craven
District-Wide Coordinator,
Toronto DSB

Shirley Dalrymple
Dr. John Denison HS,
York DSB

Judy Dussiaume
Curriculum Coordinator,
Rainbow DSB

Beverly Farahani
Kingston CVI,
Limestone DSB

Shawn Godin
Cairine Wilson SS
Ottawa-Carleton DSB

Mary Howe
Coordinator,
London Catholic DSB

Elizabeth Pattison
Westlane SS,
Niagara DSB

Tom Steinke
Consultant,
Ottawa-Carleton Catholic DSB

Kathy Wilkinson
Collingwood CI,
Simcoe County DSB

Reviewer Panel

Ian Anderson
Ancaster HS,
Hamilton-Wentworth DSB

Karin Banerd
Smith Falls DCI,
Upper Canada DSB

John Battaglia
Catholic Central HS,
Windsor-Essex CDSB

Alex Belloni
Mother Teresa HS,
Ottawa-Carleton CSSB

Mary Bourassa
Lisgar CI,
Ottawa-Carleton DSB

Pamela Bradshaw
Lambton-Kent CVI,
Lambton-Kent DSB

Louise Brighton
Mother Teresa CHS,
Toronto CDSB

Sonia Brown
Cobourg East DCI,
Kawartha Pine Ridge DSB

Karen Bryan
North Dundas DHS,
Upper Canada DSB

Mike Cafferata
Agincourt CI,
Toronto DSB

Tom Chapman
Consultant,
Hastings & Prince Edward DSB

Angela Con
Educational Services Resource
Teacher,
Kawartha Pine Ridge DSB

Mike Daoust
Brebeuf College,
Toronto CDSB

Mary Ellen Diamond
Consultant,
Niagara RCSB

Frank Di Pietro
Consultant,
Windsor-Essex CDSB

Rob Fleischauer
Centre Wellington DHS,
Upper Grand DSB

Domenic Greto
Brother Andre CHS,
York CDSB

Andy Hallikas
Fort Frances SS,
Rainy River DSB

Sue Hessey
Learning Coordinator,
Thames Valley DSB

Pat Kehoe
Mother Teresa HS,
Ottawa-Carleton CSSB

Antonietta Lenjosek
St. Mark HS,
Ottawa-Carleton CSSB

Marcia Linklater
Meadowvale SS,
Peel DSB

Clara Madonia
Don Bosco HS,
Toronto CDSB

Frank Maggio
Consultant,
Halton CDSB

Irene McEvoy
Lorne Park SS, Peel DSB

Bob McRoberts
Dr. G.W. Williams SS,
York DSB

Colleen Morgulis
Monsignor Paul Dwyer CHS,
Durham CDSB

Rob Nielen
Innisdale SS,
Simcoe County DSB

Marisa Palma
St. Elizabeth HS,
York CSSB

Reno Palombi
Consultant,
Algoma DSB

Sue Pyke
Richview CI,
Toronto DSB

Vince Rizzotto
Cardinal Newman CSS,
Hamilton-Wentworth CDSB

Gayle Rodger
Northern CI,
Lambton-Kent DSB

Cathy Romiens
Vincent Massey HS,
Greater Essex DSB

John Santarelli
Cathedral HS,
Hamilton-Wentworth CDSB

Rinaldo Schiabel
Chaminade College,
Toronto CDSB

Alex Shum
York Memorial CI,
Toronto DSB

Silvana Simone
Emery CI,
Toronto DSB

Tony Stancati
Michael Power HS,
Toronto CDSB

Frank Stranges
John Paul II HS,
London DCSB

Lisa Thornton
Lindsay CVI,
Trillium Lakelands DSB

Peter Wei
North Toronto CI,
Toronto DSB

Betsy Wimbs
R. H. King Academy,
Toronto DSB

Bill Woodcock
Consultant,
Lambton-Kent DSB

Charles Wyszkowski
Consultant,
Durham DSB

Gene Yawny
St. Theresa's HS,
Simcoe Muskoka CDSB

Anne Yeager
Orangeville DSS,
Upper Grand DSB

Contents

Functions and Relations sections are shown in navy.

Part 2: Functions

Functions and Relations sections are shown in navy.

Part 3: Trigonometric Functions

Functions and Relations sections are shown in navy.

LOCI AND CONICS

Part 4: Loci and Conics

Functions and Relations sections are shown in navy.

Introduction to Nelson Mathematics 11

Nelson Mathematics 11 is designed to help you develop your skill at solving real problems using mathematical skills and logical reasoning. There are questions that give you a chance to practise familiar mathematical skills like solving equations, graphing data, and modelling. You will also have opportunities to tackle problems that require you to develop your own strategy for solving them. Throughout the book, you will be encouraged to use a variety of methods to communicate what you have learned to others.

Variety of Approaches

The lessons in *Nelson Mathematics 11* provide the opportunity to explore concepts on your own or through working with others. Some lessons provide several solved examples to help you build an understanding of a concept; others guide you through the investigation of a concept.

There are five kinds of lessons in *Nelson Mathematics 11*:

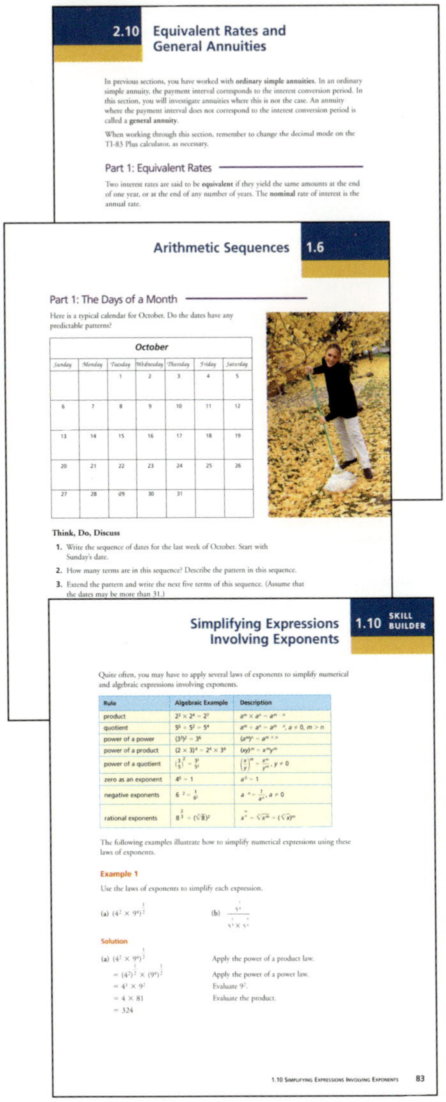

Concept Lessons

Concepts and ideas are presented through the use of Solved Examples and Key Ideas. Practise, Apply, Solve questions provide practice and an opportunity to consolidate your understanding.

Concept Lessons with Think, Do, Discuss Questions

Concepts and ideas are explored through real-life contexts. Your teacher may act as a coach and guide your class through the questions to build your understanding of new concepts and skills or you may be asked to answers these questions in groups or on your own. The Key Ideas provide a summary of the important ideas discussed. To clarify your understanding, several solved examples are presented, along with questions from the Practise, Apply, Solve questions.

Skill Builder Lessons

These lessons focus on the development of mathematical skills. The purpose of these lessons is to extend and improve your skills in mathematics involving familiar and unfamiliar concepts. Skills are taught through the use of solved examples and then reinforced through the Key Ideas and the Practise, Apply, Solve questions.

Technology Lessons

Technology lessons help you develop your skills with the use of technology, including graphing calculators, digital probes, spreadsheets, and graphing software. Step by step instructions and screen shots are provided.

Exploration Lessons

Exploration lessons often introduce and explore a new concept. These activities provide a hands-on experience that can be done in class or on your own at home.

Performance Tasks

These tasks range from short problem-solving questions to longer experiments and investigations. Your teacher may assign some of these activities so both of you can see how well you understand the concepts of the chapters. These can be done in class or as take-home tasks. You could also do these activities on your own for extra practice and review.

For some of these activities, you will work on your own, while for others you will likely work in a group. Along with quizzes, tests, and exams these activities provide an opportunity for you to demonstrate your understanding of the most important ideas in the grade 11 Functions and Relations course and Functions course.

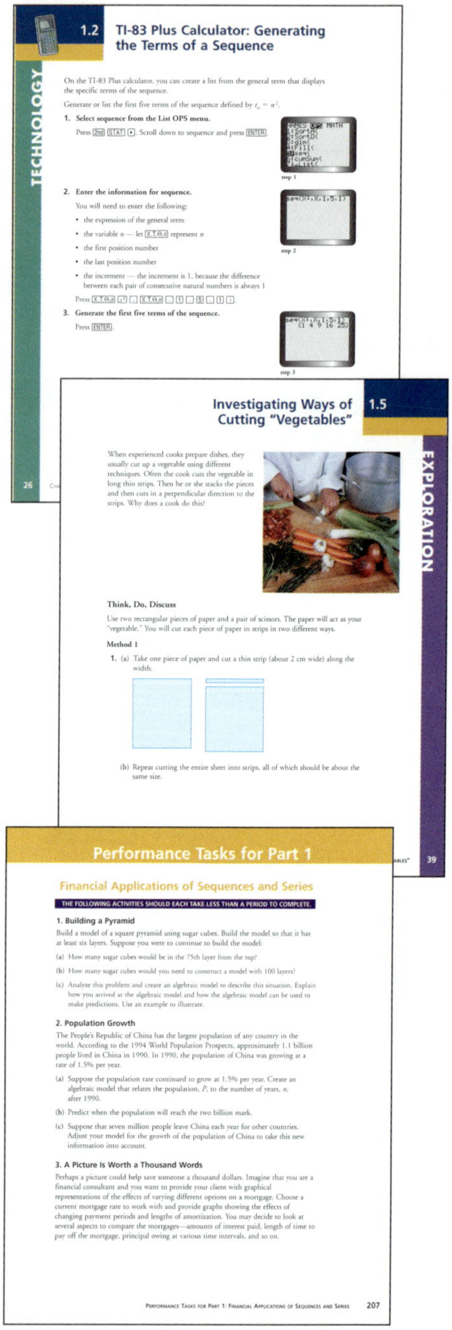

TECHNOLOGY

1.2 TI-83 Plus Calculator: Generating the Terms of a Sequence

On the TI-83 Plus calculator, you can create a list from the general term that displays the specific terms of the sequence.

Generate or list the first five terms of the sequence defined by $t_n = n^2$.

1. Select sequence from the List OPS menu.

Press [2nd] [STAT] [▸]. Scroll down to sequence and press [ENTER].

step 1

2. Enter the information for sequence.

You will need to enter the following:

- the expression of the general term
- the variable n — let [X,T,Θ,n] represent n
- the first position number
- the last position number
- the increment — the increment is 1, because the difference between each pair of consecutive natural numbers is always 1

Press [X,T,Θ,n] [x²] [,] [X,T,Θ,n] [,] [1] [,] [5] [,] [1] [)].

step 2

3. Generate the first five terms of the sequence.

Press [ENTER].

step 3

26

1.5 Investigating Ways of Cutting "Vegetables"

EXPLORATION

When experienced cooks prepare dishes, they usually cut up a vegetable using different techniques. Often the cook cuts the vegetable in long thin strips. Then he or she stacks the pieces and then cuts in a perpendicular direction to the strips. Why does a cook do this?

Think, Do, Discuss

Use two rectangular pieces of paper and a pair of scissors. The paper will act as your "vegetable." You will cut each piece of paper in strips in two different ways.

Method 1

1. (a) Take one piece of paper and cut a thin strip (about 2 cm wide) along the width.

(b) Repeat cutting the entire sheet into strips, all of which should be about the same size.

39

Performance Tasks for Part 1

Financial Applications of Sequences and Series

THE FOLLOWING ACTIVITIES SHOULD EACH TAKE LESS THAN A PERIOD TO COMPLETE.

1. Building a Pyramid

Build a model of a square pyramid using sugar cubes. Build the model so that it has at least six layers. Suppose you were to continue to build the model:

(a) How many sugar cubes would be in the 75th layer from the top?

(b) How many sugar cubes would you need to construct a model with 100 layers?

(c) Analyze this problem and create an algebraic model to describe this situation. Explain how you arrived at the algebraic model and how the algebraic model can be used to make predictions. Use an example to illustrate.

2. Population Growth

The People's Republic of China has the largest population of any country in the world. According to the 1994 World Population Prospects, approximately 1.1 billion people lived in China in 1990. In 1990, the population of China was growing at a rate of 1.5% per year.

(a) Suppose the population rate continued to grow at 1.5% per year. Create an algebraic model that relates the population, P, to the number of years, n, after 1990.

(b) Predict when the population will reach the two billion mark.

(c) Suppose that seven million people leave China each year for other countries. Adjust your model for the growth of the population of China to take this new information into account.

3. A Picture Is Worth a Thousand Words

Perhaps a picture could help save someone a thousand dollars. Imagine that you are a financial consultant and you want to provide your client with graphical representations of the effects of varying different options on a mortgage. Choose a current mortgage rate to work with and provide graphs showing the effects of changing payment periods and lengths of amortization. You may decide to look at several aspects to compare the mortgages—amounts of interest paid, length of time to pay off the mortgage, principal owing at various time intervals, and so on.

PERFORMANCE TASKS FOR PART 1: FINANCIAL APPLICATIONS OF SEQUENCES AND SERIES 207

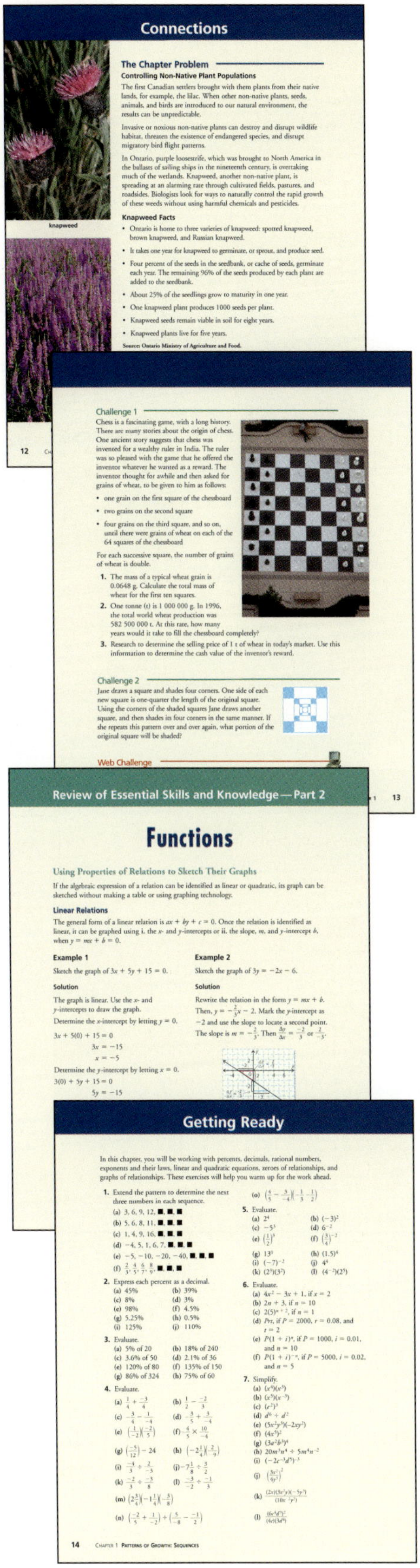

Special Features of *Nelson Math 11*

Connections

Mathematics is not just something you do in mathematics class. You use it in other classes and in your daily life. It will also be important as you make a career choice. At the start of each chapter, there are Chapter Problems that apply math to various careers and situations. There are also two Challenge questions that require you to use your problem solving skills combined with what you learned in the chapter. A third Web Challenge requires you to use the Internet.

Features That Help You Prepare

Review of Essential Skills and Knowledge

This feature reviews concepts from previous grades to help you prepare for the work ahead.

1. Cover up the solution to each example.
2. Try to answer the example on your own. Show all of your work.
3. Compare your solution with the one in the book.
4. If you need to, ask another student or your teacher for help.
5. Once you understand the examples, do the Practice questions. Compare your answers to those in the book.

Getting Ready

These pages review important ideas from previous grades and chapters. Use this section to determine if you are ready to start the new work for this chapter. If you cannot do these questions, be sure to ask the teacher or another student for help.

Features That Help You Review

Check Your Understanding

These questions will help you decide, on your own, whether you understand the important ideas of a chapter. Think about each question and write the answer in your notebook. As you do this, you will be creating your own summary of the chapter. You can use your answers to these questions, along with the Chapter Review, to prepare for quizzes, tests, and exams.

Review and Practice

This feature lets you reinforce your understanding of the concepts and skills you have developed. Refer to the Key Ideas and Solved Examples when answering these questions. You can use these questions for review and study.

Chapter Review Test

Use this test to review and find out if you are ready for a class test or exam.

Cumulative Review Test

There is a Cumulative Review Test at the end of Chapters 2, 4, and 6. Each test incorporates concepts and ideas from the chapters that precede it. At the end of Chapter 7, there is also a year-end test that covers material from the entire book. You can use these tests as another source of review and as extra practice for exams.

Icons

These two icons identify an opportunity to use technology.

You will use a graphing calculator or a data probe.

You will use graphing software, *The Geometer's Sketchpad*, or a computer to develop a spreadsheet.

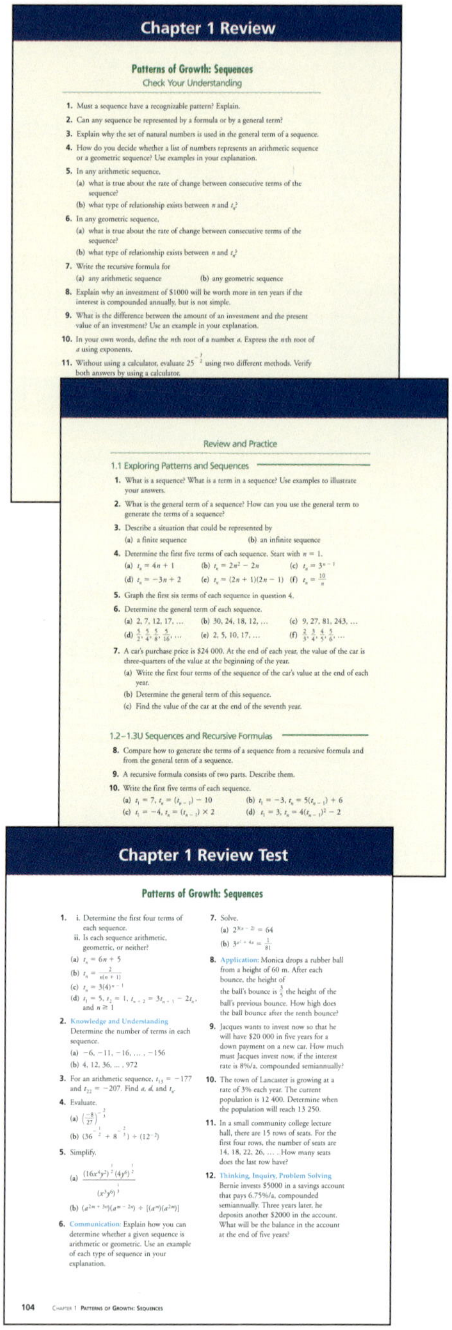

Chapter 1 Review

Patterns of Growth: Sequences

Check Your Understanding

1. Must a sequence have a recognizable pattern? Explain.
2. Can any sequence be represented by a formula or by a general term?
3. Explain why the set of natural numbers is used in the general term of a sequence.
4. How do you decide whether a list of numbers represents an arithmetic sequence or a geometric sequence? Use examples in your explanation.
5. In any arithmetic sequence,
(a) what is true about the rate of change between consecutive terms of the sequence?
(b) what type of relationship exists between n and t_n?
6. In any geometric sequence,
(a) what is true about the rate of change between consecutive terms of the sequence?
(b) what type of relationship exists between n and t_n?
7. Write the recursive formula for
(a) any arithmetic sequence (b) any geometric sequence
8. Explain why an investment of $1000 will be worth more in ten years if the interest is compounded annually, but is not simple.
9. What is the difference between the amount of an investment and the present value of an investment? Use an example in your explanation.
10. In your own words, define the nth root of a number a. Express the nth root of a using exponents.
11. Without using a calculator, evaluate $25^{-\frac{1}{2}}$ using two different methods. Verify both answers by using a calculator.

Review and Practice

1.1 Exploring Patterns and Sequences

1.2–1.3U Sequences and Recursive Formulas

Chapter 1 Review Test

Patterns of Growth: Sequences

Financial Applications of Sequences and Series

Pattern Recognition

When the independent variable in a relation changes by a steady increment, the dependent variable often changes according to a pattern.

<table>
<tr><th>Type of Pattern</th><th>Description</th><th>Example</th></tr>
<tr><td>Linear</td><td>The first differences between dependent variables are constant.</td><td>
<table>
<tr><td>Number of Books (× 1000)</td><td>1</td><td>2</td><td>3</td><td>4</td><td>5</td></tr>
<tr><td>Cost of Books ($) (× 1000)</td><td>60</td><td>70</td><td>80</td><td>90</td><td>100</td></tr>
<tr><td>First Differences (× 1000)</td><td>10</td><td>10</td><td>10</td><td>10</td><td></td></tr>
</table>
In a linear relation, each first difference is always the same. Here, each first difference is $10 000.</td></tr>
<tr><td>Quadratic</td><td>The first differences between dependent variables change, but the second differences are constant.</td><td>
<table>
<tr><td>Time (s)</td><td>0</td><td>1</td><td>2</td><td>3</td><td>4</td><td>5</td></tr>
<tr><td>Height of Ball (m)</td><td>5</td><td>30.1</td><td>45.4</td><td>50.9</td><td>46.6</td><td>32.5</td></tr>
<tr><td>First Differences</td><td>25.1</td><td>15.3</td><td>5.5</td><td>–4.3</td><td>–14.1</td><td></td></tr>
<tr><td>Second Differences</td><td>–9.8</td><td>–9.8</td><td>–9.8</td><td>–9.8</td><td></td><td></td></tr>
</table>
In this case, the first differences are not the same, so the relation is nonlinear. In a quadratic relation, each second difference is always the same. Here, each second difference is –9.8.</td></tr>
<tr><td>Exponential</td><td>There is a common multiplier between dependent variables.</td><td>
<table>
<tr><td>Time (h)</td><td>0</td><td>1</td><td>2</td><td>3</td><td>4</td></tr>
<tr><td>Number of Bacteria</td><td>1000</td><td>2000</td><td>4000</td><td>8000</td><td>16 000</td></tr>
<tr><td>Common Multipier</td><td>× 2</td><td>× 2</td><td>× 2</td><td>× 2</td><td></td></tr>
</table>
</td></tr>
</table>

Practice

1. Examine each pattern.

(a) 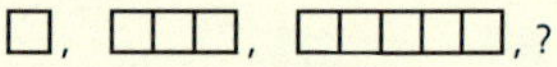

(b) 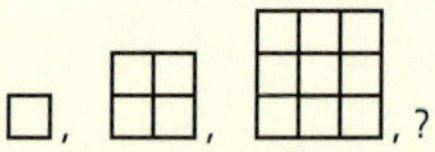

(c) 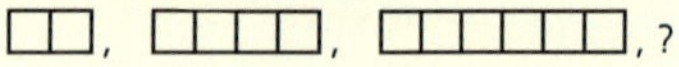

(d) 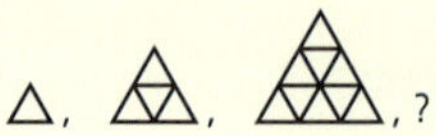

(e) 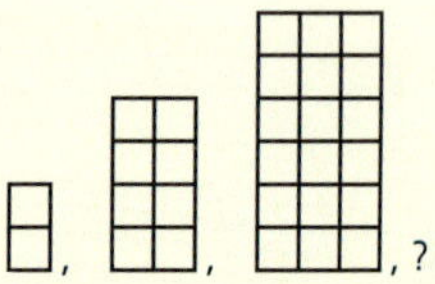

(f) 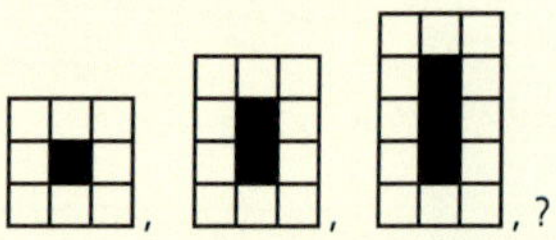

i. Draw the next diagram.
ii. Write the four numbers that represent the four diagrams, in terms of the number of squares or triangles.
iii. Determine the fifth number.

2. Suppose each diagram in question 1 were made from toothpicks.

i. What numbers represent each pattern of four diagrams, in terms of the number of toothpicks?
ii. How many toothpicks will be in the fifth diagram?

3. Examine the data in each table.

i. Is the pattern of the dependent variable linear, quadratic, or exponential?
ii. State the next value of y.

(a)

x	3	4	5	6
y	9	11	13	15

(b)

x	0	1	2	3
y	1	0.5	0.25	0.125

(c)

x	2	4	6	8
y	−13	−49	−109	−193

(d)

x	0	2	4	6
y	1	4	16	64

4. Neville has 49 m of fencing to build a dog run. Here are some dimensions he considered to maximize the area. Describe the type of pattern displayed by (a) the width and (b) the area.

Length (m)	1	2	3	4	5
Width (m)	23.5	22.5	21.5	20.5	19.5
Area (m²)	23.5	45.0	64.5	82.0	97.5

5. What pattern does the change in mass of a radioactive material each year show?

Time (a)	0	1	2	3
Mass (g)	500	250	125	62.5

7. What pattern does the change in cost of renting a pickup truck show?

Distance (km)	0	100	200	300	400
Rental Cost ($)	35.00	41.00	47.00	53.00	59.00

8. Predict the next number in each pattern.

(a) $-3, 5, -7, 9, -11, ■$

(b) $0.3, -0.09, 0.027, -0.0081, ■$

(c) $-4, -16, -36, -64, ■$

(d) $\frac{1}{8}, \frac{11}{24}, \frac{19}{24}, \frac{27}{24}, \frac{35}{24}, ■$

Operations with Rational Numbers

Set of rational numbers $\mathbf{Q} = \left\{\frac{a}{b} \mid a, b \in \mathbf{I}, b \neq 0\right\}$. For all operations, begin by changing all mixed numbers to improper fractions.

Addition and Subtraction

Write equivalent fractions with a common denominator. Add or subtract numerators.

$$\frac{a}{b} + \frac{c}{d} = \frac{ad + bc}{bd}$$

Multiplication

Reduce to lowest terms and multiply.

$$\left(\frac{a}{b}\right)\left(\frac{c}{d}\right) = \frac{ac}{bd}$$

Example 1

Evaluate $-1\frac{2}{5} + 3\frac{7}{10}$.

Solution

$$\begin{aligned}-1\frac{2}{5} + 3\frac{7}{10} &= \frac{-7}{5} + \frac{37}{10}\\ &= \frac{(-7)(2) + (37)(1)}{10}\\ &= \frac{-14 + 37}{10}\\ &= \frac{23}{10}\\ &= 2\frac{3}{10}\end{aligned}$$

Division

Multiply by the reciprocal of the divisor.

$$\begin{aligned}\frac{\frac{a}{b}}{\frac{c}{d}} &= \left(\frac{a}{b}\right)\left(\frac{d}{c}\right)\\ &= \frac{ad}{bc}\end{aligned}$$

Example 2

Evaluate $\dfrac{\left(\frac{2}{3}\right)\left(\frac{-3}{4}\right)}{2\frac{1}{2}}$.

Solution

$$\begin{aligned}\frac{\left(\frac{2}{3}\right)\left(\frac{-3}{4}\right)}{2\frac{1}{2}} &= \frac{\left(\frac{\cancel{2}^{1}}{\cancel{3}_{1}}\right)\left(\frac{-\cancel{3}^{1}}{\cancel{4}_{2}}\right)}{2\frac{1}{2}}\\ &= \frac{\frac{-1}{2}}{\frac{5}{2}}\\ &= \left(\frac{-1}{\cancel{2}_{1}}\right)\left(\frac{\cancel{2}^{1}}{5}\right)\\ &= -\frac{1}{5}\end{aligned}$$

Practice

1. Evaluate.

(a) $\frac{1}{2} - \frac{-2}{3}$

(b) $\frac{3}{5} - \frac{2}{3}$

(c) $\frac{-7}{11} + \frac{1}{3}$

(d) $\frac{5}{-6} + \frac{2}{-4}$

(e) $\frac{2}{-3} - 2\frac{5}{6}$

(f) $\frac{-3}{4} + 3\frac{2}{5}$

(g) $-8\frac{1}{4} + 3\frac{1}{2}$

(h) $\frac{7}{10} - \frac{-3}{4} + \frac{3}{5}$

(i) $1\frac{3}{4} + 2\frac{1}{5} - 4\frac{2}{3}$

(j) $\frac{-5}{7} + \frac{2}{3} - \frac{-1}{2}$

2. Evaluate.

(a) $\left(\frac{-2}{-3}\right)\left(\frac{9}{-10}\right)$

(b) $\left(\frac{1}{-2}\right)\left(\frac{2}{-5}\right)$

(c) $\left(\frac{-5}{12}\right)\left(\frac{4}{-15}\right)$

(d) $\left(2\frac{1}{2}\right)\left(-5\frac{2}{3}\right)$

(e) $\left(\frac{9}{4}\right)\left(\frac{-8}{27}\right)$

(f) $\left(-3\frac{1}{11}\right)\left(1\frac{1}{10}\right)$

(g) $\left(5\frac{3}{7}\right)\left(\frac{-7}{19}\right)$

(h) $\left(\frac{-2}{-9}\right)\left(-3\frac{1}{4}\right)$

(i) $\left(-4\frac{1}{3}\right)\left(-2\frac{3}{4}\right)$

(j) $\left(\frac{-2}{3}\right)\left(\frac{15}{-18}\right)\left(\frac{9}{5}\right)\left(\frac{-7}{8}\right)$

3. Evaluate.

(a) $\frac{2}{-3} \div \frac{-4}{3}$

(b) $\frac{-3}{8} \div \frac{-2}{3}$

(c) $-1\frac{1}{2} \div \frac{9}{4}$

(d) $2\frac{5}{7} \div \frac{-38}{21}$

(e) $-6\frac{1}{8} \div \frac{7}{-16}$

(f) $\dfrac{\frac{-2}{3}}{\frac{4}{9}}$

(g) $\dfrac{\frac{3}{-5}}{\frac{21}{-20}}$

(h) $\dfrac{\frac{5}{9}}{\frac{-10}{27}}$

(i) $\dfrac{\frac{-4}{5}}{\frac{8}{-15}}$

(j) $\left(2\frac{1}{3}\right) \div \left(-3\frac{2}{3}\right)$

4. Evaluate.

(a) $\frac{2}{-5} - \left(\frac{-1}{10} + \frac{-1}{2}\right)$

(b) $\frac{3}{5} - \left(2\frac{1}{2} - \frac{2}{3}\right)$

(c) $-3\frac{4}{7} - \left(\frac{2}{5} - 2\frac{2}{3}\right)$

(d) $\frac{-4}{9}\left(\frac{3}{8} - \frac{1}{12}\right)$

(e) $-2\frac{5}{8}\left(-1\frac{2}{3} + 4\frac{3}{4}\right)$

(f) $3\frac{4}{5} \div \left(2\frac{1}{4} - \frac{2}{3}\right)$

(g) $\left(2\frac{1}{8}\right)\left(-1\frac{3}{4}\right)\left(3\frac{2}{3}\right)$

(h) $\left(-1\frac{1}{8}\right)\left(2\frac{3}{4}\right) \div \left(3\frac{2}{3}\right)$

(i) $\left(\frac{5}{12}\right) \div \left(-1\frac{3}{4}\right)\left(3\frac{2}{3}\right)$

(j) $\left(1\frac{3}{8}\right)\left(-1\frac{3}{4}\right) \div \left(-3\frac{2}{3}\right)\left(2\frac{3}{4}\right)$

5. Evaluate the expression.

(a) $\dfrac{\frac{-4}{5} - \frac{3}{5}}{\frac{1}{5} - \frac{-1}{3}}$

(b) $\dfrac{\frac{1}{4} - \frac{-1}{3}}{\frac{-5}{12} - \frac{3}{-4}}$

(c) $\dfrac{1\frac{2}{3} - 2\frac{3}{4}}{-2\frac{3}{5} - 1\frac{1}{4}}$

(d) $\dfrac{6\frac{2}{5} - 8\frac{2}{3}}{-3\frac{5}{7} - 2\frac{3}{14}}$

Exponent Laws

exponent

3^4 and a^n are called powers

base

4 factors of 3

$3^4 = (3)(3)(3)(3)$

n factors of a

$a^n = (a)(a)(a)\ \dots\ (a)$

Operations with powers follow a set of procedures or rules.

Rule	Description	Algebraic Description	Example
Zero as an Exponent	When an exponent is zero, the value of the power is 1.	$a^0 = 1$	$120^0 = 1$
Negative Exponents	A negative exponent is the reciprocal of the power with a positive exponent.	$a^{-n} = \frac{1}{a^n}$	$3^{-2} = \frac{1}{3^2}$ $= \frac{1}{9}$
Multiplication	When the bases are the same, keep the base and add exponents.	$(a^m)(a^n) = a^{m+n}$	$(5^4)(5^{-3}) = 5^{4+(-3)}$ $= 5^{4-3}$ $= 5^1$ $= 5$
Division	When the bases are the same, keep the base and subtract exponents.	$\frac{a^m}{a^n} = a^{m-n}$	$\frac{4^6}{4^{-2}} = 4^{6-(-2)}$ $= 4^{6+2}$ $= 4^8$
Power of a Power	Keep the base and multiply exponents.	$(a^m)^n = a^{mn}$	$(3^2)^4 = 3^{(2)(4)}$ $= 3^8$

Example

Simplify $\frac{(x^5y^7)^{-2}(x^2y)}{(x^{-2}y^{-4})^3}$ and evaluate for $x = 7$ and $y = -3$.

Solution

$$\frac{(x^5y^7)^{-2}(x^2y)}{(x^{-2}y^{-4})^3} = \frac{x^{(5)(-2)}y^{(7)(-2)}x^2y}{x^{(-2)(3)}y^{(-4)(3)}}$$

$$= \frac{x^{-10}y^{-14}x^2y}{x^{-6}y^{-12}}$$

$$= x^{-10+2-(-6)}\,y^{-14+1-(-12)}$$

$$= x^{-10+2+6}\,y^{-14+1+12}$$

$$= x^{-2}y^{-1}$$

Substitute $x = 7$ and $y = -3$.

$$= (7)^{-2}\,(-3)^{-1}$$

$$= \left(\frac{1}{7^2}\right)\left(\frac{1}{-3}\right)$$

$$= -\frac{1}{147}$$

Practice

1. Evaluate to three decimal places where necessary.

(a) 4^2 (b) 5^0

(c) 3^{-2} (d) -3^2

(e) $(-3)^2$ (f) 2^{-3}

(g) $\left(\frac{1}{2}\right)^3$ (h) $\left(\frac{2}{3}\right)^{-2}$

(i) $(-1)^{75}$ (j) $(-1)^{92}$

(k) $(0.5)^2$ (l) $(-0.2)^{-3}$

(m) $(0.5)^4$ (n) $(3.1)^{-3}$

(o) $(-3.62)^{-5}$ (p) $1200(1.05)^9$

2. Express each power with a positive exponent and then simplify to an exact value.

(a) $3^0 + 5^0$ (b) $2^{-1} + 3^{-1}$

(c) $5 - 4^{-1}$ (d) $\left(\frac{1}{2}\right)^{-1}\left(\frac{2}{3}\right)^{-1}$

(e) $2^{-2} + 2^{-3}$ (f) $\left(\frac{1}{2}\right)^{-1} + \left(\frac{1}{3}\right)^{-1}$

(g) $12(2^{-1} - 3^{-1})$ (h) $\dfrac{2^{-1} + 3^{-1}}{\left(\frac{1}{3}\right)^2}$

3. Evaluate to an exact answer.

(a) $\dfrac{81^3}{9^7}$ (b) $\dfrac{-125^5}{625^3}$

(c) $(64^{-5})(8^9)$ (d) $\dfrac{(343^2)(243^2)}{(27^4)(49^4)}$

4. Simplify.

(a) $(x)^5(x)^3$ (b) $(m)^{-2}(m)^4(m)^{-3}$

(c) $(y)^{-5}(y)^2$ (d) $(a^b)^c$

(e) $(x^3)^4$ (f) $\dfrac{c^8}{c^7}$

(g) $\dfrac{t^5}{t^{-2}}$ (h) $\dfrac{(x^5)(x^{-3})}{x^{-2}}$

(i) $(n^{-5})^{-1}$ (j) $(m^2n^3)^4$

(k) $((m^{-3})^4)^{-2}$ (l) $\left(\dfrac{x^2}{y^{-3}}\right)^3$

5. Simplify.

(a) $(x^2y^4)(x^{-3}y^2)$

(b) $(-2m^3)^2(3m^2)^3$

(c) $\dfrac{(5x^2)^{-2}}{(5x^2)^{-3}}$

(d) $(4u^3v^2)^{-2} \div (-2u^2v^3)^{-3}$

6. Simplify and then evaluate.

(a) $\dfrac{[(m^3)(n^{-2})]^{-1}}{m^{-5}n}$, $m = 5$ and $n = -2$

(b) $\dfrac{(27^{-m})^{-3}}{(9^n)^{-2}}$, $m = 1$, $n = 2$

Expanding, Simplifying, and Factoring Algebraic Expressions

Type	Description	Example
Collecting Like Terms $2a + 3a = 5a$	Add or subtract the coefficients of the like terms.	$3a - 2b - 5a + b$ $= 3a - 5a - 2b + b$ $= -2a - b$
Distributive Property $a(b + c) = ab + ac$	Multiply each term of the binomial by the monomial.	$-4a(2a - 3b)$ $= -8a^2 + 12ab$
Product of Two Binomials $(a + b)(c + d)$ $= ac + ad + bc + bd$	Multiply the first term of the first binomial by the second binomial and then multiply the second term of the first binomial by the second binomial. Collect like terms if possible.	$(2x^2 - 3)(5x^2 + 2)$ $= 10x^4 + 4x^2 - 15x^2 - 6$ $= 10x^4 - 11x^2 - 6$
Common Factoring $ab + ac = a(b + c)$	Find the largest common factor of each term.	$10x^4 - 8x^3 + 6x^5$ $= 2x^3(5x - 4 + 3x^2)$
Factoring Trinomials $ax^2 + bx + c$, when $a = 1$	Write as the product of two binomials. Determine two numbers whose sum is b and whose product is c.	$x^2 + 4x - 21$ $= (x + 7)(x - 3)$
Factoring Trinomials $ax^2 + bx + c$, when $a \neq 1$	Look for a common factor. If none exists, write as the product of two binomials using trial and error. Check by expanding and simplifying.	$3x^2 + 4x - 4$ $= (3x - 2)(x + 2)$ Check: $(3x)(x) + (3x)(2)$ $+ (-2)(x) + (-2)(2)$

Example

Factor $12w^2 - 26w + 12$.

Solution

$12w^2 - 26w + 12$ There is a common factor of 2.

$= 2(6w^2 - 13w + 6)$ To have $+6$, both factors must be the same sign. To have $-13w$, both factors must be negative.

$= 2(3w - 2)(2w - 3)$

Practice

1. Simplify.

(a) $3x + 2y - 5x - 7y$

(b) $-6m + 5n - 3p - 3m + n$

(c) $5x^2 - 4x^3 + 6x^2$

(d) $6 - 5x + 3y - 8x + 2 - 7y$

(e) $(4x - 5y) - (6x + 3y) - (7x + 2y)$

(f) $(4x^3 + 3y^2) - (7y^2 + 5x^3) + (2x^3 - 5y^2)$

(g) $m^2n + p - (2p - 3m^2n)$

(h) $-(x^3 - y^3) + (3x^3 + 2y^3)$

2. Expand.

(a) $3(2x + 5y - 2)$

(b) $-5(x - y - 2z)$

(c) $-2m(m - n)$

(d) $5x(x^2 - x + y)$

(e) $-2a(5a - 4a^2 - 3a^3)$

(f) $-7y(2x^2 - 3y^2)$

(g) $m^2(3m^2 - 2n)$

(h) $-3u^3v^2(-6u^{-2}v^4 + 5u^4v^{-3})$

(i) $x^5y^3(4x^2y^4 - 2xy^5)$

3. Expand and simplify.

(a) $3x(x + 2) + 5x(x - 2)$

(b) $-7h(2h + 5) - 4h(5h - 3)$

(c) $2m^2n(m^3 - n) - 5m^2n(3m^3 + 4n)$

(d) $-3xy^3(5x + 2y + 1) + 2xy^3(-3y - 2 + 7x)$

4. Expand and simplify.

(a) $(3x - 2)(4x + 5)$

(b) $(7 - 3y)(2 + 4y)$

(c) $(5x - 7y)(4x + y)$

(d) $(3x^3 - 4y^2)(5x^3 + 2y^2)$

(e) $(3mn^2 - 2m)(5mn^2 + 4m)$

(f) $(4m^5n^3 - 3m^2n)(3m^5n^3 + 5m^2n)$

5. Factor.

(a) $4 - 8x$

(b) $9mn - 12n$

(c) $6x^2 - 5x$

(d) $3m^2n^3 - 9m^3n^4$

(e) $28x^2 - 14xy$

(f) $5mn - 7mn^3$

6. Factor each expression.

(a) $x^2 - x - 6$

(b) $x^2 + 7x + 10$

(c) $x^2 - 9x + 20$

(d) $x^2 - 3x - 28$

(e) $3y^2 + 18y + 24$

(f) $2t^2 - 16t - 30$

(g) $m^2 - 9$

(h) $25n^2 - 64p^2$

7. Factor.

(a) $6y^2 - y - 2$

(b) $12x^2 + x - 1$

(c) $5a^2 + 7a - 6$

(d) $6m^2 - 7m + 2$

(e) $10x^2 + 9x - 9$

(f) $3x^2 - 13x - 10$

(g) $25n^2 - 30n + 9$

(h) $12x^2 - 18x - 12$

(i) $60x^2 + 8x - 4$

Solving Linear and Quadratic Equations Algebraically

Linear Equations

To solve a linear equation, first eliminate any fraction by multiplying all terms by the lowest common denominator. Eliminate any brackets using the distributive property, then isolate the variable. A linear equation has only one solution.

Example 1

Solve $-3(x + 2) - 3x = 4(2 - 5x)$.

Solution

$$\begin{aligned} -3(x + 2) - 3x &= 4(2 - 5x) \\ -3x - 6 - 3x &= 8 - 20x \\ -3x - 3x + 20x &= 8 + 6 \\ 14x &= 14 \\ x &= \frac{14}{14} \\ x &= 1 \end{aligned}$$

Example 2

Solve $\frac{y - 7}{3} = \frac{y - 2}{4}$.

Solution

$$\begin{aligned} \frac{y - 7}{3} &= \frac{y - 2}{4} \\ 12\left(\frac{y - 7}{3}\right) &= 12\left(\frac{y - 2}{4}\right) \\ 4(y - 7) &= 3(y - 2) \\ 4y - 28 &= 3y - 6 \\ 4y - 3y &= -6 + 28 \\ y &= 22 \end{aligned}$$

Quadratic Equations

To solve a quadratic equation, first rewrite it in the form $ax^2 + bx + c = 0$. Then factor the left side, if possible. Set each factor equal to zero and solve. A quadratic equation can have no roots, one root, or two roots. Not all quadratic equations can be solved this way.

Example 3

Solve $x^2 + 3x = 10$.

Solution

$$\begin{aligned} x^2 + 3x &= 10 \\ x^2 + 3x - 10 &= 0 \\ (x + 5)(x - 2) &= 0 \end{aligned}$$

Then $x + 5 = 0$ or $x - 2 = 0$

$x = -5$ or $x = 2$

Example 4

Solve $-x = 3 - 2x^2$.

Solution

$$\begin{aligned} -x &= 3 - 2x^2 \\ 2x^2 - x - 3 &= 0 \\ (2x - 3)(x + 1) &= 0 \end{aligned}$$

Then $2x - 3 = 0$ or $x + 1 = 0$

$2x = 3$ or $x = -1$

$x = \frac{3}{2}$

Practice

1. Solve.

(a) $6y - 8 = 4x + 10$

(b) $2x + 7.8 = 9.4$

(c) $13 = 5m - 2$

(d) $13.5 - 2m = 5m + 41.5$

(e) $35 = -1 - 6m$

(f) $8(y - 1) = 4(y + 4)$

(g) $4(5 - r) = 3(2r - 1)$

(h) $12(n - 3) - 5(n + 2)$
$= 2(n - 4) + 7$

2. Determine the root of each equation.

(a) $\frac{x}{5} = 20$

(b) $\frac{2}{5}x = 8$

(c) $4 = \frac{3}{2}m + 3$

(d) $\frac{5}{7}y = 3 + 12$

(e) $3y - \frac{1}{2} = \frac{2}{3}$

(f) $4 - \frac{m}{3} = 5 + \frac{m}{2}$

(g) $\frac{3}{5}x + \frac{2}{3} = 2 - \frac{1}{3}x$

(h) $\frac{1}{5}(3x + 1) = 2$

(i) $\frac{1}{2}(x + 1) = \frac{1}{4}(x - 1)$

(j) $\frac{5m - 1}{6} = \frac{2m + 3}{3}$

3. Solve.

(a) $(x - 3)(x + 2) = 0$

(b) $(2x + 5)(3x - 1) = 0$

(c) $(m + 4)(m + 3) = 0$

(d) $(3 - 2x)(4 + 3x) = 0$

(e) $(2y + 5)(3y - 7) = 0$

(f) $(5n + 3)(4 - 3n) = 0$

4. Determine the roots.

(a) $x^2 - x - 2 = 0$

(b) $x^2 + x - 20 = 0$

(c) $m^2 + 2m - 15 = 0$

(d) $6x^2 - x - 2 = 0$

(e) $6t^2 + 5t - 4 = 0$

(f) $2x^2 + 4x - 30 = 0$

5. Solve.

(a) $4x^2 = 8x - 1$

(b) $4x^2 = 9$

(c) $6x^2 - x = 1$

(d) $5x^2 - 6 = -7x$

(e) $12x^2 = 2 + 5x$

(f) $-4x + 1 = -2x^2$

(g) $3x^2 + 5x - 1 = 2x^2 + 6x + 5$

(h) $7x^2 + 2(2x + 3) = 2(3x^2 - 4) + 13x$

6. (a) What is the height of a triangle with an area of 15 cm^2 and a base of 5 cm?

(b) A rectangular lot has a perimeter of 58 m and is 13 m wide. How long is the lot?

7. A model rocket is shot straight into the air. Its height in metres at t seconds is given by $h = -4.9t^2 + 29.4t$. When does the rocket reach the ground?

8. The population of a city is modelled by $P = 0.5t^2 + 10t + 200$, where P is the population in thousands and t is the time in years, with $t = 0$ corresponding to the year 2000. When is the population 350 000?

Chapter 1

Patterns of Growth: Sequences

Patterns are fundamental to mathematics. Identifying patterns will allow you to make accurate predictions about the future and to analyze past events. You may see patterns in nature, music, art, architecture, and, of course, mathematics. You can model some patterns using algebraic relationships. For example, in this chapter, you will calculate interest, which grows in a predictable pattern, using formulas.

In this chapter, you will

- determine mathematical relationships for representing predictable patterns
- examine recursive relationships
- investigate and use arithmetic sequences to solve problems
- investigate and use geometric sequences to solve problems
- solve problems involving simple interest and compound interest
- revisit the laws of exponents and extend them to include rational exponents
- solve exponential equations

Visit the Nelson Mathematics student Web site at **www.math.nelson.com**. You'll find links to interactive examples, online tutorials, and more.

Connections

knapweed

purple loosestrife

The Chapter Problem

Controlling Non-Native Plant Populations

The first Canadian settlers brought with them plants from their native lands, for example, the lilac. When other non-native plants, seeds, animals, and birds are introduced to our natural environment, the results can be unpredictable.

Invasive or noxious non-native plants can destroy and disrupt wildlife habitat, threaten the existence of endangered species, and disrupt migratory bird flight patterns.

In Ontario, purple loosestrife, which was brought to North America in the ballasts of sailing ships in the nineteenth century, is overtaking much of the wetlands. Knapweed, another non-native plant, is spreading at an alarming rate through cultivated fields, pastures, and roadsides. Biologists look for ways to naturally control the rapid growth of these weeds without using harmful chemicals and pesticides.

Knapweed Facts

- Ontario is home to three varieties of knapweed: spotted knapweed, brown knapweed, and Russian knapweed.
- It takes one year for knapweed to germinate, or sprout, and produce seed.
- Four percent of the seeds in the seedbank, or cache of seeds, germinate each year. The remaining 96% of the seeds produced by each plant are added to the seedbank.
- About 25% of the seedlings grow to maturity in one year.
- One knapweed plant produces 1000 seeds per plant.
- Knapweed seeds remain viable in soil for eight years.
- Knapweed plants live for five years.

Source: Ontario Ministry of Agriculture and Food.

Non-Native Plant Problem

Suppose 100 knapweed seeds are accidentally carried into a field on hikers' clothing or shoes. If there are no other factors that will affect their growth, then how many knapweed plants and seeds will be produced in the field over ten years? When will the number of plants exceed five hundred trillion?

For help with this problem, see pages 25, 35, 50, 60, 82, and 96.

Challenge 1

Chess is a fascinating game, with a long history. There are many stories about the origin of chess. One ancient story suggests that chess was invented for a wealthy ruler in India. The ruler was so pleased with the game that he offered the inventor whatever he wanted as a reward. The inventor thought for awhile and then asked for grains of wheat, to be given to him as follows:

- one grain on the first square of the chessboard
- two grains on the second square
- four grains on the third square, and so on, until there were grains of wheat on each of the 64 squares of the chessboard

For each successive square, the number of grains of wheat is double.

1. The mass of a typical wheat grain is 0.0648 g. Calculate the total mass of wheat for the first ten squares.
2. One tonne (t) is 1 000 000 g. In 1996, the total world wheat production was 582 500 000 t. At this rate, how many years would it take to fill the chessboard completely?
3. Research to determine the selling price of 1 t of wheat in today's market. Use this information to determine the cash value of the inventor's reward.

Challenge 2

Jane draws a square and shades four corners. One side of each new square is one-quarter the length of the original square. Using the corners of the shaded squares Jane draws another square, and then shades its four corners in the same manner. If she repeats this pattern over and over again, what portion of the original square will be shaded?

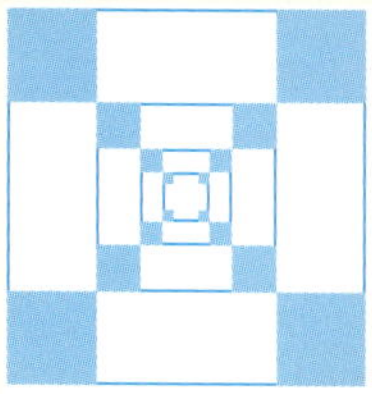

Web Challenge

For a related Internet activity, go to **www.math.nelson.com.**

Getting Ready

In this chapter, you will be working with percents, decimals, rational numbers, exponents and their laws, linear and quadratic equations, zeroes of relationships, and graphs of relationships. These exercises will help you warm up for the work ahead.

1. Extend the pattern to determine the next three numbers in each sequence.

(a) 3, 6, 9, 12, ■, ■, ■

(b) 5, 6, 8, 11, ■, ■, ■

(c) 1, 4, 9, 16, ■, ■, ■

(d) −4, 5, 1, 6, 7, ■, ■, ■

(e) −5, −10, −20, −40, ■, ■, ■

(f) $\frac{2}{3}, \frac{4}{5}, \frac{6}{7}, \frac{8}{9}$, ■, ■, ■

2. Express each percent as a decimal.

(a) 45% (b) 39%
(c) 8% (d) 3%
(e) 98% (f) 4.5%
(g) 5.25% (h) 0.5%
(i) 125% (j) 110%

3. Evaluate.

(a) 5% of 20 (b) 18% of 240
(c) 3.6% of 50 (d) 2.1% of 36
(e) 120% of 80 (f) 135% of 150
(g) 86% of 324 (h) 75% of 60

4. Evaluate.

(a) $\frac{1}{4} + \frac{-3}{4}$ (b) $\frac{1}{2} - \frac{-2}{3}$

(c) $-\frac{3}{4} - \frac{1}{-4}$ (d) $-\frac{3}{5} + \frac{3}{-4}$

(e) $\left(\frac{1}{-2}\right)\left(\frac{-2}{5}\right)$ (f) $-\frac{4}{5} \times \frac{10}{-4}$

(g) $\left(\frac{-5}{12}\right) - 24$ (h) $\left(-2\frac{1}{4}\right)\left(\frac{2}{-9}\right)$

(i) $\frac{-4}{3} \div \frac{2}{-3}$ (j) $-7\frac{1}{8} \div \frac{3}{2}$

(k) $\frac{-2}{3} \div \frac{-3}{8}$ (l) $\frac{-3}{-2} \div \frac{-1}{3}$

(m) $\left(2\frac{3}{4}\right)\left(-1\frac{1}{4}\right)\left(-\frac{3}{8}\right)$

(n) $\left(\frac{-2}{5} + \frac{1}{-2}\right) \div \left(\frac{5}{-8} - \frac{-1}{2}\right)$

(o) $\left(\frac{4}{5} - \frac{3}{-4}\right)\left(-\frac{1}{3} - \frac{1}{2}\right)$

5. Evaluate.

(a) 2^4 (b) $(-3)^2$
(c) -5^3 (d) 6^{-2}
(e) $\left(\frac{1}{2}\right)^3$ (f) $\left(\frac{3}{4}\right)^{-2}$
(g) 13^0 (h) $(1.5)^4$
(i) $(-7)^{-2}$ (j) 4^4
(k) $(2^3)(3^2)$ (l) $(4^{-2})(2^5)$

6. Evaluate.

(a) $4x^2 - 3x + 1$, if $x = 2$

(b) $2n + 3$, if $n = 10$

(c) $2(5)^{n+2}$, if $n = 1$

(d) Prt, if $P = 2000$, $r = 0.08$, and $t = 2$

(e) $P(1 + i)^n$, if $P = 1000$, $i = 0.01$, and $n = 10$

(f) $P(1 + i)^{-n}$, if $P = 5000$, $i = 0.02$, and $n = 5$

7. Simplify.

(a) $(x^4)(x^3)$

(b) $(x^5)(x^{-3})$

(c) $(e^2)^3$

(d) $d^6 \div d^2$

(e) $(5x^2y^3)(-2xy^2)$

(f) $(4x^5)^2$

(g) $(3a^2b^3)^4$

(h) $20m^3n^4 \div 5m^4n^{-2}$

(i) $(-2c^{-3}d^5)^{-3}$

(j) $\left(\frac{3x^2}{4y^3}\right)^2$

(k) $\frac{(2x)(3x^2y)(-5y^3)}{(10x^{-2}y^2)}$

(l) $\frac{(6c^4d^3)^2}{(4c)(3d^4)}$

8. Simplify.

(a) $2x + 3x - 8x$
(b) $3x^2 - 5y^3 - 6x^2 + 7y^3$
(c) $(3x + 5) + (2 - 4x) - (2x - 1)$
(d) $5(2x + 3y)$
(e) $2(3a - 5b) + 4(3a - 3b)$
(f) $3a(5b - 6c + 2) + 4c(2a - b + 1)$
(g) $(x + 5)(x - 2)$
(h) $(2x - 4)^2$
(i) $(3x - 2y)(8x + 4y)$
(j) $(2x + 5)(2x - 5)$

9. Factor fully.

(a) $6x^2 + 9x - 12xy$
(b) $a^2 - 81$
(c) $x^2 + 8x + 12$
(d) $a^2 - 10a + 25$
(e) $10x^2 + 17x + 3$
(f) $6c^2 - 2c - 28$

10. Solve.

(a) $3x + 15 = 5x - 5$
(b) $5(2x - 6) = 3(2x + 1) - 10x - 5$
(c) $2x^2 = 50$
(d) $(x - 5)(x + 3) = 0$
(e) $x^2 - x - 12 = 0$
(f) $3x^2 + 4x = 2$
(g) $(2x + 1)^2 = 1$
(h) $5a^2 - 3a + 2 = 2a^2 + a - 2$

11. Determine the first differences and identify the relationship as linear or nonlinear.

(a)

x	y	First Differences
1	8	
2	11	
3	14	
4	17	
5	20	
6	23	

(b)

t	d	First Differences
6	35	
7	48	
8	63	
9	80	
10	99	
11	120	

(c)

x	y	First Differences
−3	$\frac{1}{8}$	
−2	$\frac{1}{4}$	
−1	$\frac{1}{2}$	
0	1	
1	2	
2	4	

(d)

t	h	First Differences
3	−2	
4	−4	
5	−6	
6	−8	
7	−10	
8	−12	

12. i. Sketch a graph of each relationship.
ii. Use the graph to determine the zeroes of the relationship.

(a) $y = 2x + 6$
(b) $y = x^2 - 4$
(c) $y = x^2 + 3x - 18$
(d) $y = -x^2 - 5x - 6$

1.1 Exploring Patterns and Sequences

Here are six different relationships. Some of them contain a hidden pattern. Try to uncover the hidden pattern.

A. Harry sells vacuum cleaners and earns \$400 each month. For each vacuum cleaner he sells, he earns an additional \$110.

B. Marka deposits \$500 only once in a savings account that pays 5% interest at the end of each year.

C. Andrew drops a rubber ball from a height of 2 m. After each bounce, the height of the ball's bounce is one-half the height of the ball's previous bounce.

D. David tosses a coin repeatedly. Each time he tosses the coin, he records 1 if the coin comes up heads and 0 if the coin comes up tails.

E. A square number can be represented by an arrangement of dots. Each square number is the total number of dots in each diagram. Here are the first four square numbers:

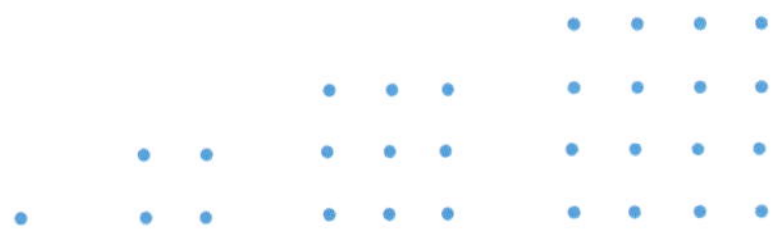

F. In a fractal, a pattern repeats itself in the same shape. The Sierpinski triangle is an example of a **fractal**. Divide one equilateral triangle into four, congruent triangles by joining the midpoints of the sides of the larger triangle and remove the centre triangle. You can repeat these steps many times. Here are the first four stages of the Sierpinski triangle:

stage 1 stage 2 stage 3 stage 4

Think, Do, Discuss

1. Copy and complete each table. List the five numbers that you enter for each table separately.

A.

Number of Vacuum Cleaners Sold	1	2	3	4	5
Total Earnings ($)					

_____, _____, _____, _____, _____

B.

At End of Each Year	1	2	3	4	5
Money in Savings Account ($)					

_____, _____, _____, _____, _____

C.

Bounce	1	2	3	4	5
Height of Ball After Each Bounce (m)					

_____, _____, _____, _____, _____

D.

Toss	1	2	3	4	5
Heads = 1, Tails = 0					

_____, _____, _____, _____, _____

E.

Diagram	1	2	3	4	5
Square Number					

_____, _____, _____, _____, _____

F.

Stage	1	2	3	4	5
Total Number of Triangles					

_____, _____, _____, _____, _____

2. Which of the relationships are predictable? unpredictable?

3. If possible, describe in words the pattern in each relationship.

4. If possible, use the pattern to find the next three numbers in each list.

5. Do any of these relationships come to an end? Explain.

6. For each relationship and if possible, find an algebraic expression that describes the value of each term according to its position in the list. Let n represent the position of the term in the list, where n is a natural number, $\{1, 2, 3, \ldots\}$.

7. Use the algebraic expression you found in step 6 to determine the tenth number in each list.

8. If n is the independent variable, then graph each predictable relationship. Can you join the points with a line or a curve? Explain.

Focus 1.1

Key Ideas

- A **sequence** is an ordered list of numbers. Each number is called a **term.**
- When a sequence follows a specific pattern, you can describe each term of the sequence by its position in the list. For example, in the sequence, 3, 6, 9, 12, 15, 18, … , each term is a multiple of 3. The sixth term of the sequence is 18.

position	1	2	3	4	5	6
term	3	6	9	12	15	18

- The general form of a sequence is t_1, t_2, t_3, … , t_n, … . The subscript of each term identifies the position of the term in the sequence. As a result, n belongs to the set of natural numbers, {1, 2, 3, 4, 5, … }.
- A sequence that has a last term is a **finite sequence.** A sequence that has no last term, but continues on indefinitely, is an **infinite sequence.**

  The sequence 2, 6, 18, 54, 162 is finite.

  The sequence 1, 3, 4, 7, 11, … is infinite. The ellipsis, … , shows that the sequence continues on with the same pattern indefinitely.
- The most interesting sequences have patterns. This type of sequence can be described by a rule, or an algebraic expression. You can use the rule to generate one, several, or all of the terms of the sequence. This rule is called the **general term** of the sequence and it is represented by t_n. For example, the general term of the sequence 3, 6, 9, 12, 15, 18, … is $t_n = 3 \times n$.
- You can graph a sequence by plotting points, (position, term), on the *x*-*y* plane. You cannot join the plotted points with a straight line or a curve because the first element of each ordered pair is always a natural number. The graph of a sequence is then called **discrete.**

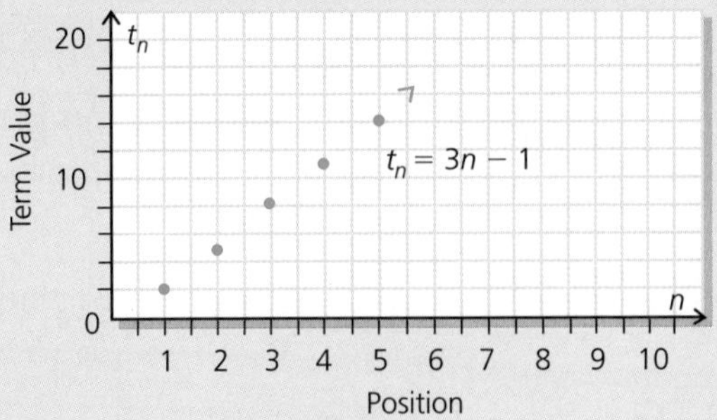

Example 1

Find, if possible, the next four terms of each sequence. If you cannot find the next four terms, then explain why.

(a) The sequence of the number of seats in each of the first four rows in an auditorium, beginning with the first row, is 17, 22, 27, and 32.

(b) The sequence of points in the last four football games that the Hamilton Tiger Cats played is 13, 21, 35, and 17.

Solution

(a) The numbers increase constantly by 5. The next four terms are then 37, 42, 47, and 52.

(b) The number of points scored in any game depends on many factors. Because the terms do not have a predictable pattern, the next four terms of this sequence cannot be determined.

Example 2

Determine the first four terms of each sequence.

(a) $t_n = 3n^2 - 4$ (b) $t_n = 5^{n-1}$ (c) $t_n = \frac{n-2}{n+2}$

Solution

To find the first four terms of each sequence, substitute 1, 2, 3, and 4 for n.

(a) $t_n = 3n^2 - 4$

$t_1 = 3(1)^2 - 4 = -1$ $t_2 = 3(2)^2 - 4 = 8$ $t_3 = 3(3)^2 - 4 = 23$ $t_4 = 3(4)^2 - 4 = 44$

The first four terms are -1, 8, 23, and 44.

(b) $t_n = 5^{n-1}$

$t_1 = 5^{1-1} = 5^0 = 1$ $t_2 = 5^{2-1} = 5^1 = 5$ $t_3 = 5^{3-1} = 5^2 = 25$ $t_4 = 5^{4-1} = 5^3 = 125$

The first four terms are 1, 5, 25, and 125.

(c) $t_n = \frac{n-2}{n+2}$

$t_1 = \frac{1-2}{1+2} = -\frac{1}{3}$ $t_2 = \frac{2-2}{2+2} = \frac{0}{4} = 0$ $t_3 = \frac{3-2}{3+2} = \frac{1}{5}$ $t_4 = \frac{4-2}{4+2} = \frac{2}{6} = \frac{1}{3}$

The first four terms are $-\frac{1}{3}$, 0, $\frac{1}{5}$, and $\frac{1}{3}$.

Example 3

Determine whether each sequence is finite or infinite.

(a) all positive integers divisible by 5

(b) the leap years from 2000 to the end of the twenty-first century

Solution

(a) The sequence is 5, 10, 15, 20, … . You can multiply each term by 5 to get the next term, and you could do this repeatedly, without end. This sequence is then infinite.

(b) The year 2000 is a leap year. Then every fourth year after 2000 is a leap year. The last leap year in the century is 2096. The sequence is 2000, 2004, 2008, 2012, … , 2096. Because the sequence has a last term, it is finite.

Example 4

The area of the largest equilateral triangle in the diagram, triangle 1, is 4096 cm^2. The second triangle is the result of joining the midpoints of the sides of the first triangle. The third and other triangles were also drawn in this way.

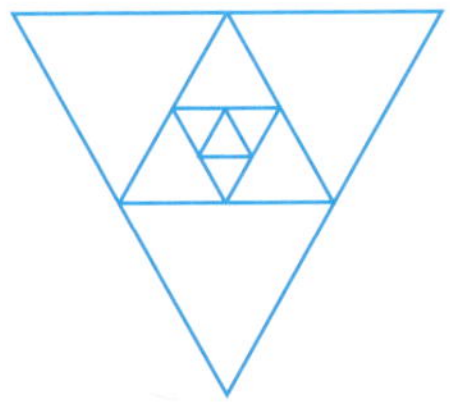

stage 3

(a) Create a sequence by determining the area of each of the first four triangles.

(b) Find the general term of this sequence.

(c) What is the area of the eighth triangle?

(d) Graph this sequence.

Solution

(a) When you join the midpoints of any equilateral triangle, you divide the triangle into four, congruent, equilateral triangles. Therefore, the area of each of the four triangles is one-quarter the area of the larger triangle. Find the area of *each* smaller triangle by dividing the area of the larger triangle by 4, starting with the area 4096 cm^2.

Triangle	1	2	3	4
Area (cm^2)	4096	$\frac{4096}{4} = 1024$	$\frac{1024}{4} = 256$	$\frac{256}{4} = 64$

(b) The sequence is 4096, 1024, 256, 64, … . You could also generate each term by dividing the first term, 4096, by a multiple of 4, or a power of 4. Each exponent is 1 less than the position, n, of the term.

$$4096, \frac{4096}{4}, \frac{4096}{16}, \frac{4096}{64}, \ldots$$

$$\frac{4096}{4^0}, \frac{4096}{4^1}, \frac{4096}{4^2}, \frac{4096}{4^3}, \ldots$$

The general term is $t_n = \frac{4096}{4^{n-1}}$.

(c) Find the area of the eighth triangle by determining t_8.

$$\begin{aligned} t_8 &= \frac{4096}{4^{8-1}} \\ &= \frac{4096}{4^7} \\ &= \frac{4096}{16\ 384} \\ &= 0.25 \end{aligned}$$

The area of the eighth triangle is 0.25 cm^2.

(d) The independent variable in this relationship is n, the term's position, and the dependent variable is t_n, the term's value. In any sequence, n is a natural number. Therefore, the points in the graph cannot be connected by a line or by a curve.

n	t_n
1	4096
2	1024
3	256
4	64
5	16

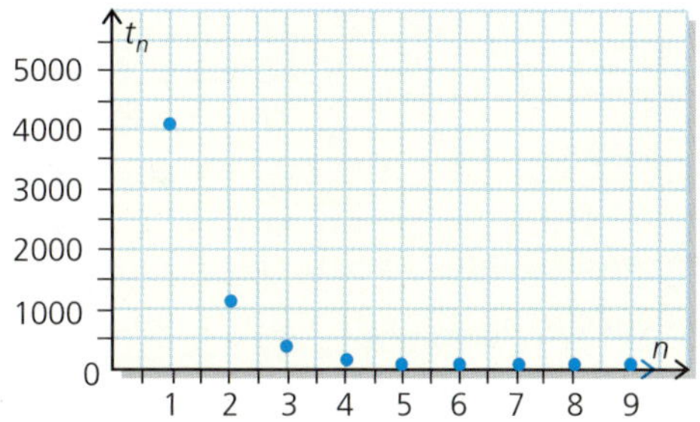

Practise, Apply, Solve 1.1

A

1. Find the next four terms of each sequence.

(a) 1, 5, 25, 125, … (b) 16, 12, 8, 4, … (c) 8, 14, 20, 26, …

(d) $1, \frac{1}{4}, \frac{1}{9}, \frac{1}{16}, \ldots$ (e) 9, 98, 987, 9876, … (f) −3, 6, −12, 24, …

(g) 5, 4, 9, 13, 22, … (h) 6, 16, 36, 66, … (i) 1, 2, 2, 4, 8, …

(j) 1, 8, 27, 64, … (k) 0.3, 0.5, 0.7, 0.9, … (l) 12, 6, 3, 1.5, …

2. Find the next four terms of each sequence. If you cannot find the next four terms, then explain why.

(a) the dates in January when it snows: 2, 3, 8, 12, …

(b) the house numbers on the right side of a street: 1024, 1026, 1028, 1030, …

(c) the number of goals scored by the Toronto Maple Leafs in each of their home games: 1, 5, 4, 2, …

(d) the number of bacteria in a petri dish each hour: 48, 96, 192, 384, …

(e) Paula's annual salary: \$42 000.00, \$43 680.00, \$45 427.20, \$47 244.29, …

(f) the number of students waiting at your bus stop each day: 16, 12, 17, 17, …

3. Determine the first five terms of each sequence. Start with $n = 1$.

(a) $t_n = n + 4$ (b) $t_n = n^2 - 2$ (c) $t_n = 2^n$

(d) $t_n = 5n - 2$ (e) $t_n = (n + 2)(n - 2)$ (f) $t_n = \frac{5}{n}$

(g) $t_n = 3(-2)^{n+1}$ (h) $t_n = (-1)^n$ (i) $t_n = -3n + 7$

4. Determine t_{10} of each sequence.

(a) $t_n = 5n - 12$ (b) $t_n = 3(2^{n-5})$ (c) $t_n = \frac{n}{n+1}$

(d) $t_n = n^2 - 10n$ (e) $t_n = \sqrt{4.9n}$ (f) $t_n = \frac{2^{n-6}}{n-2}$

B

5. Determine the general term of each sequence.

(a) 3, 7, 11, 15, … (b) 36, 42, 48, 54, … (c) 4, 12, 36, 108, …

(d) $\frac{2}{3}, \frac{2}{9}, \frac{2}{27}, \frac{2}{81}, \ldots$ (e) 5, −5, 5, −5, 5, … (f) $1, \sqrt{2}, \sqrt{3}, 2, \ldots$

(g) 65, 61, 57, 53, … (h) $\frac{2}{3}, \frac{3}{4}, \frac{4}{5}, \frac{5}{6}, \ldots$ (i) $1, \frac{1}{4}, \frac{1}{9}, \frac{1}{16}, \ldots$

6. **Knowledge and Understanding:** Determine the first five terms, as well as t_{10}, for the sequence defined by $t_n = (5 - n)^n$.

7. Graph the first five terms of each sequence.

(a) $t_n = 3n - 1$ (b) $t_n = 3^{5-n}$ (c) $t_n = -2n + 4$

(d) $t_n = \sqrt{n + 5}$ (e) $t_n = \frac{3}{n+1}$ (f) $t_n = (2n - 1)(3n)$

8. A circle can be cut into pieces, not necessarily equal, using straight lines. The circle can be cut into two pieces with one line, four pieces with two lines, and so on.

number of pieces 2 4 ? ?

(a) Determine the next three terms of this sequence.

(b) Find t_{10}.

(c) Describe your method for finding t_{10}.

9. (a) Use a calculator to determine the first ten terms of the sequence

$$\sqrt{2}, \sqrt{\sqrt{2}}, \sqrt{\sqrt{\sqrt{2}}}, \sqrt{\sqrt{\sqrt{\sqrt{2}}}} \ldots .$$

(b) Describe the pattern of the sequence.

(c) Predict t_{1000} of this sequence.

10. **Communication:** Explain why the graph of a sequence cannot be a line or a curve.

11. (a) Write four different sequences that each begin with 3, 6, … .

(b) Describe the pattern in each sequence.

(c) Determine the general term for each sequence.

12. Determine t_2, t_5, and t_{10} of each sequence.

(a) $t_n = 5n - 15$ (b) $t_n = n^4$ (c) $t_n = \frac{5}{n}$

(d) $t_n = (3n + 4)^2$ (e) $t_n = 2^{n+1}$ (f) $t_n = (-1)^{n+3}$

(g) $t_n = \frac{n-1}{2n+2}$ (h) $t_n = 3n^2 + 2n - 1$ (i) $t_n = (n-1)^3$

13. Determine whether each sequence is finite or infinite. Explain your answer.

(a) a pattern around the rim of a drinking glass

(b) the digits in the decimal equivalent of π

(c) the positive even numbers

(d) the square roots of all counting numbers

(e) the positive integer powers of 5, between 0 and 1 000 000

14. **Application:** Nikki invests \$1000 in a money market account that earns 4.5% of \$1000 each year.

(a) Determine the balance in her account at the end of the first, second, and third years.

(b) Find the general term for the balance in the account. Let n represent the year.

(c) Find the balance in the account after ten years.

15. Sarah builds each cube with unit cubes.

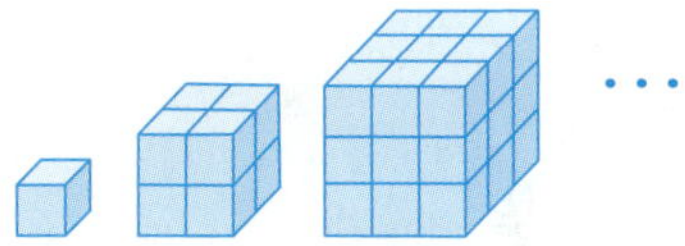

(a) Write the sequence of the unit cubes in each cube.

(b) Determine the next three terms of the sequence.

(c) Write the general term of this sequence.

(d) How many unit cubes would Sarah need to build the 15th cube?

16. Mark drops a ball from a height of 20 m. After each bounce, the height of the ball's bounce is one-half the height of the ball's previous bounce.

(a) Write the sequence that shows the height of the ball's bounce after each of its first five bounces.

(b) Determine the general term of this sequence.

(c) What is the height of the ball's bounce after the tenth bounce?

(d) Is this sequence finite or infinite? Explain your choice.

17. Marty's grandmother gives him 25¢ every time he visits. He visits her every Saturday.

(a) Write the sequence that shows the accumulated money that Marty receives for the first five Saturday visits.

(b) Determine the general term of this sequence.

(c) How much will Marty receive annually from his grandmother?

18. **Thinking, Inquiry, Problem Solving:** An atom consists of electrons that orbit the nucleus of the atom. There may be from one to seven orbitals of electrons, and each orbital holds a maximum number of electrons. For the first four orbitals, these numbers are 2, 8, 18, and 32, respectively.

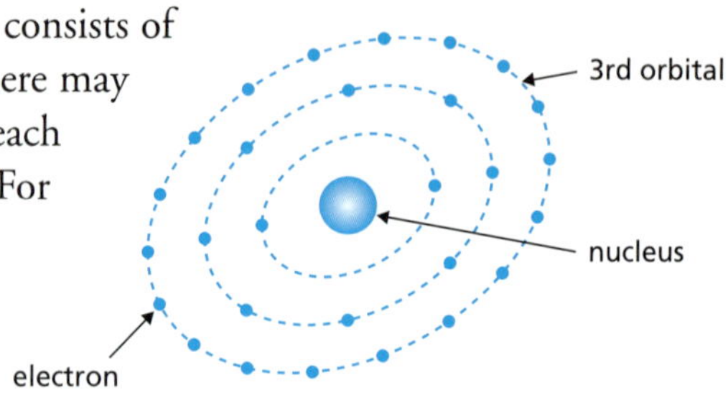

(a) Determine the maximum number of electrons in the outermost orbital.

(b) Determine the general term of this sequence.

19. **Check Your Understanding:** The number of bacteria in a culture doubles at the end of each hour. Ten bacteria are introduced into a petri dish.

(a) Create a table of the number of bacteria in the petri dish at the end of each hour for the first 5 h.

(b) Extend the pattern in the table to determine the number of bacteria in the petri dish at the end of the eighth hour.

(c) Find an algebraic expression that represents the number of bacteria in the petri dish at the end of the nth hour.

(d) Use the algebraic expression to determine the number of bacteria at the end of the tenth hour.

C

20. Consider the sequence 6, 12, 18, 24, … . Which of the following numbers are terms of this sequence?

216, 575, 492, 750, 824

21. Erica builds each individual shape with unit cubes.

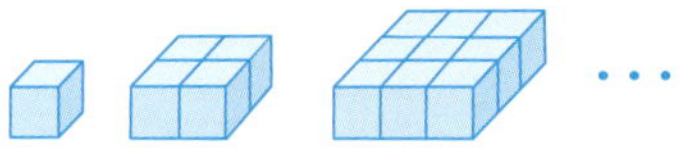

(a) Write the sequence that represents the surface area of each shape.

(b) Find the next three terms of the sequence.

(c) Determine the general term of the sequence.

(d) What is t_{20}?

22. Paul builds each shape with unit cubes.

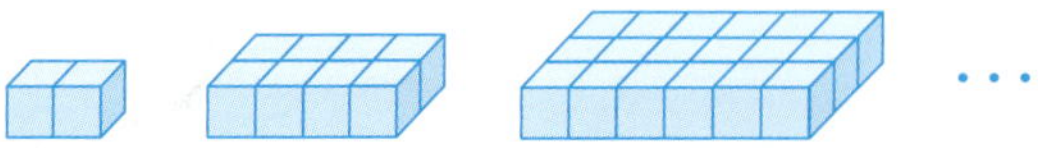

(a) Write the sequence that represents the volume of each shape.

(b) Find the next three terms of the sequence.

(c) Determine the general term of the sequence.

(d) What is t_{20}?

23. (a) Build or draw each stage of the diagram by starting with the first square and then adding to it. Use one toothpick or one short line for each side of the smallest square. Determine the next two terms of the sequence.

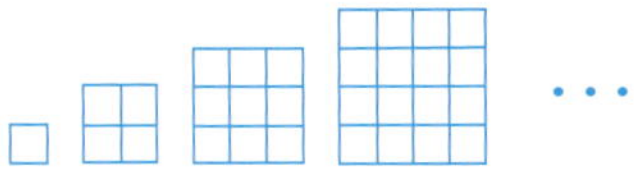

(b) As you build or draw each stage, describe any patterns.

(c) How many toothpicks or short lines will the tenth diagram have?

The Chapter Problem—Controlling Non-Native Plant Populations

In this section, you studied sequences. Apply what you learned to answer these questions about the Chapter Problem on page 12.

CP1. How many of the original 100 knapweed seeds will germinate?

CP2. How many knapweed seeds will be added to the seedbank?

CP3. Of the seeds that do germinate, how many will grow to maturity in the first year?

CP4. How many new seeds will the mature plants add to the seedbank?

CP5. Use your answers for questions 1 to 4 to complete the table.

Year	Number of Seeds in the Seedbank	Number of Seeds that Germinate	Number of Remaining Seeds	Total Number of Plants	Number of New Seeds Produced
0	100	4	96	1	1000
1	1096				
2					
3					
4					
5					

CP6. Describe any pattern in the Total Number of Plants column.

CP7. Describe any pattern in the Number of Seeds in the Seedbank column.

TECHNOLOGY

1.2 TI-83 Plus Calculator: Generating the Terms of a Sequence

On the TI-83 Plus calculator, you can create a list from the general term that displays the specific terms of the sequence.

Generate or list the first five terms of the sequence defined by $t_n = n^2$.

1. Select sequence from the List OPS menu.

Press [2nd] [STAT] [▸]. Scroll down to sequence and press [ENTER].

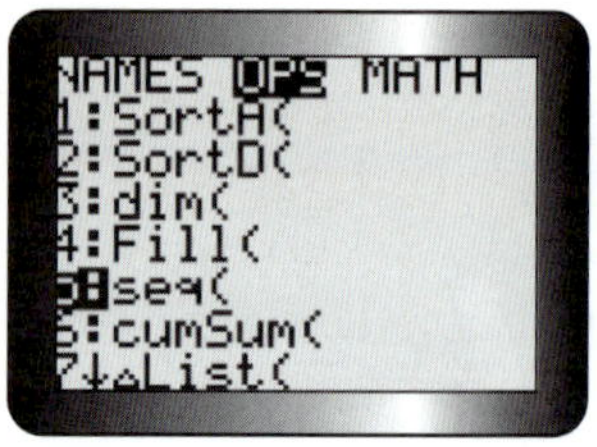

step 1

2. Enter the information for sequence.

You will need to enter the following:

- the expression of the general term
- the variable n — let [X,T,Θ,n] represent n
- the first position number
- the last position number
- the increment — the increment is 1, because the difference between each pair of consecutive natural numbers is always 1

Press [X,T,Θ,n] [x^2] [,] [X,T,Θ,n] [,] [1] [,] [5] [,] [1] [)].

step 2

3. Generate the first five terms of the sequence.

Press [ENTER].

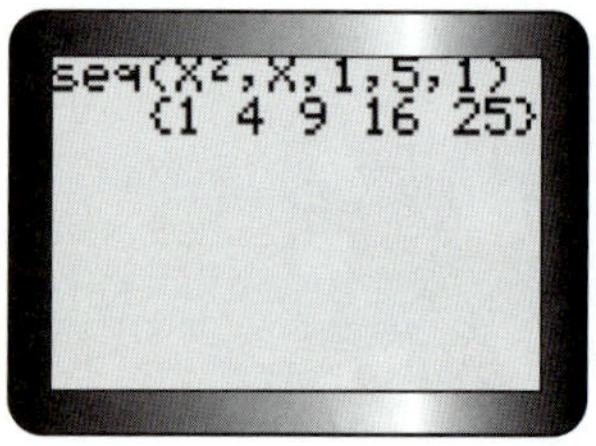

step 3

Practice 1.2

List the first ten terms of each sequence.

(a) $t_n = 2n + 4$ (b) $t_n = n^3$ (c) $t_n = \frac{n+2}{n}$ (d) $t_n = \sqrt{n}$

(e) $t_n = -5n - 2$ (f) $t_n = (0.5)^n$ (g) $t_n = 2(3)^n$ (h) $t_n = n^n$

Sequences and Recursive Formulas

1.3U

Functions and Relations

Part 1: Depreciation

A new car is rarely resold for its original purchase price. As soon as a new car is driven away from a dealership, the value of the car decreases. This decrease in value is called **depreciation**. The show room price of a new car is \$26 000. The salesperson estimates that the value of the car will depreciate by an average of 10% each year.

Think, Do, Discuss

1. Determine the dollar amount of depreciation for the first year.
2. Determine the value of the car at the end of the first year.
3. What percent of the original purchase price does the value in step 2 represent?
4. Determine the value of the car at the end of the second year.
5. Write the first five terms of the sequence that represents the value of the car at the end of each year for the first five years.
6. Let t_n represent any term of this sequence. How could you represent the term before t_n?
7. For this sequence, write a formula that uses the previous term to calculate any term, except the first term.
8. At the end of which year will the car's value be about one-half of its original purchase price?

Part 2: The Fibonacci Sequence

There are many examples of sequences in nature, and in our everyday lives. A female honeybee hatches from an egg laid by a female honeybee, after the egg has been fertilized by the male. So each female honeybee has two parents. However, a male honeybee hatches from an unfertilized egg and has only one parent, a female honeybee. The tree diagram shows six generations of a typical male honeybee.

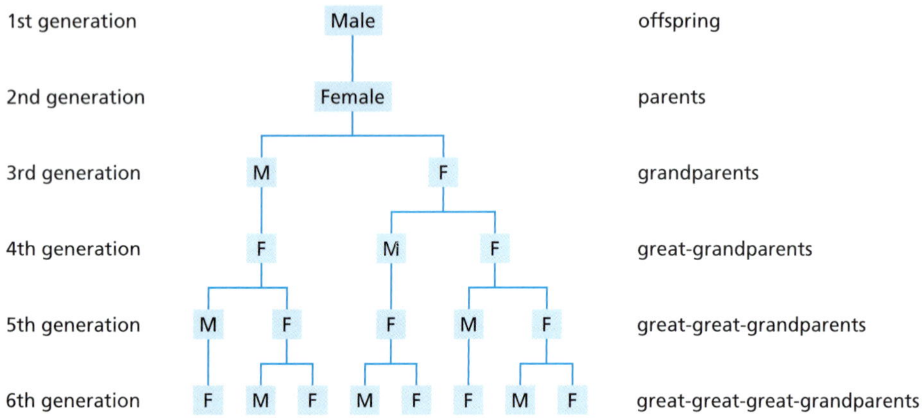

Think, Do, Discuss

1. Starting with the first generation, write the sequence of the number of honeybees in each generation.
2. Identify the pattern in this sequence.
3. Use this pattern to determine the next five terms of the sequence.
4. Let t_n represent any term in this sequence. How could you represent the term before t_n? How could you represent the term before the term that is before t_n?
5. Given that $t_1 = 1$, $t_2 = 1$, and n is a natural number, determine a formula for the general term of this sequence.
6. This sequence is known as the **Fibonacci sequence**, and it occurs in many different situations in nature. Could you easily calculate the 50th term of this sequence? Explain.
7. Create a tree diagram that represents six generations of a female honeybee. Write the sequence that represents the number of honeybees in each generation.
8. Does this sequence have the same pattern as the sequence in step 1? Is this sequence a Fibonacci sequence?
9. Determine a formula for this sequence.
10. Use your formula to find the next five terms of this sequence.
11. For 11 generations of honeybees, who has more ancestors, a male honeybee or a female honeybee?

Focus 1.3U

Key Ideas

- In a **recursive sequence**, a new term is generated from the previous term or terms. For example, 1, 2, −1, 3, −4, 7, −11, ... is a recursive sequence because each term, beginning with the third term, is the result of subtracting t_{n-1} from t_{n-2}.
- A **recursive formula** shows how to find each term from the previous term or terms. For example,

  $t_1 = 1,\ t_2 = 2,\ t_n = t_{n-2} - t_{n-1}$, where $n \in N$

  To find t_n, subtract t_{n-1} from t_{n-2}. The first two terms are given. The sequence is 1, 2, −1, 3, −4, 7, −11, ...
- A recursive formula refers to at least one known term. The first term, and sometimes several other terms, appear with the formula. Examine the formula carefully before applying it.

Example 1

Write the first four terms of each sequence.

(a) $t_1 = 2,\ t_n = 3t_{n-1} + 5$ (b) $t_1 = -1,\ t_2 = 1,\ t_n = 2t_{n-2} + 4t_{n-1}$

Solution

(a) The first term is given. To find the next term, multiply the previous term by 3 and add 5.

$t_1 = 2$

$$\begin{aligned} t_2 &= 3t_{2-1} + 5 \\ &= 3t_1 + 5 \\ &= 3(2) + 5 \\ &= 6 + 5 \\ &= 11 \end{aligned} \qquad \begin{aligned} t_3 &= 3t_{3-1} + 5 \\ &= 3t_2 + 5 \\ &= 3(11) + 5 \\ &= 33 + 5 \\ &= 38 \end{aligned} \qquad \begin{aligned} t_4 &= 3t_{4-1} + 5 \\ &= 3t_3 + 5 \\ &= 3(38) + 5 \\ &= 114 + 5 \\ &= 119 \end{aligned}$$

The first four terms are 2, 11, 38, and 119.

(b) The first two terms are given. To find the third term, multiply the first term by 2, multiply the second term by 4, and add.

$t_1 = -1 \qquad t_2 = 1$

$$\begin{aligned} t_3 &= 2t_{3-2} + 4t_{3-1} \\ &= 2t_1 + 4t_2 \\ &= 2(-1) + 4(1) \\ &= -2 + 4 \\ &= 2 \end{aligned} \qquad \begin{aligned} t_4 &= 2t_{4-2} + 4t_{4-1} \\ &= 2t_2 + 4t_3 \\ &= 2(1) + 4(2) \\ &= 2 + 8 \\ &= 10 \end{aligned}$$

The first four terms are −1, 1, 2, and 10.

Example 2

Write a recursive formula for each sequence.

(a) 2, 6, 18, 54, … (b) 1, 2, 4, 7, 11, 16, … (c) 4, 5, 20, 100, 2000, …

Solution

(a) To find any term, except the first one, multiply the previous term by 3.

$t_1 = 2 \qquad t_2 = 3t_1 \qquad t_3 = 3t_2 \qquad t_n = 3(t_{n-1})$

(b) To find the second term, add 1. To find the third term, add 2. Each number added is 1 less than the position of the term.

$t_1 = 1 \qquad t_2 = t_1 + 1 = t_1 + (2 - 1) \qquad t_3 = t_2 + 2 = t_2 + (3 - 1) \qquad t_n = t_{n-1} + (n - 1)$

(c) To find any term, except for the first two terms, multiply the two previous terms.

$t_1 = 4 \qquad t_2 = 5 \qquad t_3 = t_2 \times t_1 \qquad t_4 = t_3 \times t_2 \qquad t_n = (t_{n-1})(t_{n-2})$

Example 3

Todd fractured his wrist while he was Rollerblading. To relieve the pain, his doctor suggested that he take 500 mg of aspirin every 6 h. At this rate, only 26% of the aspirin remains in his body by the time he takes a new dose.

(a) Find the first six terms of the sequence that represents the amount of aspirin remaining in Todd's body after each dose of aspirin.

(b) Write a recursive formula for this sequence.

(c) Graph the sequence.

(d) Describe what happens to the amount of aspirin remaining in Todd's body as he takes more aspirin.

Solution

(a) The initial dose, or first amount, is 500 mg. The second amount is 500 mg, with 26% of the first amount remaining in his body.

$$\begin{aligned} 500 + 0.26(500) &= 500 + 130 \\ &= 630 \end{aligned}$$

The second amount of aspirin is 630 mg.

The third amount is 500 mg, with 26% of the second amount remaining in his body.

$$\begin{aligned} 500 + 0.26(630) &= 500 + 163.8 \\ &= 663.8 \end{aligned}$$

Continue this pattern:

The fourth amount is $500 + 0.26(663.8) = 672.588$ mg.

The fifth amount is $500 + 0.26(672.588) = 674.872\ 88$ mg.

The sixth amount is $500 + 0.26(674.87288) = 675.466\ 948\ 8$ mg.

The first six terms of the sequence are 500, 630, 663.8, 672.588, 674.872 88, and 675.466 948 8.

(b) The recursive formula for this sequence is $t_1 = 500$, $t_n = 500 + 0.26(t_{n-1})$.

(c)

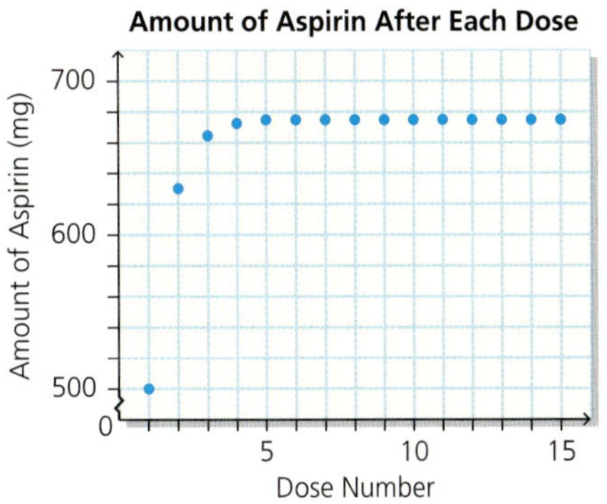

(d) It is apparent from the graph that, as Todd takes more aspirin, the amount that remains in his body increases and then becomes constant at a certain level. Create a spreadsheet to estimate the constant amount of aspirin remaining in Todd's body. Enter and format the information shown in cells A1, B1, and B2. Enter 1 to 10 in column A, beginning with A2, as shown.

	A	B
1	Dose Number	Amount of Aspirin (mg)
2	1	500
3	2	=500+0.26*B2
4	3	
5	4	
6	5	
7	6	
8	7	
9	8	
10	9	
11	10	

Select cells B3 to B11 and use the **Fill Down** command to complete the column.

	A	B
1	Dose Number	Amount of Aspirin (mg)
2	1	500
3	2	630
4	3	663.8
5	4	672.588
6	5	674.87288
7	6	675.4669488
8	7	675.6214067
9	8	675.6615657
10	9	675.6720071
11	10	675.6747218

The amount of aspirin remaining in Todd's body becomes constant at about 675.67 mg.

Practise, Apply, Solve 1.3U

A

1. Write the first five terms of each recursive sequence.

(a) The first term is 3. Any other term is 9 more than the previous term.

(b) The first term is 6. Any other term is the product of the previous term and 4.

(c) The first term is 36. Any other term is one-half of the previous term.

(d) The first term is 22. Any other term is 2 less than the previous term.

(e) The first term is 3 and the second term is 4. Any other term is the product of the two previous terms.

(f) The first term is -5 and the second term is 7. Any other term is the sum of the two previous terms.

2. Write the first five terms of each sequence.

(a) $t_1 = 4, t_n = t_{n-1} + 5$

(b) $t_1 = -3, t_n = 2t_{n-1} - 2$

(c) $t_1 = 8, t_n = t_{n-1} \div 2$

(d) $t_1 = 4, t_n = (t_{n-1})^2$

(e) $t_1 = 5, t_n = \frac{t_{n-1}}{n}$

(f) $t_1 = 1, t_2 = 2, t_n = (t_{n-1})(t_{n-2})$

(g) $t_1 = 2, t_2 = -1, t_n = (t_{n-1}) + (t_{n-2})$

(h) $t_1 = 1, t_2 = 1, t_n = 2(t_{n-1}) - 3(t_{n-2})$

3. Write a recursive formula for each sequence.

(a) 2, 7, 12, 17, …

(b) -2, 4, -8, 16, …

(c) 10, 5, 2.5, 1.25, …

(d) 2, 4, 16, 256, …

(e) 243, 81, 27, 9, 3, …

(f) 34, 25, 16, 7, …

4. Write a recursive formula for each sequence in question 1.

5. A new boat depreciates by 15% of its original value each year.

(a) What is the boat worth as a percent of the purchase price one year after it is bought?

(b) The boat was bought for $35 000. Write its value at the end of each year for the next five years as a sequence.

(c) Write a recursive formula for this sequence.

B

6. A farmer grows trees for a nursery. The farm has 4200 trees. Each year, the farmer harvests 20% of the trees and replants 850 trees.

(a) Write a recursive formula for the total number of trees on the farm each year.

(b) What happens to the total number of trees on the farm over time?

7. Knowledge and Understanding: If $t_1 = 6$, $t_2 = 4$, $t_3 = 2$, and $t_n = (t_{n-3} + t_{n-2}) \times t_{n-1}$, find t_7.

8. Graph the first five terms of each recursive sequence.

(a) $t_1 = 3$, $t_n = t_{n-1} + 2$

(b) $t_1 = -5$, $t_n = 2t_{n-1}$

(c) $t_1 = 8$, $t_n = t_{n-1} \div 2$

(d) $t_1 = 2$, $t_n = 10 - t_{n-1}$

9. Tarek applies for a job and is hired. His starting salary is \$40 000 for the first year. Each following year, his salary will be increased by \$1250.

(a) Write a recursive formula for the sequence of Tarek's annual salaries.

(b) Use the formula to find the first five terms of this sequence.

(c) Find Tarek's salary ten years from now. Is it convenient to use the recursive formula in this situation? Explain.

10. Here are the first three stages of a fractal called the Koch snowflake. To create the snowflake, start with an equilateral triangle. For stage 2, begin by dividing one side of the triangle into three and replace the middle segment with two lines that each have the same length as the middle segment. You can repeat these steps to create successive stages.

stage 1 stage 2 stage 3

(a) Each side of the original equilateral triangle is 18 cm. Copy and complete the table.

	Number of Segments	Length of Each Segment (cm)	Perimeter (cm)
stage 1	3	18	54
stage 2			
stage 3			

(b) Write a recursive formula for each of the three sequences in the table in (a).

(c) Find the number of segments in stage 6.

(d) Find the length of each segment in stage 7.

(e) What is the perimeter of the snowflake in stage 8?

11. When a bungee jumper jumps off a platform, the bungee cord stretches 50 m. For each successive bounce, the cord stretches 80% of the previous length.

(a) Write a recursive formula for the sequence of the length of the bungee chord after each bounce.

(b) Determine the first five terms of this sequence.

(c) Calculate the total distance travelled by the bungee jumper for the first five bounces.

12. Communication: Create a sequence in which each term after the second term is a function of the previous two terms. Write a recursive formula for your sequence and use it to find the first ten terms.

13. Nadia has a viral infection and must take 250 mg of medicine every 3 h. Only 30% of the medicine remains in her body by the time she takes the next dose. At what level (by mass) will the medicine remaining in her body become constant?

14. Consider the sequence 2, 6, 12, 20, 30, … .

(a) Find the next term in the sequence by using the pattern in the differences between consecutive pairs of terms.

(b) Write a recursive formula for this sequence.

15. Application: The fourth term of a sequence is 281. The recursive formula for the sequence is $t_n = 3(t_{n-1}) + 5$, for $n = 2, 3, \ldots$. What is the first term of the sequence?

16. In some lotteries, a million-dollar grand prize is paid in 20 annual payments of \$50 000 each. The winner receives the first \$50 000 on the day he or she claims the prize. The organizers of the lottery put just enough money into an account to pay the annual payments, and, after the 19th payment, the balance of the account is \$0. The account has an annual interest rate of 5%. Let a_0 represent the initial amount of money put into the account and a_n represent the amount of money in the account after the nth payment.

(a) Write a recursive formula for a_n.

(b) Use your calculator to find a_{19}, if $a_0 = \$604\ 266.05$.

(c) What is the advantage in paying the winner under these conditions?

17. The population of a small town doubles every five years.

(a) Today the population is 3500. Write a recursive formula for the sequence that represents the town's population every five years.

(b) Determine the population 25 years from now.

18. Every person has two parents, four grandparents, eight great-grandparents, and so on.

(a) Write a recursive formula for the sequence of the number of ancestors going back each generation for any person.

(b) How many ancestors does each person have going back for eight generations?

19. If $t_1 = 2$, $t_2 = 4$, and $t_3 = 6$, find the next three terms of the sequence defined by $t_n = \frac{(t_{n-1})(t_{n-2})}{(t_{n-3})}$.

20. **Thinking, Inquiry, Problem Solving:** In Ontario, many homes have filtration systems to remove impurities from the water. The water supplied to a particular home contains 4 mg of impurities, but the water is continuously recycled through a filtration system, and 52% of the impurities are removed each hour. How long will it take for the water to contain less than 0.02 mg of impurities?

21. **Check Your Understanding:** If you were asked to find the 88th term of a sequence and were given both the general term of the sequence and a recursive formula, which would you use? Give an example to support your decision.

C

22. Determine a recursive formula for the sequence 5, 9, 18, 34, 59, … .

23. A theatre has 20 seats in the first row, 22 in the second row, 26 in the third row, 32 in the fourth row, and so on.

(a) Write a recursive formula for the sequence that represents the number of seats in each row, beginning with the first row.

(b) The theatre has ten rows of seats. How many seats are in the last row?

(c) How many seats are in the theatre?

24. To draw a diagonal in a regular polygon, join a pair of non-adjacent vertices. How many diagonals does a decagon have altogether?

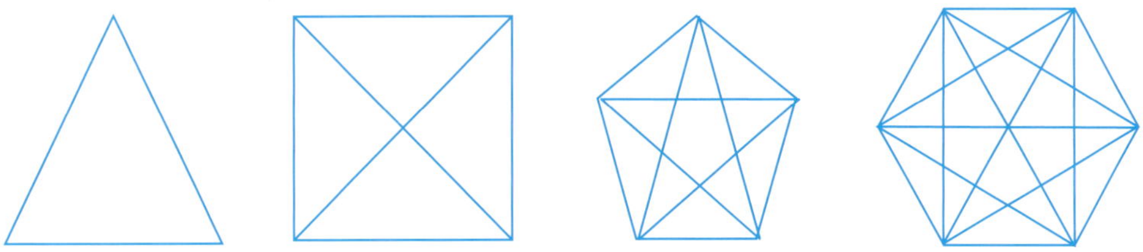

3 sides 4 sides 5 sides 6 sides

The Chapter Problem—Controlling Non-Native Plant Populations

In this section, you have studied recursive sequences. Apply what you have learned to answer these questions about the Chapter Problem on page 12.

CP8. Recall that the knapweed plant lives for five years and that the seeds of the plant are viable in soil for eight years. Use this information to extend the table on page 25 to include years 6 to 10.

CP9. Write a recursive formula for the sequence of the total number of plants in each year.

CP10. Write a recursive formula for the sequence of the number of seeds in the seedbank each year.

1.4 TI-83 Plus Calculator: Graphing Sequences

TECHNOLOGY

Part 1: Creating a Table and Graphing — The General Term

Using the TI-83 Plus calculator, you can first create a table for a sequence and then graph. You will need the general term.

Create and graph the sequence defined by $t_n = 3n - 1$.

1. Change the graphing mode from function to sequence.

The graphing modes are listed on the fourth line of the MODE menu. Press [MODE] and scroll down and across to **Seq**. Press [ENTER].

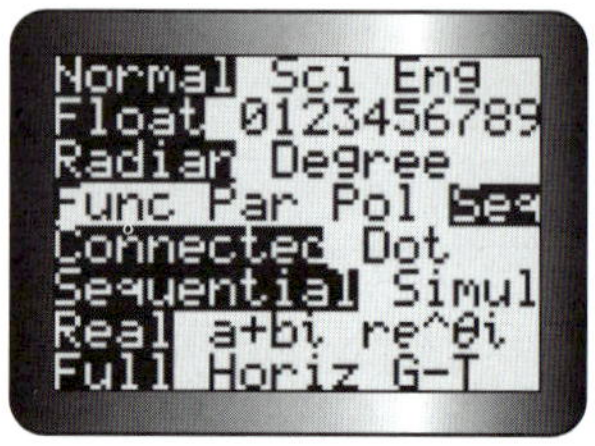

step 1

2. Enter the general term into the sequence editor.

Press [Y=]. In this editor, **u**(n), **v**(n), and **w**(n) represent the general terms of sequences. You can change the minimum value of n (n**Min**). In most cases, you will not need to change the value 1, because, when n = 1, the first term is generated. Scroll down to **u**(n) and position the cursor to the right of the equal sign. Press [3] [X,T,Θ,n] [–] [1].

step 2

3. Adjust the window to display the required number of terms.

Press [WINDOW]. The setting n**Min** indicates the smallest n-value for the calculator to evaluate, while n**Max** indicates the largest n-value for the calculator to evaluate. **PlotStart=1** means that the graph starts at the first term. **PlotStep=1** means that each consecutive term will be plotted. You can change these settings, but use these window settings for this example.

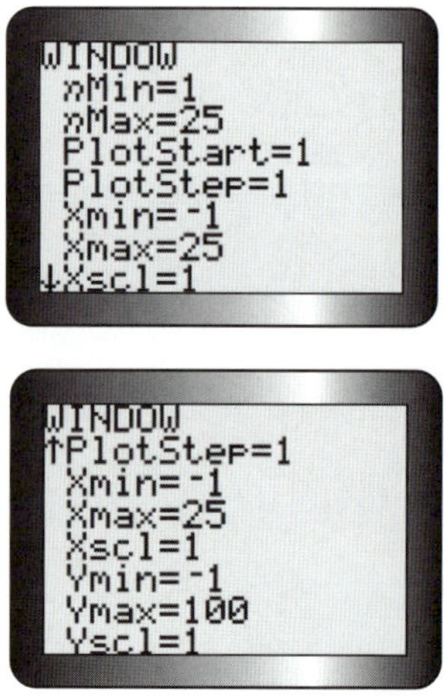

step 3

4. Graph the sequence.

Press [GRAPH].

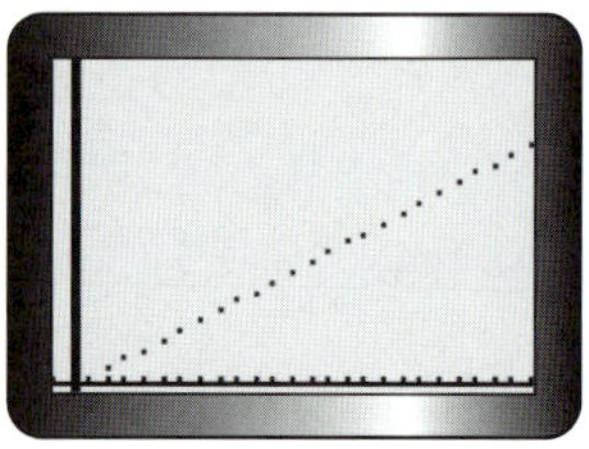

step 4

5. **Trace along the graph to identify specific terms of the sequence.**

   Press [TRACE]. Use [▶] and [◀] to move from point to point. The n-value, or position, and the x- and y-coordinates of each term are displayed at each point. The y-coordinate represents the value of the term.

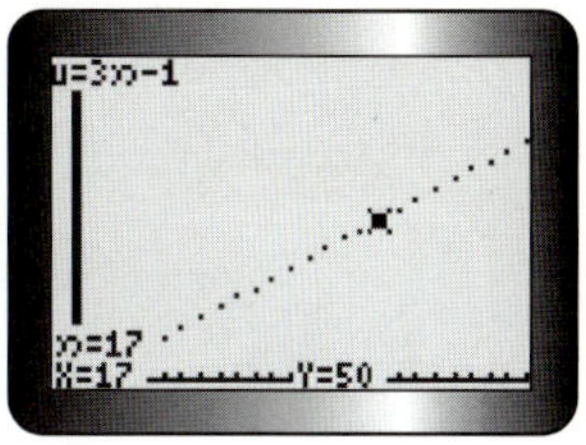

step 5

6. **View the terms of the sequence in a table.**

   (a) Press [2nd] [WINDOW]. Set **TblStart** to 1 and **ΔTbl** to 1.

   (b) Press [2nd] [GRAPH] to display the table. Use the cursor keys to scroll through the table.

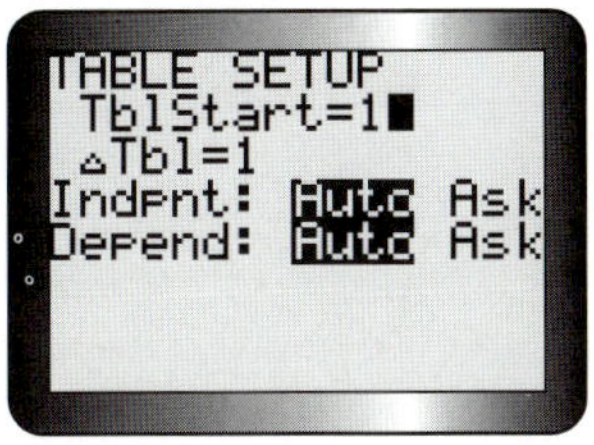

step 6a

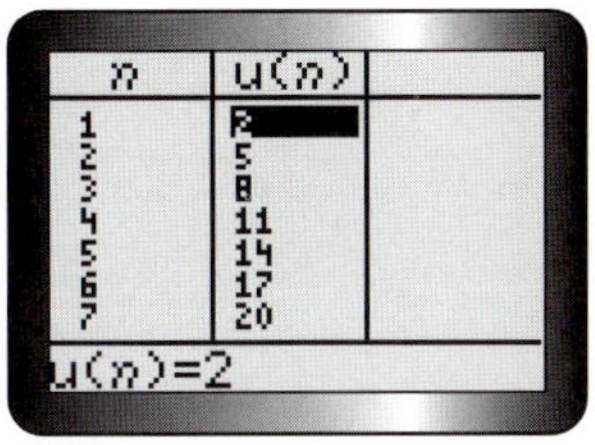

step 6b

Note: To see the graph and the table at the same time, use split-screen mode. Press [MODE], then scroll down and across to **G-T** (on the last line of the MODE menu). Press [ENTER] [GRAPH].

Part 2: Creating a Table and Graphing — The Recursive Formula

Using the TI-83 Plus calculator, you can graph recursive sequences in the same way, with one exception: you must specify an initial value or values for **u(*n*Min)** in the sequence editor.

Graph the sequence $t_1 = 500$, $t_n = 500 + 0.26t_{n-1}$.

1. **Enter the recursive formula in the sequence editor and set the initial value.**

   Press [Y=]. Then, for the sequence **u(*n*)**, press [5] [0] [0] [+] [0] [.] [2] [6] [2nd] [7] [(] [X,T,Θ,n] [−] [1] [)].

   Set the initial value to 500. Position the cursor to the right of the equal sign for **u(*n*Min)** and press [2nd] [(] [5] [0] [0] [2nd] [)] [ENTER].

step 1

Note: You do not have to enter the braces ([2nd] [(] and [2nd] [)]) around the initial value, or the first term. However, if you were to enter, for example, $t_1 = 0$ and $t_2 = 1$, then you would press [2nd] [(] [1] [,] [0] [2nd] [)].

2. **Set the window.**

   Press WINDOW and enter the values shown.

step 2

3. **Draw the graph.**

   Press GRAPH.

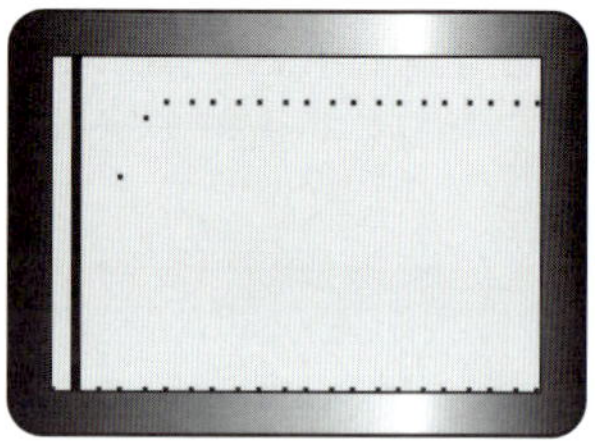

step 3

4. **View the terms of the sequence in a table.**

   Press 2nd WINDOW. Set **TblStart** to 1 and **ΔTbl** to 1. Press 2nd GRAPH to display the table. Use the cursor keys to scroll through the table.

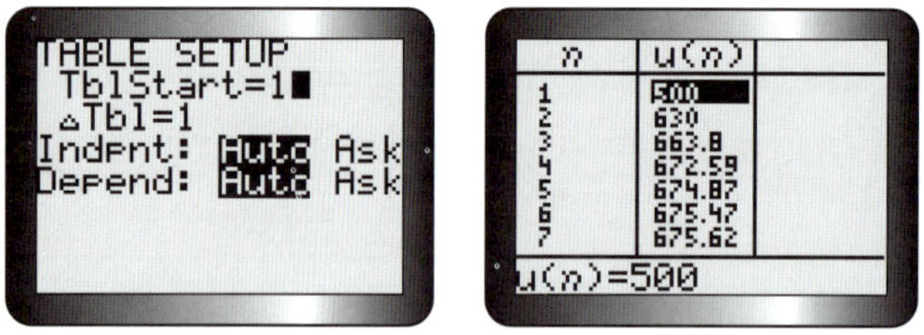

step 4

Practice 1.4

Part 1

i. Graph the first 25 terms of each sequence.
ii. Determine the 10th, 15th, and 20th terms of each sequence.
iii. Check your answers. Use either TRACE or look at the table (2nd GRAPH).

(a) $t_n = 6n + 3$ (b) $t_n = n^2$ (c) $t_n = \frac{1}{n}$ (d) $t_n = \sqrt{n}$

(e) $t_n = 2n^3 - n$ (f) $t_n = -n$ (g) $t_n = 10(1.1)^n$ (h) $t_n = 10(2)^{-n}$

Part 2

i. Graph the first ten terms of each recursive sequence.
ii. Determine the fifth and tenth terms of each sequence.
iii. Check your answers. Use either TRACE or look at the table (2nd GRAPH).

(a) $t_n = t_{n-1} + 4, t_1 = 3$ (b) $t_n = 5t_{n-1}, t_1 = 6$

(c) $t_n = -2t_{n-1} + 3, t_1 = 5$ (d) $t_n = 2t_{n-1}, t_1 = 2$

(e) $t_n = \frac{1}{2}(t_{n-1}), t_1 = 100$ (f) $t_n = t_{n-1} - t_{n-2}, t_1 = 5, t_2 = 7$

Investigating Ways of Cutting "Vegetables"

When experienced cooks prepare dishes, they usually cut up a vegetable using different techniques. Often the cook cuts the vegetable in long thin strips. Then he or she stacks the pieces and then cuts in a perpendicular direction to the strips. Why does a cook do this?

Think, Do, Discuss

Use two rectangular pieces of paper and a pair of scissors. The paper will act as your "vegetable." You will cut each piece of paper in strips in two different ways.

Method 1

1. (a) Take one piece of paper and cut a thin strip (about 2 cm wide) along the width.

(b) Repeat cutting the entire sheet into strips, all of which should be about the same size.

Method 2

2. (a) Take the other piece of paper and cut it in half along the width.

(b) Stack the halves. Cut the pile in half, along the width.

(c) Continue stacking and cutting, until you have created strips that are about the same width as the strips you created in method 1.

(d) Copy and complete the table.

Number of Cuts	Number of Pieces Using Method 1	Number of Pieces Using Method 2
1		
2		
3		
⋮	⋮	⋮

3. Compare the number of pieces created after each cut using both methods. How does the number of pieces change with each cut? Describe the pattern.

4. For each method, find the next three terms of the sequence of the number of pieces for each cut.

5. Suppose you had to cut over 1000 strips. What is the least number of cuts you would have to make?

6. Determine a recursive formula for each sequence in step 3.

7. Determine the general term of each sequence.

8. Discuss how the sequences are alike and how they are different.

Arithmetic Sequences 1.6

Part 1: The Days of a Month

Here is a typical calendar for October. Do the dates have any predictable patterns?

October						
Sunday	*Monday*	*Tuesday*	*Wednesday*	*Thursday*	*Friday*	*Saturday*
		1	2	3	4	5
6	7	8	9	10	11	12
13	14	15	16	17	18	19
20	21	22	23	24	25	26
27	28	29	30	31		

Think, Do, Discuss

1. Write the sequence of dates for the last week of October. Start with Sunday's date.
2. How many terms are in this sequence? Describe the pattern in this sequence.
3. Extend the pattern and write the next five terms of this sequence. (Assume that the dates may be more than 31.)
4. Determine the **first differences** between pairs of consecutive terms of this sequence. What do you notice? What type of relationship exists between n and the value of the term?
5. Graph this sequence. What is the rate of change between each pair of consecutive terms in this sequence?
6. Determine the general term for this sequence.
7. Write the sequence of dates for all the Tuesdays of the month.

8. Repeat steps 2 to 6 for the sequence in step 7.

9. Describe how to locate, in the calendar, a sequence where the rate of change between each pair of consecutive terms is 8.

10. Describe how to locate, in the calendar, a sequence where the rate of change between each pair of consecutive terms is 6.

Part 2: Simple Interest

Ed is planning to buy a sofa, not with cash, but through a financing plan. After Ed makes a down payment, he must pay a finance charge, which is a percent of the balance owing and depends on the length of time that Ed will take to pay the balance owing. The finance charge is an example of **simple interest**.

Interest is the cost of using money. A bank pays interest for using money in, for example, savings accounts. You pay interest when you use or borrow money.

Interest is calculated as a percent of an amount of money, called the **principal**, which is used for a specific period. The interest is calculated at the end of a period and is added to the principal. However, at the end of the next period, simple interest is again calculated, but **only** on the principal. As a result, the interest earned each period is constant, and the balance grows by the same amount each year.

The formula for **simple interest** is

$$I = Prt$$

where I is the simple interest,
P is the principal (the amount of money borrowed or invested),
r is the annual interest rate, and
t is the time in years.

The balance in an account or the balance owing on a loan at the end of t years, T, is the sum of the original principal, P, and the interest earned or charged, I.

$$\begin{aligned} T &= P + I \\ &= P + Prt \\ &= P(1 + rt) \end{aligned}$$

Examining Simple Interest

On the day Juan is born, his grandparents deposit \$10 000 in a savings account that pays simple interest. The annual interest rate is 5%. If they do not make any other deposits, what is the balance in the account on the day Juan turns 18?

Think, Do, Discuss

1. Calculate the interest earned at the end of the first year.
2. Determine the balance in the account on Juan's first birthday.
3. Calculate the interest earned at the end of the second year.
4. Determine the balance in the account on Juan's second birthday.
5. Write the sequence that represents the balance in the account on each birthday from the 1st to the 18th.
6. What is the balance in the account on Juan's 18th birthday? How much of the balance is interest?
7. Explain the pattern in this sequence. What is the rate of change between each pair of consecutive year-end balances?
8. Graph this sequence.
9. Is the growth of the balance in the account linear or nonlinear? Explain.
10. Let n represent the number of years. Determine
    (a) the general term (b) the recursive formula for this sequence
11. Suppose Juan leaves the money in the account until he retires at 65. What would be the balance in the account on his 65th birthday?
12. Mary deposits \$5000 in an account that earns simple interest at a rate of 8%/a. If she makes no other deposits, determine the sequence that represents the balance at the end of each year for ten years. Determine the general term of this sequence.

Focus 1.6

Key Ideas

- In an **arithmetic sequence**, the **common difference**, d, is a constant value. For the general arithmetic sequence $t_1, t_2, t_3, t_4, \ldots, t_n, \ldots, d = t_n - t_{n-1}$. Here are some examples of arithmetic sequences:

  $2, 6, 10, 14, 18, \ldots$, and $d = 4$

  $5, 2, -1, -4, -7, \ldots$, and $d = -3$

  $0, 0.25, 0.5, 0.75, 1.0, 1.25, \ldots$, and $d = 0.25$

  $\frac{1}{8}, \frac{1}{2}, \frac{7}{8}, 1\frac{1}{4}, 1\frac{5}{8}, \ldots$, and $d = \frac{3}{8}$

- The common difference in an arithmetic sequence corresponds to the rate of change between any two consecutive terms of the sequence. The first differences are constant. Therefore, the terms of an arithmetic sequence change at a constant rate. So, in any arithmetic sequence, the relationship between n and t_n is linear.

- The **general term** of an arithmetic sequence is

$$t_n = a + (n - 1)d$$

where t_n is the nth term,
a is the first term, or t_1, and
d is the common difference.

- An example of an arithmetic sequence is the annual balance in an account that pays simple interest. This investment grows at a constant or linear rate.

Example 1

Identify which sequences are arithmetic. If a sequence is arithmetic, determine the common difference and the general term.

(a) $-9, -6, -3, 0, \ldots$ (b) $11, 22, 44, 88, \ldots$

Solution

For each sequence, find the differences between each pair of consecutive terms. If the differences are the same, the sequence is arithmetic.

(a) For this sequence,

$$-6 - (-9) = 3, -3 - (-6) = 3, \text{ and } 0 - (-3) = 3$$

Because the common difference is 3, the sequence is arithmetic. Now find the general term.

$$\begin{aligned} t_n &= a + (n - 1)d && \text{Substitute known values.} \\ &= -9 + (n - 1)3 \\ &= -9 + 3n - 3 \\ &= 3n - 12 \end{aligned}$$

The general term is $t_n = 3n - 12$.

(b) For this sequence,

$$22 - 11 = 11, 44 - 22 = 22, \text{ and } 88 - 44 = 44$$

Because the differences are not common, this sequence is not arithmetic, and the general term cannot be found.

Example 2

Determine the 25th term of the sequence $-17, -10, -3, 4, \ldots$.

Solution

For this sequence,

$$-10 - (-17) = 7, -3 - (-10) = 7, \text{ and } 4 - (-3) = 7$$

This sequence is arithmetic, with $d = 7$ and $a = -17$. Find the general term.

$$\begin{aligned} t_n &= a + (n - 1)d && \text{Substitute.} \\ &= -17 + (n - 1)7 && \text{Expand.} \\ &= -17 + 7n - 7 && \text{Simplify.} \\ &= -24 + 7n \end{aligned}$$

Substitute $n = 25$ in the general term to find the 25th term.

$$\begin{aligned} t_n &= -24 + 7n \\ t_{25} &= -24 + 7(25) \\ &= 151 \end{aligned}$$

Example 3

Determine the number of terms in the finite arithmetic sequence 3, 15, 27, ... , 495.

Solution

In this arithmetic sequence, $a = 3$ and $d = 12$. Substitute to find the general term.

$$\begin{aligned} t_n &= a + (n - 1)d \\ &= 3 + (n - 1)12 \\ &= 3 + 12n - 12 \\ &= -9 + 12n \end{aligned}$$

To find the number of terms, substitute the value of the last term for t_n and solve for n.

$$\begin{aligned} t_n &= -9 + 12n \\ 495 &= -9 + 12n \\ 495 + 9 &= 12n \\ 504 &= 12n \\ 42 &= n \end{aligned}$$

This sequence has 42 terms.

Example 4

Irma deposits \$750.00 in a savings account that earns simple interest. This table shows the balance at the end of each year for four years.

Year	1	2	3	4
Year-End Balance (\$)	783.75	817.50	851.25	885.00

Determine the following.

(a) the annual interest rate

(b) the general term for the balance at the end of the nth year

(c) the balance at the end of the 15th year

Solution

(a) Each year, the account earns the same amount of interest. This amount is

$$\$783.75 - \$750.00 = \$33.75$$

In this case, $I = \$33.75$, $P = \$750$, and $t = 1$. Use the formula $I = Prt$ to find r.

$$\begin{aligned} I &= Prt && \text{Substitute.} \\ 33.75 &= 750r(1) \\ 33.75 &= 750r && \text{Solve for } r. \\ \frac{33.75}{750} &= r \\ 0.045 &= r \end{aligned}$$

The annual interest rate is 4.5%.

(b) The year-end balances form an arithmetic sequence with $a = 783.75$ and $d = 33.75$.

$$\begin{aligned} t_n &= a + (n - 1)d \\ &= 783.75 + (n - 1)33.75 \\ &= 783.75 + 33.75n - 33.75 \\ &= 750 + 33.75n \end{aligned}$$

(c) To find the balance in the account at the end of the 15th year, let $n = 15$.

$$\begin{aligned} t_n &= 750 + 33.75n \\ t_{15} &= 750 + 33.75(15) \\ &= 750 + 506.25 \\ &= 1256.25 \end{aligned}$$

OR

Find the interest earned over 15 years and add it to the principal.

$$\begin{aligned} I &= Prt \\ &= 750 \times 0.045 \times 15 \\ &= 506.25 \\ \text{amount} &= P + I \\ &= 750 + 506.25 \\ &= 1256.25 \end{aligned}$$

The balance in the account at the end of the 15th year is \$1256.25.

Example 5

Charlie opened a savings account as a child. He opened the account with only one deposit. At the end of the tenth year, there was \$300 in the account and, at the end of the 15th year, there was \$325 in the account. The account earns simple interest. Determine the annual interest rate and the original deposit.

Solution

Because the interest is simple, the year-end balances are the terms of an arithmetic sequence. The balance at the end of the tenth year is t_{10} and the balance at the end of the 15th year is t_{15}. So $t_{10} = 300$, $t_{15} = 325$, and $t_n = a + (n - 1)d$.

$$t_{15} = 325$$
$$325 = a + (15 - 1)d$$
$$325 = a + 14d$$

$$t_{10} = 300$$
$$300 = a + (10 - 1)d$$
$$300 = a + 9d$$

Solve the system of equations by elimination.

$$\begin{aligned} 325 &= a + 14d \quad ① \\ 300 &= a + 9d \quad ② \quad \text{Subtract.} \\ \hline 25 &= 5d \quad \text{Solve for } d. \\ 5 &= d \end{aligned}$$

To find a, let $d = 5$ in equation ①.

$$\begin{aligned} 325 &= a + 14d \\ 325 &= a + 14(5) \\ 325 &= a + 70 \\ 325 - 70 &= a \\ 255 &= a \end{aligned}$$

If $a = 255$, then the balance in the account at the end of the first year was \$255. The interest earned at the end of the first year was \$5. Then the original deposit was \$255 − \$5 = \$250.

To find the interest rate, substitute $P = \$250$, $I = \$5$, and $t = 1$ in the formula for simple interest.

$$\begin{aligned} I &= Prt \\ 5 &= 250 \times r \times 1 \\ \frac{5}{250} &= r \\ 0.02 &= r \end{aligned}$$

The annual interest rate is 2%.

Practise, Apply, Solve 1.6

A

1. **i.** Determine whether each sequence is arithmetic.
ii. If a sequence is arithmetic, then determine the rate of change between pairs of consecutive terms.

(a) 4, 11, 15, 19, … (b) 32, 23, 14, 5, … (c) 5, 6, 5, 6, …
(d) 2, 8, 32, 144, … (e) 22, 33, 44, 55, … (f) $\frac{1}{4}, \frac{1}{2}, \frac{3}{4}, 1, \ldots$

2. **i.** Determine whether each general term defines an arithmetic sequence.
ii. For each arithmetic sequence, determine the rate of change between pairs of consecutive terms.

(a) $t_n = 3n - 2$ (b) $t_n = 5^{n-1}$ (c) $t_n = -4n + 7$
(d) $t_n = (n + 1)(n - 1)$ (e) $t_n = \frac{1}{2}n + 2$ (f) $t_n = \frac{n + 2}{n}$

3. For each of the following arithmetic sequences, determine
   i. the common difference **ii.** the general term **iii.** t_{10}
   (a) 5, 10, 15, 20, …
   (b) $-30, -24, -18, -12, \ldots$
   (c) 13, 11, 9, 7, …
   (d) $\frac{1}{3}, \frac{2}{3}, 1, 1\frac{1}{3}, \ldots$
   (e) 0.2, 0.35, 0.5, 0.65, …
   (f) $-3, -3, -3, -3, \ldots$
4. Determine the recursive formula for each arithmetic sequence in question 3.
5. Find the general term for the arithmetic sequence in which
   (a) the first term is 7 and the consecutive terms increase by 6
   (b) the first term is -9 and the consecutive terms decrease by 2
   (c) the first term is 25 and the consecutive terms decrease by 6
   (d) the first term is 121 and the consecutive terms increase by 12
6. **Knowledge and Understanding:** An arithmetic sequence is $-5, 4, 13, 22, \ldots$.
   (a) Find the next three terms.
   (b) Find t_n.
   (c) What is t_{200}?

B

7. For each sequence, find
   i. t_n, the general term **ii.** t_{24}
   (a)
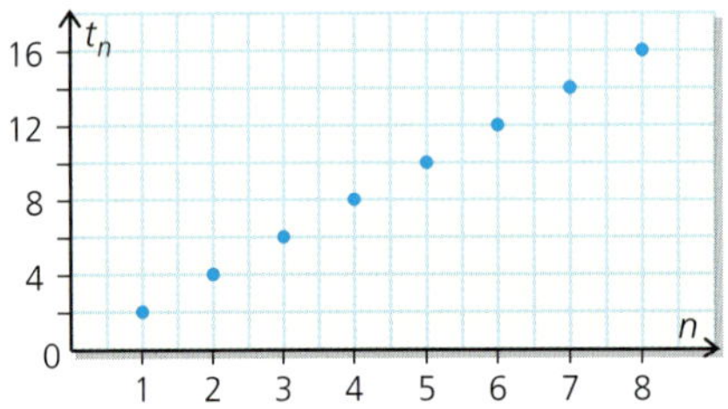

   (b)
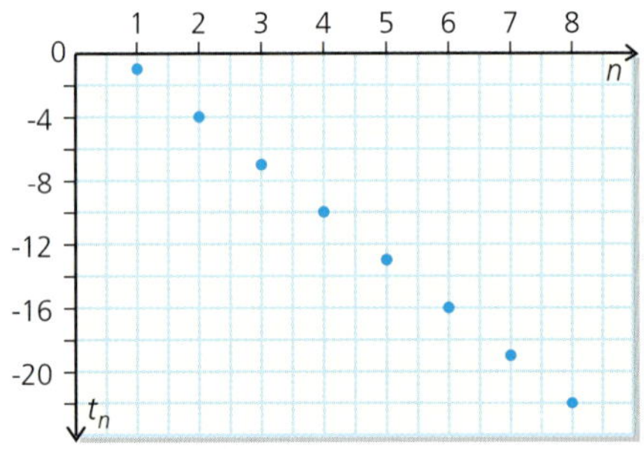

   (c)
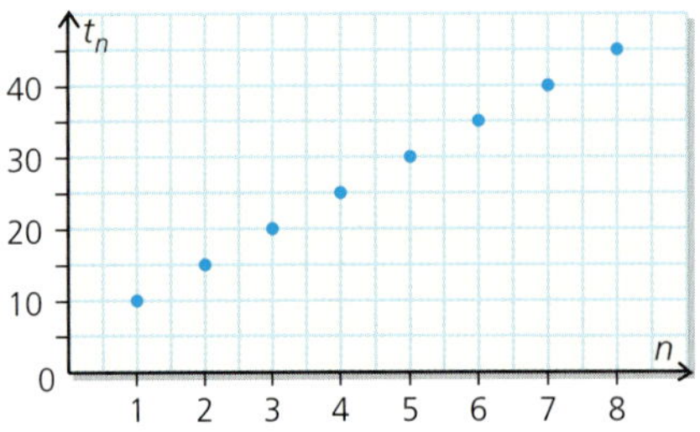

   (d)
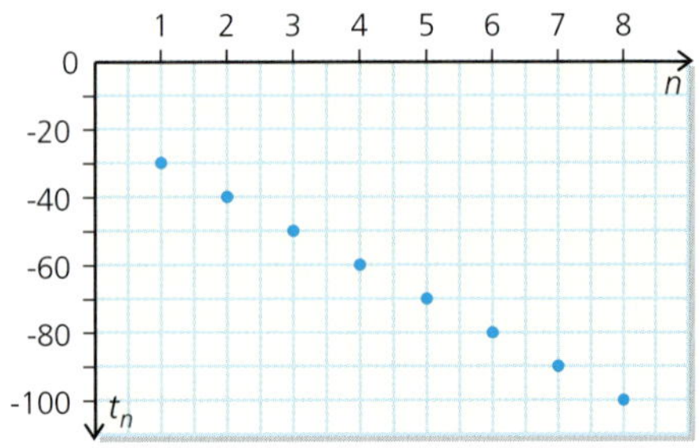

8. Graph each sequence.

(a) $t_n = 4n - 6$
(b) $t_n = -5n + 3$
(c) $t_n = -n - 1$
(d) $t_n = \frac{1}{2}n + 4$
(e) $t_n = \frac{n + 1}{2}$
(f) $t_n = 10n - 2$
(g) $t_n = 3(n - 1)$
(h) $t_n = -2n + 4$

9. **Communication:**

(a) Graph the sequence defined by $t_n = -12 + 3n$.

(b) Use the graph to determine which term has a value of 21.

(c) Use the general term to determine which term has a value of 21.

(d) Compare the methods in (b) and (c). Which method gives the more reliable answer? Explain.

10. Calculate the simple interest in each situation.

(a) \$500 invested at 4%/a for 2 years

(b) \$3000 borrowed at 3.5%/a for 5 years

(c) \$4250 invested at 6%/a for 38 months

(d) \$5000 borrowed at 5.75%/a for 45 weeks

(e) \$900 invested at 8%/a for 60 days

11. Determine the number of terms in each arithmetic sequence.

(a) 8, 11, 14, 17, … , 71
(b) −10, −14, −18, −22, … , −138
(c) 6, 17, 28, 39, … , 435
(d) 21, 17, 13, 9, … , −35
(e) 8, 15, 22, 29, … , 99
(f) −92, −84, −76, −68, … , 52

12. Bob opens a savings account with a deposit of \$2000. The interest rate is 4.5%/a. He does not make any other deposits.

(a) By what amount will the year-end balance in the account increase each year?

(b) Write the sequence of the year-end balances for the first five years.

(c) Determine the general term of this sequence.

(d) Graph this sequence.

(e) At the end of one year, the balance in the account is \$3350. For how many years has the original deposit earned interest?

13. Carlo bought a house for \$175 000. His real estate agent told him that houses in the neighbourhood appreciate (increase) in value by \$5500 annually. When could he sell his house for at least twice the purchase price?

14. A pile of bricks has 85 bricks in the bottom row, 81 bricks in the second row, 77 bricks in the third row, and so on. There is only one brick in the top row.

(a) How many bricks are in the 13th row?

(b) How many rows are there in the pile?

15. **Application:** The most famous of all comets is Halley's comet, named for English astronomer Edmund Halley (1656–1742). He was the first to surmise that comets seen in 1531, 1607, and 1682 were, in fact, the same comet. He also correctly predicted the comet's return in 1758. The period of Halley's comet is about 76 years.

(a) Develop a formula to predict when Halley's comet will be visible from Earth.

(b) Predict when Halley's comet will be visible from Earth in our century.

(c) Predict when Halley's comet will be visible twice in a century in this millennium.

(d) Can you use this model to make precise predictions? Explain.

16. Write the recursive formula to generate the terms of any arithmetic sequence. Let a be the first term and d be the common difference.

17. For each of the following arithmetic sequences, determine a, d, and t_n.

(a) $t_6 = 23, t_{11} = 38$ (b) $t_8 = -49, t_{15} = -84$ (c) $t_{12} = 52, t_{16} = 80$

(d) $t_4 = 12, t_{21} = 20.5$ (e) $t_5 = 52, t_{17} = 124$ (f) $t_3 = 24, t_{19} = -88$

18. **Thinking, Inquiry, Problem Solving:** Suppose you earn 25¢ on September 1, 50¢ on September 2, 75¢ on September 3, and so on. How much money will you earn by the end of the month?

19. **Check Your Understanding**

(a) Determine t_n and t_{25} for the sequence 17, 23, 29, 35, … .

(b) List the properties that make a sequence arithmetic.

C

20. A water well-drilling company charges $40 for drilling the first metre, $44.50 for the second metre, $49 for the third metre, and so on. How much would the company charge to drill a 10-m well?

21. Show that the sequence $c, \frac{c+d}{2}, d$ is arithmetic.

22. Find the general term of the sequence $5x - 3, 3x - 4, x - 5, -x - 6, \ldots$.

23. How many multiples of 3 are between 40 and 1000?

The Chapter Problem—Controlling Non-Native Plant Populations

Apply what you learned to answer the following questions about the Chapter Problem on page 12.

CP11. Is the plant sequence you found in CP9 arithmetic? Explain.
CP12. Is the seed sequence you found in CP10 arithmetic? Explain.

Geometric Sequences 1.7

Part 1: Doubling

Many microorganisms are introduced into our bodies through everyday activities, breathing, eating, and drinking water. Some microorganisms are beneficial and some are not.

One such bacterium is *Escherichia Coli* or *E. coli*. *E. coli* bacteria live in the intestine and help your body to absorb certain vitamins. However, one strain of *E. coli* bacteria is particularly harmful. The rate at which bacteria cells divide and reproduce determines the time it takes for the bacteria to affect your health.

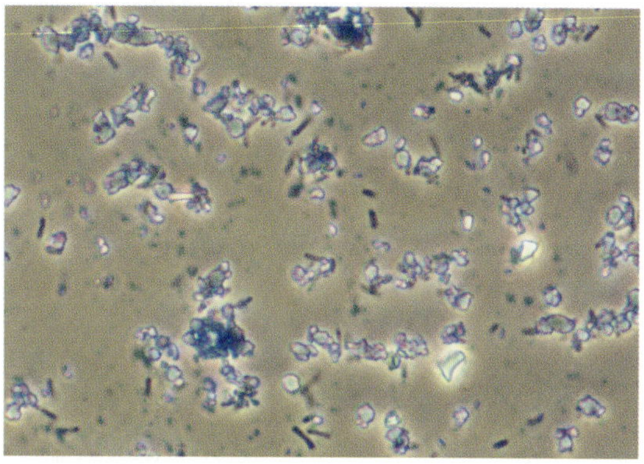

***Escherichia coli* bacteria**

E. coli bacteria are very small. About 50 cells lined up end to end would be roughly as thick as a strand of your hair. As few as 100 cells would cause infection. Each bacterium divides in two about every one-half hour to one hour.

Think, Do, Discuss

1. Assume that 100 *E. coli* bacteria double in number every hour. Copy and complete the table to show how many bacteria are present after each hour for 8 h.

Time (h)	0	1	2	3	4	5	6	7	8
Number of Bacteria	100	200							

2. Write the number of bacteria after each hour for 8 h as a sequence. The first term is 100.

3. Determine the first differences between pairs of consecutive terms of this sequence. Interpret the first differences.

4. Graph this sequence. Describe the rate of change between pairs of consecutive terms.

5. Divide each term, except the first, by the previous term. What do you notice? What is the significance of this value?

6. Rewrite each term of the sequence that you wrote in step 2 as an expression of the original 100 bacteria and the value that you calculated in step 5.

7. Write the general term for this sequence.

8. Determine the number of bacteria after 24 h.

Part 2: Half-life

Half-life is the time required for a radioactive material to decay to one-half of its original mass. Uranium-238, used in nuclear reactors, has a very long half-life, 4.5×10^9 years. Only a small fraction of uranium-238 has decayed since the Earth was formed. However, carbon-11, used in medical applications, has a half-life of only 20 min.

Pickering Nuclear Reactor in Ontario

Think, Do, Discuss

1. After a medical procedure, Harry's body has absorbed 100 mg of carbon-11. Copy and complete the table to show the mass of carbon-11 after each 20-min interval for 3 h.

20-Min Interval	0	1	2	3	4	5	6	7	8	9
Mass of Carbon-11 (mg)	100	50								

2. Write the mass of carbon-11 after each 20-min interval for 3 h as a sequence. The first term is 100.
3. Determine the first differences between pairs of consecutive terms of this sequence. Interpret the first differences.
4. Graph this sequence. Describe the rate of change between pairs of consecutive terms.
5. Divide each term, except the first, by the previous term. What do you notice? What is the significance of this value?
6. Rewrite each term of the sequence that you wrote in step 2 as an expression of the original 100 mg and the value that you calculated in step 5.
7. Write the general term for this sequence.
8. Determine the mass of carbon-11 remaining after 24 h.

Focus 1.7

Key Ideas

- In a **geometric sequence**, the ratio of any term, except the first one, to the previous term, is constant for all pairs of consecutive terms. This constant or **common ratio** is represented by r.

  In the general geometric sequence $t_1, t_2, t_3, t_4, \ldots, t_n, \ldots, r = \frac{t_n}{t_{n-1}}$.

  Here are some examples of geometric sequences.

  $4, 8, 16, 32, 64, \ldots$, and $r = 2$

  $-3, 6, -12, 24, -48, \ldots$, and $r = -2$

  $100, 10, 1, 0.1, 0.01, \ldots$, and $r = 0.1$

  $\frac{1}{2}, \frac{1}{8}, \frac{1}{32}, 1, 128, \ldots$, and $r = \frac{1}{4}$

- The general term of a geometric sequence is

  $t_n = ar^{n-1}$

  where t_n is the nth term,
  a is the first term, or t_1, and
  r is the common ratio.

- If $r > 1$, then the terms increase. If $0 < r < 1$, then the terms decrease.
- The relationship between n and t_n of any geometric sequence is nonlinear.

Example 1

For each sequence,

i. determine if it is arithmetic, geometric, or neither
ii. determine the next three terms
iii. find the general term and use it to determine t_{10}
iv. graph the sequence

(a) 4, 12, 36, 108, … (b) 100, 98, 96, 94, …

Solution

(a) i. Starting with the second term, divide each term by the term before it.

$$\frac{12}{4} = 3, \frac{36}{12} = 3, \frac{108}{36} = 3$$

This sequence is geometric and has a common ratio of 3.

ii. To find the next three terms, multiply each new term by the common ratio.

$$108 \times 3 = 324, 324 \times 3 = 972, \text{and } 972 \times 3 = 2916$$

The next three terms are 324, 972, and 2916.

iii. The general term is $t_n = ar^{n-1}$, with $a = 4$ and $r = 3$.

$$t_n = 4(3)^{n-1}$$

$$\begin{aligned} t_{10} &= 4(3)^{10-1} \\ &= 4(3)^9 \\ &= 78\,732 \end{aligned}$$

iv.

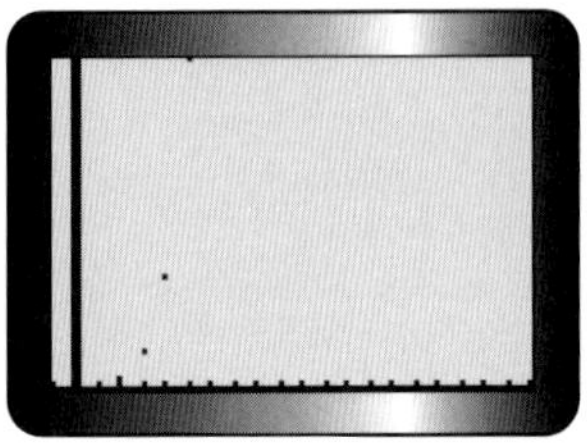

(b) **i.** Starting with the second term, subtract each term from the previous term.

$$98 - 100 = -2,\ 96 - 98 = -2,\ 94 - 96 = -2$$

This sequence is arithmetic and has a common difference of -2.

ii. To find the next three terms, add the common difference to each new term.

$$94 + (-2) = 92,\ 92 + (-2) = 90,\ 90 + (-2) = 88$$

The next three terms are 92, 90, and 88.

iii. The general term is $t_n = a + (n - 1)d$, with $a = 100$ and $d = -2$.

$$\begin{aligned} t_n &= 100 + (n - 1)(-2) \\ &= 100 - 2n + 2 \\ &= 102 - 2n \end{aligned}$$

$$\begin{aligned} t_{10} &= 102 - 2(10) \\ &= 82 \end{aligned}$$

iv.

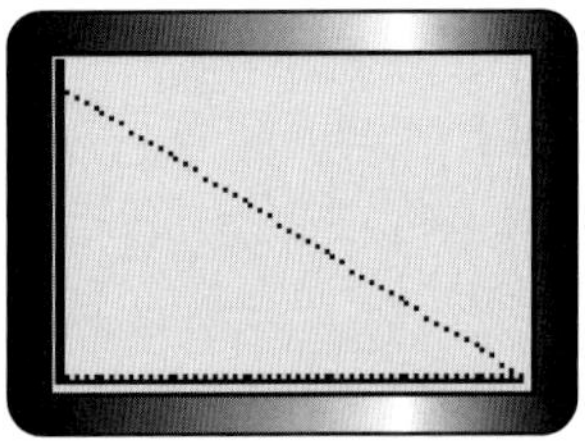

Example 2

A new provincial lottery offers two choices to the grand prize winner. Option A is a lump-sum payment of \$25 000 000. Option B is a yearly payment on the winner's birthday that starts with \$1 and doubles each year thereafter for the rest of the winner's life. Suppose you win this lottery on your 20th birthday. Which option would you choose?

Solution

The payments under option B are \$1, \$2, \$4, \$8, \$16, … .
This sequence is geometric, with $a = 1$ and $r = 2$.

$$t_n = ar^{n-1}$$
$$t_n = 1(2)^{n-1}$$

Use a table to examine the pattern in more detail.

r (year)	t_n (payment, \$)	*r* (year)	t_n (payment, \$)	*r* (year)	t_n (payment, \$)
1	1	10	512	19	262 144
2	2	11	1 024	20	524 288
3	4	12	2 048	21	1 048 576
4	8	13	4 096	22	2 097 152
5	16	14	8 192	23	4 194 304
6	32	15	16 384	24	8 388 608
7	64	16	32 768	25	16 777 216
8	128	17	65 536	26	33 554 432
9	256	18	131 072	27	67 108 864

Clearly, at the end of 27 years, option B surpasses option A in winnings. Keep in mind that the total earnings under option B is the sum of all the terms in the sequence. Consider the payment on the 60th birthday by itself.

$$\begin{aligned} t_{60} &= 1(2)^{60-20-1} \\ &= 1(2)^{39} \\ &= 5.497\ 558\ 139 \times 10^{11} \end{aligned}$$

The payment on the 60th birthday would be \$549 755 813 900.

Example 3

Since 1967, the average annual salary of major league baseball players has risen by about 17% each year. In 1967, the average annual salary was \$19 000.

(a) Predict the average annual salary of a baseball player in 2007.

(b) Verify your answer using graphing technology.

Solution

(a) Each year, the new average annual salary is the salary of the previous year, plus an increase of 17% of that amount, or 117% of the previous salary.

For 1968, 19 000 × 1.17 = 22 230
For 1969, 22 230 × 1.17 = 26 009.10

Year	1967	1968	1969	1970	1971	1972
Average Salary ($)	19 000	22 230	26 009.10	30 430.65	35 603.86	41 656.51

The average salary each year is a geometric sequence, where $a = 19\ 000$ and $r = 1.17$. For a geometric sequence, $t_n = ar^{n-1}$. In this case, $t_n = 19\ 000(1.17)^{n-1}$ and $n = 1$ corresponds to 1967. Therefore, in 2007,

$$\begin{aligned} n &= 2007 - (1967 - 1) \\ &= 41 \end{aligned}$$

$$\begin{aligned} t_{41} &= 19\ 000(1.17)^{41-1} \\ &= 19\ 000(533.868\ 712\ 7) \\ &= 10\ 143\ 505.54 \end{aligned}$$

The model predicts an average annual salary of $10 143 505.54 in 2007.

(b) Using the TI-83 Plus calculator, select the sequence graphing mode ([MODE]) and enter the general term in the sequence editor ([Y=]). Adjust the window ([WINDOW]) and [GRAPH]. [TRACE] to find the value of the 41st term.

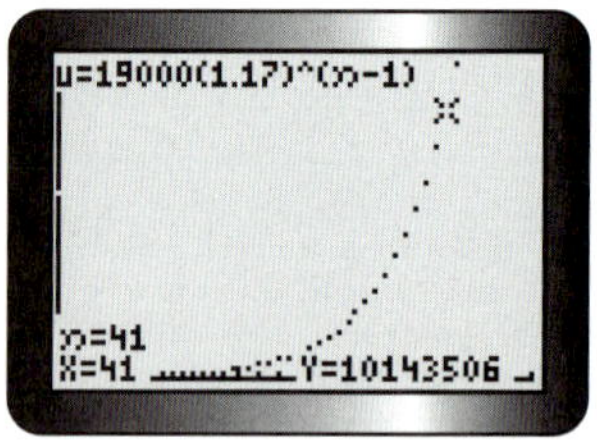

Example 4

The half-life of iodine-131 is eight days.

(a) What will remain of 12 mg of iodine-131 after 112 days?

(b) Verify your answer using graphing technology.

Solution

(a)

Eight-Day Interval	0	1	2	3
Mass Remaining (mg)	12	12 × 0.5 = 6	6 × 0.5 = 3	3 × 0.5 = 1.5

The mass remaining after each interval forms the sequence 12, 6, 3, 1.5, … . This sequence is geometric, with $a = 12$ and $r = 0.5$. For a geometric sequence, $t_n = ar^{n-1}$. In this case, $t_n = 12(0.5)^{n-1}$ and $n = 1$ corresponds to the initial mass of 12 mg. In 112 days, the number of eight-day intervals is $\frac{112}{8}$ or 14. Since $t_1 = 12$, then t_{15} is the mass remaining after the 14th interval.

$$
\begin{aligned}
t_{15} &= 12(0.5)^{15-1} \\
&= 12(0.000\ 061\ 035) \\
&= 0.000\ 732\ 42
\end{aligned}
$$

After 112 days, 0.000 732 42 mg of iodine-131 will remain.

(b) Using the TI-83 Plus calculator, select the sequence graphing mode ([MODE]) and enter the general term in the sequence editor ([Y=]). Adjust the window ([WINDOW]) and [GRAPH]. [TRACE] to find the value of the 15th term.

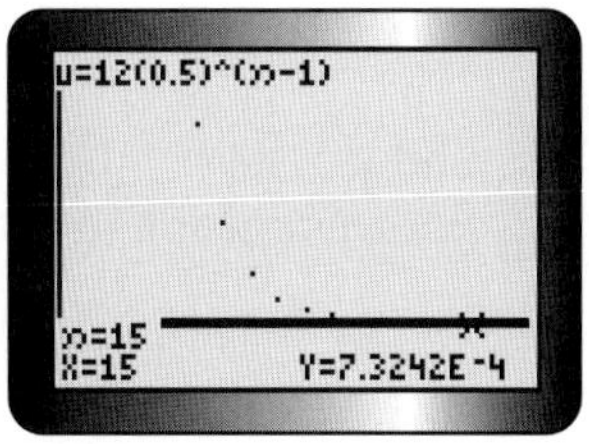

Practise, Apply, Solve 1.7

A

1. i. Identify which sequences are geometric.
ii. For each geometric sequence, determine the common ratio.

(a) 4, 12, 36, 108, … (b) −5, 15, −45, 135, … (c) 17, 24, 31, 38, …

(d) 2, 8, 32, 128, … (e) 56, 45, 34, 23, … (f) $\frac{1}{4}, \frac{1}{8}, \frac{1}{16}, \frac{1}{32}, \ldots$

2. i. Determine which general terms represent geometric sequences.
ii. Determine the common ratio of each geometric sequence.

(a) $t_n = 3^{n-1}$ (b) $t_n = (n + 3)(n - 5)$ (c) $t_n = -2n^2 - 5n + 1$

(d) $t_n = 2(6)^{n+1}$ (e) $t_n = \frac{1}{3n - 2}$ (f) $t_n = 5(-1)^n$

3. For each of the following geometric sequences, determine
i. the common ratio ii. the general term iii. t_8

(a) 3, 15, 75, 375, … (b) −12, −144, −1728, −20 736, …

(c) 4, 2, 1, $\frac{1}{2}$, … (d) 6, −12, 24, −48, …

(e) 0.2, 0.02, 0.002, 0.0002, … (f) 5, 5, 5, 5, …

4. Determine the recursive formula for each sequence in question 3.

5. Find the general term of the geometric sequence in which
(a) the first term is 3 and the common ratio is 7
(b) the first term is −4 and the common ratio is $-\frac{1}{4}$
(c) the first term is 125 and the common ratio is −0.2
(d) the first term is −6 and the common ratio is 3

6. **i.** Determine whether each sequence is arithmetic, geometric, or neither.
ii. If a sequence is arithmetic or geometric, then find t_n.

(a) 30, 40, 50, 60, …

(b) 4, 16, 64, 256, …

(c) 2, 6, 7, 21, 22, …

(d) 30, 6, 1.2, 0.24, …

(e) 145, 130, 115, 100, …

(f) 1.21, 1.44, 1.69, 1.96, …

B

7. For each geometric sequence, find

(a) t_n, the general term

(b) t_{10}

i.

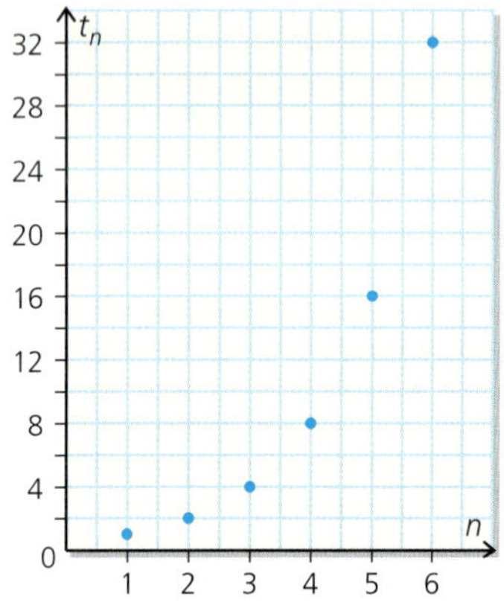

ii.

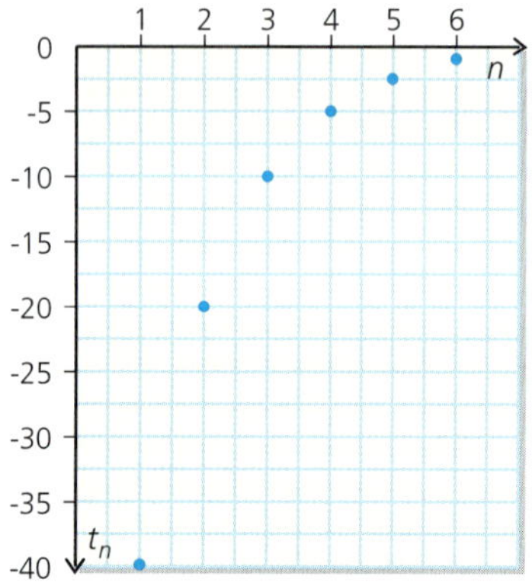

iii.

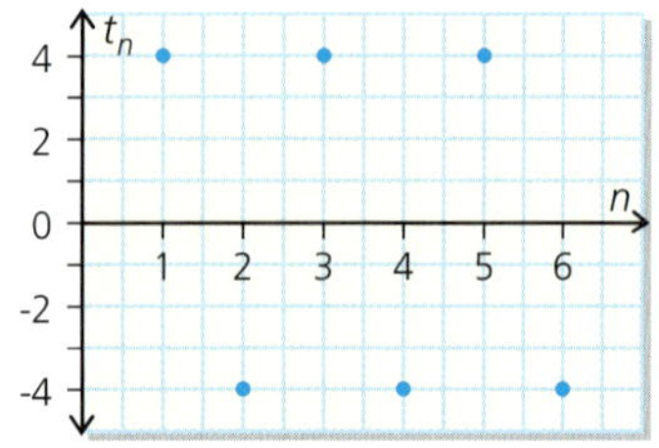

iv.

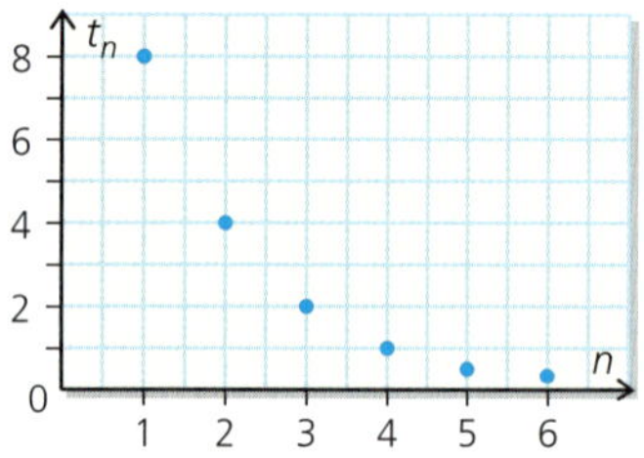

8. Graph each sequence.

(a) $t_n = 5^{n-1}$

(b) $t_n = -2(3)^{n-1}$

(c) $t_n = 10\left(\frac{1}{2}\right)^n$

(d) $t_n = 3(-2)^{n+1}$

(e) $t_n = 4(5)^{n+2}$

(f) $t_n = (2)^{2n}$

(g) $t_n = 0.5(4)^{n-2}$

(h) $t_n = -(10)^{n+1}$

9. **Knowledge and Understanding:** Consider the sequence $1, -\frac{2}{3}, \frac{4}{9}, -\frac{8}{27}, \ldots$.

(a) Determine the general term of this sequence.

(b) Find t_8.

10. Suki bought a car for \$28 500 and its value depreciates by 12% each year.

(a) Write the sequence of the car's value at the end of each year for the next five years. Start with the purchase price.

(b) Determine the general term of this sequence.

(c) Determine the car's value at the end of the eighth year.

11. Todd accepts a job with a graphic design firm. His starting salary is \$34 000, and each year he will receive an annual increase of 2.5%.

(a) Write the sequence of his annual salary for the next five years. Start with Todd's initial salary.

(b) Determine the general term of this sequence.

(c) Determine Todd's annual salary at the end of his tenth year.

12. A rare coin is bought at an antique auction in 1998 for \$500. Each year, its value appreciates by 6% of its purchase price. Determine the coin's value in 2010.

13. The half-life of a radioactive substance is 10 min. How much of 500 g of this substance will remain after 8 h?

14. A colony of bacteria doubles in number every 20 min. The initial population of the colony is 20 bacteria. How many bacteria are there after 4 h?

15. Since 1900, the world's population has grown at an average rate of 1.35% per year. In 1900, the world's population was 1.65 billion.

(a) Determine the general term of the sequence that models this relationship.

(b) Use the model to predict the world's population in 2010.

16. **Communication:** A printing company buys a photocopying machine for \$250 000. The machine's value depreciates at a rate of 25% per year. Explain how this situation involves a geometric sequence.

17. Examine each stage.

(a) Find the first four terms of the sequence that represents the number of shaded triangles at each stage.

(b) How many shaded triangles does stage 8 have?

(c) Find the first four terms of the sequence that represents the perimeter of the shaded figure at each stage. Use the fact that the largest triangle is equilateral, and each side is one unit long.

(d) Determine the perimeter of the shaded figure in stage 7.

18. Write the recursive formula for any geometric sequence. Let a be the first term and r be the common ratio.

19. **Application:** The value of a new sports utility vehicle depreciates at a rate of 8% per year. If the vehicle was bought for \$45 000, when is it worth less than 40% of its original value?

20. For each geometric sequence, find a, r, and t_n.

(a) $t_6 = -4, t_7 = -20$ (b) $t_2 = 8, t_4 = 32$ (c) $t_4 = 54, t_7 = 1458$

21. **Check Your Understanding**

(a) Determine t_n and t_{10} for the sequence 4, 28, 196, 1372, … .

(b) The third and fourth terms of a geometric sequence are 12 and 4, respectively. Determine the first and second terms. Explain your answer.

C

22. Write the first five terms of a sequence that is both arithmetic and geometric.

23. **Thinking, Inquiry, Problem Solving:** A square measures 12 cm by 12 cm. Connect the midpoints of the square to make a smaller square and four triangles. Shade one triangle. Repeat these steps five more times. At this stage, determine the total area of the shaded region.

24. The first three terms of the sequence 8, a, b, 36 form an arithmetic sequence, but the last three terms form a geometric sequence. Find all the possible values of a and b.

25. Find the tenth term of the sequence $\frac{a^2}{b}, -a, b, \frac{-b^2}{a}, \ldots$.

The Chapter Problem—Controlling Non-Native Plant Populations

In this section, you have studied geometric sequences. Apply what you have learned to answer these questions about the Chapter Problem on page 12.

CP13. Are either of the plant or seed sequences you found in CP9 and CP10 geometric? Explain.

CP14. Find the general term for the plant sequence.

CP15. Find the general term for the seed sequence.

Compound Interest: Amount and Present Value

1.8

Part 1: Investigating Compound Interest

Recall that in Part 2 of section 1.6, Juan's grandparents opened a simple interest savings account for him when he was born. On the same day, Juan's parents also open a savings account for him. Juan's father deposits $10 000 in a savings account with an annual interest rate of 5%. The account pays **compound interest** on the balance at the end of each year.

At the end of the first year, interest is calculated on the principal and added to the balance in the account. The balance in the account at the beginning of the second period is the principal, plus the interest. At the end of the second year, interest is again calculated on the balance in the account, but, unlike simple interest, the interest is calculated on the principal, **plus** interest. In this way, the interest is compounded.

If there are no other deposits, what will be the balance in the account on Juan's 18th birthday?

Think, Do, Discuss

1. Calculate the interest earned at the end of the first year in the account opened by his parents.
2. Determine the balance in the account on Juan's first birthday.
3. Calculate the interest earned at the end of the second year.
4. Determine the balance in the account on Juan's second birthday.
5. Copy and complete the table on the next page. You could complete this table by hand, use a spreadsheet, or use the sequence editor of the TI-83 Plus calculator ([2nd] [LIST] [ENTER]).

Year	Balance at the Start of the Year ($)	Interest ($)	Balance at the End of the Year ($)
0	10 000		
1			
2			
⋮			
17			
18			

6. What is the balance in the account on Juan's 18th birthday? How much of this amount is interest?

7. Write the sequence that represents the balance in the account from the 1st birthday to the 18th birthday.

8. Do the terms of this sequence increase by a constant value?

9. Graph this sequence.

10. Does the amount of money in the account grow at a linear or nonlinear rate? Explain.

11. Using the sequence you found in step 7, divide each term by the previous term. What do you notice?

12. What type of sequence have you created?

13. Write each term of the sequence in step 7 as an expression of the value in step 11 and the original principal of $10 000.

14. Let n be a natural number that represents the number of years. Determine the general term of this sequence.

15. Both Juan's parents and grandparents opened savings accounts, each with $10 000. Explain why the balance in the compound interest account is much greater than the balance in the simple interest account on Juan's 18th birthday.

16. If Juan left the money in the compound interest account until he retired at 65, what would be the balance in the account on his 65th birthday?

17. Elena deposits $5000 in an account that earns compound interest. The annual interest rate is 8%. Write the sequence that represents the yearly balance in the account each year for ten years. Determine the general term of this sequence.

Part 2: Defining Compound Interest—Amount

In Part 1 of this section, you calculated the interest for each year. Compound interest can also be calculated for these periods:

- **semiannually**: 2 times per year, at the end of every six months
- **quarterly**: 4 times per year, at the end of every three months
- **monthly**: 12 times per year, at the end of each month

Each of these periods, for example, six months, three months, or one month, is called a **conversion period**. The interest rate for each conversion period is a fraction of the annual interest rate, r.

$$i = \frac{r}{\text{number of conversion periods per year}}$$

When solving a compound interest problem, draw a **time line** to organize information. A time line is simply a line divided into equal sections. Each section represents a conversion period. Julie invests \$500 for three years at 10%/a, compounded quarterly.

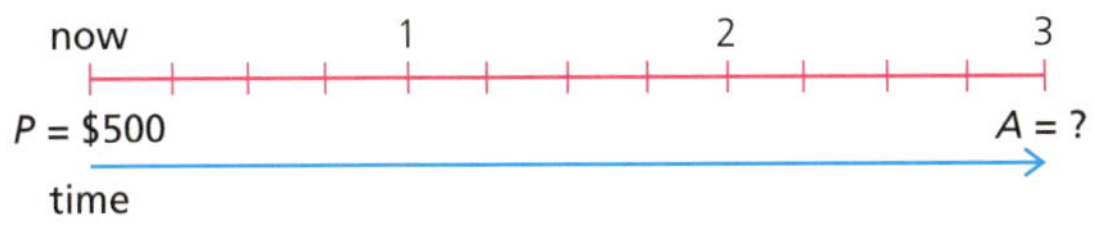

The left end point represents the present, "now," and the right end point represents the end of the period, the end of the third year. The principal is on the left and the amount, to which the investment will grow, is on the right. There are four conversion periods in each year, and the time line has 12 sections.

For a long period, for example, 20 years, you need draw only part of the line, but include a break in the line, as shown. Joe invests \$1000 for 20 years at 10%/a, compounded semiannually. Here is the time line, where each year is divided into two equal sections and there is a break between year 2 and year 19.

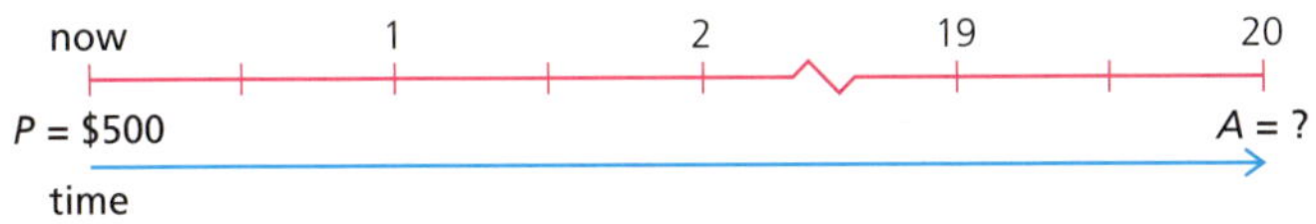

Examining the Amount Under Different Conditions

You have inherited \$10 000 and have decided to invest the total inheritance in a savings account that pays 12%/a. You wish to invest the money for ten years, but you have four different options:

- **Option A:** Interest is compounded annually.
- **Option B:** Interest is compounded semiannually.
- **Option C:** Interest is compounded quarterly.
- **Option D:** Interest is compounded monthly.

Think, Do, Discuss

Steps 1 to 7 relate to option A.

1. How often is interest paid each year? Draw a time line.
2. How long is each conversion period?
3. What is the interest rate for each conversion period?
4. How many times will interest be paid for this investment?
5. Write the sequence that represents the balance in the account at the end of each conversion period.
6. By what factor does each new term increase? Determine the general term of this sequence.
7. Determine the balance in the account at the end of ten years.
8. Repeat steps 1 to 7 for options B, C, and D.
9. Graph each option on the same set of axes. Plot only the points that correspond to the balances in the account **at the end of each year** for each option.
10. Which option offers the best return on your initial investment? Explain your answer.

Part 3: Defining Compound Interest—Present Value

Marcus has just graduated from college, and he plans to buy a new car three years from now. He will need \$24 000 at that time. How much money must he invest today at 6%/a, compounded annually, to save the required amount?

Think, Do, Discuss

1. In this problem, which value is unknown, the future amount or the principal?
2. Draw a time line. Where should \$24 000 be placed on the time line?
3. Substitute the known values in the formula $A = P(1 + i)^n$ and solve for P.
4. What sum of money must Marcus invest today to have \$24 000 three years from now?
5. Express the formula $A = P(1 + i)^n$ in terms of P.
6. Use what you know about negative exponents to rewrite the formula for P so that n is negative.

Focus 1.8

Key Ideas

- In this section, interest is added or compounded to the principal before the interest for the next period is calculated. The formula for **compound interest** is

$$A = P(1 + i)^n$$

where A is the amount, the **future value** of an investment, or a loan,
P is the original principal invested or borrowed,
i is the interest rate per conversion period, and
n is the number of conversion periods.

- You can calculate compound interest in several ways:

annually	once per year	i = annual interest rate	n = number of years
semiannually	2 times per year	i = annual interest rate ÷ 2	n = number of years × 2
quarterly	4 times per year	i = annual interest rate ÷ 4	n = number of years × 4
monthly	12 times per year	i = annual interest rate ÷ 12	n = number of years × 12

- The formula for compound interest is similar to the general term of a geometric sequence. Compare $A = P(1 + i)^n$ to $t_n = ar^{n-1}$.
- The amount that must be invested now, P, that will grow to a specific amount, A, in the future is called the **present value**. The formula for present value is

$$P = \frac{A}{(1 + i)^n} \text{ or } P = A(1 + i)^{-n}$$

where P is the present value,
A is the amount that the investment will grow to in the future,
i is the interest rate for each conversion period, and
n is the total number of conversion periods.

- A time line is useful for solving a compound interest problem, because you can use it to organize information and clarify whether the problem deals with present value or future value (amount).

Example 1

Martina invests \$5000 in a savings account that pays 5.25%/a, compounded annually. She does not make another deposit.

(a) Create the geometric sequence of the year-end balances in the account.

(b) Determine the amount in the account after 20 years.

Algebraic Solution

(a) $r = 5.25\%$ or 0.0525 and $P = \$5000$

The amount at the end of the first year is

$$\begin{aligned} A &= P + I \\ &= P + Prt \\ &= P(1 + rt) \end{aligned}$$

$$\begin{aligned} A &= 5000(1 + 0.0525 \times 1) \\ &= 5000(1.0525)^1 \\ &= 5262.50 \end{aligned}$$

This amount becomes the new principal at the beginning of the second year and earns interest at the same rate.

The amount at the end of the second year is

$$\begin{aligned} A &= 5262.50(1.0525) \text{ or } 5000(1.0525)^2 \\ &= 5538.78 \end{aligned}$$

The amount at the end of the third year is

$$\begin{aligned} A &= 5538.78(1.0525) \text{ or } 5000(1.0525)^3 \\ &= 5829.57 \end{aligned}$$

The general term is

$$t_n = 5000(1.0525)^n$$

The terms are $5000(1.0525)^1, 5000(1.0525)^2, 5000(1.0525)^3, \ldots$.
Therefore, the sequence is 5262.50, 5538.78, 5829.57, … .

(b) Draw a time line.

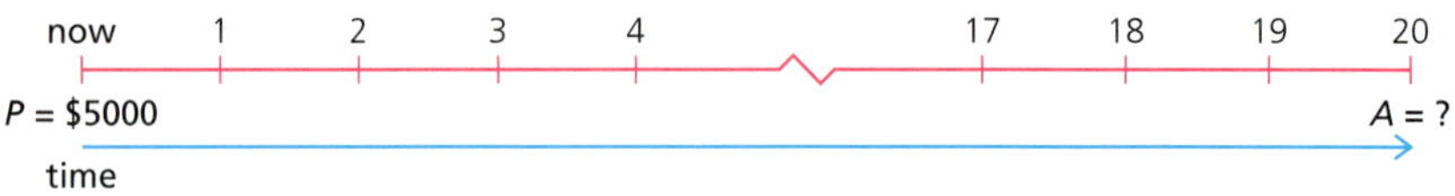

$A = P(1 + i)^n$, where $P = \$5000$, $i = 5.25\%$ or 0.0525, and $n = 20$

$$\begin{aligned} A &= 5000(1 + 0.0525)^{20} \\ &= 5000(1.0525)^{20} \\ &= 13\,912.72 \end{aligned}$$

At the end of the 20th year, there will be \$13 912.72 in the account.

Spreadsheet Solution

(a) Enter the headings in cells A1 to D1 and enter the values in cells A2 and B2, as shown. Enter the formulas, as shown, in cells A3, B3, C3, and D3.

	A	B	C	D
1	Year	Balance at the start of the year	Interest	Balance at the end of the year
2	1	$5,000	=0.0525*B2	=B2+C2
3	=A2+1	=D2	=0.0525*B3	=B3+C3
4				
5				

Select cells A3 to D5 and use **Fill Down**. Note: You may choose to format the cells differently.

	A	B	C	D
1	Year	Balance at the start of the year	Interest	Balance at the end of the year
2	1	$5,000.00	$262.50	$5,262.50
3	2	$5,262.50	$276.28	$5,538.78
4	3	$5,538.78	$290.79	$5,829.57
5	4	$5,829.57	$306.05	$6,135.62

The values in column B represent the terms of the sequence.
The sequence is 5262.50, 5538.78, 5829.57, … .

(b) Expand the spreadsheet in (a).

Select cells A5 to D21 and **Fill Down**.

	A	B	C	D
1	Year	Balance at the start of the year	Interest	Balance at the end of the year
2	1	$5,000.00	$262.50	$5,262.50
3	2	$5,262.50	$276.28	$5,538.78
4	3	$5,538.78	$290.79	$5,829.57
5	4	$5,829.57	$306.05	$6,135.62
6	5	$6,135.62	$322.12	$6,457.74
7	6	$6,457.74	$339.03	$6,796.77
8	7	$6,796.77	$356.83	$7,153.60
9	8	$7,153.60	$375.56	$7,529.17
10	9	$7,529.17	$395.28	$7,924.45
11	10	$7,924.45	$416.03	$8,340.48
12	11	$8,340.48	$437.88	$8,778.36
13	12	$8,778.36	$460.86	$9,239.22
14	13	$9,239.22	$485.06	$9,724.28
15	14	$9,724.28	$510.52	$10,234.80
16	15	$10,234.80	$537.33	$10,772.13
17	16	$10,772.13	$565.54	$11,337.67
18	17	$11,337.67	$595.23	$11,932.89
19	18	$11,932.89	$626.48	$12,559.37
20	19	$12,559.37	$659.37	$13,218.74
21	20	$13,218.74	$693.98	$13,912.72

The value in cell D21 is the balance in the account at the end of the 20th year. (This is also the value at the beginning of the 21st year.)

Example 2

Natalie invests \$18 000 at 8%/a, compounded semiannually.

(a) Determine the value of the investment after four years.

(b) Find the interest at this time.

Solution

(a) The interest is compounded. Find the amount at the end of the fourth year. Draw a time line.

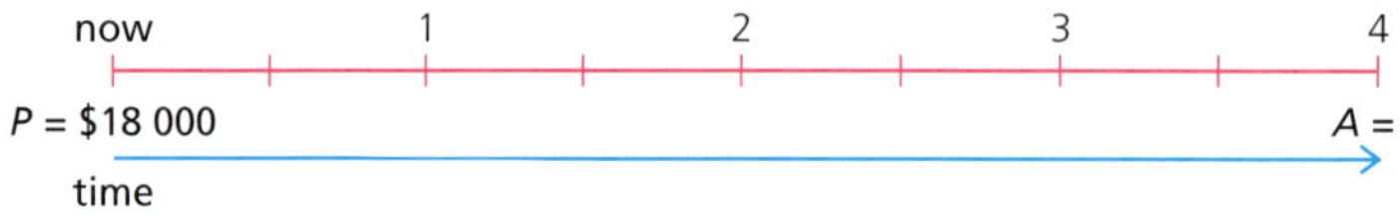

$A = P(1 + i)^n$, where $P = \$18\ 000$, $i = \frac{8\%}{2} = 4\%$ or 0.04, and $n = 2 \times 4 = 8$

$$\begin{aligned} A &= 18\ 000(1.04)^8 \\ &= 24\ 634.24 \end{aligned}$$

At the end of the fourth year, the value of the investment is \$24 634.24.

(b)
$$\begin{aligned} \text{interest} &= \text{amount} - \text{principal} \\ &= 24\ 634.24 - \$18\ 000 \\ &= 6634.24 \end{aligned}$$

The interest is \$6634.24.

Example 3

Alwynn invests \$500 in an account that earns 6%/a, compounded monthly. Peter also invests \$500 at the same time, but in a different account that earns 6%/a, simple interest.

(a) Determine the difference between their investments at the end of the fifth year.

(b) Using graphing technology, compare the balance in each account at the end of each month for ten years.

(c) Discuss how the two investments are different.

Solution

(a) For Alwynn's investment, $A = P(1 + i)^n$, where $P = \$500$, $i = \frac{6\%}{12} = 0.5\%$ or 0.005, and $n = 5 \times 12 = 60$.

$$\begin{aligned} A &= 500(1.005)^{60} \\ &= 674.43 \end{aligned}$$

For Peter's investment, $A = P + Prt$, where $P = \$500$, $r = 6\%$ or 0.06, and $t = 5$

$$A = \$500 + 500(0.06)(5)$$
$$= \$650$$

Alwynn's investment is worth more after five years.
The difference is \$674.43 − \$650 or \$24.43.

(b) To graph the monthly balances, determine the interest rate for each month, which is, for both cases, 0.005.

For Alwynn's investment, graph $t_n = 500(1.005)^n$.
For Peter's investment, graph $t_n = 500 + 500(0.005)n$.
In both cases, n is a natural number from 1 to 120 (120 months = 10 years).

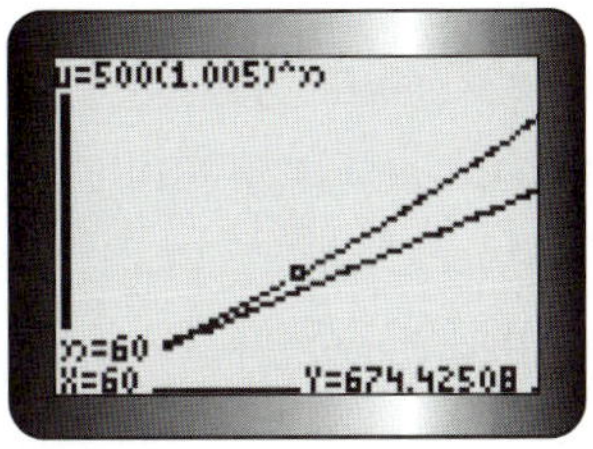

Alwynn's account

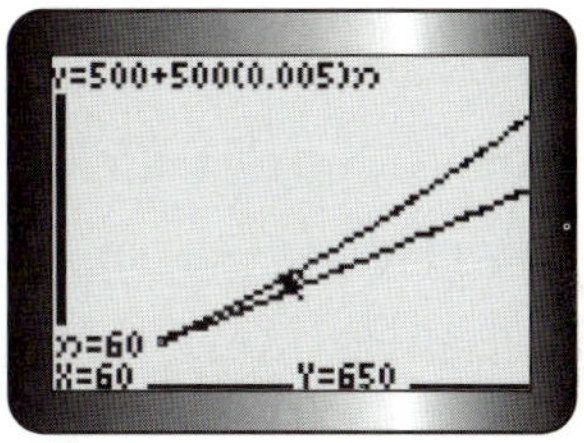

Peter's account

(c) From the graphs, Alwynn's investment is growing at a much faster rate than Peter's. As time passes, the difference between the monthly balances will increase. Peter's monthly balance grows at a constant rate, while Alwynn's monthly balance grows by increasing amounts from month to month.

Example 4

Determine the present value of an investment that will be worth \$5000 in ten years. The interest rate is 4.8%/a, compounded quarterly.

Solution

Draw a time line.

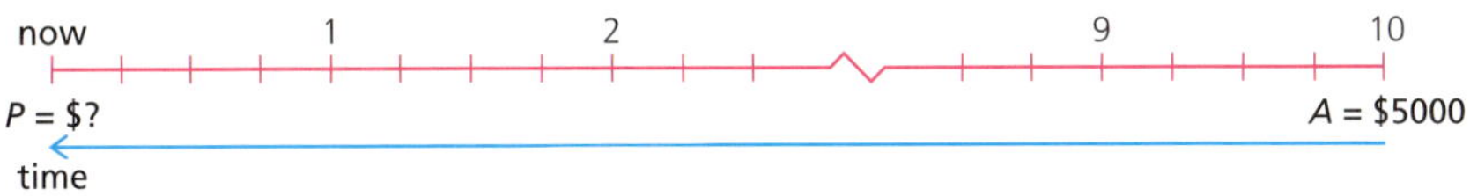

$P = A(1 + i)^{-n}$, where $A = \$5000$, $i = \frac{4.8\%}{4} = 1.2\%$ or 0.012, and $n = 10 \times 4 = 40$

$$P = \$5000(1.012)^{-40}$$
$$= \$5000(0.620\ 553\ 886\ 4)$$
$$= \$3102.77$$

Note: To calculate $(1.1012)^{-40}$ using the TI-83 Plus calculator, enter [1] [.] [1] [0] [1] [2] [^] [(-)] [4] [0]. For most scientific calculators, enter [1] [.] [1] [0] [1] [2] [y^x] [+/−] [4] [0] [=].

Practise, Apply, Solve 1.8

A

1. For each situation, determine

  i. the interest rate for each conversion period

  ii. the number of conversion periods

(a) an investment at 6%/a, compounded annually, for 5 years

(b) a loan at 8%/a, compounded semiannually, for 9 years

(c) a deposit at 4.4%/a, compounded quarterly, for 7 years

(d) a loan at 6%/a, compounded monthly, for 3 years

(e) an investment at 5%/a, compounded annually, for 5 years

(f) a deposit at 8.2%/a, compounded quarterly, for 16 months

(g) an investment at 4.5%/a, compounded semiannually, for 42 months

(h) a loan at 5.2%/a, compounded weekly, for 2 years

(i) a deposit at 5.475%, compounded daily, for 3 years

2. Evaluate to four decimal places.

(a) $(1.1)^{12}$ (b) $(1.05)^{-20}$ (c) $(1.025)^{36}$

(d) $(1.002)^{-45}$ (e) $200(1.04)^{24}$ (f) $5000(1.12)^{-5}$

(g) $6525(1.03)^{-22}$ (h) $10\ 000(1.006)^{36}$

3. In the formula $A = P(1 + i)^n$, what does each variable represent?

(a) A (b) P (c) i (d) n

4. For each situation, determine

  i. the amount **ii.** the interest earned

(a) $4000 borrowed for 4 years at 3%/a, compounded annually

(b) $7500 invested for 6 years at 6%/a, compounded monthly

(c) $15 000 borrowed for 5 years at 2.4%/a, compounded quarterly

(d) $28 200 invested for 10 years at 5.5%/a, compounded semiannually

(e) $850 financed for 1 year at 3.65%/a, compounded daily

(f) $2225 invested for 47 weeks at 5.2%/a, compounded weekly

5. For each situation, determine

  i. the present value of **ii.** the interest earned on

(a) an investment that will be worth $5000 in 3 years. The interest rate is 4%/a, compounded annually.

(b) an investment that will be worth $13 500 in 4 years. The interest rate is 6%/a, compounded monthly.

(c) a loan of $11 200 due in 5 years, with interest of 4.4%/a, compounded quarterly.

(d) an investment that will be worth \$128 500 in 8 years. The interest rate is 6.5%/a, compounded semiannually.

(e) a loan of \$850 due in 400 days, with interest of 5.84%/a, compounded daily.

(f) an investment that will be worth \$6225 in 100 weeks. The interest rate is 13%/a, compounded weekly.

6. Communication: Explain the difference between the amount of an investment and its present value. Provide an example.

B

7. Margaret can finance the purchase of a new \$949.99 refrigerator in two ways:

- **Plan A:** no money down, finance at 5%/a for 2 years
- **Plan B:** no money down, finance at 5%/a, compounded quarterly for 2 years

Which plan should she choose? Justify your answer.

8. Find the balance of the investment if \$1000 is compounded annually, at 5%/a, for

(a) 10 years. (b) 20 years. (c) 30 years.

9. About when will the amount with compound interest in question 8 be twice the original principal?

10. On the day his son is born, Mike wishes to invest a single sum of money that will grow to \$10 000 when his son turns 21. If Mike invests the money at 4%/a, compounded semiannually, how much must he invest today?

11. Knowledge and Understanding: How much will \$7500 be worth if it is invested now for 10 years at 6%/a, compounded annually? Verify your calculation by determining the present value of the investment.

12. Jeannie bought a \$1000 Canada Savings Bond at work. Each month, \$83.33 is deducted from her monthly paycheque to finance the bond. The bond pays 5%/a, compounded annually, and matures seven years from the date of the first payment. Determine the value of the bond.

13. Barry bought a boat two years ago and at that time paid a down payment of \$10 000 cash. Today he must make the second and final payment of \$7500, which includes the interest charge on the balance owing. Barry financed this purchase at 6.2%/a, compounded semiannually. Determine the purchase price of the boat.

14. Tiffany deposits \$9000 in an account that pays 10%/a, compounded quarterly. After three years, the interest rate changes to 9%/a, compounded semiannually. Calculate the value of her investment two years after this change.

15. Exactly six months ago, Lee borrowed \$2000 at 9%/a, compounded semiannually. Today he paid \$800, which includes principal and interest. What must he pay to close the debt at the end of the year (six months from now)?

16. Today Sigrid has $7424.83 in her bank account. For the last two years, her account has paid 6%/a, compounded monthly. Before then, her account paid 6%/a, compounded semiannually, for four years. If she made only one deposit six years ago, determine the original principal.

17. Explain, with an example, why compounded interest is comparable to a geometric sequence.

18. **Application:** On June 1, 1996, Anna invested $2000 in a money market fund that paid 6%/a, compounded monthly. After five years, her financial advisor moved the accumulated amount to a new account that paid 8%/a, compounded quarterly. Determine the balance in her account on January 1, 2008.

19. Bernie deposited $4000 into the "Accumulator Account" at his bank. During the first year, the account pays 4%/a, compounded quarterly. As an incentive to the bank's customers, this account's interest rate is increased by 0.2% each year. Calculate the balance in Bernie's account after three years.

20. On the day Sarah was born, her grandparents deposited $500 in a savings account that earns 4.8%/a, compounded monthly. They deposited the same amount on her 5th, 10th, and 15th birthdays. Determine the balance in the account on Sarah's 18th birthday.

21. **Thinking, Inquiry, Problem Solving:** On the first day of every month, Josh deposits $100 in an account that pays 4%/a, compounded monthly.

    (a) Determine the balance in his account after one year.

    (b) What single sum of money invested today, at the same interest rate, will accumulate to the same amount under Josh's original investment scheme?

22. **Check Your Understanding:** Matt invests $500 at 8%/a, compounded semiannually. On the same day, Justin invests $500 at 8%/a, compounded quarterly. Who will have more money after five years? Explain, including appropriate calculations.

C

23. Determine the interest rate that would cause an investment to double in seven years if interest is compounded annually.

24. If $500 was invested at 8%/a, compounded annually, in one account, and $600 was invested at 6%/a, compounded annually, in another account, then when would the amounts in both accounts be equal?

25. For compound interest, does doubling the interest rate cause the amount to double? Explain.

Rational Exponents 1.9

Part 1: Investigating Fractional Conversion Periods

You have seen that the principal of an investment earning compound interest grows exponentially, according to the relationship $A = P(1 + i)^n$. So far, you have calculated an amount at the end of a conversion period. Can the amount be determined for part of a conversion period?

Think, Do, Discuss

1. Marjorie invested \$1000 in a mutual fund that earns interest at 21%/a, compounded annually. Copy and complete the table. Determine the values of the investment at the beginning of the period, at the end of the first year, and at the end of the second year.

Year	0		1		2
Amount (\$)	$1000(1.21)^0 =$		$1000(1.21)^1 =$		$1000(1.21)^2 =$

2. Suppose Marjorie wishes to determine the value of her investment at the end of six months. How could six months be represented as a fraction of a year?
3. In your table, enter the year and the expression for the amount of the investment at the end of six months.
4. Use your calculator to evaluate $(1.21)^{\frac{1}{2}}$. What value do you get? Store this value in your calculator's memory.
5. Multiply 1000 by the number stored in memory. What does this value represent?
6. Multiply the product in step 5 by the value stored in memory. What does this value represent?
7. Multiply the value stored in memory by itself. To what exponent must $(1.21)^{\frac{1}{2}}$ be raised to obtain 1.21? Describe the mathematical relationship between $(1.21)^{\frac{1}{2}}$ and 1.21.
8. Suppose Marjorie wishes to determine the value of her investment at the end of 18 months. How could 18 months be represented as a fraction of a year?

9. In the table you copied from page 73, enter the year and the expression for the amount of the investment at the end of 18 months.

10. Evaluate 1000 × (number stored in memory) × (number stored in memory) × (number stored in memory). What does the product represent?

11. To what exponent must $(1.21)^{\frac{1}{2}}$ be raised to obtain $(1.21)^{\frac{3}{2}}$?

Describe the mathematical relationship between $(1.21)^{\frac{1}{2}}$ and $(1.21)^{\frac{3}{2}}$.

12. Anthony invests \$1000 at 9.2727%/a, compounded annually. Determine an expression that represents the amount of the investment at the end of 4 months, 8 months, and 12 months, respectively. Use your calculator to evaluate each expression.

13. Use your calculator to evaluate $(1.092\ 727)^{\frac{1}{3}}$. How many times must this result be multiplied by itself to get 1.092 727?

14. To what exponent must $(1.092\ 727)^{\frac{1}{3}}$ be raised to obtain 1.092 727?

Describe the mathematical relationship between $(1.092\ 727)^{\frac{1}{3}}$ and 1.092 727.

15. Determine the value of Anthony's investment after 32 months.

Part 2: Defining Rational Exponents

You know that an exponent can be an integer. For example,

$$3^2 = 3 \times 3 \\ = 9 \qquad 3^{-2} = \frac{1}{3 \times 3} \\ = \frac{1}{9} \qquad 3^0 = 1$$

But what does a rational-number exponent mean?

Defining $x^{\frac{1}{2}}$

Apply the exponent law for the power of a power.

$$\left(x^{\frac{1}{2}}\right)^2 = x^{\frac{1}{2} \times 2} \\ = x^1 \\ = x$$

Since $x^{\frac{1}{2}}$ squared equals x, then $x^{\frac{1}{2}}$ must be defined as $\sqrt{x}$.

Therefore,

$$\sqrt{x} \times \sqrt{x} = x \quad \text{and} \quad x^{\frac{1}{2}} \times x^{\frac{1}{2}} = x^{\frac{1}{2} + \frac{1}{2}} \\ = x$$

Therefore, $x^{\frac{1}{2}} = \sqrt{x}$. $\sqrt{x}$ is read "the square root of x."

Defining $x^{\frac{1}{3}}$

Again, apply the exponent law for the power of a power.

$$\begin{aligned}\left(x^{\frac{1}{3}}\right)^3 &= x^{\frac{1}{3}+\frac{1}{3}+\frac{1}{3}} \\ &= x^1 \\ &= x\end{aligned}$$

Since $x^{\frac{1}{3}}$ cubed equals x, then $x^{\frac{1}{3}}$ must be defined as $\sqrt[3]{x}$.

Therefore, $\sqrt[3]{x} \times \sqrt[3]{x} \times \sqrt[3]{x}$ and

$$\begin{aligned}x^{\frac{1}{3}} \times x^{\frac{1}{3}} \times x^{\frac{1}{3}} &= x^{\frac{1}{3}+\frac{1}{3}+\frac{1}{3}} \\ &= x\end{aligned}$$

Therefore, $x^{\frac{1}{3}} = \sqrt[3]{x}$. $\sqrt[3]{x}$ is read "the cube root of x."

Defining $x^{\frac{1}{n}}$

By a similar argument, if n is an integer and $n \neq 0$, then

$x^{\frac{1}{n}} = \sqrt[n]{x}$. $\sqrt[n]{x}$ is read "the nth root of x."

Example 1

Evaluate each power.

(a) $49^{\frac{1}{2}}$ (b) $(-64)^{\frac{1}{3}}$ (c) $8^{-\frac{1}{3}}$ (d) $\left(\frac{1}{36}\right)^{\frac{1}{2}}$

Solution

(a) $\begin{aligned}49^{\frac{1}{2}} &= \sqrt{49} \\ &= 7\end{aligned}$

(b) $\begin{aligned}(-64)^{\frac{1}{3}} &= \sqrt[3]{-64} \\ &= -4\end{aligned}$

(c) $\begin{aligned}8^{-\frac{1}{3}} &= \frac{1}{8^{\frac{1}{3}}} \\ &= \frac{1}{\sqrt[3]{8}} \\ &= \frac{1}{2}\end{aligned}$

(d) $\begin{aligned}\left(\frac{1}{36}\right)^{\frac{1}{2}} &= \sqrt{\frac{1}{36}} \\ &= \frac{1}{6}\end{aligned}$

Defining $x^{\frac{2}{3}}$

Use the exponent law for power of a power to express $x^{\frac{2}{3}}$ in two ways.

$$\begin{aligned}x^{\frac{2}{3}} &= x^{\frac{1}{3}\times 2} \\ &= (\sqrt[3]{x})^2\end{aligned} \qquad \text{or} \qquad \begin{aligned}x^{\frac{2}{3}} &= x^{2\times\frac{1}{3}} \\ &= \sqrt[3]{x^2}\end{aligned}$$

Defining $x^{\frac{m}{n}}$

If m and n are integers and $n \neq 0$, then $x^{\frac{m}{n}} = (\sqrt[n]{x})^m = \sqrt[n]{x^m}$.

Example 2

Evaluate.

(a) $8^{\frac{2}{3}}$ (b) $-25^{\frac{5}{2}}$ (c) $81^{-\frac{3}{4}}$

Solution

(a) $8^{\frac{2}{3}} = (\sqrt[3]{8})^2 = 2^2 = 4$

(b) $-25^{\frac{5}{2}} = -(\sqrt{25})^5 = -(5)^5 = -3125$

(c) $81^{-\frac{3}{4}} = \frac{1}{81^{\frac{3}{4}}} = \frac{1}{(\sqrt[4]{81})^3} = \frac{1}{(3)^3} = \frac{1}{27}$

Consolidate Your Understanding

1. What exponent can you use to represent the nth root of a number?

2. Use the exponent law for power of a power to express $27^{\frac{2}{3}}$ in two ways.

Focus 1.9

Key Ideas

- The rational exponent of $\frac{1}{n}$ indicates the nth root of the base. If $n > 1$ and $n \in N$, then $x^{\frac{1}{n}} = \sqrt[n]{x}$.
- If the numerator of a rational exponent is *not* 1 and if m and n are both positive integers, then
  - $x^{\frac{m}{n}} = \sqrt[n]{x^m}$ $x^{\frac{m}{n}}$ means the nth root of the mth power of x.
  - $x^{\frac{m}{n}} = (\sqrt[n]{x})^m$ $x^{\frac{m}{n}}$ means the mth power of the nth root of x.

  Note that $x^{\frac{m}{n}} = \sqrt[n]{x^m} = (\sqrt[n]{x})^m$.

- Evaluate negative rational exponents in the same way as you would evaluate negative integer exponents. If m and n are both positive integers, then

$$x^{-\frac{m}{n}} = \frac{1}{x^{\frac{m}{n}}} = \frac{1}{\sqrt[n]{x^m}} \text{ or } \frac{1}{(\sqrt[n]{x})^m}$$

- These symbols $\sqrt{}$, $\sqrt[3]{}$, $\sqrt[4]{}$, … are called radical signs. $\sqrt{x}$ and $\sqrt[4]{81}$ are examples of **radicals**.

Example 3

Evaluate each power.

(a) $16^{\frac{3}{4}}$

(b) $27^{-\frac{2}{3}}$

Solution

(a) $16^{\frac{3}{4}} = (\sqrt[4]{16})^3$
$= 2^3$
$= 8$

For most scientific calculators, enter
[1] [6] [y^x] [(] [3] [÷] [4] [)] [=].

(b) $27^{-\frac{2}{3}} = (\sqrt[3]{27})^{-2}$
$= 3^{-2}$
$= \frac{1}{3^2}$
$= \frac{1}{9}$

Using the TI-83 Plus calculator, enter
[2] [7] [^] [(-)] [(] [2] [÷] [3] [)] [ENTER]
[MATH] [1] [ENTER].

Example 4

Suppose \$4000 is invested at 5%/a, compounded annually. Determine the amount after 123 days.

Solution

Draw a time line to organize the information.

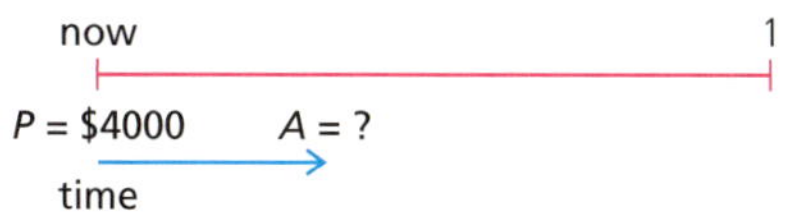

$A = P(1 + i)^n$, where $P = \$4000$, $i = 5\%$ or 0.05, and $n = \frac{123}{365}$.

$$A = 4000(1.05)^{\frac{123}{365}}$$
$$= 4000(1.016\ 577\ 524)$$
$$= 4066.31$$

The amount after 123 days is \$4066.31.

Example 5

Determine the present value of an investment that will be worth \$8000 in 6 years 8 months. The interest rate is 6%/a, compounded quarterly.

Solution

Draw a time line to organize the information.

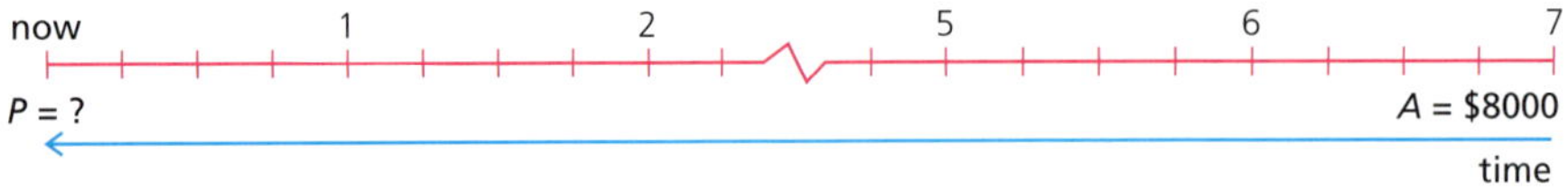

$P = A(1 + i)^{-n}$, where $A = \$8000$, $i = \frac{6\%}{4} = 1.5\%$ or 0.015, and $n = \frac{80}{3}$

$$\begin{aligned} P &= 8000(1.015)^{-\frac{80}{3}} \\ &= 8000(0.672\ 314\ 080\ 1) \\ &= 5378.51 \end{aligned}$$

The present value of the investment is \$5378.51.

Example 6

Barb put four new 1.5-V batteries in her portable radio. She went to bed listening to her favourite FM station and fell asleep with the radio on. The radio uses 2% of the charge each hour. If she turned the portable radio off 7.5 h after she had turned it on, determine the remaining charge in the batteries.

Solution

The radio uses 2% of the charge each hour, which means that 98% remains. Since the batteries are new, there are 6 V of charge initially.

Time (h)	0	1	2	3	4
Voltage (V)	6	6×0.98 $= 5.88$	5.88×0.98 $= 5.7624$	5.7624×0.9 $\doteq 5.6472$	5.6472×0.98 $\doteq 5.5343$

The remaining charge after each hour is a geometric sequence, with $a = 6$ and $r = 0.98$. The general term is $t_n = 6(0.98)^{n-1}$.
Evaluate t_n for $n = 8.5$ or $\frac{17}{2}$, since 7.5 h corresponds to $t_{8.5}$.

$$\begin{aligned} \text{remaining charge} &= 6(0.98)^{\frac{15}{2}} \\ &= 6(0.859\ 400\ 432\ 1) \\ &\doteq 5.156 \end{aligned}$$

When Barb turns off the radio, there are 5.156 V remaining in the batteries.

Practise, Apply, Solve 1.9

Answer questions 1 to 4 without the aid of a calculator.

A

1. Evaluate each expression.

(a) 4^3 (b) $(-6)^2$ (c) -3^2 (d) $(-9)^3$ (e) 15^0

(f) $\left(\frac{1}{2}\right)^3$ (g) $\left(\frac{2}{3}\right)^4$ (h) $\left(-\frac{2}{3}\right)^3$ (i) $\left(\frac{3}{4}\right)^{-2}$ (j) $\left(-\frac{1}{4}\right)^{-3}$

2. Evaluate each expression.

(a) $\sqrt{121}$ (b) $\sqrt[3]{8}$ (c) $\sqrt[4]{16}$ (d) $\sqrt[3]{125}$ (e) $\sqrt[5]{1024}$

3. Evaluate each expression.

(a) $4^{\frac{1}{2}}$ (b) $(-8)^{\frac{1}{3}}$ (c) $-81^{\frac{1}{4}}$ (d) $27^{\frac{1}{3}}$ (e) $125^{\frac{1}{3}}$

(f) $\left(\frac{1}{16}\right)^{\frac{1}{2}}$ (g) $(216)^{-\frac{1}{3}}$ (h) $(125)^{-\frac{1}{3}}$ (i) $\left(\frac{4}{9}\right)^{\frac{1}{2}}$ (j) $(16)^{-\frac{1}{4}}$

4. Evaluate each expression.

(a) $16^{\frac{3}{2}}$ (b) $8^{\frac{2}{3}}$ (c) $-16^{\frac{3}{4}}$ (d) $27^{\frac{4}{3}}$ (e) $81^{\frac{5}{4}}$

(f) $\left(\frac{1}{8}\right)^{\frac{2}{3}}$ (g) $(27)^{-\frac{2}{3}}$ (h) $(125)^{-\frac{4}{3}}$ (i) $\left(\frac{4}{25}\right)^{\frac{3}{2}}$ (j) $(32)^{-\frac{3}{5}}$

5. Evaluate to two decimal places. Use a calculator.

(a) $11^{\frac{1}{2}}$ (b) $(-24)^{\frac{1}{3}}$ (c) $-100^{\frac{1}{4}}$ (d) $50^{\frac{1}{3}}$ (e) $165^{\frac{1}{5}}$

(f) $(0.58)^{\frac{1}{2}}$ (g) $(1.05)^{-\frac{1}{3}}$ (h) $(200)^{-\frac{1}{3}}$ (i) $(12.65)^{\frac{1}{6}}$ (j) $(17.6)^{-\frac{1}{4}}$

6. Evaluate to two decimal places. Use a calculator.

(a) $25^{\frac{3}{2}}$ (b) $55^{\frac{2}{3}}$ (c) $1.25^{\frac{3}{4}}$ (d) $12.8^{\frac{2}{5}}$ (e) $167^{\frac{3}{4}}$

(f) $\left(\frac{5}{6}\right)^{\frac{1}{3}}$ (g) $(1034)^{-\frac{2}{3}}$ (h) $(44)^{-\frac{4}{3}}$ (i) $\left(\frac{16}{25}\right)^{\frac{3}{2}}$ (j) $(85)^{-\frac{2}{5}}$

B

7. Determine the amount in each situation.

(a) \$6000 borrowed for 4 months at 3%/a, compounded annually
(b) \$2500 invested for 1 year and 3 months at 4%/a, compounded semiannually
(c) \$12 300 borrowed for 22 months at 4.4%/a, compounded quarterly
(d) \$13 560 invested for 100 days at 6.5%/a, compounded annually
(e) \$3750 financed for 13 months at 3.65%/a, compounded semiannually
(f) \$6320 invested for 6 days at 5.2%/a, compounded weekly

8. Determine the present value

(a) of an investment that will be worth \$3000 in 300 days. The interest rate is 5%/a, compounded annually.

(b) of an investment that will be worth \$10 500 in 4 months. The interest rate is 6%/a, compounded semiannually.

(c) of a loan of \$7400 that will be due in 37 months. The interest rate is 6%/a, compounded quarterly.

(d) of a loan of \$100 000 that will be due in 2 years 5 months. The interest rate is 6.5%/a, compounded semiannually.

(e) of an investment that will be worth \$150 in 8 months. The interest rate is 8.2%/a, compounded annually.

(f) of an investment that will be worth \$3400 in 15 months. The interest rate is 11%/a, compounded semiannually.

9. A car depreciates in value according to the model $V = 25\ 000(0.85)^n$, where V is the value of the car at the end of the nth year.

(a) What was the purchase price of the car?

(b) At what annual rate is the value of the car depreciating?

(c) What is the value of the car at the end of 3 years?

(d) What is the value of the car at the end of 4 years 4 months?

10. A rare stamp, bought for \$500, increases in value by 6% each year.

(a) Determine an algebraic expression to model the stamp's value over time.

(b) Determine the stamp's value five years after it was bought.

(c) Determine the stamp's value 300 days after it was bought.

11. Carbon-16 has a half-life of 20 min.

(a) A sample of carbon-16 has an initial mass of 700 mg. Determine an algebraic expression that models the sample's mass over time.

(b) Determine the sample's mass after 3 h.

(c) What is the sample's mass after 5 min?

12. **Knowledge and Understanding:** To find the depreciation rate, r, of an item, use the formula for declining balances, $r = 1 - \left(\frac{S}{C}\right)^{\frac{1}{n}}$, where S is the salvage value, in dollars, C is the original cost, in dollars, and n is the useful life of the item, in years. Determine the depreciation rate for a truck that was purchased for \$125 000. The salvage value after three years is \$85 000.

13. Many soft drinks contain about 40 mg of caffeine in one 355-mL can. Every 5 h, the mass of caffeine in an adult's bloodstream reduces by half.

(a) Determine an algebraic expression that models the mass of caffeine in an adult's bloodstream over time.

(b) Determine the mass of caffeine in an adult's bloodstream 15 h after he or she drinks a can of cola.

(c) What is the mass of caffeine in an adult's bloodstream 2 h after he or she drinks a can of cola?

14. Simplify.

(a) $(25x^2)^{\frac{1}{2}}$ (b) $(-27x^3)^{\frac{1}{3}}$ (c) $(16x^4)^{\frac{1}{4}}$ (d) $(-16x^4)^{-\frac{1}{2}}$

(e) $(243x^5)^{\frac{1}{5}}$ (f) $[(x+2)^4]^{\frac{1}{4}}$ (g) $(-64x^8)^{\frac{1}{4}}$ (h) $[(2x+5)^7]^{\frac{1}{7}}$

15. Communication: Create a flow chart that gives the correct sequence of keystrokes to evaluate $(-125)^{-\frac{5}{3}}$ on a scientific calculator.

16. Simplify.

(a) $(25x^4)^{\frac{3}{2}}$ (b) $(27a^3b^3)^{\frac{2}{3}}$ (c) $\left(\frac{8x^3}{125}\right)^{\frac{2}{3}}$ (d) $\left(\frac{27}{64y^3}\right)^{\frac{2}{3}}$

17. Simplify.

(a) $(16x^2)^{-\frac{3}{2}}$ (b) $(49c^6)^{-\frac{3}{2}}$ (c) $\left(\frac{-8x^3}{216}\right)^{-\frac{1}{3}}$ (d) $\left(\frac{16}{81y^8}\right)^{-\frac{3}{4}}$

18. Application: Four years two months ago, Sami invested a sum of money at 5%/a, compounded semiannually. Today there is \$921.35 in the account. How much did Sami invest?

19. A new 1.5-V battery is put in a watch. The battery loses 1% of its charge each day, and the watch needs 0.001 V to run.

(a) Determine whether the watch will still run after 500 days.

(b) Determine the voltage in the battery after 3 h.

20. The length, L, of the longest board that can be carried horizontally around the right-angle corner of two intersecting hallways is $L = \left(a^{\frac{2}{3}} + b^{\frac{2}{3}}\right)^{\frac{3}{2}}$, where a and b represent the width, in centimetres, of the hallways. What is the longest piece of plywood a carpenter can carry horizontally around the corner of two intersecting hallways if one hallway is 150 cm wide and the other is 200 cm wide? Round to the nearest hundredth.

21. **Check Your Understanding**

(a) Evaluate $(32)^{-\frac{3}{5}}$ using two different methods. Do not use a calculator.

(b) Use a scientific calculator to verify your answers.

C

22. Thinking, Inquiry, Problem Solving: Leon invested a sum of money ten years ago. Today the investment has grown to \$7146.03. He invested the original amount for 4 years 6 months at 8%/a, compounded quarterly. Then he reinvested this amount at 6%/a, compounded monthly.

    (a) How much did Leon originally invest?

    (b) Suppose instead that he had invested the principal for ten years in an account that paid 10%/a, compounded semiannually. What must be the interest rate to generate the same amount, \$7146.03?

23. The time, t, in minutes, of a communications satellite's orbit of the Earth is $t = (1.66 \times 10^{-4})(6370 + h)^{1.5}$, where h is the height, in kilometres, of the satellite above the Earth.

    (a) Determine the time for a satellite that is 450 km above the Earth to orbit the Earth once.

    (b) If television satellites must orbit the Earth at the same rate that the Earth rotates, then determine how high above the Earth's surface a television satellite must be for this to happen.

The Chapter Problem—Controlling Non-Native Plant Populations

In this section, you have used rational exponents. Apply what you have learned to answer these questions about the Chapter Problem on page 12.

CP16. Use your model to predict the number of plants present after 5 years.

CP17. Use your model to predict the number of seeds present after 2 years 3 months.

CP18. What factors make question CP17 unreasonable for this situation?

Did You Know?

Go is a game played on a board with 19 horizontal and vertical lines. Players take turns trying to capture territory by placing pebbles where the lines intersect. The winner of the game has the most occupied territory and pieces.

Computers can now beat the greatest chess players, but they cannot yet beat the best Go players. This is because there are too many moves for even the fastest computers to calculate.

Simplifying Expressions Involving Exponents

1.10 SKILL BUILDER

Quite often, you may have to apply several laws of exponents to simplify numerical and algebraic expressions involving exponents.

Rule	Algebraic Example	Description
product	$2^3 \times 2^4 = 2^7$	$a^m \times a^n = a^{m+n}$
quotient	$5^6 \div 5^2 = 5^4$	$a^m \div a^n = a^{m-n}$, $a \neq 0$, $m > n$
power of a power	$(3^3)^2 = 3^6$	$(a^m)^n = a^{m \times n}$
power of a product	$(2 \times 3)^4 = 2^4 \times 3^4$	$(xy)^m = x^m y^m$
power of a quotient	$\left(\frac{3}{5}\right)^2 = \frac{3^2}{5^2}$	$\left(\frac{x}{y}\right)^m = \frac{x^m}{y^m}$, $y \neq 0$
zero as an exponent	$4^0 = 1$	$a^0 = 1$
negative exponents	$6^{-2} = \frac{1}{6^2}$	$a^{-n} = \frac{1}{a^n}$, $a \neq 0$
rational exponents	$8^{\frac{2}{3}} = (\sqrt[3]{8})^2$	$x^{\frac{m}{n}} = \sqrt[n]{x^m} = (\sqrt[n]{x})^m$

The following examples illustrate how to simplify numerical expressions using these laws of exponents.

Example 1

Use the laws of exponents to simplify each expression.

(a) $(4^2 \times 9^4)^{\frac{1}{2}}$

(b) $\dfrac{5^{\frac{1}{4}}}{5^{\frac{1}{3}} \times 5^{\frac{3}{4}}}$

Solution

(a) $(4^2 \times 9^4)^{\frac{1}{2}}$ — Apply the power of a product law.

$= (4^2)^{\frac{1}{2}} \times (9^4)^{\frac{1}{2}}$ — Apply the power of a power law.

$= 4^1 \times 9^2$ — Evaluate 9^2.

$= 4 \times 81$ — Evaluate the product.

$= 324$

(b) $\dfrac{5^{\frac{1}{4}}}{5^{\frac{1}{3}} \times 5^{\frac{3}{4}}}$ — Apply the product law.

$= \dfrac{5^{\frac{1}{4}}}{5^{\frac{1}{3}+\frac{3}{4}}}$ — Apply the quotient law.

$= 5^{\frac{1}{4}-\left(\frac{1}{3}+\frac{3}{4}\right)}$ — Determine a common denominator.

$= 5^{\frac{3}{12}-\left(\frac{4}{12}+\frac{9}{12}\right)}$ — Simplify.

$= 5^{\frac{3}{12}-\frac{13}{12}}$ — Evaluate.

$= 5^{-\frac{10}{12}}$

$= 5^{-\frac{5}{6}}$ — Express using positive exponents.

$= \dfrac{1}{5^{\frac{5}{6}}}$

$= \dfrac{1}{\sqrt[6]{5^5}}$ — Simplify.

$= \dfrac{1}{\sqrt[6]{3125}}$

You can simplify algebraic expressions using the laws of exponents.

Example 2

Simplify each expression.

(a) $\left(\dfrac{\sqrt[4]{x^7}}{\sqrt{x}}\right)^8$

(b) $\dfrac{(x^{2n+1})(x^{3n-1})}{(x^{2n})^3}$

Solution

(a) $\left(\dfrac{\sqrt[4]{x^7}}{\sqrt{x}}\right)^8$ — Rewrite with rational exponents.

$= \left(\dfrac{x^{\frac{7}{4}}}{x^{\frac{1}{2}}}\right)^8$ — Apply the quotient law.

$= \left(x^{\frac{7}{4}-\frac{1}{2}}\right)^8$ — Determine a common denominator.

$= \left(x^{\frac{7}{4}-\frac{2}{4}}\right)^8$ — Simplify.

$= \left(x^{\frac{5}{4}}\right)^8$ — Apply the power of a power law.

$= x^{\frac{40}{4}}$ — Simplify.

$= x^{10}$

(b) $\frac{(x^{2n+1})(x^{3n-1})}{(x^{2n})^3}$ Apply the product and power of a power laws.

$= \frac{x^{2n+1+3n-1}}{x^{2n\times 3}}$ Simplify.

$= \frac{x^{5n}}{x^{6n}}$ Apply the quotient law.

$= x^{5n-6n}$ Simplify.

$= x^{-n}$ Express using positive exponents.

$= \frac{1}{x^n}$

Key Ideas

- When simplifying expressions involving exponents (positive, negative, and rational) follow the laws and rules for exponents and the order of operations (BEDMAS).
- Express all answers using positive exponents.
- Express all answers in radical form.

Practise, Apply, Solve 1.10

A

1. Simplify.

(a) $(x^4)(x^3)$ (b) $(c^4)^5$ (c) $x^6 \div x^3$ (d) $(ab)^3$

(e) $(d^4)(d^2)(d^{-3})$ (f) $b^{-3} \div b^2$ (g) $(2x^3)^2$ (h) $\left(\frac{2x}{-3y^2}\right)^3$

2. Write each expression as a power of 2.

(a) $2^4 \times 2^5$ (b) $2^n \times 2^m$ (c) $(2^4)^x$ (d) 4^3

(e) 8^n (f) $2^6 \div 2^{-2}$ (g) $4^4 \div 2^m$ (h) 16^{3x-1}

3. Evaluate.

(a) 3^5 (b) 7^0 (c) 8^{-2} (d) $(-3)^4$ (e) $-16^{-\frac{3}{4}}$

(f) $16^{\frac{1}{4}}$ (g) $32^{\frac{2}{5}}$ (h) $4^{\frac{3}{2}}$ (i) $125^{-\frac{1}{3}}$ (j) $100^{-\frac{1}{2}}$

(k) $-27^{\frac{1}{3}}$ (l) $256^{\frac{3}{4}}$ (m) $27^{\frac{2}{3}}$ (n) $128^{-\frac{3}{7}}$ (o) $64^{\frac{2}{3}}$

4. Rewrite using positive exponents.

(a) $(x^{-3})^2$ (b) $\sqrt[3]{x}$ (c) $\sqrt[4]{c^5}$ (d) $\sqrt[3]{a^{-2}}$ (e) $(\sqrt{c^{-3}})^2$

5. Simplify.

(a) $\frac{(xy)^4}{xy}$ (b) $\frac{3(ab)^4}{(-a^2)^2}$ (c) $(a^3b)^2\left(\frac{-a}{b}\right)^3$ (d) $(-d^3)^4\left(\frac{c}{d}\right)^6$

(e) $\left(\frac{-1}{b}\right)^2(a^3b)^2$ (f) $\frac{(a^4b^2)^3}{(a^2b^2)^2}$ (g) $\left(\frac{x}{-y}\right)^3(-xy)^4$ (h) $\left(\frac{x^3}{y^4}\right)^4\left(\frac{y^2}{x^4}\right)^3$

B

6. Simplify.

(a) $49^{\frac{1}{2}} + 16^{\frac{1}{4}}$ (b) $27^{\frac{2}{3}} - 81^{\frac{3}{4}}$

(c) $16^{\frac{3}{4}} + 16^{\frac{3}{4}} - 81^{-\frac{1}{4}}$ (d) $128^{-\frac{5}{7}} - 16^{-0.75}$

(e) $16^{\frac{3}{2}} + 16^{-0.5} + 8 - 27^{\frac{2}{3}}$ (f) $81^{\frac{1}{2}} + \sqrt[3]{8} - 32^{\frac{4}{5}} + 16^{\frac{3}{4}}$

(g) $9^{\frac{1}{2}} - \sqrt[4]{16} + 16^{\frac{1}{2}} - 2(2^{-3})$ (h) $\left(\frac{1}{8}\right)^{\frac{1}{3}} - \sqrt[3]{\frac{27}{125}} + 4\left(8^{-\frac{2}{3}}\right)$

7. Evaluate using the laws of exponents.

(a) $2^3 \times 4^{-2} \div 2^2$ (b) $(2^2 \times 3)^{-1}$ (c) $\left(\frac{3^{-1}}{2^{-1}}\right)^{-2}$

(d) $4^{-1}(4^2 + 4^0)$ (e) $\frac{2^5}{3^{-2}} \times \frac{3^{-1}}{2^4}$ (f) $(5^0 + 5^2)^{-1}$

(g) $\frac{3^{-2} \times 2^{-3}}{3^{-1} \times 2^{-2}}$ (h) $\frac{4^{-2} + 3^{-1}}{3^{-2} + 2^{-3}}$ (i) $\frac{5^{-1} - 2^{-2}}{5^{-1} + 2^{-2}}$

8. Rewrite each expression, without using fractions.

(a) $\frac{x}{y^2}$ (b) $\frac{m^3}{n^2}$ (c) $\frac{2x^3}{y^5z^2}$ (d) $\frac{10a^2b}{2c^2}$

(e) $\frac{30m^2}{-6n^4}$ (f) $\frac{1}{x^{-2}}$ (g) $\frac{m^{-5}}{n^{-4}}$ (h) $\frac{8x^3y^{-2}}{4z^{-3}}$

9. Express using only positive exponents.

(a) a^4b^{-3} (b) $\frac{4a^{-2}b^3}{c^{-2}}$ (c) $\frac{5a^{-2}b^{-3}}{ab^{-2}}$ (d) $\frac{2a^2b^{-3}}{3bc^{-4}}$ (e) $\frac{(4a)^{-2}}{(3b)^{-1}}$

10. Find the value of each expression for $a = 1$, $b = 3$, and $c = 2$.

(a) ab^c (b) a^cb^c (c) $(ab)^{-c}$ (d) $(b \div c)^{-a}$

(e) $(-a \div b)^{-c}$ (f) $(a^{-1}b^{-2})^c$ (g) $(a^bb^a)^c$ (h) $[(b)^{-a}]^{-c}$

11. Simplify and then determine the number or numbers represented by each variable.

(a) $n^3 = 64$ (b) $c^3 = 512$

(c) $d^4 = 625$ (d) $(n^2)^5 \div n^5 = 243$

(e) $x^{15} \div x^2 = 12^{13}$ (f) $(t^2)^2 \times t^0 = 10\,000$

(g) $m^3 \times m^2 = 3125$ (h) $\left(\frac{m^7}{m^6}\right)^2 = 196$

(i) $n^{10} \div n^8 = 576$ (j) $(x^8)(x^2) \div (x^7) = 1$

(k) $(p \times p^2)^3 = 3^9$ (l) $(x^2)^2 \div x^3 = 15$

12. State whether each expression is true or false.

(a) $9^{\frac{1}{2}} + 4^{\frac{1}{2}} = (9 + 4)^{\frac{1}{2}}$ (b) $\left(9^{\frac{1}{2}}\right)\left(4^{\frac{1}{2}}\right) = (9 \times 4)^{\frac{1}{2}}$

(c) $\left(\frac{1}{a} + \frac{1}{b}\right)^{-1} = a + b$ (d) $\left(\frac{1}{a} \times \frac{1}{b}\right)^{-1} = ab$

(e) $\left(x^{\frac{1}{3}} + y^{\frac{1}{3}}\right)^6 = x^2 + y^2$ (f) $\left[\left(x^{\frac{1}{3}}\right)\left(y^{\frac{1}{3}}\right)\right]^6 = x^2y^2$

13. Simplify.

(a) $\sqrt{x^2}$ (b) $\sqrt[3]{c^3}$ (c) $\sqrt[3]{z^9}$

(d) $\sqrt[4]{d^8}$ (e) $\left(\frac{2}{3}\right)^{\frac{5}{3}}\left(\frac{2}{3}\right)^{\frac{1}{3}}$ (f) $\left(4^{\frac{1}{3}}\right)^{\frac{6}{4}}$

(g) $\left(2x^{-\frac{1}{3}}y^{\frac{3}{4}}\right)^2$ (h) $\left(-3u^{\frac{3}{5}}v^{-\frac{1}{5}}\right)^2$ (i) $\dfrac{18y^{\frac{4}{3}}z^{-\frac{1}{3}}}{24y^{-\frac{2}{3}}z}$

(j) $\dfrac{a^{\frac{3}{4}} \times a^{\frac{1}{2}}}{a^{\frac{3}{2}}}$ (k) $\left(c^{\frac{3}{2}}\right)^{\frac{1}{3}}$ (l) $\left(k^{-\frac{1}{2}}\right)^{\frac{2}{5}}$

14. Simplify.

(a) $\dfrac{x^{\frac{1}{2}} \times x^{\frac{2}{3}}}{x^{\frac{1}{4}}}$ (b) $\dfrac{x^{\frac{5}{6}} \times x^{\frac{2}{3}}}{x^{\frac{1}{2}}}$ (c) $\left(y^{\frac{1}{2}}\right)^2 \div (16y^6)^{\frac{1}{2}}$

(d) $\left(\dfrac{\sqrt[4]{y^4}}{\sqrt{y^2}}\right)^3$ (e) $\left(\dfrac{x^3}{81}\right)\left(\dfrac{81^{\frac{3}{4}}}{x}\right)$ (f) $\dfrac{(x^2y^4)^{\frac{1}{2}}(x^4y^2)^{\frac{1}{2}}}{\left(x^{\frac{1}{2}}y^{\frac{1}{2}}\right)^6}$

15. Simplify.

(a) $(x^2)^{5-r}$ (b) $(a^{4+2r})(a^{-3r-5})$

(c) $(b^{2m+3n}) \div (b^{m-n})$ (d) $x^{3(7-r)}x^r$

(e) $(a^{10-p})\left(\frac{1}{a}\right)^p$ (f) $[(3x^4)^{6-m}]\left(\frac{1}{x}\right)^m$

16. Simplify.

(a) $(3x^3)^2$ (b) $(4x^2y^{-4})^{-2}$ (c) $(16x^{10}y^4)^{\frac{1}{2}}$

(d) $(2x^{-2})^2(3x^4)^{-3}$ (e) $\dfrac{(2x^{-1})^{-2}}{2(y^{-1})^{-2}}$ (f) $\left(\dfrac{3x^2}{y^{-1}}\right)^{-2}\left(\dfrac{2y^2}{3x}\right)^3$

17. Check Your Understanding: Simplify $\left(\dfrac{3x^3}{2y^4}\right)^2\left(\dfrac{2y^2}{3x^4}\right)^{-3}$.

C

18. Solve.

(a) $x^3 = 27$ (b) $x^{\frac{1}{2}} = 5$ (c) $c^{\frac{2}{3}} = 64$ (d) $3a^{\frac{4}{5}} = 48$

19. Solve.

(a) $\left(\frac{1}{16}\right)^{\frac{1}{4}} - \sqrt[3]{\frac{8}{27}} = \sqrt{x^2}$ (b) $\sqrt[3]{\frac{1}{8}} - \sqrt[4]{x^4} + 15 = \sqrt[4]{16}$

20. If $a = 2$ and $b = -1$, which expression has the greater value?

A: $\dfrac{a^{-2b}a^{-b+2}}{(a^{-2})^b}$ B: $\dfrac{(a^b)^{-3}a^{-(1-2b)}}{(a^{-b})^3}$

1.11 Solving Exponential Equations

In an exponential equation, at least one of the exponents is, or has, a variable. Some examples of exponential equations are $2^x = 8$, $5^{x-3} = 10^{2x}$, and $5210 = 4000(1.05)^n$.

Part 1: Approximating a Solution

Martin invested \$1000 at 8%/a, compounded annually. Today the investment is worth \$4660.96. For how long has the money been invested?

Think, Do, Discuss

1. Use the formula for compound interest to write an equation for this situation.
2. How would you describe this equation?
3. Use the expression on the right side of the equal sign to complete the table.

Years (n)	0	2	4	6	8	10	12	14
Amount (\$)								

4. Using the information in the table, graph this relationship. In this case, can you draw a **curve of best fit** through the points? Explain.
5. Can you use the graph in step 4 to solve the problem? What must you do with the graph so that you may solve the problem?
6. Adjust the graph accordingly and determine for how long the money has been invested.
7. Are you confident that your answer is accurate? Explain.
8. Using the exponent key on your calculator, guess and check to solve the equation in step 1.
9. Which method, graphing or using a calculator, gives an exact solution? Explain.

Part 2: Exponential Equations with the Same Base

An Algebraic Solution

You can use algebra to determine an exact solution for an exponential equation when the powers on each side of the equation have the same base.

In the equation $a^x = a^y$, the bases are the same. For this equation to be true, the exponents must be equal. That is, if $a^x = a^y$, then $x = y$.

Example 1

Solve.

(a) $3^{2x} = 81$ (b) $5^{2x-1} = \frac{1}{125}$ (c) $36^{2x+4} = \sqrt{1296^x}$

Solution

(a)

$3^{2x} = 81$ Express 81 as a power of 3.

$3^{2x} = 3^4$ The same bases must have equal exponents.

$\therefore\ 2x = 4$ Solve for x.

$x = 2$

Verify that $x = 2$.

L.S.	R.S.
3^{2x}	81
$= 3^{2(2)}$	
$= 3^4$	
$= 81$	

Since L.S. = R.S., the solution is correct.

(b)

$5^{2x-1} = \frac{1}{125}$ Express $\frac{1}{125}$ as a power of 5.

$5^{2x-1} = 5^{-3}$ The same bases must have equal exponents.

$\therefore\ 2x - 1 = -3$ Solve for x.

$2x = -3 + 1$

$2x = -2$

$x = -1$

(c)

$36^{2x+4} = \sqrt{1296^x}$ Express the left side as a power of 6 and the right side using a rational exponent.

$(6^2)^{2x+4} = 1296^{\frac{x}{2}}$ Express the right side as a power of 6.

$6^{2(2x+4)} = (6^4)^{\frac{x}{2}}$ Apply the power of a power law and multiply the exponents.

$6^{4x+8} = 6^{2x}$ The same bases must have equal exponents.

$\therefore\ 4x + 8 = 2x$ Solve for x.

$4x - 2x = -8$

$2x = -8$

$x = -4$

Solving Exponential Equations Involving Quadratic Equations

Some exponential equations can be more difficult to solve. In the following examples, quadratic equations must be used to solve the original exponential equation.

Example 2

Solve.

(a) $2^{x^2 + 2x} = \frac{1}{2}$ (b) $2^{2x} - 2^x = 12$

Solution

(a)

$2^{x^2 + 2x} = \frac{1}{2}$	Express the right side as a power of 2.
$2^{x^2 + 2x} = 2^{-1}$	The same bases must have equal exponents.
$\therefore \quad x^2 + 2x = -1$	Rearrange the quadratic equation so the right side is 0.
$x^2 + 2x + 1 = 0$	Factor the left side.
$(x + 1)(x + 1) = 0$	Set each factor equal to zero.
$x + 1 = 0$ or $x + 1 = 0$	
$x = -1$ or $x = -1$	

(b)

$2^{2x} - 2^x = 12$	Apply the power of a power law.
$(2^x)^2 - 2^x = 12$	Rearrange the quadratic equation so that the right side is 0.
$(2^x)^2 - 2^x - 12 = 0$	Let $a = 2^x$.
$a^2 - a - 12 = 0$	Factor the left side.
$(a - 4)(a + 3) = 0$	Solve each factor.
$a - 4 = 0$ or $a + 3 = 0$	
$a = 4$ or $a = -3$	Substitute 2^x for a.
$2^x = 4$ or $2^x = -3$	Solve $2^x = 4$. The equation $2^x = -3$ has no solution, since any positive base raised to any exponent results in a positive value.
$2^x = 2^2$	
$\therefore \quad x = 2$	

Finding the Number of Terms in a Geometric Sequence

Use an exponential equation to determine the number of terms in any finite geometric sequence.

Example 3

Determine the number of terms in the sequence 4, 20, 100, … , 1 562 500.

Solution

This sequence is geometric, with $a = 4$ and $r = 5$.

$$\begin{aligned}
t_n &= ar^{n-1} \\
t_n &= 4(5)^{n-1} && \text{Let } t_n = 1\,562\,500. \\
1\,562\,500 &= 4(5)^{n-1} && \text{Divide both sides by 4.} \\
\frac{1\,562\,500}{4} &= \frac{4(5)^{n-1}}{4} \\
390\,625 &= 5^{n-1} && \text{Express 390 625 as a power of 5.} \\
5^8 &= 5^{n-1} \\
\therefore\ 8 &= n - 1 && \text{Solve for } n. \\
8 + 1 &= n \\
9 &= n
\end{aligned}$$

The sequence has nine terms.

Exponential Growth and Decay Problems

Exponential growth and radioactive decay (half-life) involve exponential equations.

Example 4

Radioactive material decays according to the relationship $M = c\left(\frac{1}{2}\right)^{\frac{t}{h}}$, where

M is the mass of the decayed radioactive material, in grams,
c is the original mass of the radioactive material, in grams,
$\frac{1}{2}$ is the decay factor,
t is the time, as specified, and
h is the half-life of the radioactive material.

Radon has a half-life of 25 days. How much time does it take for a sample of 200 g to decay to 12.5 g?

Solution

$M = c\left(\frac{1}{2}\right)^{\frac{t}{h}}$, and $M = 12.5$ g, $c = 200$ g, and $h = 25$ days

$$\begin{aligned}
12.5 &= 200\left(\frac{1}{2}\right)^{\frac{t}{25}} && \text{Divide both sides by 200.} \\
\frac{12.5}{200} &= \frac{200\left(\frac{1}{2}\right)^{\frac{t}{25}}}{200} && \text{Simplify.} \\
\frac{1}{16} &= \left(\frac{1}{2}\right)^{\frac{t}{25}} && \text{Express each side as a power of 2.} \\
2^{-4} &= (2^{-1})^{\frac{t}{25}} && \text{Apply the power of a power law to the right side and multiply the exponents.} \\
2^{-4} &= 2^{-\frac{t}{25}} && \text{The same bases must have equal exponents.} \\
-4 &= -\frac{t}{25} && \text{Solve for } t. \\
25(-4) &= 25\left(-\frac{t}{25}\right) \\
-100 &= -t \\
100 &= t
\end{aligned}$$

The radon decays to 12.5 g in 100 days.

Part 3: Solving an Exponential Equation Using Graphing Technology

When you cannot find an exact solution, use graphing technology to find a very close approximation.

Example 5

A bacteria culture doubles in size every 30 min. If the initial population of the culture is 10 bacteria, how long will the population take to reach 1 000 000?

Solution

The sequence 10, 20, 40, 80, … is geometric.

$t_n = ar^{n-1}$ Substitute the values of a and r.

$t_n = 10(2)^{n-1}$ Substitute 1 000 000 for t_n.

$1\ 000\ 000 = 10(2)^{n-1}$ You could graph $y = 10(2)^{n-1}$ and then TRACE to find the value of n. But use the zero operation to get a more accurate answer. First divide both sides by 10 and rearrange the equation so that one side is 0.

$100\ 000 = (2)^{n-1}$ Subtract 100 000 from both sides.

$0 = (2)^{n-1} - 100\ 000$ You must find the zero of the graph of $y = (2)^{n-1} - 100\ 000$ to find the solution.

Graph $y = (2)^{n-1} - 100\ 000$ and use the graph to determine the value of n when $y = 0$, that is, determine the zero. For the TI-83 Plus calculator, ensure that the selected graphing mode is **function** (MODE).

1. Enter the equation.

step 1

2. Adjust the window.

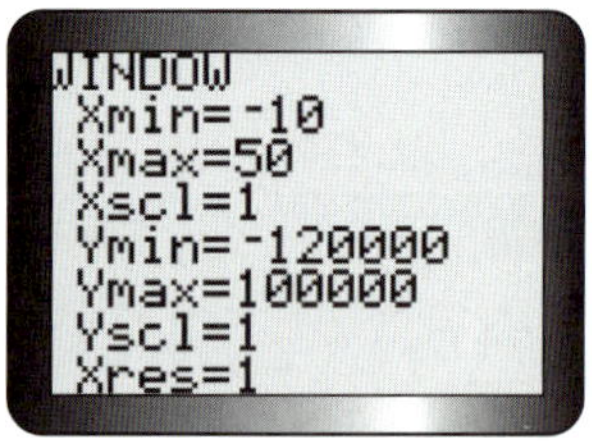

step 2

3. Draw the graph.

Press GRAPH.

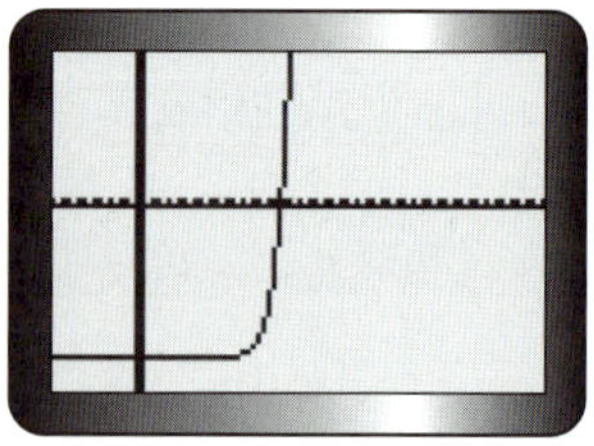

step 3

4. Determine the zero using the zero operation.

Press 2nd TRACE 2 ENTER. Respond to **Left Bound?** by moving the cursor to any point along the curve below the x-axis. Respond to **Right Bound?** by moving the cursor to any point along the curve above the x-axis. Respond to **Guess?** by pressing ENTER.

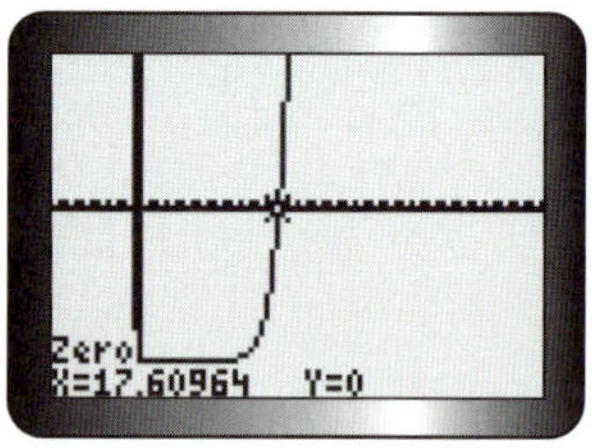

step 4

The population of the culture grows to 1 000 000 between the 17th and 18th terms of the sequence. Since the time between terms, the doubling period, is 30 min, then the time taken to reach 1 000 000 is

$$17.609\,64 \times 30 = 528.2892$$

The population of the bacteria colony takes 528.2892 min or 8 h 48 min 17 s to grow to 1 000 000.

Consolidate Your Understanding

1. Write an example of an exponential equation. Explain how an exponential equation is different from
   (a) a linear equation
   (b) a quadratic equation
2. What must be true of the expressions on both sides of an exponential equation to solve it algebraically?
3. How can you verify your solutions for an exponential equation?
4. Do all exponential equations have exact solutions? Explain.

Focus 1.11

Key Ideas

- In an **exponential equation**, at least one of the exponents is, or has, a variable. For example, $3^{4x + 2} = 27^{x - 2}$ is an exponential equation.
- You can determine an approximate solution to any exponential equation by graphing and then by interpolating or extrapolating.
- You can also determine an approximate solution to any exponential equation by using a scientific or graphing calculator to guess and check.
- If both sides of an exponential equation have the same base, you can solve this exponential equation algebraically. The algebraic solution in this case is exact. If the bases are the same, then the exponents are equal. That is, if $m^x = n^y$ and $m = n$, then $x = y$.
- If you use graphing technology to create a graph, then the solutions to the equation tend to be more accurate than the solutions found from a hand-drawn graph.
- You should verify the solutions to an exponential equation by substitution.

Practise, Apply, Solve 1.11

A

1. Express each as a power of 3.

(a) 27 (b) 81 (c) $\frac{1}{9}$ (d) 9^{2x} (e) $\left(\frac{1}{27}\right)^x$

2. Determine which value of x is the solution to the equation.

(a) $3^{2x-5} = 27$
  i. $x = 1$
  ii. $x = 4$

(b) $4^{x+3} = 64$
  i. $x = 1$
  ii. $x = 0$

(c) $5^{x+2} = \frac{1}{25}$
  i. $x = 0$
  ii. $x = -4$

(d) $2^{5x+2} = \sqrt{2}$
  i. $x = -\frac{3}{10}$
  ii. $x = -\frac{1}{2}$

3. Determine the exact solutions algebraically.

(a) $2^x = 2^7$ (b) $5^x = 5^3$ (c) $3^{x+6} = 3^{12}$ (d) $10^{2x-1} = 10^3$

(e) $2^{2x-1} = 2^{x+9}$ (f) $7^{3x+2} = 7^{2x+5}$ (g) $4^{2x} = 4^8$ (h) $5^x = 5^{3x-12}$

4. Find the exact roots of each equation.

(a) $2^x = 32$ (b) $3^x = 27$ (c) $3^x = 9^{x-1}$ (d) $5^x = 3125$

(e) $4(2^x) = 32$ (f) $5^x = \frac{1}{125}$ (g) $6^x = \sqrt[3]{6}$ (h) $3^{-x} = \frac{1}{81}$

5. Determine the approximate solutions using your calculator and guessing and checking. Round to two decimal places.

(a) $2^x = 20$ (b) $5^x = 35$ (c) $3^x = 100$ (d) $10^x = 800$

(e) $2^{2x} = 50$ (f) $7^{3x} = 150$ (g) $4^{2x-1} = 80$ (h) $200 = 5^{3x+2}$

B

For questions 6 to 9, determine the exact solutions algebraically.

6. Solve each equation without using a calculator.

(a) $4^x = 8\sqrt{2}$ (b) $3^x = \sqrt[5]{9}$ (c) $125^x = 25\sqrt{5}$ (d) $8x = 16\sqrt[3]{2}$

7. (a) Solve. $\left(\frac{1}{9}\right)^{x+2} = \left(\frac{1}{27}\right)^{x+3}$

(b) Verify your answer in (a).

8. Solve each equation.

(a) $2^{7-x} = \frac{1}{2}$ (b) $2^{x-2} = 4^{x+2}$ (c) $\left(\frac{1}{4}\right)^{x-2} = \left(\frac{1}{8}\right)^{x+1}$

(d) $9^{2x+1} = 81(27^x)$ (e) $2^{2x+2} + 7 = 71$ (f) $(2^{x+1})(4^{x+1})(8^{x+1}) = 128^x$

9. Determine the solution or solutions of each equation.

(a) $2^{x^2} = 32(2^{4x})$ (b) $3^{x^2} = 27(3^{2x})$ (c) $9^{x+2} = \left(\frac{1}{27}\right)^{x+2}$

(d) $2^{r^2+6r} = 2^{-8}$ (e) $3^{x^2+20} = \left(\frac{1}{27}\right)^{3x}$ (f) $(8)^{x^2} = (4)^{4-5x}$

(g) $(2^{x-4})^x = 32$ (h) $9^{x^2+1} = (27^x)(3^{2x})$ (i) $2^{x^2} = (16^{x-1})(2^x)$

10. Determine the number of terms in each geometric sequence.

(a) 2, 6, 18, … , 39 366 (b) 5, 10, 20, … , 10 240

(c) −2, −10, −50, … , −6250 (d) 16, 8, 4, … , $\frac{1}{64}$

(e) 3, 6, 12, … , 384 (f) 4, 24, 144, … , 186 624

11. Determine the approximate solutions using graphing technology. Round to two decimal places.

(a) $3^x = 30$ (b) $5^z = 10$ (c) $5.6^y = 60$ (d) $(1.04)^x = 2$

(e) $25^{-x} = 10$ (f) $12^{2x} = 500$ (g) $4.1^{3x} = 40$ (h) $5^{2x-1} = 45$

12. A bacteria culture doubles in size every 15 min. How long will it take for a culture of 20 bacteria to grow to a population of 163 840?

13. **Knowledge and Understanding:** Determine the exact solution of $9^{2x+1} = 81(27^x)$.

14. The use of wind turbines to generate electrical energy in Europe has increased exponentially. The energy produced by wind turbines between 1980 and 1995 can be modelled by the equation $y = 6.489(1.580)^x$, where x is the number of years since 1980 and y is the number of gigawatt-hours of energy produced.

(a) Determine the amount of energy produced in 1980.

(b) Determine the amount of energy produced in 1992.

(c) In what year was 398.191 107 2 GW-h produced?

(d) Determine when 500 GW-h of energy were produced.

15. If $500 is deposited in an account paying 8%/a, compounded semiannually, how long will it take for the deposit to increase to $900?

16. **Communication:** You can solve an exponential equation algebraically or by using a graph. Explain how you would decide which method to use. Include examples.

17. Thorium-227 has a half-life of 18.4 days. How much time will a 50-mg sample take to decompose to 10 mg?

18. **Thinking, Inquiry, Problem Solving:** When a plant or an animal dies, it stops absorbing carbon-14 from the atmosphere. Carbon-14 is an unstable radioactive isotope and decays over time. By measuring the amount of carbon-14 remaining in a sample from a plant or animal fossil, scientists can accurately predict the age of the specimen.

(a) Research to find the half-life of carbon-14.

(b) Estimate the age of the fossil of a leaf that contains 0.10% of the original amount of carbon-14.

19. If a sum of money is invested at 9%/a, compounded monthly, how much time will the investment take to double?

20. **Application:** Erica has a new job with a starting salary of \$32 000. She has been guaranteed an annual raise of 6% each year over the next ten years. When will her annual salary be more than \$50 000?

21. When a driver leaves the lights of a parked car turned on, the battery begins to discharge. A 12-V car battery loses about 8% of its charge each hour. The car must have at least 9 V of power to turn the starter's motor. How much time does the driver have to turn off the lights and still be able to start the car?

22. **Check Your Understanding:** Solve $31\,250 = 2(5)^{3x-12}$ algebraically. Verify your answer by finding the zero of the corresponding relationship using graphing technology.

C

23. Solve.

(a) $2^{2x} - 33(2^x) + 32 = 0$ (b) $25^x - 30(5^x) + 125 = 0$

24. Solve. Round to two decimal places.

(a) $9^{x^2-3x} = \frac{1}{27}$ (b) $(5^{x^2})(625) = \left(\frac{1}{125}\right)^{2x}$

25. Samantha invests \$1000 at 6%/a, compounded quarterly. Mark invests \$1500 at 5%/a, compounded quarterly. When will the balances in their accounts be equal?

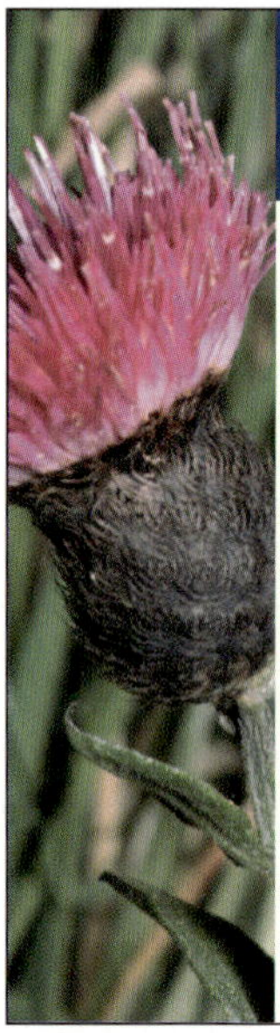

The Chapter Problem—Controlling Non-Native Plant Populations

In this lesson, you have studied exponential equations. Use what you have learned to answer these questions about the Chapter Problem on page 12.

CP19. Use your model to predict the number of plants and seeds that exist after ten years.

CP20. How do the values in question CP19 compare with those in the table? Explain the similarities or differences.

CP21. Use your model, along with graphing technology, to determine when the number of plants exceeds 500 trillion.

CP22. If the site will support 105 mature knapweed plants per square metre, how many hectares would be affected after ten years? (1 ha = 10 000 m^2)

Chapter 1 Review

Patterns of Growth: Sequences

Check Your Understanding

1. Must a sequence have a recognizable pattern? Explain.
2. Can any sequence be represented by a formula or by a general term?
3. Explain why the set of natural numbers is used in the general term of a sequence.
4. How do you decide whether a list of numbers represents an arithmetic sequence or a geometric sequence? Use examples in your explanation.
5. In any arithmetic sequence,
   (a) what is true about the rate of change between consecutive terms of the sequence?
   (b) what type of relationship exists between n and t_n?
6. In any geometric sequence,
   (a) what is true about the rate of change between consecutive terms of the sequence?
   (b) what type of relationship exists between n and t_n?
7. Write the recursive formula for
   (a) any arithmetic sequence (b) any geometric sequence
8. Explain why an investment of $1000 will be worth more in ten years if the interest is compounded annually, but is not simple.
9. What is the difference between the amount of an investment and the present value of an investment? Use an example in your explanation.
10. In your own words, define the nth root of a number a. Express the nth root of a using exponents.
11. Without using a calculator, evaluate $25^{-\frac{3}{2}}$ using two different methods. Verify both answers by using a calculator.
12. List and describe the steps for simplifying the expression $\left(\frac{1}{c}\right)^{n+m}(c^3)^m$.
13. How can you decide whether an exponential equation should be solved algebraically or by graphing?
14. Solve $6(3^{2x-1}) = 486$ algebraically. Verify your answer by solving this equation using graphing technology.

Review and Practice

1.1 Exploring Patterns and Sequences

1. What is a sequence? What is a term in a sequence? Use examples to illustrate your answers.

2. What is the general term of a sequence? How can you use the general term to generate the terms of a sequence?

3. Describe a situation that could be represented by

(a) a finite sequence (b) an infinite sequence

4. Determine the first five terms of each sequence. Start with $n = 1$.

(a) $t_n = 4n + 1$ (b) $t_n = 2n^2 - 2n$ (c) $t_n = 3^{n-1}$

(d) $t_n = -3n + 2$ (e) $t_n = (2n + 1)(2n - 1)$ (f) $t_n = \frac{10}{n}$

5. Graph the first six terms of each sequence in question 4.

6. Determine the general term of each sequence.

(a) 2, 7, 12, 17, … (b) 30, 24, 18, 12, … (c) 9, 27, 81, 243, …

(d) $\frac{5}{2}, \frac{5}{4}, \frac{5}{8}, \frac{5}{16}, \ldots$ (e) 2, 5, 10, 17, … (f) $\frac{2}{3}, \frac{3}{4}, \frac{4}{5}, \frac{5}{6}, \ldots$

7. A car's purchase price is \$24 000. At the end of each year, the value of the car is three-quarters of the value at the beginning of the year.

(a) Write the first four terms of the sequence of the car's value at the end of each year.

(b) Determine the general term of this sequence.

(c) Find the value of the car at the end of the seventh year.

1.2–1.3U Sequences and Recursive Formulas

8. Compare how to generate the terms of a sequence from a recursive formula and from the general term of a sequence.

9. A recursive formula consists of two parts. Describe them.

10. Write the first five terms of each sequence.

(a) $t_1 = 7, t_n = (t_{n-1}) - 10$ (b) $t_1 = -3, t_n = 5(t_{n-1}) + 6$

(c) $t_1 = -4, t_n = (t_{n-1}) \times 2$ (d) $t_1 = 3, t_n = 4(t_{n-1})^2 - 2$

11. Write a recursive formula for each sequence.

(a) 2, 5, 8, 11, … (b) 18, 11, 4, −3, … (c) 3, 9, 81, 6561, …

(d) 2, 4, 6, 10, … (e) $1, \frac{2}{3}, \frac{4}{9}, \frac{8}{27}, \ldots$ (f) 4, 6, 12, 36, …

12. Graph the first five terms of each recursive sequence.

(a) $t_1 = 6, t_n = (t_{n-1}) + 3$ (b) $t_1 = -4, t_n = 3(t_{n-1})$

(c) $t_1 = 8, t_n = t_{n-1} \div 2$ (d) $t_1 = 2, t_n = 10 - t_{n-1}$

13. Dennis must take 250 mg of sinus medication every 12 h. Only 25% of the medication remains in his body by the time he takes the next dose.

(a) At what level will the mass of medication become constant?

(b) How long will it take for the medication to reach this level?

1.4–1.6 Arithmetic Sequences

14. Explain how to use the first differences between pairs of consecutive terms of a sequence to determine if the sequence is arithmetic.

15. (a) Write the general term of any arithmetic sequence.

(b) Explain the meaning of each variable in the formula in (a).

16. Graph an arithmetic sequence in which

(a) the first term is 4 and the terms increase by 3

(b) the first term is 10 and the terms decrease by 2

17. For each of the following arithmetic sequences, find

i. the common difference **ii.** the general term **iii.** t_{15}

(a) 6, 12, 18, 24, … (b) −40, −25, −10, 5, … (c) 36, 31, 26, 21, …

(d) $\frac{1}{4}, \frac{1}{2}, \frac{3}{4}, 1, 1\frac{1}{4}, \ldots$ (e) 1.2, 1.9, 2.6, 3.3, … (f) 4, 36, 68, 100, …

18. Graph each sequence.

(a) $t_n = -n + 5$ (b) $t_n = 7n - 4$ (c) $t_n = -3n + 7$ (d) $t_n = \frac{n + 4}{2}$

19. Ralph deposits $5000 in a savings account that pays simple interest at 3.25%/a. He makes no other deposits.

(a) By what amount will the year-end balance increase each year?

(b) Write the sequence of the year-end balances over five years.

(c) Determine the general term.

(d) Graph this sequence.

(e) At the end of one year, the balance in the account is $5975. For how long has the original deposit earned interest?

20. Two terms have been given for each arithmetic sequence. Determine a, d, and t_n for each sequence.

(a) $t_5 = 24$, $t_9 = 36$
(b) $t_6 = -41$, $t_{15} = -95$
(c) $t_{11} = 91$, $t_{20} = 172$
(d) $t_2 = -8$, $t_{12} = -158$

1.7 Geometric Sequences

21. Explain how to determine whether a sequence is geometric.

22. Graph a geometric sequence whose terms are

(a) increasing
(b) decreasing

23. (a) Write the general term of any geometric sequence.

(b) Explain the meaning of each variable in the formula in (a).

24. For each of the following geometric sequences, determine

i. the common ratio **ii.** the general term **iii.** t_{12}

(a) 2, 14, 98, 686, ...
(b) −3, −12, −48, −192, ...
(c) 160, 80, 40, 20, ...
(d) 7, −21, 63, −189, ...
(e) 0.4, 0.08, 0.016, 0.0032, ...
(f) 6561, 2187, 729, 243, ...

25. A transport truck that was bought for $149 500 depreciates in value by 15% each year.

(a) Starting with the purchase price, write the sequence of the truck's value at the end of each year for the next five years.

(b) Determine the general term of this sequence.

(c) Determine the truck's value at the end of the seventh year.

1.8 Compound Interest: Amount and Present Value

26. Explain why more money accumulates if the interest is compounded than if the interest is simple.

27. (a) Write the compound interest formula for determining the amount of an investment.

(b) Explain the meaning of each variable in the formula in (a).

28. Show how to use the formula for amount to determine present value.

29. For each situation, determine

i. the amount ii. the interest earned

(a) \$5000 borrowed for 7 years at 6%/a, compounded annually

(b) \$10 500 invested for 4 years, at 4.8%/a, compounded monthly

30. For each situation, determine

i. the present value of ii. the interest earned on

(a) a loan of \$21 500 that will be due in 6 years. The interest rate is 8%/a, compounded quarterly.

(b) a loan of \$100 000 that will be due in 5 years. The interest rate is 5%/a, compounded semiannually.

31. Linh deposits \$12 000 in an account that pays 6%/a, compounded semiannually. After five years, the interest rate changes to 6%/a, compounded monthly. Calculate the value of the money eight months after the change in the interest rate.

32. Mandy and her fiancé plan to buy a new house three years from now. They intend to make a down payment of \$20 000. The Eastern Bank offers an account with an interest rate of 8%/a, compounded monthly. How much money must they invest today to reach their goal?

1.9 Rational Exponents

33. Copy and complete each exponent law.

(a) $x^{\frac{1}{n}} = ■$ (b) $x^{\frac{m}{n}} = ■$ (c) $x^{-\frac{m}{n}} = ■$

34. Evaluate each power.

(a) $9^{\frac{1}{2}}$ (b) $(-27)^{\frac{1}{3}}$ (c) $-16^{\frac{1}{4}}$ (d) $8^{\frac{1}{3}}$ (e) $32^{\frac{1}{5}}$

(f) $\left(\frac{1}{64}\right)^{\frac{2}{3}}$ (g) $(27)^{-\frac{1}{3}}$ (h) $(8)^{-\frac{4}{3}}$ (i) $\left(\frac{4}{9}\right)^{\frac{3}{2}}$ (j) $(32)^{-\frac{4}{5}}$

35. Use a calculator to evaluate each power to two decimal places.

(a) $26^{\frac{1}{2}}$ (b) $(-20)^{\frac{1}{3}}$ (c) $-88^{\frac{1}{4}}$ (d) $35^{\frac{1}{3}}$ (e) $200^{\frac{1}{5}}$

(f) $\left(\frac{3}{4}\right)^{\frac{1}{3}}$ (g) $(945)^{-\frac{2}{3}}$ (h) $(38)^{-\frac{4}{3}}$ (i) $(1.35)^{\frac{3}{2}}$ (j) $(26.55)^{-\frac{2}{5}}$

36. Determine each amount.

(a) \$5000 borrowed for 10 months at 5%/a, compounded annually

(b) \$5500 invested for 2 years 9 months, at 6%/a, compounded semiannually

37. Determine the present value

(a) of a loan of \$1500 that is due in 20 weeks. The interest rate is 6%/a, compounded quarterly.

(b) of a loan of \$100 000 that is due in 3 years 8 months. The interest rate is 7%/a, compounded semiannually.

38. A rare coin was bought for \$1200; its value increases by 5% each year. Determine

(a) an algebraic model for the coin's value over time

(b) the coin's value ten years after it was bought

(c) the coin's value 28 months after it was bought

1.10 Simplifying Expressions Involving Exponents

39. State each of the eight exponents laws, then illustrate each with an example.

40. Evaluate.

(a) $25^{\frac{1}{2}} + 16^{\frac{3}{4}}$ (b) $8^{\frac{2}{3}} - 81^{\frac{3}{4}} + 4^2$ (c) $81^{-\frac{3}{4}} + 16^{-\frac{3}{4}} - 16^{-\frac{1}{2}}$

41. Evaluate each expression for $x = -3$ and $y = 1$.

(a) $\frac{2x^2y^{-2}}{x^3}$ (b) $(3x^2y^{-3})^{-3}$ (c) $\frac{3x^{-3}y^2}{x^3y^{-1}}$ (d) $\frac{x^{-2} - y}{y^{-1} + x^2}$

42. Simplify.

(a) $(2a^2b^2)^2(3a^4b)^{-2}$ (b) $(-4x^2y^{-3}z^4)^2$ (c) $(5x^3y^{-2})^3 \div (5x^{-2}y^3)^{-1}$

43. Simplify.

(a) $(a^{10 + 2p})(a^{-p - 8})$ (b) $(2x^2)^{3 - 2m}\left(\frac{1}{x}\right)^{2m}$

(c) $[(c)^{2n - 3m}](c^3)^m \div (c^2)^n$ (d) $(x^{4n - m})\left(\frac{1}{x^3}\right)^{m + n}$

1.11 Solving Exponential Equations

44. Give an example of an exponential equation.

45. When may you solve an exponential equation algebraically?

46. List the steps for solving an exponential equation using graphing technology.

47. Solve each expression algebraically.

(a) $3^{2x - 1} = 27$ (b) $(2^{2x})(2^{x - 1}) = 32$

(c) $5^{3x + 2} = \frac{1}{5}$ (d) $6^{2x - 3} = \sqrt{6}$

48. Solve each expression using graphing technology. Round to two decimal places.

(a) $5^x = 50$ (b) $6^z = 12$ (c) $2.5^c = 100$ (d) $1.05^x = 1.5$

49. Solve.

(a) $(2)^{x^2} = (2)^{-12 - 7x}$ (b) $(3^{x + 2})^x = \frac{1}{3}$

(c) $9^{x^2 + 1} = (3^{3x - 1})(3^{2x})$ (d) $4^{x^2} = (16^{1 - x})\left[\left(\frac{1}{4}\right)^x\right]$

50. Determine the number of terms in each geometric sequence.

(a) 3, 12, 48, … , 49 152 (b) −7, −14, −28, … , −3584

51. How long will it take for \$1000 invested at 8%/a, compounded quarterly, to triple in value?

Chapter 1 Summary

In this chapter, you have used the mathematical relationships arising from patterns to solve problems about investment, growth, and half-life. You have found the general term of an arithmetic sequence, $t_n = a + (n - 1)d$; a geometric sequence, $t_n = ar^{n - 1}$; and a recursive sequence.

You have calculated simple interest and compound interest, and used time lines, spreadsheets, and calculators to calculate the present value of invested money, $P = A(1 + i)^{-n}$, and the future value of invested money, $A = P(1 + i)^n$.

In addition, you have applied the exponent laws and rules to solve exponential equations involving rates of growth and decay.

Chapter 1 Review Test

Patterns of Growth: Sequences

1. i. Determine the first four terms of each sequence.
ii. Is each sequence arithmetic, geometric, or neither?

(a) $t_n = 6n + 5$

(b) $t_n = \frac{2}{n(n+1)}$

(c) $t_n = 3(4)^{n-1}$

(d) $t_1 = 5$, $t_2 = 1$, $t_{n+2} = 3t_{n+1} - 2t_n$, and $n \geq 1$

2. Knowledge and Understanding
Determine the number of terms in each sequence.

(a) $-6, -11, -16, \ldots, -156$

(b) $4, 12, 36, \ldots, 972$

3. For an arithmetic sequence, $t_{13} = -177$ and $t_{22} = -207$. Find a, d, and t_n.

4. Evaluate.

(a) $\left(\frac{-8}{27}\right)^{-\frac{2}{3}}$

(b) $(36^{-\frac{1}{2}} + 8^{-\frac{2}{3}}) \div (12^{-2})$

5. Simplify.

(a) $\dfrac{(16x^4y^2)^{\frac{1}{2}}(4y^6)^{\frac{1}{2}}}{(x^3y^6)^{\frac{1}{3}}}$

(b) $(a^{2m+3n})(a^{m-2n}) \div [(a^m)(a^{2m})]$

6. Communication: Explain how you can determine whether a given sequence is arithmetic or geometric. Use an example of each type of sequence in your explanation.

7. Solve.

(a) $2^{3(x-2)} = 64$

(b) $3^{x^2+4x} = \frac{1}{81}$

8. Application: Monica drops a rubber ball from a height of 60 m. After each bounce, the height of the ball's bounce is $\frac{3}{5}$ the height of the ball's previous bounce. How high does the ball bounce after the tenth bounce?

9. Jacques wants to invest now so that he will have \$20 000 in five years for a down payment on a new car. How much must Jacques invest now, if the interest rate is 8%/a, compounded semiannually?

10. The town of Lancaster is growing at a rate of 3% each year. The current population is 12 400. Determine when the population will reach 13 250.

11. In a small community college lecture hall, there are 15 rows of seats. For the first four rows, the number of seats are 14, 18, 22, 26, … . How many seats does the last row have?

12. Thinking, Inquiry, Problem Solving
Bernie invests \$5000 in a savings account that pays 6.75%/a, compounded semiannually. Three years later, he deposits another \$2000 in the account. What will be the balance in the account at the end of five years?

Chapter 2 Series and Financial Applications

Everyday, people spend or borrow money to acquire goods. Businesses and financial institutions offer loans, mortgages, credit cards, and other forms of credit. When people borrow money, they pay interest, which is the cost of using money.

When people save and invest money, they earn interest. You will investigate and learn more about the effects that compound interest and time have on the deposits of savings, repayment of loans, and credit purchases.

In this chapter, you will

- investigate and use arithmetic series
- investigate and use geometric series
- use computer spreadsheets to analyze and represent the repayment of a loan or the deposits of savings over time
- investigate the relationship between a geometric series and the value of an ordinary simple annuity, which is a series of regular payments or deposits that earn interest over a period of time
- analyze and solve problems involving future value
- analyze and solve problems involving present value
- use technology to further investigate financial situations involving compound interest and to generate amortization tables for loans and mortgages
- explore the effects of changing the value of the payment, interest rate, and principal on the amortization of Canadian mortgages

Visit the Nelson Mathematics student Web site at **www.math.nelson.com**. You'll find links to interactive examples, online tutorials, and more.

Connections

The Chapter Problem

Financial Planning

Many people do not have the time or expertise to manage their investments or finances, so they hire a professional financial advisor. The advisor may

- help the client to plan and follow a budget
- help the client to reach short- and long-term financial goals
- set up education funds for the client's children
- give advice on investments, such as registered retirement savings plans (RRSP), guaranteed investment certificates (GICs), mutual funds, stocks, or bonds
- manage the client's assets after retirement and estate planning

Investment Problem

You are a financial planner and you have a new client. Mr. Sacchetto is a math teacher who is celebrating his 37th birthday and his son Bart's fourth birthday.

- Mr. Sacchetto wishes to establish an education fund for his son by depositing \$25 at the end of each month until Bart's 18th birthday.
- He intends to renew his mortgage today at 8.4%/a, compounded semiannually. He still owes \$77 000, and 20 years remain in the term of the mortgage. He would like to make monthly payments.
- Mr. Sacchetto owes \$8986 on his car. To pay this debt, he makes payments of \$300 at the end of each month. The interest rate is 10.2%/a, compounded monthly.
- Mr. Sacchetto wants to retire on his 55th birthday with \$120 000 in savings. At that time, he wishes to begin withdrawing a regular amount from these savings at the end of each month. For this reason, he wishes to set up a registered income fund (RIF) that will be depleted, or used up, on his 75th birthday.

As his advisor, he asks you to develop a financial plan for him. Throughout the chapter, you will be asked questions that will assist you in developing the plan.

For help with this problem, see pages 116, 126, 142, 155, 167, 182, and 195.

Challenge 1

Joe and Anne wish to buy a house that costs $148 000. They know very little about mortgages or how to qualify for a mortgage. Here are some of their questions.

- What does it mean to "qualify" for a mortgage?
- What is the minimum down payment required for a mortgage?
- What are some of the advantages of making a larger down payment?
- Can all or a portion of an RRSP be used as collateral or as a deposit?
- What are the terms and conditions of a mortgage?
- Is it possible to make extra payments or to increase the payments? Is it also possible to change the terms of a mortgage or to make an "early renewal"?
- What are the current interest rates on mortgages? What is an affordable monthly mortgage payment?

Learn more about Canadian mortgages and write a report that addresses these questions. You may find it helpful to visit a local bank or credit union. Visit Nelson Thomson Learning's Web site at www.math.nelson.com for more information.

Challenge 2

A **perpetuity** is an annuity that pays out a specified amount beginning on a fixed date and continuing forever. One example of a perpetuity is the series of interest payments from a sum of money invested permanently. Investigate perpetuities further. Determine how much is needed to establish a scholarship fund that pays scholarships of $1200 every three months forever if the endowment can be invested at 8%/a, compounded quarterly, and if the first scholarship is paid

(a) three months from now **(b)** two years from now

Web Challenge

For a related Internet activity, go to **www.math.nelson.com**.

Getting Ready

In this chapter, you will learn more about sequences, as explored in Chapter 1. You will identify arithmetic and geometric sequences and find the general term, t_n. You will work with decimals, rational numbers, and rational exponents. You will also simplify expressions involving exponents and solve exponential equations.

These exercises will help you warm up for the work ahead.

1. Find the first five terms of each of the following sequences. Start with $n = 1$.

(a) $t_n = 3n - 7$

(b) $t_n = 5(n - 3) + 6$

(c) $t_n = 3(2)^{n-1}$

(d) $t_n = -4(n - 1) + 11$

(e) $t_n = 8\left(\frac{1}{2}\right)^{n-1}$

(f) $t_n = \frac{1}{2}(-2)^{n-1}$

(g) $t_n = 50(1.10)^n$

(h) $t_n = 1000(1.06)^{n-1}$

(i) $t_n = -8(n - 1) + 15$

2. Determine if each sequence is arithmetic, geometric, or neither.

(a) 5, 16, 27, 38, …

(b) 3, −6, 12, −24, …

(c) 10, −15, 20, −25, …

(d) 81, 27, 9, 3, …

(e) 3, 5, 8, 12, …

(f) 61, 55, 49, 43, …

(g) 1000, 1100, 1210, 1331, …

(h) $\frac{3}{4}, \frac{5}{7}, \frac{7}{10}, \frac{9}{12}$

(i) 7, 3, −1, −4, …

3. For each sequence that is either arithmetic or geometric in question 2, find the general term, t_n.

4. Evaluate without using a calculator.

(a) $64^{\frac{1}{2}}$

(b) $16^{\frac{5}{4}}$

(c) $64^{-\frac{1}{3}}$

(d) $\left(\frac{3}{4}\right)^{-2}$

5. Use a calculator to evaluate to four decimal places.

(a) $12^{\frac{1}{2}}$

(b) $(-36)^{\frac{1}{3}}$

(c) $(1.16)^{-3}$

(d) $(1.05)^{-\frac{1}{3}}$

(e) $(1.05)^{\frac{36}{52}}$

(f) $(5842)^{-\frac{2}{3}}$

(g) $(1.08)^{\frac{13}{4}}$

(h) $(1212)^{-\frac{101}{365}}$

6. Solve.

(a) $5^{2x-7} = 5^{5x+12}$

(b) $3^{4x} = 27^{x+1}$

(c) $5(2)^x = 160$

(d) $\left(\frac{3}{2}\right)^{-x} = \frac{32}{243}$

7. Evaluate to two decimal places.

(a) $1000(1.10)^2$

(b) $675(1.02)^{36}$

(c) $8500(1.008)^{-12}$

(d) $400(1.06)^{\frac{35}{4}}$

(e) $100\left(\frac{(1.12)^{10} - 1}{0.12}\right)$

(f) $500 \times \frac{1 - (1.008)^{-240}}{0.008}$

8. Calculate the simple interest in each situation.

(a) \$4000 invested at 6.5%/a for 6 years

(b) \$1000 borrowed at 9%/a for 28 months

(c) \$3300 invested at 8%/a for 150 days

(d) \$28 000 borrowed at 11%/a for 100 weeks

9. Determine the number of terms in each arithmetic sequence.

(a) 6, 13, 20, 27, … , 97

(b) 18, 14, 10, 6, … , −38

10. An antique postage stamp appreciates by 9% of its value each year. The stamp was worth \$0.34 in 1969. What is its value in 2012?

11. A new car that was purchased for \$25 600 depreciates in value by 12% each year. Determine its value at the end of seven years.

12. Determine the amount and the interest earned for

(a) \$3600 invested for 9 years at 5.8%/a, compounded annually

(b) \$18 000 borrowed for 5 years at 8.4%/a, compounded monthly

(c) \$7700 invested for 56 months at 6.4%/a, compounded quarterly

(d) \$13 500 borrowed for 2 years at 7.3%/a, compounded daily

13. Determine the present value and the interest earned for each of the following.

(a) \$3600 is due in 9 years if it is invested at 4.8%/a, compounded annually

(b) \$800 is due in 5 years if it is borrowed at 7.6%/a, compounded semiannually

(c) \$22 700 is due in 6 years if it is invested at 5.4%/a, compounded monthly

(d) \$5300 is due in 36 months if it is borrowed at 9.36%/a, compounded weekly

14. On his daughter's tenth birthday, Mr. Huceluk invests a single sum of money that will grow to \$12 000 when she turns 19. The money is invested at 9%/a, compounded monthly. How much must he invest on her tenth birthday to reach his goal?

15. Jane borrowed \$6800 at 9.8%/a, compounded quarterly, to purchase a jet ski. At the end of nine months, she paid \$2100, which includes principal and interest. What must she pay at the end of three years after the purchase to close the debt?

16. A culture of bacteria doubles in size every 20 min. How long will it take for the population to reach 60 000, if the initial population was six bacteria?

17. Kadie invested \$3000 at 6%/a, compounded quarterly. How long will it take for the investment to be worth \$8500?

18. Determine the number of terms in each geometric sequence.

(a) 2, 6, 18, … , 13 122

(b) 5, 10, 20, 40, … , 10 240

2.1 Arithmetic Series

Over 200 years ago, a teacher in Germany wanted to keep his students busy for a while, so he asked them to add all the whole numbers from 1 to 100. Within a few moments, ten-year-old Karl Friedrich Gauss had the correct answer, while his classmates struggled with the problem for several hours. (They all got the wrong answer.)

Here is Gauss's solution. Suppose you write out the terms of the sum horizontally. Now write the sum in reverse order, underneath the first line. Add each vertical pair of terms.

$$\begin{array}{ccccccccccccccc} 1 & + & 2 & + & 3 & + & 4 & + & 5 & + \ldots + & 98 & + & 99 & + & 100 \\ 100 & + & 99 & + & 98 & + & 97 & + & 96 & + \ldots + & 3 & + & 2 & + & 1 \\ \hline 101 & + & 101 & + & 101 & + & 101 & + & 101 & + \ldots + & 101 & + & 101 & + & 101 \end{array}$$

$101 \times 100 = 10\,100$ The sum has 100 terms, so multiply 101 by 100.

$10\,100 \div 2 = 5050$ Each term of the sum from 1 to 100 appears twice, so divide the result by 2.

Therefore $1 + 2 + 3 + \ldots + 100 = 5050$.

You will use this method in the following problem.

An auditorium is being built in the shape of a semicircle with 12 seats in the first row, 15 seats in the second row, 18 seats in the third row, 21 seats in the fourth row, and so on.

Think, Do, Discuss

1. Recall working with sequences in Chapter 1. What type of sequence describes the seating? Explain. How many seats are in the tenth row? Find the general term, t_n, that represents the number of seats in the nth row.
2. How would you find the total number of seats in the first seven rows? Would this method be efficient for finding the number of seats in the first 30 rows? Explain.
3. The sum of the terms of a sequence is called a **series**. The sum of the first seven rows of seats is S_7, where $S_7 = t_1 + t_2 + t_3 + t_4 + t_5 + t_6 + t_7$. The sum of the first 30 rows of seats is S_{30}. Express S_7 as the sum of seven terms, using the general term, t_n, you found in step 1. Write this sum in your notebook.

4. Use Gauss's method to guide you through the following steps.
   (a) Rewrite the sum for S_7 in reverse order so that t_7 is below t_1, t_6 is below t_2, and so on.
   (b) Add each pair of terms, for example, $t_7 + t_1$. What is the sum of each pair?
   (c) How many pairs of terms are there? Calculate the sum of the pairs of terms and let this sum be equal to $2S_7$.
   (d) What must you do to $2S_7$ to determine S_7, which is the number of seats in the first seven rows? Verify your solution by adding the terms in S_7.
5. How many seats are in the 30th row? Use what you learned in the previous steps to find the total number of seats in the first 30 rows.
6. Suppose you know the first term and the last term of an arithmetic sequence. Suggest a formula for finding S_n, the sum of any **arithmetic series.**

Focus 2.1

Key Ideas

- A **series** is the sum of the terms of a sequence. The sum of the first n terms of a sequence is S_n, where

$$S_n = t_1 + t_2 + t_3 + t_4 + \ldots + t_{n-1} + t_n$$

- An arithmetic sequence has the general term $t_n = a + (n - 1)d$, where a is the **first term** and d is the **common difference** between terms. The sum of this sequence is called an **arithmetic series** and is

$$S_n = a + (a + d) + (a + 2d) + (a + 3d) + \ldots + [a + (n - 2)d] + [a + (n - 1)d]$$

- Find the sum of the series, S_n, by adding the first term, t_1, and the last term, t_n, together, multiplying by the number of terms, n, and then dividing the result by 2.
- The sum of the n terms of an arithmetic series is

$$S_n = \frac{n(t_1 + t_n)}{2}$$

- Substitute a for t_1 and substitute $a + (n - 1)d$ for t_n in $S_n = \frac{n(t_1 + t_n)}{2}$. The result produces the sum of the first n terms of an arithmetic series,

$$S_n = \frac{n}{2}[2a + (n - 1)d]$$

Use this formula when you know the first term of the series, the common difference, and the number of terms.

Example 1

For the series $2 + 11 + 20 + 29 + \dots$, find

(a) t_{20} (b) S_{20}

Solution

(a) The series is arithmetic, and $a = 2$, $d = 9$, and $n = 20$.

$$t_n = a + (n - 1)d$$

Therefore, $t_{20} = 2 + 19(9) = 173$.

(b) Since the first and the last terms are known, use $S_n = \frac{n(t_1 + t_n)}{2}$ to find S_{20}.

$$\begin{aligned} S_{20} &= \frac{20(2 + 173)}{2} \\ &= 10(175) \\ &= 1750 \end{aligned}$$

Example 2

A military unit buys 10 spare parts during the first month of a contract, 15 spare parts in the second month, 20 spare parts in the third month, 25 spare parts in the fourth month, and so on. The acquisitions officer wants to know the total number of spare parts the unit will have after 24 months.

Solution

The sequence of the number of spare parts bought each month is 10, 15, 20, 25, … . For this arithmetic sequence, $a = 10$ and $d = 5$. Find the sum of the first 24 terms.

$$S_n = \frac{n}{2}[2a + (n - 1)d] \qquad \text{Substitute } a = 10,\ d = 5, \text{ and } n = 24.$$

$$\begin{aligned} S_{24} &= \frac{24}{2}[2(10) + (24 - 1)(5)] \qquad \text{Simplify.} \\ &= 12(20 + 115) \\ &= 1620 \end{aligned}$$

The unit will have a total of 1620 spare parts after 24 months.

Example 3

Samantha deposited \$128 in her account. Each week, she deposits \$7 less than the previous week until she makes her last deposit of \$9. Find the total value of her deposits.

Solution

The arithmetic series $128 + 121 + 114 + \dots + 16 + 9$ represents the sum of her weekly deposits. To calculate the sum, first find the number of terms in the series.

$t_n = a + (n - 1)d$	Substitute $a = 128$, $d = -7$, and $t_n = 9$.
$9 = 128 + (n - 1)(-7)$	Expand.
$9 = 128 - 7n + 7$	Solve for n.
$-126 = -7n$	
$18 = n$	

There are 18 terms in the series.

Now find the sum.

$S_n = \frac{n(t_1 + t_n)}{2}$	Substitute $n = 18$, $t_1 = 128$, and $t_n = 9$.
$S_{18} = \frac{18(128 + 9)}{2}$	Simplify.
$= 1233$	

Samantha deposited \$1233 in her account.

Example 4

The fifth term of an arithmetic series is 9, and the sum of the first 16 terms is 480. Find the first three terms of the series.

Solution

For an arithmetic sequence, $t_n = a + (n - 1)d$. In this case, $n = 5$ and $t_5 = 9$.

Therefore, $9 = a + 4d$ ①

For an arithmetic series, $S_n = \frac{n}{2}[2a + (n - 1)d]$. In this case, $n = 16$ and $S_{16} = 480$.

$$480 = \frac{16}{2}(2a + 15d)$$

$$480 = 8(2a + 15d)$$

$$60 = 2a + 15d \quad ②$$

To find a and d, solve the linear system of equations ① and ②.

$9 = a + 4d$	①	
$60 = 2a + 15d$	②	Multiply equation ① by 2 to obtain ③.
$18 = 2a + 8d$	③	
$60 = 2a + 15d$	②	Subtract ② from ③.
$-42 = -7d$		
$6 = d$		

Substitute $d = 6$ in equation ① to obtain the value of a.

$$9 = a + 4(6) \quad ①$$

$$a = -15$$

The first three terms of the series are -15, -9, and -3.

Practise, Apply, Solve 2.1

A

1. Determine whether each series is arithmetic.

(a) $5 + 8 + 11 + 14 + 17 + \dots$

(b) $1 + 2 + 3 + 5 + 8 + 13 + \dots$

(c) $-83 - 77 - 71 - 65 - 59 - \dots$

(d) $a + 2a + 4a + 8a + 16a + \dots$

2. For each series, calculate t_{10} and S_{10}.

(a) $2 + 10 + 18 + 26 + \dots$

(b) $100 + 85 + 70 + 55 + \dots$

(c) $-18 - 11 - 4 + 3 + \dots$

(d) $\frac{1}{6} + \frac{1}{2} + \frac{5}{6} + \frac{7}{6} + \dots$

3. **Communication:** You could add whole numbers from 1 to 10 by evaluating $\frac{10 \times 11}{2}$, and you could add the whole numbers from 1 to 50 by evaluating $\frac{50 \times 51}{2}$. How would you add the whole numbers from 1 to 200? Explain how the terms in these expressions are obtained.

4. Find the sum of the whole numbers from

(a) 1 to 30 (b) 1 to 60

(c) 1 to 1000 (d) 1 to 24

5. Find the sum of each arithmetic series, given the first and the last terms.

(a) $t_1 = 7$ and $t_{12} = 51$ (b) $t_1 = 88$ and $t_{15} = 4$

(c) $t_1 = -784$ and $t_{20} = 869$ (d) $t_1 = -2$ and $t_{30} = 85$

6. Find the sum of each series.

(a) $3 + 7 + 11 + \dots + t_{15}$ (b) $11 + 22 + 33 + \dots + t_{20}$

(c) $4 - 1 - 6 - \dots - t_{27}$ (d) $\frac{1}{2} + \frac{5}{8} + \frac{3}{4} + \dots + t_{14}$

B

7. **Knowledge and Understanding:** Find S_{21} for the series $2.8 + 3.2 + 3.6 + 4.0 + \dots$.

8. Find the sum of each arithmetic series.

(a) $13 + 24 + 35 + \dots + 156$

(b) $15 + 11 + 7 + \dots - 37$

(c) $-77 - 70 - 63 - \dots + 252$

(d) $\frac{1}{6} + \frac{1}{3} + \frac{1}{2} + \dots + \frac{5}{3}$

9. In an arithmetic series of 50 terms, the 17th term is 53 and the 28th term is 86. Find the sum of the series.

10. In an arithmetic series of 20 terms, the seventh term is 34 and the ninth term is 48. Find the sum of the series.

11. In an arithmetic series, the 15th term is 43 and the sum of the first 15 terms is 120. Add the first 20 terms of the series.

12. In an arithmetic series, the 12th term is 15 and the sum of the first 15 terms is 105. Add the first three terms of the series.

13. **Application:** An usher was asked to count the number of seats in an auditorium. The auditorium had 25 rows of seats. He counted the 59 seats in the last row at the back and noticed that each subsequent row toward the front row had two fewer seats than the row before it. How many seats are in the auditorium?

14. The sum of the first n odd numbers is 400. What is the value of n?

15. The arithmetic series $5 + 9 + 13 + \ldots + t_n$ has a sum of 945. How many terms does the series have?

16. In a lecture hall, there are 13 seats in the first row. The next six rows increase by two seats each. Each of the remaining rows increases by three seats each. There are 12 rows in all. How many seats are in the lecture hall?

17. A skydiver jumped out of a plane. She fell 4.9 m in the first second, 14.7 m in the second second, 24.5 m in the third second, and so on, in the same pattern, until she opened her parachute. How far did she fall between the eighth second and the thirteenth second?

18. **Check Your Understanding:** Explain, in your own words, when it is better to use $S_n = \frac{n(t_1 + t_n)}{2}$ instead of $S_n = \frac{n}{2}[2a + (n - 1)d]$. What values must you know to find each sum?

C

19. Michelle purchased a used car for \$17 000. Once Michelle drove away from the lot, the car's value depreciated by 20%. For each subsequent year, the car's value depreciated by \$450. What was the total depreciation after six years?

20. A hockey arena has 10 920 seats. The first row of seats around the rink has 220 seats. The number of seats in each subsequent row increases by 16.

(a) How many rows of seats does the arena have?

(b) The arena's owners would like to expand the arena by adding four more rows of seats. What will be the new capacity of the arena?

21. Three squares are added to a 1 by 1 square to form a 2 by 2 square. How many squares must be added to the 2 by 2 square to produce a 3 by 3 square? Use an arithmetic series to prove that an n by n square has a total of n^2 squares.

22. **Thinking, Inquiry, Problem Solving:** The sum of the terms of the general arithmetic series is $S_n = a + (a + d) + (a + 2d) + (a + 3d) + \ldots + [a + (n - 2)d] + [a + (n - 1)d]$. Use the method in the Think, Do, Discuss, which begins with rewriting the terms of the series in reverse order, to show that $S_n = \frac{n}{2}[2a + (n - 1)d]$.

23. Evaluate $(1 + 5 + 9 + 13 + \ldots + 201) - (3 + 7 + 11 + 15 + \ldots + 203)$.

24. Evaluate $300 - 299 + 298 - 297 + 296 - \ldots + 100 - 99$.

The Chapter Problem—Financial Planning

CP1. Visit a local bank or credit union, or search the Internet to obtain information about registered retirement savings plans (RRSPs), guaranteed investment certificates (GICs), registered education savings plans (RESPs), and registered income funds (RIFs). Briefly describe each type of savings plan and explain its purpose.

Karl Friedrich Gauss (1777–1855)

Karl Friedrich Gauss is one of the three greatest mathematicians who ever lived. The other two are Archimides and Isaac Newton. By age 24, Gauss had made essential advances in many areas of math and science, including geometry, number theory, probability theory, astronomy, and electricity. Read about this remarkable man in *Men of Mathematics,* by E.T. Bell, or use the Internet to do research on him. Why is there a statue of Gauss in his birthplace standing on a star with 17 points?

Investigating a Sequence Using the TI-83 Plus Calculator and the TI Calculator-Based Ranger (CBR)

2.2

EXPLORATION

In this activity, you will explore the changing height of a bouncing ball and develop a sequence that will predict the maximum height of the ball after each bounce. You will also find the total vertical distance that the ball travels after a number of bounces.

Equipment

- TI CBR (Calculator-Based Ranger)
- TI-83 Plus graphing calculator
- ball (a racquetball or a large rubber ball)

Procedure

1. Connect the CBR to the calculator. Turn on both the calculator and the CBR.
2. Press [APPS] on the calculator.
3. Select **2:CBL/CBR** and press any key. Then select **3:RANGER** and press [ENTER].
4. From the main menu of the RANGER program, select **3:APPLICATIONS.**
5. For the units, select **1:METERS**. Under the applications menu, select **3:BALL BOUNCE.**
6. Follow the directions on your calculator's screen. Choose one person to release the ball and another to operate the CBR. Release the ball, making sure that the CBR is at least 0.5 m above the ball. Press the **TRIGGER** key on the CBR just before the ball hits the ground.
7. Your graph should have at least five bounces. If this is not the case or you are not satisfied with the results of your experiment, press [ENTER]. Then select **5:REPEAT SAMPLE**, and try the experiment again.
8. When you are satisfied with your data, sketch the graph of height versus time.

Analyzing the Data

1. Use [▶] and [TRACE] to find the approximate maximum height of the ball, y, after the first bounce. After each bounce, n, record the maximum height of the ball, y, in your notebook, using a table. Use these values to calculate the total vertical distances, as described in the table, travelled by the ball.

EXPLORATION

Bounce, n	Maximum Height of the Ball After Bounce n, y(m)	$\frac{\text{Maximum Height After this Bounce}}{\text{Maximum Height After Previous Bounce}} \times 100$ (%)	Total Vertical Distance Travelled by the Ball Between this Bounce and the Next Bounce (m)	Total Vertical Distance Travelled Since $t = 0$ (m)
1				
2				
3				
4				
5				

2. Press [ENTER] to return to the **PLOT MENU** and select 7:**QUIT** to exit the RANGER program.

3. Plot the data points representing the maximum height of the ball on a scatter plot. Press [STAT], select **1:Edit** to enter the bounce number, n, in **L1** and the maximum height of the ball after each bounce, y, in **L2**. Press [2nd] [Y=]. Press [ENTER] to select **Plot1**. Press [ENTER] again. For **Type**, select the second graph; for **Xlist**, select L1; for **Ylist**, select L2; and select the square for **Mark**. To see a plot of this data, press [ZOOM] [9].

4. Write the sequence that represents the maximum height of the ball after each bounce. Describe this type of sequence. Use the third column in your table to help you determine the general term, t_n, that models this sequence.

5. Rewrite your model for t_n by substituting x for n. Press [Y=] and enter the equation of your model. Press [ENTER] and then [GRAPH]. Describe how well the model fits the data.

6. Use [TRACE] and the graph of your model to predict the maximum height after each bounce from $n = 1$ to $n = 8$. Record your predictions in your notebook.

7. Use your model to calculate the total vertical distance travelled by the ball after the first

(a) five bounces

(b) eight bounces

(c) Compare the answer you found in (a) to the total vertical distance that you calculated for the table.

8. Suppose you dropped a large super ball from a great height. Explain the difficulty of using this method to calculate the total vertical distance travelled by the ball after the first 20 bounces.

9. Repeat this exploration to determine how the maximum height and the total vertical distance travelled by the ball is affected by different surfaces, for example, a concrete floor, different balls, or different initial heights.

Geometric Series 2.3

A large telemarketing call centre will be closed on Monday due to an ice storm, and the employees are notified on Sunday. The company has already set up an emergency phone "tree." The company's president calls three employees. Then each of these three employees calls three other people, and so on.

Think, Do, Discuss

1. Start with the company's president at the top, and draw a diagram of the phone tree for the first four rounds of calls. The diagram represents the sequence of the number of employees notified at each round.
2. How many employees were notified by the president, who made the first round of calls? How many employees were notified during the second round of calls? the third round of calls? the fourth round of calls?
3. The number of employees notified during each round of calls forms a sequence. What do you call this sequence? Explain. Determine the general term, t_n, to represent the number of employees notified during the nth round.
4. Write the sequence that represents the number of employees notified for the first seven rounds of calls. Find the total number of employees notified after the first seven rounds of calls.
5. The sum of the terms of a geometric sequence is a **geometric series**. The sum of the sequence in step 4 is S_7, where $S_7 = t_1 + t_2 + t_3 + t_4 + t_5 + t_6 + t_7$. Write the series, substituting the appropriate values for t_1 to t_7.
6. To develop a formula for the sum of the geometric series, begin by multiplying both sides of the equation in step 5 by the common ratio, $r = 3$. Write the terms in $3S_7$ so that t_1 of $3S_7$ is below t_2 of S_7 and t_2 of $3S_7$ is below t_3 of S_7, and so on. Compare S_7 to $3S_7$. What is the same? What is different? Would there be so many common terms if you had multiplied S_7 by a number other than the common ratio of $r = 3$? Explain.
7. Subtract S_7 from $3S_7$. What values remain on the right side? Which terms of the geometric sequence do these values represent?
8. $2S_7$ is now the sum of only two terms. What must you do to both sides so that the left side is S_7? Find S_7. What does this sum represent?
9. Use the method in steps 7 and 8 to determine the total number of employees notified after ten rounds of calls.

10. The general term of a geometric sequence is $t_n = 3(4)^{n-1}$. Use the method in steps 5 to 8 to find S_8, the geometric series, or sum, of the first eight terms.

11. A geometric sequence has the general term $t_n = ar^{n-1}$, and a and r are known. Suggest a formula for finding S_n, the geometric series of this sequence.

12. List the first five terms of the series if the first term is a and the common ratio, r, is 1. What is the sum of these five terms, S_5?

Focus 2.3

Key Ideas

- The general term of a geometric sequence is $t_n = ar^{n-1}$, where a is the first term of the sequence and r is the common ratio.
- The sum of the terms of a geometric sequence is a **geometric series**. The sum is written

$$S_n = a + ar + ar^2 + ar^3 + \ldots + ar^{n-2} + ar^{n-1}$$

- The sum of the first n terms of a geometric series can also be written

$$S_n = \frac{t_{n+1} - t_1}{r - 1},\ r \neq 1$$

- In any geometric sequence, $t_{n+1} = r(t_n) = r(ar^{n-1}) = ar^{1+n-1} = ar^n$, and $t_1 = a$. Substituting these values in $\frac{t_{n+1} - t_1}{r - 1}$ gives

$$\begin{aligned} S_n &= \frac{ar^n - a}{r - 1} \\ &= \frac{a(r^n - 1)}{r - 1},\ r \neq 1 \end{aligned}$$

Example 1

Find S_8, the sum of the first eight terms of each series.

(a) $2 - 6 + 18 - 54 + \ldots$

(b) $200 + 100 + 50 + 25 + \ldots$

Solution

(a) The series is geometric, and $a = 2$ and $r = -3$.

Method 1: Use $S_n = \frac{t_{n+1} - t_1}{r - 1}$.

To find S_8, first find $t_{n+1} = ar^n$.

$t_9 = ar^8 = 2(-3)^8 = 13\,122$

In this case, $t_1 = 2$ and $r = -3$.

$$\begin{aligned} S_8 &= \frac{13\,122 - 2}{-3 - 1} \\ &= \frac{13\,120}{-4} \\ &= -3280 \end{aligned}$$

Method 2: Use $S_n = \frac{a(r^n - 1)}{r - 1}$.

In this case, $a = 2$, $r = -3$, and $n = 8$.

$$\begin{aligned} S_8 &= \frac{2[(-3)^8 - 1]}{-3 - 1} \\ &= \frac{2(6561 - 1)}{-3 - 1} \\ &= \frac{13\,120}{-4} \\ &= -3280 \end{aligned}$$

(b) The series is geometric, and $a = 200$, $r = \frac{1}{2}$, and $n = 8$.

$$S_n = \frac{a(r^n - 1)}{r - 1}$$ Substitute the values of a, r, and n.

$$S_8 = \frac{200\left[\left(\frac{1}{2}\right)^8 - 1\right]}{\frac{1}{2} - 1}$$ Simplify.

$$\doteq \frac{200(-0.996\ 093\ 75)}{-\frac{1}{2}}$$

$$= 398.4375$$ (**Hint:** To get the fractional equivalent of a decimal using the TI-83 Plus calculator, press MATH 1 ENTER.)

$$= \frac{6375}{16}$$

Example 2

A new lottery offers to pay the grand prize winner in one of two ways:

Option A: \$10 000 000 now

Option B: A payment each day for 30 days: \$0.01 on the first day, \$0.02 on the second day, \$0.04 on the third day, \$0.08 on the fourth day, and so on

For the grand prize winner, which option results in the biggest grand prize?

Solution

Option B can be represented by the following series:

$$S_{30} = 0.01 + 0.02 + 0.04 + 0.08 + \ldots + t_{30}$$

The series is geometric, and $a = 0.01$, $r = 2$, and $n = 30$.

$$S_n = \frac{a(r^n - 1)}{r - 1}$$ Substitute the values of a, r, and n.

$$S_{30} = \frac{0.01(2^{30} - 1)}{2 - 1}$$ Simplify.

$$= 0.01(1\ 073\ 741\ 823)$$

$$= 10\ 737\ 418.23$$

At the end of 30 days, the grand prize winner would have \$10 737 418.23. Option B offers the greatest grand prize.

Example 3

Find the sum of the geometric series $\frac{1}{16} + \frac{1}{4} + 1 + 4 + \ldots + 65\,536$.

Solution

First find the number of terms in the geometric series, where $t_n = ar^{n-1}$.

Let $t_n = 65\,536$, $a = \frac{1}{16}$, and $r = 4$. Solve for n.

$65\,536 = \frac{1}{16}(4)^{n-1}$	Multiply both sides by 16.
$1\,048\,576 = 4^{n-1}$	Use trial and error to rewrite 1 048 576 as a power of 4.
$4^{10} = 4^{n-1}$	Since the bases are the same, the exponents must be equal.
$\therefore\ 10 = n - 1$	
$11 = n$	

Determine the sum.

$S_n = \dfrac{a(r^n - 1)}{r - 1}$	Substitute $a = \frac{1}{16}$, $r = 4$, and $n = 11$.
$S_{11} = \dfrac{\frac{1}{16}(4^{11} - 1)}{4 - 1}$	Simplify.
$= \dfrac{\frac{1}{16}(4\,194\,303)}{3}$	
$= \dfrac{4\,194\,303}{16 \times 3}$	
$= 87\,381.3125$	

Example 4

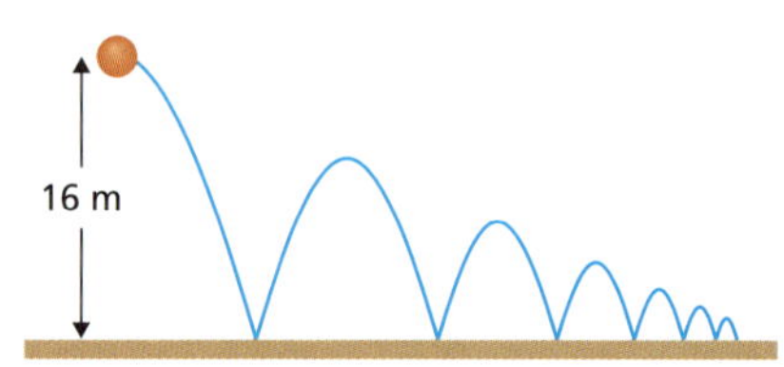

Amy drops a ball from a height of 16 m. Each time the ball touches the ground, it bounces up to $\frac{5}{8}$ of the maximum height of the previous bounce. Determine the total vertical distance the ball has travelled when it touches the ground on the seventh bounce. Express your answer to two decimal places.

Solution

Calculate the total vertical distance the ball has travelled by finding the sum of the downward distances and the sum of the upward distances. The upward vertical distance is the same as the downward vertical distance for each bounce. Therefore, the total vertical distance travelled is twice the sum of the downward distances, less 16 m, which is the height from which the ball is dropped. The sum of the downward distances is S_7, the sum of the geometric sequence, with $a = 16$, $r = \frac{5}{8}$, and $n = 7$.

$$S_n = \frac{a(r^n - 1)}{r - 1}$$ Substitute the values for a, r, and n.

$$S_7 = \frac{16\left[\left(\frac{5}{8}\right)^7 - 1\right]}{\frac{5}{8} - 1}$$ Simplify.

$$\doteq \frac{-15.403\,953\,55}{-0.375}$$

$$= 41.08$$

The total downward distance is about 41.08 m and the total upward distance is 41.08 − 16 = 25.08 m. The total vertical distance travelled by the ball is 66.16 m.

Practise, Apply, Solve 2.3

A

1. i. Determine whether each of the following series is arithmetic, geometric, or neither.
ii. For each series that is geometric, determine the common ratio.

(a) $400 + 200 + 100 + 50 + \ldots$

(b) $15\,000 + 12\,000 + 9600 + 7680 + \ldots$

(c) $24 - 28 + 32 - 36 + 40 - \ldots$

(d) $-3000 + 4500 - 6750 + 10\,125 - \ldots$

(e) $\frac{1}{4} - \frac{1}{8} + \frac{1}{16} - \frac{1}{32} + \ldots$

(f) $12 + 16 + 21 + 27 + 34 + \ldots$

2. For each of the following geometric series, determine
i. the general term, t_n
ii. the general sum, S_n
iii. S_8 to two decimal places, where appropriate

(a) $2 + 6 + 18 + 54 + \ldots$

(b) $1 - \frac{2}{3} + \frac{4}{9} - \frac{8}{27} + \ldots$

(c) $6 - 12 + 24 - 48 + \ldots$

(d) $81 + 27 + 9 + 3 + \ldots$

(e) $0.4 + 0.04 + 0.004 + 0.0004 + \ldots$

(f) $8 - 8 + 8 - 8 + \ldots$

3. For each of the given geometric series, find the indicated sum. Give your answers to two decimal places, where appropriate.

(a) S_7; $5 - 10 + 20 - \ldots$

(b) S_{10}; $54 + 18 + 6 + \ldots$

(c) S_8; $-300 + 4500 - 67\,500 + \ldots$

(d) S_9; $2 + 2\sqrt{2} + 4 + 4\sqrt{2} + \ldots$

(e) S_n; $1 + x + x^2 + \ldots$

(f) S_n; $5w + 10w^2 + 20w^3 + \ldots$

4. **Knowledge and Understanding:** For the geometric series $6 - 18 + 54 - \ldots$, find

(a) the eighth term

(b) the sum of the first eight terms

B

5. Evaluate each geometric series.

(a) $7 + 14 + 28 + \dots + 3584$

(b) $-3 - 6 - 12 - 24 - \dots - 768$

(c) $1 + \frac{5}{2} + \frac{25}{4} + \dots + \frac{15\,625}{64}$

(d) $96\,000 - 48\,000 + 24\,000 - \dots + 375$

(e) $1000 + 1000(1.06) + 1000(1.06)^2 + \dots + 1000(1.06)^{12}$

6. The fifth term of a geometric series is 405 and the sixth term is 1215. Find the sum of the first nine terms.

7. A large school board established a phone tree to contact all of its employees in case of emergencies or inclement weather. Each of the three superintendents calls three employees who each in turn calls three other employees, and so on. How many rounds of phone calls are needed to notify all 9840 employees?

8. **Communication:** Ed begins working as a reporter for a local newspaper. He earns \$1200 for the first month. Each subsequent month, his pay increases by 10%. Describe two different methods for calculating Ed's total pay for the last six months of his first year.

9. Moira wants to share a joke with her friends by e-mail. She sends an e-mail to five friends and asks them to forward her e-mail to five other people, and so on.

(a) Draw a tree diagram to represent the first three rounds of e-mails.

(b) No one receives two copies of the joke. How many people will receive an e-mail of the joke

i. for the first round of e-mails?

ii. for the second round of e-mails?

iii. for the third round of e-mails?

(c) Write an equation to represent the total number of people who receive the e-mail after n rounds of e-mails.

(d) Determine the total number of people who receive the e-mail after eight rounds. What is the likelihood that this event would occur? Justify your answer.

10. When you shut off a circular saw, it continues to turn for a while. Each second, the speed or revolutions per second, r/s, is $\frac{2}{3}$ of the speed of the previous second. At the beginning of the ninth second, the saw has turned a total of 258 times. What was the speed of the saw at the beginning of the first second when it was first shut off? Express your answer to one decimal place.

11. Roger just received his first annual pension cheque of \$19 500. Each subsequent year, the value of the cheque will be 1.02 times the previous year's cheque, to account for 2% inflation.

(a) How much can Roger expect his seventh cheque to be worth?

(b) Determine the total amount he will have received after his tenth cheque.

12. **Application:** A new computer software company earns a profit of \$245 000 in its first year. The company expects the profit to increase by 15% each year for each subsequent year.

(a) What profit can the company expect to earn in its seventh year?

(b) Find the total profit the company will earn in its first ten years.

13. A super ball is dropped from a height of 15 m. After each bounce, the maximum height of the ball is 70% of the ball's maximum height of the previous bounce. What is the total vertical distance that the ball has travelled when it touches the ground after the fifth bounce? Express your answer to two decimal places.

14. A community group has a telethon each year, which is aired on the community cable channel. This year, \$4500 was raised. The fundraisers wish to increase the money raised by 12% each year.

(a) How much would they need to raise from the telethon five years from now to meet their goal?

(b) How much could the fundraisers expect to raise in total after seven years?

15. **Thinking, Inquiry, Problem Solving:** The sum of the terms of any general geometric series is $S_n = a + ar + ar^2 + ar^3 + \ldots + ar^{n-2} + ar^{n-1}$. Multiply S_n by the common ratio, r, to obtain an expression for $rS_n - S_n$. Use this expression to prove that $S_n = \frac{a(r^n - 1)}{r - 1}$.

16. A sweepstakes has \$4 000 000 in prizes. The first ticket drawn wins \$15, the second ticket drawn wins \$45, the third ticket drawn wins \$135, and so on.

(a) How many tickets can be drawn without giving away more than the allotted prize money?

(b) How much money is left after all the prizes are awarded?

17. **Check Your Understanding**

(a) Use the method in the Think, Do, Discuss of this section to prove that the sum of the series 2 + 8 + 32 + 128 + 512 + 2048 + 8192 is 10 922.

(b) Verify your solution using $S_n = \frac{a(r^n - 1)}{r - 1}$.

C

18. In a geometric series, $t_1 = 3$ and $S_3 = 21$.

(a) Write an expression to represent the second and third terms.

(b) Use the expressions that you found in (a) to help you determine the common ratio. Explain how there can be two solutions.

19. Show that the sum of n terms of the series $2 + 1 + \frac{1}{2} + \frac{1}{4} + \ldots + t_n$ is always less than 4, where n is any natural number.

20. Neither of these series is arithmetic nor geometric, but, by analyzing their patterns, you can find each sum. Find each sum.

(a) $2 - 4 + 6 - 8 + 10 - \ldots - 100$

(b) $1 + 2 + 4 + 5 + 7 + 8 + \ldots + 95 + 97 + 98$

21. The series $\frac{1}{2} + \frac{1}{4} + \frac{1}{8} + \frac{1}{16} + \ldots$ is an example of an infinite geometric series.

(a) Determine the sum of this series.

(b) Is it possible to find the sum of *any* infinite geometric sequence? Explain.

(c) Under what conditions is it possible to find the sum of an infinite geometric sequence?

The Chapter Problem—Financial Planning

In this section, you studied geometric series. Apply what you learned to answer these questions about the Chapter Problem on page 106.

CP2. Bart's education fund earns interest at 6%/a, compounded monthly. Find the value of the first $25 deposit after

(a) 1 month (b) 2 months (c) 3 months

(d) 4 months (e) 36 months

CP3. Show why the sequence of the monthly values of the $25 deposit is a geometric sequence. Determine an expression for t_n, the value of the first deposit after n months.

CP4. Find the sum of the first eight terms of the sequence in CP3.

Did You Know?

The mighty pyramids of Egypt were built thousands of years ago. But when exactly? In *Nature* magazine, Kate Spence has suggested an answer to this question. Spence begins with the fact that one side of the Great Pyramid of Cheops is off true north by exactly 0.05°. The Egyptians did not have compasses, so they may have used the stars to orient the pyramid. Over many centuries, the positions of the stars change because the Earth wobbles slightly on its axis. Spence has shown that in 2478 BCE a straight line drawn between the stars Kochab and Mizar would have been off true north by exactly 0.05°. Thus, Spence concludes that the Great Pyramid was begun in 2478 BCE.

Using a Spreadsheet to Represent the Value of a Deposit

You just invested $5000 in a term deposit that pays 8%/a, compounded annually. You could graph the annual balance by hand or use a graphing calculator. However, a spreadsheet can create a table of the annual balance and the graph.

Create a Table of the Annual Balance

You may find that the spreadsheet software that you are using may have different commands or techniques for achieving the same results.

1. Create a spreadsheet with four columns, labelled Period, Balance, Interest at 8%/a, and Year-end Balance in cells A1, B1, C1, and D1, respectively.
2. In cells A2 and B2, enter 1 and 5000, respectively. In cell C2, enter the expression for interest, **=B2*.08**, and press [ENTER] to calculate the value.
3. The year-end balance is the sum of the balance at the beginning of the year and the interest earned. In cell D2, enter the expression **=B2+C2** and press [ENTER].
4. In cell A3, enter the expression **=A2+1** and press [ENTER]. The balance at the end of each year is the balance at the beginning of the next year. In cell B3, enter the expression **=D2** and press [ENTER]. In cell C3, enter the expression for interest, **=B3*.08** and press [ENTER]. In cell D3, enter the expression **=B3+C3** and press [ENTER].
5. Select cells A3 across to D3 and down to D8. Use the Fill Down command to complete the table.
6. You can display financial data in different ways. Select cells B2 to D8 and click the **$** button or icon. Each number will appear with a dollar sign, a comma, and will be rounded to two decimal places.

	A	B	C	D
1	Period	Balance	Interest at 8%/a	Year-end Balance
2	1	$5,000.00	$400.00	$5,400.00
3	2	$5,400.00	$432.00	$5,832.00
4	3	$5,832.00	$466.56	$6,298.56
5	4	$6,298.56	$503.88	$6,802.44
6	5	$6,802.44	$544.20	$7,346.64
7	6	$7,346.64	$587.73	$7,934.37
8	7	$7,934.37	$634.75	$8,569.12

7. To find the sum of the cells in a row or column, use the **SUM** function or the Σ button. To find the total interest earned over seven years, enter the expression =SUM(C2:C8) in cell C9.

Graph the Annual Balance

Now create a graph. Select the data in the table you wish to graph and choose the **Chart** command. Select **XY – Scatter**. Check your spreadsheet software menus to find the proper commands. You can also add labels, axes, scales, and titles to the graph, similar to the ones shown.

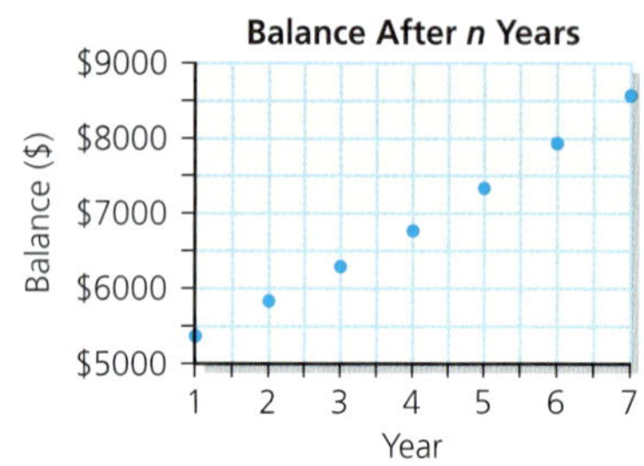

Practice 2.4

Use a spreadsheet to create a table and a graph that display the value of each investment over ten years.

(a) $2000 at 4%/a, compounded yearly

(b) $8000 at 8%/a, compounded quarterly

(c) In the spreadsheet, calculate the total interest earned over the first eight years for the investments in (a) and (b).

(d) $30 000 at 6%/a, compounded monthly

(e) $5000 at 6%/a, compounded semiannually

TECHNOLOGY

Future Value and Amortization Tables 2.5

Part 1: Future Value of Annuities

Mr. Watts wishes to help pay for his 12-year-old granddaughter's future university expenses. Mr. Watts decides to deposit \$3000 at the end of each year, for seven years, in a savings account that pays interest at 7.5%/a, compounded annually. What will be the total value of this investment at the end of each year?

Queen's University

This type of investment, where fixed amounts are deposited or paid at regular intervals over a set period of time, is called an **annuity**. The **payment interval** is the time between successive payment dates. The annuity is called an **ordinary annuity** because the payments are made at the end of the payment intervals.

One way to represent an annuity is with a spreadsheet. Here are some of the values and formulas that Mr. Watts has entered in a spreadsheet to represent his annuity.

	A	B	C	D	E
1	Period	Balance	Interest at 7.5%/a	Payment	New Balance
2	1	0	=B2*0.075	\$3,000	=B2+C2+D2
3	=A2+1	E2	=B3*0.075	=\$D\$2	=B3+C3+D3

He obtained the following table and graph.

	A	B	C	D	E
1	Period	Balance	Interest at 7.5%/a	Payment	New Balance
2	1	\$0.00	\$0.00	\$3,000.00	\$3,000.00
3	2	\$3,000.00	\$225.00	\$3,000.00	\$6,225.00
4	3	\$6,225.00	\$466.88	\$3,000.00	\$9,691.88
5	4	\$9,691.88	\$726.89	\$3,000.00	\$13,418.77
6	5	\$13,418.77	\$1,006.41	\$3,000.00	\$17,425.17
7	6	\$17,425.17	\$1,306.89	\$3,000.00	\$21,732.06
8	7	\$21,732.06	\$1,629.90	\$3,000.00	\$26,361.97

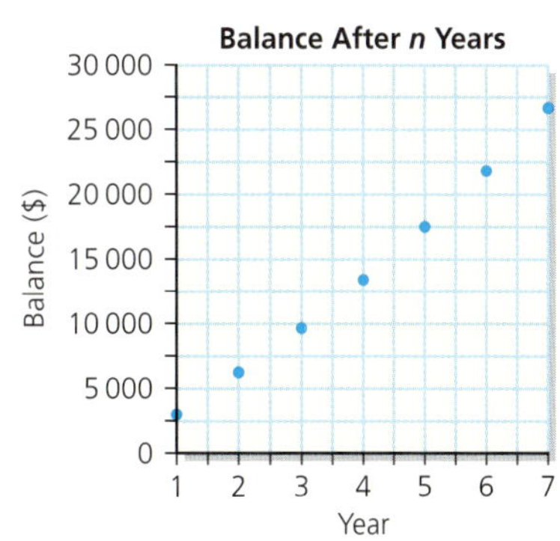

Think, Do, Discuss

1. Why is the interest \$0 for the first period?
2. Explain how the new balance is calculated each year, or period.
3. Describe how the balance at the beginning of each period is determined.
4. In cell D3, the expression **=\$D\$2** appears. Examine this column in the spreadsheet. What do you notice? Mr. Watts used the **Fill Down** command to complete the columns. What happens to the cell references in the spreadsheet? What effect do the \$ signs in **=\$D\$2** have on the values in the Payment column?
5. Reproduce Mr. Watts' spreadsheet and the graph.
6. What is the balance in the account at the end of seven years? This balance is called the **amount**, or accumulated value, of an annuity. Describe two ways for finding the "accumulated" interest. Use the SUM function or the Σ toolbar button to determine the total interest earned.
7. Change the payment in cell D2 to determine the payment that will yield
   (a) \$30 000 after seven years (b) \$15 000 after seven years
8. Change the interest rate to (a) 5%/a and (b) 10%/a. What is the balance in the account after seven years for each change in interest rate? Determine the total interest earned for each of these rates. Compare the interest rates to the total interest earned. What do you notice?
9. The annual payment is \$3000. What must be the minimum annual interest rate, to one decimal place, so that the balance in the account after seven years is \$30 000?
10. Describe how you would modify the spreadsheet to find the annual balance for seven years if Mr. Watts made each payment at the beginning of the year. This type of annuity is called an **annuity due**. Modify your spreadsheet and compare it with your original spreadsheet.
11. What factors would affect the total future value of an annuity? List as many factors as possible.

Part 2: The Amortization Table

One day, you may want to buy an expensive item, such as a home, but you may not have the cash to do so. Then you can take out a loan or mortgage from a financial institution, for example, a credit union. You usually agree to repay, or amortize, the value of the loan, plus interest, by making regular equal payments for the **term**, or **amortization period**, of the loan. A portion of each **blended payment** is **interest**. The other portion is applied to reduce the **principal**, that is, the amount borrowed. In this way, a portion of each payment reduces the amount borrowed.

An **amortization table**, or schedule, shows

- the regular blended payment
- the portion of each payment that is interest
- the portion of each payment that reduces the principal
- the outstanding balance after each payment.

Here is the amortization table for the repayment of a $4000 loan. The monthly payment is $520. The interest rate is 12%/a, compounded monthly. The loan would be paid after eight months if the eighth payment was adjusted to $542.88 ($520 + $22.88). The loan would also be paid after nine months with a final payment of $23.11 ($22.88 + $0.23).

	A	B	C	D	E
1	Payment Number	Payment	Interest Paid	Principal Paid	Outstanding Balance
2	0				$4,000.00
3	1	$520.00	$40.00	$480.00	$3,520.00
4	2	$520.00	$35.20	$484.80	$3,035.20
5	3	$520.00	$30.35	$489.65	$2,545.55
6	4	$520.00	$25.46	$494.54	$2,051.01
7	5	$520.00	$20.51	$499.49	$1,551.52
8	6	$520.00	$15.52	$504.48	$1,047.03
9	7	$520.00	$10.47	$509.53	$537.50
10	8	$520.00	$5.38	$514.62	$22.88
11	9	$520.00	$0.23	$519.77	$(496.89)

Lise takes out a $9500 loan to purchase a used car. The interest rate is 9%/a, compounded monthly. She agrees to repay the loan in one year by making the same payment of $830.79 at the end of every month.

Here is part of a spreadsheet that shows the amortization table of this loan.

	A	B	C	D	E
1	Payment Number	Payment	Interest Paid	Principal Paid	Outstanding Balance
2	0	——	——	——	9500
3		830.79			

Think, Do, Discuss

1. Enter the information in the spreadsheet in a new spreadsheet. What expression would you enter in cell A3 to increase the payment number?
2. The interest rate is 9%/a, compounded monthly. What is the interest rate of the interest conversion period? Does the payment interval correspond to the interest conversion period? Explain.
3. Calculate the interest paid for the first month *on the principal*. Write an expression for this calculation and enter it in cell C3. How is the interest calculated for subsequent periods?
4. Subtract the interest for the first month from the payment. What remains? Write an expression to represent the remaining value and enter it in cell D3.
5. What is the outstanding balance at the end of the first month? Describe how to calculate the outstanding balance for a given period. Write an expression for the outstanding balance and enter it in cell E3.
6. Enter the values and expressions for the third row in your spreadsheet. Are any of these values constant? Explain. Use the **Fill Down** command to complete the amortization table.
7. What is the outstanding balance after the 12th payment? How do you know that the loan has been completely paid? How can you adjust the last payment so that the outstanding balance will be $0? Make the adjustment.
8. Use the features of the spreadsheet to obtain a scatter plot that shows the outstanding balance at the end of each month.
9. Use the **SUM** function or the Σ toolbar button to find the total payments, the total interest paid, and the total principal paid. Do these values make sense? Explain.
10. Estimate how long it would take Lise to repay the loan if she reduced each payment by almost one-half to $415.40. Modify the spreadsheet to determine how long it would take her to repay the loan.
11. Suppose each payment is still $830.79, but the interest rate changes to 12%/a, compounded monthly. How much more would Lise have to pay in interest? What would be her last payment?
12. Lise may have chosen to purchase a new car of the same make. To buy the new car, she would have had to borrow $28 000. How long would it take her to repay this loan under the original terms? How much interest altogether would she pay?
13. Suppose the monthly payment is $415.40. How long would it take for Lise to repay this $28 000 loan? How much total interest would Lise pay?
14. What would you tell someone who is purchasing a car about minimizing the total interest paid on a car loan?

Focus 2.5

Key Ideas

- An **annuity** is a series of payments, or deposits, at regular intervals.
- The **payment interval** is the time between successive payment dates.
- The **term** of an annuity is the time from the beginning of the first payment interval to the end of the last payment interval.
- The **periodic payment** of an annuity is the amount deposited or paid for each payment interval.
- In an **ordinary annuity**, the payment is made at the end of each payment interval. In an **annuity due**, the payment is made at the beginning of each payment interval. The annuity is called a **simple annuity** when the payment interval corresponds to the interest conversion period. For example, if the interest conversion period of the loan is a month, then the payment interval is a month. If the interest conversion period of the loan is three months (quarterly), then the payment interval is three months (quarterly).
- The annuity is called a **general annuity** when the payment interval does not correspond to the interest conversion period. This annuity will be examined in a later section.
- The **amount** of an annuity is the final value at the end of the term of the annuity. The amount includes all of the periodic payments and the compound interest.
- A spreadsheet allows you to change the parameters of an annuity problem and analyze the effects of the changes.
- Many people will take out a **loan** or **mortgage** to borrow a large sum of money to buy an expensive item, such as a car or a home. The components of a loan or mortgage are the **principal**—the amount borrowed—the interest rate, the interest conversion period, and the **periodic payment.**
- The periodic payment may be described as a **blended payment**, because a portion of the payment is interest and a portion of the payment reduces the principal. The **amortization period** of a loan or mortgage is the time taken for the debt to be paid in full if all the blended payments are made punctually.
- An **amortization table** shows the amount of the regular blended payment, the interest portion of each payment, the principal portion of each payment, and the outstanding balance after each payment. A spreadsheet is useful for creating amortization tables. A spreadsheet is also useful for analyzing the effects of changing the parameters of a loan problem.

Example 1

Samantha has a part-time job and is saving money for a trip to Europe. She deposits \$600 at the end of every three months in a savings plan that pays 8%/a, compounded quarterly. Determine the quarterly balances for the first 30 months.

Solution: Using a Spreadsheet

Both the \$600 deposit and interest are paid quarterly. The quarterly interest rate is 2%. Adjust the spreadsheet that you created for the Think, Do, Discuss of Part 1. In cell C2, enter the expression **=B3*.02** and, in cell D2, enter **600**.

	A	B	C	D	E
1	Period	Previous Balance	Interest at 8%/a	Payment Made	New Balance
2	1	0	=B2*0.02	600	=B2+C2+D2
3	=A2+1	=E2	=B3*0.02	=D2	=B3+C3+D3

Use the **Fill Down** command to complete the table for ten payments that take place over 30 months.

	A	B	C	D	E
1	Period	Balance	Interest at 8%/a	Payment Made	New Balance
2	1	\$0.00	\$0.00	\$600.00	\$600.00
3	2	\$600.00	\$12.00	\$600.00	\$1,212.00
4	3	\$1,212.00	\$24.24	\$600.00	\$1,836.24
5	4	\$1,836.24	\$36.72	\$600.00	\$2,472.96
6	5	\$2,472.96	\$49.46	\$600.00	\$3,122.42
7	6	\$3,122.42	\$62.45	\$600.00	\$3,784.87
8	7	\$3,784.87	\$75.70	\$600.00	\$4,460.57
9	8	\$4,460.57	\$89.21	\$600.00	\$5,149.78
10	9	\$5,149.78	\$103.00	\$600.00	\$5,852.78
11	10	\$5,852.78	\$117.06	\$600.00	\$6,569.83

Example 2

Rodrigo plans to buy a new car in three years. At the end of three years, he would like to pay \$12 000 in cash. How much must he put in an account at the end of every month to achieve his goal? The account pays interest at 7.5%/a, compounded monthly.

Solution

The term of Rodrigo's annuity is 3 years, or 36 periods. The interest rate is 7.5%/a, or 0.625%/month. Adjust the spreadsheet that you created for the Think, Do, Discuss of Part 1. Estimate a reasonable monthly payment, for example, \$300.

	A	B	C	D	E
1	Period	Balance	Interest at 7.5%/a	Payment Made	New Balance
2	1	0	=B2*0.00625	600	=B2+C2+D2
3	=A2+1	=E2	=B3*0.00625	=\$D\$2	=B3+C3+D3

Complete the table.

	A	B	C	D	E
1	Period	Balance	Interest at 7.5%/a	Payment Made	New Balance
2	1	$0.00	$0.00	$300.00	$300.00
3	2	$300.00	$1.88	$300.00	$601.88
4	3	$601.88	$3.76	$300.00	$905.64
5	4	$905.64	$5.66	$300.00	$1,211.30
6	5	$1,211.30	$7.57	$300.00	$1,518.87
7	6	$1,518.87	$9.49	$300.00	$1,828.36
.	.	.	.	.	.
.	.	.	.	.	.
.	.	.	.	.	.
34	33	$10,590.85	$66.19	$300.00	$10,957.05
35	34	$10,957.05	$68.48	$300.00	$11,325.53
36	35	$11,325.53	$70.78	$300.00	$11,696.31
37	36	$11,696.31	$73.10	$300.00	$12,069.41
38	37	$12,069.41	$75.43	$300.00	$12,444.85

The monthly payment should be lower, because the balance after 36 periods is more than $12 000. Try other values for the payment so that the final balance after 36 months is as close as possible to $12 000. The closest balance, after 36 months, is shown in this portion of another spreadsheet.

Rodrigo should deposit $298.28 each month.

	A	B	C	D	E
34	33	$10,530.13	$65.81	$298.28	$10,894.23
35	34	$10,894.23	$68.09	$298.28	$11,260.59
36	35	$11,260.59	$70.38	$298.28	$11,629.25
37	36	$11,629.25	$72.68	$298.28	$12,000.22
38	37	$12,000.22	$75.00	$298.28	$12,373.50

Example 3

An ad in an electronics store window reads, "Big-screen television: Was $3270: now $2890, or $500 down and $122.81 for 24 months on approved credit." What is the annual interest rate, compounded monthly, of the store's payment plan?

Solution

The problem represents an annuity with an initial value of $2390. Find the interest rate that would reduce the outstanding balance to $0 after 24 payments. Estimate a reasonable monthly interest rate, for example, 1.5%/month, or 18%/a, and create a spreadsheet. Notice that, in cell E2, the payment in cell D2 is subtracted from the balance, since the payment reduces the debt. Use the **Fill Down** command, as necessary, to complete the spreadsheet.

	A	B	C	D	E
1	Period	Balance	Interest at 18%/a	Payment Made	New Balance
2	1	2390	=B2*0.015	122.81	=B2+C2–D2
3	=A2+1	=E2	=B3*0.015	=D2	=B3+C3–D3

	A	B	C	D	E
22	21	$379.17	$5.69	$122.81	$262.04
23	22	$262.04	$3.93	$122.81	$143.16
24	23	$143.16	$2.15	$122.81	$22.05
25	24	$22.50	$0.34	$122.81	–$99.97
26	25	$99.97	–$1.50	$122.81	–$224.28
27	26	–$224.28	–$3.36	$122.81	–$350.45

The loan is paid in full before the 24th payment, which means that the interest rate is too low. Try other interest rates. Notice that 1.75%/month is the best estimate, as shown.

	A	B	C	D	E
22	21	$470.53	$8.23	$122.81	$355.95
23	22	$355.95	$6.23	$122.81	$239.37
24	23	$239.37	$4.19	$122.81	$120.75
25	24	$120.75	$2.11	$122.81	$0.05
26	25	$0.05	$0.00	$122.81	–$122.76
27	26	–$122.76	–$2.15	$122.81	–$247.72

The store's interest charge is 1.75%/month, or 21%/a, compounded monthly.

Example 4

Mina took out a mortgage of $75 800 to purchase a house in Massey. She agrees to repay the mortgage over 20 years with equal monthly blended payments of $653.02 each. The interest rate is 8.4%/a, compounded monthly. Her final payment must be increased by $0.25 to pay off the mortgage.

(a) How much interest will she pay over the life of the mortgage?

(b) Determine the outstanding balance for each of the first ten months.

(c) How much more interest would her purchase cost if her mortgage rate had been 9%/a?

Solution

(a) You could use the SUM function of the spreadsheet to find the sum of the interest column in an amortization table. Alternatively, find the interest by multiplying the payment by the total number of payments and subtracting the principal. Remember that $0.25 is added to the last payment.

$$\begin{aligned}\text{total interest} &= \$653.02 \times 20 \times 12 - \$75\,800 + \$0.25 \\ &= \$80\,925.05\end{aligned}$$

(b) Create an amortization spreadsheet.

	A	B	C	D	E
1	Payment Number	Payment	Interest Paid	Principal Paid	Outstanding Balance
2	0	——	——	——	$75,800.00
3	=A2+1	653.02	=E2*0.007	=B3–C3	=E2–D3

	A	B	C	D	E
1	Payment Number	Payment	Interest Paid	Principal Paid	Outstanding Balance
2	0				$75,800.00
3	1	$653.02	$530.60	$122.42	$75,677.58
4	2	$653.02	$529.74	$123.28	$75,554.30
5	3	$653.02	$528.88	$124.14	$75,430.16
6	4	$653.02	$528.01	$125.01	$75,305.15
7	5	$653.02	$527.14	$125.88	$75,179.27
8	6	$653.02	$526.25	$126.77	$75,052.51
9	7	$653.02	$525.37	$127.65	$74,924.85
10	8	$653.02	$524.47	$128.55	$74,796.31
11	9	$653.02	$523.57	$129.45	$74,666.86
12	10	$653.02	$522.67	$130.35	$74,536.51

(c) Change the expression in cell C3 to **=E2*.0075** and scroll down the spreadsheet until the outstanding balance is close to $0.

	A	B	C	D	E
272	270	$653.02	$22.24	$630.78	$2,334.30
273	271	$653.02	$17.51	$635.51	$1,698.78
274	272	$653.02	$12.74	$640.28	$1,058.50
275	273	$653.02	$7.94	$645.08	$413.42
276	274	$653.02	$3.10	$649.92	–$236.50
277	275	$653.02	–$1.77	$654.79	–$891.29

If the interest rate is 9%/a, Mina would need to make 273 payments of $653.02 each and one final payment of $416.52 ($413.42 + $3.10) to pay the mortgage.

The total interest paid at 9%/a is

$$273 \times \$653.02 + \$416.52 - \$75\ 800 = \$102\ 890.98$$

The total interest paid at 8.4%/a is $80 925.05

A 0.6% increase in the mortgage rate to 9% would cost Mina an additional $21 965.93 in interest. This is a substantial difference. This example suggests that people should research mortgage rates to find the lowest possible interest rate.

Practise, Apply, Solve 2.5

A

Refer to Example 1 on page 134 to answer questions 1 and 2.

1. (a) What is Samantha's periodic payment?

(b) Is her savings plan an example of an ordinary annuity or an annuity due? Explain.

(c) Why is her savings plan a simple annuity?

(d) Determine the interest earned and the new balance after the 11th payment.

(e) How would you modify the spreadsheet if Samantha already had $1500 in her savings plan prior to making deposits?

2. (a) Without using a spreadsheet, determine Samantha's quarterly balances for the first two years if she deposited $600 at the beginning of each month for three months.

(b) What type of annuity is described in (a)?

(c) How much more interest would she have earned over the two years?

(d) Describe how you would modify the spreadsheet for the change in payment.

Refer to Example 2 on page 134 to answer questions 3 and 4.

3. (a) What is the payment interval of Rodrigo's annuity?

(b) Why are there 36 payment intervals in this example?

(c) How much interest is earned in the 34th payment interval?

(d) In the final spreadsheet, the balance at the end of the 36th period is $12 000.22. Explain why the payment cannot be adjusted to give a balance of exactly $12 000.

(e) How would you modify the spreadsheet so that the interest rate is 6%/a, compounded monthly?

4. For a monthly payment of $300, the balance will grow to $12 069.41 in three years. For a monthly payment of $298.28, the balance will grow to $12 000.22 in three years.

(a) Explain the difference between the balances.

(b) Find the interest earned for each situation and determine the difference.

B

5. **Communication:** Phong wants to purchase a motorcycle. He can borrow $6500 at 10%/a, compounded quarterly, if he agrees to repay the loan by making equal quarterly payments for four years. Estimate a reasonable quarterly payment. Explain your answer.

6. For four years, you deposit $250 at the end of every three months in an annuity earning 10%/a, compounded quarterly.
   (a) What is the term of the annuity?
   (b) What is the payment interval?
   (c) How many payments would you make altogether?
   (d) What is the interest rate for the conversion period?

7. **Knowledge and Understanding:** Meredith borrows $3600 to help pay for nurse's college. She will repay the loan by making equal blended payments of $625 each at the end of every six months. The interest rate is 11%/a, compounded semiannually.
   (a) Without using a spreadsheet, construct an amortization table for the loan repayment.
   (b) What is the final payment if she takes all of the four years to repay the loan?
   (c) What is the last payment if she chooses to repay the loan in seven payments?

8. Verify your work in question 7 by using a spreadsheet to create an amortization table of Meredith's loan.

9. Mr. Abourbih has $12 000 in a savings account that pays 5%/a, compounded quarterly. Mr. Abourbih intends to deposit $500 at the end of every three months in the account for five years.
   (a) Use a spreadsheet to determine the balance in the account over the five years.
   (b) How much more would the balance be at the end of five years if each deposit were $550?
   (c) How much more would the balance be at the end of five years if the interest rate were 6.5%/a, compounded quarterly?
   (d) How much do you think you could realistically save every three months? How much are your current savings?
   (e) Use the values in (d) to determine how much you could save over the same five years.

10. Prima just started grade 9 and would like to save $12 000 over the next four years to help pay for her first year of university.
   (a) Determine, to the nearest cent, how much she should deposit at the end of every three months in an account that pays 6%/a, compounded quarterly, to attain her goal.
   (b) Determine how much she should deposit at the end of each month for four years if the account pays 6%/a, compounded monthly.
   (c) Compare the payments in (a) and (b). Explain why the payment in (a) is not quite three times the payment in (b).

11. Kacee borrows $1800 to buy a computer. She will repay the loan by making equal blended payments of $165.25 each at the end of each month. The interest rate is 18%/a, compounded monthly.

(a) What is the interest rate per conversion period?

(b) Without using a spreadsheet, create an amortization of her loan.

(c) Verify the amortization in (b) by using a spreadsheet.

(d) Graph the amortization of her loan.

12. Determine the annual interest rate, compounded monthly, of the payment plan for the computer.

Laptop Computer
$2700 cash
OR
$500 down and
$144.60 per month
for 18 months o.a.c.

13. **Thinking, Inquiry, Problem Solving:** Two twin sisters, Bev and Cindy, just celebrated their 15th birthdays. Bev decides to start making regular annual deposits of $1000 each at 7%/a, compounded annually, beginning today and ending on her 26th birthday. At that time, she will not make any more deposits. On her 26th birthday, Cindy decides to start making regular annual deposits of $1000 each at the same interest rate. Determine when or if Cindy's investment will be equal to Bev's investment. Include tables and arguments in your solution.

14. Lakshmi Samson is saving to buy a house. After every six months, she deposits $1800 in an account that pays 8%/a, compounded semiannually.

(a) How much money will she have saved in six years?

(b) After making the first deposit of $1800, she increases each subsequent payment by 10%. How much money will she have saved in six years?

15. **Application:** Stephanie buys a boat by paying 10% down and by financing the balance with a bank loan at 15%/a, compounded monthly. She arranges to amortize the loan by making monthly payments of $225 each for three years. Determine what Stephanie paid for the boat.

16. Ms. Reynen is thinking about retirement plans that would enable her to retire at age 60. She may deposit \$1000 each year in an registered retirement savings plan (RRSP), beginning at age 30. Or she may deposit \$3000 each year in an RRSP, beginning at age 50. Both plans offer the same annual compound interest rate. Analyze the effect that the interest rate would have on the value of each plan when Miss Reynen turns 60. Report your findings.

17. On his way to work, Mr. Pretz sees this ad for a pickup truck.

Used 2000 Pickup
\$16,200 cash
OR
\$3,000 down and
\$633.77/month for 24 months

(a) Determine the annual interest rate, compounded monthly, of the payment plan.

(b) Mr. Pretz is interested in buying the truck. He knows that he can get a loan from his bank to finance the cash price of the truck. The interest rate is 8%/a, compounded monthly. What monthly payment would enable him to repay the bank loan in two years?

(c) Why is the payment in (b) greater than the advertised payment?

(d) Mr. Pretz decides to make the \$3000 down payment and finance the remaining amount through a bank loan as in (b). Determine how much money he will save by financing the loan through his bank instead of through the truck dealer.

18. The Larsen family has just financed the purchase of a motor home for \$48 000. They agree to repay the loan by making equal monthly blended payments of \$595 each at 8.4%/a, compounded monthly.

(a) Create an amortization of their loan.

(b) How long will it take to repay the loan?

(c) How much will be the final payment?

(d) Determine how much interest they will pay over the life of the loan.

(e) Use technology to graph the amortization of the loan.

(f) How much sooner would the loan be paid if they had made a 10% down payment?

(g) How much would the Larsens have saved in interest had they obtained a loan at 7.2%/a, compounded monthly?

19. Check Your Understanding

(a) Without using a spreadsheet, show how an annuity that pays 6.6%/a, compounded monthly, will grow over eight months. A periodic payment of $200 is paid at the end of each month.

(b) Determine the value of the annuity if the monthly payment is made at the beginning of each month. Explain the differences between the two payment options.

C

20. Ansley wants to borrow $40 000. She must decide how to repay the loan. She could either make quarterly payments of $3000 each at 12%/a, compounded quarterly, or make monthly payments of $1000 each at 12%/a, compounded monthly.

(a) Describe the advantages and disadvantages of each option.

(b) What advice would you give Ansley? Justify your advice.

21. Fatuma has decided to invest $3000 at the end of each year for the next five years in a savings account that pays 8%/a, compounded semiannually. Use a spreadsheet to determine the amount of the annuity.

The Chapter Problem—Financial Planning

In this section, you studied the use of spreadsheets to analyze financial situations. Apply what you learned to answer these questions about the Chapter Problem on page 106.

CP5. Bart's education fund earns 6%/a, compounded monthly. Create a spreadsheet to represent the monthly balance in the fund. Use it to determine the balance after the 20th payment.

CP6. How many payments will take place by the time Bart reaches his 18th birthday? Determine the accumulated value of Bart's education fund on his 18th birthday.

CP7. Create an amortization table to represent the repayment of Mr. Sacchetto's car loan. Print the table.

CP8. When will the car loan be paid? What is the amount of the final payment?

CP9. Can you create an amortization table to represent the repayment of Mr. Sacchetto's mortgage? Explain.

TI-83 Plus Calculator: Finding the Sum and the Cumulative Sum of a Series

2.6

TECHNOLOGY

In Chapter 1, you learned how to create the terms of a sequence using the TI-83 Plus calculator given the general term of the sequence. You can also find the sum of the terms of this sequence — the series — using the TI-83 Plus calculator.

Find the sum and the cumulative sum of the first five terms of the sequence defined by $t_n = n^2$.

Part 1: Finding the Sum of the Terms of a Series

1. Generate the first five terms of the sequence.

(a) Select **sequence** from the List OPS menu. Press [2nd] [STAT] [▶]. Scroll down to **5:seq** and press [ENTER].

(b) Enter the expression of the general term, the variable, the starting value of the variable, the ending value of the variable, and the increment, 1. Press [ENTER] to generate the first five terms, as shown.

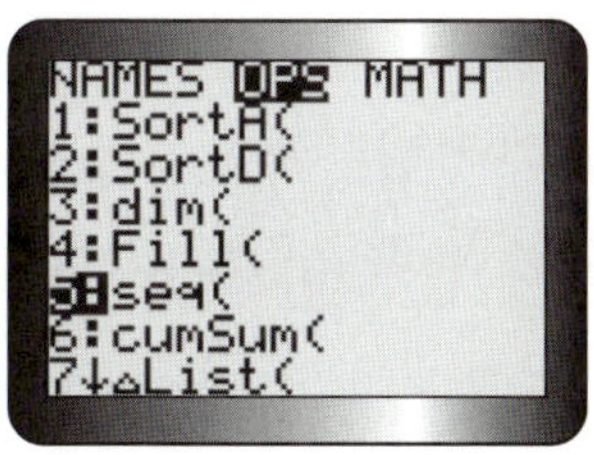

step 1a

step 1b

2. Select sum from the List MATH menu.

Press [2nd] [STAT] [▶] [▶] and scroll down to **5:sum**. Press [ENTER].

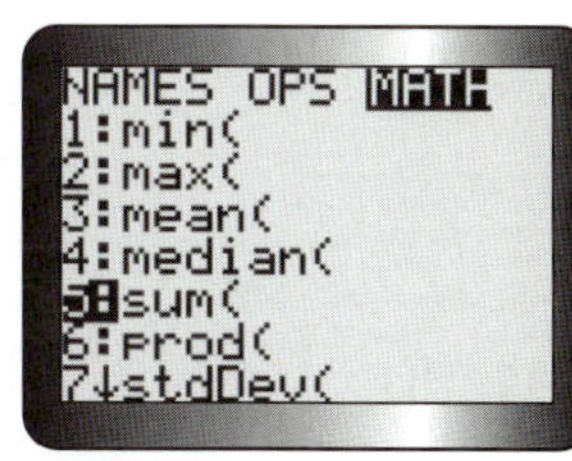

step 2

3. Find the sum of the series.

Use **Ans**, last answer, to insert the terms in **sum**. Press [2nd] [(-)] [)] [ENTER]. The sum is displayed.

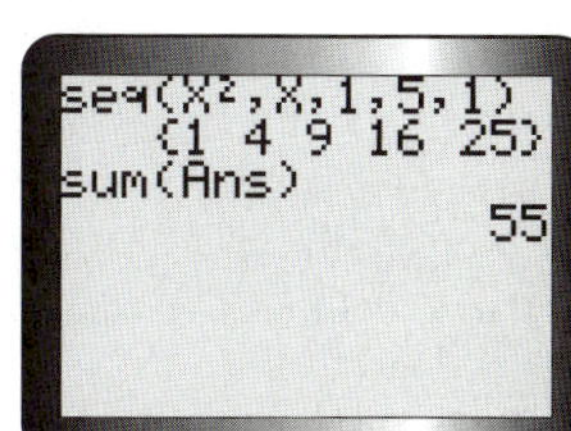

step 3

Part 2: Finding the Cumulative Sum of the Terms of a Series

The cumulative sum displays the progression of sums of the terms of a series.

1. **Generate the terms of the sequence again.**

   Follow step 1 of Part 1.

2. **Select cumulative sum from the LIST OPS menu.**

   Press [2nd] [STAT] [▶] and scroll down to **6:cumSum**. Press [ENTER].

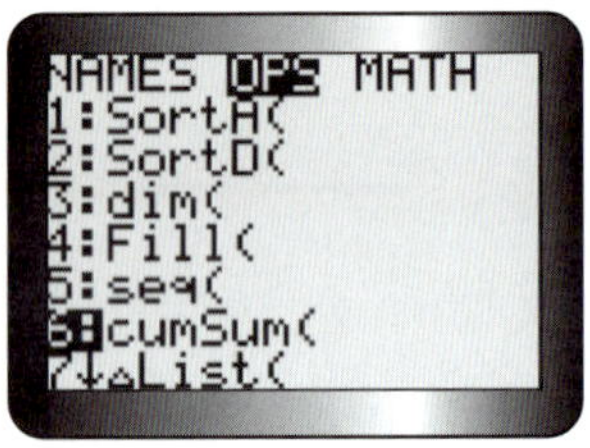

step 2

3. **Find the cumulative sums of the terms of the sequence.**

   Press [2nd] [(-)] [)] [ENTER]. The cumulative sums are displayed.

step 3

$$\begin{cases} 1 = 1 \\ 5 = 1 + 4 \\ 14 = 1 + 4 + 9 \\ 30 = 1 + 4 + 9 + 16 \\ 55 = 1 + 4 + 9 + 16 + 25 \end{cases}$$

Practice 2.6

1. For each of the following sequences, find the sum of the first ten terms.

   (a) $t_n = 5n + 1$ (b) $t_n = n^3$ (c) $t_n = 3(2)^{n-1}$

   (d) $t_n = -5n + 3$ (e) $t_n = 1000(1.1)^n$ (f) $t_n = n$

   (g) $t_n = 100(1.05)^n$ (h) $t_n = 25 + 4(n - 1)$

2. Find the cumulative sums of the first ten terms for each of the sequences in question 1.

Using Series to Analyze Financial Situations: Future Value

2.7

In section 2.5, you represented the future value of an ordinary simple annuity by finding the new balance after each payment and then adding the new balances. The amount of the annuity is the accumulated value of all the periodic payments, including interest.

In this section, you will investigate a method for finding the amount, or accumulated value, of an annuity by applying your knowledge of series.

Part 1: Representing an Ordinary Simple Annuity with a Series

In section 2.5, Mr. Watts wanted to help pay for his 12-year-old granddaughter's future university expenses. Mr. Watts decided to deposit $3000 at the end of each year, for seven years, in a savings account that pays 7.5%/a, compounded annually. Find the amount of the annuity at the end of seven years.

The amount of each deposit is shown in the **time line.** This time line shows the seven periods and all of the periodic payments. Each symbol, from F1 to F7, represents the amount, or accumulated value, of **each** deposit at the end of seven years.

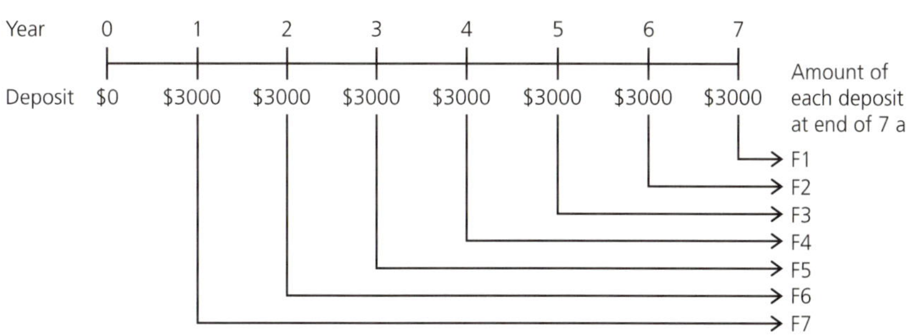

Think, Do, Discuss

1. Each of the symbols from F1 to F7 represents the amount, or future value, of the payment at the end of seven years. What is the amount of the last deposit, F1?

2. At the end of the sixth year, Mr. Watts deposits \$3000. For how many periods is this deposit in the account? Write an expression to represent F2, the future value of the deposit made at the end of the sixth year.

3. Repeat step 2 for each of the other deposits, F3 to F7.

4. Copy and complete the time line.

5. Write the series that represents the future values or amounts of all the deposits at the end of seven years. Use the expressions that you found in steps 1 to 3. Begin with F1.

6. Describe this type of series. What is the first term? Describe the first term in the context of the investment. What is the common ratio? Describe the common ratio in the context of the investment. How many terms are in the series?

7. Recall the formula for the sum of this type of series. Find the sum of the future values of the deposits. Compare your solution to the one you found in the Think, Do, Discuss of Part 1 in section 2.5.

Part 2: Developing a Formula for the Amount of an Ordinary Simple Annuity

Andrea wants to find an algebraic expression to represent the amount, or accumulated value, of an ordinary simple annuity. She lets R be the regular periodic payment of the annuity and lets n be the total number of interest conversion periods, or the total number of payments. She drew the following time line.

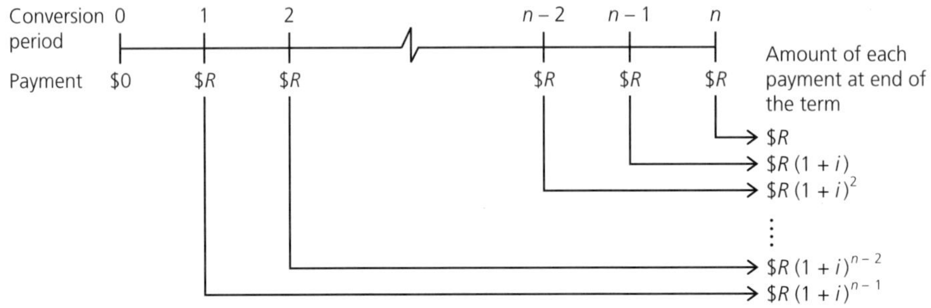

Think, Do, Discuss

1. What does i represent in the time line? Explain why the exponent in the future value of the first payment is $n - 1$.

2. Given Andrea's time line, write the series of terms, S_n, that represents the future value or amount of each payment of the annuity, beginning with the nth payment. What type of series is S_n?

3. What is the first term of the series? What is the common ratio? Substitute these values in the formula you used in step 7 of Part 1. Simplify the denominator.

4. Use this formula again to find the amount of an annuity if the amount of each payment is \$1000, payable at the end of every six months for three years. The interest rate is 10%/a, compounded semiannually.

Focus 2.7

Key Ideas

- The **amount**, or accumulated value, of an annuity is the sum of all the future values of all payments at the end of the term of the annuity.
- Show the amount of an ordinary simple annuity in a **time line**. A time line includes the payment intervals, the periodic payments or deposits, and the amount of each payment or deposit at the end of the term.

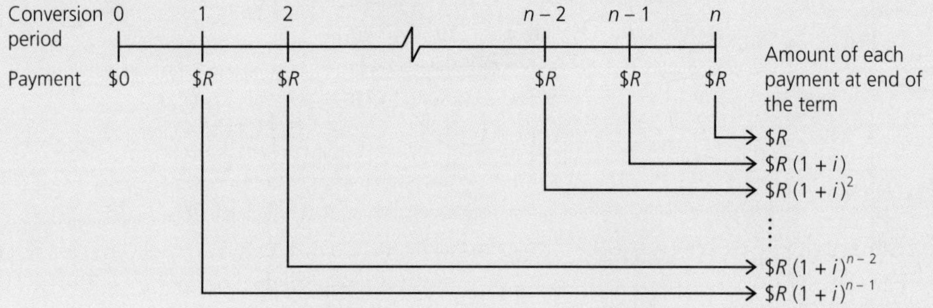

- The **amount** — the accumulated value or the future value — of an ordinary simple annuity can be written as the geometric series

$$R + R(1 + i) + R(1 + i)^2 + \ldots + R(1 + i)^{n-2} + R(1 + i)^{n-1}$$

where R represents the regular payment

n represents the number of interest conversion periods or the total number of payments

i represents the interest rate per conversion period

- An accumulated or future value of an ordinary simple annuity is the sum of a geometric series, $S_n = \dfrac{a(r^n - 1)}{r - 1}$, where $a = R$, $r = 1 + i$, and n is the number of payments.
- Another formula for calculating the accumulated or future value of an ordinary simple annuity, S_n or FV, is

$$\begin{aligned} FV &= S_n \\ &= R \times \frac{(1 + i)^n - 1}{i}. \end{aligned}$$

Example 1

For ten years, Shelagh deposits \$750 at the end of every three months in a savings account that pays 8%/a, compounded quarterly.

(a) Draw a time line to represent the annuity.

(b) Write the series that represents the annuity.

(c) Find the amount of the annuity and the total interest earned.

(d) Verify your results using **sequence** (from the List OPS menu) and **sum** (from the List MATH menu) on the TI-83 Plus calculator.

Solution

(a) The quarterly interest rate is 2% = 0.02 and the number of periods is $4 \times 10 = 40$.

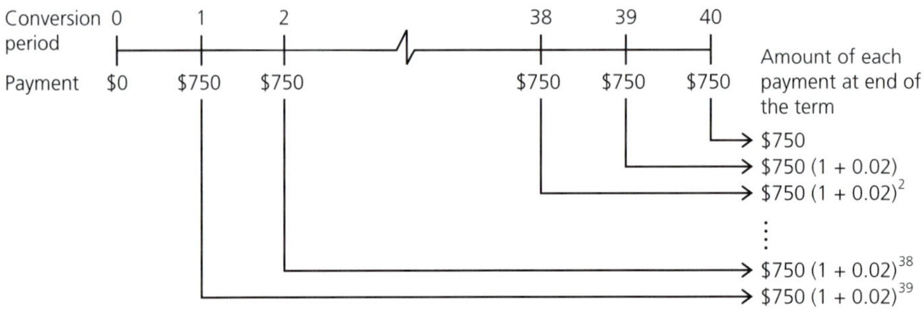

(b) The series is $S_{40} = 750 + 750(1 + 0.02) + 750(1 + 0.02)^2 + \ldots + 750(1 + 0.02)^{38} + 750(1 + 0.02)^{39}$.

(c) **Method 1:** Using $S_n = \dfrac{a(r^n - 1)}{r - 1}$

The series is geometric, and $a = 750$, $r = 1.02$, and $n = 40$.

$$S_n = \frac{a(r^n - 1)}{r - 1}$$

Substitute the values for a, r, and n.

$$S_n = \frac{750(1.02^{40} - 1)}{1.02 - 1} \quad \text{Simplify.}$$

$$= 45\,301.49$$

The amount of the annuity is \$45 301.49.

Find the total interest earned on the annuity by subtracting the total payments from the accumulated value.

$$\text{total interest} = \$45\,301.49 - (40 \times \$750)$$
$$= \$15\,301.49$$

Method 2: Using $FV = R \times \frac{(1 + i)^n - 1}{i}$

The series represents the future value or amount of an ordinary simple annuity, where $R = 750$, $i = 0.02$, and $n = 40$.

$$FV = R \times \frac{(1 + i)^n - 1}{i} \qquad \text{Substitute the values for } R, i, \text{ and } n.$$

$$= 750 \times \frac{(1.02)^{40} - 1}{0.02} \qquad \text{Simplify.}$$

$$= 45\,301.49$$

The total interest earned is \$45 301.49, as found in Method 1.

(d) The series is the first 40 terms of a geometric sequence with the general term $t_n = 750(1.02)^{n-1}$. The sum of the sequence is \$45 301.49.

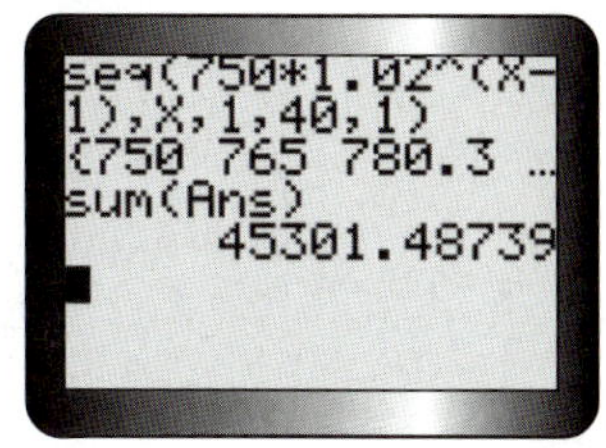

Example 2

Roberta is an electrical engineer. She hopes to retire at 55, with savings. She plans to make equal monthly deposits, at the end of each month, for 20 years in a trust account that has a guaranteed interest rate of 9%/a, compounded monthly. She wants to have \$300 000 in the account at the end of 20 years.

(a) Draw a time line to represent the annuity.

(b) Write the series that represents the annuity.

(c) What amount must be her monthly deposit?

Solution

(a) Find the monthly payment, R. The accumulated value is \$300 000, the interest rate per conversion period, i, is 0.0075, and the total number of periods, n, is 12×20 or 240.

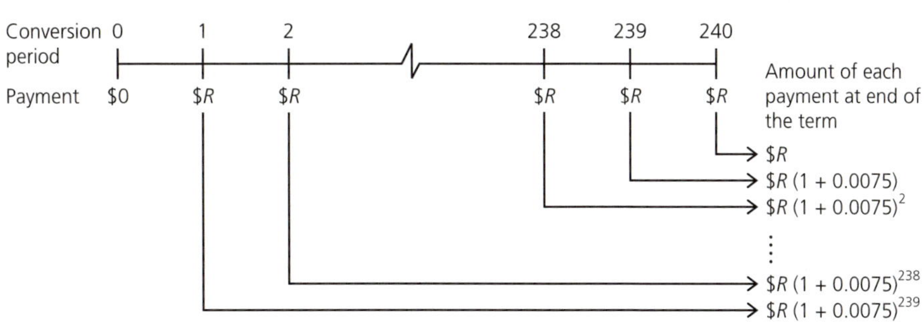

(b) The series is $S_{240} = R + R(1 + 0.0075) + R(1 + 0.0075)^2 + \ldots + R(1 + 0.0075)^{238} + R(1 + 0.0075)^{239}$ and $S_{240} = 300\ 000$.

(c) Use $S_{240} = \frac{a(r^{240} - 1)}{r - 1}$, where $a = R$, $r = 1.0075$, and $S_{240} = 300\ 000$, or use $FV = R \times \frac{(1 + i)^n - 1}{i}$, where $n = 240$, $i = 0.0075$, and $FV = 300\ 000$.

Solve for R.

$$300\ 000 = R \times \left(\frac{(1.0075)^{240} - 1}{0.0075}\right)$$

Evaluate the expression in brackets.

$$300\ 000 \doteq R(667.886\ 869\ 9) \quad \text{Solve for } R.$$

$$449.18 \doteq R$$

Roberta must deposit \$449.18 each month.

Example 3

Rebecca has just celebrated her 12th birthday. She decides to save her \$100 monthly allowance and will deposit \$1200 at the end of each year in an account that pays 11%/a, compounded annually.

(a) Draw a time line to represent the annuity.

(b) Write the series that represents the annuity.

(c) Determine how old Rebecca will be when her annuity is worth \$20 000.

Solution

(a) The number of periods is unknown. The regular deposits are \$1200 each and the interest rate per conversion period is 11% = 0.11. The future value of the annuity must be \$20 000.

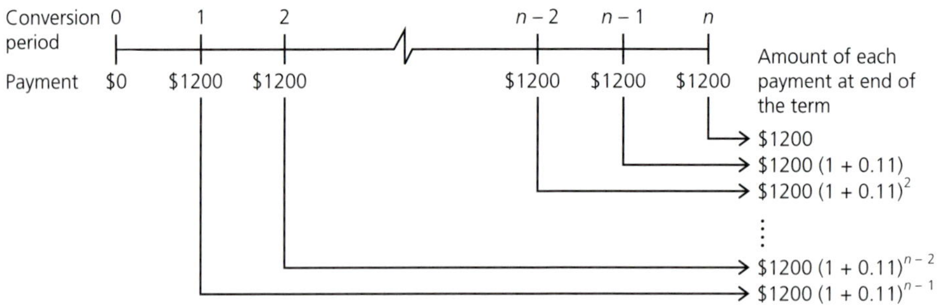

(b) The series is $S_n = 1200 + 1200(1.11) + 1200(1.11)^2 + \ldots + 1200(1.11)^{n-2} + 1200(1.11)^{n-1}$ and $S_n = 20\ 000$.

9. (a) Draw a time line and find the amount of each annuity in question 8 if the periodic payment is made at the beginning of each payment interval.
   (b) Verify your solutions using technology.

10. Tara and Tobey are planning to buy a home in three years. They would like to accumulate enough money for a $30 000 down payment. They will deposit the same sum of money at the end of each month in an account that pays 6%/a, compounded monthly.
   (a) Draw a time line to represent the annuity.
   (b) Write the series that represents the annuity.
   (c) Determine the monthly deposit required to meet their goal.

11. At the end of every six months, Marcia deposited $100 in a savings account that paid 4%/a, compounded semiannually. She made the first deposit when her son was six months old and she made the last deposit on her son's 21st birthday. The money remained in the account until her son turned 25, when Marcia gave him the money. How much did he receive?

12. At the end of each month, $50 is deposited in an account for 25 years. Then the accumulated money remains in the account for an additional 5 years. Find the amount in the account at the end of this time. The interest rate is 4.8%/a, compounded monthly.

13. Marcel would like to take a vacation to Mexico during March break, which is nine months from today. The trip will cost $1600. Marcel saves and deposits $195 at the end of each month for the next eight months at 9%/a, compounded monthly. Will he have enough money to pay for his trip?

14. **Communication:** Explain why the two formulas for finding the accumulated value of a simple annuity would not work if the interest conversion period did not coincide with the payment interval.

15. During the school year, Quentin has a part-time job working at the library. He deposits $75 at the end of each month for three years in an education fund that pays 6%/a, compounded monthly.
   (a) Draw a time line to represent the annuity.
   (b) Write the series that represents the annuity.
   (c) Determine how much is in the fund after three years.
   (d) Verify your solution using technology. Graph the monthly balance over the three years.
   (e) Determine how many payments are needed so that $5200 will accumulate in the fund.

16. Rhys deposits \$2000 at the end of every three months in an account that pays 6%/a, compounded quarterly.

(a) Determine how many payments he will need to make so that the value of the account is worth at least \$45 000.

(b) Use technology to verify your solution and to graph the quarterly balances up to a value of \$45 000.

17. Samantha has just celebrated her seventh birthday. Her aunt Lise decides to start an education fund in Samantha's name and deposits \$450 at the end of every three months in a fund that pays 8.4%/a, compounded quarterly.

(a) Draw a time line to represent the annuity.

(b) Write the series that represents the annuity.

(c) Determine how old Samantha will be when the fund is worth \$24 000.

(d) How much less time would it take for the fund to accumulate to \$24 000 if Lise made deposits of \$530 each?

18. **Application:** Mario deposits \$25 at the end of each month for four years in an account that pays 9.6%/a, compounded monthly. He then makes no further deposits and no withdrawals. Find the balance after ten years.

19. Darcey is a pastry chef. He would like to accumulate \$80 000 in savings before he retires 20 years from now. He intends to make the same deposit at the end of each month in a registered retirement savings plan that pays 6.3%/a, compounded monthly.

(a) Draw a time line to represent the annuity.

(b) Write the series that represents the annuity.

(c) Determine the periodic payment that will enable him to reach his goal.

(d) He decides to wait five years before making the monthly deposits. What periodic payment would he have to make to reach the same goal?

(e) About how much more money did he have to invest by waiting five years?

20. Gwyneth has \$4320 in her savings account and she deposits \$800 at the end of every three months. The account earns 6%/a, compounded quarterly. What will be the balance in the account after five years?

21. **Thinking, Inquiry, Problem Solving:** Eire was wondering which of these options is better — to double the interest of an annuity, or to double the term of an annuity. Work with a partner to determine if one option is better than the other and explain your findings.

22. **Check Your Understanding**

(a) In Example 2, Roberta made monthly deposits for 20 years to attain her financial goal. How would her monthly deposit be affected if she had started making deposits five years earlier, that is, if she made deposits for 25 years? Explain.

(b) Find the periodic payment, if Roberta had started making deposits five years earlier. How much less would she have had to pay?

23. Fatuma has decided to invest $3000 at the end of each year for the next five years in a savings account that pays 8%/a, compounded semiannually.

(a) Draw a time line to represent the accumulated value of each payment.

(b) Determine the amount of the annuity.

24. Mr. Friday is preparing his will. He wants to leave the same amount of money to his son and to his daughter. His daughter is careful with money, but his son spends it carelessly, so he decides to give them the money in different ways. The interest rate is 6%/a, compounded monthly. How much must his estate pay his son each month over 20 years so that the accumulated value will be equal to the $50 000 cash his daughter will receive upon his death? Assume that the daughter's inheritance earns the same interest rate over the 20 years.

The Chapter Problem—Financial Planning

In this section, you studied future value. Apply what you learned to answer these questions about the Chapter Problem on page 106.

CP10. Confirm the accumulated value of Bart's education fund on his 18th birthday, including the payment on his 18th birthday. Use the formula for the accumulated value of an ordinary simple annuity.

CP11. Can you determine the periodic payment for the registered income fund (RIF) given what you know about the accumulated value of an annuity? Explain.

CP12. Mr. Sacchetto intends to make a deposit at the end of every three months in a savings account that earns 8%/a, compounded quarterly, to meet his retirement goal of having $120 000 in savings at age 55.

(a) Draw a time line to represent the accumulated values of Mr. Sacchetto's deposits in the savings account.

(b) List the series that represents the accumulated values of the RIF.

(c) For his savings account, determine the quarterly deposit that Mr. Sacchetto must make to meet his retirement goal.

(d) Determine how much more money in total he would have to deposit if the account pays only 6%/a, compounded quarterly.

2.8 Using Series to Analyze Financial Situations: Present Value

In the previous section, you learned how to calculate the amount, or future value, of an ordinary simple annuity. The amount is the sum of the accumulated values of all the payments.

When people think about their retirement, they often hope to have a regular income from a pension or from an annuity. A **registered income fund** (RIF) is one type of annuity. This fund is a lump sum of money that is invested now so that a regular income may be drawn from the fund over a long period at some time in the future. For example, Blake wants to receive a $1000 payment at the end of the next five years, so he invests an amount that is less than $1000 today. The amount that he invests is less than the future value because the investment earns interest during the term.

The amount that is invested now to yield a larger amount in the future is called the **present value**. In this section, you will calculate the present value of an annuity by adding the present values of all the payments.

Part 1: Representing the Present Value of an Ordinary Simple Annuity with a Series

The St. Charles College Math Club wants to establish a math scholarship to reward its top graduating math student. The $1000 scholarship will be awarded at the end of each year for the next five years. The club has some money to pay for the future scholarship payments. Calculate how much money is needed now by finding the present value of each of the five $1000 awards and then adding the present values. The trust account pays 9%/a, compounded annually.

Here is the time line that shows the payments as present values.

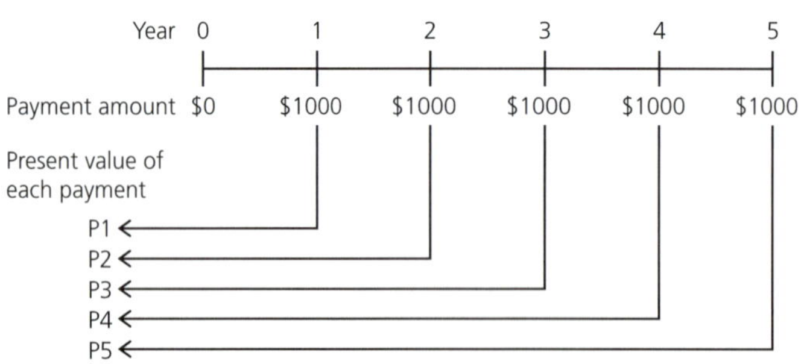

Think, Do, Discuss

1. Is $1000 required now to cover the cost of the $1000 scholarship that will be awarded at the end of the first year? Explain.

2. The interest rate is 9%/a, compounded annually. Determine an expression that would represent the amount that is needed now to provide the first $1000 scholarship payment at the end of the first year. Express the present value of the payment as a product rather than as a quotient by using negative exponents.

3. Determine an expression for the present value of the second $1000 scholarship. Express this present value as a product.

4. Repeat step 3 to find expressions for the present values of the third, fourth, and fifth payments.

5. Copy and complete the time line.

6. Use the expressions you found above, *beginning with the present value of the fifth payment,* P5, to write the series that represents the accumulated sum of all the present value payments. Do not find the value of each term.

7. What is the first term? What do you multiply the first term by to get the second term? What is this type of series? What is the common ratio? How many terms does the series have?

8. Use the formula you learned earlier in this chapter to find the sum of the present values of the payments. How much money would the club need to raise and then deposit in the trust account to sustain the scholarship over five years?

Part 2: Developing a Formula for the Present Value or Amount of an Ordinary Simple Annuity

Andrea wants to find an algebraic expression to represent the present, or discounted, value of an ordinary simple annuity. She lets R be the regular periodic payment of the annuity. She lets n be the total number of interest conversion periods, or the total number of payments. She drew the following time line.

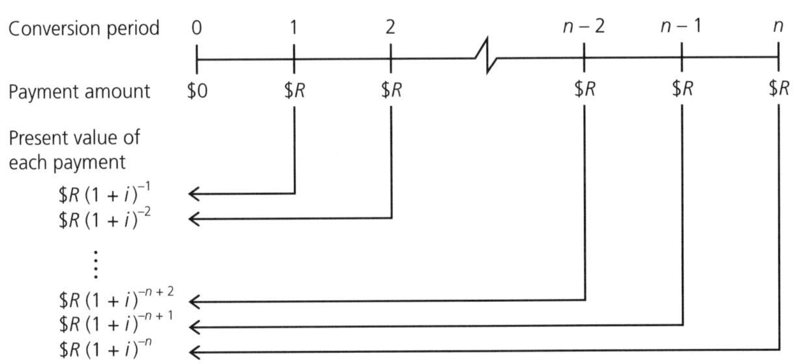

Think, Do, Discuss

1. What does i represent in the time line? Explain why the exponent in the present value of the first payment is -1. Explain why the exponent in the present value of the last payment is $-n$.

2. Given Andrea's time line, write the series of terms, PV, that represents the present or discounted value of each payment of the annuity, *beginning with the last payment.* What type of series is PV?

3. What is the first term of the series? What is the common ratio? Substitute these values in the formula you used in step 8 of Part 1.

4. You can simplify the equation in step 3, but before you do, what do you notice about the bases of the powers in this equation? What do you do to the exponents when you multiply these powers? Use the distributive property to simplify your equation. The result is the present value, PV, of an ordinary simple annuity.

5. A math scholarship awards \$500 at the end of each year for ten years. Use the formula you developed in step 4 to find the present value that should be deposited in a trust account that pays 11%/a, compounded annually, to sustain the scholarship.

Focus 2.8

Key Ideas

- The **present value**, or **discounted value**, of an annuity is the value at the beginning of the term of the annuity. The present value is the sum of all the present values of the payments.
- This time line represents the **present value** of an ordinary simple annuity.

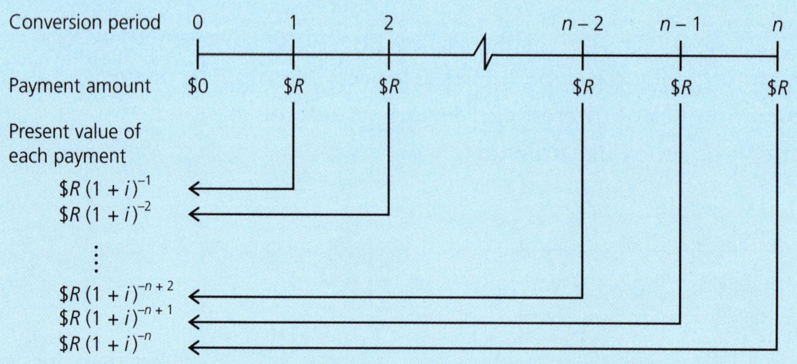

- The present or discounted value of an ordinary simple annuity can be written as the geometric series

$$R(1 + i)^{-n} + R(1 + i)^{-n+1} + R(1 + i)^{-n+2} + \ldots + R(1 + i)^{-2} + R(1 + i)^{-1}$$

where R represents the regular payment

n represents the number of interest conversion periods or the total number of payments

i represents the interest rate per conversion period

- The present or discounted value of an ordinary simple annuity is the sum of a geometric series, $S_n = \frac{a(r^n - 1)}{r - 1}$, where $a = R(1 + i)^{-n}$, $r = 1 + i$, and n is the number of payments.
- Find the present or discounted value of an ordinary simple annuity, A or PV, using

$$\begin{aligned} A &= PV \\ &= R \times \frac{1 - (1 + i)^{-n}}{i} \end{aligned}$$

Example 1

Claire has just won a lottery. She is offered two prize options: \$125 000 cash today or payments of \$1000 each at the end of each month for 20 years. Claire expects a return of 9%/a, compounded monthly, if she invests the cash prize.

(a) Draw a time line to represent the present value of the payment option.

(b) Write the series that represents the annuity.

(c) Which option should Claire choose?

Solution

(a) The monthly interest rate is $0.75\% = 0.0075$ and the term is $12 \times 20 = 240$.

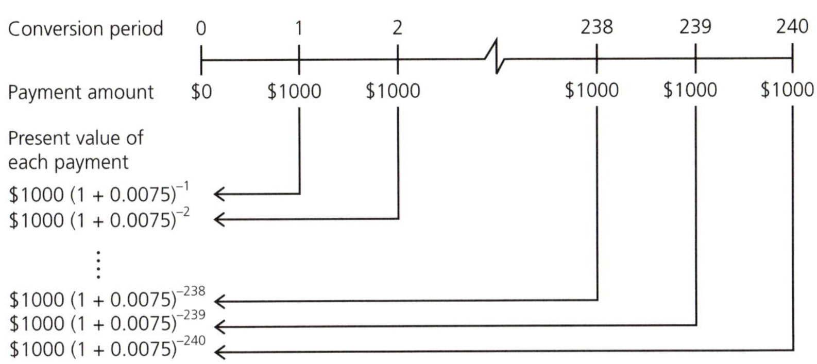

(b) The series is $S_{240} = 1000(1.0075)^{-240} + 1000(1.0075)^{-239}$
$+ 1000\,(1.0075)^{-238} + \dots + 1000(1.0075)^{-2} + 1000(1.0075)^{-1}$.

(c) **Method 1:** Using $S_n = \frac{a(r^n - 1)}{r - 1}$

It is possible to misinterpret this problem by comparing the cash value today, \$125 000, to the total money paid under the payment option, $\$1000 \times 12 \times 20 = \$240\ 000$.

The series is geometric, and $a = 1000(1.0075)^{-240}$, $r = 1.0075$, and $n = 240$.

$$S_n = \frac{a(r^n - 1)}{r - 1} \qquad \text{Substitute the values for } a, r, \text{ and } n.$$

$$S_{240} = 1000(1.0075)^{-240}\left[\frac{(1.0075)^{240} - 1}{1.0075 - 1}\right] \qquad \text{Simplify.}$$

$$\doteq 1000(0.166\ 412\ 844\ 8)\ (667.886\ 869\ 9)$$

$$= 111\ 144.95$$

The present value of the payment option is \$111 144.95. Claire should choose the \$125 000 if she may invest it at 9%/a, compounded monthly.

Method 2: Using $PV = R \times \frac{1 - (1 + i)^{-n}}{i}$

The series represents the present or discounted value of an ordinary simple annuity where $R = 1000$, $i = 0.0075$, and $n = 240$.

$$PV = R \times \frac{1 - (1 + i)^{-n}}{i} \qquad \text{Substitute the values for } R, i, \text{ and } n.$$

$$= 1000 \times \frac{1 - (1.0075)^{-240}}{0.0075} \qquad \text{Simplify.}$$

$$= 111\ 144.95$$

Using the formula for the present or discounted value also yields \$111 144.95.

Example 2

The Sybulski family purchase a motor home. They borrow \$30 000 at 9.6%/a, compounded monthly, and they will make payments at the end of each month. They have two choices for the term: seven years or ten years.

(a) Draw a time line to represent the present value of the seven-year annuity.

(b) Write the series that represents the seven-year annuity.

(c) Find the monthly payment under each term.

(d) How much would they save in interest by selecting the shorter term?

Solution

(a) The monthly interest rate is $9.6\% \div 12 = 0.8\%$ or 0.008 and the number of periods is $12 \times 7 = 84$ for the seven-year term.

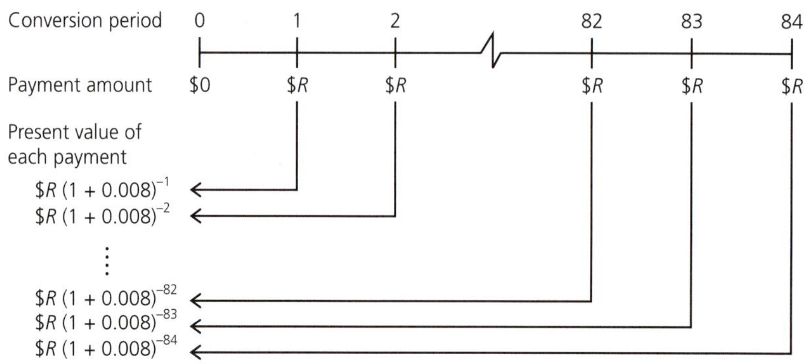

(b) The series is $S_{84} = R(1.008)^{-84} + R(1.008)^{-83} + R(1.008)^{-82} + \dots + R(1.008)^{-2} + R(1.008)^{-1}$, where $S_{84} = 30\ 000$.

(c) Use $PV = R \times \frac{1 - (1 + i)^{-n}}{i}$. The present value of the loan is \$30 000. Find the monthly payment, R, under both terms.

For a seven-year term, $PV = 30\ 000$, $i = 0.8\%$ or 0.08, and $n = 84$.

$$PV = R \times \frac{1 - (1 + i)^{-n}}{i}$$ Substitute the values for PV, i, and n.

$$30\ 000 = R \times \frac{1 - (1.008)^{-84}}{0.008}$$ Simplify and solve for R.

$$R = 491.86$$

For a ten-year term, the values for PV and i are the same, but $n = 12 \times 10 = 120$.

$$PV = R \times \frac{1 - (1 + i)^{-n}}{i}$$ Substitute the values for PV, i, and n.

$$30\ 000 = R \times \frac{1 - (1.008)^{-120}}{0.008}$$ Simplify and solve for R.

$$R = 389.84$$

For a seven-year term, the payment would be \$491.86. For a ten-year term, the payment would be \$389.84.

(d) The total repayment cost of the seven-year term is \$491.86 × 84 = \$41 316.24 and \$389.84 × 120 = \$46 780.80 for the ten-year term. The family would save \$5464.56 in interest by choosing the shorter term.

Example 3

Mr. Fabiilli deposits \$3000 in an RRSP each year. The interest rate for the RRSP is 10.5%/a, compounded annually. He contributes to this RRSP for 20 years, at the end of which time he retires. Upon retiring, Mr. Fabiilli decides to transfer this RRSP to a RIF. How much can he withdraw from the fund at the end of every three months if the fund earns 9%/a, compounded quarterly, and if he wishes to deplete the fund after 15 years? Use time lines to help you solve the problem.

Solution

First find the accumulated or future value of this RRSP in 20 years. Here is the time line, where $R = 3000$, $n = 20$, and $i = 10.5\%$ or 0.105.

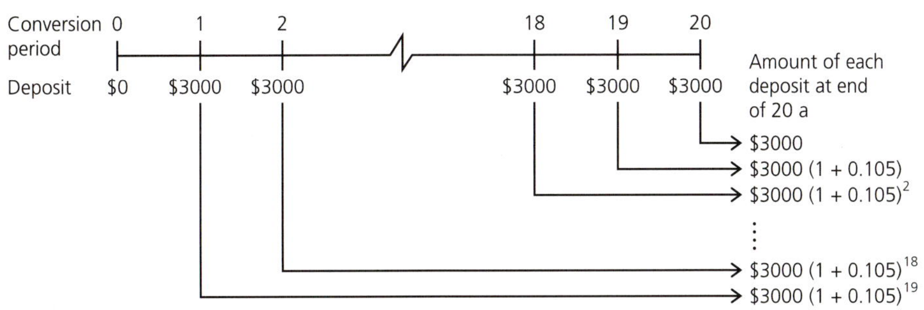

The accumulated or future value of the deposits is the geometric series,
$S_{20} = 3000 + 3000(1.105) + 3000(1.105)^2 + \ldots + 3000(1.105)^{18} + 3000(1.105)^{19}$.

Use either $S_n = \frac{a(r^n - 1)}{r - 1}$, and $a = 3000$, $r = 1.105$, and $n = 20$ or $FV = R \times \frac{(1 + i)^n - 1}{i}$, and $R = 3000$, $i = 0.105$, and $n = 20$ to find the accumulated value of his deposits.

$$\begin{aligned} S_{20} &= 3000 \times \frac{(1.105)^{20} - 1}{0.105} \\ &= 181\,892.42 \end{aligned}$$

The future value of the RRSP will be $181 892.42.

Now find the quarterly payment that would yield the present value of $181 892.42. Here is the time line, where $n = 4 \times 15$ or 60, and $i = \frac{0.09}{4}$ or 0.0225.

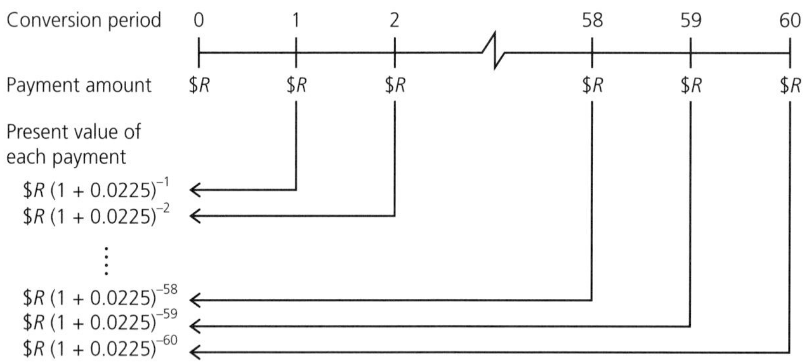

The present value of the deposits is the geometric series $S_{60} = R(1.0225)^{-60} + R(1.0225)^{-59} + R(1.0225)^{-58} + \ldots + R(1.0225)^{-2} + R(1.0225)^{-1}$, where $S_{60} = 181\,892.42$.

Solve for R.

Use the present value formula $PV = R \times \frac{1 - (1 + i)^{-n}}{i}$, where $PV = 181\,892.42$, $n = 4 \times 15$ or 60, and $i = \frac{0.09}{4}$ or 0.0225.

$$181\,892.42 = R \times \frac{1 - (1.0225)^{-60}}{0.0225} \qquad \text{Simplify and solve for } R.$$

$$R = 5554.14$$

Therefore, Mr. Fabiilli can withdraw $5554.14 from the fund at the end of every three months.

Practise, Apply, Solve 2.8

A

1. Evaluate to six decimal places.

(a) $(1.08)^{-10}$ (b) $(1.12)^{-6}$ (c) $(1.03)^{-24}$

(d) $(1.005)^{-60}$ (e) $(1.075)^{-20}$ (f) $(1.05)^{-48}$

2. Evaluate to two decimal places.

(a) $100(1.1)^{-24} \times \frac{(1.1)^{24} - 1}{1.1 - 1}$ (b) $900 \times \frac{1 - (1.075)^{-120}}{0.075}$

(c) $3000(1.05)^{-10} \times \frac{(1.05)^{10} - 1}{1.05 - 1}$ (d) $750 \times \frac{1 - (1.007)^{-240}}{0.007}$

3. Evaluate.

(a) $100(1.075)^{-24} + 100(1.075)^{-23} + 100(1.075)^{-22} + \ldots + 100(1.075)^{-2} + 100(1.075)^{-1}$

(b) $750(1.001)^{-240} + 750(1.001)^{-239} + 750(1.001)^{-238} + \ldots + 750(1.001)^{-2} + 750(1.001)^{-1}$

(c) $1500(1.035)^{-10} + 1500(1.035)^{-9} + 1500(1.035)^{-8} + \ldots + 1500(1.035)^{-2} + 500(1.035)^{-1}$

4. For each annuity

i. find the present or discounted value of each payment at the beginning of the term

ii. write the present or discounted values of the payments as a series

iii. find the present or discounted value of the annuity

(a) The rate of interest is 9%/a, compounded annually.

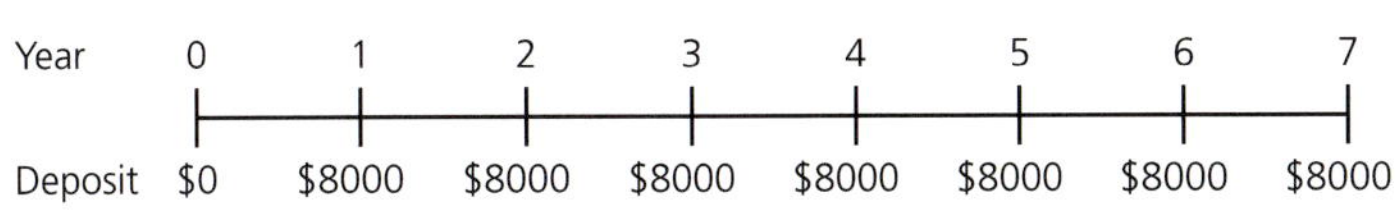

(b) The rate of interest is 8%/a, compounded semiannually.

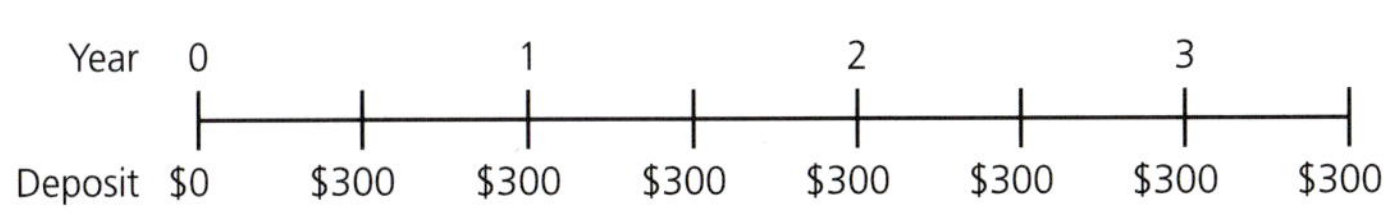

(c) The rate of interest is 8%/a, compounded quarterly.

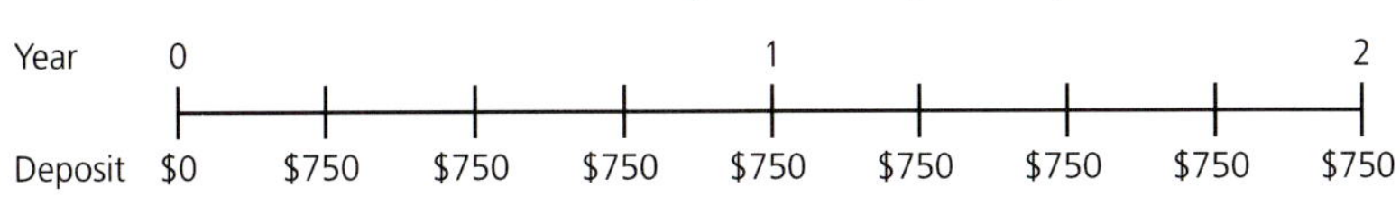

5. (a) Draw a time line to represent the present value of this annuity: $1200 is deposited at the *beginning* of every three months for three years in an account that pays 9%/a, compounded quarterly.
(b) Describe this type of annuity.
(c) Write the present values of all the payments as a series.
(d) Find the present value of the annuity.

B

6. For each of the following
   i. draw a time line to represent the present value of the annuity
   ii. write the series that represents the present value of the annuity
   iii. find the present value of the annuity
(a) $8000 is deposited at the end of every year for 11 years at 7%/a, compounded annually
(b) $650 is paid at the end of every 3 months for 6 years at 8%/a, compounded quarterly
(c) $60 is deposited at the end of every week for 3 years at 13%/a, compounded weekly
(d) $3800 is paid at the end of every 6 months for 8 years at 6.5%/a, compounded semiannually

7. The Ontario Association for Mathematics Education wishes to establish a math scholarship to reward the top mathematics educator in the province. The scholarship will be worth $2000. The association will deposit a lump sum in a trust account that pays 7.5%/a, compounded annually, for ten years. Determine how much must be deposited now if the first award will be given
(a) one year from now (b) immediately (c) 4 years from now
Include a time line and a series to represent each case.

8. Lily wants to buy a snowmobile. She can borrow $7500 at 10%/a, compounded quarterly, if she repays the loan by making equal quarterly payments for four years.
(a) Draw a time line to represent the annuity.
(b) Write the series that represents the present value of the annuity.
(c) Find the quarterly payment that Lily must make.

9. Nader plans to buy a used car. He can afford to make payments of $280 each month for a maximum of three years. The best interest rate he can find is 9.8%/a, compounded monthly. What is the most he can spend on a vehicle?

10. How much must Marie deposit now in a fund paying 6%/a, compounded semiannually, if she withdraws $1000 every six months, starting six months from today, for the next ten years?

11. **Knowledge and Understanding:** Roxanne buys a DVD/CD player for $50 down and ten monthly payments of $40 each. The first payment is due next month.

    (a) The interest rate is 18%/a, compounded monthly. What is the selling price of the player?

    (b) What is the interest charge?

12. Shimon wants to purchase a speedboat that sells for $22 000, including all taxes. The dealer offers either a $2000 discount if Shimon pays the total amount in cash or a finance rate of 2.4%/a, compounded monthly, if Shimon makes equal monthly payments for five years.

    (a) Determine the monthly payment that Shimon must make if he chooses the second offer.

    (b) What is the total cost of the dealer's finance plan for the speedboat?

    (c) To pay for the boat with cash now, Shimon knows that he can borrow the money from the bank at 6%/a, compounded monthly, over the same five-year period. Which offer should Shimon choose? Justify your answer.

13. René buys a computer system for $80 down and 18 monthly payments of $55 each. The first payment is due next month.

    (a) The interest rate is 15%/a, compounded monthly. What is the selling price of the computer system?

    (b) What is the finance charge?

14. The Peca family buy a cottage on Manitoulin Island for $69 000. They plan to deposit $5000 and then finance the remaining amount with a loan at 9%/a, compounded monthly. The loan payments are monthly. They may choose either a seven-year term or a ten-year term.

    (a) Find the monthly payment required for each term.

    (b) How much would they save in interest by selecting the shorter term?

    (c) What other factors should the Pecas consider when making their financing decision?

15. **Application:** A car dealer advertises a new sports car. The selling price is $32 000. The dealer offers this finance plan: the interest rate is 2.4%/a, compounded monthly, for five years with monthly payments. You can save $3000 by paying cash for the sports car. Suppose you could obtain a loan from a financial institution at 5.4%/a, compounded monthly. What is the best way to buy the car? Show your work.

16. In Example 3, the interest rate for the RRSP is 10.5%/a and the interest rate for the RIF is 9%/a. Determine how much Mr. Fabiilli would be able to withdraw from the RIF at the end of every three months if the interest rate for the RRSP is 9%/a and the interest rate on his RIF is 7.5%/a.

17. **Communication:** In Example 3 of section 2.5, a spreadsheet was used to solve the following problem: "An ad in an electronics store window reads, 'Big-screen television: Was \$3270: now \$2890 or \$500 down and \$122.81 for 24 months on approved credit.' What is the annual interest rate, compounded monthly, of the store's payment plan?" Discuss the merits and difficulties of trying to solve this problem using the present value of an annuity.

18. At the end of each year, Mr. Fox deposits \$2600 in an RRSP. The interest rate is 7.2%/a, compounded annually. He contributes to this RRSP for 20 years, at the end of which time he retires. Upon retiring, Mr. Fox decides to transfer all of this RRSP to an RIF. The interest rate for the RIF is 8.4%/a, compounded quarterly.

(a) Mr. Fox wishes to deplete the fund after 15 years. Then what will be the quarterly payment from the RIF?

(b) What would be the RIF payment if Mr. Fox had started contributing to his RRSP five years earlier, that is, if he had contributed to the RRSP for a total of 25 years?

Use time lines to help you solve this problem.

19. A lottery offers winners two prize choices. Option A is \$1000 each week for life and Option B is \$660 000 in one lump sum. The current expected rate of return for a large investment is 6.76%/a, compounded weekly.

(a) Which option would you suggest to a winner who expects to live for another 25 years?

(b) At what point in time is Option A better than Option B?

20. **Check Your Understanding:** The present value of the last payment of an ordinary simple annuity is $2500(1.05)^{-36}$.

(a) Describe two annuities, each with a different conversion period, that can be represented by the present value of this last payment.

(b) Find the present values of all the payments for each annuity in (a).

C

21. **Thinking, Inquiry, Problem Solving:** Carissa claims that she has found a different method for finding the present value of a ordinary simple annuity. Instead of finding the present value of each payment, she finds the accumulated or future value of each payment. She then finds the sum of the future values of the payments. Finally, she finds the present value of this total sum.

(a) Using Carissa's method and referring to Example 1 of section 2.7, find the present value of the annuity where \$750 is deposited at the end of every three months in a savings account that pays 8%/a, compounded quarterly, for ten years.

(b) Create another example to show that her claim is true. Include time lines.

(c) In step 3 of the Think, Do, Discuss in Part 2, you developed the present value formula $\frac{R(1 + i)^{-n}[(1 + i)^n - 1]}{i}$. Use this formula to prove that Carissa's claim works for *all* simple ordinary annuities.

22. Kyla has just graduated from university. She must repay her student loans that total \$17 000. She can afford to make monthly payments of \$325 each. The bank's interest rate is 7.2%/a, compounded monthly. Determine how long it will take Kyla to repay her student loan.

23. Kumar wants to buy a used jeep that costs \$7500. He borrows the \$7500 at 11.4%/a, compounded monthly. Kumar decides that he can afford to pay \$280 each month toward the loan. How long will it take to Kumar to repay is loan? Use a spreadsheet to verify your answer.

The Chapter Problem—Financial Planning

In this section, you studied the present value of an annuity. Apply what you learned to answer these questions about the Chapter Problem on page 106.

CP13. Can you apply the formula for the present value of an ordinary simple annuity to determine Mr. Sacchetto's new monthly mortgage payment? Explain.

CP14. At age 55, Mr. Sacchetto may choose between two RIF options for investing the \$120 000 savings. Option A provides monthly payments from an RIF that pays 7.2%/a, compounded monthly. Option B provides monthly payments from an RIF that pays 7.25%/a, compounded quarterly.

(a) Can you use the formula for the present value of an ordinary simple annuity to solve for the RIF payment under each option? Explain.

(b) For option A, draw a time line to represent the present value of the payments he would receive.

(c) Determine the monthly RIF payment he would receive under option A.

CP15. Use the formula for the present value of an ordinary simple annuity to estimate the term of Mr. Sacchetto's car loan.

2.9 TI-83 Plus Calculator: Analyzing Financial Situations Using the TVM Solver

In this section, you will analyze annuities using the time-value-of-money (TVM) solver of the TI-83 Plus calculator.

Part 1: Introducing the TVM Solver

Press [MODE] and change the fixed decimal mode to 2, because most of the values that you are working with here represent dollars and cents. Scroll down to **Float**, across to 2, and press [ENTER].

Press [APPS] and then select **1:Finance**. From the Finance CALC menu, select **1:TVM Solver**. The screen that appears should be similar to the second one shown, but the values may be different.

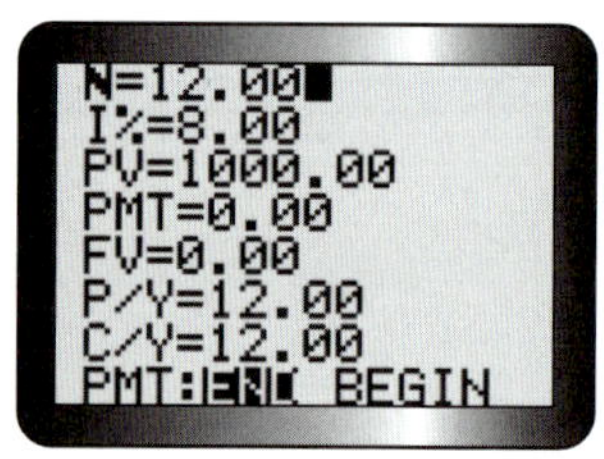

You will notice eight variables on the screen.

N	total number of payment periods, or the number of interest conversion periods for simple annuities
I%	annual interest rate as a percent, not as a decimal
PV	present or discounted value
PMT	regular payment amount
FV	future or accumulated value
P/Y	number of payment periods per year
C/Y	number of interest conversion periods per year
PMT	Choose **BEGIN** if the payments are made at the beginning of the payment intervals. Choose **END** if the payments are made at the end of the payment intervals.

You may enter different values for the variables. Enter the value for money that is *paid* as a negative number, since the investment is a cash outflow; enter the value of money that is *received* as a positive number, since the money is a cash inflow. When you enter a whole number, you will see that the calculator adds the decimal and two zeros.

To solve for a variable, move the cursor to that variable and press [ALPHA] [ENTER], and the calculator will calculate this value. A small shaded box to the left of the line containing the variable will appear.

Part 2: Determining Future Value and Present Value

Example 1

Find the future value or amount of $7500 invested for nine years at 8%/a, compounded monthly.

Solution

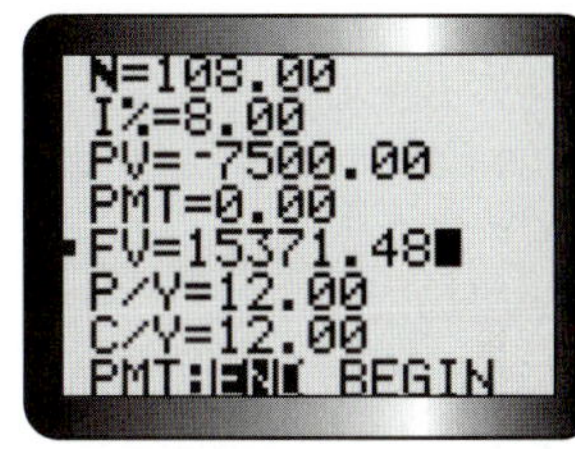

The number of interest conversion periods, **N**, is $9 \times 12 = 108$, **I%** $= 8$, and **PV** $= -7500$. The value for present value, **PV**, is negative, because the investment represents a cash outflow. **PMT** $= 0$ and **FV** $= 0$. The payments per year, **P/Y**, and the compounding periods per year, **C/Y**, are both 12. Open the **TVM Solver** and enter these values. Scroll to the line containing **FV**, the future value, and press [ALPHA] [ENTER].

The investment will be worth $15 371.48 after nine years.

Example 2

Maeve would like to have $3500 at the end of five years, so she can visit Europe. How much money should she deposit now in a savings account that pays 9%/a, compounded quarterly, to finance her trip?

Solution

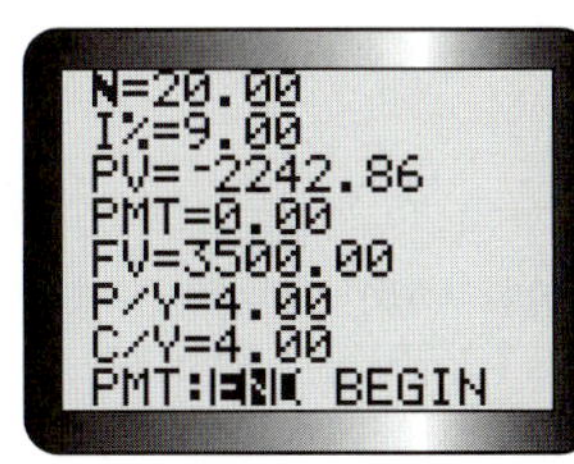

Open the **TVM Solver** and enter the values shown in the screen, except the value for **PV**. The value for **FV** is positive, because the future value of the investment will be "paid" to Maeve, representing a cash inflow. Scroll to the line containing **PV** and press [ALPHA] [ENTER] to get $-\$2242.86$. The solution for **PV** is negative, because Maeve must pay this money and the payment is a cash outflow.

Part 3: Determining the Future or Accumulated Value of an Ordinary Simple Annuity

Example 3

Celia deposits $1500 at the end of each year in a savings account that pays 4.5%/a, compounded annually. What will be the balance in the account after five years?

Solution

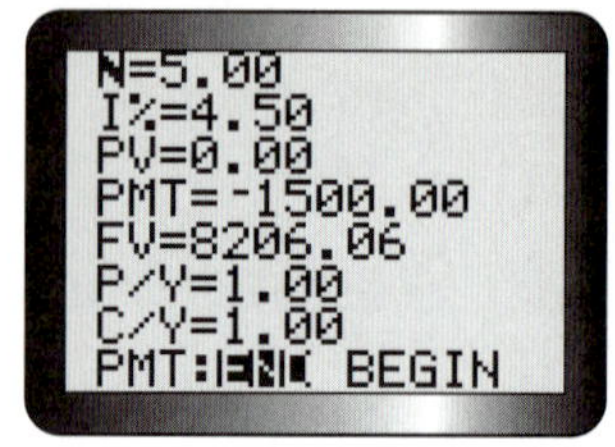

N = 5 and **I%** = 4.5. Because there is no money in the account at the beginning of the term, **PV** = 0. **PMT** = −1500. The payment, **PMT**, is negative, because Celia makes a payment, which is a cash outflow. **P/Y** = 1 and **C/Y** = 1. Open the **TVM Solver** and enter these values.

Scroll to the line containing **FV** and press [ALPHA] [ENTER].

The balance in Celia's account at the end of the year will be $8206.06.

Example 4

Mr. Bartolluci would like to have $150 000 in his account when he retires in 15 years. How much should he deposit at the end of each month in an account that pays 7%/a, compounded monthly?

Solution

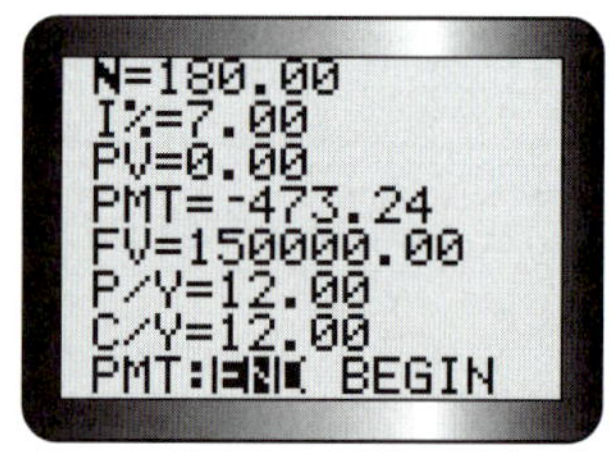

Open the **TVM Solver** and enter the values shown, except for **PMT**. Note that **N** = 12 × 15 = 180, and the future value, **FV**, is positive, since he will receive the money at some future time. Scroll to the line containing **PMT** and press [ALPHA] [ENTER].

Mr. Bartolluci must deposit $473.24 at the end of each month for 15 years. The payment appears as −473.24, because it is a cash outflow.

Part 4: Determining Present or Discounted Value of an Ordinary Simple Annuity

Example 5

Northern Lights High School wishes to establish a scholarship fund. A $500 scholarship will be awarded at the end of each school year for the next eight years. If the fund earns 9%/a, compounded annually, what does the school need to invest now to pay for the fund?

Solution

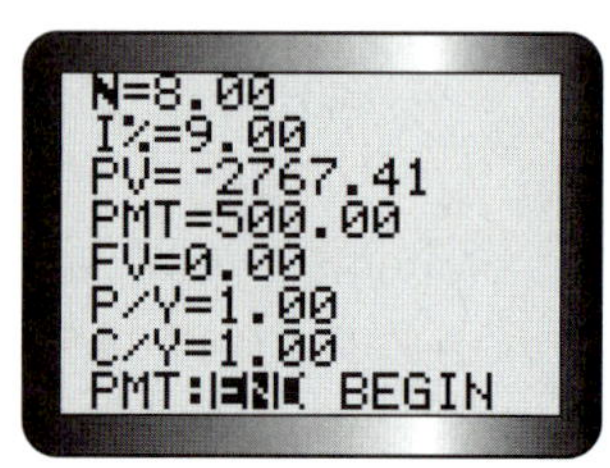

Open the **TVM Solver** and enter 8 for **N**, 9 for **I%**, and 500 for **PMT**. The value for **PMT** is positive, because someone will receive $500 each year. Enter 0 for **FV**, since the fund will be depleted at the end of the term. Enter 1 for both **P/Y** and **C/Y**. Scroll to the line containing **PV** and press [ALPHA] [ENTER].

The school must invest $2767.41 now for the scholarship fund. The present value appears as −2767.41, because the school must pay this money to establish the fund. The payment is a cash outflow.

TECHNOLOGY

Example 6

Monica buys a snowboard for $150 down and pays $35 at the end of each month for 1.5 years. If the finance charge is 16%/a, compounded monthly, find the selling price of the snowboard.

Solution

Open the **TVM Solver** and enter the values as shown in the screen, except the value for **PV**. The payment, **PMT**, is positive, because the payments are a cash inflow for the snowboard's seller. Scroll to the line containing **PV** and press [ALPHA] [ENTER].

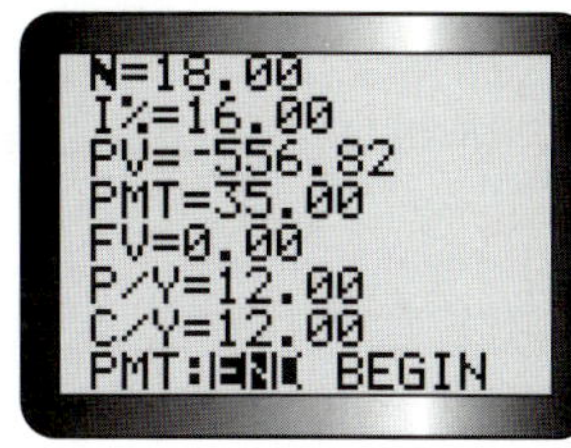

The present value is $556.82. The present value appears as a negative value on the screen, because it represents what Monica would have to pay now if she were to pay cash.

The selling price is the sum of the positive present value and the down payment. Since the down payment is also a payment, add both numbers. The total cash price is $PV + \$150 = \$706.82$. Under this finance plan, Monica will pay $\$35 \times 18 + \$150 = \$780$.

Practice 2.9

Use the TVM Solver to solve each of the following problems.

(a) Guy purchases a $10 000 GIC that earns 5%/a, compounded annually. What will the GIC be worth after eight years?

(b) What amount would you have to invest today at 6%/a, compounded semiannually, so that the investment will be worth $8000 after four years?

(c) For ten years, $750 is deposited at the end of every three months in a savings account that pays 8%/a, compounded quarterly. Find the future value or amount of the annuity.

(d) Gurtrude would like to have $3800 at the end of four years, so she can go to college. How much money should she deposit in a savings account that pays 3.5%/a, compounded quarterly, to finance her education?

(e) Trudy is planning for her retirement from her job as a chemist. When she retires, she would like to receive $300 at the end of each month for 15 years from a retirement income fund (RIF) that earns 5%/a, compounded monthly. How much money would she need to establish the RIF at the beginning of her retirement?

(f) Ramona has $53 380 in her savings account and she withdraws $240 at the end of every three months. If the account earns 5%/a, compounded quarterly, what will be her bank balance after three years?

2.10 Equivalent Rates and General Annuities

In previous sections, you have worked with **ordinary simple annuities**. In an ordinary simple annuity, the payment interval corresponds to the interest conversion period. In this section, you will investigate annuities where this is not the case. An annuity where the payment interval does not correspond to the interest conversion period is called a **general annuity**.

When working through this section, remember to change the decimal mode on the TI-83 Plus calculator, as necessary.

Part 1: Equivalent Rates

Two interest rates are said to be **equivalent** if they yield the same amounts at the end of one year, or at the end of any number of years. The **nominal** rate of interest is the annual rate.

Example 1

Suppose that \$1 is deposited in an account that earns 10%/a, compounded annually. Also suppose that another \$1 is deposited in another account that earns interest, but the interest is compounded quarterly. What is the interest rate of the second account so that the value in each account at the end of one year is the same?

Solution

Draw a time line to organize the given information.

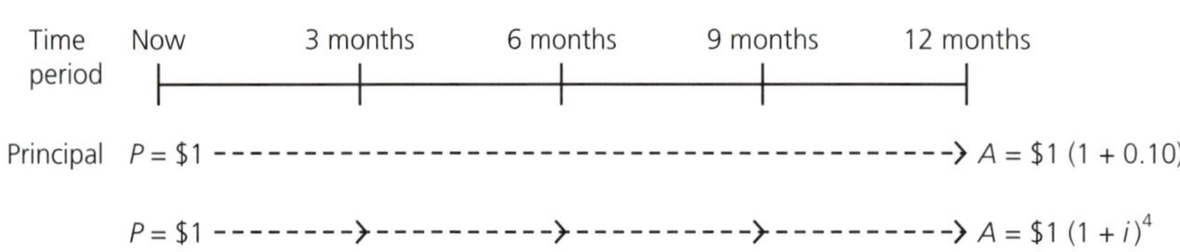

Let i be the **quarterly** interest rate. Then $4 \times i$ is the *nominal* interest rate, compounded quarterly.

One dollar invested at 10%/a, compounded annually, will accumulate at the end of one year to $\$1(1 + 0.10)^1 = \$1.10$.

One dollar invested at $4i$ %/a, compounded quarterly, will accumulate at the end of one year to $\$1(1 + i)^4 = \$(1 + i)^4$.

The accumulated values must be equal. Let $\$1(1 + i)^4$ equal \$1.10 and solve for i.

$$(1 + i)^4 = 1.10 \qquad \text{Take the fourth root of each side.}$$
$$1 + i = \sqrt[4]{1.10}$$
$$1 + i \doteq 1.024\,113\,689 \qquad \text{Isolate } i.$$
$$i = 0.024\,113\,689$$

Then $4 \times 0.024\,113\,689 \doteq 0.0965$.

The interest rate that is equivalent to 10%/a, compounded annually, is 9.65%/a, compounded quarterly.

Example 2

What is the nominal interest rate, compounded quarterly, that is equivalent to 15%/a, compounded monthly?

Solution

Draw a time line to organize the information. Let i be the equivalent quarterly interest rate. Suppose again that \$1 is invested in two accounts at the beginning of the year.

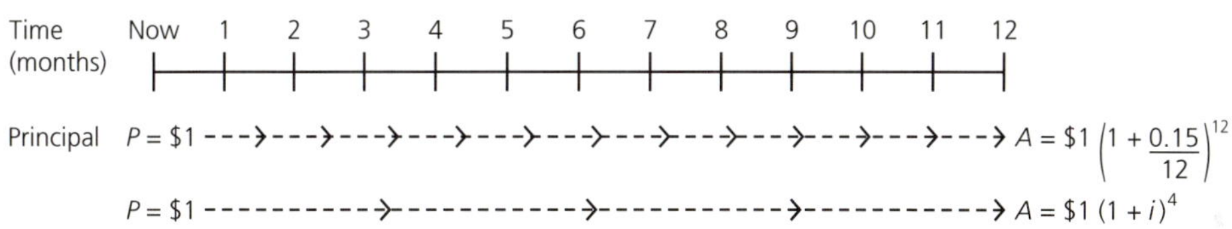

Let i represent the quarterly rate.

At the end of one year, \$1, compounded quarterly, will accumulate to $(1 + i)^4$.

At the end of the same year, \$1, compounded monthly, at 15%/a, will accumulate to $\left(1 + \frac{0.15}{12}\right)^{12}$.

Let $(1 + i)^4$ equal $\left(1 + \frac{0.15}{12}\right)^{12}$ and solve for i.

$$(1 + i)^4 = \left(1 + \frac{0.15}{12}\right)^{12}$$
$$(1 + i)^4 = (1.0125)^{12} \qquad \text{Take the fourth root of each side.}$$
$$1 + i = \sqrt[4]{(1.0125)^{12}}$$
$$1 + i = 1.0125^3 \qquad \text{Isolate } i.$$
$$i \doteq 0.037\,970\,703\,1$$

Then $4 \times 0.037\,970\,703\,1 \doteq 0.151\,88$.

The interest rate per conversion period is about 3.797%. The nominal rate is $4 \times 0.037\,970\,703\,1$, or about 15.188%/a, compounded quarterly. This rate is equivalent to 15%/a, compounded monthly.

Part 2: Calculating the Future Value or the Present Value of an Ordinary General Annuity

In an ordinary general annuity, the payment interval does not coincide with the interest conversion period. To solve a problem involving an ordinary general annuity, you must first find the nominal interest rate that coincides with the payment interval. Then solve as if the problem were an ordinary simple annuity.

Example 3

Leno deposits \$1500 at the end of each year for ten years in a registered home ownership plan (RHOSP) that earns 10%/a, compounded quarterly.

(a) Draw a time line to represent the annuity.

(b) Write the series that represents the annuity.

(c) How much money will have accumulated in the plan at the end of ten years?

(d) Verify your answer using technology.

(e) What would be the accumulated value if the plan earned 10%/a, compounded annually? Comment on the difference.

Solution

(a) Draw a time line that shows the payment intervals, not the interest conversion periods. Therefore, $n = 10$.

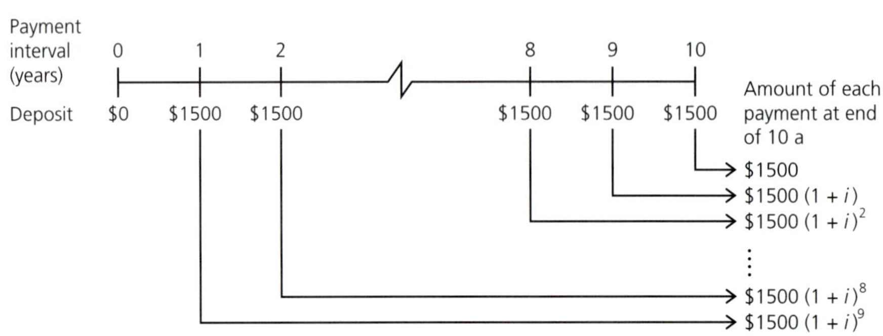

(b) The payments are annual, but the interest is compounded quarterly. Before you can write the sequence, you need to find the nominal interest rate that is equivalent to 10%/a, compounded quarterly. Let i be 2.5%. Then

$$1 + i = 1.025^4$$
$$i = 1.025^4 - 1$$
$$i \doteq 0.103\ 812\ 891$$

The geometric series is $S_{10} = 1500 + 1500(1.103\ 812\ 891) + 1500(1.103\ 812\ 891)^2 + \ldots + 1500(1.103\ 812\ 891)^8 + 1500(1.103\ 812\ 891)^9$.

(c) Find the sum of the series using $S_n = \frac{a(r^n - 1)}{r - 1}$, where $a = 1500$, $r = 1.103\ 812\ 891$, and $n = 10$. Or, find the accumulated value of the ordinary simple annuity using $FV = R \times \frac{(1 + i)^n - 1}{i}$, where $R = 1500$, $n = 10$, and $i = 0.103\ 812\ 891$.

$$S_{10} = FV = 1500 \times \frac{(1.103\ 812\ 891)^{10} - 1}{0.103\ 812\ 891}$$

Note: It is important to use as many digits as possible when calculating. Avoid rounding numbers until your final calculation.

$$FV = \$24\ 347.61$$

At the end of ten years, \$24 347.61 will have accumulated in Leno's plan. This amount represents a good down payment for the purchase of a home.

(d) Use the **TVM Solver** of the TI-83 Plus calculator to verify the solution. Do not find the equivalent nominal rate. You can enter the information that you have directly into the **TVM Solver**, and you will see why in the next few steps.

Press [MODE] and change the fixed decimal mode to 2, because most of the values in this section represent dollars and cents.

Open the **TVM Solver**. Enter the following:

N = 10, since there are ten payment intervals

I% = 10, the annual interest rate

PV = 0

PMT = −1500. This value is negative, because the payment is an outflow of Leno's cash.

FV = 0

P/Y = 1, since only one deposit is made annually

C/Y = 4, since interest is compounded quarterly

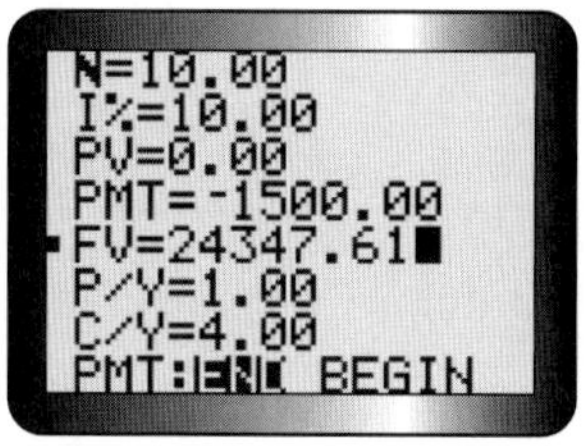

Scroll to the line containing **FV** and press [ALPHA] [ENTER]. The future or accumulated value is \$24 347.61, as it is in (a). Notice that the value is positive, because it represents an inflow of cash for Leno.

(e) Find the accumulated value of the ordinary simple annuity with $R = 1500$, $n = 10$, and $i = 0.10$.

$$FV = R \times \frac{(1 + i)^n - 1}{i}$$ Substitute the values for R, n, and i.

$$= 1500 \times \frac{(1.10)^{10} - 1}{0.10}$$ Simplify.

$$= 23\ 906.14$$

The accumulated value is \$23 906.14, if the plan earned interest at 10%/a, compounded annually. This value is \$441.47 less than the value earned if the interest is compounded quarterly over ten years.

The length or frequency of the interest conversion period has some effect on the accumulated value. But this effect seems small when compared to the effects that the interest rate and the size of payment have on the accumulated value of an annuity.

Example 4

Jade Coyne wishes to purchase a used car from her uncle. She will pay him \$18 000 by making weekly payments. They agree that Jade will pay interest at 7.2%/a, compounded monthly. Jade would like to repay the loan in three years.

(a) Draw a time line to represent the repayment of the loan.

(b) Write the series that represents the repayment of the loan.

(c) What is the weekly payment?

(d) Use technology to determine how much sooner Jade could repay the loan if the weekly payment is increased by \$20.

Solution

(a) Draw a time line that shows the payment intervals, not the interest conversion periods. Therefore, $n = 3 \times 52$ or 156.

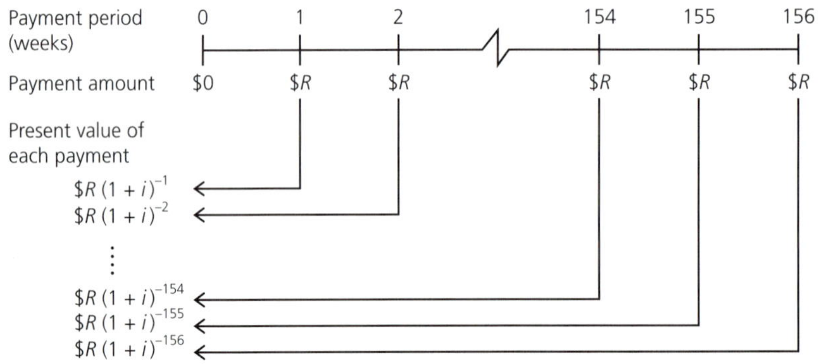

(b) Find the interest rate, i, compounded weekly, that is equivalent to 7.2%/a, compounded monthly. $7.2\% \div 12 = 0.6\%$

$$(1 + i)^{52} = (1.006)^{12} \qquad \text{Take the 52nd root of each side.}$$
$$1 + i = \sqrt[52]{(1.006)^{12}}$$
$$1 + i = (1.006)^{\frac{12}{52}}$$
$$i = (1.006)^{\frac{3}{13}} - 1$$
$$i \doteq 0.001\,381\,431\,4$$

The series is $S_{156} = R(1.001\,381\,431\,4)^{-156} + R(1.001\,381\,431\,4)^{-155} + R(1.001\,381\,431\,4)^{-154} + \ldots + R(1.001\,381\,431\,4)^{-2} + R(1.001\,381\,431\,4)^{-1}$, where $S_{156} = 18\,000$.

(c) **Finding the Weekly Payment Using Formulas**

You could find the sum of the geometric series using $S_n = \frac{a(r^n - 1)}{r - 1}$, with $a = R(1.001\ 381\ 431\ 4)^{-156}$, $n = 156$, $S_{156} = 18\ 000$, and $r = 1.001\ 381\ 431\ 4$. Then solve for R.

Alternatively, you can find the weekly deposit, R, using the formula for the present value of an ordinary simple annuity.

$PV = 18\ 000$, $n = 156$, and $i = 0.001\ 381\ 431\ 4$

$$PV = R \times \frac{1 - (1 + i)^{-n}}{i}$$ Substitute the values for PV, n, and i.

$$18\ 000 = R \times \frac{1 - (1.001\ 381\ 431\ 4)^{-156}}{0.001\ 381\ 431\ 4}$$ Simplify and solve for R.

$$R = \$128.34$$

Finding the Weekly Payment Using Technology

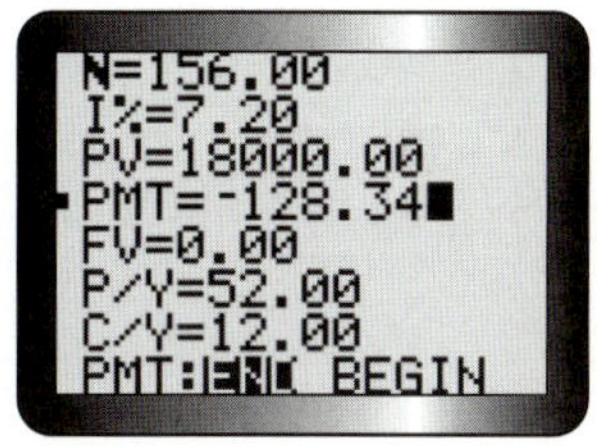

Solve for the payment, R, using the **TVM Solver**. Enter the values as shown in the screen, except for **PMT**. Scroll to the line containing **PMT** and press [ALPHA] [ENTER].

The payment is \$128.34. The value is negative in the screen because the payment is an outflow of cash for Jade.

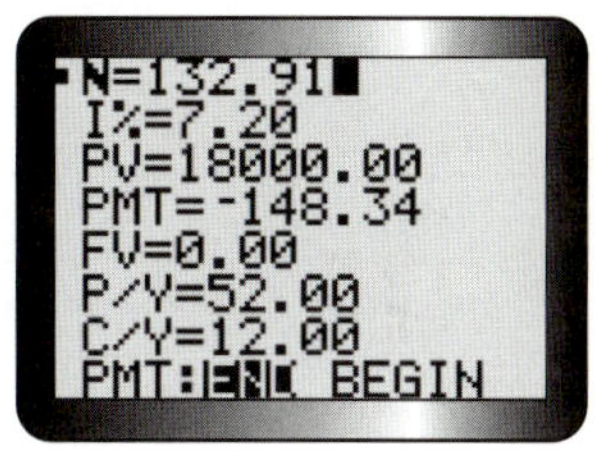

(d) Open the **TVM Solver** and adjust the payment to **PMT** $= -148.34$. Scroll to the line containing **N** and press [ALPHA] [ENTER].

Jade will repay the loan after about 133 weeks, or 23 weeks sooner, if she increases the monthly payment by \$20.

Consolidate Your Understanding

1. An investment earns 12%/a, compounded semiannually. Would the equivalent nominal rate, compounded quarterly, be greater than or less than 12%/a? Explain why.

2. Write a problem so that the answer to the problem is $(1 + i)^2 = \left(1 + \frac{0.09}{4}\right)^4$.

3. Solve for i in question 2.

Focus 2.10

Key Ideas

- An annuity where the payment interval does not correspond to the interest conversion period is called a **general annuity.**
- Two interest rates are said to be **equivalent** if they yield the same accumulated values at the end of one year.
- The **nominal** rate of interest is the annual rate.
- Solve an ordinary general annuity by first finding the nominal interest rate that coincides with the payment interval. Then solve the problem as you would for an ordinary simple annuity.
- Use the time-value-of-money (TVM) solver of the TI-83 Plus calculator to solve simple and general annuity problems. The **TVM Solver** allows you to specify both the **P/Y**, the payments per year, and **C/Y**, the number of interest conversion periods per year. For this reason, it is not necessary to find the equivalent rate when solving a general annuity.

Practise, Apply, Solve 2.10

A

1. Simplify.

(a) $\sqrt{(1+i)^2}$ (b) $\sqrt[4]{(1+i)^4}$ (c) $\sqrt[7]{(1+i)^7}$ (d) $\sqrt[3]{(1+i)^3}$

2. Evaluate to four decimal places.

(a) $\sqrt{(1.06)^4}$ (b) $\sqrt[3]{(1.08)^{12}}$ (c) $\sqrt[4]{(1.0125)^{12}}$ (d) $\sqrt[2]{(1.04)^{18}}$

3. Solve for i.

(a) $1+i=(1.025)^4$ (b) $1+i=(1.01)^{12}$ (c) $(1+i)^2=1.10$
(d) $(1+i)^{12}=1.015$ (e) $(1+i)^4=(1.06)^2$ (f) $(1+i)^{12}=(1.025)^4$
(g) $(1+i)^{52}=(1.03)^4$ (h) $(1+i)^2=(1.0055)^{52}$

4. Find the equivalent nominal interest rate, compounded annually and rounded to two decimal places, for each of the following.

(a) 8%/a, compounded semiannually (b) 8%/a, compounded quarterly
(c) 10.4%/a, compounded weekly (d) 8.76%/a, compounded daily
(e) 18%/a, compounded quarterly (f) 21%/a, compounded monthly

5. Find the nominal rate that is equivalent to 18%/a, compounded quarterly, if interest is paid

(a) annually (b) semiannually (c) monthly
(d) weekly (e) daily

B

6. For each of the following,

i. draw a time line to represent the amount of each annuity
ii. write the series that represents the amount of the annuity
iii. find the amount of each on the date of the last payment

(a) \$5000 is deposited at the end of every year for 10 years at 8%/a, compounded semiannually

(b) \$800 is deposited at the end of every 3 months for 5 years at 8%/a, compounded annually

(c) \$150 is deposited at the end of every week for 2 years at 11%/a, compounded semiannually

(d) \$3300 is deposited at the end of every 6 months for 7 years at 10%/a, compounded quarterly

(e) \$1000 is deposited at the end of every month for 3 years at 9%/a, compounded annually

7. Michelle wants to purchase a new stereo sound system for \$3800. She can put \$300 down and finance the outstanding balance. The interest rate is 18%/a, compounded annually. What monthly payment will allow her to pay for the purchase in 18 months? Include a time line.

8. **Knowledge and Understanding:** Natalie and Preston would like to accumulate \$25 000 at the end of 3.5 years for a future down payment on a house in Prescott. How much should they deposit at the end of each week in a savings account that pays 7.2%/a, compounded monthly, to meet their goal?

(a) Draw a time line to represent the annuity.

(b) Write the series that represents the amount of the annuity.

(c) Determine the weekly deposit.

9. Recall question 9 in section 2.8. Nader plans to buy a used car. He can afford to pay \$280 at the end of each month for three years. The best interest rate he can find is 9.8%/a, compounded monthly. For this interest rate, the most he could spend on a vehicle is \$8702.85.

(a) Determine the amount he could spend on the purchase of a car if the interest rate is 9.8%/a, compounded annually.

(b) Explain why the change in the compounding period has such a small effect on the amount he can afford to spend on a car.

10. **Communication:** The following screens were obtained from the **TVM Solver** of the TI-83 Plus calculator. Write a problem that would describe each screen.

(a)

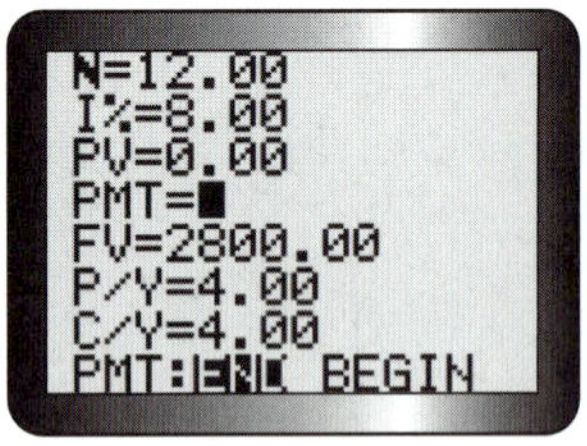

(b)

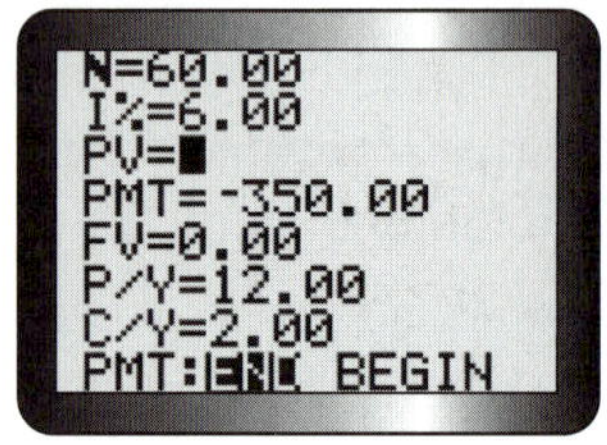

11. **Application:** Daniel buys an engagement ring for his fiancée, Lise. He pays \$3400 by putting \$500 down and financing the rest at 9.6%/a, compounded annually. He hopes to completely pay this debt in three years. What must he pay at the end of each month? Verify your answer using technology.

If possible, use technology to solve questions 12 to 18. Use the ***TVM Solver*** *on the TI-83 Plus calculator. Or visit the Nelson Thomson Learning Web site at www.math.nelson.com and use one of the several online loan calculators.*

Jack and Jill Hill are saving money to purchase their first home. Their intent is to deposit \$832 at the end of each month for six years in a savings account that pays 7.2%/a, compounded annually. They have hired you to analyze the effects of changing the conditions of their long-term savings plan to maximize the money they can save. Questions 12 to 16 will assist you in your analysis.

12. First analyze the effect of changing the compounding period.

(a) Determine the future value of their savings plan at the end of six years, if the savings account pays

i. 7.2%/a, compounded annually
ii. 7.2%/a, compounded semiannually
iii. 7.2%/a, compounded monthly
iv. 7.2%/a, compounded weekly
v. 7.2%/a, compounded daily

(b) Based on your analysis, describe the effect of changing the compounding period on their savings plan.

13. Analyze the effect of altering the frequency of the deposits.

(a) The Hills deposit \$832 at the end of each month. What is the equivalent year-end deposit? Use your answer to find the future value of the annual deposits after six years.

(b) What is the equivalent semiannual deposit? Find the future value of their savings plan after six years using the semiannual deposit.

(c) Determine the equivalent weekly deposit. Use it to find the future value of their savings plan after six years.

(d) Determine the equivalent daily deposit. Use it to find the future value of their savings plan after six years.

(e) Based on your analysis, report the effect that the frequency of the deposits has on their savings plan.

14. Analyze the effect of changing the interest rate.

(a) Determine the future value of their savings plan at the end of six years if the interest earned on the monthly deposits of $832 is

i. 7.8%/a, compounded annually
ii. 8.4%/a, compounded annually
iii. 6%/a, compounded annually

(b) Based on your analysis, report the effect of changing the interest rate on their savings plan.

15. Analyze the effect of changing the size of the deposit.

(a) Determine the future value of their savings plan at the end of six years if the monthly deposits of $832 are

i. increased by 10%
ii. decreased by 10%
iii. changed to $800

(b) Based on your analysis, report the effect of changing the size of the deposit on their savings plan.

16. Analyze the effect of the total number and timing of the deposits.

(a) Determine the future value of their savings plan at the end of six years if the monthly deposits of $832 each are made at the beginning of each month, instead of at the end of each month.

(b) Determine the future value of their savings plan at the end of six years if the Hills wait one year before deciding to make their month-end deposits of $832 each.

(c) Determine the future value of their savings plan at the end of six years if the Hills decide to stop making deposits at the end of the fifth year.

(d) Determine the future value of their savings plan if the Hills decide to make deposits for 6.5 years by starting the plan six months earlier.

(e) Based on your analysis, report on the effect of changing the total number and timing of the deposits on their savings plan.

17. Based on what you have analyzed, create a report that you could present to the Hills. In your report, outline the best and most important strategies they should follow to save as much money as possible for their home purchase.

18. An ad for a big-screen television reads, "Was $3270. Now $2890 cash, or $500 down and $122.81 for 24 months on approved credit." Use the financial functions of the TI-83 Plus calculator to answer the following.

(a) What is the annual rate of interest, compounded monthly, of the payment plan?

(b) What is the total interest?

19. **Check Your Understanding:** Explain why 12%/a, compounded monthly, is not the same as 12%/a, compounded quarterly.

C

20. Lee wishes to purchase a downhill ski package that includes the skis, poles, bindings, and boats. The selling price is \$1894. The finance plan includes a \$150 down payment and payments of \$113 each at the end of the month for 1.5 years. Find the annual interest charge, if the interest charge is

(a) compounded monthly (b) compounded annually

21. Thinking, Inquiry, Problem Solving

(a) Imagine that you have a loan and the interest rate on the loan doubles. You wish to keep the same amortization period, but should you double the payment? Justify your reasoning with examples.

(b) Imagine that you are going to borrow money. You decide to double the amount that you want to borrow. Should you double the payment if you wish to keep the same amortization period? Justify your reasoning with examples.

The Chapter Problem—Financial Planning

In this section, you studied general annuities. Apply what you learned to solve these questions about the Chapter Problem on page 106.

CP16. What interest rate, compounded monthly, is equivalent to 8.4%/a, compounded semiannually? Without technology, use this rate to find Mr. Sacchetto's new monthly mortgage payments. Recall that he owes \$77 000 and has 20 years remaining in the term. Determine the principal still owing on his mortgage after five years.

CP17. Use the **TVM Solver** to verify the new payment and outstanding balance.

CP18. Recall that, at age 55, Mr. Sacchetto may choose between two RIF options for investing the \$120 000 savings. Option A provides monthly payments from an RIF that pays 7.2%/a, compounded monthly. Option B provides monthly payments from an RIF that pays 7.25%/a, compounded quarterly. Without using the **TVM Solver**, determine the monthly RIF payment Mr. Sacchetto would receive if he selects Option B.

CP19. Write the values that you would enter for **N**, **I%**, **PV**, **FV**, **P/Y**, and **C/Y** into the **TVM Solver** to find the monthly RIF payment Mr. Sacchetto would receive if the fund pays 7.25%/a, compounded quarterly. Verify your solution for question CP18.

CP20. Which RIF payment option should he choose?

TI-83 Plus Calculator: Creating Repayment Schedules

In this section, you will create a repayment schedule, by applying some of the financial functions from the Finance CALC menu.

Part 1: Introducing Other Functions in the Finance CALC Menu

You have used the **TVM Solver** to find, for example, future value and present value. The calculator can use the information that you have entered into the **TVM Solver** to perform other functions. Here are three other functions:

ΣInt(*A*, *B*, *roundvalue*) calculates the sum of the interest paid from period *A* to period *B*

ΣPrn(*A*, *B*, *roundvalue*) calculates the sum of the principal paid from period *A* to period *B*

bal(*x*, *roundvalue*) calculates the balance owing after period *x*

The calculator rounds values as it calculates. You will need to tell the calculator the value for rounding, *roundvalue*. The greater *roundvalue* is, the greater the accuracy of the calculations. In this section, the *roundvalue* is 6, which is also the value that banks use.

Part 2: Using the TVM Solver and Other Finance CALC Menu Functions

Press [MODE] and change the fixed decimal mode to 2, because most of the values in this section represent dollars and cents.

Example 1

Eleanor finances the purchase of a new pickup truck by borrowing \$18 000. She will repay the loan with monthly payments. The term of the loan is five years. The interest rate is 14%/a, compounded monthly.

(a) How much is the monthly payment?

(b) How much will she pay in interest?

(c) How much will she still owe on the loan after the 30th payment, that is, at the halfway point in repaying the loan?

(d) What portion of the 30th payment reduces the principal?

TECHNOLOGY

Solution

(a) Press [APPS] and select **1:Finance**. Then press [ENTER] to select **1:TVM Solver** from the Finance CALC menu. Enter **N** = 60, because 12 × 5 = 60. Enter **I%** = 14, **PV** = 18000, **FV** = 0, **P/Y** = 12, and **C/Y** = 12. Notice that the present value, **PV**, is a positive number, because Eleanor receives (a cash inflow) $18 000 from the bank.

Scroll to the line containing **PMT** and press [ALPHA] [ENTER]. The monthly payment is $418.83.

The payment appears as a negative value, because Eleanor pays this amount each month. The actual value is −418.828 515 3, which the calculator rounded to −418.83.

(b) Use **ΣInt**(*A*, *B*, *roundvalue*) to calculate the total interest that Eleanor will pay.

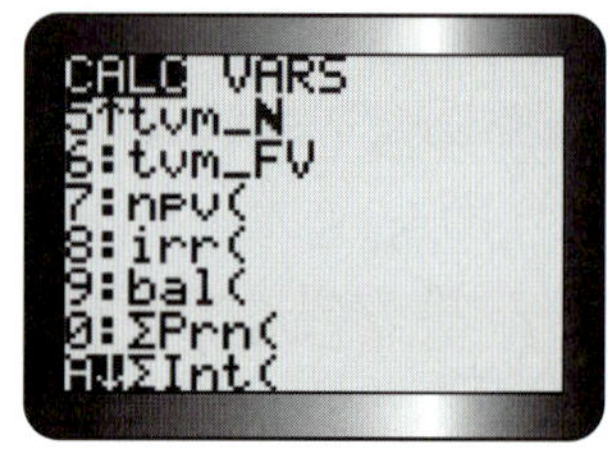

Press [2nd] [MODE] to return to the home screen. Press [APPS] and then select **1:Finance** from the Finance CALC menu. Select **ΣInt** by scrolling down or by pressing [ALPHA] [A]. Press [ENTER].

Press [1] [,] [6] [0] [,] [6] [)] [ENTER]. The sum of the interest paid from the first period to the 60th period is calculated.

By the end of the loan, Eleanor will have paid $7129.71 in total interest. Eleanor will have paid $7129.71 + $18 000 = $25,129.71 in interest and principal for the truck.

Note that the product of the payment, $418.83, and the total number of payments, 60, is $25 129.80. The difference of $0.09 is due to rounding, because 418.828 515 3 was rounded to 418.83.

(c) Find the balance on the loan after the 30th payment. *roundvalue* must be consistent, that is, 6.

From the Finance CALC menu, select **bal** by scrolling or by pressing [9]. Press [3] [0] [,] [6] [)] [ENTER].

Eleanor still owes $10 550.27 after the 30th payment. Why is this amount not $9000?

(d) Find the portion of the 30th payment that reduces the principal by calculating the sum of the principal paid from the 30th payment to the 30th payment. In other words, you are calculating the sum of only one item, the 30th period. *roundvalue* is again 6. From the Finance CALC menu, select **ΣPrn** by scrolling or by pressing [0]. Press [3] [0] [,] [3] [0] [,] [6] [)] [ENTER].

The portion of the 30th payment that reduces the principal is $292.33. The other portion of this payment, $126.50, is interest.

Part 3: Using the Finance Functions to Create Repayment Schedules

Use the functions described in parts 1 and 2 to create repayment schedules or amortization tables.

Example 2

Recall that Eleanor borrows $18 000 to purchase a pickup truck. She will repay the loan with monthly payments. The term of the loan is five years. The interest rate is 14%/a, compounded monthly.

(a) What will be the monthly outstanding balance on the loan after each of the first seven months?

(b) Create a repayment schedule for the first seven months of the loan.

(c) Use the repayment schedule to verify that the loan is completely paid after five years or 60 payments.

Solution

(a) Find the outstanding balance after each payment for the first seven months. You will combine **sequence** (List OPS menu) and **bal**.

From the home screen, press [2nd] [STAT] [▶] [5] to select **sequence**. Then press [APPS] [ENTER] 9 to select **bal**. Press [X,T,Θ,n] [,] [6] [)] [,] [X,T,Θ,n] [,] [1] [,] [7] [,] [1] [)]. Press [ENTER] to calculate the sequence of balances, beginning with the first month, 1, and ending with seventh month, 7. The increment for this sequence is 1, which is the last value entered. Recall that the increment is the change from payment number to payment number. Scroll right ([▶]) to see the other balances.

(b) Create a repayment, or an amortization, schedule for the first seven months by comparing the interest, principal, and balance in a table.

Begin by opening the equation editor. Press [Y=]. Clear **Y1** to **Y3**, if necessary. Store the interest portion of each payment in **Y1**. Move the cursor to the right of **Y1=**. Press [APPS] [ENTER] and select **ΣInt**. Press [X,T,Θ,n] [,] [X,T,Θ,n] [,] [6] [)] [ENTER].

To store the principal portion of each payment in Y2, press [APPS] [ENTER] and select **ΣPrn**. Press [X,T,Θ,n] [,] [X,T,Θ,n] [,] [6] [)] [ENTER].

To store the outstanding balance after each payment in Y3, press [APPS] [ENTER] [9] to select **bal**. Press [X,T,Θ,n] [,] [6] [)] [ENTER].

Before viewing the table, press [2nd] [WINDOW]. Set **TblStart** to 1 and **ΔTbl** to 1. The table will start with payment 0 and the payment number will increase by 1 at each step.

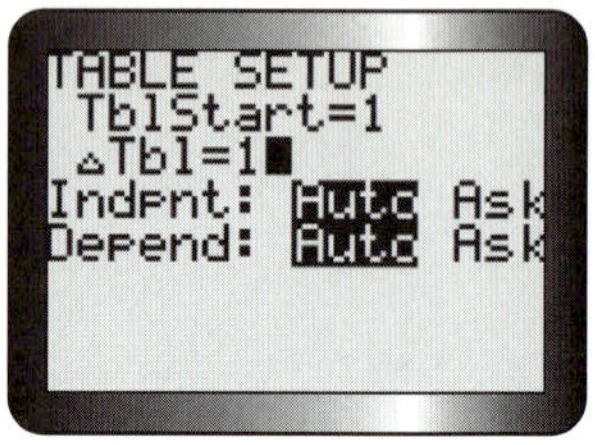

Press [2nd] [GRAPH] to see the amortization table. Notice that the interest portion and the principal portion of each payment appear as negative values. Each payment, which is a combination of interest and principal, is a cash outflow for Eleanor.

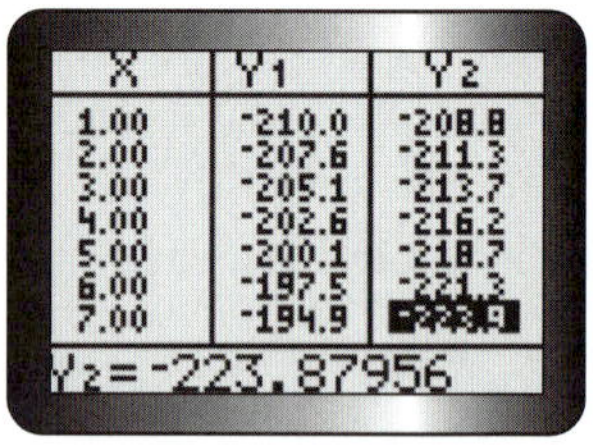

Scroll right to see the values for **Y3**, the outstanding balance.

The outstanding balance after seven payments is \$16 486.03.

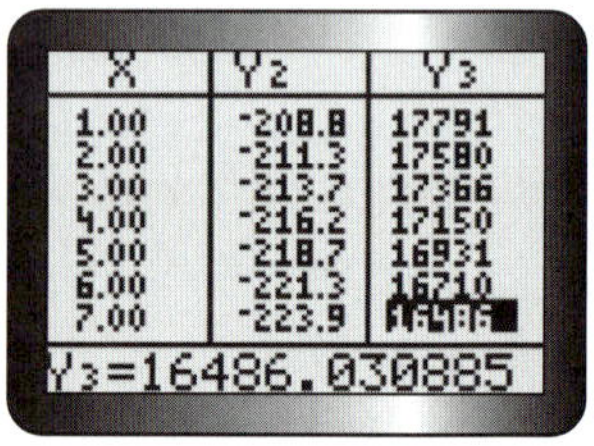

(c) Scroll or reset the table's start value to see other entries in the amortization table. Scroll up to the beginning of the table. Notice that a substantial portion of the \$418.83 payment is interest. Scroll down the table. At the end of the amortization, most of the payment is applied to the principal. The final outstanding balance is **2.5E−5** or 2.5×10^{-5}. As a decimal, this value is \$0.000 025. Therefore, the amortization period of 60 payments is correct. The loan will be paid completely after five years or 60 payments.

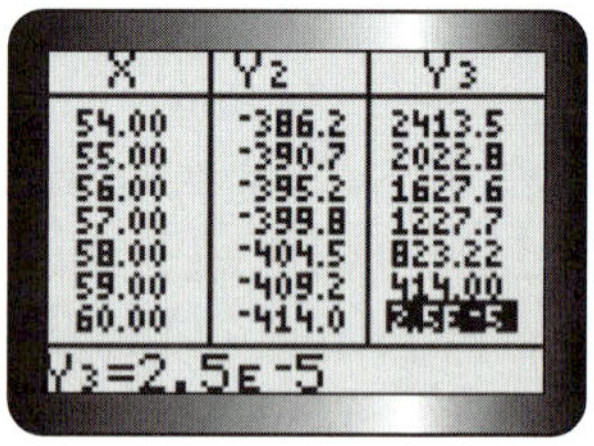

Practice 2.11

Alysa borrows \$2650 to buy a laptop computer. She will repay this loan with 18 monthly payments. The interest rate is 21%/a, compounded monthly.

(a) What is the monthly payment?

(b) How much interest will she pay?

(c) How much does she owe after the tenth payment?

(d) How much of this tenth payment reduces the principal?

(e) Use the financial functions of the TI-83 Plus calculator to create an amortization table for the repayment of her entire loan.

Using Technology to Analyze Canadian Mortgages

2.12

By regulation, the annual interest rates of the majority of Canadian mortgages are compounded, *at most*, semiannually. However, the payment interval is much more frequent. Monthly, weekly, or bi-weekly payment intervals are the most popular.

Mortgage amortizations in Canada can be represented by general annuities. The periodic payment is usually determined using a repayment or amortization period of 20 years or 25 years. But the interest rate is not guaranteed for either length of time. The rate is usually guaranteed, or fixed, for a specific time, such as six months, one year, two years, three years, or five years. At the end of this time, the term and interest rate may be **renegotiated**.

Some mortgages are completely **open**. The word "open" means that the interest rate is not fixed but changes as the bank's prime lending rate changes. Many mortgages allow you to make extra payments during the term or to increase the periodic payment by as much as 20% per year. Many financial institutions offer loan and mortgage calculators on their Web sites. Visit the Nelson Thomson Learning Web site at www.math.nelson.com for links to some of these sites.

Example 1

Carmen took out a mortgage of $75 800 to purchase a farmhouse outside of Kingston. She will repay the mortgage with equal monthly blended payments. The interest rate is 8.4%/a, compounded semiannually. The term is 20 years.

(a) Determine the monthly payment.

(b) How much interest will Carmen pay over the life of the mortgage?

Solution: Using the TVM Solver

(a) Solve for the payment, R, using the **TVM Solver**. Enter the values, except for the value for PMT, shown in the screen. Scroll to the line containing **PMT** and press [ALPHA] [ENTER]. The value of the payment is negative, because the payment is an outflow of Carmen's cash.

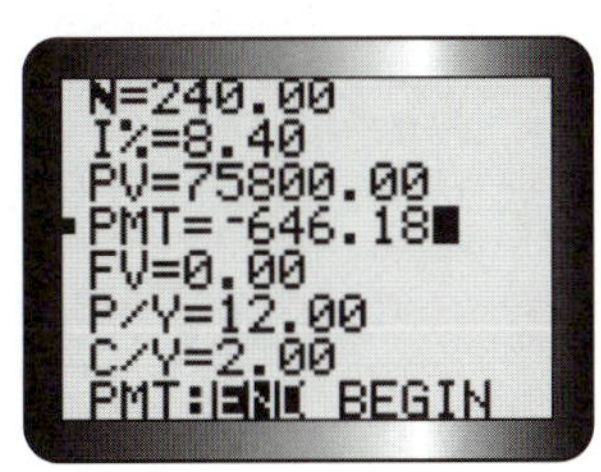

The monthly payment is $646.18.

(b) The total interest that Carmen will pay is the sum of the interest payments from the first payment to the 240th payment. Use **ΣInt** from the Finance CALC menu.

Carmen will pay \$79 283.89 in interest over the life of the mortgage.

Solution: Using a Spreadsheet

(a) First find the interest rate, i, compounded monthly, that is equivalent to 8.4%/a, compounded semiannually.

$$8.4\% \div 2 = 4.2\%$$

$$(1 + i)^{12} = (1.042)^2 \qquad \text{Take the 12th root of each side.}$$

$$1 + i = \sqrt[12]{(1.042)^2}$$

$$1 + i = (1.042)^{\frac{1}{6}}$$

$$i = (1.042)^{\frac{1}{6}} - 1$$

$$i \doteq 0.006\,880\,553\,5$$

Create a spreadsheet to produce the amortization table. As you did in section 2.5, change the payment value until you find the value that results in a balance of \$0 after 240 payments.

	A	B	C	D	E
1	Payment Number	Payment	Interest Paid	Principal Paid	Outstanding Balance
2	0	———	———	———	\$75,800.00
3	=A2+1	\$646.18	=E2*0.0068805535	=B3–C3	=E2–D3

(b) As in section 2.5, use the **SUM** function or the **Σ** toolbar button to determine the total interest paid.

Solution: Using Algebra

(a) Use $i = 0.006\,880\,553\,5$, the value calculated above, because the interest is compounded semiannually, but the payments are monthly.

Now find the weekly deposit, R, using the formula for present value, PV, of an ordinary simple annuity.

$$PV = 75\,800,\ n = 20 \times 12 \text{ or } 240, \text{ and } i = 0.006\,880\,553\,5$$

$$PV = R \times \frac{1 - (1 + i)^{-n}}{i} \qquad \text{Substitute the values for } PV,\ n, \text{ and } i.$$

$$75\,800 = R \times \frac{1 - (1.006\,880\,553\,5)^{-240}}{0.006\,880\,553\,5} \qquad \text{Simplify and solve for } R.$$

$$R = 646.18$$

Carmen's monthly payment is \$646.18.

(b) Find the total interest that Carmen will pay by multiplying the monthly payment by the number of payments and subtracting the principal.

$$\text{total interest paid} = \$646.18 \times 240 - \$75\ 800$$
$$= \$79\ 283.20$$

To find a more accurate answer for the interest paid, use the unrounded value of R, 646.182 868 9, in your calculation.

$$\text{total interest paid} = \$646.182\ 871 \times 240 - \$75\ 800, \text{ or about } \$79\ 283.89.$$

Notice that the difference is \$0.69.

Example 2

Analyze the effect of changing the payment from \$646.18 monthly to \$161.55 weekly on the term of Carmen's loan. Discuss your findings.

Solution: Using the TVM Solver

$\$646.18 \div 4 = \$161.55$

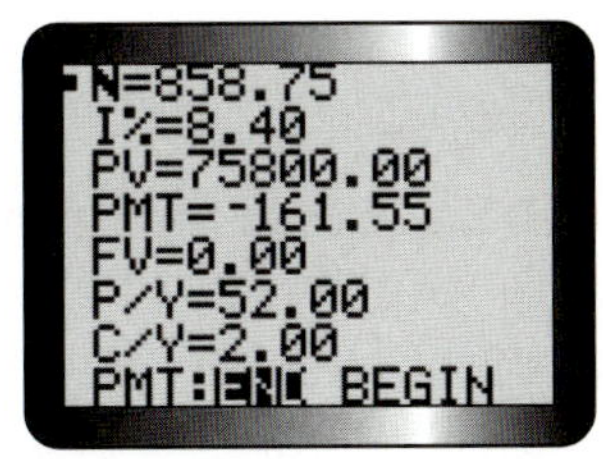

Adjust the payment, **PMT**, to −161.55 and the payments per year, **P/Y**, to 52. Solve for **N**. Carmen will pay the mortgage in full in just under 859 weeks by making weekly payments of \$161.55 each. For a monthly payment of \$646.18, the term is $52 \times 20 = 1040$ weeks. Carmen can reduce the amortization period by 181 weeks, or almost 3.5 years, by reducing the payment and paying more frequently.

Find the total interest paid using **ΣInt**. The total interest paid is about \$62 930.91, which is about \$16 353 less than \$79 283.89.

Enter **ΣInt**, **ΣPrn**, and **bal** into Y1, Y2, and Y3, respectively. Set **Tblstart** to 854. Look at the amortization table. As you can see in the table, the loan is paid in full after 859 weeks. The final payment can be adjusted to $\$161.55 - \$40.54 = \$121.01$.

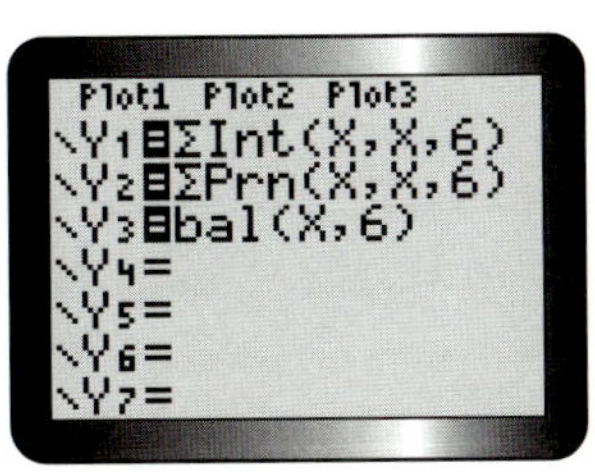

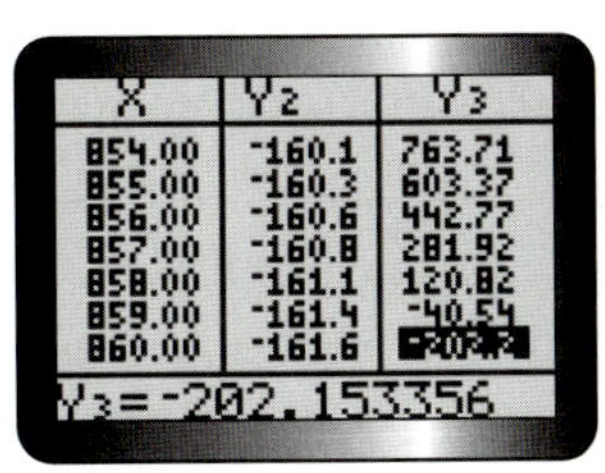

The significant savings in interest, \$16 353, is achieved by changing the monthly payment of \$646.18 to a weekly payment of \$161.55. This change suggests that the frequency of payments has a substantial effect on the amortization.

Take a closer look at the payment amount. Dividing \$646.18 by 4 to get \$161.55 is based on the assumption that there are four monthly payments. You may assume further that there are $4 \times 12 = 48$ payments in a year. However, the payment of \$161.55 is weekly, which means that there are 52 payments for the year. In this way, four additional payments are gained for the year, and these payments further reduce the principal owed. You will address this topic in more detail in the Practise, Apply, Solve of this chapter.

Solution: Using a Spreadsheet

First find the interest rate, i, compounded weekly, that is equivalent to 8.4%/a, compounded semiannually.

$$8.4\% \div 2 = 4.2\%$$

$$(1 + i)^{52} = (1.042)^2 \qquad \text{Take the 52nd root of each side.}$$

$$1 + i = \sqrt[52]{(1.042)^2}$$

$$1 + i = (1.042)^{\frac{1}{26}}$$

$$i = (1.042)^{\frac{1}{26}} - 1$$

$$i \doteq 0.001\,583\,635\,1$$

The equivalent weekly interest rate is 0.001 583 635 1, as a decimal.

Adjust the spreadsheet in Example 1 to reflect the changes in the interest rate and the payment. Notice that the mortgage is repaid after the 859th payment. Again this final payment can be adjusted to \$161.55 − \$40.54 = \$121.01. Find the total interest paid, \$62 930.91, by using the SUM function or the $\sum$ toolbar button.

	A	B	C	D	E
854	852	\$161.55	\$1.97	\$159.58	\$1,083.63
855	853	\$161.55	\$1.72	\$159.83	\$923.80
856	854	\$161.55	\$1.46	\$160.09	\$763.71
857	855	\$161.55	\$1.21	\$160.34	\$603.37
858	856	\$161.55	\$0.96	\$160.59	\$442.78
859	857	\$161.55	\$0.70	\$160.85	\$281.93
860	858	\$161.55	\$0.45	\$161.10	\$120.82
861	859	\$161.55	\$0.19	\$161.36	−\$40.54
862			\$62 930.91		

Consolidate Your Understanding

1. Compare using the **TVM Solver** and using a spreadsheet for solving mortgage and general annuity problems. Does one form of technology have more advantages than the other?
2. Compare using a spreadsheet and using the TI-83 Plus calculator for producing repayment schedules and amortization tables. Does one form of technology have more advantages than the other?
3. Discuss some of the factors that could affect the time it might take for someone to amortize a mortgage.

Focus 2.12

Key Ideas

- By regulation, the interest rate on any Canadian mortgage can be compounded, **at most**, semiannually. The repayment of a mortgage in Canada can be represented by a general annuity, because the payment interval of a Canadian mortgage does not coincide with the interest conversion period.
- First find the equivalent interest rate that coincides with the payment interval, before creating an amortization table for a Canadian mortgage.
- An alternative to solving general annuities algebraically is the **TVM Solver** of the TI-83 Plus calculator.
- You may use both the TI-83 Plus calculator and a spreadsheet effectively to produce amortization schedules, or tables, of loans.
- You may use both the **TVM Solver** and a spreadsheet effectively to analyze the effects of changing the conditions of a mortgage or the effects of changing the conditions of long-term savings plans.
- Many financial institutions offer loan and mortgage calculators on their Web sites to assist clients with investment decisions.

Practise, Apply, Solve 2.12

A

1. Solve for i to eight decimal places.

(a) $(1 + i)^{12} = (1.05)^2$ (b) $(1 + i)^{12} = (1.035)^2$

(c) $(1 + i)^{24} = (1.04)^2$ (d) $(1 + i)^{52} = (1.06)^2$

(e) $(1 + i)^{365} = (1.055)^2$ (f) $(1 + i)^{52} = (1.055)^2$

2. Find the equivalent nominal rate, compounded monthly, for each of the following mortgage rates.

(a) 7.0%/a, compounded semiannually (b) 8.5%/a, compounded semiannually

(c) 9.9%/a, compounded semiannually (d) 12%/a, compounded semiannually

3. Visit a local financial institution or visit the Nelson Thomson Learning Web site at www.math.nelson.com to research the different types of mortgages available. Write a report that describes the differences and similarities of these mortgages. Give some advantages and disadvantages of each type. Your report should address some of the following topics or phrases: length of term, fully open, limited open, fully closed, pre-payment options, lump-sum payment options, and variable or fixed rates.

4. In Example 2, the monthly payment of \$646.18 changes to a weekly payment of \$161.55.

(a) Show that these payments do not yield equivalent amounts at the end of one year.

(b) Find, to the nearest cent, the weekly payment that is equivalent to a monthly payment of \$646.18.

(c) Analyze the effect of changing the \$646.18 monthly payment to the weekly payment in (b) on the term of Carmen's loan. Discuss your findings.

(d) Review your work and the solution of Example 2. Which of the following has a greater effect on the repayment of a mortgage, the frequency of payment or the size of the payment?

5. Describe, in your own words, how the interest is calculated for a Canadian mortgage.

B

Use technology to solve questions 6 to 19. Use the TVM Solver on the TI-83 Plus calculator, a spreadsheet, or visit the Nelson Thomson Learning Web site at www.math.nelson.com to use one of several online mortgage calculators.

6. **Knowledge and Understanding:** Lynn may apply for a mortgage of \$80 000 at 8.8%/a, compounded semiannually.

(a) Calculate and compare the monthly mortgage payment for a term of
  i. 25 years **ii.** 20 years

(b) How much will Lynn save in interest by choosing the shorter term?

(c) What would you suggest to Lynn?

7. Mr. Bowhey may buy a cottage near Algonquin Provincial Park by taking out a \$60 000 mortgage. He expects to make a total monthly payment of \$624 and he assumes the interest rate will be fixed at 8.0%/a, compounded semiannually, until the cottage is fully paid for.

(a) Use the **TVM Solver** of the TI-83 Plus Calculator to find the term of the mortgage, in months and to two decimal places, if
  i. the monthly payment is \$624
  ii. the semimonthly payment is \$312 (\$624 ÷ 2)
  iii. the weekly payment is \$144 (\$624 × 12 ÷ 52)

(b) Based on your solutions, does the frequency of the payments have a significant effect on the term of the mortgage?

8. Mr. Bowhey (see question 7) decides to make weekly payments of \$624 ÷ 4, or \$156.

(a) Find the term of the mortgage in months. Express your answer to two decimal places.

(b) Determine how much interest Mr. Bowhey would save by choosing to make weekly payments of \$156 instead of \$144.

9. The Tang family is about to purchase a new home for \$203 000. They intend to make a down payment of \$43 000 and mortgage the remaining amount over 25 years. They obtain a fixed five-year term mortgage rate of 8.6%/a, compounded semiannually.

(a) Determine the monthly payment.

(b) Find the outstanding balance on the mortgage at the end of each of the first five years.

(c) Determine how much principal has been repaid and how much interest has been paid at the end of the five-year term.

(d) Assume that the interest rates do not change. Determine the total interest the Tangs can expect to pay over 25 years and the total cost of their home.

10. (a) For question 9, determine the monthly payment if the Tangs were able to obtain a mortgage rate of 7.8%/a. How much would they save in total interest over 25 years?

(b) Assume that the Tangs pay the payment in question 9 (a). How much sooner will they be able to completely pay their mortgage?

11. The Tangs decide to increase the monthly payment in question 9 (a) by 10% at the end of each of the first two years.

(a) Determine the new monthly payments for year 2 and year 3 to year 5.

(b) Determine the new outstanding balance on the mortgage at the end of each of the first five years.

(c) How much sooner will the house be paid for if the Tangs continue to make the same monthly payment that is made in year 3 to year 5?

12. Mrs. Rice purchases a cottage on Lake Nipissing for \$61 500. She puts 20% down and takes out a mortgage to finance the remaining amount. The term of the mortgage is seven years and the interest rate is 6.8%/a, compounded semiannually.

(a) Determine the monthly payment.

(b) Create an amortization table of her mortgage and obtain a graph of its amortization.

(c) How much of the 12th payment is

i. principal? ii. interest?

(d) How much of the 50th payment is

i. principal? ii. interest?

(e) What is the total cost of her cottage, including the total interest?

(f) Suppose Mrs. Rice had managed to make a 25% down payment. Determine the total cost of her cottage, including all the interest.

13. **Communication:** Friends of your parents plan to visit them to discuss mortgages. They plan to purchase a home soon and intend to amortize the mortgage over 25 years. They would like suggestions and strategies for minimizing the amortization period. Write a report outlining your suggestions and strategies for minimizing the total cost of paying for their home. Use what you have discovered in this section and from your own independent research, including visits to financial institutions.

14. Mr. Los is planning to purchase a home. He decides to deposit \$440 at the end of each month in an account that pays 6%/a, compounded yearly. At the end of four years, he uses his savings for a down payment on a \$156 000 home. He obtains a mortgage for the balance at a rate of 8%/a, compounded semiannually. He can afford semi-monthly payments of \$525 each. Assume the interest rates remain constant. How long it will take him to repay the mortgage?

15. In question 14, Mr. Los decides to start saving for the purchase of the house 1.5 years sooner. Then he will save for 5.5 years. He also decides that he can afford semi-monthly payments of \$545 each. How much sooner will he be able to repay the mortgage? How much less will be the total cost of his home?

16. **Application:** In 1979, a new home could be purchased for \$85 000 by paying \$5000 down and financing the remaining amount. Typically a mortage was amortized over 20 years. The initial term was three years and the interest rate was 10%/a, compounded semiannually.

(a) Find the monthly payment and the balance owing at the end of the term.

(b) In the early 1980s, mortgage rates increased dramatically. When it was time to renew the term in 1982, the mortgage rate had grown to 22%/a, compounded semiannually. Determine the new payment required to maintain the mortgage.

(c) Determine the percent by which the original payment was increased to maintain the 20-year amortization.

(d) Explain why bankruptcy rates were extremely high in the early 1980s.

17. **Thinking, Inquiry, Problem Solving:** A major Canadian bank advertises a 3% "cash-back" mortgage offer that may be used to reduce the principal on a mortgage. The offer is only valid for a five-year fixed rate mortgage where the interest rate is 7.4%/a, compounded semiannually, with monthly payments over a 25-year amortization. A competing bank does not make this offer, but it offers a five-year fixed rate mortgage at 7%/a, compounded semiannually, with monthly payments. Which option should you choose if your mortgage is for \$120 000?

18. Visit a bank or credit union or visit the Nelson Thomson Learning Web site at www.math.nelson.com to get information on the different mortgage rates available. Select and record the highest and lowest rates that you find.

(a) Is there a relationship between the mortgage interest rates and the conditions and terms? Explain.

(b) Predict how long it would take to repay a $100 000 mortgage using both rates if you repay the loan with monthly payments of $600.

(c) Determine how long it would take to repay a $100 000 mortgage using the highest and lowest rates that you found if you made monthly payments of $600. Compare the results with your predictions.

19. Check Your Understanding: List three factors that determine the monthly payment on a mortgage. For each factor, explain how they affect the payment.

The Chapter Problem—Financial Planning

In this section, you studied Canadian mortgages. Apply what you learned to answer these questions about the Chapter Problem on page 106.

CP21. Use technology to create an amortization table for the repayment of his mortgage for the first two years.

CP22. Determine how much principal he still owes on the mortgage after five years.

CP23. Determine the total amount of interest paid and the amount of principal repaid after the 30th payment.

CP24. At the end of the second year of his mortgage, Mr. Sacchetto wins $7500 at bingo. He decides to make a lump-sum payment on the mortgage at the end of the second year. How much sooner will the mortgage be repaid if he continues to make payments equal to the payment in question CP19?

Chapter 2 Review

Series and Financial Applications

Check Your Understanding

1. What is the difference between a sequence and a series?
2. How can you decide whether a sum of terms represents an arithmetic series or a geometric series? Use examples in your explanation.
3. Use Gauss's method to prove that the sum of all natural numbers from 1 to 60 is 1830.
4. Describe the steps and calculations for amortizing a \$2000 loan. The monthly payment is \$320. The interest rate is 6%/a, compounded monthly.
5. At the end of each year, Charlotte deposits \$1000 in a savings account for five years. The interest rate is 4%/a, compounded annually. Explain and show how the amount of the sum of the deposits can be found by using the equation for the sum of a geometric series.
6. Each of the following represents an annuity. Write a problem that would describe each annuity.
   (a) $400 + 400(1.06) + 400(1.06)^2 + \ldots + 400(1.06)^{22} + 400(1.06)^{23}$
   (b) $100(1.02)^{-48} + 100(1.02)^{-47} + 100\,(1.02)^{-46} + \ldots + 100(1.02)^{-2} + 100(1.02)^{-1}$
7. Find the sum of each series in question 6 using the formula for the sum of a geometric series.
8. Draw a time line for each of the following annuities.
   (a) the accumulated value of \$200 deposited at the end of every 3 months for 4 years at 10%/a, compounded quarterly
   (b) the present value of \$350 deposited at the end of every month for 1.5 years at 9%/a, compounded monthly
   (c) the accumulated value of \$500 deposited at the end of every 6 months for 2 years at 12%/a, compounded quarterly
9. Represent each annuity in question 8 as a geometric sum. Find the accumulated value of each sum.
10. The amount of an annuity with monthly payments will be worth more at 12%/a, compounded weekly, rather than at 12.5%/a, compounded annually. Explain and show why this statement is true.
11. A family asks for your advice for minimizing the total cost of purchasing, and then repaying the mortgage of, a new home. Name at least four things that you would advise them to do.

Review and Practice

2.1 Arithmetic Series

1. Explain what each variable in the general term of an arithmetic sequence represents.
2. What is a series? Write the formula for finding the sum of the first n terms of an arithmetic series.
3. Find the sum of each of the following arithmetic series.
   (a) $32 + 43 + 54 + \ldots$ to 17 terms
   (b) $19 + 14 + 9 + \ldots$ to 23 terms
   (c) $-68 - 61 - 54 - \ldots + 58$
   (d) $\frac{1}{3} + \frac{1}{2} + \frac{2}{3} + \frac{5}{6} + \ldots + \frac{9}{2}$
4. In an arithmetic series of 28 terms, the 7th term is 41, and the 18th term is 96. Find the sum of the series.
5. In an arithmetic series, the 11th term is -12 and the sum of the first 15 terms is -315. Find the first 4 terms of the series.
6. Erika has \$347 in her safety deposit box. At the end of the week, she deposits \$5. Each subsequent week, she deposits \$3 more than she deposited the previous week. How much money will be in the deposit box at the end of 20 weeks?

2.2–2.3 Geometric Series

7. Explain what each term in the general term of a geometric sequence represents.
8. Use the general term in question 7 to write the geometric series of the first n terms. What is the formula for adding the first n terms of a geometric series?
9. Add each geometric series.
   (a) $4 + 20 + 100 + \ldots$ to 9 terms
   (b) $19 - 38 + 76 - \ldots$ to 13 terms
   (c) $192\ 000 - 96\ 000 + 48\ 000 - \ldots + 1500$
   (d) $300 + 300(1.1) + 300(1.1)^2 + \ldots + 300(1.1)^{11}$
10. Mrs. Lee has just received her first annual pension cheque of \$22 800. The payment increases each year by 2.5% to account for inflation.
    (a) What will be the amount of the tenth pension cheque?
    (b) How much can she expect to receive in total after ten years?
11. A sweepstakes gives away \$1 000 000 in prizes. The first ticket drawn wins \$10, the second ticket drawn wins \$30, the third ticket drawn wins \$90, and so on.
    (a) How many tickets can the sweepstakes afford to draw?
    (b) How much money is left after all the prizes are awarded?

2.4–2.5 Using Spreadsheets to Analyze and Represent Financial Situations: Future Value and Amortization Tables

12. Describe an annuity, and the difference between an ordinary annuity and an annuity due.

13. Describe the amortization period, or term, of a loan or mortgage. What is the purpose of an amortization table? Describe the components of an amortization table.

14. Ewen would like to volunteer as an aid worker in a third-world country after graduating from high school. He deposits $110 at the end of every month in a savings plan that pays 6%/a, compounded monthly.

(a) What is the monthly rate of interest?

(b) Explain why Ewen's savings plan is an ordinary simple annuity.

(c) Use a spreadsheet to find the value of his savings after two years.

(d) How much interest is earned by his savings?

(e) After the first deposit, Ewen decides to increase each deposit by $4 every month. Determine the new balance after two years.

15. Madonna buys a stereo by financing $2400 at 18%/a, compounded monthly. Each month, she pays $130 until the debt is paid in full.

(a) Without using a spreadsheet, construct an amortization table for the first eight months. How much does she still owe after eight months?

(b) Use a spreadsheet to create an amortization of the loan.

(c) How long will it take her to repay the loan? What will be the final payment?

(d) Determine the total cost of the stereo purchase.

(e) What monthly payment would let her repay the loan in 18 months?

16. Using a spreadsheet, determine the annual interest rate, compounded monthly, of the finance plan for the computer system shown in the ad.

Computer System

Includes free digital camera, CD burner, 20" screen, and much more.

Take home price $2,890.00

OR

$450 down and $158.02 per month for 18 months

17. Amanda has just started grade 10. She wants to save $7500 over the next three years to help pay for her first year of college. Use a spreadsheet to find, to the nearest cent, how much she would have to deposit at the end of every three months in an account. The account pays 7%/a, compounded quarterly.

2.6–2.7 Using Series to Analyze Financial Situations: Future Value

18. The future value of an ordinary simple annuity can be written as the geometric series $R + R(1 + i) + R(1 + i)^2 + \ldots + R(1 + i)^{n-2} + R(1 + i)^{n-1}$. Describe what each variable represents.

19. Give two equations for finding the accumulated value of any ordinary simple annuity.

20. Since the birth of his daughter, Kay, Mr. Kemp has deposited \$450 at the end of every three months in an education savings plan. The interest rate is 8%/a, compounded quarterly. What will be the fund's value when Kay turns 17?

(a) Draw a time line to represent the annuity.

(b) Write the series that represents the annuity.

(c) Find the amount in the savings plan when Kay turns 17 and the total interest earned.

21. Singh Lee wants to travel to China in 20 months. The trip will cost \$3200. How much should she deposit at the end of each month in an account that pays 9%/a, compounded monthly, to raise \$3200?

(a) Draw a time line to represent the annuity.

(b) Write the series that represents the annuity.

(c) Find how much Singh Lee must deposit at the end of each month.

22. The Pilons are buying a home in the future. They want to accumulate enough money for a \$30 000 down payment. They plan on depositing \$475 at the end of each month in an account that pays 6%/a, compounded monthly.

(a) Draw a time line to represent the annuity.

(b) Write the series that represents the annuity.

(c) Determine how long it will take them to save for the down payment.

(d) Determine the monthly deposit needed to buy a home at the end of the next four years.

2.8 Using Series to Analyze Financial Situations: Present Value

23. Describe, in your own words, the difference between the present value of an ordinary simple annuity and the future value of an ordinary simple annuity.

24. The present value of an ordinary simple annuity can be written as the geometric series $R(1 + i)^{-n} + R(1 + i)^{-n+1} + R(1 + i)^{-n+2} + \ldots + R(1 + i)^{-2} + R(1 + i)^{-1}$. Use the sum of a geometric series, $S_n = \frac{a(r^n - 1)}{r - 1}$, to show that this value can also be found using $PV = R \times \frac{1 - (1 + i)^{-n}}{i}$.

25. For each of the following,

i. draw a time line to represent the present value of the annuity
ii. write the series that represents the present value of the annuity
iii. find the present value of the annuity

(a) \$3000 deposited at the end of every year for 9 years at 5%/a, compounded annually

(b) \$500 paid at the end of every 3 months for 5 years at 6%/a, compounded quarterly

26. Rolly bought a Windsurfer for \$350 down and 18 monthly payments of \$75 each. The first payment is due at the beginning of next month.

(a) The interest rate is 21%/a, compounded monthly. What is the selling price of the Windsurfer?

(b) What is the finance cost?

27. C.C. Ryder wants to buy a motorcycle. He can borrow \$9200 at 10%/a, compounded quarterly, and repay the loan with equal quarterly payments for four years.

(a) Draw a time line to represent the annuity.

(b) Write the series that represents the present value of the annuity.

(c) Find the quarterly payment that Mr. Ryder must make.

2.9–2.10 Equivalent Rates and General Annuities

28. What is the difference between a simple annuity and a general annuity?

29. Find the nominal rate that is equivalent to 15%/a, compounded quarterly, if interest is paid

(a) annually (b) monthly (c) weekly

30. Nevia wishes to save some money to purchase a used jeep. She can save $270 each month. She deposits her savings at the end of each month for three years in an account that pays 5%/a, compounded annually.

(a) Draw a time line to represent the annuity.

(b) Write the series that represents the future value of the annuity.

(c) Find the amount she will have after three years.

(d) After three years, she uses her savings as a down payment on a jeep that costs $14 800. She finances the remaining balance over two years at 8%/a, compounded semiannually. Determine the monthly payment.

31. Yolanda wants to buy a snow machine for $8700. The store will let Yolanda finance the purchase at 18%/a, compounded annually. Yolanda plans to repay the purchase in four years by making a payment at the end of each month.

(a) Draw a time line to represent the repayment of the loan.

(b) Write the series that represents the present values of all the payments.

(c) Determine the monthly payment. Verify your solution using technology.

32. The Cooper family borrows $17 300 to purchase a house trailer for camping. They decide to repay the loan by making bi-weekly payments for three years. The interest rate is 9%/a, compounded monthly.

(a) Determine the bi-weekly payment that lets them repay the loan in three years.

(b) Use technology to determine how much sooner the Coopers could repay the loan if they increased the bi-weekly payment by $50.

(c) Use technology to determine the bi-weekly payment that enables them to repay the loan in three years if the interest rate is 9%/a, compounded annually.

2.11–2.12 Using Technology to Analyze Canadian Mortgages

33. A couple is considering a $98 000 mortgage at 7.6%/a, compounded semiannually.

(a) Calculate and compare the monthly mortgage payment for a term of

i. 25 years **ii.** 20 years

(b) How much will be saved in interest by choosing the shorter term?

(c) What would you suggest to the couple?

34. Mrs. Graywolf took out a \$43 800 mortgage to purchase a cottage in Temagami. She will repay the mortgage over eight years with equal monthly blended payments. The interest rate is 8.4%/a, compounded semiannually.

(a) Determine the monthly payment.

(b) Create an amortization table of the mortgage.

(c) Determine how much interest she will pay over the life of the mortgage.

35. The Willis family wants to buy their first home for \$137 800. They have \$22 000 for a down payment. They can afford a weekly mortgage payment of \$225. The interest rate is 8.8%/a, compounded semiannually.

(a) Determine how long it would take to repay the mortgage.

(b) What is the cost of the house, including the interest charge?

(c) How much would be saved in interest if the weekly payment were \$250?

36. The Wong family purchase a new home for \$233 000. They put \$51 000 down and mortgage the remainder for a term of 25 years. They obtain a fixed five-year mortgage. The interest rate is 8.6%/a, compounded semiannually.

(a) Determine the monthly payment needed to repay the loan.

(b) Find the outstanding balance at the end of each of the first five years.

(c) How much of the 20th and 120th payment is applied to the principal?

(d) At the end of the five-year mortgage, the Wongs make an \$18 000 lump-sum payment before renewing the mortgage for a fixed three-year term at 7.4%/a, compounded semiannually. Find the new monthly payment.

(e) How much do the Wongs still owe after eight years?

Chapter 2 Summary

In this chapter, you have seen that a series is the sum of the terms of a sequence and found the general term of an arithmetic series and a geometric sequence. You have used spreadsheets to find the future value and present value of a deposit or an annuity. You have also seen how payments are amortized over a period of time and how Canadian mortgages operate.

Chapter 2 Review Test

Series and Financial Applications

1. Find the sum of each series.
   (a) $-11 - 3 + 5 + 13 + \ldots + 125$
   (b) $6 - 18 + 54 - \ldots + 39\ 366$

2. A hockey arena has a total seating capacity of 15 690. The first row of seats around the rink has 262 seats. The number of seats in each subsequent row increases by 18.
   (a) How many rows of seats are in the arena?
   (b) By what percent would the capacity increase if three more rows were added after the last row?

3. **Application:** A lottery plans to give out \$5 000 000 in prizes. The first ticket drawn wins \$20, the second ticket drawn wins \$50, the third ticket drawn wins \$125, and so on. Can the lottery afford to give out 14 prizes?

4. Romika buys a laptop computer by borrowing \$1400 at 15.6%/a, compounded monthly. She repays the loan by paying \$110 at the end of each month.
   (a) Create an amortization table for the first six payments.
   (b) How much of the fourth payment reduces the principal of the loan?

5. **Knowledge and Understanding**
   Calvin buys a new electric guitar and amplifier for a total cost of \$2300. He paid a deposit of \$200 and borrowed the balance at 16.2%/a compounded monthly. He agrees to repay the loan by making equal monthly payments over 2.5 years.
   (a) Draw a time line to represent the repayment of the loan.
   (b) Write the series that represents the present values of the payments.
   (c) Find the monthly payment that Calvin must make.

6. **Thinking, Inquiry, Problem Solving**
   Penny decides on her 25th birthday to start planning for her future by depositing \$3200 at the end of each year in an investment that pays 9%/a, compounded annually, until her 45th birthday. She then leaves the money in the investment to collect interest until her 55th birthday.
   (a) Determine how much money she will have on her 55th birthday.
   (b) Penny's best friend, Susie, decides to wait until her 35th birthday to start planning for her future. Susie can get the same rate of return on her investment. Find the yearly payment that she would be required to make until her 55th birthday so that her investment is equivalent to Penny's investment.

7. Marisa has just won the Mega Bucks Sweepstakes. She must decide between two prize options: \$50 000 cash today or receive \$1250 at the end of every three months for 20 years. Marisa expects a return of 8%/a, compounded quarterly, if she invests the cash prize.
   (a) Draw a time line to represent the present value of the payment option.
   (b) Write the series that represents the annuity.
   (c) Which option should Marisa choose and why?

8. **Communication:** The Walton family want to purchase a home. They are considering a mortgage of \$116 800 at 7.6%/a, compounded semiannually.
   (a) Determine the bi-weekly payment if the term of the mortgage is 20 years.
   (b) How much will the Waltons pay in interest over the life of the mortgage?
   (c) What would you suggest to the Waltons for minimizing the interest they must pay?

Cumulative Review Test 1

Financial Applications of Sequences and Series

1. A sequence is defined by the general term $t_n = 2n^2 - 4n$.

(a) Determine the first four terms of the sequence.

(b) Find t_{15}.

(c) Graph the first eight terms of the sequence.

(d) Which term has a value of 880?

2. Martina has won the grand prize in the "Cash Forever" lottery. She will receive \$50 000 the first year and receive an annual increase of \$2000 each year, on top of the \$50 000 annual payment.

(a) Write the first five terms of the sequence of her annual payments.

(b) Determine the general term of this sequence.

(c) Find her annual payment in the tenth year.

(d) Determine her total winnings over the next 20 years.

3. For each sequence, determine

i. the general term **ii.** t_{15} **iii.** S_{25}

(a) $-18, -54, -162, \ldots$

(b) $30, 26, 22, \ldots$

4. Determine the number of terms in each sequence.

(a) $-2, 4, 10, \ldots, 364$

(b) $3, \frac{3}{2}, \frac{3}{4}, \ldots, \frac{3}{1024}$

5. (a) Determine the amount of a \$12 000 investment at 6%/a compounded quarterly for four years.

(b) Determine the present value of \$8000 due in 5 years if money is worth 5% compounded semiannually.

6. Evaluate. Round to the nearest hundredth where necessary.

(a) $25^{\frac{3}{2}}$ (b) $-27^{-\frac{2}{3}}$

(c) $20^{\frac{4}{5}}$ (d) $200(1.08)^{-10}$

7. Simplify.

(a) $\dfrac{(25x^6y^4)^{\frac{1}{2}}(9x^4y^2)^{\frac{1}{2}}}{\left(-x^{\frac{1}{2}}y^{\frac{1}{2}}\right)^6}$

(b) $\dfrac{(49x^{-8}y^2)^{-\frac{1}{2}}(27x^{-3}y^{12})^{\frac{2}{3}}}{\sqrt[4]{16x^8y^{-4}}}$

8. Solve.

(a) $2^{3x+2} = \frac{1}{32}$ (b) $3^{2x^2+9x} = 243$

9. How long will it take for \$5000 invested at 6% compounded monthly to grow to \$6545.42?

10. Pavendeep bought a hot tub by financing \$4800 through Wet Coast Spas at 15%/a compounded monthly. He agrees to make monthly payments of \$220 until it is paid in full.

(a) Without the use of a spreadsheet, construct an amortization table for the first six months. What does he still owe after six months?

(b) Use a spreadsheet to create an amortization of the loan.

(c) How long will it take him to repay the complete loan? What will be the final payment?

(d) What is the total cost of buying the hot tub?

(e) What monthly payment amount would enable him to repay the loan in 12 months?

11. Monique is saving for a new car. She wants to have enough money for a $10 000 down payment. She plans to deposit $450 at the end of each month into an account that pays 8%/a compounded monthly.

(a) Draw a time line diagram to represent the annuity.

(b) Write out the series that represents the annuity.

(c) Determine how long it will take her to save for the down payment.

(d) Monique buys the new car she wants. After making the down payment, she still owes $18 350. Determine her monthly car payment if she finances this amount at 4.8%/a compounded monthly.

12. Simon wants to buy a home entertainment system for $4600. The store will finance the purchase at a rate of 15%/a compounded annually. Simon plans to repay the system in four years with monthly payments at the end of each month.

(a) Draw a time line diagram to represent the repayment of the loan.

(b) Write out the series that represents the present value of all the payments.

(c) Determine his monthly payment.

(d) Verify your solution using technology.

13. The Watsons are buying a cottage for $145 900. They have $25 000 for a down payment and can afford a monthly mortgage payment of $1200. They have negotiated a mortgage rate of 7.6%/a compounded semiannually.

(a) How long would it take them to repay their mortgage?

(b) How much will their cottage end up costing them when interest charges are included?

(c) How much would they save in interest costs if they increase their monthly payments by 50%?

Functions and Relations

14U. Determine the first six terms of the sequence defined by $t_1 = -5$ and $t_n = -3(t_{n-1}) + 8$.

15U. Marcus has a bacterial infection and must take 350 mg of medication every six hours. By the time he takes the next dose, 32% of the medication remains in his body.

(a) Determine a recursive formula that models this situation.

(b) What will the amount of medication in his body level off to?

(c) How long will it take for the medication to reach this level?

Performance Tasks for Part 1

Financial Applications of Sequences and Series

THE FOLLOWING ACTIVITIES SHOULD EACH TAKE LESS THAN A PERIOD TO COMPLETE.

1. Building a Pyramid

Build a model of a square pyramid using sugar cubes. Build the model so that it has at least six layers. Suppose you were to continue to build the model:

(a) How many sugar cubes would be in the 75th layer from the top?

(b) How many sugar cubes would you need to construct a model with 100 layers?

(c) Analyze this problem and create an algebraic model to describe this situation. Explain how you arrived at the algebraic model and how the algebraic model can be used to make predictions. Use an example to illustrate.

2. Population Growth

The People's Republic of China has the largest population of any country in the world. According to the 1994 World Population Prospects, approximately 1.1 billion people lived in China in 1990. In 1990, the population of China was growing at a rate of 1.5% per year.

(a) Suppose the population rate continued to grow at 1.5% per year. Create an algebraic model that relates the population, P, to the number of years, n, after 1990.

(b) Predict when the population will reach the two billion mark.

(c) Suppose that seven million people leave China each year for other countries. Adjust your model for the growth of the population of China to take this new information into account.

3. A Picture Is Worth a Thousand Words

Perhaps a picture could help save someone a thousand dollars. Imagine that you are a financial consultant and you want to provide your client with graphical representations of the effects of varying different options on a mortgage. Choose a current mortgage rate to work with and provide graphs showing the effects of changing payment periods and lengths of amortization. You may decide to look at several aspects to compare the mortgages—amounts of interest paid, length of time to pay off the mortgage, principal owing at various time intervals, and so on.

4. Retirement Plans

Sara and Ritu have just finished school and have started their first full-time jobs. Sara has decided that she is going to start putting \$100/month away in a Retirement Plan. Ritu thinks that Sara is crazy because Sara is only 22 and should enjoy her money now and worry about saving for retirement later. Ritu is not going to worry about saving money until she is 45.

(a) Suppose both young women retire at age 60. How much money will Ritu have to contribute monthly, to retire with the same savings as Sara? Assume that they can invest their money at 9% compound monthly.

(b) Write a convincing argument for one of the young women's positions.

THE FOLLOWING ACTIVITIES COULD EACH TAKE MORE THAN A PERIOD TO COMPLETE.

5. Buying a Car

Harpreet is going to buy her first car for \$17 500. She will make a down payment \$3500 and finance the rest at 9% compounded monthly. She will make regular monthly payments for four years. She estimates that her car will depreciate in value at a rate of 18% per year. Provide a complete analysis of this situation by determining the amount of her monthly payments, the total interest that she will be paying, and the value of her car when she has completed her payments. Include graphs, charts, and tables with your analysis.

6. Prescribing Medicine

When doctors prescribe medication for their patients, several factors influence the amount of medication prescribed and the timing of the doses. Investigate the effect on a patient who must take a 30-mg dose of a painkiller every 4 h. The half-life of the drug for a particular patient is 2 h. This means that it takes 2 h for half of the drug to be metabolized while the other half remains in the patient's system.

(a) Use charts, graphs, and algebraic models to investigate this situation.

(b) The patient must take this medication for ten days. Predict how much of this medication will be in the patient's system after ten days.

(c) If the patient stops taking the medication after ten days, how much of the medication will be in the patient's system ten days after the medication is stopped?

Functions

Using Properties of Relations to Sketch Their Graphs

If the algebraic expression of a relation can be identified as linear or quadratic, its graph can be sketched without making a table or using graphing technology.

Linear Relations

The general form of a linear relation is $ax + by + c = 0$. Once the relation is identified as linear, it can be graphed using **i.** the x- and y-intercepts or **ii.** the slope, m, and y-intercept b, when $y = mx + b = 0$.

Example 1

Sketch the graph of $3x + 5y + 15 = 0$.

Solution

The graph is linear. Use the x- and y-intercepts to draw the graph.

Determine the x-intercept by letting $y = 0$.

$$3x + 5(0) + 15 = 0$$
$$3x = -15$$
$$x = -5$$

Determine the y-intercept by letting $x = 0$.

$$3(0) + 5y + 15 = 0$$
$$5y = -15$$
$$y = -3$$

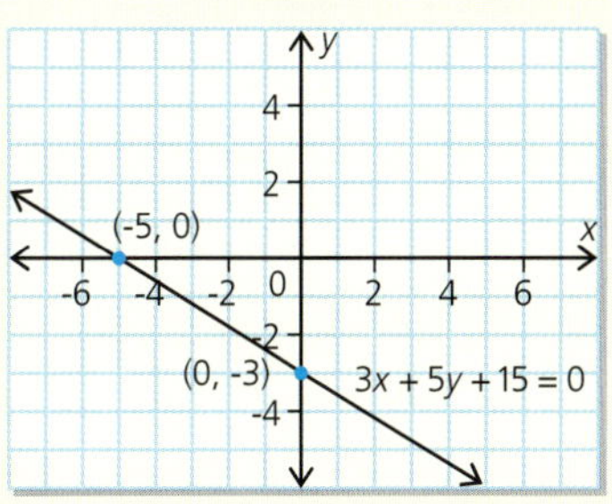

Example 2

Sketch the graph of $3y = -2x - 6$.

Solution

Rewrite the relation in the form $y = mx + b$. Then, $y = -\frac{2}{3}x - 2$. Mark the y-intercept as -2 and use the slope to locate a second point. The slope is $m = -\frac{2}{3}$. Then $\frac{\Delta y}{\Delta x} = \frac{-2}{3}$ or $\frac{2}{-3}$.

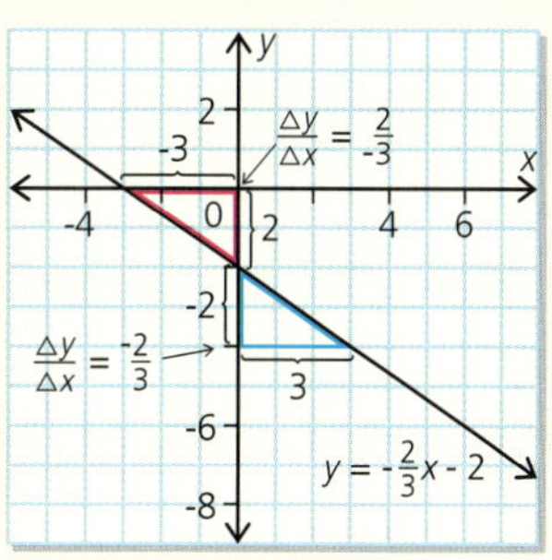

Quadratic Relations in Standard Form

The standard form of a quadratic relation is $y = ax^2 + bx + c$. The graph is a parabola. If $a > 0$, the parabola opens upward; if $a < 0$, the parabola opens downward.

Example 3: Graphing Using Symmetry

Sketch the graph of $y = -3x^2 - 2x + 7$.

Solution

$y = -3x^2 - 2x + 7$ — $a = -3$, so the parabola opens downward.

$y = x(-3x - 2) + 7$ — Factor partially.

Let $x = 0$ or $-3x - 2 = 0$ to find two points on the curve. When $x = 0$, then $y = 7$. When $-3x - 2 = 0$, then $x = -\frac{2}{3}$, and $y = 7$. The axis of symmetry is halfway between $(0, 7)$ and $\left(-\frac{2}{3}, 7\right)$.

Therefore, $x = \dfrac{0 + \left(\frac{-2}{3}\right)}{2} = -\dfrac{1}{3}$

To find the vertex, substitute $x = -\frac{1}{3}$ into $y = -3x^2 - 2x + 7$.

$$y = -3\left(-\frac{1}{3}\right)^2 - 2\left(-\frac{1}{3}\right) + 7 = 7\frac{1}{3}$$

The curve opens downward, so the vertex occurs at $\left(-\frac{1}{3}, 7\frac{1}{3}\right)$.

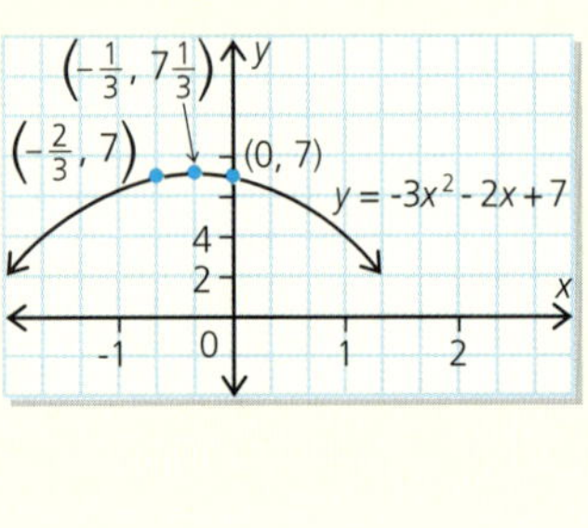

Quadratic Relations in Vertex Form

The vertex form of a quadratic relation is $y = a(x - h)^2 + k$, where (h, k) is the vertex. This is also the coordinates of the maximum point when $a < 0$ and of the minimum point when $a > 0$.

Example 4: Graphing Using Vertex Form

Sketch the graph of $y = 2(x + 2)^2 + 3$.

Solution

The equation is in vertex form, and we see that the vertex is $(-2, 3)$. Determine one point on the curve and use symmetry to find a second point.

When $x = 0$,

$$y = 2(0 + 2)^2 + 3$$
$$= 11$$

So, $(0, 11)$ is a point on the curve. Another point, $(-4, 11)$, is symmetric to the axis of symmetry. Now sketch.

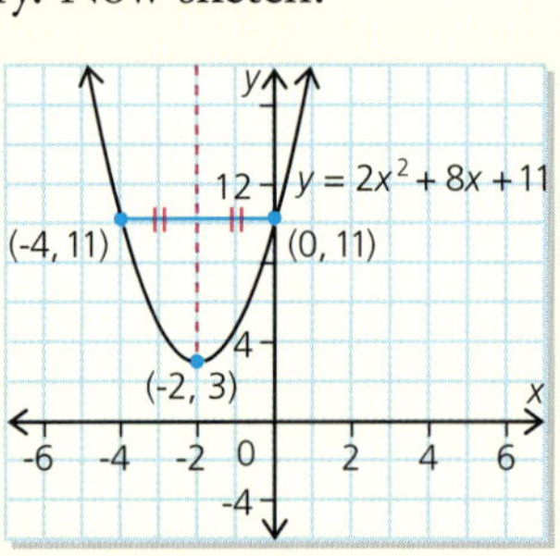

In this case, $(-2, 3)$ is the minimum point. The relation has a minimum value of 3, when $x = -2$.

Practice

1. Sketch each graph using intercepts.

(a) $4x - 6y = 12$

(b) $-5x + 3y = 15$

(c) $3x - 8y + 24 = 0$

(d) $\frac{1}{2}x - \frac{3}{4}y = 9$

2. Sketch the graphs using the slope and y-intercept.

(a) $y = -3x + 7$

(b) $y = -\frac{3}{4}x - 2$

(c) $2x + 3y = 6$

(d) $\frac{2}{3}y = 6x + 1$

3. Sketch the graphs using partial factoring.

(a) $y = 2x^2 - 6x + 5$

(b) $y = -3x^2 + 9x - 2$

(c) $y = 5x^2 - 3 + 5x$

(d) $y = 3 + 4x - 2x^2$

4. Sketch the graphs using the zeros of the curve.

(a) $y = x^2 + 4x - 12$

(b) $y = x^2 - 7x + 10$

(c) $y = 2x^2 - 5x - 3$

(d) $y = 6x^2 - 13x - 5$

5. Sketch the graph.

(a) $y = (x - 2)^2 + 3$

(b) $y = (x + 4)^2 - 10$

(c) $y = 2(x - 1)^2 + 3$

(d) $y = -3(x + 1)^2 - 4$

6. A football is kicked into the air. Its height, h, in metres, after t seconds is approximated by $h = -5(t - 2.3)^2 + 27.45$. What is the maximum height reached by the football?

7. A computer game company models the profit on its latest game using $P = -3\left(x - \frac{19}{3}\right)^2 - \frac{525}{12}$, where x is the number of games sold in hundred thousands, and P is the profit in millions of dollars. What is the maximum profit the company can expect to earn using this model?

Completing the Square to Convert to the Vertex Form of a Parabola

A quadratic relation in standard form, $y = ax^2 + bx + c$, can be rewritten in vertex form as $y = a(x - h)^2 + k$ by creating a perfect square in the original and then factoring the square.

Steps to Complete the Square	Example: $y = 2x^2 + 12x - 5$
• Remove the common constant factor from both the x^2- and x-term.	$y = 2(x^2 + 6x) - 5$
• Determine the constant that must be added (and subtracted) to create a perfect square. This is half the coefficient of the x-term, squared.	$y = 2(x^2 + 6x + 9 - 9) - 5$
• Group the three terms of the perfect square. Multiply the subtracted value and move it outside the bracket.	$y = 2(x^2 + 6x + 9) - 2(9) - 5$
• Factor the perfect square and collect like terms.	$y = 2(x + 3)^2 - 23$

Practice

1. Write each trinomial as a perfect square.

(a) $x^2 + 2x + 1$ (b) $x^2 + 4x + 4$

(c) $x^2 + 6x + 9$ (d) $x^2 + 10x + 25$

(e) $x^2 - 12x + 36$ (f) $x^2 - 14x + 49$

(g) $x^2 - 18x + 81$

(h) $x^2 - 20x + 100$

2. Complete the square, and write in vertex form.

(a) $y = x^2 + 2x + 2$

(b) $y = x^2 + 4x + 6$

(c) $y = x^2 - 12x + 40$

(d) $y = x^2 - 18x + 80$

3. Express in vertex form by completing the square. State the equation of the axis of symmetry and the coordinates of the vertex.

(a) $y = 2x^2 - 4x + 7$

(b) $y = 5x^2 + 10x + 6$

(c) $y = -3x^2 - 12x + 2$

(d) $y = -\frac{1}{2}x^2 + 5x + 2$

(e) $y = -0.1x^2 - 0.5x + 0.4$

(f) $y = -\frac{3}{4}x^2 + 5x - 2$

4. Complete the square to find the roots.

(a) $x^2 - 10x + 9 = 0$

(b) $9x^2 - 12x - 5 = 0$

(c) $2x^2 + 3x - 20 = 0$

5. A baseball is hit from a height of 1 m. Its height in metres, h, after t seconds is $h = -4.9t^2 + 10t + 1$.

(a) What is the maximum height of the ball?

(b) When does the ball reach this height?

6. A town's population is $P = 0.16t^2 + 7.2t + 100$, where P is the population in thousands and t is the time in years, with $t = 0$ being the year 2000. When will the population reach its minimum? What is the minimum?

Solving Quadratic Equations: The Quadratic Formula

The solutions, or roots, of a quadratic equation in the form $ax^2 + bx + c = 0$ are given by $x = \frac{-b \pm \sqrt{b^2 - 4ac}}{2a}$.

The discriminant, $b^2 - 4ac$, can be used to determine the nature of the roots.

- If $b^2 - 4ac > 0$, there are two real roots.
- If $b^2 - 4ac = 0$, there is one real root.
- If $b^2 - 4ac < 0$, there are two imaginary, or non-real, roots.

Example 1

Solve $3x^2 - 2x = 6$ to two decimal places.

Solution

Rewrite $3x^2 - 2x = 6$ in the form $ax^2 + bx + c = 0$. Then $3x^2 - 2x - 6 = 0$, where $a = 3$, $b = -2$, and $c = -6$.

$$x = \frac{-b \pm \sqrt{b^2 - 4ac}}{2a}$$

Substitute known values.

$$x = \frac{-(-2) \pm \sqrt{(-2)^2 - 4(3)(-6)}}{2(3)}$$

$$x = \frac{2 \pm \sqrt{76}}{6}$$

Then, $x = 1.79$ and $x = -1.12$ to two decimal places.

Example 2

Determine the number and type of roots of $5m^2 = 3m - 7$.

Solution

Rewrite $5m^2 = 3m - 7$ in the form $ax^2 + bx + c = 0$. Then $5m^2 - 3m + 7 = 0$, where $a = 5$, $b = -3$, and $c = 7$. Determine the number and type of roots by examining $b^2 - 4ac$.

$$\begin{aligned} b^2 - 4ac &= (-3)^2 - 4(5)(7) \\ &= -131 \end{aligned}$$

Then $b^2 - 4ac < 0$, so there are two imaginary or non-real roots.

Practice

Evaluate all answers to two decimal places where necessary.

1. Indicate whether each equation has two real roots, one real root, or two imaginary or non-real roots.

(a) $3m^2 - 2m + 9 = 0$

(b) $15x^2 - 6 = x$

(c) $9m^2 - 24m = -16$

(d) $36 + 25n^2 = -60n$

(e) $20x^2 + 9x - 18 = 0$

(f) $5x^2 = 6x - 7$

2. Solve each equation using the quadratic formula.

(a) $10x^2 - x - 7 = 0$

(b) $15m^2 + 27m + 20 = 0$

(c) $28p^2 - 71p = -45$

(d) $42y^2 + y = 30$

(e) $32 - 76x + 45x^2 = 0$

(f) $35 + 9x - 18x^2 = 0$

3. A water balloon is catapulted into the air so that its height, h, in metres, after t seconds is $h = -4.9t^2 + 25t + 1.9$.

(a) When is the balloon 13 m high?

(b) How long does the balloon take to hit the ground?

4. The underside of a bridge is a parabolic arch defined by $h = -0.1d^2 + 2d$, where h is the height in metres above the bottom of the bridge and d is the distance in metres from the left side of the bridge. How far from the left side of the bridge is the height 5 m? Give the answer to one decimal.

Transformations of Quadratic Relations

The graph of any quadratic relation can be created by altering or repositioning the graph of the base curve $y = x^2$. To do so, write the relation in vertex form, $y = a(x - h)^2 + k$. The base curve, $y = x^2$, is translated vertically or horizontally, stretched or compressed vertically, or reflected about the x-axis, depending on the values of a, h, and k.

<table>
<tr><th>Relation</th><th>Type of Transformation</th><th>Graph</th><th>Explanation</th></tr>
<tr><td>$y = x^2$</td><td>Base parabola</td><td>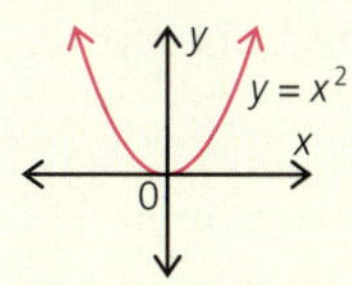
</td><td>This is the base curve upon which other transformations are applied.</td></tr>
<tr><td>$y = x^2 + k$</td><td>Vertical Translation
The curve shifts up if $k > 0$ and down if $k < 0$.</td><td>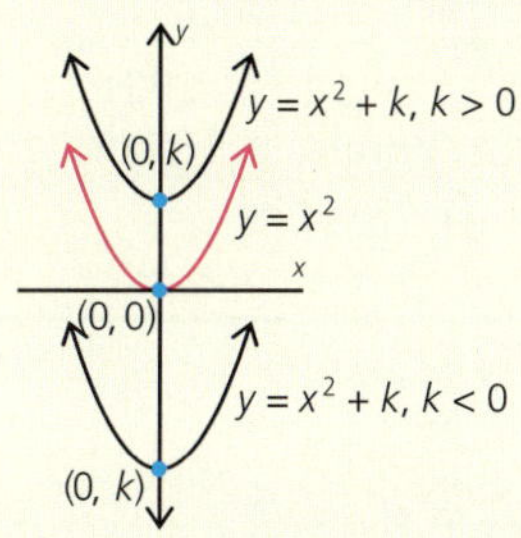
</td><td>Add k to the y-coordinate of every point on the base curve. The resultant curve is congruent to the base curve.</td></tr>
<tr><td>$y = (x - h)^2$</td><td>Horizontal Translation
The curve shifts to the right if $h > 0$ and to the left if $h < 0$.</td><td>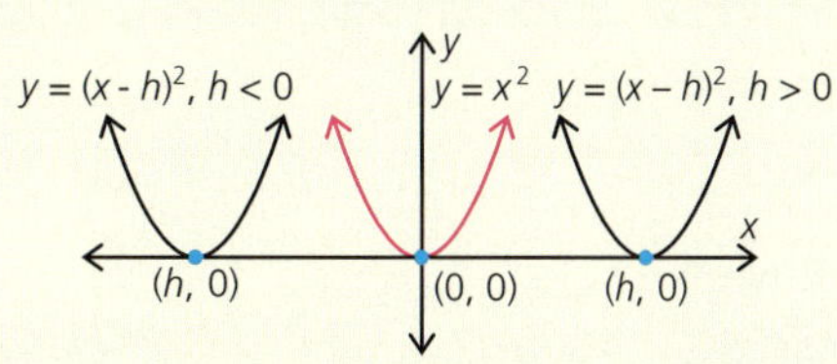
</td><td>Subtract h from the x-coordinate of every point on the base curve.</td></tr>
<tr><td>$y = ax^2$</td><td>Reflection
The curve is reflected about the x-axis if $a < 0$.</td><td>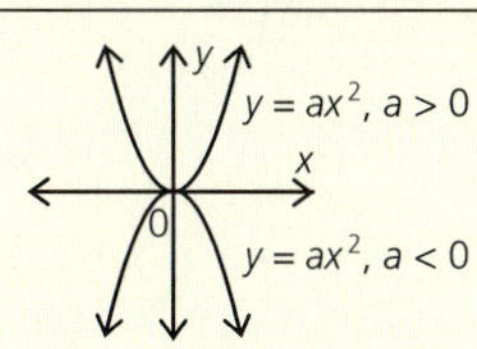
</td><td>Multiply the y-coordinate of every point on the base curve by a.</td></tr>
<tr><td></td><td>Vertical Stretch
The curve has a narrow opening if $a > 1$.</td><td>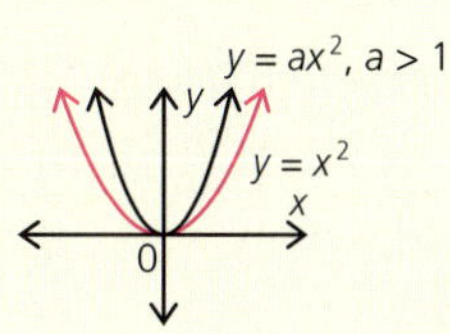
</td><td></td></tr>
<tr><td></td><td>Vertical Compression
The curve has a wide opening if $0 < a < 1$.</td><td>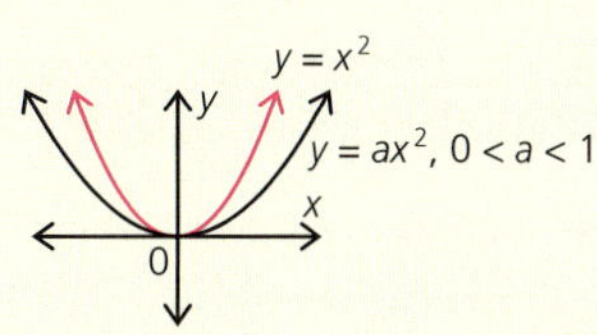
</td><td></td></tr>
</table>

Example

Use transformations to graph $y = -2(x + 3)^2 - 4$.

Solution

Step 1: Begin with the graph of the base curve, $y = x^2$ (black). Select three points on the curve to help define its shape. From the form $y = a(x - h)^2 + k$, see that $a = -2$, $h = -3$, and $k = -4$.

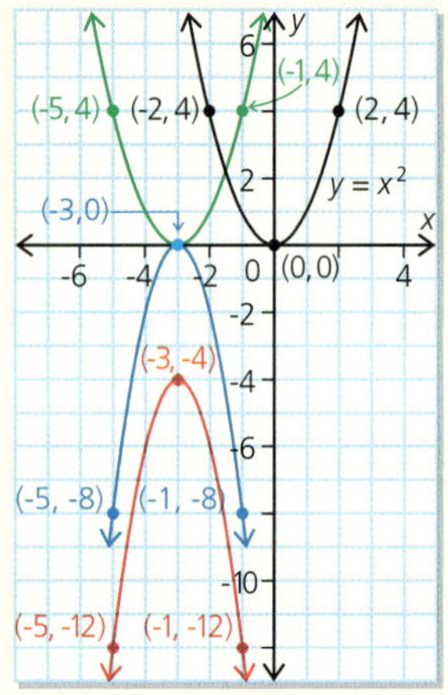

Step 2: $h = -3$, so shift the entire parabola 3 units to the left (green).

Step 3: $a = -2$, so multiply every y-coordinate by -2. The parabola is reflected and its opening becomes narrower (blue).

Step 4: $k = -4$, so shift the entire parabola 4 units down. This is the final graph (red).

Practice

In questions 1 and 2, the coordinates of a point on the parabola $y = x^2$ are given. State the new coordinates under each transformation.

1. (a) $(2, 4)$; shift up 3
   (b) $(-2, 4)$; shift down 5
   (c) $(-1, 1)$; shift left 4
   (d) $(1, 1)$; shift right 6
   (e) $(3, 9)$; vertical stretch of $-\frac{1}{3}$
   (f) $(2, 4)$; vertical stretch of 2

2. (a) $(-2, 4)$; shift left 2 and up 5
   (b) $(-1, 1)$; shift right 4, vertical stretch 3, and reflect about x-axis
   (c) $(3, 9)$; vertical compression by 3, shift left 5, and shift down 2
   (d) $(0, 0)$; shift left 5, vertical stretch 3, shift up 4, and reflect about x-axis

3. Points $(-2, 4)$, $(0, 0)$, and $(2, 4)$ are on the parabola $y = x^2$. Use your knowledge of transformations to determine the equation of the parabola using these coordinates.
   (a) $(-2, 6)$, $(0, 2)$, $(2, 6)$
   (b) $(-2, 12)$, $(0, 0)$, $(2, 12)$
   (c) $(2, 4)$, $(4, 0)$, $(6, 4)$
   (d) $(-2, -6)$, $(0, -2)$, $(2, -6)$

In questions 4 and 5, sketch each graph using transformations on $y = x^2$.

4. (a) $y = x^2 + 3$ (b) $y = x^2 - 4$
   (c) $y = (x - 3)^2$ (d) $y = (x + 4)^2$
   (e) $y = 2x^2$ (f) $y = \frac{1}{2}x^2$

5. (a) $y = 2(x - 1)^2 + 3$
   (b) $y = -3(x + 1)^2 + 2$
   (c) $y = \frac{1}{2}(x - 2)^2 - 1$
   (d) $y = -\frac{1}{3}(x + 2)^2 - 4$

Chapter 3 Introducing Functions

The relationship between two or more quantities is one of the most fundamental concepts in mathematics. In earlier grades, you have studied relations in many different contexts. In this chapter, you will learn that some of these relations are called functions and you will examine functions in more detail.

You will find functions used in digital network design, speech recognition software, encryption, music and sound synthesis, marketing, economic forecasting, investment planning, medicine, environmental sciences, and logistics. Calculators, spreadsheet software, databases, and almost all other software applications use predefined functions.

In this chapter, you will

- learn the meaning of "function"
- use function notation for evaluating functions, representing inverse functions, and representing transformations
- investigate the properties of $f(x) = \sqrt{x}$ and $f(x) = x^2$
- investigate and explain the relationship between a function and its inverse
- solve inequalities
- describe the relationship between the graph of a function and its image under transformations
- describe the domain and range of functions under transformations

Visit the Nelson Mathematics student Web site at **www.math.nelson.com**. You'll find links to interactive examples, online tutorials, and more.

Connections

This is the Enigma machine, which the Germans used to send coded messages during World War II. However, the Germans did not know that the British cracked the code, and were able to read the secret messages. Historians say that this shortened the war by about two years.

Alfred J. Menezes

The Chapter Problem

Cryptography

If you have bought something over the Internet, then you have probably had to enter a credit card number when placing your order. The Internet is a vast web of interconnected servers. Your order may have passed through *many* different computers on its way to the company from which you made the purchase. It may be possible for someone to intercept the order and "read" the credit card number. Billions of transactions are made every day on the Web. It is necessary to protect the privacy of the details of transactions from people who would misuse this information.

Cryptography is the study of coding messages. A message is coded so that only the people to whom the message is sent can "read" the message. On the Internet, "public-key encryption" is one method for coding messages such as a credit card number. Public-key encryption has two parts, a public key for coding a message and a private key for decoding it. One key is used to code a message and then that key itself is coded. The coded key is the public key that is sent.

Professor Alfred J. Menezes is a pioneer in the development of elliptic curve coding systems. He teaches at the University of Waterloo, and does consulting work with Certicom. His work is critical in the development of secure wireless communications, in which Canadian companies are becoming world leaders.

Suppose you wanted to send a coded message to a friend. To code the message, assign each letter a number between 1 and 26. Then multiply each number by 17 and divide by 26. Add 1 to the remainder.

For example, the message "HI" can be coded as "GX."

H is 8, $8 \rightarrow 8(17) = 136 \rightarrow 6$ (since $136 = 5(26) + 6$) $\rightarrow 7$, which is G.

I is 9, $9 \rightarrow 9(17) = 153 \rightarrow 23 \rightarrow 24$, which is X.

To "decode" this message, convert each number back into a letter. Danielle uses this code to send the message X WVKH NRCG to a friend. How could the code be made more complicated? Is it possible to break any code?

Design your own code to send the message "Codes are cool." Do research and find other examples of codes used in different contexts.

For help with this problem, see pages 240, 260, 277, and 291.

Challenge 1

In some codes, letters are switched with other letters. One way to break this kind of code is to examine the frequencies of the letters used in everyday language and then to compare these frequences with the frequencies of the letters used in the coded message. The location of the letters in a word can also help you to decide which letters are vowels.

Decode the following:

LQPITCVWNCVKQPU! AQW JCXG HKIWTGF VJKU QPG QWV!
RTGVVA LQQN, GJ?

Challenge 2: Error-Correcting Codes

Suppose you heard someone say, "The makle eaves are playing at the Corel Centre this weekend … ." You would probably understand that what the person really said was, "The Maple Leafs are playing at the Corel Centre this weekend." Your brain has a built-in error-correcting decoder! However, there is a limit to the number of errors that the decoder can correct.

Suppose you heard someone else say, "The mable eaves are staying at the morel sinner this weekend." You might not be able to decipher the correct message. A good code produces a unique output for each input.

The bars, or optical code, printed on an envelope for mailing in Canada is a code containing the essential address information, so that optical readers can quickly direct the letter to the right location. The bars contain an error-correcting code that can "make up" for an error in the input, such as part of the bar being torn away or smudged.

Research error-correcting codes. Find a way to code "HI," so that at least one error could be corrected.

To complete these challenges, you may need to discuss a research plan with your teacher or other students. You may also need to research beyond the resources in your classroom.

Web Challenge

For a related Internet activity, go to **www.math.nelson.com.**

Getting Ready

In this chapter, you will be working with algebraic expressions, linear and quadratic relations, and transformations. These exercises will help you warm up for the work ahead.

1. Determine the value of each expression if $x = -4$ and $y = 5$.

(a) $-x + 4y$

(b) $4x^2 - 3x + 2$

(c) $6x^2 - 2y^2$

(d) $(2x + 3y)(5x - 2y)$

(e) $-3x^2y^3 + 2x^3y^2$

(f) $\frac{xy + y^2}{y}$

(g) $\frac{x^2 - x + 10}{y^2 - 4y}$

(h) $\frac{(x - 3)^2}{(-2 - y)^2}$

2. Create a table for each relation and then graph the relation.

(a) $y = 3x + 2$ (b) $4x - 2y = 8$

(c) $y = x^2 + 2$ (d) $y = x^2 + 6x + 2$

(e) $y = 2(x - 3)^2 + 1$

(f) $y = -(x + 3)(x - 5)$

3. Solve each linear equation.

(a) $2x - 5 = 7$

(b) $3x - 4 - 5x = -3x - 2$

(c) $5(3 + 2d) = -5$

(d) $-4(2c + 3) = 8$

(e) $3(2m - 5) + 4(3m + 2) = 11$

(f) $7(4 - 3g) = -8(2g - 1)$

(g) $\frac{3x}{4} = -6$

(h) $\frac{3c}{4} - \frac{2c}{3} = 6$

(i) $\frac{y + 2}{3} = \frac{2y + 3}{5}$

4. Replace ■ with either $<$ or $>$ to make each statement true.

(a) $-13 - (-2)^2$ ■ $-12 - (-2)(-3)$

(b) $-2 - (-2)(3)$ ■ $-4 - (-3)$

(c) $8 \div (-2) + 6$ ■ $-15 \div 3$

(d) $(-1)^2 - (-2)^2$ ■ $(-4)^2 - (-5)^2$

5. CARZ rents cars at a fixed daily rate and charges \$0.25/km. The cost of renting a car for one day and driving it for 240 km is \$105.

(a) Is distance or cost the dependent variable?

(b) What is the rate of change in this situation?

(c) Write an equation for the rental cost in terms of the distance driven.

(d) Graph the relation.

(e) Determine the cost to rent a car for one day if it is driven 440 km.

(f) Determine the distance driven if the total rental cost is \$125.

6. Express each of the following in the form $y = mx + b$.

(a) $2y = 4x + 10$

(b) $3x + 2y = 12$

(c) $4x + 6y - 10 = 0$

(d) $\frac{1}{2}x + \frac{3}{4}y = 1$

(e) $\frac{3}{5}x - 2 = 6y$

(f) $\frac{x}{3} + \frac{y}{5} = -1$

7. A football is punted into the air. Its height, h, in metres, after t seconds is $h = -4.9(t - 2.4)^2 + 29$.

(a) What was the height of the ball when it was kicked?

(b) What was the maximum height of the ball?

(c) How high was the ball after 2 s?

(d) Was the ball still in the air after 5 s? Justify your answer.

8. Express each equation in vertex form by completing the square.

(a) $y = x^2 + 6x$

(b) $y = 2x^2 + 4x$

(c) $y = 2x^2 - 4x + 5$

(d) $y = -3x^2 + 6x - 7$

(e) $y = 2x^2 + 20x + 43$

(f) $y = -5x^2 + 10x - 11$

9. For each of the following quadratic relations, state

i. the coordinates of the vertex

ii. the equation of the axis of symmetry

iii. the direction of opening

(a) $y = (x - 2)^2 + 4$

(b) $y = -2(x + 3)^2 - 5$

(c) $y = 4x^2 + 8x - 5$

(d) $y = -2x^2 + 10x - 3$

10. What transformations must you apply to $y = x^2$ to create each new graph? List the transformations in the order you would apply them.

(a) $y = -x^2 + 4$

(b) $y = (x - 5)^2$

(c) $y = (x + 3)^2 - 1$

(d) $y = -2(x - 4)^2 - 5$

11. Sketch by hand the graph of the relation. Start with the graph of $y = x^2$ and use the appropriate transformations.

(a) $y = x^2 + 2$

(b) $y = (x + 3)^2$

(c) $y = -2x^2$

(d) $y = \frac{1}{2}x^2$

(e) $y = (x + 1)^2 + 3$

(f) $y = -3(x - 2)^2 + 12$

12. What transformations must be applied to the graph of $y = x^2$ to produce the graph of $y = 2x^2 - 12x + 7$?

13. For each set of data,

i. determine if the relationship is linear or quadratic by examining the first differences and the second differences

ii. create a scatter plot and draw the curve of best fit

(a)

Age of Car (years)	0	1	2	3	4
Resale Value ($)	25 000	22 000	19 360	17 036.80	14 992.38

(b)

Time (s)	0	1	2	3	4
Height of Ball (m)	1.0	16.10	21.40	16.90	2.60

14. Solve for x. Determine all possible solutions.

(a) $x^2 = 36$

(b) $x^2 + 4x = 21$

(c) $2x^2 - 1 = 97$

(d) $-3x^2 + 18x = 27$

3.1 Investigating a Special Kind of Relationship

EXPLORATION

In earlier grades, you may have studied the relationship between footprint length and height. The data in **L1** and **L2** in the first screen were collected from seven students in a grade 11 math class. How can you predict the height of someone whose footprint is 28 cm long?

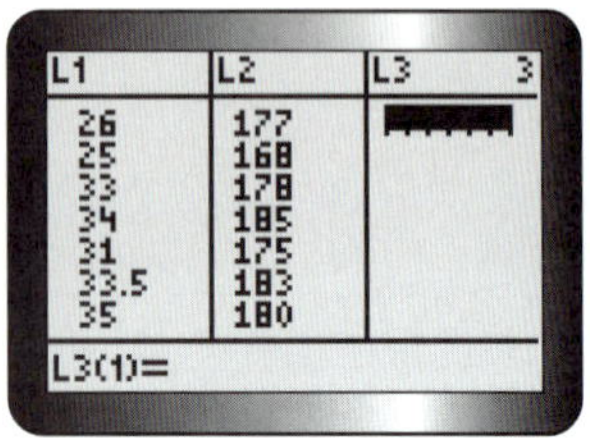

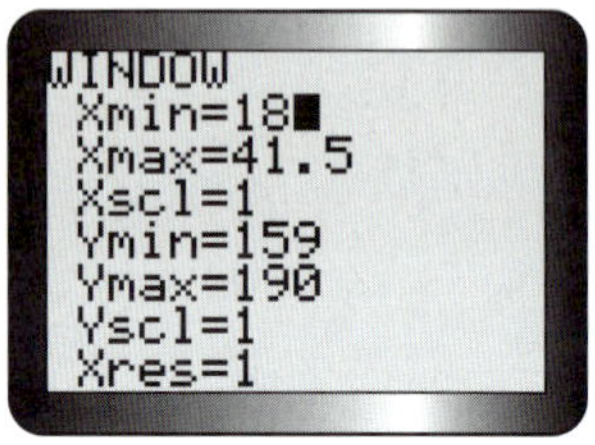

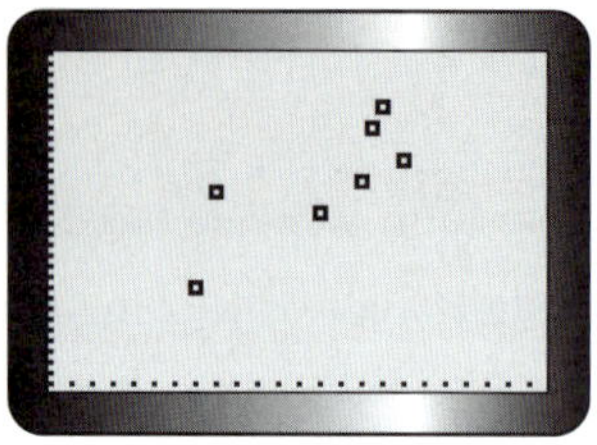

Think, Do, Discuss

1. (a) This data illustrates a relationship between footprint length and height. Which variable is independent in this case?

(b) Using a TI-83 Plus calculator, enter the data into lists and create a scatter plot. Zoom in, if needed, so that your screen looks like the third screen above.

(c) Someone in the group has a footprint that is 31 cm long. What can you say about that person's height?

(d) Now you know one value of the independent variable. Does this value determine a unique value for the dependent variable?

2. It appears that there might be a relationship between footprint length and height for all the students in the class. For this relationship, footprint is the input and height is the output. It appears that a student's height can be found using the length of his or her footprint.

(a) Think of a line that runs just above all the data points. Think of another line that lies just below all the data points. Enter the equations for these lines into the equation editor and graph. It might be reasonable to expect that data about other students in the class may lie between these two lines. Write your two equations.

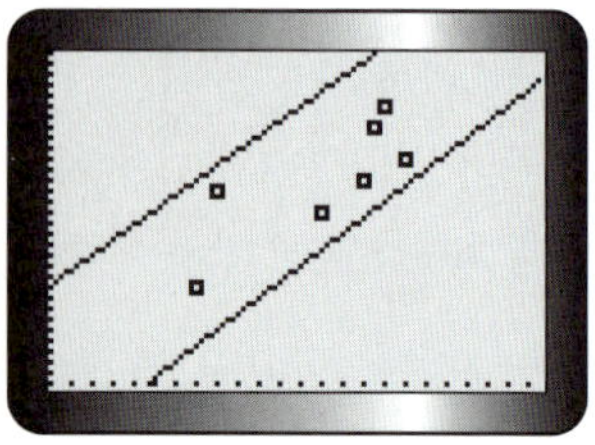

(b) Estimate a reasonable range for Asif's height if his footprint is 31 cm long.

i. Draw a vertical line through $x = 31$ by doing the following:

- Press [2nd] [PRGM] to open the DRAW menu.
- Select **4:Vertical**. Scroll left or right until $x = 31$.

ii. Use your graph to estimate a reasonable range for Asif's height by doing the following:

- Scroll up or down to move the cursor to each line.
- Record the y-coordinate for the top line as Asif's greatest possible height. Record the y-coordinate for the bottom line as Asif's least possible height.

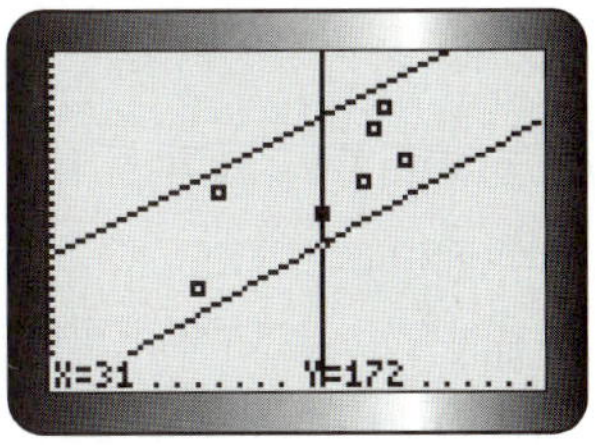

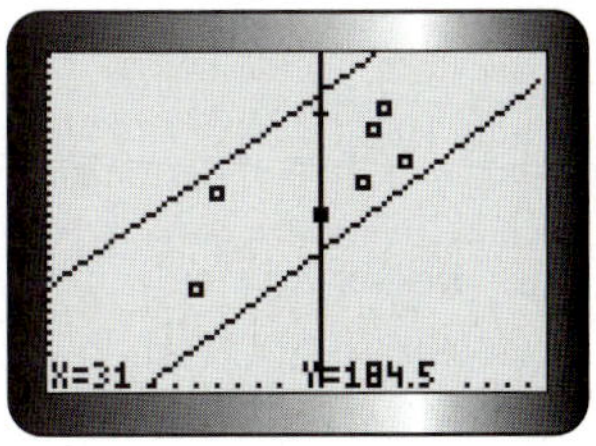

(c) What can you say about Asif's height? How could you make your prediction more accurate?

(d) The two lines you have drawn and all of the points between these lines define a model for the relationship between footprint length and height for the whole class. Suppose that you are given a value of the independent variable. Does this model *uniquely* determine a value for the dependent variable?

(e) A 31-cm long footprint is found in the snow. How can you use this model to predict the person's height? How might you change the model to make a more accurate prediction?

3. Another model for the relationship between footprint length and height is the line of best fit and its equation.

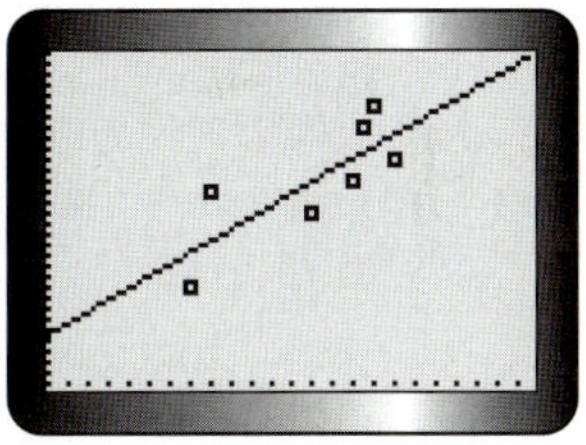

(a) Let ℓ be the length of the footprint for any student in the class. Then let h be the corresponding height. Think of an equation for the line of best fit and graph it on the scatter plot. Record your equation for the line of best fit.

(b) Use your equation to estimate the height of a student in the class whose footprint is 31 cm long.

(c) Imagine that you know a value of the independent variable. Does this model uniquely determine a value for the dependent variable?

(d) Determine the correlation coefficient, r, for the line of best fit. What does the correlation coefficient tell you about this model for the relationship?

The relationship between footprint length and height for the seven students:

Consider the data for the seven students. You could identify each student by his or her footprint since the length of each footprint is different. This relationship is called a **function** because there is only one height for each footprint.

The relationship between footprint length and height for all students in the grade 11 class:

You have the data about a few students, but you cannot predict the relationship between footprint length and height for all the students in the class with complete accuracy. There may be several students in the class whose footprint is 28 cm long, but with different heights. In this situation, there are several different heights for one footprint length, so this relationship is not a function.

The linear model for the relationship using the equation of the line of best fit:

You could describe the linear model as a rule, for example, "Multiply the length of the footprint by 1.1 and then add 143.6 cm to determine the height." Using this model, you can estimate that the person whose footprint is 28 cm long will be 174 cm tall.

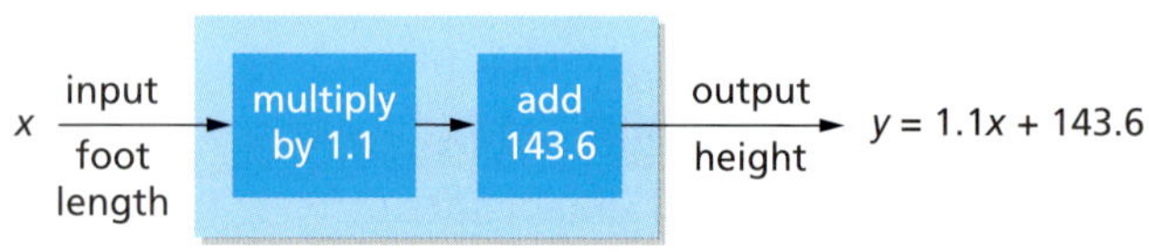

In this model, height is a **function** of the length of the footprint, because height depends on the length of the footprint. The equation can be used to estimate a person's height, given the length of his or her footprint.

4. For set of data,

i. create a scatter plot
ii. determine a linear model and a quadratic model. Which model is more appropriate?
iii. decide a reasonable range for the *y*-coordinate if the *x*-coordinate is 4
iv. estimate the *y*-coordinate if the *x*-coordinate is 4

(a)

x	y
−1	5
2	−3
5	−4
8	0
9	3
12	15

(b)

x	y
−1	6
2	3
5	1
8	−2
9	−3
12	−5

(c)

x	y
−1	−4
2	2
5	7
8	11
9	12
12	15

(d)

x	y
−1	0
2	1
5	3
8	4
9	5
12	6

Functions: Concept and Notation 3.2

In this section, you will develop the concept of a function. You will also learn how to write a function and how to work with functions.

Part 1: The Function

A vending machine behaves like a function. In other words, you get a predictable and reliable output from a vending machine depending on what you put into it.

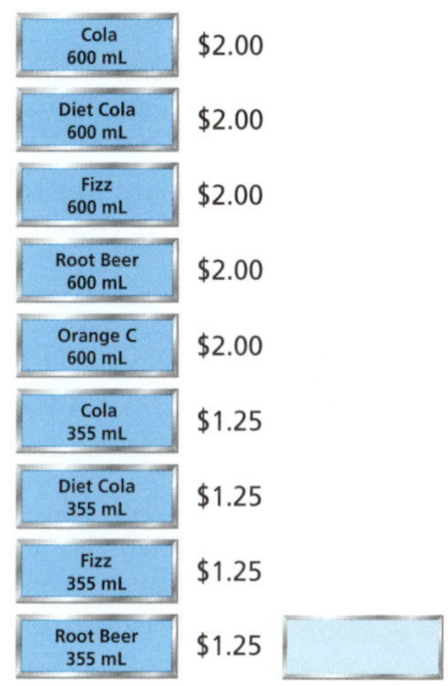

A soft-drink vending machine allows the customer to put in nickels, dimes, quarters, loonies, or toonies, and then make a choice.

When you input the correct combination of coins and push a button, you expect to get the correct soft drink. The "input" for this function is a number of coins and a button on the machine. The "output" is a soft drink.

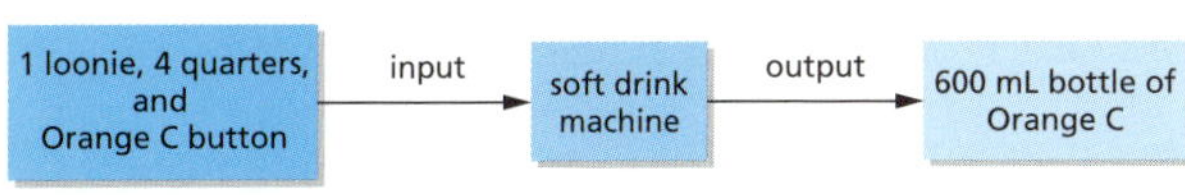

A different input might produce the same output. For example:

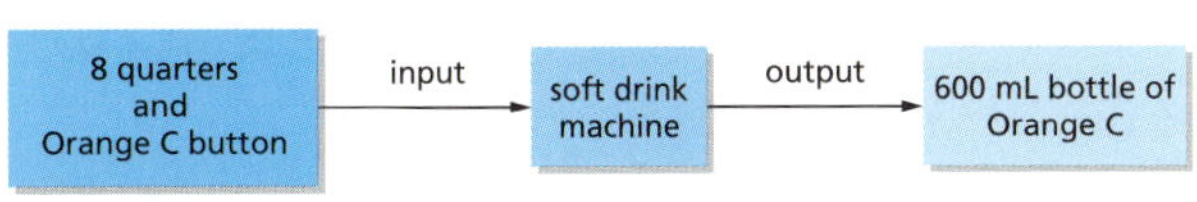

However, you would not expect the same inputs to produce different outputs. For example, suppose that you input two loonies and pushed the Orange C button. Would you expect to get a bottle of Fizz?

The combination of coins and the soft-drink button used are the **independent variables**. The soft drink received is the **dependent variable**. The machine operates as a **function** because the machine produces a guaranteed output for a specific input. In other words, a unique value of the dependent variable is produced for a specific set of values of the independent variables. The soft drink received is a function of the combination of coins and the soft-drink button pushed.

A **function** produces a unique value of the dependent variable for each value of the independent variable.

The set of all possible values of the independent variable is called the **domain** of the function. The set of all possible values of the dependent variable is called the **range** of the function.

There are some vending machines that are not functions. One example is a machine that rewards a child with a surprise toy when the child inserts a loonie.

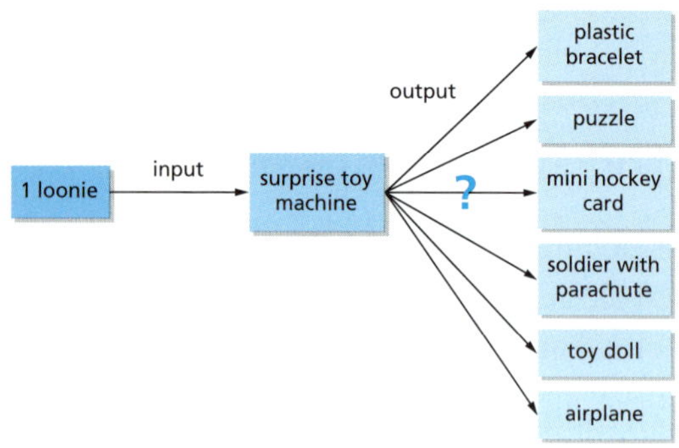

The prize is not a function of the coin inserted in the machine since there are a variety of toys that the child could receive for $1. One value of the independent variable produces more than one value of the dependent variable.

Example 1

For the soft-drink machine,

(a) what is the domain of the function? (b) what is the range of the function?

Solution

(a) The domain is the set of all possible combinations of coins, which total $2 or $1.25, and a specific button.

(b) The range is the set of all possible types of drinks that the machine contains.

Example 2

The table and the graph show the cost of mailing a first-class letter in Canada in 2001.

Mass of Letter	Mailing Cost
less than 30 g	47¢
30 g to 50 g	75¢
over 50 g but less than 100 g	94¢
over 100 g but less than 200 g	$1.55
200 g to 500 g	$2.05

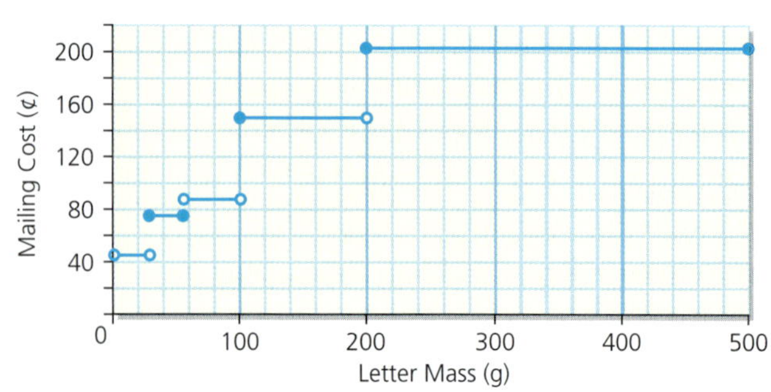

(a) What is the cost of mailing a letter with mass

i. 20 g? ii. 100 g?

(b) State the domain of the relation in set notation.

(c) State the range of the relation.

(d) Why must this relation be a function?

Solution

(a) Estimate each cost using the graph. Find the exact cost in the table.

i. It costs 47¢ to mail a 20-g letter.
ii. It costs \$1.55 to mail a 100-g letter.

(b) In the graph, the first interval starts at 0 g and the last interval ends with 500 g, so the domain is the set of all real numbers greater than 0 but less than or equal to 500. Use set notation to describe the domain, or range, with symbols. Let m be the mass in grams. Then the domain is $\{m \mid 0 < m \leq 500, m \in \mathbf{R}\}$, which is read, "the set of all values m, such that m is greater than 0 and less than or equal to 500, and m is an element of the set of real numbers."

(c) The range is the set of all possible prices. From the table, the range is {47¢, 75¢, 94¢, \$1.55, \$2.05}. From the graph, you can only estimate these values.

(d) Consumers would not pay different prices for two letters with the same mass. Each different mass has a unique price.

Part 2: Function Notation

In section 3.1, you determined the line of best fit for data about a group of students in a grade 11 math class. The equation $h = 1.1\ell + 143.6$ is one possible model for the relation between height and foot length for students in this class. Using function notation, you can write this equation as $f(\ell) = 1.1\ell + 143.6$. The name of the function is f, and $f(\ell)$ refers to the output of the function. $f(\ell)$ is the value of the function f at ℓ and is read "f at ℓ" or "f of ℓ."

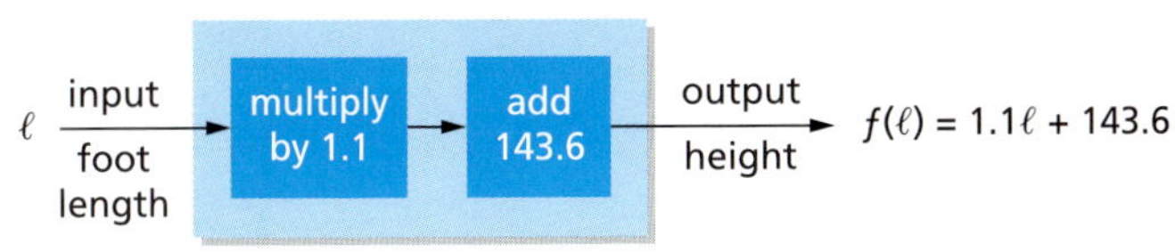

Example 3

Determine the height of a student whose footprint is 31 cm long.

Solution

$f(31)$ will be the output of f when the input is 31. To calculate $f(31)$, replace ℓ with 31 and evaluate.

$$f(\ell) = 1.1\ell + 143.6$$
$$f(31) = 1.1(31) + 143.6$$
$$= 177.7$$

The student whose footprint is 31 cm long may be 177.7 cm tall.

Example 4

Peter throws a ball in the air, and Hazel uses a Calculator-Based Ranger (CBR) to record the height of the ball as it goes up and then down. They use quadratic regression to find the equation of the curve of best fit, $f(t) = -4.9t^2 + 1.9t + 1.1$, where $f(t)$ is the height in metres after t seconds. The CBR was 1.2 m above the ground during the experiment. Hazel didn't start recording until 0.3 s after Peter released the ball.

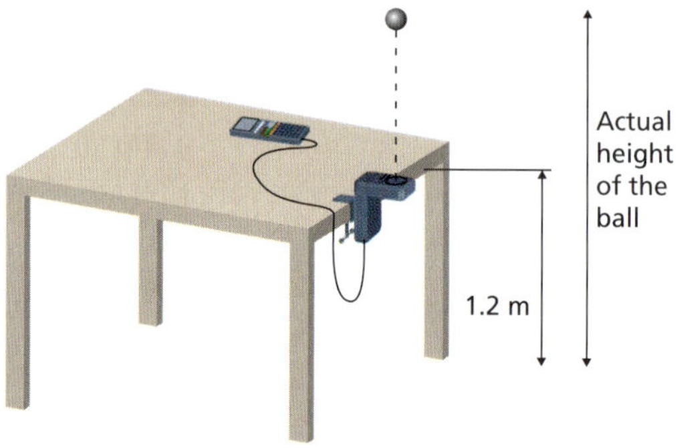

(a) Calculate the height at which Peter releases the ball.

(b) Calculate the height of the ball after 1 s.

(c) Rewrite the function so that the height of the ball above the ground is a function of the time since Peter released the ball.

(d) Use the new function to verify your answers from (a) and (b).

Solution

(a) The graph of f shows the height of the ball. Note that the CBR started recording data 0.3 s after Peter threw the ball. When $t = 0$, the ball had already been in the air for 0.3 s. To calculate the height of the ball when it was released, find $f(-0.3)$.

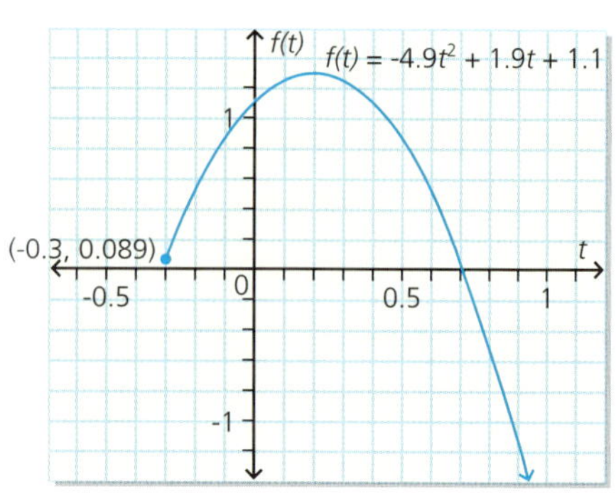

$$f(-0.3) = -4.9(-0.3)^2 + 1.9(-0.3) + 1.1$$
$$= -4.9(0.09) - 0.57 + 1.1$$
$$= 0.089$$

Peter released the ball 0.089 m above the CBR, which is 1.2 m above the floor.

$$0.089 + 1.2 = 1.289$$

When Peter released the ball, it was about 1.3 m above the floor.

(b) The CBR started recording data 0.3 s after Peter threw the ball. Since $1 - 0.3 = 0.7$, use $t = 0.7$ s. The total height of the ball after 1 s is the sum of $f(0.7)$ and 1.2 m, the height at which the CBR is attached to the table.

$$\begin{aligned} f(0.7) + 1.2 &= -4.9(0.7)^2 + 1.9(0.7) + 1.1 + 1.2 \\ &= -4.9(0.49) + 1.33 + 2.3 \\ &= 1.229 \end{aligned}$$

After 1 s, the ball is about 1.2 m above the ground.

(c) Let $h(t)$ be the height of the ball in metres t seconds after Peter releases the ball. Subtract 0.3 from the value of t in $f(t)$ and add 1.2 to the height.

$$\begin{aligned} h(t) &= f(t - 0.3) + 1.2 \\ &= -4.9(t - 0.3)^2 + 1.9(t - 0.3) + 1.1 + 1.2 \\ &= -4.9(t^2 - 0.6t + 0.09) + 1.9t - 0.57 + 2.3 \\ &= -4.9t^2 + 2.94t - 0.441 + 1.9t + 1.73 \\ &= -4.9t^2 + 4.84t + 1.289 \end{aligned}$$

(d) For (a), $t = 0$ when Peter released the ball.

$$\begin{aligned} h(0) &= -4.9(0)^2 + 4.84(0) + 1.289 \\ &= 1.289 \end{aligned}$$

For (b), $t = 1$ when the ball is released after 1 s.

$$\begin{aligned} h(1) &= -4.9(1)^2 + 4.84(1) + 1.289 \\ &= 1.229 \end{aligned}$$

The answers obtained using $h(t)$ are the same as those for (a) and (b).

Part 3: The Vertical Line Test

In section 3.1, you investigated the relationship between the footprint length and height. All of the seven students had footprints of different lengths. Al remeasures the footprint that is 33.5 cm long and finds that it is actually 33 cm long. Here are the revised lists and a new scatter plot.

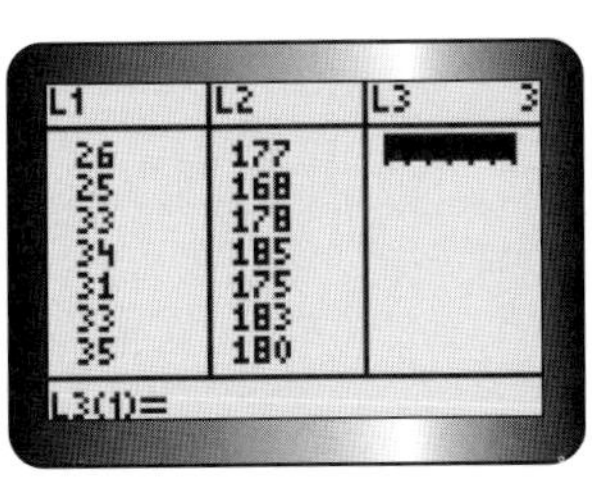

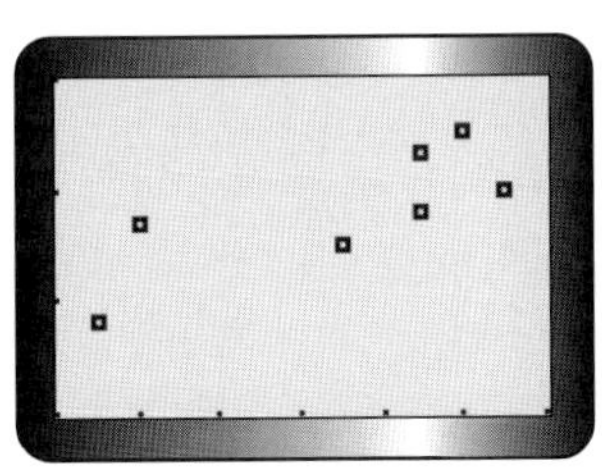

Think, Do, Discuss

1. (a) Why is it no longer possible to identify every person in the group only by the length of his or her footprint?
   (b) How do you know this relation is not a function?

2. (a) Place a ruler on the vertical axis (the height axis). Move the ruler slowly to the right. As you move the ruler to the right, note the number of points on the graph of the relation that lie along the edge of the ruler at any one time.

   (b) Which two points lie on the same line? Explain why these two points show that this relation is not a function.

   (c) Draw a line through these two points. Describe the direction of this line.

   (d) In your own words, describe a test to determine whether a relation is a function using its graph.

Consolidate Your Understanding

1. How can you tell if a relation is a function?
2. Why is it useful when a relation is a function?
3. How can you determine the domain and range of a function from its graph?
4. A function is given by $f(x) = 3x - 5$. Describe this function as a rule.
5. What does $f(2)$ mean?
6. How can you tell from the graph of a relation whether it is a function or not? Explain.

Focus 3.2

Key Ideas

- The set of all possible input values of a relation is called the **domain**. The set of all possible output values is called the **range**.
- A function is a relation in which each element of the domain corresponds to exactly one element of the range.
- You may describe a relation and a function as
  - a set of ordered pairs. For example, $\{(0, 1), (3, 4), (2, -5)\}$.
  - a table. For example,

x	y
1	5
2	7
3	9

  - a description in words. For example, there is a relationship between the age and the height of students in your class.
  - a rule. For example, the output is 4 more than the input.
  - an equation. For example, $y = 2x + 1$.

- an input/output diagram. For example,

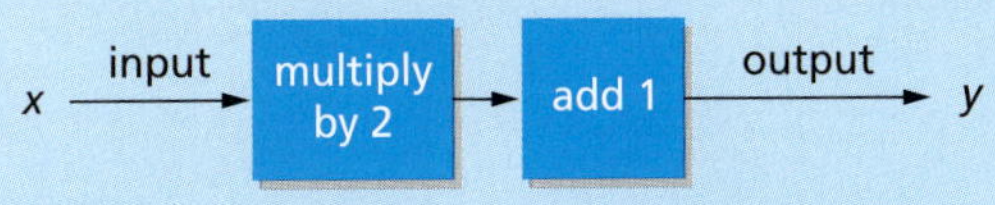

- function notation. For example, $f(x) = 2x + 1$.
- an arrow diagram. For example,

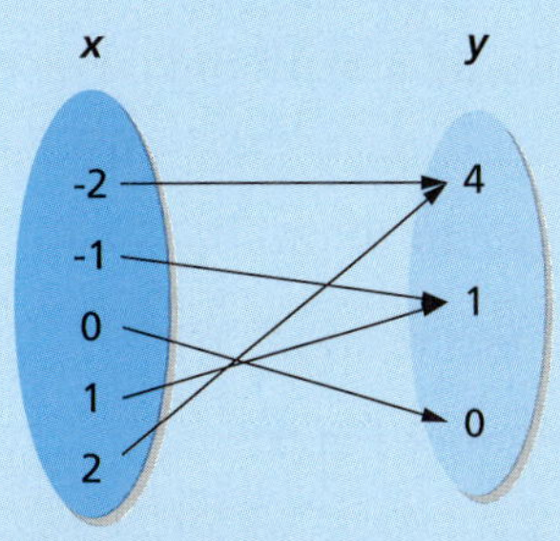

- a graph or a scatter plot. For example,

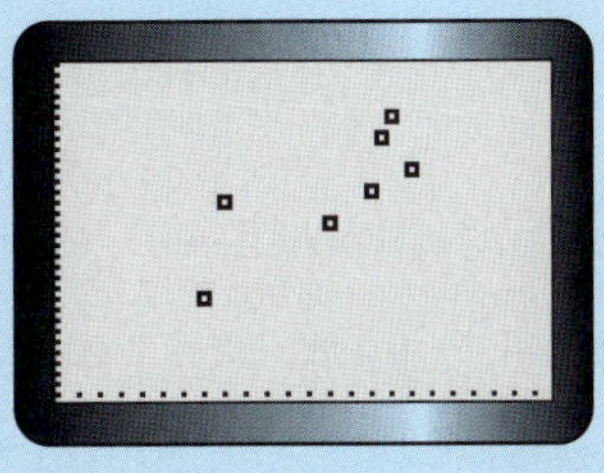

- $f(x)$ is called function notation and is read "f at x" or "f of x."
- $f(x)$ represents an expression for determining the value of the function f for any value of x.
- $f(3)$ represents the value of the function (the output) when x (the input) is 3. $f(3)$ is the y-coordinate of the point on the graph of f with x-coordinate 3.
- y usually represents the output. Then $y = f(x)$ is the equation of a function f.
- The **vertical line test** can be used to determine if the graph of a relation is a function.

  The relation is not a function if you can draw a vertical line through two or more points on the graph of the relation. The relation is a function if you cannot draw a vertical line through two or more points on the graph.

Example 5

How old are you right now?

(a) Would the answer to this question produce a function? Explain.

(b) Let the domain be the set of all the students in your class. Then what is the range?

Solution

(a) Yes, because every person you ask has only one possible age.

(b) The range is probably {15, 16, 17}.

Example 6

A relation is shown in the arrow diagram. The input is a student's name and the output is a score out of 10 on a math quiz. For example, Seyran scored 8 out of 10 on the math quiz.

(a) Write this relation as a set of ordered pairs.

(b) State the domain of this relation.

(c) Is this relation a function? Explain.

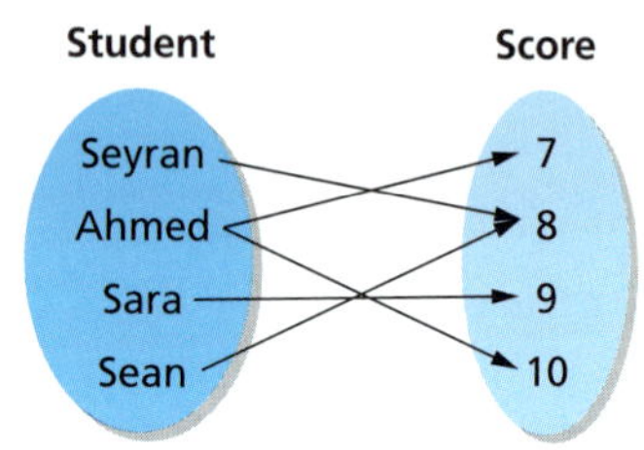

Solution

(a) {(Seyran, 8), (Ahmed, 7), (Ahmed, 10), (Sara, 9), (Sean, 8)}.

(b) The domain is {Seyran, Ahmed, Sara, Sean}.

(c) The arrow diagram shows that Ahmed had two scores, because he redid the math quiz after he scored a low mark the first time. So there are two values in the range for one value in the domain. This relation is not a function.

Example 7

The equation $y = 4x + 1$ describes a relation.

(a) The input for this relation is any real number. Describe a rule for calculating the output value.

(b) Graph this relation.

(c) Is this relation a function? Explain.

Solution

(a) The equation shows that x is the input and $4x + 1$ is the output. Multiply the input by 4, and then add 1 to get the output.

(b) This relation is a line with slope 4 and y-intercept 1.

(c) Each value of x yields only one value of y, so this relation is a function. Verify using the vertical line test.

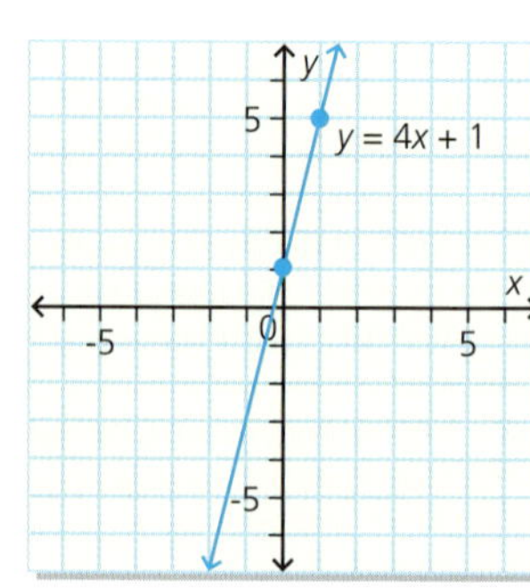

Example 8

For the function $g(x) = x^2 - 4x$,

(a) evaluate $g(-3)$

(b) simplify $g(a + 1)$

(c) graph g

(d) find the domain and range of g

Solution

(a) $$\begin{aligned} g(-3) &= (-3)^2 - 4(-3) \\ &= 9 + 12 \\ &= 21 \end{aligned}$$

(b) $$\begin{aligned} g(a + 1) &= (a + 1)^2 - 4(a + 1) \\ &= a^2 + 2a + 1 - 4a - 4 \\ &= a^2 - 2a - 3 \end{aligned}$$

(c) Express the equation in vertex form by completing the square.

$$\begin{aligned} g(x) &= x^2 - 4x \\ &= x^2 - 4x + 4 - 4 \\ &= (x - 2)^2 - 4 \end{aligned}$$

The vertex is $(2, -4)$, and the parabola opens up. Factor the original function to get $g(x) = x(x - 4)$. The x-intercepts are 0 and -4.

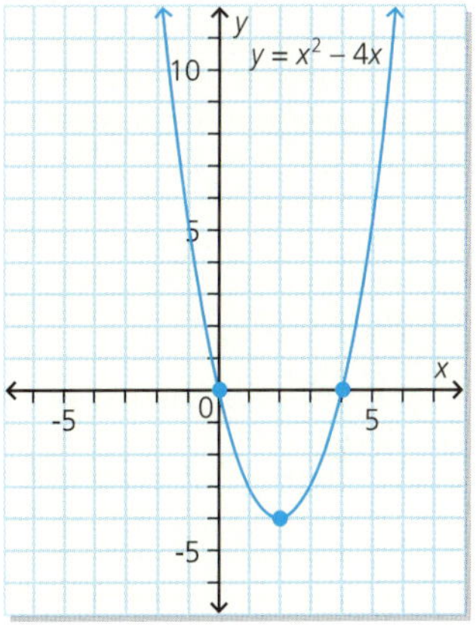

(d) Any real number may be input for g, so the domain is **R**. The value of y is not less than -4, so the range is $\{y \mid y \geq -4, y \in \mathbf{R}\}$.

Example 9

The graph represents an infinite number of points that belong to a relation.

Use the vertical line test to explain why this relation is not a function.

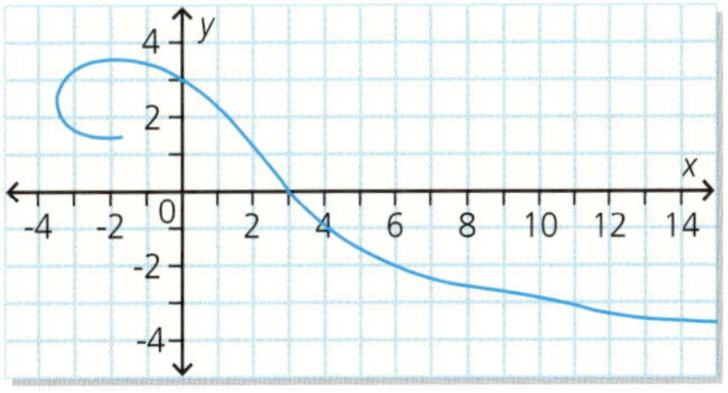

Solution

At $x = -2.5$, the vertical line passes through two values of y, about 1.5 and 3.2, so this relation is not a function.

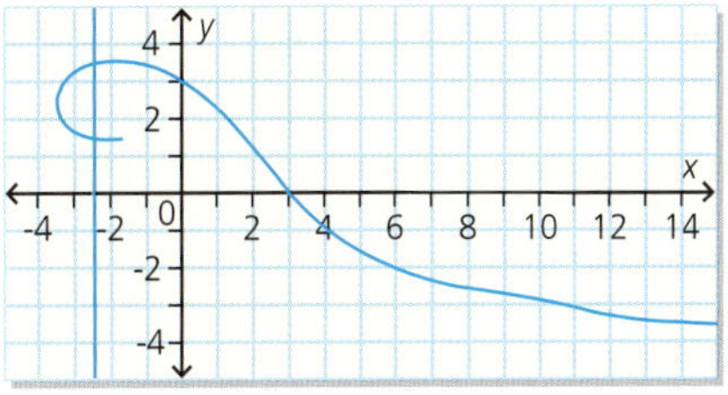

Practise, Apply, Solve 3.2

A

1. The scatter plot shows a relation. The marks on each axis indicate single units.

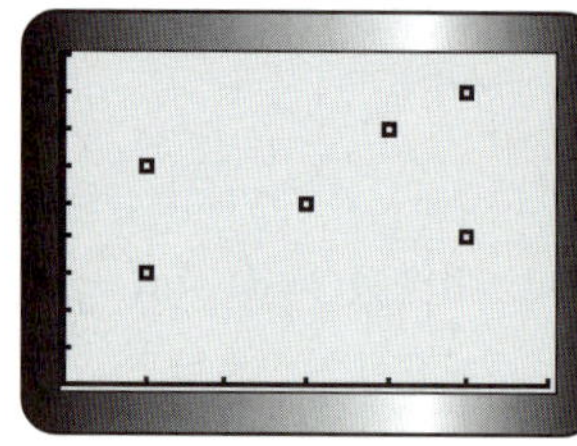

(a) State the domain and range of this relation.

(b) Draw an arrow diagram to illustrate the relation.

(c) Is this relation a function? Explain.

2. For each of the following, state

i. the domain and range

ii. whether it defines a function or not, and justify your answer

(a) $\{(1, 2), (3, 1), (4, 2), (7, 2)\}$

(b) $\{(1, 2), (1, 3), (4, 5), (6, 1)\}$

(c) $\{(1, 0), (0, 1), (2, 3), (3, 2)\}$

(d)

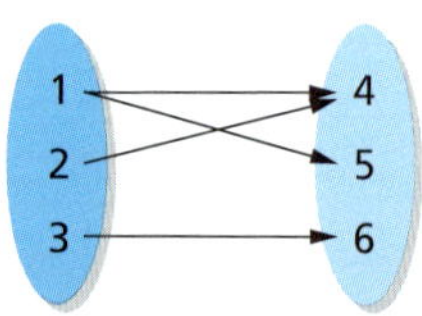

(e)

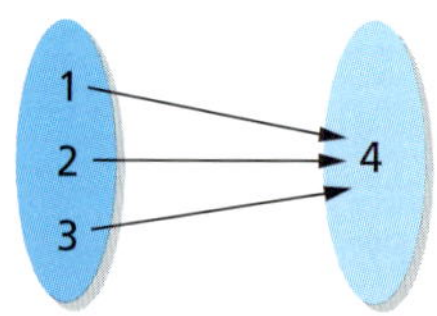

(f)

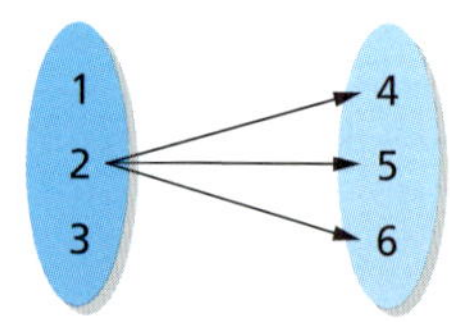

3. Consider the $\sqrt{}$ key on your calculator. Recall that $\sqrt{}$ means the positive square root.

(a) What is the output if the input is 25?

(b) Does the output have more than one value for any input value?

(c) Why must this operation be a function? Explain.

(d) Are there any numbers that cannot be used as input?

(e) State the domain of this function.

4. Consider the rule "Take the square root of the input number to get the output number."

(a) What is the output if the input is 25?

(b) Does the output have more than one value for any input value?

(c) Is this relation a function? Explain.

(d) Are there any numbers that cannot be used as input?

B

5. The graph of $y = f(x)$ is shown.

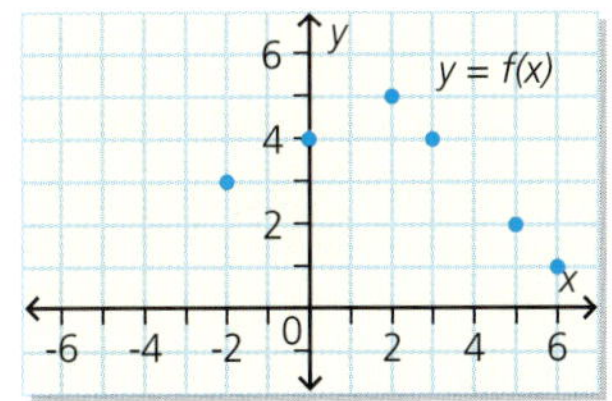

i. State the domain and range of f.

ii. Evaluate.

(a) $f(3)$ (b) $f(5)$

(c) $f(5 - 3)$ (d) $f(5) - f(3)$

iii. In part ii, why is the function in (d) not the same as the answer in (c)?

iv. $f(2) = 5$. What is the corresponding ordered pair? What does 2 represent? What does $f(2)$ represent?

6. For $g(x) = 3 - 2x$, find

(a) $g(3)$ (b) $g(0)$ (c) $g(-2)$ (d) $2g(1)$

(e) $g(-2) - 3$ (f) $g(-2 - 3)$ (g) $g(a)$

7. State whether each graph shows a function. Justify your answer.

(a)

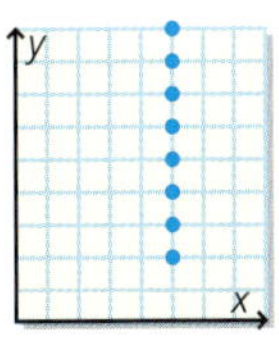

(b)

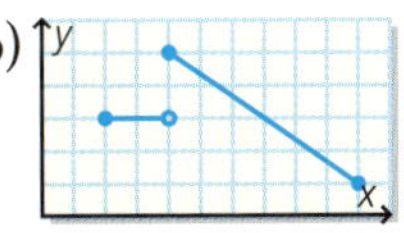

(c)

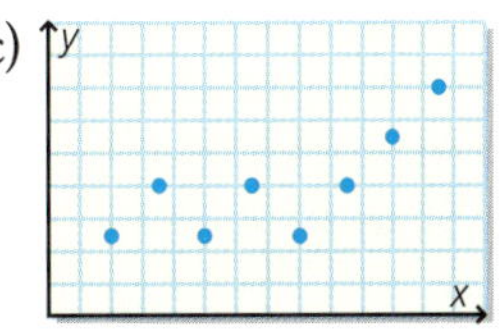

(d)

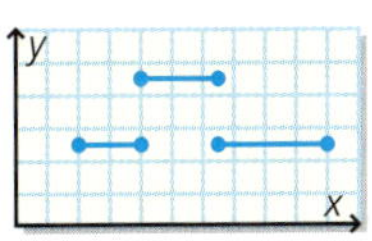

(e)

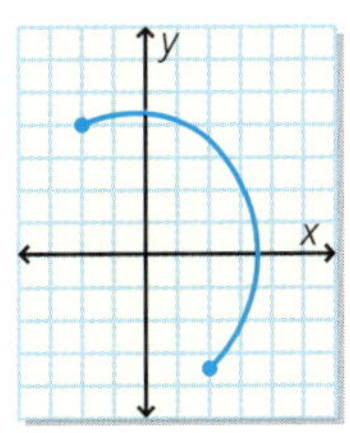

(f)

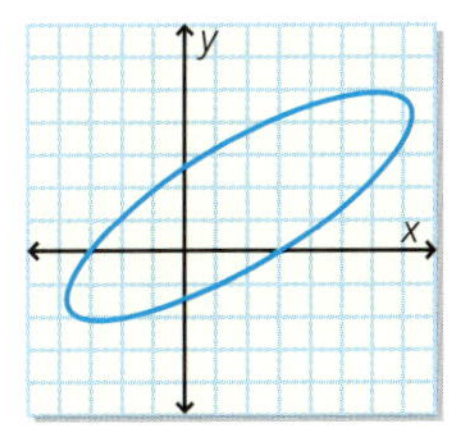

(g)

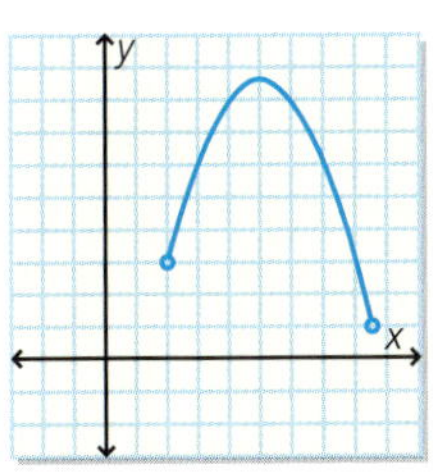

(h)

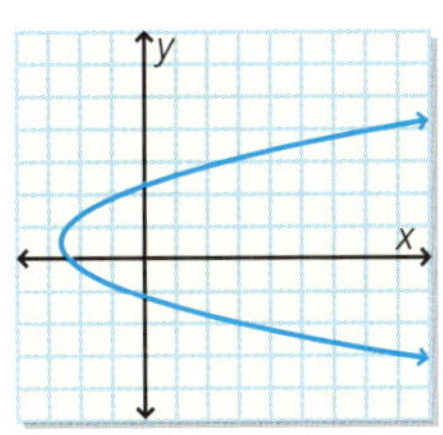

(i)

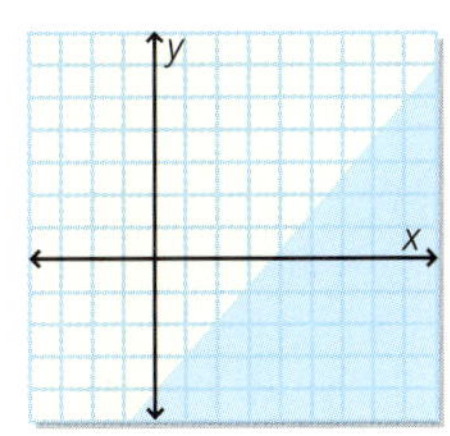

8. Consider the function $g(t) = 3t + 5$.

i. Create a table and graph the function.

ii. Determine each value.

(a) $g(0)$ (b) $g(1)$ (c) $g(2)$

(d) $g(3)$ (e) $g(1) - g(0)$ (f) $g(2) - g(1)$

(g) $g(3) - g(2)$ (h) $g(1001) - g(1000)$ (i) $g(a + 1) - g(a)$

(j) $\frac{g(4) - g(0)}{4 - 0}$

iii. In part ii, what are the answers to (e), (f), and (g), as a group, commonly called? Why is the answer to (j) the same as those for (e), (f), (g), (h), and (i)?

9. **Knowledge and Understanding:** For each of the following,

i. sketch the relation
ii. state the domain and range
iii. explain why the relation is a function

(a) $y = \frac{1}{x}$ (b) $y = 6 - 2x$

(c) $x + 3y = 6$ (d) $y = x^2 + 3$

10. Bill called a garage to ask for a price quote on tires. Bill told the clerk what size of tire he needed, and the clerk told him the price. When Bill called back later that same day, another clerk told him a different price. How could this happen? Explain why this situation is not a function. How could you adapt this situation to make it a function?

11. The adjacent table lists all of the ordered pairs belonging to a function *g*.

i. Determine the equation of the line that passes through these points.
ii. Write $g(x)$.
iii. Evaluate.

(a) $g(5)$ (b) $g(5 - 3)$

(c) $g(5) - g(3)$ (d) $2g(3) - 5$

x	*y*
1	5
2	7
3	9
4	11
5	13

12. Consider the function $f(s) = s^2 - 6s + 9$.

i. Create a table for the function.
ii. Determine each value.

(a) $f(0)$
(b) $f(1)$
(c) $f(2)$
(d) $f(3)$
(e) $f(4)$
(f) $f(1) - f(0)$
(g) $f(2) - f(1)$
(h) $f(3) - f(2)$
(i) $f(4) - f(3)$
(j) $[f(2) - f(1)] - [f(1) - f(0)]$
(k) $[f(3) - f(2)] - [f(2) - f(1)]$
(l) $[f(4) - f(3)] - [f(3) - f(2)]$
(m) $[f(1002) - f(1001)] - [f(1001) - f(1000)]$

iii. In part ii, what are the answers to (f), (g), (h), and (i), as a group, commonly called? What are the answers to (j), (k), and (l), as a group, commonly called?

13. The graph shows $f(x) = 2(x - 3)^2 - 1$.

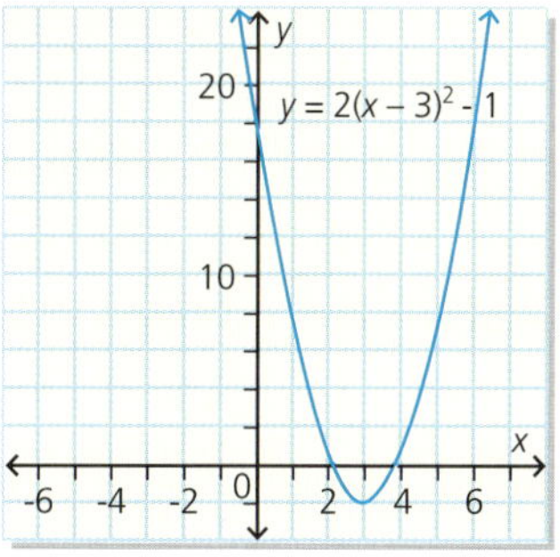

(a) Evaluate $f(-2)$.

(b) What does $f(-2)$ represent on the graph of f?

(c) State the domain and range of the relation.

(d) How do you know that f is a function from its graph?

(e) How do you know that f is a function from its equation?

14. Consider the relation $y = x^2 - 3x$.

(a) Are there any values of the independent variable for which the dependent variable is not unique?

(b) Is this relation a function? Explain.

15. A relation is defined by $x^2 + y^2 = 25$.

(a) Sketch a graph of the relation.

(b) Is this relation a function? Explain.

16. For each of the following,

i. graph the relation
ii. state the domain and range
iii. is the relation a function? Why or why not?

(a) $y = 3x - 1$ (b) $y = 10 - 4.9x^2$ (c) $y = 3(x - 2)^2 - 5$

(d) $y = \frac{1}{x^2}$ (e) $x^2 - y = 3x$ (f) $y = x(x - 4)$

(g) $5x + 3y = 15$

17. State the domain and range of the function $y = \sqrt{x - 1} + 2$.

18. The cost of renting a banquet hall depends on the size of the room and the number of meals served. A graph of the number of meals versus cost is shown.

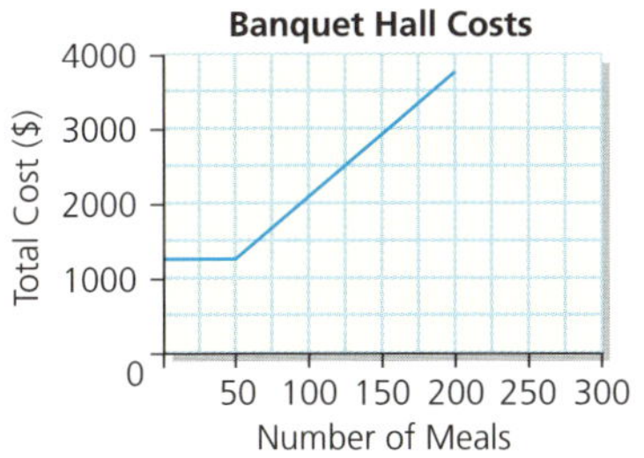

(a) What problems would the banquet hall have if this relation were not a function?

(b) What is the domain and range of this function?

(c) Why does the domain have an upper limit?

(d) Why is the graph a reasonable representation of the cost to rent a banquet hall?

19. **Communication:** A ball is thrown, and its height is recorded a number of different times. The ball reaches a maximum height of 20 m after 1.5 s.

(a) Sketch the relation. Time is the independent variable and height is the dependent variable.

(b) State a reasonable domain and range for the relation.

(c) Is this relation a function? Explain.

(d) A student decided to use height as the independent variable and time as the dependent variable. Sketch a graph of this relation.

(e) Why is this relation not a function?

20. A freight delivery company charges \$4/kg for any order less than 100 kg and \$3.50/kg for any order of at least 100 kg.

(a) Why must this relation be a function?

(b) What is the domain of this function? What is its range?

(c) Graph this function.

(d) What suggestions can you offer to the company for a better pricing structure? Support your answer.

21. **Thinking, Inquiry, Problem Solving:** A women's clothing store owner wants to create a payment plan to motivate employees to sell as much as possible. However, the owner wants to give the employees some security during slow times when there are few customers. She has three possible plans as follows:

Plan A: a flat salary of \$300/week

Plan B: a payment of \$200/week, plus 5% commission on sales

Plan C: 7.5% commission on sales

(a) What is a reasonable domain for this relation? What is a reasonable range?

(b) Why is it important to the employees for this relation to be a function?

(c) Create a plan that combines these payment plans for the best results. Justify your decisions.

22. **Application:** The amount owed on a loan depends on several variables. Assume that the interest is compounded annually.

(a) Graph the amount owed versus the interest rate for a loan of \$10 000 over five years.

(b) Describe the domain and range of this function.

23. Sara asked each of her family members to measure his or her foot length. Then she graphed the relationship between foot length and age, using age as the independent variable.

(a) Will this relationship be a function? Explain.

(b) Sara asked all of her friends to measure the foot lengths of their family members. Then she combined the data. Will this relationship be a function? Explain.

(c) Sara modelled the relationship with a line of best fit. Is this model a function? Explain.

(d) Is foot length a function of age? Explain.

24. Check Your Understanding: Create your own examples of a relation that is not a function and another that is a function, using descriptions, graphs, tables, or equations. Explain the difference between the relation and the function.

C

25. Binary numbers are used by computers and other digital devices. A binary number has only 0s and 1s. The binary number 1101 is equivalent to the decimal number 13. To convert a binary number to a decimal number, use the following process. Start at the left.

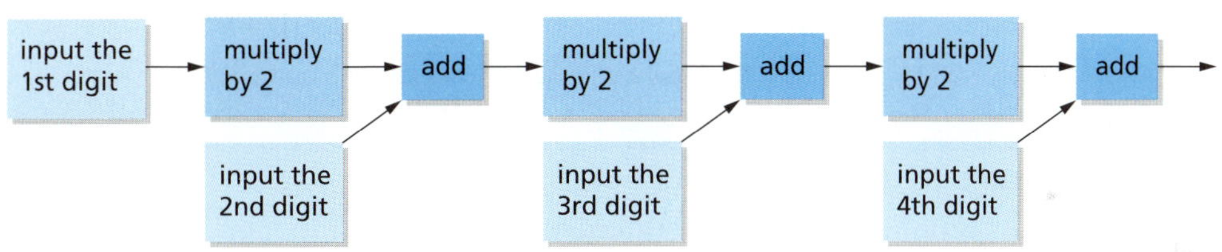

(a) Use this process to decode the binary number 1101.

(b) Why is this process a function?

(c) The diagram below shows how to convert any binary number into a decimal number. Use this process to convert each of the following into a decimal number.

i. 10101 **ii.** 11 **iii.** 1000

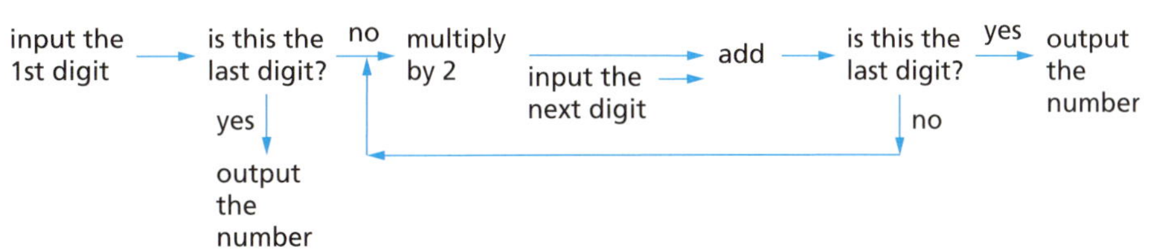

(d) Suppose the domain of this function is the set of all one-, two-, three-, or four-digit binary numbers. What is the range of the function?

(e) How many binary digits, or bits, are needed to represent all of the letters and symbols on a keyboard?

26. Many calculators can generate a random number. Using a TI-83 Plus calculator, press [MATH] and scroll right to **PRB**. Select **1:rand** by pressing [ENTER]. Press [ENTER] again to get a random number. To get another random number, you can repeat these steps or just press [ENTER] to repeat the command.

(a) Generate five random numbers in a row and record these in a list.

(b) Why does it appear that **rand** is not a function? Why is this not a problem?

(c) It is also possible to store numbers in **rand**. To store the value 0, press [0] [STO▸] [MATH]. Scroll right to **PRB** and select **1:rand** by pressing [ENTER]. Now generate and write another list of random numbers. Compare your list to those of other students. What do you notice?

(d) Enter the first number from your list in (a) and store it in **rand**. Generate and write another list of random numbers and compare them to the numbers in your first list.

(e) Generate several lists of three random numbers by storing 0.4, 0.8, 1.2, 1.6, 2.0, 2.4, and 2.8 in **rand**. What do you notice?

(f) Describe how your random number generator seems to work.

(g) Is **rand** a function? Explain. Why might this be a problem?

The Chapter Problem—Cryptography

In this section, you were introduced to the idea of a function. Apply what you have learned to answer these questions about the Chapter Problem on page 218.

CP1. The coding method described in the Chapter Problem is an example of a function. Why?

CP2. What is the domain of this function? Why?

CP3. What is the range of this function? Why?

CP4. What does it mean "to break the code"?

Solving Inequalities

3.3 SKILL BUILDER

In mathematics, you must be able to represent intervals and identify smaller sections of a relation or a set of numbers. You can use the following inequality symbols:

$>$	greater than	$<$	less than
$\geq$	greater than or equal to	$\leq$	less than or equal to

When you write one of these symbols between two or more expressions, the result is called an **inequality**, for example, $3x - 1 < 8$.

To solve an inequality you have to find all the possible values of the variable that satisfy the inequality.

For example, $x = 2$ satisfies $3x - 1 < 8$, but so does $x = 2.9$, $x = -1$, and $x = -5$.

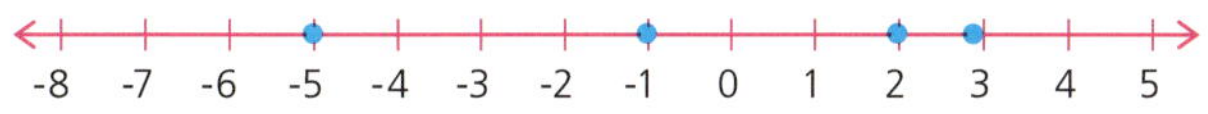

In fact, every real number less than 3 satisfies this inequality. The thicker part of the number line below represents this solution. To show that 3 is not included in the solution, use an open dot at this value. A solid dot shows that a value is included in the solution.

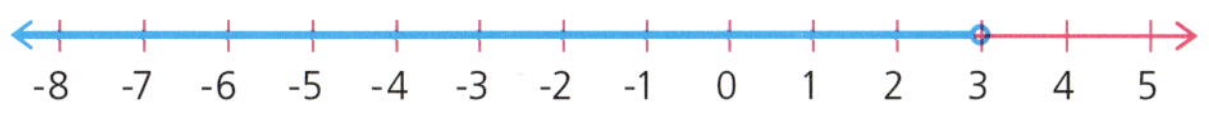

The solution to $3x - 1 < 8$ can be written in set notation as $\{x \mid x < 3, x \in \mathbf{R}\}$. This is read "the set of x such that x is less than 3, where x is an element of the set of real numbers."

Example 1

Write each set in set notation.

(a)

(b)

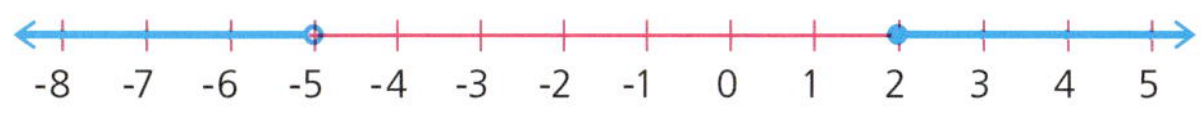

Solution

(a) $\{x \mid -5 < x \leq 2, x \in \mathbf{R}\}$

(b) $\{x \mid x < -5 \text{ or } x \geq 2, x \in \mathbf{R}\}$

Example 2

Graph each set on a number line.

(a) $\{x \mid -5 < x \leq 2, x \in \mathbf{N}\}$

(b) $\{x \mid -1 < x \leq 1, x \in \mathbf{R}\}$

(c) $\{x \mid x^2 \leq 9, x \in \mathbf{R}\}$

(d) $\{x \mid x^2 > 4, x \in \mathbf{R}\}$

Solution

(a) Recall that $\mathbf{N} = \{1, 2, 3, 4, 5, \dots\}$.

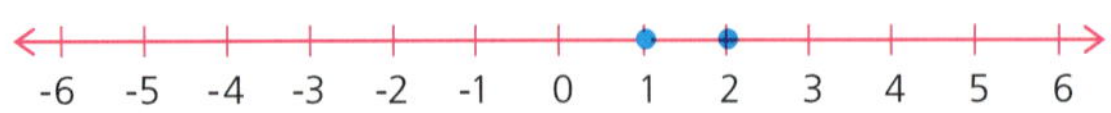

(b)
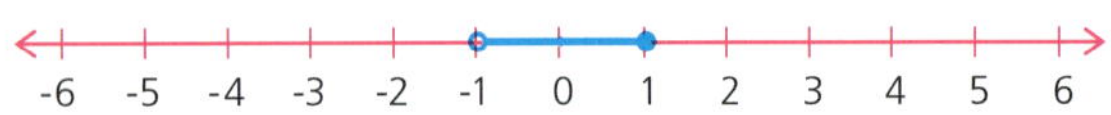

(c) For $x^2 \leq 9$, $x \leq 3$ and $x \geq -3$.

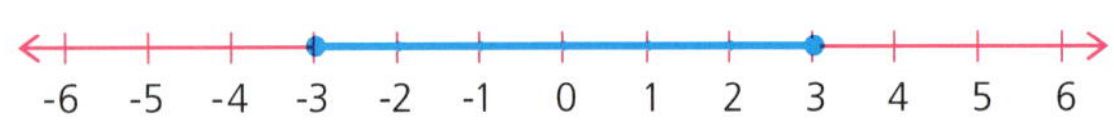

(d) For $x^2 > 4$, $x > 2$ or $x < -2$.

In earlier grades, you learned to solve linear equations algebraically

- by adding or subtracting the same quantity from both sides, or
- by multiplying or dividing both sides by a nonzero quantity

To solve a linear inequality such as $3x - 1 < 8$ algebraically, the rules are similar, but not identical.

Start with the inequality $3 < 4$.

Add 7 to both sides, then $10 < 11$. The left side is still less than the right side.

Add -7 to both sides, then $-4 < -3$. The left side is still less than the right side.

Multiply both sides by 2, then $6 < 8$. The left side is still less than the right side.

Multiply both sides by -2, then $-6 > -8$. The left side is **greater** than the right side now.

Divide both sides by 2, then $1.5 < 2$. The left side is still less than the right side.

Divide both sides by -2, then $-1.5 > -2$. The left side is **greater** than the right side now.

The same rules apply to an inequality that has more than two expressions, for example, $-2 \leq 3 < 4$.

Add or subtract the same number from all three parts of this inequality. Notice that the inequality signs do not change.

Multiply or divide all three parts of this inequality by the same number. Notice that the inequality signs change if each part is multiplied or divided by a negative number.

Example 3

Solve and graph each solution set on a number line, $x \in \mathbf{R}$.

(a) $1 - x \leq -3$ (b) $\frac{2a}{3} + 4 > 2$ (c) $-4 < \frac{1 - 3x}{2} < 1$

Solution

(a)

$1 - x \leq -3$	Add x to both sides.
$1 \leq -3 + x$	Add 3 to both sides.
$4 \leq x$	

This is equivalent to $x \geq 4$.

The solution set is $\{x \mid x \geq 4, x \in \mathbf{R}\}$.

(b)

$\frac{2a}{3} + 4 > 2$	Subtract 4 from both sides.
$\frac{2a}{3} > -2$	Multiply both sides by 3.
$2a > -6$	Divide both sides by 2.
$a > -3$	

The solution set is $\{a \mid a > -3, a \in \mathbf{R}\}$.

(c)

$-4 < \frac{1 - 3x}{2} < 1$	Multiply each expression by 2.
$-8 < 1 - 3x < 2$	Subtract 1 from each expression.
$-9 < -3x < 1$	Divide each expression by -3 and reverse the inequality signs.

$3 > x > -\frac{1}{3}$ or $-\frac{1}{3} < x < 3$

The solution set is $\{x \mid -\frac{1}{3} < x < 3, x \in \mathbf{R}\}$.

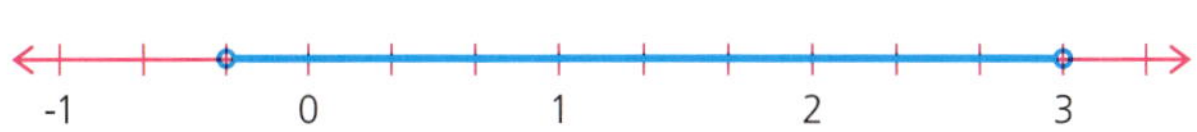

Example 4

The graph of $f(x) = 3x - 1$ is shown.

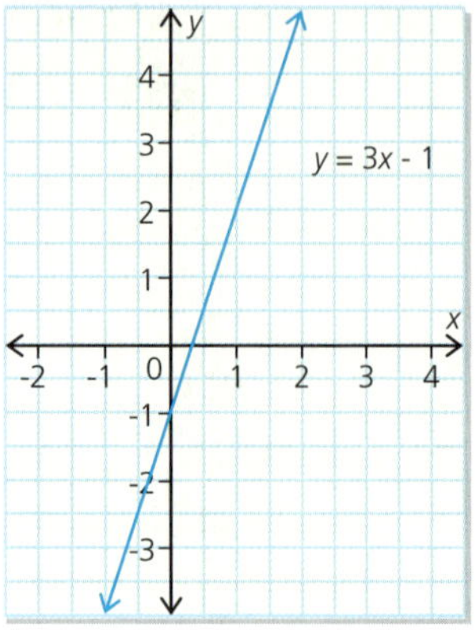

(a) What can you say about $f(x)$ if $x > 2$?

(b) For $2 < f(x) < 8$, what is the restriction on x?

Solution

(a) In the graph of $y = f(x)$, the green area represents $x > 2$. Follow the arrow up and then over to the y-axis. The yellow area represents $y > 5$ or $f(x) > 5$.

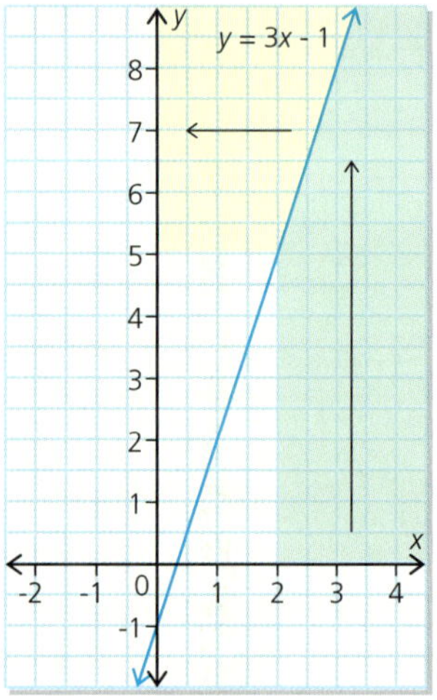

You can also find the **restriction** on y, where $y = 3x - 1$, algebraically. Start with $x > 2$.

$x > 2$	Multiply both sides by 3.
$3x > 6$	Subtract 1 from both sides.
$3x - 1 > 5$	

Then $f(x) > 5$.

(b) For $2 < f(x) < 8$, the y-coordinates must be between 2 and 8, which is represented in the graph by the yellow area. Follow the arrow right and then down to the x-axis. The green area shows that x must be between 1 and 3.

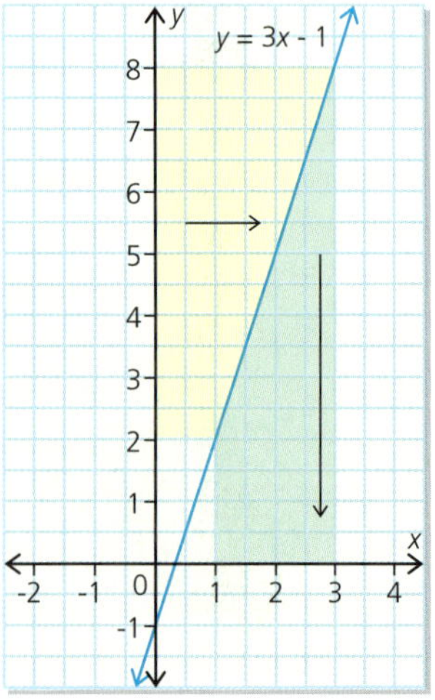

You can also find the restriction on x algebraically.

If $2 < f(x) < 8$,

then,	$2 < 3x - 1 < 8$	Add 1 to each expression.
	$3 < 3x < 9$	Divide each expression by 3.
	$1 < x < 3$	

Example 5

Find the range of the function if $-2 < x \leq 7$ and $f(x) = 3x + 1$.

Solution

$-2 < x \leq 7$	Multiply each expression by 3.
$-6 < 3x \leq 21$	Add 1 to each expression.
$-5 < 3x + 1 \leq 22$	Replace $3x + 1$ with $f(x)$.
$-5 < f(x) \leq 22$	

The range of the function is the set of all real numbers greater than -5 but less than or equal to 22. So the range is $\{y \mid -5 < y \leq 22, y \in \mathbf{R}\}$.

Focus 3.3

Key Ideas

- To solve an inequality means to find all the possible values of the variable that satisfy the inequality.
- To solve an inequality algebraically, isolate the variable by
  - adding or subtracting the same quantity from both sides
  - multiplying or dividing both sides by a positive quantity
  - multiplying or dividing both sides by a negative quantity and reverse the inequality signs

Practise, Apply, Solve 3.3

A

1. Graph each of the following on a number line.
"Or" means that if either test is satisfied, then the value belongs to the set.
"And" requires that both tests are satisfied before the value is included in the set.

(a) $\{x \mid 3 < x \leq 5, x \in \mathbf{N}\}$
(b) $\{x \mid x \geq -1, x \in \mathbf{R}\}$
(c) $\{s \mid s < -3s \in \mathbf{R}\}$
(d) $\{t \mid 1 < t < 2, t \in \mathbf{R}\}$
(e) $\{x \mid -3 \leq x < 1, x \in \mathbf{R}\}$
(f) $\{u \mid 3 \geq u \geq 1, u \in \mathbf{R}\}$
(g) $\{x \mid x < -3 \text{ or } x > 2, x \in \mathbf{R}\}$
(h) $\{x \mid x < 5 \text{ and } x \geq 2, x \in \mathbf{R}\}$
(i) $\{x \mid x^2 \leq 16, x \in \mathbf{R}\}$
(j) $\{s \mid s^2 > 9, s \in \mathbf{R}\}$

2. Describe each of the following in set notation.

(a)
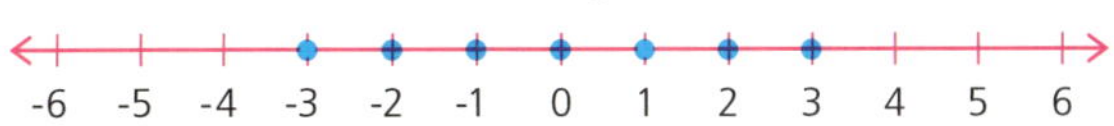

(b)
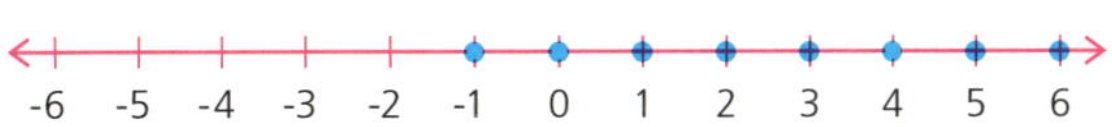

(c)
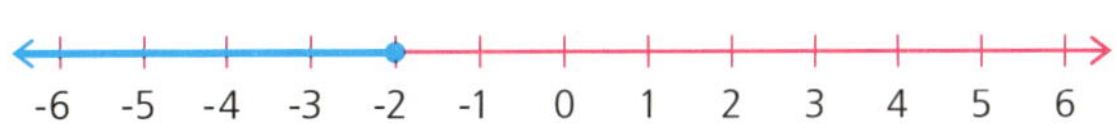

(d)
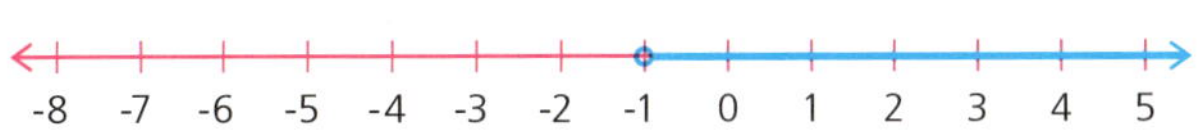

(e)

(f)
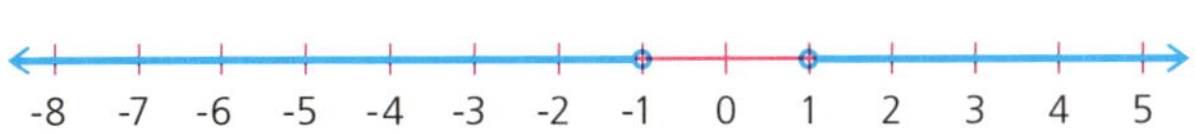

(g)

In questions 3 to 5, all variables belong to the set of real numbers.

3. Solve and graph each solution set.

(a) $3a - 2 \leq 7$

(b) $3 - 7t > 17$

(c) $5 - 2x > x - 7$

(d) $2(s + 3) - 3(s - 5) \geq 12$

(e) $10 < 5 - (2x - 1)$

(f) $x^2 > 1$

(g) $r^2 \leq 25$

(h) $t + 1 < \frac{3t - 1}{2}$

4. Solve and graph.

(a) $1 \leq x + 3 < 4$

(b) $-1 \leq \frac{x}{3} - 1 < 2$

(c) $4 < \frac{4 - 2b}{-3} < 8$

(d) $2x^2 - 7 \leq 11$

5. Solve.

(a) $\frac{5 - 4b}{3} < 5$

(b) $2 \geq 5 - \frac{2}{3}x \geq 1$

(c) $\frac{3(1 - 2x)}{4} - \frac{1}{2}x < 1$

B

6. A function is defined by $f(x) = 5 - 2x$.

(a) Graph $y = f(x)$.

(b) For $x \leq 1$, determine the range of f graphically.

(c) Verify your answer to (b) algebraically.

(d) For $5 < f(x) \leq 17$, determine the domain of f graphically.

(e) Verify your answer to (d) algebraically.

7. A function is $g(x) = 2(x - 3)^2 + 4$.

(a) Determine the range of g when $x > 4$.

(b) Determine the range of g when $0 \leq x \leq 6$.

(c) Determine the domain of g when $f(x) \leq 12$.

8. There is another way to solve Example 3(a) algebraically. Write an alternative solution.

9. Find the domain and range of f if $-2 < x < 3$ and $f(x) = x(x - 2)$.

10. The function $h(t) = -4.9t(t - 5)$ models the height, h, of a golf ball above the ground in metres, t seconds after the ball is hit. Find the domain of the function.

C

11. Each inequality is written in poor mathematical form. Rewrite each inequality correctly.

(a) $3 < x < -2$

(b) $2 < x > -3$

(c) $5 > x < 2$

12. A parabola with vertex $A(1, 2)$ must pass between $B(5, 10)$ and $C(5, 34)$. Determine the restrictions on the coefficient of x^2 in the equation of the parabola.

The Inverse Function 3.4

Part 1: Defining the Inverse Function

In grade 10, you used trigonometry to find sides and angles in triangles. For a right triangle, $\sin\theta = \frac{\text{opposite}}{\text{hypotenuse}}$. You saw that on a calculator, [SIN] can be used to find the value of this ratio for a given angle. You also saw that on a calculator, [SIN⁻¹] can be used to find which angle has the value of a given ratio. [SIN⁻¹] is the reverse of [SIN]. In other words, [SIN⁻¹] is the **inverse function** of [SIN]. In this section, you will learn about the concepts, notation, and properties of inverse functions.

Think, Do, Discuss

Skating on the Rideau Canal in Ottawa

1. The formula for converting a temperature in degrees Celsius into degrees Fahrenheit is $F = \frac{9}{5}C + 32$.
An American visitor to Canada uses this simpler rule to convert from Celsius to Fahrenheit: double the Celsius temperature, then add 30.

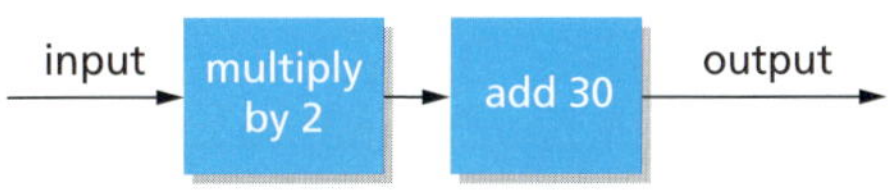

(a) Copy and complete the table using the visitor's rule.

Temperature (°C)	Temperature (°F)
10	50
15	
20	
25	
30	

(b) What is the independent variable? the dependent variable?

(c) Does this rule define a function? Explain.

(d) Let f represent the rule. What ordered pair, (0, ■), belongs to f?

(e) Let x represent the temperature in degrees Celsius. Write the equation for this rule in function notation.

(f) Graph the relation. Use the same scale of -40 to 100 on each axis.

(g) In the table, $f(10) = 50$, which corresponds to a point on the graph of $y = f(x)$. What is the x-coordinate of this point? What is its y-coordinate?

2. A Canadian visited Florida and used this rule to convert the temperature from degrees Fahrenheit into degrees Celsius. To convert 50°F into a temperature in degrees Celsius, the Canadian subtracted 30 and divided the result by 2 to get 10°C.

(a) Copy and complete the table using this rule.

Temperature (°F)	Temperature (°C)
50	10
60	
70	
80	
90	

(b) What is the independent variable? the dependent variable?

(c) This relationship is called the **inverse** of the function in step 1. The first function converts from degrees Celsius into degrees Fahrenheit. The inverse function is the "reverse" of the original function because it converts from degrees Fahrenheit into degrees Celsius. Compare the tables in steps 1(a) and 2(a). Describe how you could use a table for a relation to get a table for its inverse relation.

(d) In mathematics, f is often used to denote the original function, and f^{-1} is used to denote the **inverse** function. Notice that $(10, 50) \in f$ and $(50, 10) \in f^{-1}$. Describe how you can find an ordered pair that belongs to the inverse function if you know an ordered pair that belongs to the original function.

(e) What operations will reverse or "undo" the original rule? Write the rule that the Canadian could use to convert temperature from degrees Fahrenheit into degrees Celsius.

(f) Let x represent the temperature in degrees Fahrenheit. Write the equation for this rule in function notation.

(g) Graph the inverse relation on the same axes you drew in step 1(f).

(h) Draw the line with equation $y = x$ on the same axes. Fold your graph paper along the line $y = x$. What do you notice about the graphs of f and f^{-1}?

(i) In the table, $f^{-1}(50) = 10$, which corresponds to a point on the graph of $y = f^{-1}(x)$. What is the x-coordinate of this point? What is the y-coordinate? What is the corresponding point on the graph of $y = f(x)$?

(j) What are the coordinates of the point of intersection of the graphs of $y = f(x)$ and $y = f^{-1}(x)$? What is the significance of this point?

Part 2: Determining an Algebraic Expression for the Inverse Function

In this section, you will explore different ways of finding the equation of $f^{-1}(x)$. In many applications of functions, it is important to convert easily from input to output and from output to the original input. But solving for $f^{-1}(x)$ may be difficult or even impossible in some cases.

When you get ready for school, you probably follow these steps to put on your shoes.

→ put on your socks → pull on your shoes → tie your laces →

When you take off your shoes, you perform the *inverse* steps in the *opposite* sequence.

← take off your socks ← pull off your shoes ← untie your laces ←

Finding an inverse relation is very similar. To find an inverse relation, do the inverse operations in the opposite sequence.

In section 3.1, you found a model for the relationship between footprint length and height by using footprint length as the input and height as the output. An equation for the line of best fit is $y = 1.1x + 143.6$, where x is the footprint length in centimetres and y is the height in centimetres.

Could you use this relationship to estimate footprint length if you knew a person's height? Suppose the person is 170 cm tall.

$$170 = 1.1x + 143.6$$
$$26.4 = 1.1x$$
$$x = 24$$

A person who is 170 cm tall may have a footprint that is 24 cm long.

So you can use the length of a person's footprint to estimate the person's height. You can also reverse the process. That is, you can use a person's height to estimate the length of the person's footprint.

To get the inverse relation, reverse the operations and their order. So the independent variable (footprint length) becomes the dependent variable and the dependent variable becomes the independent variable.

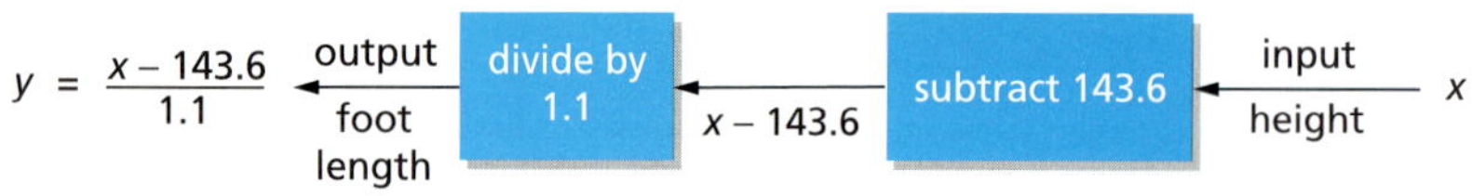

The equation for the inverse relation is $y = \frac{x - 143.6}{1.1}$.

The equations $y = 1.1x + 143.6$ and $y = \frac{x - 143.6}{1.1}$ both describe the relationship between footprint length and height, but the quantities for the independent and dependent variables have been interchanged.

You can also find the equation of the inverse relation algebraically.

First interchange the independent and dependent variable in the original relation. Then solve for y.

original relation: $y = 1.1x + 143.6$

inverse relation: $x = 1.1y + 143.6$

These equations look almost the same. Solve the inverse relation for y, the output value.

$$x = 1.1y + 143.6 \quad \text{Subtract 143.6 from both sides.}$$
$$x - 143.6 = 1.1y \quad \text{Divide both sides by 1.1.}$$
$$\frac{x - 143.6}{1.1} = y$$

The inverse relation is $f^{-1}(x) = \frac{x - 143.6}{1.1}$ and it gives footprint length as a function of height.

To find the footprint length of someone who is 170 cm tall, substitute $x = 170$ in the inverse relation.

$$\begin{aligned} f(170) &= \frac{170 - 143.6}{1.1} \\ &= \frac{26.4}{1.1} \\ &= 24 \end{aligned}$$

A person who is 170 cm tall may have a footprint that is 24 cm long.

Example 1

(a) For $f(x) = 4x - 8$, determine $f^{-1}(x)$.

(b) Find $f(2)$.

(c) Find $f^{-1}(0)$.

(d) Compare your answers for (b) and (c). Explain what you notice.

Solution

(a) Rewrite $f(x) = 4x - 8$ as $y = 4x - 8$.

To determine $f^{-1}(x)$, interchange x and y and then solve for y.

$$x = 4y - 8$$
$$x + 8 = 4y$$
$$\frac{x + 8}{4} = y$$

$\therefore f^{-1}(x) = \frac{x + 8}{4}$

(b) $f(2) = 4(2) - 8$
$= 8 - 8$
$= 0$

(c) $f^{-1}(0) = \frac{0 + 8}{4}$
$= \frac{8}{4}$
$= 2$

(d) In (b), $(2, 0) \in f$. In (c), $(0, 2) \in f^{-1}$. These points seem to correspond, and this makes sense because the x- and y-coordinates have been interchanged.

Example 2

The equation for g is $2x + 3y = 6$. Determine $g(x)$ and $g^{-1}(x)$.

Solution

To determine $g(x)$, first solve for y.

$2x + 3y = 6$	Subtract $2x$ from both sides.
$3y = 6 - 2x$	Divide both sides by 3.
$y = 2 - \frac{2}{3}x$	

$\therefore g(x) = 2 - \frac{2}{3}x$

Then find $g^{-1}(x)$.

g is defined by:	$2x + 3y = 6$	Interchange x and y.
g^{-1} is defined by:	$2y + 3x = 6$	Solve for y.
	$2y = 6 - 3x$	
	$y = 3 - \frac{3}{2}x$	

$\therefore g^{-1}(x) = 3 - \frac{3}{2}x$

Consolidate Your Understanding

1. How can you find the equation of the inverse relation if you know the equation of the relation?
2. How is finding $f^{-1}(x)$ different from finding the inverse of a relation?
3. Describe how you would find $f^{-1}(x)$ if you were given $f(x)$.

Key Ideas

- The **inverse** of a relation and a function maps each output of the original relation back onto the corresponding input value. The inverse is the "reverse" of the original relation, or function.
- f^{-1} is the name for the inverse relation.
- $f^{-1}(x)$ represents the expression for calculating the value of f^{-1}.
- If $(a, b) \in f$, then $(b, a) \in f^{-1}$.
- Given a table of values for a function, interchange the independent and dependent variables to get a table for the inverse relation. The domain of f is the range of f^{-1}. The range of f is the domain of f^{-1}.
- The graph of $y = f^{-1}(x)$ is the reflection of $y = f(x)$ in the line $y = x$.
- The graphs of $y = f(x)$ and $y = f^{-1}(x)$ intersect at points on the line $y = x$.
- $(x, f(x))$ represents any point on the graph of $y = f(x)$.
- $(x, f^{-1}(x))$ represents any point on the graph of $y = f^{-1}(x)$.
- To determine the equation of the inverse in function notation, interchange x and y and solve for y.

Example 3

The table shows all of the ordered pairs belonging to function g.

x	y
1	5
2	7
3	9
4	11
5	13

(a) Determine $g(x)$.

(b) Write the table for the inverse relation.

(c) Evaluate $g(5)$.

(d) Evaluate $g^{-1}(5)$.

(e) What are the coordinates of the point that corresponds to $g^{-1}(5)$ on the graph of g^{-1}?

(f) What are the coordinates of the point on the graph of g that corresponds to $g^{-1}(5)$?

(g) Determine $g^{-1}(x)$.

Solution

(a) The points form a line with slope 2 (each time x increases by 1, y increases by 2). Extrapolate to find that the y-intercept is 3, so the equation of the line is $y = 2x + 3$, where $x \in \{1, 2, 3, 4, 5\}$.

$\therefore g(x) = 2x + 3$, where $x \in \{1, 2, 3, 4, 5\}$

(b) The table for g^{-1} is shown. Note that the x- and y-coordinates are reversed.

x	y
5	1
7	2
9	3
11	5
13	5

(c) From the table for g, $g(5) = 13$.

(d) From the table for g^{-1}, $g^{-1}(5) = 1$.

(e) $g^{-1}(5)$ corresponds to $(5, 1)$ on the graph of g^{-1}.

(f) $g^{-1}(5)$ corresponds to $(1, 5)$ on the graph of g.

(g) For g, multiply x by 2 and then add 3. To reverse these operations, subtract 3 and then divide by 2.

$\therefore g^{-1}(x) = \frac{x-3}{2}$, where $x \in \{5, 7, 9, 11, 13\}$

Example 4

The graph of $y = f(x)$ is shown.

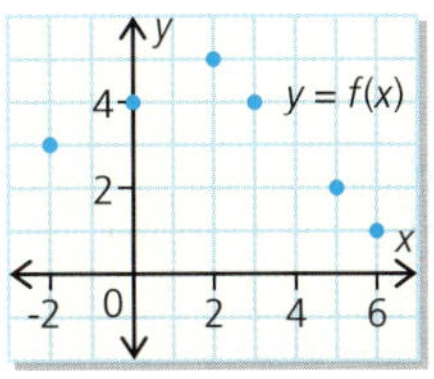

i. State the domain and range of f.

ii. Draw an arrow diagram for f^{-1}.

iii. Evaluate.
(a) $f(2)$ (b) $f(4)$ (c) $f^{-1}(1)$ (d) $f^{-1}(4)$

iv. Graph $y = f^{-1}(x)$.

v. Is f^{-1} a function? Explain.

vi. State the domain and range of f^{-1}.

Solution

i. The domain is $\{-2, 0, 2, 3, 5, 6\}$ and the range is $\{1, 2, 3, 4, 5\}$.

ii.

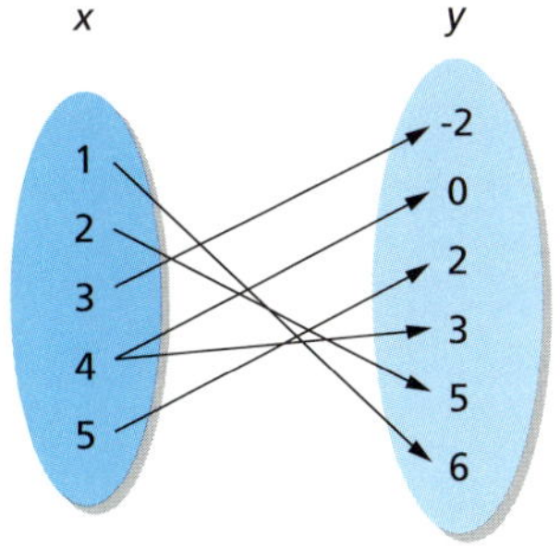

iii. (a) $f(2) = 5$, since $(2, 5)$ is on the graph

(b) $f(4)$ is undefined, because there is no point on the graph with x-coordinate 4. The value 4 is not in the domain of f.

(c) $f^{-1}(1) = 6$, because $f(6) = 1$

(d) There are two possible values of $f^{-1}(4)$ because $f(3) = 4$ and $f(0) = 4$.
$f^{-1}(4) = 3$ or $f^{-1}(4) = 0$

iv. Switch x and y in each ordered pair of f and plot these new points.

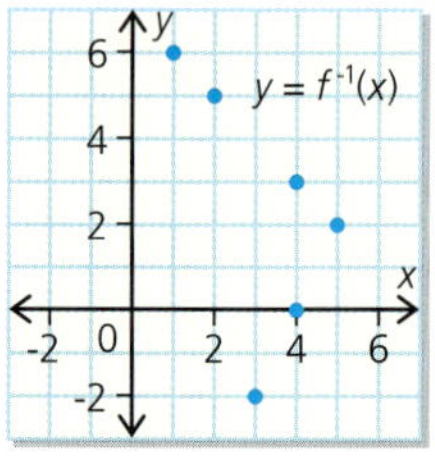

v. f is a function because each input value has a unique output value. However, the points (0, 4) and (3, 4) belong to f, so (4, 0) and (4, 3) belong to f^{-1}. f^{-1} is not a function, because one input value, 4, has two output values, 0 and 3.

vi. The domain of f^{-1} is {1, 2, 3, 4, 5} and the range is {−2, 0, 2, 3, 5, 6}.

Example 5

A relation is $h(x) = -4x + 6$, where $\{x \mid -2 \le x \le 3, x \in \mathbf{R}\}$.

(a) Sketch the graph of $y = h(x)$.

(b) Sketch the graph of $y = h^{-1}(x)$.

(c) State the domain and range of h.

(d) State the domain and range of h^{-1}.

(e) Are h and h^{-1} functions? Explain.

Solution

(a)

x	y
−2	14
−1	10
0	6
1	2
2	−2
3	−6

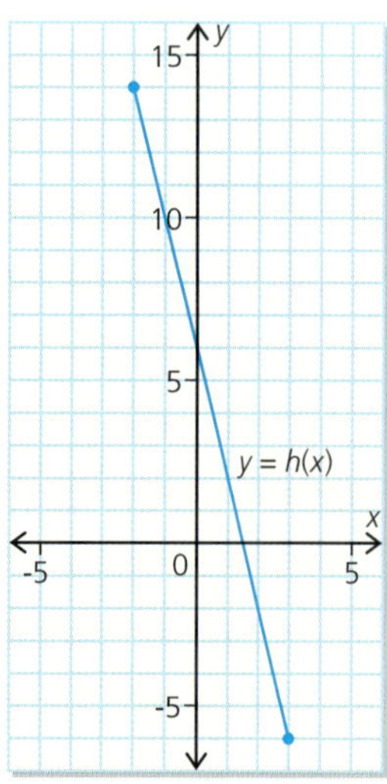

(b) Interchange x and y and plot the new points.

x	y
14	−2
10	−1
6	0
2	1
−2	2
−6	3

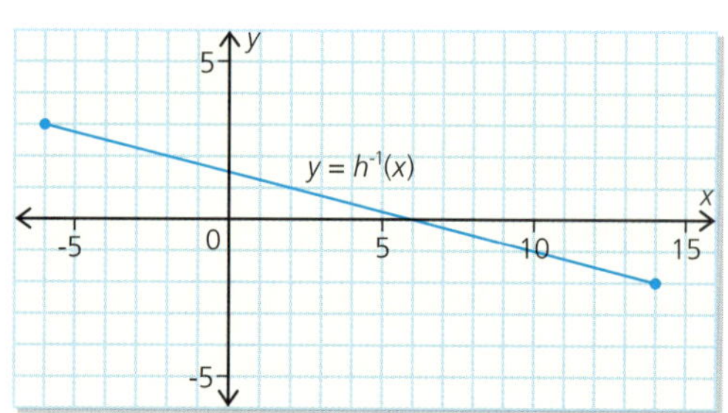

(c) The domain of h is $\{x \mid -2 \leq x \leq 3, x \in \mathbf{R}\}$.
The range of h is $\{y \mid -6 \leq y \leq 14, y \in \mathbf{R}\}$.

(d) The domain of h^{-1} is $\{x \mid -6 \leq x \leq 14, x \in \mathbf{R}\}$.
The range of h^{-1} is $\{y \mid -2 \leq y \leq 3, y \in \mathbf{R}\}$.

(e) Both h and h^{-1} are functions. Both pass the vertical line test. For each relation, each value in the domain corresponds with one unique value in the range.

Practise, Apply, Solve 3.4

A

1. For each set of ordered pairs,

i. graph the relationship and its inverse
ii. is the relationship a function? Is the inverse a function? Explain.

(a) $\{(0, 1), (1, 3), (2, 5), (3, 7)\}$

(b) $\{(0, 3), (1, 3), (2, 3), (3, 3)\}$

(c) $\{(1, 1), (1, 2), (1, 3), (1, 4)\}$

2. For each of the following,

i. draw an arrow diagram for the inverse relationship
ii. state whether or not each inverse defines a function, and justify your answer

(a)

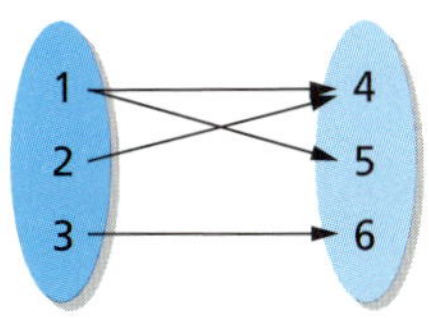

(b)

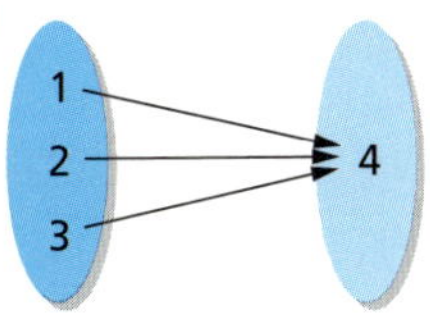

(c)

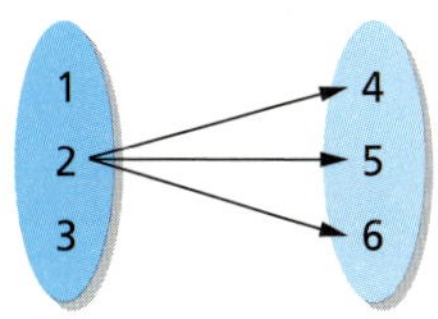

3. The graph of the function f is shown.

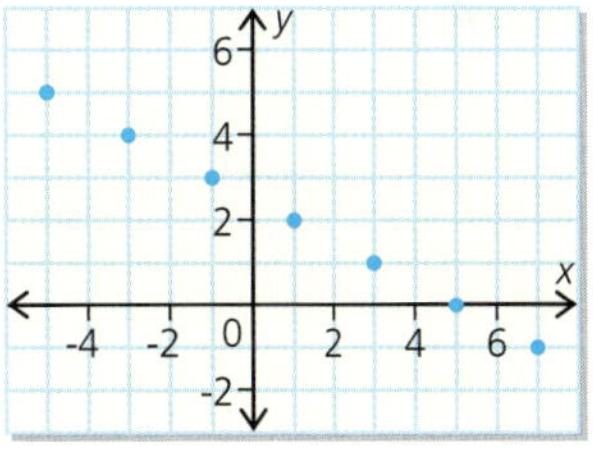

(a) Create a table of first differences for f.

(b) Create a table of first differences for f^{-1}.

(c) Graph f^{-1}.

(d) Determine the slope of the line that passes through the points belonging to f.

(e) Determine the slope of the line that passes through the points belonging to f^{-1}.

(f) Determine $f(x)$.

(g) Determine $f^{-1}(x)$.

(h) Compare your answers to (f) and (g). Explain.

4. Graph the inverse of each relation.

(a)

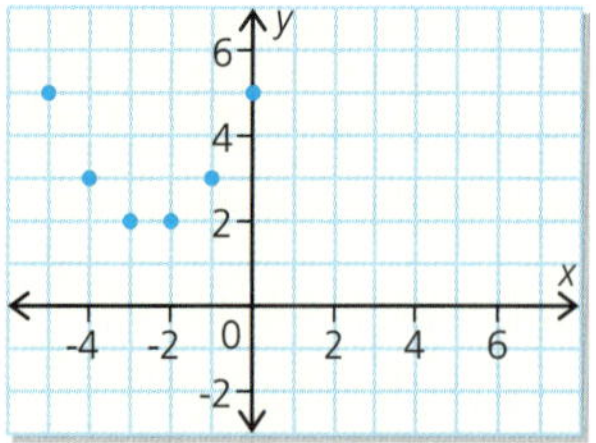

(b)

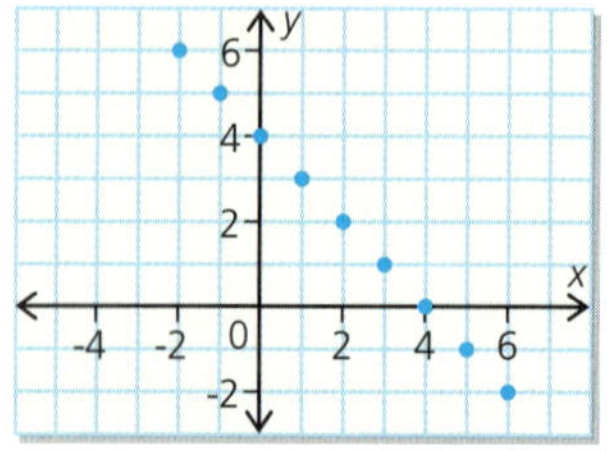

(c)

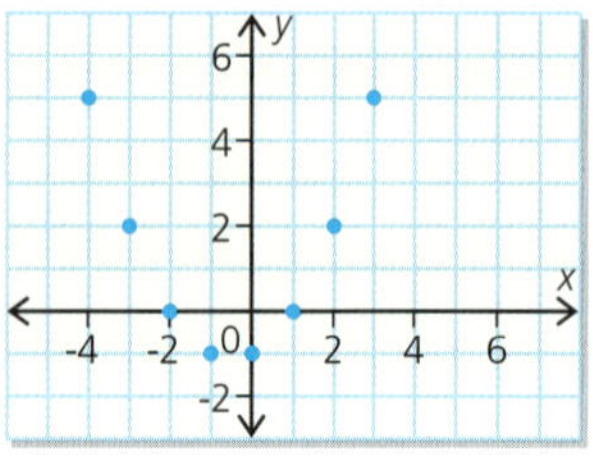

(d)

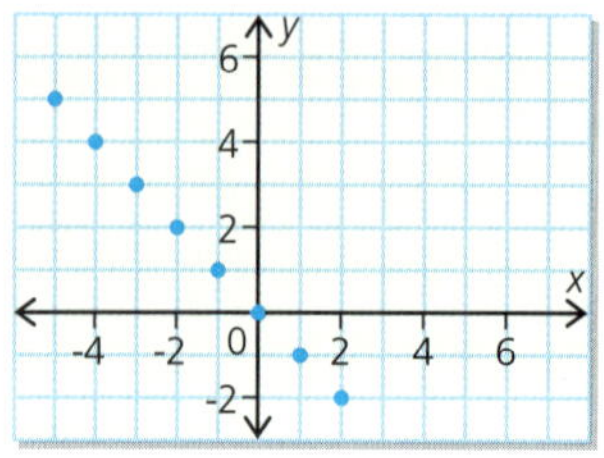

(e)

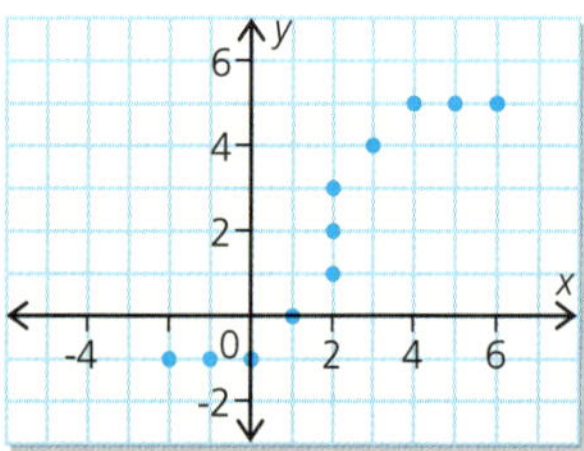

(f)

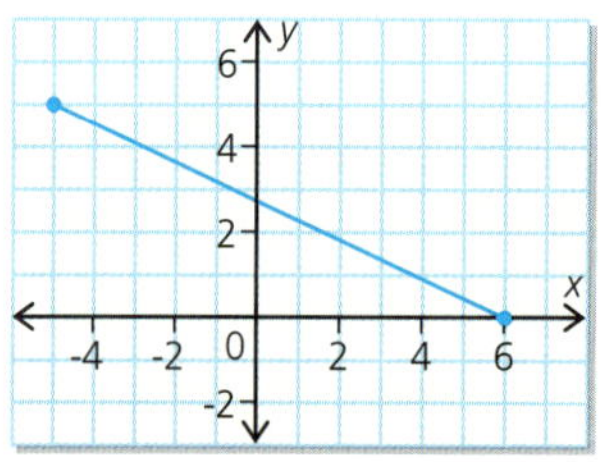

(g)

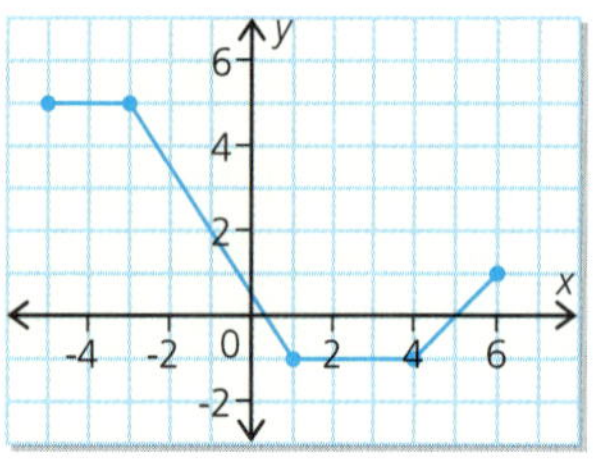

(h)

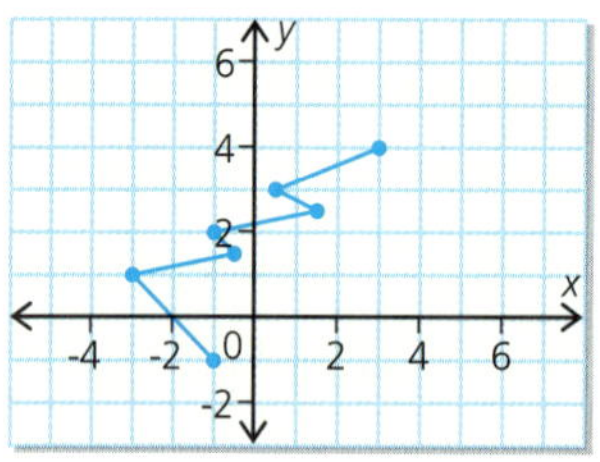

5. For each part in question 4, identify the points that are common to both the relation and its inverse. Explain.

B

6. The graph of a relation, $y = f(x)$, is shown.

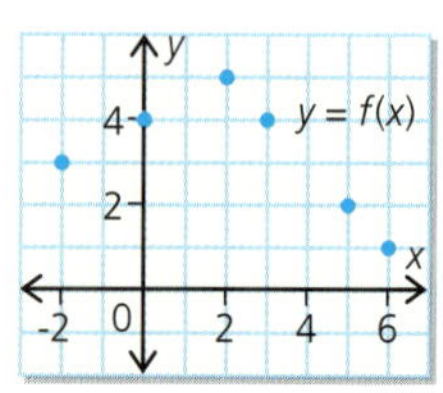

i. Graph $y = f^{-1}(x)$.

ii. State the domain and range of f^{-1}.

iii. Evaluate.

(a) $f(3)$ (b) $f^{-1}(3)$ (c) $f(2)$

(d) $f^{-1}(2)$ (e) $f^{-1}(5)$ (f) $f^{-1}(4)$

iv. Is f^{-1} a function? Explain.

v. What point on the graph of f^{-1} corresponds to $f^{-1}(1) = 6$? What coordinate does the value 1 represent at that point? What coordinate does $f^{-1}(1)$ represent?

7. For $g(t) = 3t - 2$, determine each of the following.

(a) $g(0)$
(b) $g^{-1}(-2)$
(c) $g(5)$
(d) $g^{-1}(13)$
(e) $g^{-1}(t)$
(f) $g^{-1}(0)$
(g) $g^{-1}(5)$
(h) $g^{-1}(a)$
(i) $g^{-1}(x - 2)$
(j) $g^{-1}(3a - 2)$
(k) $3g^{-1}(t)$
(l) $3g^{-1}(t) - 2$
(m) $g^{-1}(8) - g^{-1}(7)$
(n) $g^{-1}(14) - g^{-1}(13)$
(o) $g^{-1}(a + 1) - g^{-1}(a)$
(p) $\dfrac{g(13) - g(7)}{13 - 7}$
(q) $\dfrac{g^{-1}(13) - g^{-1}(7)}{13 - 7}$

8. For $f(x) = \frac{2}{3}(x - 5)$, determine each of the following.

(a) $f(-4)$
(b) $f^{-1}(-2)$
(c) $f^{-1}(6)$
(d) $f^{-1}(x)$
(e) $f(x)$
(f) $\frac{2}{3}(f^{-1}(-6) - 5)$
(g) $f^{-1}\left(\frac{8}{3}\right)$
(h) $f^{-1}(a)$
(i) $f^{-1}(a + 1)$
(j) $f^{-1}(a + 1) - f^{-1}(a)$
(k) $\dfrac{2(f^{-1}(t) - 5)}{3}$
(l) $\dfrac{f^{-1}(12) - f^{-1}(4)}{12 - 4}$
(m) $\dfrac{f(17) - f(8)}{17 - 8}$
(n) $\dfrac{f^{-1}(a) - f^{-1}(b)}{a - b}$

9. **Knowledge and Understanding:** The relation f is defined by $2x + 3y = 7$. Graph f and f^{-1}.

(a) Determine $f(x)$.
(b) Determine $f^{-1}(x)$.
(c) Solve $f(x) = 5$.
(d) $f(x) = 5$ corresponds to what point on the graph of f?
(e) $f(x) = 5$ corresponds to what point on the graph of f^{-1}?
(f) Show your answers to (d) and (e) on your graphs.
(g) Solve $f^{-1}(x) = 5$.
(h) $f^{-1}(x) = 5$ corresponds to what point on the graph of f?
(i) $f^{-1}(x) = 5$ corresponds to what point on the graph of f^{-1}?
(j) Show your answers to parts (h) and (i) on your graphs.
(k) Solve $f(x) = f^{-1}(x)$.
(l) $f(x) = f^{-1}(x)$ corresponds to what point on the graph of f?
(m) $f(x) = f^{-1}(x)$ corresponds to what point on the graph of f^{-1}?
(n) Show your answers to (l) and (m) on your graphs.

10. An American visitor to Canada uses this rule to convert from centimetres into inches, "multiply by 4 and then divide by 10." Let the function f be the method for converting centimetres to inches, according to this rule.

(a) Write f^{-1} as a rule.
(b) Describe a situation where the rule for f^{-1} might be useful.

(c) Determine $f(x)$.

(d) Determine $f^{-1}(x)$.

(e) One day, 15 cm of snow fell. Use function notation to represent this amount in inches.

(f) Kelly is about 5 feet 6 inches tall. Use function notation to represent her height in centimetres.

11. For $g(x) = -x + 5$,

(a) find $g(7)$ (b) find $g^{-1}(7)$ (c) find $g^{-1}(x)$

(d) graph g and g^{-1} on the same axes (e) explain your results

12. For $f(x) = 3 - 2x$,

i. graph $f(x)$ and its inverse on the same axes

ii. solve

(a) $f(x) = 0$ (b) $f^{-1}(x) = 0$ (c) $f(x) = x$

(d) $f^{-1}(x) = x$ (e) $f^{-1}(x) = f(x)$

iii. For each part in ii, explain what you are asked to do in terms of the graph of f and f^{-1}.

13. Communication: An electronics store pays its employees by commission. The relation $p(s) = 100 + 0.05s$ is used to find an employee's weekly pay, p, in dollars, where s represents the employee's weekly sales in dollars.

(a) Describe the function as a rule.

(b) Determine $p^{-1}(s)$.

(c) Describe the inverse function as a rule.

(d) Describe a situation where the employee might use the inverse function.

(e) State a reasonable domain and range for p^{-1}.

14. The graph shows the cost of mailing a first-class letter in Canada in 2001.

(a) Graph the inverse relation.

(b) Is the inverse relation a function? Explain.

(c) What is the mass of a letter if there is a 94¢ stamp on the letter?

Letter Mass	Mailing Cost
less than 30 g	47¢
30 g to 50 g	75¢
over 50 g but less than 100 g	94¢
over 100 g but less than 200 g	$1.55
200 g to 500 g	$2.05

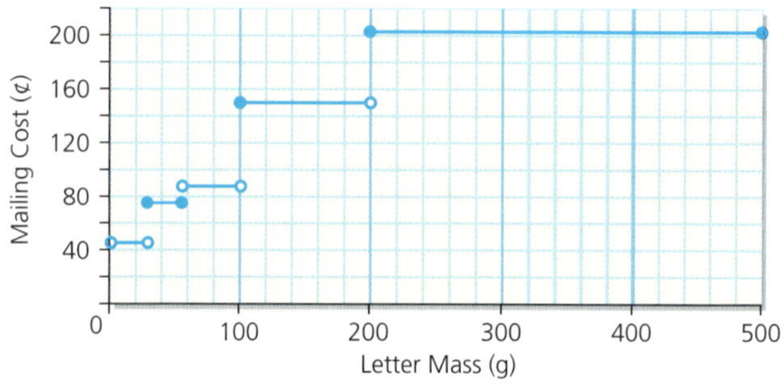

15. Ali did his homework at school with a graphing calculator. He determined that the equation of the line of best fit for some data was $y = 2.63x - 1.29$. Once he got home, he realized he had mixed up the independent and dependent variables. Write the correct equation for the relation in the form $y = mx + b$.

16. Tiffany is paid \$8.05/h, plus 5% of her sales over \$1000, for a 40-h work week. For example, suppose Tiffany sold \$1800 worth of merchandise. Then she would earn \$8.05(40) + 0.05(\$800) = \$362.

(a) Graph the relation between total pay for a 40-h work week and her sales for the work week.

(b) Write this relation in function notation.

(c) Graph the inverse relation.

(d) Write the inverse relation in function notation.

(e) Write an expression using function notation that represents her sales if she earned \$420 one work week. Then evaluate.

17. **Thinking, Inquiry, Problem Solving:** The manager of the meat department at a grocery store noted that sales of ground beef depended on the price. The table records a range of prices and the corresponding sales.

Price per Kilogram (\$)	4.39	4.07	4.65	4.59	3.94
Mass Sold (kg)	1000	2500	700	800	2700

(a) Draw a scatter plot for the relation on your graphing calculator.

(b) Determine an equation of the line of best fit for this relation and write the relation in function notation.

(c) Create a scatter plot for the inverse relation.

(d) Determine the equation of the line of best fit for the inverse relation using technology. Write the inverse relation in function notation.

(e) Determine an equation of a linear model for the inverse relationship using your answer from (b).

(f) Graph the equations that you wrote for (d) and (e) on the same axes. Compare and contrast the graphs. Explain what you notice.

(g) Use a linear model to estimate how much beef will be sold if the price is \$4.75/kg.

(h) Use a linear model to estimate how much beef will be sold if the price is \$5.00/kg. Explain.

(i) Use a linear model to estimate the price the manager should charge if he hopes to sell 4000 kg of beef in one week.

18. A Canadian address can be converted into a six-character postal code, such as N2V 3C2.

(a) Why must this conversion be a function?

(b) Explain why the inverse is not a function.

19. In section 3.2, a binary number was converted into a decimal number. Design a process for the inverse relation, that is, converting a decimal number into a binary number.

20. Application: For security, a credit card number is coded in the following way, so that it can be sent as a message. "Subtract each digit from 9."
    (a) Code the credit card number 4332 178 256.
    (b) A coded credit card number is 207 456 127. What is the original credit card number?
    (c) Find $f(x)$ if x represents a single input digit.
    (d) Find $f^{-1}(x)$.
    (e) Graph the functions $y = f(x)$ and $y = f^{-1}(x)$ on the same axes.

21. To code words as numbers, Watson used this rule:
    A is 1, B is 2, C is 3, ... , Z is 26, and a blank is 0. For example, "HI" becomes "89" and "A BALL" becomes "10211212."
    (a) Code the word "BOY" using this rule.
    (b) Explain why this relation is a function.
    (c) Decode "21520201513."
    (d) Why is this rule not a good way to encode words?

22. Check Your Understanding: In section 3.2, the soft-drink vending machine was an example of a function.
    (a) What is the independent variable for the inverse relation?
    (b) What is the dependent variable for the inverse relation?
    (c) What is the domain of the inverse relation?
    (d) What is the range of the inverse relation?
    (e) Is the inverse relation a function? Explain.

The Chapter Problem—Cryptography

In this section, you worked with the inverse function. Apply what you learned to answer these questions about the Chapter Problem on page 218.

CP5. Graph the coding function.
CP6. How does this graph show that the relation is a function?
CP7. Is the inverse relation a function? Why must the inverse relation be a function for any encryption method?
CP8. Graph the inverse relation on the same axes in a different colour.
CP9. Use the graph of the inverse relation to decode the message.
CP10. What features of this coding technique make it easy to decode?

TI-83 Plus Calculator: Graphing Functions and Inverse Functions

In section 3.4, you examined a rule for converting a temperature in degrees Celsius into degrees Fahrenheit. The rule is, "double the temperature in degrees Celsius, and then add 30." The following table shows some approximate temperatures.

Temperature (°C)	Temperature (°F)
10	50
15	60
20	70
25	80
30	90

Method 1: Using Lists, Stat Plots, and the Equation Editor

1. (a) Graph the data in the table as a scatter plot. On the TI-83 Plus calculator, enter the data into lists and create a scatter plot, **Plot1**. Use the window settings shown in the screen.

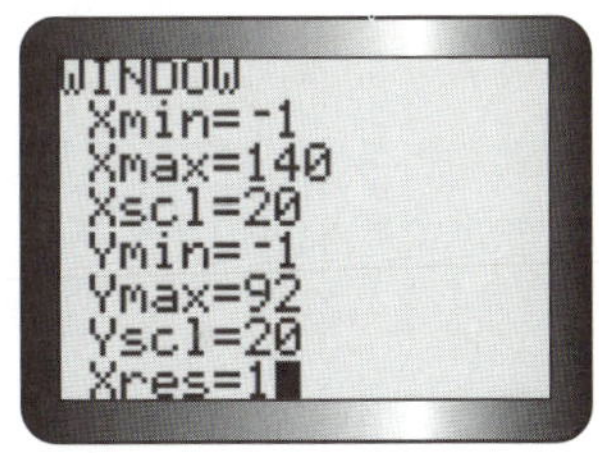

step 1a

(b) The function includes all possible temperatures, so the graph should be a line. The rule is, "multiply x by 2, and then add 30 to get y," so the equation for the function is $y = 2x + 30$. Enter the function into **Y1** and graph. The line should pass through all of the points in the scatter plot.

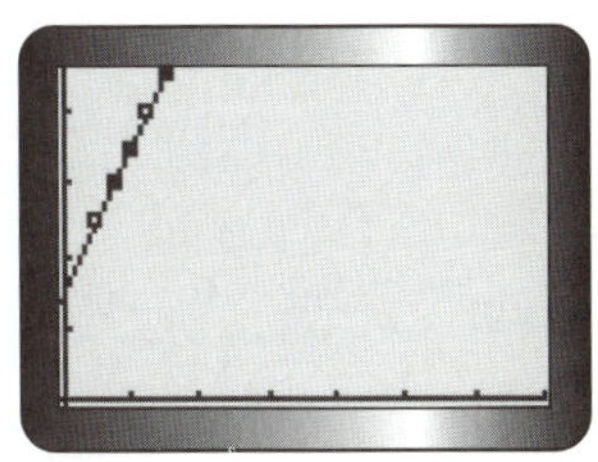

step 1b

(c) Plot the inverse by switching the lists. Create a second scatter plot. Turn on **Plot2** and use the settings shown in the screen. Display the graph by pressing [GRAPH].

step 1c

(d) Find the inverse function by interchanging x and y and solving for y.

$$x = 2y + 30$$
$$x - 30 = 2y$$
$$\frac{x - 30}{2} = y$$

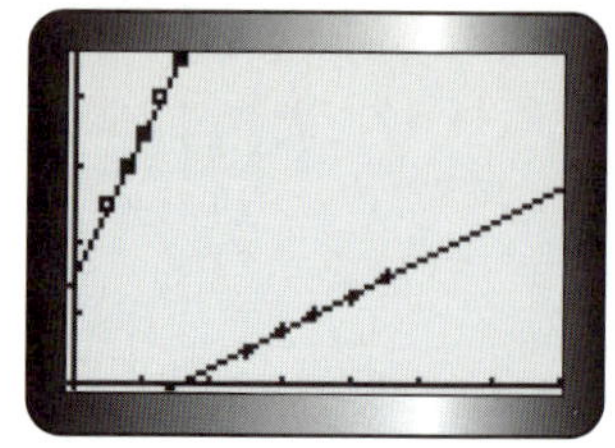

step 1d

Enter this function in **Y2** and graph. The line should pass through all of the new points plotted.

(e) Enter $y = x$ into **Y3** and graph. Describe the relationship between the three lines.

Method 2: Using Parametric Equations

Sometimes is is difficult to determine the defining equation of the inverse. Sometimes graphing in function mode will not directly produce the graph of the inverse function. **Parametric equations** allow you to graph any function and its inverse.

For example, graph the function $y = 2x + 30$ for $x \in \{10, 15, 20, 25, 30\}$.
For a parametric equation, both x and y must be expressed in terms of a parameter, T.
Replace x with T. Then $x = T$ and $y = 2T + 30$.
Next, set restrictions on T so that it will take the values 10, 15, 20, 25, and 30.

1. (a) First clear the calculator. Press [MODE]. Change the settings so that your screen matches the one shown.

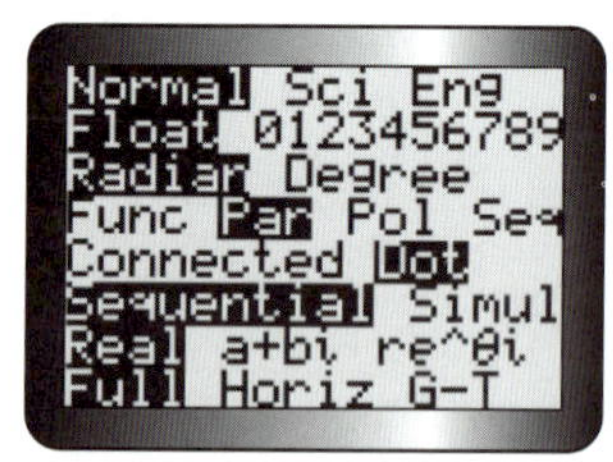

step 1a

(b) Press [WINDOW]. Enter the values shown for **Tmin**, **Tmax**, **Tstep**, and **Xmax**. The remaining window settings are the same as in method 1.

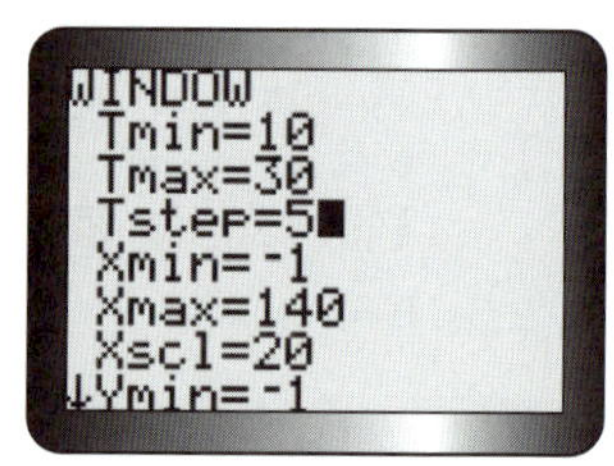

step 1b

(c) Press [Y=]. Enter T into X_{1T} by pressing [X,T,Θ,n].
Enter [2] [X,T,Θ,n] [+] [3] [0] into Y_{1T}. Press [GRAPH].

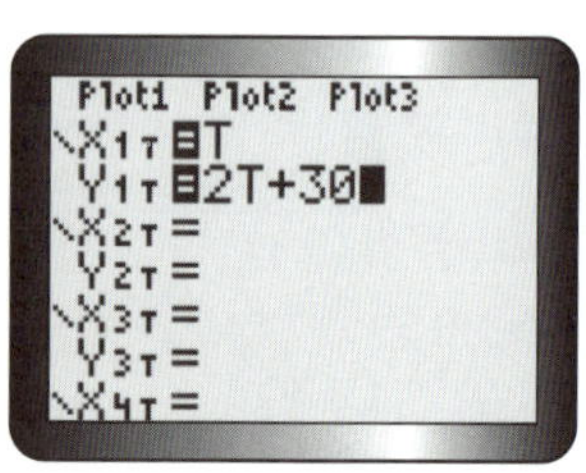

step 1c (a)

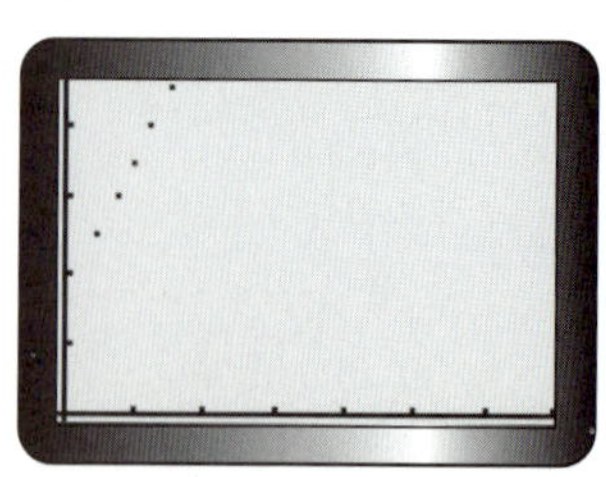

step 1c (b)

(d) What is the domain of the graphed function? What is its range?

(e) Use TRACE to verify that the points are correct.

(f) To graph the inverse relation, reverse the expressions in X_{1T} and Y_{1T}. Enter "$2T + 30$" into $\mathbf{X_{2T}}$ and "T" into $\mathbf{Y_{2T}}$. Press GRAPH.

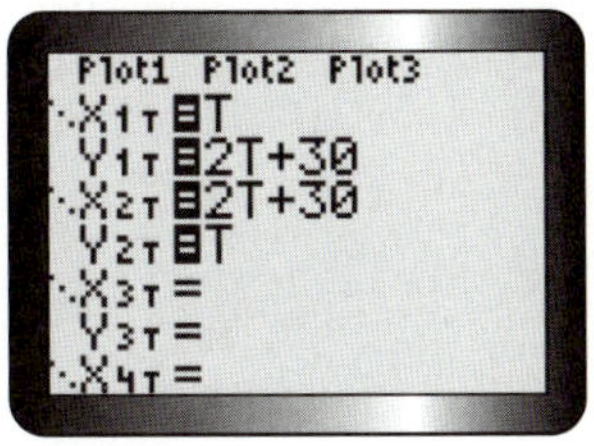

step 1f (a)

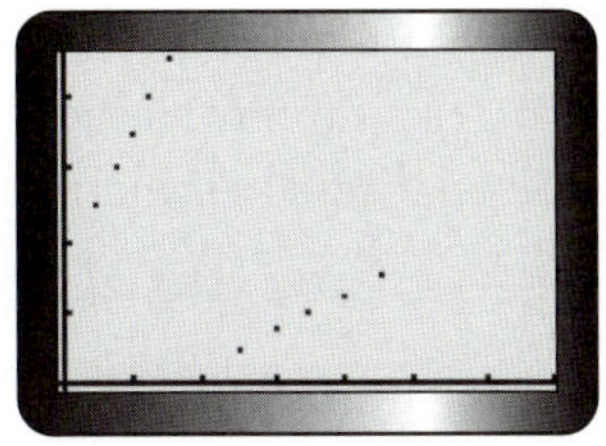

step 1f (b)

(g) What is the domain of the inverse function? What is its range?

(h) To graph more values, change the window. Set **Tmin=−1**, **Tmax=140**, and **Tstep=.5**. Graph.

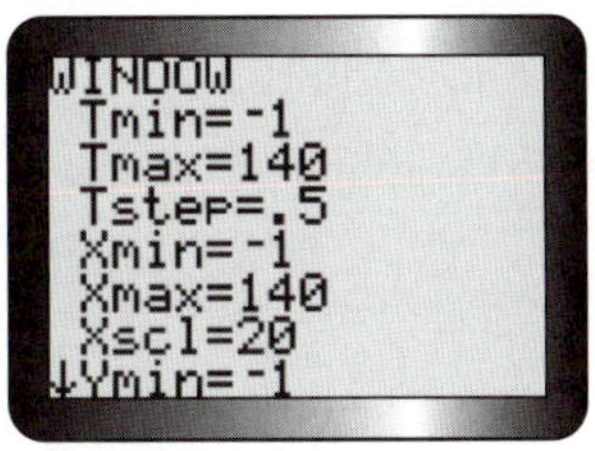

step 1h (a)

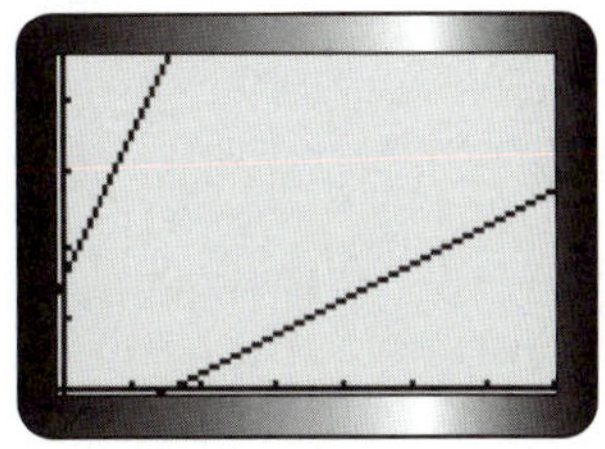

step 1h (b)

(i) Now graph the line $y = x$. Since x and y are equal, set X_{3T}=T and Y_{3T}=T.

(j) Describe the relation between the three lines on your screen.

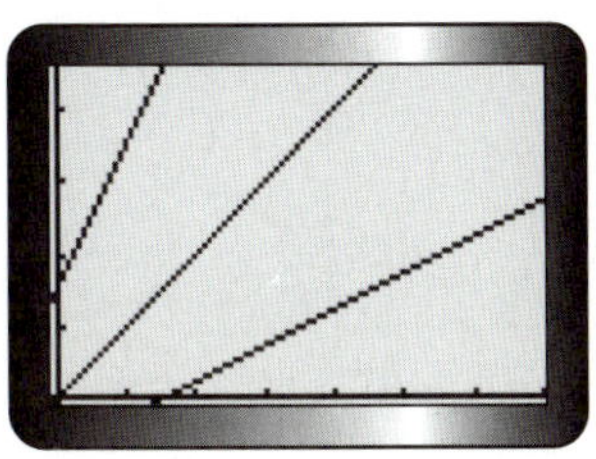

step 1j

2. (a) To graph $f(x) = 3(x - 1)^2 - 2$, clear the equations from the equation editor and set X_{1T} =T and Y_{1T}=3(T−1)^2 − 2.
Change the window to display both T-values and x-values from −2.4 to 7, **Tstep** to 0.1, and y-values from −2.2 to 4.
Change the plotting mode from **Dot** back to **Connected**.

(b) Use TRACE to determine the domain and range of f.

(c) Graph the inverse on the same axes.

(d) Use TRACE to determine the domain and range of the inverse.

(e) Use TRACE to determine the coordinates of the vertex of each parabola.

(f) f is a function, but f^{-1} is not. Explain.

TECHNOLOGY

Practice 3.5

1. For each function,

i. graph the function and its inverse using parametric equations in an appropriate window

ii. state the domain and range of the function

iii. state the domain and range of the inverse relation

iv. state whether the inverse relation is a function. Explain.

(a) $f(x) = -2(x + 1)^2 + 3$

(b) $g(x) = \sqrt{x}$

(c) $f(x) = \sqrt{x - 2}$

(d) $y = x^3$

(e) $g(x) = \frac{1}{x}$

(f) $f(x) = \frac{1}{3 - x}$

(g) $y = \frac{1}{\sqrt{x - 2}}$

(h) $f(x) = \sqrt{9 - (x - 2)^2}$

(i) $g(x) = \sin(3x)$

(j) $f(x) = 1 + \cos(3x)$

2. **i.** To graph $f(x) = 3(x - 1)^2 - 2$ for $-0.3 \le x \le 2$,

- enter the parametric equations and settings as in step 2 in method 2
- use **Tmin=−0.3** and **Tmax=2** to draw that section of the graph

ii. Graph the inverse.

iii. State the domain and range of f and f^{-1}.

iv. Graph each function and repeat ii and iii.

(a) $f(x) = \frac{1}{3 - x}, -1 \le x \le 2$

(b) $g(x) = \sqrt{9 - (x - 2)^2}, -1 \le x \le 2$

(c) $y = 2x + 0.5 \sin(10x), 0.4 \le x \le 2.3$

(d) $f(x) = -1.2x \sin(x - 0.2), 0 \le x \le 5$

Investigating Properties of Inverse Functions

3.6

In this section, you will explore the properties of certain inverse functions.

Part 1: Investigating the Relationships Between $y = \sqrt{x}$ and $y = x^2$

The teacher asked Tom, "What is the inverse of $y = x^2$?" He replied, "$y = \sqrt{x}$." Tom explained that the opposite of squaring a value is the taking of the value's square root. His explanation was correct, but the conclusion, $y = \sqrt{x}$, was not. The input/output diagrams for each function are shown.

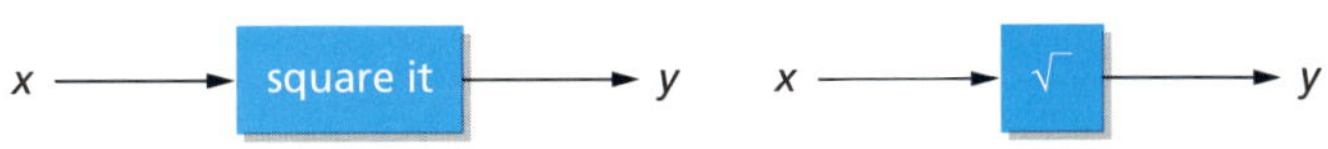

These input/output diagrams verify Tom's answer.

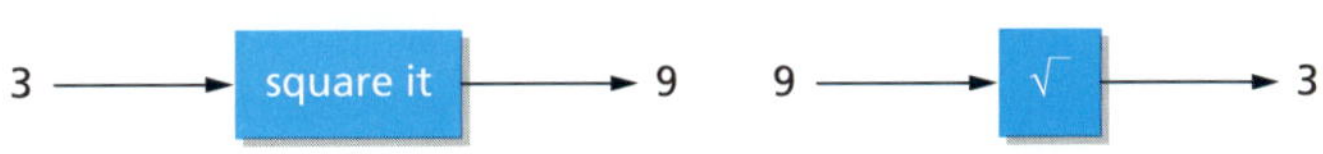

But these input/output diagrams suggest that Tom's answer is incorrect.

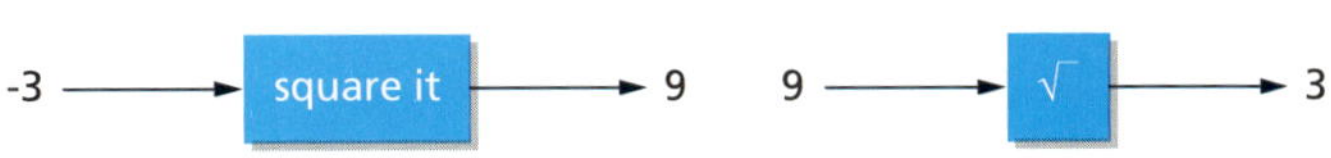

Since point $(-3, 9)$ belongs to the function, then $(9, -3)$ should belong to its inverse. But this point does not satisfy $y = \sqrt{x}$, so this relation cannot be the inverse of $y = x^2$. To get the output of -3, you could use the equation $y = -\sqrt{x}$.

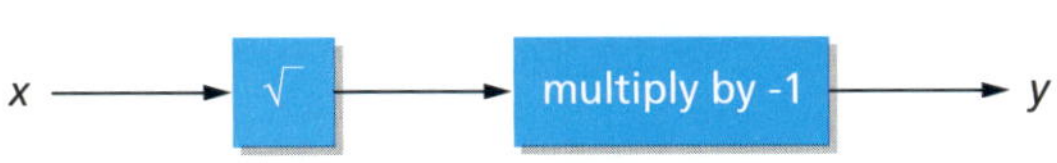

Then, with an input of 9, the output is $-(3)$ or -3.

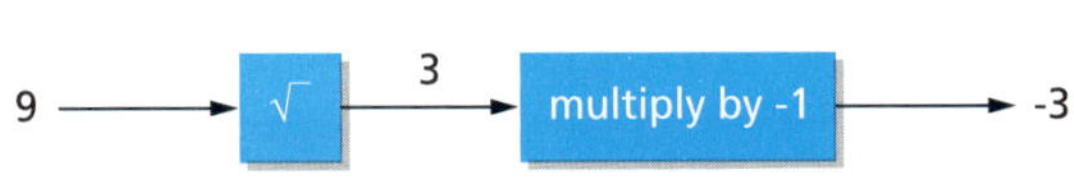

The inverse of $y = x^2$ must include $y = \sqrt{x}$ and $y = -\sqrt{x}$.

Think, Do, Discuss

1. (a) Copy and complete the tables. List the coordinates of points that belong to $y = \sqrt{x}$ in the left table. Use values for x that include 0. List the corresponding points, with the coordinates reversed, for $y = x^2$ in the right table.

x	$y = \sqrt{x}$

x	$y = x^2$

(b) Graph $y = \sqrt{x}$ and its inverse using the same colour. Use the same scale for each axis, if possible.

2. (a) Copy and complete the tables. List the coordinates of points that belong to $y = -\sqrt{x}$ in the left table. Use values for x that include 0. List the corresponding points, with the coordinates reversed, for $y = x^2$ in the right table.

x	$y = -\sqrt{x}$

x	$y = x^2$

(b) Graph $y = -\sqrt{x}$ and its inverse using the same colour on the same axes as in step 1(b).

3. Graph $y = x$ on the same axes using a different colour. Your graph should look like this one.

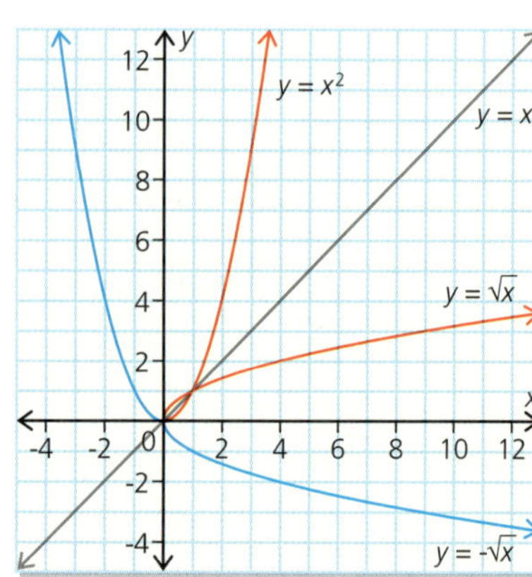

The red part of $y = x^2$ is called the **right branch** of the parabola, while the blue section is the **left branch**.

4. Fold the graph paper along the line $y = x$, and hold the paper up to the light.

(a) Which part of the graph is the inverse of $y = \sqrt{x}$? Explain.

(b) Which part of the graph is the inverse of $y = -\sqrt{x}$? Explain.

(c) Which part of the graph is the inverse of $y = x^2$? Explain.

5. State the domain and range of each function. Explain your findings.

(a) $y = x^2$ (b) $y = \sqrt{x}$ (c) $y = -\sqrt{x}$

6. (a) Does $y = x^2$ define a function? Explain.

(b) Does $y = \sqrt{x}$ define a function? Explain.

(c) Does $y = -\sqrt{x}$ define a function? Explain.

(d) Is the inverse of $y = x^2$ a function? Explain.

(e) Is the inverse of $y = \sqrt{x}$ a function? Explain.

(f) Is the inverse of $y = -\sqrt{x}$ a function? Explain.

7. (a) What restriction could you place on the domain of $y = x^2$ so that its inverse is $y = \sqrt{x}$?

(b) What restriction could you place on the domain of $y = x^2$ so that its inverse is $y = -\sqrt{x}$?

(c) What is the equation of the inverse of $y = x^2$?

(d) What restriction could you place on the range of the inverse of $y = x^2$ so that it would be a function, without changing its domain? Explain.

(e) Is there another restriction that you could place on the range of the inverse of $y = x^2$ so that it would be a function, without changing its domain? Explain.

Part 2: Restricting the Domain of a Quadratic Function So That the Inverse Is a Function

Think, Do, Discuss

1. (a) Set your calculator to degree mode. Then evaluate each of the following.

i. sin 30° **ii.** sin 150° **iii.** sin 390° **iv.** sin 510°

(b) For $f(x) = \sin(x)$, all of the ordered pairs (30°, ■), (150°, ■), (390°, ■), and (510°, ■) belong to f.

(c) Use your answers from (a) to list ordered pairs that belong to f^{-1}.

(d) What is the value of $f^{-1}(0.5)$?

(e) f^{-1} should be the inverse of sine. Use your calculator to evaluate $\sin^{-1}(0.5)$.

(f) Explain what the calculator has calculated.

2. (a) Sketch any parabola that has vertex (3, 1) and opens up.

(b) Sketch its inverse.

(c) How much of the graph of the inverse would you have to erase so that it would pass the vertical line test?

(d) Redraw the graph of the inverse so that it passes the vertical line test. What is the range of the inverse?

Stating this inequality places a restriction on the inverse relation to ensure it is a function.

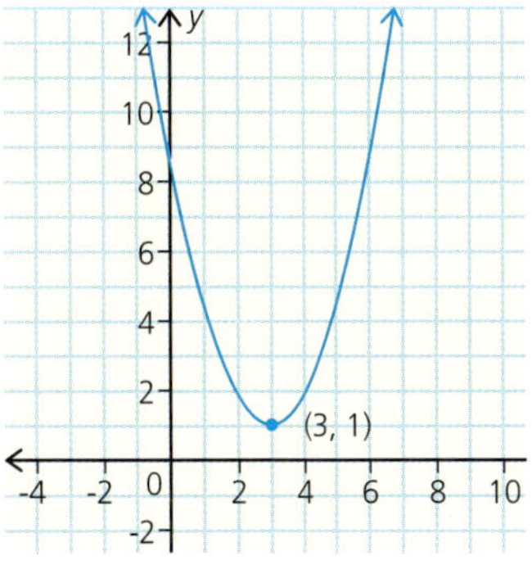

(e) How would you rewrite the domain of the original function so that its inverse passes the vertical line test?

Stating the new domain with a restriction on the original function guarantees that the inverse is a function.

(f) State the new domain and range of the function and its inverse.

(g) Why does the vertex help you to see an appropriate restriction?

(h) What other restriction could you place on the domain of the parabola?

3. For $y = 3(x + 1)^2 + 4$,

(a) state the coordinates of the vertex of this parabola

(b) describe its location and direction of the opening

(c) what restriction could you place on the domain of the function to ensure that the inverse is also a function?

4. (a) What values of y satisfy $y^2 = 16$?

(b) Solve $y^2 = 7$.

(c) Solve $y^2 = x$ for y.

(d) The equation of the inverse of $f(x) = x^2$ is $x = y^2$. Determine f^{-1}. Why is the inverse not a function?

(e) What restriction could you place on the domain of f so that the inverse is a function? In this case, what is f^{-1}?

5. (a) Solve $y^2 = 25$.

(b) Solve $(y + 1)^2 = 25$.

(c) Solve $2(y + 1)^2 = 50$.

(d) Solve $2(y + 1)^2 - 3 = 47$.

(e) Solve $2(y + 1)^2 - 3 = x$ for y.

(f) Determine f^{-1} if $f(x) = 2(x + 1)^2 - 3$.

6. (a) Solve $\sqrt{y} = 3$.

(b) Why does $\sqrt{y} = -3$ have no solution?

(c) What must be true about x if $\sqrt{y} = x$?

(d) Solve for y if $\sqrt{y} = x$.

(e) The inverse of $y = \sqrt{x}$ is $x = \sqrt{y}$. Solve for y.

Focus 3.6

Key Ideas

- The graphs of $y = x^2$, $y = \sqrt{x}$, and $y = -\sqrt{x}$ are shown.

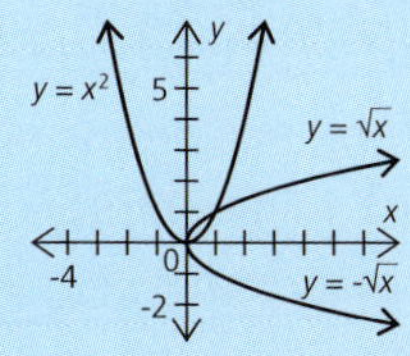

  - The domain of $y = x^2$ is **R** and its range is $\{y \mid y \geq 0, y \in \mathbf{R}\}$.
  - The domain of $y = \sqrt{x}$ is $\{x \mid x \geq 0, x \in \mathbf{R}\}$ and its range is $\{y \mid y \geq 0, y \in \mathbf{R}\}$.
  - The domain of $y = -\sqrt{x}$ is $\{x \mid x \geq 0, x \in \mathbf{R}\}$ and its range is $\{y \mid y \leq 0, y \in \mathbf{R}\}$.
  - $y = x^2$ defines a function, but its inverse does not.
  - The inverse of $y = x^2$ is $y = \pm\sqrt{x}$.
  - Both $y = \sqrt{x}$ and $y = -\sqrt{x}$ define functions.
  - The graph of $y = x^2$ reflected in the line $y = x$ produces the graph of $y = \pm\sqrt{x}$.
- Taking the square root of both sides of $y = x^2$ yields a positive square root and a negative square root. Both of these roots are part of the solution. Each square root often describes one branch of a parabola.
- Note the restrictions on the domain and the range of the original function, which may not be given.
- To ensure that the inverse of a function is also a function, you may have to restrict the domain or the range of the original function.
- The vertex of a parabola points to the beginning of a domain or a range. Note the vertex and the direction of opening when you write the restrictions on a domain or range.
- To determine the vertex of a parabola, complete the square.

Example 1

(a) What is $f^{-1}(x)$ if $f(x) = \sqrt{x}$?

(b) Graph f and f^{-1}.

(c) Where do f and f^{-1} intersect?

Solution

(a) The domain and range of $f(x) = \sqrt{x}$ are restricted to real numbers greater or equal to 0, so the inverse must also have the same restriction. Therefore, $f^{-1}(x) = x^2, x \geq 0$.

Notice that the parabola has only one branch, because the domain is restricted. The parabola would have both branches if x could be any real number.

(b) Using parametric equations, let $X_{1T} = T$ and $Y_{1T} = \sqrt{T}$ to get the graph of f. To get the graph of f^{-1}, let $X_{2T} = \sqrt{T}$ and $Y_{2T} = T$, with no restriction on the parameter. You can write the inverse as $f^{-1}(x) = x^2, x \geq 0$. So let $X_{2T} = T$ and $Y_{2T} = T^2$, but restrict T so that it is greater than or equal to 0. Set **Tmin=0** to restrict T.

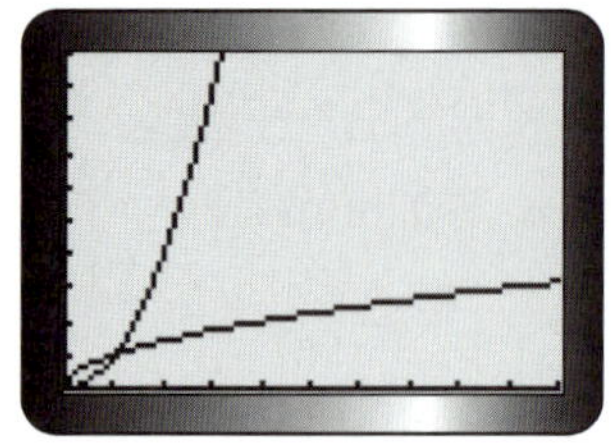

Without using parametric equations, graph f by first entering "$\sqrt{x}$" into **Y1** and graph f^{-1} by first entering "$x^2(x \geq 0)$" into **Y2**. Get ≥ by pressing [2nd] [MATH] and selecting **4:≥** from the TEST menu.

(c) In the graph, f and f^{-1} intersect at (1, 1) and at (0, 0). Notice that both points are on the line $y = x$.

Example 2

For $f(x) = (x - 1)^2 - 2$,

(a) graph f and f^{-1}

(b) state the domain and range of f

(c) state the domain and range of f^{-1}

(d) find the equation of f^{-1}

(e) are f and f^{-1} both functions? Explain.

Solution

(a) The vertex of f is $(1, -2)$. For $x = 3$ or $x = -1$, $y = 2$, so two other points on the parabola are (3, 2) and $(-1, 2)$. Sketch f using these points. The vertex of f^{-1} is $(-2, 1)$ and two other points on the parabola are (2, 3) and $(2, -1)$. Use these points to sketch f^{-1}.

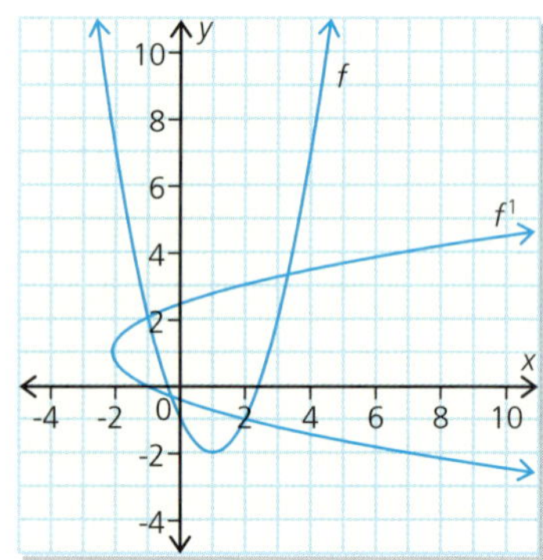

You can also use *Zap-a-Graph* to graph the parabola $y = (x - 1)^2 - 2$. Select **Reflect in y = x** under the **Transform** menu to get the graph of the inverse.

Another option is to use parametric equations on a graphing calculator to graph both relations.

(b) Since the vertex is $(1, -2)$, the domain of f is **R**, and its range is $\{y \mid y \geq -2, y \in \mathbf{R}\}$.

(c) Interchange the variables to get the inverse. The domain of f^{-1} is $\{x \mid x \geq -2, x \in \mathbf{R}\}$ and its range is **R**.

(d) The equation for the original function is $y = (x - 1)^2 - 2$. To find the equation of f^{-1}, interchange x and y and solve for y.

$$x = (y - 1)^2 - 2$$
$$x + 2 = (y - 1)^2$$
$$\pm\sqrt{x + 2} = y - 1$$
$$\pm\sqrt{x + 2} + 1 = y$$

$\therefore f^{-1}$ is defined by $y = \pm\sqrt{x + 2} + 1$

(e) f is a function because every value of x produces a unique value for y. However, f^{-1} is not a function because it fails the vertical line test for every value of $x > -2$.

Example 3

For $g(x) = \sqrt{2 - x}$,

(a) graph g and g^{-1}

(b) determine the domain and range of g

(c) state the domain and range of g^{-1}

(d) find $g^{-1}(x)$

Solution

(a) Use technology or graph by hand.

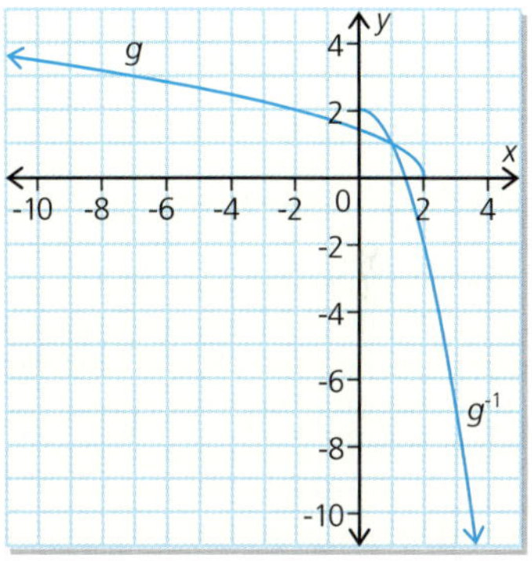

(b) You can get the domain and range of g from the graph, but you can also determine them as follows:
$\sqrt{2 - x}$ must be a real number, so x must be less than 2.
$\sqrt{2 - x}$ cannot be a negative number, but it can be any other real number. The domain of g is $\{x \mid x \le 2, x \in \mathbf{R}\}$ and its range is $\{y \mid y \ge 0, y \in \mathbf{R}\}$.

(c) Interchange the variables to get the inverse. Then the domain of g^{-1} is $\{x \mid x \ge 0, x \in \mathbf{R}\}$ and its range is $\{y \mid y \le 2, y \in \mathbf{R}\}$.

(d) g^{-1} is the right branch of a parabola that has vertex (0, 2) and opens down. The equation of g^{-1} is $y = -x^2 + 2$, but x must be greater than or equal to 0. The restriction yields only the right branch of the parabola. Therefore, $g^{-1}(x) = -x^2 + 2, x \ge 0$.

Example 4

Dean was asked to find the inverse of $f(x) = 3(x - 1)^2 - 2$, and he wrote $y = \sqrt{\frac{x + 2}{3}} + 1$.

(a) Use graphs to help explain Dean's answer. Is the answer correct?

(b) What other function should you graph to complete the graph of f^{-1}?

(c) Is f^{-1} a function? Explain.

(d) What is the correct equation for f^{-1}?

(e) Determine a restriction on the range of the inverse to ensure that f^{-1} is also a function. Do not change the domain.

Solution

(a) Using a TI-83 Plus calculator, press MODE and make sure that the graphing mode is **Func**.

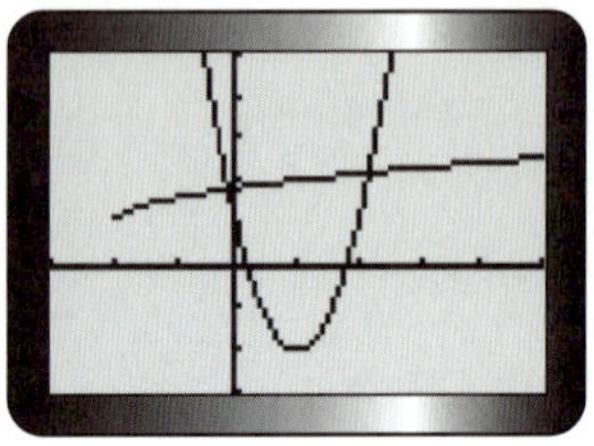

To graph $f(x) = 3(x - 1)^2 - 2$ and $f^{-1}(x) = \sqrt{\frac{x+2}{3}} + 1$, enter the equations into **Y1** and **Y2**, respectively, in the equation editor. The graph of f is a parabola, but Dean's answer for f^{-1} represents only one branch of a parabola. This relation is not the inverse of f.

(b) Once $y = -\sqrt{\frac{x+2}{3}} + 1$ is graphed, then the graph of the inverse is complete.

(c) $y = \pm\sqrt{\frac{x+2}{3}} + 1$ is not a function, even though it is the inverse of $f(x) = 3(x - 1)^2 - 2$. Dean's answer is a function because the relation passes the vertical line test.

(d) The correct equation for the inverse is $y = \pm\sqrt{\frac{x+2}{3}} + 1$. The graph of this function includes both branches of the parabola.

(e) For the inverse, only one branch of the parabola can be a function. Then $y \geq 1$, or $y \leq 1$. The domain of the inverse is $\{x \mid x \geq -2, x \in \mathbf{R}\}$. To make the inverse a function, without changing the domain, simply choose one of the branches of the parabola. For $y \geq 1$, the domain is still $\{x \mid x \geq -2, x \in \mathbf{R}\}$. The range is $\{y \mid y \geq 1, y \in \mathbf{R}\}$, and f^{-1} is a function.

Example 5

For $f(x) = 3x^2 + 6x + 5$,

(a) determine the vertex of the parabola

(b) restrict the domain so that f^{-1} is a function

(c) find $f^{-1}(x)$ using that restriction

Solution

(a) Complete the square to find the vertex.

$f(x) = 3x^2 + 6x + 5$	Factor the coefficient of x^2 from the terms with variables.
$= 3(x^2 + 2x) + 5$	Add and subtract the square of half the coefficient of x.
$= 3(x^2 + 2x + 1 - 1) + 5$	To remove the last constant from the brackets, multiply the last constant by the coefficient.
$= 3(x^2 + 2x + 1) - 3 + 5$	Factor the perfect square and simplify.
$= 3(x + 1)^2 + 2$	

The vertex of the parabola is $(-1, 2)$.

(b) The parabola opens up. To ensure that the inverse is also a function, choose one branch of the parabola. Then the restriction on the domain is $x \geq -1$.

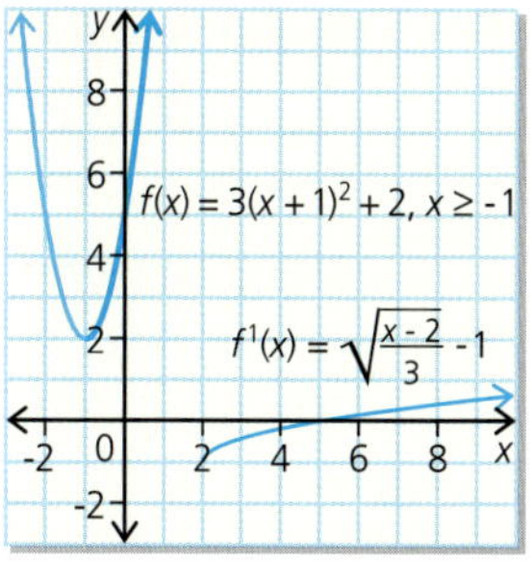

(c) The equation of f is $y = 3(x + 1)^2 + 2$ and $x \geq -1$.

To get the equation for f^{-1}, interchange the variables and solve for y. The range is $y \geq -1$.

$$\therefore x = 3(y + 1)^2 + 2 \qquad \text{Solve for } y.$$
$$x - 2 = 3(y + 1)^2$$
$$\frac{x-2}{3} = (y + 1)^2$$
$$\pm\sqrt{\frac{x-2}{3}} = y + 1$$

But $y \geq -1$, so

$$\sqrt{\frac{x-2}{3}} = y + 1$$
$$y = \sqrt{\frac{x-2}{3}} - 1$$
$$\therefore f^{-1}(x) = \sqrt{\frac{x-2}{3}} - 1$$

Practise, Apply, Solve 3.6

A

1. The graph of f is shown.

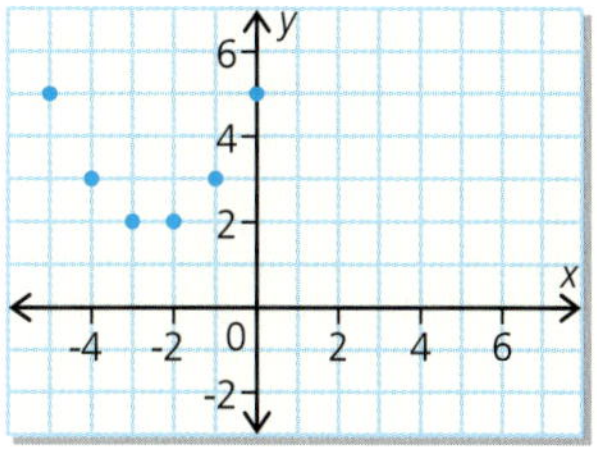

(a) Graph f^{-1}.

(b) Write a subset of f^{-1} that has the same domain as f^{-1}, but represents a function.

2. The graph of g is shown.

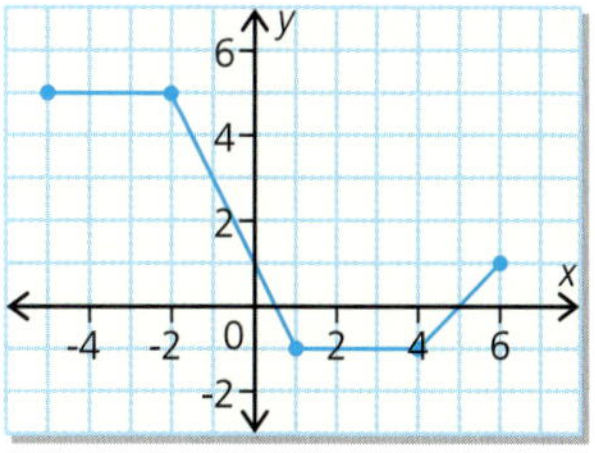

(a) Graph g^{-1}.

(b) State the domain and range of g.

(c) State the domain and range of g^{-1}.

(d) What restriction could you place on the domain of the function so that the inverse is a function and has the same domain as g^{-1}?

3. For each relation,

i. state restrictions on the domain or range of the relation that make it a function

ii. graph the inverse relation

iii. if necessary, restate the restrictions on the domain or range of the original relation to make its inverse a function

(a) 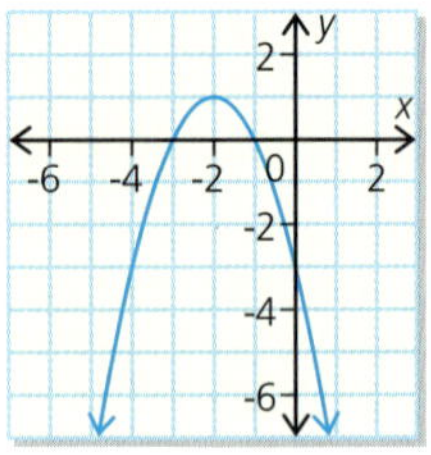

(b) 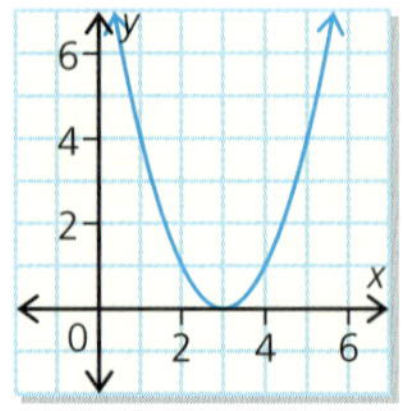

(c) 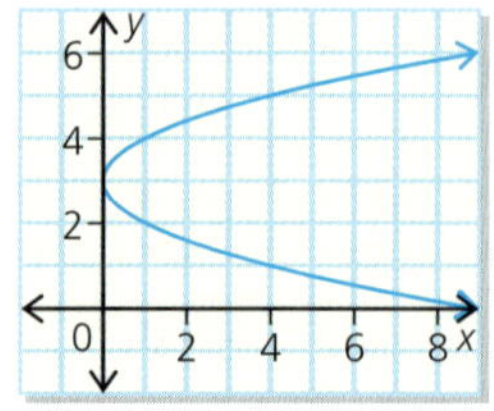

(d) 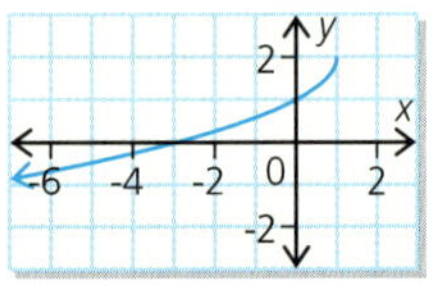

(e) 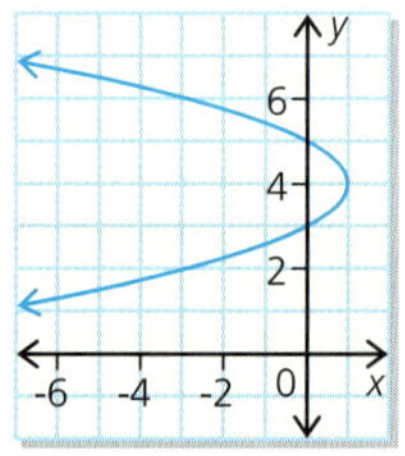

(f) 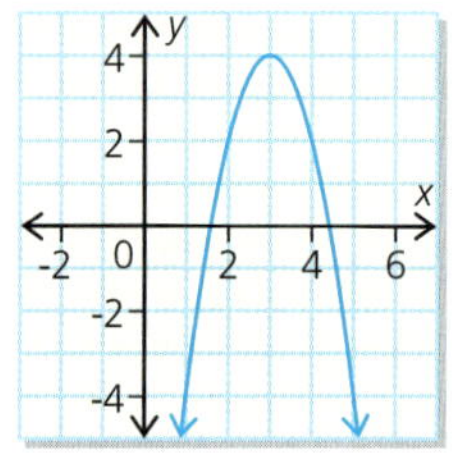

B

4. Each graph shows a function f that is a parabola or a branch of a parabola.

i. Determine $f(x)$.

ii. Graph f^{-1}.

iii. State restrictions on the domain or range of f to make its inverse a function.

iv. Determine the equations for f^{-1}.

(a) 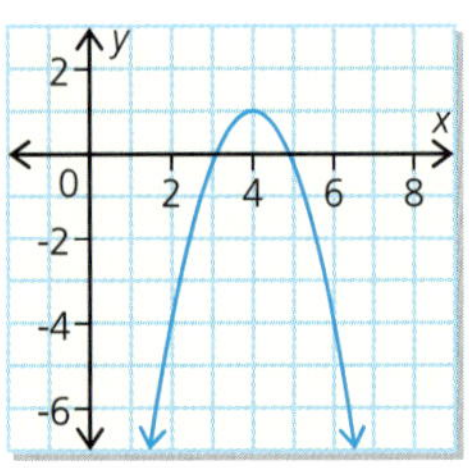

(b) 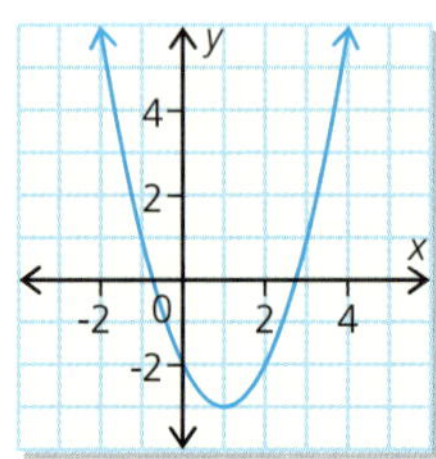

(c) 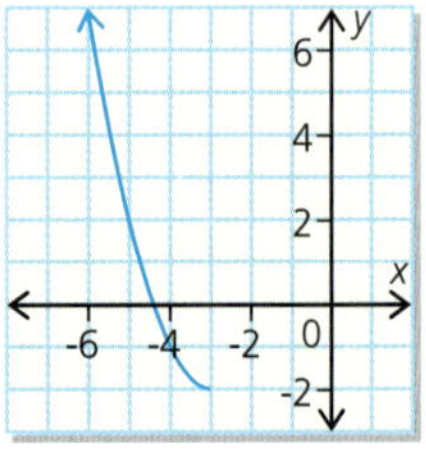

(d) 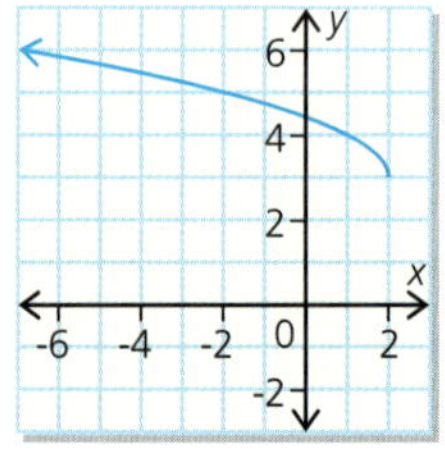

5. (a) Sketch the graph of $f(x) = -2(x + 1)^2 + 3$ by hand.

(b) Sketch the graph of its inverse.

(c) Restrict the domain of f so that both f and its inverse are functions.

6. (a) Graph $g(x) = -\sqrt{x}$ by hand.

(b) Graph its inverse on the same axes.

(c) State the domain and range of g^{-1}.

(d) Determine the equation for g^{-1}.

7. (a) Graph $g(x) = 3 + \sqrt{x}$ using parametric equations on the TI-83 Plus.

(b) Graph its inverse.

(c) Determine the equation for g^{-1}.

(d) Use your expression for g^{-1} to graph its inverse.

(e) Compare your graphs from (b) and (d). What restriction did you need to place on T to ensure there are no "extra" points?

8. (a) Graph $f(x) = \sqrt{x - 2}$ using parametric equations on the TI-83 Plus.

(b) Graph its inverse.

(c) Determine the equation for f^{-1}.

(d) Use your expression for f^{-1} to graph the inverse.

(e) Compare your graphs from (b) and (d). What restriction did you need to place on T to ensure there are no "extra" points?

9. Given $f(x) = 7 - 2(x - 1)^2$, $x \geq 1$. Graph f and f^{-1}, and then determine

(a) $f(3)$ (b) $f^{-1}(x)$ (c) $f^{-1}(5)$

(d) $f^{-1}(2a + 7)$ (e) $7 - 2(f^{-1}(x) - 1)^2$

10. **Knowledge and Understanding:** For $f(x) = -x^2 + 6x + 5$,

(a) determine the vertex of the parabola

(b) restrict the domain so that f^{-1} is a function

(c) find f^{-1} using that restriction

11. For $-2 < x < 3$ and $f(x) = 3x^2 - 6x$, determine

(a) the domain and range of f

(b) f^{-1}

12. Graph $f(x) = -\sqrt{x} + 5$ and determine

(a) the domain and range of f

(b) f^{-1}

13. Describe the relation between $y = x^2$ and $y = \sqrt{x}$.

14. The height of a golf ball after Lori Kane hits it is shown in the table below.

Time (s)	0	0.5	1	1.5	2	2.5
Height (m)	0	12.375	22.5	30.375	36.0	39.375

(a) Use first differences and second differences to extend the table.

(b) Graph the data and the curve of best fit for the relationship.

(c) Graph the inverse relation and its curve of best fit.

(d) Is the inverse a function? Explain.

15. **Communication:** A student writes, "The inverse of $y = -\sqrt{x + 2}$ is $y = x^2 - 2$."
Explain why this statement is not true.

16. Do you have to restrict either the domain or the range of the function $y = \sqrt{x + 2}$ to make its inverse a function? Explain.

17. **Application:** In section 3.4, question 20, each digit of a credit card number, the input, was coded by subtracting the digit from 9. Each input, x, is any single digit, so $0 \leq x \leq 9$. The range is the set of integers between 0 and 9. This code is very convenient, but easy to decode. A student developed a different code: "Multiply the input digit by a number that is 2 less than the digit." Let f be the coding function.

(a) Determine $f(x)$.

(b) Determine the equation for f^{-1}.

(c) Is f^{-1} a function? Explain.

(d) Suppose the input digits are restricted to the integers between 2 and 5. What is the range of f?

(e) Suppose that the output digits must be between 1 and 16. What restrictions should be placed on the input digits?

(f) What restrictions would you place on both f and f^{-1} so that they are functions? (**Hint:** There can be as many digits as possible.) Why is this restriction important?

18. **Check Your Understanding:** Given the graph of a function, how would you graph its inverse? How can you ensure that its inverse is a function?

C

19. **Thinking, Inquiry, Problem Solving:** The meat department manager discovers he could sell $m(x)$ kg of ground beef in a week, where $m(x) = 14\,700 - 3040x$, if he sold it at $\$x$/kg. He pays his supplier \$3.21/kg for the beef.

(a) Determine an algebraic expression for $P(x)$, where P represents the total profit from selling ground beef for one week.

(b) Find the equation for P^{-1}.

(c) Write an expression in function notation that represents the price that will earn \$1900 in profit, and then evaluate. Explain.

(d) Determine the price that will maximize profit.

(e) The supply cost drops to \$3.10/kg. What price should the manager set? How much profit will be earned at this price?

(f) Create a table by recording the optimal profit for several different supply costs.

(g) Why might a change in supply cost also change the volume of sales?

20. Find the range of $f(x) = \frac{1}{x}$, where $-2 < x < 3$.

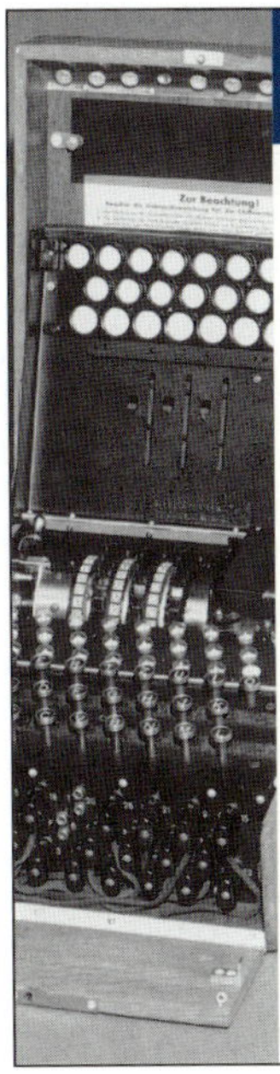

The Chapter Problem—Cryptography

Apply what you have learned about inverse functions to answer these questions about the Chapter Problem on page 218.

CP11. What is the restriction on the domain of the coding function in the Chapter Problem on page 218? Why?

CP12. What is the restriction on the range of the coding function? Why?

CP13. What was there about the coding function that guaranteed the range would work out appropriately?

CP14. A student suggested this code: instead of multiplying by 17, square the number, divide by 26, and add 1 to the remainder.

(a) Graph this function.

(b) Why would this code not work?

(c) What is necessary for any code to work?

3.7 Transformations and Function Notation

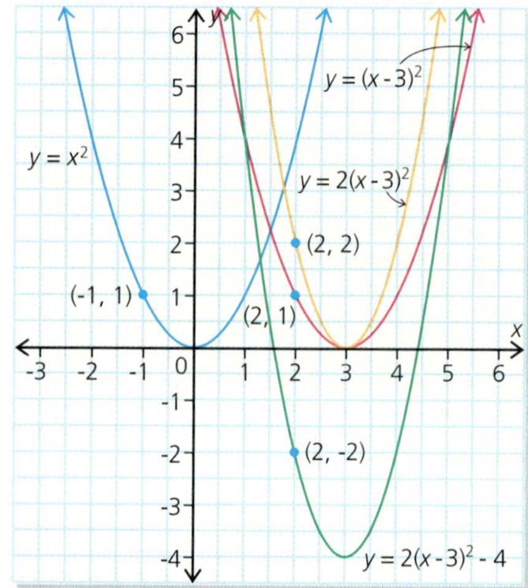

In grade 10, you used transformations to sketch the graph of a quadratic relation such as $y = 2(x - 3)^2 - 4$. First graph the curve $y = x^2$ and then translate this graph 3 units to the right, stretch it vertically by a factor of 2, and then translate it 4 units down.

This graph shows the effect of these transformations on point $(-1, 1)$. The horizontal translation of $+3$ takes the point to $(2, 1)$. The vertical stretch of factor 2 takes it to $(2, 2)$. Finally the vertical translation of -4 takes it down to $(2, -2)$.

Applying these transformations to all the points that lie on the graph of $y = x^2$ results in the graph of $y = 2(x - 3)^2 - 4$.

In this lesson, you will investigate how you can transform the graph of any function $y = f(x)$ to obtain the graph of any function in the form $y = af[k(x - p)] + q$.

Part 1: The Graph of $y = af(x - p) + q$ Compared to the Graph of $y = f(x)$

Think, Do, Discuss

1. Using a TI-83 Plus, press ZOOM 6 to set the standard window.
2. (a) Graph the base function $y = \sqrt{x}$. Enter this function into **Y1** in the equation editor.
   (b) What is the domain? What is the range?
   (c) What transformation would you apply to the graph of $y = \sqrt{x}$ to obtain the graph of $y = \sqrt{x - 5}$? Sketch your prediction on graph paper.
   (d) Graph $y = \sqrt{x - 5}$ using a graphing calculator to check your answer. Enter this function into **Y2** in the equation editor.
   (e) What is the domain of $y = \sqrt{x - 5}$? Explain. What is its range? Explain.
   (f) One point on the graph of $y = \sqrt{x}$ is $(4, 2)$. What is the corresponding point on the graph of $y = \sqrt{x - 5}$? Explain the transformation.
   (g) Evaluate $y = \sqrt{x - 5}$ for $x = 9$. How does this answer correspond to your answer to (f)?

3. (a) What transformations would you apply to the graph of $y = \sqrt{x}$ to obtain the graph of $y = 3\sqrt{x - 5}$? Sketch your prediction on graph paper.

(b) Graph $y = 3\sqrt{x - 5}$ using a graphing calculator to check your answer. Enter this function into **Y3** in the equation editor.

(c) What is the domain of $y = 3\sqrt{x - 5}$? Explain. What is its range? Explain.

(d) One point on the graph of $y = \sqrt{x}$ is (4, 2). What is the corresponding point on the graph of $y = 3\sqrt{x - 5}$? Explain the transformation.

(e) Evaluate $y = 3\sqrt{x - 5}$ for $x = 9$. How does this correspond to your answer to (e)?

4. (a) What transformations would you apply to the graph of $y = \sqrt{x}$ to obtain the graph of $y = 3\sqrt{x - 5} + 4$? Sketch your prediction on graph paper.

(b) Graph $y = 3\sqrt{x - 5} + 4$ using the graphing calculator to check your answer. Enter this function into **Y4** in the equation editor.

(c) What is the domain of $y = 3\sqrt{x - 5} + 4$? Explain. What is its range? Explain.

(d) One point on the graph of $y = \sqrt{x}$ is (4, 2). What is the corresponding point on the graph of $y = 3\sqrt{x - 5} + 4$? Explain the transformation.

(e) Evaluate $y = 3\sqrt{x - 5} + 4$ for $x = 9$. How does this answer correspond to your answer to (d)?

(f) The "base" function in all of these examples is the square root. In (e), what operation did you do before taking the square root? Which transformation did this operation correspond to? Was this transformation vertical or horizontal?

(g) In (e), what did you do after finding the square root? Which transformations did these operations correspond to? Were the transformations vertical or horizontal?

(h) The input/output diagram shows how to evaluate $y = 3\sqrt{x - 5} + 4$ for $x = 9$. On this diagram, which operations correspond to vertical transformations? to horizontal transformations?

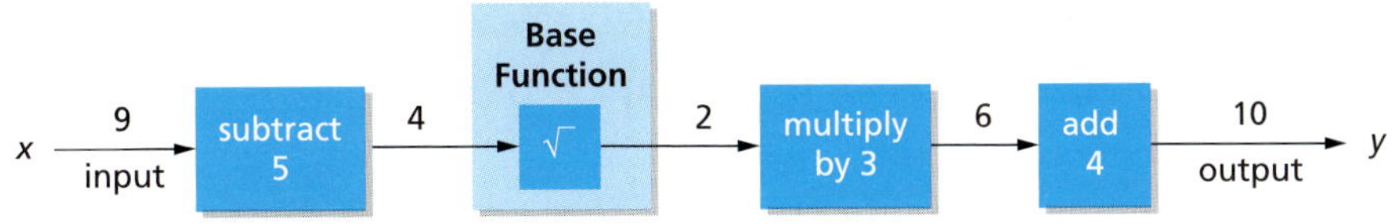

(i) Notice that the coordinates of point (4, 2) appear in the diagram above. The 4 is to the left of the base function and the 2 is to the right of the base function. Why does this make sense?

(j) Move to the right of the base function in this diagram. What is the order of the operations? In what order should you apply the transformations?

(k) Move to the left of the base function in this diagram. What is the operation? What transformation does this operation correspond to?

(l) Find other values of x that would produce integer values of y. How can you get integral answers for y without guessing?

5. Using graphing technology, explore the effects of varying a, p, and q in $y = a\sqrt{x - p} + q$ on the graph of $y = \sqrt{x}$. For each graph, record the following in your notebook:

- the equation
- the values of a, p, and q
- the domain and range of the function
- a description of the transformations that must be applied to the graph of $y = \sqrt{x}$ to obtain the graph of $y = a\sqrt{x - p} + q$

6. (a) Use graphing technology to graph $y = x^3$. What is the domain? What is the range? Is this relation a function?

(b) Explore the effects of varying a, p, and q in $y = a(x - p)^3 + q$ on the graph of $y = x^3$. For each graph, record the following in your notebook:

- the equation
- the values of a, p , and q
- the domain and range of the function
- a description of the transformations that must be applied to the graph of $y = x^3$ to obtain the graph of $y = a(x - p)^3 + q$

Part 2: The Graph of $y = f(kx)$ Compared to $y = f(x)$

Think, Do, Discuss

1. (a) Clear all the equations from the equation editor. Graph the function base $y = x^2$. Enter this equation into **Y1**. What is the domain? What is the range?

(b) On the same set of axes, graph $y = (2x)^2$. Enter this equation into **Y2**. How does the new graph compare to the graph of $y = x^2$? What is the domain? What is the range?

(c) The input/output diagram shows how to evaluate $y = (2x)^2$ for $x = 3$. What is the corresponding point on the graph of $y = x^2$? Explain.

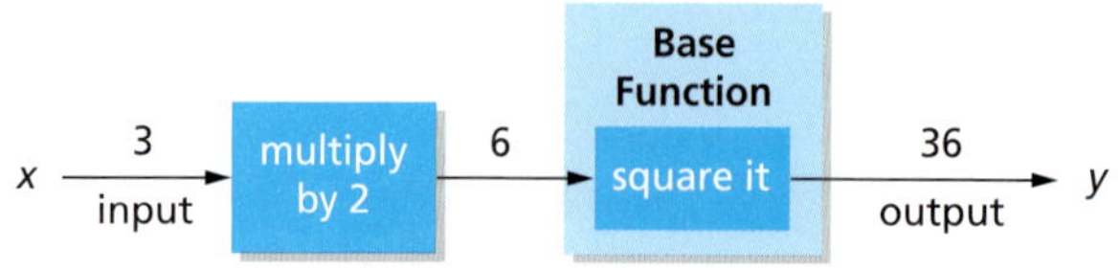

(d) Create a table for $y = (2x)^2$. Create another table of corresponding points for $y = x^2$.

x	$y = (2x)^2$
3	36
0	
1	
2	
4	
5	

... corresponds to ...

x	$y = x^2$
6	36

(e) Suppose that you had started with the table for $y = x^2$. Describe how you would find the corresponding points on the graph of $y = (2x)^2$. This transformation is called a horizontal stretch of factor $\frac{1}{2}$.

(f) Press [2nd] [GRAPH] to examine the table for both graphs. Is your work for (d) and (e) correct?

(g) Explore what happens to the graph and table when you change the coefficient k in $y = (kx)^2$ from 2 to some other number. Try numbers between 0 and 1, greater than 1, and less than 0.

2. Explore the effect of varying k in $y = \sqrt{kx}$ on the graph of $y = \sqrt{x}$. For each graph, record the following:

- the equation
- the value of k (use numbers between 0 and 1, greater than 1, and less than 0)
- an input/output diagram for the equation
- a table for $y = \sqrt{x}$ and the corresponding points for $y = \sqrt{kx}$
- the domain and range of the function
- a description of the transformations that must be applied to $y = \sqrt{x}$ to obtain the graph of $y = \sqrt{kx}$

3. Explore the effect of varying k in $y = (kx)^3$ on the graph of $y = x^3$. For each graph, record the following:

- the equation
- the value of k
- an input/output diagram for the equation
- a table for $y = x^3$ and the corresponding points for $y = (kx)^3$
- the domain and range of the function
- a description of the transformations that must be applied to $y = x^3$ to obtain the graph of $y = (kx)^3$

Part 3: The Graph of $y = af[k(x - p)] + q$ Compared to $y = f(x)$

Think, Do, Discuss

1. (a) Clear all the equations from the equation editor. Graph the function $y = \sqrt{x}$. Enter this equation into **Y1**.

(b) The input/output diagram shows how to evaluate $y = 3\sqrt{-2(x - 5)} + 4$ for $x = 3$. What is the corresponding point on the graph of $y = \sqrt{x}$? Explain.

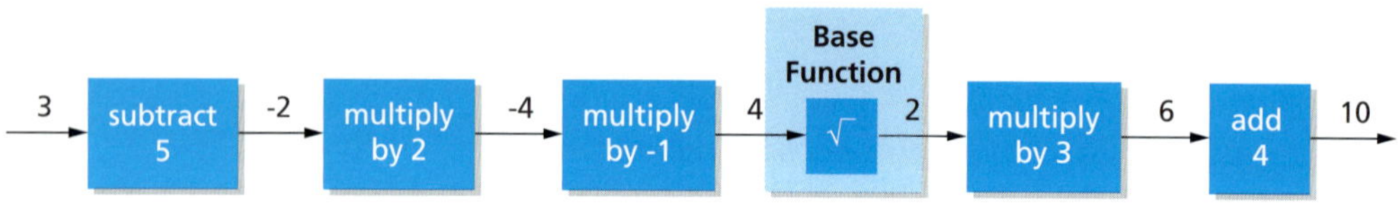

(c) Notice that the coordinates of point (4, 2) appear in this diagram. The 4 is to the left of the base function and the 2 is to the right of the base function. Why does this make sense?

(d) Move to the right of the base function in this diagram. What is the order of the operations? In what order should you apply the transformations?

(e) Move to the left of the base function in this diagram. What is the order of the operations? What transformations do these operations correspond to? In what order should you apply these transformations?

(f) Find other values of x that would produce integer values of y. How can you get integral answers for y without guessing?

(g) What transformations are applied to the graph of $y = \sqrt{x}$ to obtain the graph of $y = 3\sqrt{-2(x - 5)} + 4$? Sketch your prediction on graph paper.

(h) Graph $y = 3\sqrt{-2(x - 5)} + 4$ using a calculator to check your answer.

(i) What is the domain of $y = 3\sqrt{-2(x - 5)} + 4$? What is its range? Explain.

Focus 3.7

Key Ideas

- To graph $y = af[k(x - p)] + q$ from the graph of $y = f(x)$, consider the following:
  - ♦ The value of a determines the vertical stretch and whether there is a reflection in the x-axis or not. For $a > 0$, the graph of $y = f(x)$ is stretched vertically by factor a. For $a < 0$, the graph is reflected in the x-axis and stretched vertically by factor a.
  - ♦ The value of k determines the horizontal stretch and whether there is a reflection in the y-axis or not. For $k > 0$, the graph of $y = f(x)$ is stretched horizontally by factor $\frac{1}{k}$. For $k < 0$, the graph is reflected in the y-axis and stretched horizontally by factor $\frac{1}{k}$.

- For $p > 0$ and $q > 0$, the graph is translated p units to the right and q units up. For $p < 0$ and $q < 0$, the graph is translated p units to the left and q units down.
- The input/output diagram shows the sequence and type of transformations for transforming the graph of $y = f(x)$ into the graph of $y = af[k(x - p)] + q$.

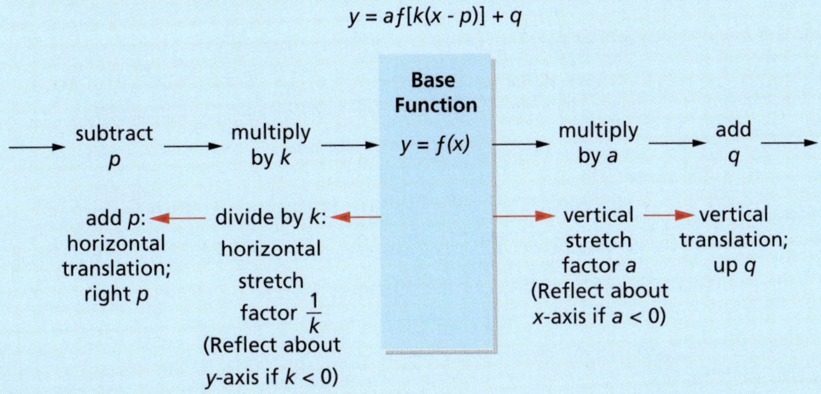

The red arrows show the order for applying the transformations to the base function.

Note that arranging the equation so that the multiplication operation is immediately before and after the base functions allows us to perform all stretches and flips before translations.

Example 1

(a) Draw an input/output diagram to show the order of operations for the function $y = -f[2(x + 1)] + 3$.

(b) Sketch its graph on the same axes as $y = f(x)$.

(c) Create a table to verify that your graph is correct.

(d) State the domain and range of the functions $y = f(x)$ and $y = -f[2(x + 1)] + 3$.

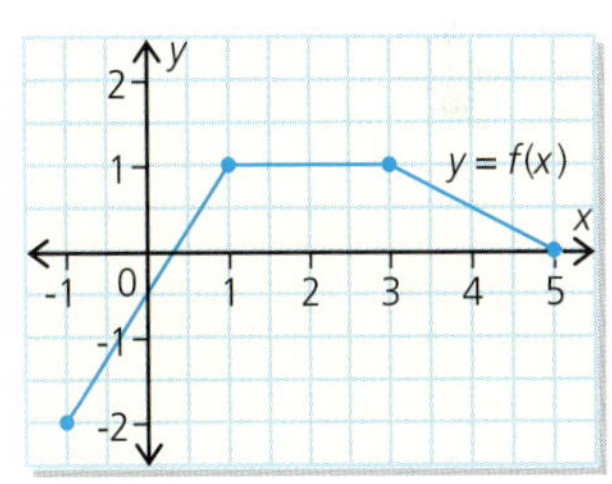

Solution

(a)

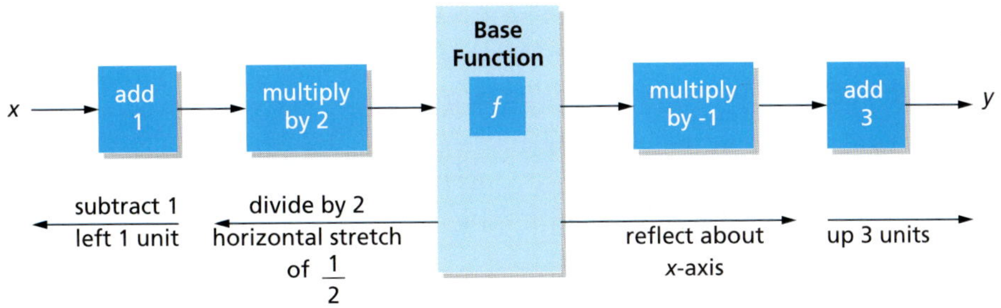

(b) The graphs show the results after each transformation is applied. The horizontal stretch of factor $\frac{1}{2}$ gives $y = f(2x)$. A reflection in the x-axis gives $y = -f(2x)$. A horizontal translation of -1 results in $y = -f[2(x + 1)]$.

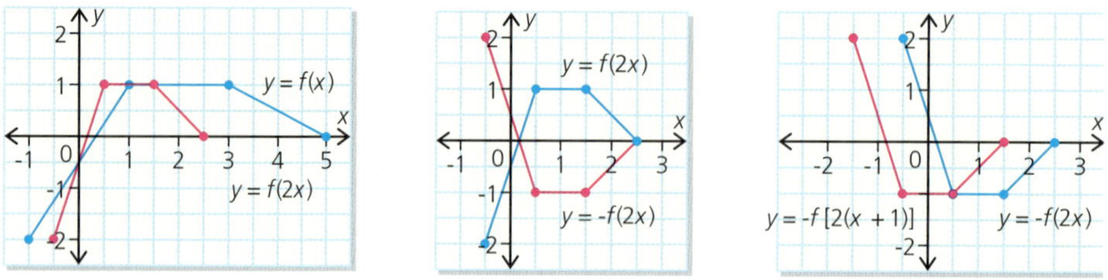

A vertical translation of 3 gives the graph of $y = -f[2(x + 1)] + 3$. The final graph shows $y = f(x)$ and $y = -f[2(x + 1)] + 3$ on the same axes.

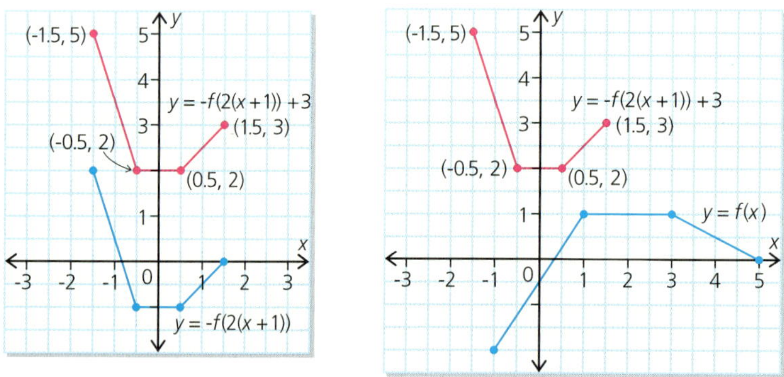

(c)

x	**Add 1.** $x + 1$	**Multiply by 2.** $2(x + 1)$ **original** x	**Apply** f. $f[2(x + 1)]$ **original** y	**Multiply by** -1. $-f[2(x + 1)]$	**Add 3.** $y = -f[2(x + 1)] + 3$
-1.5	-0.5	-1	$f(-1) = -2$	2	5
-0.5	0.5	1	$f(1) = 1$	-1	2
0.5	1.5	3	$f(3) = 1$	-1	2
1.5	2.5	5	$f(5) = 0$	0	3
0	1	2	$f(2) = 1$	-1	2
1	2	4	$f(4) = 0.5$	-0.5	2.5

The table shows that $(-1.5, 5)$, $(-0.5, 2)$, $(0.5, 2)$, $(1.5, 3)$, $(0, 2)$, and $(1, 2.5)$ are all points on the new graph.

(d) For $y = f(x)$, the domain is $\{x \mid -1 \le x \le 5, x \in \mathbf{R}\}$ and the range is $\{y \mid -2 \le y \le 1, y \in \mathbf{R}\}$. From the graph of $y = -f[2(x + 1)] + 3$, see that the domain is $\{x \mid -1.5 \le x \le 1.5, x \in \mathbf{R}\}$ and the range is $\{y \mid 2 \le y \le 5, y \in \mathbf{R}\}$.

Notice that without the graph you could still determine the domain and range of the function by applying the transformations as follows:

Begin with the domain of $y = f(x)$: $-1 \leq x \leq 5$.

After a horizontal compression of factor $\frac{1}{2}$: $-0.5 \leq x \leq 2.5$

After a translation of 1 unit left: $-1.5 \leq x \leq 1.5$.

The vertical transformations do not affect the domain.

For the range of $y = f(x)$: $-2 \leq y \leq 1$

After a reflection in the x-axis: $2 \geq y \geq -1$ or $-1 \leq y \leq 2$

After a translation of 3 units up: $2 \leq y \leq 5$

The horizontal transformations do not affect the range.

Example 2

Describe the sequence of transformations for creating the graph of $y = 5[f(2x + 6) + 4]$ from the graph of $y = f(x)$.

Solution

Rearrange $y = 5[f(2x + 6) + 4]$ to the equivalent form $y = 5f[2(x + 3)] + 20$. The input/output diagram for this function is shown.

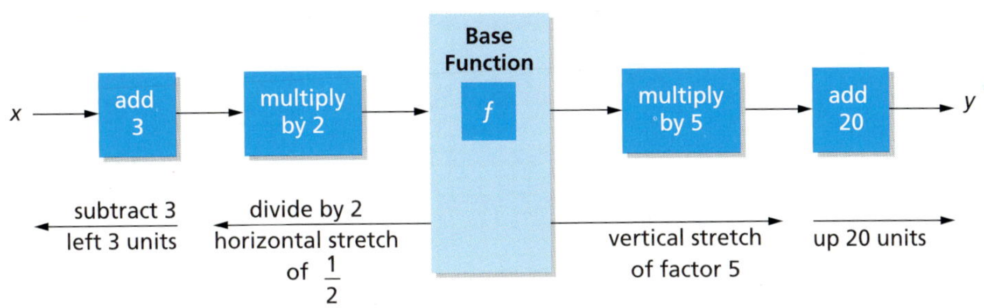

Begin by stretching $y = f(x)$ horizontally by factor $\frac{1}{2}$ and vertically by factor 5. Then translate the graph 3 units to the left and 20 units up.

Practise, Apply, Solve 3.7

A

1. Communication: Comment on this statement.

The basic shape of the final graph after transformations is the same as the shape of the original graph.

2. The ordered pairs (1, 5), (2, 3), and (3, 7) belong to a function f. The input/output diagram for a function g is shown. State the coordinates of three points on g.

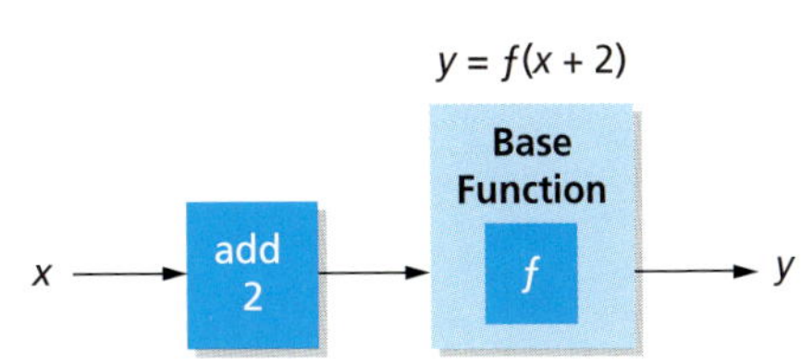

B

3. Given $g = \{(1, 2), (2, 5), (3, 7), (4, 8)\}$, list the ordered pairs that belong to the function.

(a) $y = 2g(x)$ (b) $y = g(x) + 2$ (c) $y = g(x + 2)$ (d) $y = g(2x)$

4. $f = \{(0, 3), (1, 1), (2, 4), (3, -1)\}$. After two transformations, the new function is $g = \{(0, 0), (5, -2), (10, 1), (15, -4)\}$.

(a) Graph f and g.

(b) Write one possible sequence of transformations that were applied to f to give g.

(c) Draw an input/output diagram to show the sequence of the operations that result in g.

(d) Write an equation for $g(x)$ in terms of f.

(e) Write a sequence of two transformations to change g into f.

(f) Draw an input/output diagram to show the sequence of the operations to change g into f.

(g) Write an equation for $f(x)$ in terms of g.

5. The graph of f is on the left and the graph of g is on the right.

(a) Find the sequence of transformations that were applied to the graph of f to get the graph of g.

(b) Draw an input/output diagram to show the sequence of transformations.

(c) Write an equation for $g(x)$ in terms of f.

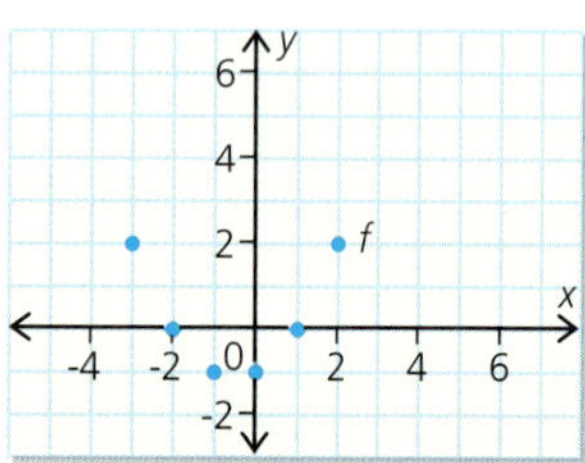

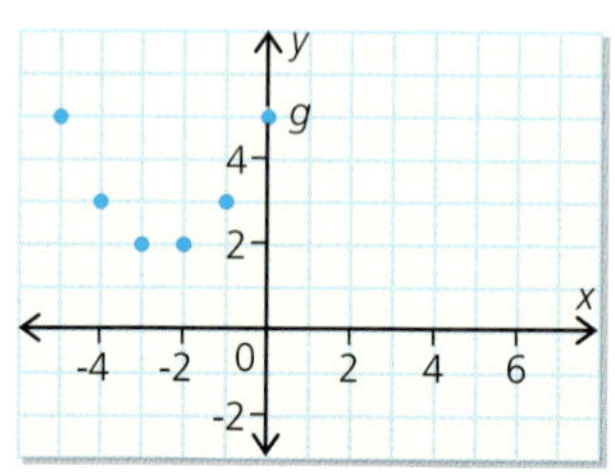

6. f is illustrated by the arrow diagram.

(a) Draw an input/output diagram for $y = 2f(x - 3)$.

(b) List the transformations in the correct sequence that you would apply to f to get $y = 2f(x - 3)$.

(c) Graph f and $y = 2f(x - 3)$ on the same axes.

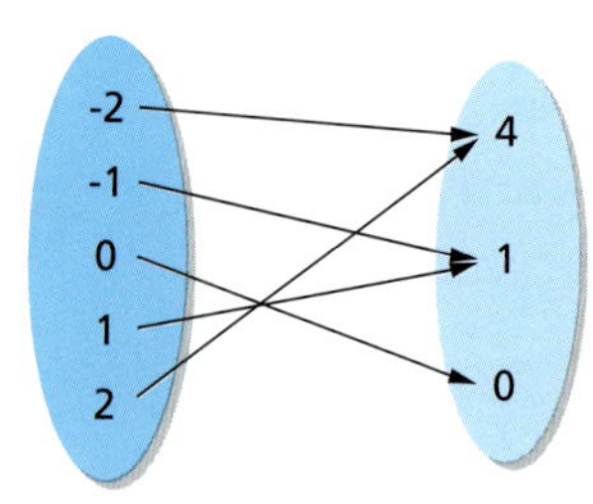

7. The graph of $y = f(x)$ is shown. Match the correct equation to each graph. Justify your choices.

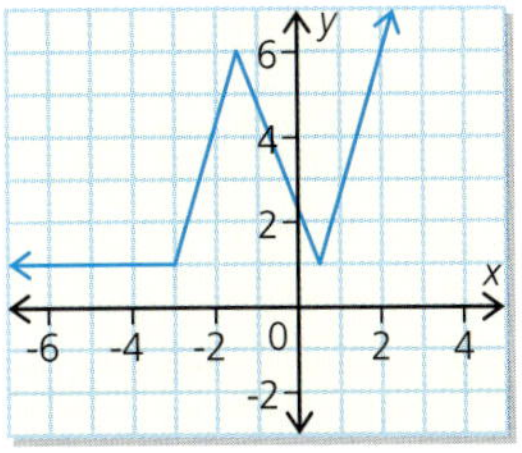

i. $y = f(x - 3)$	**ii.** $y = f(0.5x)$
iii. $y = -f(x)$	**iv.** $y = f(-x)$
v. $y = f(x + 3)$	**vi.** $y = f(2x)$
vii. $y = 2f(x)$	**viii.** $y = 0.5f(x)$
ix. $y = f(x) + 3$	**x.** $y = f(x) - 3$

(a)

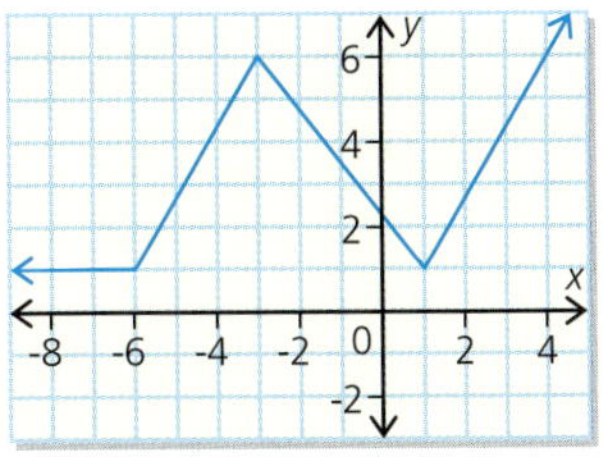

(b)

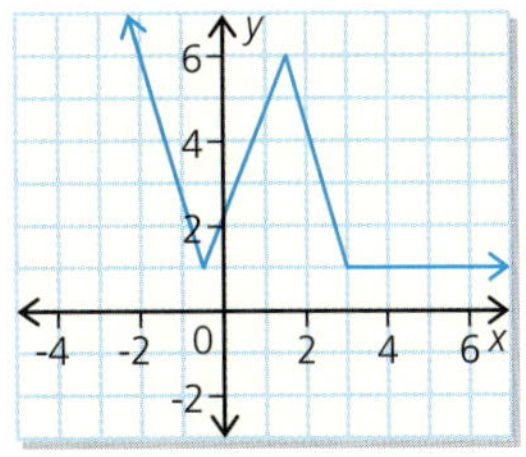

(c)

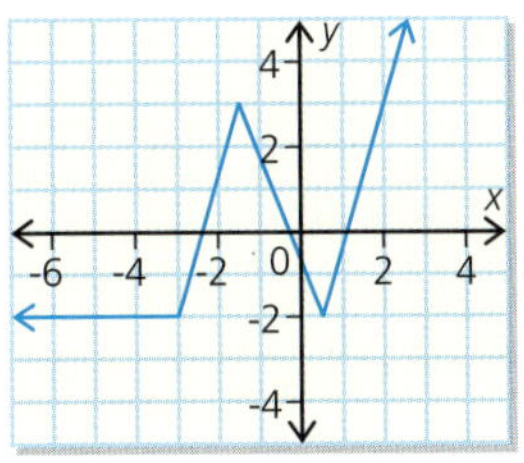

(d)

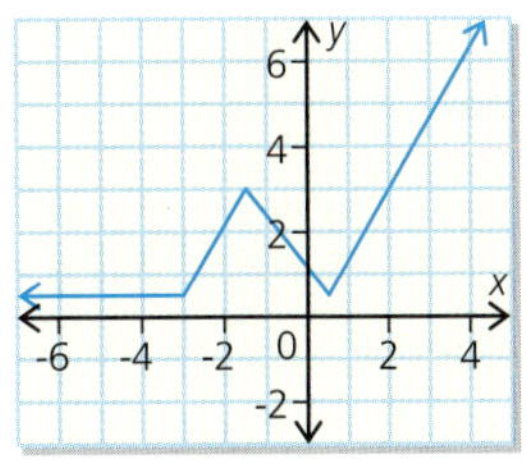

(e)

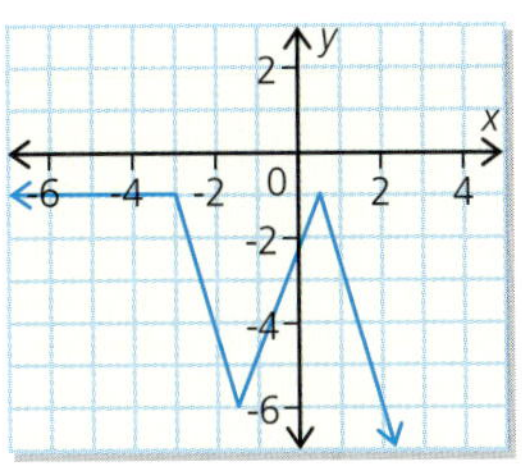

(f)

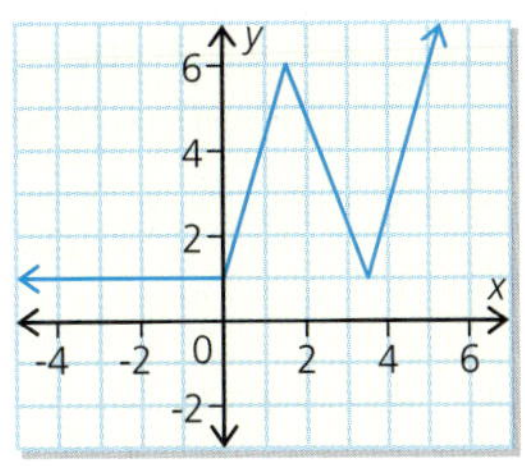

8. The graph of $y = f(x)$ is shown. Match each equation to its corresponding graph. Justify your choices.

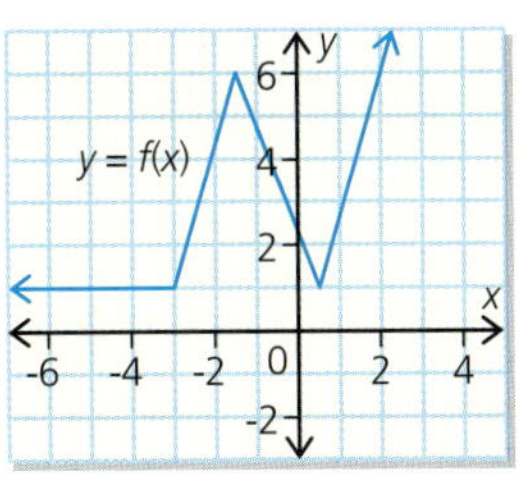

i. $y = 0.5f(2x)$	**ii.** $y = 2f(0.5x)$
iii. $y = 0.5f(0.5x)$	**iv.** $y = 2f(2x)$
v. $y = 2f(x + 3)$	**vi.** $y = f(2x) + 3$
vii. $y = 3f(x + 2)$	**viii.** $y = f(x + 3) + 2$
ix. $y = f(x - 2) - 3$	**x.** $y = f(x + 2) + 3$
xi. $y = -f(x) - 3$	**xii.** $y = f(-x) - 3$
xiii. $y = -f(x + 3)$	**xiv.** $y = f(-x - 3)$
xv. $y = 0.5f(3x + 5)$	**xvi.** $y = 2f\left(\frac{x}{3} - 2\right) - 5$
xvii. $y = 0.5f[3(x - 2)] - 5$	**xviii.** $y = 0.5f[3(x + 2)] + 5$

(a)

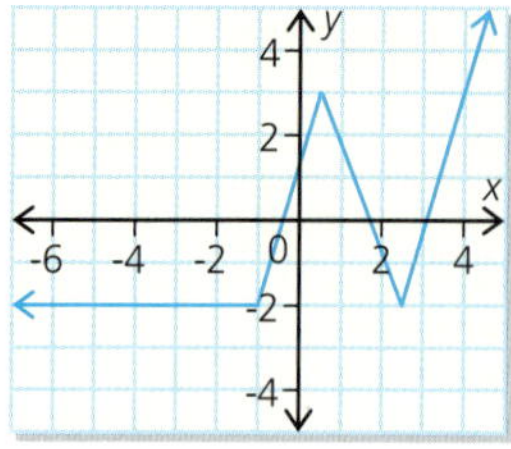

(b)

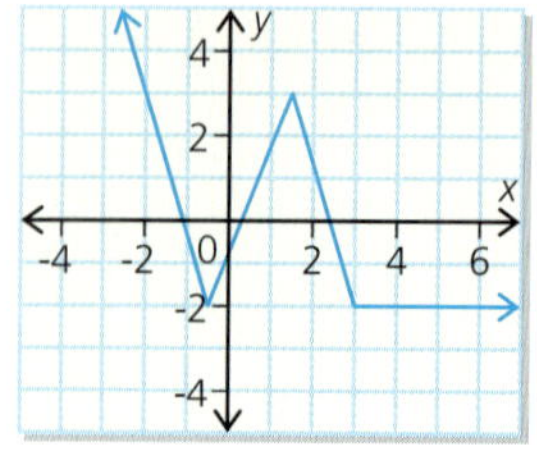

(c)

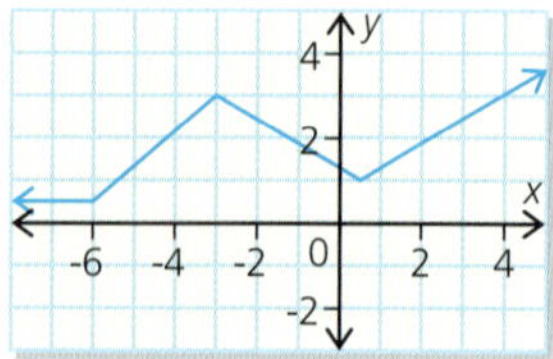

(d)

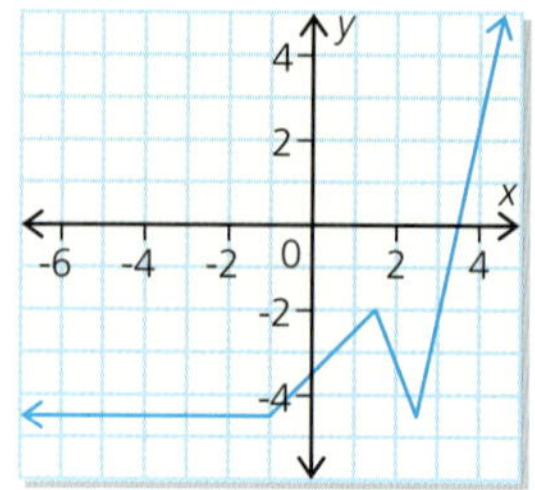

9. i. Graph $f(x) = \frac{1}{x}$ using graphing technology.

ii. Describe the transformations that you would apply to the graph of f to transform f into each of the following.

(a) $y = \frac{1}{x - 2}$ (b) $y = \frac{1}{x + 1}$ (c) $y = \frac{1}{x} + 2$

(d) $y = \frac{1}{x} - 6$ (e) $y = 0.5\left(\frac{1}{x}\right)$ (f) $y = \frac{2}{x}$

(g) $y = \frac{1}{0.5x}$ (h) $y = \frac{1}{2x}$ (i) $y = -\frac{1}{x}$

iii. Verify your answers in ii with graphing technology.

iv. State the domain and range of each function in ii.

v. Why are the graphs of (f) and (g) the same?

10. Consider $g(x) = x^2$.

(a) Draw an input/output diagram for $y = -3g(x - 2) + 1$.

(b) A point on the graph of g is (4, 16), what is the corresponding point on the transformed function?

(c) List the transformations in the sequence that you would apply to the graph of $y = g(x)$ to graph $y = -3g(x - 2) + 1$.

(d) State the domain and range of the transformed function. Justify your answer.

11. The input/output diagram shows function g in terms of function f.

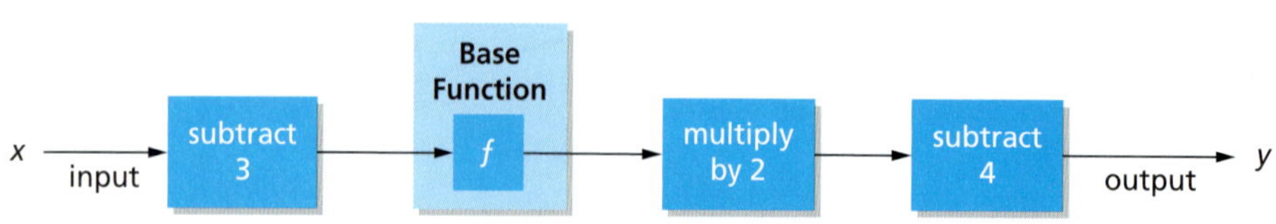

(a) Evaluate $g(4)$ if $f(x) = x^3$.

(b) Point $(2, 0) \in f$. What point belongs to g?

(c) Graph g if $f(x) = x^2$.

12. The graph of $g(x) = \sqrt{x}$ is reflected in the y-axis, stretched vertically by factor 3, and then translated 5 units right and 2 units down.

(a) Draw the graph of the new function.

(b) Write the equation of the new function.

13. The graph of $f(x) = x^3$ is translated left 5 units and up 3 units.

(a) Use a graphing calculator to graph f.

(b) Determine the equation of the translated function. Verify your answer by graphing your equation.

14. The graph of $y = f(x)$ is reflected in the y-axis, stretched vertically by factor 3, and then translated up 2 units and 1 unit to the left.

(a) Draw the input/output diagram.

(b) Write the equation for the new function in terms of f.

15. **Knowledge and Understanding:** Given the graph of $y = f(x)$, draw the graph of $y = 2f(-3x + 6) + 2$.

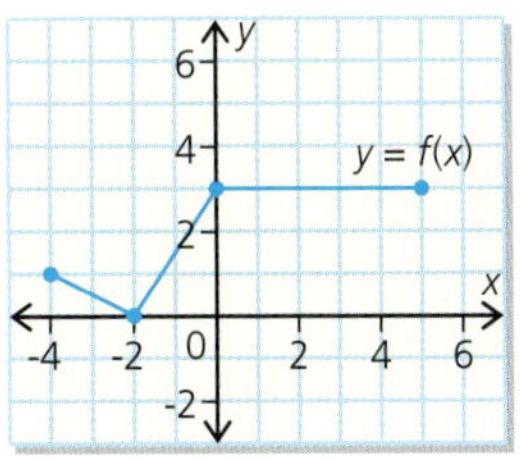

16. **Application:** A function f has domain $\{x \mid x \geq -4, x \in \mathbf{R}\}$ and range $\{y \mid y < -1, y \in \mathbf{R}\}$. Determine the domain and range of each function.

(a) $y = 2f(x)$

(b) $y = f(-x)$

(c) $y = 3f(x + 1) + 4$

(d) $y = -2f(-x + 5) + 1$

17. **Thinking, Inquiry, Problem Solving:** A squash ball was dropped from different heights. The height and the time taken for the ball to hit the ground was recorded.

Height (m)	Time (s)
1.5	0.7
2	0.8
2.5	0.86
3	0.93
1	0.6

(a) Create a scatter plot for the data.

(b) Find the equation in the form $y = a\sqrt{x}$ that most closely fits the data.

(c) What other transformation might be needed to make the graph fit the data more closely?

(d) Modify your equation until it fits the data as closely as possible.

18. Three transformations are applied to $y = x^2$: a vertical stretch of factor 2, a translation of 3 units right, and a translation of 4 units down.

(a) Is the order of the transformations important?

(b) Is there any other sequence of these transformations that could produce the same result?

19. The graph of $y = f(x)$ is transformed into $y = 3f(2x - 4)$.

(a) Describe the transformations in the correct sequence.

(b) Describe another sequence of three transformations that would produce the same final graph.

20. The transformations in Example 1 were performed in the following order: horizontal stretch factor $\frac{1}{2}$, reflection in the x-axis, translation 1 unit left, and then translation 3 units up.

(a) List all the possible sequences of these transformations that would produce the same final graph from the original function. Explain.

(b) Are there any other sequences of different transformations that would produce the same final graph from the original function? Explain.

21. **Check Your Understanding:** Describe how you determine which transformations are needed to graph a function that is expressed in terms of another function.

C

22. The graphs of $y = x^2$ and another parabola are shown.

(a) Determine a combination of transformations that would produce the second parabola from the first.

(b) Determine a possible equation for the second parabola.

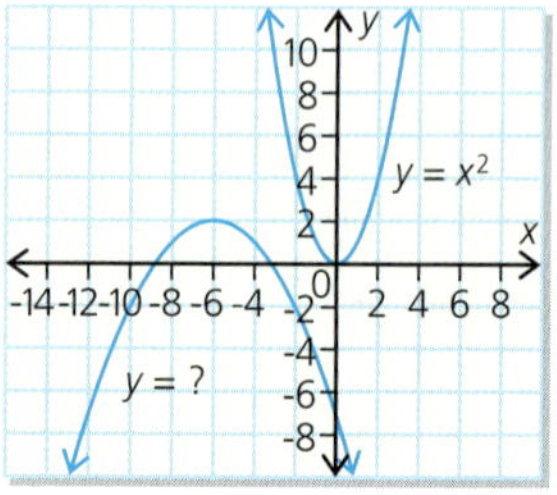

23. Ari recorded the following data from a science experiment.

Length (cm)	3.1	3.5	4	4.5	5	5.5	6
Time (s)	0.6	3.4	5.3	5.9	6.8	7.6	8.3

(a) When he graphed the data, he found that the graph resembled the graph of $y = \sqrt{x}$. Determine the equation to model the data by trial and error on the graphing calculator.

(b) Determine an algebraic model by first finding the equation for the inverse function.

(c) Compare your answers from (a) and (b).

24. A quadratic function has vertex $(3, -1)$ and another point $(5, 2)$. The base function is $f(x) = x^2$.

(a) To find the equation of the parabola, transform f so that the two points are on the graph of the transformed function. You know that $(2, 4)$ lies on f. Point $(2, 4)$ is transformed into $(5, 2)$. Determine the necessary transformations and the quadratic equation of the transformed function.

(b) $(1, 1)$ is another point on f and it is the point that is transformed into $(5, 2)$. Determine the necessary transformations and the required quadratic equation.

(c) Compare your answers from (a) and (b). Explain.

The Chapter Problem—Cryptography

Apply what you have learned about transformations to answer these questions about the Chapter Problem on page 218.

CP15. You could write the code in question CP14 in function notation as follows:

$$f(x) = \text{mod}(17x, 26) + 1, x \in \{1, 2, 3, \ldots, 26\}$$

where mod(a, b) is the remainder when a is divided by b.
For example,

mod(17, 5) = 2 because 17 divided by 5 is 3 with remainder 2.

(a) Suppose that the equation is $y = 17x + 1$. What is the equation for the inverse function (the decoder)?
(b) The last operation is "add 1." What do you know about $f^{-1}(x)$?
(c) What is the purpose of taking the remainder after dividing by 26?
(d) Suppose you multiply a certain number by 17 and divide the result by 26. The remainder is 1. What is the number?
(e) $f^{-1}(x)$ is very much like $f(x)$, but involves the number you found in (d). Determine $f^{-1}(x)$.
(f) Verify your answer for all possible values of x.
(g) Use $f^{-1}(x)$ to decode the message in the Chapter Problem on page 218.

Chapter 3 Review

Introducing Functions

Check Your Understanding

1. What is a function? Give an example of a relation that is a function and another example of a relation that is not a function.
2. A function can be described or defined in a number of ways. List the different ways and explain how you would use each to determine if a relation is a function.
3. How can you use the graph of a relation to decide if the relation is a function?
4. How do you find the domain and range of a relation?
5. How do you write the domain and the range in set notation?
6. How are the rules for solving a linear inequality algebraically different from the rules for solving a linear equation?
7. How do you write the solution to a linear inequality?
8. Describe a non-algebraic method for solving a linear inequality.
9. What is the inverse of a relation?
10. How do you graph the inverse of a relation using the graph of the relation?
11. How do you determine the equation of the inverse from the equation of a relation?
12. Why might $f^{-1}(x)$ be different from the equation of the inverse?
13. Point (a, b) is on the graph of f. Express each of the coordinates of the point using function notation.
14. Why might it be difficult to graph the inverse of a relation on a graphing calculator in function mode (**Func**)? What can you do instead?
15. Compare the domain and range of a relation with the domain and range of the inverse relation.
16. Why might the inverse of a function not be a function? How can you check whether the inverse of a function is a function?
17. Why is the inverse of $y = x^2$ not $y = \sqrt{x}$? Explain.
18. The equation of a function is expressed in terms of a base function and involves multiplication. What type of transformation could be applied to the graph of the base function to get the graph of the new function?

19. The equation of a function is expressed in terms of a base function and involves addition. What type of transformation could be applied to the graph of the base function to get the graph of the new function?

20. How does expressing a function in terms of a base function help you to determine its domain and range?

Review and Practice

3.1–3.2 Functions: Concept and Notation

1. A relation is $\{(1, 9), (2, 7), (3, 5), (4, 3)\}$.
   (a) State the domain and range.
   (b) Draw an arrow diagram for the relation.
   (c) Graph the relation.
   (d) Determine an equation for the relation.
   (e) Express this relation in function notation.
   (f) Explain why this relation is a function.
   (g) Create another ordered pair so that the relation is no longer a function.

2. For each of the following graphs, identify the domain and range, and decide if the relation is a function. Justify your answer.

(a)

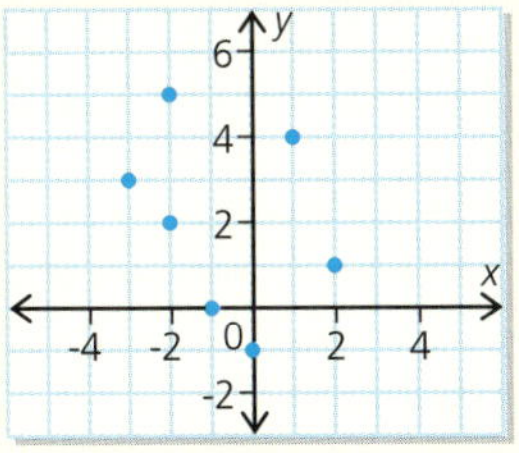

(b)

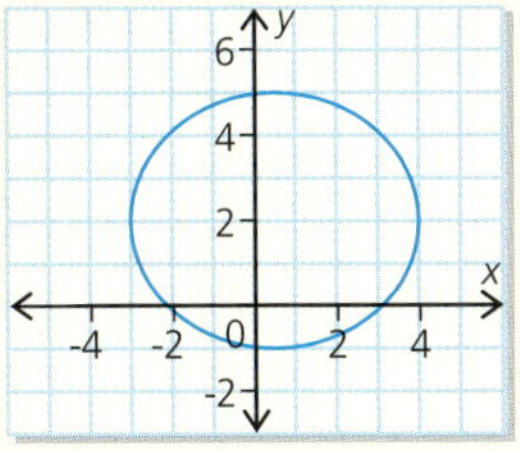

(c)

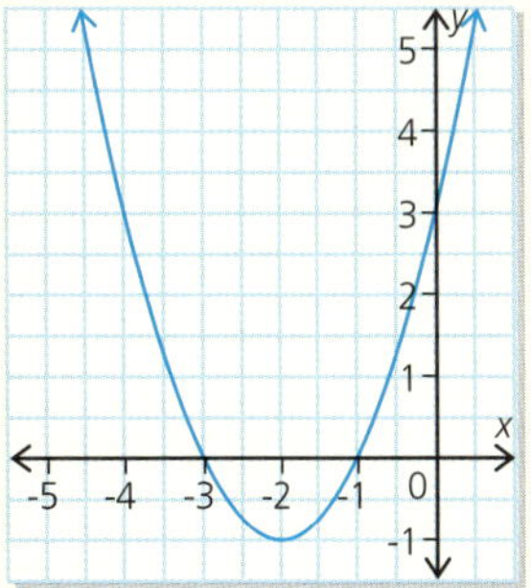

3. A relation f is $f(x) = 2x^2 - 6x$.
   (a) Evaluate $f(-2)$.
   (b) Graph f.
   (c) Is f a function? Explain.
   (d) $(5, 20) \in f$. Rewrite using function notation.
   (e) Solve $f(x) = 0$.

4. For $g(s) = \sqrt{9 - s}$,
   (a) graph g
   (b) state the domain and range of g

5. A student has a part-time job at an electronics store. She earns \$85 for working 12 h each week, plus 5% of her sales over \$1000 each week.
   (a) Why is it important that this relation is a function?
   (b) What is a reasonable domain and range for this function? Justify your answer.
   (c) Let this function be g. Find $g(5000)$.
   (d) Graph g.

3.3 Solving Inequalities

6. Graph each of the following on a number line.
   (a) $\{x \mid -2 \leq x < 4, x \in \mathbf{R}\}$
   (b) $\{x \mid x < 4, x \in \mathbf{N}\}$
   (c) $\{x \mid x^2 > 1, x \in \mathbf{R}\}$

7. Describe each in set notation.
   (a)
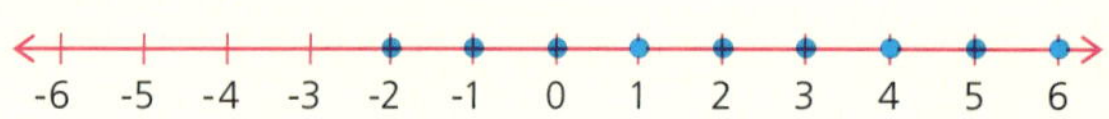

   (b)

8. The function f is $f(x) = \dfrac{4 - 2x}{5}$.
   (a) The range of f is $\{y \mid y > 2, y \in \mathbf{R}\}$. Find the domain.
   (b) The domain of f is $\{x \mid -8 \leq x < 2, x \in \mathbf{R}\}$. Find the range.

9. For $g(x) = -(x + 1)^2 + 4$,
   (a) graph g
   (b) find the domain of g if $g(x) > 0$

3.4 The Inverse Function

10. The graph of $y = f(x)$ is shown.

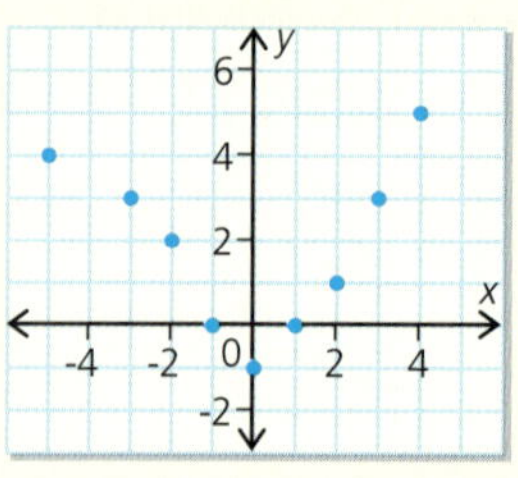

   (a) State the domain and range of f.
   (b) Express f^{-1} as a set of ordered pairs.
   (c) Graph f and f^{-1} on the same axes.
   (d) Find $f(1)$.
   (e) Find $f^{-1}(1)$.
   (f) Find $f^{-1}(0)$.
   (g) Find $f(-4)$.

11. The graph of $y = g(x)$ is shown. Graph g^{-1}.

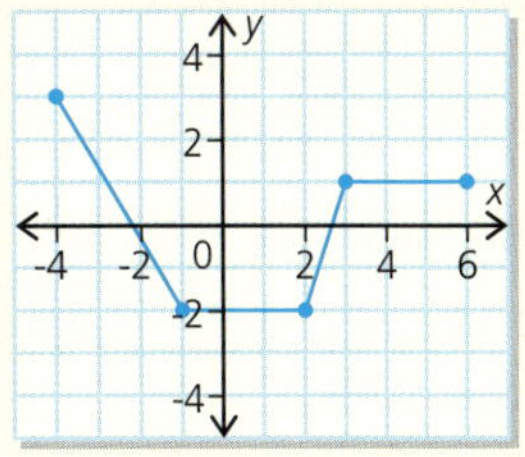

12. Find the equation for f^{-1} if $f(x) = \frac{x+3}{2}$.

13. A printing company charges \$100 to set up the artwork and \$11.50 for every T-shirt printed. g is the relation between the total charge for the printing in dollars, excluding taxes, and the number of shirts printed.

(a) Express g in function notation.

(b) Determine $g^{-1}(x)$.

(c) Describe g^{-1} as a rule.

(d) State a reasonable domain and range for g^{-1}.

(e) Write a question that would require the evaluation of $g^{-1}(1000)$.

3.5–3.6 Investigating Properties of Inverse Functions

14. Describe the relation between $y = \sqrt{x}$ and $y = x^2$.

15. The graph of $y = f(x)$ is shown. Write a subset of f that has the same domain as f^{-1} so that f^{-1} is a function.

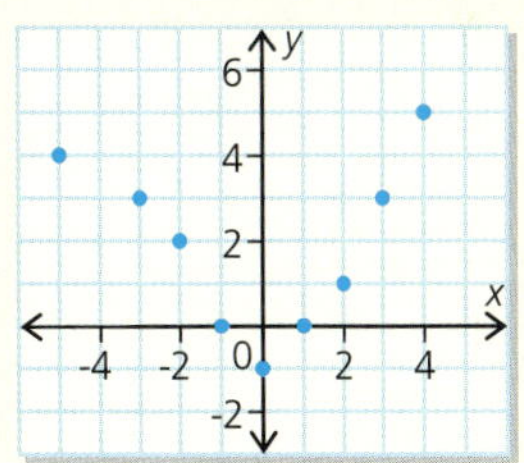

16. A function g is $g(x) = 4(x - 3)^2 + 1$.

(a) Graph g and g^{-1} using technology.

(b) At what points do the graphs of g and g^{-1} intersect?

(c) Determine an equation for g^{-1}.

(d) Solve for y in the equation that defines g^{-1}.

(e) State restrictions on the domain or range of g so that its inverse is a function.

(f) Suppose the domain of g is $\{x \mid 2 \leq x \leq 5, x \in \mathbf{R}\}$. Would the inverse be a function? Justify your answer.

17. For $f(x) = \sqrt{3 - 2x}$,

(a) graph f and f^{-1} using technology

(b) determine an equation for f^{-1}

(c) solve for y in the equation that defines f^{-1}

3.7 Transformations and Function Notation

18. Sketch the graph of $f(x) = \sqrt{x}$. On the same axes, sketch the graph of each function.

(a) $y = 2f(x)$ (b) $y = f(2x)$ (c) $y = f(x + 2)$

(d) $y = f(x) + 2$ (e) $y = -f(x)$ (f) $y = f(-x)$

19. $f = \{(0, 5), (1, 4), (2, 7), (3, 14)\}$ and $g(x) = 3f(-x + 1) + 7$.

(a) Evaluate $g(-1)$.

(b) Evaluate $g(1)$.

(c) Evaluate $g(3)$.

(d) Write g as a set of ordered pairs.

20. A function g is $g(x) = \frac{1}{2}f[3(x + 2)] - 4$.

(a) Draw an input/output diagram for g.

(b) List the transformations in the correct sequence to transform f into g.

(c) Suppose the domain of f is $\{x \mid 2 \leq x < 5, x \in \mathbf{R}\}$ and the range of f is $\{y \mid y \geq -2, y \in \mathbf{R}\}$. Determine the domain and range of g.

21. The graph of $y = g(x)$ is shown.

$$f(x) = -g\left(\frac{1}{2}x - 3\right) + 1$$

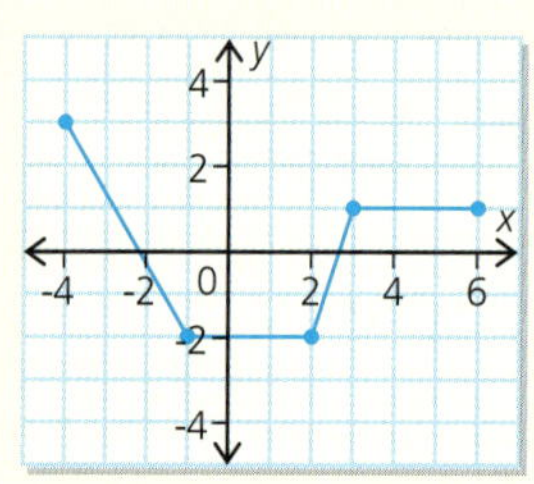

(a) Draw an input/output diagram for f.

(b) Determine the domain and range of f.

(c) Evaluate $f(4)$.

(d) Graph f.

Chapter 3 Summary

In this chapter, you saw what a function is and how to evaluate a function. You also saw how to find the inverse of functions and to describe the image of a function under various transformations.

Chapter 3 Review Test

Introducing Functions

1. Knowledge and Understanding
For each case,
i. determine $f(5)$
ii. state the domain and range
iii. state whether it is a function or not, and justify your answer

(a)

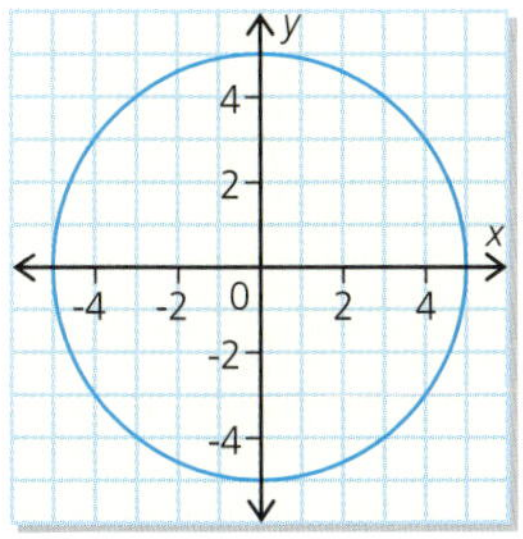

(b) $y = f(x)$

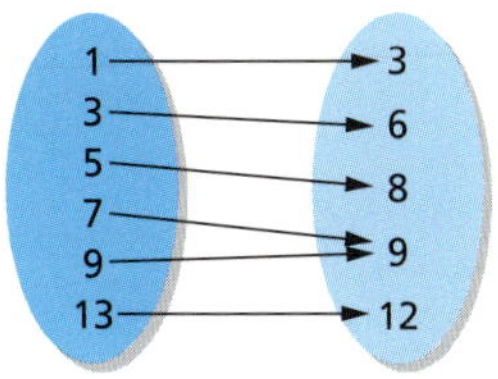

(c) $f = \{(1, 2), (1, 5), (4, 7), (5, -2), (8, 10)\}$

(d) $f(x) = 3x - 7$

(e) $f(x) = \sqrt{x - 3}$

(f) $f(x) = (x + 3)^2 - 5$

2. **i.** Solve each inequality.
ii. Graph each solution set for $x \in \mathbf{R}$.

(a) $-3(3x - 2) + 4x \geq -2x + 5(2x - 4)$

(b) $\frac{2x}{3} + \frac{3(x - 5)}{2} \leq x$

3. Determine the equation of the inverse, f^{-1}, for each function.

(a) $f(x) = 5x + 6$

(b) $f(x) = \sqrt{x + 4}$

(c) $f(x) = x^2 - 5$

4. Communication: Will the inverse of a given function also be a function? Clearly explain your reasoning and use an example to support your argument.

5. Explain why the vertical line test is a good test of whether or not the graph of a relation is a function.

6. A relation is defined by $g(x) = -x^2 + 6x - 4$.

(a) Graph $g(x)$.

(b) State the domain and range of $g(x)$.

(c) Determine the equation of g^{-1}.

(d) Graph g^{-1} using the same set of axes used in (a).

(e) State the domain and range of g^{-1}.

(f) Which relation, $g(x)$ or g^{-1}, is a function? Explain.

7. Application: A baseball club pays a peanut vendor \$50 per game for selling bags of peanuts for \$2.50 each. The club also pays the vendor a commission of \$0.05 per bag.

(a) Determine a function that describes the income the vendor makes for each baseball game. Define the variables in your function.

(b) Determine a function that describes the revenue the vendor generates each game for the baseball club. Define the variables in your function.

(c) Determine the number of bags of peanuts the vendor must sell before the baseball club makes a profit from his efforts.

8. (a) For the graph of $y = f(x)$, state the transformations that must be applied to $f(x)$ to obtain the graph of $y = -2f(-2x - 2) + 3$.

(b) Graph $y = -2f(-2x - 2) + 3$.

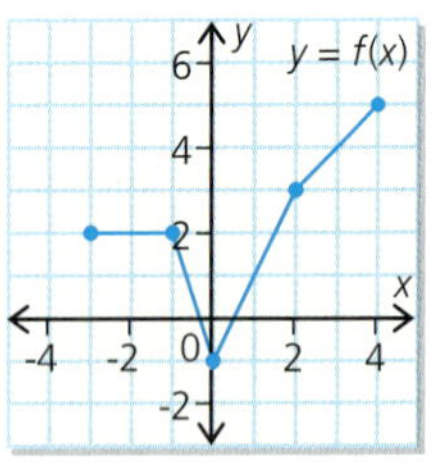

9. **Thinking, Inquiry, Problem Solving**
Make a conjecture with respect to the points of intersection between a function and its inverse. Verify your conjecture using

(a) a linear function and its inverse

(b) a quadratic function and its inverse

(c) a root function and its inverse

Chapter 4

Quadratic Functions and Rational Expressions

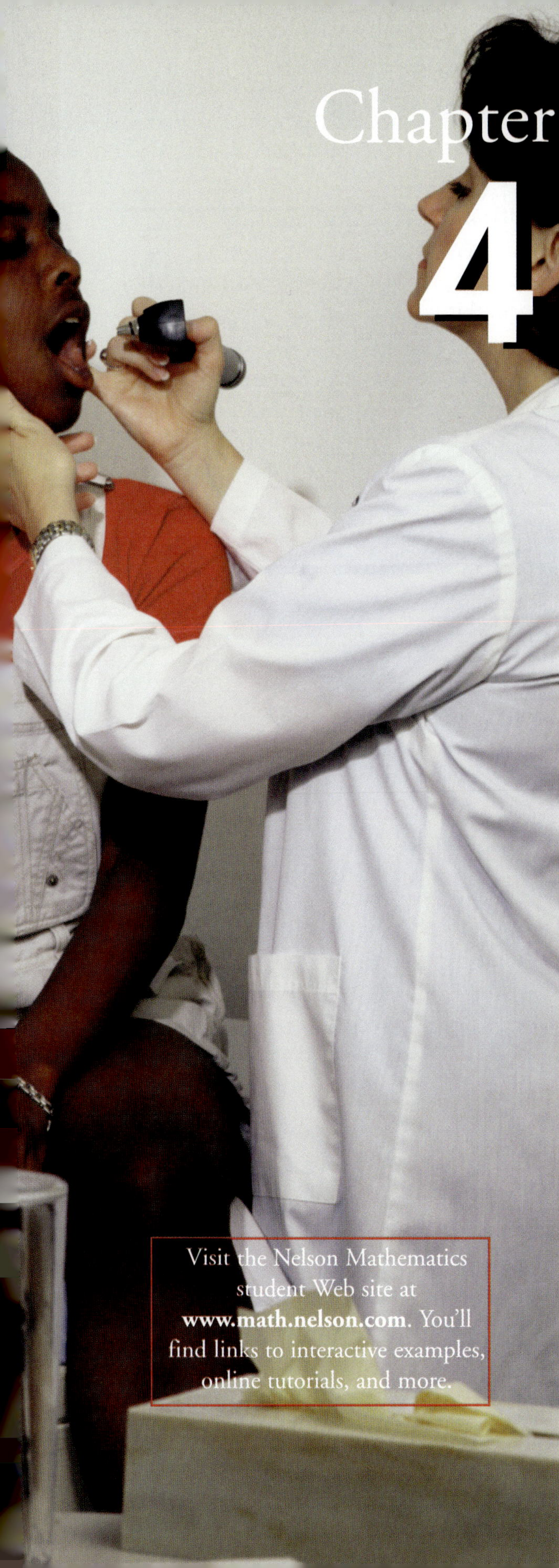

You have used linear and quadratic functions to model real-world situations. However, some situations, for example, in medicine, the life sciences, and business, are better modelled by rational functions.

Rational functions behave differently from other functions you have studied. You will need new algebraic skills to work with these functions.

In this chapter, you will

- review and extend your understanding of the quadratic function
- solve optimal value problems, with and without a graphing calculator
- relate the roots of quadratic equations to the zeros for the corresponding quadratic functions
- solve quadratic equations that do not have real roots by using complex numbers
- investigate and manipulate complex numbers
- graph the reciprocal function $f(x) = \frac{1}{x}$, investigate other examples of inverse variation, and fit a power function to inverse variation data
- use the graph of a function to sketch the graph of its reciprocal
- use a graphing calculator to explore the behaviour of functions near vertical and horizontal asymptotes
- add, subtract, multiply and divide rational expressions, and state restrictions on the variables
- add, subtract, and multiply polynomials

Visit the Nelson Mathematics student Web site at **www.math.nelson.com**. You'll find links to interactive examples, online tutorials, and more.

Connections

The Chapter Problem

Fundraising

Northern Heights Secondary School will celebrate its 25th anniversary next year. As part of the celebration, the student council decided to raise $7000 for supplies for a local food bank. Megan, who is the treasurer of the student council, suggests selling commemorative T-shirts to students. She has contacted three T-shirt suppliers about costs. Each supplier charges a fee for designing and making the template for the logo, and each supplier's cost per T-shirt is different, as shown in the table.

Supplier	Logo Design and Template	Cost per T-shirt
Custom Cottons	$250	$3.90
Tailored Tees	$400	$2.80
Tops to Go	$120	$4.50

Megan has also surveyed 100 randomly chosen students. She asked each student what prices he or she would be willing to pay for a T-shirt. The school's student population is 1582.

Number of Students	93	78	64	42	21	15	9
Price of T-shirt ($)	5.00	7.50	10.00	12.50	15.00	17.50	20.00

Which supplier should Megan choose? Will the target of $7000 be reached? Prepare a proposal for the student council. In your proposal, recommend one supplier. Support your choice with a graphical analysis of the expected profit.

For help with this problem, see pages 317, 327, 333, 355, and 371.

Challenge 1

Find a function that has two parallel asymptotes that are

(a) vertical

(b) horizontal

(c) oblique

Two parallel asymptotes divide the x-y plane into three regions.

For each type of parallel asymptotes—vertical, horizontal, and oblique—try to find a function that occupies

i. three regions of the x-y plane
ii. two regions of the x-y plane
iii. one region of the x-y plane

Write each function and sketch its graph.

Challenge 2

Find the dimensions of the isosceles triangle with the smallest area and whose incircle has radius 2 units.

Web Challenge

For a related Internet activity, go to **www.math.nelson.com**.

Getting Ready

In this chapter, you will be working with linear, quadratic, and other types of functions, algebraic expressions, and roots of equations. These exercises will help you warm up for the work ahead.

1. Evaluate.

(a) $-\frac{1}{4} + \frac{4}{5} - \frac{9}{10}$

(b) $\frac{5}{-6} - 3\frac{1}{3} + \frac{4}{9}$

(c) $\frac{9}{-4} \times \frac{-2}{7}$

(d) $\left(-4\frac{1}{6}\right)\left(-5\frac{1}{4}\right)$

(e) $-5 \div \left(\frac{-5}{6}\right)$

(f) $\left(-\frac{3}{7}\right) + \left(-1\frac{1}{5}\right)$

(g) $\frac{-5}{7} \times \frac{28}{5} \div \frac{-4}{3}$

(h) $\left(-\frac{1}{3}\right)^2 \div 1\frac{2}{9} \times \frac{11}{12}$

(i) $4 - \left(2\frac{1}{4} - \frac{-3}{8}\right)^2$

(j) $\dfrac{\frac{1}{-4} - \frac{-1}{3}}{\frac{5}{-12} - 1\frac{3}{4}}$

(k) $\frac{-3}{16} \times 3\frac{1}{5} \div \left(-1\frac{1}{3}\right)^2$

(l) $\left(\frac{4}{5} - \frac{3}{-4}\right)\left(\frac{-1}{3} - \frac{1}{4}\right)$

2. Simplify.

(a) $(4x)(3y)(-2z)$ (b) $(-5ab^2)(-6c^2)$

(c) $\frac{-27pqr}{-3qr}$ (d) $\frac{28m^3n}{14n^2}$

(e) $(-5c^2)(2bd^2)(-3a^2)$

(f) $\frac{36a^2b^2c^3d}{9a^2bd}$

3. Expand and simplify.

(a) $-4x(x^2 - 2x + 3y)$

(b) $5xy(3x - 2y + xy)$

(c) $-3a(7a^3 - 4a^2 + 2a)$

(d) $5x(x + 1) + 6x(2x - 3)$

(e) $-7y(2y - 5) - 2y(5y + 1)$

(f) $-y(4y - 3) - 3y^2$

(g) $3x^2 - 2x^2(1 - x)$

(h) $x^2(x^2 + 2x + 3) - 2x(x^2 + 2x + 3)$

4. Divide.

(a) $\frac{10a^2b + 15bc^2}{-5b}$

(b) $\frac{30x^2y^3 - 20x^2z^2 + 50x^2}{10x^2}$

(c) $\frac{xy - xyz}{xy}$

(d) $\frac{16mnr - 24mnp + 40kmn}{8mn}$

5. Expand and simplify.

(a) $(x - 2)^2$

(b) $(x + 1)(x - 4)$

(c) $(2x - 3)(x + 2)$

(d) $(4x - 5)(3x + 2)$

(e) $(4a - 3)(4a + 3)$

(f) $(x + 1)^2 - (x - 1)^2$

(g) $\left(\frac{1}{2}x + \frac{1}{3}\right)\left(3x - \frac{1}{2}\right)$

(h) $(0.3x - 0.6)(0.2x + 0.5)$

6. Determine the value of y.

(a) $y = (10 - x)(25 + 3x)$, if $x = 5$

(b) $y = 75 + 30x - 3x^2$, if $x = 0.01$

(c) $y = \frac{x + 3}{1 - x}$, if

i. $x = 10\ 000$ and **ii.** $x = -10\ 000$

(d) $y = \frac{x^2 - 2x + 1}{x - 1}$, if

i. $x = 1000$ and **ii.** $x = -1000$

(e) $y = \frac{2x}{x^2 - 9}$, if

i. $x = 2.99$ and **ii.** $x = 3.01$

7. Factor each expression. First remember to look for common factors.

(a) $5xy - 2x$

(b) $12m^2n^3 + 18m^3n^2$

(c) $15p^3q^2r^2 + 21p^4q^3r$

(d) $x^2 - 9x + 20$

(e) $y^2 - 4y - 32$

(f) $3x^2 + 24x + 45$

(g) $21x^2 + 21x - 42$

(h) $x^2 - 49$

(i) $50x^2 - 72$

(j) $9x^2 - 6x + 1$

(k) $2x^2 + x - 6$

(l) $10a^2 + a - 3$

8. Sketch the graph of each relation.

(a) $y = \frac{3}{4}x + 1$ (b) $y = -3x - 2$

(c) $x = 7.5$ (d) $y = -1.2$

(e) $2x + 5y = 10$

(f) $5x - 3y - 15 = 0$

9. Find the equation of the line that

(a) is parallel to the x-axis and passes through point $(2, -1)$

(b) has slope $-\frac{2}{3}$ and passes through point $(4, -1)$

(c) has x-intercept 2 and y-intercept 5

10. Sketch the graph for each relation. Do not make a table or use graphing technology. In each case, determine the coordinates of the vertex and the y-intercept.

(a) $y = (x - 3)(x - 5)$

(b) $y = -(x - 2)(x + 3)$

(c) $y = -2(3 - x)(5 - x)$

(d) $y = -x^2 + 5$

(e) $y = \frac{1}{2}(x + 4)^2 - 5$

(f) $y = -3(x - 2)^2 + 12$

(g) $y = x^2 - 4x + 7$

11. Solve each equation by factoring.

(a) $x^2 + 4x - 21 = 0$

(b) $x^2 + 12 = -8x$

(c) $6x^2 = 5 - 13x$

12. The population of a town is modelled by $P = 6t^2 + 110t + 3000$, where P is the population and t is the time in years. When $t = 0$, the year is 2000. According to this model,

(a) what will the population be in 2015?

(b) when will the population be 32 000?

(c) can the population ever be 0? Explain your answer.

13. Solve by completing the square.

(a) $x^2 + 6x - 1 = 0$

(b) $x^2 - 8x + 5 = 0$

(c) $2x^2 - 4x - 7 = 0$

(d) $-4x^2 + 6x = 3$

14. Solve using the quadratic formula. Round answers to two decimal places.

(a) $2x^2 - x - 3 = 0$

(b) $-2x^2 + 8x - 3 = 0$

(c) $3m^2 + 10m - 7 = 0$

(d) $2x^2 - 1.3x - 4.44 = 0$

15. Determine the number of real roots for each quadratic equation.

(a) $x^2 + 9 = 0$

(b) $x^2 + 5x - 8 = 0$

(c) $3x^2 + 2x + 6 = 0$

(d) $-3(x + 2)^2 + 10 = 0$

SKILL BUILDER 4.1

Extending Algebra Skills: Completing the Square

The same relationship can be expressed in several different algebraic forms. You have seen that quadratic relations can be written several ways:

$y = -2x^2 + 16x - 24$	$y = -2(x - 6)(x - 2)$	$y = -2(x - 4)^2 + 8$
(standard form)	(factored form)	(vertex form)

Each form provides different information about the relationship and its graph. You must be able to move algebraically from one form to another.

You have already completed the square to express a quadratic function in vertex form; however, when you work with real data, the coefficients in the model are often not integers. You will need to use rational numbers to complete the square in these cases.

Example 1

Put $f(x) = -3x^2 + 13x - 11$ in **vertex form**, $f(x) = a(x - h)^2 + k$, by completing the square. State the coordinates of the vertex.

Solution

Complete the square.

$f(x) = -3x^2 + 13x - 11$ — Factor the coefficient of x^2 from the first two terms.

$f(x) = -3(x^2 - \frac{13}{3}x) - 11$ — Add and subtract the square of half the coefficient of x inside the brackets.

$f(x) = -3\left[x^2 - \frac{13}{3}x + \left(-\frac{13}{6}\right)^2 - \left(-\frac{13}{6}\right)^2\right] - 11$ — The first three terms inside the square brackets form a perfect square. Multiply the fourth term by the coefficient of x^2. Then move this term outside the brackets.

$f(x) = -3\left[x^2 - \frac{13}{3}x + \left(-\frac{13}{6}\right)^2\right] - (-3)\left(-\frac{13}{6}\right)^2 - 11$ — Factor the perfect square.

$f(x) = -3\left(x - \frac{13}{6}\right)^2 + \frac{169}{12} - 11$ — Simplify.

$f(x) = -3\left(x - \frac{13}{6}\right)^2 + \frac{37}{12}$

The vertex form of $f(x) = -3x^2 + 13x - 11$ is $f(x) = -3\left(x - \frac{13}{6}\right)^2 + \frac{37}{12}$.

The vertex is $\left(\frac{13}{6}, \frac{37}{12}\right)$.

Example 2

Find the coordinates of the vertex for the graph of $f(x) = -0.16x^2 + 9.76x - 9.408$ by completing the square.

Solution

$f(x) = -0.16x^2 + 9.76x - 9.408$	Factor the coefficient of x^2 from the first two terms.
$f(x) = -0.16(x^2 - 61x) - 9.408$	Add and subtract the square of half the coefficient of x inside the brackets.
$f(x) = -0.16[x^2 - 61x + (-30.5)^2 - (-30.5)^2] - 9.408$	Group the three terms that form the perfect square. Then multiply the fourth term by -0.16 and move it outside the bracket.
$f(x) = -0.16[x^2 - 61x + (-30.5)^2] - (-0.16)(-30.5)^2 - 9.408$	Factor.
$f(x) = -0.16(x - 30.5)^2 + 148.84 - 9.408$	Simplify.
$f(x) = -0.16(x - 30.5)^2 + 139.432$	

The coordinates of the vertex are (30.5, 139.432).

Focus 4.1

Key Ideas

- The same relationship can be expressed in several different algebraic forms.
- Transform the equation of a quadratic function in standard form, $f(x) = ax^2 + bx + c$, to vertex form, $f(x) = a(x - h)^2 + k$, by **completing the square.**

$f(x) = ax^2 + bx + c$	Factor the coefficient of x^2 from the first two terms.
$f(x) = a\left(x^2 + \frac{b}{a}x\right) + c$	Add and subtract the square of half the coefficient of x inside the brackets.
$f(x) = a\left[x^2 + \frac{b}{a}x + \left(\frac{b}{2a}\right)^2 - \left(\frac{b}{2a}\right)^2\right] + c$	Group the three terms that form the perfect square. Multiply the fourth term by a and move it outside the brackets.
$f(x) = a\left[x^2 + \frac{b}{a}x + \left(\frac{b}{2a}\right)^2\right] - a\left(\frac{b}{2a}\right)^2 + c$	Factor the perfect square and simplify.
$f(x) = a\left(x + \frac{b}{2a}\right)^2 - \frac{b^2}{4a} + c$	

Practise, Apply, Solve 4.1

A

1. Factor the coefficient of x^2 from each expression.

(a) $2x^2 - 6x$ (b) $3x^2 + 2x$ (c) $-4x^2 + 2x$

(d) $\frac{1}{2}x^2 - 5x$ (e) $-1.2x^2 - 6.6x$ (f) $\frac{2}{3}x^2 + \frac{5}{6}x$

(g) $-\frac{4}{3}x^2 - 2x$ (h) $2.7x^2 - 0.9x$ (i) $-6x^2 + \frac{3}{5}x$

2. Find the value of d that makes each expression a perfect square.

(a) $x^2 + 3x + d$ (b) $x^2 - 7x + d$ (c) $x^2 + \frac{2}{3}x + d$

(d) $x^2 - \frac{3}{5}x + d$ (e) $x^2 - 2.5x + d$ (f) $x^2 + 0.45x + d$

(g) $x^2 - 22.4x + d$ (h) $x^2 - \frac{5}{9}x + d$ (i) $x^2 + \frac{x}{100} + d$

3. Express each function in vertex form by completing the square.

(a) $f(x) = x^2 - 4x + 3$ (b) $f(x) = x^2 + 6x - 8$

(c) $f(x) = 3x^2 - 6x + 1$ (d) $f(x) = x^2 - x$

(e) $f(x) = x^2 + 3x + 5$ (f) $f(x) = -x^2 + 5x - 2$

(g) $f(x) = x^2 - 2.6x - 2.7$ (h) $f(x) = x^2 + 5.4x - 1.8$

(i) $f(x) = x^2 - 3.4x - 2.8$

4. Express $g(x) = 2x^2 + 5x + 4$ in vertex form. Explain your steps.

B

5. Express each equation in vertex form by completing the square.

(a) $f(x) = x^2 - 3x + 2$ (b) $f(x) = 2x^2 + 5x - 4$

(c) $f(x) = 3x^2 - 4x + 1$ (d) $f(x) = 5x^2 - x - 5$

(e) $f(x) = -2x^2 + 3x + 5$ (f) $f(x) = -4x^2 - 7x - 2$

(g) $f(x) = 1.4x^2 - 4.9x - 2.7$ (h) $f(x) = -3.6x^2 + 5.4x - 1.67$

(i) $f(x) = \frac{1}{2}x^2 - 4x + 1$ (j) $f(x) = \frac{2}{3}x^2 - 5x - 2$

(k) $f(x) = -\frac{3}{2}x^2 - \frac{7}{8}x + \frac{1}{2}$ (l) $f(x) = -\frac{4}{5}x^2 + \frac{2}{3}x - \frac{3}{10}$

6. i. Find the coordinates of the vertex by completing the square.
ii. State the domain and the range of $f(x)$.
iii. Sketch the graph for each quadratic function.

(a) $f(x) = x^2 + 10x + 24$ (b) $f(x) = 4x^2 + 8x + 7$

(c) $f(x) = -2x^2 + 5x - \frac{1}{8}$ (d) $f(x) = \frac{1}{2}x^2 - 3x + 4$

(e) $f(x) = -2x^2 + 7x - 12$ (f) $f(x) = -2x^2 + 7x$

7. The function $d(x) = 5x^2 - 3x + 1$ is quadratic.

(a) Write the equation in vertex form.

(b) Write the equation of the axis of symmetry.

(c) Write the coordinates of the vertex.

(d) What is the maximum or minimum value of d?

(e) What is the domain of d?

(f) What is the range of d?

(g) Sketch the graph of d.

8. A football is punted into the air. Its height h, in metres, after t seconds is given by $h(t) = 1 + 24.5t - 4.9t^2$.

(a) Find the maximum height of the ball by completing the square. Round your answer to the nearest hundredth of a metre.

(b) When does the ball reach its maximum height?

9. For each function, determine the coordinates of the vertex.

(a) $f(x) = 2x^2 - \frac{5}{6}x - \frac{1}{2}$

(b) $f(x) = -3x^2 - \frac{2}{3}x + \frac{3}{4}$

(c) $f(x) = \frac{1}{2}x^2 + 4x - 8$

(d) $f(x) = -6x^2 + \frac{6}{7}x - \frac{3}{7}$

10. What transformations must you apply to the graph of $y = x^2$ to obtain the graph of $y = 0.4x^2 - 2x + 3.5$? Show all your work and explain each step.

11. Researchers found that the relationship between the yield of a crop and the amount of watering could be modelled by $y = -1478 + 3345x - 446x^2$, where y is the yield, in kilograms per hectare (kg/ha), and x is the annual amount of water, in hectare-metres (ha-m). How much water produces the greatest yield?

C

12. What numbers could t be if t^2 must be less than $12t - 20$?

13. State the domain and range.

(a) $g(x) = x^2 + 3x - 4$

(b) $h(x) = -2x^2 + 5x - 1$

(c) $f(x) = \frac{1}{2}x^2 - \frac{2}{3}x + \frac{3}{4}$

(d) $k(x) = 0.1x^2 - 0.5x + 0.3$

14. **Check Your Understanding:** Why should you be able to write the equation of the same quadratic function in several different equivalent forms? What are the steps for changing the equation of a quadratic function from standard form into vertex form? Use an example to explain.

4.2 Maximum and Minimum Values of Quadratic Functions

Companies that manufacture and sell items must do research before and after producing an item. Some of this research relates to manufacturing and its costs. Other research concerns, for example, the demand for the item, the selling price, and consumer preferences. While shopping in a mall, you may have been approached by someone conducting "market research." Market research is one way of collecting data.

Data are collected through research and this data may be analyzed in different ways. Most companies want to maximize their profits, so some of the analysis is used to estimate, or model, a profit function. Profit functions are typically quadratic, and you will see why in the following simplified example.

Part 1: Changing a Quadratic Profit Function from Standard Form to Vertex Form by Completing the Square

Think, Do, Discuss

1. The selling price of an item depends, in part, on how many items the company expects to sell. The relation between the price of an item, p, and the number of items sold, x, is called the **demand function**, $p(x)$. Through research, RAYZ Manufacturing collected the following data, where x is the number of pairs of sunglasses sold in thousands and p is the price of one pair in dollars.

Pairs of Sunglasses Sold, x (thousands)	0.7	1.4	1.8	2.1	2.9	3.2
Price, p ($)	30.00	27.50	25.00	22.50	20.00	17.50

   Describe the relation between the price and the number of items sold. How does the price change as the number of items sold increases? Does this change make sense to you? Explain your answer.

2. Enter the data into a graphing calculator. Then perform a linear regression to obtain the demand function, $p(x)$. Round the coefficients to whole numbers.

3. Write the **revenue function**, $R(x)$, based on your demand function. Recall that the revenue is the income from sales.

$$\begin{aligned} R(x) &= \text{number of pairs of glasses sold} \times \text{price of each item} \\ &= x \times \text{demand function} \\ &= x \times p(x) \\ &= ? \end{aligned}$$

4. Research for this item shows that the **cost function** is $C(x) = 3x + 35$. Obtain the **profit function** using $P(x) = R(x) - C(x)$. Simplify the right side by expanding and then collecting like terms. What kind of function is the profit function? Describe the graph of $y = P(x)$.

5. Complete the square of the profit function to determine how many pairs of glasses should be sold to maximize profits.

6. Sketch the graph of the profit function. What are the coordinates of the y-intercept? Which form of the equation, standard form or vertex form, did you use to find the y-intercept? Explain the significance of the x-intercepts. For the graph of a profit function, the x-intercepts are called the **break-even points**. Explain this description.

7. Use the profit function, along with the quadratic formula, to find the break-even quantities. Remember that x is in thousands.

8. Use a graphing calculator to check your graph. Check the vertex coordinates and the break-even points using the maximum and zero operations in the **CALC** menu.

Part 2: Finding the Vertex without Completing the Square

Since different forms of a quadratic function are useful for different reasons, you must be able to change from one form to another using algebra. As you have seen, working with decimals and fractions makes completing the square difficult. However, if you are dealing only with quadratic functions, then there is a way to avoid the complicated algebra.

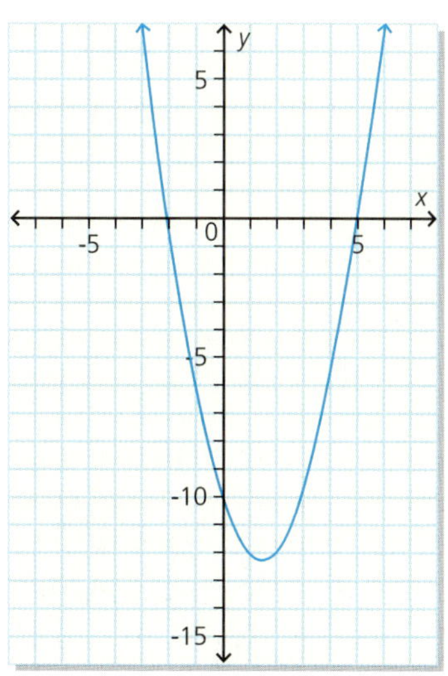

Think, Do, Discuss

1. In Chapter 3, you did some work on transforming functions. If you apply a vertical translation to a parabola, how do the coordinates of the vertex change? Consider the parabola shown here. Its equation is $y = a(x + 2)(x - 5)$. What is the x-coordinate of the vertex? How do you know what the x-coordinate is?

2. Use the coordinates of the y-intercept to find the value of a. Then expand the equation of the parabola so that it is in the form $y = ax^2 + bx + c$.

3. What vertical translation would make the parabola pass through the origin? What is the equation of the translated parabola?

4. Express the new equation in factored form. What are the new x-intercepts? Why is the x-coordinate of the vertex for the new parabola the same as that for the original parabola? Use these new x-intercepts to explain your answer.

5. Now consider the graph of the profit function, $P(x) = -5x^2 + 31x - 35$, from Part 1. What vertical translation would make the graph pass through the origin? What is the equation of the translated parabola?

6. Express the new equation in factored form. Where are the new x-intercepts? What is the x-coordinate of the vertex? Use the original equation to find the y-coordinate of the vertex for the graph of the profit function. Compare your answer to your result in Part 1.

Focus 4.2

Key Ideas

- The graph of a quadratic function is a parabola.
- If $a > 0$, the parabola opens up and the minimum value of the function occurs at the vertex. If $a < 0$, the parabola opens down and the maximum value of the function occurs at the vertex.
- There are three main forms for the equation of a quadratic function.

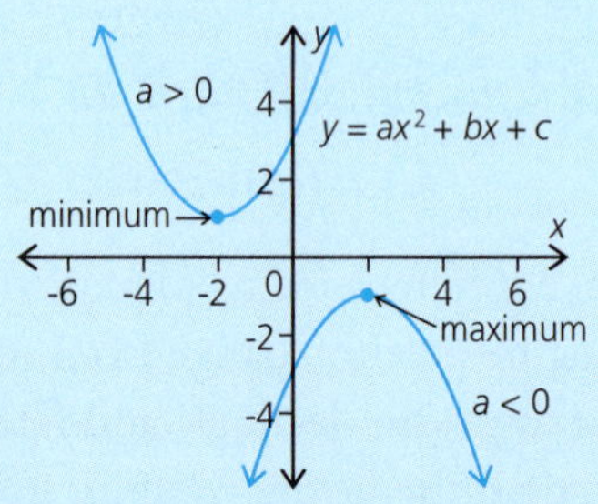

  - In standard form, $f(x) = ax^2 + bx + c$, the y-intercept, $(0, c)$, is clearly visible.
  - In factored form, $f(x) = a(x - p)(x - q)$, the x-intercepts, $(p, 0)$ and $(q, 0)$, are clearly visible.
  - In vertex form, $f(x) = a(x - h)^2 + k$, the coordinates of the vertex, (h, k), are clearly visible, and the maximum or minimum value of the function is k.
- You can change the equation of a quadratic function from standard form to vertex form by **completing the square**.
- The parabola for $f(x) = ax^2 + bx$ is a vertical translation of the parabola for $g(x) = ax^2 + bx + c$. For the factored form, $f(x) = x(ax + b)$, the midpoint between the x-intercepts, $(0, 0)$ and $\left(-\frac{b}{a}, 0\right)$, is the x-coordinate of the vertex, $-\frac{b}{2a}$, for parabolas for both $f(x)$ and $g(x)$. Find the y-coordinate of the vertex for $g(x) = ax^2 + bx + c$ by substituting $-\frac{b}{2a}$ for x in the equation. Therefore, for any function $g(x) = ax^2 + bx + c$, the vertex will have the coordinates $\left[-\frac{b}{2a}, g\left(-\frac{b}{2a}\right)\right]$.

Example 1

Research for a given orchard has shown that, if 100 pear trees are planted, then the annual revenue is \$90 per tree. If more trees are planted they have less room to grow and generate fewer pears per tree. As a result, the annual revenue per tree is reduced by \$0.70 for each additional tree planted. No matter how many trees are planted, the cost of maintaining each tree is \$7.40 per year. How many pear trees should be planted to maximize the profit from the orchard for one year?

Solution

Let x represent the number of additional trees planted.

The number of trees in the orchard is $100 + x$, and the annual revenue per tree, in dollars, is $90 - 0.70x$.

Let $R(x)$ be the total annual revenue from all the trees.

$$\begin{aligned} R(x) &= (100 + x)(90 - 0.70x) \\ &= 9000 - 70x + 90x - 0.70x^2 \\ &= 9000 + 20x - 0.70x^2 \end{aligned}$$

Let $C(x)$ be the cost function. It costs \$7.40 to maintain each tree, so the cost of maintaining all the trees in the orchard is \$7.40$(100 + x)$, or $C(x) = 740 + 7.4x$.

$$\text{profit} = \text{revenue} - \text{cost}$$

$$\begin{aligned} P(x) &= R(x) - C(x) \\ &= (9000 + 20x - 0.70x^2) - (740 + 7.4x) \\ &= -0.70x^2 + 12.6x + 8260 \qquad \text{Complete the square.} \\ &= -0.70(x^2 - 18x) + 8260 \\ &= -0.70(x^2 - 18x + 81 - 81) + 8260 \\ &= -0.70(x^2 - 18x + 81) + 56.7 + 8260 \\ &= -0.70(x - 9)^2 + 8316.7 \end{aligned}$$

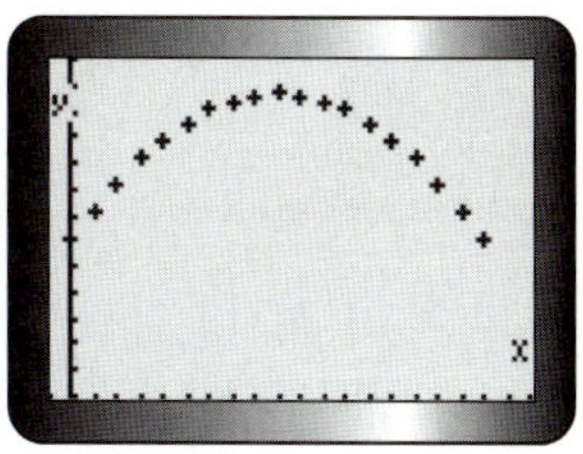

The graph of the profit function is a parabola that opens down. The profit reaches a maximum value at the vertex, (9, 8316.7). To maximize profit, nine additional trees must be planted. A total of 109 pear trees should be planted in the orchard to maximize profit.

The variable x in this solution is discrete because x represents the number of additional trees, which must be a whole number. A graph of $P(x)$ is shown.

Example 2

The demand function for a new product is $p(x) = -5x + 39$, where p represents the selling price of the product and x is the number sold in thousands. The cost function is $C(x) = 4x + 30$.

(a) How many items must be sold for the company to break even?

(b) What quantity of items sold will produce the maximum profit?

Solution

profit = revenue − cost

$$\begin{aligned} P(x) &= x \times p(x) - C(x) \\ &= x(-5x + 39) - (4x + 30) \\ &= -5x^2 + 39x - 4x - 30 \\ &= -5x^2 + 35x - 30 \\ &= -5(x^2 - 7x + 6) \\ &= -5(x - 1)(x - 6) \end{aligned}$$

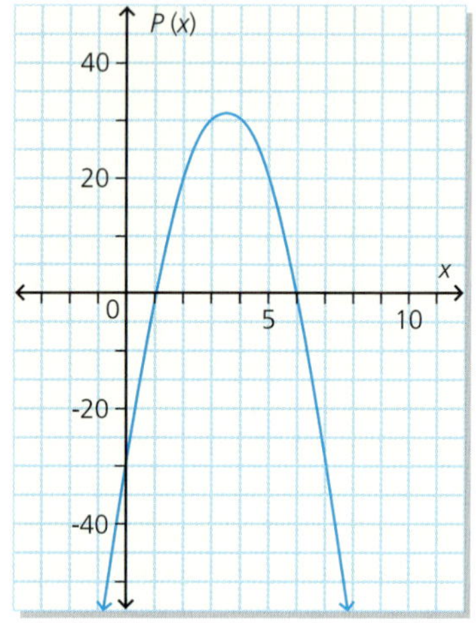

(a) The company breaks even if revenue equals cost, or $P(x) = 0$. Find the zeros, or x-intercepts, for $P(x)$. The factored form of the function shows that the x-intercepts are 1 and 6. The company will break even if 1000 items or 6000 items are sold, since x is the number of items sold in thousands.

(b) The maximum value of the profit function is at the vertex. The x-value of the vertex is the quantity that will produce maximum profit. The vertex lies on the axis of symmetry for the function, halfway between the two x-intercepts. The x-value halfway between 1 and 6 is $\frac{1 + 6}{2} = 3.5$. Profit will be maximized if 3500 items are sold.

Example 3

The cost per hour of running a bus between Burlington and Toronto is modelled by the function $C(x) = 0.0029x^2 - 0.48x + 142$, where x is the speed of the bus in kilometres per hour, and the cost, C, is in dollars. Determine the most cost-efficient speed for the bus and the cost per hour at this speed.

Solution

At the most cost-efficient speed, the hourly cost is a minimum value.

To find this speed and corresponding hourly cost, find the coordinates of the vertex. Instead of completing the square, consider a vertical translation of the cost function.

The value of x that minimizes $0.0029x^2 - 0.48x + 142$ is the same as the value of x that minimizes $0.0029x^2 - 0.48x$ or $x(0.0029x - 0.48)$.

The x-intercepts for the translated function are 0 and $\frac{0.48}{0.0029} \doteq 165.52$. The x-coordinate of the vertex is halfway between these values at $x = 0 + \frac{165.52}{2}$ or about 82.76. The most cost-efficient speed for the inter-city bus is about 83 km/h.

The cost per hour at this value is $C(82.76) = 0.0029(82.76)^2 - 0.48(82.76) + 142$
$\doteq 122.14.$

The hourly cost at this speed is about \$122.14.

Example 4

A farming cooperative collected data showing the effect of different amounts of fertilizer, x, in hundreds of kilograms per hectare (kg/ha), on the yield of carrots, y, in tonnes (t).

(a) Given the data in the table, predict the maximum yield of carrots.

Fertilizer, x (kg/ha)	0	0.25	0.50	0.75	1.00	1.25	1.50	1.75	2.00
Yield, y(t)	0.16	0.46	0.63	0.91	0.96	1.08	1.05	0.88	0.78

(b) Enter the data into a graphing calculator and use quadratic regression to estimate y as a function of x.

(c) How much fertilizer would you recommend the farmers use? Explain.

Solution

(a) From the table, the maximum yield is about 1.08 t for 125 kg of fertilizer.

(b) Enter the data into lists and create a scatter plot.

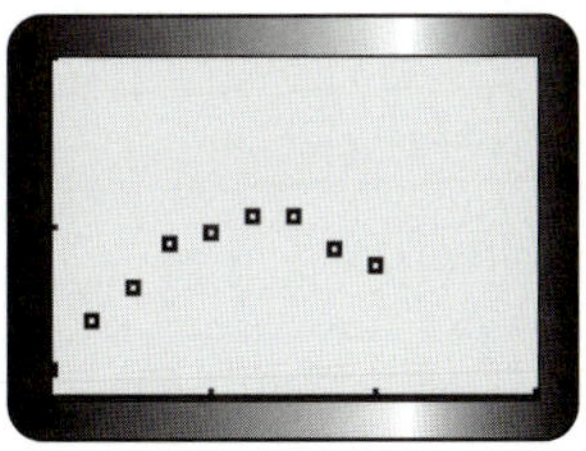

Use quadratic regression and store the resulting function in **Y1**. The function relating x and y is $y \doteq -0.53x^2 + 1.38x + 0.14$. (Coefficients are rounded to two decimal places.)

(c) Trace along the graph or choose **4:maximum** from the **CALC** menu to find the coordinates of the vertex.

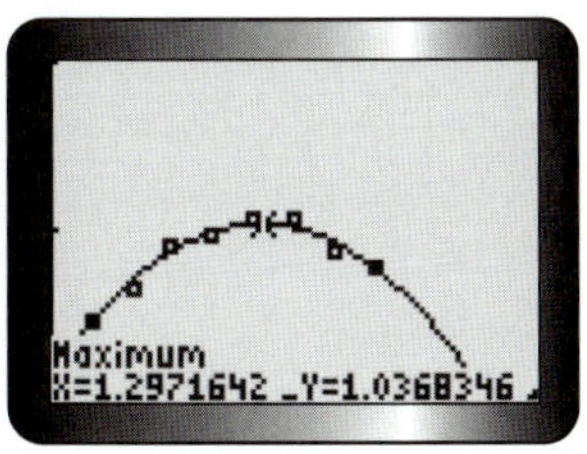

The coordinates of the vertex of the fitted parabola are about (1.30, 1.04). To maximize the yield of carrots, the farmers should use 130 kg of fertilizer per hectare.

Practise, Apply, Solve 4.2

A

1. **i.** Complete the square to find the coordinates of the vertex for the graph of each function.
ii. State whether each function has a maximum or a minimum value.
iii. Determine the value of x that produces the maximum or minimum value.
iv. State the maximum or minimum value.

(a) $f(x) = x^2 - 5x - 8$
(b) $f(x) = -2x^2 + 16x - 17$
(c) $f(x) = -4x^2 - 6x - 5$
(d) $f(x) = -\frac{1}{2}x^2 + 2x - 9$

2. Without changing the form of the equation, find the coordinates of the vertex for the graph of each function and then sketch the graph.

(a) $f(x) = (x - 3)(x - 8)$
(b) $f(x) = -2(x - 1)(x + 2)$
(c) $f(x) = -0.7(1.1 - x)(3.2 + x)$
(d) $f(x) = -\frac{5}{6}\left(x - \frac{2}{3}\right)\left(x + \frac{1}{6}\right)$

3. Without completing the square, find the coordinates of the vertex and state whether the function has a maximum or minimum value.

(a) $f(x) = 2x^2 - 6x$
(b) $h(t) = -5t^2 + 15t$
(c) $s(t) = -4.9t^2 + 19.6t + 22$
(d) $f(x) = 2.5x^2 - 15x - 24$

4. For each of the following demand functions, x is the number of items sold in thousands and $p(x)$ is the price of each item. Determine

i. the revenue function
ii. the maximum revenue

(a) $p(x) = -x + 7$
(b) $p(x) = -3x + 11$
(c) $p(x) = -0.4x + 14$

5. For each pair of revenue and cost functions, determine

i. the profit function
ii. the value of x that maximizes profit

(a) $R(x) = -x^2 + 24x$, $C(x) = 12x + 28$
(b) $R(x) = -2x^2 + 32x$, $C(x) = 14x + 45$
(c) $R(x) = -3x^2 + 26x$, $C(x) = 8x + 18$
(d) $R(x) = -2x^2 + 25x$, $C(x) = 3x + 17$

B

6. **Knowledge and Understanding:** The demand function for a new product is $p(x) = -5x + 21$, where x represents the number of items in thousands and p represents the price in dollars. The cost function is $C(x) = 4x + 14$.

(a) State the corresponding revenue function.
(b) Determine the corresponding profit function.
(c) Complete the square to determine the value of x that will maximize profits.
(d) Find the break-even quantities.
(e) Sketch the graph of the profit function.

7. The cost per hour of running an assembly line in a manufacturing plant is a function of the number of items produced per hour. The cost function is $C(x) = 0.28x^2 - 0.7x + 1$, where $C(x)$ is the cost per hour in thousands of dollars and x is the number of items produced per hour in thousands. Determine the most economical production level.

8. A T-ball baseball player hits a baseball from a tee that is 0.6 m tall. The flight of the ball can be modelled by $h(t) = -4.9t^2 + 6t + 0.6$, where h is the height in metres and t is the time in seconds. When does the ball reach its maximum height? Determine the maximum height of the ball. Answer to one decimal place.

9. The sum of two numbers is 10. What is the largest product of these numbers?

10. Prove that the value of $2x^2 - 8x + 9$ cannot be less than 1.

11. **Communication:** Suppose that $f(x)$ and $g(x)$ are both quadratic functions with graphs that open down. Explain how you know what type of function $y = f(x) + g(x)$ must be. In which direction does the graph open? Where is the maximum point of this function in relation to the maximum points for the first two functions? Explain your answers.

12. (a) An orchard owner has maintained records that show that, if 25 apple trees are planted in one acre, then each tree yields an average of 500 apples.The yield decreases by 10 apples per tree for each additional tree that is planted. How many trees should be planted for maximum total yield?

    (b) The cost of maintaining each tree is \$6.50 and the owner can expect to sell his apples for 15¢ each. How many trees should he plant for maximum revenue?

13. Through research, Pizza Pizzazz obtained the demand data in the table, where x represents the number of large pizzas sold per month, and p is the price they plan to charge per pizza.

Number of Pizzas Sold, x (thousands)	4.7	5.8	7.3	8.4	8.8	9.8
Price, p (\$)	20	18	16	14	12	10

    (a) Enter the data into a graphing calculator. Perform a linear regression to obtain a demand function, that relates the price to the number of pizzas sold. Round the coefficients to whole numbers.

    (b) Write the revenue function, based on your demand function.

    (c) Research also shows that the cost function is $C(x) = 9x + 44$. Determine a profit function and use it to find how many pizzas should be sold each month to maximize profits.

14. Students at an agricultural school collected data showing the effect of different annual amounts of water—rainfall, plus irrigation—x, in hectare-metres (ha-m), on the yield of broccoli, y, in hundreds of kilograms per hectare (100 kg/ha).

(a) Given the data in the table, predict the maximum yield of broccoli.

Rainfall, x (ha-m)	0.30	0.45	0.60	0.75	0.90	1.05	1.20	1.35	1.50
Yield, y (100 kg/ha)	35	104	198	287	348	401	427	442	418

(b) Use quadratic regression on a graphing calculator to estimate y as a function of x.

(c) What is the optimal annual amount of water? Under these conditions, what is the expected yield of broccoli?

15. Vitaly and Jen have 24 m of fencing to enclose a vegetable garden at the back of their house. What are the dimensions of the largest rectangular garden they could enclose with this length of fencing?

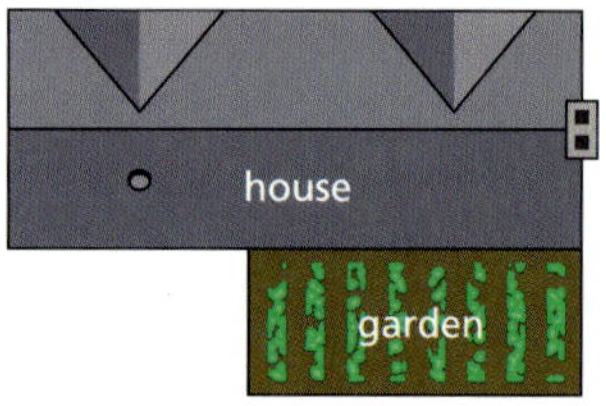

16. A 135-kg steer gains 3.5 kg/day and costs 80¢/day to keep. The market price for beef cattle is \$1.65/kg, but the price falls by 1¢/day. When should the steer be sold to maximize profit?

17. **Thinking, Inquiry, Problem Solving:** A family of functions is described by $y = ax^2 + bx$. The graphs of the functions are all parabolas, and each parabola passes through the origin. How do you know that this last sentence is true given the equation? If a is fixed and b varies, then the graphs of these parabolas would still pass through the origin, but the graphs are also related in another way.

(a) Choose any positive, or negative, value for a and create eight equations of the form $y = ax^2 + bx$ by choosing different values for b.

(b) Find the coordinates of the vertex for each of the eight parabolas.

(c) All of the eight vertices are related. Find the relation.

(d) Repeat (a), (b), and (c) for a different value of a.

(e) Write a brief report and include, if possible, a general case.

18. **Check Your Understanding**

(a) What are the three main forms for the equation of a quadratic function?

(b) Provide an example of a quadratic function in each of these three forms.

(c) Explain the significance of each form and when it should be used.

(d) Give practical examples of the use of each form.

C

19. A rock is thrown straight up in the air, from an initial height, h_0, in metres, with initial velocity, v_0, in metres per second. The height in metres above the ground after t seconds is given by $h(t) = -4.9t^2 + v_0t + h_0$. Find an expression for the time it takes the rock to reach its maximum height.

20. Application: Mark is designing a pentagonal-shaped play area for a daycare facility. He has 30 m of nylon mesh to enclose the play area. The triangle in the diagram is equilateral. Find the dimensions of the rectangle plus the triangle, to the nearest tenth of a metre, that will maximize the area he can enclose for the play area.

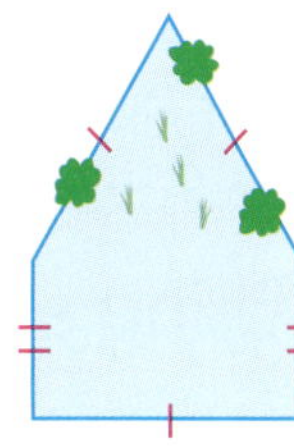

21. The diagram of a practice field shows a rectangle with a semicircle at each end. The track-and-field coach wants two laps around the field to be 1000 m. The physical education department needs a rectangular field that is as large as possible.

(a) Determine the dimensions of the track that will maximize the entire enclosed area. Do these dimensions meet the needs of the track coach and the physical education department? Explain.

(b) If only the rectangular portion of the field is maximized, can the track team run the 100-m dash along a straight part of the track? Justify your answer.

The Chapter Problem—Fundraising

Apply what you have learned in this section to answer these questions about the Chapter Problem on page 300.

CP1. Use the survey data on page 300 and the total number of students to estimate the number of T-shirts that should sell at each price.

CP2. Enter your data from CP1 into a graphing calculator. Do a linear regression to obtain a demand function relating price to the number of T-shirts sold. Round the coefficients to two decimal places.

CP3. Write the revenue function, based on your demand function from CP2.

CP4. Graph the revenue function and describe its shape. What is its domain?

4.3 Zeros of Quadratic Functions

You have seen that a quadratic function, $f(x)$, may have no zeros, one zero, or two zeros. The zeros, or x-intercepts, occur when $f(x) = 0$. There are several ways to find the number of zeros for a quadratic function.

Part 1: Using a Graph to Find the Number of Zeros

Find the number of zeros in the graph of a quadratic function by finding the number of times the graph crosses or touches the x-axis.

Example 1

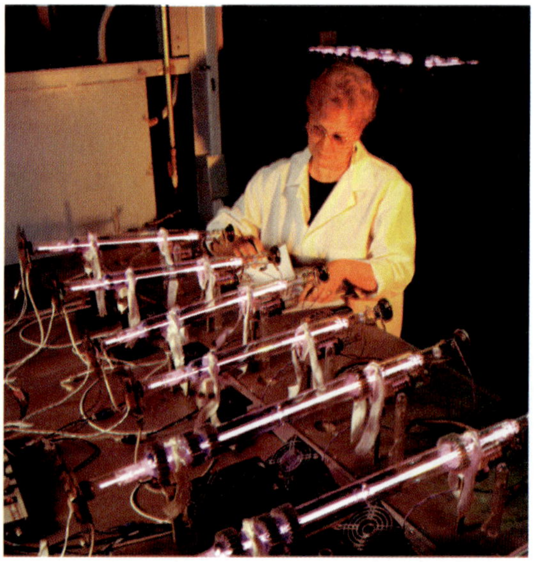

The demand function for a new mechanical part is $p(x) = -0.5x + 7.8$, where p is the price in dollars and x is the quantity sold in thousands. The new part can be manufactured by three different processes, A, B, or C. The cost function for each process is as follows:

Process A: $C(x) = 4.6x + 5.12$
Process B: $C(x) = 3.8x + 5.12$
Process C: $C(x) = 5.3x + 3.8$

Use a graphing calculator to investigate the break-even quantities for each process. Which process would you recommend to the company?

Solution

The profit function for each process is as follows:

Process A: $$P_A(x) = x(-0.5x + 7.8) - (4.6x + 5.12) = -0.5x^2 + 3.2x - 5.12$$

Process B: $$P_B(x) = x(-0.5x + 7.8) - (3.8x + 5.12) = -0.5x^2 + 4x - 5.12$$

Process C: $$P_C(x) = x(-0.5x + 7.8) - (5.3x + 3.8) = -0.5x^2 + 2.5x - 3.8$$

The company will break even when the profit is 0, that is, $P(x) = 0$.

Here are the graphs of these profit functions:

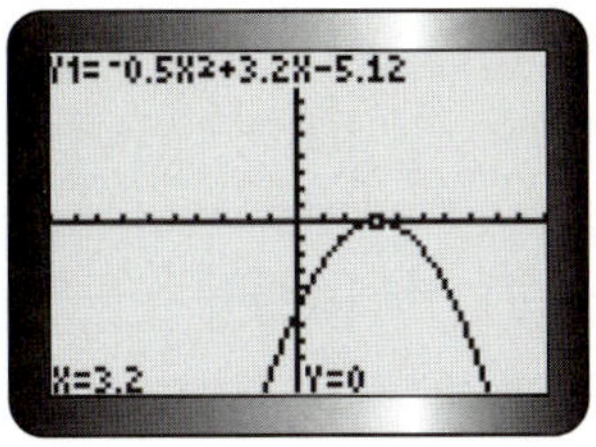

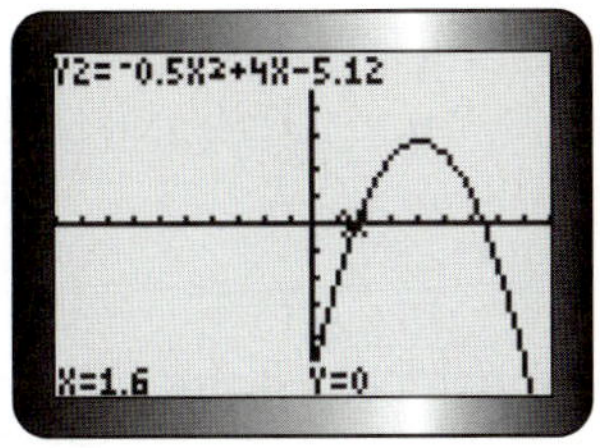

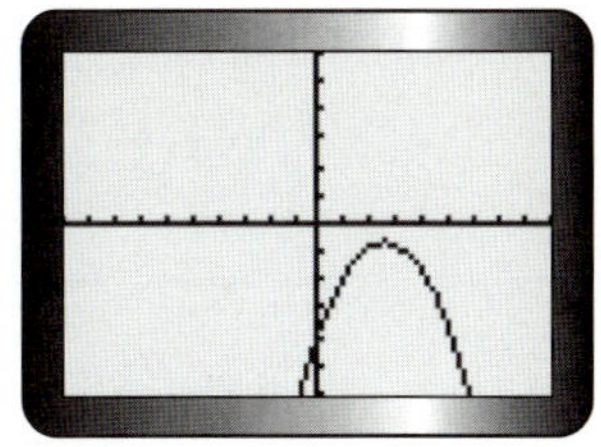

For process A, the corresponding graph of the profit function has only one x-intercept. If $x = 3.2$, then $P_A(x) = 0$. If 3200 parts were sold, then the company would not make a profit, but would break even.

For process B, the corresponding graph of the profit function has two x-intercepts. If $x = 1.6$, or $x = 6.4$, then $P_B(x) = 0$. If 1600 parts are sold, then the company breaks even. The profit increases to a maximum if 4000 parts are sold. Then the profit tapers to 0 if 6400 parts are sold.

For process C, the corresponding graph of the profit function has no x-intercepts. $P_C(x) \neq 0$. The company would not make a profit; instead, it would lose money.

The company would profit most by using process B.

Part 2: Finding the Number of Zeros Algebraically

The three forms of a quadratic function are the **factored form,** $f(x) = a(x - p)(x - q)$, the **vertex form,** $f(x) = a(x - h)^2 + k$, and the **standard form,** $f(x) = ax^2 + bx + c$. You can find the number of zeros for a function that is in any of these forms.

Finding the Number of Zeros For a Quadratic Function in Factored Form

The zeros are clearly visible in any quadratic function in factored form. A zero occurs on the graph of the relation whenever any of the factors in the relation equals 0.

The quadratic function $f(x) = a(x - p)(x - q)$ has two zeros at $x = p$ and $x = q$.

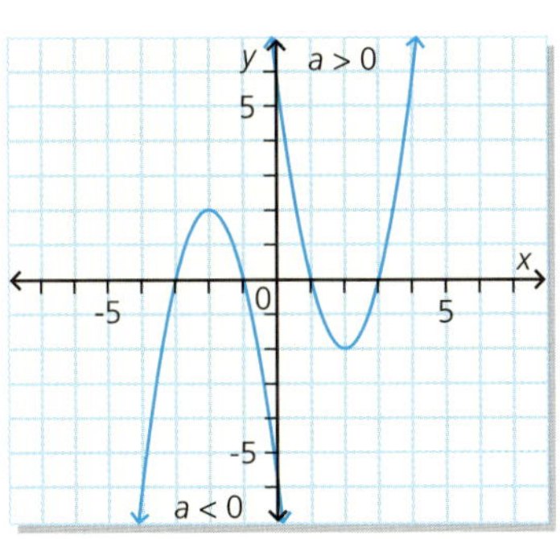

The quadratic function $g(x) = a(x - p)^2$ has one zero at $x = p$.

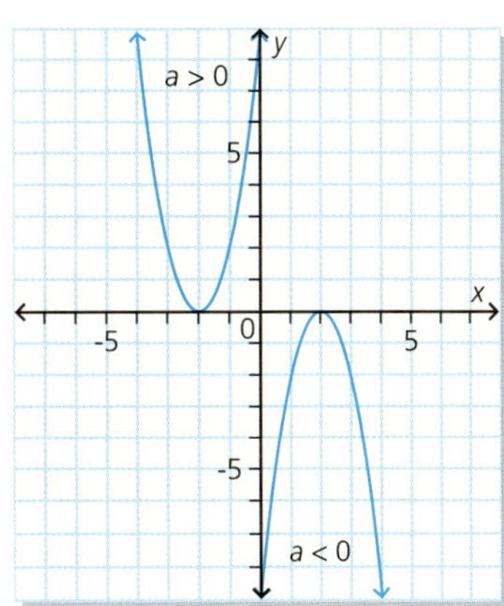

Example 2

Without drawing the graph, find the number of zeros for each function.

(a) $f(x) = -0.4(x - 1)(x + 7)$ (b) $g(x) = 3(x - 2.4)^2$

Solution

(a) Since $f(x) = -0.4(x - 1)(x + 7)$ is in factored form, the zeros are visible.

If $f(x) = 0$, then $x - 1 = 0$ or $x + 7 = 0$

$x = 1$ $x = -7$

The function $f(x)$ has two zeros.

(b) The zero is also visible in $g(x) = 3(x - 2.4)^2$.

If $g(x) = 0$, then $x - 2.4 = 0$

$x = 2.4$

The function $g(x)$ has one zero.

Finding the Number of Zeros for a Quadratic Function in Vertex Form

A quadratic function in vertex form shows the direction of the parabola's opening and the location of the vertex in terms of the x-axis.

For $f(x) = a(x - h)^2 + k$, $a > 0$ the parabola opens **up**.
The value of k determines the number of zeros.

If $k < 0$, then $f(x)$ has two zeros. The vertex (h, k) lies below the x-axis.

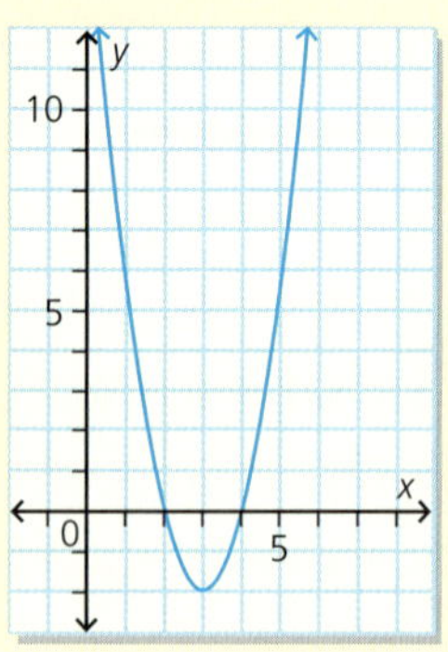

If $k = 0$, then $f(x)$ has one zero. The vertex (h, k) lies on the x-axis.

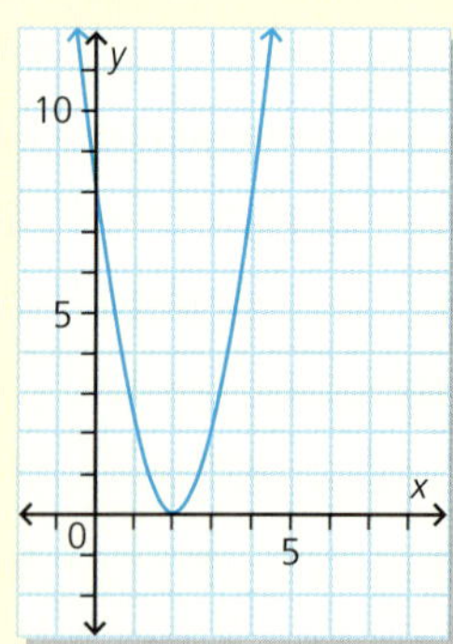

If $k > 0$, then $f(x)$ has no zeros. The vertex (h, k) lies above the x-axis.

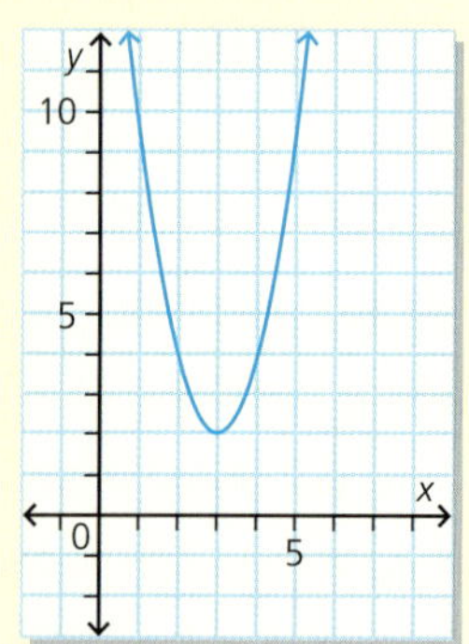

For $f(x) = a(x - h)^2 + k$, **$a < 0$** the parabola opens **down**.
The value of k determines the number of zeros.

If $k > 0$, then $f(x)$ has two zeros. The vertex (h, k) lies above the x-axis.

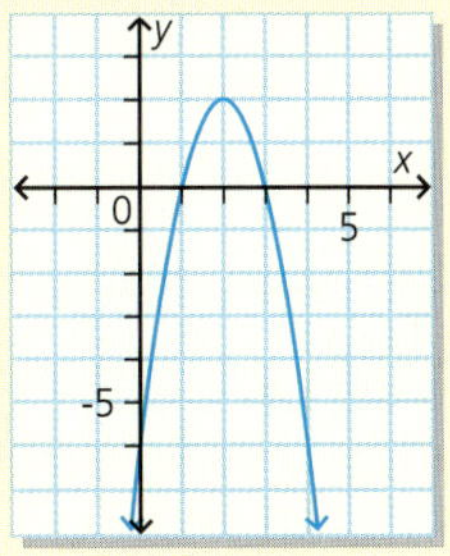

If $k = 0$, then $f(x)$) has one zero. The vertex (h, k) lies on the x-axis.

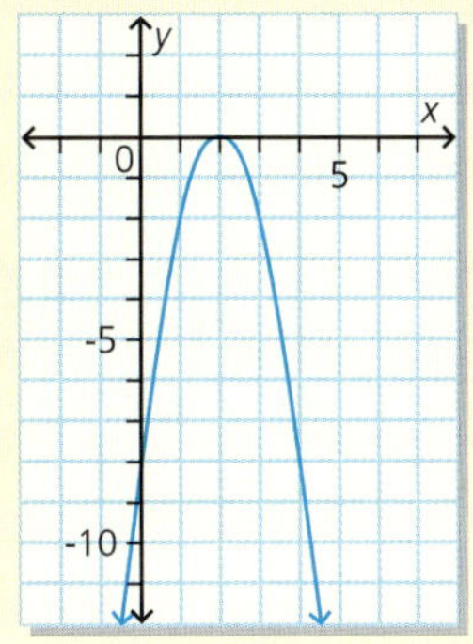

If $k < 0$, then $f(x)$ has no zeros. The vertex (h, k) lies below the x-axis.

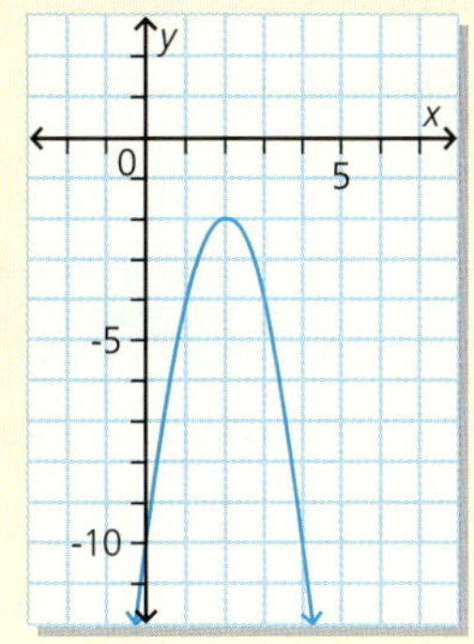

A quadratic function in vertex form, $f(x) = a(x - h)^2 + k$, has

- two zeros if a and k have opposite signs
- one zero if $k = 0$
- no zeros if a and k have the same signs

Example 3

Without drawing the graph, find the number of zeros for each function.

(a) $g(x) = 1.3(x - 4)^2 + 2.2$

(b) $h(x) = -1.7(x + 2)^2 + 4.5$

(c) $f(x) = 3(x - 2.4)^2$

Solution

(a) Since $g(x) = 1.3(x - 4)^2 + 2.2$ is in vertex form with $a > 0$ and $k > 0$, the parabola opens up and the vertex (4, 2.2) lies above the x-axis. $g(x)$ has no zeros. Alternatively, since a and k have the same signs, $g(x)$ has no zeros.

(b) Since $h(x) = -1.7(x + 2)^2 + 4.5$ is in vertex form with $a < 0$ and $k > 0$, the parabola opens down and the vertex $(-2, 4.5)$ lies above the x-axis. $h(x)$ has two zeros. Alternatively, since a and k have opposite signs, $h(x)$ has two zeros.

(c) Since $f(x) = 3(x - 2.4)^2$ is in vertex form with $a > 0$ and $k = 0$, the parabola opens up and the vertex (2.4, 0) lies on the x-axis. $f(x)$ has one zero. Alternatively, since $k = 0$, $f(x)$ has one zero.

Finding the Number of Zeros for a Quadratic Function in Standard Form

To find the zeros of the function $f(x) = ax^2 + bx + c$, you would solve $f(x) = 0$ or the equation $ax^2 + bx + c = 0$, which has roots $x = \dfrac{-b \pm \sqrt{b^2 - 4ac}}{2a}$.

The expression $b^2 - 4ac$ in the quadratic formula is called the **discriminant**. The discriminant tells the number of zeros for a quadratic function.

If $b^2 - 4ac > 0$, the quadratic function has two zeros.	If $b^2 - 4ac = 0$, the quadratic function has one zero.	If $b^2 - 4ac < 0$, the quadratic function has no zeros.
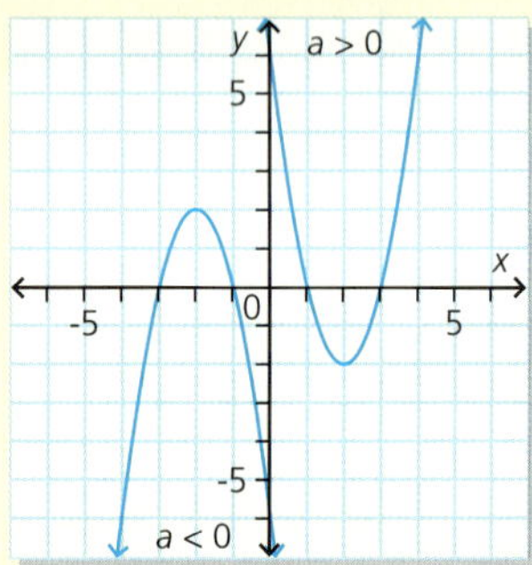	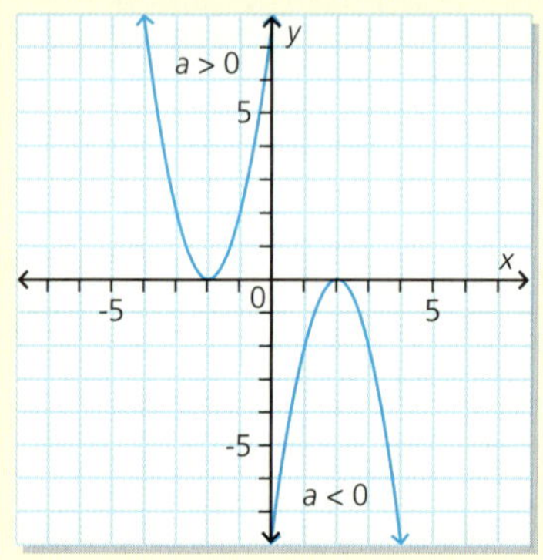	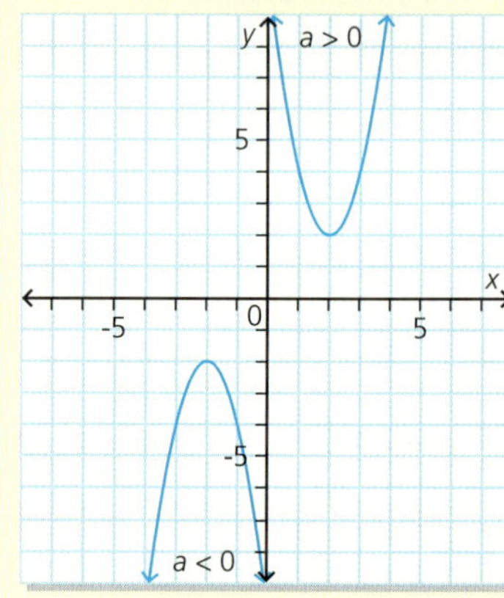

Example 4

Without drawing the graph, determine the number of zeros for each function.

(a) $h(x) = -4.9x^2 + 24.5x - 30.625$ (b) $g(x) = 3.2x^2 + 11.4x + 26.6$

(c) $f(x) = 2.1x^2 + 3.5x - 1.2$

Solution

Each function is in standard form. Calculate the value of $b^2 - 4ac$.

(a)
$$\begin{aligned} b^2 - 4ac &= (24.5)^2 - 4(-4.9)(-30.625) \\ &= 0 \end{aligned}$$

Since $b^2 - 4ac = 0$, the function $h(x)$ has one zero.

(b)
$$\begin{aligned} b^2 - 4ac &= (11.4)^2 - 4(3.2)(26.6) \\ &= -210.52 \end{aligned}$$

Since $b^2 - 4ac < 0$, the function $g(x)$ has no zeros.

(c)
$$\begin{aligned} b^2 - 4ac &= (3.5)^2 - 4(2.1)(-1.2) \\ &= 22.33 \end{aligned}$$

Since $b^2 - 4ac > 0$, the function $f(x)$ has two zeros.

The Number of Roots of a Quadratic Equation

A quadratic equation in the form $ax^2 + bx + c = 0$ has real roots that correspond to the zeros of the function $f(x) = ax^2 + bx + c$. A quadratic equation may have no real roots, one real root, or two distinct real roots.

Example 5

For what value(s) of k does the equation $kx - 8 = 2x^2$ have

(a) two distinct real roots? (b) one real root? (c) no real roots?

Solution

(a) For two distinct real roots, $b^2 - 4ac > 0$.

$kx - 8 = 2x^2$ Rearrange the equation.

$-2x^2 + kx - 8 = 0$ Substitute a, b, and c into the discriminant.

$k^2 - 4(-2)(-8) > 0$

$k^2 > 64$ Take the square roots.

$k < -8$ or $k > 8$

(b) For one real root, $b^2 - 4ac = 0$. Use the equation $-2x^2 + kx - 8 = 0$.

$-2x^2 + kx - 8 = 0$ Substitute a, b, and c into the discriminant.

$k^2 - 4(-2)(-8) = 0$

$k^2 = 64$ Take the square roots.

$k = -8$ or $k = 8$

(c) For no real roots, $b^2 - 4ac < 0$. Use the equation $-2x^2 + kx - 8 = 0$.

$-2x^2 + kx - 8 = 0$ Substitute a, b, and c into the discriminant.

$k^2 - 4(-2)(-8) < 0$

$k^2 < 64$ Take the square roots.

$k > -8$ and $k < 8$

$\therefore -8 < k < 8$

Consolidate Your Understanding

1. What are the zeros of a function? How are the zeros related to the x-intercepts of the graph of the function?

2. How many zeros does a quadratic function have? How can you determine the number of zeros

   (a) from the graph? (b) from the factored form?

   (c) from the vertex form? (d) from the standard form?

3. (a) Draw a sketch that shows all the ways that $f(x) = ax^2 + bx + c$ can intersect the x-axis.

   (b) Draw a sketch that shows all the ways that $f(x) = ax^2 + bx + c$ cannot intersect the x-axis.

4. How are the roots of a quadratic equation related to the zeros of a quadratic function?

Focus 4.3

Key Ideas

- A quadratic function may have no zeros, one zero, or two zeros.

<table>
<tr><th>No Zeros</th><th>One Zero</th><th>Two Zeros</th></tr>
<tr>
<td>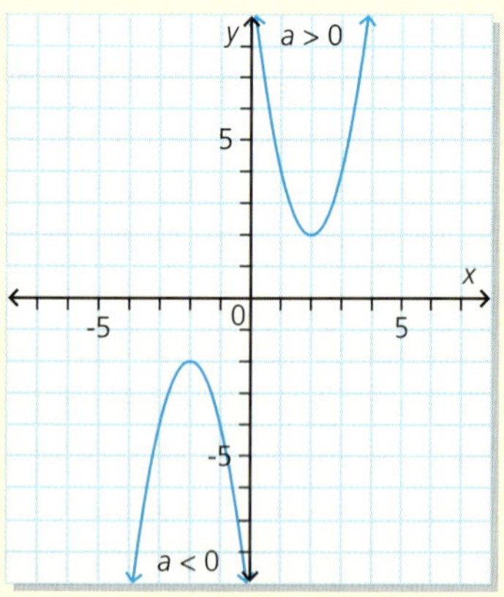
</td>
<td>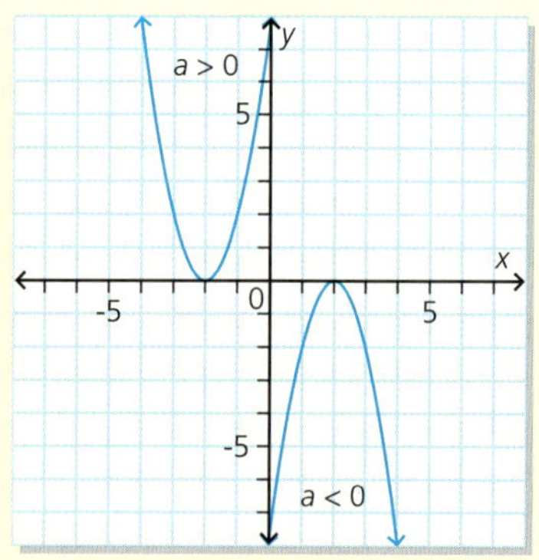
</td>
<td>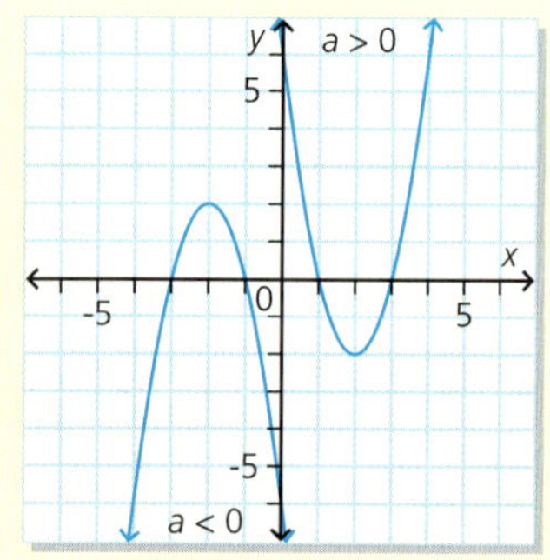
</td>
</tr>
<tr>
<td>If the graph of a quadratic function does not cross the x-axis, then the function has no zeros. If the parabola opens up, the vertex must be above the x-axis. If the parabola opens down, the vertex must be below the x-axis.</td>
<td>If the graph of a quadratic function just touches the x-axis, then the function has exactly one zero. In this case, the vertex of the parabola is on the x-axis.</td>
<td>If the graph of a quadratic function crosses the x-axis, then the function has two zeros. If the parabola opens up, the vertex must be below the x-axis. If the parabola opens down, the vertex must be above the x-axis.</td>
</tr>
</table>

- You can also find the number of zeros of a quadratic function using the equation of the function.
  - ♦ If the function equation is in factored form, then the zeros are clearly visible.
    - For $f(x) = a(x - p)(x - q)$, there are two zeros at $x = p$ and $x = q$.
    - For $f(x) = a(x - p)^2$, there is one zero at $x = p$.

- If the function is in the vertex form, $f(x) = a(x - h)^2 + k$, then it has two zeros if a and k have opposite signs; no zeros if a and k have the same signs; one zero if $k = 0$.
- If the function is in standard form, $f(x) = ax^2 + bx + c$, then you can use the discriminant $b^2 - 4ac$ to find the number of zeros. The function has two zeros if $b^2 - 4ac > 0$; one zero if $b^2 - 4ac = 0$; no zeros if $b^2 - 4ac < 0$.

- The quadratic equation $ax^2 + bx + c = 0$ has real roots that correspond to the zeros of the function $f(x) = ax^2 + bx + c$. A quadratic equation has no real roots, one real root, or two distinct real roots.

Practise, Apply, Solve 4.3

A

1. Find the number of zeros for each function by sketching its graph.

(a) $f(x) = 2(x - 1.2)^2 - 5$
(b) $f(x) = -1.5(x + 3)^2 + 1.2$
(c) $f(x) = -4(x - 3.6)^2$
(d) $f(x) = 0.5(x - 3.2)^2 + 2$

2. Each of the following functions is in the form $f(x) = a(x - h)^2 + k$. Use the values of a and k to find the number of zeros for each function.

(a) $f(x) = -2(x - 3)^2 - 4$
(b) $f(x) = -3(x + 2.5)^2 + 3.2$
(c) $f(x) = 4(x + 2)^2$
(d) $f(x) = 6.2(x - 3.5)^2 + 4.4$

3. For each of the following functions, which are in standard form, find the value of $b^2 - 4ac$. Use this value to find the number of zeros.

(a) $f(x) = 2x^2 + 3x + 1$
(b) $f(x) = -3x^2 + 5x - 3$
(c) $f(x) = 5x^2 - 4x + 2$
(d) $f(x) = 9x^2 - 14.4x + 5.76$

4. Without solving the equation, find the number of roots for each equation.

(a) $3x^2 - 2x + 1 = 0$
(b) $-2(x - 1.3)^2 + 5 = 0$
(c) $-3(x - 4)(x + 1) = 0$
(d) $-7(x - 4)^2 = 0$

5. Without drawing the graph, say whether the graph of each function intersects the x-axis at one point, intersects the x-axis at two points, or does not intersect the x-axis at all.

(a) $f(x) = x^2 - 6x + 7$
(b) $f(x) = 9 - x^2$
(c) $f(x) = (4 + x)^2$
(d) $f(x) = -2(x - 1)^2 - 1$

B

6. **Knowledge and Understanding:** The demand function for a new product is $p(x) = -4x + 42.5$, where x is the quantity sold in thousands and p is the price in dollars. The company that manufactures the product is planning to buy a new machine for the plant. There are three different types of machine. The cost function for each machine is shown.

   Machine A: $C(x) = 4.1x + 92.16$
   Machine B: $C(x) = 17.9x + 19.36$
   Machine C: $C(x) = 8.8x + 55.4$.

   Investigate the break-even quantities for each machine. Which machine would you recommend to the company?

7. For what value(s) of k does the function $f(x) = kx^2 - 4x + k$ have no zeros?

8. The function $g(x) = 4x^2 - 4x + m$ has exactly one zero. What is the value of m?

9. For what values of k does the equation $3x^2 + 4x + k = 0$ have no real roots? one real root? two real roots?

10. The graph of function $f(x) = x^2 - kx + k + 8$ touches the x-axis at one point. What is the value of k?

11. Is it possible for $p^2 + 48$ to equal $-14p$? Explain your answer.

12. **Communication:** Can the graph of a quadratic function cross the x-axis in three different places? Explain your answer.

13. **Application:** The operating costs, y, in thousands of dollars, to produce x personal CD players (x in thousands), at a manufacturing plant are shown in the table. Round the coefficients to one decimal place. If the revenue is $60 per CD player, at what level of production will the plant break even?

Number of CD Players, x (thousands)	2	4	6	8	10	12
Operating Costs, y (thousands of dollars)	148	225	287	361	439	521

14. One day, while working on a downtown construction site, Eugenia accidentally dropped her cell phone into the large excavation on the site. Fortunately, the cell phone landed on a pile of soft earth and was not damaged. She asked Tony, the construction manager, who was working nearby to throw the cell phone back up to her.

The height of an object thrown vertically up is modelled by

$$s(t) = s_0 + v_0t - \frac{1}{2}gt^2$$

where s_0 is the initial height above the ground, v_0 is the initial velocity, g is the acceleration due to gravity, t is the time, and $s(t)$ is the height above the ground at time t.

If Tony is 10 m *below* ground level, and the acceleration due to gravity is 9.8 m/s^2, with what initial velocity must he throw the cell phone for it to reach Eugenia? Explain any assumptions you make and show your calculations, graphs, or both to justify your answer.

15. **Thinking, Inquiry, Problem Solving**

(a) The line $y = x - 1$ intersects the circle $x^2 + y^2 = 25$ at two points. This line is called a **secant**. Find the coordinates of the two points of intersection.

(b) For what value(s) of k will the line $y = x + k$ be a tangent to the circle $x^2 + y^2 = 25$? A **tangent** is a line that touches a circle at exactly one point.

16. **Check Your Understanding:** Suppose you are given a quadratic revenue function and a linear cost function. How could you find the break-even point(s) graphically? algebraically? What solutions might you expect? Give examples and explain any connections between the algebra and the graphs.

C

17. Investigate the number of zeros for the function $f(x) = (k + 1)x^2 + 2kx + k - 1$ for different values of k. For what values of k will the function have no zeros? one zero? two zeros?

18. The area of a right triangle is 15 cm^2 and the hypotenuse is 9 cm long. Find the lengths of the other two sides. (**Hint:** If you know $x^2 + y^2$ and xy, then you can find $(x + y)^2$ and $(x - y)^2$.)

The Chapter Problem — Fundraising

Apply what you have learned in this section to answer these questions about the Chapter Problem on page 300.

CP5. Use the data in the first table on page 300 to write a cost function for each supplier.

CP6. Use your revenue function from CP3 and the cost function for the first supplier in question CP5 to find the corresponding profit function.

CP7. Graph your profit function from question CP6. State the domain and determine the break-even points.

CP8. Repeat questions CP6 and CP7 for the other suppliers.

CP9. Which supplier would you recommend?

4.4 Introducing Complex Numbers

Part 1: Familiar Number Systems

The figures on this clay tablet represent numbers that an ancient Sumerian used to record sheep and goats. The numbers that are commonly used to calculate, count, and measure have evolved over time to meet the needs of people with new kinds of problems to be solved. In the following problems, note how the numbers change.

Think, Do, Discuss

1. Lia has some CDs and buys four more. She now has 28 CDs. How many CDs did she have originally? Write an equation. Let the variable be the original number of CDs. What is the solution? What kind of numbers did you use in your solution?
2. Craig builds seven lawn chairs in two days. How many chairs does he build in a day? Write an equation. Let the variable be the original number of chairs that Craig builds in a day. Solve your equation. What kind of numbers did you use in your solution?
3. Stuart buys nine CDs. He then has a total of nine CDs. How many CDs did he have originally? Write an equation. Let the variable be the original number of CDs. What is the solution? This number was not introduced into use until the tenth century!
4. The temperature rose 10°C and is now 6°C. What was the initial temperature? Write an equation. Let the initial temperature be the variable. Solve the equation. What kind of numbers did you use in your solution?
5. Kim wants to create a square enclosure for her vegetable garden with an area of 2 m^2. How much chicken wire will she need for fencing the garden? Write an equation. Let the variable be the length of each side of the square enclosure. Solve the equation. What type of number did you use in your solution?
6. The above questions refer to the following sets of numbers:

   the set of natural numbers, **N**, $\{1, 2, 3, 4, \dots\}$

   the set of whole numbers, **W**, $\{0, 1, 2, 3, 4, \dots\}$

   the set of integers, **I**, $\{\dots -3, -2, -1, 0, 1, 2, 3, \dots\}$

   the set of rational numbers, **Q**, $\left\{\frac{a}{b}: a, b \in \text{I}, b \neq 0\right\}$

   the set of irrational numbers, $\bar{\text{Q}}$. An irrational number cannot be expressed as the ratio of two integers, for example, $\sqrt{2}, \sqrt{3}, \sqrt{5}, \dots$.

Are these sets distinct, or do some numbers belong to more than one set? Give examples to illustrate your answer. Draw a diagram to show how the sets connect with each other.

Part 2: Defining the Set of Complex Numbers

The sets described in Part 1 are members of the set of **real numbers**. The set of real numbers, **R**, has both rational and irrational numbers.

A quadratic function whose graph does not cross or touch the x-axis has no zeros. Take for example, the function $f(x) = 0.5x^2 - 4x + 10$ and the corresponding quadratic equation $0 = 0.5x^2 - 4x + 10$. In the set of real numbers, this equation has no real roots. However, if we extend the number system, you can find roots for this and other equations.

Think, Do, Discuss

1. Sketch the graph of the function $f(x) = x^2 + 2x + 2$. How many zeros does $f(x)$ have?
2. Try to find the zeros of the function $f(x) = x^2 + 2x + 2$ by letting $f(x) = 0$ and using the quadratic formula.
3. Why are you unable to find the zeros?
4. Let a non-real number be i, such that $i^2 = -1$. Then you can write any negative number as a multiple of i^2. For example, you could write -4 as $4i^2$ and write -31 as $31i^2$, and so on. Now you can solve the equation $x^2 + 4 = 0$.

$$\begin{aligned} x^2 + 4 &= 0 \\ x^2 &= -4 \\ x^2 &= 4i^2 \\ x &= \pm 2i \end{aligned}$$

   What are the solutions of $x^2 + 25 = 0$? of $x^2 + 3 = 0$?
5. The number i has been called an **imaginary number**. This name is easy to remember, but it is misleading because the number i does exist. Some quadratic equations have solutions that have real and imaginary parts. Try to solve the equation $x^2 + 2x + 2 = 0$. Use the number i to help you obtain two roots.
6. The roots in step 5 should be in the form $a + bi$ and $a - bi$. These numbers are called **complex numbers**. Notice that complex numbers have a real part, a, and an imaginary part, $\pm bi$. Would you describe real numbers as complex? Explain your answer.

Focus 4.4

Key Ideas

- We use the set of real numbers, *R*, most frequently to describe the relationships in the world around us. The set of real numbers contains all rational and irrational numbers. It also contains the sets of natural numbers, whole numbers, and integers.

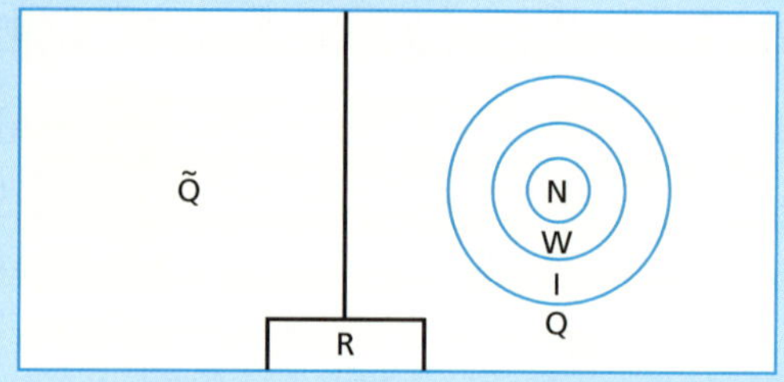

- You can write any complex number in the form $a + bi$, where a and b are real numbers and i is a non-real number such that $i^2 = -1$.
- Since you can write any real number in the form $a + 0i$, then the complex numbers, *C*, include all the real numbers.

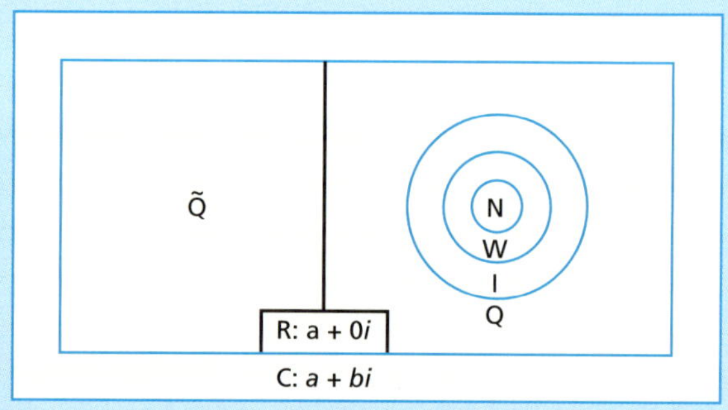

- Using complex numbers, you can find the square root of any real number—positive, zero, or negative.
- A quadratic equation, with no real roots, has two complex roots in the form $a + bi$ and $a - bi$. These roots form a **conjugate pair**. If $b^2 - 4ac < 0$, then a quadratic equation has two complex conjugate roots.

Example 1

Solve for x, where x is a complex number. Round to two decimal places, if necessary.

(a) $x^2 + 36 = 0$ (b) $2x^2 + 50 = 0$ (c) $5x^2 + 60 = 0$

Solution

(a)
$$\begin{aligned} x^2 + 36 &= 0 \\ x^2 &= -36 \\ x^2 &= 36(-1) \\ x^2 &= 36i^2 \\ x &= \pm\sqrt{36i^2} \\ x &= \pm 6i \end{aligned}$$

(b)
$$\begin{aligned} 2x^2 + 50 &= 0 \\ 2x^2 &= -50 \\ x^2 &= -25 \\ x^2 &= 25i^2 \\ x &= \pm\sqrt{25i^2} \\ x &= \pm 5i \end{aligned}$$

(c)
$$\begin{aligned} 5x^2 + 60 &= 0 \\ 5x^2 &= -60 \\ x^2 &= -12 \\ x^2 &= 12i^2 \\ x &= \pm\sqrt{12i^2} \\ x &\doteq \pm 3.46i \end{aligned}$$

Example 2

Find the complex roots of the equation $4x^2 - 2x + 3 = 0$.

Solution

Substituting $a = 4$, $b = -2$, and $c = 3$ in the quadratic formula gives

$$x = \frac{-b \pm \sqrt{b^2 - 4ac}}{2a}$$

$$x = \frac{-(-2) \pm \sqrt{(-2)^2 - 4(4)(3)}}{2(4)}$$

$$x = \frac{2 \pm \sqrt{4 - 48}}{8}$$

$$x = \frac{2 \pm \sqrt{-44}}{8}$$

$$x = \frac{2 \pm \sqrt{44i^2}}{8}$$

$$x \doteq \frac{2 \pm 6.63i}{8}$$

The complex roots of the equation are $x \doteq 0.25 + 0.83i$ and $x \doteq 0.25 - 0.83i$.

Example 3

One root of a quadratic equation is $2 + 5i$. Find the other root and express the quadratic equation in factored form.

Solution

If a quadratic equation has complex roots, then the roots form a conjugate pair. If one root is $2 + 5i$, then the other root is $2 - 5i$. The quadratic equation with roots $2 + 5i$ and $2 - 5i$ in factored form is

$$[x - (2 + 5i)] \times [x - (2 - 5i)] = 0, \text{ or } (x - 2 - 5i)(x - 2 + 5i) = 0$$

Practise, Apply, Solve 4.4

A

1. For each number, identify the set(s) of numbers to which it belongs.

(a) -3 (b) $\frac{3}{4}$ (c) $5 + 3i$ (d) $\sqrt{7}$

(e) 6.35 (f) $5.\overline{23}$ (g) $-\frac{2}{3}$ (h) 1

2. Write each of the following as a complex number. Round to two decimal places, where necessary.

(a) $\sqrt{-16}$ (b) $\sqrt{-121}$ (c) $-\sqrt{-9}$

(d) $\sqrt{-18}$ (e) $-\sqrt{-28}$ (f) $\pm\sqrt{-50}$

3. Write the complex conjugate of each complex number.

(a) $1 + i$
(b) $2 - 3i$
(c) $-3 - 4i$
(d) $-7 + 5i$
(e) $11 - 11i$
(f) $2 + \sqrt{2}i$

4. Determine whether the given complex number is a solution to the equation.

(a) $x^2 = -16, 4i$
(b) $x^2 = -14, 7i$
(c) $x^2 + 6 = 5, i$
(d) $x^2 + 10 = 16, 3i$

5. Solve for x, where x is a complex number. Round to two decimal places, if necessary.

(a) $x^2 + 4 = 0$
(b) $x^2 + 64 = 0$
(c) $3x^2 + 27 = 0$
(d) $-2x^2 = 98$
(e) $x^2 + 32 = 0$
(f) $-3x^2 - 150 = 0$

6. Solve each quadratic equation, where x is a complex number. Round to two decimal places, if necessary.

(a) $x^2 - 4x + 5 = 0$
(b) $x^2 - 2x + 17 = 0$
(c) $-x^2 + 4x = 13$
(d) $2x^2 + 2x + 1 = 0$
(e) $2x^2 = x - 1$
(f) $3x(x + 2) = -18$

B

7. For each quadratic equation, in the form $ax^2 + bx + c = 0$, determine the value of the discriminant, $b^2 - 4ac$. What does this value tell you about each equation?

(a) $x^2 + 2x + 5 = 0$
(b) $x^2 - 2x - 3 = 0$
(c) $5x^2 - 4x + 2 = 0$
(d) $3x^2 - 24x + 48 = 0$

8. Solve each equation in question 7. Round to two decimal places, if necessary.

9. **Knowledge and Understanding:** Find the roots, real or complex, of each quadratic equation, using an appropriate method. Express all answers to two decimal places.

(a) $x^2 + 5x - 24 = 0$
(b) $3(x - 2)^2 - 15 = 0$
(c) $3x^2 - 6x + 1 = 0$
(d) $x^2 - 2x + 5 = 0$

10. In each of the following, one root of a quadratic equation is given. State the other root and write the equation in factored form.

(a) $2i$
(b) $2 - i$
(c) $1 + 3i$
(d) $-1 - i$
(e) $3 - 4i$
(f) $5i - 12$

11. Find the complex factors of each expression.

(a) $x^2 + 4x + 5$
(b) $x^2 + 4x + 13$
(c) $x^2 - x + 1$
(d) $x^2 - 2x + 26$

12. Solve for x, where x is a complex number. Express answers to two decimal places.

(a) $3x^2 + 2x + 1 = 0$
(b) $2x^2 - 3x + 7 = 0$
(c) $3x^2 - 2x + 10 = 0$
(d) $5x^2 + x + 7 = 0$

13. Find two numbers with a sum of 4 and a product of 13.

14. Find two numbers with a sum of 5 and a product of 7.

15. **Application:** The monthly sales, n, in thousands of units, of a new perfume can be modelled by the function $n(t) = -0.75t^2 + 6t + 51$, where $t = 0$ corresponds to the first month of sales. Can the company expect to sell 65 000 units in any one month over the next year? Justify your answer graphically and algebraically.

16. **Communication:** Explain how complex numbers are different from real numbers. Describe the real number system and use examples to illustrate your explanation.

17. **Thinking, Inquiry, Problem Solving:** Investigate, using a graphing calculator, adding, subtracting, and multiplying complex numbers. You will need to change the real mode setting (MODE) from **real** to **a+bi**. Is the sum of two complex numbers a complex number? Is the product of two complex numbers always a complex number? Give examples to justify your answers.

18. **Check Your Understanding:** Explain what complex numbers are and how they help in the solution of quadratic equations. Use examples to illustrate your explanations.

C

19. Find all the roots, real and complex, of the equation $x^4 - 81 = 0$.

20. Is it possible to put complex numbers in order? If so, then how would you order complex numbers? If not, then why not?

21. Verify that $(x + 1)(x^2 - x + 1) = x^3 + 1$. Find all the roots, real and complex, of the equation $x^3 + 1 = 0$.

The Chapter Problem—Fundraising

In this section, you found complex roots for quadratic equations that did not have real roots. Apply what you have learned to answer these questions about the Chapter Problem on page 300.

CP10. Examine each profit function you obtained in CP6. Will the student council be able to raise \$7000 by selling T-shirts?

CP11. Determine the maximum amount the student council could raise on the basis of each supplier.

CP12. Find the number of T-shirts sold in each case in CP11.

CP13. Which T-shirt supplier would you choose? Explain your choice.

SKILL BUILDER 4.5U

Functions and Relations

Adding, Subtracting, and Multiplying Complex Numbers

Because complex numbers have two parts, the real part and the imaginary part, they are ideal for describing real-life quantities that have two components. For example, in electronics, the resistance of a circuit is expressed as impedance. Impedance has two parts, resistance, R, and a reactance, X. Impedance is represented by the complex number, $R + Xi$.

In this section, you will learn how to add, subtract, and multiply complex numbers. You may be interested to know that a calculator uses complex arithmetic algorithms to perform many simple operations.

Adding and Subtracting Complex Numbers

When adding or subtracting two complex numbers, use the laws of algebra and treat the symbol i as if it were a variable.

Example 1

(a) Add $(5 - 2i)$ and $(-3 + 7i)$.

(b) Find the sum of $(-4 - 3i)$ and its complex conjugate.

Solution

(a) $(5 - 2i) + (-3 + 7i)$

real

$= 5 - 2i - 3 + 7i$

imaginary

$= 5 - 3 - 2i + 7i$

$= 2 + 5i$

(b) $(-4 - 3i) + (-4 + 3i)$

$= -4 - 3i - 4 + 3i$

$= -4 - 4 - 3i + 3i$

$= -8 + 0i$

The sum is a real number.

Example 2

(a) Simplify $(7 - 4i) - (2 + 3i)$.

(b) Subtract $(3 - 5i)$ from its complex conjugate.

Solution

(a) $(7 - 4i) - (2 + 3i)$

$= 7 - 4i - 2 - 3i$

$= 7 - 2 - 4i - 3i$

$= 5 - 7i$

(b) $(3 + 5i) - (3 - 5i)$

$= 3 + 5i - 3 + 5i$

$= 3 - 3 + 5i + 5i$

$= 0 + 10i$

$= 10i$

The difference is an imaginary number.

Multiplying Complex Numbers

Use the distributive law to multiply complex numbers.

Example 3

(a) Simplify.

i. i^2 ii. $(i^2)^5$ iii. i^7

(b) Multiply $(4 + 3i)$ by $(2 - i)$.

(c) Expand and simplify $(-3 - 2i)^2$.

Solution

(a) i. By definition, $i^2 = -1$.

ii. $$\begin{aligned}(i^2)^5 &= (-1)^5 \\ &= -1\end{aligned}$$

iii. $$\begin{aligned}i^7 &= i^6 \times i \\ &= (i^2)^3 \times i \\ &= (-1)^3 \times i \\ &= -i\end{aligned}$$

(b) $$\begin{aligned}&(4 + 3i)(2 - i) \\ &= 8 - 4i + 6i - 3i^2 \\ &= 8 + 2i - 3(-1) \\ &= 8 + 3 + 2i \\ &= 11 + 2i\end{aligned}$$

Note: $i^2 = -1$

(c) $$\begin{aligned}&(-3 - 2i)^2 \\ &= (-3 - 2i)(-3 - 2i) \\ &= 9 + 6i + 6i + 4i^2 \\ &= 9 + 12i + 4(-1) \\ &= 9 - 4 + 12i \\ &= 5 + 12i\end{aligned}$$

Multiplying Complex Conjugates

The letter z is often used to denote a complex number, and $\bar{z}$ is the complex conjugate of z. If $z = a + bi$, then $\bar{z} = a - bi$.

Example 4

(a) Find the product of $(5 - 2i)$ and its complex conjugate.

(b) If $z = a + bi$, then find $z\bar{z}$.

Solution

(a) $$\begin{aligned}&(5 - 2i)(5 + 2i) \\ &= 25 + 10i - 10i - 4i^2 \\ &= 25 + 0i - 4(-1) \\ &= 29 + 0i \\ &= 29\end{aligned}$$

(b) $$\begin{aligned}&(a + bi)(a - bi) \\ &= a^2 - abi + abi - b^2i^2 \\ &= a^2 + 0i - b^2(-1) \\ &= a^2 + b^2 + 0i \\ &= a^2 + b^2\end{aligned}$$

Notice that the result of multiplying two complex conjugates is always a real number.

Focus 4.5U

Key Ideas

- To add or subtract complex numbers, combine the real terms and the imaginary terms separately.

$$(a + bi) + (c + di) = (a + c) + (b + d)i$$

$$(a + bi) - (c + di) = (a - c) + (b - d)i$$

- To multiply two complex numbers, use the distributive law.

$$\begin{aligned}(a + bi)(c + di) &= ac + adi + bci + bdi^2 \\ &= (ac - bd) + (ad + bc)i\end{aligned}$$

- If $z = a + bi$ is a complex number, then $\bar{z}$ is the complex conjugate of z, and $\bar{z} = a - bi$.
- The product of two complex conjugates is always a real number, since $z\bar{z} = a^2 + b^2$.
- Two complex numbers are equal if, and only if, their real parts are equal and their imaginary parts are equal. That is, $a + bi = c + di$ if, and only if, $a = c$ and $b = d$.
- A complex number is zero if, and only if, the real term and the imaginary term are both 0. That is, $a + bi = 0$ if, and only if, $a = 0$ and $b = 0$.

Practise, Apply, Solve 4.5U

A

1. Add the pairs of complex numbers.

(a) $2 + 6i$ and $5 - i$
(b) $4 - 3i$ and $1 + i$
(c) $3 + 7i$ and $-4 - 9i$
(d) $-1 + 3i$ and $2 - 13i$
(e) $5i$ and $1 - 2i$
(f) $3 + \sqrt{2}i$ and $\sqrt{2}i$

2. Subtract the second number from the first in each part of question 1.

3. Simplify each of the following.

(a) $(2 + i)(3 + 5i)$
(b) $(5 - 3i)(7 + i)$
(c) $(4 - 3i)(-2 - i)$
(d) $i(5 + i)$
(e) $(2 + i)^2$
(f) $(2 + 3i)(2 - 3i)$

4. Find $z\bar{z}$ for each value of z.

(a) $z = 1 + i$
(b) $z = 3 - 2i$
(c) $z = -4 + 2i$

5. Simplify.

(a) $(3 + 4i) + (2 + 3i)$ (b) $(5 + i) - (3 - 2i)$

(c) $(2i)^2$ (d) i^4

(e) $\frac{1}{i^2}$ (f) $\frac{1}{(1 + i)(1 - i)}$

(g) $(1 + 2i)^2$ (h) $i(4 - 5i)^2$

(i) $(2 - i)(1 + 2i)(1 - i)$ (j) $\left(\frac{\sqrt{2}}{2} + \frac{\sqrt{2}}{2}i\right)^2$

(k) $(6 - 4i)^2 - (1 - 3i)^2 + 5i$ (l) $\sqrt{-4} + \sqrt{-25}$

B

6. For each pair of roots, find a quadratic equation. Express your equation in the form $ax^2 + bx + c = 0$.

(a) $2i, -2i$ (b) $1 + 3i, 1 - 3i$

(c) $3 + 4i, 3 - 4i$ (d) $-\frac{1}{2} + \frac{\sqrt{3}}{2}i, -\frac{1}{2} - \frac{\sqrt{3}}{2}i$

7. One root of a quadratic equation is $3 - i$. Determine the other root and write a quadratic equation that has these roots. Express your answer in the form $ax^2 + bx + c = 0$.

8. Show by substitution that $x = 2 + i$ is a solution of the equation $x^2 - 4x + 5 = 0$, where x is a complex number.

9. If $f(x) = 2x^2 + 3x - 2$, then find $f(2 - i)$.

10. Find $g(3 - 4i)$ if $g(x) = -3x^2 - 2x + 4$.

11. Write a quadratic equation that has complex solutions of the form $a + bi$, where $a \neq 0$ and $b \neq 0$. Solve the equation. Show by substitution that the solutions you found are correct.

12. Suppose that $a + bi = 0$ and that $a \neq 0$ and $b \neq 0$. Rearrange the equation $a + bi = 0$ to isolate i. Explain why this rearrangement contradicts what you know about i.

13. If $z = a + bi$, then find the values of a and b for which $z + \bar{z} = 10$ and $z - \bar{z} = 14i$.

14. **Check Your Understanding:** If $z = -2 + 3i$ and $w = 4 - i$, then find $z + w$, $z - w$, zw, w^2, and $z\bar{z}$.

C

15. Find the square roots of the complex number $5 + 12i$.

16. If $a + bi$ is a root of the quadratic equation $x^2 + cx + d = 0$, then show that $a^2 + b^2 = d$ and $2a + c = 0$.

4.6 Reciprocal Functions

Part 1: Comparing Hourly Rates

Stuart is trying to decide which of two job offers to accept for summer employment. He could work as a shipper at the local lumber store, where he would be paid $11.50/h. The other job is with a student-operated house-painting business where he would earn $450 for each house that is painted.

Think, Do, Discuss

1. What information does Stuart need to calculate the hourly rate for painting houses?
2. If Stuart takes 40 h to paint a house, what is the hourly rate?
3. Suppose Stuart wants to determine the hourly rate of pay if he takes less than 40 h to paint a house, or if he takes more than 40 h to paint a house. Copy and complete the table to show the hourly rate, y, for the hours worked, x, to paint one house.

Hours Worked, x (h)	1	10	15	20	25	30	35	40	45	50	55
Hourly Rate, y ($/h)											

4. What happens to the hourly rate as the number of hours increases? Explain why the hourly rate is represented by y and why the number of hours worked is represented by x.
5. Write an equation for the relationship between the hourly rate, y, and the number of hours worked, x. Enter the equation into a graphing calculator and graph it. Restrict the domain to only positive x-values.
6. Describe the graph. According to the graph, what happens to y as x becomes very small, that is, close to 0? What happens to y as x becomes very large?
7. How would the graph change if the rate of pay increased to $550 per house?
8. For each line in the table, calculate the product xy. What do you notice? Why does this happen? This type of relationship is called **inverse variation**. What other quantities vary in this way?
9. What factors, other than the speed at which Stuart can paint, might influence the time it takes to paint a house? Which job would you advise Stuart to take? Explain your answer.

Part 2: The Reciprocal Function $f(x) = \frac{1}{x}$

In Part 1, the value of one variable in the relation increased while the value of the other variable decreased. The products of corresponding x- and y-values were constant. This relation can be described by $xy = k$, or $y = \frac{k}{x}$, and is called **inverse variation.** There are many real-life quantities that vary in this way. They can be modelled by functions in the form $f(x) = \frac{k}{x}$. The simplest of these functions is $f(x) = \frac{1}{x}$.

Think, Do, Discuss

1. $f(x) = \frac{1}{x}$ is a **reciprocal function**. Explain why this name is appropriate.

2. Enter the function into a graphing calculator and adjust the window (**Xmin**=−5, **Xmax**=5, **Ymin**=−5, and **Ymax**=5). Then graph. Describe the shape of the graph and any special features. This graph is called a **hyperbola**.

Use the Table feature of the graphing calculator to do the next few questions.

3. What happens to the value of y as x becomes very large, for example, greater than 1000? What happens to y as x becomes very small, for example, less than −1000? Describe the graph for both situations. Does the graph meet or cross the x-axis? How do you know?

4. What is true about the value of y when **(a)** x is close to 1? **(b)** x is close to −1?

5. What happens to the value of y as x decreases from 1 to 0? as x increases from −1 to 0?

6. In the table, what is the y-value for $x = 0$? What does this y-value mean? What is the domain for the function $f(x) = \frac{1}{x}$? What is the range?

7. As x gets closer and closer to 0, the graph approaches the y-axis but never meets it. The y-axis is an example of a **vertical asymptote**. The graph also has a **horizontal asymptote**. What is its equation? How do the equations of the asymptotes relate to the domain and the range of f? Since the asymptotes are perpendicular for this hyperbola, it is called a **rectangular hyperbola.**

8. Find the equation for the inverse of $f(x) = \frac{1}{x}$, that is, $f^{-1}(x)$. What do you notice? Does this result seem reasonable from the graph? Explain your answer.

9. The **inverse** of a function is written as $f^{-1}(x)$. However, $[f(x)]^{-1}$ refers to the **reciprocal function**. Explain the difference between the inverse of a function, $f^{-1}(x)$, and the reciprocal of a function, $\frac{1}{f(x)}$. Use examples of each function and discuss the domain and the range in each case.

10. Using your knowledge of transformations, how would the graph of each function compare to the graph of $f(x) = \frac{1}{x}$? Check using a graphing calculator.

(a) $f(x) = \frac{5}{x}$ [**Hint:** $\frac{5}{x} = 5\left(\frac{1}{x}\right)$] (b) $f(x) = \frac{100}{x}$ (c) $f(x) = \frac{-1}{x}$

11. Write each function in question 10 as a power of x. In this form they are *power functions.*

Part 3: Making Connections Between the Graphs of Functions and Their Reciprocals

Can you tell from the graph of a function how the graph of the reciprocal of that function will look? In this investigation, you will compare the graph of $y = f(x)$ with the graph of $y = \frac{1}{f(x)}$ to discover some common properties.

Think, Do, Discuss

1. On a graphing calculator, adjust the window to (**Xmin=−5**, **Xmax=5**, **Ymin=−5**, and **Ymax=5**).

Graph $y = x$ and $y = \frac{1}{x}$ on the same axes. At what points do the graphs intersect? What are the y-coordinates of the points of intersection? Explain why these values make sense.

2. Where is the zero for the function $y = x$? What feature of the graph of $y = \frac{1}{f(x)}$ exists at this x-value? Explain why this makes sense.

3. What do you notice about the quadrants in which each graph occurs? When $y = x$ is close to the x-axis, where is $y = \frac{1}{f(x)}$? When $y = x$ is far away from the x-axis, where is $y = \frac{1}{f(x)}$?

4. Repeat steps 1 to 3 for each pair of functions. When you enter the reciprocal functions into a graphing calculator, you will need to include brackets around each denominator. For example, enter the function $y = \frac{1}{x+1}$ as **Y2=1/(X+1)**.

(a) $y = x + 1$ and $y = \frac{1}{x+1}$

(b) $y = x - 2$ and $y = \frac{1}{x-2}$

(c) $y = 2x + 5$ and $y = \frac{1}{2x+5}$

(d) $y = 3x - 4$ and $y = \frac{1}{3x-4}$

5. On paper, sketch the graph of $y = 2x - 1$. Using your answers for steps 1 to 4 as a guide, sketch the graph of $y = \frac{1}{2x-1}$. Use a calculator to verify your sketch.

6. On a graphing calculator, change the window to (**Xmin=−4.7**, **Xmax=4.7**, **Ymin=−5**, and **Ymax=5**). Graph the functions $y = (x - 3)(x + 1)$ and $y = \frac{1}{(x-3)(x+1)}$ on the same axes. You will need an extra pair of brackets around the product in the denominator of the reciprocal function: **Y2=1/((X−3)(X+1))**.

(a) At what points do the graphs intersect?

(b) What features of the graph of the reciprocal function exist at the zeros of the quadratic function?

(c) Compare the shape of the graph of the reciprocal function with the shape of the parabola. Consider the lines of symmetry, the quadrants that each graph occupies, and the position of each graph.

7. Repeat step 6 for each of the following pairs of functions.

(a) $y = (x + 2)(x - 1)$, $y = \dfrac{1}{(x + 2)(x - 1)}$

(b) $y = (1 - x)(4 + x)$, $y = \dfrac{1}{(1 - x)(4 + x)}$

(c) $y = (x - 2)^2$, $y = \dfrac{1}{(x - 2)^2}$

8. Sketch the parabola for the function $y = x^2 + x - 6$. First factor. Where are the vertical asymptotes of the graph of $y = \dfrac{1}{x^2 + x - 6}$? Draw the asymptotes.

9. What points will the two graphs in question 8 have in common? Mark these points on the sketch. For the graph above the x-axis, decide what will happen to the graph of the reciprocal function to the right and left of the common points. Use the distance of the parabola from the x-axis as a guide. Sketch those parts of the graph for $y = \dfrac{1}{x^2 + x - 6}$.

10. Determine the coordinates of the vertex. Use the y-coordinate of the vertex to find the value of $\dfrac{1}{x^2 + x - 6}$ corresponding to this y-value. Mark this point on the sketch. Then decide what will happen to the graph of the reciprocal function on each side of the common points *below* the x-axis. Sketch this final part of the graph for $y = \dfrac{1}{x^2 + x - 6}$. Use a graphing calculator to verify your sketch.

Focus 4.6

Key Ideas

- A relation has two variable quantities. If one quantity increases as the other decreases, and the product of the two quantities remains constant, then the quantities vary **inversely**. The relation displays inverse variation.
- An inverse variation can be described by the equations $xy = k$, $y = \dfrac{k}{x}$, or $y = kx^{-1}$.
- The simplest function that displays inverse variation is $f(x) = \dfrac{1}{x}$.
- The graph of $y = \dfrac{1}{x}$ shown here is called a **hyperbola**.

  This hyperbola has two congruent parts, one in each of the first and third quadrants. In real-world applications, often only one branch is needed.

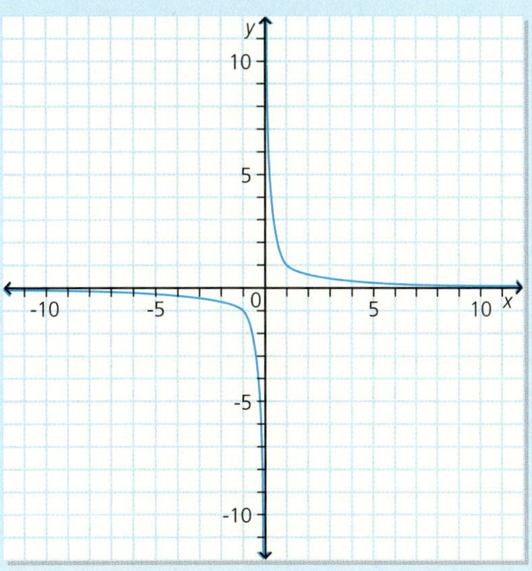

- The domain of $f(x) = \frac{1}{x}$ is the set of real numbers except 0, $D = \{x \mid x \in \mathbf{R}, x \neq 0\}$. The range is also the set of real numbers except 0, $R = \{y \mid y \in \mathbf{R}, y \neq 0\}$.
- The inverse of $f(x) = \frac{1}{x}$ is $f^{-1}(x) = \frac{1}{x}$
- An **asymptote** is a line that a function approaches but does not touch or intersect. The graph of $y = \frac{1}{x}$ has a **vertical asymptote** with equation $x = 0$ and a **horizontal asymptote** with equation $y = 0$. In this case, the vertical asymptote occurs at the break in the domain of the function, and the horizontal asymptote occurs at the break in the range. Because these two asymptotes are perpendicular, the hyperbola is called a **rectangular hyperbola**. In other types of hyperbolas, the asymptotes are not necessarily perpendicular.
- You can deduce the shape of the graph of $y = \frac{1}{f(x)}$ from the graph of $y = f(x)$ using the following properties:

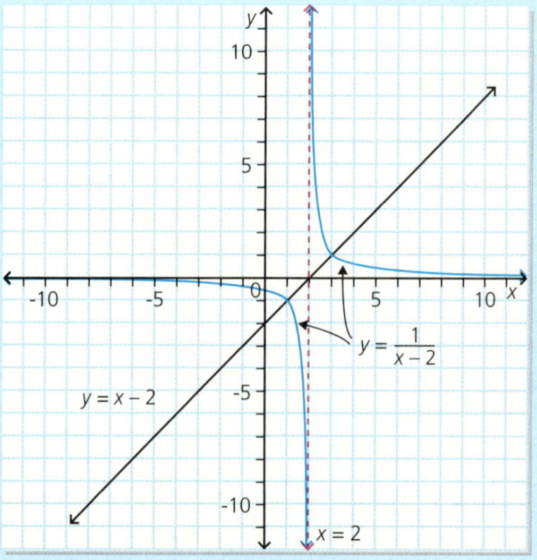

  - At each zero of $f(x)$, the graph of $y = \frac{1}{f(x)}$ has a vertical asymptote.
  - The graph of $y = \frac{1}{f(x)}$ always passes through the points where $f(x) = 1$ or $f(x) = -1$.
  - When $f(x)$ is close to 1, $\frac{1}{f(x)}$ is also close to 1.

    When $f(x)$ is close to -1, $\frac{1}{f(x)}$ is also close to -1.
  - Both graphs occur in the same quadrants.

    When $f(x)$ is positive, $\frac{1}{f(x)}$ is positive.

    When $f(x)$ is negative, $\frac{1}{f(x)}$ is negative.
  - As $f(x)$ gets larger, $\frac{1}{f(x)}$ gets smaller. As $f(x)$ gets smaller, $\frac{1}{f(x)}$ gets larger.

Example 1

The distance from Ottawa to Sault Ste. Marie is about 850 km. Create a table showing the time, x, in hours, for the journey at an average speed, y, of 30, 40, 50, 60, 70, 80, and 90 km/h. Sketch a graph to show the relationship between x and y. Write an equation for the relation. What is the effect on the time if the average speed is doubled?

Solution

Time, x (h)	Average Speed, y (km/h)
28.3	30
21.2	40
17.0	50
14.2	60
12.1	70
10.6	80
9.4	90

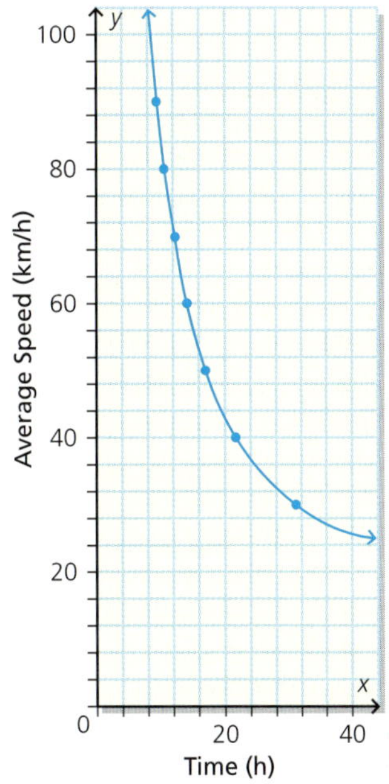

An equation for the relation is $y = \frac{850}{x}$, or $xy = 850$.

In the table, you can see that the time at an average speed of 60 km/h is half the time at 30 km/h, and the time at 80 km/h is half the time at 40 km/h.

If $y = \frac{850}{x}$, then $2y = \frac{850}{x} \times 2$.

$= \frac{850}{\frac{x}{2}}$ The effect of doubling the average speed is to halve the time of the journey.

Example 2

Sketch the graph of the function $f(x) = \frac{1}{2x + 3}$ by first sketching the graph of $f(x) = 2x + 3$.

Solution

The line $y = 2x + 3$ has slope 2 and y-intercept 3. The x-intercept is -1.5. The value of y is 1 when $x = -1$. The value of y is -1 when $x = -2$.

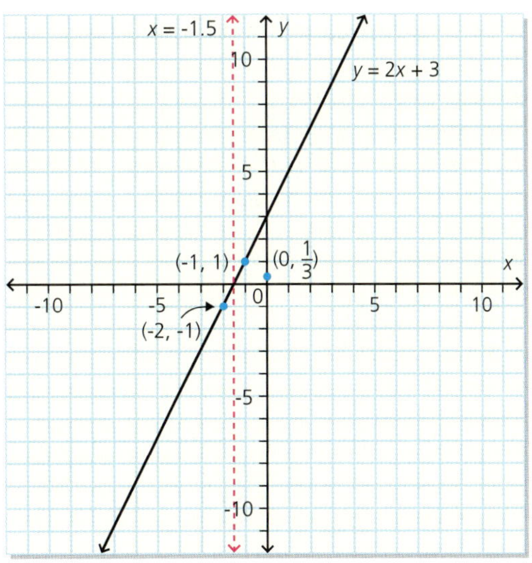

Given this information, you know the graph of $y = \frac{1}{2x + 3}$

- has a vertical asymptote with equation $x = -1.5$
- passes through points $(-1, 1)$ and $(-2, -1)$
- has y-intercept $\frac{1}{3}$

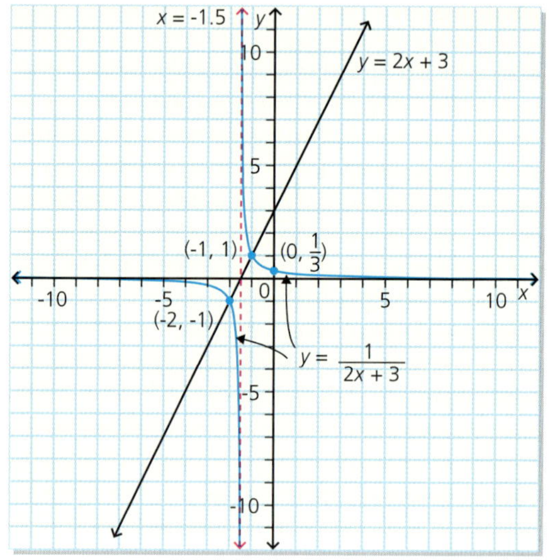

Also, given the line $y = 2x + 3$, you know the graph of $y = \frac{1}{2x + 3}$

- is in the first quadrant for $x > 0$
- is in the second quadrant for $-1.5 < x < 0$
- is in the third quadrant for $x < -1.5$

Finally the graph of $y = \frac{1}{2x + 3}$ will be far from the x-axis when the line $y = 2x + 3$ is close to the x-axis. The graph of $y = \frac{1}{2x + 3}$ will be close to the x-axis when the line $y = 2x + 3$ is far from the x-axis.

Example 3

Sketch the graph of $y = \frac{1}{2x^2 - 7x - 4}$ by first graphing $y = 2x^2 - 7x - 4$.

Solution

The graph of $y = 2x^2 - 7x - 4$ is a parabola that opens up. From the factored form, $y = (2x + 1)(x - 4)$, you know that the graph crosses the x-axis at $x = -\frac{1}{2}$ and $x = 4$. The x-coordinate of the vertex is $\frac{-0.5 + 4}{2} = 1.75$. The y-coordinate of the vertex is $2(1.75)^2 - 7(1.75) - 4 = -10.125$.

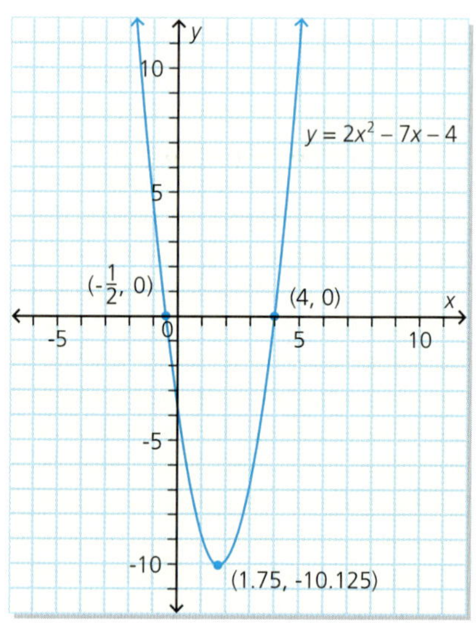

Given this information, you know that the graph of $y = \frac{1}{2x^2 - 7x - 4}$

- has vertical asymptotes at $x = -\frac{1}{2}$ and $x = 4$
- has three parts to it
- crosses the parabola where $y = 1$ and $y = -1$
- has a high point between the asymptotes at $\left(1.75, \frac{1}{-10.125}\right)$ or about $(1.75, -0.1)$

Finally, the graph of $y = \frac{1}{2x^2 - 7x - 4}$

- has y-intercept $\frac{1}{-4} = -0.25$
- is close to the x-axis when the parabola is far from the x-axis and is far from the x-axis when the parabola is close to the x-axis

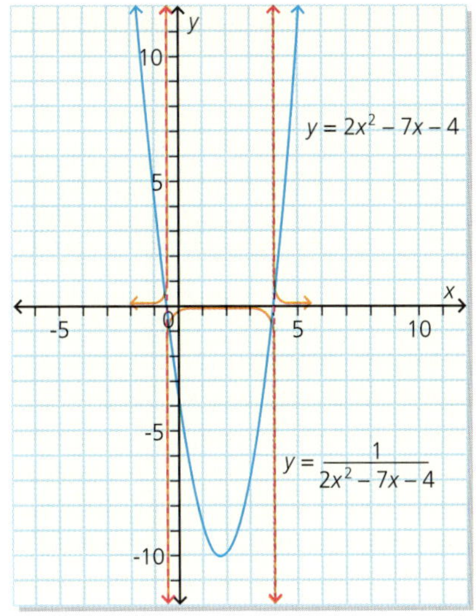

Practise, Apply, Solve 4.6

A

1. Which of the following tables display inverse variation? Explain your answer.

(a)

x	y
2	24
3	16
4	12
6	8

(b)

x	y
10	360
8	450
6	600
4	900

(c)

x	y
3	9
6	36
9	81
12	144

2. Write an equation for each relation in question 1.

3. **i.** Determine the reciprocal $y = \frac{1}{f(x)}$ for each of the following functions.
ii. Determine the equations of the vertical asymptotes of $y = \frac{1}{f(x)}$.
iii. Verify your results from (ii) using graphing technology.

(a) $f(x) = 2x$ (b) $f(x) = x + 5$ (c) $f(x) = x - 4$
(d) $f(x) = 2x + 5$ (e) $f(x) = -3x + 6$ (f) $f(x) = (x - 3)^2$
(g) $f(x) = x^2 - 3x - 10$ (h) $f(x) = 3x^2 - 4x - 4$

4. Copy and complete the table. Sketch the graphs of $y = f(x)$ and $y = \frac{1}{f(x)}$. Find equations for $y = f(x)$ and $y = \frac{1}{f(x)}$.

x	−4	−3	−2	−1	0	1	2	3	4	5	6	7
f(x)	16	14	12	10	8	6	4	2	0	−2	−4	−6
$\frac{1}{f(x)}$												

5. Sketch the graph of the reciprocal function for each of the following functions.

(a)

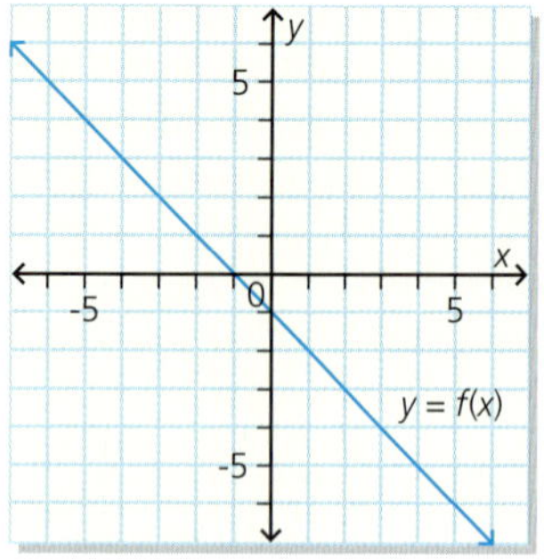

(b)

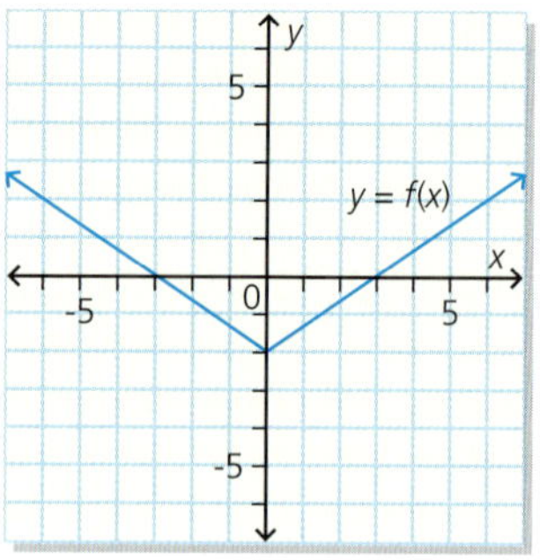

(c)

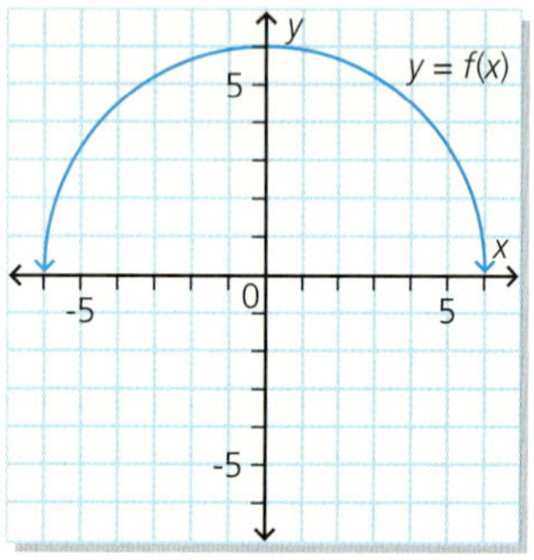

(d)

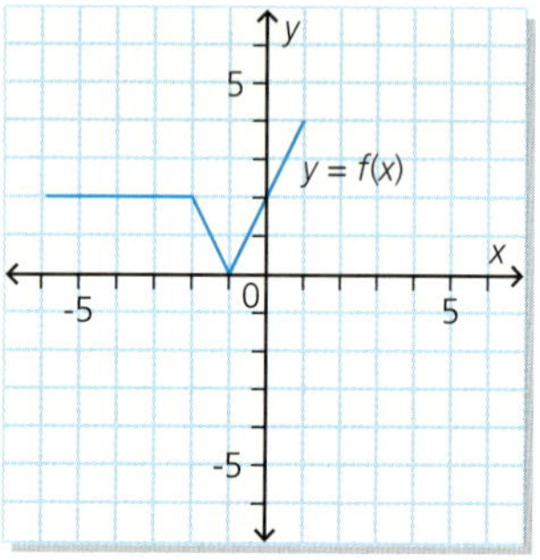

6. In the table, one value of *y* is incorrect. Sketch the graph to identify and correct the error. Determine an equation for the relationship between *x* and *y*.

x	3	4	5	6	7
y	105	87.5	63	52.5	45

B

7. The relationship between the time it takes for a car to accelerate to a given speed from rest and the acceleration is an inverse variation. It takes 6 s to reach a certain speed when the acceleration is 10 m/s^2. Find the time it takes to reach the same speed when the acceleration is 12 m/s^2. Write an equation to describe the relationship.

8. The current I, in amps (A), flowing through a light bulb can be given by $I = \frac{W}{V}$, where W is the power, in watts (W), and V is the voltage, in volts (V).

(a) How much current flows through a bulb marked 60 W, 100 V when it is lit?

(b) What total power could be obtained from a 110-V supply that is protected by a 15-A fuse?

(c) Describe the relationship between I and W for a fixed voltage supply.

9. (a) Sketch the graph of the function $f(x) = \frac{1}{x+2}$ by first sketching the graph of $f(x) = x + 2$.

(b) State the domain and the range of $f(x) = \frac{1}{x+2}$. What is the inverse function?

10. **Knowledge and Understanding:** Sketch each pair of graphs on the same axes. For each reciprocal function, state the domain and the range and find the equation of the inverse function.

(a) $y = x - 1$ and $y = \frac{1}{x-1}$ (b) $y = 5 - x$ and $y = \frac{1}{5-x}$

11. Sketch each pair of graphs on the same axes. State the domain and estimate the range for each reciprocal function.

(a) $y = 2x - 5, y = \frac{1}{2x-5}$

(b) $y = 3x + 4, y = \frac{1}{3x+4}$

(c) $y = -x, y = \frac{1}{-x}$

12. Sketch the graph of $y = \frac{1}{2x^2 + 5x - 3}$ by first graphing $y = 2x^2 + 5x - 3$.

13. For each case, draw the graph of $y = f(x)$ and $y = \frac{1}{f(x)}$ on the same axes.

(a) $f(x) = x^2 - 4$ (b) $f(x) = (x - 2)^2 - 3$

(c) $f(x) = x^2 - 3x + 2$ (d) $f(x) = (x + 3)^2$

(e) $f(x) = x^2 + 2$ (f) $f(x) = -(x + 4)^2 + 1$

14. **Communication:** Explain how you would use a sketch of the graph of $y = x^2 - 3x - 10$ to sketch the graph of $y = \frac{1}{x^2 - 3x - 10}$.

15. For each function, draw $f(x)$, $\frac{1}{f(x)}$, and $f^{-1}(x)$ on the same axes. State the domain and the range.

(a) $f(x) = 2x + 1$ (b) $f(x) = x^2 - 1$ (c) $f(x) = \sqrt{x - 4} - 3$

16. **Check Your Understanding:** Describe the properties of the function $f(x) = \frac{1}{x}$ and how it is related to the function $f(x) = x$. For what real-world situations would a function of the form $f(x) = \frac{k}{x}$ be a useful model? If you were given some data, how would you determine if the model was appropriate?

C

17. The data in the table are modelled by a relation in the form $y = \frac{k}{x} + b$.

x	1	2	4	7	10
y	5.5	4	3.3	2.9	2.8

(a) Calculate $\frac{1}{x}$ for each value of x in the table.

(b) Plot the ordered pairs $\left(\frac{1}{x}, y\right)$ and fit a line through the points.

(c) Find the slope and y-intercept. Write the equation of the original relationship.

18. **Thinking, Inquiry, Problem Solving:** In the graph of $f(x) = \frac{1}{x}$, you can estimate the shaded area under the graph from $x = 1$ to $x = 3$ by counting the shaded squares.

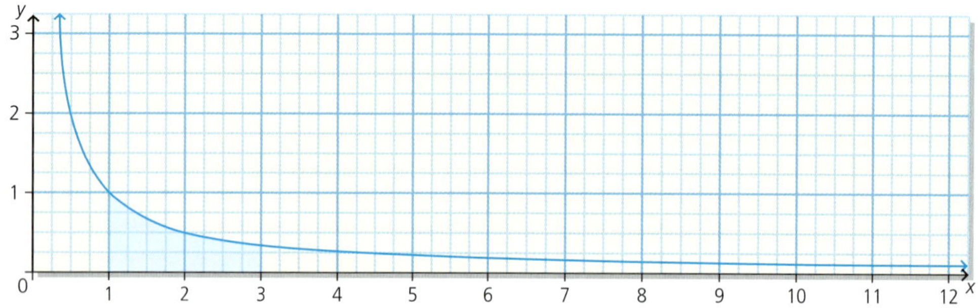

Call this area $A(3)$. From the graph, $A(3) \doteq 1.1$ (17 small squares). Copy and complete the table.

x	1	2	3	4	5	6	7	8	9	10	12
A(x)											

You should find that $A(2) + A(3) \doteq A(6)$. Complete the following statements.

(a) $A(3) + A(4) \doteq A(\blacksquare)$

(b) $A(2) + A(4) \doteq A(\blacksquare)$

(c) $A(10) - A(2) \doteq A(\blacksquare)$

(d) $A(9) \doteq (\blacksquare) \times A(3)$

Use the table to estimate each of the following.

i. $A(18)$ **ii.** $A(25)$ **iii.** $A(2.5)$ **iv.** $A(4.5)$

19. **Application:** Determine the equation of the function in the graph.

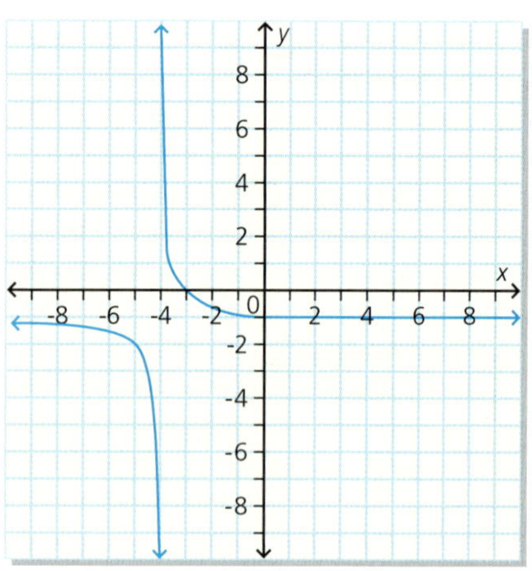

Exploring the Behaviour of Functions Near the Asymptotes

4.7

EXPLORATION

All of the reciprocal functions in the previous section had vertical and horizontal asymptotes. You can better understand the behaviour of the function near the asymptotes by looking at a table in a graphing calculator.

Examining the Function's Behaviour Near a Vertical Asymptote

1. Adjust the window. Press WINDOW and enter these values: **Xmin=−9.4**, **Xmax=9.4**, **Ymin=−5**, and **Ymax=5**. Enter the reciprocal function $f(x) = \frac{1}{x-3}$. Press GRAPH. The graph has a vertical asymptote at $x = 3$, and the x-axis is a horizontal asymptote.

2. (a) You can examine what happens as the graph approaches the vertical asymptote by looking at the table as x approaches the value 3. Open the **TABLE SETUP** screen by pressing 2nd WINDOW and enter the values shown here.

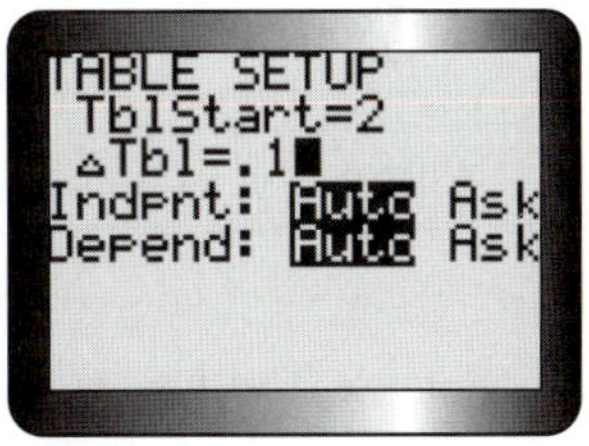

step 2a

(b) Display the table by pressing 2nd GRAPH. Notice that the x-values begin at 2.0 and increase in increments of 0.1. Scroll down, using ▼, and observe the corresponding y-values. When you get to 3, there is no y-value, the word **ERROR** appears instead.

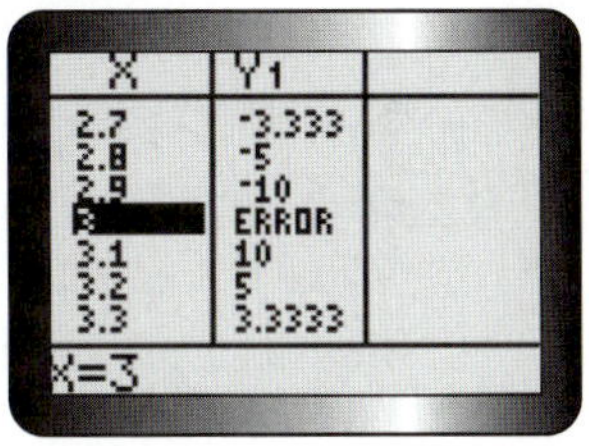

step 2b

3. (a) You can get closer to the asymptote by adjusting the values in the TABLE SETUP screen. Press 2nd WINDOW. Change **TblStart** to 2.91 and **ΔTbl** to .01. **ΔTbl** defines the increment for the independent variable. Display the table again and scroll down. How do the y-values change as x approaches 3?

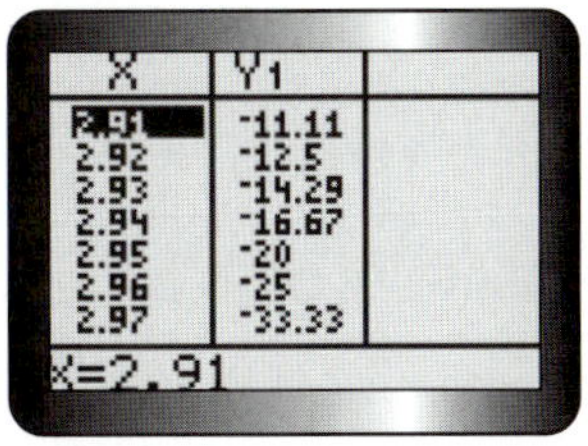

step 3a

(b) Get even closer by repeating step 3 and changing **TblStart** to 2.991 and **ΔTbl** to .001. As you scroll down the table, notice that the y-values move quickly away from 0. In the table, what is the smallest y-value at the point closest to the asymptote?

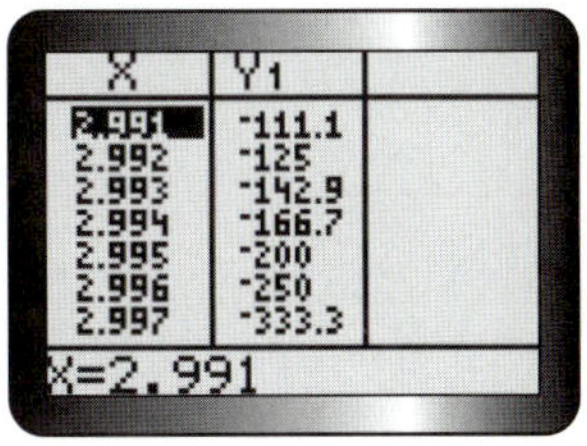

step 3b

4. If you continue scrolling past **ERROR**, then you are looking at points on the other side of the asymptote. Notice that the sign of y has changed. The y-value is just as far from zero, but is on the other side of zero.

Examining the Function's Behaviour Near a Horizontal Asymptote

5. The graph approaches a horizontal asymptote when x is far from zero. Examine this part of the table. Press [2nd][WINDOW] and set **TblStart** to 100 and **ΔTbl** to 100. Press [2nd] [GRAPH]. Scroll down the table and look at the y-values.

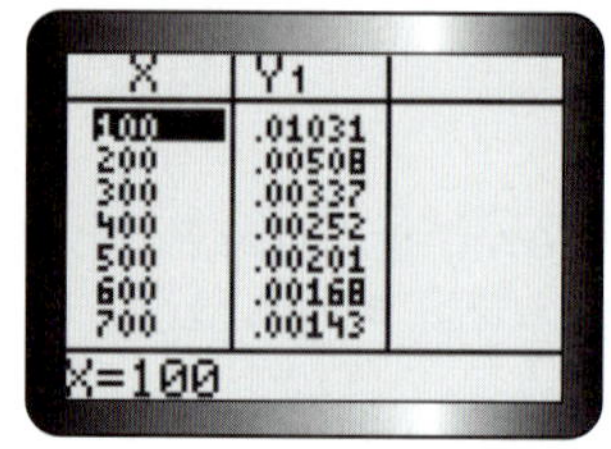

step 5

6. Repeat step 5. Set **TblStart** to -100 and leave **ΔTbl** at 100. Scroll **up** to see what happens to y as x moves farther and farther away from the origin. As x moves farther away from the origin, in both directions along the x-axis, the y-values approach 0. The equation of the horizontal asymptote is $y = 0$.

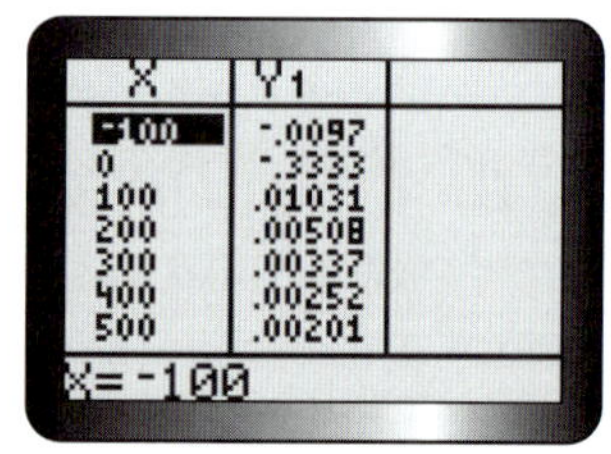

step 6

7. For each function,
   i. enter the function into the graphing calculator
   ii. use a table to examine the behaviour of the graph near the vertical asymptote(s)
   iii. sketch the graph near the vertical asymptote(s)
   iv. use the table to examine the behaviour of the graph where x is far from 0. Write the equation of the horizontal asymptote. Remember to check positive and negative x-values.

(a) $f(x) = \frac{2x}{x - 4}$

(b) $g(x) = \frac{3x}{2 - x}$

(c) $h(x) = \frac{x^2 + 3}{x^2 - 5}$

(d) $h(x) = \frac{x^2 - 4}{x^2 + 5x + 6}$

(e) $g(x) = \frac{1}{x^2 - 1}$

(f) $f(x) = \frac{2x}{x^2 + 4x + 3}$

(g) $b(x) = \frac{x + 1}{x - 2}$

(h) $m(x) = \frac{x}{x^2 - x - 6}$

Simplifying Rational Expressions 4.8

You have seen that a function such as $f(x) = 2x + 5$ has a reciprocal function, $g(x)$, where $g(x) = \frac{1}{f(x)}$. In this case, $g(x) = \frac{1}{2x + 5}$. The expression $\frac{1}{2x + 5}$ is also an example of a rational expression. Rational expressions occur not only in rational functions but also in problem solving and further theoretical work in mathematics.

Think, Do, Discuss

1. Compare these two lists.

Expressions that are rational	Expressions that are not rational
$\frac{x^2}{x^2 - 4}$	$\frac{x}{\sqrt{x - 1}}$
$x + 2 - \frac{4}{x}$	$1 - x - \frac{2}{\sqrt{x}}$
$4x^4 + 3x^2 - 2x - 1$	$3x^4 - 2x^{\frac{3}{2}} + 4x - 1$
$\frac{1}{h}\left(\frac{1}{x + h} - \frac{1}{x}\right)$	$\frac{1}{h}\left(\frac{1}{\sqrt{x + h}} - \frac{1}{\sqrt{x}}\right)$
$\frac{x^2 - 2x + 1}{x^2 - x} \div \frac{x - 1}{x}$	$\frac{x^{\frac{1}{2}} - 2}{x - 4} \div \frac{x^{\frac{1}{2}} + 2}{x^{\frac{1}{2}} + 2}$

Given these examples, describe a **rational expression**. Explain your answer.

2. Rational expressions represent variable quantities and since they have variables in the denominator, you must ensure that the variables do not take values that would make the denominator equal to zero. Therefore, you must restrict the values of the variables. For example, $\frac{x}{x + 2}$ is defined only when $x \neq -2$. What are the restrictions for $\frac{5y}{x(y - 3)^2}$?

3. Simplifying rational expressions is the same as simplifying rational numbers. For example, $\frac{12}{16} = \frac{{}^{1}\cancel{4} \times 3}{{}_{1}\cancel{4} \times 4} = \frac{3}{4}$. How would you simplify the expression $\frac{6x - 9}{4x - 6}$?

4. When you simplify a rational number, the simplified number has exactly the same value as the original number. The two numbers are exactly equivalent and interchangeable. When you reduce a rational expression, the reduced expression must have the same restrictions as the original expression. For what values of x is the expression $\frac{(3x - 5)}{(x - 4)(3x - 5)}$ not defined? Explain your answer. You must state all the restrictions on a variable before reducing a rational expression. What is the reduced expression?

5. What are the restrictions for $\frac{12xy^3}{9x^2y}$? Simplify the expression.

6. What are the restrictions for $\frac{18x(x-2y)}{12x(2x-y)}$? Simplify the expression.

7. What is the first step in deciding whether the expression $\frac{3x^2-7x+4}{x^2-1}$ is simplified? Simplify the expression, if possible, and state any restrictions.

Focus 4.8

Key Ideas

- A rational expression is a sum, difference, product, or quotient of terms, each of which could be written as a quotient of polynomials. A rational expression must have at least one rational term. No variable in a rational expression can be under a fractional exponent.
- Simplifying a rational expression is the same as simplifying a rational number. You may divide the numerator and denominator of a rational expression by any nonzero factor of the numerator or denominator.
- A rational expression cannot be defined when its denominator is 0.
- When stating or simplifying a rational expression, exclude any value(s) of the variables that would make the denominator 0. In other words, state the restrictions on the variables.
- An expression in the form $\frac{f(x)h(x)}{g(x)h(x)}$ is equal to $\frac{f(x)}{g(x)}$, provided $g(x) \neq 0$ and $h(x) \neq 0$.
- When a rational expression is simplified, it is often necessary to factor the numerator, or denominator, or both.

Example 1

For each of the following, state the restrictions on the value(s) of the variable(s).

(a) $\frac{6x^2z}{2xy}$ (b) $\frac{5x-15}{x^2-9}$ (c) $\frac{m^2+5m-6}{6m^3-5m^2-4m}$

Solution

For each case, find the value(s) of the variable(s) that make the denominator 0.

(a) For $2xy = 0$, $x = 0$ or $y = 0$. The restrictions are $x \neq 0$ and $y \neq 0$.

(b) Let $x^2 - 9 = 0$, then factor.

$$(x-3)(x+3) = 0$$
$$x = \pm 3$$

The restrictions are $x \neq \pm 3$.

(c) Let $6m^3 - 5m^2 - 4m = 0$, then factor.

$$m(6m^2 - 5m - 4) = 0$$
$$m(2m+1)(3m-4) = 0$$
$$m = 0 \text{ or } m = -\frac{1}{2} \text{ or } m = \frac{4}{3}$$

The restrictions are $m \neq -\frac{1}{2}$, 0, or $\frac{4}{3}$.

Example 2

Simplify and state any restrictions.

(a) $\frac{3x - 12}{x^2 - x - 12}$

(b) $\frac{xy - x^2}{x^2y - y^3}$

Solution

(a) $\frac{3x - 12}{x^2 - x - 12} = \frac{3(x - 4)}{(x + 3)(x - 4)}, x \neq -3, 4$

$= \frac{3}{x + 3}, x \neq -3, 4$

(b) $\frac{xy - x^2}{x^2y - y^3} = \frac{x(y - x)}{y(x^2 - y^2)}, y \neq 0$

$= \frac{-x(x - y)}{y(x + y)(x - y)}, x \neq \pm y$

$= \frac{-x}{y(x + y)}, y \neq 0, \text{ and } x \neq \pm y$

Example 3

An expression for calculating the drug dose for young children is $\frac{(t^3 - 2t^2 - 3t)a}{24t^2 - 72t}$, where t is the age of the child in years and a is the adult dose in milligrams. The adult dose for a pain-killing drug is 300 mg. What is the drug dose for

(a) a two-year-old child?

(b) a three-year-old child?

Solution

Calculating will be much easier after simplifying the formula.

Begin by factoring the numerator and the denominator.

$$\frac{(t^3 - 2t^2 - 3t)a}{24t^2 - 72t} = \frac{t(t^2 - 2t - 3)a}{24t(t - 3)}$$

$$= \frac{t(t - 3)(t + 1)a}{24t(t - 3)}$$

$$= \frac{(t + 1)a}{24}, t \neq 0, 3$$

(a) If $a = 300$ and $t = 2$, then $\frac{(2 + 1)300}{24} = 37.5$

The dose is 37.5 mg.

(b) Since $t \neq 3$, you cannot substitute the value 3 in the formula. However, use $t = 2.9999$ or $t = 3.0001$ to estimate the dose.

In either case, $\frac{(2.9999 + 1)300}{24} \doteq 50$, or $\frac{(3.0001 + 1)300}{24} \doteq 50$.

The estimated dose for a three-year-old child is 50 mg.

Practise, Apply, Solve 4.8

A

1. For each rational expression, state the restrictions on the value(s) of the variable(s).

(a) $\frac{3x - 2}{x - 1}$

(b) $\frac{4y}{2y - 1}$

(c) $\frac{-3m^2n^2}{6m^2n}$

(d) $\frac{-4x^2(x-3)}{2x(x-3)}$ (e) $\frac{2p-1}{(p-4)(p+2)}$ (f) $\frac{-8(a+b)}{2(a+b)}$

(g) $\frac{4(m+3)}{8m(m+3)}$ (h) $\frac{3(2x+1)}{5(2x-3)}$ (i) $\frac{3a(a+2)}{4a(3a+4)}$

2. (a) Factor $4x + 12$. (b) Factor $5x + 15$.

(c) Use your answers from (a) and (b) to simplify $\frac{4x+12}{5x+15}$. What restrictions apply to x?

3. Identify which of the following are equivalent to $\frac{a+b}{b-a}$.

(a) $-\frac{a+b}{a-b}$ (b) $-\frac{a+b}{b-a}$ (c) $-\frac{a+b}{-(b-a)}$ (d) $-\frac{b+a}{a-b}$

4. Simplify.

(a) $\frac{x+y}{y+x}$ (b) $-\frac{(y-x)}{y-x}$ (c) $\frac{x-y}{-(y-x)}$

(d) $\frac{-(y+x)}{-(x+y)}$ (e) $\frac{-(y-x)}{x-y}$ (f) $\frac{x-y}{y-x}$

5. Simplify and state the restrictions.

(a) $\frac{x-2}{(x+5)(x-2)}$ (b) $\frac{4y(3y-4)}{(3y-4)(3y+4)}$ (c) $\frac{(x-1)(3x+5)}{(x-1)(2x+1)}$

6. (a) Factor $k^2 - 4$. (b) Factor $3k^2 + 5k - 2$.

(c) Simplify $\frac{k^2-4}{3k^2+5k-2}$. State the restrictions.

7. (a) Factor $6p^2 + 30p + 36$ as fully as possible.

(b) Factor $3p^2 - 3p - 18$ fully.

(c) Simplify $\frac{6p^2+30p+36}{3p^2-3p-18}$. State the restrictions.

8. Simplify each rational expression and state the restrictions on the variables.

(a) $\frac{2b+8}{5b+20}$ (b) $\frac{3x^2-2x}{3x^2-6x}$ (c) $\frac{m^2-4m}{3m^2-12m}$ (d) $\frac{15x-5x^2}{x^2-3x}$

(e) $\frac{x^2-4}{x^2-5x+6}$ (f) $\frac{p^2-p-20}{3p-15}$ (g) $\frac{y^2-7y+12}{y^2-y-12}$ (h) $\frac{a^2+a-20}{a^2-11a+28}$

9. **Knowledge and Understanding:** Simplify and state the restrictions.

(a) $\frac{36x^2y}{-16xy^2}$ (b) $\frac{6x+24}{4x+16}$ (c) $\frac{9m^2-4}{9m^2-3m-2}$ (d) $\frac{x^2-10xy+25y^2}{x^2-25y^2}$

10. Simplify and state the restrictions.

(a) $\frac{6m^2-2m-4}{4m^2-4}$ (b) $\frac{2a^2+5a-3}{2a^2-7a+3}$ (c) $\frac{40+6x-18x^2}{9x^2-9x-10}$ (d) $\frac{9x^2-1}{9x^3+6x^2+x}$

11. **Communication:** What does the word *restrictions* mean in connection with a rational expression, and why must you state the restrictions? Explain using examples.

12. (a) What is the relation between the expressions $x - y$ and $y - x$?

(b) Simplify $\frac{x^2+xy-2y^2}{y^2-x^2}$ and state the restrictions on the variables.

13. Simplify and state the restrictions.

(a) $\frac{4a^2-b^2}{b-2a}$ (b) $\frac{x^2-2x+1}{1-x}$ (c) $\frac{k^2-10k+25}{25-k^2}$

14. Two expressions for calculating the drug dose for young children are $\frac{(2t^3 + t^2 - t)a}{48t^2 - 24t}$ and $\frac{(3t^2 - 2t)a}{3t^2 + 34t - 24}$, where t is the age of the child in years and a is the adult dose. If the adult dose for a pain-killing drug is 250 mg, then what is the dose, to the nearest unit, for

(a) a one-year-old child?

(b) an eight-month-old child?

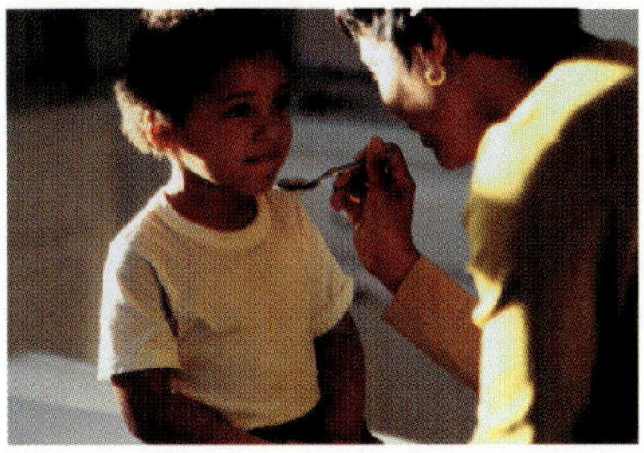

15. **Thinking, Inquiry, Problem Solving:** Find a simplified expression to represent the ratio $\frac{\text{surface area}}{\text{volume}}$ for a cylindrical can with height h and base radius r. What affects the ratio more, a change in the height or a change in the base radius? Justify your answer.

16. **Check Your Understanding:** Craig simplified $\frac{a^2 - 5b^2}{2a^2 - 9ab - 5b^2}$ to $\frac{a - 5b}{2a - b}$. Is Craig correct? If not, explain where he made his error.

C

17. Under what conditions is $\frac{-4x^3 - 7x^2 - 3x}{12x + 13x^2 - 4x^3} = \frac{2x^3 + x^2 - x}{2x^3 - 9x^2 + 4x}$ true?

18. **Application:** The concentration of pain-killing drug A in the bloodstream, t hours after it is taken orally, is given by $\frac{5t^4 - 10t^2}{t^5 - 4t}$, and the concentration of pain-killing drug B in the bloodstream, t hours after it is taken orally, is given by the expression $\frac{3t^2 - 12t}{2t^3 - 8t^2 + 5t - 20}$. Simplify both expressions. Which drug, A or B, needs to be taken more often? Justify your answer.

The Chapter Problem—Fundraising

CP14. If $C(x)$ is the cost of producing x items, then the average cost function is $AC(x) = \frac{C(x)}{x}$. Find the average cost function for your chosen supplier. Graph this function and state the domain.

CP15. How many T-shirts must be sold so that the average cost per T-shirt is less than \$5?

CP16. If $P(x)$ is the profit earned from producing and selling x items, then the average profit is modelled by the function $AP(x) = \frac{P(x)}{x}$. Find the average profit function for your chosen supplier. Graph this function and state the domain.

CP17. At what point is the average profit a maximum?

4.9 Multiplying and Dividing Rational Expressions

Multiplying and dividing rational expressions is the same as multiplying and dividing rational numbers.

Think, Do, Discuss

1. How do you multiply two rational numbers? Explain using the product $\frac{5}{48} \times \frac{72}{85}$ as an example. Give the answer as a rational number in lowest terms.

2. At what point is it easier to remove the common factors, before multiplying or after? Explain.

3. Apply the same steps to find the product $\frac{x(x+1)}{x^2-1} \times \frac{2(x-1)^2}{5x^2}$. Look for common factors and reduce, where possible. Since you are working with rational expressions, what must you be careful to state at each step?

4. How do you divide two rational numbers? Explain using the quotient $\frac{25}{28} \div \frac{10}{21}$ as an example. Give the answer as a rational number in lowest terms.

5. Apply the same steps to find the quotient $\frac{4x^2}{x^2+6x-7} \div \frac{x}{x^2-1}$. As before, look for common factors and reduce, where possible. Why are there more restrictions to include when dividing rational expressions?

Focus 4.9

Key Ideas

- To multiply rational expressions
  - factor the numerators and denominators
  - state all the restrictions on the variables
  - divide out any factors that are common to the numerator and denominator
  - multiply the numerators, then multiply the denominators, and write the result as a single rational expression
- To divide two rational expressions
  - factor the numerators and denominators
  - note any restrictions on the variables
  - take the reciprocal of the second rational expression and change $\div$ to $\times$
  - state any new restrictions

- ♦ remove any factors common to the numerator and denominator
  - ♦ multiply the numerators and then multiply the denominators
  - ♦ write the product as a single rational expression and state all restrictions
- If $f(x)$, $g(x)$, $m(x)$, and $n(x)$ are rational expressions, then

$$\frac{f(x)}{g(x)} \times \frac{m(x)}{n(x)} = \frac{f(x)m(x)}{g(x)n(x)}, \text{ provided } g(x) \neq 0 \text{ and } n(x) \neq 0$$

$$\frac{f(x)}{g(x)} \div \frac{m(x)}{n(x)} = \frac{f(x)}{g(x)} \times \frac{n(x)}{m(x)} = \frac{f(x)n(x)}{g(x)m(x)}, \text{ provided } g(x) \neq 0,\ n(x) \neq 0, \text{ and } m(x) \neq 0$$

Example 1

Simplify.

(a) $\dfrac{9x^2}{4xy} \times \dfrac{12xy^2}{3x}$

(b) $\dfrac{2a + 6}{7} \times \dfrac{3}{a^2 - 9}$

(c) $\dfrac{2x^2 + 5x + 2}{4x^2 - 8x - 5} \times \dfrac{2x^2 - 11x + 15}{3x^2 + 7x + 2}$

Solution

Follow these steps for multiplying rational expressions: factor, state restrictions, remove common factors, and then multiply.

(a)
$$\frac{9x^2}{4xy} \times \frac{12xy^2}{3x} = \frac{(3x)\cancel{(3x)}^{1}}{\cancel{4xy}_{1}} \times \frac{\cancel{(4xy)}^{1}(3y)}{\cancel{3x}_{1}}$$ Remove the common factors.

$$= \frac{3x}{1} \times \frac{3y}{1}$$ Multiply.

$$= 9xy,\ x \neq 0 \text{ and } y \neq 0$$

(b)
$$\frac{2a + 6}{7} \times \frac{3}{a^2 - 9} = \frac{2\cancel{(a+3)}^{1}}{7} \times \frac{3}{(a-3)\cancel{(a+3)}_{1}}$$

$$= \frac{2}{7} \times \frac{3}{a - 3}$$

$$= \frac{6}{7(a - 3)},\ a \neq \pm 3$$

(c)
$$\frac{2x^2 + 5x + 2}{4x^2 - 8x - 5} \times \frac{2x^2 - 11x + 15}{3x^2 + 7x + 2} = \frac{{}^{1}\cancel{(2x+1)}\cancel{(x+2)}^{1}}{{}_{1}\cancel{(2x+1)}\cancel{(2x-5)}_{1}} \times \frac{\cancel{(2x-5)}^{1}(x-3)}{\cancel{(x+2)}_{1}(3x+1)}$$

$$= \frac{1}{1} \times \frac{(x - 3)}{(3x + 1)}$$

$$= \frac{x - 3}{3x + 1},\ x \neq -2, -\frac{1}{3}, -\frac{1}{2}, \frac{5}{2}$$

Example 2

Simplify.

(a) $\dfrac{2x+8}{3x} \div \dfrac{4x+16}{2x^2}$ (b) $\dfrac{x^2+3x+2}{x^4-4x^2} \div \dfrac{x^2-x-2}{5x^3-9x^2-2x}$

Solution

Follow these steps for dividing rational expressions: factor, state restrictions, take the reciprocal of the second expression and change ÷ to ×, state additional restrictions, remove common factors, and then multiply.

(a) Factor.

$$\frac{2x+8}{3x} \div \frac{4x+16}{2x^2} = \frac{2(x+4)}{3x} \div \frac{4(x+4)}{2x(x)}$$ Multiply by the reciprocal.

$$= \frac{\cancel{2(x+4)}^{1}}{3\cancel{x}^{1}} \times \frac{\cancel{2x(x)}^{1}}{\cancel{4(x+4)}^{1}}$$ Remove common factors.

$$= \frac{1}{3} \times \frac{x}{1}$$ Multiply.

$$= \frac{x}{3},\ x \neq 0,\ -4$$

(b) $$\frac{x^2+3x+2}{x^4-4x^2} \div \frac{x^2-x-2}{5x^3-9x^2-2x} = \frac{(x+1)(x+2)}{x^2(x^2-4)} \div \frac{(x+1)(x-2)}{x(5x^2-9x-2)}$$

$$= \frac{(x+1)(x+2)}{(x)(x)(x+2)(x-2)} \div \frac{(x+1)(x-2)}{x(5x+1)(x-2)}$$

$$= \frac{{}^{1}\cancel{(x+1)}\cancel{(x+2)}^{1}}{{}_{1}\cancel{(x)}(x)\cancel{(x+2)}_{1}(x-2)} \times \frac{{}^{1}\cancel{x}(5x+1)\cancel{(x-2)}^{1}}{{}_{1}\cancel{(x+1)}\cancel{(x-2)}_{1}}$$

$$= \frac{1}{x(x-2)} \times \frac{(5x+1)}{1}$$

$$= \frac{5x+1}{x(x-2)},\ x \neq -1,\ -\frac{1}{5},\ 0,\ \pm 2$$

Example 3

Find the value of $\dfrac{3m^2-7m-6}{6m^2+3m} \times \dfrac{9m-6}{2m^2-5m-3} \div \dfrac{9m^2-4}{4m^2+4m+1}$ if $m = -0.2$.

Solution

Simplify the expression before substituting the value for m.

$$\frac{3m^2-7m-6}{6m^2+3m} \times \frac{9m-6}{2m^2-5m-3} \div \frac{9m^2-4}{4m^2+4m+1}$$

$$= \frac{(3m+2)(m-3)}{3m(2m+1)} \times \frac{3(3m-2)}{(2m+1)(m-3)} \div \frac{(3m-2)(3m+2)}{(2m+1)(2m+1)}$$

$$= \frac{{}^{1}\cancel{(3m+2)}\cancel{(m-3)}^{1}}{{}_{1}\cancel{3}m\cancel{(2m+1)}_{1}} \times \frac{{}^{1}\cancel{3}\cancel{(3m-2)}^{1}}{\cancel{(2m+1)}_{1}\cancel{(m-3)}_{1}} \times \frac{{}^{1}\cancel{(2m+1)}\cancel{(2m+1)}^{1}}{\cancel{(3m-2)}_{1}\cancel{(3m+2)}_{1}}$$

$$= \frac{1}{m} \times \frac{1}{1} \times \frac{1}{1}$$

$$= \frac{1}{m},\ m \neq -\frac{2}{3},\ -\frac{1}{2},\ 0,\ \frac{2}{3},\ 3$$

If $m = -0.2$, then $\dfrac{1}{m} = \dfrac{1}{-0.2} = -5$.

Practise, Apply, Solve 4.9

A

1. Simplify. Remember to state any restrictions.

(a) $\frac{3x}{8} \times \frac{2y}{9}$ (b) $\frac{6}{a} \times \frac{5a^2}{3b}$ (c) $\frac{9x^2y}{4y} \times \frac{12xy}{3x^2y}$

(d) $\frac{14pq}{5q^2} \times \frac{10q^3}{21pq^2}$ (e) $\frac{-8x^2}{10y} \times \frac{5y^3}{-2x^2}$

2. (a) $\frac{8a}{9} \div \frac{2b}{3}$ (b) $\frac{3m^2}{n} \div \frac{2m}{n}$ (c) $\frac{-56a^2b^2}{24a^3b} \div \frac{16ab^3}{18b}$

(d) $\frac{36pqr^2}{-26p^3qr} \div \frac{-24pq^2r}{39pr}$ (e) $\frac{-5a^3}{3b^2} \div \frac{-10a^2b}{3b^2}$

3. Simplify.

(a) $\frac{3x}{x-2} \times \frac{4(x-2)}{6x}$ (b) $\frac{5y(y+3)}{4y} \times \frac{(y-5)}{(y+3)}$ (c) $\frac{(2a-1)}{3a(a+4)} \times \frac{a(a+4)}{(2a-1)}$

(d) $\frac{10x}{x+2} \div \frac{5}{2(x+2)}$ (e) $\frac{4b(b+1)}{(b-1)} \div \frac{12(b+1)}{(b+4)}$ (f) $\frac{(3s+1)}{2s-1} \div \frac{3s(s+1)}{2s-1}$

4. Express each product in lowest terms.

(a) $\frac{12y}{3y-9} \times \frac{4y-12}{6y^2}$ (b) $\frac{6p-12}{5p+5} \times \frac{2p+2}{3p-6}$ (c) $\frac{x^2-y^2}{x^2-16} \times \frac{x-4}{x-y}$

5. Simplify each quotient.

(a) $\frac{k+1}{k^2-1} \div \frac{k}{k-1}$ (b) $\frac{x^2-4}{x+3} \div \frac{x-2}{x^2-9}$ (c) $\frac{1-3q}{2q+1} \div \frac{1-9q^2}{4q^2-1}$

6. **Communication:** Explain why there may be more restrictions when you divide rational expressions than when you multiply the same two expressions. Use an example to illustrate your explanation.

B

For questions 7 to 9, simplify each expression.

7. (a) $\frac{x^2+2x+1}{x} \times \frac{x^2-x}{x^2-1}$ (b) $(x+1) \times \frac{1}{3x^2-3}$

(c) $\frac{2x^2-x-3}{x^2-1} \times \frac{x^2+x-2}{2x^2+x-6}$ (d) $\frac{x^2+10x+25}{x^2-8x+16} \times \frac{x^2-16}{x^2-25}$

(e) $\frac{x^2+5x+6}{x^2-4} \times \frac{x^2-6x+8}{x^2-x-12}$ (f) $\frac{2x^2-5x-3}{x^2-9} \times \frac{2x^2+5x-3}{2x^2+5x+2}$

8. (a) $\frac{x^2-9}{x^2-49} \div \frac{x+3}{x+7}$ (b) $\frac{x^2-1}{2x^2+3x+1} \div \frac{x+1}{2x+1}$

(c) $\frac{3x+9}{2x^4} \div \frac{x^2+5x+6}{4x^2}$ (d) $\frac{x^2+4x-5}{x^2-3x} \div \frac{x^2-1}{x^2-6x+9}$

(e) $\frac{x^2-2x-15}{12x+9} \div \frac{x+3}{6}$ (f) $\frac{x-2}{x^3} \div \frac{x^2-3x+2}{x^2}$

9. (a) $\frac{x^2-1}{x^2+6x+9} \div \frac{x^2+2x-3}{x^2+6x+9}$ (b) $\frac{m^2+3m+2}{m^2-3m} \times \frac{3-m}{m^2+7m+6}$

(c) $(4x^2-9y^2) \div \frac{3xy+2x^2}{2}$ (d) $\frac{1+4z+4z^2}{z} \times \frac{3z^4}{12z^2-3}$

(e) $\frac{a^2+10a+25}{a^2+2a-15} \times \frac{a^2-5a+6}{a^2+3a-10}$ (f) $\frac{21p-3p^2}{16p^2+4p^3} \div \frac{14-9p+p^2}{12+7p+p^2}$

10. **Knowledge and Understanding:** Simplify.

(a) $\dfrac{5x^2 + 15x}{x^2 - 2x - 15} \times \dfrac{x^2 - 7x + 10}{10x - 20}$ (b) $\dfrac{k^2 + k - 20}{k^2 - 16} \div \dfrac{k^2 + 3k - 10}{k^2 + 2k - 8}$

11. If $f(x) = \dfrac{x^2 - 16}{4x - x^2}$, then find

(a) $f(1)$ (b) $f(-1)$ (c) $f(5)$ (d) $f(-2)$

(e) $f(3)$ (f) $f(-3)$ (g) which values of x are not allowed?

12. **Application:** An estimate of the cost, in billions of dollars, to keep the atmosphere in Canada x percent free of a chemical toxin is given by

$C(x) = \dfrac{x - 2}{100x - x^2} \div \dfrac{x^2 + 18x - 40}{5x^2 + 100x}$.

Find the cost of keeping the atmosphere

(a) 90% free of the chemical toxin

(b) 99% free of the chemical toxin

(c) 99.9% free of the chemical toxin

13. **Check Your Understanding:** Charlene could not evaluate the expression $\dfrac{15x^2 + 7x - 2}{2x^2 - x - 15} \div \dfrac{6x^2 - 11x - 10}{4x^2 - 25}$ for $x = 2.5$. Simplify the expression and explain why.

C

14. Simplify.

(a) $\dfrac{a^2 - b^2}{a^2 + b^2} \times \dfrac{a^2 + ab}{b^2 - a^2} \div a$

(b) $\dfrac{x^3 + 4x^2}{x^2 - 1} \times \dfrac{x^2 - 5x + 6}{x^2 - 3x} \div \dfrac{x^2 + 2x - 8}{x^2 - 1}$

15. Find the value of each of the following if $x = 2$.

(a) $\dfrac{x + 1}{x - 1} \times \dfrac{x + 3}{1 - x^2} \div \dfrac{(x + 3)^2}{1 - x}$

(b) $\dfrac{x^2 + 6x + 5}{x^2 + 7x + 12} \times \dfrac{x^2 + 2x - 8}{x^2 - 25} \div \dfrac{x^2 - x - 2}{x^2 - 2x - 15}$

16. **Thinking, Inquiry, Problem Solving**

If $\dfrac{(x - 1)f(x)}{3x^2 + 5x - 2} \times \dfrac{x^2 + 2x}{2x^2 - x - 1} \div \dfrac{x^2 g(x)}{6x^2 + x - 1} = \dfrac{3}{x}$, find a relationship between $f(x)$ and $g(x)$.

17. Simplify. State any restrictions on the variables.

(a) $\dfrac{2x^2 - 3x - 2}{6x^2 - x - 2} \times \dfrac{3x^2 - 5x + 2}{4x^2 - 1} \div \dfrac{x^2 - 1}{6x^2 + 7x + 2}$

(b) $\dfrac{6a^2 - 7ab - 3b^2}{4a^2 + 19ab - 5b^2} \div \dfrac{9b^2 - 4a^2}{4a^2 - 1} \times \dfrac{8a^2 + 10ab - 3b^2}{4a^2 + 4a + 1}$

(c) $\dfrac{\dfrac{m^2 - mn}{6m^2 + 11mn + 3n^2} \div \dfrac{m^2 - n^2}{2m^2 - mn - 6n^2}}{\dfrac{4m^2 - 7mn - 2n^2}{3m^2 + 7mn + 2n^2}}$

Dividing Complex Numbers

4.10U SKILL BUILDER

Functions and Relations

It is not possible to divide by a complex number directly, because the denominator has two independent terms. Overcome this difficulty using the product property of conjugate complex numbers. In other words, recall that $z\bar{z}$ is always a real number.

Example 1

Express in the form $a + bi$.

(a) $\dfrac{2 + 3i}{5 - 2i}$ (b) $\dfrac{2}{1 - i}$ (c) $\dfrac{3 + i}{i}$

Solution

In each case, multiply by $\frac{\bar{z}}{\bar{z}}$, where z is the complex number in the denominator. This is the same as multiplying by 1.

(a) In this case, $5 + 2i$ is the complex conjugate of $5 - 2i$. Multiply the numerator and denominator by $5 + 2i$.

$$\begin{aligned}
&\frac{2 + 3i}{5 - 2i} \\
&= \frac{2 + 3i}{5 - 2i} \times \frac{5 + 2i}{5 + 2i} \\
&= \frac{(2 + 3i)(5 + 2i)}{(5 - 2i)(5 + 2i)} \\
&= \frac{10 + 4i + 15i + 6i^2}{25 + 10i - 10i - 4i^2} \\
&= \frac{10 + 19i + 6(-1)}{25 - 4(-1)} \\
&= \frac{4 + 19i}{29} \\
&= \frac{4}{29} + \frac{19}{29}i
\end{aligned}$$

(b)
$$\begin{aligned}
&\frac{2}{1 - i} \\
&= \frac{2}{1 - i} \times \frac{1 + i}{1 + i} \\
&= \frac{2(1 + i)}{(1 - i)(1 + i)} \\
&= \frac{2 + 2i}{1 - i^2} \\
&= \frac{2 + 2i}{1 - (-1)} \\
&= \frac{2 + 2i}{2} \\
&= 1 + i
\end{aligned}$$

(c)
$$\begin{aligned}
&\frac{3 + i}{i} \\
&= \frac{3 + i}{i} \times \frac{-i}{-i} \\
&= \frac{(3 + i)(-i)}{i(-i)} \\
&= \frac{-3i - i^2}{-i^2} \\
&= \frac{-3i - (-1)}{-(-1)} \\
&= \frac{1 - 3i}{1} \\
&= 1 - 3i
\end{aligned}$$

Example 2

Find the reciprocal of each of the following.

(a) $1 - 2i$ (b) $a + bi$

Solution

(a)
$$\begin{aligned}
\frac{1}{1 - 2i} &= \frac{1}{1 - 2i} \times \frac{1 + 2i}{1 + 2i} \\
&= \frac{1 + 2i}{1 - 4i^2} \\
&= \frac{1 + 2i}{5} \quad \text{or} \quad \frac{1}{5} + \frac{2}{5}i
\end{aligned}$$

(b)
$$\begin{aligned}
\frac{1}{a + bi} &= \frac{1}{a + bi} \times \frac{a - bi}{a - bi} \\
&= \frac{a - bi}{a^2 - b^2i^2} \\
&= \frac{a - bi}{a^2 + b^2} \quad \text{or} \quad \frac{a}{a^2 + b^2} - \frac{b}{a^2 + b^2}i
\end{aligned}$$

Example 3

Solve for z.

(a) $(3 + 4i) = z(1 + i)$

(b) $(2 - i) + 3z = (1 + i)z$

Solution

(a)

$$\begin{aligned}(3 + 4i) &= z(1 + i)\\ \frac{(3 + 4i)}{(1 + i)} &= z\\ \frac{(3 + 4i)}{(1 + i)} \times \frac{(1 - i)}{(1 - i)} &= z\\ \frac{3 + i - 4i^2}{1 - i^2} &= z\\ \frac{3 + i + 4}{1 + 1} &= z\\ \frac{7 + i}{2} &= z\\ \frac{7}{2} + \frac{1}{2}i &= z\end{aligned}$$

(b)

$$\begin{aligned}(2 - i) + 3z &= (1 + i)z\\ 2 - i + 3z &= z + zi\\ 2 - i &= -2z + zi\\ 2 - i &= z(-2 + i)\\ \frac{2 - i}{-2 + i} &= z\\ \frac{(2 - i)(-2 - i)}{(-2 + i)(-2 - i)} &= z\\ \frac{-4 + i^2}{4 - i^2} &= z\\ \frac{-4 + (-1)}{4 - (-1)} &= z\\ \frac{-5}{5} &= z\\ -1 + 0i &= z\end{aligned}$$

Focus 4.10U

Key Ideas

- Simplify a quotient of complex numbers by making the denominator a real number.
- To divide complex numbers, multiply the numerator and the denominator by the conjugate of the denominator.

$$\begin{aligned}\frac{a + bi}{c + di} &= \frac{a + bi}{c + di} \times \frac{c - di}{c - di}\\ &= \frac{(a + bi)(c - di)}{c^2 + d^2}\end{aligned}$$

Practise, Apply, Solve 4.10U

In these questions a *and* b *are real numbers, unless stated otherwise.*

A

1. Write the complex conjugate for each complex number.

(a) $1 - i$

(b) $-1 + 2i$

(c) $\sqrt{3} - i$

(d) $-2 + \sqrt{2}i$

(e) $-\frac{1}{2} - \frac{\sqrt{3}}{2}i$

(f) $x + yi$

2. Write the reciprocal for each complex number in question 1. Then express each reciprocal in the form $a + bi$.

3. Express in the form $a + bi$.

(a) $\frac{30}{3+i}$ (b) $\frac{2}{1+i}$ (c) $\frac{4i}{1-i}$ (d) $\frac{10i}{1-2i}$ (e) $\frac{2+3i}{1-i}$

(f) $\frac{3-i}{1+2i}$ (g) $\frac{4i-3}{3+2i}$ (h) $\frac{4+i}{i}$ (i) $\frac{-2+5i}{-i}$ (j) $\frac{x+yi}{x-yi}$

4. If $z_1 = \sqrt{3} + i$ and $z_2 = \sqrt{3} - i$, then express $\frac{z_1}{z_2}$ in the form $a + bi$.

5. If $z = 3 - i$ and $w = 1 + 2i$, then express $\frac{z}{2w}$ in the form $a + bi$.

B

6. If $z_1 = 1 - i$ and $z_2 = 7 + i$, then express $\frac{z_1 - z_2}{z_1 z_2}$ in the form $a + bi$.

7. Express $\frac{1-i}{(3-i)^2}$ in the form $a + bi$.

8. Compare dividing complex numbers with dividing real numbers. In what ways are the methods similar? different? Is it possible to apply the method for dividing complex numbers to dividing real numbers? Explain your answer using examples.

9. Is it necessary to state restrictions on the variable when dividing complex numbers? Give examples with your explanation.

10. (a) If $z = 3 + 4i$, then express $z + \frac{25}{z}$ in its simplest form.

(b) If $z = a + bi$, then find the real and imaginary parts of $z + \frac{1}{z}$.

11. Solve for z and express in the form $a + bi$.

(a) $(5 - 2i) = z(1 - i)$ (b) $(3 + 2i) + z = (1 - i)z$

(c) $4z - z(3 + i) = -1 + 3i$ (d) $z(5 - 3i)^2 = 4 + 3i$

12. Find the real and imaginary parts of each of the following.

(a) $\frac{2}{3+i} + \frac{3}{2+i}$ (b) $\frac{1}{a+bi} - \frac{1}{a-bi}$

13. For the complex numbers $z_1 = \frac{a}{1+i}$, $z_2 = \frac{b}{1+2i}$, where a and b are real numbers, $z_1 + z_2 = 1$. Determine the values of a and b.

14. The complex number z satisfies $\frac{z}{z+2} = 2 - i$. Find the real and imaginary parts of z.

15. **Check Your Understanding:** State the product property of complex conjugates. Show how to use this property to express a quotient of complex numbers as a single complex number in the form $a + bi$. Include an example.

C

16. Solve for the complex numbers z and w, in the form $a + bi$.

$z + (1 + i)w = 1 - 2i$

$(1 + 2i)z - 2iw = 9 + 6i$

4.11 Adding and Subtracting Rational Expressions

Part 1: Investigating Rowing Speed

In recent years, Canadian rowing teams have performed well in international competitions. As with any sport, many hours of training and practice are required for success. To win a race, the members of a rowing team, or crew, work to increase their rowing speed.

Since river conditions vary from place to place, the rowing speed in still water is the speed for comparison and improvement. In this investigation, you will calculate the rowing speed in still water given the following information.

- During a training session, a crew takes 40 min to row 5 km upstream and then return.
- The river flows at a speed of 4 km/h.

Think, Do, Discuss

1. How does the flow of the river affect the boat when it is being rowed upstream? downstream?
2. Suppose the crew's rowing speed in still water is x km/h. Write an expression for the upstream rowing speed.
3. If you know the distance and the speed, then how can you calculate time? Write an expression for the time the crew takes to row upstream.
4. Now write an expression for the downstream rowing speed. Then write an expression for the time taken by the crew to row downstream.
5. How long did the round trip take? Write an equation that connects your answers to steps 3 and 4. Make sure that the values in the equation use the same units. To determine the rowing speed on still water, you will need to solve this equation.

Part 2: Adding and Subtracting Rational Expressions

Adding and subtracting rational expressions is similar to adding and subtracting rational numbers.

Think, Do, Discuss

1. Make two columns on a piece of paper. At the top of the left column, write "Rational Numbers" and, at the top of the right column, write "Rational Expressions." In the left column, add $\frac{2}{7} + \frac{3}{7}$. In the right column, use the same method to add $\frac{2}{x} + \frac{3}{x}$. Try to match the steps as you work. What is the same about the two sums? What must you state about x in the right column?

2. In the left column, add $\frac{3}{8} + \frac{1}{8}$. Reduce the answer to lowest terms. In the right column, use the same method to add $\frac{a}{2b} + \frac{3a}{2b}$. Reduce this answer to lowest terms. Remember to state any restriction(s).

3. In the left column, subtract $\frac{5}{6} - \frac{4}{3}$. Remember to use the lowest common denominator (LCD). In the right column, try to subtract $\frac{7}{4y} - \frac{5}{2y}$, using the same steps. What is the LCD in this case? What is the restriction?

4. Subtract $\frac{3}{4} - \frac{2}{3}$ in the left column. Show the steps for changing each fraction so that the denominators are common. Follow the same steps to subtract $\frac{3}{x} - \frac{2}{y}$. The result will not look simpler, but this form may be useful for some purposes.

5. To find the LCD for the sum $\frac{4}{15} + \frac{7}{10}$, factor each of the denominators. Express 15 and 10 as products of prime factors. Write the LCD as a product of prime factors. Find the sum in the left column. Use the same steps to add $\frac{4}{st} + \frac{7}{rt}$ in the right column.

You have now practised all the methods for adding and subtracting rational expressions. Even if a rational expression may have a binomial or a trinomial in the numerator or denominator, apply the same steps: factor, find the LCD, and reduce to lowest terms.

6. Simplify $\frac{a}{ab + b^2} - \frac{b}{a^2 + ab}$. Use the method in step 5. Begin by factoring the denominators. What is the LCD? By what factor do you multiply $\frac{a}{b(a + b)}$ so that it will have the common denominator? Do the same for $\frac{b}{a(a + b)}$. Now that the expressions have the same denominators, find the difference. Notice that the resulting numerator can be factored. Factor the numerator and simplify the expression. Did you remember to state the restrictions?

7. In Part 1, you should have obtained the equation $\frac{5}{x-4} + \frac{5}{x+4} = \frac{2}{3}$. To add the two rational expressions on the left side of this equation, follow the method in step 4. Treat each binomial as a single variable. What is the common denominator? By what factor do you multiply $\frac{5}{x-4}$ so that the denominator will be the common denominator? Do the same for $\frac{5}{x+4}$. Add the numerators and simplify.

8. You should now have the equation $\frac{10x}{x^2-16} = \frac{2}{3}$. Multiply both sides by $(x^2 - 16)$. Then multiply both sides by 3. Rearrange and solve the resulting quadratic equation. What was the crew's rowing speed in still water?

Focus 4.11

Key Ideas

- When rational expressions are added or subtracted, they must have a common denominator.
- If the denominators are the same, then simply add or subtract the numerators.

$$\frac{f(x)}{g(x)} + \frac{h(x)}{g(x)} = \frac{f(x)+h(x)}{g(x)} \qquad \frac{f(x)}{g(x)} - \frac{h(x)}{g(x)} = \frac{f(x)-h(x)}{g(x)}$$

- To find a common denominator, factor the denominators. Then create the LCD from the factors.
- The LCD is not always the product of the two denominators.
- Once you have added or subtracted, it may be possible to factor the numerator and simplify the expression further.
- Always reduce the sum or difference to lowest terms.
- State the restrictions on the variables.

Example 1

Simplify.

(a) $\frac{2}{ab^2} + \frac{4}{a^2b}$ (b) $4 - \frac{3}{xy} + \frac{x}{y^2}$ (c) $\frac{3}{x^2-4} - \frac{5}{x+2}$ (d) $\frac{1}{x^2-6x+9} - \frac{1}{x^3-9x}$

Solution

(a) $\frac{2}{ab^2} + \frac{4}{a^2b}$

$= \frac{2}{ab^2} \times \frac{a}{a} + \frac{4}{a^2b} \times \frac{b}{b}$

The LCD is a^2b^2.

$= \frac{2a}{a^2b^2} + \frac{4b}{a^2b^2}$

$= \frac{2a+4b}{a^2b^2}$

$= \frac{2(a+2b)}{a^2b^2}, a \neq 0, b \neq 0$

(b) $4 - \frac{3}{xy} + \frac{x}{y^2}$

$= 4 \times \frac{xy^2}{xy^2} - \frac{3}{xy} \times \frac{y}{y} + \frac{x}{y^2} \times \frac{x}{x}$

The LCD is xy^2.

$= \frac{4xy^2}{xy^2} - \frac{3y}{xy^2} + \frac{x^2}{xy^2}$

$= \frac{4xy^2 - 3y + x^2}{xy^2}, x \neq 0, y \neq 0$

(c) $\frac{3}{x^2 - 4} - \frac{5}{x + 2}$

$= \frac{3}{(x - 2)(x + 2)} - \frac{5}{x + 2}$

The LCD is $(x - 2)(x + 2)$.

$= \frac{3}{(x - 2)(x + 2)} - \frac{5}{(x + 2)} \times \frac{(x - 2)}{(x - 2)}$

$= \frac{3}{(x - 2)(x + 2)} - \frac{5(x - 2)}{(x + 2)(x - 2)}$

$= \frac{3 - 5(x - 2)}{(x - 2)(x + 2)}$

$= \frac{3 - 5x + 10}{(x - 2)(x + 2)}$

$= \frac{13 - 5x}{(x - 2)(x + 2)}$

$= \frac{13 - 5x}{x^2 - 4}, x \neq \pm 2$

(d) $\frac{1}{x^2 - 6x + 9} - \frac{1}{x^3 - 9x}$

$= \frac{1}{(x - 3)^2} - \frac{1}{x(x^2 - 9)}$

$= \frac{1}{(x - 3)^2} - \frac{1}{x(x - 3)(x + 3)}$

The LCD is $x(x - 3)^2(x + 3)$.

$= \frac{1}{(x - 3)^2} \times \frac{x(x + 3)}{x(x + 3)} - \frac{1}{x(x - 3)(x + 3)} \times \frac{(x - 3)}{(x - 3)}$

$= \frac{x(x + 3)}{x(x - 3)^2(x + 3)} - \frac{(x - 3)}{x(x - 3)^2(x + 3)}$

$= \frac{x^2 + 3x - x + 3}{x(x - 3)^2(x + 3)}$

$= \frac{x^2 + 2x + 3}{x(x - 3)^2(x + 3)}, x \neq 0, \pm 3$

Example 2

Simplify.

(a) $\frac{x + 3}{x - 4} - \frac{x - 1}{x + 2}$

(b) $\frac{x + 1}{x^2 + 2x - 3} - \frac{x + 2}{x^2 + 4x - 5}$

Solution

(a) $\frac{x + 3}{x - 4} - \frac{x - 1}{x + 2}$

$= \frac{x + 3}{x - 4} \times \frac{x + 2}{x + 2} - \frac{x - 1}{x + 2} \times \frac{x - 4}{x - 4}$

$= \frac{(x^2 + 5x + 6)}{(x - 4)(x + 2)} - \frac{(x^2 - 5x + 4)}{(x - 4)(x + 2)}$ The LCD is $(x - 4)(x + 2)$.

$= \frac{x^2 + 5x + 6 - x^2 + 5x - 4}{(x - 4)(x + 2)}$

$= \frac{10x + 2}{(x - 4)(x + 2)}$

$= \frac{2(5x + 1)}{(x - 4)(x + 2)}, x \neq -2, 4$

(b) $\frac{x + 1}{x^2 + 2x - 3} - \frac{x + 2}{x^2 + 4x - 5}$

$= \frac{x + 1}{(x + 3)(x - 1)} - \frac{x + 2}{(x + 5)(x - 1)}$

$= \frac{x + 1}{(x + 3)(x - 1)} \times \frac{x + 5}{x + 5} - \frac{x + 2}{(x + 5)(x - 1)} \times \frac{x + 3}{x + 3}$ The LCD is $(x + 3)(x - 1)(x + 5)$.

$= \frac{x^2 + 6x + 5}{(x + 3)(x - 1)(x + 5)} - \frac{x^2 + 5x + 6}{(x + 5)(x - 1)(x + 3)}$

$= \frac{x^2 + 6x + 5 - x^2 - 5x - 6}{(x + 3)(x - 1)(x + 5)}$

$= \frac{x - 1}{(x + 3)(x - 1)(x + 5)}$

$= \frac{1}{(x + 3)(x + 5)}, x \neq -5, -3, 1$

Example 3

Ero and Jamal set off at the same time on a 30-km walk for charity. Ero, who has trained all year for this event, walks 1.4 km/h faster than Jamal, but sees a friend on the route and stops to talk for 20 min. Even with this delay, Ero finishes the walk 2 h ahead of Jamal. How fast was each person walking, and how long did it take for each person to finish the walk?

Solution

Since speed and time are related, choose one variable to represent either speed or time. Let x km/h represent Jamal's walking speed. Then express the other **unknown** quantities in terms of x. Organize the information in a table.

$$\text{Speed} = \frac{\text{Distance}}{\text{Time}} \quad \text{so} \quad \text{Time} = \frac{\text{Distance}}{\text{Speed}}.$$

	Distance (km)	Speed (km/h)	Time (h)
Ero	30	$x + 1.4$	$\frac{30}{x + 1.4}$
Jamal	30	x	$\frac{30}{x}$

Ero took 2 h 20 min less time than Jamal to walk 30 km. The difference between the times in the Time column must be $2\frac{1}{3}$ h. Write this statement as an equation.

$$\frac{30}{x} - \frac{30}{x + 1.4} = \frac{7}{3}$$

Note that the restrictions of $x \neq 0, -1.4$ do not apply here, since $x > 0$.

$$\frac{30}{x} \times \frac{x + 1.4}{x + 1.4} - \frac{30}{x + 1.4} \times \frac{x}{x} = \frac{7}{3}$$

$$\frac{30(x + 1.4) - 30x}{x(x + 1.4)} = \frac{7}{3}$$

$$\frac{30x + 42 - 30x}{x(x + 1.4)} = \frac{7}{3}$$

$$\frac{42}{x(x + 1.4)} = \frac{7}{3}$$

$$x(x + 1.4) \times \frac{42}{x(x + 1.4)} = \frac{7}{3} \times x(x + 1.4)$$

$$42 = \frac{7}{3}x(x + 1.4)$$

$$3 \times 42 = \frac{7}{3}x(x + 1.4) \times 3$$

$$126 = 7x(x + 1.4) \qquad \text{Divide by 7.}$$

$$18 = x(x + 1.4)$$

$$18 = x^2 + 1.4x$$

$$0 = x^2 + 1.4x - 18$$

$$x = \frac{-1.4 \pm \sqrt{1.4^2 - 4(1)(-18)}}{2(1)}$$ Use the quadratic formula.

$$x = \frac{-1.4 \pm 8.6}{2}$$ Ignore the negative root, since $x > 0$.

$$x = 3.6$$

Jamal walked at 3.6 km/h and Ero walked at $3.6 + 1.4 = 5$ km/h.

Jamal's total walking time was $\frac{30}{3.6} = 8.\overline{3}$ or 8 h 20 min. Ero's total walking time was $\frac{30}{5} = 6$ h, but he took 6 h 20 min to complete the route because he stopped for 20 min during the walk.

Practise, Apply, Solve 4.11

A

1. State the LCD for each pair of expressions.

(a) $\frac{3}{x}, \frac{5}{y}$ (b) $\frac{-2}{ab}, \frac{1}{b}$ (c) $\frac{4}{x-1}, \frac{2}{x}$

(d) $\frac{b}{b+2}, \frac{3b}{b+1}$ (e) $\frac{5}{x^2}, \frac{7}{xy}$ (f) $\frac{m-1}{2m+3}, \frac{m}{m-3}$

(g) $\frac{11x}{yz^2}, \frac{8x}{y^2z}$ (h) $\frac{3s}{(s-1)(s+1)}, \frac{s+2}{s-1}$ (i) $\frac{4}{x^2-4}, \frac{3}{x+2}$

2. Find each sum.

(a) $\frac{2}{a} + \frac{7}{b}$ (b) $\frac{3}{x} + \frac{2}{x^2}$ (c) $\frac{4}{xy} + \frac{5}{yz}$

(d) $\frac{7}{x^2y} + \frac{4}{xy^2}$ (e) $\frac{6x}{y} + \frac{3}{y^2}$ (f) $\frac{2x}{x+1} + \frac{5}{x}$

(g) $\frac{3}{5y} + \frac{2}{y+2}$ (h) $\frac{2}{x+3} + \frac{3}{x+1}$ (i) $\frac{x}{x-1} + \frac{2x}{x+3}$

3. Find each difference.

(a) $\frac{3}{4x} - \frac{1}{3x}$ (b) $\frac{3}{y^2} - \frac{2}{y}$ (c) $\frac{2}{3x} - \frac{4}{x}$

(d) $\frac{10}{x^2y} - \frac{6}{xy^2}$ (e) $\frac{9}{4ab^2} - \frac{5}{6a^2b}$ (f) $\frac{6}{y+1} - \frac{3}{y-1}$

(g) $\frac{3x}{x+5} - \frac{2x}{x-3}$ (h) $\frac{t+3}{t-1} - \frac{2t}{t+1}$ (i) $\frac{4}{x(x+2)} - \frac{3}{x}$

4. Simplify.

(a) $\frac{-2}{x} + \frac{5}{x^2} - \frac{8}{3x}$ (b) $\frac{6}{pq} - \frac{4}{q} - \frac{8}{p^2q}$

(c) $\frac{2x}{yz} - \frac{3x}{y} - \frac{9x}{y^2z}$ (d) $\frac{2a}{(a+1)(a+3)} + \frac{5}{(a+3)}$

(e) $\frac{1}{(x+2)^2} - \frac{3}{(x+2)}$ (f) $\frac{1}{2(x+4)} - \frac{3x}{(x+4)^2} + \frac{1}{2}$

5. Simplify.

(a) $\frac{x}{3x - 6} + \frac{3}{2x - 4}$ (b) $\frac{3x - 1}{x^2 + 3x} + \frac{2}{5x}$ (c) $\frac{6}{y} + \frac{3}{y^2 - 2y}$

(d) $\frac{4p}{p^2 + 3p} - \frac{2}{p + 3}$ (e) $\frac{2x + 1}{x^2 - x - 2} + \frac{3}{x - 2}$ (f) $\frac{4a}{a^2 - 9} - \frac{2}{a + 3}$

(g) $\frac{1}{y + 4} - \frac{y - 3}{y^2 + 3y - 4}$ (h) $\frac{3m + 1}{2m - 3} + \frac{m}{m^2 - 9}$

B

6. Simplify and state each result in lowest terms.

(a) $\frac{x}{x^2 - 1} - \frac{1}{x^2 - 1}$ (b) $\frac{x - 3}{x^2 - 7x + 10} - \frac{x + 2}{x^2 - 25}$

(c) $\frac{3a}{6a^2 - a - 2} + \frac{2a}{10a^2 - a - 3}$ (d) $\frac{1}{h}\left(\frac{1}{3x + h} - \frac{1}{3x}\right)$

(e) $\frac{k + 1}{2k^2 - 7k + 6} - \frac{k - 3}{2k^2 - k - 3}$ (f) $\frac{1}{a - 3} + \frac{1}{a^2 - 9} - \frac{1}{a^2 - 2a - 3}$

7. **Communication:** Explain why it is better to find the LCD instead of multiplying the denominators when adding or subtracting rational expressions. Use an example to illustrate your points.

8. **Knowledge and Understanding:** Simplify.

(a) $\frac{5x - 7y}{12x} + \frac{2x - 9y}{8y}$ (b) $\frac{1}{2x + 8} - \frac{3x}{(x + 4)^2} + \frac{1}{2}$

9. Simplify.

(a) $\frac{x - 2}{x^2 - 7x + 10} + \frac{x + 2}{x^2 - 4x - 5}$

(b) $\frac{x - 3}{x^2 + x - 12} - \frac{x - 2}{x^2 + 3x - 4}$

(c) $\frac{3k}{6k^2 + 13k - 5} + \frac{2k + 1}{6k^2 + 7k - 3}$

(d) $\frac{4 - 5q}{24q^2 + 2q - 12} - \frac{5 - 4q}{12q^2 - 15q - 18}$

(e) $\left(\frac{3x - 2}{2x^2 - 5x - 3} - \frac{x + 2}{x^2 - 9}\right) \div \frac{2x - 3}{2x^2 + 7x + 3}$

(f) $\frac{a - 2}{6a^2 - 7a - 5} \div \frac{2a}{3a^2 - 5a} - \frac{3a + 2}{2a^2 + 11a + 5}$

10. Find the zeros of each function. (**Hint:** Rewrite $f(x)$ by putting all terms over a common denominator.)

(a) $f(x) = 3x - 1 + \frac{1}{x + 1}$ (b) $f(x) = 6x - 17 + \frac{28}{x + 2}$

11. Solve for x.

(a) $\frac{x - 2}{x} + \frac{4}{5x} = -\frac{1}{5}$ (b) $\frac{2x + 3}{x - 1} - \frac{3}{x} = 2$

(c) $\frac{1}{x} = \frac{2}{x + 1} + \frac{1}{1 - x}$ (d) $\frac{3x}{x^2 - 1} = \frac{x}{x + 1} - 4$

(e) $\frac{15}{x^2 - 1} = \frac{4}{x - 1} - \frac{3}{x + 1}$ (f) $\frac{x}{x - 2} + 2 = \frac{5x}{x + 2} + \frac{3x + 1}{x^2 - 4}$

12. On the 42-km go-cart course at Sportsworld, Arshia drives 0.4 km/h faster than Sarah, but she has engine trouble part way around the course and has to stop to get the go-cart fixed. This stop costs Arshia one-half hour, and so she arrives 15 min after Sarah at the end of the course. How fast did each girl drive and how long did each girl take to finish the course? Answer to one decimal place.

13. Rowing at 8 km/h, in still water, Rima and Bhanu take 16 h to row 39 km down a river and 39 km back. Find the speed of the current to two decimal places.

14. A river flows at 2 km/h, and John takes 6 h to row 16 km up the river and 16 km back. How fast did he row?

15. **Application:** Jaime bought a case of concert T-shirts for \$450. She kept two for herself and sold the rest for \$560, making a profit of \$10 on each shirt. How many shirts were in the case?

16. Stuart agrees to a house-painting job for \$900. He takes 4 days longer than expected, and he has earned \$18.75 less per day than expected. In how many days did he expect to complete the house?

17. A grade 11 class, on a field trip to Montreal, had lunch in a restaurant. The bill came to \$239.25. Four students had birthdays that day, and it was agreed that these four should not have to pay for lunch. The other students had to pay \$1 more than if all the students had paid. How many students had lunch?

18. **Check Your Understanding:** Explain the steps for adding or subtracting rational expressions. Use $\frac{x-2}{x^2-4x-32} - \frac{x-1}{x^2-2x-48}$ as an example and explain each step fully.

C

19. **Thinking, Inquiry, Problem Solving:** Find A and B such that $\frac{2x-1}{(x+1)(3x+2)} = \frac{A}{x+1} + \frac{B}{3x+2}$.

20. Find A, B, and C such that $\frac{(x-1)}{(x+1)(x-2)^2} = \frac{A}{x+1} + \frac{B}{x-2} + \frac{C}{(x-2)^2}$.

21. It takes Paulina x hours to travel a kilometres. If she increases her speed by b kilometres per hour, the journey will take her c hours less time. Find x.

The Chapter Problem—Fundraising

Apply what you have learned in this section to answer these questions about the Chapter Problem on page 300.

CP18. Write a proposal, for this fundraiser, that the representative could present to the school council. Include all of your graphs and analyses.

SKILL BUILDER 4.12

Extending Algebra Skills: Working with Polynomials

A polynomial is an algebraic expression in the form $a_0 + a_1x + a_2x^2 + a_3x^3 + \ldots + a_nx^n$, where $a_0, a_1, a_2, a_3, \ldots, a_n$ are real numbers and the exponents are non-negative integers. A polynomial with exactly one term is called a **monomial**, a polynomial with two terms is a **binomial**, and a polynomial with three terms is a **trinomial**.

It is often necessary to combine two or more polynomials. For example, a profit function is obtained by subtracting a cost function from a revenue function. The revenue function, itself, is a product of the demand function and a number of items.

Some special products, which occur frequently when combining polynomials, are as follows:

- $(a + b)(a - b) = a^2 - b^2$
- $(a + b)^2 = a^2 + 2ab + b^2$
- $(a - b)^2 = a^2 - 2ab + b^2$

You will also frequently use these exponent laws.

- $a^m \times a^n = a^{m+n}$
- $(a^m)^n = a^{m \times n}$
- $(xy)^m = x^my^m$

Adding and Subtracting Polynomials and Multiplying a Polynomial by a Monomial

To add or subtract polynomials, combine like terms. Apply the distributive property of multiplication over addition when multiplying a polynomial by a monomial.

Example 1

Simplify.

(a) $(-3x^2 - x + 1) + (-x^2 + 2x - 1)$
(b) $(x^4 - 2x^3 - 3) - (2x^4 + x^2 + 2x - 1)$
(c) $5 - 2[3x^2 + x(1 - x)]$
(d) $3x(x^2 + 4x - 2) - 3(x^2 - 5x)$

Solution

(a) $(-3x^2 - x + 1) + (-x^2 + 2x - 1)$ — Remove brackets.
$= -3x^2 - x + 1 - x^2 + 2x - 1$ — Combine like terms.
$= -4x^2 + x$

(b) $(x^4 - 2x^3 - 3) - (2x^4 + x^2 + 2x - 1)$ — Remove brackets.
$= x^4 - 2x^3 - 3 - 2x^4 - x^2 - 2x + 1$ — Combine like terms.
$= -x^4 - 2x^3 - x^2 - 2x - 2$

(c) $5 - 2[3x^2 + x(1 - x)]$ Expand $x(1 - x)$ using the distributive property.
$= 5 - 2(3x^2 + x - x^2)$ Collect like terms inside the brackets.
$= 5 - 2(2x^2 + x)$ Expand.
$= 5 - 4x^2 - 2x$ Arrange terms in ascending, or descending, powers of x.
$= 5 - 2x - 4x^2$

(d) $3x(x^2 + 4x - 2) - 3(x^2 - 5x)$ Expand.
$= 3x^3 + 12x^2 - 6x - 3x^2 + 15x$ Combine like terms.
$= 3x^3 + 9x^2 + 9x$

Multiplying Polynomials

The process of multiplying is called **expanding**. When multiplying polynomials, multiply each term of one polynomial by each term of the other polynomial.

Example 2

Simplify.

(a) $(2 - 5y)(3 - 2y + y^2)$
(b) $(3 - 4z - 5z^2)(2 - 3z + z^2)$
(c) $4(a - 5)(a + 4) - (a + 3)(a + 1)$
(d) $2(x - 3)(x + 3) - 4(x - 1)^2$

Solution

(a) Apply the distributive property.

$(2 - 5y)(3 - 2y + y^2)$
$= 6 - 4y + 2y^2 - 15y + 10y^2 - 5y^3$ Combine like terms.
$= 6 - 19y + 12y^2 - 5y^3$

(b) $(3 - 4z - 5z^2)(2 - 3z + z^2)$
$= 6 - 9z + 3z^2 - 8z + 12z^2 - 4z^3 - 10z^2 + 15z^3 - 5z^4$
$= 6 - 17z + 5z^2 + 11z^3 - 5z^4$

(c) $4(a - 5)(a + 4) - (a + 3)(a + 1)$ Apply the distributive property.
$= 4(a^2 - a - 20) - (a^2 + 4a + 3)$ Expand.
$= 4a^2 - 4a - 80 - a^2 - 4a - 3$ Combine like terms.
$= 3a^2 - 8a - 83$

(d) $2(x - 3)(x + 3) - 4(x - 1)^2$ Apply the distributive property.
$= 2(x^2 - 9) - 4(x^2 - 2x + 1)$ Expand.
$= 2x^2 - 18 - 4x^2 + 8x - 4$ Combine like terms.
$= -2x^2 - 8x - 22$

Focus 4.12

Key Ideas

- In a polynomial expression, the numerical coefficients are real numbers and the exponents are non-negative integers.
- Some polynomials have special names.
  - A **monomial** is a polynomial with one term.
  - A **binomial** is a polynomial with two terms.
  - A **trinomial** is a polynomial with three terms.
- The degree of a polynomial in one variable is the value of the highest exponent of the variable in the polynomial.
  - A polynomial in one variable of degree 0 is called a **constant**, for example, 5 and -3.2.
  - A polynomial in one variable of degree 1 is called **linear**, for example, $2x - 1$ and $4 - 7.2x$.
  - A polynomial in one variable of degree 2 is called **quadratic**, for example, $3x^2 + 2x + 1$ and $2 - 9x^2$.
  - A polynomial in one variable of degree 3 is called **cubic**, for example, $2x^3 - 5$ and $5 - 4x + 3x^2 - 2x^3$.
- To add or subtract polynomials, combine like terms.
- Apply the distributive property when multiplying polynomials.
  - To multiply a polynomial by a monomial, multiply each term in the polynomial by the monomial.
  - To multiply two polynomials, multiply each term of one polynomial by each term of the other polynomial.

Practise, Apply, Solve 4.12

A

1. Simplify.

(a) $(x^2 - 2x - 1) + (3x^2 + x + 2)$

(b) $(x^2 - x + 5) + (-x^2 + x - 3)$

(c) $(-3x^2 - 2x + 2) + (2x^2 - x - 5)$

(d) $(x^3 - 4x^2 + 1) - (x^2 - 2x + 4)$

(e) $(2x^4 - 2x^2 - 7) - (3x^4 - x^3 + x^2 - 4)$

(f) $(x^5 + x^4 + x^3 - 4x^2 - x + 5) - (-x^4 - x^3 + 2x + 4)$

(g) $(-2x^2 + 5x - 3) + (x^2 - 6x + 1) - (-3x^2 - 2x - 4)$

2. Simplify.

(a) $3x(x - 2) - 4x(x + 1)$

(b) $-x(2x - 5) - 3x(4 - x)$

(c) $2x^2(x + 3) + 4x^2(x - 1)$

(d) $-2x(x^2 - 5x - 2) - x(2x^2 - x - 4)$

(e) $-4x(x^3 - 3x^2 + 1) + x(3x^2 - 2x - 4)$

(f) $2x^2(3x^3 - 5x + 2) - x^3(2x^3 + 2x - 5)$

3. State the degree of each simplified polynomial in question 2.

4. Simplify.

(a) $4[2x - (3 - 5x)] + 3[3x - (4 + x)]$

(b) $5[x - (2x + 3)] - 2[4x - (x + 1)]$

(c) $x[5x - (3x - 8)] + 2x[3x - (4 - x)]$

(d) $-3x[x - (5 - 2x)] - x[-2x - (x - 6)]$

(e) $2a[a - 2a(a - 2)] + 3a[a + 4a(1 - a)]$

(f) $-a[5a - a(1 - 2a)] - 3a[a - 4a(a + 1)]$

5. Simplify.

(a) $(x + 2)(x^2 - x - 2)$

(b) $(1 - x)(x^3 - x^2 + 3x)$

(c) $(x^2 + 1)(x^2 - 3x + 5)$

(d) $(2 - x^2)(3 + x^2 - x^3)$

(e) $(x^2 - 3)(x^3 - 3x^2 + 2x - 1)$

(f) $(1 - x^3)(2 + 3x - 6x^2 + 2x^3 - x^4)$

B

6. Simplify.

(a) $(x + 3)(x - 1) - (x - 5)(x - 2)$

(b) $2(x + 1)(x - 4) - 4(x - 2)(x + 2)$

(c) $3(2 - x)(x - 4) + (x - 1)^2$

(d) $2(3x - 2)^2 - 4(x - 1)(2x + 5)$

(e) $(2x^2 - 1)^2 - (4 - x^2)^2$

(f) $2x(5x^2 - 2)^2 - 3x(2 - x^2)^2$

7. Simplify.

(a) $(x - 1)(x + 3)(x + 1) + (2x - 1)(x - 2)$

(b) $(x - 3)(x + 2)(x + 3) - (3 - x)^2$

(c) $(2a + 7)^2(a - 2) + 2(a^2 - 1)(4a + 3)$

(d) $(t - 1)(2t - 1)(3t + 4) - (1 - t)^2(t + 4)$

(e) $3(x - 2)(x + 3)^2 - (3x - 1)(2x + 1)^2$

(f) $(x - 1)^2(x + 3)^2 - (x + 1)^2(x - 2)^2$

8. Simplify.

(a) $(x^2 - 3x + 5) - (2x^2 - 5x - 7)$

(b) $x(2x - 3)^2 - 2x(x - 4)$

(c) $(1 - x + x^2 - x^3 - x^4)(1 + x)$

9. Jake wrote the following.

$$(x + 1)^2 - (x + 2)(x - 3) = x^2 + 2x + 1 - x^2 - x - 6$$
$$= x - 5$$

What mistake(s) did he make? Write a correct simplification, and explain how to avoid making Jake's error.

10. Expand each expression.

(a) $(2a - 3)(a^3 - 2a^2 + a - 1)$

(b) $(y^2 + 3y - 5)(2y^2 - y + 6)$

(c) $(x^2 - x + 1)^2$

(d) $(x - 1)^2(x + 3)^2$

11. **Check Your Understanding:** Create an expression that contains the difference of a product of two binomials and a product of a monomial and a trinomial. Simplify your expression and state the degree of the resulting polynomial.

C

12. Simplify.

(a) $(a^2 + 2a - 1)^2 + (a^2 - 2a + 1)^2$

(b) $(a^2 - ab + b^2)^2 - (a^2 - 2ab + b^2)^2$

13. For any five consecutive integers, prove that

(a) the square of the middle integer is always 4 more than the product of the first and fifth integers

(b) the product of the second and fourth integers is always 3 more than the product of the first and fifth integers

14. If $x + y + z = 1$ and $x^2 + y^2 + z^2 = 3$, then find the value of $xy + xz + yz$.

15. If $5x^4 - 14x^3 + 18x^2 + 40x + 16 = (x^2 - 4x + 8)(ax^2 + bx + c)$, then find a, b, and c and all solutions of the equation
$5x^4 + 18x^2 + 16 = 14x^3 - 40x$.

16. For $x^3 - 1 = (x - 1)(ax^2 + bx + c)$, find the values of a, b and c. Find the three roots of the equation $x^3 = 1$.

Chapter 4 Review

Quadratic Functions and Rational Expressions

Check Your Understanding

1. Describe three different forms for the equation of a quadratic function. Explain the importance and uses of each form. Describe the algebraic methods for moving from one form to another.
2. What shape is the graph of a quadratic function? What information do the coordinates of the vertex of the graph provide? How can you determine the vertex coordinates when the equation is in standard form? in factored form?
3. How are the zeros of a function related to the graph of the function? How many zeros does a quadratic function have? Describe how you would determine the number of zeros from the equation of a quadratic function in (a) factored form, (b) vertex form, and (c) standard form.
4. Describe the sets of numbers that make up the set of real numbers. What are complex numbers and how are they related to real numbers? What are complex conjugates and how are they connected to quadratic equations?
5. How do you add or subtract complex numbers? How do you multiply complex numbers? What happens when you add complex conjugates? What happens when you multiply complex conjugates? How do you divide complex numbers? Give an example for each.
6. What is inverse variation? Give an example of two quantities that vary inversely and write an equation that describes the relationship between them. State the domain and the range and sketch the graph of this relation.
7. How can you use the graph of a function to obtain the graph of its reciprocal function? Explain the steps using an example.
8. What is a rational function? How are the graphs of reciprocal and rational functions different from the graphs of the other functions you have studied? Describe their features with examples.
9. Explain how you would simplify a rational expression. Include a discussion of restrictions. Why must you state the restrictions before reducing an expression?
10. When you add or subtract rational expressions, what steps do you take to find the lowest common denominator? Explain with an example.
11. Write an example of a polynomial expression, state its degree, and explain how you determined the degree. What special names are given to polynomials with one, two, or three terms? Is your polynomial one of these special types? Explain.

Review and Practice

4.1 Skill Builder: Extending Algebra Skills: Completing the Square

1. What is the vertex form of a quadratic function? How does this form relate to completing the square? What other equivalent forms may a quadratic function have? Give an example of each form.

2. Describe the steps for changing a quadratic function in standard form to vertex form by completing the square.

3. Express each function in vertex form by completing the square.

(a) $f(x) = x^2 - 6x + 7$

(b) $f(x) = x^2 - 5x + 1$

(c) $f(x) = 2x^2 + 7x - 3$

(d) $f(x) = -4x^2 - 3x + 2$

(e) $f(x) = -1.6x^2 - 2.4x - 1$

(f) $f(x) = \frac{2}{3}x^2 - \frac{4}{9}x + 2$

4. For each quadratic function, find the coordinates of the vertex by completing the square, state the domain and the range of $f(x)$, and sketch the graph.

(a) $f(x) = x^2 + 8x + 13$

(b) $f(x) = -2x^2 + 5x$

(c) $f(x) = \frac{1}{2}x^2 - 5x + 15$

5. The height, h, in metres, of a baseball after Bill hits it with a bat is described by the function $h(t) = 0.8 + 29.4t - 4.9t^2$, where t is the time in seconds after the ball is struck. What is the maximum height of the ball? At what time does the ball reach this maximum height? How high above the ground was the ball when it was hit?

4.2 Maximum and Minimum Values of Quadratic Functions

6. What features of the graph of a quadratic function are most easily determined from the function in

(a) in standard form?

(b) in factored form?

(c) in vertex form?

Give an example for each form.

7. How are the graphs of $f(x) = ax^2 + bx$ and $g(x) = ax^2 + bx + c$ related? How does this help you find the maximum or minimum value for each function?

8. How can you tell from the equation of a quadratic function whether the function has a maximum or minimum value? For each of the following functions, and without changing the form of the equation,

i. state whether the function has a maximum or a minimum value

ii. find the value of x that produces the maximum or minimum value

iii. find the maximum or minimum value of the function

(a) $f(x) = -2(x - 1)^2 + 6$

(b) $f(x) = (x - 3)(x + 7)$

(c) $h(t) = -5t^2 + 20t$

(d) $g(x) = -0.1(3.2 - x)(2.1 + x)$

(e) $f(x) = 3.2(x - 1.1)^2 - 4.5$

(f) $C(x) = 0.04x^2 + 18x + 198$

9. The demand function for a new product is $p(x) = -5x + 22$, where x is the number of items sold in thousands and p is the price in dollars. The cost function is $C(x) = 3x + 15$.

(a) State the corresponding revenue function.

(b) Find the corresponding profit function.

(c) Complete the square to find the value of x that will maximize profits.

(d) Find the break-even quantities.

(e) Sketch the graph of the profit function.

10. It costs a bus company \$225 to run a minibus on a ski trip, plus \$30 per passenger. The bus has seating for 22 passengers, and the company charges \$60 per fare if the bus is full. For each empty seat, the company has to increase the ticket price by \$5. How many empty seats should the bus run with to maximize profit from this trip?

4.3 Zeros of Quadratic Functions

11. Sketch the graph of a quadratic function that has no zeros. Explain how you know that the function you have sketched has no zeros. Repeat for a quadratic function that has (a) one zero, and (b) two zeros.

12. What is the discriminant and how may you use it to find the number of zeros for the function $f(x) = ax^2 + bx + c$? Give an example of a function in standard form with (a) no zeros, (b) one zero, and (c) two zeros.

13. For a quadratic function in the form $y = a(x - h)^2 + k$, how may you use the values of a and k to find the number of zeros? Give an example of a function written in vertex form with (a) no zeros, (b) one zero, and (c) two zeros.

14. Without drawing the graph,

i. find the number of zeros for each function

ii. indicate whether the graph touches the x-axis at one point, intersects the x-axis at two points, or does not meet the x-axis

(a) $f(x) = 3x^2 + 4x + 1$
(b) $g(x) = -2(x + 3.6)^2 + 4.1$
(c) $h(x) = -5(x + 1.3)^2$
(d) $m(x) = 4(x + 1)^2 + 0.5$
(e) $n(x) = -x^2 - 6x - 9$
(f) $p(x) = -3.2(x + 1.1)(x - 2.4)$

15. Find the value(s) of k so that the graph of each function has

i. two x-intercepts
ii. one x-intercept
iii. no x-intercepts

(a) $f(x) = kx^2 - 8x + 2$
(b) $f(x) = 2x^2 + kx + 50$
(c) $f(x) = 9x^2 + kx + 4$
(d) $f(x) = x^2 + (k + 1)x + 1$

4.4 Introducing Complex Numbers

16. Draw a diagram to show how the sets of numbers used in mathematics relate to each other and are connected to the set of real numbers and to the set of complex numbers.

17. How are complex numbers different from real numbers? What form do complex numbers take and when do you use them?

18. Under what circumstances will a quadratic equation have complex roots? How are these roots connected?

19. Identify *all* sets of numbers to which each number belongs.

(a) 0.85
(b) -7
(c) $\sqrt{-3}$
(d) $\frac{5}{9}$
(e) $2 + 5i$
(f) $\sqrt{5}$
(g) $2.\overline{45}$
(h) $\frac{-3}{7}$
(i) 0
(j) $\sqrt{9}$

20. Write the complex conjugate of each complex number.

(a) $2 - i$
(b) $1 + 3i$
(c) $-4 - 5i$
(d) $-5 + 6i$
(e) $13 - 13i$
(f) $3 + \sqrt{3}i$

21. Solve each quadratic equation for x, where $x \in \mathrm{C}$. Round to two decimal places, where necessary.

(a) $x^2 + 81 = 0$
(b) $-2x^2 = 72$
(c) $x^2 - 2x + 3 = 0$
(d) $x^2 - 4x + 20 = 0$
(e) $2x^2 = 3x - 2$
(f) $3x(x + 4) = -14$

4.5U Skill Builder: Adding, Subtracting, and Multiplying Complex Numbers

22. Give an example to show how to add or subtract complex numbers. What happens when you add two complex conjugates?

23. Give another example to show how to multiply complex numbers. What happens when you multiply two complex conjugates?

24. Simplify each of the following.

(a) $(3i)^2$
(b) i^5
(c) $(2 - i)(5 + 2i)$
(d) $(-3 - 4i)(2 - 3i)$
(e) $(-1 + 7i)(-1 - 7i)$
(f) $-i(3 - 5i)$
(g) $(-1 + 4i)^2$
(h) $\frac{1}{(2 + i)(2 - i)}$
(i) $(7 - 2i)^2 - (2 - 3i)^2 + 2i$
(j) $(5 + 3i) + (8 - 2i) - (6 - 3i)$

25. Find $z + \bar{z}$, $z - \bar{z}$, and $z\bar{z}$ for each value of z.

(a) $z = 3 - i$
(b) $z = 3 + 4i$
(c) $z = -5 + 2i$

26. If $f(x) = -2x^2 - x + 2$, then find $f(3 - 2i)$.

27. In each case, one root of a quadratic equation is given. Find the other root and write a quadratic equation that has these roots. Express the answer in the form $ax^2 + bx + c = 0$.

(a) $3i$
(b) $1 - 2i$
(c) $-\frac{1}{2} - \frac{\sqrt{3}}{2}i$

4.6–4.7 Reciprocal Functions

28. Explain why the function $f(x) = \frac{1}{x}$ is said to display inverse variation. What special features does the graph of this function have? What is the name for this type of graph? Describe the domain and the range for $f(x) = \frac{1}{x}$.

29. What properties of the graph of $y = f(x)$ can help you graph $y = \frac{1}{f(x)}$?

30. (a) Which of the following tables display inverse variation? Explain your answer.

i.

x	y
2	30
3	20
5	12
8	7.5

ii.

x	y
12	240
9	320
5	576
2	1440

iii.

x	y
2	7
4	31
6	71
8	127

(b) Write an equation for each relation.

31. The time a car takes to accelerate to a certain speed from rest and the acceleration vary inversely. The car takes 5 s to reach a certain speed when the acceleration is 12 m/s^2. Find the time the car takes to reach the same speed when the acceleration is 15 m/s^2. Write an equation to model the relation between time and acceleration. Sketch the graph of the relation.

32. In each case, graph $y = f(x)$ and use it to graph $y = \frac{1}{f(x)}$ on the same axes.

(a) $f(x) = x^2 - 1$ (b) $f(x) = (x - 3)^2 - 4$ (c) $f(x) = (x + 1)^2$

(d) $f(x) = x^2 + 3$ (e) $f(x) = -(x + 2)^2 + 3$ (f) $f(x) = \sqrt{2 - x} - 4$

33. For each function, draw $f(x)$, $\frac{1}{f(x)}$, and $f^{-1}(x)$ on the same axes. Also, state the domain and the range.

(a) $f(x) = 2x - 1$ (b) $f(x) = x^2 - 3$ (c) $f(x) = \sqrt{x - 2} - 3$

4.8 Simplifying Rational Expressions

34. What is a rational expression? How does factoring help when simplifying a rational expression?

35. When is a rational expression not defined? How does this condition affect simplifying rational expressions?

36. Simplify and state any restrictions.

(a) $\frac{3x + 9}{-5x - 15}$ (b) $\frac{48p^3q^2}{-18pq^3}$ (c) $\frac{16x^2 - 9}{4x^2 + x - 3}$

(d) $\frac{a^2 - 2a - 8}{a^2 - a - 12}$ (e) $\frac{10x^2 - 11x - 6}{10x^2 + 19x + 6}$ (f) $\frac{x^2 - 6x + 9}{9 - x^2}$

(g) $\frac{2x^2 - 5xy + 2y^2}{y^2 - 3xy + 2x^2}$

37. (a) The concentration of pain-killing drug in the bloodstream t hours after it is taken orally is given by the expression $\frac{5t^5 + 10t^3}{t^6 + 4t^4 + 4t^2}$. Find the concentration, to one decimal place, after $\frac{1}{2}$ h, 1 h, and 2 h.

(b) The drug may be taken again once the concentration drops below 1. How long does it take for the concentration to drop to this level?

4.9 Multiplying and Dividing Rational Expressions

38. Explain the steps for multiplying rational expressions. Give reasons for each step. What other steps are needed for dividing rational expressions?

39. Why are there extra restrictions when dividing rational expressions?

40. Simplify and state any restrictions.

(a) $\frac{6x}{8y} \times \frac{2y^2}{3x}$ (b) $\frac{10m^2}{3n} \times \frac{6mn}{20m^2}$ (c) $\frac{2ab}{5bc} \div \frac{6ac}{10b}$ (d) $\frac{5p}{8pq} \div \frac{3p}{12q}$

41. Simplify and state any restrictions.

(a) $\frac{3}{x^2 - 9} \div \frac{3x - 6}{x - 3}$ (b) $\frac{1}{10a - 2a^2} \div \frac{a}{4a - 20}$

(c) $\frac{3}{y^2 - 2y - 15} \times \frac{y^2 - 9}{6y - 18}$ (d) $\frac{x^2 + 4x - 21}{x^2 - 6x - 16} \times \frac{x^2 - 8x + 15}{x^2 + 9x + 14}$

42. If $f(x) = \frac{x^2 - 9}{3x - x^2}$ and $g(x) = \frac{x^2 - 5x + 6}{2x^2 - 4x}$, then find

(a) $f(1)$ (b) $f(-1)$ (c) $g(5)$ (d) $g(-2)$

(e) $f(3)$ (f) $f(-3)$ (g) $\frac{f(x)}{g(x)}$

For what values of x is each function not defined?

43. Simplify and state any restrictions.

(a) $\frac{x^2}{2xy} \times \frac{x}{2y^2} \div \frac{(3x)^2}{xy^2}$

(b) $\frac{x^2 - 5x + 6}{x^2 - 1} \times \frac{x^2 - 4x - 5}{x^2 - 4} \div \frac{x - 5}{x^2 + 3x + 2}$

(c) $\frac{1 - x^2}{1 + y} \times \frac{1 - y^2}{x + x^2} \div \frac{y^3 - y}{x^2}$

(d) $\frac{x^2 - y^2}{4x^2 - y^2} \times \frac{4x^2 + 8xy + 3y^2}{x + y} \div \frac{2x + 3y}{2x - y}$

(e) $\frac{a^2 + 5ab + 6b^2}{a^2 - 5ab + 6b^2} \times \frac{a^2 - 2ab - 3b^2}{a^2 + ab - 2b^2} \div \frac{a^2 + 4ab + 3b^2}{a^2 - ab - 2b^2}$

4.10U Skill Builder: Dividing Complex Numbers

44. What property of complex conjugates do you use to simplify reciprocals and quotients of complex numbers?

45. Explain how to divide complex numbers. Use an example to show the steps.

46. For each complex number,

i. write the complex conjugate

ii. write the reciprocal

iii. express each reciprocal in the form $a + bi$, where a and b are real

(a) $2 - i$ (b) $-1 + i$ (c) $\sqrt{2} - \sqrt{2}i$

(d) $-3 + \sqrt{3}i$ (e) $-\frac{1}{2} + \frac{\sqrt{3}}{2}i$

47. Express in the form $a + bi$.

(a) $\frac{4}{1 - i}$ (b) $\frac{5}{2 + i}$ (c) $\frac{6i}{1 + i}$ (d) $\frac{8}{1 - 3i}$

(e) $\frac{3 - i}{2 + i}$ (f) $\frac{5i - 2}{2 + 3i}$ (g) $\frac{5 - i}{i}$ (h) $\frac{-3 + 4i}{-i}$

(i) $\frac{a + bi}{a - bi}$ (j) $\frac{(1 - i)(3 + 2i)}{1 + i}$ (k) $\frac{(4 - i)(2 + 3i)}{(2 - i)^2}$

48. (a) If $z = \sqrt{3} + i$, then express $z + \frac{9}{z}$ in its simplest form.

(b) If $z = x + yi$, then find the real and imaginary parts of $z + \frac{1}{z}$.

49. Solve for z and express in the form $a + bi$.

(a) $(4 - 3i) = z(1 + i)$ (b) $6z - z(4 - i) = -2 + 6i$

4.11 Adding and Subtracting Rational Expressions

50. When two rational expressions are added or subtracted, what must be true about the two denominators if the LCD is not the product of them? Give an example. Then find the sum or difference, showing the steps for finding the LCD.

51. When you are finding a sum or difference of rational expressions, why is it important to note restrictions on the variables *before* you reduce the resulting expression?

52. Simplify. Remember to state any restrictions, and reduce the answer to lowest terms.

(a) $\frac{4}{5x} - \frac{2}{3x}$

(b) $\frac{3}{ab^2} + \frac{5}{a^2b}$

(c) $\frac{5}{x+1} - \frac{2}{x-1}$

(d) $\frac{4x}{(x+3)^2} - \frac{3}{(x+3)}$

(e) $\frac{1}{x^2+3x-4} + \frac{1}{x^2+x-12}$

(f) $\frac{1}{x^2-5x+6} - \frac{1}{x^2-9}$

(g) $\frac{x^2-4y^2}{x^2+2xy} + \frac{x^2-2xy+4y^2}{2xy}$

(h) $\frac{1}{x^2+2x-3} + \frac{1}{x^2-1} - \frac{2}{x^2+4x+3}$

(i) $\frac{x^2-1}{(x+1)^2} - \frac{x^2-5x+6}{x^2-4x+4} + \frac{x+3}{x^2+4x+3}$

(j) $\frac{a-b}{ab} - \frac{a-2b}{ab+b^2} - \frac{2a+b}{a^2-ab}$

53. Find the zeros of each function. First rewrite the equation in a different form.

(a) $f(x) = 4x - 12 + \frac{9}{x+2}$

(b) $f(x) = 9x - 15 + \frac{40}{x+3}$

54. Solve for x.

(a) $\frac{3}{x-5} + \frac{2x}{x-3} = 5$

(b) $\frac{3x}{x-1} + 4 = \frac{x}{x+1}$

(c) $\frac{1}{1-x} - \frac{1}{1+x} = \frac{4x}{1+x^2}$

(d) $\frac{5}{x+2} + \frac{x(x+3)}{x^2-4} = \frac{x}{x-2}$

55. In a motorcycle race, one lap of the course is 650 m. At the start of the race, Genna sets off 4 s after Tom does, but she drives her motorcycle 5 m/s faster and finishes the lap 2.5 s sooner than he does.

(a) Find the speed at which each of them is driving.

(b) Find the time taken by each of them to cover the distance.

4.12 Skill Builder: Extending Algebra Skills: Working with Polynomials

56. Write three examples of polynomials and state the degree of each one. What is special about the exponents in a polynomial? How do you find the degree of a polynomial?

57. Use your polynomials from question 56 to show how polynomials are added, subtracted, and multiplied.

58. Create an expression that contains a sum and a difference and involves all of the following: (a) a product of a binomial and a trinomial, (b) a product of three binomials, and (c) the square of a trinomial.

Simplify your expression. Then state the degree of the resulting polynomial.

59. Simplify.

(a) $(5x^4 - x^2 - 2) - (x^4 - 2x^3 + 3x^2 - 5)$

(b) $(-x^2 + x - 6) + (x^2 - 4x + 1) - (2x^2 - x - 5)$

(c) $-3x(x^2 - 2x - 4) - x(x^2 - 3x - 2)$

(d) $4x^2(2x^3 - x + 3) - x^3(3x^3 + 5x - 1)$

(e) $x[2x - (3x - 4)] + 4x[2x - (3 - x)]$

(f) $x[2x - (5x - 4)] + 4x[x - (6 - x)]$

60. Simplify.

(a) $(x^2 + 4)(x^2 - 2x + 3)$

(b) $3x(3x^2 - 1)^2 - 2x(1 - x^2)^2$

(c) $(t - 2)(3t - 1)(4t + 3) - (2 - t)^2(t + 5)$

(d) $(x - 3)^2(x + 1)^2 - (x + 2)^2(x - 4)^2$

(e) $(3x - 2)(x^3 + 4x^2 - 2x - 1)$

(f) $(a^2 + 4a - 3)(3a^2 - 2a + 4)$

(g) $(x^2 - 3x + 2)^2$

(h) $(x - 4)^2(x + 1)^2$

61. Prove that the triangle with sides $\frac{1}{2}(n^2 + 1)$, $\frac{1}{2}(n^2 - 1)$, and n contains a right angle.

Chapter 4 Summary

In this chapter, you reviewed and extended your knowledge of quadratic functions and began to work with complex numbers. You learned how to graph the reciprocal function $f(x) = \frac{1}{x}$ and how to use the graph of a function to sketch its reciprocal. You have also added, subtracted, multiplied, and divided rational expressions.

Chapter 4 Review Test

Quadratic Functions and Rational Expressions

1. (a) If $z = -3 + 2i$ and $w = 2 - i$, then find $z + w$, $z - w$, $z\bar{z}$, and $\frac{z}{2w}$.

(b) Find $f(2 - 5i)$, where $f(x) = -2x^2 - 3x + 1$.

2. Simplify each of the following.

(a) $\frac{28x^3y}{-21xy^2}$

(b) $\frac{7}{x^2 - 4} - \frac{3}{x^2 + 5x + 6}$

(c) $\frac{a^2 - b^2}{a} \times \frac{3ab}{a^2 + 4ab + 3b^2} \div \frac{a^2 - ab}{a + 3b}$

(d) $(x - y)^3 + (x + y)^3 + 3(x + y)(x - y)^2 + 3(x - y)(x + y)^2$

3. (a) Find the coordinates of the vertex. State whether the function has a maximum or minimum value.

i. $f(x) = -3x^2 + 8x$

ii. $g(x) = (x - 1)(x + 5)$

iii. $h(t) = -4.9t^2 + 24.5t + 6$

(b) A car rental agency has 150 cars. The owner finds that, at a price of \$48 per day, he can rent all the cars. For each \$2 increase in price, the demand is less and 4 fewer cars are rented. For each car that is rented, there are routine maintenance costs of \$5 per day. What rental charge will maximize profit?

4. Application: Juliet has dropped her locket from her balcony so that Romeo, standing below, can put a note into it. He must then throw the locket back up to Juliet. The height of an object thrown vertically up is modelled by the quadratic function $s(t) = s_0 + v_0t - \frac{1}{2}gt^2$, where s_0 is the initial height above ground, v_0 is the initial velocity, g is the acceleration due to gravity, t is the time, and $s(t)$ is the height above the ground at time t. The balcony rail is 9 m above the ground, and the acceleration due to gravity is 9.8 m/s^2. Assume that the time it takes for the locket to fall 9 m is the same as the time it takes for Romeo to throw it back up to Juliet. What initial velocity must he give the locket if it is to reach Juliet? Show calculations or graphs, or both, to justify your answer.

5. Knowledge and Understanding

(a) For what values of k does the equation $kx^2 + k = 8x - 2kx$ have

i. two distinct real roots?

ii. one real root?

iii. no real roots?

(b) One root of a quadratic equation is $1 - 2i$. State the other root and write the equation in the form $ax^2 + bx + c = 0$.

6. The route for a fundraising marathon is 16 km long. Participants may walk, jog, run, or cycle. Make a table to show the estimated times for completing the marathon at the different speeds. Write an equation to describe the relation between speed and time and sketch its graph. What is the name of this relation?

7. **Communication:** Sketch the graph of $y = 3x - 4$ and use it to sketch the graph of $y = \frac{1}{3x - 4}$ on the same axes. State the domain and the range for the reciprocal function. Explain the properties of functions and their reciprocals that helped you sketch the second graph.

8. A formula for calculating the drug dose for young children is $\frac{(t^3 - 4t^2 - 5t)a}{22t^2 - 110t}$, where t is the age of the child in years and a is the adult dose. If the adult dose for a certain antibiotic is 200 mg, what dose does the formula indicate for a

   (a) 1-year-old child?

   (b) 5-year-old child?

   Answer to one decimal place.

9. Marissa and Jovanna enter a 200-km bicycle race. Marissa cycles 5 km/h faster than Jovanna, but her bicycle gets a flat tire, which takes one-half hour to repair. If the two girls finish the race in a tie, then how fast was each girl cycling? Answer to one decimal place.

10. **Thinking, Inquiry, Problem Solving** Prove that the triangle whose sides are $n^2 + 1$, $n^2 - 1$, and $2n$ is a right triangle.

Cumulative Review Test 2

Functions

1. For each relation,

i. identify the domain and range

ii. tell whether it is a function or not. Justify your answer.

(a) 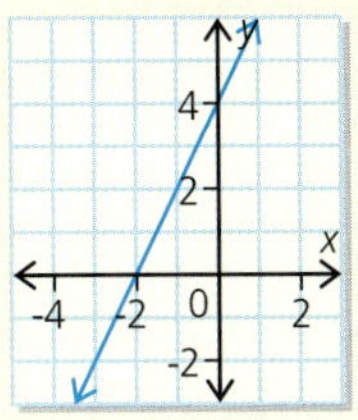

(b) 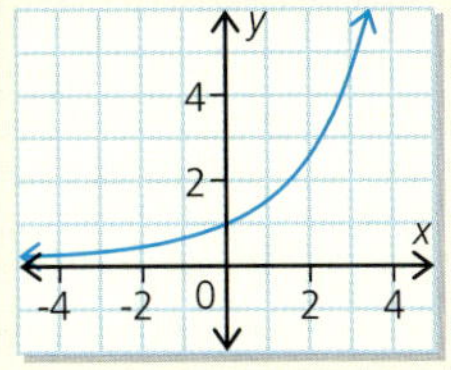

(c) 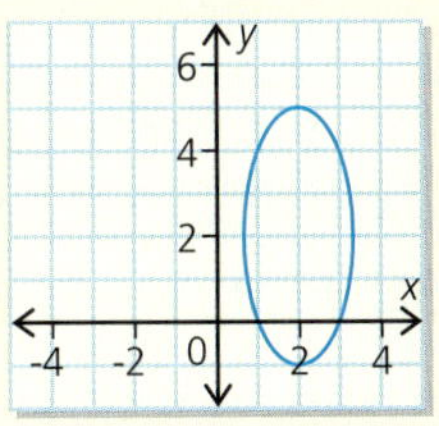

(d) 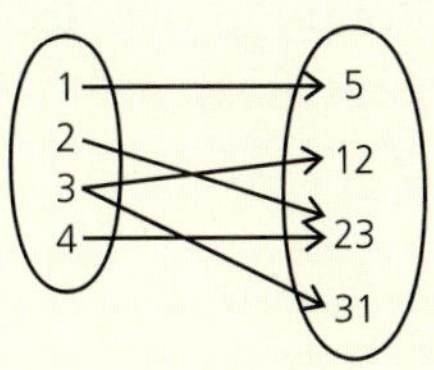

(e) $\{(-1, 4), (0, 2), (3, 5), (3, 6), (4, 9), (5, 9)\}$

(f) $f(x) = \sqrt{2x + 5}$

(g) $x = -(y + 2)^2 - 3$

(h) $x^2 + y^2 = 9$

2. Given that $f(x) = -3x + 8$, determine

(a) $f(4)$

(b) the value(s) of x where $f(x) = 14$

(c) $f^{-1}(6)$

(d) the value(s) of x where $f(x) = f^{-1}(x)$

3. Graph each of the following on a number line.

(a) $\{x \mid -4 < x < 3, x \in \mathbf{I}\}$

(b) $\{x \mid x \geq 2, x \in \mathbf{R}\}$

(c) $\{x \mid x^2 \leq 3, x \in \mathbf{R}\}$

4. Assume that $g(x) = 12x - 9$ and $-33 < g(x) < 123$. Find the domain of $g(x)$.

5. The graph of $y = f^{-1}(x)$ is shown.

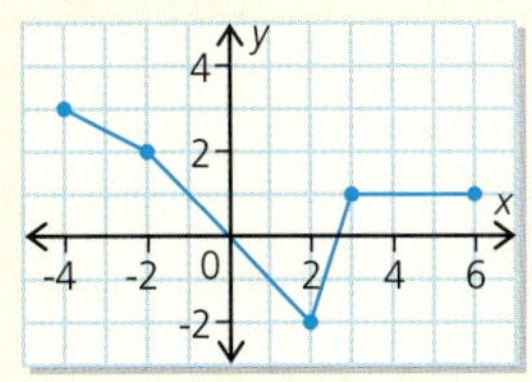

(a) Draw the graph of f.

(b) Is f a function? Explain.

6. For each quadratic function

i. find the coordinates of the vertex by completing the square

ii. state the domain and the range

iii. sketch the graph

(a) $f(x) = x^2 + 10x - 22$

(b) $f(x) = 3x^2 + 8x$

(c) $f(x) = \frac{2}{3}x^2 + 4x - 8$

7. For each function

i. determine the equation of g^{-1}

ii. sketch g and g^{-1} on the same set of axes

iii. state the domain and range of g and of g^{-1}

(a) $g(x) = 2x^2 + 12x - 14$

(b) $g(x) = \sqrt{4x + 8}$

8. Graph each equation. In each case, begin by graphing $f(x) = x^3$ on the same axes.

(a) $y = 3f(x)$
(b) $y = f\left(\frac{1}{2}x\right)$
(c) $y = f(x - 2)$
(d) $y = f(x) + 2$
(e) $y = -f(x)$
(f) $y = f(-x)$

9. The graph of $y = g(x)$ is shown, and $f(x) = \frac{1}{2}g(2x - 4) - 1$.

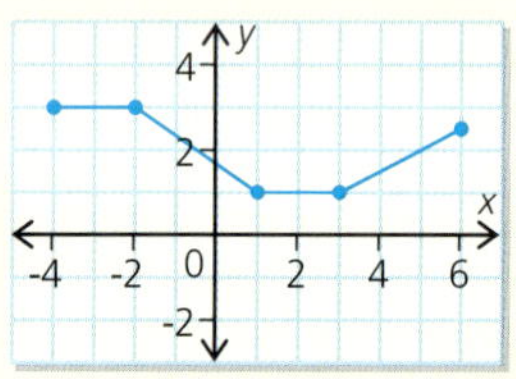

(a) Draw an input/output diagram for f.
(b) Determine the domain and range of f.
(c) Evaluate $f(4)$.
(d) Graph f.

10. The demand function for a new product is $p(x) = -4x + 28$, where x is the number of items sold in thousands and p is the price in dollars. The cost function is $C(x) = 4x + 12$.

(a) State the corresponding revenue function.
(b) Find the corresponding profit function.
(c) Complete the square to find the value of x that will maximize profits.
(d) How many items must be sold for the company to break even?
(e) Sketch the graph of the profit function.

11. When priced at \$40 each, a toy has annual sales of 5000 units. The manufacturer estimates that each \$1 increase in cost will decrease sales by 100 units. Find the unit price that will maximize the total revenue.

12. Without drawing the graph,

i. find the number of zeros for each function
ii. indicate whether the graph touches the x-axis at one point, intersects the x-axis at two points, or does not meet the x-axis

(a) $f(x) = 4x^2 + 12x + 9$
(b) $g(x) = -2(x - 0.5)^2 + 12.5$
(c) $h(x) = -3(x + 1.9)^2$

13. Solve each quadratic equation for x, where $x \in \mathbf{C}$. Round to two decimal places, where necessary.

(a) $2x^2 + 5x - 3 = 0$
(b) $3x^2 + 48 = 0$
(c) $3x^2 - 2x + 3 = 0$
(d) $5x^2 - 4x + 20 = 0$

14. Draw $f(x)$, $\frac{1}{f(x)}$, and f^{-1} on the same axes. State the domain and the range for each of the three functions for each part.

(a) $f(x) = 4x + 3$
(b) $f(x) = 4x^2 - 9$
(c) $f(x) = x + 3 - 5$

15. For each rational function, find

i. find the zeros

ii. find the asymptotes

iii. find the domain

iv. graph the function and estimate the range

(a) $f(x) = \dfrac{2x + 4}{x - 1}$

(b) $g(x) = \dfrac{-2x}{x^2 - 6x + 9}$

(c) $h(x) = \dfrac{x^2 - x - 30}{x + 2}$

16. Simplify.

(a) $(2x^4 - 3x^2 - 6)$
$+ (6x^4 - x^3 + 4x^2 + 5)$

(b) $(x^2 - 4)(2x^2 + 5x - 2)$

(c) $-7x(x^2 + x - 1)$
$- 3x(2x^2 - 5x + 6)$

(d) $-2x^2(3x^3 - 7x + 2)$
$- x^3(5x^3 + 2x - 8)$

(e) $-2x[5x - (2x - 7)]$
$+ 6x[3x - (1 + 2x)]$

(f) $(x + 2)^2(x - 1)^2 - (x - 4)^2(x + 4)^2$

(g) $(x^2 + 5x - 3)^2$

17. Simplify. State any restrictions.

(a) $\dfrac{2x + 4}{x^2 - 4}$

(b) $\dfrac{18p^2q^2}{-6p^{-1}q^3}$

(c) $\dfrac{25x^2 - 9}{4x^2 + x - 3} \times \dfrac{8x - 6}{5x^2 + 8x + 3}$

(d) $\dfrac{a^2 - 3a - 10}{a^2 - a + 12} \div \dfrac{a^2 - 5a - 15}{a^2 + 7a + 12}$

(e) $\dfrac{a^2 + 6ab + 8b^2}{a^2 + 14ab + 20b^2} \times \dfrac{a^2 + 5ab - 6b^2}{a^2 - ab - 6b^2}$
$\div \dfrac{a^2 + 8ab + 12b^2}{a^2 + 2ab - 15b^2}$

(f) $\dfrac{2}{b + 7} + \dfrac{3}{4 - 3b}$

(g) $\dfrac{3}{x^2 - x - 12} - \dfrac{2}{x^2 - 16}$

(h) $\dfrac{a + b}{a} - \dfrac{a - b}{ab + b^2} - \dfrac{2a + b}{b}$

Functions and Relations

18U. Simplify.

(a) $(-4i)^2$

(b) $2i^9$

(c) $(2 - 7i)(2 + 7i)$

(d) $(-3 - 4i) + (2 - 3i) - (4 - 5i)$

(e) $\dfrac{3 - 5i}{8 + 3i}$

(f) $[(-i + (3 - 5i)]^3$

(g) $\dfrac{(-1 + 4i)^2}{(2 + i)(3 + i)}$

(h) $\dfrac{(6 - 3i) - (7 + 2i)}{(2 + 3i) + (2 - i)}$

Performance Tasks for Part 2

Functions

THE FOLLOWING ACTIVITIES SHOULD EACH TAKE LESS THAN A PERIOD TO COMPLETE.

1. Studying Functions

Analyze two of the following functions in depth. Include:

i. the domain and range
ii. the relationship to the base graph, including applied transformations
iii. any lines of symmetry
iv. the inverse of the function

Include diagrams and graphs as well as written and algebraic responses in your analysis.

(a) $y = 2\sqrt{x + 4}$

(b) $y = 3x^2 - 24x + 50$

(c) $y = 3 - \sqrt{x}$

2. The Cost of Money

The value of a Canadian dollar in U.S. dollars often changes. Suppose one U.S. dollar is worth \$1.48 Canadian.

(a) Express the relationship as an equation.

(b) Graph the equation and its inverse, by hand and using technology.

(c) Explain the meaning of the inverse relationship and find its equation.

(d) Suppose a Canadian shopping at a U.S. store sees a sign that Canadian dollars will be discounted by 40%. Is this a good deal? Explain.

Research Extension (Extra Time)

(e) Find the current values of the U.S. and Canadian dollars and create the exchange equations.

3. Exponential Equations

Demonstrate how to solve exponential equations both graphically and algebraically. Use these equations as models:

(a) $2^{-2x} = 4$ (b) $2^{4x-2} = 8^x$ (c) $4^{x+3} = 8^{2x}$

4. Graphing Complex Numbers

A complex number in the form $x + yi$ can be graphed as the ordered pair (x, y).

(a) Graph the complex number $2 + 3i$ as an ordered pair (2, 3). Label this point A.

(b) Graph the complex number $-3 + 4i$ as an ordered pair. Label this point B.

(c) Label the origin O. Draw line segments OA and OB.

(d) Draw two lines, one through A parallel to OB, and one through B parallel to OA.

(e) Find the intersection point of the two lines you drew in (d).

(f) What relationship does this point have to points A and B?

(g) Make a conjecture and test it using several different complex numbers as points.

5. Graphing Equations

Part I

(a) Match each equation to its graph. The scales are the same on all graphs. Explain your reasoning in each case.

(b) State the domain and range of each relation. Note: You should be able to do this question without graphing technology.

i. $y = -2(x - 2)^2 + 3$

ii. $y = 2^x + 1$

iii. $y = 2(x + 1)^2 - 2$

iv. $y = -3\sqrt{x - 1} + 2$

v. $y = \frac{4}{x}$

vi. $y = 2\sqrt{x + 1}$

A

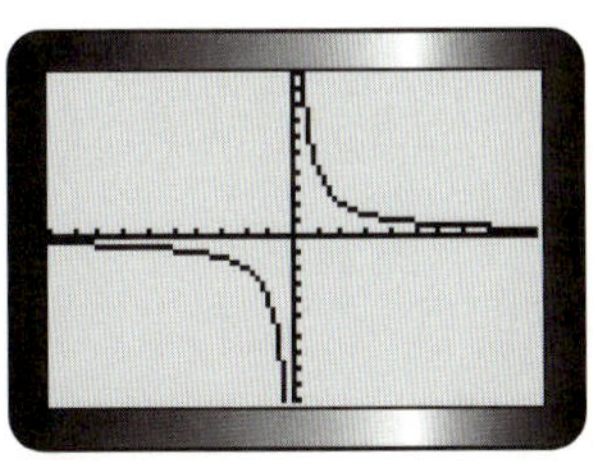

B

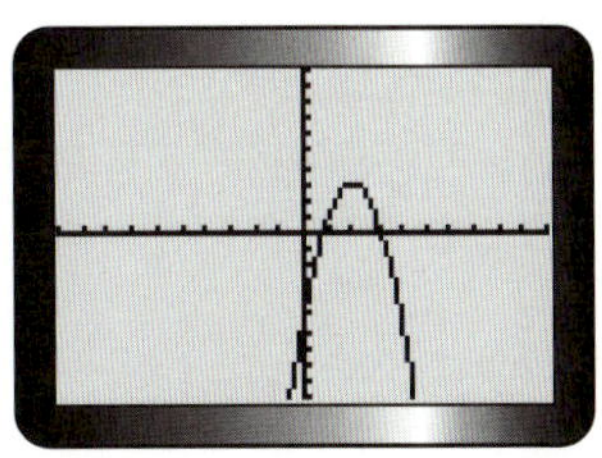

C

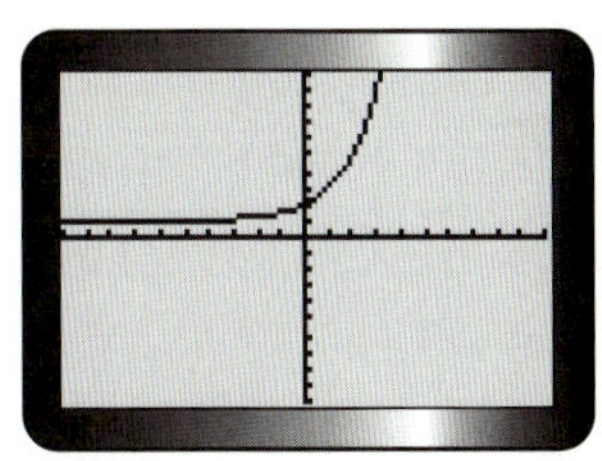

D

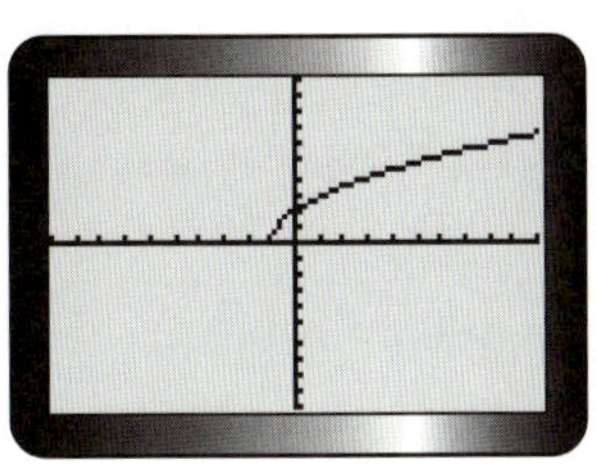

E

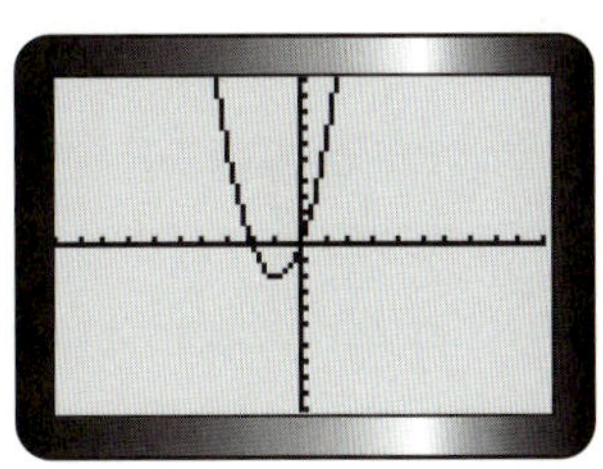

F

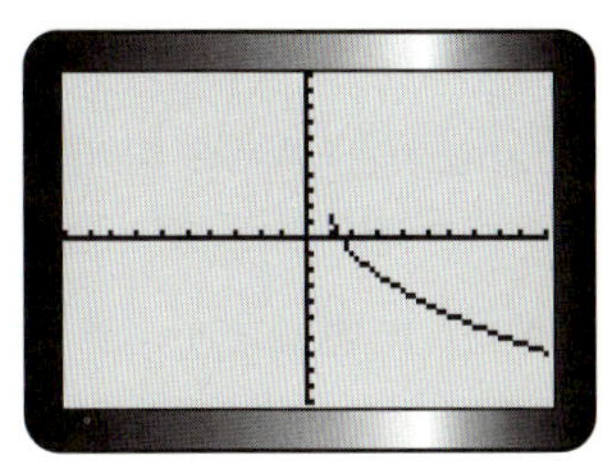

Part II

Create an equation for the following graph. (Note that in this calculator screen, the *x* and *y*-axes both go from –10 to 10.) Explain how you determined the equation.

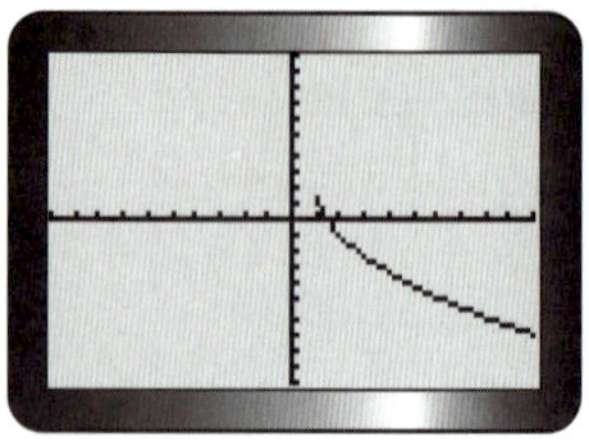

6. Chartering a Flight

Westown Secondary School band wants to fly to Vancouver for a music competition. The Fly-Rite charter company gives the band this information.

Number on Trip	25	40	50	60	80	100
Cost per Person	\$960	\$600	\$480	\$400	\$300	\$240

Another company, Straight-Away Charters, charges a flat fee of \$10 000, plus \$200 per person.

(a) Copy and complete the table.

Number on Trip	30	40	50	75	100
Cost per Person		\$450			

(b) Graph both relations on the same set of axes. Use "number on trip" as the independent variable and "cost per person" as the dependent variable.

(c) Describe and compare the relations.

(d) Create an equation to describe each relation.

(e) How many students would need to take the trip for the costs to be equal? Verify your answer algebraically.

(f) Straight-Away increases its per-person charge to \$250 per person. How would this increase effect your graph?

(g) Given the new rate, discuss whether Fly-Rite or Straight-Away offers the better deal.

7. Fractals

Fractal geometry creates many interesting designs and patterns. One of the techniques used in fractal geometry is called an iterative technique. This technique starts with a single value, such as 2, that is substituted and evaluated in a given function, such as $f(x) = 2x + 1$. The result, in this case 5, is then also substituted in the given function $f(x)$. In this case, the result of the second iteration would be 11.

(a) Find the first three iterates (values after three iterations) when the initial value of x is 2 and the function is $f(x) = x^2 - 1$.

(b) Fractals are also generated by using a complex number as the initial value. Use $z = 2 + 3i$ as the initial value and $f(z) = z^2 + (-1 + 2i)$ and determine the values for the first three iterates. Clearly show how you are obtaining the values.

(c) The result after the first iteration of $g(z) = 2z + (4i - 5)$ is $-7 + 5i$. What was the initial value?

Research Extension (Extra Time)

(d) Now that you have the mathematics behind fractals, research and report how fractal designs use this technique to generate patterns.

THE FOLLOWING ACTIVITIES SHOULD EACH TAKE MORE THAN A PERIOD TO COMPLETE.

8. Presenting Math

Create a presentation to teach other students everything they need to know about at least one of the following transformations: translations, reflections, or stretches. Your presentation should

i. include visuals and the use of technology for graphing

ii. clearly link the graph of a relation under a transformation with the algebraic expression for that relation

iii. make use of at least three different base graphs chosen from: $y = x$, $y = x^2$, $y = \sqrt{x}$, $y = \sin x$, or $y = \cos x$

9. Demonstrating Math

You have been chosen to demonstrate what you have learned in math class for the upcoming parents' night. You know that many of the parents of your friends in the class struggled to help with homework on "word problems." You are to create a presentation to demonstrate how to use quadratic modelling to solve problems. Your presentation should include well-organized instructions, steps, and hints as to how to use both algebraic and graphical solutions. You should use at least two of these problems as samples to guide the presentation.

(a) A total of 800 m of fencing material is used to enclose a rectangular field and to divide the field into four portions by fences parallel to one of the sides of the field. Find the maximum area that can be enclosed in this rectangle and state the dimensions of the rectangle.

(b) A charter company will provide a plane for a fare of $200 each for 80 or fewer passengers. For each passenger over the 80-person mark, the fare is decreased by $2 per person for everyone. What number of passengers would produce the greatest revenue for the company?

10. How Fast?

Kim and Julie are joining Nicole at her parents' cottage for the weekend. The cottage is 150 km away from their neighbourhood. Kim can leave directly after school but Julie will be leaving after band practice, an hour and a quarter later. Kim took her time and drove slowly, averaging 20 km/h slower than Julie. They both arrived there at the same time. At what speeds were they travelling?

Trigonometric Functions

The Trigonometry of Right Triangles

By the Pythagorean relationship, $a^2 + b^2 = c^2$ for any right angle triangle, where c is the length of the hypotenuse, and a and b are the lengths of the other two sides.

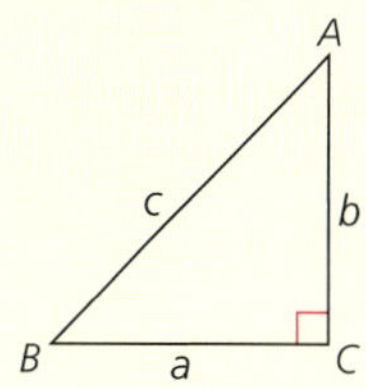

In any right angle triangle, there are three primary trigonometric ratios associated with the measure of an angle to the ratio of two sides. For example, for ΔABC, in figure 1,

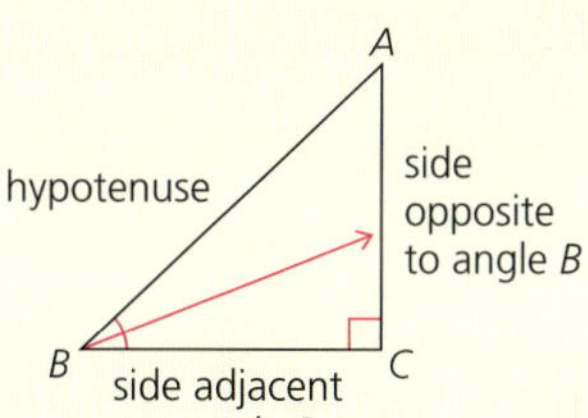

For $\angle B$

$\sin B = \frac{\text{opposite}}{\text{hypotenuse}}$

$\cos B = \frac{\text{adjacent}}{\text{hypotenuse}}$

$\tan B = \frac{\text{opposite}}{\text{adjacent}}$

figure 1

Similarly, in figure 2,

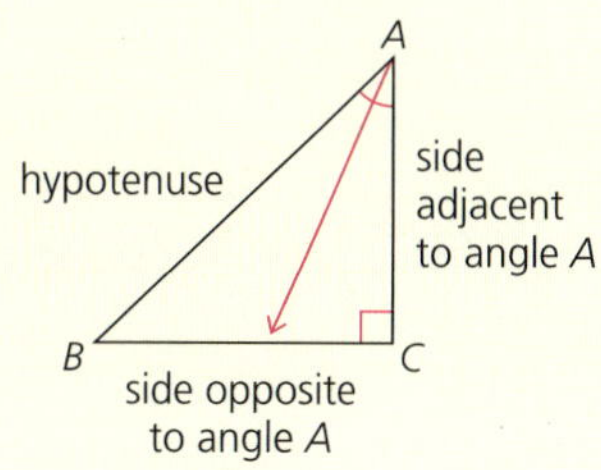

For $\angle A$

$\sin A = \frac{\text{opposite}}{\text{hypotenuse}}$

$\cos A = \frac{\text{adjacent}}{\text{hypotenuse}}$

$\tan A = \frac{\text{opposite}}{\text{adjacent}}$

figure 2

Note how the opposite and adjacent sides change in figures 1 and 2 with angles A and B.

Example 1

State the primary trigonometric ratios of $\angle A$.

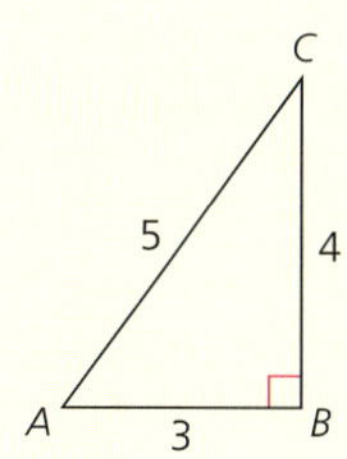

Solution

Sketch the triangle, then label the opposite side, the adjacent side, and the hypotenuse.

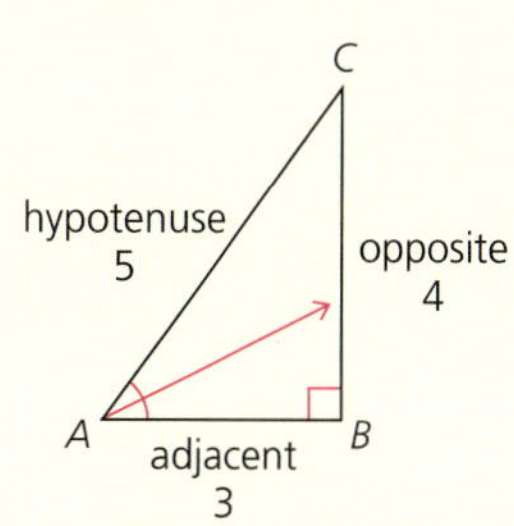

$$\sin A = \frac{\text{opposite}}{\text{hypotenuse}} = \frac{4}{5}$$

$$\cos A = \frac{\text{adjacent}}{\text{hypotenuse}} = \frac{3}{5}$$

$$\tan A = \frac{\text{opposite}}{\text{adjacent}} = \frac{4}{3}$$

Example 2

A ramp must have a rise of one unit for every eight units of run. What is the angle of inclination for the ramp?

Solution

The slope of the ramp is $\frac{\text{rise}}{\text{run}} = \frac{1}{8}$. Draw a labelled sketch.

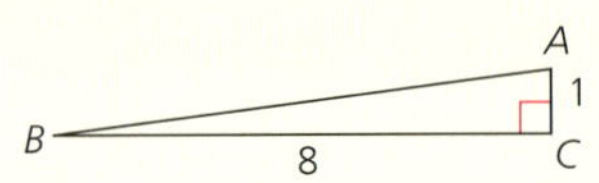

Calculate the measure of $\angle B$ to determine the angle of inclination.

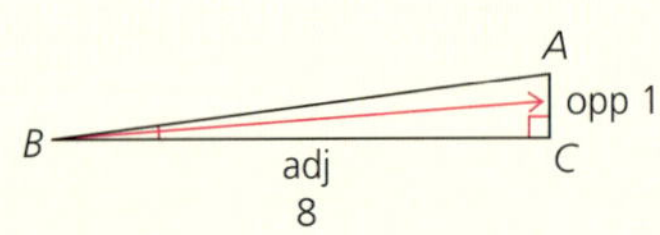

The trigonometric ratio that associates $\angle B$ to the opposite and adjacent sides is the tangent. Therefore,

$$\tan B = \frac{\text{opposite}}{\text{adjacent}}$$
$$= \frac{1}{8}$$
$$B = \tan^{-1}\left(\frac{1}{8}\right)$$
$$\doteq 7°$$

The angle of inclination is about 7°.

Example 3

Determine x to the nearest centimetre.

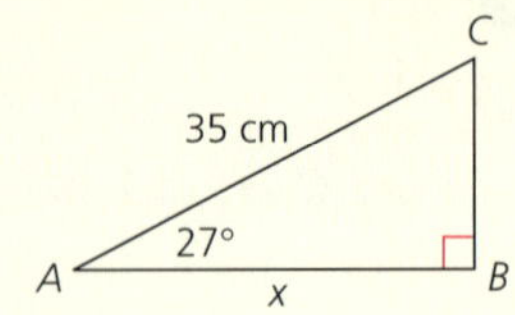

Solution

Label the sketch. The cosine ratio associates $\angle A$ to the adjacent side and the hypotenuse.

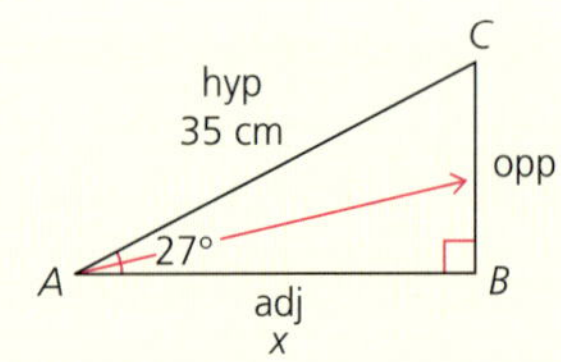

Then,

$$\cos A = \frac{\text{adjacent}}{\text{hypotenuse}}$$
$$= \frac{x}{35}$$
$$x = 35 \cos 27°$$
$$\doteq 31$$

Then, x is about 31 cm.

Practice

1. A rectangular lot is 15 m by 22 m. How long is the diagonal to the nearest metre?

2. State the primary trigonometric ratios for $\angle A$.

(a)

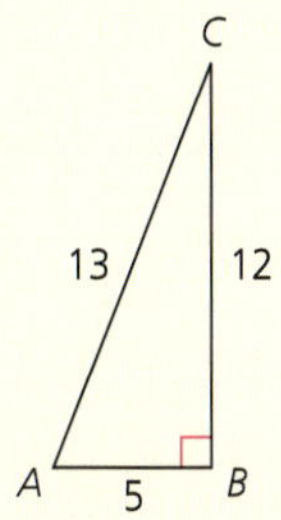

(b)

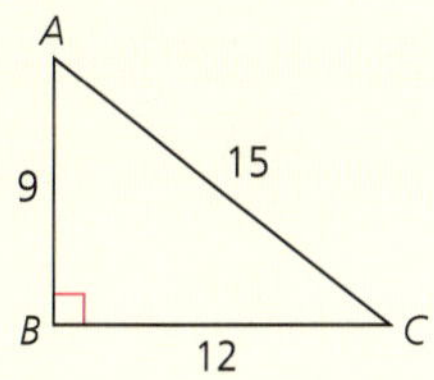

(c)

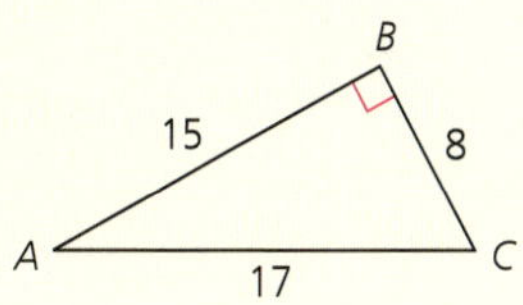

(d)

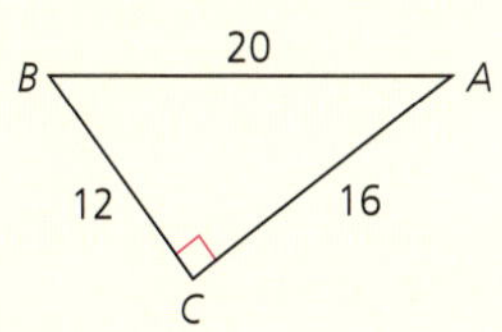

3. Solve for x to one decimal place.

(a) $\sin 39° = \frac{x}{7}$ (b) $\cos 65° = \frac{x}{16}$

(c) $\tan 15° = \frac{x}{22}$ (d) $\tan 49° = \frac{31}{x}$

4. Solve for $\angle A$ to the nearest degree.

(a) $\sin A = \frac{5}{8}$ (b) $\cos A = \frac{13}{22}$

(c) $\tan B = \frac{19}{22}$ (d) $\cos B = \frac{3}{7}$

5. Determine x to one decimal place.

(a)

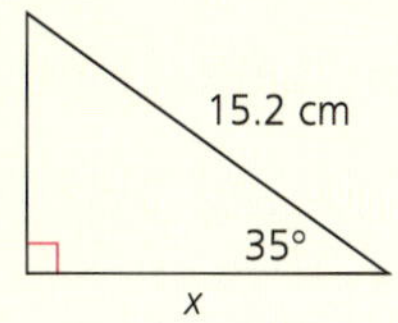

(b)

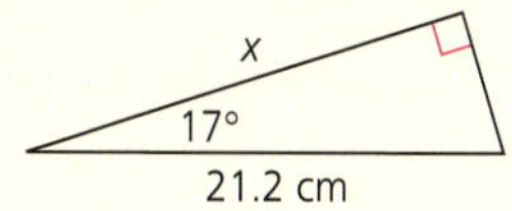

(c)

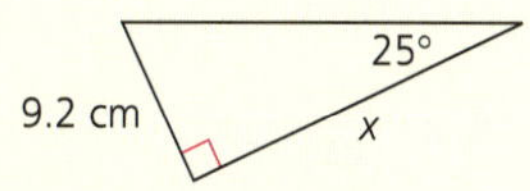

(d)

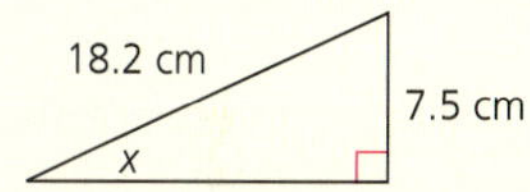

6. In ΔABC, $\angle B = 90°$ and $AC = 13$ cm. Determine

(a) BC if $\angle C = 17°$

(b) AB if $\angle C = 26°$

(c) $\angle A$ if $BC = 6$ cm

(d) $\angle C$ if $BC = 9$ cm

7. A tree casts a shadow 9.3 m long when the angle of the sun is 43°. How tall is the tree?

8. Janine stands 30.0 m from the base of a communications tower. The angle of elevation from her eyes to the top of the tower is 70°. How high is the tower if her eyes are 1.8 m above the ground?

9. A surveillance camera is mounted on the top of an 80 m tall building. The angle of elevation from the camera to the top of another building is 42°. The angle of depression from the camera to the same building is 32°. How tall is the other building?

Trigonometry of Acute Triangles: the Sine Law and the Cosine Law

An acute triangle contains three angles less than 90°.

Sine Law

The sine law states that for ΔABC,

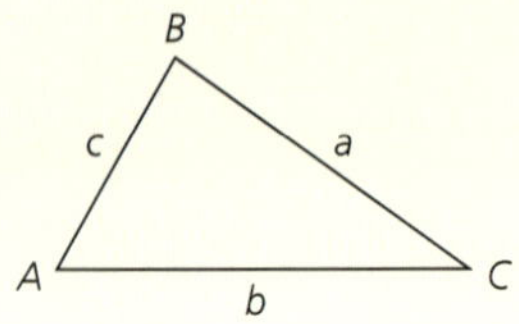

- $\frac{\sin A}{a} = \frac{\sin B}{b} = \frac{\sin C}{c}$ or $\frac{a}{\sin A} = \frac{b}{\sin B} = \frac{c}{\sin C}$

To use the sine law, two angles and one side (AAS) or two sides and an opposite angle (SSA) must be given.

Cosine Law

The cosine law states that for ΔABC,

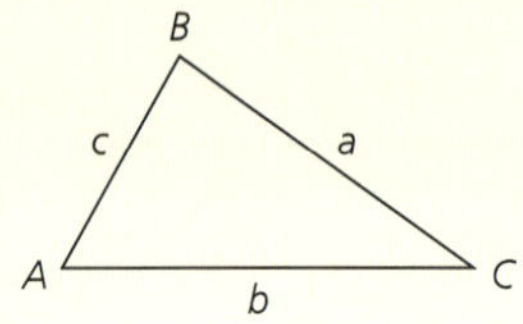

- $c^2 = a^2 + b^2 - 2ab \cos C$ or
- $a^2 = b^2 + c^2 - 2bc \cos A$ or
- $b^2 = a^2 + c^2 - 2ac \cos B$

To use the cosine law, two sides and the contained angle (SAS) or three sides (SSS) must be given.

Example 1

Determine the length of XZ to one decimal place.

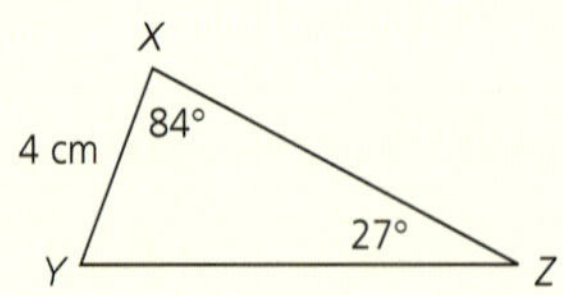

Solution

In this triangle, $\angle X = 84°$, $\angle Z = 27°$, and $z = 4$ cm.

$$\begin{aligned}\angle Y &= 180° - (84° + 27°)\\ &= 180° - 111°\\ &= 69°\end{aligned}$$

This is not a right triangle, so the primary trigonometric ratios do not apply. Two angles and one side are known, so the sine law can be used.

$$\frac{\sin Y}{y} = \frac{\sin Z}{z}$$

$$\frac{\sin 69°}{y} = \frac{\sin 27°}{4}$$

$$y = \frac{4 \sin 69°}{\sin 27°}$$

$$\doteq 8.2$$

Then XZ is about 8.2 cm.

Example 2

Determine the length of ZY to one decimal place.

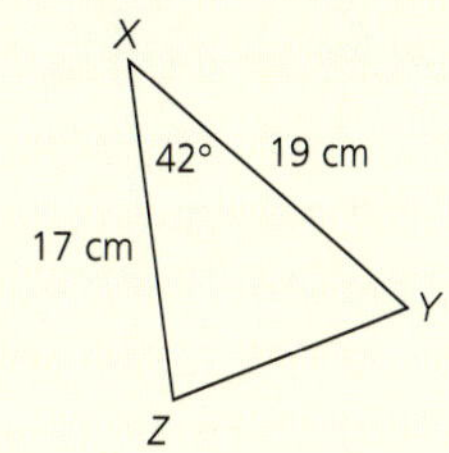

Solution

In this triangle, $\angle X = 42°$, $y = 17$ cm, and $z = 19$ cm.

There is not enough information to use the primary trigonometric ratios or the sine law. However, two sides and the contained angle are known, so the cosine law can be used.

$$x^2 = y^2 + z^2 - 2yz \cos X$$
$$x^2 = 17^2 + 19^2 - 2(17)(19) \cos 42°$$
$$x = \sqrt{17^2 + 19^2 - 2(17)(19) \cos 42°}$$
$$x \doteq 13$$

Therefore, ZY is about 13 cm.

Practice

1. Solve to one decimal place.

(a) $\dfrac{\sin 35°}{c} = \dfrac{\sin 42°}{12}$

(b) $\dfrac{15}{\sin 43°} = \dfrac{13}{\sin B}$

(c) $19^2 = 15^2 + 13^2 - 2(15)(13) \cos A$

(d) $c^2 = 12^2 + 17^2 - 2(12)(17) \cos 47°$

(e) $\dfrac{\sin A}{12.3} = \dfrac{\sin 58°}{14.2}$

(f) $\dfrac{\sin 14°}{3.1} = \dfrac{\sin 27°}{b}$

2. Determine x to one decimal place.

(a)

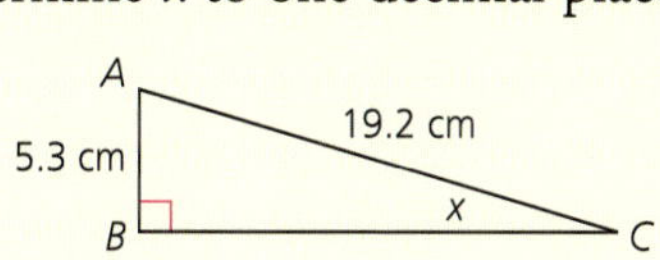

(b)

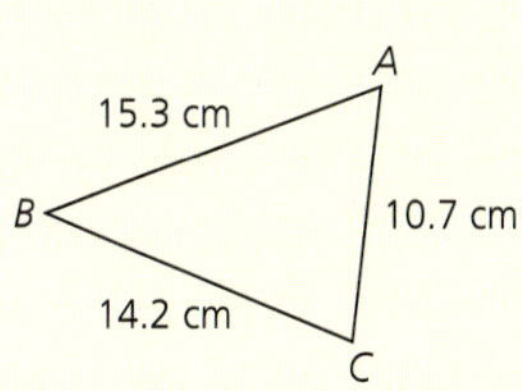

(c)

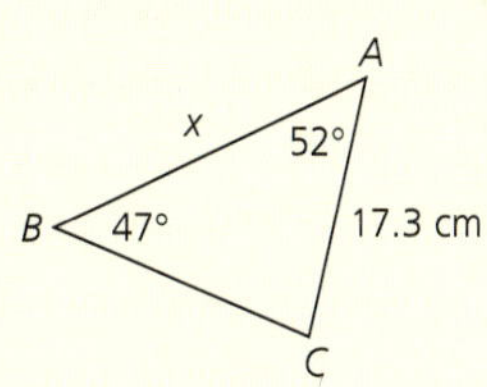

(d)

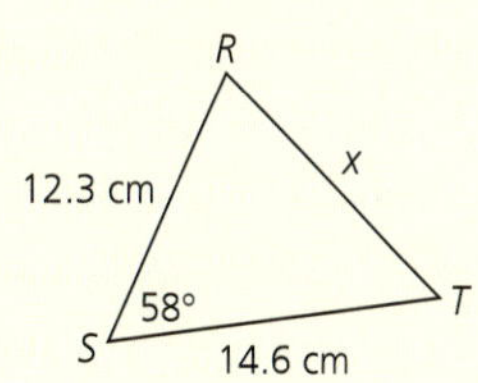

(e)

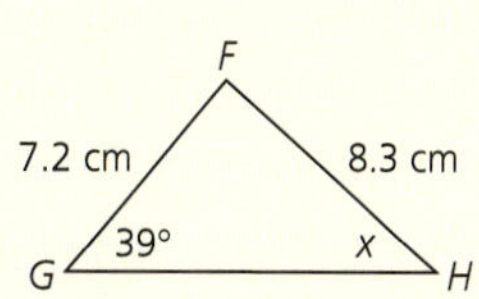

(f)

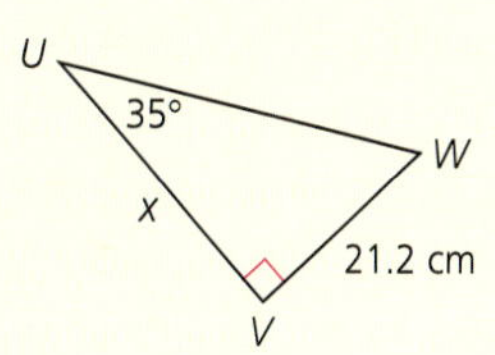

3. Solve each triangle for all missing sides and angles.

(a) ΔCAT, with $c = 5.2$ cm, $a = 6.8$ cm, and $\angle T = 59°$

(b) ΔABC, with $a = 4.3$ cm, $b = 5.2$ cm, and $c = 7.5$ cm

(c) ΔDEF, with $DE = 14.3$ cm, $EF = 17.2$ cm, and $\angle D = 39°$

4. A swamp separates points L and R. To determine the distance between them, Ciana stands at L and looks towards R. She turns about 45° and walks 52 paces from L to point P. From P, she looks at R and estimates that $\angle LPR$ is about 60°. How many paces is it from L to R?

5. An observation helicopter using a laser device determines the helicopter is 1800 m from a boat in distress. The helicopter is 1200 m from a rescue boat. The angle formed between the helicopter and the two boats is 35°. How far apart are the boats?

6. Neil designs a cottage that is 15 m wide. The roof rafters are the same length and meet at an angle of 80°. The rafters hang over the supporting wall by 0.5 m. How long are the rafters?

Chapter 5 Modelling Periodic Functions

Many events in nature happen over and over again. For instance, the tides rise and fall each day as the Earth turns and the moon's gravity pulls at the ocean waters. The moon waxes and wanes from a full moon to a new moon each month. Many animals and birds migrate great distances and are often seen at the same time of the year at very specific locations as they travel on their journey. The sound waves produced by a vibrating vocal chord or a vibrating string help to identify a specific person's voice or the type of musical instrument being played. All of these are examples of periodic phenomena.

In this chapter, you will

- investigate periodic phenomena and study their properties
- model periodic data using graphs and functions involving trigonometry
- extend the notion of trigonometry from angles and sides in a triangle to include any real number on the coordinate plane
- identify specific trigonometric functions
- investigate transformations of trigonometric functions
- solve problems that can be modelled using trigonometric functions
- solve trigonometric equations with and without technology
- use technology to develop models to assist in problem solving

Visit the Nelson Mathematics student Web site at **www.math.nelson.com**. You'll find links to interactive examples, online tutorials, and more.

Connections

The Chapter Problem

How Much Daylight?

Naomi is a fishing guide in the Far North. She keeps track of the number of hours of daylight each day where she works. She uses this data to give her customers the best opportunity to maximize their catches and still stay within catch limits.

She averaged the number of hours of daylight each month, starting in January, and recorded the data shown.

Month	J	F	M	A	M	J	J	A
Average Daylight Each Day (h)	5.5	8.0	11.0	13.5	16.3	19	19.5	18.5

Month	S	O	N	D	J	F	M	A
Average Daylight Each Day (h)	15.8	13.0	10.7	7.8	5.5	7.9	11.2	13.5

Month	M	J	J	A	S	O	N	D	J
Average Daylight Each Day (h)	16.5	19.2	19.6	17.9	14.8	12.6	10.5	7.5	5.7

In this chapter, you will learn about modelling periodic functions to answer these questions.

1. (a) Explain how Naomi could use this data to help her customers maximize their fishing experience.

(b) Show that the data is periodic and it can be modelled by a trigonometric function.

(c) Determine the trigonometric model that describes this situation. Use the model to predict the average number of hours of daylight 252 months later. Use the model to determine which months from the start of the millennium have an average of about 10 h of daylight.

Challenge 1

Average monthly temperature depends on location. Use the Internet to find the average monthly temperature for your town or city for a two-year period. If you cannot find this information for your municipality, look for a location close to where you live.

Organize the data so that a scatter plot, a curve of best fit, and a mathematical model can be found. Describe in detail the mathematical model and its curve of best fit as they relate to the context of the problem.

Challenge 2

Many recreation centres have wave action pools. Research how the waves are made. Explain how the waves are generated, how the length of a wave is determined, and how the height of the crest and the depth of the trough of a wave are maintained. Construct a working model of a wave action pool and develop an equation that models the situation.

Web Challenge

For a related Internet activity, go to **www.math.nelson.com**.

Getting Ready

In this chapter, you will learn more about the trigonometry of right triangles. As well, you will investigate a special type of nonlinear model that applies to many cyclical, real-life situations.

These exercises will help you warm up for the work ahead.

1. Solve for x to one decimal place.

(a)

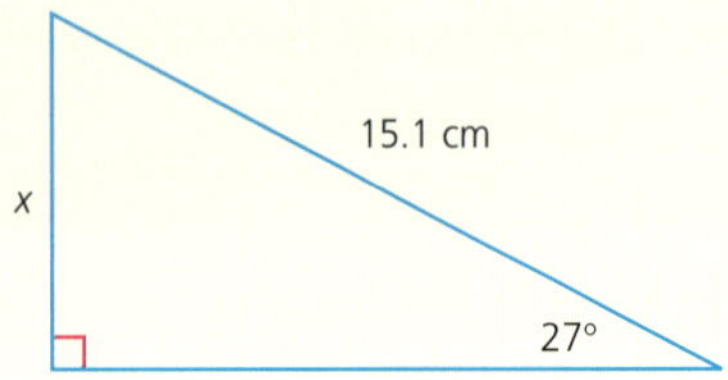

(b)

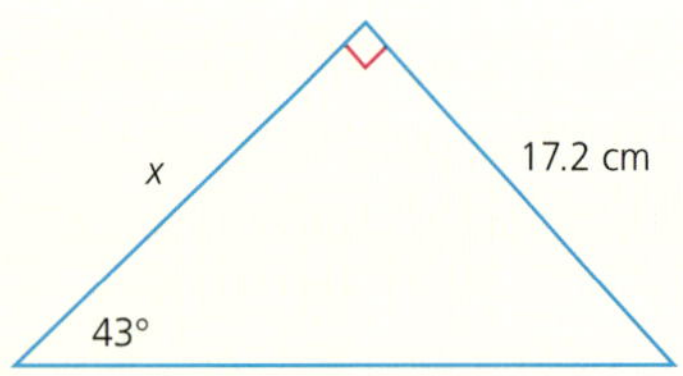

(c)

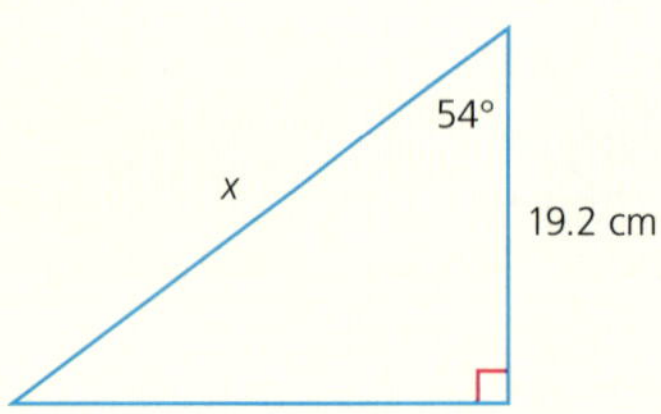

2. Evaluate to three decimal places.

(a) $27 \sin 50°$ (b) $106 \cos 87°$

(c) $23 \cos 63°$ (d) $76.5 \sin 45°$

(e) $5.3 \tan 23°$ (f) $2.8 \tan 80°$

3. Solve for angle θ to the nearest degree, $0° \leq \theta \leq 90°$.

(a) $\sin \theta = \frac{1}{2}$ (b) $\cos \theta = \frac{\sqrt{3}}{2}$

(c) $\tan \theta = \sqrt{3}$ (d) $\sin \theta = 0.937$

(e) $\cos \theta = 0.253$ (f) $\tan \theta = 57.287$

4. Solve for θ to the nearest degree.

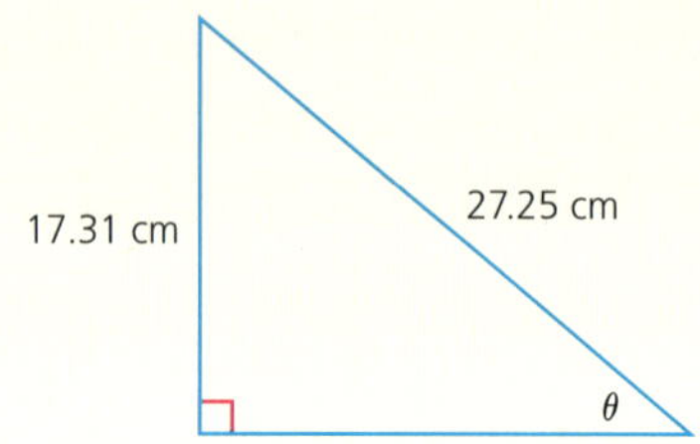

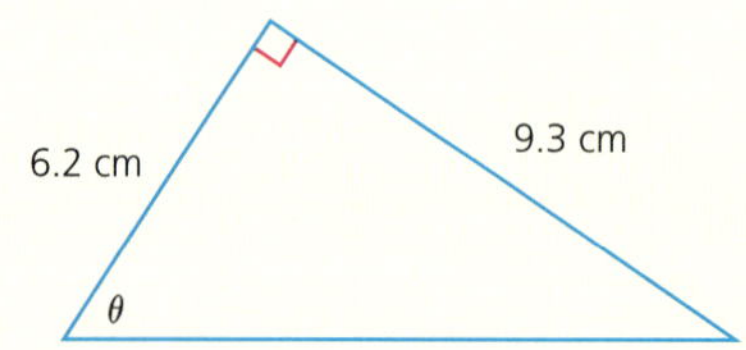

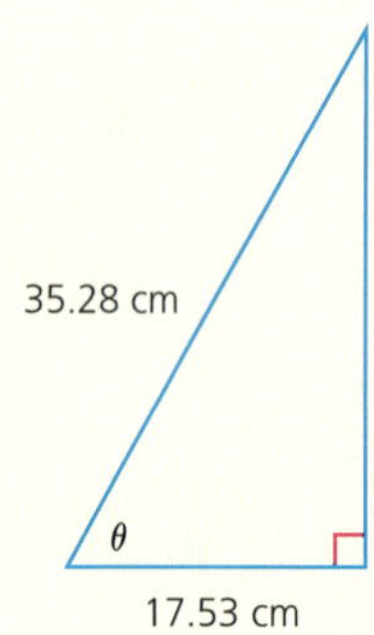

5. A rectangular field is 30 m by 25 m. Calculate the length of the diagonal to one decimal place.

6. Point $P(6, 7)$ is on the circumference of a circle centred at the origin. What is the radius of the circle?

7. Write the simplified general term for each sequence.

(a) 1, 3, 5, 7, …

(b) −7, −3, 1, 5, …

(c) 17, 26, 35, 44, …

(d) −3.25, −2.75, −2.25, −1.75, …

(e) $\frac{7}{8}, \frac{1}{2}, \frac{1}{8}, -\frac{1}{4}, \ldots$

(f) 0°, 180°, 360°, 540°, …

(g) −135°, 45°, 225°, 405°, …

(h) −90°, −30°, 30°, 90°, …

8. Let $f(x) = x^2$. Use transformations on $y = f(x)$ to sketch each graph.

(a) $y = f(x) + 2$ (b) $y = f(x) - 3$

(c) $y = 2f(x)$ (d) $y = 0.5f(x)$

(e) $y = f(x - 1)$ (f) $y = f(x + 2)$

(g) $y = -f(x)$ (h) $y = f(2x)$

9. The graph of $y = f(x)$ is shown. Sketch the graph of $y = -3f[(2(x - 1)] + 1$.

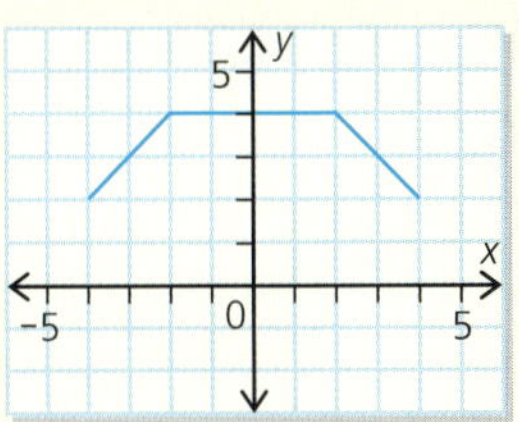

10. State the coordinates of the maximum or the minimum value and identify the zeros of each function.

(a)

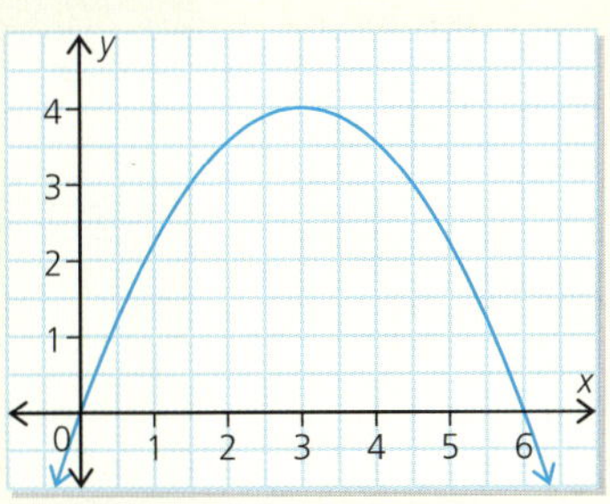

(b)

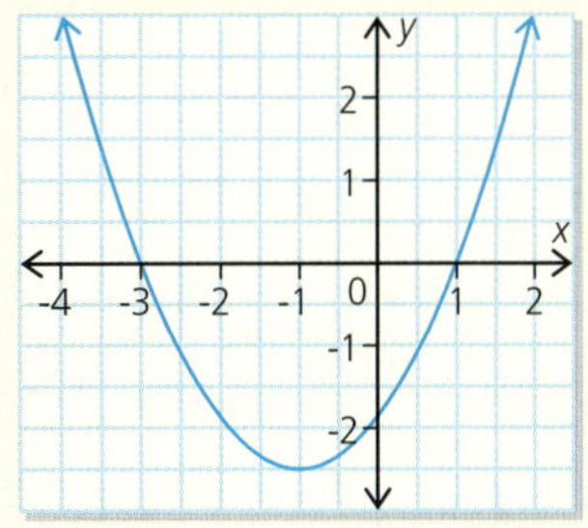

(c)

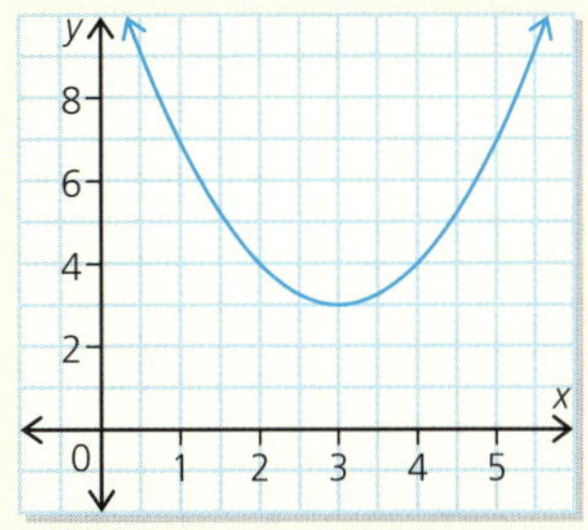

(d)

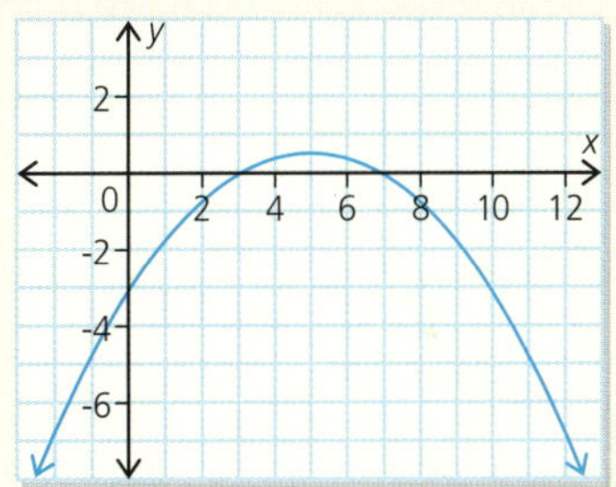

11. Solve each equation.

(a) $4x = 1$

(b) $3x + 2 = 1$

(c) $5m + 3 = 6$

(d) $3n = n + 1$

(e) $5v - \sqrt{3} = 3v$

(f) $z - 1 = -z$

(g) $5p + 1 = 3p$

(h) $3x + 5 = 4x - 7$

5.1 Periodic Phenomena

Part 1: Investigating Periodic and Non-Periodic Models

Consider what kind of mathematical model would apply in each case.

1. A model rocket is launched. The table records its height above ground.

Time (s)	0	1	2	3	4	5	6
Height (m)	0	25	40	45	40	25	0

2. A technician counts the number of bacteria in a petri dish every hour for 6 h.

Time (h)	0	1	2	3	4	5	6
Bacteria Count	1500	2900	6100	12 400	25 100	49 800	100 500

3. A coach measures the velocity of air as a gymnast inhales and exhales after working out.

Time (s)	1.0	1.5	2.0	2.5	3.0	3.5	4.0	4.5	5.0
Velocity of Air (L/s)	1.75	1.24	0	−1.24	−1.75	−1.24	0	1.24	1.75

Time (s)	5.5	6.0	6.5	7.0	7.5	8.0	8.5	9.0
Velocity of Air (L/s)	1.24	0	−1.24	−1.75	−1.24	0	1.24	1.75

Think, Do, Discuss

1. (a) Draw and label a separate scatter plot for each situation.
   (b) Which situation can be modelled with an exponential relation? Justify your answer. Draw the curve of best fit and comment on how well the model fits the data.
   (c) Which situation can be modelled with a quadratic relation? Justify your answer. Draw the curve of best fit and comment on how well the model fits the data.
   (d) Which situation is neither exponential nor quadratic but is still nonlinear? Draw a curve of best fit to match the data points. How well does the curve fit the model?

2. Use your graphs from step 1 to answer these questions.
   (a) How high is the rocket after 4.5 s?
   (b) About how many bacteria should there be after 8 h?
   (c) What is the velocity of the air after 6.75 s? Is the air being inhaled or exhaled at this time? Explain.

Steps 3 to 6 refer to the gymnast's record of breathing.

3. (a) How long does it take for one complete cycle of inhaling and exhaling?
   (b) What is the maximum velocity of the air? What is the minimum velocity?
4. (a) What is the velocity of air for the gymnast after 13 s? after 16 s?
   (b) Explain how the graph was extended to extrapolate the required information.
5. (a) Describe the shape of the graph of the gymnast's breathing.
   (b) Explain why the shape of the curve is reasonable for this case.
6. As time goes on, the gymnast will relax. What changes would you expect to see in the graph?

Part 2: Repeating Functions

Look up at the moon on a clear night. Sometimes the moon is full and the night sky is bright. At other times, there is a new moon with no visible light and the sky is dark. The moon is said to wax from dark to bright and wane back to dark.

Fraction of the Moon Visible at Midnight
Days 1 to 66 of the Year 2000

Day of the Year	1	2	3	4	5	6	10	15	20	21
Fraction of Moon Visible	0.25	0.18	0.11	0.06	0.02	0.00	0.11	0.57	0.99	1.00

Day of the Year	25	30	35	40	45	50	55	60	65	66
Fraction of Moon Visible	0.80	0.32	0.02	0.14	0.64	1.00	0.77	0.31	0.01	0.00

Source: US Naval Observatory, Washington.

Think, Do, Discuss

1. (a) Draw and label a scatter plot of the data.
   (b) Draw the curve of best fit.
2. (a) Starting with day 1, how many days does it take for the shortest complete pattern of the graph to repeat?
   (b) Starting with day 6, how many days does the graph take to repeat?
   (c) On what other day could the graph begin and still repeat?

3. (a) Extend the pattern of the graph to include the 95th day of the new millennium. Was the phase of the moon closer to a full moon or a new moon? Explain.

   (b) Extend the graph to predict the fraction of the moon that was visible on the summer solstice, June 21. Was the moon waxing or waning? Explain.

Part 3: Properties of Repeating Functions

Graphs of periodic functions are self-replicating. That is, they repeat themselves over and over again. What are some other properties of periodic functions?

Think, Do, Discuss

1. Redraw the graph of the phases of the moon for the first three months of the year.
2. What is the maximum value of the curve? the minimum value? Explain the meaning of maximum and minimum in this case.
3. (a) Draw a straight, horizontal line through the graph that is halfway between the maximum and minimum values. This line is called the **axis of the curve** or **axis of the shape**. Write the equation of the axis of the curve using the maximum and minimum values.

   (b) The **amplitude** of a periodic function is the magnitude of the distance from this line to either the maximum or minimum value. How can the maximum and minimum values be used to calculate the amplitude?

   (c) Draw one complete cycle of the graph that begins on the line and ends on the line. Draw a different cycle that also begins and ends on the line. Explain how the two cycles are alike and not alike.

Focus 5.1

Key Ideas

- Repeating data forms a periodic function.
- A periodic function has a self-repeating graph.
- The **cycle** of a graph is the smallest complete repeating pattern of the graph.

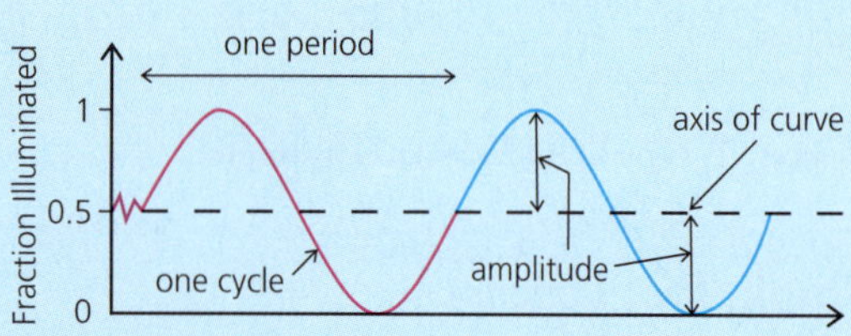

- The length of one cycle is called the **period.**
- The horizontal line that is halfway between the maximum and minimum values of a periodic curve is called the **axis of the curve.**
- The equation of the axis of the curve is

$$y = \frac{\text{maximum value} + \text{minimum value}}{2}$$

- The magnitude of the vertical distance from the axis of the curve to either the maximum or minimum value is called the **amplitude** of the function. The amplitude, a, is calculated as

$$a = \frac{\text{maximum value} - \text{minimum value}}{2}$$

Example 1

Determine whether each graph is periodic or not.

(a) tip of vibrating meter stick

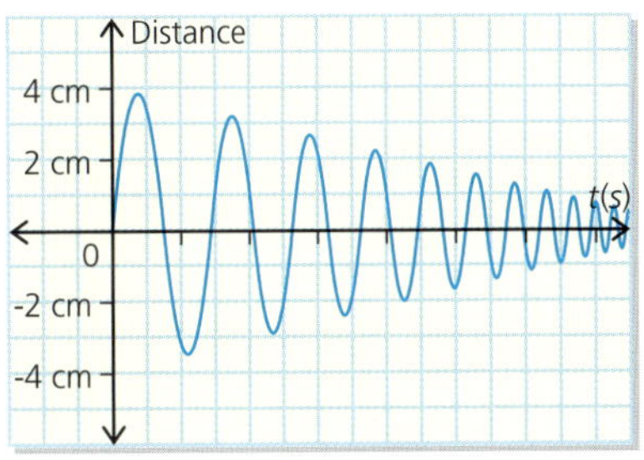

(b) movement of a piston in a combustion engine

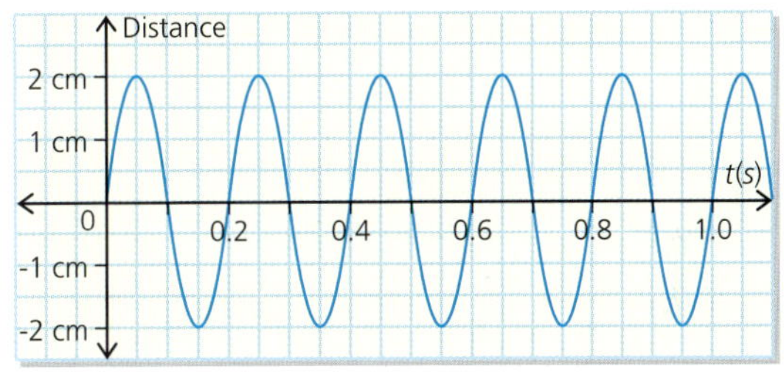

Solution

(a) The vibrating metre stick is not periodic because the graph does not repeat. The maximum and minimum values keep changing and it takes less and less time for the curve to complete one cycle.

(b) The movement of a piston is periodic because the graph repeats every 0.2 s and each cycle is exactly the same. The period is 0.2 s, the amplitude is 2 cm.

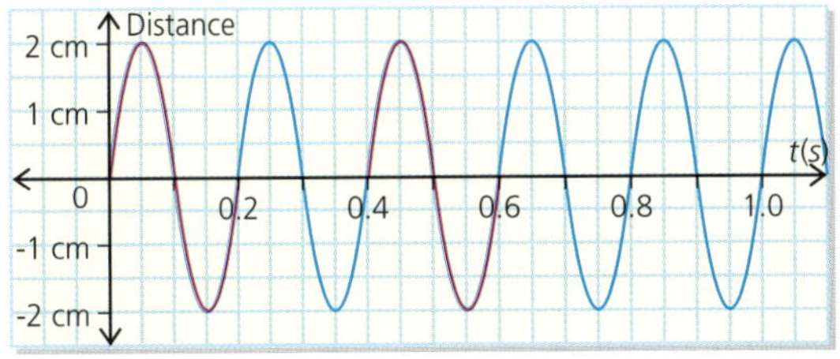

Example 2

The automatic dishwasher in a school cafeteria runs constantly through lunch. The graph shows the amount of water used as a function of time.

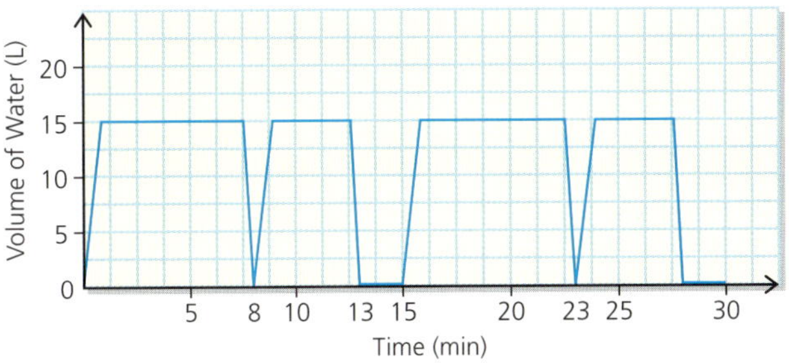

(a) Explain why the operation of the dishwasher is an example of a periodic function.

(b) What is the length of the period? What does one complete cycle mean in the context of the question?

(c) Extend the graph for one more complete cycle.

(d) How much water is used if the dishwasher runs through eight complete cycles?

Solution

(a) A periodic function has a repeating graph and each cycle is the same. The graph of the dishwasher repeats and each cycle is the same. This function is periodic.

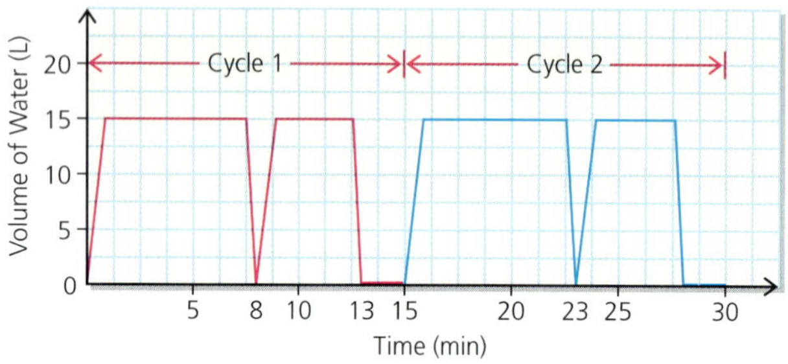

(b) The period is the length of one complete cycle. Calculate the period by subtracting the beginning time of a cycle from the ending time of a cycle.

$$15 - 0 = 15, \text{ or } 30 - 15 = 15$$

One complete cycle could mean an 8-min wash, followed by a 5-min rinse, followed by 2 min to unload and load dishes.

(c)

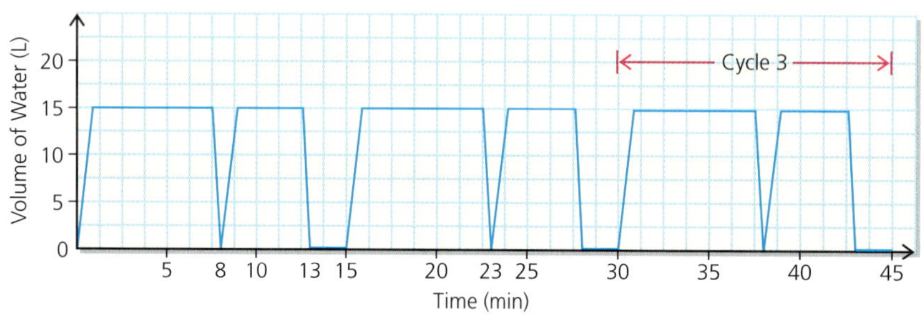

(d) The dishwasher uses 15 L to wash and another 15 L to rinse. Then eight cycles use $8(15 + 15) = 8(30)$. The washer uses 240 L.

Example 3

The Bay of Fundy, which is between New Brunswick and Nova Scotia, has the highest tides in the world. There can be no water on the beach at low tide, while at high tide the water covers the beach.

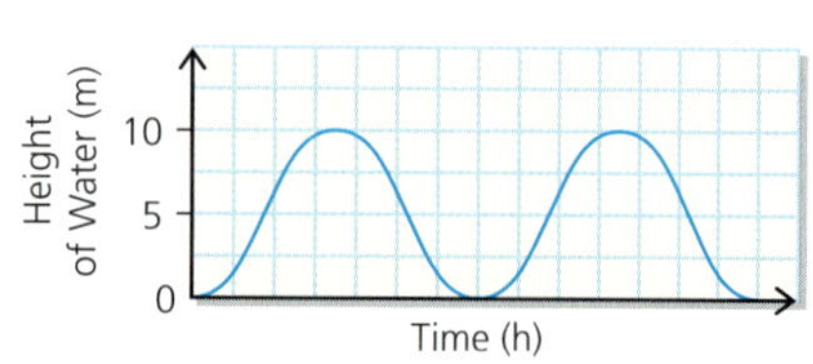

(a) Why can you use periodic functions to model the tides?

(b) What is the change in depth of water from low tide to high tide?

(c) Determine the equation of the axis of the curve.

(d) What is the amplitude of the curve?

Solution

(a) Tides resemble periodic functions because they repeat over a fixed interval of time.

(b) The water level at low tide is zero. The water level at high tide is 10 m. The change is 10 m. $10 - 0 = 10$

(c) The equation of the axis of the curve is $h = \frac{(10 + 0)}{2}$. Therefore, $h = 5$.

(d) The amplitude is

$$a = \frac{(10 - 0)}{2}$$
$$= 5$$

Practise, Apply, Solve 5.1

A

1. Match each situation with its graph. Describe what type of model best describes each situation.

(a) the height of a shot put

(b) a record of a boy's heartbeat

(c) the distance a pendulum travels from its rest position

(d) the cost of a taxi ride

(e) the growth in the number of bacteria

i.
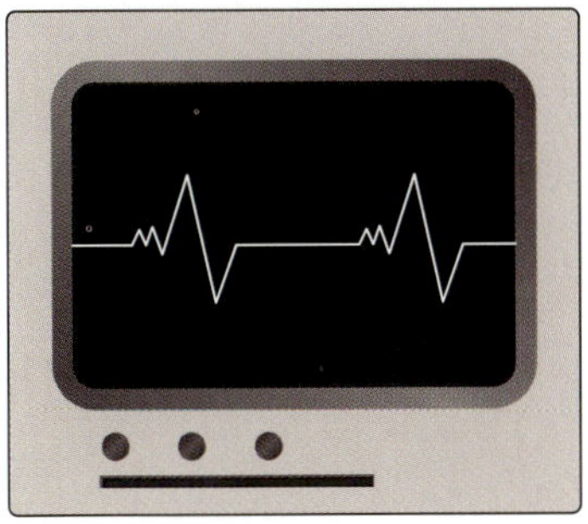

ii.
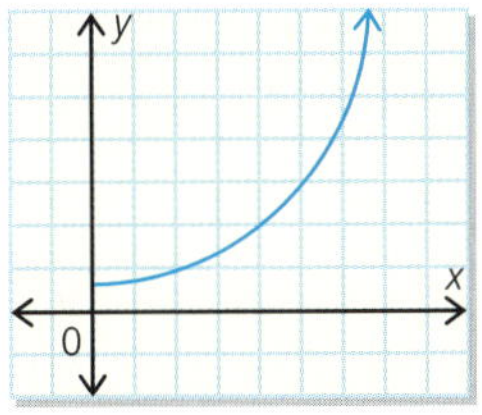

iii.
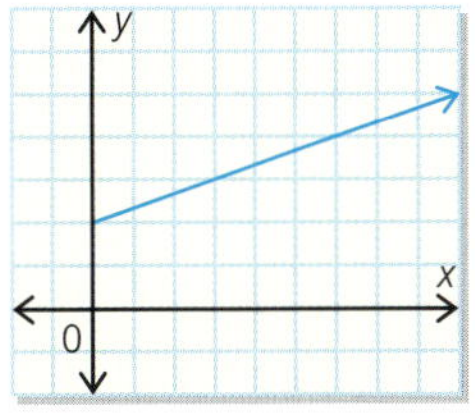

iv.
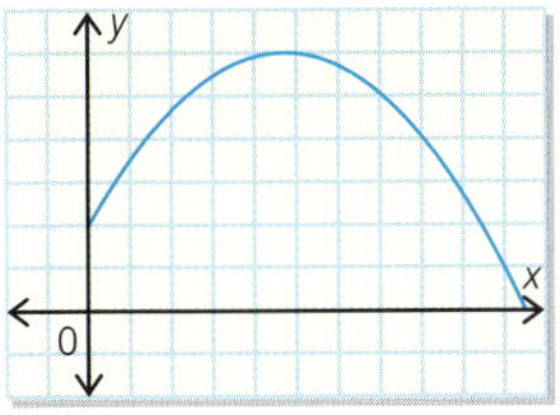

v.
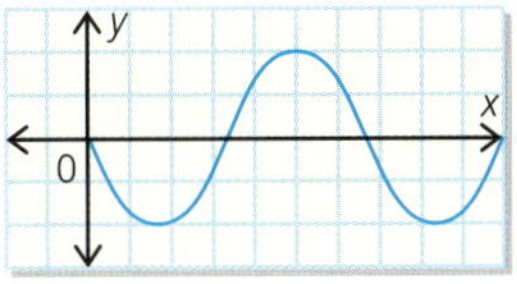

2. **Communication:** Explain why a periodic model can represent each situation.
   (a) the average monthly high temperature in Sudbury
   (b) the relationship between rabbit and coyote populations
   (c) the average monthly water level in Lake Superior
   (d) the position of the sun at sunrise in relation to due east
   (e) the vibration of a tuning fork

3. Determine whether each graph is periodic or not. Justify your answer.

(a)
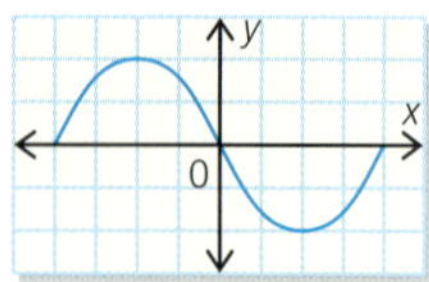

(b)
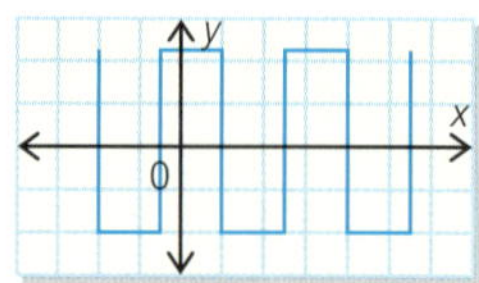

(c)
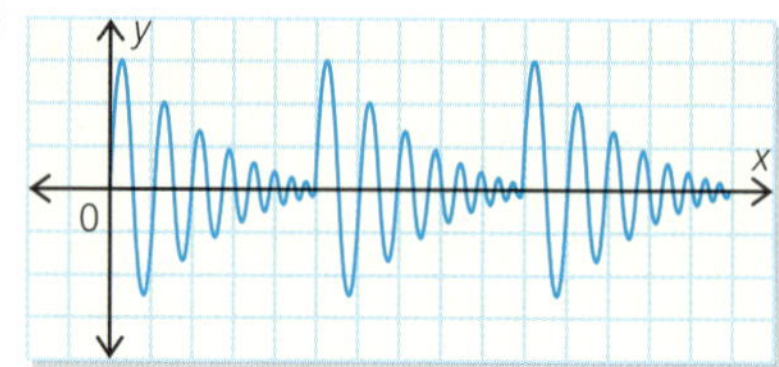

B

4. Nolan is jumping on a trampoline. The graph shows how high his feet are above the ground.
   (a) How long does it take for Nolan's jumping to become periodic? What is happening during these first few seconds?
   (b) How long is the period of the curve? Explain the meaning of period in the context of the problem.
   (c) Write an equation for the axis of the periodic portion of the curve.
   (d) What is the amplitude of the curve? Explain the meaning of amplitude in the context of the problem.

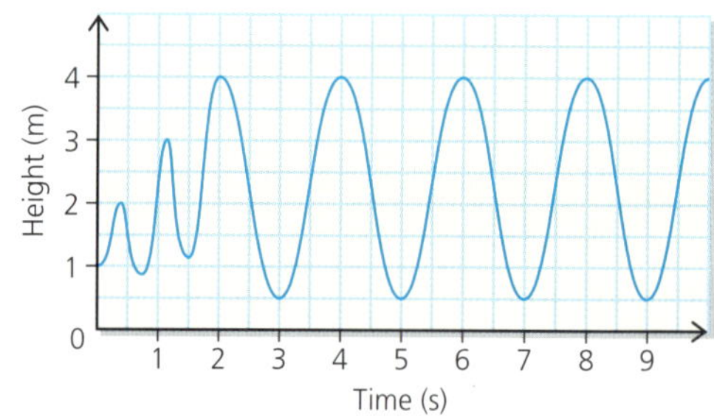

5. Sketch periodic graphs to satisfy the given properties.

Shape	Period	Amplitude	Equation of Axis	Number of Cycles
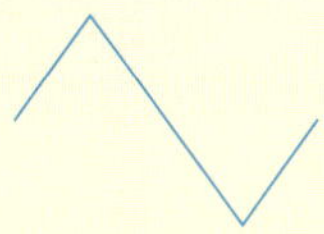	4	6	$y = 2$	2
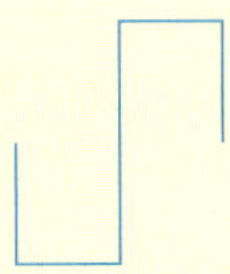	3	4	$y = 1$	3
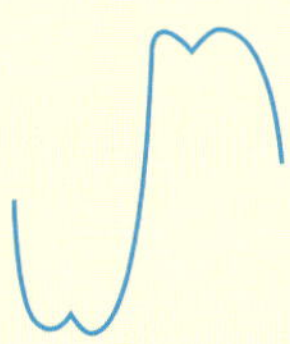	$\frac{1}{2}$	5	$y = -3$	2

6. State the period, amplitude, and the equation of the axis for each function.

(a)

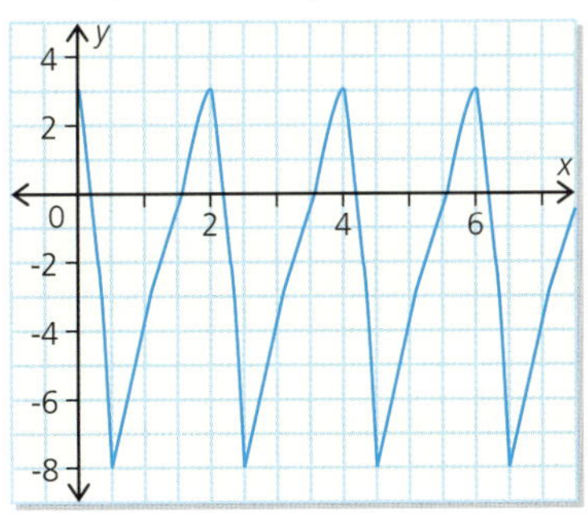

(b)

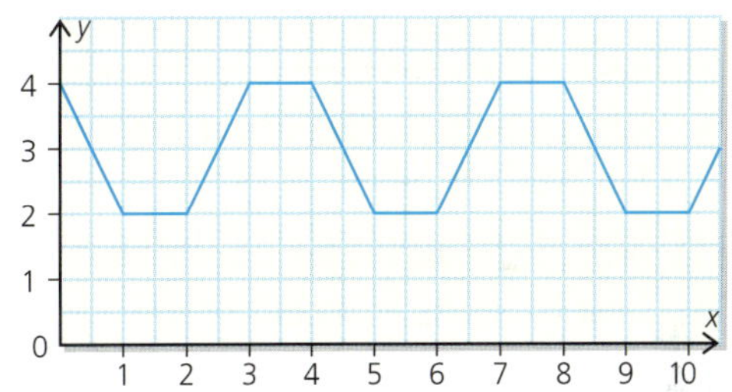

(c)

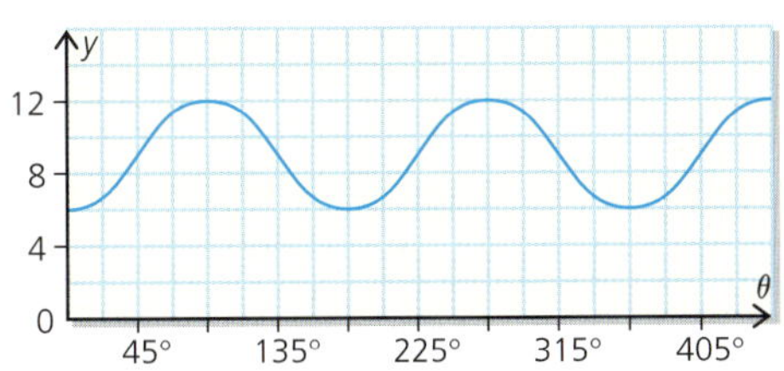

7. Draw an example of a periodic graph. Identify the properties of shape, period, amplitude, and axis of the shape. Show another student the graph and ask him or her to verify the four properties.

8. Create three differently shaped periodic graphs with amplitude 4 and period 5. Show two cycles of the graph.

9. **Application:** The graph shows the number of litres of water that a washing machine uses over several hours.

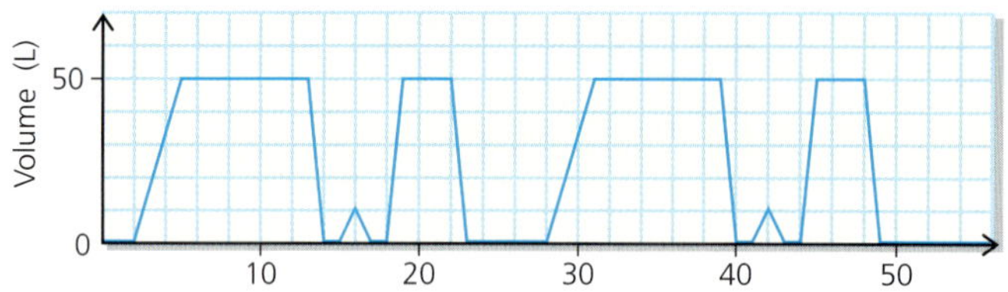

(a) There are several parts to each complete cycle of the graph. Explain what each part could mean in the context of "doing the laundry."

(b) What is the period of one complete cycle?

(c) What is the maximum volume of water used for each part of the cycle?

(d) What is the total volume of water used for one complete cycle?

(e) What volume of water represents the axis of the graph?

(f) State the amplitude of the graph.

10. **Knowledge and Understanding:** The graph shows John's height above the ground as a function of time as he rides a Ferris wheel.

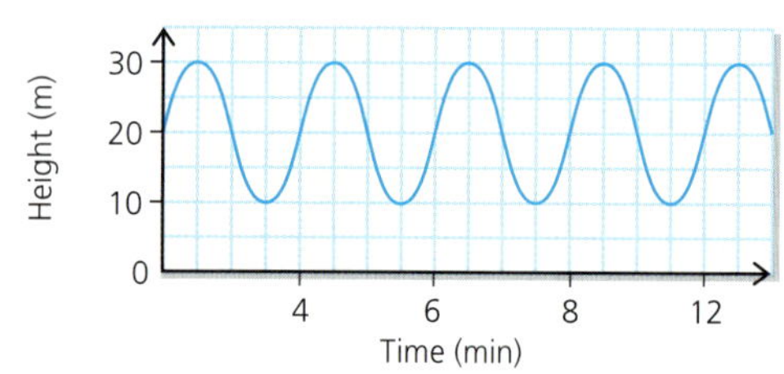

(a) State the maximum and minimum height of the ride.

(b) How long does the Ferris wheel take to make one complete revolution?

(c) What is the amplitude of the curve? How does this relate to the Ferris wheel?

(d) Determine the equation of the axis of the curve.

11. Each year, around February 18, swallows travel 12 000 km from Goya, Argentina, to San Juan, Capistrano, California. They arrive in Capistrano about March 19 and stay until about October 23. Then they leave for their month-long journey back to Goya. Explain why the migration of the swallows of Capistrano is an example of periodic phenomena.

12. **Thinking, Inquiry, Problem Solving:** A race car driver is qualifying on a 3.2 km track as shown. He tries to drive each lap exactly the same way, slowing down at the corners and accelerating through the straightaways.

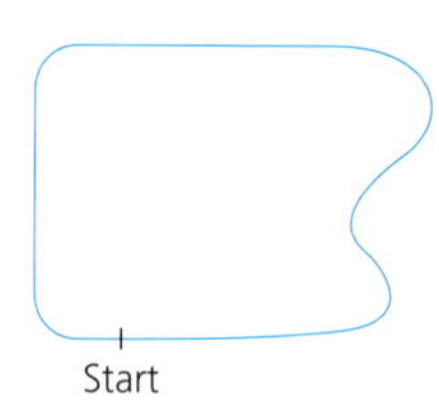

(a) Graph speed versus time for one lap around the track.

(b) Extend the graph to represent three laps around the track

(c) What does the period represent in this situation?

13. A traffic light changes colour over time as shown.

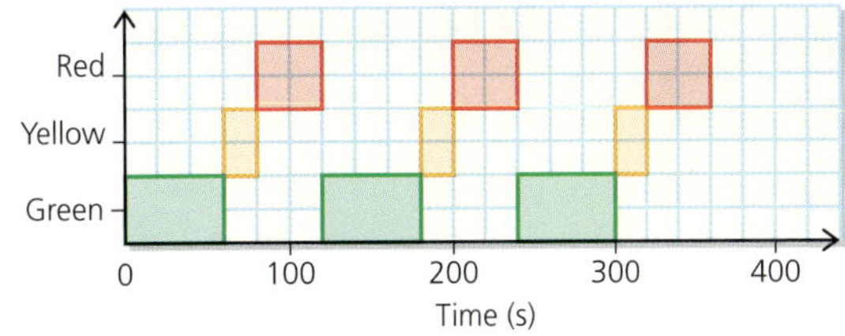

(a) Explain why the graph represents a periodic relation.

(b) Describe one complete cycle.

(c) What is the period of the graph?

(d) A 20-s advanced green arrow is added to the beginning of the cycle. What is the period now? Draw two full cycles of the graph.

14. **Check Your Understanding:** Write a definition for a periodic function. Use the concept of an independent variable and a dependent variable in your definition. Include an example of a periodic function and use your definition to explain why it is periodic.

The Chapter Problem—How Much Daylight?

In this section, you studied periodic phenomena. Apply what you learned to answer these questions about the Chapter Problem on page 404.

CP1. How can Naomi use the data in the table to schedule her guided fishing trips and maximize the possible catch within the fishing regulations on catch limits per day?

CP2. Explain why the data is periodic. What is the period of the data?

CP3. State the domain and range of the data.

CP4. (a) Graph average hours of daylight versus month. Refer to the start of the data as $t = 0$.

(b) What is the equation of the axis of the curve?

(c) What are the maximum and minimum values?

(d) What is the amplitude of the graph?

SKILL BUILDER 5.2

Understanding Angles

A triangle has three angles and no angle can be equal to or greater than 180°. Consider what happens when an angle is not part of a triangle but is in the *x*-*y* plane.

Angles and Their Location in the *x*-*y* Plane

An angle is formed when a ray is rotated about a fixed point called the **vertex**. The ray is called the **initial arm** at the beginning of the angle and the **terminal arm** at the end of the angle. Angles are often labelled with Greek letters, such as θ "theta," α "alpha," and β "beta."

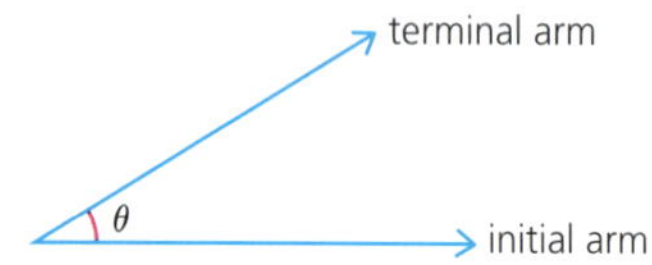

An angle θ is in **standard position** if the vertex of the angle is at the origin and the initial arm lies along the positive *x*-axis. The terminal arm can be anywhere on the arc of rotation.

Standard Form

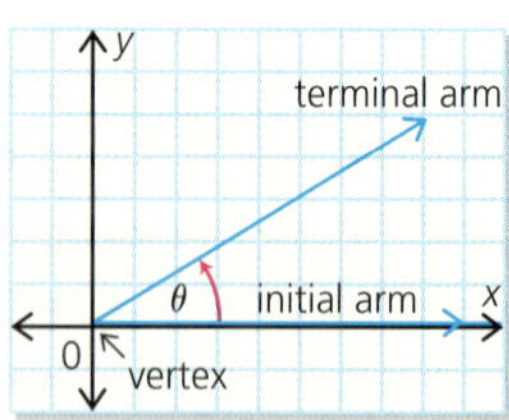

Not Standard Form

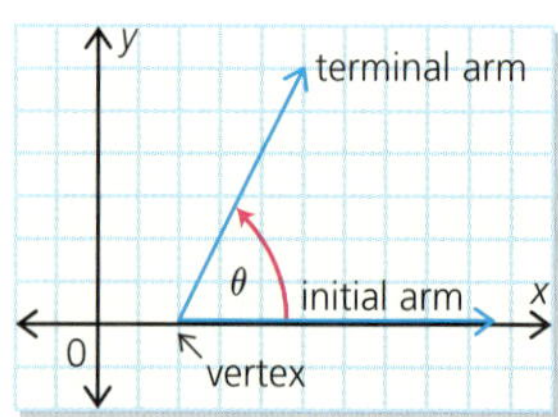

Not Standard Form

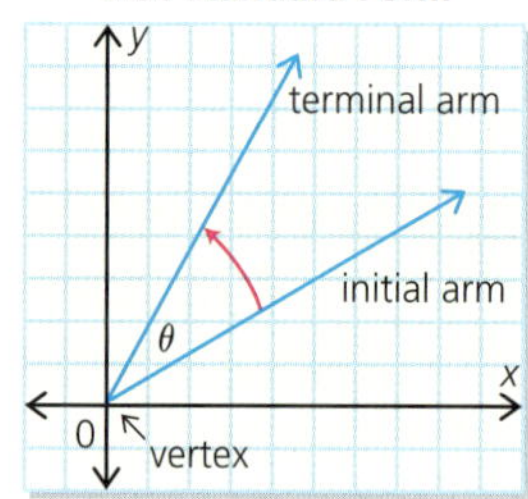

An angle can be positive or negative.

A **positive** angle is formed by a counter-clockwise rotation of the terminal arm.

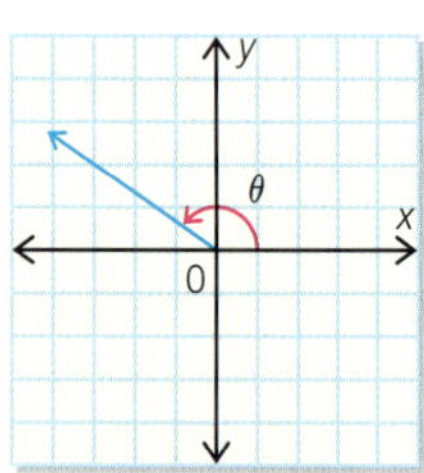

a positive angle

A **negative** angle is formed by a clockwise rotation of the terminal arm.

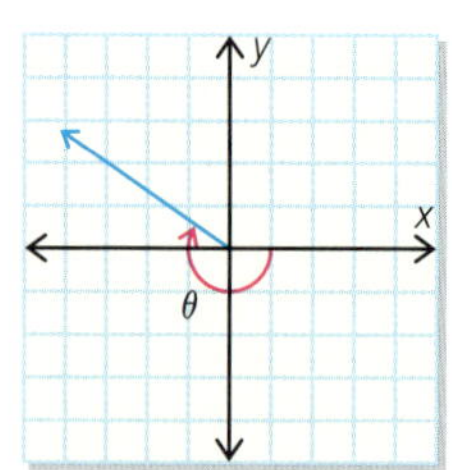

a negative angle

The *x*-*y* plane is divided into four **quadrants** by the *x*- and *y*-axes. If θ is a positive angle, then the terminal arm lies in

- quadrant I when $0° < \theta < 90°$
- quadrant II when $90° < \theta < 180°$
- quadrant III when $180° < \theta < 270°$
- quadrant IV when $270° < \theta < 360°$

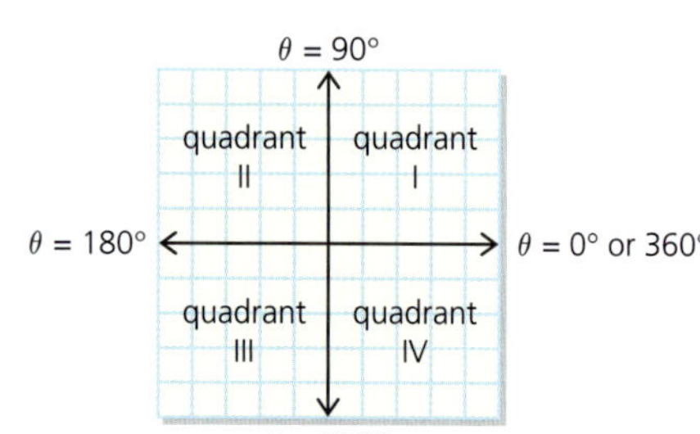

Let $P(x, y)$ be a point on the terminal arm of an angle in standard position. Since P can be anywhere in the x-y plane, the angle can terminate anywhere in the x-y plane.

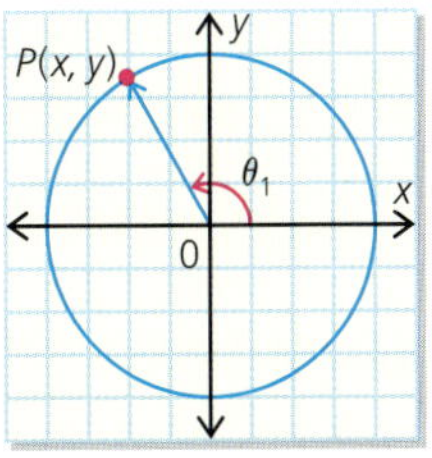

$90° < \theta_1 < 180°$
θ_1 terminates in quadrant II.

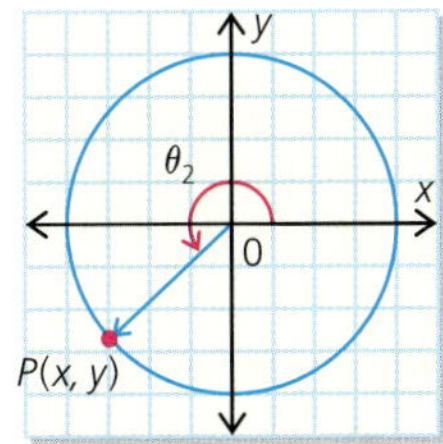

$180° < \theta_2 < 270°$
θ_2 terminates in quadrant III.

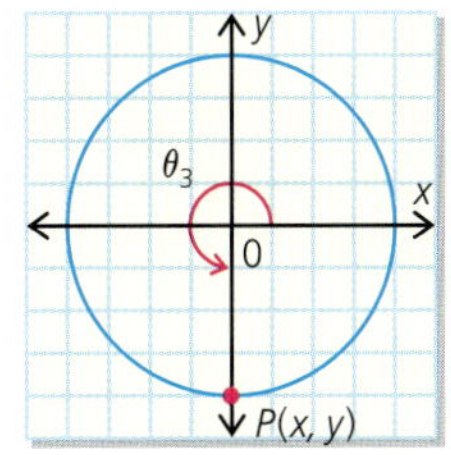

$P(x, y)$ lies in the negative y-axis.
$\theta_3 = 270°$

Coterminal angles share the same terminal arm and the same initial arm. As an example, here are four different angles with the same terminal arm and the same initial arm.

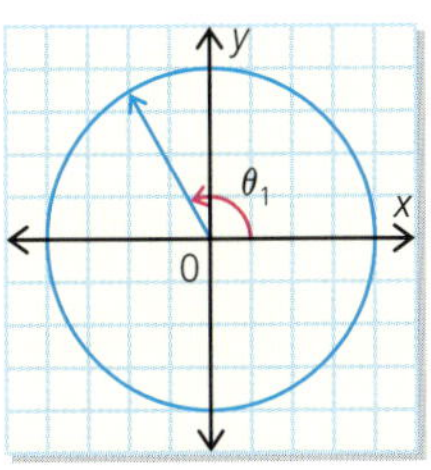

If $\theta_1 = \mathbf{120°}$, then

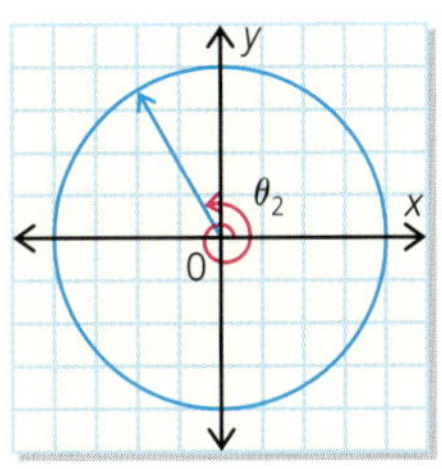

$\theta_2 = 360° + \mathbf{120°}$
$= 480°$

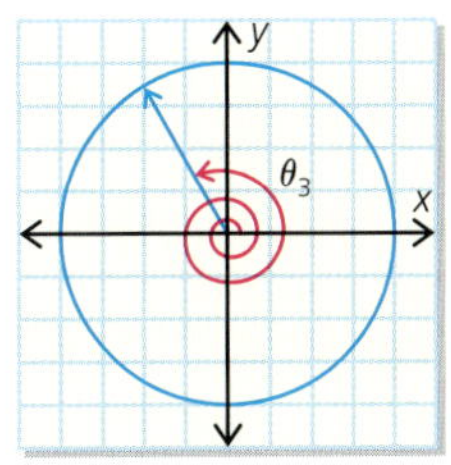

$\theta_3 = 720° + \mathbf{120°}$
$= 840°$

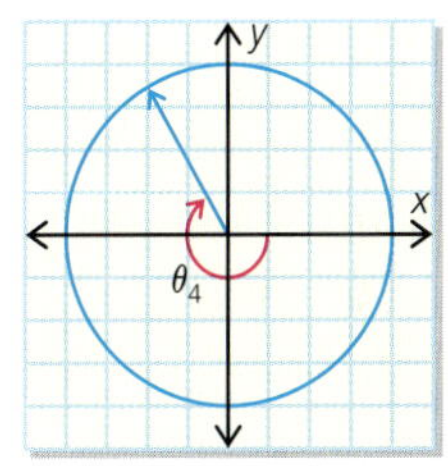

$\theta_4 = -360° + \mathbf{120°}$
$= -240°$

The **principal angle** is the angle between 0° and 360°. The coterminal angles of 480°, 840°, and −240° all share the same principal angle of 120°.

The **related acute angle** is the angle formed by the terminal arm of an angle in standard position and the x-axis. The related acute angle is always positive and lies between 0° and 90°. In this example, β represents the related acute angle for θ.

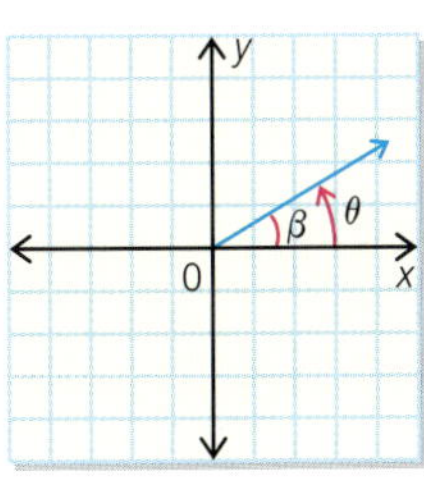

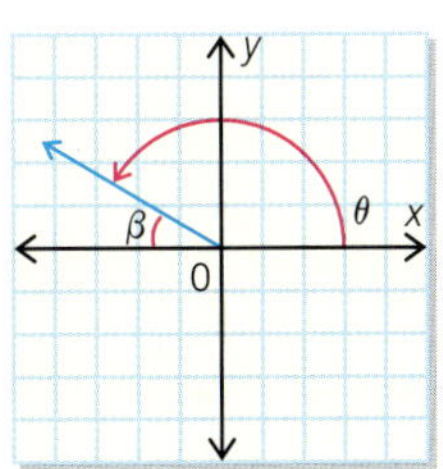

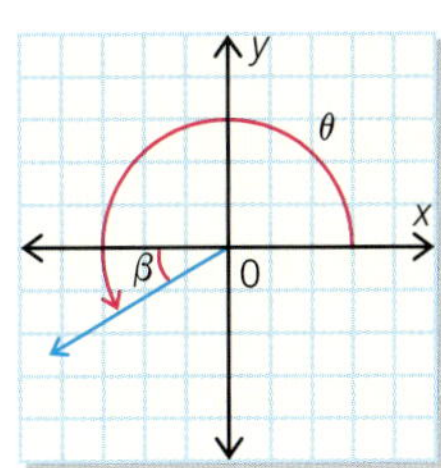

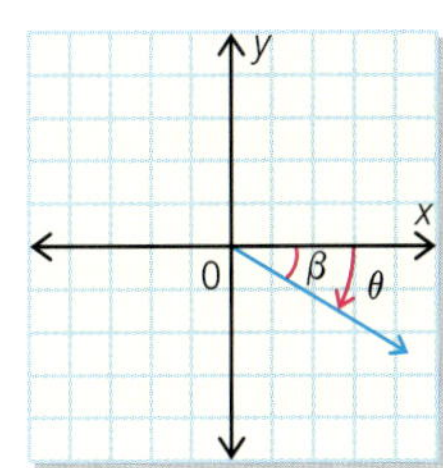

Example 1

Determine the principal angle and the related acute angle for $\theta = -225°$.

Solution

Sketch $\theta = -225°$ terminating in quadrant II. Label the principal angle and the related acute angle.

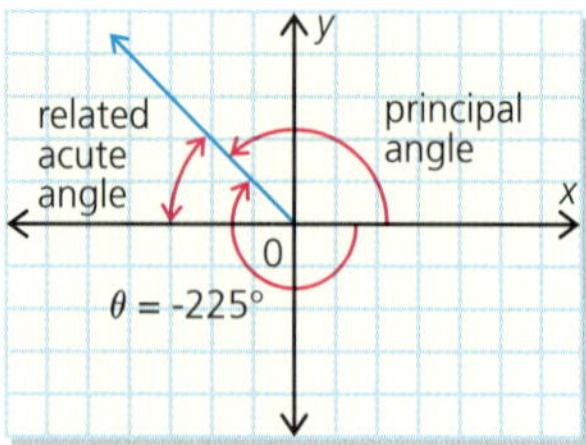

The principal angle is the smallest positive angle that is coterminal to $-225°$. In this case, $360° - 225° = 135°$. The related acute angle lies between the terminal arm and the x-axis. It is positive but less than $90°$. In this case, $|-225° - (-180°)| = 45°$. Or, using the principal angle, $180° - 135° = 45°$.

Example 2

Determine the next two consecutive positive coterminal angles and the first negative coterminal angle for $43°$.

Solution

Sketch each situation, showing the principal angle of $43°$.

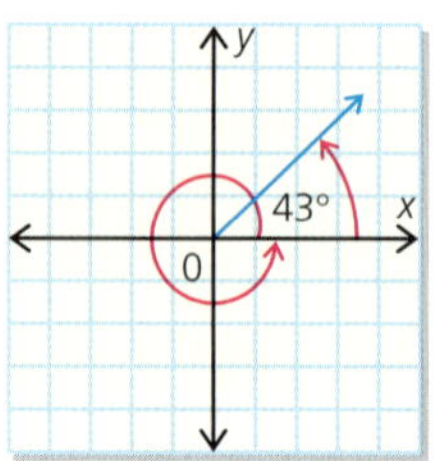

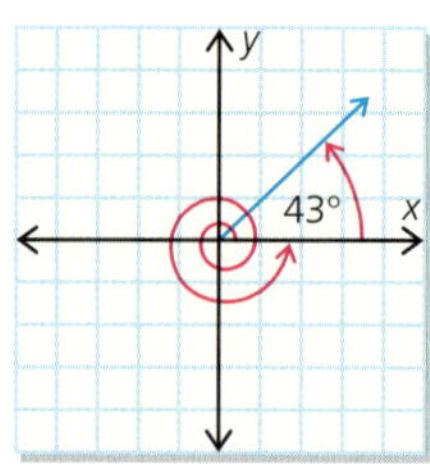

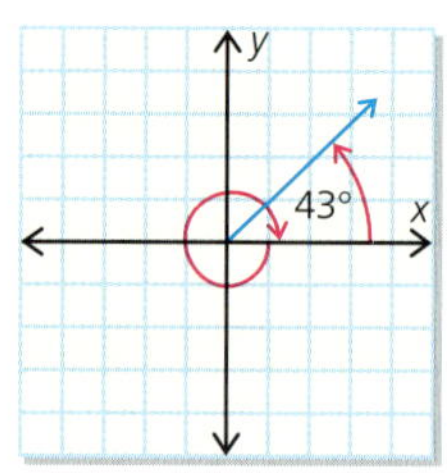

(a) The first positive coterminal angle for $43°$ is $360° + 43° = 403°$.

(b) The second coterminal angle is $360° + 360° + 43° = 763°$.

(c) The first negative coterminal angle is $-360° + 43° = -317°$.

Example 3

Point $P(-3, 4)$ is on the terminal arm of an angle in standard position.

(a) Sketch the principal angle, θ.

(b) Determine the value of the related acute angle to the nearest degree.

(c) What is the measure of θ to the nearest degree?

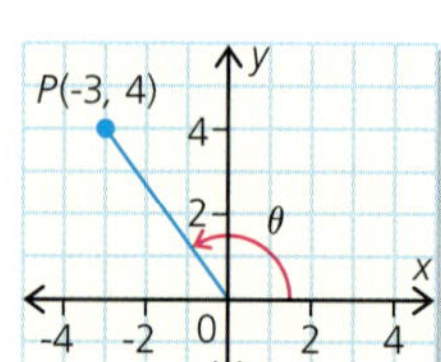

Solution

(a) Point $P(-3, 4)$ is in quadrant II, so the principal angle, θ, terminates in quadrant II.

(b) The related acute angle, β, is in the right triangle.

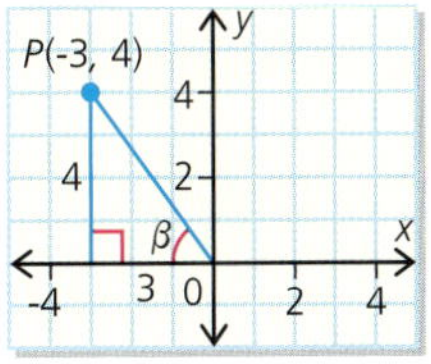

The opposite side and the adjacent side are known so the tangent ratio can be used.

$$\tan \beta = \frac{\text{opposite}}{\text{adjacent}} \qquad \text{Substitute known values.}$$

$$\tan \beta = \frac{4}{3}$$

$$\beta = \tan^{-1}\left(\frac{4}{3}\right)$$

$$\beta \doteq 53°$$

(c)

$$\begin{aligned}\theta &= 180° - \beta \\ &= 180° - 53° \\ &= 127°\end{aligned}$$

Focus 5.2

Key Ideas

- Angles can be located anywhere in the x-y plane.
- The x- and y-axes divide the x-y plane into four quadrants.
- The vertex of an angle in standard position is at the origin, and the initial arm of the angle is along the positive x-axis. The terminal arm of the angle can lie anywhere in the x-y plane.
- The initial arm of an angle rotates to its terminal position, either in a positive, counterclockwise direction or a negative, clockwise direction.
- The **principal angle** is the first positive angle less than 360°.
- The terminal arm of an angle defines an infinite number of coterminal angles. These can be positive or negative and are defined in terms of the principal angle. They are multiples of 360°; that is, $360°n$, where $n \in I$.
- The **related acute angle** is the positive angle between the terminal arm and the x-axis. It is always less than 90°.
- Any angle in standard position can be expressed in terms of its related acute angle.

Practise, Apply, Solve 5.2

A

1. Sketch each angle in standard position.

(a) 135° (b) 210° (c) 315° (d) −30°

(e) −225° (f) −330° (g) 150° (h) −120°

(i) 105° (j) −163° (k) 321° (l) −280°

2. Determine the related acute angle for each angle in question 1.

3. Sketch each angle in standard position.

(a) 379° (b) 491° (c) −545° (d) −640° (e) 593°

4. Determine whether each pair of angles is coterminal or not.

(a) 23°, 383° (b) 41°, 421° (c) −50°, 310°

(d) 38°, 398° (e) −19°, 390° (f) −41°, 319°

(g) 28°, −232° (h) −105°, −465° (i) −123°, 237°

(j) −190°, 180°

5. Calculate the next two positive coterminal angles.

(a) 132° (b) 275° (c) 305° (d) 73° (e) 270°

6. Calculate the next two negative coterminal angles.

(a) −53° (b) −138° (c) −299° (d) −180° (e) −192°

7. Match each angle with its diagram.

(a) 150° (b) −120° (c) 765° (d) −650°

(e) −220° (f) 290° (g) 560° (h) −380°

i.
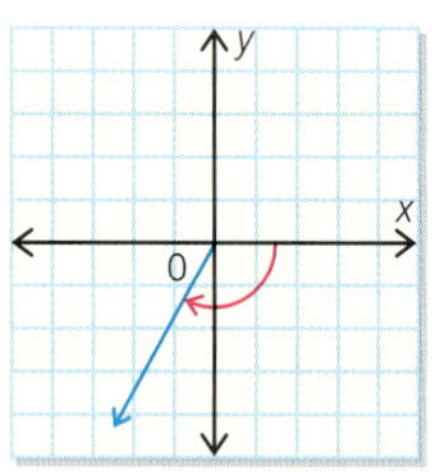

ii.
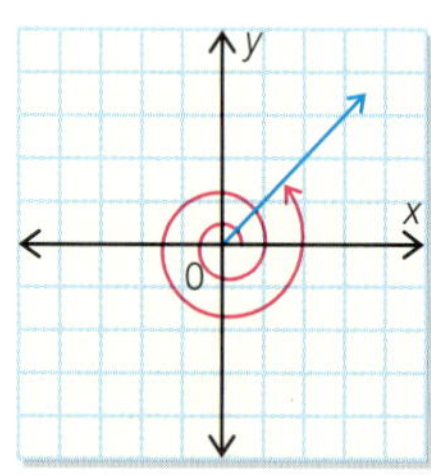

iii.
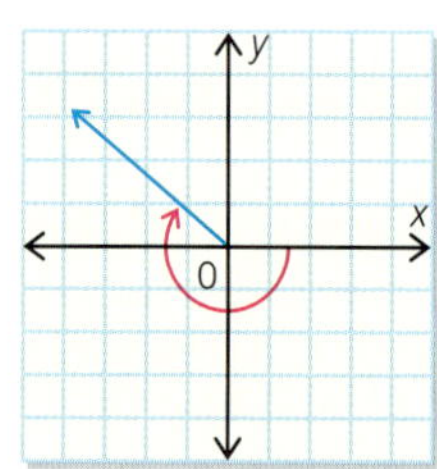

iv.
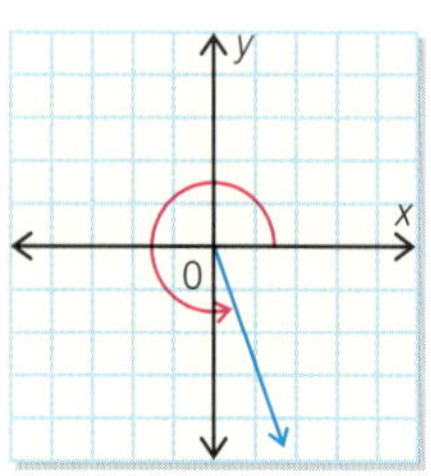

v.
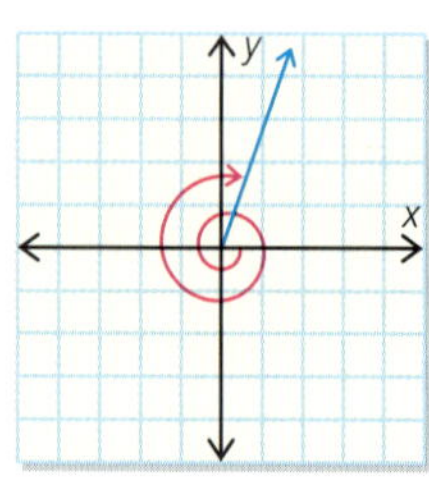

vi.
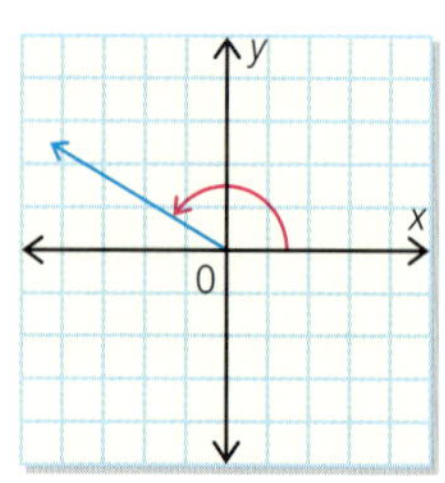

vii.

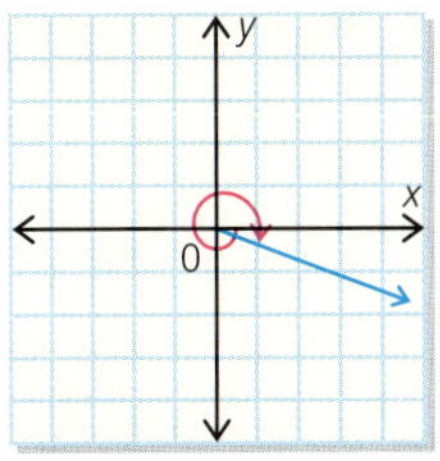

viii.

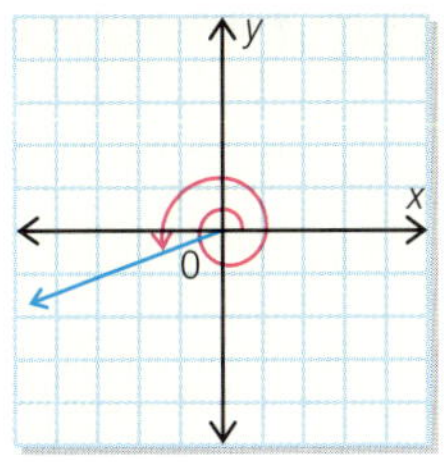

8. Determine the principal angle.

(a) $-187°$ (b) $410°$ (c) $-67°$ (d) $905°$

(e) $-282°$ (f) $-730°$ (g) $135°$ (h) $1249°$

9. State the principal angle for the given related acute angle and given quadrant.

(a) 24°, quadrant II (b) 35°, quadrant III

(c) 19°, quadrant IV (d) 63°, quadrant I

B

10. State all values of θ, where $n \in \mathbf{I}$ as shown.

(a) $\theta = 51° + 360°n, 4 \leq n \leq 6$ (b) $\theta = -71° + 360°n, -1 \leq n \leq 2$

(c) $\theta = -123° + 360°n, -2 \leq n \leq 0$ (d) $\theta = 195° + 360°n, 5 \leq n \leq 7$

11. Point $P(-9, 4)$ is on the terminal arm of an angle in standard position.

(a) Sketch the principal angle, θ.

(b) What is the measure of the related acute angle to the nearest degree?

(c) What is the measure of θ to the nearest degree?

12. Point $P(7, -24)$ is on the terminal arm of an angle in standard position.

(a) Sketch the principal angle, θ.

(b) What is the measure of the related acute angle to the nearest degree?

(c) What is the measure of θ to the nearest degree?

13. Point $P(-5, -3)$ is on the terminal arm of an angle, θ, in standard position.

(a) Sketch the principal angle, θ.

(b) What is the measure of the related acute angle to the nearest degree?

(c) What is the measure of θ to the nearest degree?

(d) What is the measure of the first negative coterminal angle?

14. **Check Your Understanding:** Point $P(-5, -9)$ is on the terminal arm of an angle θ in standard position. Explain the role of the right triangle and the related acute angle in determining the principal value of θ.

C

15. Point $P(-5, -8)$ is on the terminal arm of an angle, θ, in standard position. Determine all values of θ for $-540° \leq \theta \leq 270°$.

5.3 Trigonometric Functions

The London Eye is a Ferris wheel on the south bank of the Thames River in London, England. It is 135 m high, as high as a 40-storey building, and can carry a thousand riders at once.

Sarah and her younger brother Billy visited England and rode the London Eye. During the ride, Billy kept asking, "How high are we now?" Trigonometry can be used to model the height of Sarah and Billy at different times.

Part 1: Collecting Data for the Model

Follow these steps to gather data about Sarah and Billy's height as their capsule rotates.

Think, Do, Discuss

1. Draw a circle to model the London Eye. Centre the circle at the origin of the x- and y-axes. At the bottom of the circle, draw a horizontal line to represent the ground.
2. Draw points on the circle to indicate different positions on the ride. Choose points that are easy to estimate, such as points on the x-axis, the y-axis, and on the rotation angle halfway between the x- and y-axes in each quadrant.
   (a) How high above the ground will Sarah and Billy be when they are at the top of the ride? halfway to the top? Show these points on the diagram. What are the coordinates of each point? How can you use each coordinate to determine the height above the ground?
   (b) What acute angle corresponds to halfway between each quadrant? How many points on the ride will this angle help determine?
   (c) Draw right triangles to the circle that include each related acute angle.
   (d) How long is the hypotenuse of each right triangle? Explain your answer.
   (e) What trigonometric ratio combines the acute angle and the hypotenuse to give a second side of the triangle that represents vertical distance?
   (f) How could you use this second side length to determine Sarah and Billy's location on the London Eye with respect to the x-axis? How could you use this second side length to find their height above the ground?

(g) How many different positions on the Ferris wheel have you represented on your diagram? What principal angles in standard position do these positions represent? By using the angles in standard position, what assumption have you made about where Billy and Sarah get on the ride?

(h) Determine the height above the ground, to the nearest decimal, for each angle in standard position. Create a table in your notebook to record the data.

Angle of Rotation (degrees)									
Height Above Ground (m)									

Part 2: Extending the Primary Trigonometric Ratios Beyond Triangles

Suppose Sarah and Billy were on any Ferris wheel of radius r and their location on the wheel is $P(x, y)$, as shown. θ represents the angle of rotation.

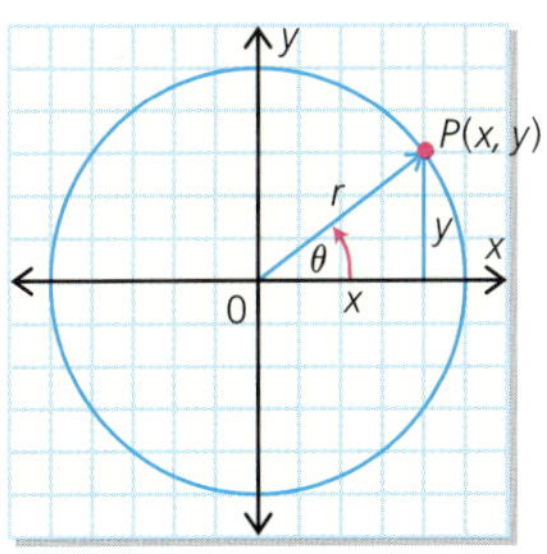

In quadrant I, the related acute angle and the angle in standard position are the same. In the right triangle for angle θ, the opposite side has length y and the adjacent side has length x. The hypotenuse of the right triangle is r, where $r = \sqrt{x^2 + y^2}$. The length r is always positive, and in quadrant I x and y are also positive.

Then,

$$\sin\theta = \frac{\text{OPP}}{\text{HYP}} = \frac{y}{r} \qquad \cos\theta = \frac{\text{ADJ}}{\text{HYP}} = \frac{x}{r} \qquad \tan\theta = \frac{\text{OPP}}{\text{ADJ}} = \frac{y}{x}$$

In general, any point, $P(x, y)$, on a circle of radius r can be expressed as a function of θ. In other words, as θ changes, corresponding changes occur in x and y, both in magnitude and sign.

Graphing the Sine and Cosine Functions

For any point $P(x, y)$ on the terminal arm of an angle θ in standard position, the trigonometric functions are defined as follows:

$$\sin\theta = \frac{y}{r},\ \cos\theta = \frac{x}{r},\text{ and }\tan\theta = \frac{y}{x},\ x \neq 0,\text{ where } r = \sqrt{x^2 + y^2}$$

Help Sarah determine her position anywhere on a Ferris wheel with respect to the centre of the wheel.

Think, Do, Discuss

1. (a) Which of the primary trigonometric functions best links the distance of a rider on the Ferris wheel from the horizontal diameter of the wheel, the size of the Ferris wheel, and the angle of rotation? Solve the equation for this distance in terms of the other two variables.

   (b) Complete the table to show this distance for the London Eye as a function of angular rotation. Use increments of 30° for one complete revolution.

Angle of Rotation	0°	30°	60°	90°	120°	...	...
Distance on Ferris Wheel from the Horizontal Diameter of the Wheel							

   (c) Graph the distance from the horizontal diameter versus the angle of rotation.

   (d) What is the greatest distance above the horizontal diameter? below the horizontal diameter? How can these values be used to determine the amplitude of the curve?

   (e) What is the period of the curve?

   (f) How would the graph look for two revolutions of the Ferris wheel? What type of model would describe the data? What equation models the distance from the horizontal diameter for any angle of rotation for the Ferris wheel?

   (g) What is Sarah and Billy's distance from the horizontal diameter when the ride has rotated 130°? 280°? 420°? 550°? What is their height above the ground for each of these positions of the Ferris wheel if it almost touches the ground?

   (h) Which coordinate is used to represent distance from the horizontal diameter?

   (i) Write an equation to model their height above the ground for any angle of rotation of the Ferris wheel.

2. (a) Which primary trigonometric function best links the distance of a rider from the vertical diameter of the Ferris wheel, the size of the wheel, and the angle of rotation? Solve the equation for this distance in terms of the other two variables.

   (b) Complete a table as in step 1(b) to show distance on the London Eye from the vertical diameter of the wheel for the given angles of rotation of the ride.

   (c) Graph the distance from the vertical diameter versus the angle of rotation.

   (d) What is the greatest horizontal distance to the right of the vertical diameter? to the left of the vertical diameter? How do these distances compare to those in step 1(d)? Explain. What is the amplitude of the curve?

   (e) What is the period of the curve?

   (f) Extend the graph to represent two revolutions of the Ferris wheel.

   (g) What is Sarah and Billy's distance from the vertical diameter when the ride has rotated 130°? 280°? 420°? 550°?

(h) Which coordinate is used to represent distance from the vertical diameter?

(i) Write an equation to model their distance from the vertical diameter at any angle of rotation.

3. (a) What x- and y-coordinates would represent Sarah and Billy's position on the London Eye at 130°? 280°? 420°? 550°? Show the coordinates on a diagram that models the Ferris wheel.

(b) What general coordinates would represent their position on this Ferris wheel for any angle of rotation θ? What coordinates would represent their position on any Ferris wheel or circular path of radius r?

(c) Draw a circle with $r = 1$ as a model of the Ferris wheel. Mark the exact coordinates of the eight positions you marked in Part 1, step 2(g) if the Ferris wheel had a radius of 1.

Graphing the Tangent Function

Sarah used the sine and cosine functions to locate her position anywhere on a circular ride. What does the graph of the tangent function look like for the Ferris wheel?

Think, Do, Discuss

1. (a) Use the data from step 1(b) and step 2(b) above to make a table to represent the tangent function. How does this data apply to the definition of the tangent function? At what points on the Ferris wheel will the tangent function not be defined? What will happen to the graph at these points?

(b) Graph the tangent function for one revolution of the Ferris wheel.

(c) What happens to the graph as the Ferris wheel starts its second revolution?

Part 3: Examining a Trigonometric Function in Terms of Time

Recall that Billy and Sarah's height on the Ferris wheel is a function of the angle of rotation of the wheel. How could you determine their position as a function of how long they are on the ride if the London Eye completes one revolution every 30 min?

Think, Do, Discuss

1. How many degrees does the Ferris wheel move every minute?
2. Assume Billy and Sarah start the ride halfway to its maximum height. Make a table that shows their height every 2 min for one revolution of the ride.
3. Graph height versus time.
4. Write an equation to model their height at any time, t.
5. What is their height at 17 min?

Part 4: Developing the CAST Rule

The trigonometric functions take on positive or negative signs, depending on in which quadrant the angle θ terminates. Using a circle and various points on the circumference of the circle, you can develop a rule for determining in which quadrants the primary trigonometric ratios are positive.

Think, Do, Discuss

1. Draw a circle and mark one point in each quadrant that is on the circumference.
2. What is the sign of the x-coordinate? the y-coordinate?
3. What is the sign of the radius?
4. Determine the sign of $\sin \theta$, $\cos \theta$, and $\tan \theta$ for each point.
5. In which quadrants is
   (a) the sine function positive?
   (b) the cosine function positive?
   (c) the tangent function positive?

Focus 5.3

Key Ideas

- The primary trigonometric functions for a point $P(x, y)$ on the terminal arm of angle θ in standard position are $\sin \theta = \frac{y}{r}$, $\cos \theta = \frac{x}{r}$, and $\tan \theta = \frac{y}{x}$, $x \neq 0$, where $r = \sqrt{x^2 + y^2}$.
- Any point $P(x, y)$ on a circle of radius r and rotated through angle θ can be expressed as the ordered pair $(r \cos \theta, r \sin \theta)$.
- For the unit circle, where $r = 1$, the rotation of point $P(x, y)$ through angle θ generates these graphs:

  The graph of $f(\theta) = \sin \theta$ is a function.
  The curve is sinusoidal.
  The graph is periodic.
  The period is 360°.
  The amplitude is 1.
  The maximum value of the curve is 1.
  The minimum value is -1.
  The zeros of the graph for this interval are 0°, 180°, and 360°.

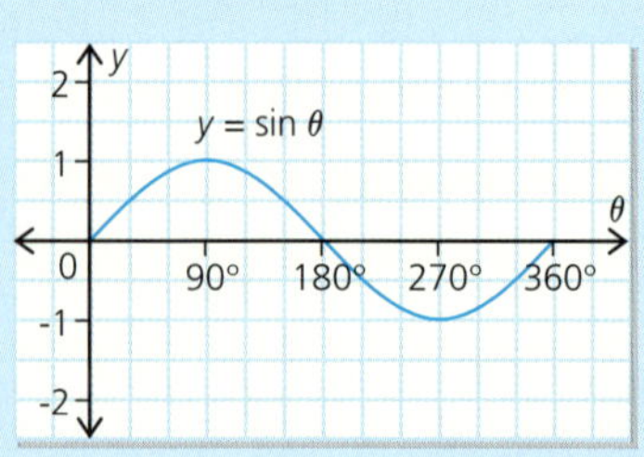

The graph of $f(\theta) = \cos\theta$ is a function.
The curve is sinusoidal.
The graph is periodic.
The period is 360°.
The amplitude is 1.
The maximum value of the curve is 1.
The minimum value is -1.
The zeros of the graph for this interval are 90° and 270°.

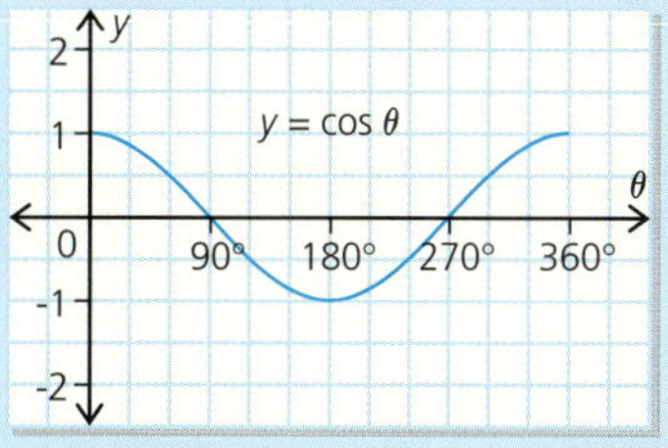

The graph of $f(\theta) = \tan\theta$ is a function.
The graph is periodic.
The period is 180°.
There is no maximum or minimum value.
The graph has asymptotes for this interval at $\theta = 90°$ and $\theta = 270°$.
The zeros of the graph for this interval are 0°, 180°, and 360°.

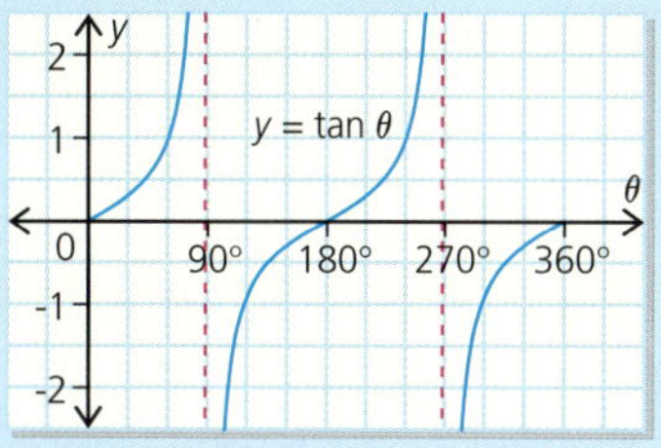

- A positive sign for trigonometric functions is summarized as the CAST rule: **C** indicates $\cos\theta$ is positive. **A** indicates all are positive. **S** indicates $\sin\theta$ is positive. **T** indicates $\tan\theta$ is positive.

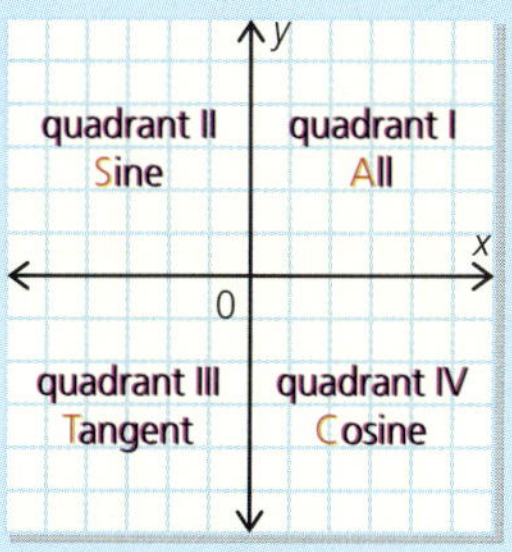

- The rotation of a point, in 45° increments, about the unit circle generates useful coordinates for graphing trigonometric functions.

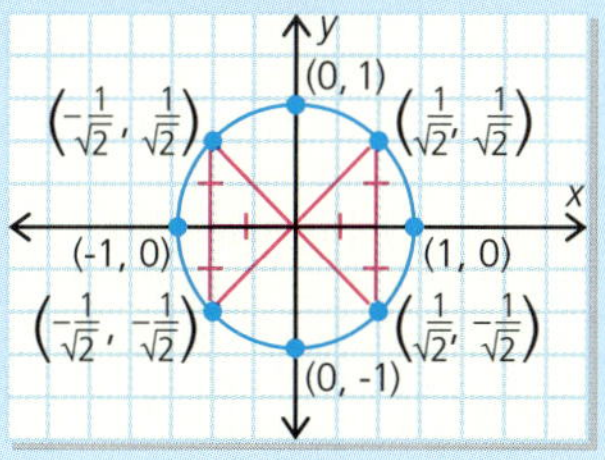

Example 1

(a) Construct a table for $y = \sin\theta$, where $-360° \le \theta \le 0°$. Use intervals of 45° and the unit circle to draw the graph by hand. Round to one decimal place.

(b) Extend the graph to include $0° \le \theta \le 720°$.

(c) State the location of all maximum and minimum values for $-360° \le \theta \le 720°$.

Solution

(a) Make a table in 45° increments using the unit circle.

θ	$-360°$	$-315°$	$-270°$	$-225°$	$-180°$	$-135°$	$-90°$	$-45°$	$0°$
$\sin\theta = \frac{y}{r}$	$\frac{0}{1} = 0$	$\frac{\left(\frac{1}{\sqrt{2}}\right)}{1} \doteq 0.7$	$\frac{1}{1} = 1$	$\frac{\left(\frac{1}{\sqrt{2}}\right)}{1} \doteq 0.7$	$\frac{0}{1} = 0$	$\frac{-\left(\frac{1}{\sqrt{2}}\right)}{1} \doteq -0.7$	$-\frac{1}{1} = -1$	$\frac{-\left(\frac{1}{\sqrt{2}}\right)}{1} \doteq -0.7$	$\frac{0}{1} = 0$

Draw the graph.

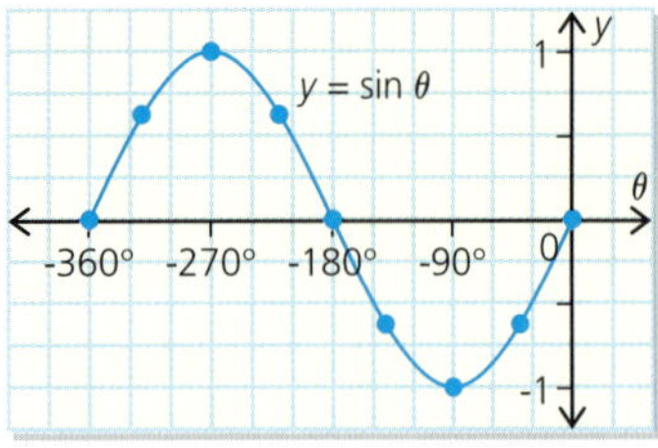

(b) The graph is sinusoidal and has a period of 360°. Extend the pattern to 720°.

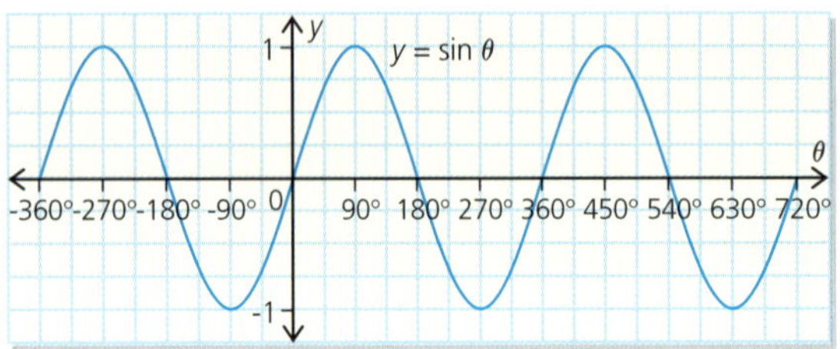

(c) The maximum values are at $-270°$, $90°$, and $450°$. The minimum values are at $-90°$, $270°$, and $630°$. These can be read directly from the graph.

Example 2

Point $P(3, -4)$ is on the terminal arm of an angle in standard position.

(a) What are the values of the primary trigonometric functions?

(b) What is the measure of the principal angle θ to the nearest degree?

Solution

(a) Draw a sketch.

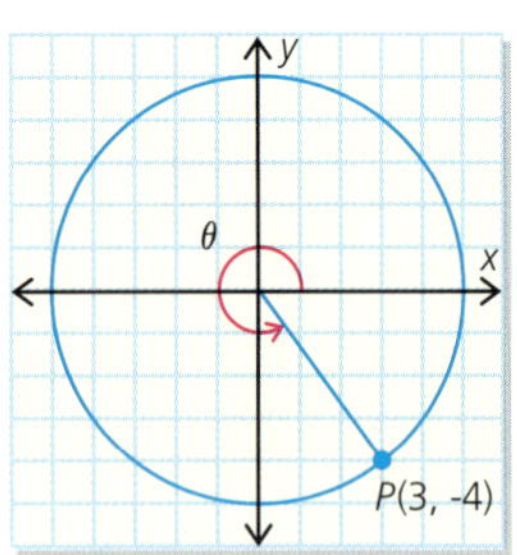

Determine the values of x, y, and r.

$$x = 3,\ y = -4, \text{ and } r = \sqrt{(3)^2 + (-4)^2}$$
$$= 5$$

Using these values, then

$$\sin\theta = \frac{y}{r} = -\frac{4}{5} \qquad \cos\theta = \frac{x}{r} = \frac{3}{5} \qquad \tan\theta = \frac{y}{x} \doteq -\frac{4}{3}$$

(b) To evaluate θ, select any one of the primary trigonometric functions and solve for θ. Using $\sin\theta = -\frac{4}{5}$ gives,

$$\theta = \sin^{-1}\left(-\frac{4}{5}\right)$$
$$\theta \doteq -53°$$

From the sketch, θ is clearly not 53°. This angle is the related acute angle. In this case, $\theta = 360° - 53°$ or 307°.

Example 3

For $\tan \theta = -\frac{7}{24}$, where $0° \leq \theta \leq 360°$,

(a) in which quadrant is it possible for θ to terminate?

(b) determine the other primary trigonometric functions for θ

(c) evaluate θ to the nearest degree

Solution

(a) Since $\tan \theta = \frac{y}{x}$ and $\tan \theta = -\frac{7}{24}$, then $\frac{y}{x} = -\frac{7}{24}$.

There are two possibilities: $x = 24$ and $y = -7$, or $x = -24$ and $y = 7$.

For the ordered pair $(24, -7)$, the angle terminates in quadrant IV.

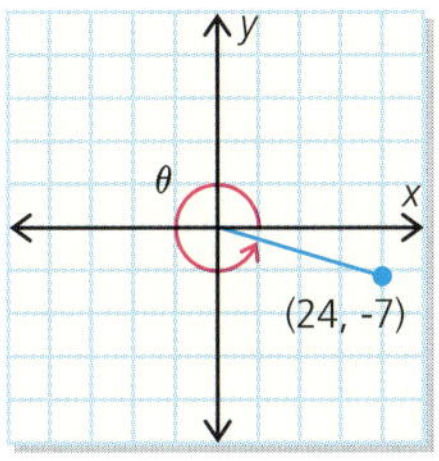

For the ordered pair $(-24, 7)$, the angle terminates in quadrant II.

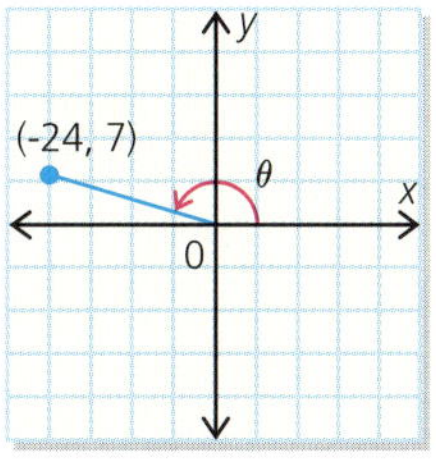

(b) For $(x, y) = (24, -7)$,

$$r = \sqrt{(24)^2 + (-7)^2} = \sqrt{576 + 49} = 25$$

$$\sin \theta = \frac{y}{r} = -\frac{7}{25} \quad \text{and} \quad \cos \theta = \frac{x}{r} = \frac{24}{25}$$

For $(x, y) = (-24, 7)$,

$$r = \sqrt{(-24)^2 + (7)^2} = \sqrt{576 + 49} = 25$$

$$\sin \theta = \frac{y}{r} = \frac{7}{25} \quad \text{and} \quad \cos \theta = \frac{x}{r} = -\frac{24}{25}$$

The solutions for both points can be combined and written in the simplified form

$$\sin \theta = \pm\frac{7}{25} \quad \text{and} \quad \cos \theta = \pm\frac{24}{25}.$$

(c) Select any one of the trigonometric functions to determine the measure of θ. Using $\sin \theta = \frac{7}{25}$, then $\theta = \sin^{-1}\left(\frac{7}{25}\right)$ or about 16°.

Clearly, 16° is not in quadrant II or in quadrant IV.
16° is the related acute angle.

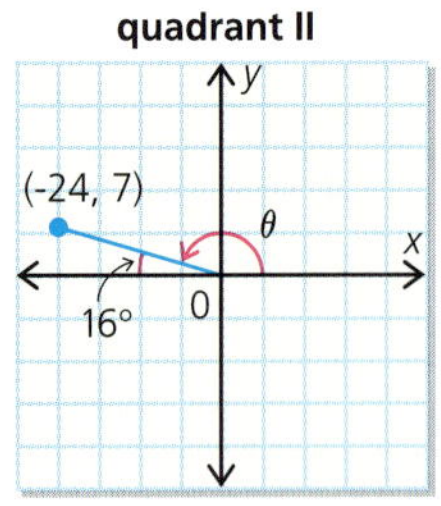

Then, for $0° \le \theta \le 360°$,

$$\begin{aligned}\theta &= 180° - 16° \\ &= 164°\end{aligned}$$

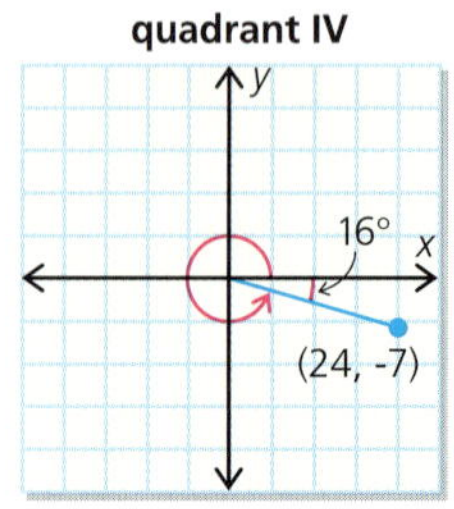

Then, for $0° \le \theta \le 360°$,

$$\begin{aligned}\theta &= 360° - 16° \\ &= 344°\end{aligned}$$

Example 4

The height, h, of a basket on a water wheel at time t is given by $h(t) = \sin{(6t)°}$, where t is in seconds and h is in metres.

(a) How high is the basket at 14 s?

(b) When will the basket first be 0.5 m under water?

Solution

(a) The values of h and t can be interpolated from a graph. Prepare a table. In this case, 5-s intervals were used, although the interval size could be different.

***t* (seconds)**	0	5	10	15	20	25	30	35	40	45	50	55	60
(6*t*)°	0°	30°	60°	90°	120°	150°	180°	210°	240°	270°	300°	330°	360°
***h*(*t*) = sin (6*t*)° (metres)**	0	0.5	0.87	1	0.87	0.5	0	−0.5	−0.87	−1	−0.87	−0.5	0

Interpolating from the graph gives a value of about 0.9 m, as shown.

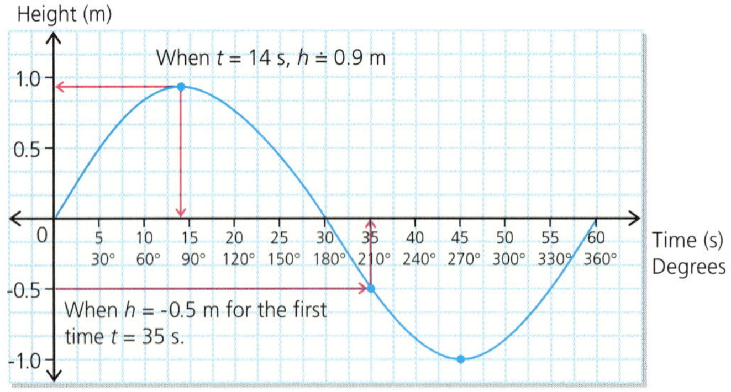

The question could also be answered by substituting into the equation.

Then,

$$\begin{aligned} h(14) &= \sin (6 \times 14)^\circ \\ &= \sin 84^\circ \\ &\doteq 0.995 \end{aligned}$$

Substitution gives a more accurate answer in this case. At 14 s, the height is almost 1 m.

(b) A height of 0.5 m under water corresponds to a height of -0.5 m in the model. Therefore,

$$h(t) = \sin (6t)^\circ$$

$$-0.5 = \sin (6t)^\circ \qquad \text{Interpolation shows that } \sin 210^\circ = -0.5.$$

The basket will be 0.5 m under water for the first time at 35 s.

Practise, Apply, Solve 5.3

A

1. Point $P(x, y)$ is on the terminal arm of an angle θ in standard position. It could be anywhere on the highlighted part of the unit circle as shown. Match each unit circle to its graph of $y = \sin \theta$.

(a)
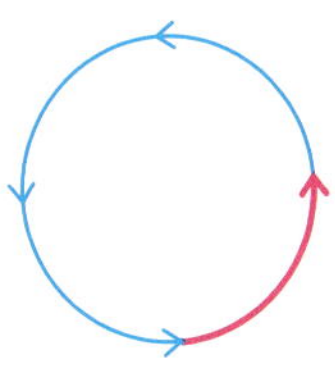

i.
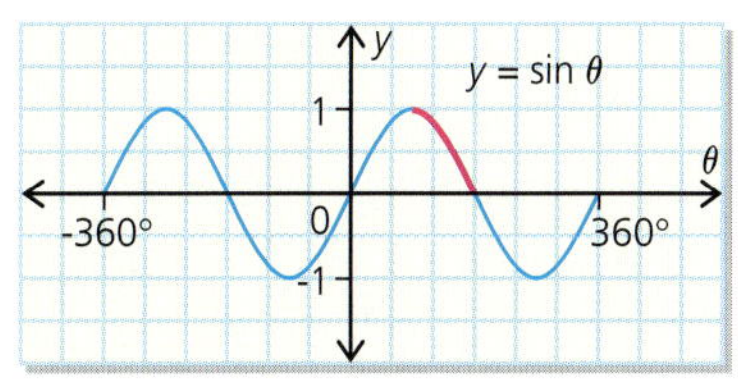

(b)
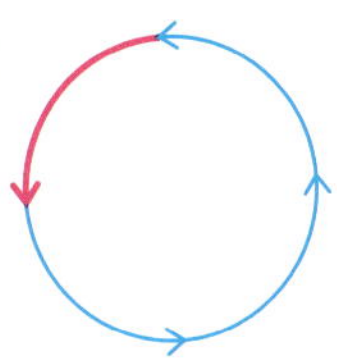

ii.
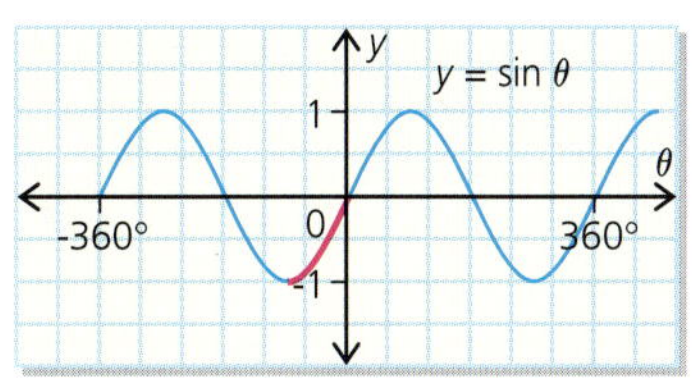

(c)
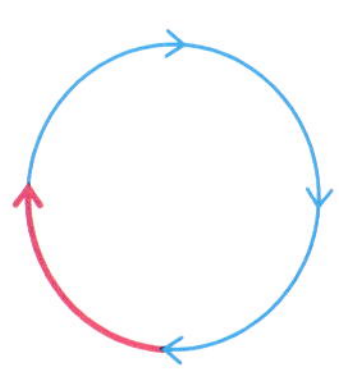

iii.
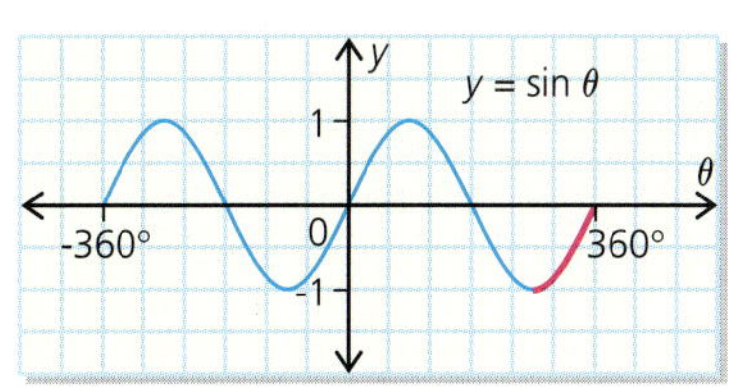

(d)
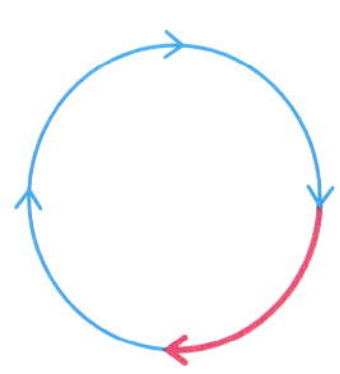

iv.
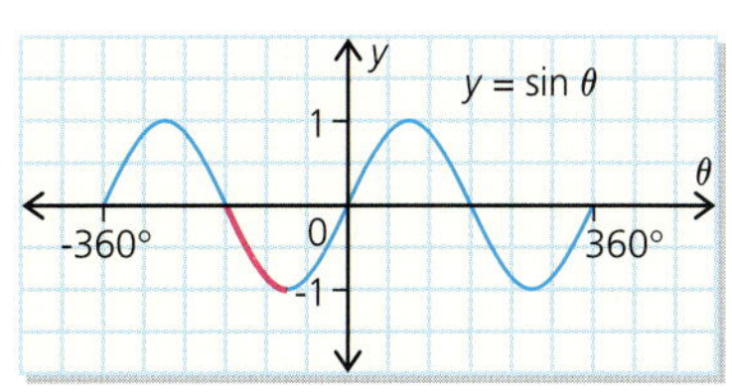

2. Repeat question 1 for the graph of $y = \cos\theta$.

(a)

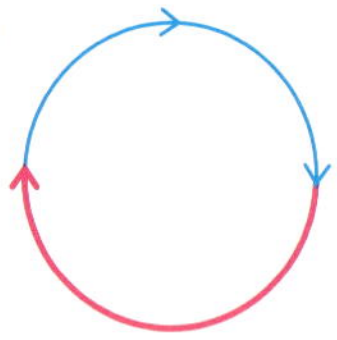

i.

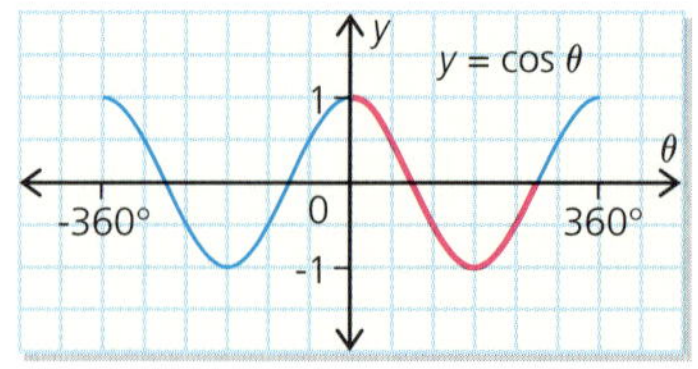

(b)

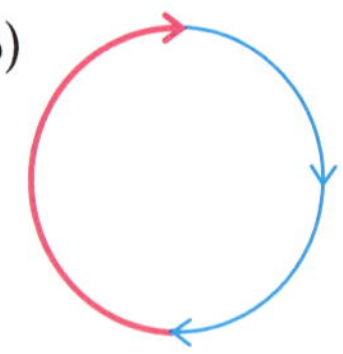

ii.

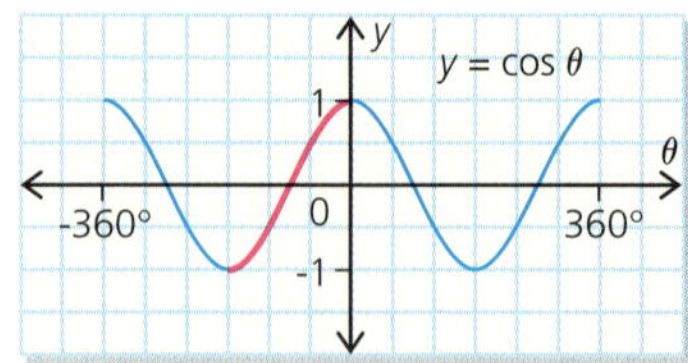

(c)

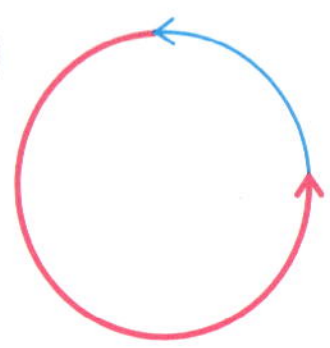

iii.

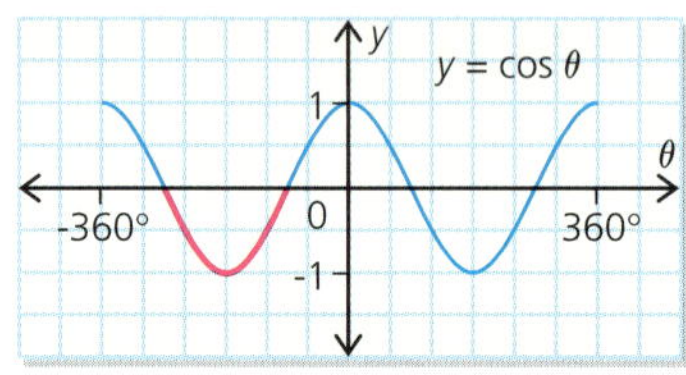

(d)

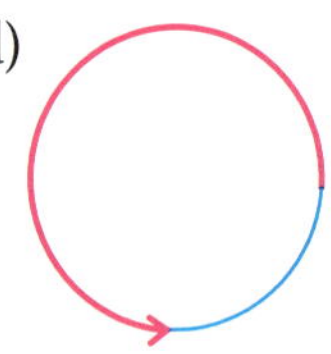

iv.

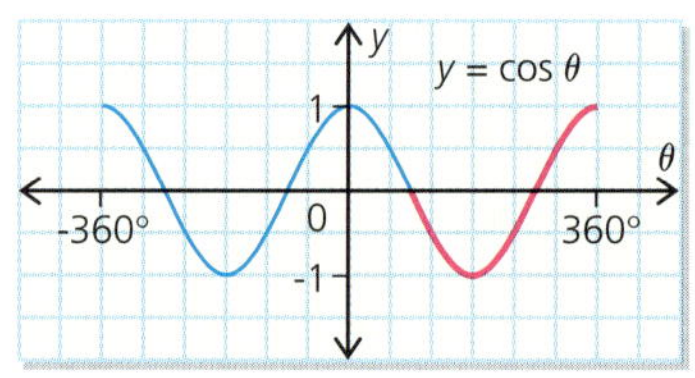

3. Repeat question 1 for the graph of $y = \tan\theta$.

(a)

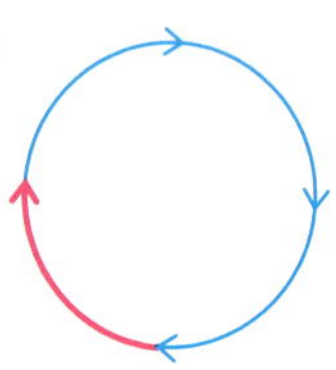

i.

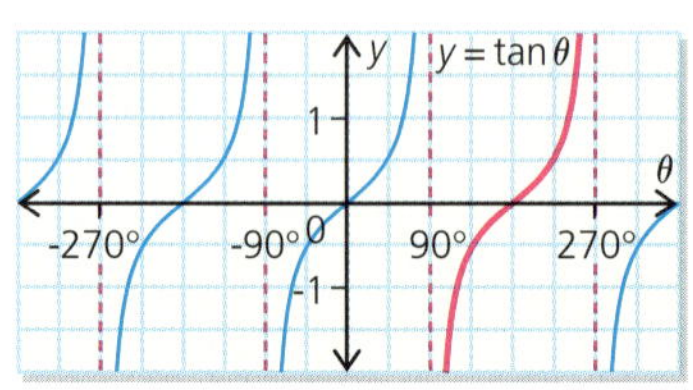

(b)

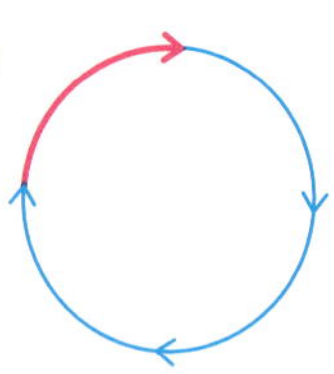

ii.

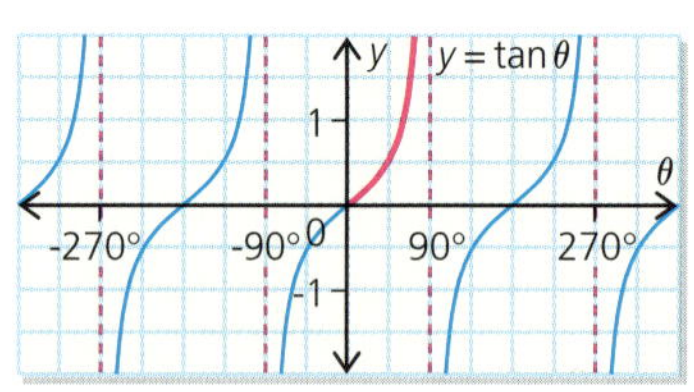

(c)

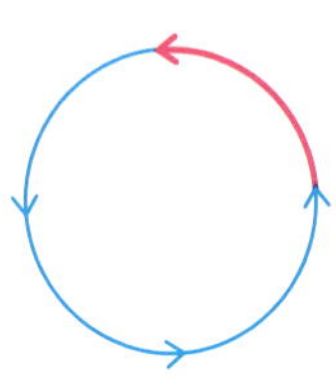

iii.

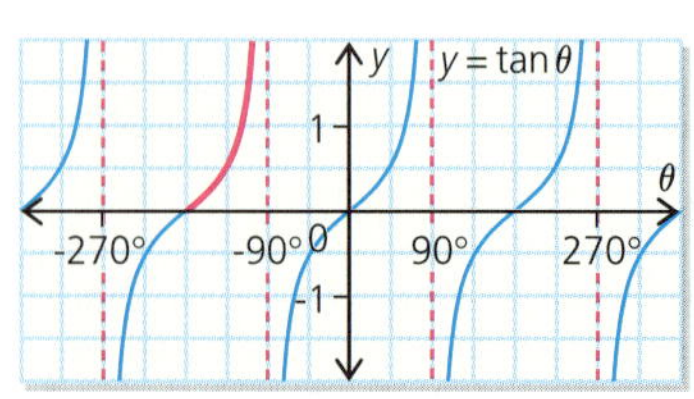

(d)

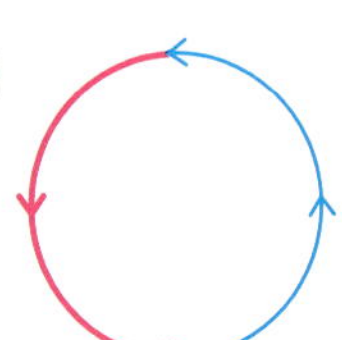

iv.

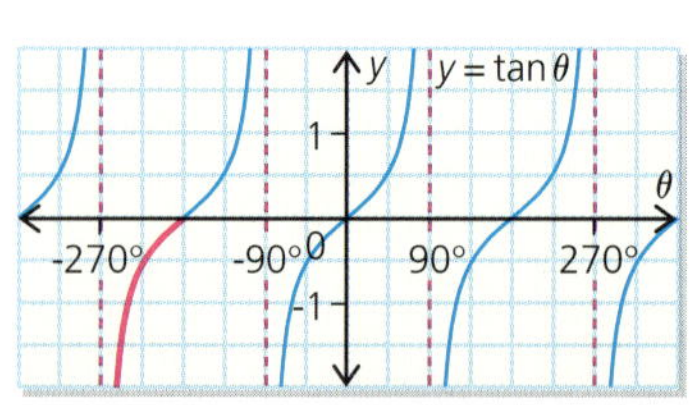

4. Use the CAST rule to state the sign of each value. Check using a calculator.

(a) tan 15° (b) sin 120° (c) cos 135° (d) tan 110°

(e) cos 205° (f) tan (−15°) (g) cos 120° (h) sin (−45°)

5. Determine the values of sin θ, cos θ, and tan θ at each point $P(x, y)$ on the terminal arm of an angle θ in standard position.

(a) (−3, −4) (b) (3, 4) (c) (5, 12) (d) (−12, 5)

(e) (7, −24) (f) (−7, 24) (g) (0, −1) (h) (−1, 0)

6. Each point is on the terminal arm of an angle θ in standard position. Find the principal value of θ to the nearest degree.

(a) (5, 11) (b) (9, −2) (c) (−4, −7) (d) (−5, 9)

B

7. Convert each point, $P(x, y)$, to the ordered pair $P(r\cos\theta, r\sin\theta)$. Round all values of r to one decimal place and all values of θ to the nearest degree.

(a) (4, 6) (b) (−3, 7) (c) (10, −23)

8. **Knowledge and Understanding:** Point (−3, −4) is on the terminal arm of an angle α (alpha) in standard position. Verify that $(\sin\alpha)^2 + (\cos\alpha)^2 = 1$.

9. Determine sin θ to three decimal places when $\tan\theta = \frac{1}{2}$ and θ is an angle in the first quadrant.

10. Determine cos α to three decimal places when $\sin\alpha = \frac{6}{\sqrt{61}}$ and α is an angle in the second quadrant.

11. Given that $\cos\alpha = -\frac{8}{17}$ and that $0° \leq \alpha \leq 360°$, find two values of α, to two decimal places.

12. **Application:** Given that $\sin\alpha = \frac{15}{17}$ and $-360° \leq \alpha \leq 360°$, find all values of α to two decimal places.

13. Consider the function $f(\theta) = \cos\theta$.

(a) Complete the table using the unit circle and sketch the graph.

θ	−360°	−270°	−180°	−90°	0°	90°	180°	270°	360°
$f(\theta)$									

(b) State the coordinates of the maximum and minimum values of $f(\theta) = \cos\theta$ within the domain of the table.

(c) What are the coordinates of the zeros of the function within this domain?

(d) Show that $f(\theta) = f(-\theta)$ for all values of θ in the table.

(e) Explain why $f(\theta) = f(-\theta)$ for all θ.

14. Consider the function $f(\theta) = \tan \theta$.

(a) Complete the table and sketch the graph.

θ	0°	30°	60°	90°	120°	150°	180°	210°	240°	270°	300°	330°	360°
$f(\theta)$													

(b) What are the coordinates of the zeros of the function within the domain of the table?

(c) Explain why the domain $\theta = n°$, $n \in \mathbf{R}$, is not sufficient for $f(\theta) = \tan \theta$. What restrictions must be added?

(d) State all zeros of the function.

(e) Extend the table to $\theta = -360°$ using the same intervals. Show that $f(\theta) = -f(-\theta)$ for all values of θ in the table.

(f) Explain why $f(\theta) = -f(-\theta)$ for all θ.

15. Evaluate $y = \cos \theta$ for $0° \le \theta \le 540°$ when $y = -0.7$. Answer to the nearest degree.

16. Evaluate $y = \sin \theta$ for $-90° \le \theta \le 540°$ when $y = -0.3$. Answer to the nearest degree.

17. (a) Evaluate $h(t) = \cos (20t)°$ for $t = 3$.

(b) What is the value of t when $h(t) = 0.3$ for $0 \le t \le 18$?

18. (a) Evaluate $h(t) = 4 \sin (30t)°$ for $t = 10$.

(b) What is the value of t when $h(t) = 3.2$ for $0 \le t \le 12$?

19. The vertical distance in metres of a rider with respect to the horizontal diameter of a Ferris wheel is modelled by $h(t) = 5 \cos (18t)°$, where t is the number of seconds.

(a) To one decimal place, what is the rider's vertical distance with respect to the horizontal diameter of the wheel when $t = 8$ s? 16 s? 30 s?

(b) When is the rider first at 4.5 m? -3.2 m?

(c) When is the third time the rider is at -2.5 m?

20. **Communication:** Draw a tangent graph that completes a full cycle from $-90°$ to 90°. Extend the domain to 630°. Show all asymptotes and label the points where the asymptotes cross the horizontal axis. Write these points as a sequence.

21. (a) Determine the sign of each primary trigonometric function for θ terminating in quadrant I. Repeat for quadrants II, III, and IV.

(b) Which trigonometric functions are positive in each quadrant?

(c) Graph each trigonometric function for $0° \le \theta \le 360°$. Shade the positive part of the graph and link the graph to your answer for (b).

22. **Check Your Understanding:** Explain why $y = \sin \theta$ and $y = \cos \theta$ have maximum and minimum values, but $y = \tan \theta$ does not.

C

23. **Thinking, Inquiry, Problem Solving:** A string is wrapped once in a counterclockwise direction around a cube with 10 cm sides as shown.

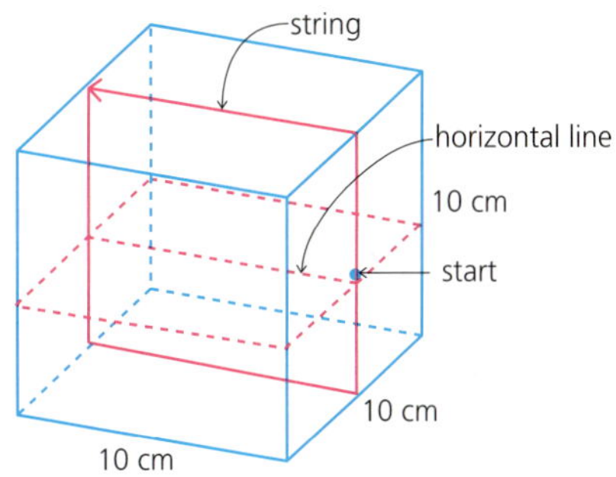

(a) Graph the location of the string around the cube with respect to its distance above or below the horizontal line indicated.

(b) How much string is used to go once around the cube? What is the period of the graph? How are the perimeter of the cube and the period length of the graph related?

(c) Extend the graph to show the string wrapped around the cube two times. How much string is used?

(d) What is the minimum value of the graph? What is the least amount of string needed for this minimum value?

24. Determine all values of θ for which $\sin \theta = \cos \theta$, for $-360° \leq \theta \leq 360°$.

25. The secondary trigonometric functions are the reciprocals of $\sin \theta$, $\cos \theta$, and $\tan \theta$. The reciprocal of $\sin \theta$ is the **cosecant** and is written **csc** θ. The reciprocal of **cos** θ is **secant** θ and is written **sec** θ. The reciprocal of **tan** θ is the cotangent θ and is written **cot** θ.

(a) Write each secondary trigonometric function in terms of its primary trigonometric function.

(b) Write each secondary trigonometric function in terms of a point $P(x, y)$ on the terminal arm of an angle θ in standard position. State all restrictions.

(c) Make a table for each secondary function and then sketch its graph for $0° \leq \theta \leq 360°$.

(d) Show how the restrictions on the domain of each function appear on the graph.

(e) State the domain and range of each secondary trigonometric function.

The Chapter Problem—How Much Daylight?

In this section, you studied trigonometric functions. Apply what you learned to answer these questions about the Chapter Problem on page 404.

CP5. Sketch the graph for all 25 months in the table.

CP6. Highlight one complete cycle for the graph that resembles a typical sine function. Highlight a cycle that resembles a typical cosine function.

CP7. What type of periodic function could be used to model the relationship between time in months and average monthly hours of daylight?

5.4 Radian Measure

So far, you have measured angles in degrees, with 360° being one revolution around a circle. There is another way to measure angles called **radian measure**. With radian measure, the arc length of a circle is compared to the radius of the circle in the ratio $\frac{\text{arc length}}{\text{radius}}$. A radian does not have a specific unit but is a real number. Radian measure has many real-life applications for periodic functions.

In radian measure,

$$\theta = \frac{\text{arc length}}{\text{radius}}$$

$$\theta = \frac{a}{r}$$

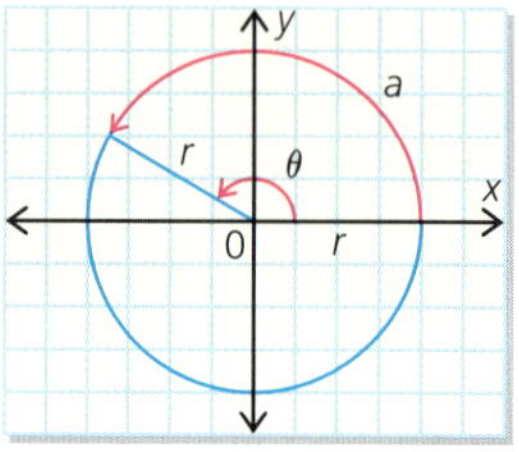

What is the radian measure for one complete revolution around a circle, that is, when $\theta = 360°$? Once around the circle is the circumference of the circle. For a complete circle, the arc length is equal to the circumference. If the radius is r, then $C = 2\pi r$.

If $\theta = \frac{a}{r}$, then

$$\theta = \frac{2\pi r}{r}$$

$$\theta = 2\pi$$

Notice that no units are attached to this value because it is a real number. The value 2π can be converted to an approximate real number. For instance, if two decimal places are required, then replace π with 3.14. Then,

$$\begin{aligned}\theta &= 2\pi \\ &\doteq 2(3.14) \\ &= 6.28\end{aligned}$$

Observe in these diagrams how degree measure and radian measure describe the same angle θ.

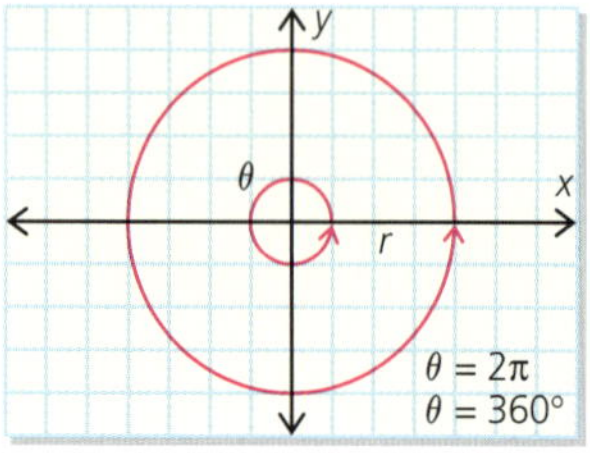

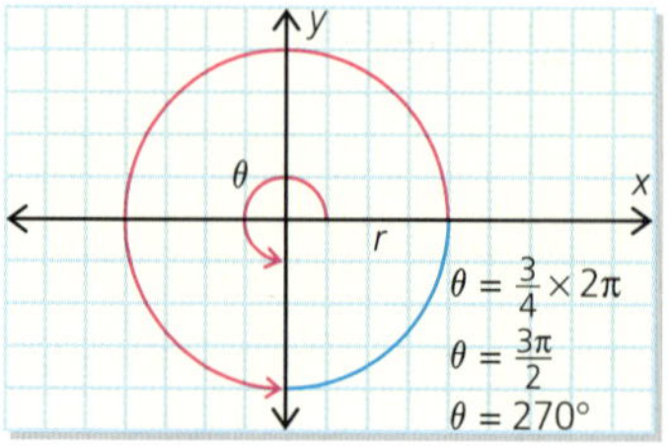

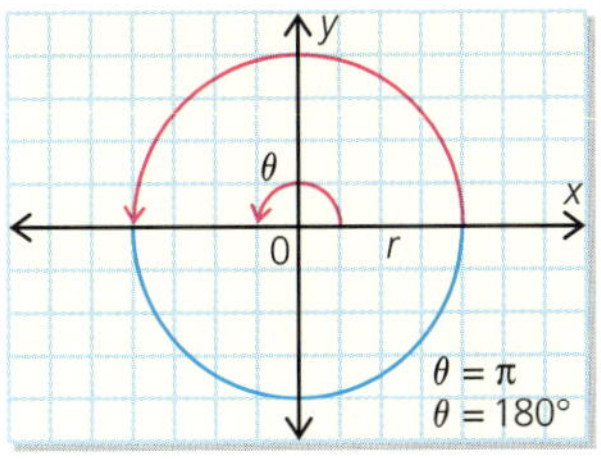

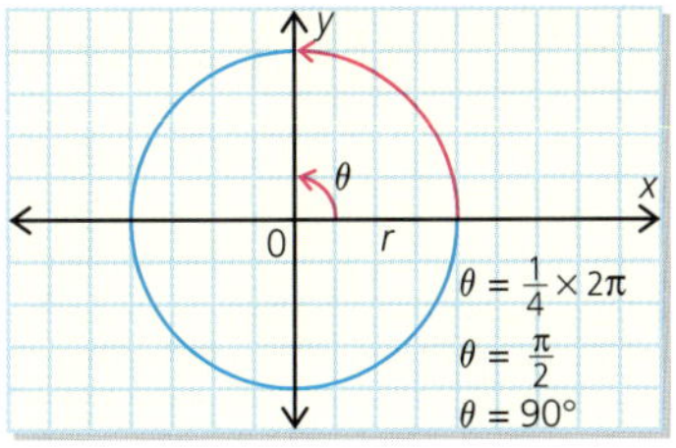

In trigonometry, it is often necessary to convert from degree measure to radian measure, and vice versa. When converting, the proportion $\frac{\text{radians}}{\pi} = \frac{\text{degrees}}{180°}$ is often useful. When using the proportion, substitute any three known values to determine the fourth value.

There are two values π can have. If the answer is in degrees, $\pi = 180°$. If it is in radians, $\pi \doteq 3.14$ radians.

Example 1

What does one radian look like and how many degrees is it equivalent to?

Solution

One radian occurs when the arc length and the radius are the same length. Use the proportion relating radians and degrees. Note that $\pi \doteq 3.14$ radians.

$$\frac{\text{radians}}{\pi} = \frac{\text{degrees}}{180°}$$
$$\frac{1}{\pi} = \frac{x}{180°}$$
$$x = \frac{180°}{\pi}$$
$$\doteq 57.3°$$

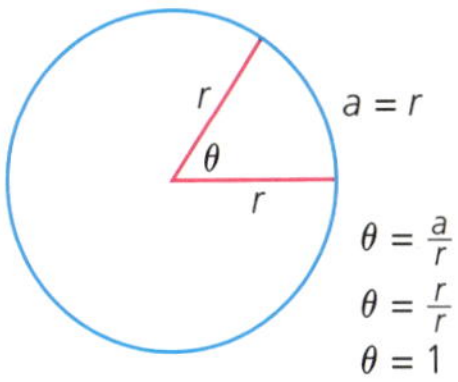

Therefore, one radian is about 57°.

Example 2

Convert 120° to radians and round to two decimals.

Solution

Use the proportion relating radians and degrees.

$$\frac{\text{radians}}{\pi} = \frac{\text{degrees}}{180°}$$
$$\frac{x}{\pi} = \frac{120°}{180°}$$
$$x = \frac{120°\pi}{180°}$$
$$x = \frac{2\pi}{3}$$

Notice that the number has no units and is now a real number. Now find the approximate value using $\pi \doteq 3.14$.

$$x = \frac{2(3.14)}{3}$$
$$\doteq 2.09$$

Check visually.

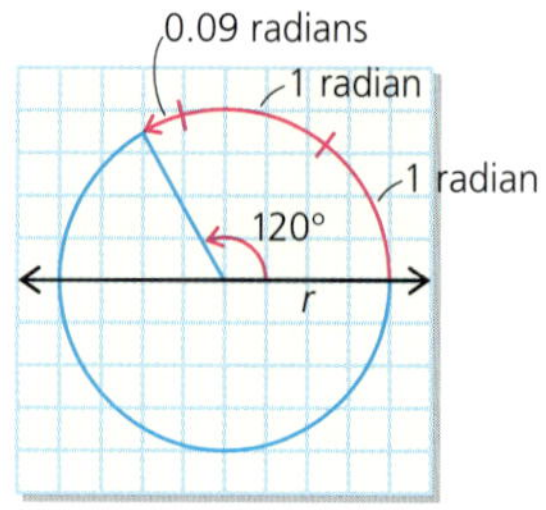

Example 3

Change $\frac{5\pi}{3}$ to degree measure.

Solution

One method is to use the proportion relating radians and degrees.

$$\frac{\text{radians}}{\pi} = \frac{\text{degrees}}{180°}$$
$$\frac{\frac{5\pi}{3}}{\pi} = \frac{x}{180°}$$
$$\frac{\frac{5}{3}}{1} = \frac{x}{180°}$$
$$x = \frac{5}{3}(180°)$$
$$x = 300°$$

Then $\frac{5\pi}{3} = 300°$.

Another method is to simply substitute $\pi = 180°$.

$$\frac{5\pi}{3} = \frac{5(180°)}{3}$$
$$\frac{5\pi}{3} = 300°$$

Check visually.

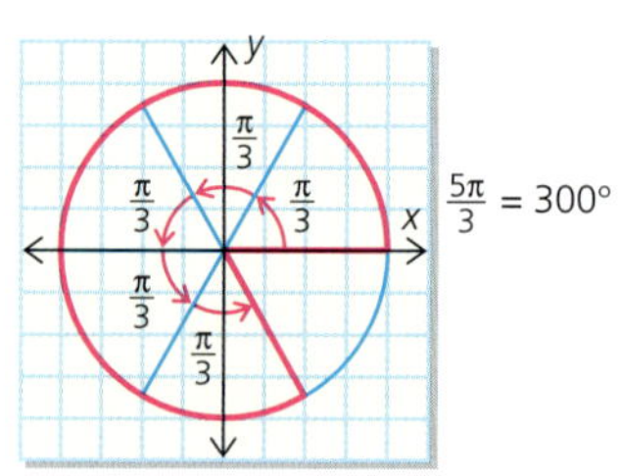

Example 4

The motion of a certain pendulum is modelled by $d = \cos\left(\frac{\sqrt{9.8}}{2}t\right)$, where d is the distance in metres of the arc length from the release point and t is the time in seconds since release.

(a) Make a table in 1-s increments for $0 \leq t \leq 10$. Round distances to the nearest metre.

(b) Use the table to draw the graph.

(c) What is the length of one cycle? Explain why the graph is periodic in the context of the question.

(d) What is the maximum displacement from rest?

(e) State the amplitude of the function.

Solution

(a) Evaluate $d = \cos\left(\frac{\sqrt{9.8}}{2}t\right)$, for $0 \leq t \leq 10$, and complete the table.

***t* (s)**	0	1	2	3	4	5	6	7	8	9	10
***d* (m)**	1	0	−1	0	1	0	−1	0	1	0	−1

(b) 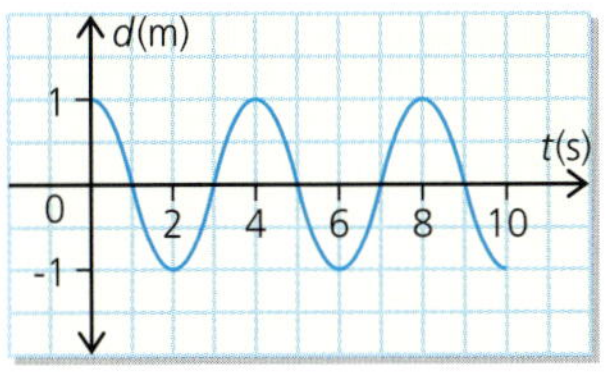

(c) One cycle is 4 s.

The graph is periodic because it repeats itself every 4 s. The pendulum swings 1 m away from rest, through rest to a point 1 m on the other side of rest, and then returns, passing through rest to its original position.

(d) The maximum displacement is 1 m.

(e) The amplitude is 1.

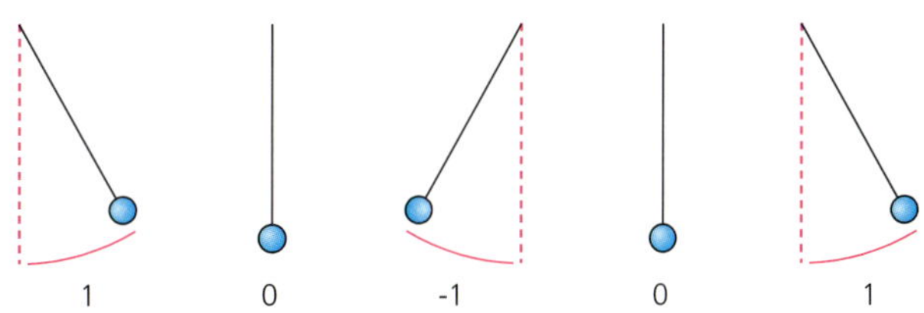

Consolidate Your Understanding

1. Show how degree measure and radian measure are related.

2. Explain the difference between $\pi = 180°$ and $\pi = 3.14$.

Focus 5.4

Key Ideas

- Angles can be measured using degrees or radians.
- A radian has no specified unit. It is simply a real number.
- π radians $= 180°$ or π radians $\doteq 3.14$ radians.
- The proportion $\frac{\text{radians}}{\pi} = \frac{\text{degrees}}{180°}$ can be used to convert between radian and degree measures.
- Radian measure has many practical applications to periodic phenomena.

Practise, Apply, Solve 5.4

A

1. A point is rotated about a circle of radius 1. Its start and finish are shown. State the rotation in radian measure and in degree measure.

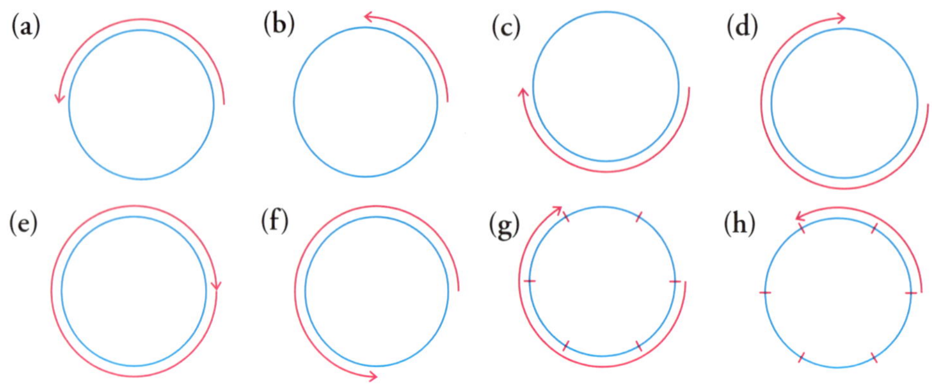

2. Sketch each rotation about a circle of radius 1.

(a) π (b) $\frac{\pi}{3}$ (c) $\frac{2\pi}{3}$ (d) $\frac{4\pi}{3}$

(e) $\frac{5\pi}{3}$ (f) $-\pi$ (g) $-\frac{\pi}{2}$ (h) $-\frac{\pi}{4}$

3. Convert to degree measure.

(a) $\frac{2\pi}{3}$ (b) $-\frac{5\pi}{3}$ (c) $\frac{\pi}{4}$ (d) $-\frac{3\pi}{4}$

(e) $\frac{7\pi}{6}$ (f) $-\frac{3\pi}{2}$ (g) $\frac{11\pi}{6}$ (h) $-\frac{9\pi}{2}$

4. Sketch the approximate location of each radian measure on a unit circle. Do not convert to degree measure.

(a) 3.14 (b) 2 (c) 1.5 (d) 4.2 (e) -5.3

5. **Knowledge and Understanding:** Convert to radian measure.

(a) 90° (b) 270° (c) $-180°$ (d) 45°

(e) $-135°$ (f) 60° (g) 240° (h) $-120°$

6. Sketch each angle in standard position and state its related acute angle.

(a) $\frac{\pi}{4}$ (b) $\frac{2\pi}{3}$ (c) $-\frac{\pi}{6}$

(d) $-\frac{3\pi}{2}$ (e) $\frac{5\pi}{4}$ (f) $\frac{5\pi}{3}$

B

7. (a) Graph $y = \sin \theta$ for $-2\pi \leq \theta \leq 2\pi$. Use a table with $\frac{\pi}{6}$ increments.

(b) What are the coordinates of all maximum and minimum points for this domain?

(c) State the location of all zeros of the function for this domain.

8. (a) Graph $y = \cos\theta$ for $-2\pi \le \theta \le 2\pi$. Use a table with $\frac{\pi}{4}$ increments.

(b) What are the coordinates of all maximum and minimum points for this domain?

(c) State the location of all zeros of the function for this domain.

9. (a) Graph $y = \tan\theta$ for $-2\pi \le \theta \le 2\pi$. Use a table with $\frac{\pi}{6}$ increments.

(b) State the equation of all asymptotes within this domain.

(c) State the location of all zeros of the function for this domain.

10. Sketch the graph within the given domain.

(a) $y = \sin\theta,\ -2\pi \le \theta \le 2\pi$ (b) $y = \sin\theta,\ -180° \le \theta \le 540°$

11. Sketch the graph within the given domain.

(a) $y = \cos\theta,\ 0° \le \theta \le 360°$ (b) $y = \cos\theta,\ -\pi \le \theta \le 3\pi$

12. Sketch the graph within the given domain.

(a) $y = \tan\theta,\ -180° \le \theta \le 180°$ (b) $y = \tan\theta,\ -\pi \le \theta \le \frac{3\pi}{2}$

13. Determine all values of θ, to the nearest degree, for $-360° \le \theta \le 360°$.

(a) $\sin\theta = -\frac{1}{2}$ (b) $\cos\theta = 0.825$ (c) $\tan\theta = 13.623$

14. Determine all values of θ, to one decimal place, for $-\pi \le \theta \le 3\pi$.

(a) $\sin\theta = \frac{7}{8}$ (b) $\cos\theta = -0.5$ (c) $\tan\theta = -4.25$

15. A water wheel of radius 1 m sits in a stream as shown.

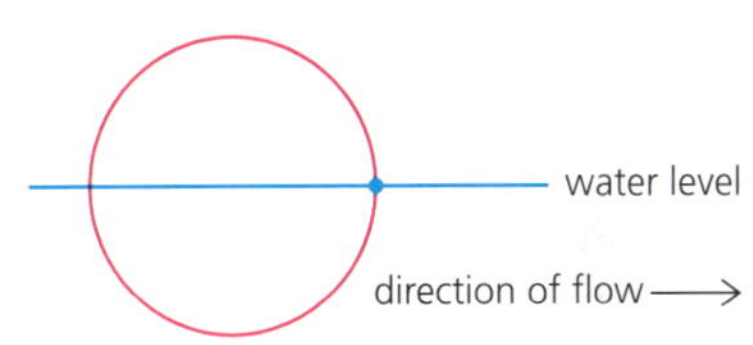

(a) Draw, for one complete revolution of the wheel, a sequence of right angle triangles to represent the position of a point on the water wheel for every rotation of $\frac{\pi}{6}$.

(b) Make a table with intervals of $\frac{\pi}{6}$ to show the displacement from the surface of the stream of the indicated point as it rotates from 0 to 2π.

(c) Use the table to graph displacement from surface versus angle of rotation.

(d) Describe the graph and write an equation that models the situation.

16. **Application:** A buoy rises and falls as it rides the waves. The equation $h(t) = \cos\frac{\pi}{5}t$ models the displacement of the buoy in metres at t seconds.

(a) Graph the displacement from 0 to 20 s, in 2.5-s intervals.

(b) Determine the period of the function from the graph. Determine the period algebraically from the equation.

(c) What is the displacement at 35 s?

(d) At what time, to the nearest second, does the displacement first reach -0.8 m?

17. **Communication:** A spring bounces up and down according to the model $d(t) = 0.5 \cos 2t$, where d is the displacement in centimetres from the rest position and t is the time in seconds. The model does not consider the effects of gravity.

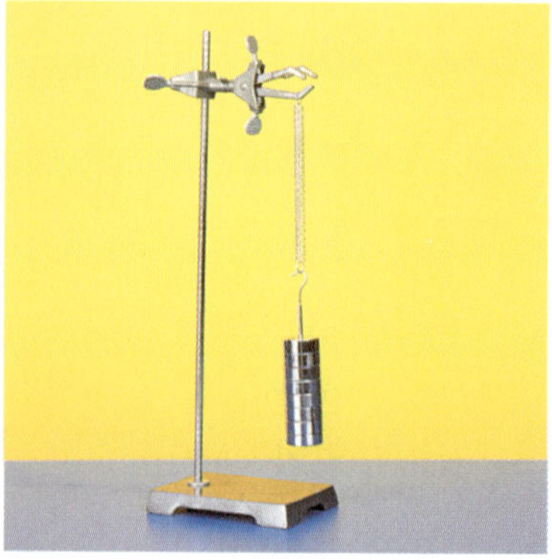

(a) Make a table for $0 \le t \le 9$, using 0.5-s intervals.

(b) Draw the graph.

(c) Explain why the function models periodic behaviour.

(d) What is the relationship between the amplitude of the function and the displacement of the spring from its rest position?

18. **Check Your Understanding:** Explain how periodic phenomena can be measured in degrees or real numbers. Give an example to support your answer.

C

19. **Thinking, Inquiry, Problem Solving:** A gear of radius 1 m turns in a counterclockwise direction and drives a larger gear of radius 3 m. Both gears have their central axis along the horizontal.

(a) Which direction is the larger gear turning?

(b) If the period of the smaller gear is 2 s, what is the period of the larger gear?

(c) Make a table in convenient intervals for each gear, to show the vertical displacement, d, of the point where the two gears first touched. Begin the table at 0 s and end it at 12 s. Graph vertical displacement versus time.

(d) What is the displacement of the point on the large wheel when the drive wheel first has a displacement of -0.5 m?

(e) What is the displacement of the drive when the large wheel first has a displacement of 2 m?

(f) What is the displacement of the point on the large wheel at 5 min?

The Chapter Problem—How Much Daylight?

CP8. Revisit your graph of the data for the two-year period in the table.

(a) Evaluate $f(3)$.

(b) Show that $f(3) = f(3 + 12)$ and explain why this should be true.

(c) Explain why there are other values that are about the same as $f(3)$.

CP9. (a) Approximate the average number of daylight hours for $f(30)$.

(b) Extend the graph to evaluate $f(-10)$.

(c) Which months correspond to $f(30)$ and $f(-10)$?

TI-83 Plus Calculator: Graphing Trigonometric Functions

You can graph trigonometric functions in both degree measure and radian measure using the TI-83 Plus calculator.

Graphing in Degrees

Graph the function $y = \sin x$ for $0° \leq x \leq 360°$.

1. **Put the calculator in degree mode.**

   Press [MODE]. Scroll down and across to **Degree**. Press [ENTER].

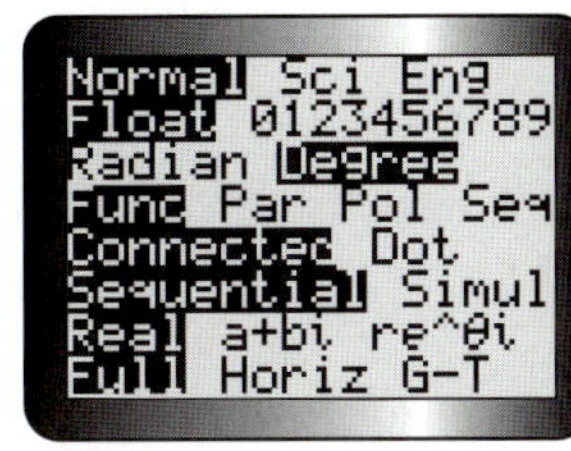

step 1

2. **Enter $y = \sin x$ into the equation editor.**

   Press [Y=] [SIN] [X,T,Θ,n] [)].

3. **Adjust the window to correspond to the given domain.**

   Press [WINDOW]. Set **Xmin=0**, **Xmax=360**, and **Xscl=90**. These settings display the graph from 0° to 360°, using an interval of 90° on the x-axis. In this case, set **Ymin=−1** and **Ymax=1**, since the sine function lies between these values. However, if this fact is not known, this step can be omitted.

step 3

4. **Graph the function using ZoomFit.**

   Press [ZOOM] [0]. The graph is displayed over the domain and the calculator determines the best values to use for **Ymax** and **Ymin** in the display window.

step 4

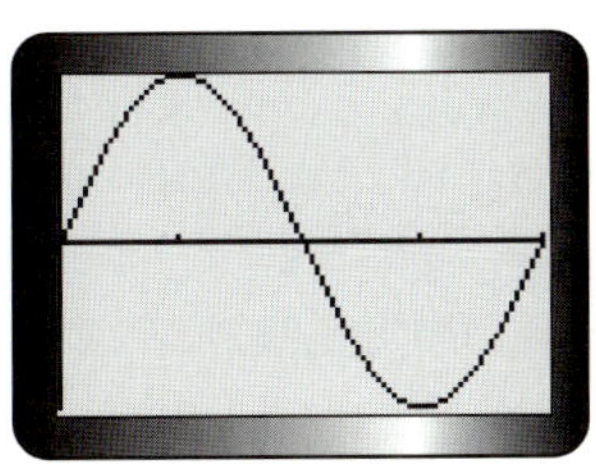

TECHNOLOGY

Graphing in Radians

Graph the function $y = \cos x$ for $0 \leq x \leq 2\pi$.

1. **Put the calculator in radian mode.**

   Press [MODE] and scroll down to **Radian**. Press [ENTER].

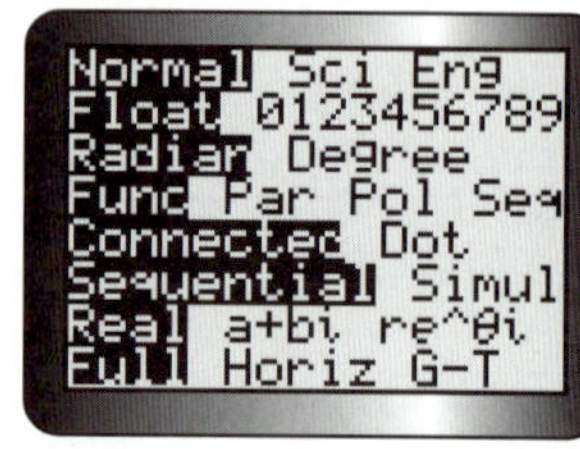

step 1

2. **Enter $y = \cos x$ into the equation editor.**

   Press [Y=] [COS] [X,T,Θ,*n*] [ )].

3. **Adjust the window to correspond to the given domain.**

   Press [WINDOW]. Set **Xmin=0**, **Xmax=2π**, and **Xscl=$\frac{\pi}{2}$**. (Press [2nd] [^] to use [π]). These settings display the graph from 0 to 2π, using an interval of $\frac{\pi}{2}$ on the x-axis. In this case, set **Ymin=−1** and **Ymax=1**, since the cosine function lies between these values. If this fact is not known, then omit this step. Note that the calculator displays the values in terms of π as decimals.

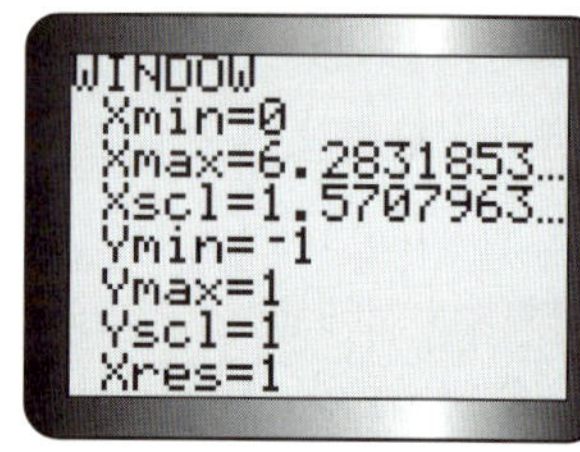

step 3

4. **Graph the function using ZoomFit.**

   Press [ZOOM] [0]. The graph is displayed over the domain and the calculator determines the best values to use for **Ymax** and **Ymin** in the display window.

   Note: You can use **ZoomTrig** (press [ZOOM] [7]) to graph the function in step 4. **ZoomTrig** will always display the graph in a window where **Xmin=−360°** (-2π), **Xmax= 360°** (2π), **Xscl= 90°** $\left(\frac{\pi}{2}\right)$, **Ymin=−4**, and **Ymax=4**.

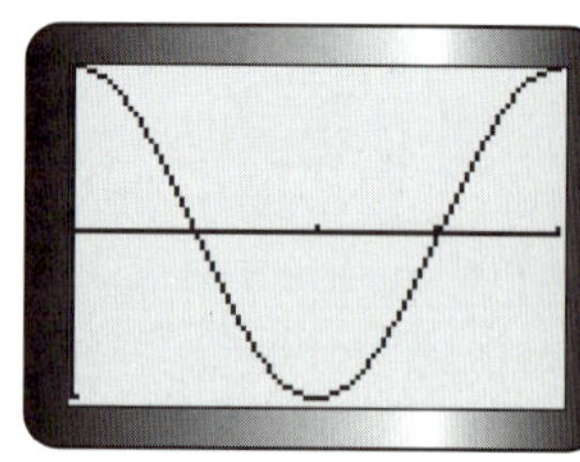

step 4

Practice 5.5

1. Graph each function using the specified domain and interval.
   (a) $y = \sin x$, $0° \leq x \leq 360°$, x-interval $= 45°$
   (b) $y = \cos x$, $0° \leq x \leq 720°$, x-interval $= 90°$
   (c) $y = \tan x$, $0° \leq x \leq 360°$, x-interval $= 90°$
   (d) $y = \sin x$, $-360° \leq x \leq 360°$, x-interval $= 60°$
   (e) $y = \cos x$, $0 \leq x \leq 2\pi$, x-interval $= \frac{\pi}{2}$
   (f) $y = \tan x$, $0 \leq x \leq 3\pi$, x-interval $= \frac{\pi}{4}$
   (g) $y = \sin x$, $-2\pi \leq x \leq 2\pi$, x-interval $= \frac{\pi}{6}$
   (h) $y = \sin x$, $-4\pi \leq x \leq 4\pi$, x-interval $= \pi$

Investigating Transformations 5.6

In section 5.3, you were able to find Sarah and Billy's location anywhere on the London Eye Ferris wheel by knowing the radius of the Ferris wheel and the angle of rotation. You also found that any point on the circumference of the wheel has coordinates $(r\cos\theta, r\sin\theta)$. You saw that the functions $y = \cos\theta$ and $y = \sin\theta$ are models for the x- and y-coordinates, respectively, as the point $P(x, y)$ moves around the unit circle.

Part 1: The Graphs of $y = a\sin\theta$ and $y = a\cos\theta$

Sarah and Billy found information on the Internet about another large Ferris wheel. This Ferris wheel is in Osaka, Japan, and its diameter is 100 m. The height of the Ferris wheel from the ground to the highest point is 112.5 m.

Think, Do, Discuss

1. (a) Suppose that the centre of the wheel is at the origin of a graph. What are the coordinates of any point on the circumference of the Ferris wheel in Osaka?

(b) State the function that models the y-coordinate for any angle of rotation, θ. Graph the function for $0 \leq \theta \leq 4\pi$, and state its amplitude.

(c) State the function that models the θ-coordinate for any angle of rotation, θ. Graph the function for $0 \leq \theta \leq 4\pi$, and state its amplitude.

2. (a) Predict the graph of $y = a\sin\theta$ for $0 \leq \theta \leq 4\pi$, for $a = 1$, 2, and 3, and for $a = \frac{1}{2}$ and $\frac{1}{4}$. Sketch each graph on the same axes. Verify your sketches with a graphing calculator.

(b) Sketch, on a new set of axes, the graph of $y = a\sin\theta$ for $0 \leq \theta \leq 4\pi$, and for $a = -1$, -2, and -3. Verify your sketches with a graphing calculator. How are these graphs different from those for $a = 1$, 2, and 3?

(c) Compare the zeros for each function.

(d) How is the amplitude of each graph affected by the value of a?

(e) What are the maximum and minimum values for each graph?

3. Repeat step 2 for $y = a\cos\theta$.

4. Explain how the value of a affects $y = a\sin\theta$ and $y = a\cos\theta$.

Part 2: The Graphs of $y = a \sin \theta + d$ and $y = a \cos \theta + d$

Think, Do, Discuss

1. (a) Sketch a model of the Osaka Ferris wheel so that the θ-axis represents the ground and the centre of the wheel is on the y-axis.
   (b) Describe the transformation of any point, $P(x, y)$, on the circumference of the circle if the centre of the Ferris wheel is not at the origin, but at the point in (a).
   (c) State the function that models the y-coordinate for any angle of rotation, θ. Graph the function for $0 \leq \theta \leq 4\pi$ and state its amplitude.
   (d) Describe the relation between the amplitude and both the maximum and minimum values.
   (e) Suppose that Sarah and Billy were riding on the Ferris wheel in Osaka. What is their height above the ground when the angle, in standard position, of the Ferris wheel is $\frac{2\pi}{3}$?
   (f) Sarah and Billy are 50 m above the ground. What is the angle of rotation, in standard position, at this point?
2. (a) Predict the graph of $y = \sin \theta + d$ for $d = -2, -1, 1,$ and 2. Sketch each graph on the same axes. Verify each sketch with a graphing calculator.
   (b) How can you determine the maximum and minimum values without drawing the graphs?
   (c) State the maximum and the minimum values for $y = 4 \sin \theta - 9$. Explain how you calculated the values.
3. (a) Sketch, on the same axes, the graph of $y = \cos \theta + d$ for $0 \leq \theta \leq 4\pi$, for $d = -2, -1, 1,$ and 2. Verify each sketch with a graphing calculator.
   (b) State the maximum and minimum values for $y = -3 \cos \theta + 5$. What is the equation of the axis of the curve? How did you find this equation?
   (c) Explain how the value of d affects $y = a \sin \theta + d$ and $y = a \cos \theta + d$.

Part 3: The Graphs of $y = a \sin k\theta + d$ and $y = a \cos k\theta + d$

Sarah and Billy ride on the Ferris wheel at the fall fair. The Ferris wheel is 10 m in diameter and it is 11 m at its highest point. One revolution of the wheel takes 2 min, and the ride lasts 4 min.

Think, Do, Discuss

1. (a) What is Sarah and Billy's height on this Ferris wheel at any angle of rotation, θ?

(b) Through how many degrees does the Ferris wheel rotate in the first second? How many degrees has the Ferris wheel rotated after 2 s? 3 s? 4 s? Through how many degrees has it rotated after t seconds?

(c) Write the angle of rotation, θ, in terms of time, t.

(d) Let time be the independent variable. Describe their position by writing two trigonometric equations. Use a graphing calculator to graph the equations for a complete ride. What mode should you set for the graphing calculator? Explain.

(e) What is the period of each graph? How might you determine the period from each equation?

2. Predict the period of the graph of $y = \sin k\theta$ for $k = 2$, 3, and 4. Verify each period by drawing each graph. Clear the previous equation from the graphing calculator before entering another equation.

3. Repeat step 2 for $k = \frac{1}{2}$ and $\frac{1}{4}$. Set the window on the graphing calculator so that you may see one complete cycle of each graph.

4. How could you find the period of $y = \sin k\theta$ from the period of $y = \sin \theta$?

5. What is the period of $y = \cos 6\theta$? Draw the graph and visually verify the period.

6. State the period of $y = -3 \cos (2\theta) + 7$.

7. Explain how the value of k affects $y = a \sin k\theta + d$ and $y = a \cos k\theta + d$.

Part 4: The Graphs of $y = a \sin k(\theta + b) + d$ and $y = a \cos k(\theta + b) + d$

Imagine that the car in which Sarah and Billy ride the Ferris wheel may hold several passengers. At the start of the ride, a number of other passengers got on with Sarah and Billy. The trigonometric functions $y = a \sin k\theta + d$ and $y = a \cos k\theta + d$ apply in this situation. This diagram represents the angle of rotation in standard position so that one arm of the angle is parallel to the x-axis.

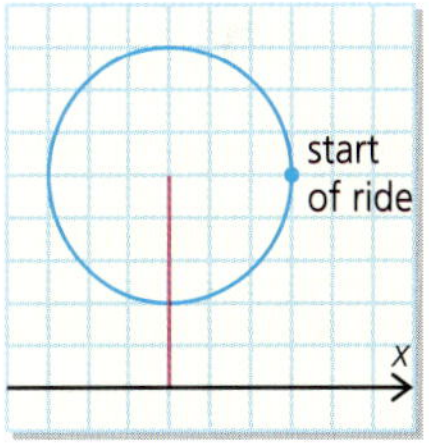

How would the sinusoidal model change if the passengers boarded the Ferris wheel at a different point on the wheel? The diagrams show two possible points on the wheel.

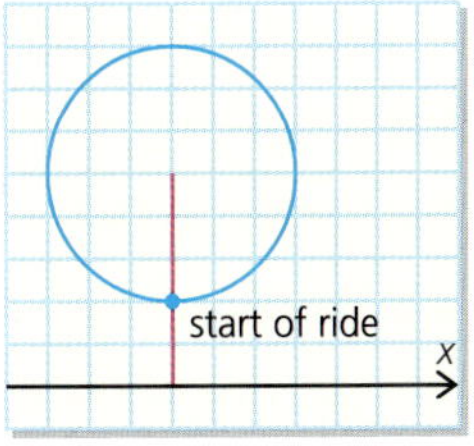

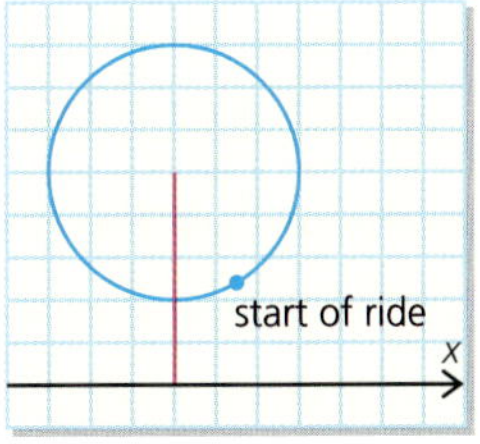

Think, Do, Discuss

1. Sarah and Billy ride the Ferris wheel at a local fair. The lowest point on the wheel is 1 m above the ground. The highest point is 13 m above the ground. The wheel is divided into quarters labelled 0, 1, 2, and 3. Extend the pattern and complete each table. Graph each set of coordinate pairs on the same axes in the *x*-*y* plane.

(a)

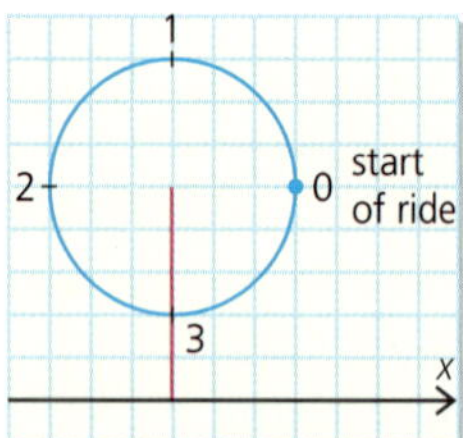

Position on Wheel	0	1	2	3	4	5	6
Height (m)							

(b)

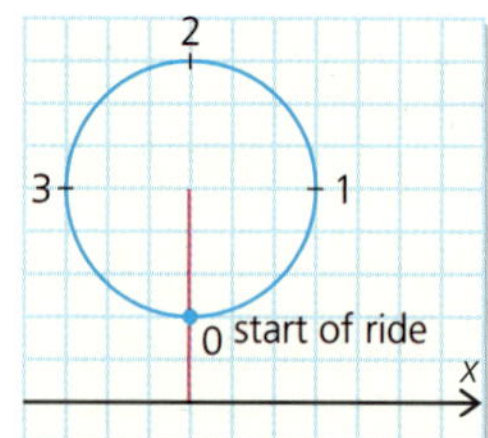

Position on Wheel	0	1	2	3	4	5	6
Height (m)							

2. (a) Highlight the first complete cycle for each curve.

(b) Find the equation of the axis for each curve. Compare the equations. What is the amplitude of each curve?

(c) Compare the maximum and minimum values of each curve.

(d) Compare the periods of the curves.

(e) How are the curves different?

(f) By how many degrees is each curve separated? Explain the difference.

(g) State the equation of the curve in step 1(a) in terms of the angle of rotation, θ. Verify that the graph of this equation matches your graph.

(h) Replace θ with $(\theta - 90°)$ in the equation. Use a graphing calculator to graph the equation and compare it to the corresponding hand-drawn graph in step 1(b).

(i) Describe the transformation of the original graph in step 1(a) to the graph in step 1(b). Explain the change in terms of the starting position.

3. Suppose the function for the height, h, in metres on the Ferris wheel is modelled by $h(\theta) = 6 \sin (\theta - 45°) + 7$.

(a) Sketch the starting point on the Ferris wheel.

(b) Graph the equation by hand.

(c) Verify your hand-drawn graph using a graphing calculator.

4. Sketch the starting point on a circle and graph each function.

(a) $h(\theta) = 6 \sin (\theta + 90°) + 7$

(b) $h(\theta) = 6 \sin (\theta + 45°) + 7$

5. (a) The Ferris wheel's speed in step 1(a) is one revolution every 1.5 min. Write the equation to represent the height if the angle at the boarding point is in the standard position. Graph the equation.

(b) Replace θ with $(\theta - 45°)$ in the equation. Graph the new equation. Describe the horizontal shift of the graph of the equation with θ to the graph of the equation with $(\theta - 45°)$. What is the starting position on the Ferris wheel? Describe this point in terms of the angle in standard position.

6. State the horizontal shift for $y = 2 \sin 3(\theta + 90°) + 5$ and compare it to the horizontal shift for $y = 2 \sin (3\theta + 90°) + 5$.

7. Explain how the value of b affects $y = a \sin k(\theta + b) + d$ and $y = a \cos k(\theta + b) + d$.

Focus 5.6

Key Ideas

- The graph of $y = a \sin k(\theta + b) + d$ is a transformation of the graph of $y = \sin \theta$. The graph of $y = a \cos k(\theta + b) + d$ is a transformation of the graph of $y = \cos \theta$. The values of a, k, b, and d determine the shape or positioning of the graph. In the following, "the graph" refers to either the graph of $y = \sin \theta$ or the graph of $y = \cos \theta$.

The value of a determines the vertical stretch or compression, called the **amplitude**. The value of a also tells whether the curve is reflected in the θ-axis.

- For $a > 1$, the graph is stretched vertically by the factor a. For $0 < a < 1$, the graph is vertically compressed by a factor of a.
- For $a < 0$, the graph is reflected in the θ-axis and stretched vertically or compressed by the factor a.

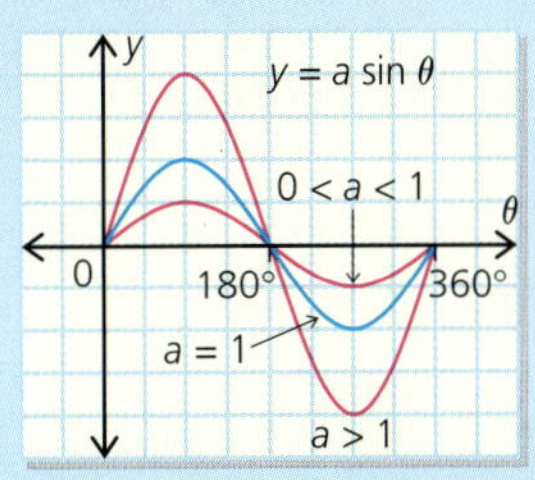

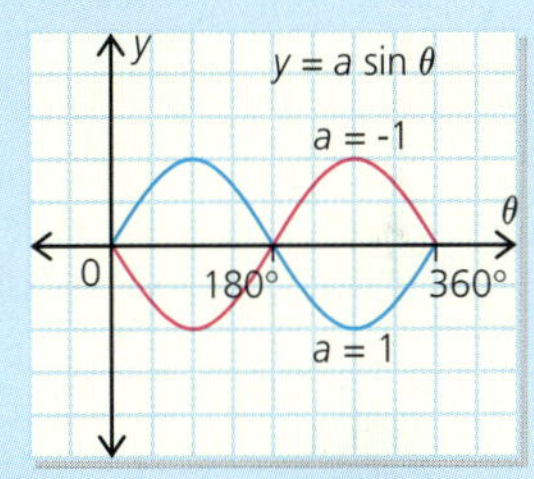

The value of k determines the horizontal stretch or compression.

- For $k > 1$, the graph is compressed horizontally by the factor $\frac{1}{k}$. For $0 < k < 1$, the graph is stretched horizontally by the factor $\frac{1}{k}$.
- The value of k determines the number of cycles in the period of the graph.

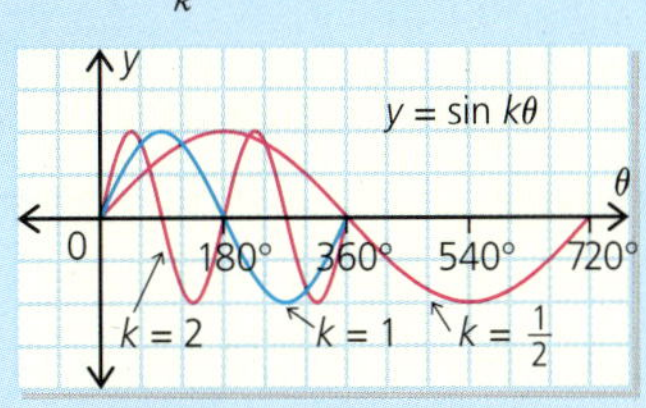

The value of b determines the horizontal translation.

- For $b > 0$, the graph is horizontally translated b units to the left.
- For $b < 0$, the graph is horizontally translated b units to the right.
- The value b is called the **phase shift**.

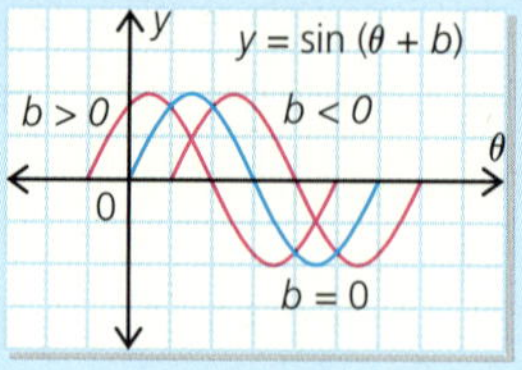

The value of d determines the vertical translation.

- For $d > 0$, the graph is vertically translated d units up.
- For $d < 0$, the graph is vertically translated d units down.

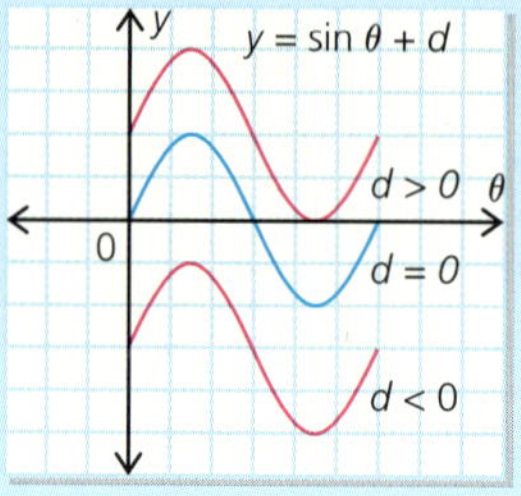

- To determine the phase shift of $y = \sin(k\theta + p)$ or $y = \cos(k\theta + p)$, rewrite the equations in the form $y = \sin k(\theta + b)$ or $y = \cos k(\theta + b)$, where $b = \frac{p}{k}$.
- To determine the period of the trigonometric function, divide the period of the base curve by k.

$$y = \sin k\theta \text{ has period } \frac{360°}{k} \text{ or } \frac{2\pi}{k}$$

$$y = \cos k\theta \text{ has period } \frac{360°}{k} \text{ or } \frac{2\pi}{k}$$

$$y = \tan k\theta \text{ has period } \frac{180°}{k} \text{ or } \frac{\pi}{k}$$

- To graph $y = a \sin k(\theta + b) + d$ and $y = a \cos k(\theta + b) + d$, apply the transformations in this order:
  1. horizontal stretch or compression
  2. horizontal translation or phase shift, left or right
  3. vertical stretch or compression
  4. reflection about the θ-axis
  5. vertical translation, up or down

Example 1

(a) Determine the period, in degrees, of $y = \sin 3\theta$.

(b) Find the period, in radians, for $y = \cos \frac{\theta}{4}$.

Solution

(a) The period of $y = \sin \theta$ is 360°. The graph of $y = \sin 3\theta$ is compressed horizontally by a factor of $\frac{1}{3}$. There are three cycles of $y = \sin 3\theta$ for one cycle of $y = \sin \theta$. Then $3\theta = 360°$.

$$3\theta = 360°$$
$$\theta = \frac{360°}{3}$$
$$\theta = 120°$$

The period of $y = \sin 3\theta$ is 120°.

(b) The period of $y = \cos \theta$ is 2π. The graph of $y = \cos \frac{\theta}{4}$ is stretched horizontally by a factor of $\frac{1}{\frac{1}{4}}$ or 4. There is $\frac{1}{4}$ cycle of $y = \cos \frac{\theta}{4}$ for one cycle of $y = \cos \theta$.

Then $\frac{\theta}{4} = 2\pi$.

$$\theta = 4(2\pi)$$
$$\theta = 8\pi$$

The period of $y = \cos \frac{\theta}{4}$ is 8π.

Example 2

State the phase shift for each function.

(a) $y = \cos (4\theta + 180°)$

(b) $y = \sin 2(\theta + 15°)$

(c) $y = \cos (3\theta - \pi)$

(d) $y = \tan (2\theta + 180°)$

Solution

(a) Rewrite $y = \cos (4\theta + 180°)$ as $y = \cos 4\left(\theta + \frac{180°}{4}\right)$.
Then $y = \cos 4(\theta + 45°)$.
The phase shift is $-45°$.

(b) $y = \sin 2(\theta + 15°)$ is already in the correct form.
The phase shift is $-15°$.

(c) $y = \cos (3\theta - \pi)$
$= \cos 3\left(\theta - \frac{\pi}{3}\right)$
The phase shift is $\frac{\pi}{3}$.

(d) Rewrite $y = \tan (2\theta + 180°)$ as $y = \tan 2(\theta + 90°)$.
The phase shift is $-90°$.

Example 3

Describe the graph of $y = -3 \sin (5\theta + \pi) + 4$ for $0 \leq \theta \leq 2\pi$ as a transformation of $y = \sin \theta$. Graph each step of the transformation process.

Solution

The equation is in the form $y = a \sin (k\theta + p) + d$, which gives the values of a, k, and d. Rewrite the equation in the form $y = a \sin k(\theta + b) + d$ to determine the value of b. The equation becomes $y = -3 \sin 5\left(\theta + \frac{\pi}{5}\right) + 4$.

Start by graphing $y = \sin \theta$.

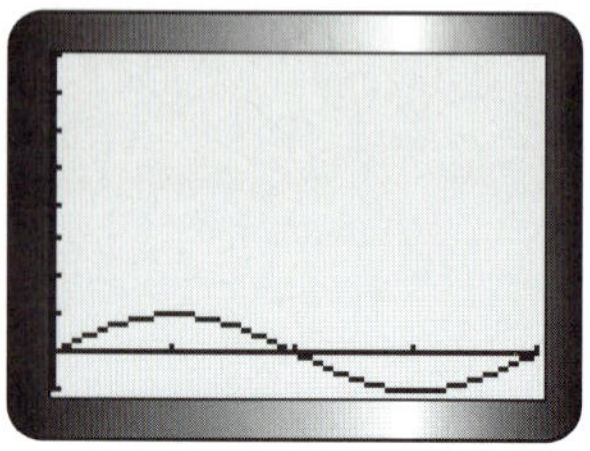

There are five cycles of the graph in the period of $y = \sin \theta$, which is 2π. The period is then $\frac{2\pi}{5}$.

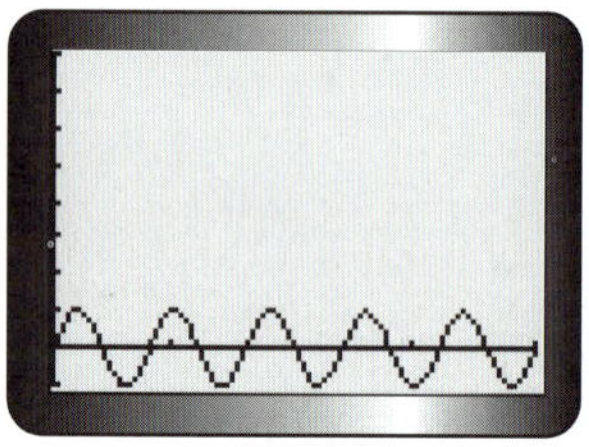

The phase shift, b, is $-\frac{\pi}{5}$. The graph shifts $\frac{\pi}{5}$ to the left.

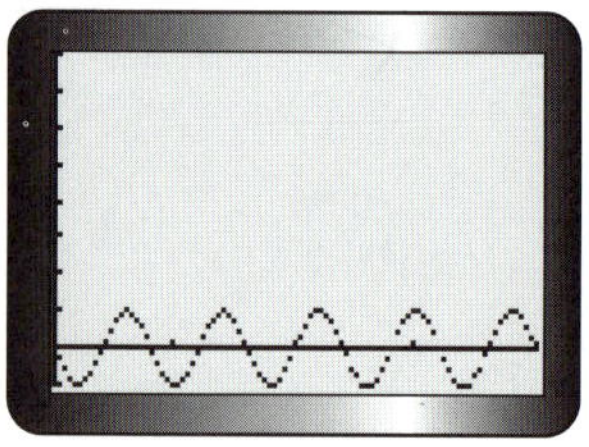

The vertical stretch, a, is 3. Stretch the curve by a factor of 3. Because a is negative, the curve is reflected about the θ-axis.

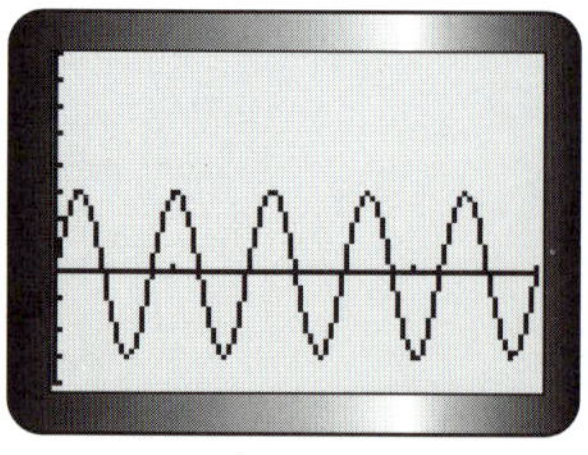

The vertical translation, d, is 4. Translate the graph 4 units up.

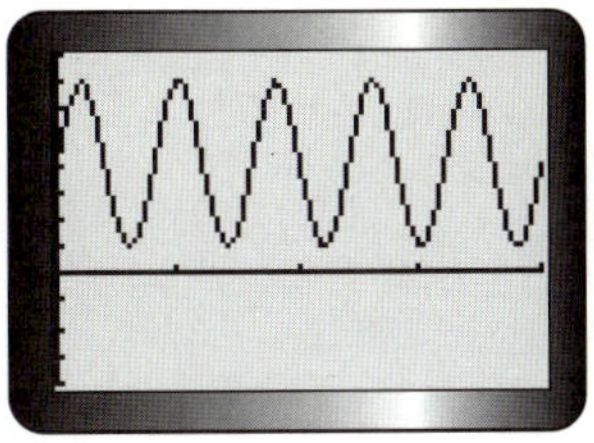

Example 4

The average monthly temperature, T, in degrees Celsius in the Kawartha Lakes was modelled by $T(t) = -22 \cos \frac{\pi}{6}t + 10$, where t represents the number of months. For $t = 0$, the month is January; for $t = 1$, the month is February, and so on.

(a) What is the period? Explain the period in the context of the problem.

(b) What is the maximum temperature? the minimum temperature?

(c) What is the range of temperatures for this model?

Solution

(a) The period of $f(\theta) = \cos \theta$ is 2π.

Then $\frac{\pi}{6}t = 2\pi$.

$$t = (2\pi)\left(\frac{6}{\pi}\right)$$

$$t = 12$$

The period of this function is 12.

The cycle of temperatures repeats itself every 12 months.

(b) The amplitude is $|-22| = 22$. The vertical translation is 10 units up. The maximum temperature is 22°C + 10°C = 32°C. The minimum temperature is −22°C + 10°C or −12°C.

(c) The temperature range is −12°C to 32°C.

Practise, Apply, Solve 5.6

A

1. Explain how each graph is different from the graph of $y = \sin \theta$, where $\theta \in \mathbf{R}$.

(a) $y = \sin \theta + 2$ (b) $y = \sin 2\theta$ (c) $y = 2 \sin \theta$ (d) $y = -2 \sin \theta$

2. For each function, explain the transformation from $y = \cos \theta$.

(a) $y = \frac{1}{2} \cos \theta$

(b) $y = \cos \frac{\theta}{2}$

(c) $y = \cos \theta + \frac{1}{2}$

(d) $y = -\frac{1}{2} \cos \theta$

3. State the period of each function in degrees.

(a) $y = \sin 3\theta$ (b) $y = \cos \frac{\theta}{4}$ (c) $y = \cos 6\theta$

(d) $y = \sin 5\theta$ (e) $y = \cos \frac{3}{2}\theta$ (f) $y = \sin \frac{\theta}{3}$

(g) $y = \tan 2\theta$ (h) $y = \tan \frac{\theta}{2}$ (i) $y = \tan \frac{\theta}{3}$

4. State the period of each function in radians.

(a) $y = \cos 4\theta$ (b) $y = \sin 6\theta$ (c) $y = \sin \frac{5}{3}\theta$ (d) $y = \cos 2\pi\theta$

(e) $y = \cos \frac{2}{5}\theta$ (f) $y = \sin \frac{2}{3}\theta$ (g) $y = \tan 3\theta$ (h) $y = \tan \frac{2\theta}{3}$

5. Match each function to its corresponding graph. Do not use technology.

(a) $y = \sin\left(\theta + \frac{\pi}{4}\right)$ (b) $y = \sin\left(\theta - \frac{\pi}{4}\right)$ (c) $y = \cos\left(\theta + \frac{\pi}{4}\right)$

i.
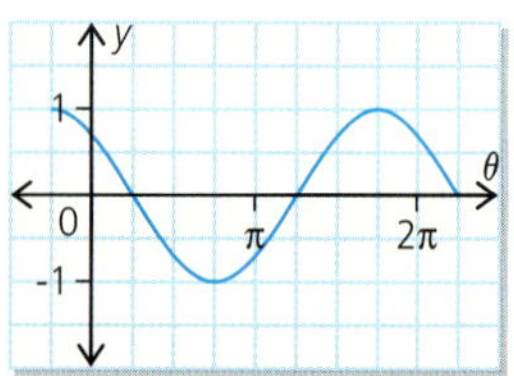

ii.
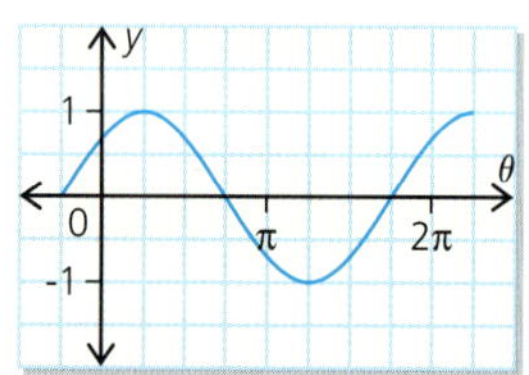

iii.
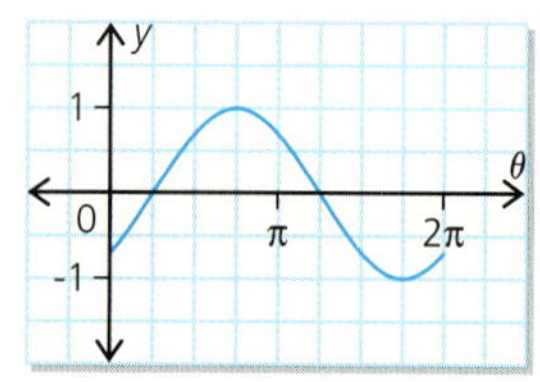

6. Match each function to its corresponding graph.

(a) $y = \sin(2\theta - 90°)$, $0° \leq \theta \leq 360°$

(b) $y = \sin(3\theta + 90°)$, $0° \leq \theta \leq 360°$

(c) $y = \sin\left(\frac{\theta}{2} + 30°\right)$, $0° \leq \theta \leq 360°$

i.
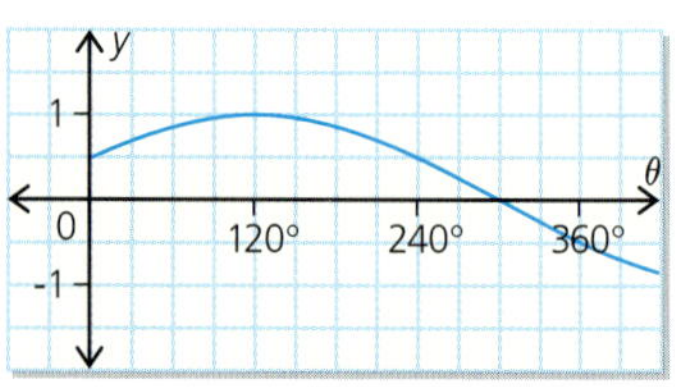

ii.
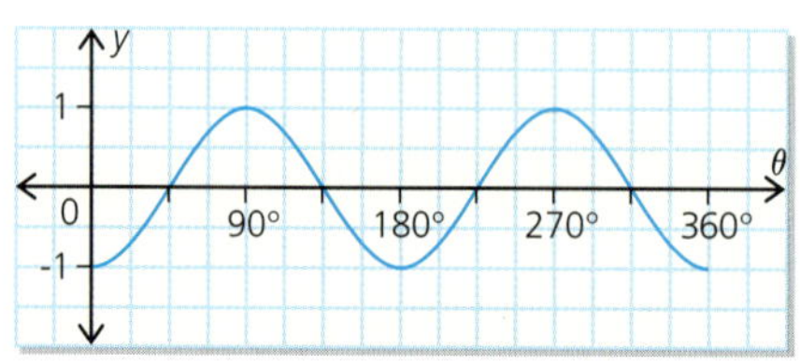

iii.
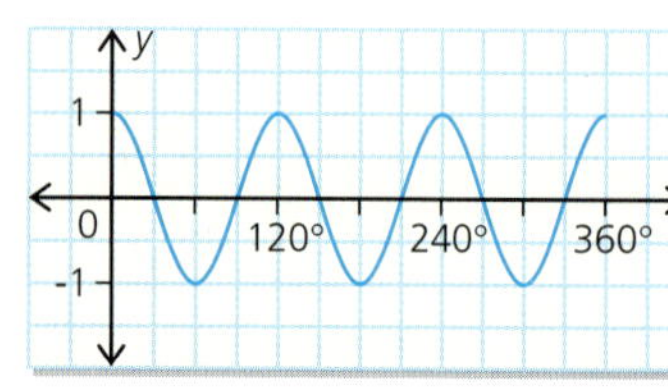

7. **Knowledge and Understanding:** State the amplitude, period, phase shift, and vertical shift for each function.

(a) $y = 3\sin(2\theta - 60°) + 1$ (b) $y = 5\cos(3\theta + 45°) - 2$

(c) $y = -2\sin\left(\frac{\theta}{3} + 15°\right) + 2$ (d) $y = \frac{1}{2}\cos\left(\frac{\theta}{2} - 7.5°\right) - 3$

(e) $y = 1 - 4\cos\left(6\theta + \frac{\pi}{3}\right)$ (f) $y = 2 + 3\sin 4\left(\theta - \frac{\pi}{2}\right)$

B

8. Sketch each graph for $0° \leq \theta \leq 360°$ by comparing it to $y = \sin\theta$. Do not use technology.

(a) $y = -\sin\theta + 2$ (b) $y = \frac{1}{2}\sin\theta - 2$ (c) $y = -2\sin\frac{\theta}{2}$

9. Sketch each graph for $0 \le \theta \le 2\pi$ by comparing it to $y = \cos\theta$. Do not use technology.

(a) $y = -\cos\theta + 2$ (b) $y = \frac{1}{2}\cos\theta - 2$ (c) $y = -2\cos\frac{\theta}{2}$

10. Sketch each graph for $0° \le \theta \le 360°$ by comparing it to $y = \tan\theta$. Do not use technology.

(a) $y = -\tan\theta$ (b) $y = \tan 2\theta$ (c) $y = \tan\frac{\theta}{2} + 1$

11. For $y = 3f(2\theta - 90°) - 1$, $f(\theta) = \sin\theta$. Evaluate y to one decimal place for each value of θ.

(a) $30°$ (b) $45°$ (c) $125°$ (d) $-225°$

12. For $y = -2f\left(3\theta + \frac{\pi}{2}\right) - 1$, $f(\theta) = \cos\theta$. Evaluate y to one decimal place for each value of θ.

(a) $\frac{\pi}{3}$ (b) $\frac{2\pi}{3}$ (c) $-\frac{\pi}{6}$ (d) $-\frac{3\pi}{4}$

13. For $y = 2f(2\theta - 45°) - 1$, $f(\theta) = \tan\theta$. Evaluate y to one decimal place for each value of θ.

(a) $15°$ (b) $90°$ (c) $60°$ (d) $-25°$

14. **Communication**

(a) Explain how the graphs of $y = \sin\theta$ and $y = \cos\theta$ are alike and different?

(b) Rewrite $y = \sin\theta$ as a cosine function.

(c) Rewrite $y = \cos\theta$ as a sine function.

15. Sketch the graph of $y = -2\cos\left(\theta + \frac{\pi}{4}\right)$, $0 \le \theta \le 2\pi$, by comparing it to $y = \cos\theta$.

16. The graph of $y = 2\sin 3\theta$ is shifted to the right $\frac{\pi}{2}$ units and down 2 units. Write the new equation.

17. The graph of $y = -3\cos\frac{\theta}{2}$ is shifted to the left $\frac{2\pi}{3}$ units and up 1 unit. Write the new equation.

18. Sketch each graph for $-360° \le \theta \le 360°$. Verify the sketch using a calculator.

(a) $y = 3\sin(2\theta - 60°) + 1$ (b) $y = 5\cos(3\theta + 45°) - 2$

(c) $y = -2\sin\left(\frac{\theta}{3} + 15°\right) + 2$ (d) $y = \frac{1}{2}\cos\left(\frac{\theta}{2} - 7.5°\right) - 3$

19. Sketch each graph for $0 \le \theta \le 2\pi$. Verify the sketch using a graphing calculator.

(a) $y = 1 - 4\cos\left(6\theta + \frac{\pi}{3}\right)$ (b) $y = 2 + 3\sin 4\left(\theta - \frac{\pi}{2}\right)$

20. How is the graph of $y = -3\cos\left(2\theta - \frac{\pi}{4}\right) + 1$ different from the graph of $y = \cos\theta$? How is the graph of $y = -3\cos\left(2\theta - \frac{\pi}{4}\right) + 1$ different from the graph of $y = \sin\theta$?

21. Application: Each person's blood pressure is different. But there is a range of blood pressure values that is considered healthy. The function $P(t) = -20 \cos \frac{5\pi}{3} t + 100$ models the blood pressure, P, in millimetres of mercury, at time, t, in seconds of a person at rest.

(a) What is the period of the function? What does the period represent for an individual?

(b) How many times does this person's heart beat each minute?

(c) Sketch the graph of $y = P(t)$ for $0 \leq t \leq 6$.

(d) What is the range of the function? Explain the meaning of the range in terms of a person's blood pressure.

22. The average monthly temperature in a region of Australia is modelled by the function $T(t) = 9 + 23 \cos \frac{\pi}{6} t$, where T is the temperature in degrees Celsius and t is the month of the year. For $t = 0$, the month is January.

(a) Prepare a table for $0 \leq t \leq 13$.

(b) Graph the data.

(c) Explain how to use the axis of the curve and the amplitude to determine the maximum and minimum values of the function.

(d) Determine the period of the function from the graph. Verify your answer algebraically.

(e) Verify the graph in (b) by using a graphing calculator.

(f) Explain how to sketch a similar graph using transformations of $y = \cos \theta$.

23. The function $D(t) = 4 \sin \left[\frac{360}{365}(t - 80)\right]^{\circ} + 12$ is a model of the number of hours of daylight, D, on a specific day, t, on the 50° of north latitude.

(a) Explain why a trigonometric function is a reasonable model for predicting the number of hours of daylight.

(b) How many hours of daylight do March 21 and September 21 have? What is the significance of each of these days?

(c) What is the significance of the number 80 in the model?

(d) How many hours of daylight do June 21 and December 21 have? What is the significance of each of these days?

(e) Explain what the number 12 represents in the model.

(f) Graph the model.

(g) What are the maximum hours of daylight? the minimum hours of daylight? On what days do these values occur?

(h) Use the graph to determine t when $D(t) = 12$. What dates correspond to t?

24. The position of the sun at sunset, north or south of due west, depends on the latitude and the day of the year. The number of degrees, P, north or south of due west for a specific latitude on a specific day, t, is modelled by the function $P(t) = 28 \sin \left(\frac{2\pi}{365} t - 1.4\right)$.

(a) What is the angle at sunset on February 28, to one decimal place? What is the angle on May 15?

(b) Graph the function.

(c) What is the maximum angle north of due west? What is the minimum angle south of due west? How could you find these angles without drawing the graph?

(d) What is the period of the function and how does it relate to the problem?

(e) What is the significance of the number 1.4 in terms of the day of the year?

25. Check Your Understanding: Recall $y = \sin \theta$ and $y = a \sin k(\theta + b) + d$.

(a) Explain the meaning of a, k, b, and d.

(b) Explain how to use the graph of $y = \sin \theta$ to sketch the graph of $y = 3 \sin (2\theta + 90)° + 1$.

(c) Sketch the graph of $y = 3 \sin (2\theta + 90)° + 1$ following your explanation from (b). Verify your sketches using a graphing calculator.

C

26. Thinking, Inquiry, Problem Solving: The population, R, of rabbits and the population, F, of foxes in a given region are modelled by the functions

$$R(t) = 10\,000 + 5000 \cos \frac{2\pi}{24} t \text{ and } F(t) = 1000 + 500 \sin \frac{2\pi}{24} t,$$

where t is the time in months. Explain, referring to each graph, how the number of rabbits and the number of foxes are related.

The Chapter Problem—How Much Daylight?

In this section, you studied transformations of trigonometric functions. Apply what you learned to answer these questions about the Chapter Problem on page 404.

CP10. Refer to the graph of the original data you made earlier.

(a) Explain how the axis of the graph and the concept of vertical shift are related. What does vertical shift mean in this problem?

(b) What choices of starting position are possible when highlighting a cycle? What is the phase shift if a typical sine function were highlighted? if a typical cosine function were highlighted? What does phase shift mean in this problem?

(c) Compare the period of this data to the period of $y = \sin \theta$ or $y = \cos \theta$. How can you use this information to find the equation representing the data?

5.7 Modelling Periodic Phenomena

In section 5.1, you worked with this table that gives the fraction of the moon that is visible at midnight as the new millennium began. You drew a scatter plot and the curve of best fit to model the waxing and waning of the moon.

Day of the Year	1	2	3	4	5	6	10	15	20	21
Fraction of Moon Visible	0.25	0.18	0.11	0.06	0.02	0.00	0.11	0.57	0.99	1.00

Day of the Year	25	30	35	40	45	50	55	60	65	66
Fraction of Moon Visible	0.80	0.32	0.02	0.14	0.64	1.00	0.77	0.31	0.01	0.00

Source: US Naval Observatory, Washington.

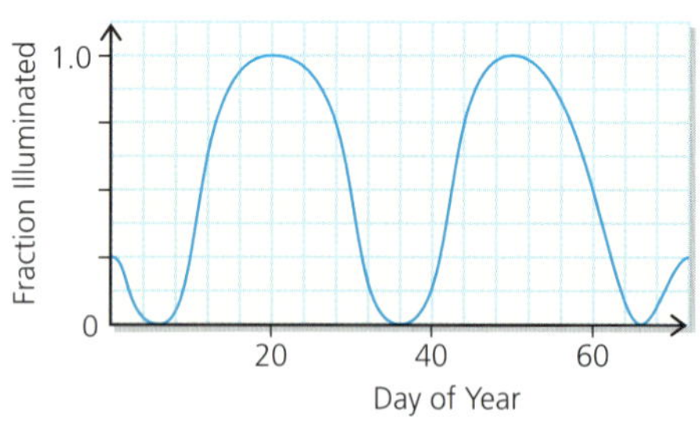

You found that this data represents a periodic phenomenon with the following properties:

- The period is about 29.5 days.
- The "full" moon is fully visible when the maximum value is 1.0. The "new" moon is not visible when the minimum value is 0.
- The axis of the curve is the horizontal line $y = 0.5$.
- The amplitude of the curve is $\frac{\text{maximum} - \text{minimum}}{2} = 0.5$.

You know that a sinusoidal model of this data is $y = a \sin k(\theta + b) + d$. Find the values of a, k, b, and d to complete the model.

The amplitude, a, is 0.5.

The period of $y = \sin \theta$ is 2π and the period of this function is 29.5 days. Then

$$k\theta = 2\pi$$
$$29.5k = 2\pi$$
$$k = \frac{2\pi}{29.5}$$

Compare the graph here to $y = \sin \theta$. The phase shift, b, is about 14 days to the left. Therefore, $b = -14$.

The equation for the axis of the curve is $y = 0.5$. Then the vertical translation, d, is 0.5.

Substituting in $y = a \sin k(\theta + b) + d$ gives $y = 0.5 \sin \frac{2\pi}{29.5}(t - 14) + 0.5$, where t represents the day of the year.

Verify this model by graphing the equation with a graphing calculator. Before graphing, set the mode to radian.

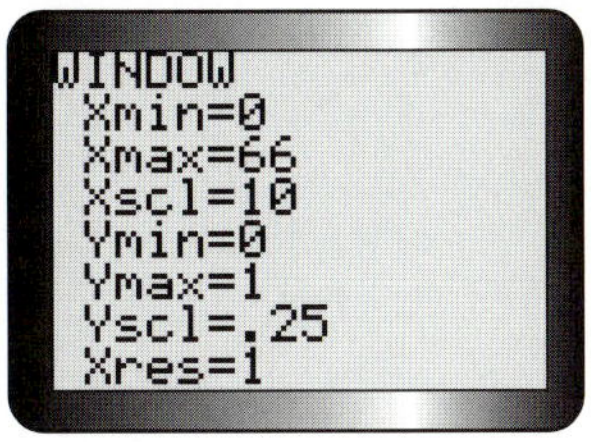

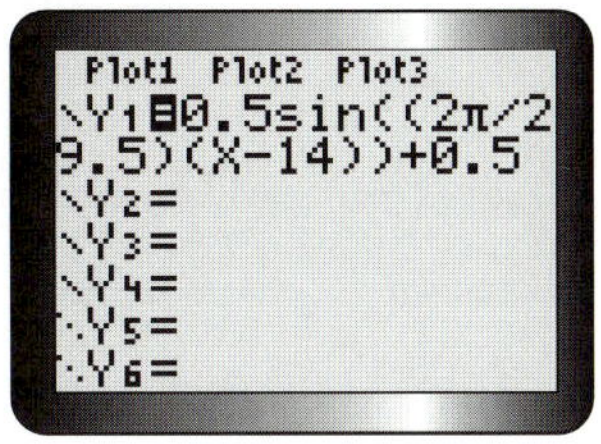

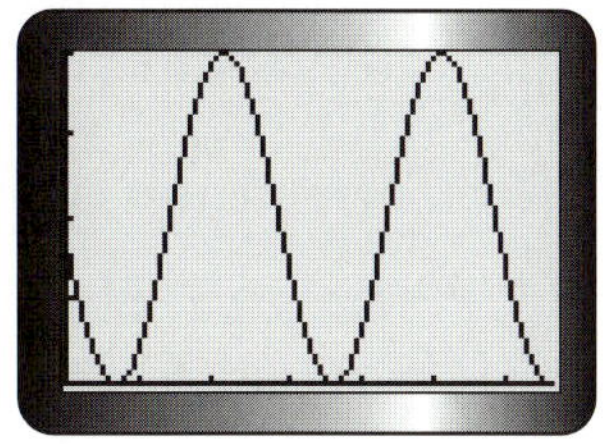

Example 1

Write the model of the waxing and waning of the moon at the turn of the millennium as a cosine function.

Solution

The cosine function has the form $y = a \cos k(t + b) + d$, and $a = 0.5$, $k = \frac{2\pi}{29.5}$, and $d = 0.5$. The variable t represents the day of the year.

To determine the value of b, examine the original graph on page 460 to identify where the cosine curve could start. The cosine pattern begins at the maximum value. In this case, $t = 21$ days. Then $b = -21$.

Therefore, the model is $y = 0.5 \cos \frac{2\pi}{29.5}(t - 21) + 0.5$.

Example 2

Determine the function that is the simplest model of the following data.

Independent Variable	−90°	−45°	0°	45°	90°	125°	180°
Dependent Variable	8	6	4	6	8	6	4

Solution

First decide what type of model could represent the data.
Draw a sketch to help you decide.

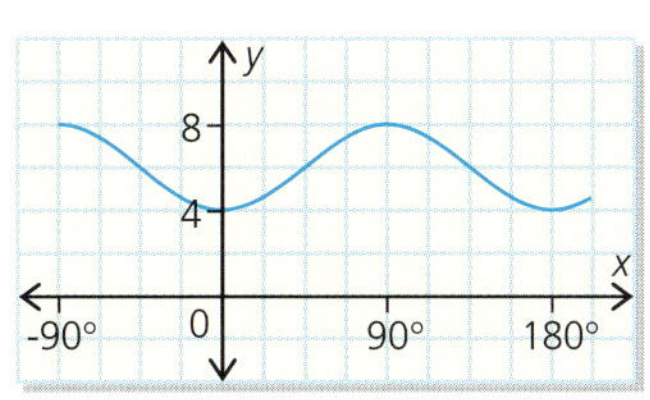

The curve in the graph appears to represent a sine function or a cosine function.

Case 1: The Sine Model

For the sine model, $y = a \sin k(\theta + b) + d$.

The maximum value is 8 and the minimum value is 4.

The axis of the graph is midway between the maximum and minimum values.

The equation of the axis $y = \frac{8 + 4}{2}$ or $y = 6$.

Then d, the vertical translation, is 6.

The amplitude, a, is half the difference between the maximum and minimum values, $\frac{8 - 4}{2} = 2$. Then $a = 2$.

The period is 180°. There are two complete cycles for each complete cycle of $y = \sin \theta$. The horizontal compression is a factor of $\frac{1}{2}$, so $k = 2$.

Another way to determine k is to solve $k\theta = 360°$ when $\theta = 180°$.

$$\begin{aligned} k\theta &= 360° \\ k(180°) &= 360° \\ k &= \frac{360°}{180°} \\ k &= 2 \end{aligned}$$

The part of this graph that corresponds to the sine function starts at 45°, which is a shift to the right. Then b is $-45°$.

Now substitute $a = 2$, $k = 2$, $b = -45°$, and $d = 6$ in $y = a \sin k(\theta + b) + d$ to get $y = 2 \sin 2(\theta - 45°) + 6$.

Case 2: The Cosine Model

For the cosine model, $y = a \cos k(\theta + b) + d$.

The horizontal compression, $k = 2$, and the vertical translation, $d = 6$, do not change.

The cosine curve reflects about the line $y = 6$. For $a = -2$, the phase angle, b, is 0.

Then the cosine model is $y = -2 \cos 2\theta + 6$.

The simplest model for this data is the one in Case 2, $y = -2 \cos 2\theta + 6$.

For both cases, the maximum and minimum values appeared in the original data. Sometimes these are not given in the data and must be projected from the graph.

Consolidate Your Understanding

1. How do you decide that a trigonometric model best represents the data?
2. How do you decide which trigonometric model to use?
3. How can you verify that the model represents the data?

Focus 5.7

Key Ideas

- You can obtain the trigonometric models $y = a \sin k(\theta + b) + d$ and $y = a \cos k(\theta + b) + d$ by first graphing periodic sinusoidal data.
- You can model and solve many real-life problems using $y = a \sin k(\theta + b) + d$ or $y = a \cos k(\theta + b) + d$.
- The values of a, k, b, and d are found by determining the transformations that must be applied to $y = \sin \theta$ or $y = \cos \theta$, respectively, to obtain the graph of the data.

Practise, Apply, Solve 5.7

A

1. Graph the data in each table. Then determine the model $y = a \sin \theta$ of the data.

(a)

θ	$-180°$	$-90°$	$0°$	$90°$	$180°$	$270°$	$360°$
y	0	-3	0	3	0	-3	0

(b)

θ	$-\pi$	$-\frac{\pi}{2}$	0	$\frac{\pi}{2}$	π	$\frac{3\pi}{2}$	2π
y	0	2	0	-2	0	2	0

2. Graph the data. Then determine the model $y = \cos k\theta$ of the data.

(a)

θ	$-90°$	$-45°$	$0°$	$45°$	$90°$	$135°$	$180°$
y	-1	0	1	0	-1	0	1

(b)

θ	-2π	$-\pi$	0	π	2π	3π	4π
y	-1	0	1	0	-1	0	1

3. Graph the data. Then determine the model $y = \sin(\theta + b)$ of the data.

(a)

θ	$30°$	$120°$	$210°$	$300°$	$390°$
y	0	1	0	-1	0

(b)

θ	$-45°$	$45°$	$135°$	$225°$	$315°$
y	0	1	0	-1	0

4. Graph the data. Then determine the model $y = \cos(\theta + b)$ of the data.

(a)

θ	$\frac{2\pi}{6}$	$\frac{5\pi}{6}$	$\frac{8\pi}{6}$	$\frac{11\pi}{6}$	$\frac{14\pi}{6}$
y	1	0	-1	0	1

(b)

θ	$-\frac{\pi}{6}$	$\frac{2\pi}{6}$	$\frac{5\pi}{6}$	$\frac{8\pi}{6}$	$\frac{11\pi}{6}$
y	1	0	-1	0	1

5. Use the ordered pairs $(-30°, 0)$, $(15°, 1)$, $(60°, 0)$, $(105°, -1)$, and $(150°, 0)$ to determine an equation in the form $y = \sin k(\theta + b)$.

6. The ordered pairs $(0°, 5)$, $(90°, 6)$, $(180°, 5)$, $(270°, 4)$, and $(360°, 5)$ satisfy the equation $y = \sin \theta + d$. Determine d.

7. The ordered pairs $(0, -8)$, $\left(\frac{\pi}{2}, -9\right)$, $(\pi, -10)$, $\left(\frac{3\pi}{2}, -9\right)$, and $(2\pi, -8)$ satisfy the equation $y = \cos \theta + d$. Determine d.

B

8. **Knowledge and Understanding:** Find the sine function $y = a \sin k(\theta + b) + d$ for each graph.

(a)

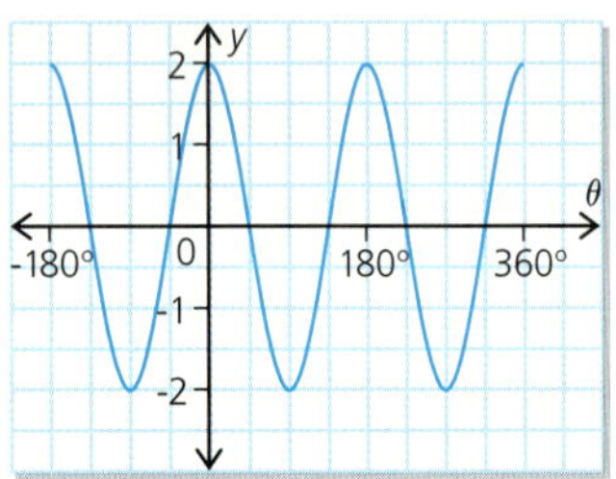

(b)

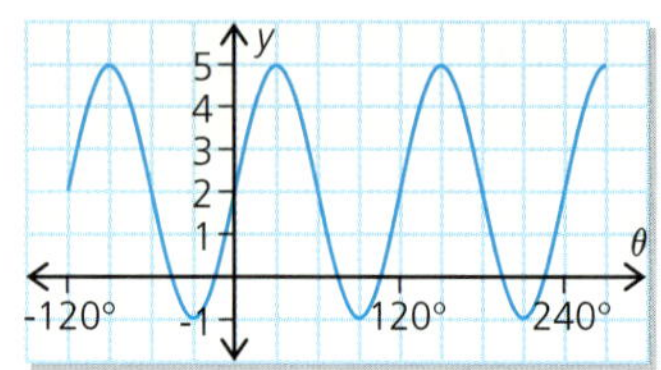

(c)

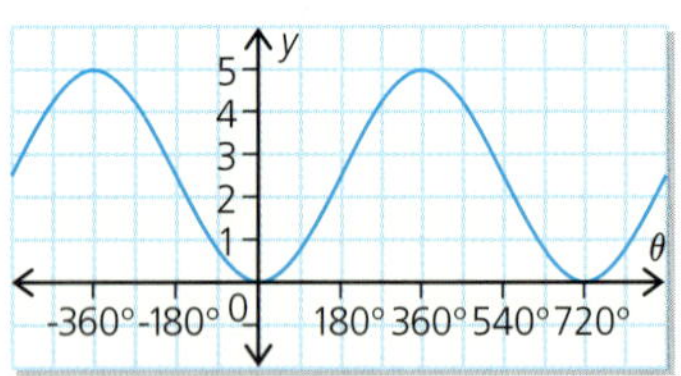

(d)

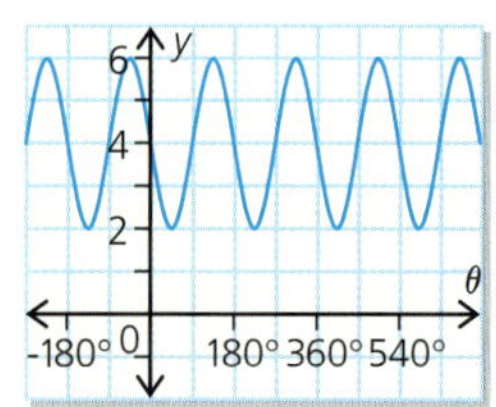

(e)

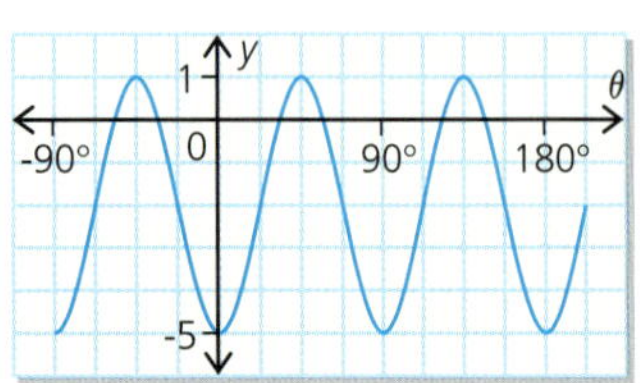

9. Find the cosine function $y = a \cos k(\theta + b) + d$ for each graph in question 8.

10. Determine the sine function that models the given information.

	Amplitude	Period	Phase Shift	Vertical Shift
(a)	3	2π	$\frac{\pi}{4}$	-1
(b)	$\frac{1}{2}$	π	$-\frac{\pi}{3}$	2
(c)	2	$\frac{\pi}{2}$	$\frac{\pi}{6}$	3
(d)	-2	4π	$\frac{\pi}{8}$	-3
(e)	$-\frac{3}{4}$	3π	$\frac{\pi}{2}$	-2

11. Sketch each pair of functions on the same axes. Follow the pattern to generalize $y = \sin k\theta$ in terms of the cosine function.

(a) $y = \sin \theta$ and $y = \cos\left(\theta - \frac{\pi}{2}\right)$, $0 \leq \theta \leq 2\pi$

(b) $y = \sin 2\theta$ and $y = \cos 2\left(\theta - \frac{\pi}{2}\right)$, $0 \leq \theta \leq 2\pi$

(c) $y = \sin 3\theta$ and $y = \cos 3\left(\theta - \frac{\pi}{2}\right)$, $0 \leq \theta \leq 2\pi$

12. For each part of question 10, rewrite the sine function as a cosine function.

13. A skyscraper sways 55 cm back and forth from "the vertical" during high winds. At $t = 5$ s, the building is 55 cm to the right of vertical. The building sways back to the vertical and, at $t = 35$ s, the building sways 55 cm to the left of the vertical. Write an equation that models the motion of the building in terms of time.

14. **Application:** In the "land of the midnight sun," it is daylight all the time during the summer. The first coordinate is the hour of the day. The second coordinate is the angle of elevation of the sun, in degrees, above the horizon at a location in Canada's Far North.

(00:00, 38.59), (01:00, 41.49), (02:00, 42.95), (03:00, 42.75), (04:00, 40.93), (05:00, 37.73), (06:00, 33.51), (07:00, 28.67), (08:00, 23.56), (09:00, 18.52), (10:00, 13.82), (11:00, 9.73), (12:00, 6.46), (13:00, 4.22), (14:00, 3.13), (15:00, 3.26), (16:00, 4.61), (17:00, 7.09), (18:00, 10.55), (19:00, 14.80), (20:00, 19.59), (21:00, 24.67), (22:00, 29.74), (23:00, 34.47), (24:00, 38.48)

(a) Draw a scatter plot of the data and the curve of best fit.

(b) What type of model describes the graph?

(c) Write an equation to model the situation. Describe the constants and the variables in the context of this problem. What restrictions must be placed on the domain?

(d) How could you use the model to calculate the elevation of the sun at 02:00 for the given location?

(e) When is the elevation of the sun above the horizon 30°?

15. The table shows the average monthly high temperature for one year in Kapuskasing.

Time (months)	J	F	M	A	M	J	J	A	S	O	N	D
Temperature (°C)	−18.6	−16.3	−9.1	0.4	8.5	13.8	17.0	15.4	10.3	4.4	−4.3	−14.8

Source: Environment Canada.

(a) Draw a scatter plot of the data and the curve of best fit. Let January be month 0.

(b) What type of model describes the graph?

(c) Write an equation to model the situation. Describe the constants and the variables in the context of this problem.

(d) Use a calculator to graph the equation. Compare the graph and the scatter plot.

(e) What is the average monthly temperature for the 38th month?

16. The depth of water in a harbour on the Bay Fundy that faces the ocean changes each hour, as shown.

Time (h)	00:00	01:00	02:00	03:00	04:00	05:00	06:00	07:00	08:00	09:00	10:00	11:00	12:00
Depth (m)	5.5	6.3	8.5	11.5	14.5	16.7	17.5	16.7	14.5	11.5	8.5	6.3	5.5

(a) Graph the data and determine an equation that models the situation.

(b) Verify the graph using a graphing calculator.

(c) Use the equation to determine the depth of water at 10:30. Verify your answer using the graph.

(d) When is the water 7 m deep?

17. The table shows the velocity of air in litres per second of Nicole's breathing while she is at rest.

Time (s)	0	0.25	0.5	0.75	1.0	1.25	1.5	1.75	2	2.25	2.5	2.75	3
Velocity (L/s)	0	0.22	0.45	0.61	0.75	0.82	0.85	0.83	0.74	0.61	0.43	0.23	0

(a) Explain why breathing is an example of a periodic function.

(b) Graph the data and determine an equation that models the situation.

(c) Use a graphing calculator to draw the scatter plot of the data. Enter your equation into the equation editor and graph. Comment on the closeness of fit between the scatter plot and the graph.

(d) For $t = 6$ s, what is the velocity of Nicole's breathing? Verify your answer using an alternative method.

(e) How many seconds have passed when the velocity is 0.5 L/s?

18. Communication: The table shows the average monthly temperature for Athens, Lisbon, and Moscow. Graph the data to show that temperature is a function of time. Write the equations that model each function. Explain the differences in the amplitude and the vertical shift for each city.

Time (months)	J	F	M	A	M	J	J	A	S	O	N	D
Temperature (°C)												
Athens	12	13	15	19	24	30	33	32	28	23	18	14
Lisbon	13	14	16	18	21	24	26	27	24	21	17	14
Moscow	−9	−6	0	10	19	21	23	22	16	9	1	−4

19. The maximum height of a Ferris wheel is 35 m. The wheel takes 2 min to make one revolution. Passengers board the Ferris wheel 2 m above the ground at the bottom of its rotation.

(a) Write an equation to represent the position of a passenger at any time, t, in seconds.

(b) How high is the passenger after 45 s?

(c) The ride lasts for 4 min. When will the passenger be at the maximum height during this ride?

20. **Check Your Understanding:** Suppose you are given the graph of a sinusoidal function. Explain how you can determine the value of each variable in the corresponding equation $y = a \sin k(\theta + b) + d$.

(a) a (b) k (c) b (d) d

C

21. **Thinking, Inquiry, Problem Solving:** The diameter of a car's tire is 50 cm. While the car is being driven, the tire picks up a nail.

(a) Model the height of the nail above the ground in terms of the distance the car has travelled since the tire picked up the nail.

(b) How high above the ground will the nail be after the car has travelled 0.5 km?

(c) The nail reaches a height of 10 cm above the ground for the sixth time. How far has the car travelled?

(d) What assumption must you make concerning the driver's habits for the function to give an accurate height?

The Chapter Problem—How Much Daylight?

In this section, you modelled periodic phenomena using trigonometry. Apply what you learned to answer these questions about the Chapter Problem on page 404.

CP11. Write an equation in the form $y = a \sin k(\theta + b) + d$ to model the average number of hours of daylight for the Far North community.

CP12. Use a graphing calculator set to an appropriate scale to graph the equation. Confirm that the graph matches your graphs that you drew for previous sections.

CP13. How many hours of daylight should be expected at month 252?

5.8 Solving Linear Trigonometric Equations

The equation $\cos \theta = 0.5$ for the interval $0 \leq \theta \leq 2\pi$ is a **linear trigonometric equation**. The solutions to this type of equation are all the values in the given domain that make the equation true. In this case, the equation has two solutions, $\theta = \frac{\pi}{3}$ and $\theta = \frac{5\pi}{3}$. Solutions can be expressed in either degree measure or radian measure. Generally, express solutions using the same notation that is used in the given domain of the equation.

Part 1: Investigating the Number of Solutions

The monthly sales of lawn equipment can be modelled by the function $S(t) = 32.4 \sin \left(\frac{\pi}{6}\right)t + 53.5$, where S is the monthly sales in thousands of units and t is the time in months, $t = 1$ corresponds to January.

Think, Do, Discuss

1. Use a graphing calculator and set the mode to radian.
2. Enter the sales function into **Y1** of the equation editor. Ensure that you enter the equation as shown above.
3. Adjust the window. What must be the minimum and maximum settings for the x- and y-axes so that you will see the first year of the function in the graph?
4. Set the window to display the graph for one year and graph the function by using **ZoomFit**. (Press [ZOOM] [0].)
5. What is the period of this function?
6. In which month are monthly sales at a maximum? at a minimum?
7. In which month will 70 000 units be sold? Write the trigonometric equation that corresponds to this situation. Enter 70 into **Y2** of the equation editor and graph.
8. How many points of intersection are there? What are they and what do they mean?
9. How many times will the company sell 70 000 units over the next three years? In which months will this occur?
10. Check your predictions by adjusting the window settings for a period of three years and then graph.

11. According to this model, how many times will the company sell 70 000 units over the next ten years?

12. How many solutions are possible for the equation $70 = 32.4 \sin\left(\frac{\pi}{6}\right)t + 53.5$? Explain.

Part 2: Solving Trigonometric Equations

The domain plays an important role in the solution of trigonometric equations. The domain limits the number of possible solutions. Without a domain, a trigonometric equation would have an infinite number of solutions due to the periodic nature of the trigonometric functions.

You can solve a trigonometric equation in several ways.

Estimating the Solutions from a Graph

Sometimes you need only an estimate of the solution. To estimate a solution, use the information in a graph.

Example 1

Solve $\sin \theta = 0.5$ for $0° \le \theta \le 360°$.

Solution

Sketch the graph of $y = \sin \theta$ for $0° \le \theta \le 360°$.

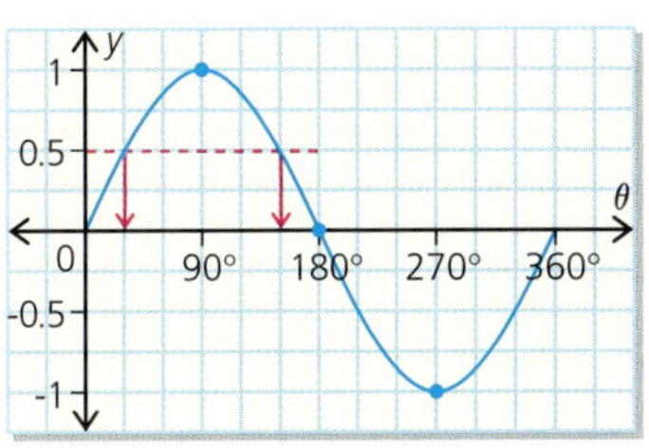

Draw a horizontal line through 0.5 on the y-axis to determine the angles that correspond with this value. From the graph, you can estimate that the solutions are $\theta = 30°$ and $\theta = 150°$.

Using a Scientific Calculator or a Graphing Calculator

You can determine all of the solutions in the given domain by using related angles and the period of the related function. Use a scientific calculator or a graphing calculator to calculate angles.

Example 2

Solve $\cos\theta = -0.8552$ for $0° \leq \theta \leq 360°$.

Solution

The domain is in degree measure. Ensure that the calculator is in degree mode. The cosine function is negative in quadrants II and III. For the given domain, there are only two solutions. Use a scientific or a graphing calculator to determine $\cos^{-1}(-0.8552)$.

$$\theta = \cos^{-1}(-0.8552)$$
$$\theta \doteq 148.78°$$

This angle is in quadrant II. The related angle is $180° - 148.78° = 31.22°$.

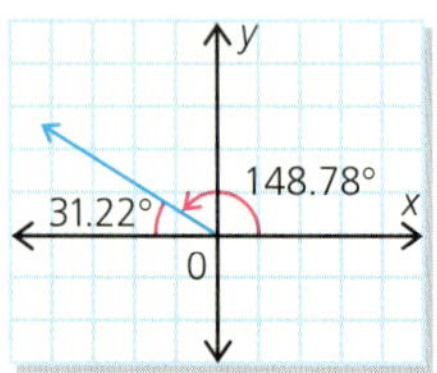

The angle in quadrant III is $180° + 31.22° = 211.22°$.

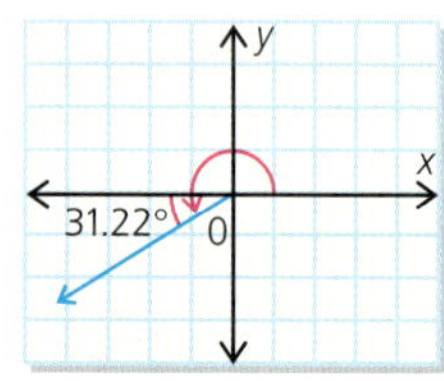

The two solutions of the equation are 148.78° and 211.22°.

Example 3

Solve $\tan\theta = 1.5$ for $0 \leq \theta \leq 2\pi$.

Solution

The domain is given in radian measure. Ensure that the calculator is in radian mode. The tangent function is positive in quadrants I and III. For the given domain, there are only two solutions. Use a scientific or a graphing calculator to determine $\tan^{-1}(1.5)$.

$$\theta = \tan^{-1}(1.5)$$
$$\theta \doteq 0.9828$$

This angle is in quadrant I.

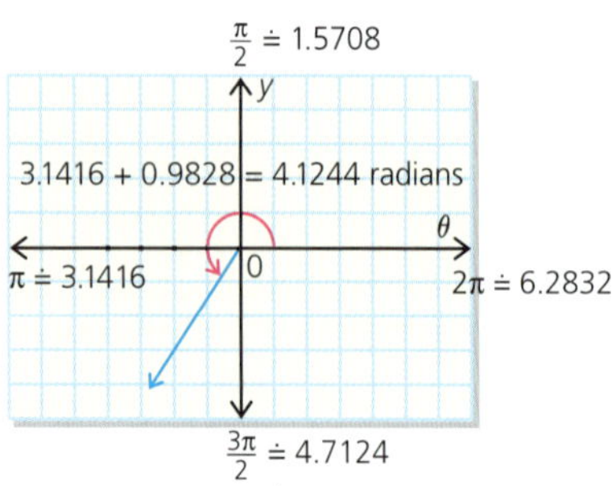

The angle in quadrant III is $\pi + 0.9828 \doteq 3.1416 + 0.9828$ or 4.1244 radians. The two solutions for this equation are 0.9828 radians and 4.1244 radians.

A few more steps are required when the period of a trigonometric equation is not 360° or 2π.

Example 4

Solve $3 \sin (2x) + 2 = 1$ for $0° \leq x \leq 360°$.

Solution

$3 \sin (2x) + 2 = 1$ Rearrange the equation by solving for $\sin (2x)$.

$$\begin{aligned} 3 \sin (2x) + 2 &= 1 \\ 3 \sin (2x) &= 1 - 2 \\ 3 \sin (2x) &= -1 \\ \sin (2x) &= -\frac{1}{3} \end{aligned}$$

Use a scientific or a graphing calculator to determine $\sin^{-1}\left(-\frac{1}{3}\right)$.

$$\sin^{-1}\left(-\frac{1}{3}\right) \doteq -19.47°$$

This angle is not in the given domain.

The sine function is negative in quadrants III and IV. The related acute angle is 19.47°.

quadrant III

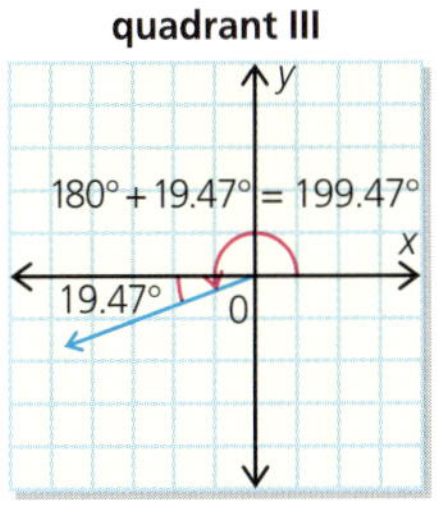

quadrant IV

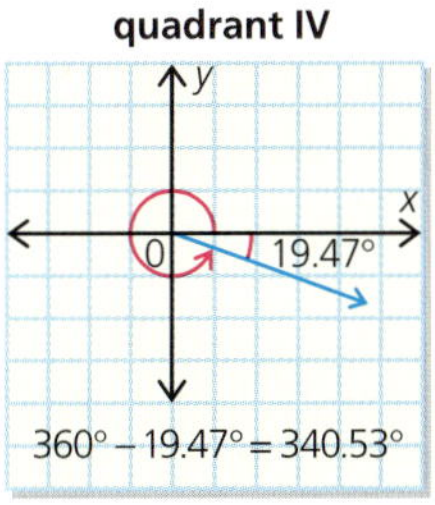

$$\begin{aligned} 2x &= 199.47° \\ x &= 99.735° \end{aligned}$$

$$\begin{aligned} 2x &= 340.53° \\ x &= 170.265° \end{aligned}$$

But the function $y = \sin (2x)$ has a period of 180°. Adding 180° to each solution yields the solutions for the second cycle, 180° to 360°. This equation has four solutions.

$x_1 = 99.735°$, $x_2 = 170.265°$, $x_3 = 99.735° + 180°$ or $279.735°$, and $x_4 = 170.265° + 180°$ or $350.265°$

Finding the Point of Intersection Between Two Functions

Example 5

Solve $2 \sin \theta - 3 = -3.5$ for $0° \leq \theta \leq 360°$.

Solution

Find the solutions to this equation by graphing two functions, $y = 2 \sin \theta - 3$ and $y = -3.5$, over the given domain on the same axes. The points of intersection between the two curves are the solutions to the original equation, $2 \sin \theta - 3 = -3.5$.
Put the calculator in degree mode.

1. Enter the functions into the equation editor.

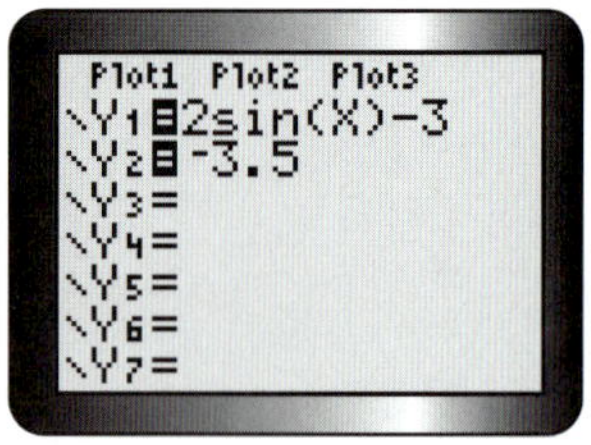

2. Set the window for the given domain.

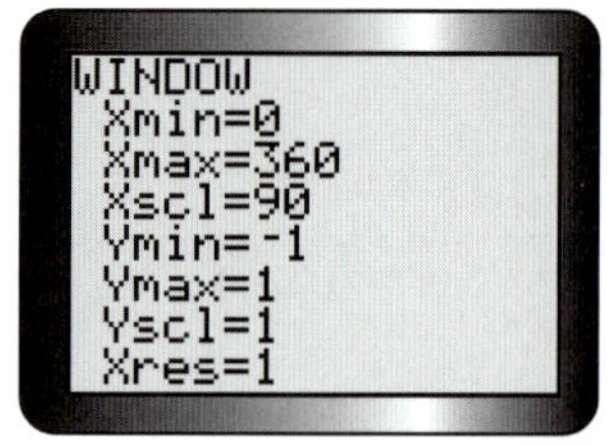

3. Graph by using ZoomFit. Press [ZOOM] [0].

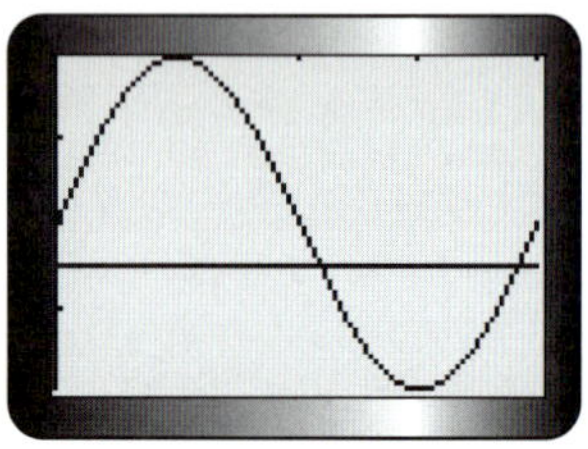

4. Determine all the points of intersection. Press [2nd] [TRACE] [5] and respond to the questions.

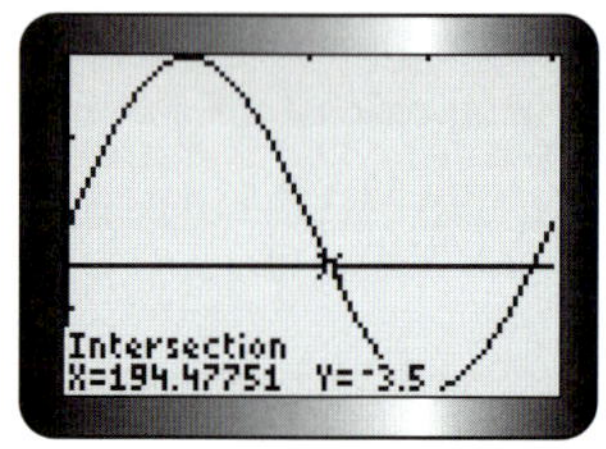

Determine the other point of intersection. The equation $2 \sin (\theta) - 3 = -3.5$ has solutions $\theta = 194.48°$ and $\theta = 345.52°$ for $0° \leq \theta \leq 360°$.

Using the Zeros of the Corresponding Function

Example 6

Solve $4 \cos (3x) = 1$ for $0 \leq x \leq 2\pi$.

Solution

Find the solutions to this equation by rearranging the original equation so that $4 \cos (3x) - 1 = 0$. Graph the corresponding function $y = 4 \cos (3x) - 1$ over the domain $0 \leq x \leq 2\pi$. The zeros or x-intercepts of $y = 4 \cos (3x) - 1$ correspond to the solutions of $y = 4 \cos (3x) - 1$.

Put the calculator in radian mode before graphing.

1. Enter the function into the equation editor.

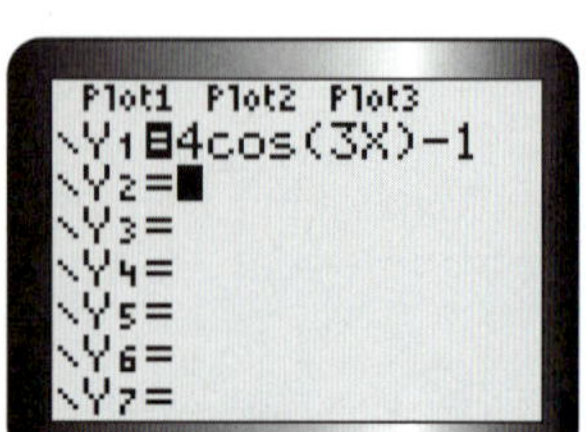

2. Set the window for the given domain. Xmin=0, Xmax=2π, Xscl=$\frac{\pi}{2}$.

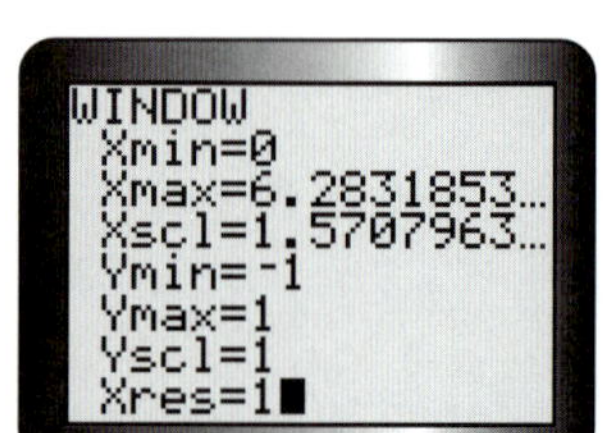

3. Graph by using **ZoomFit**. Press [ZOOM] [0].

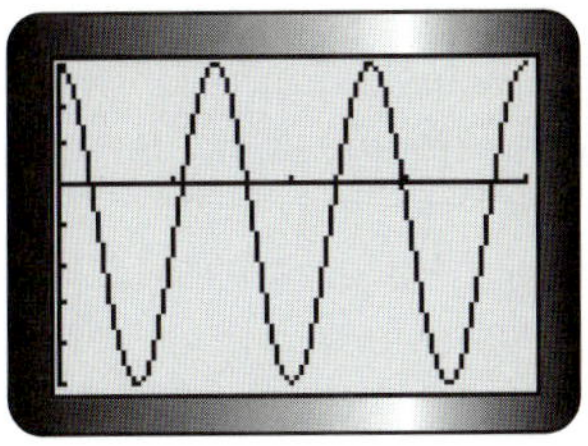

4. Determine all the zeros. Press [2nd] [TRACE] [2] and respond to the questions.

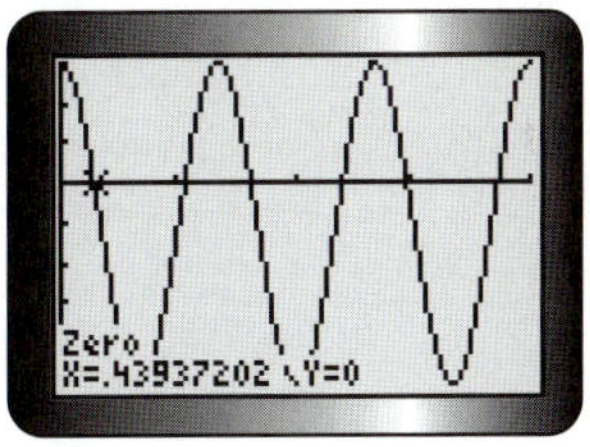

Determine the other five zeros of the function $y = 4 \cos(3x) - 1$. The equation $4 \cos(3x) = 1$ has solutions $x = 0.4394, 1.655, 2.5334, 3.7494, 4.6282$, and 5.8438, where $0 \le x \le 2\pi$.

Consolidate Your Understanding

1. Give an example of a linear trigonometric equation and its solutions for a specific domain.
2. How many solutions are possible for a linear trigonometric equation if the domain is not specified?
3. Which technique described in this section is best for solving the majority of linear trigonometric equations?
4. Does a scientific or a graphing calculator always yield *all* the solutions to a linear trigonometric equation over a given domain? Explain.
5. How can you solve *any* linear trigonometric equation?

Focus 5.8

Key Ideas

- Any equation that has $\sin x$, $\cos x$, or $\tan x$ and whose highest power is 1 is called a **linear trigonometric equation**. For example, $2 \sin x = 1$
- The solutions to a trigonometric equation are all of the values of the independent variable that make the equation a true statement and that are part of a given domain. For example, $2 \sin x = 1$ has solutions $x = \frac{\pi}{6}$ and $\frac{5\pi}{6}$, where $0 \le x \le 2\pi$ is the domain.
- A trigonometric equation can have an infinite number of solutions due to the periodic nature of trigonometric functions. The given domain limits the number of solutions. For example, the domain $0 \le x \le 2\pi$ indicates that the solutions to an equation must lie between these values.
- An approximate solution for any linear trigonometric equation can be interpolated or extrapolated from the graph of the equation.

- Use the inverse trigonometric functions on a scientific or a graphing calculator to obtain reasonable estimates of a solution. However, the solution provided by the calculator may or may not lie in the given domain. Use the related acute angle and the period of the corresponding function to determine all of the solutions in the given domain.
- Estimate the solution for any linear trigonometric equation by using graphing technology.
  - **i.** You can first write the equation as two separate functions, then determine the points of intersection between the two functions over the given domain.

    OR
  - **ii.** First rearrange the trigonometric equation so that zero is on one side, then determine the zeros or *x*-intercepts of the function over the given domain

Practise, Apply, Solve 5.8

A

1. Use the graph, where the domain is $0 \le \theta \le 2\pi$, to determine the value(s) of θ.

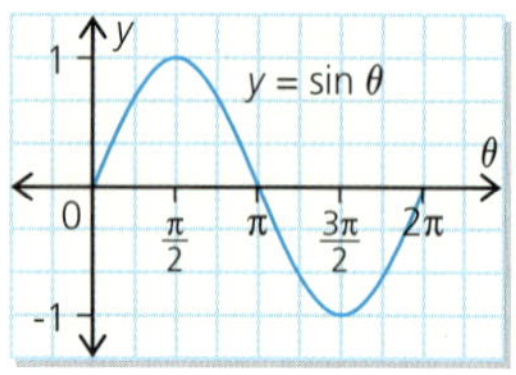

(a) $\sin \theta = 1$ (b) $\sin \theta = -1$ (c) $\sin \theta = 0.5$ (d) $\sin \theta = -0.5$

2. Use the graph, where the domain is $0 \le \theta \le 2\pi$, to determine the value(s) of θ.

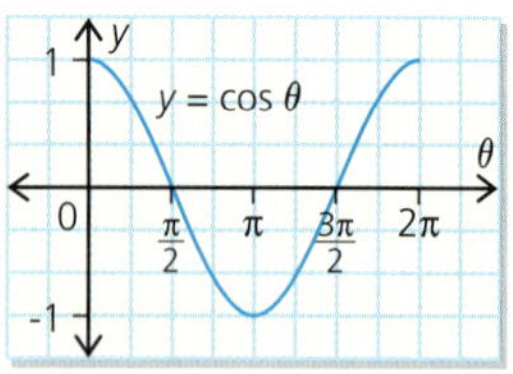

(a) $\cos \theta = 1$ (b) $\cos \theta = -1$ (c) $\cos \theta = 0.5$ (d) $\cos \theta = -0.5$

3. For $\sin x = \frac{\sqrt{3}}{2}$, $0 \le x \le 2\pi$.

(a) How many solutions are possible?

(b) In which quadrants would you find the solutions?

(c) Determine the related acute angle for this equation.

(d) Determine all the solutions to the equation.

4. For $\cos x = -0.8667$, $0° \leq x \leq 360°$.
   (a) How many solutions are possible?
   (b) In which quadrants would you find the solutions?
   (c) Determine the related angle for this equation to the nearest degree.
   (d) Determine all the solutions to the equation to the nearest degree.

5. For $\tan \theta = 2.7553$, $0 \leq \theta \leq 2\pi$.
   (a) How many solutions are possible?
   (b) In which quadrants would you find the solutions?
   (c) Determine the related angle for this equation to the nearest hundredth.
   (d) Determine all the solutions to the equation to the nearest hundredth.

B

6. Using a calculator, determine the solutions for each equation. The domain is $0° \leq x \leq 360°$. Round your answers to the nearest tenth of a degree.
   (a) $\sin x = 0.65$ (b) $\cos x = 0.8$ (c) $\tan x = 1.5$
   (d) $\sin x = 0.15$ (e) $\tan x = 0.75$ (f) $\cos x = -0.655$

7. Using a calculator, determine the solutions for each equation. The domain is $0 \leq \theta \leq 2\pi$. Round your answers to the nearest hundredth of a radian.
   (a) $\sin \theta = 0.4255$ (b) $\cos \theta = 0 .1576$ (c) $\tan \theta = 2.35$
   (d) $\sin \theta = -0.5005$ (e) $\tan \theta = -0.6341$ (f) $\cos \theta = -0.7583$

8. Using a calculator, determine the roots for each equation. The domain is $0° \leq \theta \leq 360°$.
   (a) $\tan \theta = 1$ (b) $\sin \theta = \frac{1}{\sqrt{2}}$ (c) $\cos \theta = \frac{\sqrt{3}}{2}$
   (d) $\sin \theta = -\frac{\sqrt{3}}{2}$ (e) $\cos \theta = -\frac{1}{\sqrt{2}}$ (f) $\tan \theta = \sqrt{3}$

9. Using a calculator, determine the roots for each equation. The domain is $0° \leq \theta \leq 360°$. Express your answers to one decimal place.
   (a) $2 \sin \theta = -1$ (b) $3 \cos \theta = -2$ (c) $2 \tan \theta = 3$
   (d) $-3 \sin \theta - 1 = 1$ (e) $-5 \cos \theta + 3 = 2$ (f) $8 - \tan \theta = 10$

10. **Knowledge and Understanding**
    (a) How many solutions does the equation $5 \cos x + 3 = 6$ for $0° \leq x \leq 360°$ have?
    (b) Solve the equation in (a).

11. Using a calculator, determine the solutions for each equation to two decimal places. The domain is $0 \leq x \leq 2\pi$.
    (a) $3 \sin x = \sin x + 1$ (b) $5 \cos x - \sqrt{3} = 3 \cos x$
    (c) $\cos x - 1 = -\cos x$ (d) $5 \sin x + 1 = 3 \sin x$

12. Using a calculator, determine the solutions for each equation to two decimal places. The domain is $0 \leq x \leq 2\pi$.

(a) $\sin 2x = \frac{1}{\sqrt{2}}$

(b) $\sin 4x = \frac{1}{2}$

(c) $\sin 3x = -\frac{\sqrt{3}}{2}$

(d) $\cos 4x = -\frac{1}{\sqrt{2}}$

(e) $\cos 2x = -\frac{1}{2}$

(f) $\cos\left(\frac{x}{2}\right) = \frac{\sqrt{3}}{2}$

13. **Communication:** Sketch the graph of $y = \sin 2\theta$, $0 \leq \theta \leq 2\pi$. On the graph, clearly indicate all the solutions to the trigonometric equation $\sin 2\theta = -\frac{1}{\sqrt{2}}$.

14. **Thinking, Inquiry, Problem Solving:** Search the Internet to find a sunrise and sunset calculator. Use the calculator to determine the number of hours of daylight over a one-year period for a city near your community. It may be helpful to find the numbers of hours of daylight for 15-day intervals. Use the data to create an algebraic model. Then determine on which day(s) of the year this city gets exactly 11 h of daylight.

15. A Ferris wheel has a radius of 7 m. The centre of the wheel is 8 m above the ground. The Ferris wheel rotates at a constant speed of 15°/s. The height above the ground of the only red seat can be modelled by the function $h(t) = 8 + 7 \sin (15°t)$.

(a) Determine the height of the red seat at the start of the ride.

(b) What is the maximum height of any seat?

(c) When is the red seat at its maximum height during the first rotation?

(d) What is the minimum height of any seat?

(e) When is the red seat at its minimum height during the first rotation?

(f) How long will it take for the red seat to complete two full rotations?

16. On a merry-go-round, each horse moves up and down five times in one complete revolution. Imagine that each horse rises and falls 25 cm from its centre position. The up-and-down motion of each horse can be modelled by the function $h(t) = 25 \cos (5\theta)$, where h is the horse's displacement from its centre and θ is the rotation angle of the merry-go-round. Assume the ride begins when $\theta = 0°$ for a given horse.

(a) Determine the displacement of one horse at the start of the ride.

(b) At what rotation angles will the horse be displaced 15 cm in one revolution?

(c) At what rotation angles will the horse be displaced −20 cm in one revolution?

(d) How long will it take for one complete revolution if the carousel rotates at a speed of 24°/s?

17. Solve each of the following using graphing technology. The domain is $0° \leq x \leq 360°$. Express your answers to the nearest tenth of a degree.

(a) $4 \sin x - 3 = -4$

(b) $0.5 \cos x = 0.1$

(c) $3 \tan x - 2 = 5$

(d) $2 \sin (2x) = -1$

(e) $-1 \cos (3x) = 1$

(f) $5 \tan \left(\frac{x}{2}\right) = 1$

(g) $2 \sin (x + 90°) = 1$

(h) $\cos (x - 60°) + 2 = 3$

18. Solve each of the following using graphing technology. The domain is $0 \leq x \leq 2\pi$. Express your answers to the nearest hundredth.

(a) $3 \sin x + 6 = 5$

(b) $2 \cos (0.5x) = 2$

(c) $2 \tan (2x) = 1$

(d) $4 \sin 3x = -2$

(e) $-2 \cos x = 1$

(f) $-\tan (x) = 5$

(g) $\sin (x - \pi) = 1$

(h) $2 \cos (x + 1) = 0.5$

19. **Application:** The horizontal distance, d, in metres, of a baseball's path when it is hit by a bat can be modelled by $d(\theta) = \frac{v^2}{9.8} \sin (2\theta) + 0.5$, where v is the initial speed of the ball in metres per second and θ is the angle at which the ball leaves the bat.

(a) A home run travels a horizontal distance of 142 m. The ball leaves the bat an angle of 43°. Determine the initial speed of the ball.

(b) The ball travels a horizontal distance of 59 m and leaves the bat at a speed of 30 m/s. Determine the angle at which the ball was struck if

i. it was a line drive

ii. it was a fly ball

20. The average monthly temperature of Littletown can be modelled by the function $T(t) = 14.6 \sin 0.5(t - 1) + 9.15$, where T is the temperature in degrees Celsius and $t = 0$ represents January 1, $t = 1$ represents February 1, and so on.

(a) In which month is the average monthly temperature the highest? the lowest?

(b) Use the model to predict when the temperature is 0°C.

(c) When is the temperature 20°C?

21. The daily mean temperature is the average of the highest and lowest temperatures during one day. The table shows the average daily mean temperature for each month, in degrees Celsius, for London, Ontario, over a 50-year period.

Month	J	F	M	A	M	J	J	A	S	O	N	D
Daily Mean Temperature (°C)	−6.7	−6.2	−0.5	6.2	12.6	17.7	20.3	19.3	15.3	9.1	3.3	−3.4

Source: Environment Canada

(a) Create a scatter plot of temperature versus time, where $t = 1$ represents January, $t = 2$ represents February, and so on.

(b) Draw the curve of best fit.

(c) Determine the trigonometric function that models this relationship.

(d) When will the daily mean temperature be 15°C in London, according to the function? Explain any differences between this and the table.

22. The table shows the average number of monthly hours of sunshine for Toronto.

Month	J	F	M	A	M	J	J	A	S	O	N	D
Average Monthly Sunshine (h)	95.5	112.6	150.5	187.7	229.7	254.9	278	244	184.7	145.7	82.3	72.6

Source: Environment Canada

(a) Create a scatter plot of the number of hours of sunshine versus time, where $t = 1$ represents January, $t = 2$ represents February, and so on.

(b) Draw the curve of best fit.

(c) Determine the trigonometric function that models this relation.

(d) When will the number of monthly hours of sunshine be at a maximum according to the function? When will it be a minimum according to the function?

(e) How good a model is the equation? Explain.

23. Check Your Understanding

(a) For $2 \cos \theta + 3 = 4$, how many solutions are possible if the domain is $0 \leq \theta \leq 2\pi$?

(b) Solve the equation $2 \cos \theta + 3 = 4$ for $0 \leq \theta \leq 2\pi$, without using a calculator or graphing technology.

(c) Verify the solutions you found for the equation in (b) by using graphing technology.

C

24. Solve $\cos \theta - \sin \theta = 0$ for $0 \leq \theta \leq 2\pi$, without using graphing technology.

25. Solve $\sin (2\theta - 20°) = \frac{1}{2}$ for $0° \leq \theta \leq 360°$, without using graphing technology.

The Chapter Problem—How Much Daylight?

In this section, you studied linear trigonometric equations. Apply what you learned to answer this question on the Chapter Problem on page 404.

CP14. The equation $h(t) = 7 \sin \frac{\pi}{6}(t - 2) + 12.5$ is a model for the average number of hours of daylight per month, beginning at the turn of the millennium. Solve for t if $h(t) = 13$ and $0 \leq t \leq 240$.

TI-83 Plus Calculator: Using Sinusoidal Regression to Find the Curve of Best Fit

The TI-83 Plus calculator can draw a curve of best fit for data on a scatter plot. The calculator can also provide the equation of the trigonometric function for this curve.

This table gives the mean monthly temperature in degrees Celsius for Kingston, Ontario.

Month	J	F	M	A	M	J	J	A	S	O	N	D
Mean Monthly Temperature (°C)	−8	−7	−1.4	5.6	11.7	16.5	20.3	19.5	15.2	8.8	3	−4.3

Ensure that the calculator is in radian mode.

1. Enter data into lists.

To create a scatter plot, begin by entering the data into lists. Enter the months into **L1** and the corresponding temperature values into **L2**. Use 1 for January, 2 for February, and so on. Press [STAT] [1] to edit the lists.

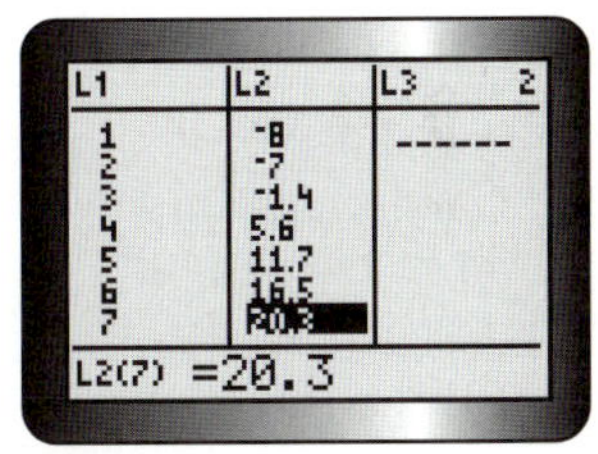

step 1

2. Open the stat plot editor and adjust the settings.

Once you have entered all the values into the appropriate lists, select the first stat plot. Press [2nd] [Y=] [1] [ENTER]. Make sure that you have the **Type**, **Xlist**, and **Ylist** set as shown.

step 2

3. View the scatter plot.

Press [ZOOM] [9]. The data is clearly nonlinear. The scatter plot resembles a sine curve or a cosine curve.

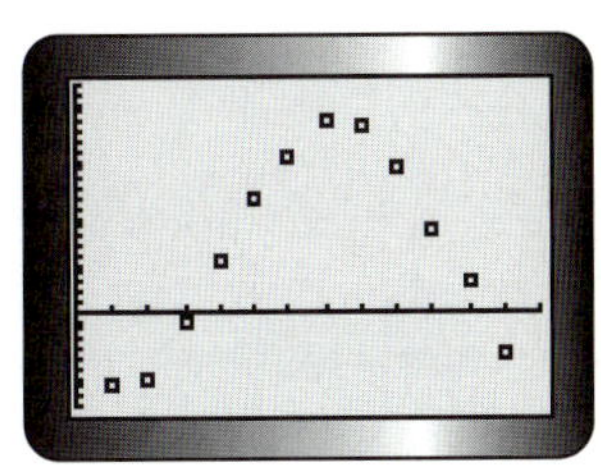

step 3

4. **Find the equation of the curve of best fit**

To find the equation of the curve of best fit, you can use **sinusoidal regression**. Press [STAT] and scroll over to **CALC**. Scroll down to **C:SinReg** and press [ENTER].

step 4

5. **Enter the names of the lists.**

Press [2nd] [1] [,] [2nd] [2] [,] [VARS]. Scroll over to **Y-VARS**, then press [1] [1]. You have stored the equation of the curve of best fit in the equation editor under **Y1**. Press [ENTER] to display the results.

step 5

6. **Display the curve of best fit.**

Press [GRAPH].

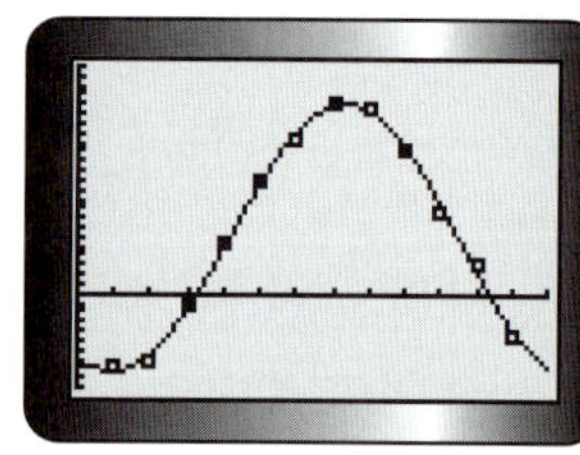

step 6

7. **Display the equation of the trigonometric function.**

Press [Y=]. The equation that best represents the data is $y = 14.2 \sin (0.5x - 2) + 5.9$.

step 7

Practice 5.9

1. The table shows an individual's blood pressure in millimetres of mercury.

Time (s)	0	0.25	0.5	0.75	1	1.25	1.5	1.75	2
Blood Pressure (mm)	100	120	100	80	100	120	100	80	100

Write the trigonometric equation that models this relationship

2. Return to section 5.7 and use **SinReg** to confirm your answers to questions 13, 14, 15, 16, and 17.

3. Answer the Chapter Problem by using sinusoidal regression and compare the graph and model to the work previously done. Account for any differences.

Using Digital Probes to Collect Periodic Data

5.10

Digital probes are small machines that collect data directly from an experiment. The data collected can be sent directly to a computer or graphing calculator for analysis and decision making.

Experiment 1: A Graph of Sound

Your task is to find the frequency of two different tuning forks. You will examine the graph and the corresponding equation that models the vibration of the tuning fork.

Equipment

- a microphone/amplifier with CBL DIN adapter
- two different tuning forks
- a rubber tuning fork hammer

You will need the BEATS and SOUND programs for the Calculator-Based Laboratory (CBL).

Procedure: Setting Up and Operating the CBL Unit

Ensure that both the unit and the graphing calculator are turned off before beginning.

1. Connect the CBL to the graphing calculator using the unit-to-unit link cable and the INPUT/OUTPUT (I/O) port located on the bottom edge of each unit.
2. Connect the microphone to Channel 1 (CH1) on the top edge of the CBL unit.
3. Turn the CBL unit and the calculator ON.
4. Start the SOUND program.

5. Take one of the tuning forks and strike it with the rubber hammer. Place the vibrating fork close to, but not touching, the microphone.
6. Press [ENTER] to start collecting data.
7. The resulting plot should appear to be sinusoidal. If it is not, then press [CLEAR] [ENTER] and repeat steps 4 to 6 until you are satisfied with the graph.

TECHNOLOGY

Analyzing the Data

1. What variables are stored in L1 and L2?
2. Describe the type of graph.
3. (a) Determine the amplitude of the graph.
   (b) Determine the period of the graph.
   (c) Determine the equation of the axis of the graph.
4. Determine the equation that models the sound wave of the first tuning fork. Check the accuracy of your model using sinusoidal regression.
5. The frequency of a tuning fork can be determined using the relationship $f = \frac{1}{T}$, where f is the frequency in hertz (Hz) and T is the period of the sound wave. Calculate the frequency of the tuning fork. (One hertz is equal to one cycle per second.)
6. Repeat the experiment for the other tuning fork and answer questions 1 to 5 for that tuning fork.

Experiment 2: A Graph of the Motion of a Ping-Pong Paddle Along a Horizontal Axis

In this experiment, you will use the CBL, or the Calculator-Based Ranger (CBR), to record data associated with the movement of a Ping-Pong paddle as someone repeatedly moves the paddle toward and away from the motion detector. Use the HIKER program with the CBL and the RANGER program with the CBR to collect and graph the data.

Procedure: Setting Up and Operating the CBL Unit or the CBR Unit (CBL/CBR)

Ensure that both the unit and the graphing calculator are turned off before beginning.

1. Connect the CBL/CBR to the calculator using the unit-to unit connector cable. Connect the cable to the INPUT/OUTPUT(I/O) port on the bottom of the calculator.

2. Connect the motion detector to the SONIC port on the CBL. This port is on the left side of the unit. (This step is not required when using the CBR.)

3. Turn the CBL/CBR and the calculator ON.

4. Place the motion detector on the edge of a table or chair. Place the motion detector so that it can detect the motion of the Ping-Pong paddle as the paddle repeatedly moves toward and away from the detector.

5. If you are using the CBL, then start the HIKER program on the calculator. The program should pause and display a message, **Press Enter To Start Graph**. Press [ENTER] and move the Ping-Pong paddle back and forth, at the same speed, about 10 cm each way 10 to 15 times. The motion detector should make a clicking sound.

If using the CBR, start the RANGER program and press [ENTER]. Select **2: SET DEFAULTS**. Press [ENTER] to choose START NOW. Then move the Ping-Pong paddle back and forth, at the same speed, about 10 cm each way 10 to 15 times.

Analyzing the Data

1. (a) Determine the amplitude of the graph.

(b) Determine the period of the graph.

(c) Determine the axis of the graph.

2. Write the equation that models the motion of the Ping-Pong paddle. Check the accuracy of your model using sinusoidal regression.

3. Repeat the experiment. Move the paddle more slowly and about 20 cm each way.

4. Compare these two graphs. How are the equations different? How are they the same?

TECHNOLOGY

Chapter 5 Review

Modelling Periodic Functions

Check Your Understanding

1. How can you tell when the graph of a set of data is periodic?

2. List five real-life situations that can be modelled by periodic functions. Explain why they are periodic.

3. (a) Sketch a sinusoidal curve.

(b) Name the primary trigonometric functions that are models of sinusoidal curves.

(c) How are the functions the same?

(d) How are the functions different?

4. Consider a set of data that can be modelled using a sinusoidal function. Describe the relationship between

(a) the maximum and minimum values and the axis of the function

(b) the maximum and minimum values and the amplitude of the curve

5. Explain the following sentence: Sinusoidal functions have period lengths that are multiples of 360° or 2π.

6. (a) Define the meaning of radian measure and explain its use.

(b) Describe how to convert between degree measure and radian measure.

7. Point $P(x, y)$ is on the terminal arm of an angle θ in standard position. State the primary trigonometric functions.

8. (a) Explain why the tangent function is not defined for all values of the independent variable.

(b) What occurs at the point where the tangent function is not defined? How does this feature help when sketching the graph?

9. Describe the transformation on $y = \cos \theta$ for each function. Use a sketch in your description.

(a) $y = \cos 2\theta$ (b) $y = -\frac{1}{2} \cos \theta$ (c) $y = \cos \frac{\theta}{2}$

(d) $y = \cos \theta + 2$ (e) $y = \cos (\theta + 2)$

10. What transformations are needed to obtain the graph of $y = a \sin k(\theta + b) + d$ from the graph of $y = \sin \theta$ under each set of conditions?

(a) $a > 1, k > 1, b < 0, d > 0$ (b) $-1 < a < 0, 0 < k < 1, b > 0, d < 0$

11. Explain how to use the domain of a periodic function to determine all values of θ when $\sin \theta = 0.5$.

Review and Practice

5.1 Periodic Phenomena

1. What feature of a function determines whether or not it is periodic?

2. Explain what each item means for a periodic curve. Show each item on a labelled diagram.

(a) cycle (b) period (c) amplitude

(d) axis of the curve (e) maximum and minimum

3. Explain why each case could be an example of a periodic phenomenon.

(a) the number of litres of ice cream consumed in Ontario each year

(b) the number of cubic metres of natural gas used each year by a factory

(c) the position of a pendulum in a grandfather clock

(d) the vibration of a guitar string

(e) the average monthly low temperature in London

(f) the sound of a fog horn

4. Sketch two cycles for each periodic relation.

(a) wash/rinse cycle of a dishwasher: period 10 min, amplitude 10 L, and axis 10 L

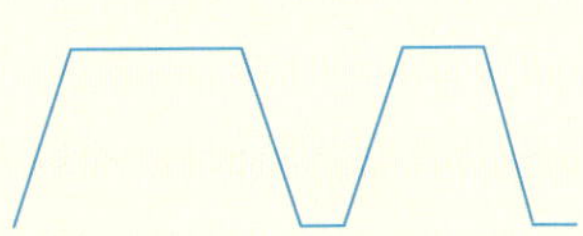

(b) tip of a windmill blade above the ground: period 50 s, amplitude 2 m, and axis 3 m

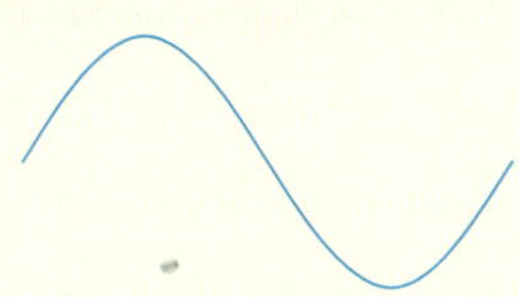

5. The graph shows Nina's height above the ground as she rides the Ferris wheel at the fair.

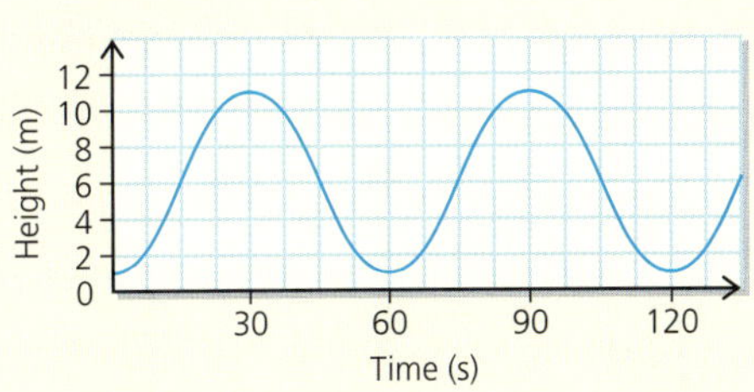

(a) State the maximum and minimum heights of the ride.

(b) How long does the wheel take to make one revolution?

(c) What is the amplitude of the curve? How does this relate to the Ferris wheel?

(d) Write an equation to represent the axis of the curve.

5.2 Understanding Angles

6. Explain each term.

(a) angle in standard position (b) positive angle (c) negative angle
(d) coterminal angle (e) principal angle (f) related acute angle

7. (a) How many degrees are possible for a positive angle, θ, that terminates in quadrant I? quadrant II? quadrant III? quadrant IV?

(b) How many radians are possible for a positive angle, θ, that terminates in quadrant I? quadrant II? quadrant III? quadrant IV?

8. Draw each angle. Show the principal angle, its measure, and the measure of the related acute angle.

(a) $-130°$ (b) $500°$ (c) $-560°$ (d) $280°$

9. State all values of θ in each case.

(a) $\theta = 62° + 360°n$, for $-2 \leq n \leq 3$, $n \in \mathbf{I}$

(b) $\theta = -137° + 360°n$, for $-1 \leq n \leq 2$, $n \in \mathbf{I}$

10. State the measure of all coterminal angles when

(a) the principal angle is $110°$ and $-360° \leq \theta \leq 540°$

(b) the principal angle is $190°$ and $-540° \leq \theta \leq 720°$

11. Point $P(-11, 14)$ is on the terminal arm of an angle θ in standard position.

(a) Mark the principal angle on a sketch. In which quadrant does the angle terminate?

(b) Determine the measure of the related acute angle to the nearest degree.

(c) What is the measure of θ to the nearest degree?

5.3 Trigonometric Functions

12. (a) State the primary trigonometric functions for any point $P(x, y)$ on the terminal arm of an angle θ in standard position.

(b) Explain how point $P(x, y)$ can be written with coordinates $P(r\cos\theta, r\sin\theta)$.

13. (a) Sketch the graph of $y = \sin\theta$ for $-360° \leq \theta \leq 360°$.

(b) State the period, amplitude, range, and axis of the curve.

(c) State the coordinates of all maximum values, minimum values, and zeros of the curve within this domain.

14. Repeat question 13 for $y = \cos\theta$.

15. (a) Sketch the graph of $y = \tan \theta$ for $-360° \leq \theta \leq 360°$.
(b) Why is the function undefined for certain values of θ?
(c) What occurs at the point where the graph is undefined?

16. Point $(-17, -20)$ is on the terminal arm of an angle θ in standard position.
(a) State the primary trigonometric functions for θ.
(b) Determine the measure of θ to the nearest degree.

17. A circular dining room at the top of a skyscraper rotates in a counterclockwise direction so diners can see the entire city. A woman sits next to the window ledge and places her purse on the ledge as shown. Eighteen minutes later she realizes that her table has moved but her purse is on the ledge where she left it. The coordinates of her position are $(x, y) = (20 \cos (7.5t)°, 20 \sin (7.5t)°)$, where t is the time in minutes and x and y are in metres. What is the shortest distance she has to walk to retrieve her purse? Round to one tenth of a metre.

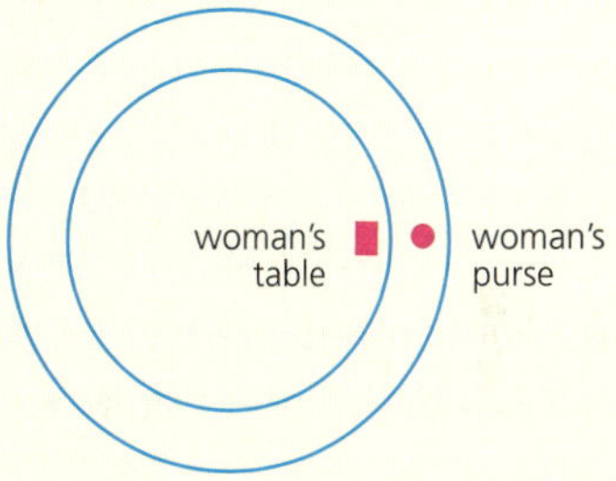

5.4–5.5 Radian Measure

18. How are degree measure and radian measure alike? different?

19. Show that $\theta = 2\pi$ for one revolution of a circle with radius r.

20. Convert each degree to exact radian measure and then evaluate to one decimal.
(a) 20° (b) −50° (c) 160° (d) 420° (e) −280°

21. Convert each radian measure to degree measure.
(a) $\frac{\pi}{4}$ (b) $-\frac{5\pi}{4}$ (c) $\frac{8\pi}{3}$ (d) $-\frac{2\pi}{3}$ (e) $\frac{11\pi}{6}$

22. Round each radian measure to the nearest degree and mark it on the unit circle.
(a) 3.2 (b) −1.4 (c) 8.3 (d) 1.5 (e) 2.2

23. Graph $y = \sin \theta$, for $-\frac{3\pi}{2} \leq \theta \leq \frac{5\pi}{2}$.

24. Determine θ to one decimal place for $-2\pi \leq \theta \leq 2\pi$.
(a) $\sin \theta = 0.75$ (b) $\cos \theta = -0.35$ (c) $\tan \theta = 6.33$

25. A ship that is docked in port and rises and falls with the waves. The model $h(t) = \sin\left(\frac{\pi}{5}\right)t$ describes the vertical movement of the ship, h, in metres at t seconds.

(a) What is the vertical position of the ship at 22 s to the nearest hundredth of a metre?

(b) What is the period of the function? What does this mean in this case?

(c) Determine all times within the first minute that the vertical position of the ship is -0.9 m to the nearest tenth of a second.

5.6 Investigating Transformations

26. Explain how to use transformations to sketch the graph of $y = a \sin k(\theta + b) + d$.

27. The average monthly temperature, T, of a town is given by $T(t) = -24 \cos \frac{\pi}{6}t + 9$.

(a) Determine the period and explain what it means in this case.

(b) How can you use the maximum and minimum values of the function $y = \cos \theta$ to determine the maximum and minimum values of T?

28. Points $\left(\frac{\pi}{2}, 1\right)$ and $(\pi, 0)$ are on the curve $y = \sin \theta$. State the new coordinates under each transformation.

(a) $y = -3 \sin \theta$

(b) $y = \sin \theta + 1$

(c) $y = \sin\left(\theta + \frac{\pi}{4}\right)$

(d) $y = \sin 2\theta$

29. Sketch the graphs using transformations of the base curve for $0 \leq \theta \leq 2\pi$.

(a) $y = 2 \sin 3\left(\theta - \frac{\pi}{6}\right) - 4$

(b) $y = -3 \cos\left(2\theta + \frac{\pi}{2}\right) + 2$

30. State the amplitude, period, phase shift and vertical shift.

(a) $y = 2 \cos\left(\frac{\theta}{2} - 60°\right) + 1$

(b) $y = -3 \sin (2\theta + 90°) - 1$

(c) $y = 1 + 2 \cos 3\left(\theta - \frac{\pi}{6}\right)$

5.7 Modelling Periodic Phenomena

31. (a) Why should a set of data be graphed before trying to fit it to a trigonometric model?

(b) List the four pieces of information needed to complete the general form of a trigonometric equation. Explain how to determine this information.

32. Determine a trigonometric model to represent each set of data.

(a)

θ	0°	30°	60°	90°	120°
$f(\theta)$	0	4	0	−4	0

(b)

t	−2	0	2	4	5.7	8.0	10.0	12
$f(t)$	5.5	6.0	5.5	4.5	4.0	4.5	5.5	6

33. The Double Scoop Ice Cream Company tracked its mean monthly production of ice cream over the last two years.

Ice Cream Production in Thousands of Litres

Month	J	F	M	A	M	J	J	A	S	O	N	D
Year 1	168	181	219	222	246	276	264	252	219	204	181	174
Year 2	169	180	220	221	245	274	265	251	219	203	180	175

(a) Explain why it is reasonable to expect ice cream production to be periodic.

(b) Determine a trigonometric model that best represents the data.

(c) Use a graphing calculator to graph your trigonometric model. Comment on the closeness of fit to the given data.

5.8 Solving Linear Trigonometric Equations

34. Identify three different ways that an approximate solution to a linear trigonometric equation can be determined.

35. Determine whether the given value is a solution to the equation.

(a) $\cos \theta = \frac{1}{2}, \theta = \frac{5\pi}{3}$ (b) $5 \sin \theta + 6 = 10, \theta = 25°$

36. Solve for x to one tenth of a degree, where $0° \leq x \leq 360°$.

(a) $\sin x = \frac{2}{3}$ (b) $\cos x = -\frac{5}{8}$ (c) $\tan x = 2.8$

(d) $3 \sin 2x = -4$ (e) $5 \cos (0.5x) - 1 = 1$ (f) $3 \tan \frac{x}{2} + 2 = 9$

37. Solve for x to one hundredth of a radian, where $0 \leq x \leq 2\pi$.

(a) $\cos x = \frac{7}{8}$ (b) $\sin x = -\frac{3}{11}$ (c) $\tan 2x = 1$

(d) $5 \sin x = -5$ (e) $5 \cos 3x - 1 = 1$ (f) $3 \tan \frac{x}{2} + 2 = 9$

38. Solve for x to one tenth of a degree, where $0° \leq x \leq 360°$. Use graphing technology.

(a) $10 \sin x - 3 = 5$ (b) $4 \cos x = -1$

(c) $2 \tan x - 1 = 5$ (d) $2 \sin (2x + 90°) = 1$

39. Solve for x to one hundredth of a radian, where $0 \leq x \leq 2\pi$. Use graphing technology.

(a) $\tan x + 7.5 = 8$ (b) $3 \cos (3x) = -3$

(c) $4 \sin (3x + \pi) + 1 = -3$ (d) $-\cos (2x + 2\pi) - 1 = 0$

40. The average monthly maximum temperature of Windsor can be modelled by $T(t) = 14.9 \sin \frac{\pi}{6}(t - 3) + 13$, where T is the temperature in Celsius and $t = 0$ represents January 1, $t = 1$ represents February 1, and so on.

(a) When is the average monthly maximum temperature highest? lowest?

(b) Use the model to predict when the temperature is 0°C.

(c) When does the temperature reach 25°C?

Chapter 5 Summary

In this chapter, you saw that a periodic function can be represented by a curve with a repeating pattern or cycle. Periodic phenomena occur in the world around us. The life cycle of plants and animals, phases of the moon, motion of waves, and vibration of sound are all examples of periodic phenomena.

Motion about a circle produces trigonometric functions that relate a point's position on the circle to its angle of rotation. These functions are the sine, cosine, and tangent functions, and are called the primary trigonometric functions. They have many real-life applications. The angles of rotation can be expressed in degree measure or radian measure. Radian measure is used when the position is a function of time or distance rather than degrees of rotation.

Trigonometric functions are transformed similarly to how quadratic functions are transformed. The equation $y = a \sin k(\theta + b) + d$ is a transformation of the base curve $y = \sin \theta$. The equation $y = \cos k(\theta + b) + d$ is a transformation of the base curve $y = \cos \theta$.

A graphical model of a situation can be drawn if enough data points are known. Once the data is seen to be periodic, an equation can be found for it. A graphing calculator can be used to plot the data points and graph the equation. As well, the **SinReg** feature of the calculator can be used to determine the equation of periodic data.

Chapter 5 Review Test

Modelling Periodic Functions

1. Identify each function as linear, quadratic, exponential, or periodic. State the period and the maximum and minimum values of each periodic function.

(a) \$1000 is invested at 10% per annum compounded semiannually for 5 years.

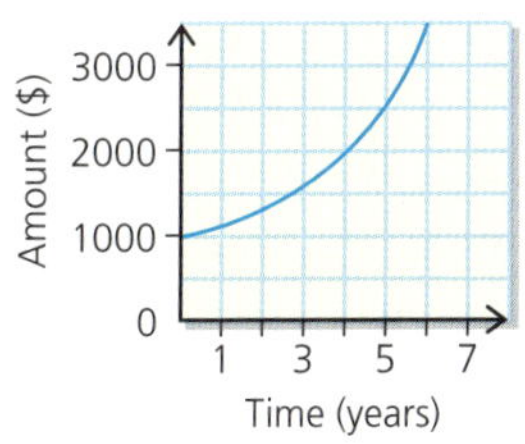

(b) The cost of printing an advertising flier is \$350, plus \$0.05 per copy.

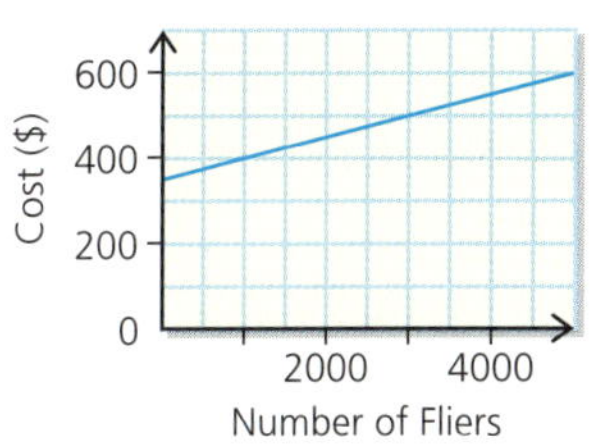

(c) A model rocket is shot vertically upward and falls back to the ground.

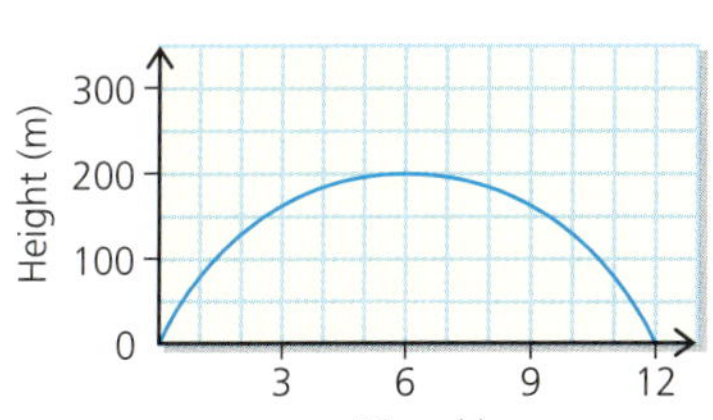

(d) A rider on a merry-go-round moves up and down with the horse as the merry-go-round travels in a circle.

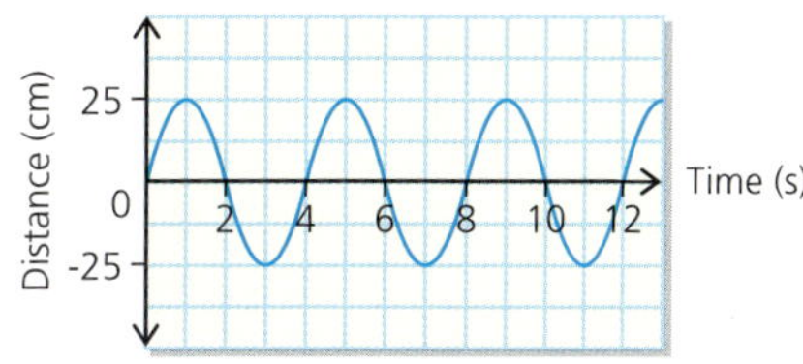

2. **Communication:** You are given a set of data that looks like a sinusoidal function. Explain how you can determine an algebraic model from the graph.

3. State all coterminal angles for θ.

(a) $\theta = 47°$, for $-360° \le \theta \le 720°$

(b) $\theta = \frac{2\pi}{3}$, for $-2\pi \le \theta \le 2\pi$

(c) $\theta = 15°$, for $0° \le \theta \le 1080°$

4. Convert to radian measure as an exact value in simplest terms.

(a) $260°$ (b) $-15°$

5. Convert to degree measure.

(a) $\frac{5\pi}{2}$ (b) $-\frac{7\pi}{2}$

6. Express $27°$ in radian measure to two decimal places.

7. Point $P(-3, 7)$ is on the terminal arm of angle θ in standard position.

(a) State the exact values of the primary trigonometric functions.

(b) Determine the value of θ to the nearest degree.

8. **Knowledge and Understanding**
Consider $y = 2 \sin 3(\theta - 30°) + 1$, for $0° \le \theta \le 360°$.

(a) State the values of the period, phase shift, amplitude, and vertical shift.

(b) Sketch five graphs on separate axes to show the progression from the base curve to the given function.

9. (a) Solve $5 \cos \theta = -0.42$ for θ to the nearest degree, where $0° \le \theta \le 360°$.

(b) Solve $\sin 3\theta = -0.6$ for θ to the nearest degree, where $0° \le \theta \le 240°$.

(c) Solve $2 \tan\left(\theta - \frac{\pi}{2}\right) = 57.3$ for θ to one decimal, where $0 \le \theta \le \pi$.

(d) Solve $4 - 3 \sin\left(\theta - \frac{\pi}{2}\right) = 6.2$ for θ to one decimal, where $0 \le \theta \le 2\pi$.

10. The average daily maximum temperature in Kenora is shown for each month.

Time (months)	J	F	M	A
Temperature (°C)	−13.1	−9.0	−1.1	8.5

Time (months)	M	J	J	A
Temperature (°C)	16.8	21.6	24.7	22.9

Time (months)	S	O	N	D
Temperature (°C)	16.3	9.3	−1.2	−10.2

Source: Environment Canada.

(a) Prepare a scatter plot of the data. Let January represent month 0.

(b) Draw a curve of best fit. Explain why this type of data could be expressed as a periodic function.

(c) State the maximum and minimum values.

(d) What is the period of the curve? Explain why this is appropriate within the context of the question.

(e) Write an equation for the axis of the curve.

(f) What is the phase shift if the cosine function acts as the base curve?

(g) Use the cosine function to write an equation that models the data.

(h) Use the equation to predict the temperature for the 38th month. How could this prediction be confirmed using the table?

11. **Application:** The function
$d(\theta) = \frac{v^2}{9.8} \sin 2\theta + 0.5$, models the horizontal distance d, in metres, that a baseball is hit. The distance depends on the initial velocity of the ball, v, in metres per second and the angle, θ, that the ball leaves the bat.

(a) A home run leaves the bat at an angle of 45° and travels 138 m. What is the initial speed of the ball?

(b) What is the angle at which the ball is struck if the ball travels 64 m and leaves the bat at a speed of 28 m/s?

12. **Thinking, Inquiry, Problem Solving**
How many solutions exist for $\sin k\theta = \frac{1}{2}$, where $\{k \in \mathbf{I} \mid k \ge 1\}$ and $0 \le \theta \le 2\pi$?

Chapter 6

Extending Skills with Trigonometry

People have used trigonometry for thousands of years. Architects and engineers have used it to design and build structures ranging from the pyramids in Egypt to the CN Tower in Toronto. Astronomers have used trigonometry to measure the distance of the planets and stars from the Earth, and travellers have used it to navigate on land, on sea, and in the air.

In Chapter 5, you used trigonometric functions to model periodic phenomena. In earlier grades, you used trigonometry to determine sides and angles of acute and right triangles. In this chapter, you will apply what you have learned to obtuse triangles and extend your skills to deal with more complex trigonometric equations.

In this chapter, you will

- extend the sine law and cosine law to obtuse triangles
- use trigonometry to model and solve problems in two and three dimensions
- determine the exact values of special trigonometric ratios
- learn about a type of equation called an identity
- prove whether a given equation is an identity or not
- solve quadratic trigonometric equations.

Connections

The Chapter Problem

What Time Is It?

In early times, people used the repeating patterns of nature to keep track of time. For instance, the sundial uses the fact that as the Earth rotates on its axis, the position of the sun changes, causing the position of shadows to change. The ancient Greeks used their knowledge of geometry to make sundials that were very complex and accurate. However, even the best sundial has its drawbacks: it cannot be used on cloudy days or at night.

Mechanical clocks were invented sometime in the 1300s. These crude devices were inaccurate and had to be constantly reset. In the 1500s, Galileo discovered that a pendulum could be used to keep uniform time. You may have seen grandfather clocks that use a pendulum to do this. Owing to friction, a swinging pendulum left on its own will eventually stop swinging. In a clock, a device called a yoke pushes the pendulum to ensure that it swings through the same angle on each swing.

When a pendulum is set in motion, it swings back and forth through an arc. Let x be the distance that the pendulum swings from the centre point and l be the length of the pendulum. Then the motion can be modelled by the function $x = M\cos\left(t\sqrt{\frac{980}{l}}\right)$, where M is the maximum value of x and t is the time, in seconds, that has elapsed since the pendulum was set in motion.

The **period** of a pendulum is the time the pendulum takes to return to its point of release. In this diagram, the period is equivalent to two swings, one to the left and the return swing to the right. When the value of M is small, the period depends entirely on the length of pendulum.

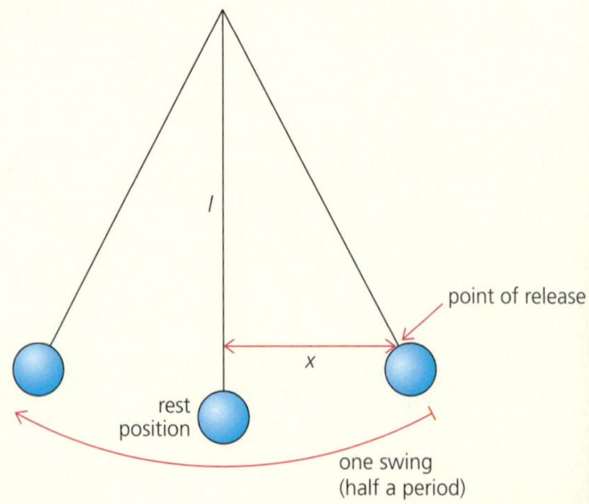

How long must the pendulum in a grandfather clock be for one swing to take exactly one second?

Challenge 1

The largest right pyramid that can be contained entirely in a cube, shares the same base and height of the cube. Determine:

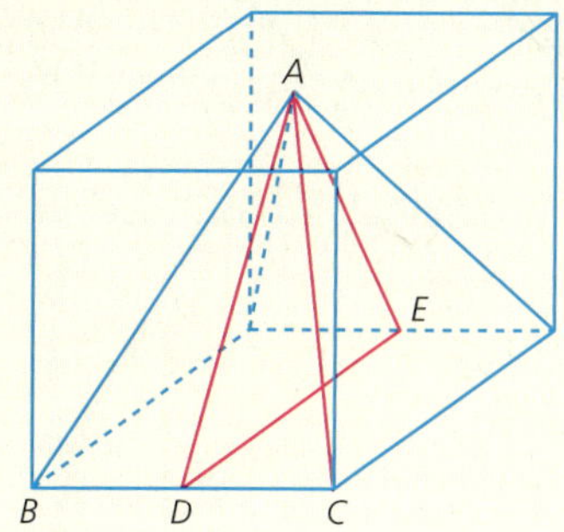

(a) all three angles in the triangular faces of the pyramid, $\angle ABC$, $\angle ACB$, and $\angle BAC$.

(b) the angle at which each triangular face of the pyramid meets with the base, $\angle ADE$.

(c) the angle at the top of the pyramid formed between opposite triangular faces, $\angle DAE$.

Challenge 2

In this chapter, you will learn about special types of equations called fundamental trigonometric identities. There are also other kinds of trigonometric identities. Two of these are called **addition formulas**. For the sine and cosine functions, where x and y are angles, the formulas are

$$\sin (x + y) = \sin x \cos y + \cos x \sin y$$

$$\cos (x + y) = \cos x \cos y - \sin x \sin y$$

(a) Use the special triangles to show that these relationships are true when $x = \frac{\pi}{3}$ and $y = \frac{\pi}{6}$.

(b) Use the addition formula to develop equivalent expressions for $\sin 2x$ and $\cos 2x$.

(c) Prove that $\frac{1 - \cos 2x + \sin 2x}{1 + \cos 2x + \sin 2x} = \tan x$.

Web Challenge

For a related Internet activity, go to **www.math.nelson.com**.

Getting Ready

In this chapter, you will be working with the sine law and the cosine law, and solving trigonometric equations. These exercises will help you warm up for the work ahead.

1. Evaluate to four decimal places.

(a) $\sin 48°$ (b) $\cos 12°$
(c) $\tan 140°$ (d) $\sin 220°$
(e) $\cos \frac{\pi}{12}$ (f) $\sin \frac{5\pi}{6}$
(g) $\tan \frac{3\pi}{2}$ (h) $\cos 4.5$

2. Express each radian measure in degrees. Answer to one decimal place.

(a) $\frac{3\pi}{4}$ (b) $\frac{11\pi}{9}$
(c) 3.5 (d) 5.85

3. Express each degree measure in radians.

(a) 45° (b) 210°
(c) 140° (d) 340°

4. In each case, P is a point on the terminal arm of θ, an angle in standard position.

i. Sketch θ.
ii. Determine the primary trigonometric ratios of θ.
iii. Determine θ to the nearest degree.

(a) $P(6, 8)$ (b) $P(-2, 4)$
(c) $P(-2, -5)$ (d) $P(1, -2)$

5. Determine θ, $0° \leq \theta \leq 360°$.

(a) $\sin \theta = 1$ (b) $\cos \theta = -1$
(c) $\tan \theta = 1$ (d) $\cos \theta = 0$
(e) $\cos \theta = 0.5$ (f) $\sin \theta = -0.5$
(g) $\sin \theta = 0$ (h) $\tan \theta = -1$

6. Solve for θ, $0° \leq \theta \leq 360°$. Answer to one decimal place.

(a) $3 \sin \theta = -1$ (b) $-3 \cos \theta = 2$
(c) $2 \tan \theta = 4$ (d) $-2 \sin \theta - 1 = 1$

7. Solve for θ, where $0 \leq \theta \leq 2\pi$. Answer to one decimal place.

(a) $-4 \cos \theta + 3 = 2$
(b) $1 + \tan \theta = 0$
(c) $6 + 5 \sin \theta = 5$
(d) $6 = 2 + 8 \cos \theta$

8. State the amplitude, period, phase shift, and vertical shift of each function.

(a) $y = \sin 3x$
(b) $y = 3 \cos \left(x + \frac{\pi}{2}\right)$
(c) $y = \frac{1}{2} \tan x - 1$
(d) $y = -2 \sin 0.5(x - 30°) + 2$
(e) $y = \tan 3x$
(f) $y = \cos \left(2x + \frac{\pi}{2}\right)$

9. Graph each equation, $0 \leq \theta \leq 2\pi$.

(a) $y = \sin \theta$ (b) $y = \cos \theta$
(c) $y = \tan \theta$ (d) $y = \cos 2\theta$
(e) $y = \sin \theta + 2$
(f) $y = -2 \sin \left(\theta - \frac{\pi}{4}\right)$
(g) $y = \tan \left(\theta + \frac{\pi}{2}\right)$
(h) $y = \sin (0.5\theta) - 1$

10. Determine the function that defines each graph.

(a)

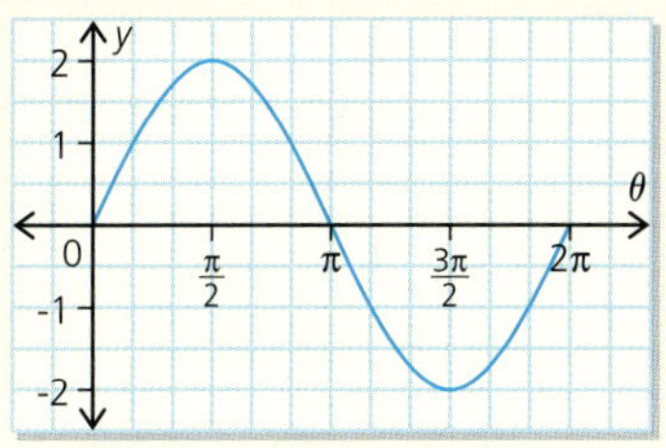

(b)

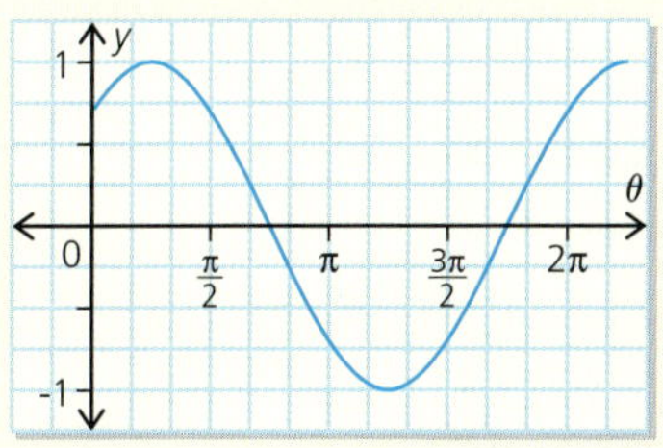

(c)

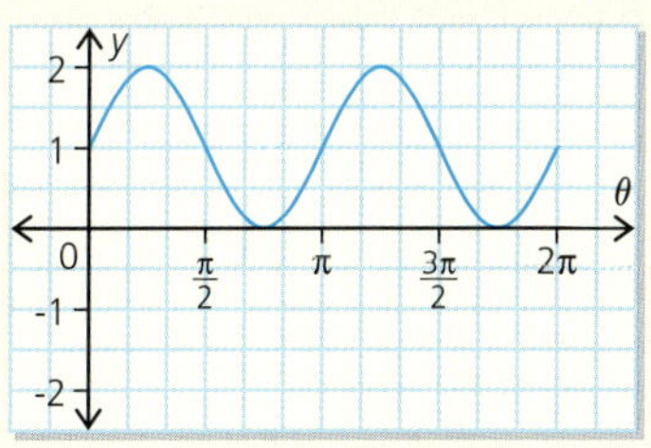

(d)

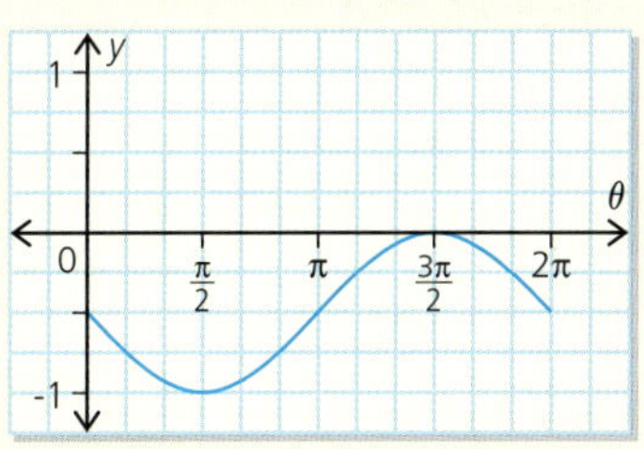

11. Find the value of each variable to the nearest tenth.

(a)

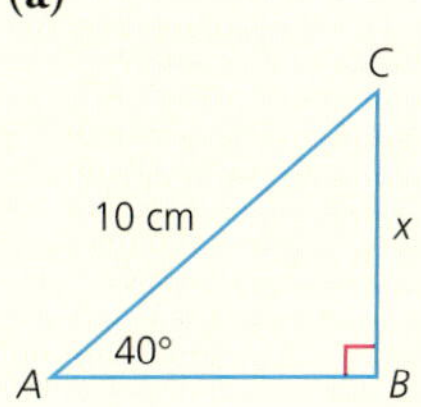

(b)

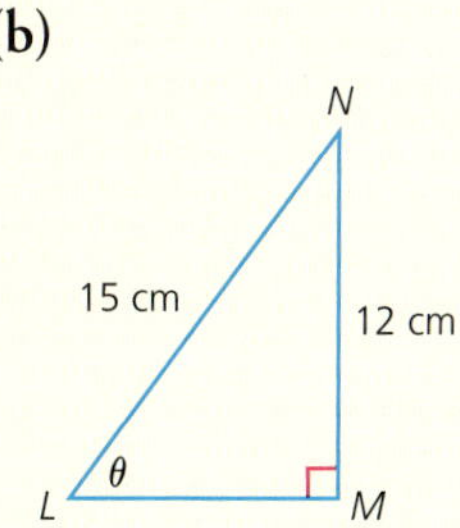

(c)

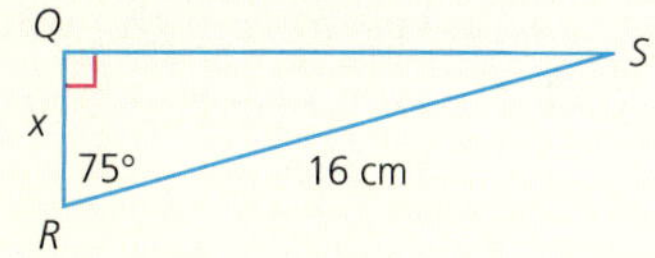

(d)

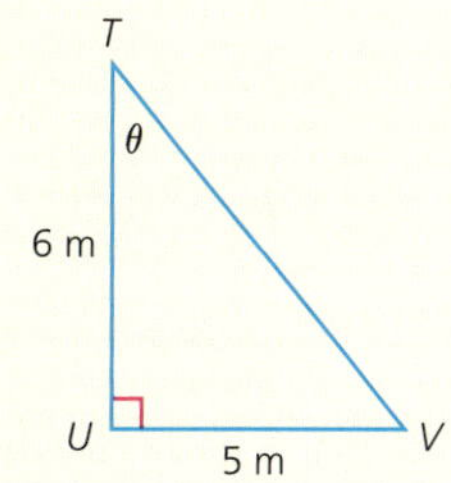

12. Use the sine law to find the value of each variable to the nearest tenth. All angles are acute.

(a)

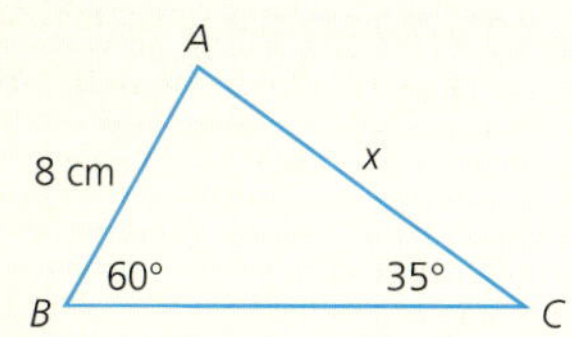

(b)

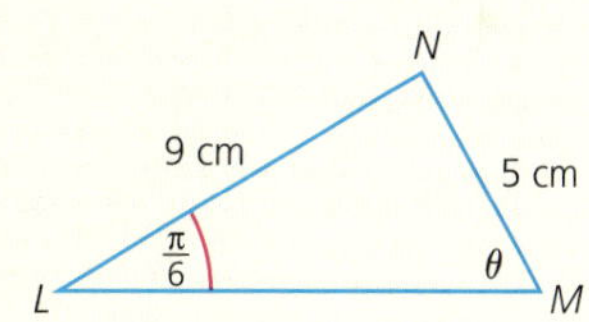

(c)

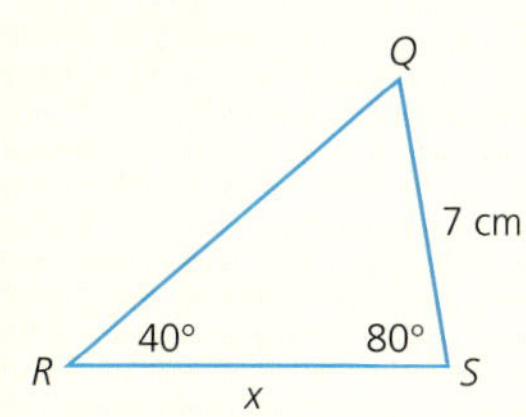

(d)

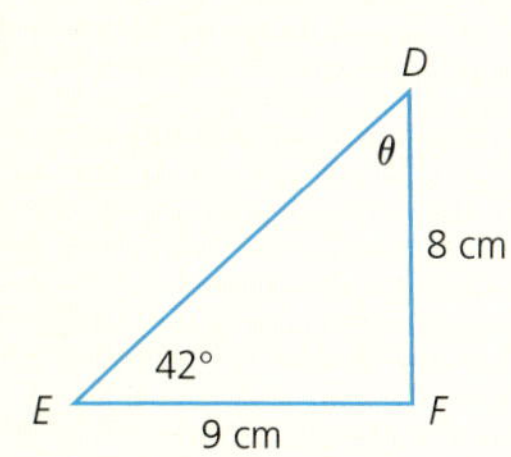

13. Use the cosine law to find the value of each variable to the nearest tenth.

(a)

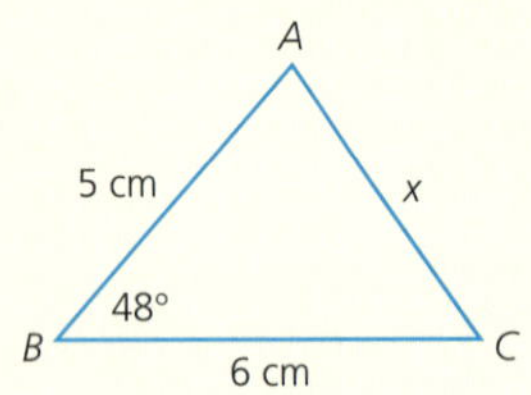

(b)

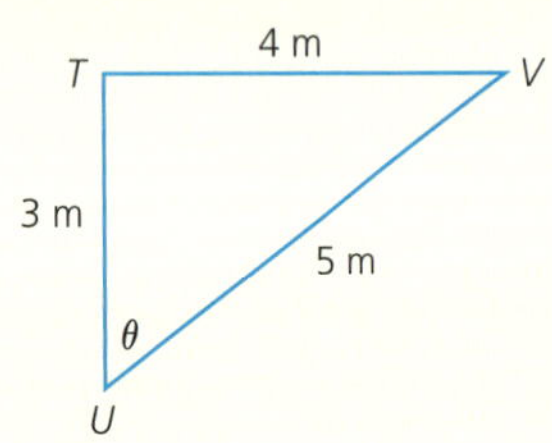

(c)

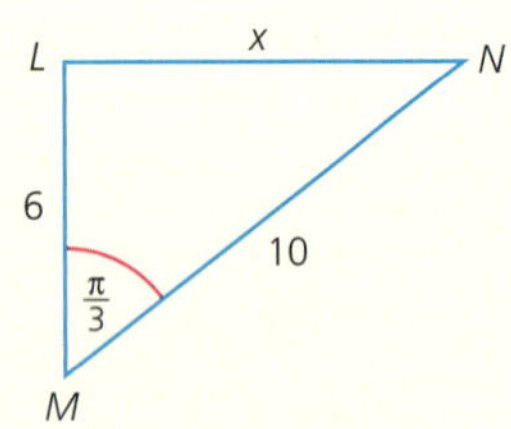

(d)

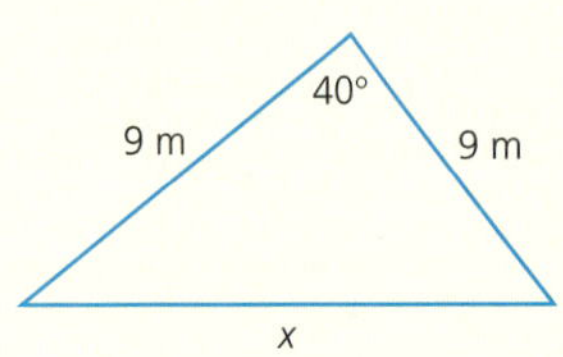

14. Solve each triangle.

(a) ΔABC, $\angle B = 90°$, $\angle C = 33°$, $AC = 4.9$ cm

(b) ΔDEF, $e = 3$ cm, $\angle F = 64°$, $\angle E = 49°$

(c) ΔGHI, $g = 7$ cm, $i = 6$ cm, $\angle H = 43°$

15. Factor fully.

(a) $x^2 - 64$

(b) $x^2 + 12x + 35$

(c) $6x^2 - 13x - 5$

(d) $4x^2 - 20x + 25$

(e) $2x^3 - 4x$

(f) $8x^2 + 10x - 3$

(g) $x^2 - 9x + 14$

(h) $x^2 - 3x - 40$

16. Determine the roots of each quadratic equation.

(a) $x^2 + 4x - 21 = 0$

(b) $x^2 - 11x + 24 = 0$

(c) $5x^2 - 8x = 0$

(d) $x^2 + 3x - 54 = 0$

(f) $2x^2 - 9x = 5$

(g) $6x^2 = 7x - 2$

Extending Trigonometry Skills with Oblique Triangles 6.1

In earlier courses, you used the sine law and the cosine law to solve acute triangles. A triangle without a right angle is called an **oblique** triangle. Recall that in an acute triangle, ΔABC, with sides a, b, and c, these relations are true.

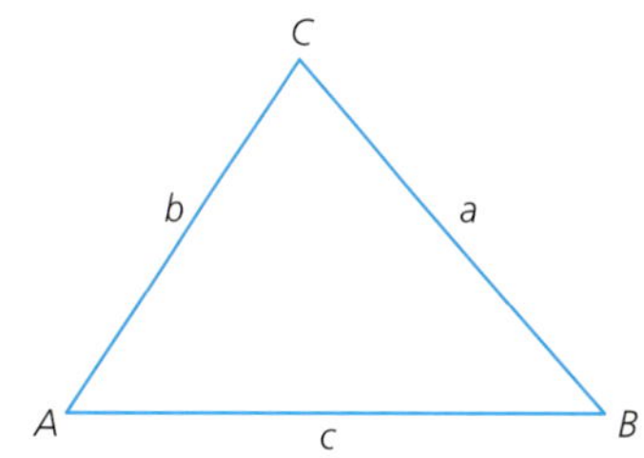

The Sine Law	The Cosine Law
$\frac{a}{\sin A} = \frac{b}{\sin B} = \frac{c}{\sin C}$	$a^2 = b^2 + c^2 - 2bc \cos A$
or	$b^2 = a^2 + c^2 - 2ac \cos B$
$\frac{\sin A}{a} = \frac{\sin B}{b} = \frac{\sin C}{c}$	$c^2 = a^2 + b^2 - 2ab \cos C$

Can the sine law and cosine law be used to solve an obtuse triangle?

Part 1: Investigating the Cosine Law and Obtuse Triangles

Don is a carpenter who often frames houses. This blueprint shows a cross section of the roof structure for the house he is now working on.

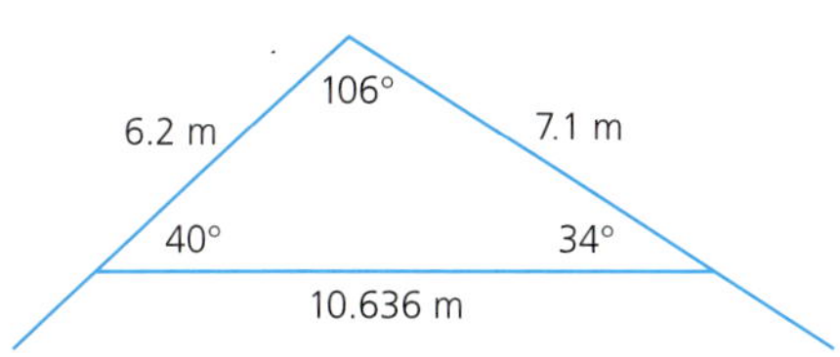

Think, Do, Discuss

1. Sketch the roof. Starting with the obtuse angle, label the vertices A, B, and C in a counterclockwise direction. Label the corresponding sides of the triangle.
2. Show that the cosine law is true for each acute angle in the diagram.
3. Determine cos 106°. How does this cosine differ from the cosines of the other two angles in the triangle?
4. How does the cosine of any obtuse angle differ from the cosine of any acute angle? Does this prevent the cosine law from being true for the obtuse angle?

5. Show that the cosine law is true for the obtuse angle.

6. Based on the results from step 5, can you say that the cosine law will work in all obtuse triangles? Explain.

7. Examine this proof of the cosine law for any obtuse triangle, where $\angle B$, or $\angle ABC$, is obtuse.

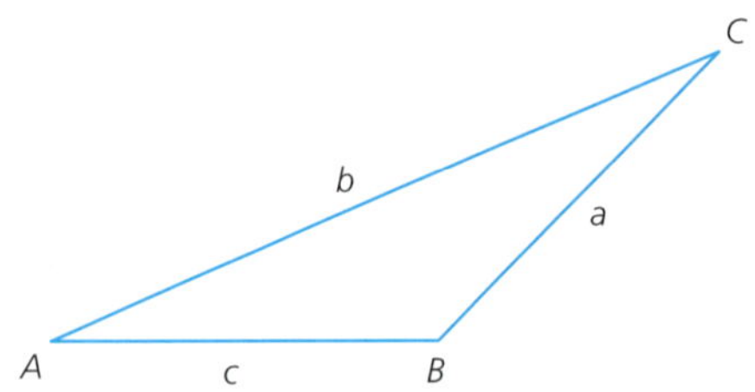

Proof that $b^2 = a^2 + c^2 - 2ac \cos B$, when $\angle B > 90°$

i. Draw h perpendicular to side c extended. Let x be the length of BD and h be the length of CD.

ii. Since $CD \perp AD$, then ΔADC and ΔBDC are right triangles. Use the Pythagorean theorem to determine an expression for h^2 in both triangles.

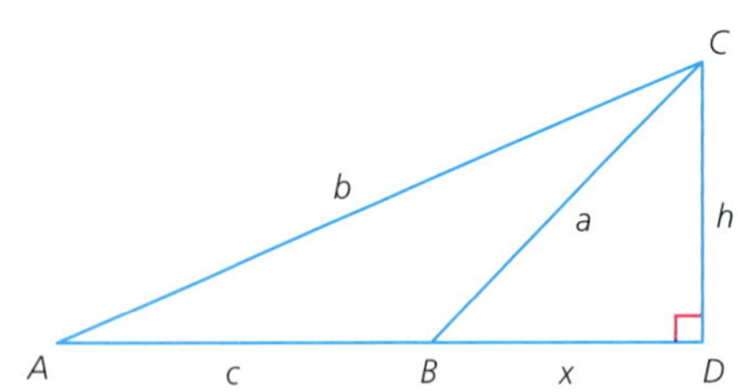

In ΔADC,

$$(c + x)^2 + h^2 = b^2$$
$$h^2 = b^2 - (c + x)^2$$
$$h^2 = b^2 - (c^2 + 2cx + x^2)$$
$$h^2 = b^2 - c^2 - 2cx - x^2 \quad ①$$

In ΔBDC,

$$a^2 = x^2 + h^2$$
$$a^2 - x^2 = h^2 \quad ②$$

iii. Since h represents the height of both triangles, equations ① and ② are equal.

$$b^2 - c^2 - 2cx - x^2 = a^2 - x^2 \quad \text{Rearrange to isolate } b^2.$$
$$b^2 = a^2 + c^2 + 2cx - x^2 + x^2 \quad \text{Simplify.}$$
$$b^2 = a^2 + c^2 + 2cx$$

iv. ΔBDC is a right triangle. Use a primary trigonometric ratio to find an expression for x.

$$\cos \angle CBD = \frac{\text{adjacent}}{\text{hypotenuse}}$$
$$\cos \angle CBD = \frac{x}{a}$$
$$a \cos \angle CBD = x$$

v. In ΔBDC,

$$\angle CBD = 180° - \angle ABC$$
$$= 180° - \angle B \qquad \text{where } \angle ABC = \angle B$$

For any obtuse angle $(180° - \theta)$, $\cos(180° - \theta) = -\cos\theta$.

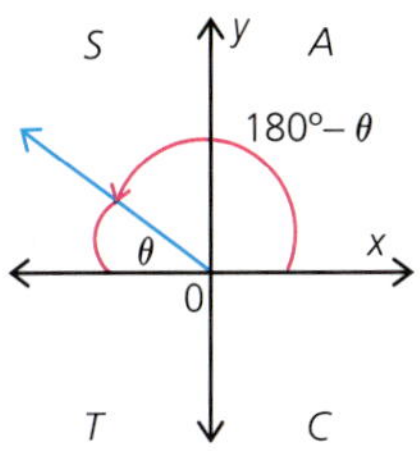

Therefore,

$$\cos \angle CBD = \cos(180° - \angle ABC)$$
$$= \cos(180° - \angle B)$$
$$= -\cos B$$

Substitute into $a \cos \angle CBD = x$, from step iv.

$$a(-\cos B) = x$$
$$-a \cos B = x$$

Substitute this expression for x into $b^2 = a^2 + c^2 + 2cx$.

$$b^2 = a^2 + c^2 + 2c(-a\cos B)$$
$$b^2 = a^2 + c^2 - 2ac\cos B$$

This is the result to be proven. Therefore, for any ΔABC, $b^2 = a^2 + c^2 - 2ac\cos B$. Similarly, by drawing perpendiculars to the other sides, you can prove that

$$a^2 = b^2 + c^2 - 2bc\cos A$$
$$c^2 = a^2 + b^2 - 2ab\cos C$$

8. In the proof above,

(a) What does h represent in ΔABC, ΔADC, and ΔBDC?

(b) Explain why the two expressions for h^2 can be set equal to each other in step iii.

(c) Explain why $\cos(180° - \theta) = -\cos\theta$ in step v.

9. What is the least information you need to know about a triangle to use the cosine law to calculate

(a) an unknown side?

(b) an unknown angle?

Part 2: Investigating the Sine Law and Obtuse Triangles

Refer to your diagram of the roof cross section from Part 1.

Think, Do, Discuss

1. Show that the sine law is true for each acute angle in the diagram.

2. Determine sin 106°. Other than value, does this sine differ from the sines of the other two angles in the triangle in any way?

3. Determine sin 74°. What do you notice?

4. When using the sine law to calculate the length of a side, is the calculation affected at all if the angle is obtuse, rather than acute or right?

5. Show that the sine law is true for the obtuse angle in the diagram.

6. Based on your results in step 5, can you say that the sine law will work in all obtuse triangles? Explain.

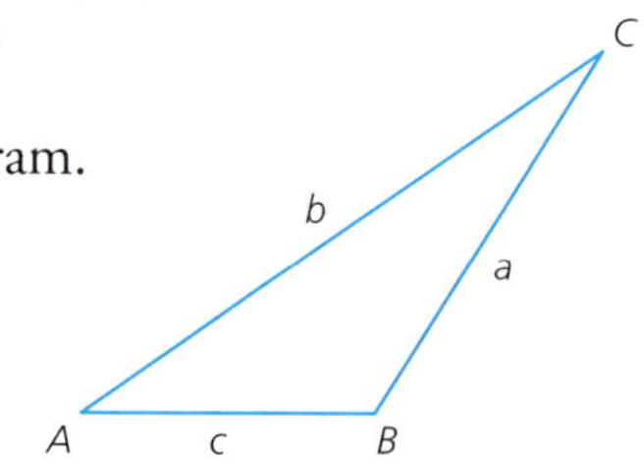

7. Examine this proof of the sine law for any obtuse triangle, where $\angle B$, or $\angle ABC$, is obtuse.

Proof that $a \sin B = b \sin A$ or $\frac{a}{\sin A} = \frac{b}{\sin B}$, where $\angle B > 90°$

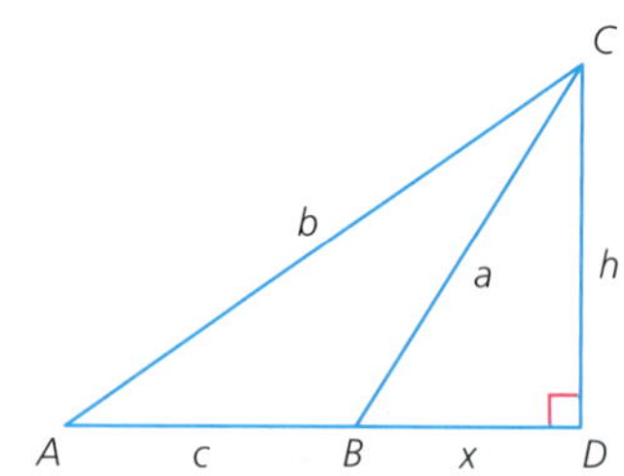

i. Draw $CD \perp AB$ extended to point D. Label CD as h.

ii. In ΔCAD,

$$\sin A = \frac{h}{b}$$
$$\therefore \quad b \sin A = h$$

In ΔCBD,

$$\sin \angle CBD = \frac{h}{a}$$
$$\angle CBD = 180° - \angle ABC$$
$$= 180° - \angle B \qquad \text{where } \angle ABC = \angle B$$

Therefore,

$$\sin \angle CBD = \sin (180° - \angle ABC)$$
$$= \sin (180° - \angle B)$$

For any obtuse angle $(180° - \theta)$, $\sin (180° - \theta) = \sin \theta$.

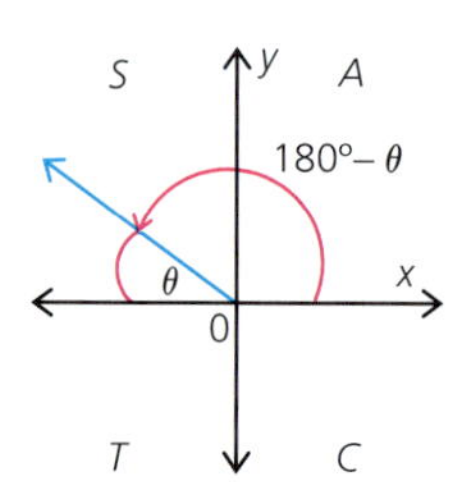

Therefore,

$$\sin \angle CBD = \sin B$$

Substitute into $\sin (\angle CBD) = \frac{h}{a}$

$$\sin B = \frac{h}{a}$$
$$\therefore \quad a \sin B = h$$

iii. Because h represents the height of both triangles, it follows that

$$a \sin B = b \sin A \text{ or } \frac{a}{\sin A} = \frac{b}{\sin B}$$

Similarly, by drawing perpendiculars to the other sides, it may be proven that

$$\frac{a}{\sin A} = \frac{b}{\sin B} = \frac{c}{\sin C}$$

8. In the proof in step 7, explain why $\sin(180° - \theta) = \sin \theta$.

9. What is the least information you need to know about the triangle to use the sine law to calculate

(a) an unknown side? (b) an unknown angle?

Part 3: A Closer Look at the Sine Law — The Ambiguous Case

You can use the sine law when you know two side lengths of a triangle and the measure of an angle opposite one of the known sides. In this situation, does the given information always define one unique triangle? Dynamic geometry software can be used in this activity.

Think, Do, Discuss

1. Draw a line segment AB at least 15 cm long. Construct line segment AC so that $\angle CAB = 40°$ and $AC = b = 10$ cm.

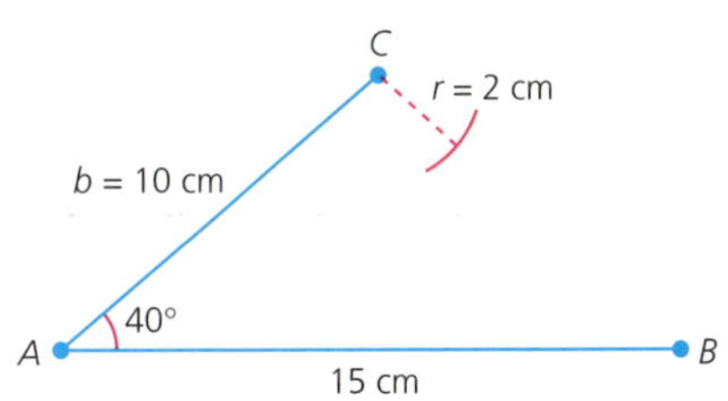

2. Construct an arc that originates from point C with a radius of 2 cm. Does the arc intersect AB?

3. Repeat step 2 using the radii from the table. Record the number of triangles that can be drawn with each radius.

Radius, r (cm)	Number of Triangles
2	
4	
6	
8	
10	

4. Determine the radius that would allow you to draw exactly one triangle.

5. Calculate the value of $b \sin A$. What does this represent in your diagram?

6. For which values of r does the arc intersect AB twice?

7. For the radii that allowed you to create two triangles, determine the height of each triangle. What do you notice?

8. Repeat steps 1–3 using $\angle A = 120°$. Under what conditions do you get a triangle? do not get a triangle?

Focus 6.1

Key Ideas

- Any triangle without a right angle is called an **oblique triangle**. The cosine law and the sine law can be used to determine angles or sides in all triangles (acute, right, and obtuse).
- In ΔABC, with sides a, b, and c,

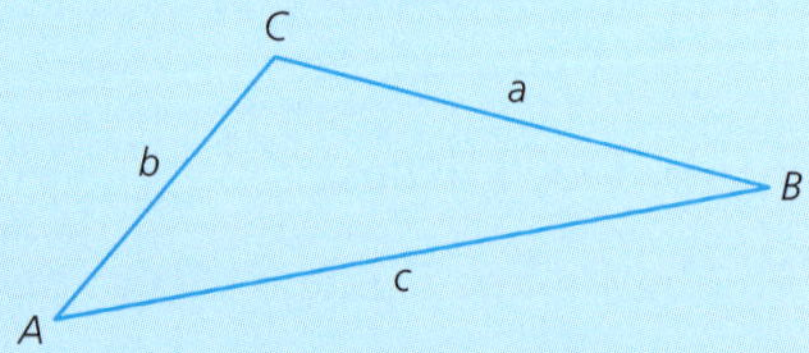

The Sine Law	The Cosine Law
$\frac{a}{\sin A} = \frac{b}{\sin B} = \frac{c}{\sin C}$	$a^2 = b^2 + c^2 - 2bc \cos A$
or	$b^2 = a^2 + c^2 - 2ac \cos B$
$\frac{\sin A}{a} = \frac{\sin B}{b} = \frac{\sin C}{c}$	$c^2 = a^2 + b^2 - 2ab \cos C$

- To solve an oblique triangle, you need to know the measure of at least one side and any two other parts of the triangle. There are four cases in which this can happen.

Given Information	What Can Be Found	Law Required
1. Two angles and any side (AAS or ASA)	side	sine law
2. Two sides and the contained angle (SAS)	side	cosine law
3. Three sides (SSS)	angle	cosine law
4. Two sides and an angle opposite one of them (SSA)	angle	sine law

Case 4 is called the **ambiguous case** because sometimes it is possible to draw more than one triangle for the given information. In this case, there are four possible outcomes if $\angle A$ is acute, and two possible outcomes if $\angle A$ is right or obtuse. These possibilities are shown for the given $\angle A$, the given sides a and b, in ΔABC. The side opposite the given angle is always a, and $b \sin A$ represents the possible height of the triangle.

<table>
<tr><th>∠A < 90° (acute)</th><th>Conditions</th><th>Number and Type of Triangles Possible</th></tr>
<tr><td>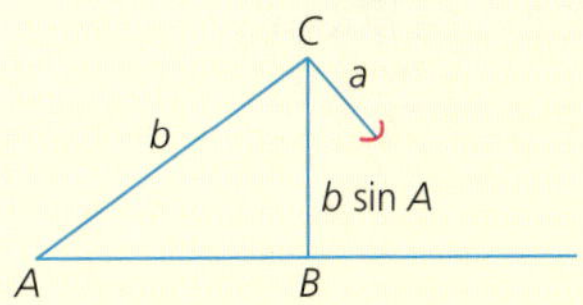</td><td>$a < b \sin A$</td><td>no triangle</td></tr>
<tr><td>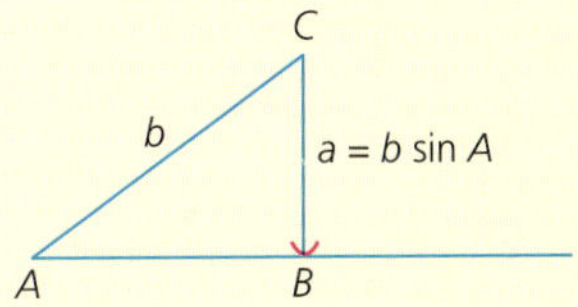</td><td>$a = b \sin A$</td><td>one right triangle</td></tr>
<tr><td>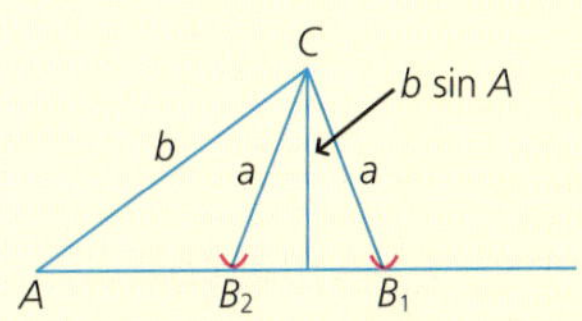</td><td>$b \sin A < a < b$</td><td>two triangles—one acute, one obtuse</td></tr>
<tr><td>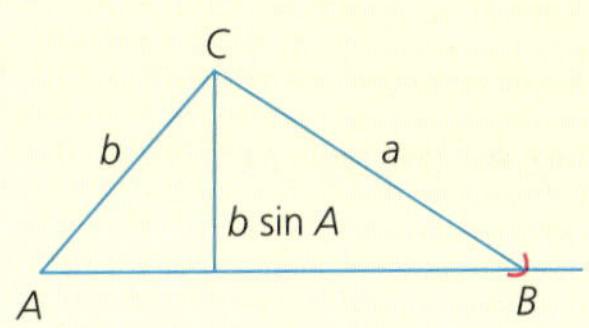</td><td>$a \geq b$</td><td>one triangle</td></tr>
</table>

<table>
<tr><th>∠A > 90° (obtuse)</th><th>Conditions</th><th>Number and Type of Triangles Possible</th></tr>
<tr><td>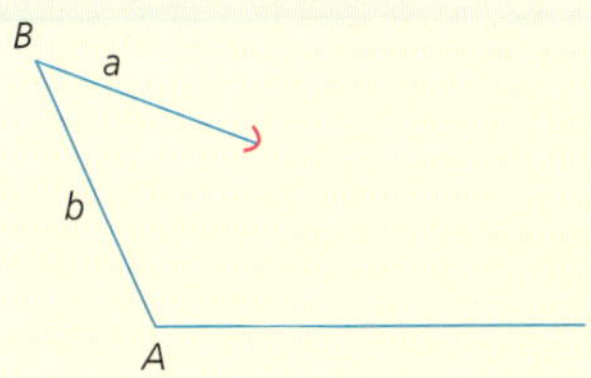</td><td>$a \leq b$</td><td>no triangle</td></tr>
<tr><td>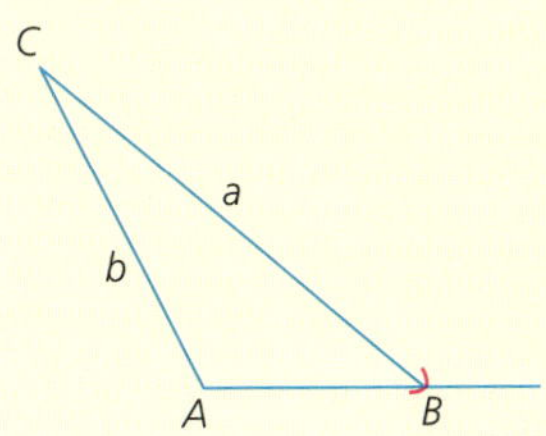</td><td>$a > b$</td><td>one obtuse triangle</td></tr>
</table>

Determining whether a given angle ($\angle A$) is acute or obtuse, and then comparing the size of a, b, and $b \sin A$ allows you to see which situation you are dealing with and, in turn, the number of possible solutions.

Example 1

Determine the measure of

(a) $\angle A$ in ΔABC to the nearest degree, if $a = 55$ cm, $b = 26$ cm, and $c = 32$ cm

(b) $\angle B$ in ΔABC to the nearest degree, if $a = 3$ m, $b = 15$ m, and $\angle A = 16°$

(c) side r in ΔRST to one decimal if $\angle S = 130°$, $s = 50$ mm, and $t = 20$ mm

Solution

(a) All three sides (SSS) are known in ΔABC. Use the cosine law to determine $\angle A$. Sketch the triangle.

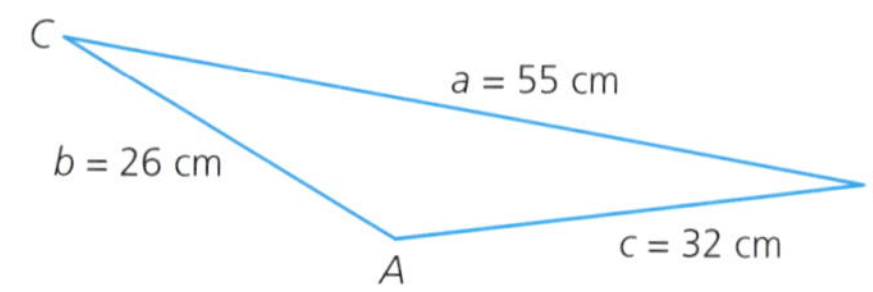

$a^2 = b^2 + c^2 - 2bc \cos A$	Substitute known values.
$55^2 = 26^2 + 32^2 - 2(26)(32) \cos A$	Solve for cos A.
$\cos A = \dfrac{55^2 - 26^2 - 32^2}{-2(26)(32)}$	Simplify.
$\cos A = -0.796\,274\,038\,5$	Determine the value of A using $\cos^{-1}$.
$\angle A = \cos^{-1}(-0.796\,274\,038\,5)$	
$\angle A \doteq 143°$	

(b) Two sides and an angle opposite one side are given (SSA). This is the ambiguous case of the sine law, where the given angle is acute. Check the relationship between a, b, and $b \sin A$.

$$a = 3,\ b = 15,\ \angle A = 16°$$
$$b \sin A = 15 \sin 16°$$
$$\doteq 4.1$$

Since $3 < 4.1$, then $a < b \sin A$. No triangle has these dimensions, so $\angle B$ cannot be determined.

Alternative solution using the sine law:

$\dfrac{a}{\sin A} = \dfrac{b}{\sin B}$	Substitute known values.
$\dfrac{3}{\sin 16°} = \dfrac{15}{\sin B}$	Solve for sin B.
$\sin B = \dfrac{15 \sin 16°}{3}$	Simplify.
$\sin B \doteq 1.378$	
$\angle B = \sin^{-1}(1.378)$	Solve for B using $\sin^{-1}$.
$\angle B = \text{ERROR}$	Trying to determine the value of B using $\sin^{-1}$ on a calculator returns an error message, because the maximum value of $\sin \theta$ is 1. $\angle B$ cannot be determined.

(c) Two sides and an angle opposite one side are known (SSA). This is the ambiguous case of the sine law, where the given angle is obtuse. In this case, $s > t$ (50 > 20), so only one obtuse triangle is possible. Sketch a diagram.

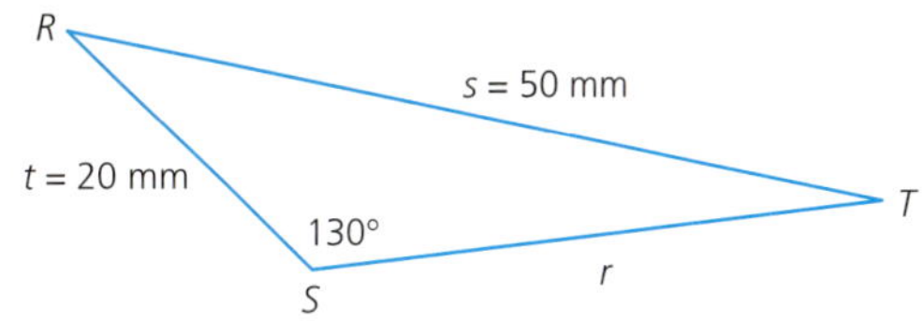

The ratio $\frac{r}{\sin R}$ has no known variables but must be eventually used to determine r. Also, $\angle R$ must be determined, but this cannot be done until $\angle T$ is known.

$$\frac{s}{\sin S} = \frac{t}{\sin T}$$ Substitute known values.

$$\frac{50}{\sin 130°} = \frac{20}{\sin T}$$ Solve for sin T.

$$\sin T = \frac{20 \sin 130°}{50}$$ Simplify.

$$\sin T = 0.306\ 417\ 777\ 2$$ Solve for T using $\sin^{-1}$.

$$\angle T = \sin^{-1}(0.306\ 417\ 777\ 2)$$

$$\angle T \doteq 17.843\ 481\ 13°$$ Do not round because this value must be used to determine r.

Determine the value of R.

$$\angle R = 180° - (130° + 17.843\ 481\ 13°)$$
$$= 32.156\ 518\ 87°$$

To determine r, use the proportion $\frac{s}{\sin S} = \frac{r}{\sin R}$.

$$\frac{50}{\sin 130°} = \frac{r}{\sin 32.156\ 518\ 87°}$$
$$r = \frac{50 \sin 32.156\ 518\ 87°}{\sin 130°}$$
$$r \doteq 34.7$$

The value of r is about 34.7 mm.

Example 2

In ΔABC, $\angle A = 40°$, $a = 22$ cm, and $b = 27$ cm. Solve ΔABC. Round each angle to the nearest degree and each length to one tenth of a centimetre.

Solution

Two sides and an angle opposite one of the sides are given (SSA). This is the ambiguous case of the sine law where the given angle is acute. Check the relationship between a, b, and $b \sin A$.

We are given $a = 22$ cm and $b = 27$ cm. The value of $b \sin A$ must be determined.

$$b \sin A = 27 \sin 40°$$
$$\doteq 17.4$$

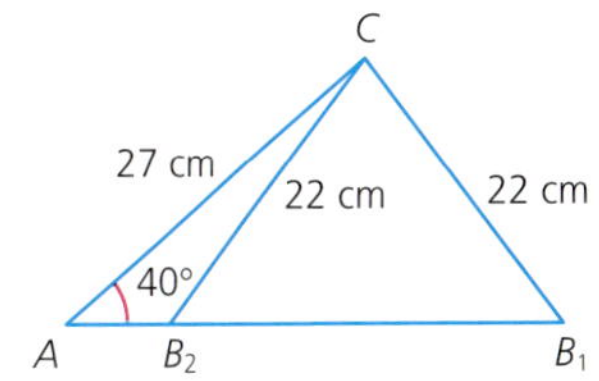

Therefore, 17.4 < 22 < 27. As a result, $b \sin A < a < b$. There are two triangles to consider, one acute and one obtuse.

Case 1: ΔABC is acute.

Draw a well-labelled diagram.

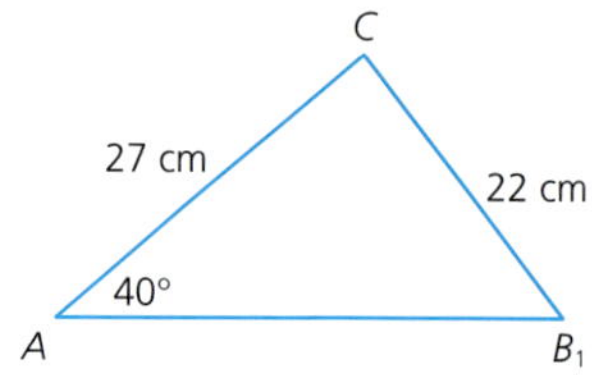

Use the sine law to find $\angle B_1$.

$$\frac{a}{\sin A} = \frac{b}{\sin B_1} \qquad \text{Substitute known values.}$$

$$\frac{22}{\sin 40°} = \frac{27}{\sin B_1} \qquad \text{Solve for } \sin B_1.$$

$$\sin B_1 = \frac{27 \sin 40°}{22} \qquad \text{Simplify.}$$

$$\angle B_1 = \sin^{-1}(0.788\ 875\ 702\ 8) \qquad \text{Determine } \angle B_1 \text{ using } \sin^{-1}.$$

$$\angle B_1 \doteq 52°$$

Determine $\angle C$.

$$\begin{aligned}\angle C &= 180° - (40° + 52°)\\ &= 180° - 92°\\ &= 88°\end{aligned}$$

Determine side c using the sine law.

$$\frac{c}{\sin C} = \frac{a}{\sin A} \qquad \text{Substitute known values.}$$

$$\frac{c}{\sin 88°} = \frac{22}{\sin 40°} \qquad \text{Solve for } c.$$

$$c = \frac{22 \sin 88°}{\sin 40°} \qquad \text{Simplify.}$$

$$c \doteq 34.2 \text{ cm}$$

Case 2: ΔABC is obtuse.

$\angle B_2$ is the supplement of $\angle B_1$ in Case 1. Therefore,

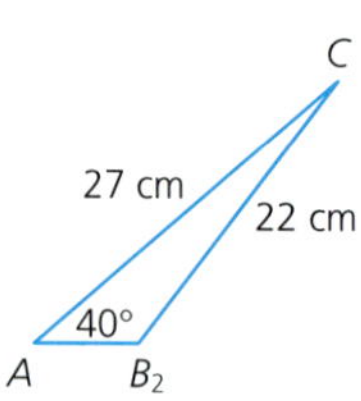

$$\begin{aligned}\angle B_2 &= 180° - 52°\\ &= 128°\end{aligned}$$

$$\begin{aligned}\angle C &= 180° - (40° + 128°)\\ &= 12°\end{aligned}$$

Determine the length of side c.

$$\frac{c}{\sin C} = \frac{a}{\sin A} \qquad \text{Substitute.}$$

$$\frac{c}{\sin 12°} = \frac{22}{\sin 40°} \qquad \text{Solve for } c.$$

$$c = \frac{22 \sin 12°}{\sin 40°} \qquad \text{Simplify.}$$

$$c \doteq 7.1 \text{ cm}$$

When ΔABC is acute, $\angle B = 52°$, $\angle C = 88°$, and $c = 34.2$ cm. When ΔABC is obtuse, $\angle B = 128°$, $\angle C = 12°$, and $c = 7.1$ cm.

Example 3

A boat travels 60 km due east. It then adjusts its course by 25° northward and travels another 90 km in this new direction. How far is the boat from its initial position to the nearest kilometre?

Solution

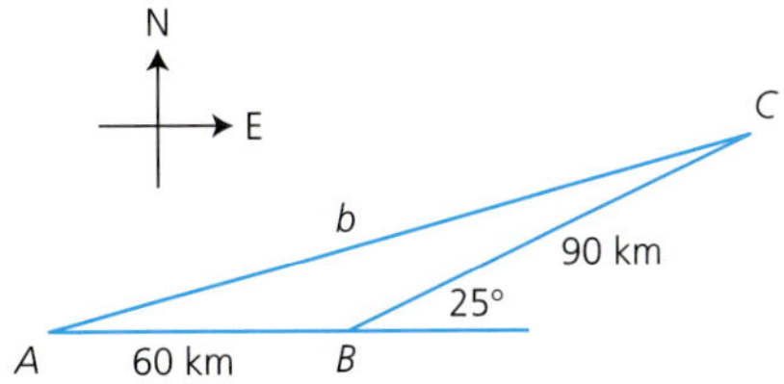

Draw a well-labelled sketch of the situation.

The distance required is side b in the diagram. In ΔABC, two sides and the angle between them are known (SAS). Use the cosine law to find side b.

$$\angle B = 180° - 25° = 155°$$

$$b^2 = a^2 + c^2 - 2ac\cos B$$ Substitute.

$$b^2 = 90^2 + 60^2 - 2(90)(60)\cos 155°$$ Simplify.

$$b^2 = 8100 + 3600 - (10\,800)(-0.906\,307\,787)$$

$$b^2 = 21\,488.1241$$

$$b = \sqrt{21\,488.1241}$$ Determine the square root and round.

$$b \doteq 147$$

The boat is about 147 km from its initial position.

Practise, Apply, Solve 6.1

A

1. Determine the measure of the indicated angle to the nearest degree.

(a)

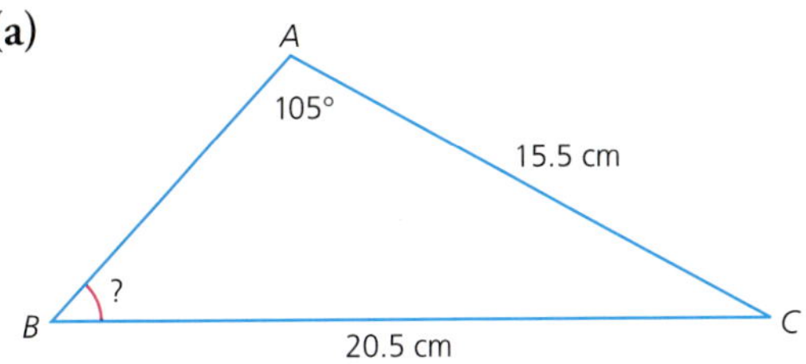

(b)

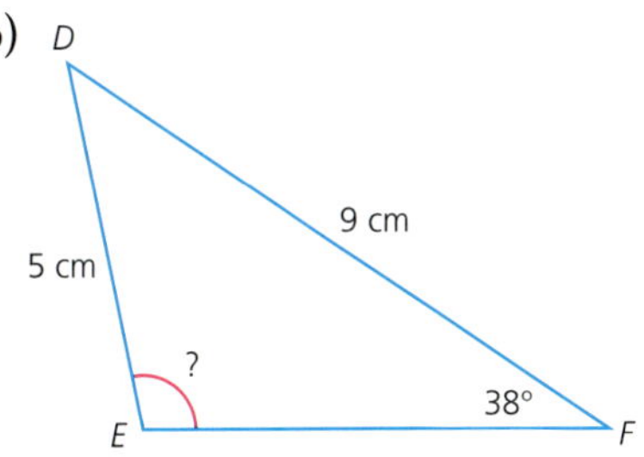

(c)

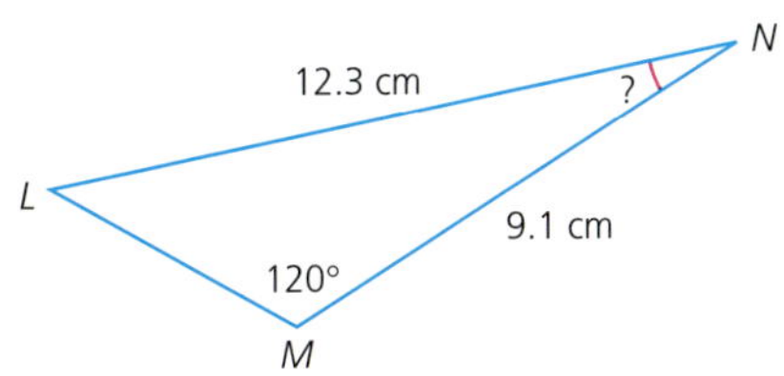

(d)

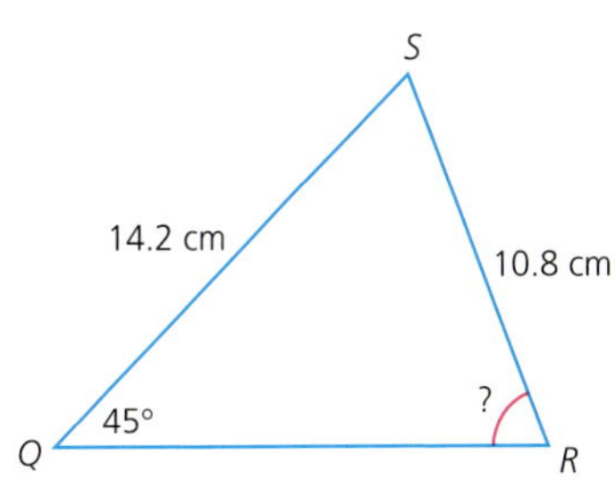

2. Determine the measure of the indicated side to one decimal place.

(a)

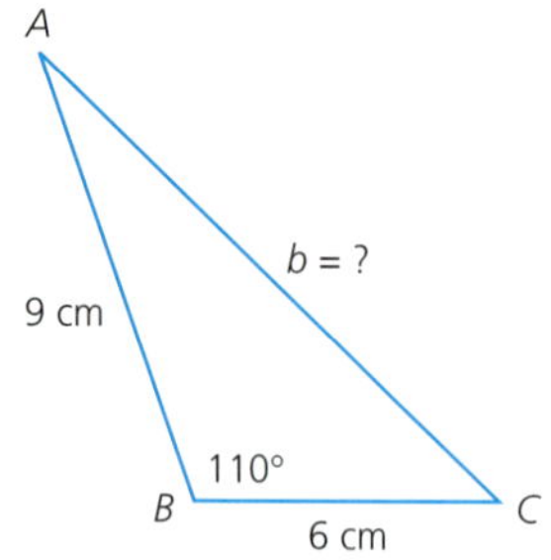

(b)

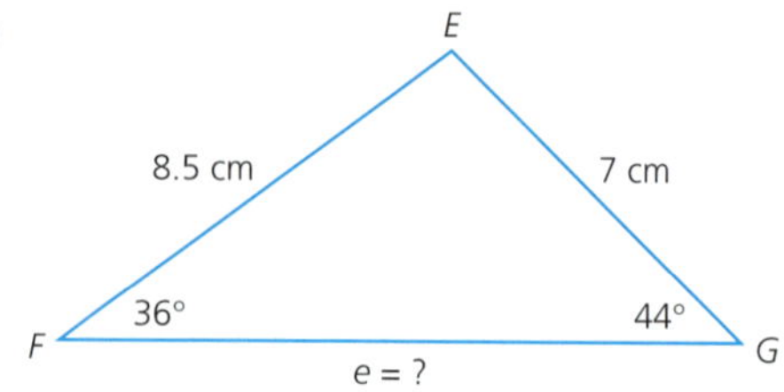

(c)

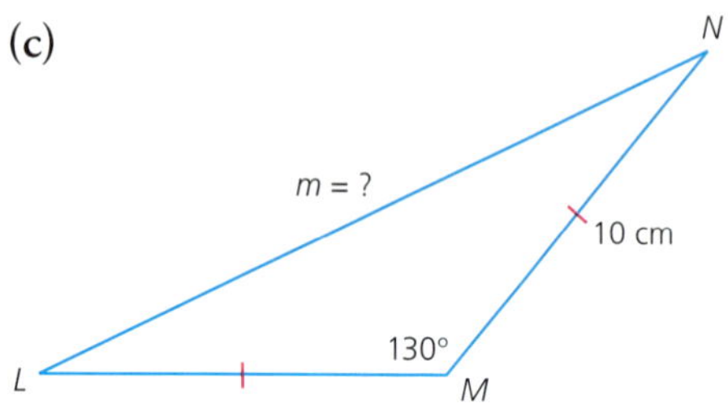

(d)

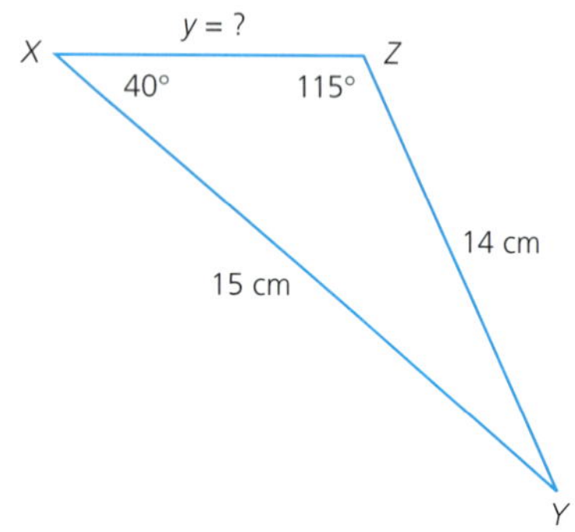

3. Determine the measure of the indicated angle to the nearest degree.

(a)

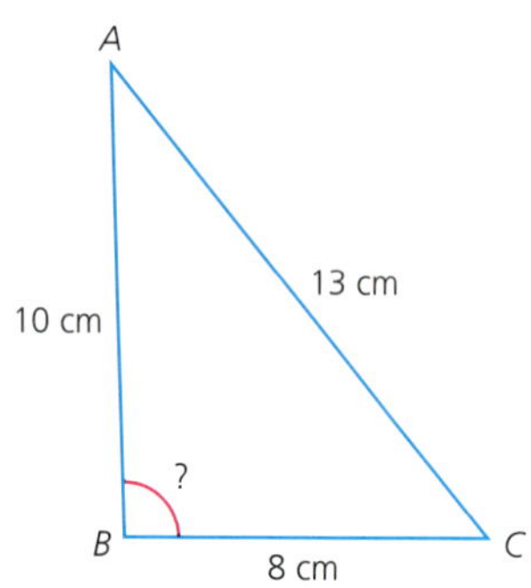

(b)

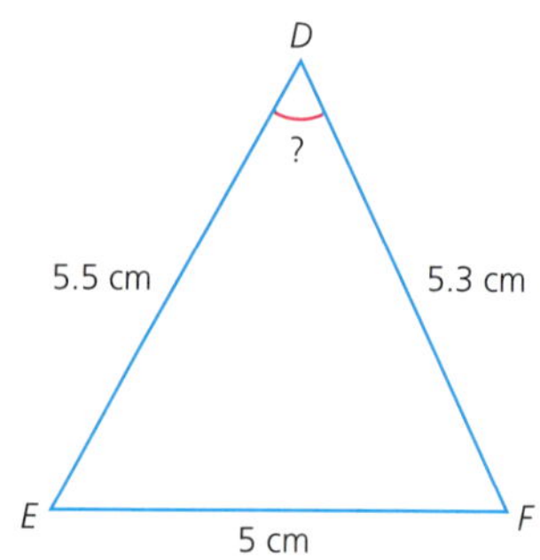

(c)

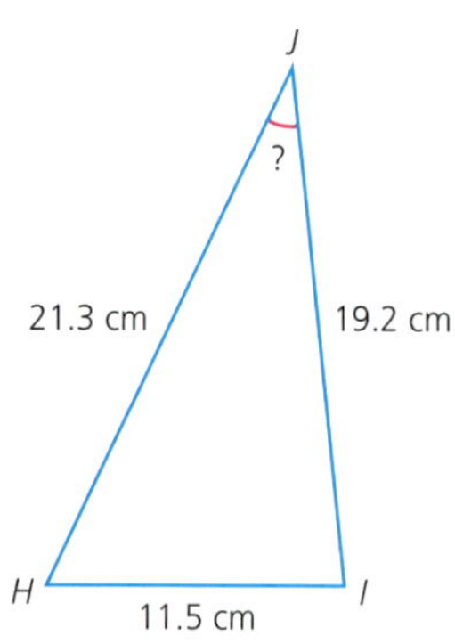

(d)

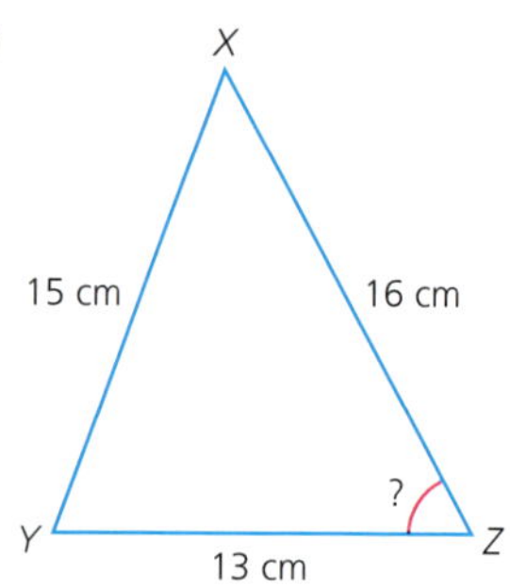

4. Determine the measure of the indicated side to one decimal place.

(a)

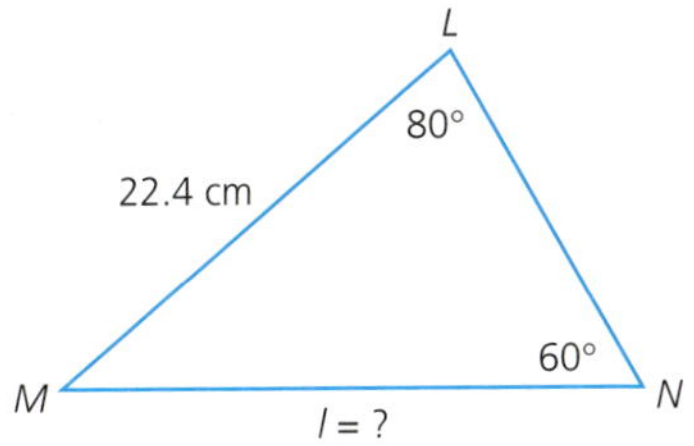

(b)

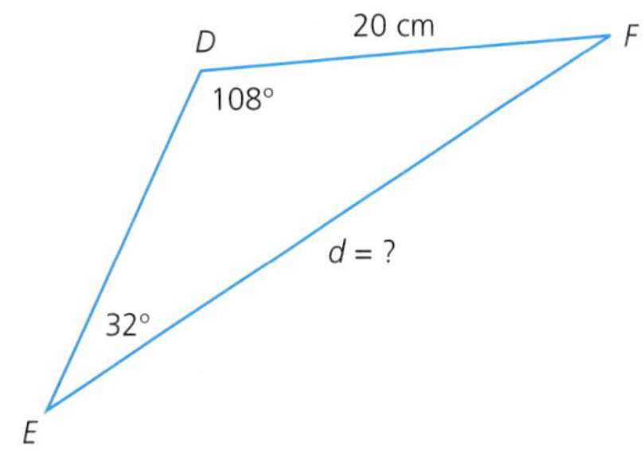

(c)

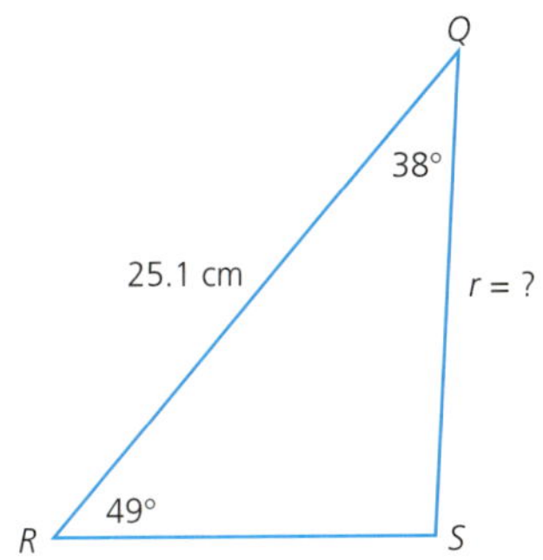

(d)

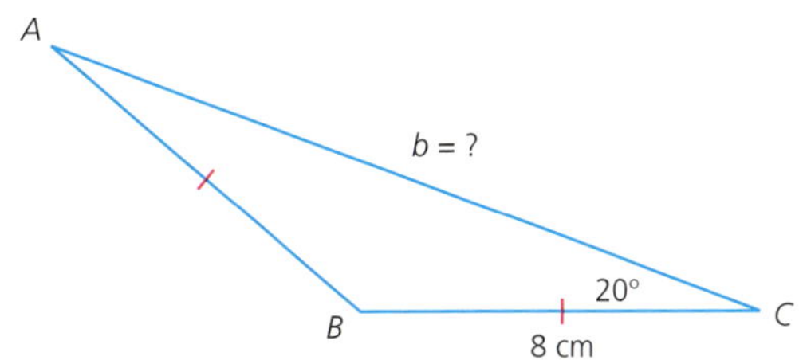

5. Each triangle is a rough sketch with the given information marked. Determine which triangles have no solution, one solution, and two solutions.

(a)

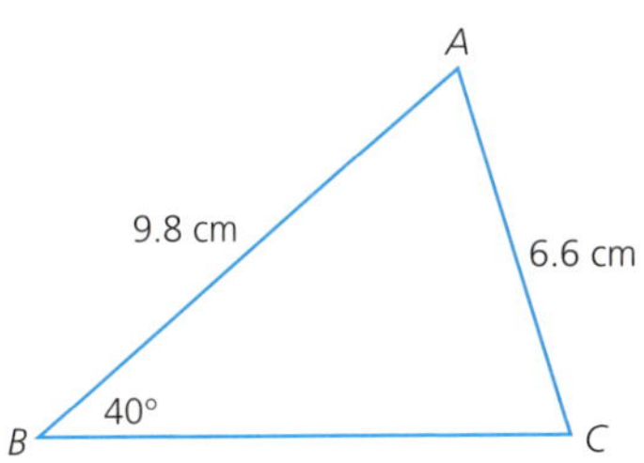

(b)

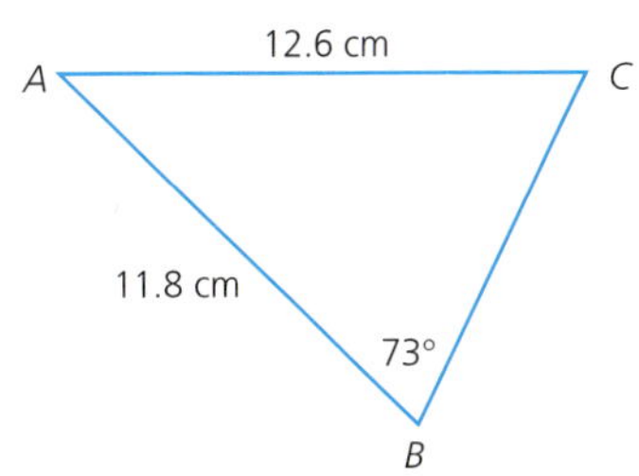

(c)

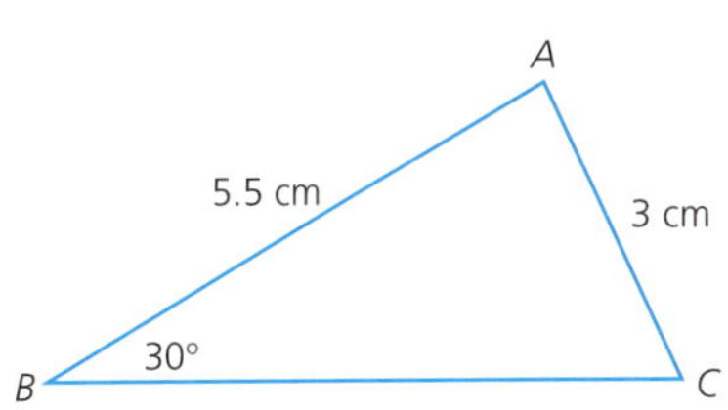

(d)

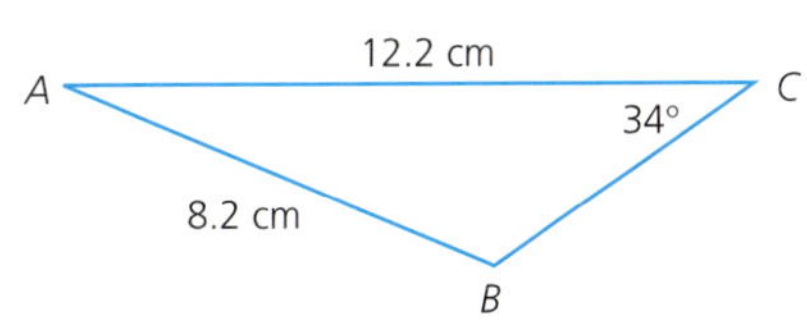

6. Given ΔABC.

i. sketch and label each triangle.

ii. calculate $b \sin A$ for each triangle.

iii. determine the number of possible solutions for the missing side, c.

iv. determine the length of side c to the nearest tenth of a unit.

(a) $a = 1.3$ cm, $b = 2.8$ cm, $\angle A = 33°$

(b) $a = 7.3$ m, $b = 14.6$ m, $\angle A = 30°$

(c) $a = 7.2$ mm, $b = 9.3$ mm, $\angle A = 35°$

(d) $a = 24.3$ cm, $b = 17.2$ cm, $\angle A = 75°$

7. Solve each triangle. Express each angle to the nearest degree and each length to the nearest tenth of a unit.

(a)

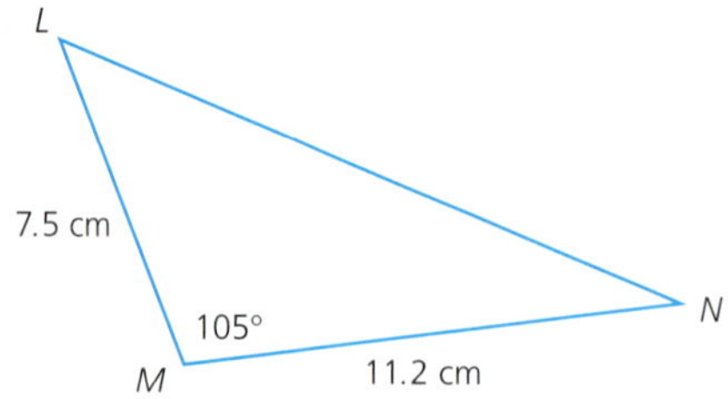

(b)

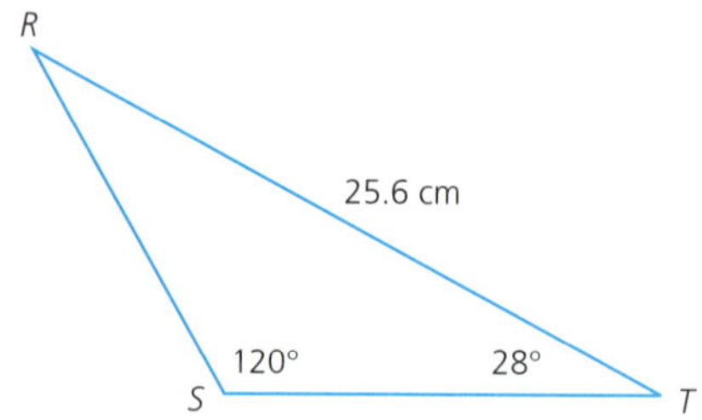

(c)

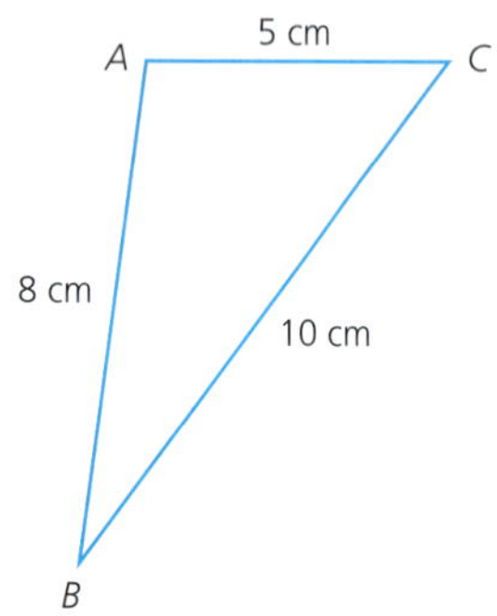

(d)

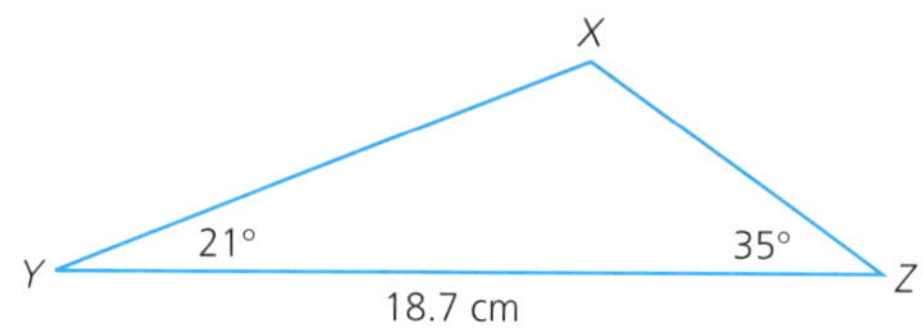

(e) ΔABC, $\angle A = 35°$, $\angle C = 40°$, $a = 12.8$ cm

(f) ΔLMN, $\angle L = 35°$, $m = 24$ cm, $n = 30$ cm

(g) ΔQRS, $\angle Q = 28°$, $\angle R = 60°$, $s = 15.2$ cm

(h) ΔDEF, $d = 12$ cm, $e = 14$ cm , $f = 16$ cm

8. Solve each triangle. Begin by sketching and labelling a diagram. Account for all possible solutions. Express each angle to the nearest degree and each length to the nearest tenth of a unit.

(a) ΔABC, $\angle A = 68°$, $a = 11.9$ cm, $b = 10.1$ cm

(b) ΔDEF, $\angle D = 52°$, $d = 7.2$ cm, $e = 9.6$ cm

(c) ΔHIF, $\angle H = 35°$, $h = 9.3$ cm, $i = 12.5$ cm

(d) ΔDEF, $\angle E = 45°$, $e = 81$ cm, $f = 12.2$ cm

(e) ΔXYZ, $\angle Y = 38°$, $y = 11.3$ cm, $x = 15.2$ cm

9. **Knowledge and Understanding:** In ΔDEF, $\angle D = 41°$, $d = 23$ cm, and $e = 27$ cm. Solve ΔDEF. Express each angle to the nearest degree and each length to one decimal place.

10. Show that the Pythagorean theorem is a special case of the cosine law. A diagram may be helpful.

11. From an airplane, a surveyor observes two points on the opposite shores of a lake, as shown. How far is it across the lake?

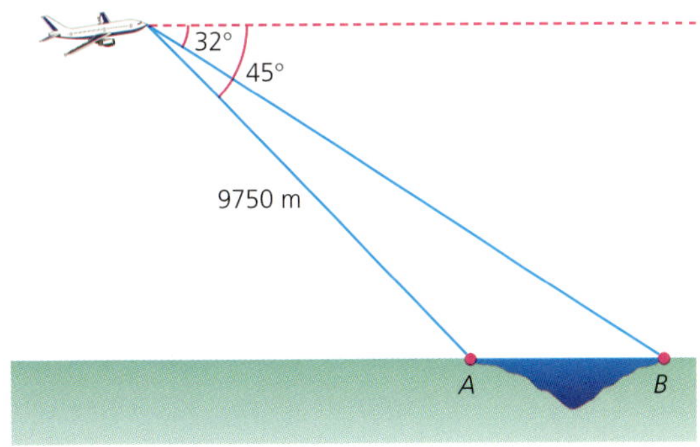

12. **Thinking, Inquiry, Problem Solving:** Mrs. Mardle says, "My lot is a triangular piece of property that is 430 m long on one side and the adjacent side is 110 m long. The angle opposite one of these sides is 35°."

(a) Is Mrs. Mardle right or wrong? Explain your reasoning.

(b) Determine the other side and angles of this lot, if possible.

13. The pitcher's mound on a softball field is 14.01 m from home plate and the bases are 18.29 m apart.

(a) How far is the pitcher's mound from first base?

(b) How far is first base from third base?

(c) How far is the pitcher's mound from second base?

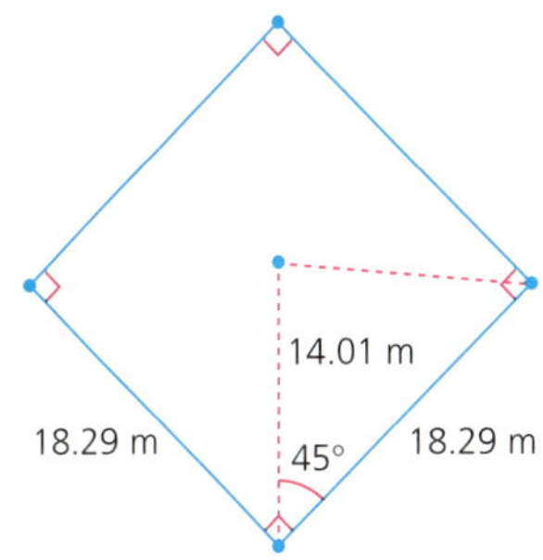

14. Determine the length of CD to the nearest tenth of a metre.

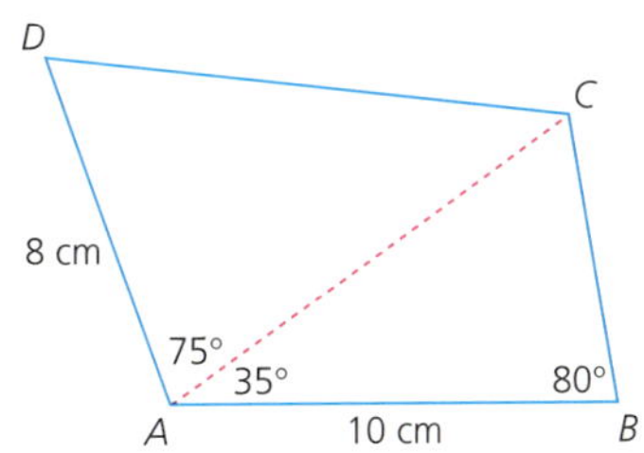

15. A paper drinking cup is in the shape of a cone. The angle at the bottom of the cone is 28.5° and each side of the cup is 10 cm. Determine the diameter of the cup.

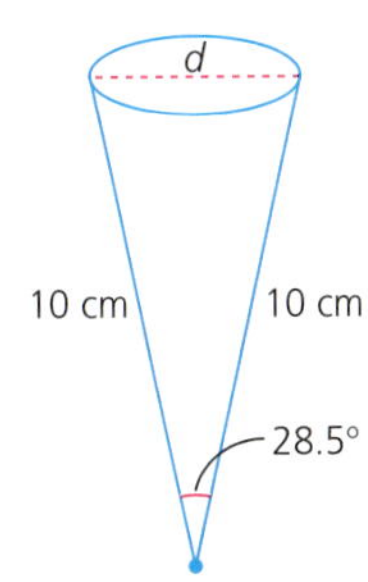

16. **Communication:** In ΔLMN, $\angle L$ is acute. Explain, with the help of a diagram, the relationship between $\angle L$, sides l and m, and the height of the triangle, for each of the following to occur.

(a) No triangle is possible.

(b) Only one triangle is possible.

(c) Two triangles are possible.

17. Two wires used to support a radio tower run along the same line but in opposite directions. They form an angle of 96° at the top of the tower. The wires are staked in the ground 25 m apart. One of the wires forms an angle of 44° with the ground.

(a) How long is each wire?

(b) How high is the tower?

18. A sailboat on Lake Huron leaves Southampton and sails 20° west of north for 20 km. At the same time, a fishing boat leaves Southampton and sails 30° west of south for 15 km. At this point, how far apart are the boats to the nearest kilometre?

19. **Application:** A radio tower, at the top of a hill, casts a shadow 36 m long down the hill. The hill is inclined at an angle of 13° and the angle of elevation of the sun is 43°. How high is the tower?

20. From two different tracking stations, a weather balloon is spotted from two angles of elevation, 57° and 83°, respectively. The tracking stations are 15 km apart. Find the altitude of the balloon.

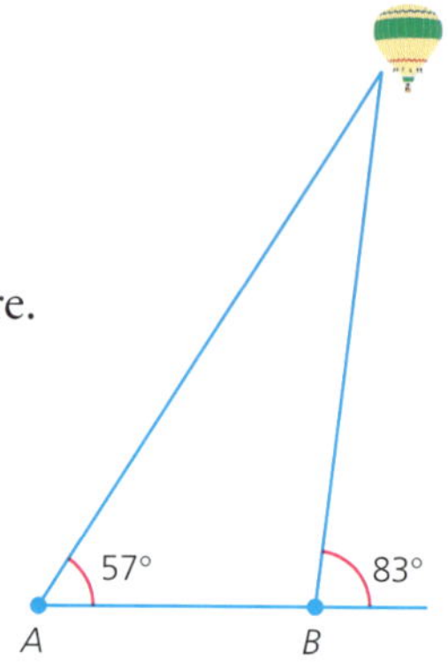

21. Find the perimeter of an isosceles triangle with a vertical angle of 100° and a base of 25 cm. Answer to the nearest tenth of a centimetre.

22. **Check Your Understanding:** An oblique triangle can be solved using the cosine law, the sine law, or a combination of both. Based on the given information, draw a triangle that represents each case. For each case, highlight all the given sides and angles on your diagram using a different colour. Under each diagram, summarize what could be found, the law that would be used, and the algebraic representation of the law.

C

23. The angles of a triangle are 120°, 40°, and 20°. The longest side is 10 cm longer than the shortest side. Find the perimeter of the triangle to the nearest hundredth of a centimetre.

24. In quadrilateral *QRST*, *QR* = 3 cm, *RS* = 4 cm, *ST* = 5 cm, and *TQ* = 6 cm. Also, diagonal *RT* is 7 cm. How long is the other diagonal to the nearest tenth of a centimetre?

25. A regular pentagon has all sides equal and all central angles equal. Calculate, to the nearest tenth, the area of the pentagon shown.

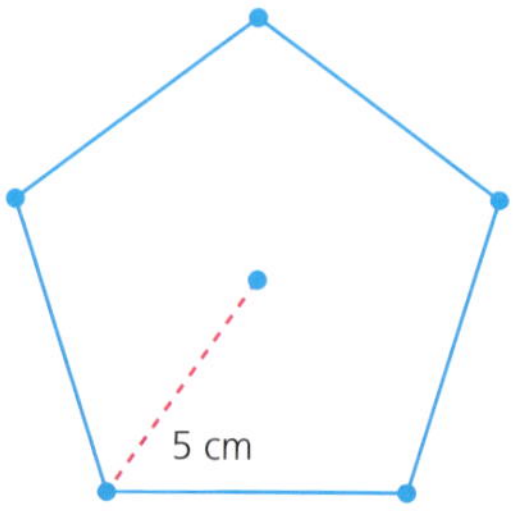

The Chapter Problem—What Time Is It?

CP1. Suppose a 50-cm long pendulum is pulled back 30 cm from the rest position. Determine the angle that the pendulum passes through on the first swing. That is, find the angle from its starting point to the point where it changes direction.

CP2. How far must the pendulum be pulled back to pass through

(a) a right angle? (b) an angle of 120°?

CP3. How long will the pendulum take to complete one swing? one period?

Solving Trigonometry Problems in Two and Three Dimensions

6.2

Part 1: Problems in Two Dimensions

A new road requires building a bridge across a river. To determine the width of the river, a surveyor stakes out a base line of 300 m along the bank of a river. She places the line so that a tree on the opposite bank of the river lies between the ends of the line. From each end of the base line, she sights the position of the tree. The lines of sight to the tree make angles of 36° and 44° with the base line. Determine the width of the river.

Think, Do, Discuss

1. When solving any type of trigonometry problem, what will help you visualize the problem?
2. Draw a well-labelled sketch of the situation in the problem. Label all vertices and sides, and label all the given information.
3. For which kinds of triangles can you use the primary trigonometric ratios? Do you need to use these in this problem?
4. What information do you need to use the cosine law to solve a problem?
5. Do you need to use the cosine law in this problem?
6. What do you need to know to use the sine law to solve a problem?
7. Do you need to use the sine law in this problem?
8. List the steps to follow to solve this problem.
9. Carry out the steps. How wide is the river to the nearest tenth of a metre?
10. Will the river always be this wide? What other factors should the surveyor think about when building a bridge that can be used through all seasons? Explain.

A Problem-Solving Model

In mathematics, and other subjects, it is often useful to use a problem-solving model. Here is one possible model.

1. **Understand the problem.**

   Draw a rough sketch. List the given information. List what must be found. List the mathematical concepts that could be used. List the steps that you think would lead to the solution.

2. **Create a mathematical model of the problem.**

   Draw a well-labelled diagram. Mark all given information on it. Determine what information you need to find. Identify the relationships you will need to use.

3. **Plan a solution.**

   Determine or explain how to use the relationships you identified in step 2.

4. **Execute the plan.**

   Perform all the calculations in your plan.

5. **Interpret and evaluate the solution.**

   Consider if your answer reasonable. Calculate the answer to the specified degree of accuracy.

6. **Generalize your results.**

   Determine if your solution can be used in similar problems.

Part 2: Problems in Three Dimensions

While on a hiking trip in Algonquin Park, two hikers separate from their group and each becomes lost. Both hikers go to wide open clearings where aircraft can see them. After several hours, the larger group contacts the park rangers to tell them of the lost hikers. A rescue helicopter, at an altitude of 200 m, spots both hikers at the same time. One is at an angle of depression of 9° and a bearing of 240°. The other is at an angle of depression of 13° and a bearing of 68°. How far apart are they?

Think, Do, Discuss

Follow the problem-solving model.

1. **Understand the problem.**

   (a) Draw a diagram. Include two vertical right triangles that share the same height. The hypotenuse of each triangle represents the lines of sight from the helicopter to each hiker and the height of the triangles is the distance between the ground and the helicopter. Draw the horizontal triangle by joining the points that represent the hikers' positions. This line is the distance between the hikers.

(b) List all the given information. Is any of it not needed?

(c) Write down what you need to know in order to find the distance between the lost hikers.

(d) List the mathematical concepts that might be useful for solving this problem. Explain how to use them.

(e) List the steps that you think would lead to the solution.

2. Create a mathematical model of the problem.

(a) Draw an accurate diagram. Label it so you can refer to the sides and angles by name.

(b) On your diagram, mark all the information that you have been given.

(c) What missing information do you need in order to determine the distance between the hikers? Will you use a vertical or horizontal triangle to find this distance?

(d) Identify the relationships that you need to use to find the missing information. Will you use vertical or horizontal triangles to find the missing information?

3. Plan a solution.

(a) What type of triangles must you use to determine the missing information? Which trigonometric ratios must be used?

(b) How can you find the angle between the two hikers?

(c) What type of triangle must you use to determine the distance between the two hikers?

(d) Do you need the sine law or cosine law in this problem?

4. Execute the plan.

(a) Determine the missing information, then determine the distance between the hikers.

5. Interpret and evaluate the solution.

(a) Describe how you can check whether your answer is reasonable.

(b) To what degree of accuracy should you calculate your answer?

6. Generalize your results.

(a) Can you always use this method to determine the distance between two objects when seen from above?

(b) Could you use this method to determine the distance between two elevated objects when seen from below?

Focus 6.2

Key Ideas

- When solving problems involving trigonometry, try to follow a problem-solving model. Consider the following:

  Draw and label a diagram with all the given information.

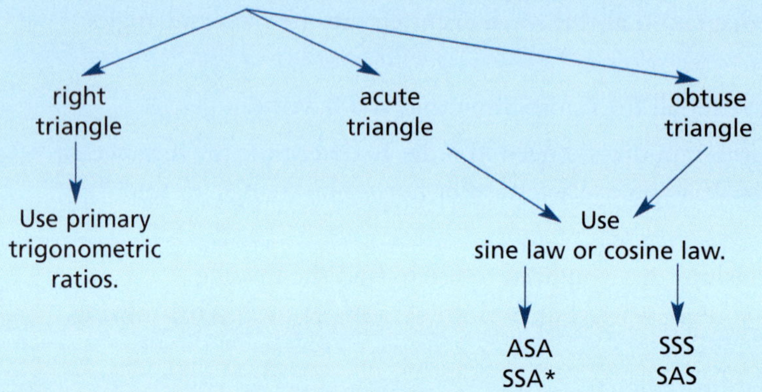

*SSA is the ambiguous case and may have 0 sets, 1 set, or 2 sets of solutions.

- If both the sine law and cosine law can be used to solve a triangle, use the sine law, since it is the easier method.
- When solving a problem in three dimensions, it is helpful to separate the information into horizontal and vertical triangles.

Example 1

Mark is a landscaper who is creating a triangular planting garden. The homeowner wants the garden to have two equal sides and contain an angle of 135°. Also, the longest side of the garden must be exactly 5 m.

(a) How long is the plastic edging that Mark needs to surround the garden?

(b) Determine the area of the garden.

Solution

(a) Draw a well-labelled diagram.

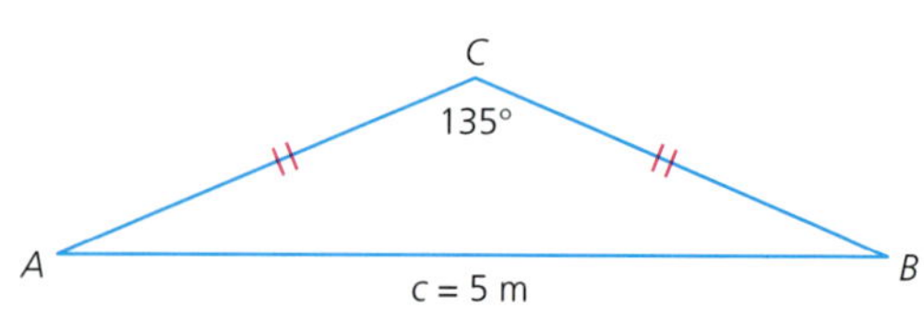

Since two sides must be equal, the triangle is isosceles. Therefore, $AC = CB$.

$$\begin{aligned}\angle A &= \angle B \\ &= (180° - 135°) \div 2 \\ &= 22.5°\end{aligned}$$

To determine the amount of edging needed, the perimeter of the triangle must be determined. Therefore, sides a and b must be determined. In this oblique triangle, two angles and a side are known (ASA). Therefore, use the sine law.

$$\begin{aligned}\frac{a}{\sin A} &= \frac{c}{\sin C}\\ \frac{a}{\sin 22.5°} &= \frac{5}{\sin 135°}\\ a &= \frac{5 \sin 22.5°}{\sin 135°}\\ a &= \frac{5(0.382\ 683\ 432\ 40)}{0.707\ 106\ 781\ 2}\\ a &\doteq 2.7\end{aligned}$$

$$\begin{aligned}\text{Perimeter} &= a + b + c\\ &= 2.7 + 2.7 + 5\\ &= 10.4\end{aligned}$$

Mark will need about 10.4 m of plastic edging.

(b) To determine the area of the garden, first determine the height of ΔABC. Draw CD, the height of the triangle, by drawing a line from vertex C to D, so $CD \perp AB$.

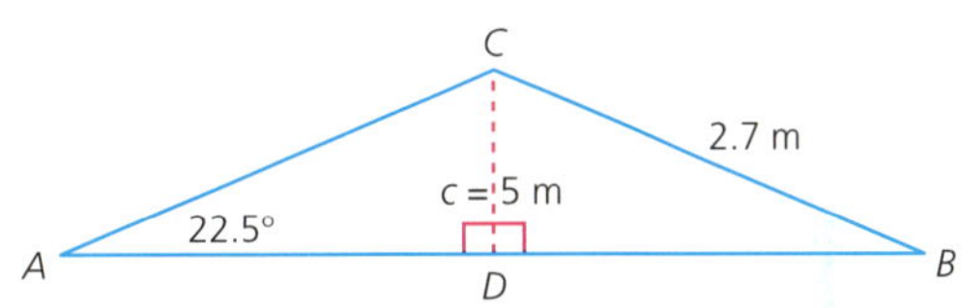

$$\begin{aligned}AC &= CB\\ &= 2.7 \text{ m}\end{aligned}$$

ΔCAD is a right triangle, so use primary trigonometric ratios. Use the sine ratio to determine CD.

$$\begin{aligned}\sin 22.5° &= \frac{CD}{2.7}\\ 2.7\,(\sin 22.5°) &= CD\\ 2.7(0.382\ 683\ 432\ 4) &= CD\\ 1.03 &\doteq CD\end{aligned}$$

$$\begin{aligned}\text{Area of } \Delta ABC &= \frac{1}{2}(bh)\\ &= \frac{1}{2}(AB)(CD)\\ &= \frac{1}{2}(5)(1.03)\\ &= 2.575\end{aligned}$$

The garden is 2.575 m^2 in area.

Example 2

The Great Pyramid at Giza in Egypt has a square base with sides of 232.6 m long. The distance from the top of the pyramid to each corner of the base was originally 221.2 m.

(a) Determine the angle each face makes with the base.

(b) Determine the size of the apex angle of a face of the pyramid.

Solution

(a) Draw a well-labelled diagram. $\angle EGF$ is the angle each face makes with the base of the pyramid, where G is the midpoint of BC. To determine this angle, two sides of ΔEFG must be determined.

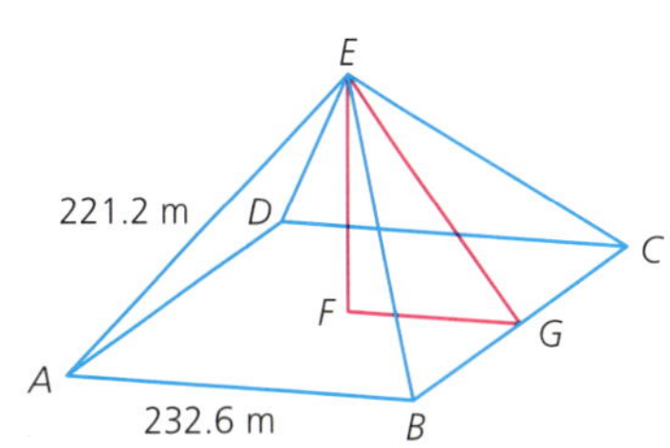

Quadrilateral *ABCD* is a square. The height of the pyramid, *EF*, occurs at the exact centre of the base. Therefore,

$$\begin{aligned} FG &= \frac{AB}{2} \\ &= \frac{232.6}{2} \\ &= 116.3 \end{aligned}$$

In ΔEBG, $EB = 221.2$ m. Also, since *G* is the midpoint of *BC*, then,

$$\begin{aligned} BG &= \frac{BC}{2} \\ &= \frac{232.6}{2} \\ &= 116.3 \end{aligned}$$

ΔEBC is isosceles and $EG \perp BC$. Therefore,

$$\begin{aligned} BG^2 + GE^2 &= EB^2 \\ 116.3^2 + GE^2 &= 221.2^2 \\ 13\ 525.69 + GE^2 &= 48\ 929.44 \\ GE^2 &= 48\ 929.44 - 13\ 525.69 \\ GE^2 &= 35\ 403.75 \\ GE &= \sqrt{35\ 403.75} \\ GE &\doteq 188.2 \end{aligned}$$

$EF \perp FG$ and ΔEGF is a right triangle. Therefore, use primary trigonometric ratios.

$$\begin{aligned} \cos(\angle EGF) &= \frac{FG}{GE} \\ \cos(\angle EGF) &= \frac{116.3}{188.2} \\ \cos(\angle EGF) &\doteq 0.617\ 959\ 617\ 4 \\ \angle EGF &= \cos^{-1}(0.617\ 959\ 617\ 4) \\ \angle EGF &\doteq 51.8° \end{aligned}$$

(b) The apex angle of each face is the vertical angle of each side of the pyramid. $\angle AEB$ is an apex angle. In ΔAEB, all three sides are known (SSS). $AE = EB$ or 221.2 m and $AB = 232.6$ m. Therefore, use the cosine law.

$$\begin{aligned} AB^2 &= AE^2 + EB^2 - 2(AE)(EB)\cos(\angle AEB) && \text{Substitute.} \\ 232.6^2 &= 221.2^2 + 221.2^2 \\ &\quad - 2(221.2)(221.2)\cos(\angle AEB) && \text{Expand.} \\ 54\ 102.76 &= 48\ 929.44 + 48\ 929.44 \\ &\quad - 97\ 858.88\cos(\angle AEB) && \text{Isolate } \cos(\angle AEB). \\ 97\ 858.88\cos(\angle AEB) &= 48\ 929.44 + 48\ 929.44 - 54\ 102.76 \\ 97\ 858.88\cos(\angle AEB) &= 43\ 756.12 \\ \cos(\angle AEB) &= \frac{43\ 756.12}{97\ 858.88} \\ \cos(\angle AEB) &= 0.447\ 134\ 894\ 7 \end{aligned}$$

Determine $\angle AEB$.

$$\cos^{-1}(0.447\ 134\ 894\ 7) = \angle AEB$$
$$63.4° = \angle AEB$$

Example 3

From the top of a 50-m high bridge, two boats are seen at anchor. One boat is S50°W and has an angle of depression of 38°. The other boat is S60°E and has a 35° angle of depression. How far apart are the boats?

Solution

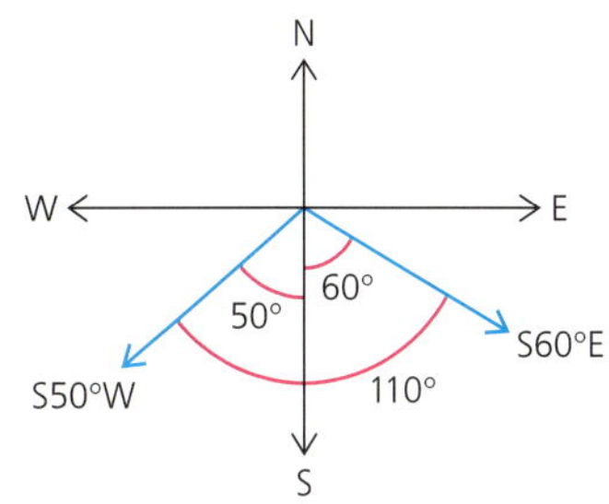

To work in three dimensions, you need an accurate sketch to help visualize the situation. First visualize the bearings on the horizontal plane.

Now visualize the vertical planes as they intersect each bearing line.

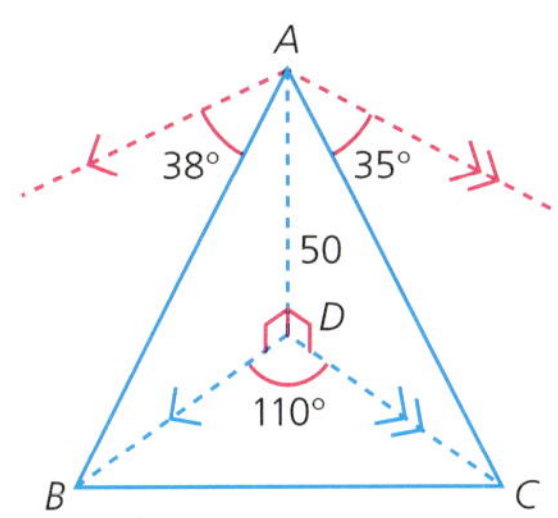

To determine BC, the distance between the boats, use ΔBCD. In this obtuse triangle, $\angle BDC$ and sides BD and CD are known (SAS). Therefore, use the cosine law. To determine BD, use right triangle ABD. To find CD, use right triangle ACD.

In ΔABD,

$$\angle BAD = 90° - 38°$$
$$= 52°$$

Therefore, $\tan 52° = \frac{BD}{50}$

$$BD = 50 \tan 52°$$
$$BD \doteq 64.0$$

In ΔACD,

$$\angle CAD = 90° - 35°$$
$$= 55°$$

Therefore, $\tan 55° = \frac{DC}{50}$

$$DC = 50 \tan 55°$$
$$DC \doteq 71.4$$

In ΔBCD,

$$BC^2 = BD^2 + DC^2 - 2(BD)(DC)\cos D$$
$$BC^2 = 64^2 + 71.4^2 - 2(64)(71.4)\cos 110°$$
$$BC^2 \doteq 4096 + 5097.96 - 9139.2(-0.342\ 020\ 143\ 3)$$
$$BC^2 = 12\ 319.750\ 49$$
$$\sqrt{BC^2} = \sqrt{12\ 319.750\ 49}$$
$$BC \doteq 110.99$$

The boats are about 111 m apart.

Practise, Apply, Solve 6.2

A

1. Morana is trolling for salmon in Lake Ontario. She sets the fishing rod so its tip is 1 m above the water and the line enters the water at an angle of 35°. Fish have been tracked at a depth of 45 m. What length of line must she let out?

2. Josh is building a garden shed that is 4 m wide. The two sides of the roof must meet at an 80° angle and be equal in length. How long must each rafter be if he allows for a 0.5-m overhang?

3. A parallelogram has sides of 12 cm and 15 cm. The contained angle is 75°. How long is

   (a) the shorter diagonal? (b) the longer diagonal?

4. The height of any isosceles triangle begins from the midpoint of the base of the triangle. Suppose ΔABC is isosceles, with the two equal sides being 10 cm and the equal angles being 40°. Determine the height and area of the triangle.

5. A regular hexagon is inscribed inside a circle with radius 10 cm. Determine the perimeter of the hexagon.

6. The blueprints for the roof of a new house call for one side to have a slope of $\frac{1}{3}$ and the other side to have a slope of $\frac{1}{2}$. Determine the measure of the angle at the peak of the roof.

B

7. Determine the measure of the indicated side or angle correct to the accuracy given in the question.

   (a)

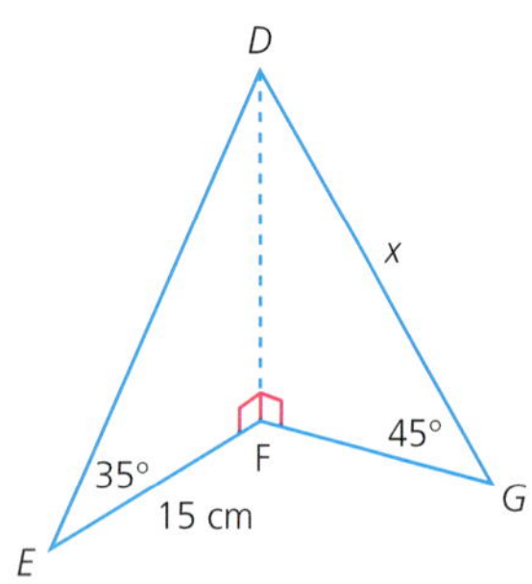

   (b)

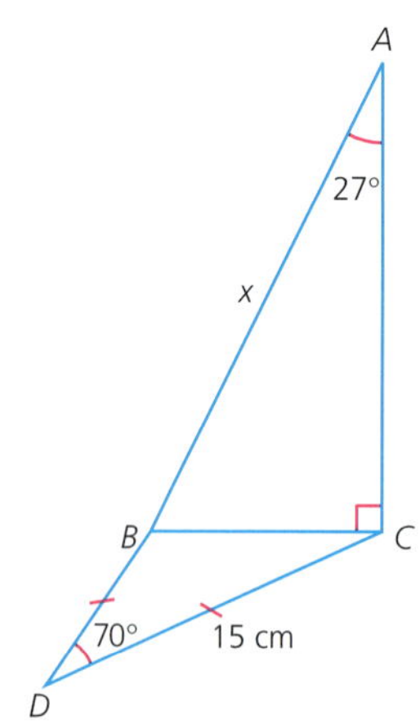

(c)

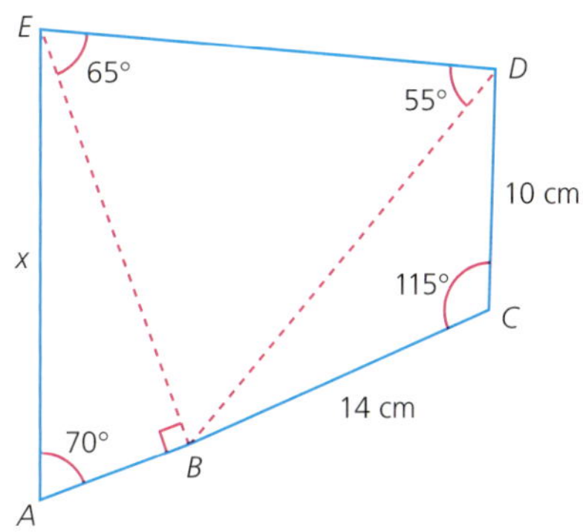

(d)

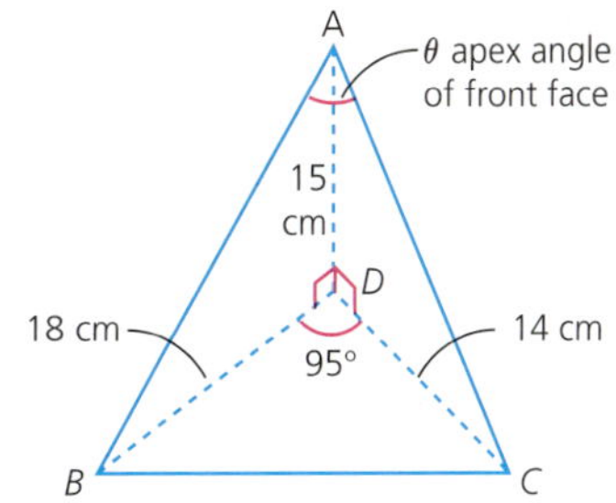

8. **Communication:** Think of a real-life problem that can be modelled by a three-dimensional diagram in which a side or distance must be determined. Describe the problem, sketch the situation, and explain what must be done to solve the problem.

9. **Knowledge and Understanding:** A roof truss is 10.4 m wide and the angles formed by the roof beams are 19° and 23°. How long is each roof beam?

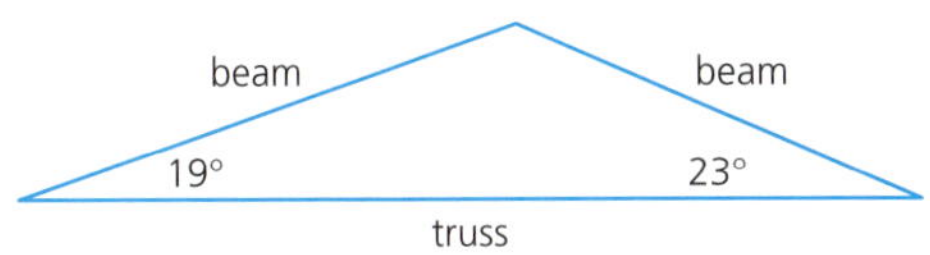

10. The Leaning Tower of Pisa leans toward the south at an angle of about 5.5°. On one day, its shadow is 90 m long, and the angle of elevation from the tip of the shadow to the top of the tower is 32°.
    (a) What is the slant height of the tower?
    (b) How high is the tip of the tower above the ground?

11. Two ships, the *Argus* and the *Baffin*, are 125.0 nautical miles apart. They both hear a homing signal from a lifeboat. The captain of the *Argus* calculates that the angle formed between the *Baffin*, itself, and the lifeboat is 36°. The captain of the *Baffin* calculates the angle between the *Argus*, itself, and the lifeboat is 42°.
    (a) How far is each ship from the lifeboat?
    (b) The *Argus* has a top speed of 9.7 nautical miles per hour. The top speed of the *Baffin* is 9.4 nautical miles per hour. Which ship should reach the lifeboat first?

12. A surveyor needs to estimate the length of a swampy area. She starts at one end of the swamp and walks in a straight line, 450 paces and turns 60° towards the swamp. She then walks in another straight line, 380 paces before arriving at the other end of the swamp. One pace is about 75 cm. Estimate the length of the swamp in metres.

13. Two planes, *Able* and *Baker*, are 31 km apart when plane *Able* is 38 km from an airstrip. The angle between the two planes, as measured from the airstrip, is 46°. Both planes are flying at the same speed. Which plane will land first? Explain.

14. **Application:** Two forest fire towers, *A* and *B*, are 20.3 km apart. The bearing from *A* to *B* is N70°E. The ranger in each tower observes a fire and radios the fire's bearing from the tower. The bearing from tower *A* is N25°E. From tower B, the bearing is N15°W. How far is the fire from each tower?

15. Two roads intersect at an angle of 48°. A car and a truck collide at the intersection, and then leave the scene of the accident on different roads. The car travels at 100 km/h, while the truck goes 80 km/h. Fifteen minutes after the accident, a police helicopter locates the car and pulls it over. Twenty minutes after the accident, a police cruiser pulls over the truck. How far apart are the car and the truck at this time?

16. A surveyor uses a diagram to help determine the height, *h*, of a mountain.

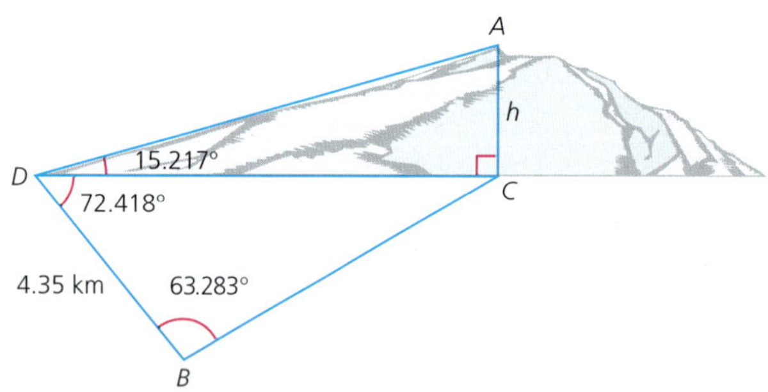

(a) Use ΔBDC to determine $\angle C$.

(b) Use ΔBDC and the sine law to determine DC.

(c) Use ΔADC to calculate h.

17. Two roads intersect at an angle of 12°. Two cars leave the intersection, each on a different road. One car travels at 90 km/h and the other car at 120 km/h. After 20 min, a police helicopter 1000 m directly above and between the cars, notes the angle of depression of the slower car is 14°. What is the horizontal distance from the helicopter to the faster car?

18. **Thinking, Inquiry, Problem Solving:** A given pyramid has a regular hexagonal base. Each side of the base is 12.5 cm and the vertical height of the pyramid is 20.0 cm. Determine

(a) the measure of the apex angle of each face

(b) the surface area of the pyramid

(c) the volume of the pyramid

19. Check Your Understanding: When you are given a problem to solve that involves trigonometry, what essential thing must you do to solve each problem? Explain how you would decide whether to use the primary trigonometric ratios, the sine law, the cosine law, or a combination of these.

C

20. Two hot air balloons are moored directly over a level road. The diagram shows the angle of elevation of the balloons from two observers 2 km apart.

(a) To the nearest tenth of a kilometre, how far apart are the balloons?

(b) Which balloon is higher, and by how many metres?

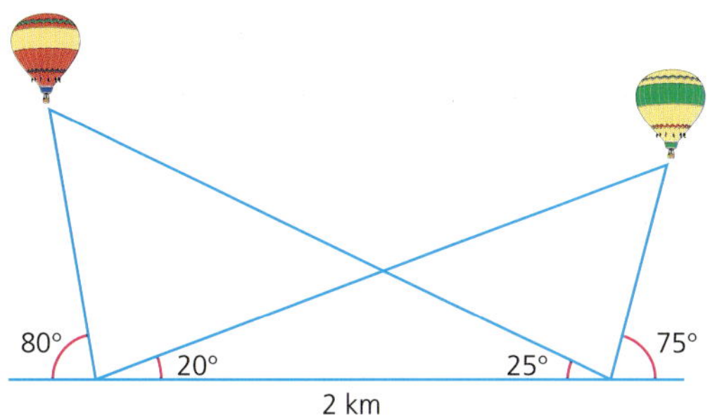

The Chapter Problem—What Time Is It?

Apply what you have learned to answer these questions about the Chapter Problem on page 494.

CP4. Assume the pendulum is 80 cm long. How far must it be pulled back from the centre or rest position (horizontal distance), to swing through an angle of $\frac{5\pi}{8}$?

CP5. How long will this pendulum take to complete one swing? one period?

CP6. Does the pendulum need to be longer or shorter than 80 cm for one swing to occur in 1 s? Explain your reasoning.

SKILL BUILDER 6.3

Using Special Triangles to Determine Exact Values

Determining the value of a trigonometric function for a given angle can be found to a high degree of accuracy using scientific and graphing calculators. However, these values are close approximations, not exact values. This is due, in large part, to rounding of irrational numbers such as $\sqrt{2}$, $\sqrt{3}$, and $\sqrt{5}$.

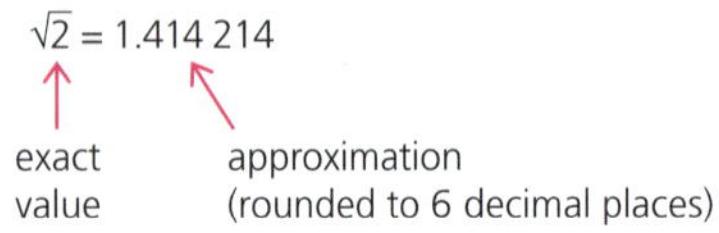

In the early stages of trigonometry, triangles were used to generate tables of values for each trigonometric function. A few of these triangles are still in use today to help generate exact values for trigonometry functions involving frequently used angles of $\frac{\pi}{6}$, $\frac{\pi}{4}$, and $\frac{\pi}{3}$.

Any right isosceles triangle has angles of $\frac{\pi}{4}$, $\frac{\pi}{4}$, and $\frac{\pi}{2}$. Since the trigonometric ratios are independent of the lengths of the sides, the simplest triangle that contains these angles can be used to generate the trigonometric ratios. This triangle has two equal sides of 1 unit in length.

Calculate the hypotenuse using the Pythagorean theorem.

$$1^2 + 1^2 = x^2$$
$$1 + 1 = x^2$$
$$2 = x^2$$
$$\sqrt{2} = x \qquad \text{Since } x \text{ is a side length it must be positive.}$$

Label the opposite side, the adjacent side, and the hypotenuse. It follows that

In radians,

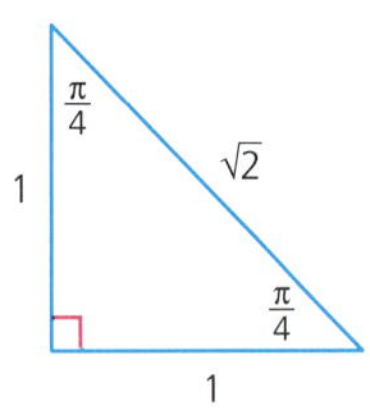

$$\sin\frac{\pi}{4} = \frac{1}{\sqrt{2}}$$
$$\cos\frac{\pi}{4} = \frac{1}{\sqrt{2}}$$
$$\tan\frac{\pi}{4} = 1$$

In degrees,

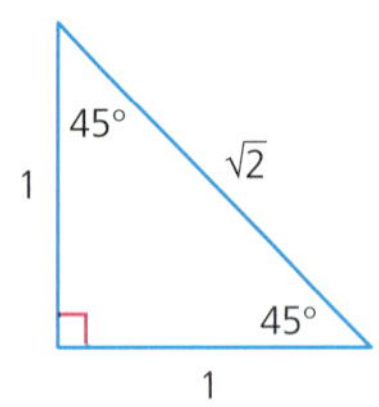

$$\sin 45^\circ = \frac{1}{\sqrt{2}}$$
$$\cos 45^\circ = \frac{1}{\sqrt{2}}$$
$$\tan 45^\circ = 1$$

An equilateral triangle contains three angles of $\frac{\pi}{3}$. Drawing the perpendicular bisector of the base creates two congruent triangles, which both contain angles of $\frac{\pi}{6}$, $\frac{\pi}{3}$, and $\frac{\pi}{2}$. The simplest case to consider is an equilateral triangle with sides of 2 units. Looking at one of these triangles, the vertical side can be found using the Pythagorean theorem.

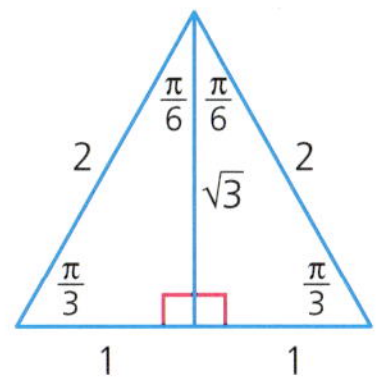

$$x^2 + 1^2 = 2^2$$
$$x^2 + 1 = 4$$
$$x^2 = 4 - 1$$
$$x^2 = 3$$
$$x = \sqrt{3}$$ Since x is a side length, it must be positive.

Label the opposite side, the adjacent side, and the hypotenuse. It follows that

$$\sin\frac{\pi}{3} = \frac{\sqrt{3}}{2} \qquad \sin\frac{\pi}{6} = \frac{1}{2}$$
$$\cos\frac{\pi}{3} = \frac{1}{2} \qquad \cos\frac{\pi}{6} = \frac{\sqrt{3}}{2}$$
$$\tan\frac{\pi}{3} = \frac{\sqrt{3}}{1} \text{ or } \sqrt{3} \qquad \tan\frac{\pi}{6} = \frac{1}{\sqrt{3}}$$

In degrees,

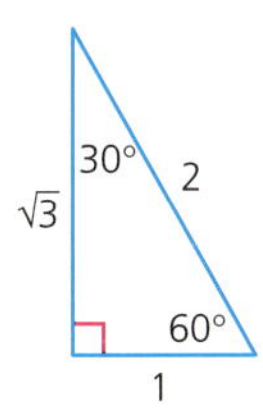

$$\sin 60° = \frac{\sqrt{3}}{2} \qquad \sin 30° = \frac{1}{2}$$
$$\cos 60° = \frac{1}{2} \qquad \cos 30° = \frac{\sqrt{3}}{2}$$
$$\tan 60° = \frac{\sqrt{3}}{1} \text{ or } \sqrt{3} \qquad \tan 30° = \frac{1}{\sqrt{3}}$$

Determining an Exact Value

The special triangles can be used to determine the exact value of an expression.

Example 1

Determine the exact value of $\sin\frac{\pi}{4}\cos\frac{\pi}{4} + \sin\frac{\pi}{3}\cos\frac{\pi}{6}$.

Solution

Use the special triangles above and substitute the appropriate ratio.

$$\begin{aligned}\sin\frac{\pi}{4}\cos\frac{\pi}{4} + \sin\frac{\pi}{3}\cos\frac{\pi}{6} &= \left(\frac{1}{\sqrt{2}}\right)\left(\frac{1}{\sqrt{2}}\right) + \left(\frac{\sqrt{3}}{2}\right)\left(\frac{\sqrt{3}}{2}\right) \\ &= \frac{1}{2} + \frac{3}{4} \\ &= \frac{2}{4} + \frac{3}{4} \\ &= \frac{5}{4} \text{ or } 1\frac{1}{4}\end{aligned}$$

Special Triangles and Related Angles

The special triangles can be used to determine the exact value of a trigonometric ratio for angles with $\frac{\pi}{6}$, $\frac{\pi}{4}$, and $\frac{\pi}{3}$ as related angles.

Example 2

Determine the exact value of $\cos \frac{5\pi}{4}$.

Solution

Sketch the angle in standard position.

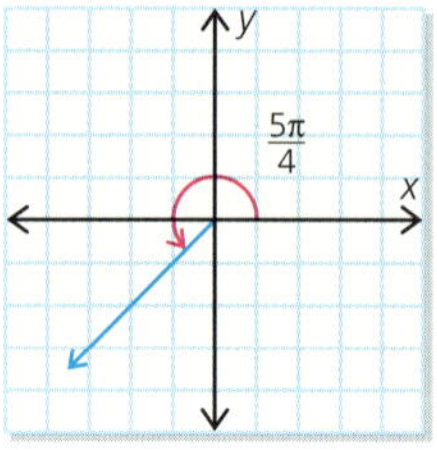

Determine the related angle and create a right triangle by drawing a vertical line from the terminal arm, perpendicular to the x-axis. Determine the values of x, y, and r using the $\frac{\pi}{4}$ special triangle and the fact that this angle lies in the third quadrant.

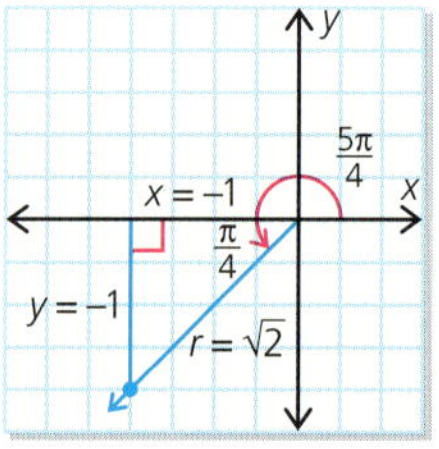

Determine the exact value.

$$\begin{aligned}\cos \frac{5\pi}{4} &= \frac{x}{r}\\ &= \frac{-1}{\sqrt{2}}\end{aligned}$$

Example 3

Determine the exact value of sin $(-210°)$.

Solution

Sketch the angle in standard position.

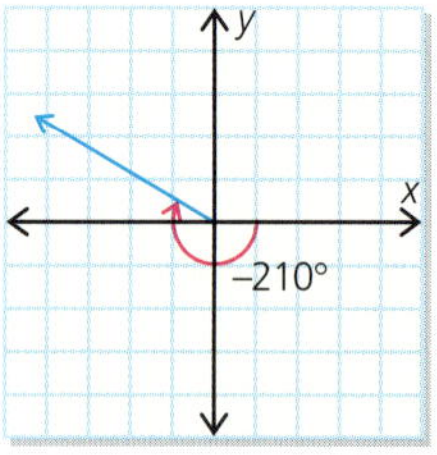

Determine the related angle and create a right triangle by drawing a vertical line from the terminal arm, perpendicular to the x-axis. Determine the values of x, y, and r using the 30° special triangle and the fact that this angle lies in the second quadrant.

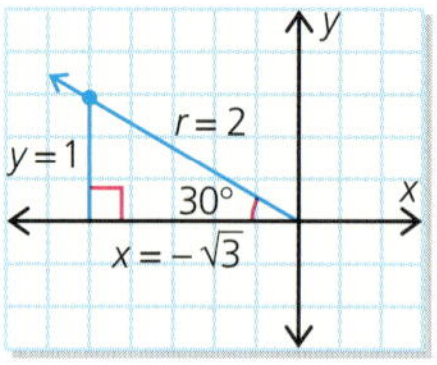

Determine the exact value.

$$\sin(-210°) = \frac{y}{r} = \frac{1}{2}$$

Example 4

Determine the exact value of $\tan \frac{11\pi}{6}$.

Solution

Sketch the angle in standard position.

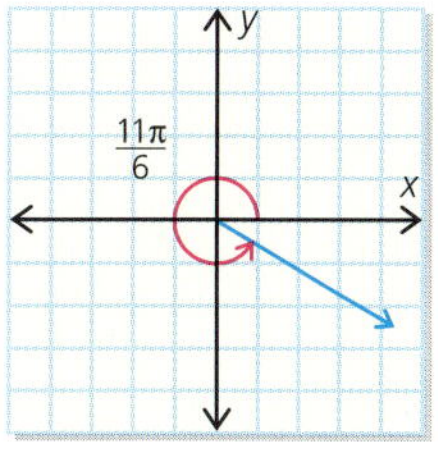

Determine the related angle and create a right triangle by drawing a vertical line from the terminal arm, perpendicular to the x-axis. Determine the values of x, y, and r using the $\frac{\pi}{6}$ special triangle and the fact that this angle lies in the fourth quadrant.

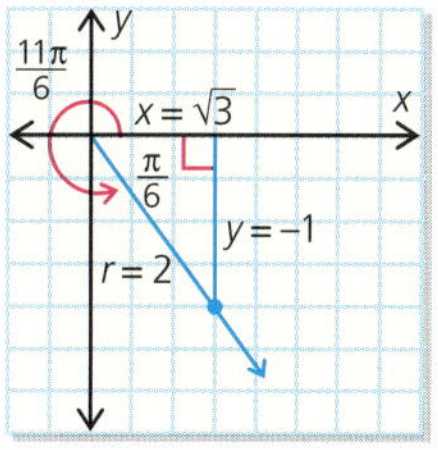

Therefore,

$$\tan \frac{11\pi}{6} = \frac{y}{x} = \frac{-1}{\sqrt{3}}$$

Using the Special Triangles to Solve Linear Trigonometric Equations

Sometimes special triangles can be used to help determine the solution.

Example 5

Solve $2 \cos \theta = \sqrt{3}, 0 \le \theta \le 2\pi$.

Solution

$$2 \cos \theta = \sqrt{3} \quad \text{Rearrange the equation by isolating } \cos \theta.$$

$$\cos \theta = \frac{\sqrt{3}}{2}$$

Since $\cos \theta = \frac{x}{r}$, then $x = \sqrt{3}$, and $r = 2$. These are sides in the $\frac{\pi}{3} - \frac{\pi}{6}$ special triangle. The cosine function is positive in quadrants I and IV. There are two possible solutions.

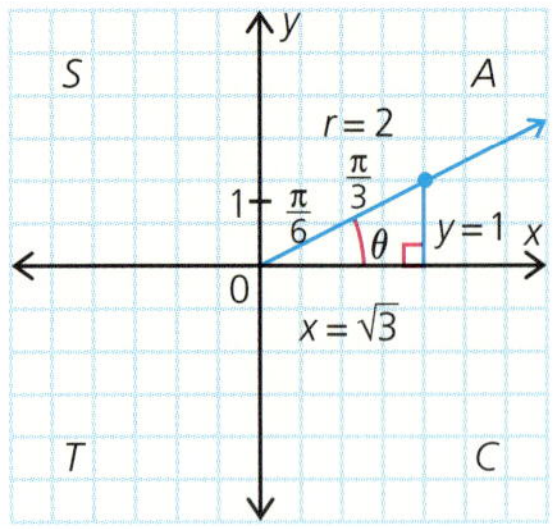

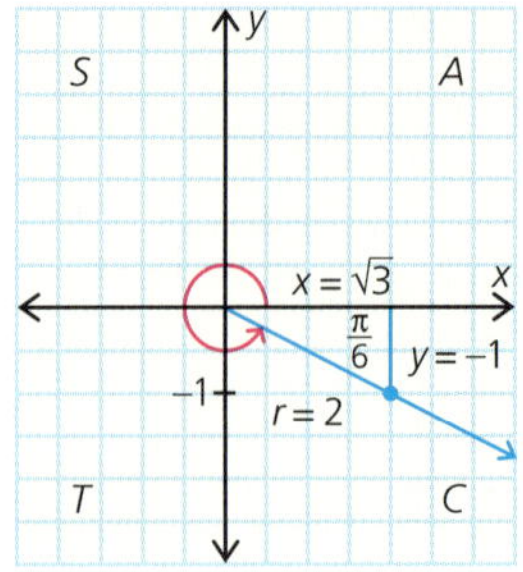

$$\theta = 2\pi - \frac{\pi}{6} = \frac{11\pi}{6}$$

The solutions are $\theta = \frac{\pi}{6}$ and $\theta = \frac{11\pi}{6}$.

Verifying a Relationship

The special triangles can also be used to show that a relationship is true, if the expression involves 30°, 45°, or 60° angles or related angles.

Example 6

Show that $\frac{\cos 150°}{\sin 150°} = \frac{1}{\tan 150°}$.

Solution

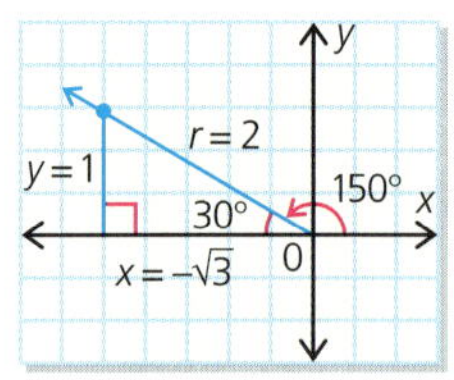

Sketch the angle in standard position. Then determine the values of x, y, and r using the 30° special triangle and the fact that the angle lies in quadrant II.

From the diagram,

$$\cos 150° = \frac{-\sqrt{3}}{2} \qquad \sin 150° = \frac{1}{2} \qquad \tan 150° = \frac{-1}{\sqrt{3}}$$

Substitute into the left and right sides of the original expression to verify.

L.S.	R.S.
$\frac{\cos 150°}{\sin 150°}$	$\frac{1}{\tan 150°}$
$= \frac{\frac{-\sqrt{3}}{2}}{\frac{1}{2}}$	$= \frac{1}{\frac{1}{-\sqrt{3}}}$
$= \left(\frac{-\sqrt{3}}{2}\right)\left(\frac{2}{1}\right)$	$= 1 \times \frac{-\sqrt{3}}{1}$
$= -\sqrt{3}$	$= -\sqrt{3}$

L.S. = R.S., therefore $\frac{\cos 150°}{\sin 150°} = \frac{1}{\tan 150°}$.

Key Ideas

- Use the triangle shown to find the exact value of the trigonometric functions for any angle in standard position where $30° \left(\frac{\pi}{6}\right)$ or $60° \left(\frac{\pi}{3}\right)$ is the related angle.

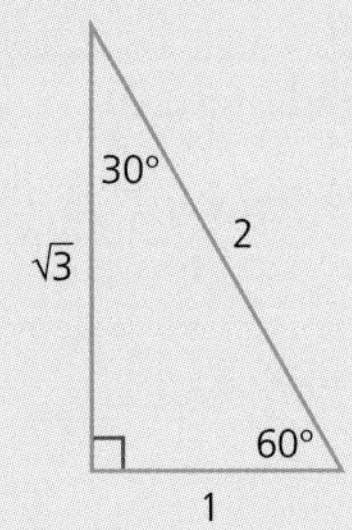

- Use the triangle shown to find the value of the trigonometric functions for any angle in standard position where $45° \left(\frac{\pi}{4}\right)$ is the related angle.

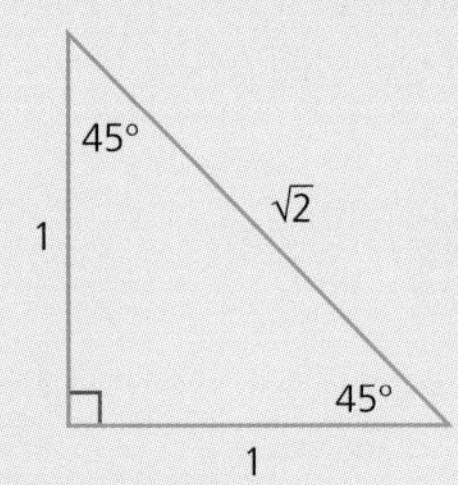

- To find the exact value of a trigonometric function for any angle that has a related angle of 30°, 45°, or 60°, follow these steps.
  1. Sketch the angle in standard position.
  2. Create a right triangle by drawing a vertical line from the terminal arm of the angle to the x-axis.
  3. Determine the measure of the related angle.
  4. Assign values for x, y, and r using the appropriate special triangle and the quadrant location of the angle.
  5. Determine the exact value using the appropriate trigonometric ratio.
- Sometimes, if a trigonometric equation involves a ratio from one of the special triangles, the solutions can be determined using $\frac{\pi}{6}$, $\frac{\pi}{4}$, or $\frac{\pi}{3}$ as related angles.

Practise, Apply, Solve 6.3

A

1. (a) Draw a triangle with angles of 30°, 60°, and 90°. Label the sides using the lengths $\sqrt{3}$, 2, and 1.

(b) Explain your reasoning for positioning each side length.

2. (a) Draw a single triangle with angles of 45°, 45°, and 90°. Label the sides using the lengths $\sqrt{2}$, 1, and 1.

(b) Explain your reasoning for positioning each side.

3. Determine the exact value.

(a) $\cos(-30°)$ (b) $\tan(-60°)$ (c) $\sin(-45°)$

4. Determine the exact value.

(a) $\tan(-150°)$ (b) $\sin(-240°)$ (c) $\cos(-315°)$

5. Determine the exact value.

(a) $\sin \frac{3\pi}{4}$ (b) $\tan \frac{4\pi}{3}$ (c) $\cos \frac{11\pi}{6}$ (d) $\tan \frac{-7\pi}{6}$

B

6. Determine the exact value.

(a) $\sin 495°$ (b) $\cos 570°$ (c) $\tan(-690°)$ (d) $\sin 675°$

7. Determine the exact value.

(a) $\cos \frac{13\pi}{4}$ (b) $\cos \frac{-19\pi}{6}$ (c) $\tan \frac{7\pi}{3}$ (d) $\cos \frac{23\pi}{6}$

8. Use special triangles to show each equation is true.

(a) $\sin 45° = \sin 135°$ (b) $\sin 225° = \sin(-45°)$

(c) $\cos(-45°) = \cos 45°$ (d) $\tan 135° = \tan(-45°)$

9. Use special triangles to show each equation is true.

(a) $\sin 60° = \sin(-240°)$ (b) $\cos(-30°) = \cos 30°$

(c) $\tan 120° = \tan(-60°)$ (d) $\sin 150° = \sin(-330°)$

10. Show that $(\sin\theta)^2 + (\cos\theta)^2 = 1$ for each angle.

(a) $\theta = 45°$ (b) $\theta = \frac{\pi}{3}$ (c) $\theta = 60°$ (d) $\theta = \frac{7\pi}{4}$

11. Show that $\tan\theta = \frac{\sin\theta}{\cos\theta}$ for each angle.

(a) $\theta = 120°$ (b) $\theta = -150°$ (c) $\theta = \frac{11\pi}{3}$ (d) $\theta = \frac{13\pi}{4}$

12. Use special triangles to determine the roots of each equation, $0° \le \theta \le 360°$.

(a) $\tan \theta = -1$

(b) $\sin \theta = \frac{1}{\sqrt{2}}$

(c) $\cos \theta = \frac{-\sqrt{3}}{2}$

(d) $\sin \theta = \frac{\sqrt{3}}{2}$

(e) $\cos \theta = \frac{1}{\sqrt{2}}$

(f) $\tan \theta = -\sqrt{3}$

(g) $\sin \theta = \frac{1}{2}$

(h) $\tan \theta = \frac{-1}{\sqrt{3}}$

(i) $\sin 2x = \frac{1}{\sqrt{2}}$

(j) $\cos 2x = \frac{1}{2}$

(k) $5 \cos x - \sqrt{3} = 3 \cos x$

(l) $\sin \frac{x}{2} = \frac{\sqrt{3}}{2}$

13. Graph $y = \sin \theta$, $-360° \le \theta \le 360°$, using 45° increments. Determine the exact coordinates when $\theta = 45° + 90°n$, $n \in \mathbf{I}$. Mark the coordinates on the graph. Explain why $y = \sin \theta$ is a function.

14. Graph $y = \cos \theta$, $-2\pi \le \theta \le 2\pi$, in increments of $\frac{\pi}{6}$. Determine the exact coordinates for $[\theta, f(\theta)]$ if the related angle is $\frac{\pi}{6}$. Mark the coordinates on the graph. Explain why $y = \cos \theta$ is a function.

15. Check Your Understanding

(a) Determine the exact measure of each unknown side length in the diagram.

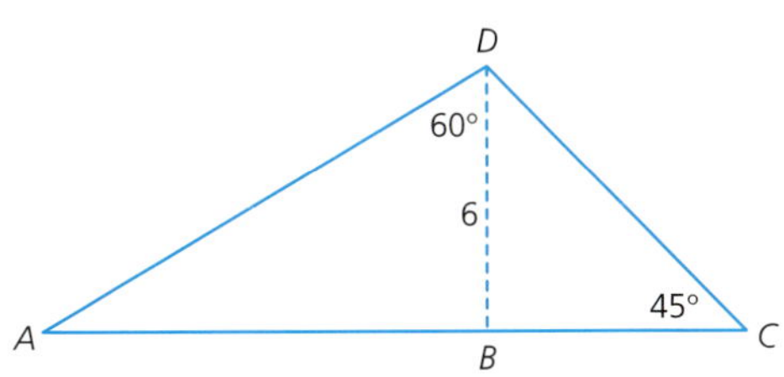

(b) Find the exact value of the sine, cosine, and tangent of $\angle A$ and $\angle C$.

6.4 Investigating Identical Expressions

EXPLORATION

In previous courses, you solved linear equations and quadratic equations. Now you can also solve linear trigonometric equations. Even though these three types of equations are solved using different strategies, some of these equations can be similar.

Defining an Identity

Think, Do, Discuss

1. With or without graphing technology, graph $y = 3(x + 2)$. On the same set of axes, graph $y = 3x + 6$.
2. How many points of intersection exist between the two relationships?
3. Solve $3(x + 2) = 3x + 6$.
4. What happens when you try to solve this equation?
5. How many solutions are possible for this equation?
6. Are there any real numbers that do not satisfy the equation? Explain.
7. Compare the left side and right side of the original equation. How would you describe the relation between these expressions?
8. Repeat steps 1 to 7 for $(x - 1)(x + 1) = x^2 - 1$.
9. Equations like the ones in steps 3 and 8 are called **identities**. Explain why this name is appropriate.
10. Are $4x + 6x = 10x$, $(x + 3)(x + 2) = x^2 + 5x + 6$, and $\sin x = \cos\left(x - \frac{\pi}{2}\right)$ identities? Explain.
11. Explain how to show graphically that a given equation is an identity.

Did You Know?

Would you like to make one million dollars? It's easy—all you have to do is prove, or disprove, Goldbach's Conjecture. In 1742, Christian Goldbach conjectured that every even number greater than 2 can be expressed as the sum of two prime numbers. Since then, mathematicians have been working hard to find out whether this conjecture is true or not. In 2000, Faber and Faber published a novel called *Uncle Petros and Goldbach's Conjecture.* To publicize the book, they offered a prize of \$1 million (U.S.) to anyone who could resolve the conjecture. There is also a practical reason for wanting to know whether the conjecture is true. If it is, then computer scientists can use it to design new methods to protect coded messages.

Trigonometric Identities

An equation that is true for all values of the variable in it is called an **identity**. For instance, the expression $4(2x + 3) = 8x + 12$ is an example of an algebraic identity because it is true for all values of x. Both sides of the expression are equivalent, or identical. If each side of the equation were separated and graphed, both graphs would be identical.

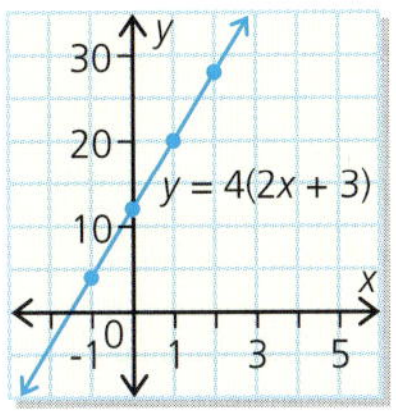

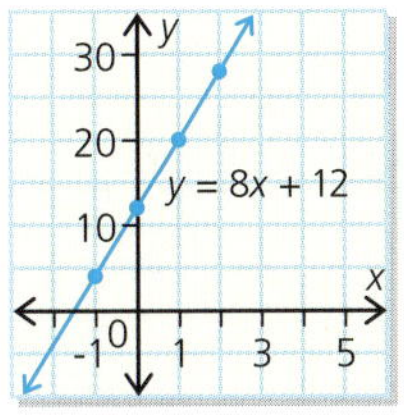

Some trigonometric equations can also be identities. However, it is not always obvious that both sides represent identical expressions. Showing that both sides of the equation represent the same expression proves that the original equation is an identity.

Fundamental Trigonometric Identities

Recall that for any angle, θ, in standard position, where $P(x, y)$ is a point on the terminal arm of the angle, the primary trigonometric ratios are

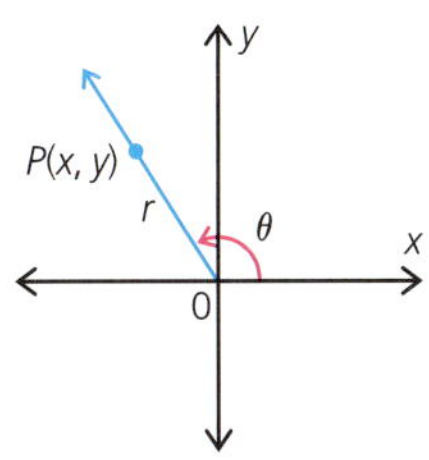

$$\sin \theta = \frac{y}{r} \qquad \cos \theta = \frac{x}{r} \qquad \tan \theta = \frac{y}{x}$$

The Quotient Identity

Examining the ratio of $\frac{\sin \theta}{\cos \theta}$ allows you to develop an equivalent expression.

$$\begin{aligned}\frac{\sin \theta}{\cos \theta} &= \frac{\frac{y}{r}}{\frac{x}{r}} \\ &= \frac{y}{\cancel{r}_1} \times \frac{\cancel{r}^1}{x} \\ &= \frac{y}{x}\end{aligned}$$

However, $\tan \theta = \frac{y}{x}$. Therefore,

$$\frac{\sin \theta}{\cos \theta} = \tan \theta \qquad ①$$

Equation ① is called a **quotient identity**. Both sides of this identity produce exactly the same graph.

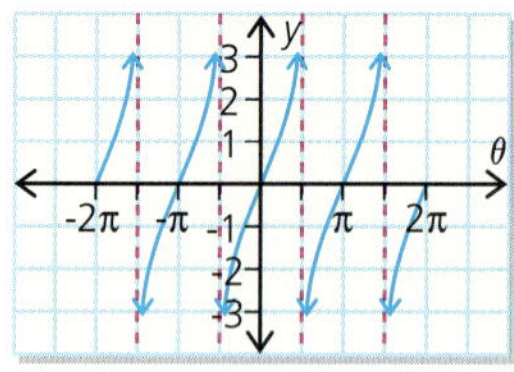

$y = \dfrac{\sin \theta}{\cos \theta}$

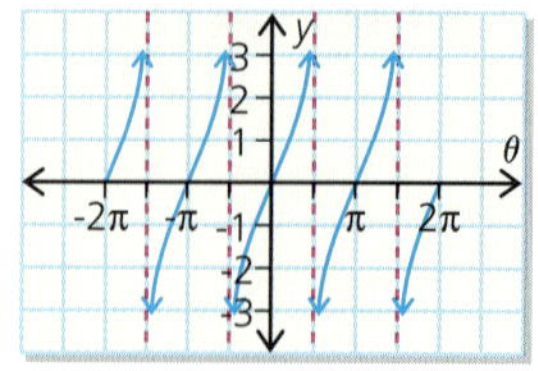

$y = \tan \theta$

For any angle θ, the two expressions produce the exact same values, with the exception of where the functions are undefined. Therefore, the equation has an infinite number of solutions.

A Pythagorean Identity

For any angle θ in standard position, $x^2 + y^2 = r^2$.

Because r is the distance from the origin to P, $r \neq 0$.

Divide the equation by r^2 to develop an equivalent expression.

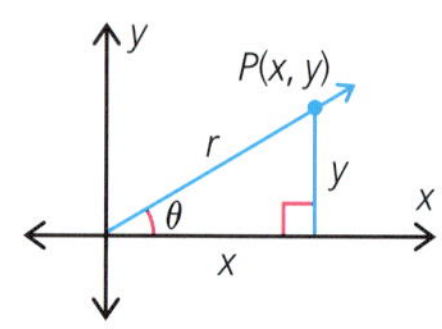

$$x^2 + y^2 = r^2$$
$$\frac{x^2}{r^2} + \frac{y^2}{r^2} = \frac{r^2}{r^2}$$
$$\frac{x^2}{r^2} + \frac{y^2}{r^2} = 1$$
$$\left(\frac{x}{r}\right)^2 + \left(\frac{y}{r}\right)^2 = 1$$
$$(\sin \theta)^2 + (\cos \theta)^2 = 1$$
$$\sin^2 \theta + \cos^2 \theta = 1 \qquad ②$$

Equation ② is called a **Pythagorean identity**. Both sides of this identity produce exactly the same graph.

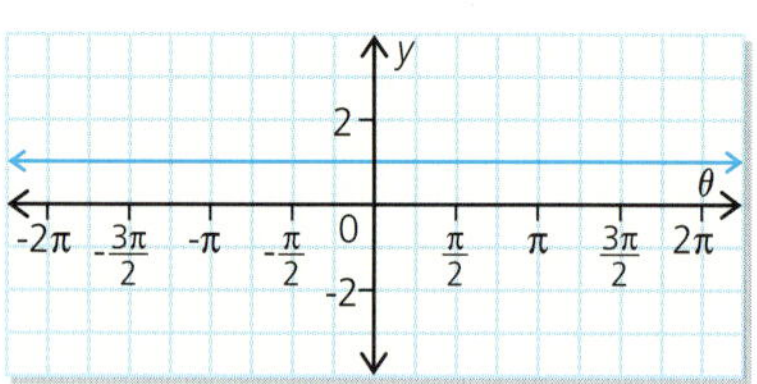

$y = \sin^2 \theta + \cos^2 \theta$

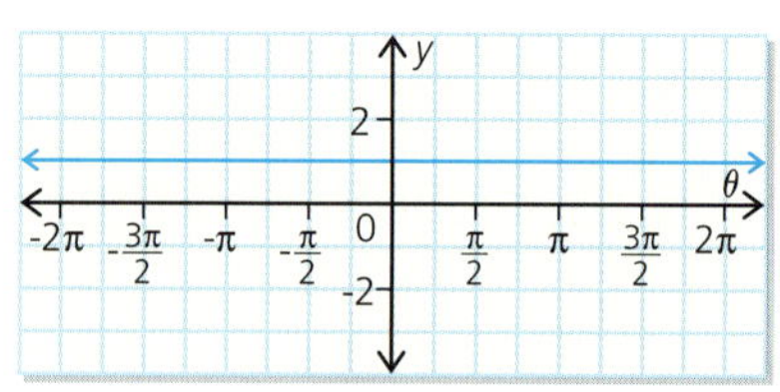

$y = 1$

For any angle, θ, the two expressions produce exactly the same value. Therefore, the equation has an infinite number of solutions. Rearranging this identity gives two other versions.

$$\sin^2 \theta = 1 - \cos^2 \theta \quad \text{and} \quad \cos^2 \theta = 1 - \sin^2 \theta$$

The quotient identity and this Pythagorean identity are often called the **fundamental trigonometric identities** because they can be used to prove that other more complicated equations are also identities. To prove that an equation is an identity, you must simplify the expression and show that the left side equals the right side.

It is often best to simplify the more complicated side first and rewrite expressions in terms of sine and cosine.

Example 1

Prove $\tan\theta\cos\theta = \sin\theta$.

Solution

L.S.	R.S.
$\tan\theta\cos\theta$	$\sin\theta$
$= \left(\frac{\sin\theta}{\cos\theta}\right)\cos\theta$	
$= \sin\theta$	

L.S. = R.S., therefore for all θ, $\tan\theta\cos\theta = \sin\theta$.

Example 2

Prove that $\tan^2\theta = \sin^2\theta\cos^{-2}\theta$.

Solution

L.S.	R.S.
$\tan^2\theta$	$\sin^2\theta\cos^{-2}\theta$
$= (\tan\theta)^2$	$= (\sin\theta)^2(\cos\theta)^{-2}$
$= \left(\frac{\sin\theta}{\cos\theta}\right)^2$	$= (\sin\theta)^2\left(\frac{1}{\cos\theta}\right)^2$
	$= \frac{(\sin\theta)^2}{(\cos\theta)^2}$
	$= \left(\frac{\sin\theta}{\cos\theta}\right)^2$

L.S. = R.S., therefore for all θ, $\tan^2\theta = \sin^2\theta\cos^{-2}\theta$.

Often, it is necessary to find a common denominator and then add or subtract expressions. In this case, always look for expressions involving $\sin^2\theta$ or $\cos^2\theta$. These are cases where the Pythagorean identity, $\sin^2\theta + \cos^2\theta = 1$, can be used. Sometimes it is necessary to factor, as Example 4 shows.

Example 3

Prove that $\tan x + \frac{1}{\tan x} = \frac{1}{\sin x\cos x}$.

Solution

L.S.	R.S.
$\tan x + \frac{1}{\tan x}$	$\frac{1}{\sin x\cos x}$
$= \frac{\sin x}{\cos x} + \frac{1}{\frac{\sin x}{\cos x}}$	$= \frac{1}{\cos x\sin x}$
$= \frac{\sin x}{\cos x} + \frac{\cos x}{\sin x}$	
$= \frac{\sin x\sin x + \cos x\cos x}{\cos x\sin x}$	
$= \frac{\sin^2 x + \cos^2 x}{\cos x\sin x}$	
$= \frac{1}{\cos x\sin x}$	

L.S. = R.S., therefore

$\tan x + \frac{1}{\tan x} = \frac{1}{\sin x\cos x}$

for all values of x.

Example 4

Prove that $\frac{\sin^2\theta}{1-\cos\theta} = 1 + \cos\theta$.

Solution

L.S.	R.S.
$\frac{\sin^2\theta}{1-\cos\theta}$	$1 + \cos\theta$
$= \frac{1-\cos^2\theta}{1-\cos\theta}$	
$= \frac{\cancel{(1-\cos\theta)}^{1}(1+\cos\theta)}{\cancel{1-\cos\theta}_{1}}$	
$= 1 + \cos\theta$	

L.S. = R.S., therefore,

$\frac{\sin^2\theta}{1-\cos\theta} = 1 + \cos\theta$ for all θ.

Key Ideas

- An **identity** is any mathematical equation that is true for all values of the variable. For example, $3(x + 1) = 3x + 3$ is an identity.
- A **trigonometric identity** is any mathematical equation with trigonometric expressions that is true for all values of the variable.

Fundamental Trigonometric Identities

Quotient Identity: $\frac{\sin x}{\cos x} = \tan x$

Pythagorean Identity: $\sin^2 x + \cos^2 x = 1$

$\sin^2 x = 1 - \cos^2 x$

$\cos^2 x = 1 - \sin^2 x$

- It is not always obvious that both sides of a trigonometric expression are equal. To prove that it is an identity, a proof that shows that both sides of the expression are equal is required.
- To prove that a given expression is an identity follow these steps.
  1. Separate the two sides of the expression.
  2. Simplify the more complicated side until it is identical to the other side or transform both sides of the expression into the same expression.
- The following strategies can be helpful for proving identities.
  1. Express all tangent functions in terms of the sine function or the cosine function.
  2. Look for expressions to which the Pythagorean identity can be applied.
  3. Where necessary, factor or find a common denominator.
- It is not always easy to prove an identity. If you get stuck or take a wrong turn, try another approach.

Practise, Apply, Solve 6.5

A

1. Use the definitions $\sin\theta = \frac{y}{r}$, $\cos\theta = \frac{x}{r}$, and $\tan\theta = \frac{y}{x}$ to prove each identity.

(a) $\frac{\cos\theta}{\sin\theta} = \frac{1}{\tan\theta}$ (b) $1 + \tan^2\theta = \frac{1}{\cos^2\theta}$ (c) $1 - \sin^2\theta = \cos^2\theta$

2. Simplify.

(a) $\sin x\left(\frac{1}{\cos x}\right)$

(b) $(\cos x)(\tan x)$

(c) $1 - \cos^2 x$

(d) $1 - \sin^2 x$

(e) $\cos^2 x + \sin^2 x$

(f) $(1 - \sin x)(1 + \sin x)$

(g) $\frac{\tan x}{\sin x}$

(h) $\frac{\frac{\sin x}{\cos x}}{\tan x}$

(i) $\left(\frac{1}{\tan x}\right)\sin x$

(j) $\frac{1 + \tan^2 x}{\tan^2 x}$

(k) $\frac{\sin x \cos x}{1 - \sin^2 x}$

(l) $\frac{1 - \cos^2 x}{\sin x \cos x}$

(m) $\frac{1}{\sin x} + \frac{1}{\cos x}$

(n) $\tan x + \frac{1}{\cos x}$

(o) $\frac{1}{\tan x} + \sin x$

3. Factor each expression.

(a) $1 - \cos^2 \theta$

(b) $1 - \sin^2 \theta$

(c) $\sin^2 \theta - \cos^2 \theta$

(d) $\sin \theta - \sin^2 \theta$

(e) $\cos^2 \theta + 2 \cos \theta + 1$

(f) $\sin^2 \theta - 2 \sin \theta + 1$

4. (a) Prove that $\frac{\cos \alpha}{\tan \alpha} = \frac{1}{\sin \alpha} - \sin \alpha$, by expressing the left side in terms of $\sin \alpha$.

(b) Prove the identity.

5. (a) Prove that $\frac{\cos^2 x}{1 - \sin x} = 1 + \sin x$ by expressing $\cos^2 x$ in terms of $\sin x$.

(b) Factor the expression in (a).

(c) Prove the identity.

B

6. Verify each identity.

(a) $\frac{\sin x}{\tan x} = \cos x$

(b) $\frac{\tan \theta}{\cos \theta} = \frac{\sin \theta}{1 - \sin^2 \theta}$

(c) $\frac{1}{\cos \alpha} + \tan \alpha = \frac{1 + \sin \alpha}{\cos \alpha}$

(d) $1 - \cos^2 \theta = \tan \theta \cos \theta \sin \theta$

7. Prove each identity.

(a) $\frac{\sin^2 x}{1 - \cos x} = 1 + \cos x$

(b) $\frac{\tan^2 \alpha}{1 + \tan^2 \alpha} = \sin^2 \alpha$

(c) $\cos^2 x = (1 - \sin x)(1 + \sin x)$

(d) $\sin^2 \theta + 2 \cos^2 \theta - 1 = \cos^2 \theta$

8. Prove each identity.

(a) $(\sin x + \cos x)^2 = 1 + 2 \sin x \cos x$

(b) $\dfrac{1}{\sin^2 \theta} + \dfrac{1}{\cos^2 \theta} = \dfrac{1}{\sin^2 \theta - \sin^4 \theta}$

(c) $\cos x + \sin x \tan x = \dfrac{1}{\cos x}$

(d) $\dfrac{\sin^2 x}{\cos^2 x} \times \dfrac{1}{\tan x} = \tan x$

9. Prove each identity.

(a) $\dfrac{\cos^2 \theta - \sin^2 \theta}{\cos^2 \theta + \sin \theta \cos \theta} = 1 - \tan \theta$

(b) $\tan^2 x - \sin^2 x = \sin^2 x \tan^2 x$

(c) $\tan^2 x - \cos^2 x = \dfrac{1}{\cos^2 x} - 1 - \cos^2 x$

(d) $\dfrac{1}{1 + \cos \theta} + \dfrac{1}{1 - \cos \theta} = \dfrac{2}{\sin^2 \theta}$

10. Which equations are not identities? Justify your conclusion.

(a) $\dfrac{1 + 2 \sin \beta \cos \beta}{\cos \beta + \sin \beta} = \sin \beta + \cos \beta$

(b) $\dfrac{\tan x \sin x}{\tan x + \sin x} = \dfrac{\tan x \sin x}{\tan x \sin x}$

(c) $(1 - \cos^2 \theta)(1 - \tan^2 \theta) = \dfrac{\sin^2 \theta - 2 \sin^4 \theta}{1 - \sin^2 \theta}$

(d) $1 - 2 \cos^2 x = \sin^4 x - \cos^4 x$

11. Prove each identity.

(a) $\cos x \tan^3 x = \sin x \tan^2 x$

(b) $\sin^2 \theta + \cos^4 \theta = \cos^2 \theta + \sin^4 \theta$

(c) $(\sin x + \cos x)\left(\dfrac{\tan^2 x + 1}{\tan x}\right) = \dfrac{1}{\cos x} + \dfrac{1}{\sin x}$

(d) $\tan^2 \beta + \cos^2 \beta + \sin^2 \beta = \dfrac{1}{\cos^2 \beta}$

12. Prove that $\dfrac{\frac{1 - \cos x}{\cos x}}{\tan x} = \dfrac{\frac{\tan x}{1 + \cos x}}{\cos x}$.

13. **Check Your Understanding:** Prove that $\sin^2 x\left(1 + \dfrac{1}{\tan^2 x}\right) = 1$.

C

14. Prove each identity.

(a) $\dfrac{1 - \cos \beta}{\sin \beta} = \dfrac{\sin \beta}{1 + \cos \beta}$

(b) $\dfrac{\sin x}{1 + \cos x} = \dfrac{1}{\sin x} - \dfrac{1}{\tan x}$

15. Prove that $\dfrac{\sin^2 \phi + 2 \cos \phi - 1}{\sin^2 \phi + 3 \cos \phi - 3} = \dfrac{\cos^2 \phi + \cos \phi}{-\sin^2 \phi}$.

16. Prove that $\sin^2 \phi - \cos^2 \phi - \tan^2 \phi = \dfrac{2 \sin^2 \phi - 2 \sin^4 \phi - 1}{1 - \sin^2 \phi}$.

Solving Quadratic Trigonometric Equations

6.6 SKILL BUILDER

Often in mathematics, it is necessary to combine skills and strategies you have used before to deal with more complicated problems. A **quadratic trigonometric equation** is a trigonometric equation with sin x, cos x, or tan x, and has 2 as its highest power. For instance, $2\sin^2 x + \sin x = 1$ is a quadratic trigonometric equation. These equations are new to you, but you can solve them by combining methods for solving quadratic equations and linear trigonometric equations.

Solving by Factoring

Recall that factoring can help solve some quadratic equations.

Example 1

Solve $x^2 - 2x = 15$.

Solution

$x^2 - 2x = 15$	Express the equation in the form $ax^2 + bx + c = 0$.
$x^2 - 2x - 15 = 0$	Factor.
$(x - 5)(x + 3) = 0$	Set each factor equal to 0 and solve.

$$x - 5 = 0 \quad \text{and} \quad x + 3 = 0$$
$$x = 5 \quad \text{and} \quad x = -3$$

This strategy can be applied to quadratic trigonometric equations.

Factoring to Solve Quadratic Trigonometric Equations

Factoring can be used to solve some quadratic trigonometric equations once the equation has been expressed in standard form.

Example 2

Solve $\sin^2 x = 1$, $0 \leq x \leq 2\pi$.

Solution

$\sin^2 x = 1$	Rearrange the equation so one side equals 0.
$\sin^2 x - 1 = 0$	Factor.
$(\sin x - 1)(\sin x + 1) = 0$	Set each factor equal to 0 and solve.

$$\sin x - 1 = 0 \quad \text{and} \quad \sin x + 1 = 0$$
$$\sin x = 1 \quad \text{and} \quad \sin x = -1$$

In the graph of $y = \sin x$, notice that $y = 1$ when $x = \frac{\pi}{2}$, and $y = -1$ when $x = \frac{3\pi}{2}$.

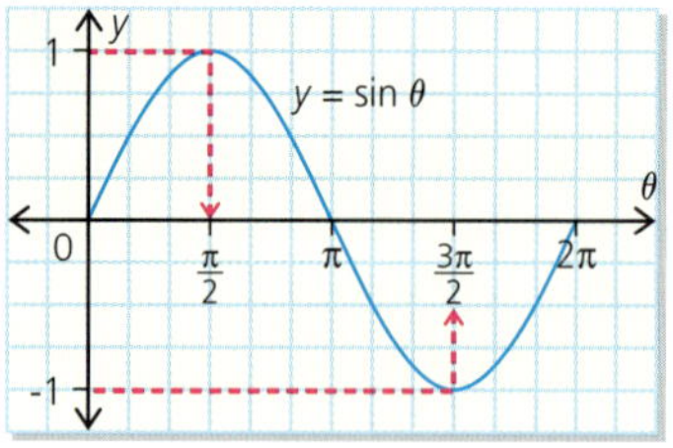

$$\sin \frac{\pi}{2} = 1 \quad \text{and} \quad \sin \frac{3\pi}{2} = -1$$

Therefore, $x = \frac{\pi}{2}$ and $\frac{3\pi}{2}$.

Using Special Triangles

Sometimes the special triangles can be used.

Example 3

Solve $2\cos^2 2\theta - 1 = -\cos 2\theta$, $0 \le \theta \le 2\pi$.

Solution

$2\cos^2 2\theta - 1 = -\cos 2\theta$	Rearrange so one side equals 0.
$2\cos^2 2\theta + \cos 2\theta - 1 = 0$	Factor.
$(2\cos 2\theta - 1)(\cos 2\theta + 1) = 0$	Set each factor equal to 0 and solve.

$$2\cos 2\theta - 1 = 0 \quad \text{and} \quad \cos 2\theta + 1 = 0$$
$$2\cos 2\theta = 1 \quad \text{and} \quad \cos 2\theta = -1$$
$$\cos 2\theta = \frac{1}{2}$$

The equation $\cos 2\theta = \frac{1}{2}$ can be solved using the $\frac{\pi}{3} - \frac{\pi}{6}$ special triangle. Cosine is positive in quadrants I and IV. In this case, $\frac{\pi}{3}$ is the related angle.

In quadrant I: $x = 1$, $r = 2$

$$\therefore 2\theta = \frac{\pi}{3}$$
$$\theta = \frac{\pi}{(3)(2)}$$
$$\theta = \frac{\pi}{6}$$

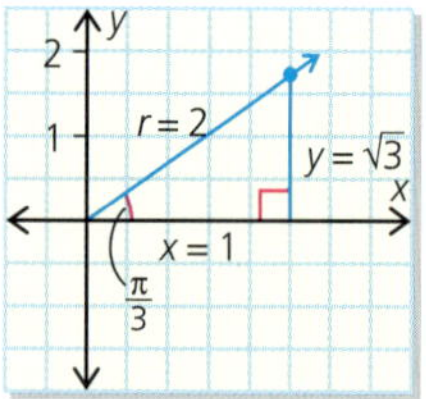

In quadrant IV: $x = 1$, $r = 2$

$$\therefore 2\theta = \frac{5\pi}{3}$$
$$\theta = \frac{5\pi}{(3)(2)}$$
$$\theta = \frac{5\pi}{6}$$

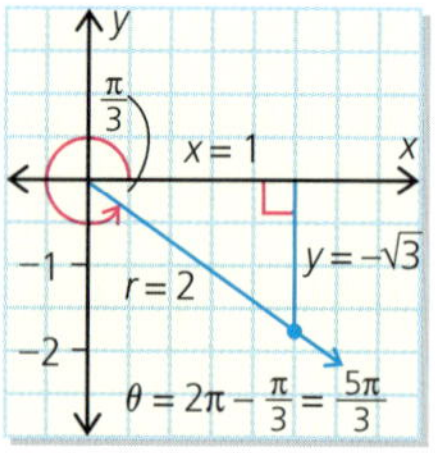

However, the period of the equation is π. Add π to the solutions to find all the solutions in the domain.

$$\theta_1 = \frac{\pi}{6} \qquad \theta_2 = \frac{\pi}{6} + \pi = \frac{7\pi}{6} \qquad \theta_3 = \frac{5\pi}{6} \qquad \theta_4 = \frac{5\pi}{6} + \pi = \frac{11\pi}{6}$$

Use the graph of $y = \cos\theta$ to solve $2\theta = -1$.

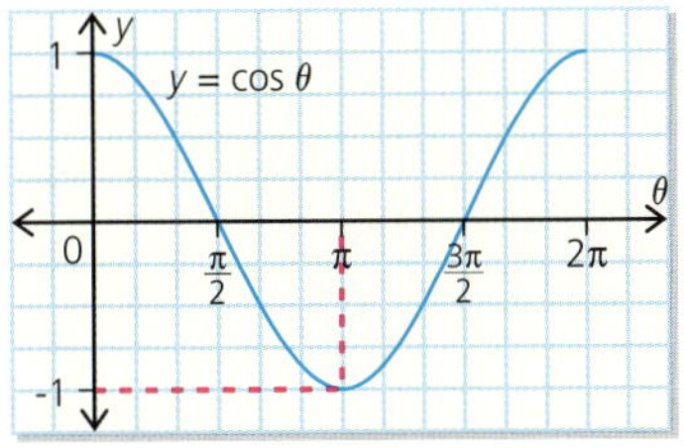

$$2\theta = \pi$$
$$\theta = \frac{\pi}{2}$$

However, the period of the equation is π. Add π to the solutions to find all the solutions in the domain.

$$\theta_5 = \frac{\pi}{2} \qquad \theta_6 = \frac{\pi}{2} + \pi$$
$$= 3\frac{\pi}{2}$$

Therefore, $2\cos^2\theta - 1 = -\cos\theta$, $0 \le \theta \le 2\pi$, has six solutions.

$$\theta_1 = \frac{\pi}{6} \qquad \theta_2 = \frac{\pi}{2} \qquad \theta_3 = \frac{5\pi}{6} \qquad \theta_4 = \frac{7\pi}{6} \qquad \theta_5 = \frac{3\pi}{2} \qquad \theta_6 = \frac{11\pi}{6}$$

Using a Calculator

Often you must use the Pythagorean identity and a calculator to solve an equation.

Example 4

Solve $8 + 13\sin x = 12\cos^2 x$, $0° \le x \le 360°$.

Solution

$8 + 13\sin x = 12\cos^2 x$	Rearrange so one side equals 0.
$-12\cos^2 x + 13\sin x + 8 = 0$	Express the equation in terms of $\sin x$ ($\cos^2 x = 1 - \sin^2 x$).
$-12(1 - \sin^2 x) + 13\sin x + 8 = 0$	Expand.
$-12 + 12\sin^2 x + 13\sin x + 8 = 0$	Simplify.
$12\sin^2 x + 13\sin x - 4 = 0$	Factor.
$(3\sin x + 4)(4\sin x - 1) = 0$	Set each factor equal to 0 and solve.

$$3\sin x + 4 = 0 \quad \text{and} \quad 4\sin x - 1 = 0$$
$$3\sin x = -4 \quad \text{and} \quad 4\sin x = 1$$
$$\sin x = -\frac{4}{3} \quad \text{and} \quad \sin x = \frac{1}{4}$$

The equation $\sin x = -\frac{4}{3}$ has no solutions, since $-1 \le \sin x \le 1$.

The equation $\sin x = \frac{1}{4}$ has two solutions, and x is an angle in quadrants I or II. Use a scientific or graphing calculator.

$$x = \sin^{-1}\left(\frac{1}{4}\right)$$

$$x \doteq 14.5°$$

The angle in quadrant II has 14.5° as its related angle.

Therefore, $x \doteq 180° - 14.5°$ or 165.5°.

The equation $8 + 13 \sin x = 12 \cos^2 x$, $0° \le x \le 360°$ has two solutions, $x \doteq 14.5°$ and $x \doteq 165.5°$.

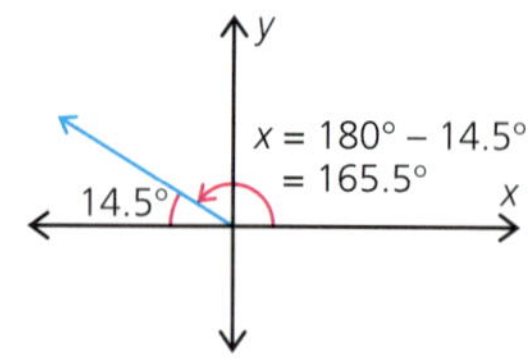

Using Graphing Technology

Graphing technology can be used to solve a quadratic trigonometric equation. This approach will work even when the equation cannot be factored.

Example 5

Solve $6 \sin^2 x + \sin x - 2 = 0$, $0 \le x \le 2\pi$, using graphing technology.

Solution

Find the solutions to this equation by graphing $y = 6 \sin^2 x + \sin x - 2$ over the domain $0 \le x \le 2\pi$ and locating the zeros, or x-intercepts.

1. Put the calculator in radian mode.

On the TI-83 Plus, press [MODE]. Then scroll down to **Radian** and press [ENTER].

2. Enter the relation into the equation editor.

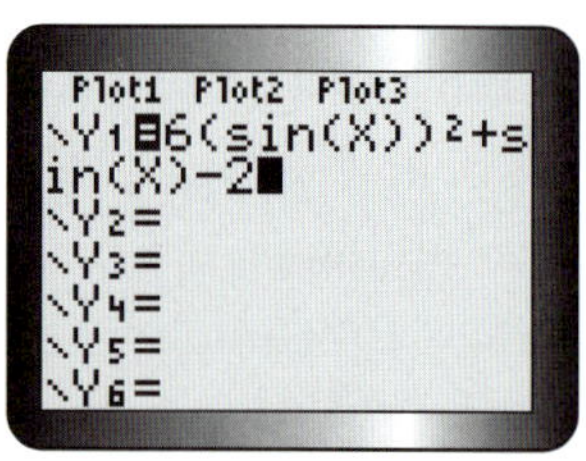

3. Set the window for the given domain.

Xmin = 0, Xmax = 2π, and Xscl = $\pi/2$.

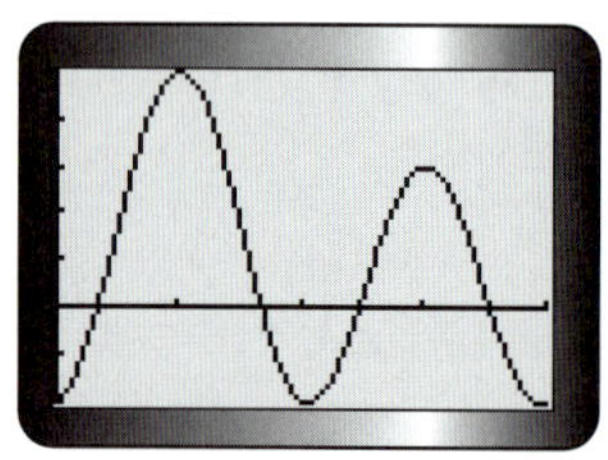

4. Graph by using zoom fit.

Press [ZOOM] [0].

5. Determine all the zeros.

Press [2nd] [TRACE] [2], then choose the left bound and right bound. Press [ENTER] on Guess.

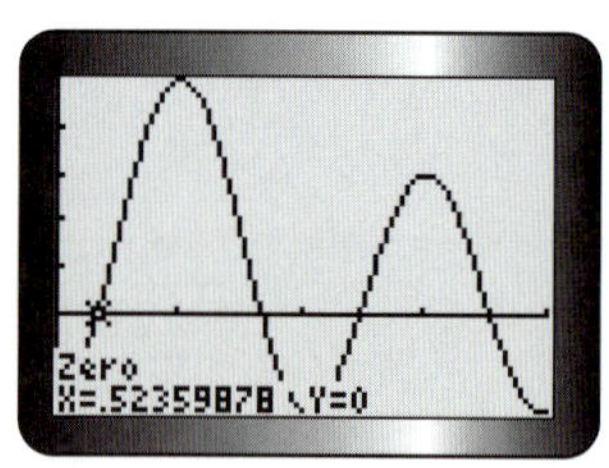

6. The three other zeros are found similarly.

The equation $6 \sin^2 x + \sin x - 2 = 0$ has solutions $x = 0.5236$, $x = 2.6180$, $x = 3.8713$, and $x = 5.5535$, $0 \leq x \leq 2\pi$.

Key Ideas

- Any trigonometric equation with $\sin x$, $\cos x$, or $\tan x$, with 2 as its highest power, is called a **quadratic trigonometric equation**. For example, $2 \sin^2 x + \sin x = 1$ is a quadratic trigonometric equation.
- A quadratic trigonometric equation must be expressed in terms of the same trigonometric ratio before it can be solved.
- Factoring often helps when solving a quadratic expression. Once the expression has been factored, set each factor equal to 0 to obtain two linear trigonometric equations that can be solved.
- It is possible that one of the factors may not lead to a solution of the original equation. This occurs when $\sin \theta > 1$, $\cos \theta > 1$, $\sin \theta < -1$, or $\cos \theta < -1$.
- The period and the domain of the corresponding functions must be considered when determining all possible solutions.
- A close approximation to the solution for any quadratic trigonometric equation can be found by graphing the corresponding trigonometric function using graphing technology and determining the zeros of the function over the given domain.

Practise, Apply, Solve 6.6

A

1. Factor.

(a) $5x^2 - 10x$

(b) $x^2 + 13x + 40$

(c) $10x^2 - 11x - 6$

(d) $x^2 - 81$

2. Factor.

(a) $\sin^2 \theta - \sin \theta$

(b) $\cos^2 \theta - 2 \cos \theta + 1$

(c) $3 \sin^2 \theta - \sin \theta - 2$

(d) $4 \cos^2 \theta - 1$

3. Verify that the value of θ is a solution of each equation.

(a) $2 \sin^2 \theta = 1, \theta = \frac{3\pi}{4}$

(b) $4 \cos^2 2\theta = 3, \theta = \frac{\pi}{12}$

(c) $2 \sin^2 \theta - \sin \theta = 1, \theta = \frac{\pi}{2}$

4. Solve each equation for x, $0° \le x \le 360°$.

(a) $\sin x \cos x = 0$

(b) $\sin x (\cos x - 1) = 0$

(c) $(\sin x + 1) \cos x = 0$

(d) $\cos x (2 \sin x - \sqrt{3}) = 0$

(e) $(\sqrt{2} \sin x - 1)(\sqrt{2} \sin x + 1) = 0$

(f) $(\sin x - 1)(\cos x + 1) = 0$

5. Solve each equation for x, $0 \le x \le 2\pi$.

(a) $(2 \sin x - 1) \cos x = 0$

(b) $(\sin x + 1)^2 = 0$

(c) $(2 \cos x + \sqrt{3}) \sin x = 0$

(d) $(2 \cos x - 1)(2 \sin x + \sqrt{3}) = 0$

(e) $(\sqrt{2} \cos x - 1)(\sqrt{2} \cos x + 1) = 0$

(f) $(\sin x + 1)(\cos x - 1) = 0$

B

6. Solve for θ to the nearest degree, $0° \le \theta \le 360°$.

(a) $\sin^2 \theta = 1$ (b) $\cos^2 \theta = 1$ (c) $\tan^2 \theta = 1$

(d) $4 \cos^2 \theta = 1$ (e) $3 \tan^2 \theta = 1$ (f) $2 \sin^2 \theta = 1$

7. (a) Write $2 \sin^2 x - \sin x - 1$ in factored form.

(b) Use the factors from (a) to solve $2 \sin^2 x - \sin x - 1 = 0$, $0 \le x \le 2\pi$.

8. (a) Write $2 \cos^2 x + \cos x - 1$ in factored form.

(b) Use the factors in (a) to solve $2 \cos^2 x + \cos x - 1 = 0$, $0° \le x \le 360°$.

9. Solve for x to the nearest degree, $0° \le x \le 360°$.

(a) $2 \sin^2 x - \sin x = 0$ (b) $\cos^2 x = \cos x$

(c) $2 \tan^2 x + \tan x - 3 = 0$ (d) $6 \sin^2 x - \sin x = 1$

(e) $\cos^2 x - 6 \cos x + 5 = 0$ (f) $4 \sin^2 x - 3 = -\sin \mathrm{x}$

10. Solve for θ to the nearest hundredth of a radian, $0 \le \theta \le 2\pi$.

(a) $2 \cos^2 \theta + \cos \theta - 1 = 0$ (b) $2 \sin^2 \theta = 1 - \sin \theta$

(c) $\cos^2 \theta = 2 + \cos \theta$ (d) $2 \sin^2 \theta + 5 \sin \theta - 3 = 0$

(e) $3 \tan^2 \theta - 2 \tan \theta = 1$ (f) $12 \sin^2 \theta + \sin \theta - 6 = 0$

11. Solve for x to the nearest degree, $0° \le x \le 360°$.

(a) $\cos^2 2x = -\cos 2x$ (b) $2 \sin^2 \left(\frac{x}{2}\right) = 1$

12. Solve for θ to the nearest hundredth of a radian, $0 \le \theta \le 2\pi$.

(a) $\cos^2 \theta - \sin^2 \theta = 1$ (b) $\sin \theta - \cos^2 \theta - 1 = 0$

(c) $2 \sin - \cos^2 \theta = 2$ (d) $13 - 15 \sin^2 \theta + \cos \theta = 0$

13. Solve for θ, using graphing technology. Answer to the nearest degree, $0° \leq \theta \leq 360°$.

(a) $3 \sin^2 \theta + 2 \sin \theta = 0$

(b) $8 \cos^2 \theta - 2 \cos \theta - 1 = 0$

(c) $4 \cos^2 \left(\frac{\theta}{2}\right) - 3 \cos \left(\frac{\theta}{2}\right) = 0$

(d) $5 \sin^2 (2\theta) + 14 \sin (2\theta) = 3$

14. Solve for x using graphing technology. Answer to the nearest hundredth, $0 \leq x \leq 2\pi$.

(a) $3 \cos^2 x = 5 \cos x$

(b) $2 \sin^2 x + 3 \sin x - 2 = 0$

(c) $4 \cos^2 x = 7 \cos x + 2$

(d) $3 \sin^2 x - 2 \sin x - 1 = 0$

15. **Check Your Understanding**

(a) Give an example of a quadratic trigonometric equation.

(b) Can factoring be used to solve all quadratic trigonometric equations? Explain.

(c) What two factors play a role when determining the number of solutions of a quadratic trigonometric equation?

C

16. Solve each equation without using graphing technology.

(a) $3 \tan^2 (2x) = 1,\ 0° \leq x \leq 360°$

(b) $\sqrt{2} \sin \theta = \sqrt{3} - \cos \theta,\ 0 \leq \theta \leq 2\pi$. (**Hint:** Square both sides of the equation and check for extraneous roots.)

The Chapter Problem—What Time Is It?

Apply what you have learned to answer these questions about the Chapter Problem on page 494.

CP7. A 70-cm long pendulum is released at a distance of 8 cm from rest.

(a) Determine the period and the time of one complete swing.

(b) Graph the function that models this situation. Explain the meaning of positive and negative values of the dependent variable, x.

(c) Determine the pendulum's distance from the rest position after 2 s.

(d) Determine four possible values for t when the pendulum is 6 cm from the centre point.

CP8. Use the model $x = M \cos \left(t\sqrt{\frac{980}{l}}\right)$ to determine an expression that represents the period of the function when $l = 70$ cm.

CP9. How long does the pendulum in a grandfather clock take to complete one full period? (A period is two complete swings.)

CP10. Use your answers from CP8 and CP9 to create an equation to determine the length of the pendulum in a grandfather clock. Solve the equation.

Chapter 6 Review

Extending Skills with Trigonometry

Check Your Understanding

1. Explain why the sine law holds true for obtuse angle triangles as well as acute angle triangles.

2. What dimensions of a triangle do you need to know to use the cosine law? the sine law?

3. If you are given a side, an angle, and the side opposite this angle, how many triangles could you create? What additional information about the triangle do you need to help you decide which case you are dealing with?

4. You are asked to determine the exact value of $\sin \frac{\pi}{4}$.

(a) Explain why you cannot use a calculator in this case.

(b) What must you use to accomplish this?

(c) To obtain an approximate value from the calculator, what mode would you use?

5. Determine, over the domain $0 \le \theta \le 2\pi$, the maximum number of solutions possible for a trigonometric equation based on

(a) the sine function with a period of 2π

(b) the sine function with a period of 4π

(c) the tangent function with a period of π

6. How many solutions does a trigonometric equation have if the domain is not specified? Explain why.

7. If an equation is also an identity, how many solutions can it have? Explain.

8. Explain how you could prove that a given equation is an identity using

(a) a graph

(b) algebra

9. Write an example of

(a) a linear trigonometric equation

(b) a quadratic trigonometric equation

10. Can all quadratic trigonometric equations be solved by factoring? Explain.

11. Approximate solutions to linear and quadratic trigonometric equations can be found using graphing technology. What must be done to the equation so that the zeros of the corresponding trigonometric function can be used to solve the original equation?

Review and Practice

6.1 Extending Trigonometry Skills with Oblique Triangles

1. Complete this table based on the given information for an oblique triangle.

Given Information	What Can Be Found	Law Required
two angles and any side (AAS or ASA)		
two sides and the contained angle (SAS)		
three sides (SSS)		
two sides and an angle opposite one of them (SSA)		

2. For the triangle shown,

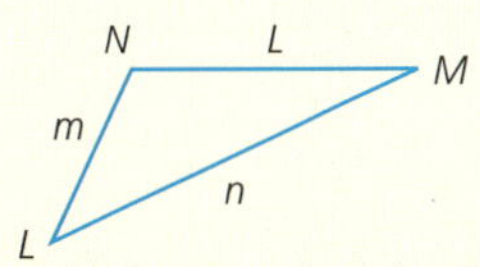

(a) Write the sine law you could use to find $\angle L$.

(b) Write the cosine law you could use to find m.

3. In ΔABC, $a = 8$ cm and $\angle A = 62°$. Find a value for b so that $\angle B$ has

(a) two possible values (b) one possible value (c) no possible value

4. Determine the measure of the indicated side or angle. Answer to one decimal place.

(a)

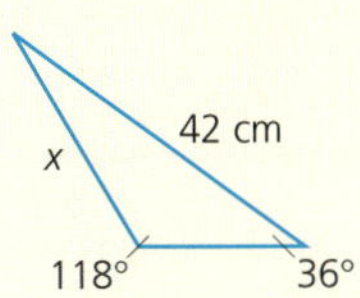

(b)

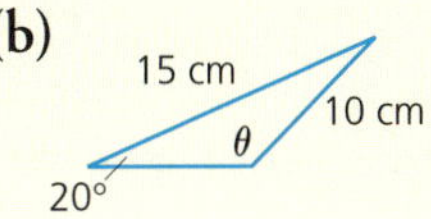

(c)

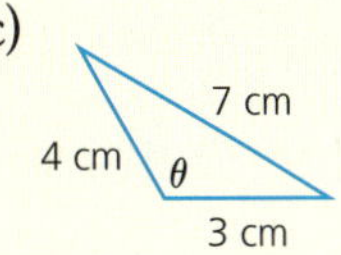

(d)

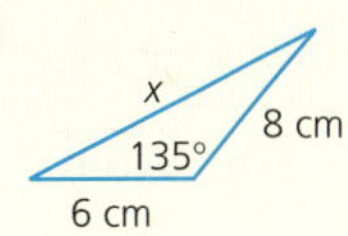

5. Solve each triangle.

(a) In ΔABC, $a = 12$ cm, $c = 11$ cm, and $\angle B = 115°$.

(b) In ΔQRS, $\angle Q = 48°$, $\angle R = 25°$, and $s = 121$ cm.

6. In ΔABC, $a = 13.4$ cm, $b = 16.6$ cm, and $\angle A = 38°$. Determine how many solutions ΔABC has. Then solve ΔABC.

6.2 Solving Trigonometry Problems in Two and Three Dimensions

7. Name three things to consider when solving a problem involving trigonometry. What should be part of every solution to a trigonometry problem?

8. A surveyor places a base line along one bank of a river. From each end of the base line, a rock is sighted on the opposite bank of the river. The base line is 160 m long and the lines of sight of the rock form angles of 42° and 71° with the base line. How wide is the river?

9. The radar operator at an airport control tower locates two planes flying toward the airport at the same altitude. One plane is 120 km from the airport at a bearing of N70°E. The other is 180 km away, on a bearing of S55°E. How far apart are the planes?

10. An engineer needs to find the height of an inaccessible cliff and takes the measurements shown. How high is the cliff?

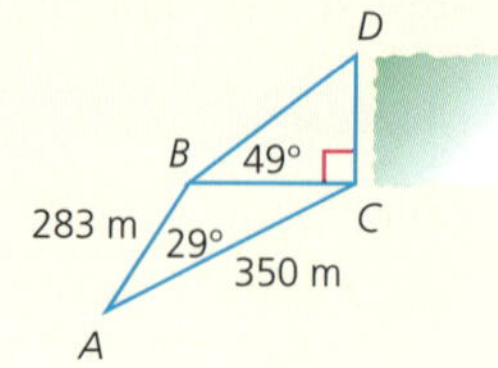

11. Two roads intersect at 15°. Two cars leave the intersection, each on a different road. One car travels at 80 km/h and the other car at 100 km/h. After 30 min, a traffic helicopter, 750 m directly above and between the cars, notes the angle of depression of the slower car is 18°. What is the horizontal distance from the helicopter to the faster car?

12. In the octahedron shown, $AB = 25$ cm, $AC = 15$ cm, and $CD = 10$ cm. Determine the size of $\angle AGB$.

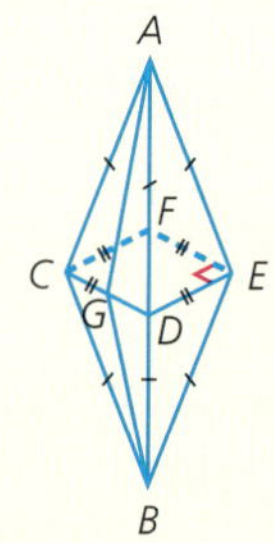

6.3 Using Special Triangles to Determine Exact Values

13. Draw a well-labelled diagram of a right triangle with an angle of 45°. Use the triangle to determine

(a) $\cos 45°$ (b) $\sin 135°$ (c) $\cos 225°$ (d) $\tan(-45°)$

14. Draw a well-labelled diagram of a right triangle with an angle of $\frac{\pi}{6}$. Use the triangle to determine

(a) $\sin \frac{\pi}{6}$ (b) $\cos \frac{\pi}{6}$ (c) $\tan \frac{5\pi}{6}$ (d) $\sin \frac{5\pi}{3}$

15. Calculate each value exactly.

(a) $\sin^2(45°) + \cos^2(60°)$

(b) $\sin \frac{-\pi}{4} \cos \frac{5\pi}{4} + \tan^2 \frac{\pi}{4}$

(c) $\cos(60°)\sin^2(240°) - \sin(-60°)$

(d) $3\sin^2 \frac{\pi}{3} - 2\cos^2 \frac{\pi}{6}$

16. Prove that $\tan \frac{3\pi}{4} + \frac{1}{\tan \frac{3\pi}{4}} = \frac{1}{\sin \frac{3\pi}{4} \cos \frac{3\pi}{4}}$.

17. For each equation, find possible values of x, $0° \le x \le 360°$.

(a) $\sin x = \frac{\sqrt{3}}{2}$ (b) $-2\cos 2x = 1$ (c) $\sqrt{3}\tan x = 1$

6.4–6.5 Trigonometric Identities

18. Write an example of a trigonometric identity.

19. How many solutions exist for the identity that you wrote in question 18? Explain.

20. Prove that $\tan x \sin x + \cos x = \frac{1}{\cos x}$.

21. Prove that $\tan x = \frac{\sin x + \sin^2 x}{\cos x\,(1 + \sin x)}$.

22. Prove that $\sin^4 x - \cos^4 x = \sin^2 x - \cos^2 x$.

23. Prove that $\frac{1 - \tan^2 \theta}{\tan \theta - \tan^2 \theta} = \frac{\tan \theta + 1}{\tan \theta}$.

6.6 Solving Quadratic Trigonometric Equations

24. How can you identify whether or not a trigonometric equation is quadratic?

25. What algebraic technique can sometimes be used to solve a quadratic trigonometric equation?

26. Solve for x, where, $0° \leq x \leq 360°$.

(a) $\cos x\,(1 - 2\sin x) = 0$

(b) $4\sin^2 x - 1 = 0$

(c) $2\cos^2 x + \cos x - 1 = 0$

(d) $3\sin^2 x + 4\sin x = 4$

(e) $1 - \cos x = 4\sin^2 x$

(f) $5\cos^2 x - 3 = 0$

27. Solve for θ, where $0 \leq \theta \leq 2\pi$.

(a) $(\sin \theta + 1)(\cos \theta - 1) = 0$

(b) $\cos^2 \theta = \frac{1}{4}$

(c) $\cos^2 2\theta = \cos 2\theta$

(d) $10\sin^2 \theta + 7\sin \theta = 6$

(e) $\tan^2 \theta = \sqrt{3}$

(f) $\cos^2 \theta - 5\sin \theta + 6 = 0$

Chapter 6 Summary

In this chapter, you saw that the sine law and the cosine law can be used to solve oblique triangles, and you used these laws to solve trigonometric problems in two and three dimensions. You also saw what an identity is and how to verify an identity. You also used skills for solving quadratic equations and linear trigonometric equations to solve a new type of equation, a quadratic trigonometric equation.

Chapter 6 Review Test

Extending Skills with Trigonometry

1. Solve each triangle. Round each value to the nearest tenth of a unit.

(a) ΔLMN; $\angle L = 75°$, $m = 110$ m, and $n = 95$ m

(b) ΔABC; $\angle A = 108°$, $b = 15.5$ cm, and $a = 20.9$ cm

2. **Knowledge and Understanding**
Solve ΔABC, where $\angle A = 38°$, $b = 25$ cm, and $a = 21$ cm

3. Determine each value exactly.

(a) $\sin \frac{\pi}{6}$ (b) $\cos 135°$

(c) $\tan \frac{-5\pi}{6}$ (d) $\sin 300°$

4. Solve for x, where $0° \leq x \leq 360°$.

(a) $2 \cos x = \sqrt{2}$

(b) $\sin^2 x = \frac{1}{4}$

5. Prove each identity.

(a) $\tan 2\beta = \frac{(1 - \cos \beta)(1 + \cos \beta)}{(1 - \sin \beta)(1 + \sin \beta)}$

(b) $\sin \theta + \tan \theta = \tan \theta\,(1 + \cos \theta)$

6. Solve $2 \cos^2 x - 13 \cos x = -6$, where $0° \leq x \leq 360°$.

7. Solve $1 - 2 \sin^2 \theta = -\cos \theta$, where $0 \leq \theta \leq 2\pi$.

8. **Application:** Find the area of this triangle.

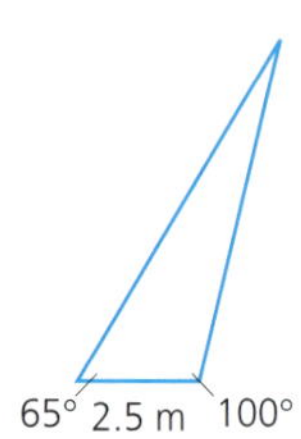

9. Bert wants to find the height of a tree across a river. To do this he lays out a base line 80 m long and measures the angles as shown. The angle of elevation from A to the top of the tree is 8°. How tall is the tree?

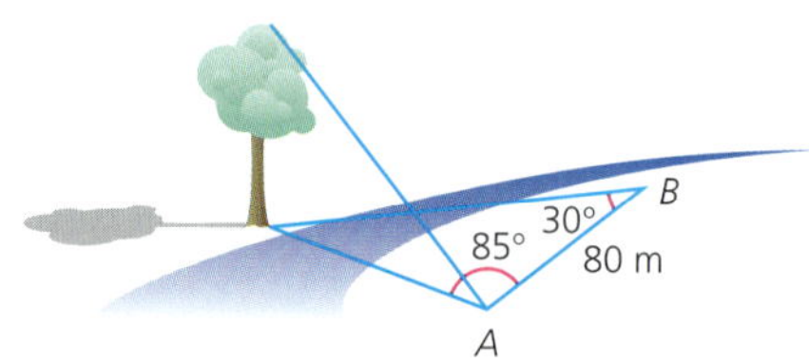

10. **Communication:** Explain when one of the factors of a quadratic trigonometric equation will not lead to a solution of the original equation. Use an example in your explanation.

11. **Thinking, Inquiry, Problem-Solving**
In the diagram, points X and Y are the midpoints of AB and BC, respectively.

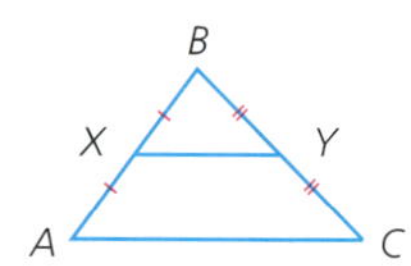

Show that $AC = 2XY$.

Cumulative Review Test 3

Trigonometric Functions

1. Draw each angle. Indicate the principal angle and its measure, plus the measure of the related acute angle.

(a) $-100°$ (b) $845°$

(c) $\frac{-7\pi}{8}$ (d) $\frac{17\pi}{6}$

2. Point $P(-3, 8)$ lies on the terminal arm of θ, an angle in standard position.

(a) Draw a diagram of θ.

(b) Determine the primary trigonometric ratios of θ.

(c) Determine the measure of θ to the nearest degree.

3. Express each angle in radians.

(a) $15°$ (b) $120°$

(c) $-270°$ (d) $216°$

4. Express each angle in degrees.

(a) $\frac{13\pi}{6}$ (b) $\frac{8\pi}{9}$

(c) $\frac{-5\pi}{4}$ (d) $\frac{13\pi}{16}$

5. For each function

i. state the amplitude, period, phase shift, and vertical shift

ii. sketch the graph

(a) $y = 3 \sin \theta - 1$

(b) $y = \tan \theta$

(c) $y = -2 \cos (\theta - 30°) + 2$

(d) $y = 3 \sin 2(\theta + 45°) - 1$

(e) $y = 0.5 \cos 3\left(\theta - \frac{\pi}{6}\right) + 4$

(f) $y = -5 \sin \left(\frac{\theta}{2} - \frac{2\pi}{3}\right) + 1$

6. A Ferris wheel has a radius of 10 m and completes one full revolution in 36 s. The riders board the ride from a platform 1 m above the ground at the bottom of the wheel.

(a) Determine an equation that models the position of a rider above the ground, at time, t, in seconds.

(b) Determine a rider's height above the ground 10 s after the ride starts.

(c) When will the rider be at the maximum height? What is this height?

7. Solve. Round answers to two decimal places.

(a) $0.5 = \sin \theta, 0 \leq \theta \leq 2\pi$

(b) $3 = 4 \sin x - 2, 0° \leq x \leq 360°$

(c) $6 = 4 - 5 \cos 3\theta, 0 \leq \theta \leq 2\pi$

(d) $9 = 4 \tan 2x, 0° \leq x \leq 360°$

8. The Lazars recently bought a cottage on a small sheltered inlet on Prince Edward Island. They wish to build a dock on an outcropping of level rocks. To determine the tide's effect at this position, they measured the depth of the water every hour over a 24-h period.

Time	1:00	2:00	3:00	4:00	5:00	6:00
Depth (m)	3.81	5.05	5.94	6.25	5.89	4.95

Time	7:00	8:00	9:00	10:00	11:00	12:00
Depth (m)	3.69	2.45	1.56	1.25	1.62	2.55

Time	13:00	14:00	15:00	16:00	17:00	18:00
Depth (m)	3.81	5.05	5.94	6.25	5.89	4.95

Time	19:00	20:00	21:00	22:00	23:00	24:00
Depth (m)	3.69	2.45	1.56	1.25	1.62	2.55

(a) Graph the data and determine an equation that models this situation over a 24-h period.

(b) What is the maximum depth of the water at this location?

(c) The hull of their boat must have a clearance of at least 1 m at all times. Is this location suitable for their dock? Explain.

9. Solve each triangle.

(a)

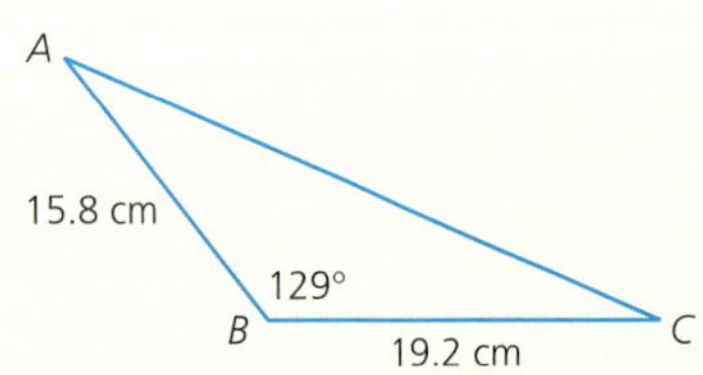

(b)

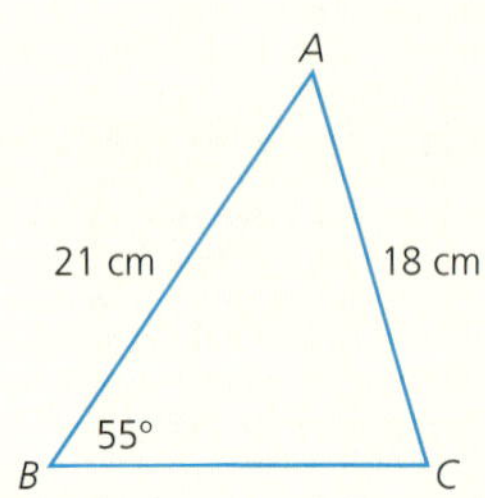

(c) ΔDEF: $d = 15$ m, $e = 18$ m, and $f = 20$ m

(d) ΔQRS: $\angle Q = 36°$, $\angle R = 27°$, and $s = 55.4$ cm

10.

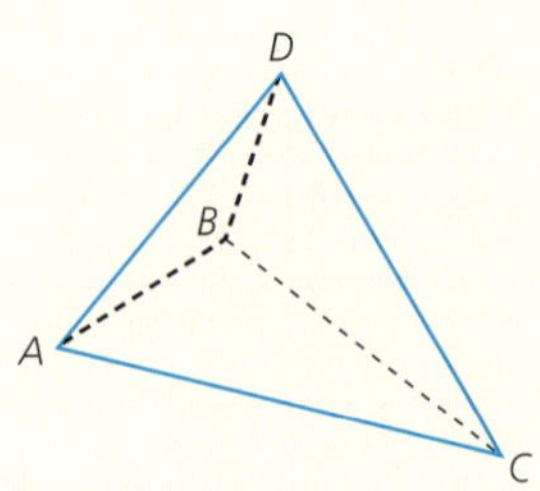

Determine the surface area to two decimal places, where: $AB = BD = 12$ cm, $AD = 16$ cm, and $AC = BC = DC = 20$ cm.

11. Two airplanes leave the same airport in opposite directions. At 2:00 P.M., the angle of elevation from the airport to the first plane is 28° and to the second plane is 19°. The elevation of the first plane is 9 km. The elevation of the second plane is 7.2 km. Find the air distance between the two airplanes.

12. Determine the exact value.

(a) $\sin \pi$ (b) $\cos \frac{7\pi}{6}$

(c) $\tan (-225°)$ (d) $\sin 300°$

(e) $\sin 45° \cos 135° + \tan 30° \tan 210°$

(f) $\cos \frac{5\pi}{3} \cos \frac{3\pi}{2} - \sin \frac{5\pi}{3} \sin \frac{3\pi}{2}$

13. Prove each identity.

(a) $\sin x + \tan x + \cos x \tan x = \tan x (2 \cos x + 1)$

(b) $\sin^2 \theta - \sin^4 \theta = \cos^2 \theta - \cos^4 \theta$

(c) $\frac{1 + \sin x}{\cos x} + \frac{\cos x}{1 + \sin x} = \frac{2}{\cos x}$

(d) $\frac{\tan^2 \alpha}{\tan^2 \alpha + 1} = \sin^2 \alpha$

14. Solve. Where necessary, round to one decimal place.

(a) $2 \sin^2 x \tan x - \tan x = 0$, $0 \leq x \leq 2\pi$

(b) $15 \sin^2 x - 7 \sin x = 2$, $0° \leq x \leq 360°$

(c) $\tan^2 x - 2 \tan x + 1 = 0$, $0 \leq x \leq 2\pi$

(d) $4 \cos^2 x - 3 = 0$, $0° \leq x \leq 360°$

15. The depth of the ocean at a swim buoy can be modelled by $y = 5 + 3 \sin \frac{\pi}{6} t$, where y is the water depth in metres and t is the time in hours. Consider a day for which $t = 0$ represents 12:00 midnight. For that day, when do high and low tides occur?

Performance Tasks for Part 3

Trigonometric Functions

THE FOLLOWING ACTIVITIES SHOULD EACH TAKE LESS THAN A PERIOD TO COMPLETE.

1. Sunrise, Sunset

Using the Internet or an almanac, find the sunrise times for each day of the year in a particular city. Plot the sunrise times for every tenth day as a function of the day of the year.

(a) Write an equation that approximately models this data.

(b) Test how well your model fits the data and use the model to predict the sunrise for some of the days that are not in the plot.

(c) Write a report that details how you arrived at the model and discusses how well the model fits the data.

2. Amusement Rides

A popular ride at an amusement park is called the "Ring of Terror." It is like a Ferris wheel but is inside a haunted house. Riders board a platform at the centre of the "ring" and the ring moves counterclockwise. When a rider is moving above the platform, he or she meets flying creatures and when the seat descends to a level below the platform, creatures emerge from a murky, slimy pit. The radius of the ring is 6 m.

(a) Graph the height of a rider with respect to the platform through three revolutions of the ride.

(b) Create an equation to model the motion of a person in the ride.

(c) How would your graph and equation change if the rider got on the ride in the pit, at the bottom of the ring? Explain.

3. Lawn Chairs

The manufacturer of a reclining lawn chair would like to have the chair be positioned at the following angles: 95° 120°, 135°, 160°, and 175°. In the figure, *AC* is 65 cm and *AB* is 45 cm. Find the positions for the notches on *BC* that will produce the required angles. Give a complete solution.

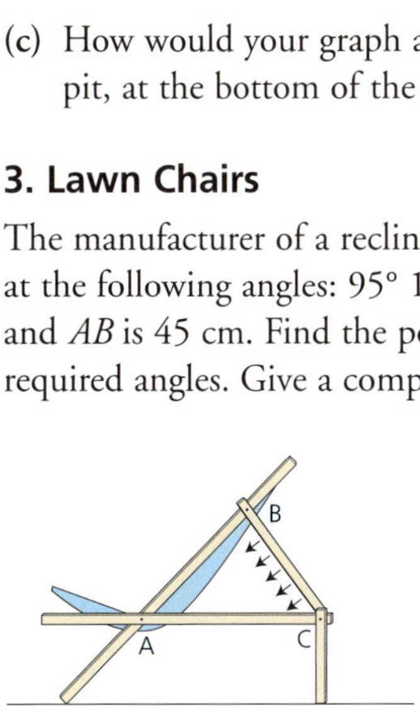

4. Solving Systems of Trigonometric Equations

Solve the following system of equations, both graphically and algebraically, for values where $-2\pi \leq x \leq 2\pi$.

$$y = \cos^2 x$$
$$y = \frac{1}{2} + \sin^2 x$$

5. How High Is the Tower?

A skier sees the top of a radio tower, due south of him, at an angle of elevation of 32°. He then skis on a bearing of 130° for 560 m and finds himself due east of the tower. Calculate

(a) the height of the radio tower

(b) the distance from the tower to the skier

(c) the angle of elevation of the top of the tower from the new position

6. Proving Identities

Use graphing technology to determine which statements are trigonometric identities. For those that are, prove the identity. For those that are not, decide for which values the statements are true.

(a) $\tan^2 x \cos^2 x = 1 - \cos^2 x$

(b) $\cos^2 x = \sin^2 x - 1$

(c) $\dfrac{1}{\cos x} + \dfrac{1}{\sin x} = 1$

(d) $\dfrac{\tan x \cos x}{\sin x} = 1$

THE FOLLOWING ACTIVITIES COULD EACH TAKE MORE THAN A PERIOD TO COMPLETE.

7. The Tide Is High.

This data was collected on the east coast of Canada on August 15 and relates the height, *h*, of a tide to the time of day, *t*.

t	4 A.M.	5 A.M.	6 A.M.	7 A.M.	8 A.M.	9 A.M.	10 A.M.	11 A.M.
***h* (m)**	0.7	1.2	2.4	4.1	5.8	7.1	7.6	7.2

t	12 P.M.	1 P.M.	2 P.M.	3 P.M.	4 P.M.	5 P.M.	6 P.M.	7 P.M.	8 P.M.
***h* (m)**	6.1	4.5	2.9	1.6	0.8	1.1	2.1	3.7	5.4

(a) Graph this data using time as the x-axis and height as the y-axis. You may need to use a 24-h clock for the time. In other words, 2 P.M. should be represented as 14.

(b) How high is high tide and how low is low tide?

(c) Determine the amplitude and period for this periodic function.

(d) Determine an equation that approximates the data. Justify all components of your equation.

(e) Determine the height of the tide at 2:00 A.M. on August 15, 11:00 P.M. on August 15, and 3:00 A.M. on August 16.

8. A Trigonometric Trip

Create a trigonometric trip. Use your surrounding area to create a problem of finding an inaccessible height or distance. Your problem should be three-dimensional and include a right triangle and the use of the cosine and sine law. Submit the problem and full solution. Perhaps the whole class could go on a trigonometric walk to take measurements and solve one another's problems.

9. Math Music

A pure tone produces a sine wave when shown on an oscilloscope. When an instrument is played, the tone is not pure. For instance, when a guitar string or piano string vibrates it does not produce a simple sine wave. It does produce other, less distinguishable harmonious waves of higher pitch called *harmonic* waves. For instance, $y = \sin(2x)$ is called the second harmonic, $y = \sin(3x)$ is called the third harmonic, and $y = \sin(4x)$ is called the fourth harmonic.

(a) Use a table to graph the second harmonic for values between $-2\pi \leq \theta \leq 2\pi$.

(b) When a note is played on a musical instrument, the fundamental pitch usually has the greatest amplitude. The second, third, and fourth harmonics can be heard but their amplitudes are usually lower than the fundamental harmonic.

Graph $y = \frac{1}{2}\sin(2x)$ to see how the amplitude is reduced.

(c) The wave of a musical instrument is actually an additive waveform produced by combining the fundamental sine wave form and different combinations of harmonics.

Graph $y = \sin x + \frac{1}{2}\sin(2x)$ by hand. Do this by graphing both $y = \sin x$ and $y = \frac{1}{2}\sin(2x)$ on the same set of axes and then adding the y-values for corresponding x-values. Use graphing technology to determine if your graph is accurate.

(d) Use graphing technology to graph each equation. Sketch the graph on paper:

i. $y = \sin x + \frac{1}{2}\sin(2x) + \frac{1}{4}\sin(4x)$

ii. $y = \sin x + \frac{1}{3}\sin(3x) + \frac{1}{5}\sin(5x) + \frac{1}{7}\sin(7x)$

Research Extension (Extra Time)

(e) By examining waves produced on an oscilloscope by a synthesizer (or other technology set-ups), match the above graphs to the instruments imitated by the synthesizer. Create an equation of your own with harmonics and see if you can determine which instrument it most closely resembles.

Loci and Conics

Analytic Geometry: Lines and Line Segments

Finding the Slope of a Line Given Two Points

The slope, m, of the line between points $A(x_1, y_1)$ and $B(x_2, y_2)$ is

$$m = \frac{\text{rise}}{\text{run}}$$
$$= \frac{\Delta y}{\Delta x} \quad \text{or} \quad m = \frac{y_2 - y_1}{x_2 - x_1}$$

Finding the Length of a Line Segment

Use the formula $d = \sqrt{(\Delta x)^2 + (\Delta y)^2}$ or $d = \sqrt{(x_2 - x_1)^2 + (y_2 - y_1)^2}$ where $A(x_1, y_1)$ and $B(x_2, y_2)$ are the endpoints of the line segment.

Finding the Midpoint of a Line Segment

The coordinates of the midpoint of the line segment joining points $A(x_1, y_1)$ and $B(x_2, y_2)$ are $\left(\frac{x_1 + x_2}{2}, \frac{y_1 + y_2}{2}\right)$.

Finding the Equation of a Line Given the Slope and a Point

Use the slope–y-intercept form of the line.

$y = mx + b$

1. Substitute the slope.
2. Substitute the coordinates of the point.
3. Solve for b.
4. Express the equation in the form $y = mx + b$.

Finding the Equation of a Circle Centred at the Origin

The equation of a circle centred at (0, 0) with radius r is $x^2 + y^2 = r^2$.

Determining if Lines Are Parallel or Perpendicular

Compare the slopes.

Two lines are parallel if they have the same slope; that is, $m_1 = m_2$.

Two lines are perpendicular if their slopes are negative reciprocals; that is, if $m_1 = -\frac{1}{m_2}$.

Practice

1. Determine the slope and length of the line segment through each pair of points.
   (a) $(3, 1), (-5, 2)$
   (b) $(-6, 4), (-5, -3)$
   (c) $\left(\frac{3}{4}, \frac{1}{2}\right), \left(\frac{1}{2}, \frac{7}{8}\right)$
   (d) $(0.5, -3.3), (4.5, 4.7)$

2. Determine the equation of the line
   (a) with slope $-\frac{2}{3}$ that passes through $(5, -2)$
   (b) with slope $\frac{3}{5}$ and y-intercept 6
   (c) that passes through $(4, -2)$ and $(-3, -7)$
   (d) with x-intercept 5 and y-intercept -8

3. Determine the equation of the circle centred at the origin with each radius.
   (a) $r = 5$
   (b) $r = \frac{8}{3}$
   (c) $r = 0.3$

4. A circle centred at the origin has a radius of 13 units. State all values of y when $x = 5$.

5. Each pair of coordinates represents points on a line. Determine whether the lines are parallel, perpendicular, or neither.
   (a) $(1, -4), (5, 4)$ and $(3, 15), (-2, 5)$
   (b) $(-3, -19), (4, 23)$ and $(6, 1), (-18, 5)$
   (c) $(15, 16), (-3, 4)$ and $(2, -7), (-4, 2)$
   (d) $(0, 7), (-3, 1)$ and $(2, -2), (-4, -5)$
   (e) $(2, 1), (-2, 13)$ and $(5, -19), (-1, -1)$

6. Identify the lines that are parallel within each grouping.
   (a) l_1: $2x + 3y - 15 = 0$
   l_2: $2x - 3y = 18$
   l_3: $3y = -2x - 21$
   (b) l_1: $4y = 3x + 8$
   l_2: $3x = 4y - 16$
   l_3: $3x + 4y = 12$

7. Identify the lines that are perpendicular within each grouping.
   (a) l_1: $x + 2y - 10 = 0$
   l_2: $6x - 3y - 21 = 0$
   l_3: $2x - y - 7 = 0$
   (b) l_1: $3y = 4x + 15$
   l_2: $8y = 3x - 8$
   l_3: $3y + 4x = 15$

8. The end points of the diameter of a circle are $(10, 24)$ and $(-10, 24)$.
   (a) What are the coordinates of the centre of the circle?
   (b) What is the radius of the circle?
   (c) Determine the equation of the circle.

9. The end points of the chord on a circle are $(-2, 1)$ and $(5, -3)$. Find the equation of the perpendicular bisector of the chord.

10. The vertices of ΔABC are $A(3, 4)$, $B(4, -3)$, and $C(-4, -1)$. Determine the equation of the altitude from vertex B to the line AC.

Solving a System of Linear Equations

Many kinds of situations can be modelled using linear equations. When two or more linear equations are used to model a problem, they are called a linear system of equations. Point $P(x_1, y_1)$ is the intersection point of the linear equations in the system. Point P is called the solution to the linear system and satisfies all equations in the system.

Solving a Linear System Graphically

Linear systems can be solved graphically, although this method does not always yield an exact solution.

Example 1

Solve the system graphically.

$$y = 2x - 8 \quad ①$$

$$x + y = 7 \quad ②$$

Solution

Draw both graphs on the same axes and locate the point of intersection.

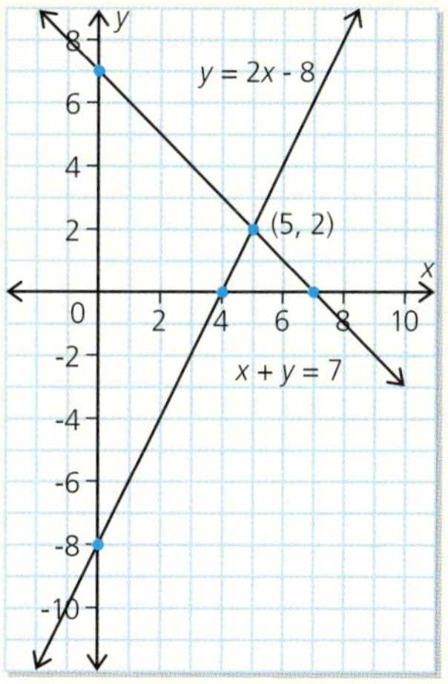

Point (5, 2) appears to be the point of intersection. Verify this result algebraically by substituting (5, 2) into equations ① and ②.

In equation ①,

L.S.	R.S.
y	$2x - 8$
$= 2$	$= 2(5) - 8$
	$= 2$

Therefore L.S. = R.S.

In equation ②,

L.S.	R.S.
$x + y$	7
$= 5 + 2$	
$= 7$	

Therefore L.S. = R.S.

Solving a System of Linear Equations Algebraically

Linear systems can also be solved using algebra. Algebra can be used in two ways to solve a linear system, elimination and substitution. The following example will be solved both ways. These methods always yield exact solutions.

Example 2

Solve the system of linear equations algebraically.

$3x + 2y + 24 = 0$ ①

$5y + 2x = -38$ ②

Solution by Elimination

$3x + 2y = -24$ ③ $2x + 5y = -38$ ④	Express both equations in the form $ax + by = c$.
To eliminate x, multiply equation ③ by 2 and equation ④ by 3. $6x + 4y = -48$ ③ × 2 → ⑤ $6x + 15y = -114$ ④ × 3 → ⑥	Choose a variable to eliminate from both equations. Multiply each equation by a number that gives the same or opposite coefficient for that variable in both equations
Equation ⑤ − Equation ⑥ $6x + 4y = -48$ ⑤ $6x + 15y = -114$ ⑥ $6x - 6x + 4y - 15y = -48 - (-114)$	Add or subtract like terms in the system to eliminate the chosen variable.
$-11y = 66$ $y = -6$	Simplify the resulting equation and solve for the remaining variable.
Substitute $y = -6$ into equation ①. $3x + 2(-6) + 24 = 0$ ① $3x = -24 + 12$ $3x = -12$ $x = -4$	Determine the other variable by substituting the solved variable into equation ① or ②.

Solution by Substitution

Solve for y in equation ①. $3x + 2y + 24 = 0$ ① $2y = -24 - 3x$ $y = -12 - \frac{3}{2}x$	Choose one of the equations and isolate one of its variables by expressing that variable in terms of the other variable.
Substitute $y = -12 - \frac{3}{2}x$ into equation ②. $5y + 2x = -38$ ② $5\left(-12 - \frac{3}{2}x\right) + 2x = -38$ $-60 - \frac{15}{2}x + 2x = -38$ $\frac{-15x + 4x}{2} = -38 + 60$ $\frac{-11x}{2} = 22$ $x = 22\left(-\frac{2}{11}\right)$ $x = -4$	Substitute the expression that you determined in place of the corresponding variable in the other equation.
Substitute x = −4 into equation ①. $3x + 2y + 24 = 0$ ① $3(-4) + 2y + 24 = 0$ $-12 + 2y + 24 = 0$ $2y = -12$ $y = -6$	Determine the other value by substituting the solved value into equations ① or ②.

Both methods yield the same solution of $(-4, -6)$.

Practice

1. Determine which ordered pair satisfies both equations.

(a) $x + y = 5$; $x = y + 1$ — (4, 1), (2, 3), (3, 2), (5, 4)

(b) $x + y = -5$; $y = -2x$ — (3, −6), (10, −5), (5, −10), (−3, −2)

2. Solve the system by drawing the graph.

(a) $3x + 4y = 12$
$2x + 3y = 9$

(b) $x + y = -4$
$2x - y = 4$

(c) $x - 3y + 1 = 0$
$2x + y - 4 = 0$

(d) $x = 1 - 2y$
$y = 2x + 3$

3. Solve for the variable indicated.

(a) $x - 3y = 12$, for x

(b) $x - 4y = 15$, for x

(c) $2x + y = 12$, for y

(d) $8x - y = 4$, for y

(e) $2y - 2x = 18$, for x

(f) $6x - 3y = 4$, for y

(g) $15x - 12y + 14 = 0$, for x

(h) $5x + 2y + 10 = 0$, for y

(i) $\frac{1}{2}x + \frac{2}{3}y = 8$, for y

4. For each linear system, state which variable could be eliminated more easily.

(a) $x + y = 4$
$x - 3y = 5$

(b) $3x - 2y = 4$
$2x + 2y = 5$

(c) $3x - 2y = 7$
$5x + 7 = -2y$

(d) $3y - 2x + 9 = 0$
$14 + 7y = 2x$

5. Determine the coordinates of the point of intersection using substitution.

(a) $3p + 2q - 1 = 0$
$p = q + 2$

(b) $2m - n = 3$
$m + 2n = 24$

(c) $2x + 5y + 18 = 0$
$x + 2y + 6 = 0$

(d) $6g - 3h = 9$
$4g = 5 + 3h$

6. Determine the coordinates of the point of intersection using elimination.

(a) $2m + 5n = 8$
$5m - 2n = 20$

(b) $3u + 21 = 5v$
$4v + 6 = -9u$

(c) $2x + 3y = 18$
$5x - 4y = -1$

(d) $3x + 2y - 22 = 0$
$5x = 4y - 22$

7. Solve each system of equations using substitution or elimination as appropriate.

(a) $2g + h = 3$
$3g + 2h = 5$

(b) $m - 3n - 11 = 0$
$2m = 6 - 10n$

(c) $3x + y = 9$
$x - 2y = -7$

(d) $2p = q + 5$
$q - 3p = 0$

Chapter 7U

Investigating Loci and Conics

Functions and Relations

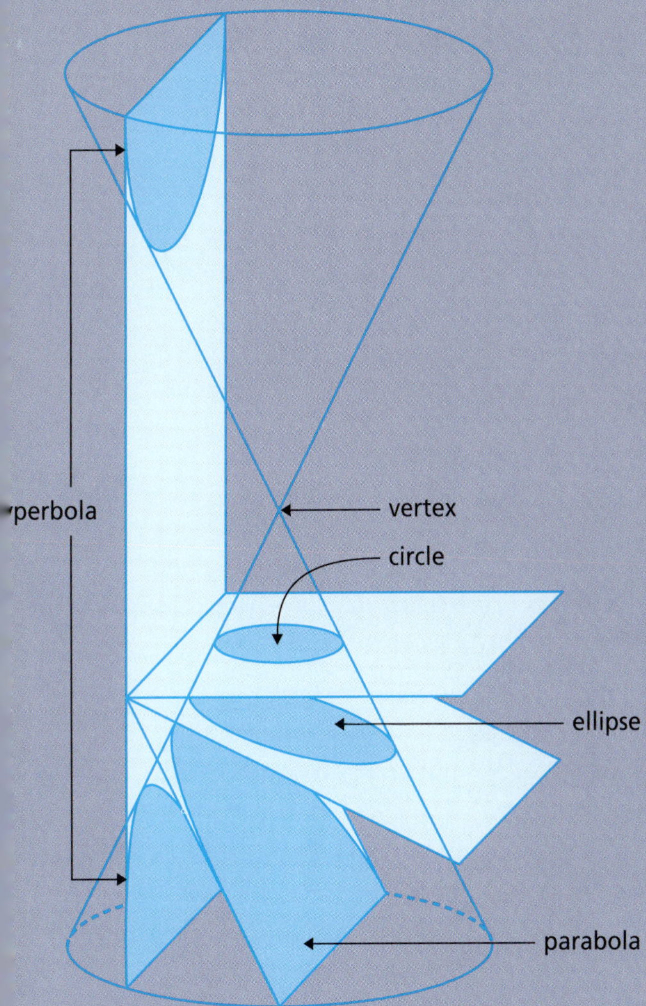

Visit the Nelson Mathematics student Web site at **www.math.nelson.com**. You'll find links to interactive examples, online tutorials, and more.

Circles, parabolas, ellipses, and hyperbolas are conic sections. Astronomers describe the orbits of planets and satellites using conical curves. Today a meteorologist may determine, for example, the circulation speed of a cone-shaped hurricane by finding the tangent to a conic section. You may see conics in satellite dishes, car headlights, and architectural structures.

A plane slicing through a cone at various angles produces a conic section. A horizontal slice produces a circle; a vertical slice produces a hyperbola. A diagonal slice, cutting through the bottom and the side of a cone, produces a parabola. Another diagonal slice, cutting through only the side of a cone, produces an ellipse.

In this chapter, you will

- construct and describe models to represent certain conditions, or a described locus of points
- use locus definitions to determine equations of conics: circles, parabolas, ellipses, and hyperbolas
- determine and explore geometric models for conics using technology and concrete materials
- investigate and determine the key features of conics
- sketch graphs of conics
- pose and solve problems about conics

Connections

The Chapter Problem

Designing a Bridge

Designing a bridge that will support a road or railway and provide a pathway underneath the bridge is a frequent task for engineers. There are many things to consider when designing a bridge. The focus of this problem is the design of an arch that will allow vehicles to pass under it. An arch may be a semicircle, a semiellipse, a parabola, or a hyperbola.

Your task is to design several different arches. Each arch must be from 5 m to 6 m high and must span a two-lane road that is 11 m wide. The arch must also allow trucks to travel in either lane of the road. The largest truck that might pass under the arch is 3 m wide and 4 m high.

You are to create at least three bridge designs in this chapter—a semicircle, a semiellipse, and a parabola—that will satisfy the above criteria. For each design, show the following:

1. a diagram of the design with dimensions
2. the equation of the curve and a graph of the curve
3. that two trucks of the given dimensions will be able to pass, side by side, under the archway. Make sure that you allow space between the trucks, as well as at the sides of the road.

Conclude by recommending the best design. As well as using your own calculations to support your recommendations, you might also research which bridge designs are more common or which arches offer the best support.

For help with this problem, see pages 583, 594, and 604.

Challenge 1

Satellite dishes are widely used in the telecommunications field. The cross section of a satellite dish may be a parabola, a hyperbola, or a semiellipse.

One simple way to understand how a satellite dish works is to experiment with a flashlight.

1. What is the shape of a flashlight's reflector? Find and verify the equation of this shape.
2. Is the light source at the focal point of the cone of light? Shine the light on the wall. How does the shape on the wall change as you change the angle of the flashlight? Creating a circle of light may be easy, but how would you change the circle to an ellipse? Can you make a parabola?
3. Trace the reflections on a piece of paper and determine the conics you have created. Justify your choice of conic by determining and verifying the equation of each.
4. Find out about a satellite dish in your area and use the dimensions of the dish to determine which conic it resembles.

Challenge 2

Computer-assisted design (CAD) has hundreds of applications. Automobile, aircraft, aerospace, and ship designers use CAD to design vehicles. Many graphics and logos are created using CAD. In a CAD drawing of a building, you would see a "wireframe" outlining the curves of a surface. Many of the curves you see in graphic designs or architectural structures are parts of conic sections. The "golden arches" of a popular fast-food restaurant resemble a pair of parabolas.

Find a picture in a magazine, or a logo, that includes a curve that you think resembles a conic—an ellipse, a parabola, or a hyperbola. Make a conjecture about the type of conic. Trace the curve on a piece of a paper. Then draw an x-y plane on graph paper. Centre the curve about the origin of the coordinate plane. Choose several points on the curve and model the curve by determining an equation. Test other points on the curve to see how well they "fit" your algebraic model or equation. Make a conclusion about the appropriateness of your model and justify your reasoning. Present your results as a poster and be sure to include the original picture or a photocopy.

Web Challenge

For a related Internet activity, go to **www.math.nelson.com**.

Getting Ready

In this chapter, you will be working with the distance formula, second-degree equations, algebraic expressions, and key features of conic sections. You will also be dealing with radicals. These exercises will help you warm up for the work ahead.

1. Determine what value must be added to each expression to form a perfect square trinomial.

(a) $x^2 + 4x + ■$

(b) $x^2 - 6x + ■$

(c) $x^2 - 5x + ■$

(d) $x^2 - x + ■$

(e) $x^2 + 3x + ■$

2. Factor each trinomial.

(a) $x^2 + 2x + 1$

(b) $x^2 + 4x + 4$

(c) $x^2 - 8x + 16$

(d) $5x^2 - 30x + 45$

(e) $2x^2 - 28x + 98$

3. State the vertex and the axis of symmetry for each parabola.

(a) $y = x^2$

(b) $y = 2x^2 - 3$

(c) $y = (x - 2)^2 + 6$

(d) $y = 3(x + 1)^2 - 1$

(e) $y = 2(x - 4)^2$

4. Sketch the graph of each parabola in question 3.

5. State the equation of each circle with centre (0, 0) and the given radius, r.

(a) $r = 5$ (b) $r = 8$

(c) $r = \sqrt{2}$ (d) $r = \sqrt{15}$

(e) $r = 3\sqrt{2}$

6. Find the distance between each pair of points.

(a) $A(3, 2)$, $B(2, 3)$

(b) $A(0, 3)$, $B(-1, 2)$

(c) $A(-4, 6)$, $B(8, 5)$

(d) $A(0, 0)$, $B(-3, 5)$

(e) $A(-2, 5)$, $B(-3, 6)$

7. State the slope and the x- and y-intercepts of each line.

(a) $2x - 3y = 6$

(b) $x + y = 8$

(c) $y = -3$

(d) $y = 2x + 1$

(e) $8x + 2y + 24 = 0$

(f) $y = 4x - 8$

(g) $x = 2$

8. Determine the equation of each line. Express each equation in the standard form, $Ax + By + C = 0$.

(a) The slope is 4 and the y-intercept is 2.

(b) The x-intercept is 3 and the y-intercept is 4.

(c) The line is parallel to the line $y = 2x - 1$ and passes through (1, 4).

(d) The line is parallel to the x-axis and passes through (3, 5).

(e) The line is perpendicular to the line $y = x - 5$ and passes through $(-2, 6)$.

9. State the following.

(a) the coordinates of the point that is 5 units below (2, 3)

(b) the coordinates of the point that is 3 units to the left of (−1, 6)

(c) the equation of the line that is parallel to, and 3 units below, the x-axis

(d) the equation of the line that is parallel to, and 2 units to the right, of the y-axis

10. Find the intersection point for each pair of lines.

(a) $y = 2x - 4$ and $y = x - 1$

(b) $y = -2x$ and $3x - 2y = -7$

(c) $y = 2x - 1$ and $y = 5$

(d) $4x - y = -3$ and $y = 9 - 2x$

11. Simplify.

(a) $(\sqrt{3})^2$

(b) $(\sqrt{2x})^2$

(c) $(\sqrt{x+5})^2$

(d) $(\sqrt{4x-3})^2$

(e) $\sqrt{7^2}$

(f) $\sqrt{x^2}$

(g) $\sqrt{(x-5)^2}$

(h) $\sqrt{(3x+9)^2}$

12. Solve for y in each equation.

(a) $2x - y = 5$

(b) $2x + 6y + 12 = 0$

(c) $y^2 = x + 5$

(d) $x = (y + 1)^2 - 3$

(e) $x = 2(y - 3)^2 + 4$

(f) $x = -(y - 2)^2 - 7$

(g) $x^2 + y^2 = 9$

13. Graph each curve and then state the domain and the range.

(a) $y = 2x + 3$

(b) $y = \sqrt{x+2}$

(c) $x^2 + y^2 = 25$

(d) $y = 3$

(e) $y = -x^2 + 2$

(f) $2x - 5y = 10$

(g) $2x^2 + 2y^2 = 32$

(h) $y = (x + 1)^2 - 4$

(i) $x = (y - 2)^2 + 3$

(j) $x = -4$

(k) $y = \frac{1}{x+2}$

(l) $y = \frac{x}{x^2 - 9}$

14. Express each equation in vertex form by completing the square.

(a) $y = x^2 + 10x - 8$

(b) $y = x^2 + 7x + 2$

(c) $y = 2x^2 + 4x - 5$

(d) $y = -3x^2 + 5x + 1$

(e) $y = 4x^2 - 9x - 6$

(f) $y = -5x^2 + x + 10$

7.1U Introducing Locus Definitions

Functions and Relations

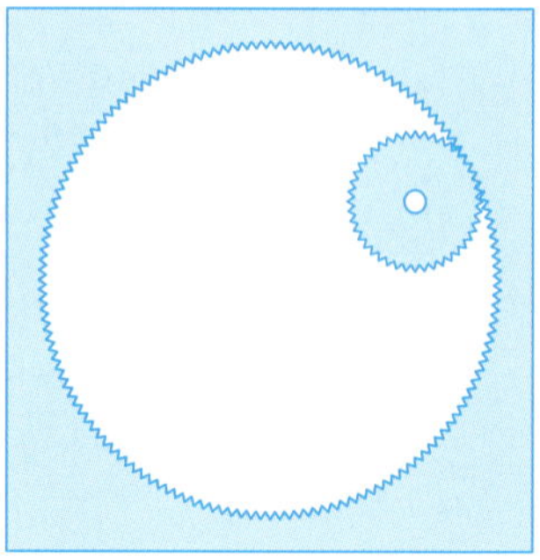

You can create interesting geometric designs with a Spirograph™. This device is a plastic frame with a large circle cut out of the middle.

The inside of the larger circle has "teeth" so that other smaller circles, or other shapes, with "teeth" can be turned inside the larger circle. You can make a design by inserting a pen in one of the holes of the smaller circle and pushing it around the inside of the large circle.

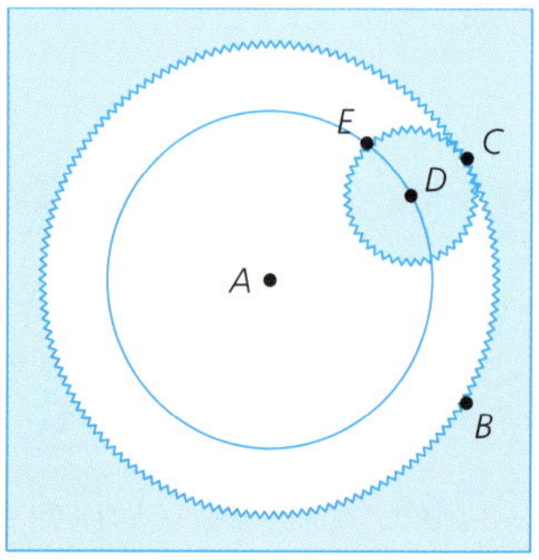

If you have used a Spirograph™ before, you may have wondered how or why different designs were created. Start with a simple example. If you were to place your pen in the hole at the centre and push the smaller circle around the inside of the large circle, what shape would you create?

In this case, you would create another circle. The circle is a set of points such that each point is a fixed distance from another larger circle. This set of points is defined as the locus of points that are a fixed distance from the outer circle.

A **locus** is a set of points that satisfy a *given condition* or conditions.

Specific conditions that define a geometric model is called a locus definition. A locus definition tells us the requirements for drawing, graphing, constructing, or creating an algebraic expression for our mathematical object.

Part 1: Locus Definitions

Think, Do, Discuss

1. If you created a circle with a Spirograph™, then you would certainly recognize that this is not the usual way of drawing a circle. You usually draw a circle with compasses, by placing one tip of a compasses' arm at a fixed point and then rotating the other arm at a fixed radius about the fixed point. Construct a circle using compasses and then define the circle using a locus definition. You might begin the definition with, "A circle is the set of points that are … ."
2. Different definitions can describe the same geometric figure. What figure would be described by the locus of points that are equidistant from the centre and edge of a circle? What specific characteristics would this figure have?
3. The typical locus definition of a circle is the set of points that are equidistant from a given point. In the three-dimensional plane, what geometric figure is the locus of points that are the same distance from a given point?

4. How would you construct a set of points, in the two-dimensional plane, that are equidistant from two given points? Use *The Geometer's Sketchpad* to explore this question. Where would these points lie? Describe the set of points geometrically.

5. Consider the locus of points that are equidistant from two lines. How would you describe this locus?

6. The locus definition may also describe a set of points that fall within a region or area. Imagine that you are with your class on a nature hike. You approach a swampy area, but you cannot tell what is swamp and what is solid ground. There are two posts in the ground. Your teacher tells you that, if the angle between you and the two posts is more than 90°, then you will walk on swampy ground. If the angle is less than 90°, then you will not walk on swampy ground. Draw a diagram or use *The Geometer's Sketchpad* to explore the problem and determine the edges of the swamp. Explore what would happen for an angle other than 90°.

Part 2: Locus Definitions That Lead to Algebraic Expressions

Recall that a locus is a set of points that satisfy a given condition or conditions. The set of points can represent a geometric figure, an area or region, or an equation.

Think, Do, Discuss

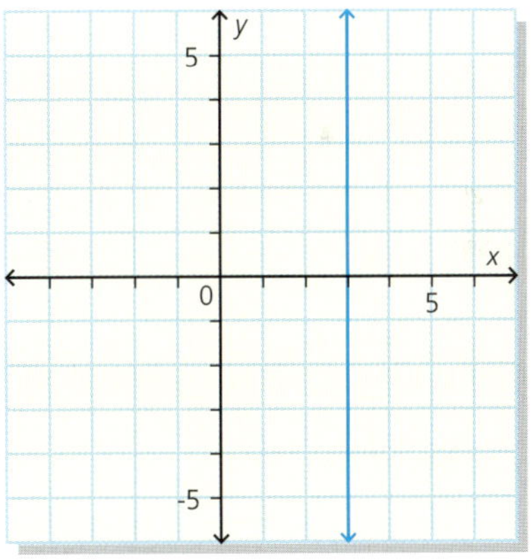

1. The adjacent diagram shows the locus of points that are 3 units to the right of the y-axis. What is the equation of this locus?

2. Describe the locus of points that are 5 units from the x-axis. Draw a diagram to help you.

3. What is the equation, or equations, for this locus of points?

4. Draw a sketch of the locus of points that are 12 units from the y-axis. Describe this locus geometrically and algebraically.

5. Describe all the points that are less than 4 units from the x-axis. Create a geometric model and an algebraic model.

6. Describe the locus of points that are 4 units from the origin. If possible, write the equation for the locus.

Focus 7.1U

Key Ideas

- A **locus** is a set of points that satisfy a *given condition* or conditions.
- You can describe many geometric figures with a locus definition.
- A locus definition may describe a geometric figure, a region, or a relation defined by an equation.
- The locus of points that are equidistant from a fixed point is a circle.
- The locus of points that are equidistant from two fixed points is the right bisector of the segment joining those points.

Example 1

Describe the locus of the points that are 3 units from the line $x = -1$. Give the equation of the locus.

Solution

Draw a diagram. Points that are 3 units from the line $x = -1$ are on both sides of the line. The points to the left of the line form a straight line with the equation $x = -4$. The points to the right form a straight line with the equation $x = 2$.

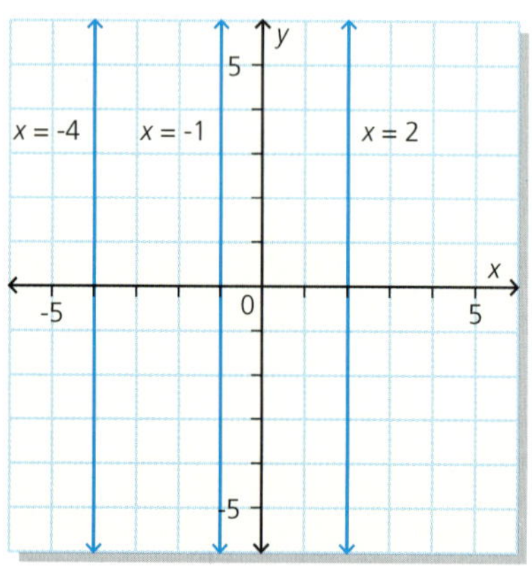

Example 2

Construct an acute angle and then draw several inscribed circles in the angle. Determine the locus of the circles' centres.

Solution

You could draw the figures using *The Geometer's Sketchpad.* By constructing several inscribed circles in $\angle KMQ$, you will see that the centres of the circles lie on the angle bisector. The locus of the circles' centres is the **angle bisector** of the angle.

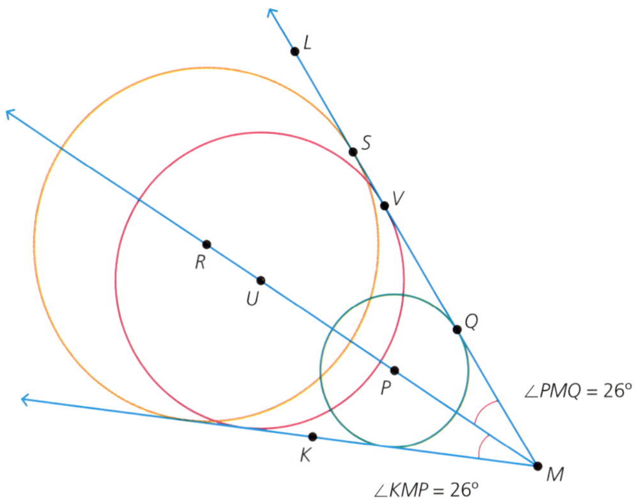

Example 3

Find the equation of the locus of points that are equidistant from points $A(-5, 2)$ and $B(1, -1)$.

Solution

Draw a diagram and let $P(x, y)$ be any point on the locus.

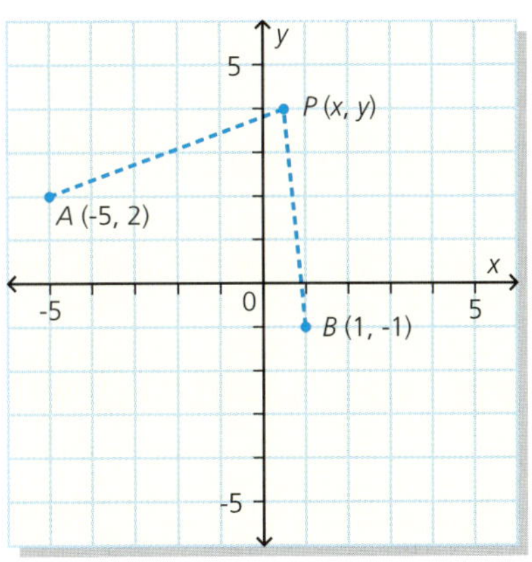

Point P is the same distance from A and from B. Then $PA = PB$.

Using the distance formula, $d = \sqrt{(x_2 - x_1)^2 + (y_2 - y_1)^2}$,

$PA = \sqrt{(x + 5)^2 + (y - 2)^2}$, and $PB = \sqrt{(x - 1)^2 + (y + 1)^2}$.

Since $PA = PB$, then

$$\sqrt{(x + 5)^2 + (y - 2)^2} = \sqrt{(x - 1)^2 + (y + 1)^2} \quad \text{Square both sides.}$$
$$(x + 5)^2 + (y - 2)^2 = (x - 1)^2 + (y + 1)^2 \quad \text{Expand.}$$
$$x^2 + 10x + 25 + y^2 - 4y + 4 = x^2 - 2x + 1 + y^2 + 2y + 1 \quad \text{Simplify.}$$
$$x^2 + 10x + 25 + y^2 - 4y + 4 - x^2 + 2x - 1 - y^2 - 2y - 1 = 0$$
$$12x - 6y + 27 = 0$$

The equation for the locus of points is $12x - 6y + 27 = 0$.

Practise, Apply, Solve 7.1U

A

1. Draw a diagram that represents the locus in each of the following situations.

(a) sitting in a seat on a Ferris wheel as it rotates

(b) going up 15 floors in an elevator

(c) going down an escalator

(d) walking from the corner of a room so that you are always the same distance from a pair of adjacent walls

2. What is the locus of each of the following? Draw a diagram to help you.

(a) all points that are 10 cm from a fixed point

(b) all points that are 3 cm above a line

(c) all points that are 2 cm from a parabola

(d) all points that are 1 cm above the surface of a sphere

3. For each set of points, describe the locus geometrically. Then graph and create an algebraic expression.

(a) 5 units from the line $y = 2$

(b) 3 units from the line $x = -2$

(c) 2 units from the line $y = 2x - 3$

(d) 4 units from the line $y = -3x + 2$

4. **Knowledge and Understanding**

(a) Find the equation for the locus of points that are 5 units from the origin.

(b) In right triangle *ABC*, the hypotenuse, *BC*, is 10 units. Determine an equation for the locus of points for the vertex *A*. What will a trace of these points look like?

5. Describe, geometrically, the locus of points that are

(a) 6 units from $(3, -1)$

(b) 3 units from $(0, 3)$

(c) 4 units from $(2, 3)$

B

6. **i.** Sketch each locus on the x-y plane.
ii. Determine the equation(s) of each locus.

(a) the points 4 units above the line $y = 3x + 6$

(b) the points 3 units below the line $2x + 4y = -8$

(c) the points 4 units from the circumference of the circle with centre (0, 0) and radius 3 units

(d) the points that lie directly 5 units to the right of the curve $y = x^2$

7. Describe and create an equation for each locus.

(a) the points that are equidistant from points (0, 2) and (0, 6)

(b) the points that are equidistant from points (0, 0) and (2, 4)

(c) the points that are equidistant from points (3, 3) and (−3, −3)

(d) the points that are equidistant from points (1, 5) and (−2, 6)

(e) the set of points that create a line parallel to the line $y = 2x + 6$, and the y-intercept is 3

(f) the set of points that create a line perpendicular to the line $y = 3x + 7$, and the locus passes through the origin

8. Sketch each locus and determine the equation. Let $P(x, y)$ be any point.

(a) The sum of the coordinates of any point is 8.

(b) The difference between the coordinates of any point is 3.

(c) The average of the coordinates of any point is 2.

(d) The product of the coordinates of any point is 20.

9. **Communication:** Create a locus definition in words for each of the following.

(a) $y = x$ (b) $x^2 + y^2 = 5$ (c) $x + y = 5$

(d) $x = -2$ (e) $y = 5$ (f) $y = \sqrt{16 - x^2}$

10. Four rods, all of equal length, are hinged at their end points to form the roaming rhombus *ROAM*. Keeping *RO* fixed, make *MA* move. What is the locus (or path) of point *M*? If *Y* is the midpoint of *MA*, what is the locus of *Y*?

11. The slope of the line joining any point, $P(x, y)$, with point (4, 2) has a slope of $\frac{3}{4}$. Determine the equation of the locus.

12. Determine the equation, or equations, of the locus whose points are equidistant from the x- and y-axes.

13. Any point, $P(x, y)$, of a locus lies 2 units to the right and 5 units below the curve $y = x^2 + 2x + 4$. Determine the equation of the locus.

14. For any point, $P(x, y)$, of a locus, the sum of the squares of the coordinates is 9.

(a) Graph the locus.

(b) Determine the equation of the locus.

15. (a) Create a set of conditions that define a locus.

(b) Use your definition to graph the locus.

(c) Determine the equation of the locus.

16. **Application:** Amy and Sara are playing in the schoolyard at recess and are hiding behind a high wall as shown. Joaquin is on the other side of the wall and is looking for them.

Show each of the following in a diagram.

(a) the points from which Joaquin can see neither Amy nor Sara

(b) the points from which Joaquin can see Sara, but not Amy

(c) the points from which Joaquin can see both Amy and Sara

17. **Check Your Understanding:** Describe and find the equation for the locus of points that are

(a) equidistant from the origin and the x-axis.

(b) equidistant from $(-2, 1)$ and $(6, 3)$

(c) equidistant from $y = 4$ and $y = -2$

(d) equidistant from points $A(3, 4)$ and $B(7, 8)$

C

18. Imagine a smaller circle, A, rolling around a larger, fixed circle, B. Describe the path of a specific point on A. You could use *The Geometer's Sketchpad* to explore this problem.

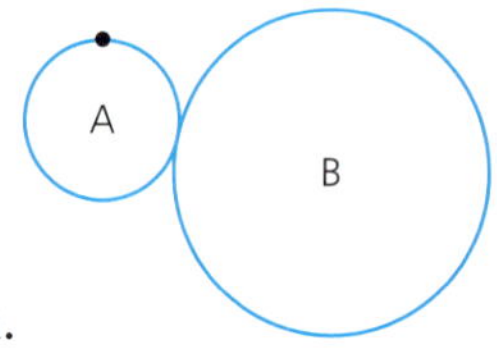

19. **Thinking, Inquiry, Problem Solving:** Create an equilateral triangle with three pushpins placed 10 cm apart in a bulletin board, covered with paper, or in a piece of corrugated cardboard. Place a 34-cm-long loop of string around the three pins.

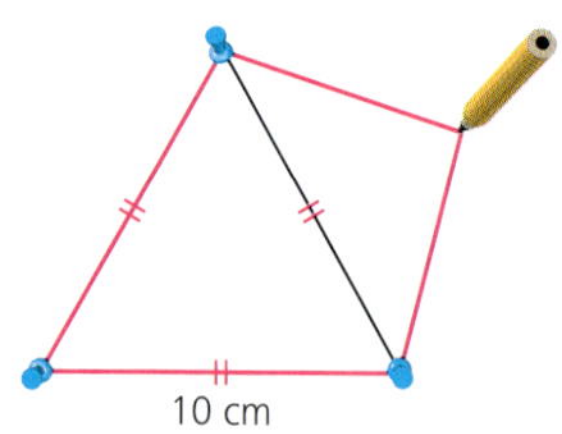

Place a pencil or a pen between the string and the triangle, pull it taut and move the pen back and forth, keeping the string taut. What type of curve do you expect to draw and why? Now move the pencil or pen and draw the curve. Does the result agree with your conjecture?

20. The blue point, B, is fixed on the arc of the circle with radius r. This circle is inside and touching another circle that has radius $2r$. The smaller circle turns inside and along the side of the larger circle. What is the locus of B? You may create a script for *The Geometer's Sketchpad* to animate this action.

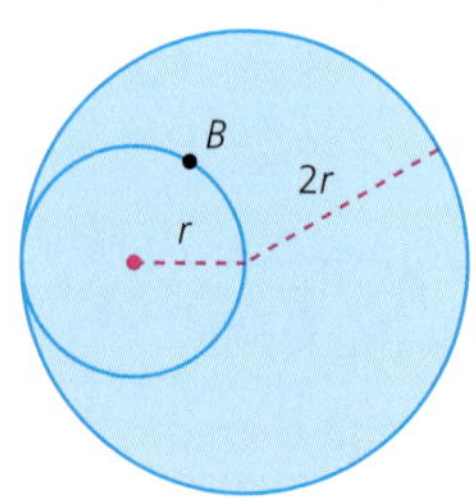

Revisiting the Circle

7.2U

Functions and Relations

The ruins of ancient Corinth include a stadium with several courses for foot races. In 1980, archaeologists found and excavated the starting line for a racecourse dating from about 500 B.C. The starting line is the arc of a circle, about 12 m long and between 1.25 m and 1.30 m wide.

Toe grooves cut into the blocks mark the 12 starting positions for the runners. These grooves provided the researchers with data points to determine the radius and centre of the circle. This led to insights about the design of racecourses in ancient Greece and about the units for length and angle used by the ancient Greeks. The archaeologists knew that they could use three points on the circle to find the equation of the circle. They used several sets of three points to verify their findings.

To find the equation of a circle, you will need the radius and the centre of the circle.

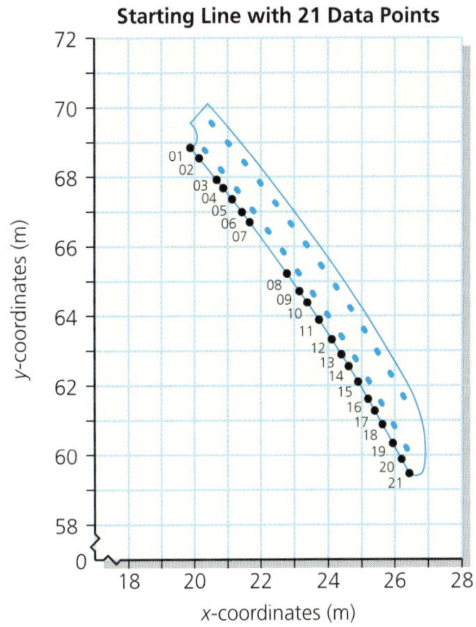

Part 1: Developing the Equation of a Circle

When you draw a circle, you most likely follow these steps:

- Choose a point to be the centre.
- Use compasses or a string to measure the radius.
- Draw a curve, which represents all the points that are a given distance from the centre of the circle.

A circle is a locus of points that are equidistant from one other point, the centre. In grade 10, the centres of most circles that you encountered were at the origin. The equation for a circle with its centre at the origin is $x^2 + y^2 = r^2$. In this section, you will determine the equation of a circle with a centre that is not (0, 0).

Think, Do, Discuss

The centre of a circle is $C(2, 3)$ and the circle's radius is 5 units.

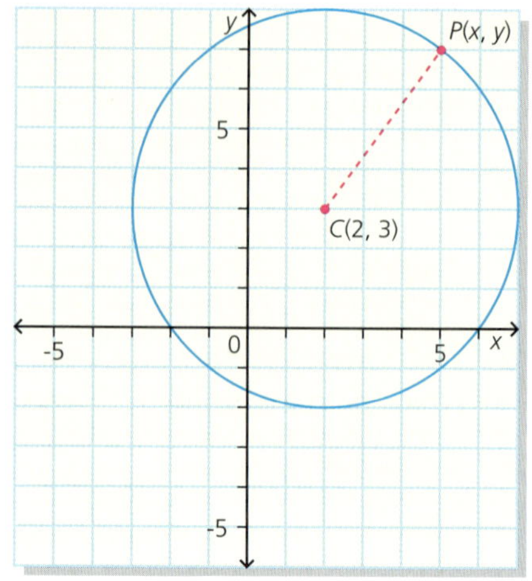

1. To find the equation of this circle, begin by recalling the distance formula. The distance from $C(2, 3)$ to $P(x, y)$ is 5 units. Substitute this information in the distance formula.
2. The distance formula has a radical sign. Take steps to "remove" this radical sign. You now have an equation for the circle that is centred at (2, 3) with a radius of 5 units.
3. What is the equation of the circle whose centre is $(3, -2)$ and whose radius is 4 units?
4. You can also create a general form for the equation of any circle. Describe the locus of points that are r units from the point $C(h, k)$. Let a point on the circle be $A(x, y)$. Write the formula for the distance from C to A.

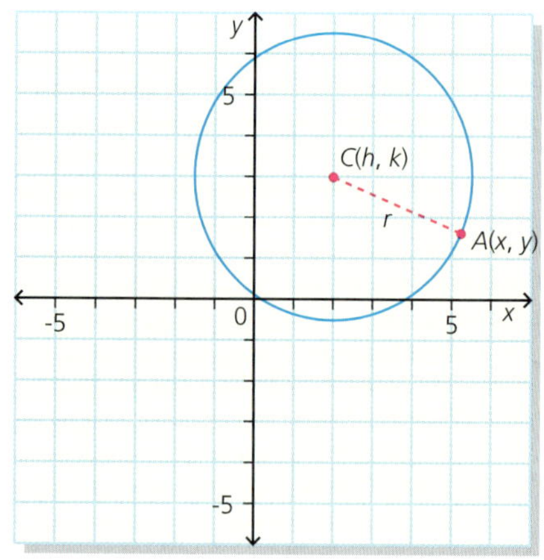

5. Since you know that the distance CA is the radius, substitute r for CA in the formula in step 4. You now have the general equation for a circle with centre (h, k) and radius r.
6. What are the centre and radius of the circle with equation $(x - 1)^2 + (y + 2)^2 = 25$?
7. What is the equation of the circle with centre (0, 3) and radius 8 units?
8. The equations thus far are in **standard form**. Expand the equation in step 6 to create an equation in the **general form** $x^2 + y^2 + 2gx + 2fy + C = 0$.
9. What are the values of g and f for this equation? What do these values tell you?
10. How would you change an equation in general form to standard form? Change the equation $x^2 + y^2 - 2x - 15 = 0$ to standard form and state the centre and the radius. Use what you learned in grade 10 about completing the square.

Part 2: Using Three Points to Find the Equation of a Circle

Think, Do, Discuss

1. You know that three points on a circle are $A(5, 4)$, $B(2, 5)$, and $C(-2, 3)$. How could you find the centre and radius of the circle?

2. You also know that the centre of the circle must be equidistant from all three points. Take two of the points, such as A and B, and describe the locus of points that are equidistant from points A and B, using geometry and by writing an equation.

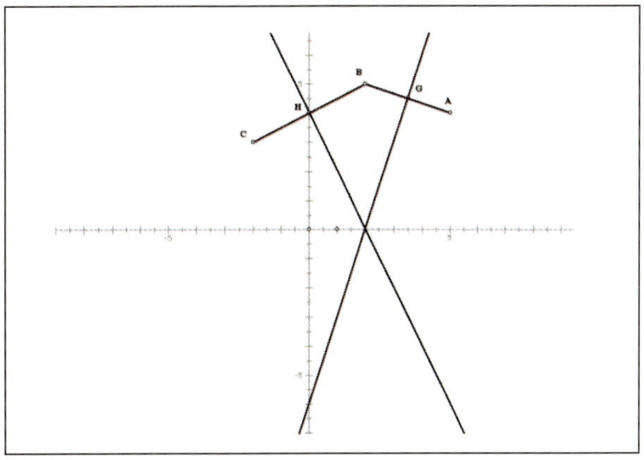

3. Describe the locus of points that are equidistant from points B and C, using geometry or by writing an equation.

4. You can continue to solve this problem geometrically or algebraically. For an algebraic solution, combine the equations that you found in steps 2 and 3. Then find the centre, using geometry or a graph. (The graph shown here was created with *The Geometer's Sketchpad*.)

5. Find the radius of the circle.

Focus 7.2U

Key Ideas

- A circle is the set or locus of all points in a plane that are equidistant from a fixed point. The fixed point is called the centre of the circle.
- The equation for a circle with centre (0, 0), the origin, and radius r units is
  $$x^2 + y^2 = r^2$$
- The equation in **standard form** for a circle with centre (h, k) and radius r is
  $$(x - h)^2 + (y - k)^2 = r^2$$
- The **general form** of the equation of a circle is
  $$x^2 + y^2 + 2gx + 2fy + C = 0$$
  This equation can be expressed in standard form by completing the square.
- A circle has an infinite number of lines of symmetry, all passing through the centre of the circle.

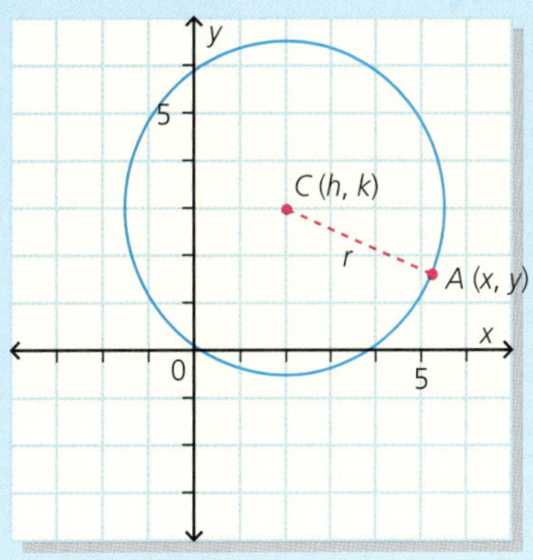

Example 1

(a) Find the equation of the circle tangent to the x-axis and with centre (3, 6).

(b) Write the equation of the locus of points that are 8 units from the point (2, −3).

Solution

(a) The equation of the circle in **standard form** is $(x - h)^2 + (y - k)^2 = r^2$.

Since the centre is (3, 6), the equation is $(x - 3)^2 + (y - 6)^2 = r^2$.

To find r, consider that the circle is tangent to the x-axis, as shown in the *The Geometer's Sketchpad* diagram.

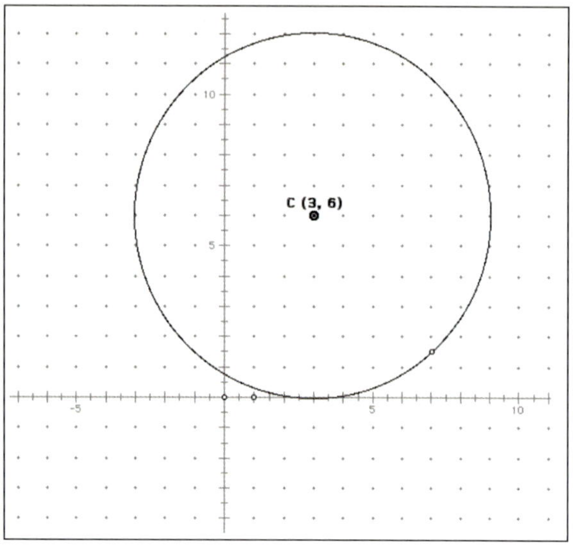

The radius is then 6 units, since the centre is 6 units from the x-axis.

The equation is
$(x - 3)^2 + (y - 6)^2 = 36$.

(b) All of the points that are 8 units from the point (2, −3) form a circle with radius 8 units and centre (2, −3). The equation of the circle is $(x - 2)^2 + (y + 3)^2 = 64$.

Example 2

Find the centre and the radius of the circle $x^2 + y^2 - 10x + 4y + 17 = 0$.

Solution

Write the equation in standard form by completing the square.

$x^2 - 10x + y^2 + 4y = -17$	Rearrange the equation.
$x^2 - 10x + ? + y^2 + 4y + ? = -17 + ? + ?$	Determine the value that must be added to create each perfect square. Add these two values to both sides of the equation.
$x^2 - 10x + 25 + y^2 + 4y + 4 = -17 + 25 + 4$	Factor and simplify.
$(x - 5)^2 + (y + 2)^2 = 12$	

The centre of the circle is (5, −2) and the radius is $\sqrt{12}$.

Example 3

Find the equation of the circle that passes through $C(0, 0)$, $D(4, -8)$, and $E(4, 0)$.

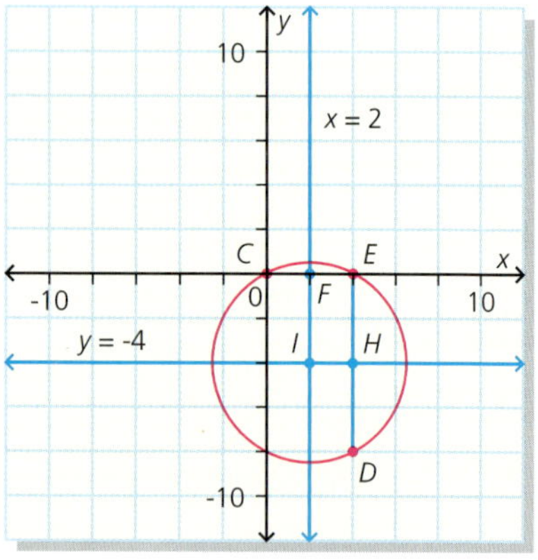

Solution

Draw a diagram. The perpendicular bisectors of CE and ED have the equations $x = 2$ and $y = -4$, respectively. The intersection point, (2, −4), of the perpendicular bisectors is the centre of the circle. To find the radius, find the distance from (2, −4) to any of the given points. Let one point be (0, 0).

$$d = \sqrt{(x_2 - x_1)^2 + (y_2 - y_1)^2}$$

In this case, *d* is the radius of the circle.

$$r = \sqrt{(x_2 - x_1)^2 + (y_2 - y_1)^2}$$
$$r = \sqrt{(2 - 0)^2 + (-4 - 0)^2}$$
$$r = \sqrt{20}$$

The equation of the circle is $(x - 2)^2 + (y + 4)^2 = 20$.

Practise, Apply, Solve 7.2U

A

1. Write the equation of the circle with

(a) centre (0, 2) and radius 4 units

(b) centre (3, 0) and radius 1 unit

(c) centre (1, 5) and radius 9 units

(d) centre (−2, 4) and radius 8 units

(e) centre (−2, −5) and radius $\sqrt{6}$ units

(f) centre (4, −6) and radius $2\sqrt{5}$ units

2. Find the centre and radius of each of the following circles.

(a) $x^2 + y^2 = 18$

(b) $(x - 2)^2 + y^2 = 9$

(c) $(x - 6)^2 + (y + 8)^2 = 81$

(d) $(x + 4)^2 + (y - 3)^2 = 32$

(e) $(x - 5)^2 + (y - 4)^2 = 27$

(f) $(x - 1)^2 + (y + 6)^2 = 40$

3. **i.** Apply the given transformations to each circle and determine the equation of the new circle.

ii. On the same axes, sketch the original circle and the new circle.

(a) $x^2 + y^2 = 9$, translated 3 units to the right and 2 units up

(b) $x^2 + y^2 = 4$, translated 4 units to the left and 3 units down

(c) $x^2 + y^2 = 1$, translated 4 units to the right and 4 units down

(d) $(x - 2)^2 + (y - 3)^2 = 9$, translated 2 units to the left and 3 units down

(e) $(x + 4)^2 + (y - 5)^2 = 9$, translated 6 units to the right and 3 units down

4. Express each equation in general form.

(a) $x^2 + y^2 = 25$

(b) $(x - 1)^2 + (y - 4)^2 = 16$

(c) $(x + 4)^2 + (y - 5)^2 = 1$

(d) $(x + 2)^2 + (y - 3)^2 = 9$

5. Express each equation in standard form.

(a) $x^2 + 8x + y^2 + 6y = 0$

(b) $x^2 + y^2 - 4x + 2y - 11 = 0$

(c) $x^2 + y^2 - 2x + 10y = -22$

(d) $x^2 + y^2 - 12x + 6y = 4$

6. **Knowledge and Understanding:** Find the radius and centre of each circle.

(a) $x^2 + y^2 - 4y = 0$

(b) $4x^2 + 4y^2 = 16$

(c) $2x^2 + 2y^2 - 6x + 4y + 1 = 0$

(d) $x^2 + y^2 - 6x + 2y + 1 = 0$

(e) $x^2 + y^2 - 8x + 6y = 11$

7. Find an equation for the locus such that

(a) all points are 2 units from the origin

(b) all points are 3 units from $(-1, 2)$

(c) all points are $\sqrt{5}$ units from $(0, 4)$

(d) all points are $2\sqrt{6}$ units from $(-2, 7)$

B

8. Find the equation of the circle that is tangent to the x-axis and has centre $(-3, 4)$.

9. **Communication:** Write the equations of the family of circles whose centres have the same x- and y-coordinates. The radius of each circle is 8 units. Describe this set of circles.

10. **Application:** Find the equation of each circle.

(a) The diameter has end points $A(-2, 4)$ and $B(2, 8)$.

(b) The diameter has end points $A(1, 2)$ and $B(3, -6)$.

(c) The centre is $(0, 0)$ and the x-intercept is 8.

(d) The centre is $(0, 2)$ and the y-intercept is -2.

(e) The centre is $(-1, 2)$ and the x-intercept is 3.

11. Is $x^2 + y^2 - 8x + 6y + 30 = 0$ the equation of a circle? Justify your answer.

12. Graph each equation. (The graph of each equation is a semicircle.)

(a) $y = \sqrt{4 - x^2}$

(b) $y = \sqrt{9 - x^2}$

(c) $y = -\sqrt{16 - x^2}$

(d) $x = \sqrt{9 - y^2}$

(e) $y = 2 + \sqrt{9 - x^2}$

(f) $y = 3 - \sqrt{25 - x^2}$

13. Find the equation of each of the following circles.

(a) centre $(0, 0)$ and passing through $(3, 4)$

(b) centre $(2, 3)$ and passing through $(4, 7)$

(c) centre $(0, 0)$ and passing through $(1, 2)$

(d) centre $(-1, 0)$ and passing through $(3, 1)$

(e) centre $(8, 2)$ and passing through $(1, 4)$

14. The centre of a circle is $(1, 2)$ and the radius is 5 units. For this circle, find the length of a chord that is 4 units above the centre and that is parallel to the x-axis.

15. **Check Your Understanding:** The general form of the equation of a circle is $x^2 + y^2 - 8x + 6y + 13 = 0$.

(a) Explain how to change this equation to standard form.

(b) Write the equation in standard form.

(c) What are the advantages of the standard form?

16. A cellular phone tower is located at point (0, 0). The tower emits a signal that is accessible in a range of 30 km. Another tower is 50 km northeast of the first tower, and its signal also has a range of 30 km. These two towers are the only ones in the area.

(a) If you are at the point (40, 20), can you make a call using a cell phone? Each linear unit represents 1 km.

(b) What is the area of the overlap of the towers' ranges?

(c) What is the minimum distance that you can be within the range of one tower, but not within the range of the other tower?

17. **Thinking, Inquiry, Problem Solving:** Find the equation of all circles, each with radius 8 units, that are tangent to the graphs of both $y = x$ and $y = -x$.

18. A point moves so that it is always twice as far from (5, 0) as it is from (2, 0). Describe the curve on which it travels and write the equation of the curve.

19. Draw the semicircle $y = \sqrt{25 - x^2}$.

(a) Locate the x-intercepts and call them A and B.

(b) Locate the y-intercept and label it C.

(c) Prove that ΔABC is a right triangle.

20. Determine the points of intersection between the circles $(x + 4)^2 + (y - 1)^2 = 25$ and $(x - 2)^2 + (y - 3)^2 = 25$. State the coordinates to the nearest hundredth.

The Chapter Problem—Designing a Bridge

In this section, you studied equations of circles. Apply what you have learned to create a semicircular arch.

CP1. What is the radius? Write the equation of the curve.

CP2. Graph the curve.

CP3. Determine if two trucks will be able to pass under the arch. Leave space between the trucks, as well as at each side of the road.

CP4. Is this a good design? Why or why not?

7.3U TI-83 Plus Calculator: Graphing Circles

To graph an equation using the graphing calculator, the equation must be in function form, with y on the left side of the equation. To graph $x^2 + y^2 = 16$ using the graphing calculator, solve for y. You must enter two equations.

1. Solve the equation for y.

$$x^2 + y^2 = 16$$
$$y^2 = 16 - x^2$$
$$\sqrt{y^2} = \pm\sqrt{16 - x^2}$$
$$\therefore \quad y = \pm\sqrt{16 - x^2}$$

$$\text{Y1} = \sqrt{16 - x^2}$$
$$\text{Y2} = -\sqrt{16 - x^2}$$

step 1

Enter the expressions for **Y1** and **Y2** into the equation editor. Adjust the window.

2. Graph the circle.

(a) If you now press GRAPH, then the graph will not look like a circle.

(b) The scales of the axes should be "square." In other words, the increments of the x- and y-axes should be the same.

Press ZOOM and select **Zsquare.**

(c) Press GRAPH.

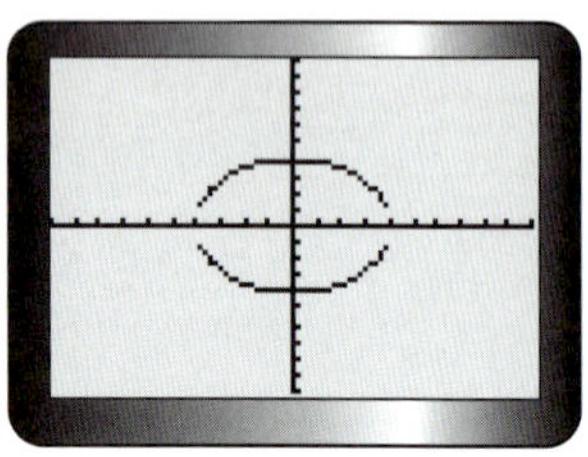
step 2a

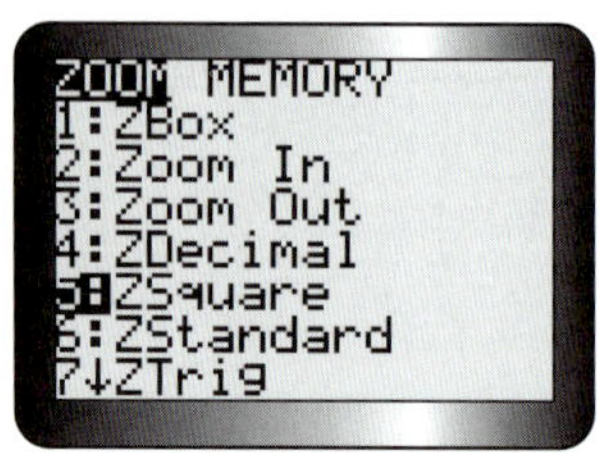

step 2b

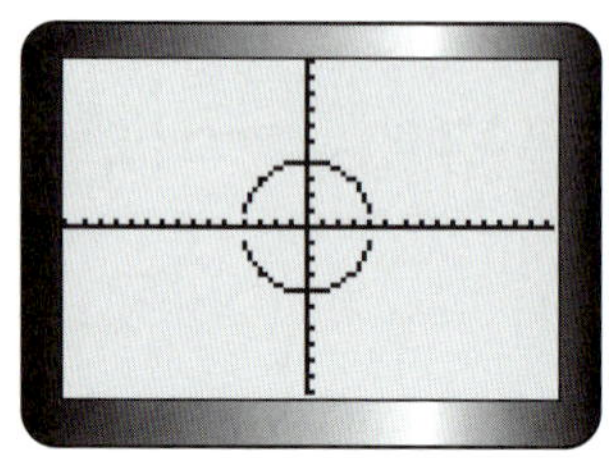
step 2c

Practice 7.3U

1. (a) To graph $x^2 + y^2 = 25$, first solve for y.

(b) Enter the expressions in (a) into the equation editor and adjust the window.

2. For each of the following changes, use your graph of $x^2 + y^2 = 25$ and conjecture how the position and size of the graph will change. Then make each change and compare the resulting graph with your conjecture.

(a) Replace x with $(x + 2)$.

(b) Replace y with $(y - 4)$.

(c) Replace 25 with 16.

(d) Replace both x and y with $(x - 1)$ and $(y + 5)$, respectively.

3. Graph each circle.

(a) $x^2 + y^2 = 9$

(b) $(x - 3)^2 + y^2 = 16$

(c) $x^2 + (y + 2)^2 = 4$

(d) $(x - 1)^2 + (y + 2)^2 = 25$

The Ellipse 7.4U

Functions and Relations

In the sixteenth century, Nicolaus Copernicus claimed that the sun, not the Earth, was the centre of the solar system. He believed that the orbits of planets were circles. A century later, Johannes Kepler (1571 – 1630) discovered that the orbits of the planets were ellipses or "stretched circles." An ellipse has two fixed points, called **focal points**, or **foci**. The sun is at one of the focal points of the Earth's orbit.

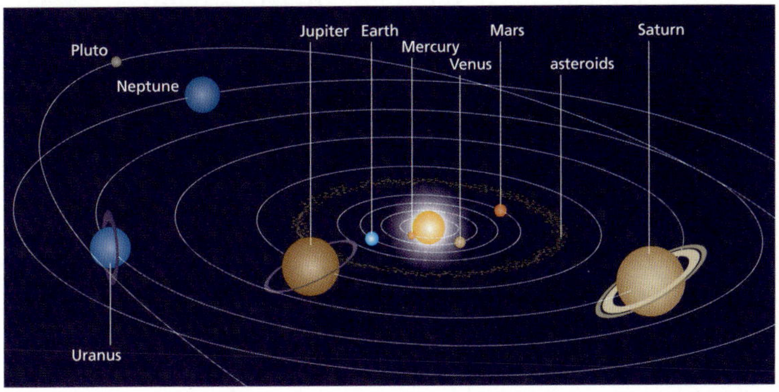

Nicolaus Copernicus (1473–1543)

Johannes Kepler (1571–1630)

Part 1: Stretching a Circle

Think, Do, Discuss

1. Graph $x^2 + 4y^2 = 16$ and describe the graph. (**Hint:** Construct a table that includes the x- and y-intercepts.)
2. What is the shape of the graph? What are the x-intercepts? the y-intercepts? Along which axis is the ellipse wider, the x-axis or the y-axis?
3. When an ellipse is centred about the origin, the line segment between the x-intercepts and the line segment between the y-intercepts are called the axes of the ellipse. The longer segment is the **major axis**, and the shorter axis is the **minor axis**. Label the major axis and the minor axis on your graph.
4. What is the length of the major axis?
5. Divide both sides of the equation in step 1 by 16. Discuss these aspects of the new equation:
   (a) the x-intercepts and the y-intercepts
   (b) the length of the major axis and the length of the minor axis

6. For the equation $\frac{x^2}{9} + \frac{y^2}{4} = 1$, predict the x- and y-intercepts. Either draw a graph or use algebra to confirm your prediction. Where is the major axis? What is the length of the major axis?

7. The **standard form** of an ellipse is $\frac{x^2}{a^2} + \frac{y^2}{b^2} = 1$, where $a > b$. What are the properties of the graph of this equation?

8. What would be different about the graph of $\frac{x^2}{b^2} + \frac{y^2}{a^2} = 1$, where $a > b$?

9. All of the above ellipses are centred about the origin. Recalling what you know about circles and given that an ellipse is a "stretched circle," find the centre of the ellipse $\frac{(x-1)^2}{9} + \frac{(y+2)^2}{4} = 1$.

10. It would be difficult to find the x- and y-intercepts of the ellipse in step 9, but it is not difficult to find the lengths of the major and the minor axes. Find the lengths of the major and the minor axes. Sketch a graph of the ellipse in step 9.

Part 2: The Locus Definition of an Ellipse

Another way of looking at an ellipse is to use a locus definition. The following construction of an ellipse is based on the locus definition of an ellipse.

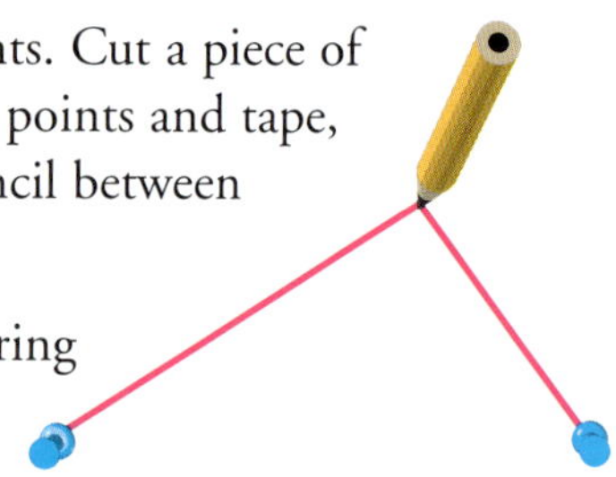

Choose two points on a sheet of paper as two fixed points. Cut a piece of string that is longer than the distance between the fixed points and tape, or tack, it to the two fixed points. Insert the tip of a pencil between the string and the fixed points, and pull the string taut.

If you move the pencil around the paper, keeping the string taut, you will draw an ellipse. Use the same length of string, but move the fixed points closer together. Notice how the new ellipse has a different shape. Leave the fixed points where they are and change the length of the string. Again, you have created a new ellipse.

The **locus definition** of an **ellipse**:
An ellipse is the set or locus of points in a plane such that the sum of the distances from two fixed points to any other point is constant.

Think, Do, Discuss

1. Explain how the diagram on the right illustrates the locus definition of the ellipse.

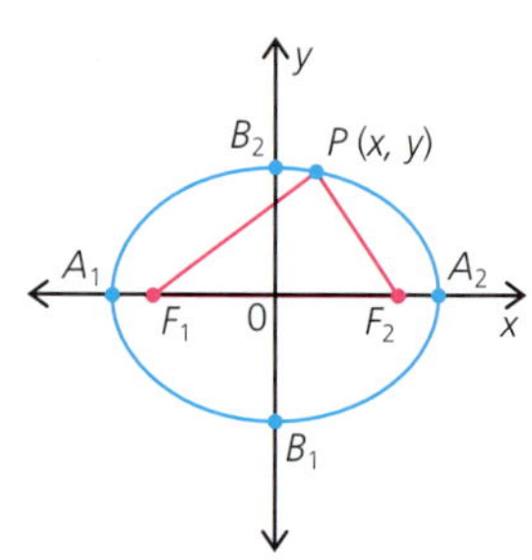

2. Describe how you would construct an ellipse so that the major axis would be horizontal. How would you construct an ellipse with a vertical major axis?

3. Imagine that the ellipse in the diagram is constructed with a piece of string that is 10 units long. What is the relationship between PF_1 and PF_2?

4. What is the length of the major axis for any ellipse?

5. Show that the length of the string is equal to the length of the major axis by moving $P(x, y)$ to point A_2.

6. Move $P(x, y)$ to point B_2. What is the length of F_1B_2?

7. Let a be the distance from the centre of the ellipse to one of the **vertices** of the major axis, A_2. (Compare this distance to one of the focal radii.) Let b be the distance from the centre to one of the **intercepts** of the minor axis, B_2, and let c be the distance from the fixed point F_2 to the centre. Use your diagram to explain why $a^2 = b^2 + c^2$.

8. For the ellipse $\frac{x^2}{25} + \frac{y^2}{16} = 1$, determine a and b and use these values to determine c. What are the coordinates of the foci for this ellipse? What is the length of string that you would need to draw this ellipse?

Focus 7.4U

Key Ideas

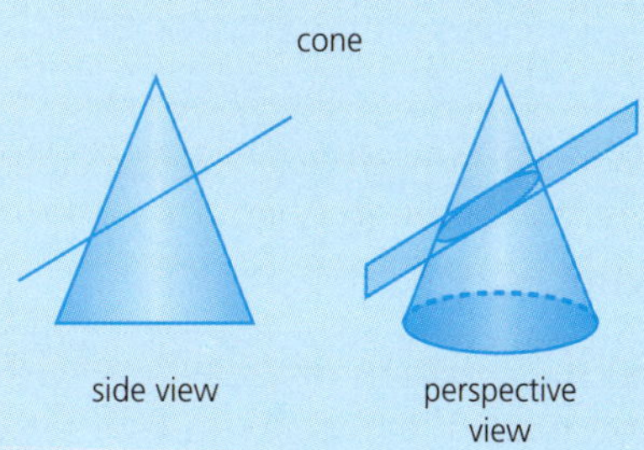

- The ellipse is created by a plane slicing through both sides of a cone at a diagonal angle.
- An ellipse is a set or locus of points in a plane such that the sum of the distances from two fixed points to any other point is constant. The sum $PF_1 + PF_2$ is a constant.

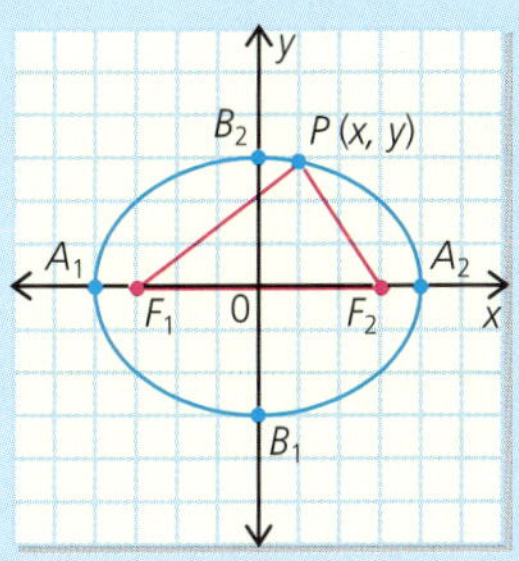

- This ellipse is centred about the origin, and its major axis lies along the x-axis.
- An ellipse has two lines of symmetry, A_1A_2 and B_1B_2, that are perpendicular to one another. The line A_1A_2 is the **major axis**, the longer axis, and B_1B_2 is the **minor axis**.
- A_1 and A_2 are called the **vertices** of the ellipse and are each $|a|$ units from the centre, (0, 0), of the ellipse. The length of the major axis is $2a$. The length of the minor axis is $2b$.
- The **standard form** of the equation for an ellipse whose centre is the origin and whose major axis is along the x-axis is

  $\frac{x^2}{a^2} + \frac{y^2}{b^2} = 1$, where $a > b$

  The vertices are $(a, 0)$ and $(-a, 0)$.

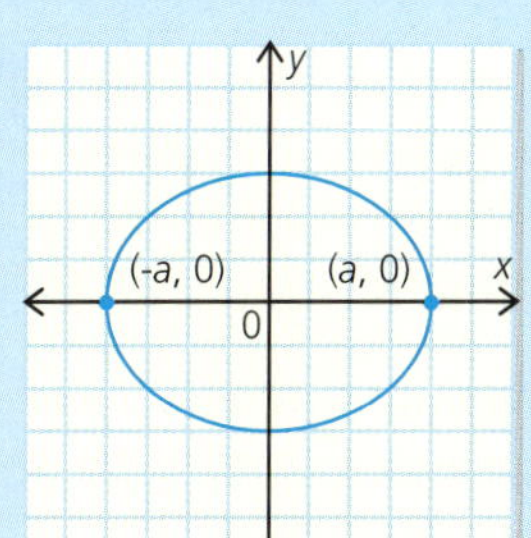

- The **standard form** of the equation for an ellipse whose centre is the origin and whose major axis is along the y-axis is

  $$\frac{x^2}{b^2} + \frac{y^2}{a^2} = 1, \text{ where } a > b$$

  The vertices are $(0, a)$ and $(0, -a)$.

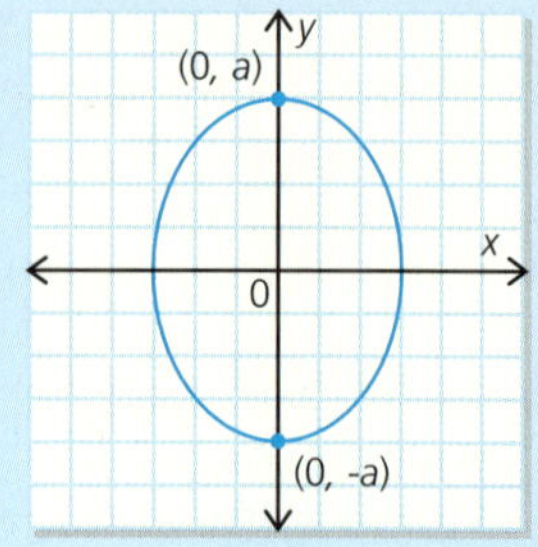

- The **foci**, or **focal points**, of the ellipse are F_1 and F_2. The foci lie on the major axis and are each $|c|$ units from the centre of the ellipse.
- In any ellipse, $a^2 = b^2 + c^2$.

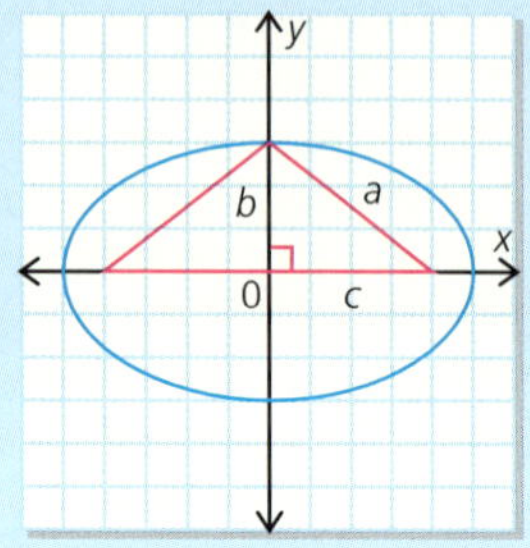

- The **standard form** of the equations for the ellipse whose centre is (h, k) is

  $$\frac{(x-h)^2}{a^2} + \frac{(y-k)^2}{b^2} = 1, \text{ for a horizontal major axis, where } a > b, \text{ or}$$

  $$\frac{(x-h)^2}{b^2} + \frac{(y-k)^2}{a^2} = 1, \text{ for a vertical major axis, where } a > b$$

Example 1

Find the equation of the ellipse with x-intercepts ± 4 and y-intercepts ± 3.

Solution

Because the positive x-intercept is larger than the positive y-intercept, let the positive x-intercept be a, and let the positive y-intercept be b. The major axis lies along the x-axis and the equation of the ellipse is

$$\frac{x^2}{16} + \frac{y^2}{9} = 1$$

Example 2

For the conic $\frac{x^2}{25} + \frac{y^2}{64} = 1$,

(a) what are the x-intercepts?

(b) what are the y-intercepts?

(c) state the coordinates of the foci

(d) find the length of the major axis

(e) graph the conic

Solution

The major axis lies along the y-axis, and $b = 5$ and $a = 8$.

(a) The x-intercepts are ± 5.

(b) The y-intercepts are ± 8.

(c) Since $a^2 = b^2 + c^2$, then $8^2 = 5^2 + c^2$.

$$\begin{aligned} 64 &= 25 + c^2 \\ c^2 &= 64 - 25 \\ c^2 &= 39 \\ \sqrt{c^2} &= \pm\sqrt{39} \\ c &= \pm\sqrt{39} \end{aligned}$$

Since the centre of the ellipse is (0, 0) and the foci lie on the major axis, the y-axis, then the foci are $(0, \sqrt{39})$ and $(0, -\sqrt{39})$.

(d) The length of the major axis is $2a$ and $a = 8$. The length is then $2(8) = 16$ units.

(e)

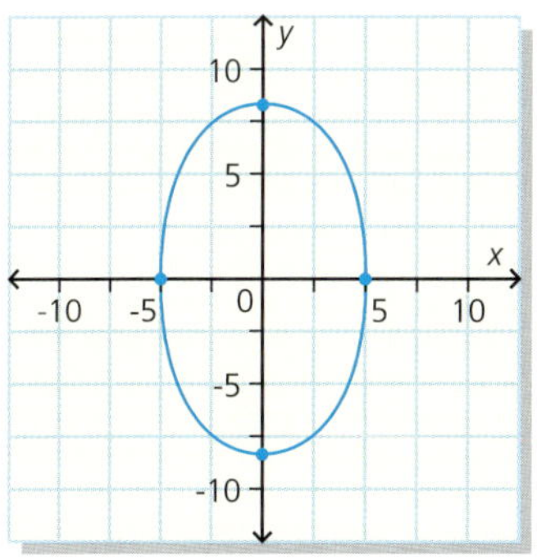

Example 3

Find the equation of the ellipse with centre (0, 0), foci (5, 0) and (−5, 0), and y-intercepts ± 6.

Solution

The foci are on the x-axis. Therefore, the major axis is horizontal. The equation is $\frac{x^2}{a^2} + \frac{y^2}{b^2} = 1$, where $a > b$, and $b = 6$ and $c = 5$. Find a.

$$\begin{aligned} a^2 &= b^2 + c^2 \\ a^2 &= 6^2 + 5^2 \\ a^2 &= 36 + 25 \\ a &= \pm\sqrt{61} \end{aligned}$$

The equation of the ellipse is

$$\frac{x^2}{61} + \frac{y^2}{36} = 1$$

Example 4

Find the centre and the length of the major and the minor axes for the ellipse $4(x - 2)^2 + 16(y + 1)^2 = 64$.

Solution

Change the form of the equation to standard form by dividing by 64.

$$\frac{4(x-2)^2}{64} + \frac{16(y+1)^2}{64} = \frac{64}{64} \qquad \text{Simplify.}$$

$$\frac{(x-2)^2}{16} + \frac{(y+1)^2}{4} = 1$$

The centre of the ellipse is $(2, -1)$, and $a = 4$ and $b = 2$.

The length of the major axis is 8 units, and the length of the minor axis is 4 units.

Example 5

The shape of an arch is a semiellipse, and its span is the major axis of the ellipse. If the span is 60 m and the height is 20 m, find the height of the arch at a point 12 m from the centre, to the nearest tenth of a metre.

Solution

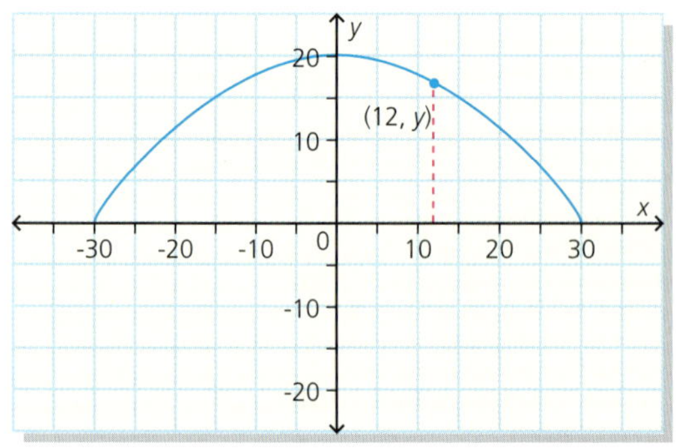

Draw a diagram and centre the ellipse about the origin, with the vertices on the x-axis.

From the diagram, $a = 30$ and $b = 20$.

The equation of the ellipse is

$$\frac{x^2}{900} + \frac{y^2}{400} = 1$$

Substitute $x = 12$ in the equation.

$$\frac{12^2}{900} + \frac{y^2}{400} = 1 \qquad \text{Expand.}$$

$$\frac{144}{900} + \frac{y^2}{400} = 1 \qquad \text{Simplify and rearrange.}$$

$$\frac{y^2}{400} = 1 - \frac{4}{25} \qquad \text{Subtract. Then multiply both sides by 400.}$$

$$y^2 = 400\left(\frac{21}{25}\right) \qquad \text{Simplify.}$$

$$y^2 = 16(21)$$

$$\sqrt{y^2} = \sqrt{16(21)}$$

$$y = \pm 4\sqrt{21} \qquad \text{The value of } y \text{ must be positive.}$$

$$y \doteq 18.3$$

The height of the arch at a point 12 m from the centre is about 18.3 m.

Practise, Apply, Solve 7.4U

A

1. For each ellipse, state the vertices and the lengths of the major and the minor axes. Then sketch the graph.

(a) $\frac{x^2}{4} + \frac{y^2}{9} = 1$

(b) $\frac{x^2}{25} + \frac{y^2}{16} = 1$

(c) $\frac{x^2}{49} + \frac{y^2}{9} = 1$

(d) $\frac{x^2}{49} + \frac{y^2}{16} = 1$

(e) $\frac{x^2}{25} + \frac{y^2}{100} = 1$

(f) $\frac{x^2}{81} + \frac{y^2}{64} = 1$

2. For each ellipse, state the centre, the lengths of the major and the minor axes, and whether the major axis is horizontal or vertical. Then sketch the graph.

(a) $\frac{(x-2)^2}{9} + \frac{y^2}{4} = 1$

(b) $\frac{(x+1)^2}{25} + (y-3)^2 = 1$

(c) $\frac{(x-3)^2}{100} + \frac{(y+4)^2}{16} = 1$

(d) $\frac{(x-1)^2}{2} + \frac{(y+2)^2}{4} = 1$

(e) $(x+1)^2 + \frac{(y+1)^2}{4} = 16$

(f) $4(x+3)^2 + 9(y-4)^2 = 36$

3. **Knowledge and Understanding:** State the lengths of the major and the minor axes, the coordinates of the foci, and sketch the graph for each of the following ellipses.

(a) $9x^2 + 4y^2 = 144$

(b) $2x^2 + y^2 = 36$

(c) $6x^2 + 4y^2 = 48$

(d) $x^2 + 8y^2 = 72$

(e) $4x^2 + 16y^2 = 64$

(f) $25x^2 + 4y^2 = 100$

4. Each ellipse is centred about the origin. Find an equation for each ellipse.

(a) major axis: along the y-axis and 9 units long; minor axis: 6 units long

(b) minor axis: 6 units long; one vertex at $(-5, 0)$

(c) foci: $(-8, 0)$ and $(8, 0)$; major axis: 20 units long

(d) one vertex at $(4, 0)$; one focus at $(-2, 0)$

(e) one vertex at $(0, 8)$; one focus at $(0, 6)$

5. For each ellipse, sketch the graph.

(a) $\frac{(x-1)^2}{4} + \frac{y^2}{9} = 1$

(b) $\frac{(x-2)^2}{9} + \frac{y^2}{4} = 1$

(c) $2x^2 + y^2 = 36$

(d) $\frac{(x+3)^2}{100} + \frac{(y-1)^2}{49} = 1$

(e) $5x^2 + 2(y-3)^2 = 80$

(f) $(x-1)^2 + 9y^2 = 9$

B

6. For each graph, find

- **i.** the coordinates of its vertices
- **ii.** the lengths of the major and the minor axes
- **iii.** the coordinates of the foci
- **iv.** the equation of the ellipse
- **v.** the domain and the range

(a)

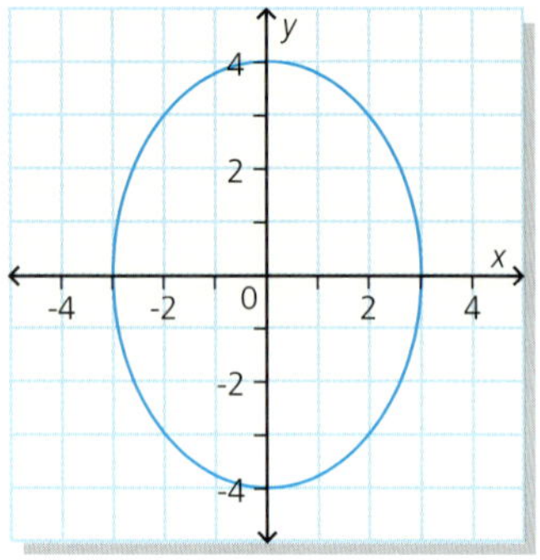

(b)

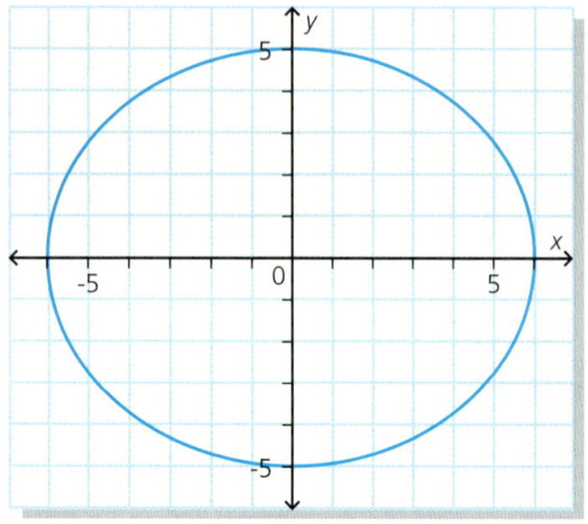

(c)

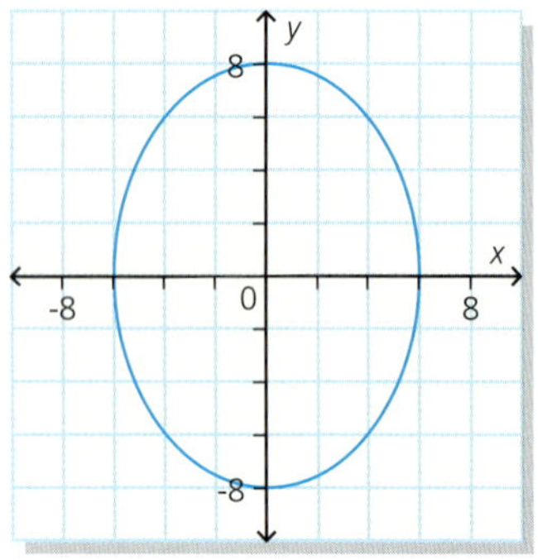

(d)

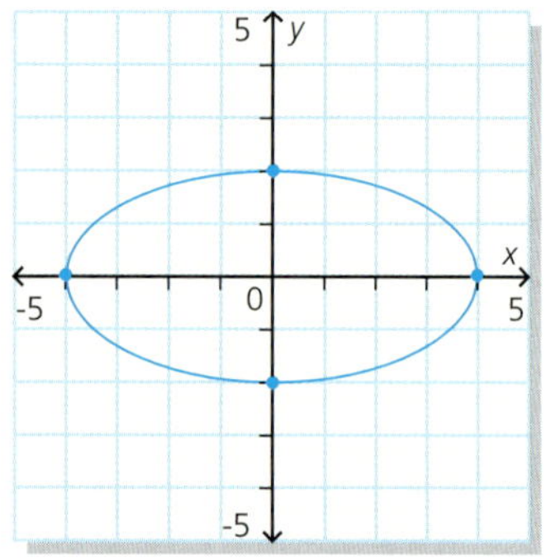

7. **Communication:** An ellipse has foci $(-49, 0)$ and $(49, 0)$ and x-intercepts ± 50. Describe the appearance of this ellipse and justify your description.

8. State the centre and the lengths of the major and the minor axes of each ellipse.

(a) $4(x - 2)^2 + (y + 1)^2 = 16$

(b) $2(x + 1)^2 + 16(y + 2)^2 = 32$

(c) $3(x + 1)^2 + 16(y - 2)^2 = 48$

(d) $5x^2 + 2(y - 3)^2 = 80$

9. In the previous section, you used a graphing calculator to draw the graph of a circle. You could use the same method to draw the graph of an ellipse using a graphing calculator. To graph $4x^2 + y^2 = 16$, arrange the equation into two parts: $y = \sqrt{16 - 4x^2}$ and $y = -\sqrt{16 - 4x^2}$. Enter the expressions into **Y1** and **Y2**, choose **Zsquare** from the Zoom menu, and [GRAPH].

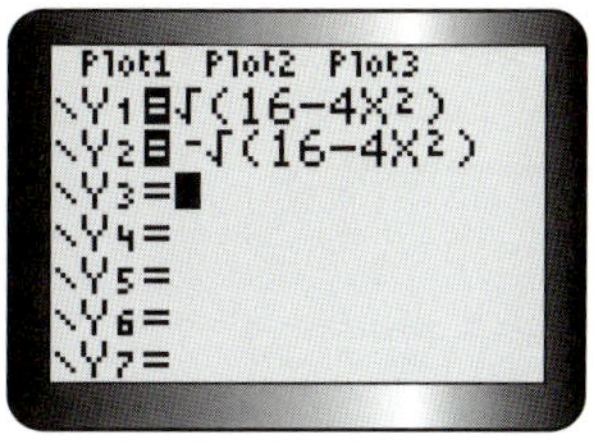

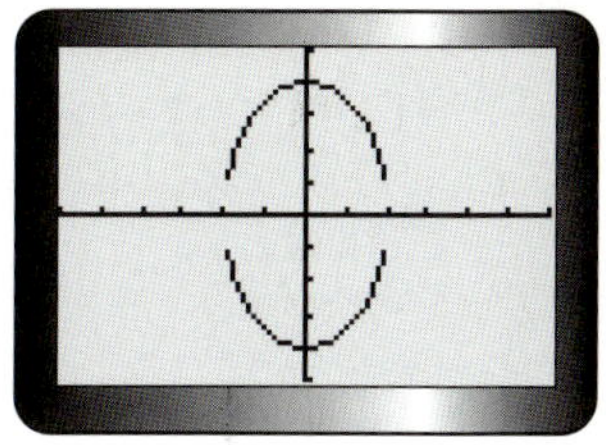

For each of the following, solve for y, then graph using technology.

(a) $2x^2 + y^2 = 32$ (b) $\frac{x^2}{5} + \frac{y^2}{9} = 1$ (c) $4(x - 1)^2 + y^2 = 16$

10. Find the equation of the ellipse with centre (0, 0) and whose foci are on the x-axis. One focus is at (5, 0), and $b = 12$.

11. Using only the locus definition of an ellipse, find the equation of the ellipse with foci (0, 4) and (0, −4). The sum of the focal radii is 10.

12. The Earth follows an elliptical path around the sun, with the sun at one of the foci. The length of the major axis of the elliptical orbit is 3×10^8 km. The focus is 2.5×10^6 km from the centre of the orbit.

(a) What is the length of the minor axis?

(b) Determine the equation of the Earth's orbit.

13. **Thinking, Inquiry, Problem Solving:** Find the equation of the ellipse that includes the points $(2, -2)$ and $\left(-\frac{2}{3}, \frac{10}{3}\right)$, and is centred at the origin.

14. You want to give your dog a chance to run in the backyard, but you do not want him to run away. You place two stakes in the ground that are 4 m apart and attach the ends of an 8 m long rope to each of the sticks. Then you attach the dog's collar to a ring that slides along the rope. Describe the region in which the dog may roam. Include the dimensions of the region.

15. Use your knowledge of completing the square to rearrange the following equations in the standard form of an ellipse.

(a) $4x^2 + y^2 - 2y - 3 = 0$ (b) $4x^2 + 9y^2 - 8x + 18y = 23$

(c) $4x^2 + y^2 - 16x + 2y + 1 = 0$ (d) $16x^2 + 9y^2 + 90y + 81 = 0$

16. State the domain and range of each of the following ellipses.

(a) $\frac{x^2}{25} + \frac{y^2}{9} = 1$ (b) $\frac{x^2}{16} + \frac{y^2}{36} = 1$

(c) $4x^2 + 25y^2 = 100$ (d) $16x^2 + 9y^2 = 144$

(e) $x^2 + 4y^2 + 4x + 8y = 8$ (f) $x^2 + 9y^2 + 2x - 18y = 26$

17. Find the equation of the ellipse with centre (0, 0) and whose foci are on the x-axis. The length of the major axis is three times the length of the minor axis, and the graph passes through point (3, 3).

18. **Check Your Understanding:** An ellipse is a "stretched circle." Could you describe a circle as an ellipse? If so, what are the foci of the circle? What are the lengths of the major and the minor axes? Would this circle satisfy the locus definition of the ellipse?

19. **Application:** A truck driver, whose truck was carrying an extra large load, was driving through a small town when he became very hungry. He spotted a fast-food restaurant with a drive-through arch in the shape of a semiellipse. While driving under the centre of the arch, he noticed that the top of his truck just touched the arch at two points. He noted that the driveway was exactly 4 m wide at the base of the arch. His truck is 3.8 m high and 3.2 m wide. He wondered whether he should radio his "buddy" to let him know that his buddy's truck might not fit under the arch. If his buddy's truck is 3.5 m wide and 3 m high, then will he be able to drive it under the arch?

20. The door of a house is in the shape of a semiellipse. The span is 100 cm wide, and the maximum height of the door is 250 cm. A sofa has to fit through the door. The sofa's dimensions are 120 cm by 80 cm by 250 cm. Will the sofa fit through the door? Justify your answer.

The Chapter Problem—Designing a Bridge

In this section, you have worked with equations of ellipses. Apply what you have learned to create a semielliptical arch.

CP5. What are the lengths of the major and the minor axes? Write the equation of the curve.

CP6. Graph the curve.

CP7. Determine whether two trucks will be able to pass, side by side, under the arch. There should be space between the trucks and at each side of the road. Adjust the major and minor axes so your arch is workable.

CP8. Is this a good design?

Did You Know?

Why is a manhole cover always circular? Could it be elliptical or square? A circle has a constant width—the diameter. So, no matter in which direction the cover is turned, it will not slip through the "manhole." You could not turn an elliptical cover in this way. Is there any other shape that has a constant width? Try experimenting with *The Geometer's Sketchpad*. Start with an equilateral triangle, ΔABC, and beginning at point A, swing an arc that is equal to AB between points B and C. Do the same for the other two points in the triangle. Would this figure work as a manhole cover? Try the same construction with a square and a regular pentagon. Which figures work and which do not?

Waxed-Paper Models

7.5U

Functions and Relations

EXPLORATION

In this activity, you will explore a paper-folding technique for creating a conic. You will need waxed paper, a pencil, and access to dynamic geometry software.

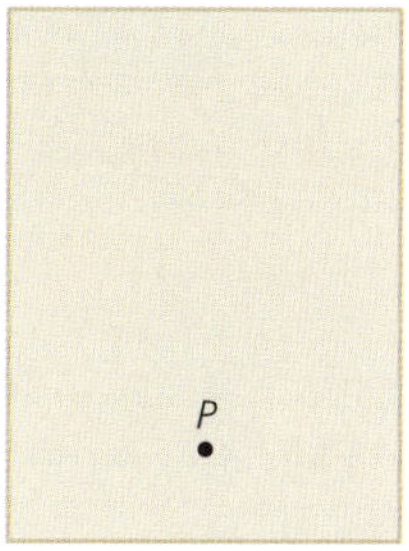

- Tear off a rectangular sheet of waxed paper. Mark a point close to the centre of the bottom edge. Mark this point *P*.
- Fold the paper, at any angle, so that the bottom edge of the paper touches point *P*. Crease the paper along the fold line and then open up the paper.
- Fold the paper again, at a different angle, so that the bottom edge of the paper touches point *P* and crease the paper. Open up the paper.
- Continue this process until you have many different creases in the waxed paper.

Think, Do, Discuss

1. What pattern emerges?
2. Compare your shape with the shapes that other students in the class have made. How are the shapes similar? How are they different? What conic does your shape resemble?
3. How does changing the position of point *P* affect the curve?
4. Explain why you could describe each line you made as a **tangent**. (A line is tangent to a curve if it touches the curve at exactly one point.)
5. How could you construct the tangent lines using what you know about geometry?
6. Use *The Geometer's Sketchpad* to recreate this waxed-paper model of your curve. Begin with a line and a point, *P*.
7. How will you construct the crease lines? (**Hint:** Choose a point on the line and connect it to *P*. What is the next step?)
8. Once you have drawn the first crease line, choose **Trace Line** from the **Display** menu to create other crease lines. Is the figure you created similar to your waxed-paper model?

9. What happens if you move the original point or line?

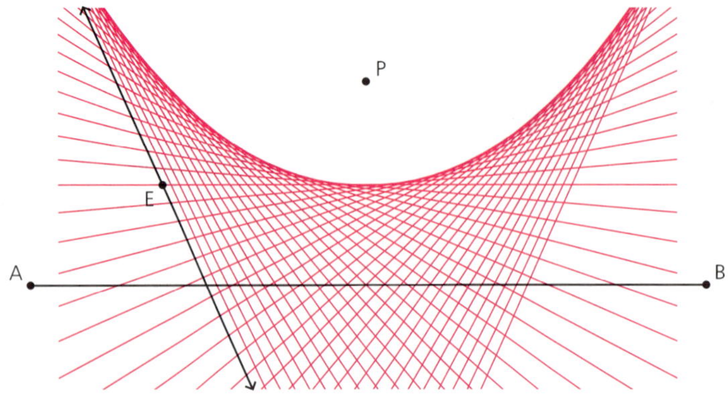

10. This shape appears to be a conic. But how can you be sure that the shape is a conic? What do you need to do?

11. You can make similar models of the conics, using waxed paper and *The Geometer's Sketchpad.* Start by cutting out a circle from another piece of waxed paper and marking a dot, or point, inside the circle, but not at the centre. Fold the paper so that the edge of the circle just touches the point. Continue creasing the paper by folding the edge at different angles.

12. What type of conic appears to be forming?

13. Try recreating the waxed-paper construction by using *The Geometer's Sketchpad.* Can you confirm your conjecture? What happens if the dot on the inside of the circle is near to the centre? very close to the edge?

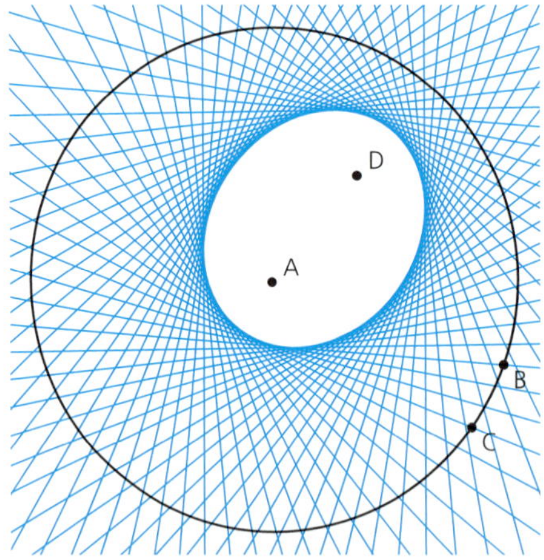

14. You can create another design by starting with a point outside the circle, rather than inside the circle. What shape do you construct?

EXPLORATION

The Parabola 7.6U

Many satellite dishes have a parabolic shape. In a parabolic reception dish, all of the rays are directed to a feedhorn, which is a fixed point or **focus** of the parabola. In this section, you will discover the role of the focus in the shape and equation of the parabola.

In grade 10, you learned that the graph of a quadratic equation, for example, $y = x^2$, is a parabola. In this section, you will look at a parabola in another way, using a locus definition that refers to both a **focus** and a fixed line, called the **directrix**.

In the previous section, you created a parabola using *The Geometer's Sketchpad.* This construction of the parabola featured a fixed point, or the focus, and a specific line, the directrix. When you folded the wax paper repeatedly, the fixed point, P, was the focus and the straight edge of the waxed paper was the directrix. The creation of the parabola was based on the locus definition of the parabola.

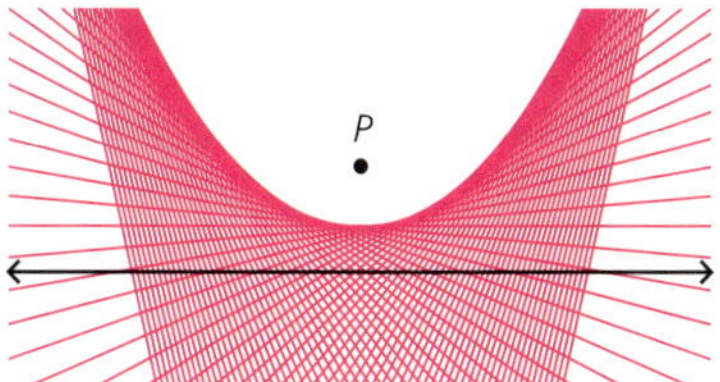

The **locus definition** of a **parabola**:
A parabola is the set or locus of points that are equidistant from a fixed point, the **focus**, and a fixed line, the **directrix**.

Part 1: Using the Locus Definition to Find the Equation of a Parabola

A parabola is the locus of all points in a plane that are the same distance from a fixed point, the **focus**, and a fixed line, the **directrix**.

Let $F(0, 2)$ be the focus and $y = -2$ be the directrix. Let $P(x, y)$ be an arbitrary point on the curve such that $PF = PT$, where PT is a perpendicular distance from the directrix to the curve.

Notice that the origin is a point on the curve since it is 2 units from both $F(0, 2)$ and the directrix.

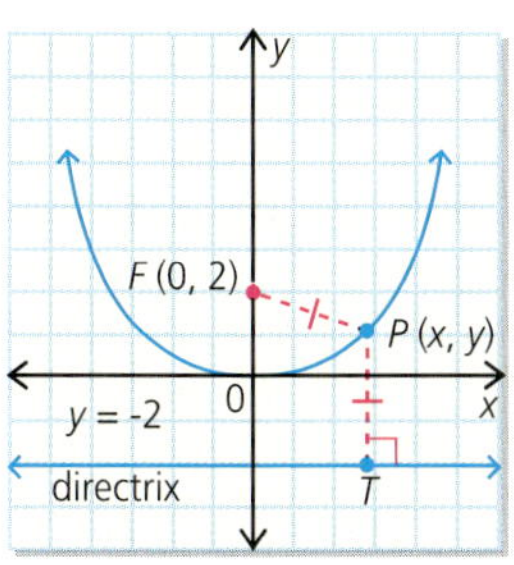

Apply the distance formula to create an equation for the curve.

$$\begin{aligned} PF &= PT && \text{Use the distance formula.} \\ \sqrt{(x-0)^2+(y-2)^2} &= \sqrt{(x-x)^2+(y+2)^2} && \text{Simplify.} \\ \sqrt{x^2+(y-2)^2} &= \sqrt{(y+2)^2} && \text{Square both sides.} \\ x^2+(y-2)^2 &= (y+2)^2 && \text{Expand.} \\ x^2+y^2-4y+4 &= y^2+4y+4 && \text{Simplify.} \\ x^2 &= 8y \end{aligned}$$

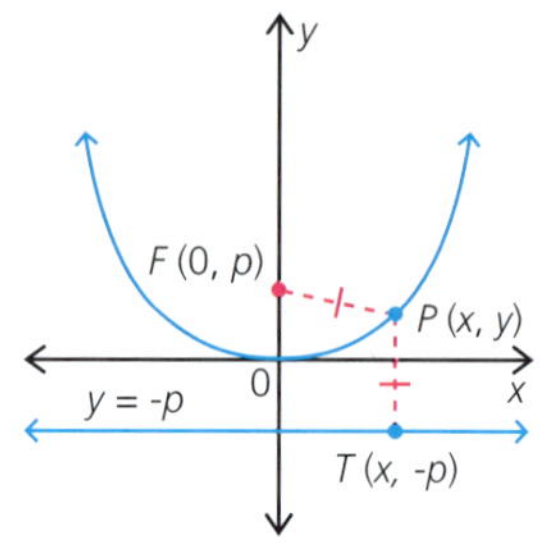

The equation $x^2 = 8y$ represents the locus of points that are equidistant from point (0, 2) and the line $y = -2$.

For any parabola, let $F(0, p)$ be the focus and let $y = -p$ be the directrix. Point $P(x, y)$ is a point on the parabola such that $PF = PT$.

Again notice that the origin is a point on the curve since it is equidistant from the focus and the directrix.

Apply the distance formula to create an equation for the curve.

$$\begin{aligned} PF &= PT && \text{Use the distance formula.} \\ \sqrt{(x-0)^2+(y-p)^2} &= \sqrt{(x-x)^2+(y-(-p))^2} && \text{Square both sides.} \\ x^2+(y-p)^2 &= (y+p)^2 && \text{Expand.} \\ x^2+y^2-2py+p^2 &= y^2+2py+p^2 && \text{Simplify.} \\ x^2 &= 4py \end{aligned}$$

The equation $x^2 = 4py$ describes a parabola with **vertex** (0, 0). The focus is $F(0, p)$ and the line $y = -p$ is the directrix. Notice that $|p|$ is the **focal length**, the distance from the vertex to the focus.

Example 1

State the directrix and the focus of the parabola $x^2 = 8y$.

Solution

The equation $x^2 = 8y$ can be written in the form $x^2 = 4py$, with $p = 2$. The focus is (0, 2) and the directrix is $y = -2$.

Example 2

State the directrix and the focus of the parabola $y^2 = 8x$.

Solution

Since y is squared rather than x, this parabola opens at the side and has the form $y^2 = 4px$. Also the focus is $(p, 0)$ and the directrix is $x = -p$. The focus of this parabola is (2, 0) and the directrix is $x = -2$.

Part 2: Translating the Parabola

In Part 1, the **vertex** of each parabola was the origin. If the vertex is not the origin, then the equation for the parabola changes.

Think, Do, Discuss

1. Begin with the equation $x^2 = 4y$. Sketch this graph.
2. Using what you know about transformations, predict the shape and features of the graph of $(x - 2)^2 = 4y$. Use a sketch or graphing technology to check your prediction. Compare your sketch with the one in step 1.
3. Predict the shape and features of the graph of $(x - 2)^2 = 4(y + 1)$. Check your prediction.
4. What is the vertex of $(x - 2)^2 = 4(y + 1)$? Describe the translation of the vertex from $x^2 = 4y$ to $(x - 2)^2 = 4(y + 1)$.
5. Graph $(x - 1)^2 = y + 2$, using this new method.
6. Graph $y = (x - 1)^2 - 2$, using techniques learned in grade 10.
7. Compare and explain the results of steps 5 and 6.
8. Predict the shape and features of the graph of $(y - 1)^2 = x$. Confirm your prediction by graphing $(y - 1)^2 = x$.
9. Equations have many different forms. The **standard form** of the parabola is $(x - h)^2 = 4p(y - k)$. The **general form** of the parabola is $x^2 + 2gx + 2fy + C = 0$. Change $(x - 3)^2 = 8y$ to its general form.

Focus 7.6U

Key Ideas

- A parabola is a conic section created by a plane slicing through the side and bottom of a cone at a diagonal angle.
- A **parabola** is the locus of all points in a plane that are the same distance from a fixed point, called the **focus**, and a fixed line, called the **directrix**.
- The **focal length** of a parabola is the distance from the vertex to the focus.
- If the vertex is (h, k), the directrix is parallel to the x-axis, and the distance from the vertex to the focus is $|p|$, then the **standard form** of the equation of a parabola is $(x - h)^2 = 4p(y - k)$. If p is positive, then the parabola opens up; if p is negative, then the parabola opens down.

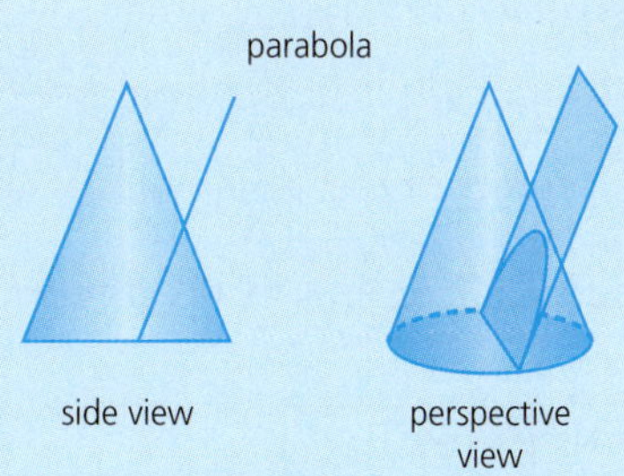

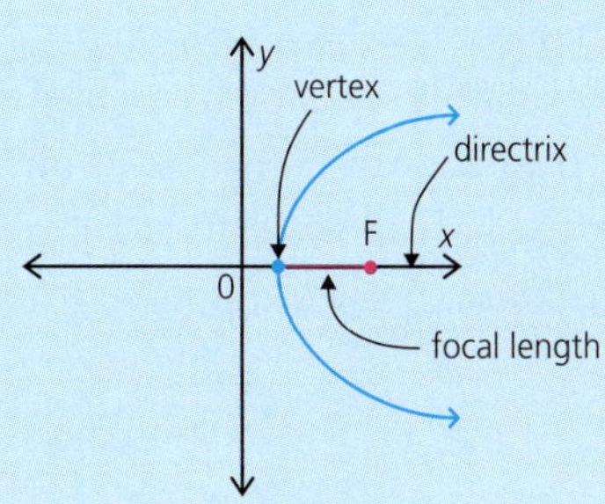

- If the vertex is (h, k), the directrix is parallel to the y-axis, and the distance from the vertex to the focus is $|p|$, then the **standard form** of the equation of a parabola is $(y - k)^2 = 4p(x - h)$. If p is positive, then the parabola opens to the right; if p is negative, then the parabola opens to the left.
- The **general form** of the equation of a parabola is $x^2 + 2gx + 2fy + C = 0$, if the directrix is parallel to the x-axis, and $y^2 + 2gx + 2fy + C = 0$, if the directrix is parallel to the y-axis.

Example 1

The general form of a parabola is $y^2 - 4x + 2y = 51$. Write the standard form of this conic and graph it.

Solution

To change the general form to the standard form of the conic, complete the square.

$$\begin{aligned} y^2 - 4x + 2y &= 51 && \text{Rearrange.} \\ y^2 + 2y &= 51 + 4x && \text{Complete the square.} \\ y^2 + 2y + 1 &= 51 + 4x + 1 \\ (y + 1)^2 &= 4x + 52 \\ (y + 1)^2 &= 4(x + 13) \end{aligned}$$

This parabola opens to the right, and its vertex is $(-13, -1)$.

Example 2

State the focus and the directrix of $x^2 = -5y$.

Solution

The equation is in the form $x^2 = 4py$.

The vertex of the parabola is at the origin, and $-5 = 4p$ or $p = -\frac{5}{4}$.

The focal length is $\frac{5}{4}$, the directrix is $y = \frac{5}{4}$, and the focus is $\left(0, -\frac{5}{4}\right)$.

Example 3

A chain of fast-food restaurants has decided to erect a large green arch, in the shape of a parabola, outside of each of its restaurants. Each arch will be 30 m high and will be 16 m wide at its widest point. A rectangular sign will be attached to each arch so that the base of the sign is 20 m from the ground. How wide, to the nearest centimetre, must the sign be if its base just fits across the arch?

Solution

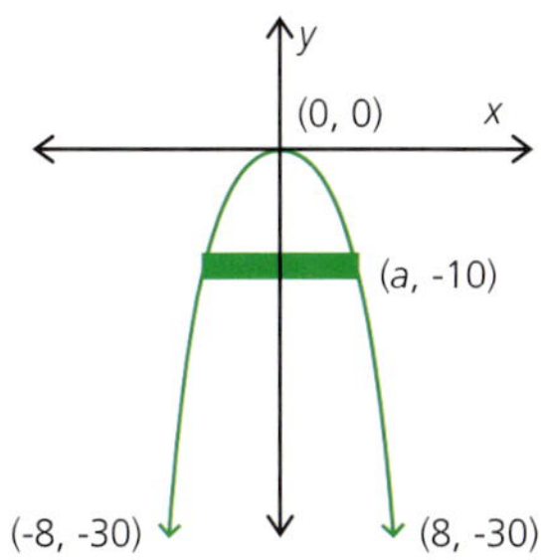

Draw a diagram and place the vertex of the parabola at the origin.

Label the graph with the given information and add information as you solve the problem. Since the parabola is symmetric, 30 m tall, and 16 m wide at the base, the two points on the curve are $(8, -30)$ and $(-8, -30)$. Then find the equation.

Since the origin is $(0, 0)$, the equation is in the form $x^2 = 4py$.

Substitute one of the points, $(8, -30)$, in the equation to find p.

$$\begin{aligned} 8^2 &= 4p(-30) && \text{Solve for } p. \\ 64 &= 4p(-30) \\ 64 &= -120p \\ \frac{64}{-120} &= p \\ \frac{-8}{15} &= p \end{aligned}$$

The equation is $x^2 = \frac{-32}{15}y$.

Use the equation to determine the width of the sign.

Since the base of the sign must sit 20 m above the ground, let $(a, -10)$ represent the bottom right corner of the sign. Substitute these coordinates in the equation.

$$\begin{aligned} a^2 &= \frac{-32}{15}(-10) && \text{Solve for } a. \\ a^2 &= \frac{320}{15} \\ a &= \pm\sqrt{\frac{320}{15}} \\ a &\doteq 4.62. \end{aligned}$$

Since a represents one-half of the width of the sign, the width of the sign is $2a$, or about 9.24 m.

Example 4

Find the equation for the locus of points that are equidistant from point $(0, 2)$ and from the line $y = -4$. State the vertex and the **focal length** of the curve.

Solution

A diagram is useful. Let $P(x, y)$ be a point on the curve and $D(x, -4)$ be a point on the directrix.

The distance from the focus to $P(x, y)$ is the same as the distance from the directrix at $D(x, -4)$ to $P(x, y)$, that is, $PF = PD$. Use the distance formula to find the equation.

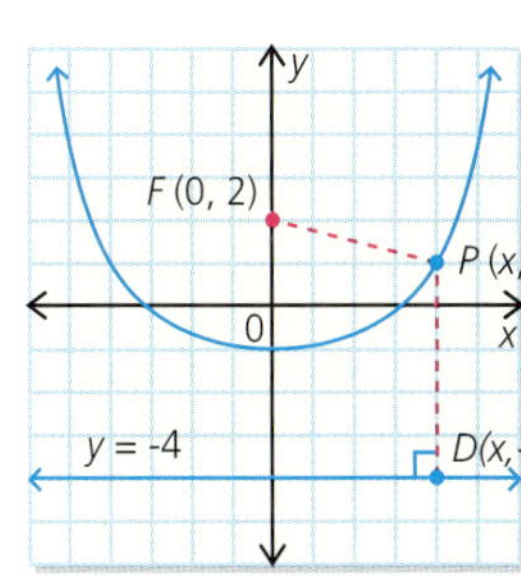

$PF = PD$	Use the distance formula.
$\sqrt{(x - 0)^2 + (y - 2)^2} = \sqrt{(x - x)^2 + [y - (-4)]^2}$	Simplify.
$\sqrt{x^2 + (y - 2)^2} = \sqrt{(y + 4)^2}$	Square both sides.
$x^2 + (y - 2)^2 = (y + 4)^2$	Expand.
$x^2 + y^2 - 4y + 4 = y^2 + 8y + 16$	Simplify.
$x^2 = 12y + 12$	Factor.
$x^2 = 12(y + 1)$	

The standard form for the equation of the locus is $x^2 = 12(y + 1)$. The vertex is $(0, -1)$, and the focal length is 3 units.

Practise, Apply, Solve 7.6U

A

1. State the focus and the directrix of each of the following parabolas.

(a) $x^2 = -16y$ (b) $y^2 = 15x$ (c) $y = x^2$

(d) $2x^2 = y$ (e) $y^2 - 8x = 0$ (f) $10x^2 = y$

2. **Knowledge and Understanding:** Find the vertex and state the direction of opening for each parabola.

(a) $16(y - 4) = x^2$ (b) $y^2 = 6(x - 2)$

(c) $x = (y + 12)^2$ (d) $y = 2(x - 3)^2$

(e) $(x - 3)^2 = -12y + 24$ (f) $x + 2 = (y - 1)^2$

3. The equation of each parabola is in general form. Write each equation in standard form. State the vertex and the direction of opening.

(a) $y^2 - 4x - 4y + 8 = 0$ (b) $x^2 - 4y - 8 = 0$

(c) $x^2 - 2x - 4y + 5 = 0$ (d) $y^2 - 2x + 6y + 11 = 0$

(e) $y^2 - 8x - 2y - 15 = 0$ (f) $x^2 - 4x - 2y - 16 = 0$

4. (a) Sketch each parabola in question 3.

(b) State the domain and the range of each parabola in question 3.

5. **Communication:** Which form of the equation of the parabola, general or standard, is more useful? Support your argument.

6. Find the equation of the locus of a point that moves so that it is equidistant from the line $x = 4$ and point $(-4, 0)$.

7. Given the following information about each parabola, find the equation of the parabola.

(a) focus $(3, 0)$, directrix $x = -3$ (b) focus $(0, -2)$, directrix $y = 2$

(c) vertex $(0, 0)$, directrix $x = 4$ (d) vertex $(0, 0)$, focus $(-0.5, 0)$

B

8. A parabola has a horizontal axis of symmetry and its vertex is (0, 0). The curve of the parabola passes through $P(-8, -4)$.

(a) Find the equation of the parabola.

(b) What are the coordinates of the focus?

(c) What is the equation of the directrix?

9. The cross section of a parabolic reflector of a headlight is shown in the diagram. The distance from B to C is 32 cm and the distance from A to D is 8 cm. Determine where the bulb should be located if it is positioned at the focus.

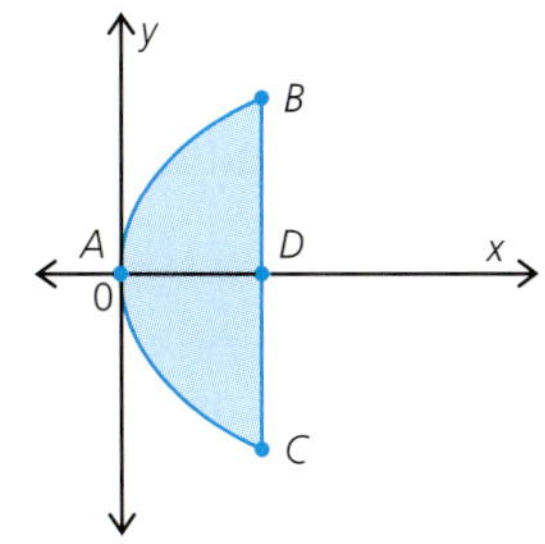

10. **Application:** Parabolic satellite dishes are deep, average, or shallow, according to the ratio of the focal length, f, to the diameter, D, of the dish at its widest part.

deep: $\frac{f}{D} < 0.3$; shallow: $\frac{f}{D} > 0.45$; average: $0.3 \leq \frac{f}{D} \leq 0.45$

Deeper dishes are preferred because they are less susceptible to interference from environmental noise. If a parabolic satellite dish is 5 m in diameter, determine the range of the focal distance for each type of dish.

(a) shallow (b) average (c) deep

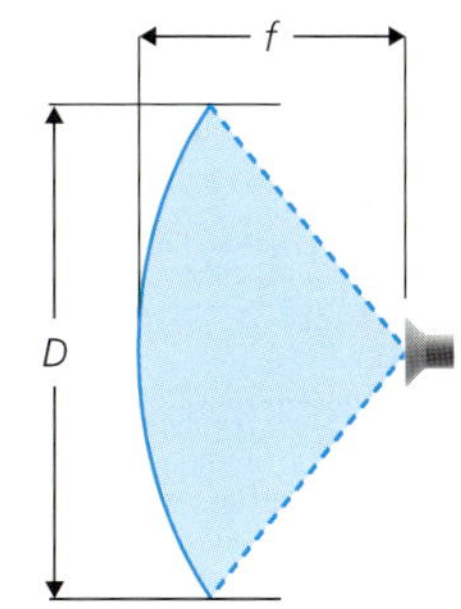

11. The bulb, or focus, of a headlight's parabolic reflector is 4 cm away from the vertex of the parabola. Imagine that the vertex is at the origin. Determine the equation of the cross section of the reflector. If the depth of the reflector is 6 cm, what is the area of the circular piece of glass that covers the open end of the reflector?

12. The receiver of a satellite dish is at the focus of the parabolic dish. The focus is 80 cm from the vertex of the dish. If the dish is 4 m in diameter, find its depth.

13. To graph $(x - 2)^2 = y + 2$ using a graphing calculator, you would have to rearrange the equation only a little. Describe how you would rearrange the equation to graph $(y - 2)^2 = x + 2$ using a graphing calculator. Graph both equations using a graphing calculator.

14. Find the equation of each parabola, given the focus and the directrix.

(a) focus (2, 0), directrix $x = -4$

(b) focus (0, 4), directrix $y = 1$

(c) focus (1, 2), directrix $y = 0$

15. Find the equation of a parabola whose vertex is (1, 2) and whose vertical directrix is 2 units to the left of the focus.

16. **Check Your Understanding:** Draw a diagram of a parabola with the vertex at the origin, labelling the focus and the directrix. Then draw a diagram of a congruent parabola with vertex $(-2, 3)$. Include the focus and the directrix in your new diagram.

17. A parabolic arch supports a bridge that is built across a stream. The arch is 24 m wide and the height of the arch is 9 m. Find the length of the supporting vertical steel girder that is 4 m from the centre of the arch.

18. Find the equation of the parabola that passes through (5, 2), that has a vertical axis of symmetry, and that has a maximum value at (4, 3).

19. **Thinking, Inquiry, Problem Solving:** In grade 10, you learned that one form of the equation of the parabola is $y = a(x - h)^2 + k$. Now you have seen that another form is $(x - h)^2 = 4p(y - k)$.
   (a) How are these equations similar? different?
   (b) How can you go from one form to the other?
   (c) What are the advantages and disadvantages of each form? Support your arguments.

20. How many points of intersection are possible between two parabolas? Draw a diagram to show each case.

21. Determine the coordinates of the points of intersection between the parabolas defined by $y = x^2 - 5x - 4$ and $y = -2x^2 + 3x - 1$.

The Chapter Problem—Designing a Bridge

In this section, you have worked with equations of parabolas. Apply what you have learned to create a parabolic arch.

CP9. Decide where you will place the axes on the parabolic arch and then write the equation of the curve.

CP10. Graph the curve.

CP11. Determine whether two trucks will be able to pass, side by side, under the arch. There should be space between the trucks and at each side of the road. You may have to adjust some of your dimensions. If so, justify your changes.

CP12. Is this a good design?

Reflective Properties of Conics

7.7U

Functions and Relations

EXPLORATION

This chapter has referred to satellites, conical reflectors in flashlights and headlights, and other reflection devices. Why are these items designed as conics? You will need to examine the reflective properties of conics to understand their significance.

You can easily create a model of a parabolic reflector. Sketch the graph of $x^2 = 8y$ on a large sheet of graph paper and mark the focus. (You could choose any other parabolic equation, but make sure the graph will fit on the paper.) Bend a thin strip of cardboard and place it accurately and securely along the parabola. Carefully roll a marble toward the curve making sure to roll the marble in a direction that is parallel to the y-axis. Roll the marble several times, starting from different points, but always roll the marble in a direction that is parallel to the y-axis.

Think, Do, Discuss

1. Does the marble's path cross the focus? Explain.
2. Draw a diagram of this model. Using the diagram, demonstrate why the marble's path crosses the focus.
3. The reflective properties of the parabola appear in the design of flashlights, car headlights, and satellite dishes. Can you find other instances of parabolic reflectors?

When you flick car headlights from bright to dim, think about conics. The bright beam is created by the light source at the focal point; its rays are parallel to the parabola's axis of symmetry. When you dim the headlights, the light source changes location and the rays point down and up. The rays pointing up are shielded—only the rays pointing down are reflected out.

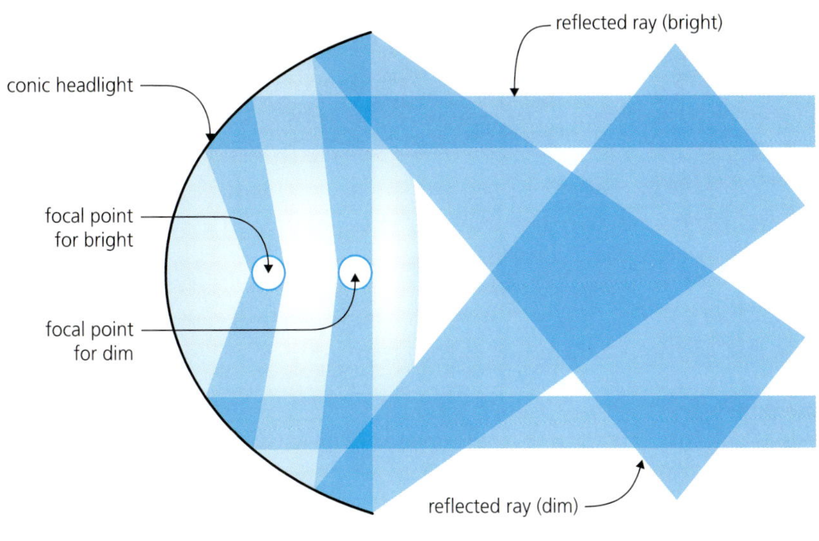

4. Try to create a model of an ellipse that is similar to the model of the parabolic reflector. This time, start with one marble at one focal point and "shoot" it toward any point on the ellipse. Shoot the marble from this focal point at several different points along the ellipse. What do you notice?

5. Draw a diagram of this model. Discuss why you think that, if you were to roll a marble from one focal point to a point on the ellipse, the marble would roll back through the other focal point.

Imagine an elliptical pool table with only one pocket located at one of the foci. If you place a ball at the other focus and roll it toward the cushion of the pool table, the ball will always be reflected to the pocket.

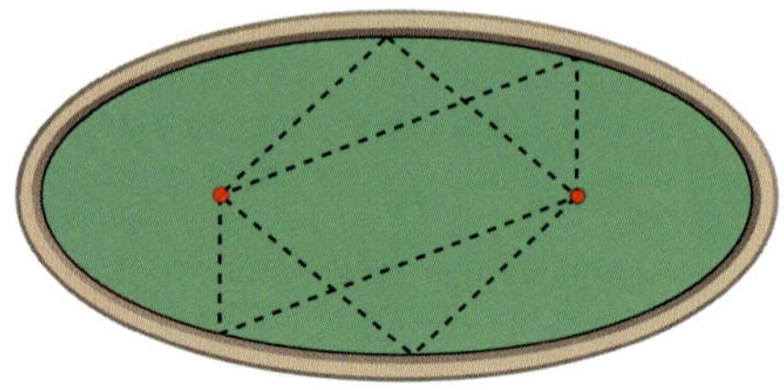

If a tangent is drawn to the curve at the point where the ball strikes the cushion, the angle at which the ball strikes the cushion is equal to the angle at which it rebounds from the cushion. In this way, the ball will always roll toward the pocket.

6. If you wanted to build an elliptical pool table with a length of 2 m and a width of 1.8 m, then where would you place the "pocket"?

Did You Know?

A "whispering gallery" is another instance of the reflective properties of an ellipse. A whispering gallery is a large room where the walls of the gallery, or the dome above it, are in the shape of an ellipse. If a person stands at one focal point of the ellipse and whispers, then someone standing at the other focal point can hear the whisper. There are many whispering galleries in the world. The ceiling in St. Paul's Cathedral in London, England is a great dome, 34 m in diameter. The dome's shape is an ellipse. If someone, facing the wall of the cathedral's whispering gallery, whispers, then the whisper is clearly audible on the opposite side of the cathedral.

One room in the National Statuary Hall in Washington, D.C., was unintentionally constructed as a whispering gallery in the nineteenth century. However, the room was unsuitable for meetings because of the echoes and was reconstructed.

The room where the city council meets in Coquitlam, British Columbia, has an elliptical dome ceiling. This room was constructed so that it would not be a whispering gallery.

Graphing Conics Using Technology

In section 7.3, you graphed circles using a graphing calculator. In several other sections, you also used a graphing calculator for graphing other conics. You can use *Zap-a-Graph* to graph a conic, without having to split the conic into parts, and to see the effect of translating a conic.

The **Define** menu is one of the menus listed in the first screen. This menu includes **Circle**, **Ellipse**, **Hyperbola**, and **Parabola**.

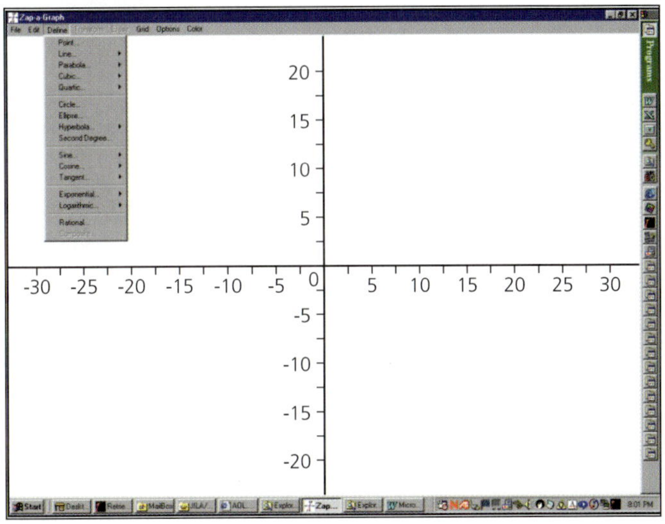

Begin by choosing **Parabola**.

1. You must then choose a form of the equation for a parabola. You should recognize most of the forms, but choose **n(y + k) = (x + h)^2**.
2. Enter these values: $n = 8$, $h = 2$, and $k = -1$.
3. Before you click **Plot**, predict the coordinates of the vertex of the parabola. Now click **Plot**. Did you correctly predict the vertex?
4. Next create an ellipse. Choose **Ellipse** from the **Define** menu and enter these values: $h = 2$, $k = 1$, $a = 6$, and $b = 4$. Then **Plot**. Does the graph confirm what you know about ellipses? You may want to change the scale on the graph by choosing **Scale** from the **Grid** menu and then entering different values.
5. Graph, or list the steps for graphing, $\frac{(x-2)^2}{36} + \frac{(y-1)^2}{16} = 1$, using a graphing calculator.
6. Graph, or list the steps for graphing, $\frac{(x-2)^2}{36} + \frac{(y-1)^2}{16} = 1$, using *Zap-a-Graph*. Compare the graphing methods in this step with those in step 5. Which method requires fewer steps?

7. Next create a hyperbola. Choose **Hyperbola** from the **Define** menu. Then choose the first option and enter the same values as you did for the ellipse in step 4 ($h = 2$, $k = 1$, $a = 6$, and $b = 4$). Plot this hyperbola and the ellipse on the same set of axes. What is common about the shapes? What is different?

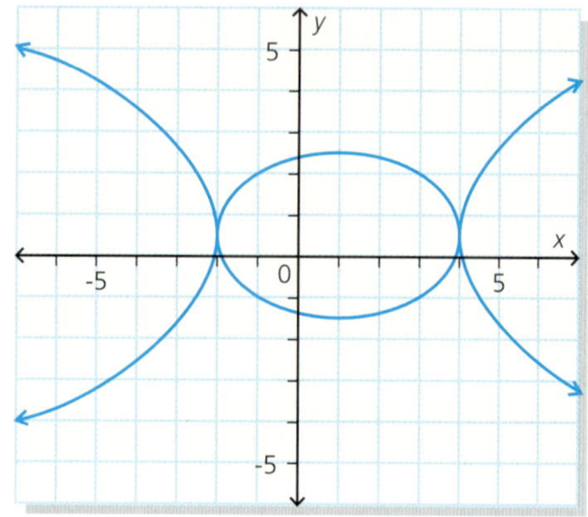

step 7

8. Before examining the hyperbola in more detail in the next section, experiment with this conic. What values of h and k would produce a hyperbola that is centred at the origin?

9. Choose **Hyperbola** from the **Define** menu. Then choose the first option. Enter these values: $h = 0$, $k = 0$, $a = 4$, and $b = 6$. Describe the graph.

10. Again choose **Hyperbola** from the **Define** menu, but choose the second form for the equation of the hyperbola. Enter the values for h, k, a, and b in step 4 ($h = 2$, $k = 1$, $a = 6$, and $b = 4$), and plot this hyperbola on the same set of axes. What is different about this graph? What is different about the equation?

11. Make a conjecture about the relationships between the equation of a hyperbola and its graph, referring to the x-intercepts, the y-intercepts, and the direction of the axis of symmetry. Test your conjectures using *Zap-a-Graph*.

Practice 7.8U

1. For each equation,
   i. determine the type of conic
   ii. describe the graph
   iii. use graphing technology to graph the conic
   iv. verify your description

   (a) $y = x^2 + 4$ (b) $x^2 + y^2 = 9$ (c) $4x^2 + y^2 = 64$
   (d) $\frac{(x-2)^2}{9} + \frac{(y+1)^2}{16} = 1$ (e) $(x + 3)^2 + y^2 = 4$ (f) $(x - 2)^2 = 2(y + 1)$

2. (a) Determine the equation of the ellipse with x-intercepts ± 3 and y-intercepts ± 2.
   (b) Graph your equation.
   (c) Verify that the graph has the given x- and y-intercepts.

3. For the equation $x^2 = 2y$,
   i. determine the new equation for each translation
   ii. graph the new equation in a different colour
   iii. determine if the new equation is correct

   (a) translation of 3 units left and 2 units up
   (b) translation of 1 unit right and 1 unit down
   (c) translation of 2 units right and 3 units up
   (d) translation of 1 unit left and 5 units down

The Hyperbola 7.9U

Functions and Relations

A hyperbola resembles a parabola, but it has two distinct sections that are formed by a plane slicing through the cone at a vertical angle.

You can also create a hyperbola using *The Geometer's Sketchpad.* Constructing a hyperbola is similar to constructing an ellipse (section 7.5). But, instead of starting with a point inside the circle, choose a point outside the circle.

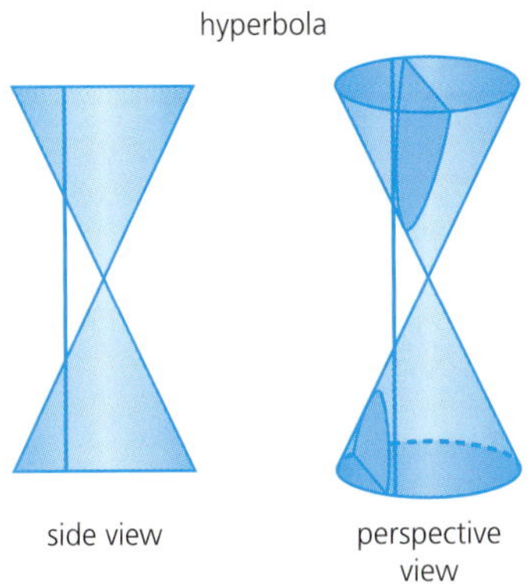

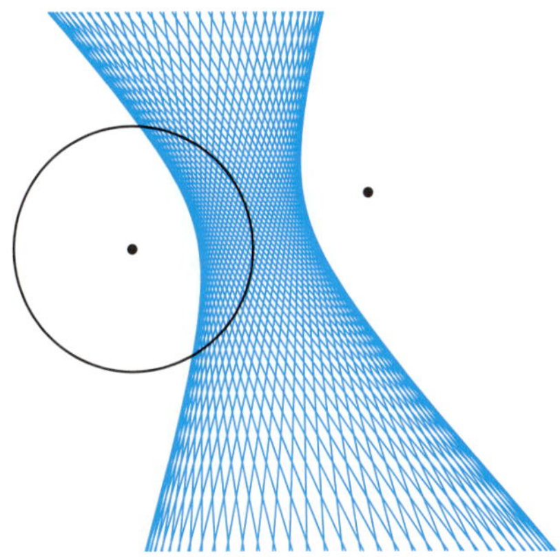

The **locus definition** of a **hyperbola**:
A hyperbola is the set or locus of points, in a plane, whose distances from two fixed points have a constant difference. The two fixed points are called the **foci**.

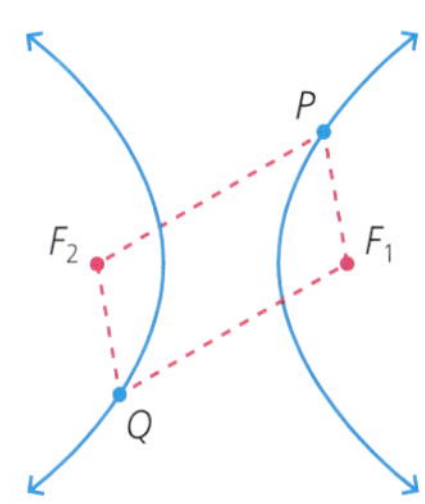

In other words, if P and Q are points on the hyperbola and F_1 and F_2 are the foci, then

$$|PF_1 - PF_2| = |QF_1 - QF_2|$$

This locus definition explains why the LORAN (LOng RAnge Navigation) navigational system relies on hyperbolas.

Two transmitters, which are some distance apart, emit radio signals at the same time. A boat's navigator records the difference between the times when the signals reach the boat.

The transmitters, A_1 and A_2, are the foci of a hyperbolic curve. The curve is the locus of all points whose distances from the foci have a constant difference, that is, the interval or the difference between the times.

The navigator refers to a map that shows a series of hyperbolic curves, called LORAN lines of position. The navigator finds the position of the boat on the map by matching the time interval to a specific curve on the map. This position is an estimate because there are many points on the curve, any one of which could be the boat's position.

By switching to another pair of LORAN transmitters, B_1 and B_2, and repeating the steps, the navigator can find another hyberbola representing the boat's position. To better estimate the boat's position, the navigator locates the intersection of the two LORAN lines, X. The boat is at one of the places marked X. Determining the position of the boat in this way is similar to finding the intersection point of two curves.

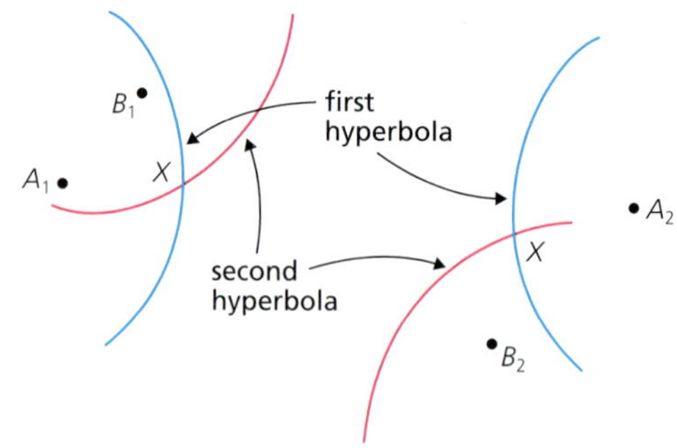

Part 1: Using the Locus Definition to Find the Equation of a Hyperbola

Find the equation for the set or locus of points whose distances from two fixed points, $F_1(-5, 0)$ and $F_2(5, 0)$, have a constant difference of 6.

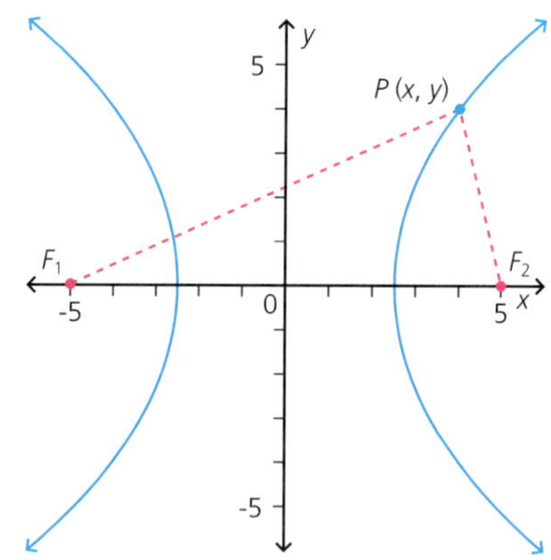

Let $P(x, y)$ be any point in the locus. The constant difference is 6.

$$\begin{aligned}
|PF_1 - PF_2| &= 6 && \text{Use the distance formula.}\\
\sqrt{(x-5)^2+y^2} - \sqrt{(x+5)^2+y^2} &= 6 && \text{Isolate a radical.}\\
\sqrt{(x-5)^2+y^2} &= 6 + \sqrt{(x+5)^2+y^2} && \text{Square both sides.}\\
(x-5)^2+y^2 &= 36 + 12\sqrt{(x+5)^2+y^2}\\
&\quad + (x+5)^2 + y^2 && \text{Expand.}\\
x^2 - 10x - 25 + y^2 &= 36 + 12\sqrt{(x+5)^2+y^2}\\
&\quad + x^2 + 10x + 25 + y^2 && \text{Isolate the radical.}\\
-20x - 36 &= 12\sqrt{(x+5)^2+y^2} && \text{Divide both sides by 4.}\\
-5x - 9 &= 3\sqrt{(x+5)^2+y^2} && \text{Square both sides.}\\
(-5x-9)^2 &= 9[(x+5)^2+y^2] && \text{Expand and simplify.}\\
25x^2 + 90x + 81 &= 9(x^2 + 10x + 25 + y^2)\\
25x^2 + 90x + 81 &= 9x^2 + 90x + 225 + 9y^2 && \text{Simplify.}\\
16x^2 - 9y^2 &= 144\\
\frac{x^2}{9} - \frac{y^2}{16} &= 1
\end{aligned}$$

Think, Do, Discuss

1. This equation, $\frac{x^2}{9} - \frac{y^2}{16} = 1$, looks similar to the equation of an ellipse. Compare this equation to the equation of an ellipse. What is different and what is the same?

2. Determine both the x- and y-intercepts of $\frac{x^2}{9} - \frac{y^2}{16} = 1$. Draw the graph by finding six other points. You also could use graphing technology, such as *Zap-a-Graph*, or rearrange the equation so that you can enter it into a graphing calculator.

3. The foci of this hyperbola are $(-5, 0)$ and $(5, 0)$. Then $c = 5$. If $\frac{x^2}{9} - \frac{y^2}{16} = 1$ is in the form $\frac{x^2}{a^2} - \frac{y^2}{b^2} = 1$, state the values of a and b.

4. Determine a relationship between a, b, and c.

5. The segment between the **vertices** is called the **transverse axis**. Find the length of the transverse axis.

6. Consider the other line of symmetry. The **conjugate axis** is perpendicular to the transverse axis and passes through the **centre** of the hyperbola. This axis is the segment between $(0, -b)$ and $(0, b)$. What is its length?

7. Predict what would change if you were to graph $\frac{x^2}{9} - \frac{y^2}{16} = -1$. What would be the x- or y-intercepts? Draw the graph to confirm your prediction. In this case, the equation is in the form $\frac{x^2}{b^2} - \frac{y^2}{a^2} = -1$. State the values of a, b, and c and state the foci of this hyperbola.

8. Create a table or use graphing technology to graph $\frac{x^2}{4} - \frac{y^2}{36} = 1$ and $\frac{x^2}{25} - \frac{y^2}{4} = -1$. Describe the graphs, stating the x- and y-intercepts.

9. Using your knowledge of transformations, describe the graph of $\frac{(x-1)^2}{4} - \frac{y^2}{36} = 1$, without graphing the equation. Verify your answer with technology.

10. Describe the graph of $\frac{(x+2)^2}{25} - \frac{(y-1)^2}{4} = 1$. Verify your answer with technology.

Part 2: Giving Shape to a Hyperbola

It is often difficult to adequately determine the shape of a specific hyperbola if you know just a few points. But it is possible to draw an accurate graph. To begin with, you can easily locate the vertices. It would also be helpful to draw the defining "boundary" lines that are called **asymptotes**. The asymptote of a hyperbola is a line that the curve approaches, but never crosses, as x or y grow larger.

Example 1

Determine the asymptotes of the hyperbola $\frac{x^2}{9} - \frac{y^2}{16} = 1$.

Solution

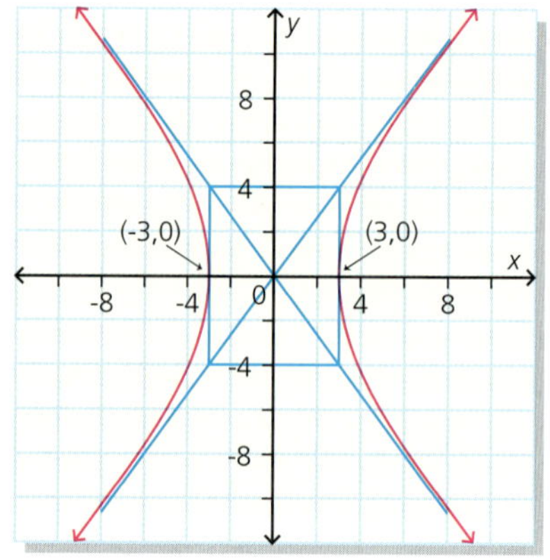

Recall that the values of a and b are 3 and 4.

To draw a graph of this hyperbola, mark the values of a and b, as shown, on the horizontal and vertical axes. Draw a rectangle, as shown. Draw and extend the diagonals of this rectangle. The extended diagonals are the asymptotes of the hyperbola.

Draw the curves of the hyperbola so that they pass through the vertices and gradually become close to, but do not touch, the asymptotes.

To determine the equations of the asymptotes, first find their slopes. The slopes are $\frac{4}{3}$ and $-\frac{4}{3}$. Since the asymptotes pass through the origin, the y-intercepts are both (0, 0). The equations of the asymptotes are $y = \frac{4}{3}x$ and $y = -\frac{4}{3}x$.

Notice that point (3, 4) is on the asymptote. If you substitute (3, 4) in the equation of the hyperbola, $\frac{x^2}{9} - \frac{y^2}{16} = 1$, you will see that this point cannot be on the hyperbola. Why?

Consolidate Your Understanding

1. Given $\frac{x^2}{a^2} - \frac{y^2}{b^2} = 1$, determine the general equations of the asymptotes by drawing a rectangle based on the values of a and b.

Focus 7.9U

Key Ideas

- The **standard form** of the equation for a hyperbola that is centred about the origin, with its foci, intercepts, and transverse axis on the x-axis, is

$$\frac{x^2}{a^2} - \frac{y^2}{b^2} = 1$$

The vertices are $(a, 0)$ and $(-a, 0)$, and the asymptotes are $y = \frac{b}{a}x$ and $y = -\frac{b}{a}x$.

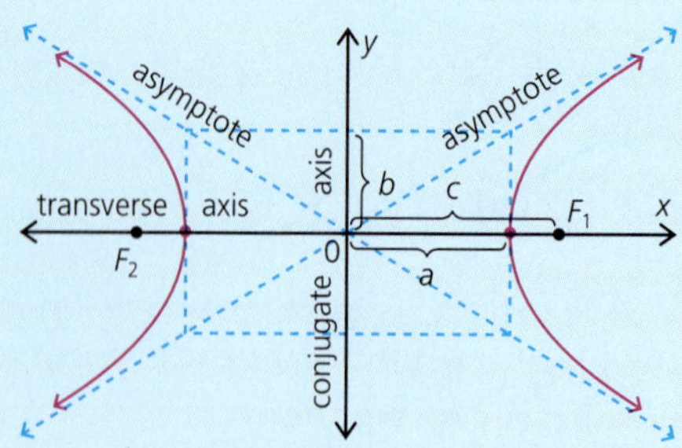

- The **standard form** of the equation for a hyperbola that is centred about the origin, with its foci, intercepts, and transverse axis on the y-axis, is

$$\frac{x^2}{b^2} - \frac{y^2}{a^2} = -1 \text{ or } \frac{y^2}{a^2} - \frac{x^2}{b^2} = 1$$

The vertices are $(0, a)$ and $(0, -a)$, and the asymptotes are

$$y = \frac{a}{b}x \text{ and } y = -\frac{a}{b}x$$

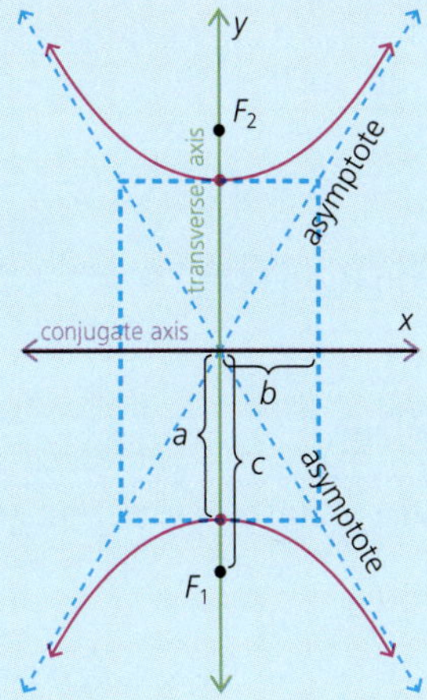

- A hyperbola has two lines of symmetry that are perpendicular to one another.
- These lines of symmetry contain the **transverse axis**, the end points of which are the vertices, and the **conjugate axis** of the hyperbola.
- If the transverse axis is along the x-axis, then the vertices are the x-intercepts of the hyperbola. If the transverse axis is along the y-axis, then the vertices are the y-intercepts.
- A hyperbola has two foci, F_1 and F_2, that lie on the transverse axis and are each $|c|$ units from the centre.
- A hyperbola is the set or locus of all points, $P(x, y)$, in a plane, whose distances from two fixed points, F_1 and F_2, have a constant difference: $|PF_1 - PF_2| = 2a$, the length of the transverse axis.
- The relationship between a, b, and c is

$$c^2 = a^2 + b^2$$

- A hyperbola that has been translated so that its centre is at (h, k) is in the form

$$\frac{(x-h)^2}{a^2} - \frac{(y-k)^2}{b^2} = 1, \text{ for a horizontal transverse axis, or}$$
$$\frac{(x-h)^2}{b^2} - \frac{(y-k)^2}{a^2} = -1, \text{ for a vertical transverse axis}$$

Example 2

Find the equation of the hyperbola with foci $(-4, 0)$ and $(4, 0)$ and vertices $(-3, 0)$ and $(3, 0)$.

Solution

Since the vertices are on the x-axis, the equation of the hyperbola will be in the form $\frac{x^2}{a^2} - \frac{y^2}{b^2} = 1$.

Since $(-4, 0)$ and $(4, 0)$ are the foci, then $c = 4$. Since $(-3, 0)$ and $(3, 0)$ are the vertices, then $a = 3$. The relationship between a, b, and c is $c^2 = a^2 + b^2$.

$$4^2 = 3^2 + b^2$$
$$16 = 9 + b^2$$
$$7 = b^2$$
$$b = \pm\sqrt{7}$$

The equation is $\frac{x^2}{9} - \frac{y^2}{7} = 1$.

Example 3

State the length of the transverse and the conjugate axes and also the vertices of the hyperbola $\frac{(x-1)^2}{4} - \frac{(y+4)^2}{16} = -1$.

Solution

Think of the equation as if the hyperbola were centred about the origin.

$$\frac{x^2}{4} - \frac{y^2}{16} = -1$$

The vertices are (0, 4) and (0, −4). The transverse axis is 8 units long. Since $b = 2$, the conjugate axis is 4 units long. You will see from the original equation that the hyperbola has been "translated" 1 unit right and 4 units down. This translation does not change the lengths of the transverse and the conjugate axes. The vertices, however, are translated with the hyperbola. The vertices are then (1, −8) and (1, 0).

Example 4

Points *A* and *B* are 1 km apart. Louise determines, because the sound of an explosion is heard at these points at different times, that the location of the explosion was 600 m closer to *A* than it was to *B*. Show that the location of the explosion is defined by a hyperbola and state its equation.

Solution

Think of points *A* and *B* as the foci of a hyperbola. Let point *E* be the location of the explosion.

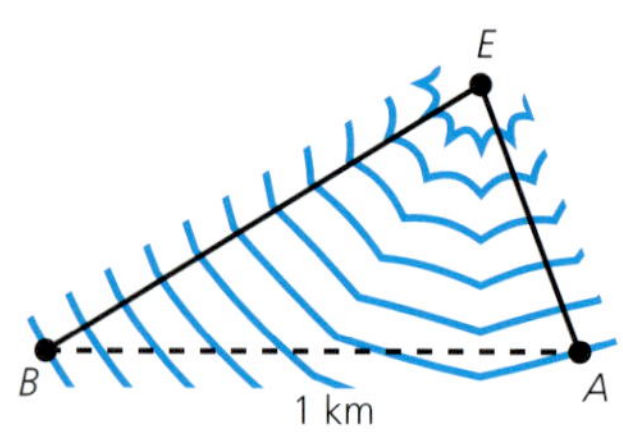

Given: $AE - EB = 600$

Since the difference between the distances is constant, you can define a hyperbola with *A* and *B* as the foci.

$AE - EB = 2a$ and $a = 300$. Since *A* and *B* are 1000 m apart, then $c = 500$.

$$a^2 + b^2 = c^2$$
$$300^2 + b^2 = 500^2$$
$$90\ 000 + b^2 = 250\ 000$$
$$b^2 = 160\ 000$$
$$b = 400$$

The equation is $\frac{x^2}{90\ 000} - \frac{y^2}{160\ 000} = 1$.

Example 5

Find the equations of the asymptotes of $4x^2 - 9y^2 = 36$.

Solution

$$4x^2 - 9y^2 = 36 \qquad \text{Divide by 36.}$$
$$\frac{x^2}{9} - \frac{y^2}{4} = 1$$

Then $a = 3$ and $b = 2$. Since the equations of the asymptotes are $y = \pm\frac{b}{a}x$, then the asymptotes in this case are $y = \frac{2}{3}x$ and $y = -\frac{2}{3}x$.

Practise, Apply, Solve 7.9U

A

1. Determine the intercepts of the following.

(a) $4x^2 - 9y^2 = 36$
(b) $2x^2 - 3y^2 = -12$
(c) $x^2 - y^2 = 18$
(d) $3y^2 - x^2 = 36$
(e) $6x^2 - 10y^2 = 120$
(f) $5x^2 - 10y^2 = 50$

2. Determine the values of a, b, and c for each of the following hyperbolas.

(a) $\frac{x^2}{5} - \frac{y^2}{20} = 1$
(b) $\frac{x^2}{36} - \frac{y^2}{9} = 1$
(c) $\frac{x^2}{5} - \frac{y^2}{20} = -1$
(d) $\frac{x^2}{4} - \frac{y^2}{16} = 1$
(e) $\frac{x^2}{8} - \frac{y^2}{12} = -1$
(f) $\frac{x^2}{144} - \frac{y^2}{81} = 1$

3. Sketch each of the following hyperbolas and label

i. the intercepts **ii.** the foci **iii.** the asymptotes

(a) $\frac{x^2}{4} - \frac{y^2}{9} = 1$
(b) $\frac{x^2}{5} - \frac{y^2}{16} = 1$
(c) $\frac{x^2}{25} - \frac{y^2}{81} = -1$
(d) $\frac{y^2}{8} - \frac{x^2}{25} = 1$
(e) $\frac{x^2}{18} - \frac{y^2}{9} = -1$
(f) $\frac{y^2}{16} - \frac{x^2}{9} = 1$

4. **Knowledge and Understanding:** Find the coordinates of the centre and the vertices for each of the following hyperbolas. Then graph the hyperbola, including the asymptotes in your sketch.

(a) $\frac{x^2}{9} - \frac{y^2}{16} = 1$
(b) $\frac{x^2}{25} - \frac{y^2}{4} = 1$
(c) $2x^2 - y^2 = 8$
(d) $81x^2 - 36y^2 = 2916$
(e) $\frac{(x-2)^2}{9} - \frac{y^2}{25} = 1$
(f) $(x + 6)^2 - 4(y - 1)^2 = 1$

5. Find the equations of the asymptotes for each hyperbola.

(a) $x^2 - y^2 = 1$

(b) $\frac{x^2}{4} - \frac{y^2}{16} = 1$

(c) $\frac{x^2}{9} - \frac{y^2}{25} = -1$

(d) $4x^2 - y^2 = 64$

6. For the hyperbola $\frac{x^2}{49} - \frac{y^2}{16} = 1$, sketch the graph and state the following.

(a) the intercepts

(b) the length of the transverse axis

(c) the locations of the foci

(d) the equations of the asymptotes

7. Each of the following hyperbolas is centred at the origin and satisfies the following conditions. Find the equation of each hyperbola.

(a) The transverse axis is 12 units long, and one focal point is $(0, 8)$.

(b) One focal point is $(0, -6)$, and one y-intercept is 3.

(c) The transverse axis is 8 units long and lies along the y-axis. The conjugate axis is 4 units long.

(d) One focal point is $(5, 0)$, and one x-intercept is -3.

8. Sketch each graph. Comment on the similarities and differences between the graphs.

(a) $x^2 - 9y^2 = 9$

(b) $x^2 - 9y^2 = -9$

(c) $9x^2 - y^2 = 9$

(d) $9x^2 - y^2 = -9$

9. **Communication:** If a hyperbola is in standard form and $a = b$, the hyperbola is said to be an **equilateral hyperbola**. Describe and show the properties of an equilateral hyperbola.

B

10. A locus contains points, $P(x, y)$, such that the difference of the distance from point P to $A(0, 3)$ and the distance from point P to $B(0, -3)$ is 4. Find the equation of this locus and sketch the graph.

11. Sketch the graph of $\frac{(x-2)^2}{9} - \frac{(y+4)^2}{9} = -1$.

12. Given the hyperbola $\frac{x^2}{9} - \frac{y^2}{25} = 1$, find the equation of each translated hyperbola.

(a) 3 units left and 2 units up

(b) 4 units right and 3 units down

(c) 2 units right

(d) 8 units left and 4 units down

13. Create a model to determine the reflective properties of hyperbolas. Design a problem that would show these reflective properties. You may need to do some research.

14. A bridge is supported by an arch in the form of the equilateral hyperbola $x^2 - y^2 = -100$. If the width at the base of the arch is 35 m, find the height of the arch at its centre.

15. Write the equation of the hyperbola whose conjugate axis is 8 units long and whose vertices are $(-2, 6)$ and $(4, 6)$.

16. Find the equation of the hyperbola with foci $(4, 4)$ and $(-2, 4)$. The transverse axis is 4 units long.

17. **Application:** Two LORAN transmitters are 100 km apart. The difference between the times that the transmitter signals take to reach a ship indicates that the ship is 30 km closer to one transmitter than it is to the other. Determine the equation of the hyperbola on which the ship is located by using the positions of the transmitters as foci.

18. **Check Your Understanding:** Show that the asymptotes of $\frac{x^2}{b^2} - \frac{y^2}{a^2} = -1$ are $y = \pm \frac{a}{b}x$.

C

19. **Thinking, Inquiry, Problem Solving:** Determine the equations of the asymptotes for $\frac{(x-2)^2}{9} - \frac{y^2}{25} = 1$. Then determine the equations of the asymptotes for $\frac{(x-h)^2}{a^2} - \frac{(y-k)^2}{b^2} = 1$.

20. Show that the conics $3x^2 - y^2 = 12$ and $x^2 + 3y^2 = 24$ have the same foci.

Did You Know?

Tycho Brahe (1546–1601)

Tycho Brahe was a Danish astronomer who observed the stars and planets before the telescope was invented. His eyesight was excellent, and his observations were very accurate. Brahe's observations were so accurate that Johannes Kepler was able to use them to show that planets do have elliptical orbits.

This photograph shows the Tycho Brahe Planetarium in Copenhagen, Denmark. The roof forms an ellipse, in memory of Brahe's work.

7.10U The General Form of Conics

Functions and Relations

The conics share several similar features. Most conics have a focus or foci. You can describe each conic by a locus definition. And you can express all conics as second-degree equations.

The equation of each conic has a general form. But all conics can have the general form $ax^2 + by^2 + 2gx + 2fy + C = 0$. This section will consolidate what you know about conics.

Part 1: Recognizing Conics in General Form

By this point, you have become very familiar with different forms of the conic sections.

Think, Do, Discuss

1. What type of conic is $9x^2 + 4y^2 = 36$? State the values of a, b, g, f, and C for the general form of this equation.
2. Change $\frac{(x-1)^2}{4} - \frac{y^2}{25} = 1$ to the general form and state the values of a, b, g, f, and C. Name the conic.
3. Predict the conic represented by $x^2 - 4x - 8y - 28 = 0$. Then rearrange the equation in standard form and determine if your prediction is correct.
4. If $ax^2 + by^2 + 2gx + 2fy + C = 0$ and $a = b = 0$ or $ab = 0$, then what is the conic?
5. If $ax^2 + by^2 + 2gx + 2fy + C = 0$ and $a = b$, then what is the conic?
6. Consider the case of $ab > 0$. What is the conic? What is the conic if $ab < 0$?
7. Name each conic.
   $4y^2 - 8y + 9x^2 - 54x + 49 = 0$
   $x^2 - 4x - y^2 - 5 - 4y = 0$
8. If $f = g = 0$, then describe the conic.

Part 2: Organizing What You Know

You can write any conic in the general form $ax^2 + by^2 + 2gx + 2fy + C = 0$. To identify the conic section represented by a given equation, write the equation in standard form. However, you can also identify the conic section by comparing it with the general form. The following table will help you organize information.

Identifying Conics by the General Form $ax^2 + by^2 + 2gx + 2fy + C = 0$

Conic Section	Standard Form	Relationship of Values in the General Form
Circle	$(x - h)^2 + (y - k)^2 = r^2$	$a = b$
Ellipse	$\frac{(x-h)^2}{a^2} + \frac{(y-k)^2}{b^2} = 1$ $\frac{(x-h)^2}{b^2} + \frac{(y-k)^2}{a^2} = 1$	$ab > 0$ $a \neq 0, b \neq 0$
Parabola	$(x - h)^2 = 4p(y - k)$ $(y - k)^2 = 4p(x - h)$	$ab = 0$, either $a = 0$ or $b = 0$
Hyperbola	$\frac{(x-h)^2}{a^2} - \frac{(y-k)^2}{b^2} = 1$ $\frac{(x-h)^2}{b^2} - \frac{(y-k)^2}{a^2} = -1$	$ab < 0$ $a \neq 0, b \neq 0$

Example 1

Identify the conic.

(a) $x^2 + y^2 - 4x - 12 = 0$

(b) $2x^2 + y^2 + 4x + 2y = 20$

Solution

For each equation, find the values of a and b for the general form $ax^2 + by^2 + 2gx + 2fy + C = 0$.

(a) In this equation, $a = b = 1$. Since $a = b$, then the conic is a circle.

(b) In this equation, $ab > 0$, and the conic is an ellipse.

Example 2

Name the conic and write it in standard form.

$$4x^2 + y^2 - 8x - 12 = 0$$

Solution

Since $ab > 0$, the conic is an ellipse. To write the equation in standard form, complete the square.

$$\begin{aligned}
4x^2 + y^2 - 8x - 12 &= 0\\
(4x^2 - 8x) + y^2 &= 12\\
4(x^2 - 2x) + y^2 &= 12\\
4(x^2 - 2x + ?) + y^2 &= 12\\
4(x^2 - 2x + 1) + y^2 &= 12 + 4\\
4(x - 1)^2 + y^2 &= 16\\
\frac{(x - 1)^2}{4} + \frac{y^2}{16} &= 1
\end{aligned}$$

The equation of the conic in standard form is $\frac{(x - 1)^2}{4} + \frac{y^2}{16} = 1$.

Consolidate Your Understanding

1. Explain how you can determine what type of conic an equation in general form represents.

2. Explain how you can tell whether a conic is centred at the origin given the general form of the equation.

Focus 7.10U

Key Ideas

- A conic that is centred about the origin has the form $ax^2 + by^2 + C = 0$.
- A conic that is not centred about the origin has the **general form**
  $ax^2 + by^2 + 2gx + 2fy + C = 0$.
- The following conditions determine the type of conic.
  - If $a = b$, then the conic is a **circle**.
  - If $ab > 0$, then the conic is an **ellipse**.
  - If $ab < 0$, then the conic is a **hyperbola**.
  - If $ab = 0$, then the conic is a **parabola**.

Practise, Apply, Solve 7.10U

A

1. Identify the conic and list the coordinates of the centre (or vertex in the case of a parabola).

(a) $(y - 2)^2 = 9(x + 1)$

(b) $\frac{(x + 1)^2}{16} - \frac{y^2}{25} = -1$

(c) $\frac{(x - 3)^2}{9} + \frac{(y - 8)^2}{12} = 1$

(d) $\frac{x^2}{16} + \frac{(y + 6)^2}{8} = 1$

(e) $(x + 1)^2 = -12(y - 1)$

(f) $\frac{(y - 2)^2}{36} - \frac{(x + 2)^2}{9} = 1$

2. **Knowledge and Understanding:** Identify the conic.

(a) $9x^2 - 4y^2 - 36x - 40y = 100$

(b) $x^2 + 25y^2 + 2x = 124$

(c) $4x^2 - 16x - y + 17 = 0$

(d) $4x^2 + 9y^2 + 9x - 3y + 4 = 0$

(e) $3x^2 + 3y^2 - 2x + 1 = 0$

(f) $3x^2 - 6y^2 - 2y + 4 = 0$

(g) $x^2 + 2y^2 - 2y + 1 = 0$

(h) $y^2 - 2y + 9x + 19 = 0$

3. For each conic,

i. identify the conic

ii. list the coordinates of the centre

iii. tell whether the foci are on a horizontal line or on a vertical line

(a) $x^2 - y^2 + 8x + 4y + 9 = 0$

(b) $12x^2 + 4y^2 - 24x = 44$

(c) $4x^2 - y^2 + 24x - 8y + 12 = 0$

4. For $3x^2 - 6x - y + 1 = 0$,

(a) determine the type of conic

(b) write the equation in standard form

(c) graph the equation

5. For $y^2 - 3x^2 - 4y + 6x + 2 = 0$,

(a) determine the type of conic

(b) write the equation in standard form

(c) graph the equation

6. For $2x^2 + 2y^2 - 8x + 12y + 24 = 0$,

(a) determine the type of conic

(b) write the equation in standard form

(c) graph the equation

7. State the type of conic and determine the general form of the equation for each conic.

(a) $\frac{x^2}{9} + \frac{(y-3)^2}{4} = 1$

(b) $(x+3)^2 + (y-1)^2 = 9$

(c) $\frac{(x+4)^2}{16} - \frac{(y-3)^2}{4} = -1$

(d) $(x-2)^2 = -6(y+1)$

(e) $\frac{(x-1)^2}{4} - \frac{(y+2)^2}{5} = 1$

(f) $(y+3)^2 = 2(x-1)$

B

8. Write each equation in standard form and sketch its graph.

(a) $4x^2 + 9y^2 - 16x + 54y + 61 = 0$

(b) $9x^2 - 4y^2 - 54x - 36y + 81 = 0$

(c) $2x^2 + 3y^2 - 12x + 12y + 24 = 0$

(d) $y^2 - 2x^2 - 2y + 6x - 12 = 0$

(e) $y^2 - 8x - 8y = 0$

9. **Communication:** A classmate claims that $2x^2 - 4x + 2y^2 + 5y - 16 = 0$ is an ellipse. Is she correct? Explain how you know.

10. A conic is given by the equation $y^2 - 5x^2 + 20x = 50$.
    (a) What are the coordinates of its centre?
    (b) Find the coordinates of the foci and the vertices.
    (c) Find the lengths of the transverse and the conjugate axes.
    (d) Find the equations of the asymptotes.
    (e) Graph the conic.

11. Determine the equation in general form for a parabola with vertex (4, 2) and focus (1, 2).

12. Determine the equation in general form for a circle with centre (2, 3) and radius 5 units.

13. Identify each conic and then graph it.
    (a) $y^2 + 6y - 4x + 25 = 0$
    (b) $9x^2 - 16y^2 - 36x + 96y + 36 = 0$
    (c) $4x^2 - 8x + y^2 - 12 = 0$
    (d) $x^2 + 4x - y + 8 = 0$
    (e) $25x^2 + 4y^2 + 100x - 16y + 16 = 0$

14. **Application:** Find the equation in general form of the conic defined by the locus of points that are equidistant from the line $x = 5$ and point (4, 1).

15. What translation maps $x^2 + y^2 + 6x + 6y + 2 = 0$ onto a circle whose centre is at the origin?

16. Determine the equation in general form for a hyperbola that is centred about the origin with one vertex at (5, 0) and one focus at (6, 0).

17. **Thinking, Inquiry, Problem Solving:** The end points of the diameter of a circle are $A(-2, 4)$ and $B(6, 2)$. Find the equation of the circle in general form.

18. **Check Your Understanding:** Explain, in your own words, the meaning of the restrictions for a and b. For instance, why does the restriction $ab < 0$ tell you that the conic is a hyperbola?

C

19. Find an equation of the hyperbola whose foci are the vertices of the ellipse $7x^2 + 11y^2 = 77$ and whose vertices are the foci of this ellipse.

20. What is the equation, in general form, of each conic?
    (a) The foci are $(-2, 0)$ and $(4, 0)$, and the sum of the focal radii is 10.
    (b) The foci are $(3, 0)$ and $(-5, 0)$, and the difference of the focal radii is 6.
    (c) The foci are $(-6, 3)$ and $(2, 3)$, and the sum of the focal radii is 10.
    (d) The foci are $(5, 4)$ and $(-7, 4)$, and the difference of the focal radii is 10.

When Lines Meet Conics

Many universities or community colleges have their own radio stations that broadcast only within a certain range or distance. You are driving to visit a campus, listening to your radio. You know that the university's radio station transmits a signal within 25 km of the station. Imagine that the transmission tower is at the origin of a graph and that you are travelling along a path that could be represented by the line $y = 2x - 10$. What are your coordinates when your radio first picks up the signal?

Solving Problems Graphically

There are several different ways to solve this problem. If you sketch this problem, it is easy to see that several solutions are possible, depending on how the line and the circle meet.

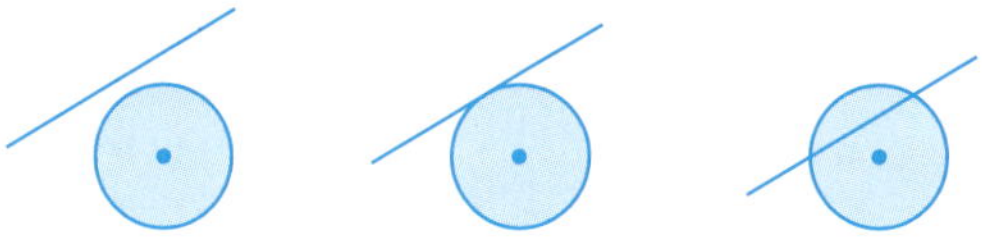

There can be no solution, one solution, or two solutions.

If you draw an accurate graph or use graphing technology, then you could easily solve the problem. To graph, you need to know the equations for the relations. The equation for the line is $y = 2x - 10$. The transmission of the signal can be represented by a circle with the equation $x^2 + y^2 = 625$. Here is a graph of both the circle and the line.

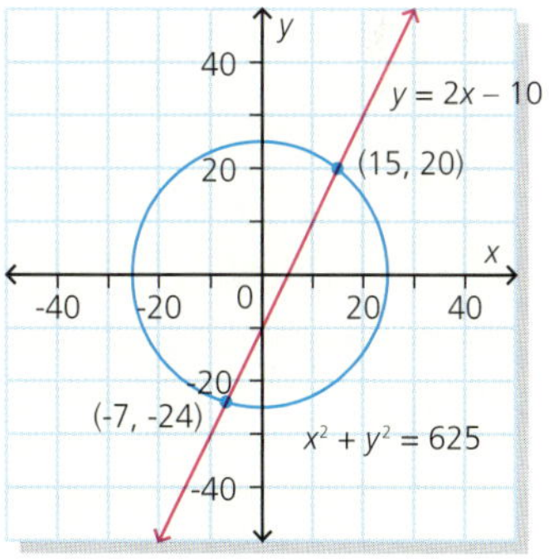

From the graph, you can see two solutions, points $(-7, -24)$ and $(15, 20)$.

Check the solutions by substituting them in each equation.

Solving Problems Algebraically

This problem can also be solved algebraically. Begin with the two equations, $x^2 + y^2 = 625$ and $y = 2x - 10$. Substitute $y = 2x - 10$ for y in the equation of the circle.

$$
\begin{aligned}
x^2 + y^2 &= 625 && \text{Substitute.}\\
x^2 + (2x - 10)^2 &= 625 && \text{Expand.}\\
x^2 + 4x^2 - 40x + 100 &= 625 && \text{Simplify.}\\
5x^2 - 40x - 525 &= 0 && \text{Factor.}\\
5(x^2 - 8x - 105) &= 0 && \text{Factor again.}\\
5(x - 15)(x + 7) &= 0 && \text{Solve.}\\
x = 15 \quad \text{or} \quad x &= -7
\end{aligned}
$$

Substitute $x = 15$ in $y = 2x - 10$.

$$
\begin{aligned}
y &= 2(15) - 10\\
y &= 30 - 10\\
y &= 20
\end{aligned}
$$

Substitute $x = -7$ in $y = 2x - 10$.

$$
\begin{aligned}
y &= 2(-7) - 10\\
y &= -14 - 10\\
y &= -24
\end{aligned}
$$

You should also verify the solutions by substituting them in the equation of the circle. The points at which you will first hear the radio signal are (15, 20) and (−7, −24).

Consolidate Your Understanding

1. Why does drawing a diagram or a sketch of the graph help you solve an intersection problem?
2. Why is it important to check your answers for both equations in the system of equations?
3. List the algebraic methods that you know for solving systems of equations.

Focus 7.11U

Key Ideas

- Systems of equations can be solved using a graph or algebra.
- To solve a system having both a quadratic equation and a linear equation, first sketch or graph the system before solving.
- Often a graphical solution will be difficult because the intersecting points may not be integer values and may be hard to determine from the graph.

Example 1

Graph the system of equations, estimate the number of solutions, and then solve the system.

$$y = x - 2$$

$$\frac{x^2}{4} + \frac{y^2}{9} = 1$$

Solution

The first equation is a line and the second equation is an ellipse. Graphing will help you to estimate the number of solutions.

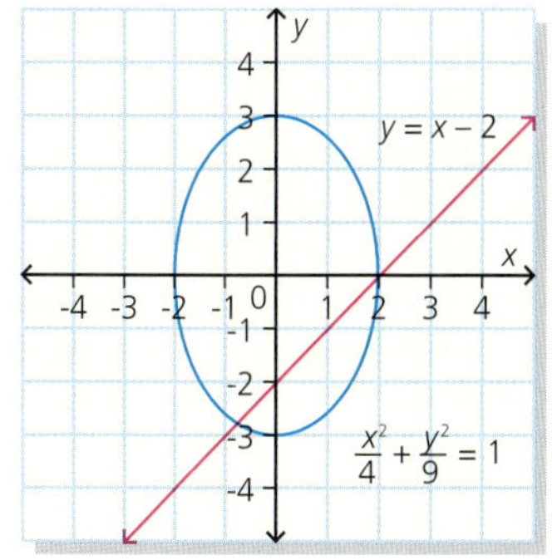

It appears that there may be two solutions. To solve the system algebraically, substitute $y = x - 2$ in the equation of the ellipse.

$$\frac{x^2}{4} + \frac{(x-2)^2}{9} = 1$$

$$9x^2 + 4(x-2)^2 = 36$$

$$9x^2 + 4(x^2 - 4x + 4) = 36$$

$$9x^2 + 4x^2 - 16x + 16 = 36$$

$$13x^2 - 16x - 20 = 0$$

Using the quadratic formula,

$$x = \frac{-(-16) \pm \sqrt{(-16)^2 - 4(13)(-20)}}{2(13)}$$

$$x = \frac{16 \pm \sqrt{256 + 1040}}{26}$$

$$x = \frac{16 \pm 36}{26}$$

$$x = 2 \text{ or } x = \frac{-10}{13}$$

If $x = 2$, then $y = 0$; if $x = \frac{-10}{13}$, then $y = \frac{-36}{13}$.

The solutions are $(2, 0)$ and $\left(\frac{-10}{13}, \frac{-36}{13}\right)$.

Example 2

Find the intersection of $y = -x^2 + 5x$ and $y = 3x + 1$.

Solution

Substitute $3x + 1$ for y in the equation $y = -x^2 + 5x$.

$-x^2 + 5x = 3x + 1$	Rearrange to isolate the variable.
$-x^2 + 2x - 1 = 0$	Divide by -1.
$x^2 - 2x + 1 = 0$	Factor.
$(x - 1)(x - 1) = 0$	Solve.
$x = 1$	

Substitute $x = 1$ in one of the original equations.

$$y = 3x + 1$$

$$y = 3(1) + 1$$

$$y = 4$$

The solution is $(1, 4)$.

Use your graphing calculator to verify the solutions.

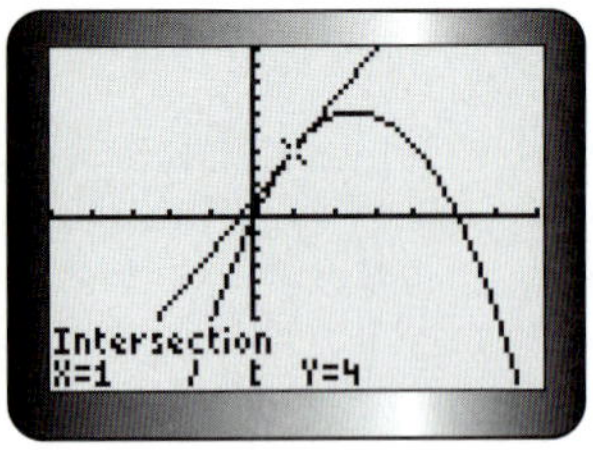

Practise, Apply, Solve 7.11U

A

1. For each system of equations, state which of the given ordered pairs are solutions to the system.

(a) $x^2 + y^2 = 25$ and $x + y = 1$ $(-3, 4), (3, -4), (4, -3), (-4, 3)$

(b) $x^2 - y^2 = 3$ and $x + y = -1$ $(1, -2), (-1, 2), (2, -1), (-2, 1)$

(c) $x^2 + y^2 = 5$ and $2x^2 + y = 0$ $(1, 2), (-1, 2), (-1, -2), (1, -2)$

Graphing technology would be useful for questions 2 to 6.

2. Graph $2x + y - 4 = 0$ and $4x^2 - y^2 = 16$.

(a) What are the coordinates of the intersection points?

(b) Verify the coordinates by substitution.

3. Graph $x^2 = \frac{1}{2}y$ and $y = -3x + 5$.

(a) What are the coordinates of the intersection points?

(b) Verify the coordinates by substitution.

4. Graph $(x - 7)^2 + (y + 4)^2 = 5$ and $2x + y - 5 = 0$.

(a) What are the coordinates of the intersection points?

(b) Verify the coordinates by substitution.

5. Graph $x - y = 0$ and $(x - 1)^2 + 4(y - 1)^2 = 20$.

(a) What are the coordinates of the intersection points?

(b) Verify the coordinates by substitution.

6. **Knowledge and Understanding**

(a) Graph $\frac{x^2}{6} + \frac{y^2}{12} = 1$ and $2x + y = 2$.

(b) Determine the intersection points.

(c) Solve the system algebraically to verify your graph.

B

7. Solve each system algebraically.

(a) $y = x + 2$ and $x^2 + y^2 = 100$

(b) $x^2 - y^2 = -4$ and $y = 5$

(c) $y = 2 - 3x$ and $x^2 = y + 2$

(d) $4x^2 + y^2 = 13$ and $2x - y = 1$

(e) $y = 2 - x$ and $x^2 + y^2 = 25$

8. **Application:** The path of a sonic boom on the Earth's surface is described by the equation $x^2 - y^2 = -45$. The path of a road is described by the equation $5x - 2y = 19$. What are the coordinates of points on the road at which the sonic boom will be heard?

9. Verify your results to this problem both graphically and algebraically. For the ellipse $4x^2 + 9y^2 = 36$, find the equation of a line that will

(a) intersect the graph at two points

(b) intersect the graph at only one point

(c) not intersect the ellipse

10. Verify your results to this problem both graphically and algebraically. For the conic $2x^2 - 3y^2 + 18 = 0$, find the equation of a line that will

(a) intersect the graph at two points

(b) intersect the graph at only one point

(c) not intersect the graph

11. Find the point(s) of intersection of $y = x + 1$ and $(x - 1)^2 + (y + 2)^2 = 9$.

12. Sketch each system and solve it algebraically.

(a) $y^2 - 8x = -8$ and $y = 2x - 10$

(b) $x^2 - 4x - y^2 - 5 - 4y = 0$ and $x - 2y = 1$

13. Show that the intersection points of the circle $(x - 2)^2 + (y + 3)^2 = 25$ and the line $4x + 3y + 1 = 0$ are the end points of the diameter of the given circle.

14. Determine the equation of the line that has two intersection points with the hyperbola $4x^2 - 16y^2 = 64$, but only one intersection point with the ellipse $4x^2 + 16y^2 = 64$.

15. A motion-detector light, which is used at night, was installed above the middle of the school gym's floor. The light can detect motion within a range defined by the equation $x^2 + y^2 = 100$. If someone walks through the path defined by the equation $x - 2y - 22 = 0$, then will the person be detected by the motion detector? Justify your answer.

16. **Check Your Understanding:** Draw diagrams to represent each scenario. Include the number of solutions and describe the algebraic solution to the problem.

(a) a circle with a line

(b) a parabola with a line

(c) an ellipse with a line

(d) a hyperbola with a line

C

17. Use a graph and algebra to show that the intersection points of $x - 2y - 4 = 0$ and $4x^2 + 16y^2 = 64$ lie on the conic defined by $x^2 + y^2 - 8x + 10y + 16 = 0$.

18. **Thinking, Inquiry, Problem Solving:** Prove that the centre of the circle given by $x^2 + y^2 - 10x - 10y + 25 = 0$ lies on the perpendicular bisector of the circle's chord defined by the equation $y = 11 - 3x$.

19. For the two conics $x^2 + 4y^2 = 49$ and $2x^2 - 3y^2 = -12$,

(a) graph the conics to determine the number of possible solutions

(b) isolate x^2 in the first expression and substitute the resulting expression in the second equation to solve

(c) does your answer for (b) support your answer in (a)?

20. Solve this system of equations using algebra and a graph.

$$y - 2 = -x^2$$
$$x^2 + y^2 = 25$$

Did You Know?

It would be so much easier to reach outer space if you could just take an elevator instead of a spaceship. Think of the benefits—no expensive rocket fuel and more people could visit space more frequently. According to an article in *The National Post,* this dream might not be a fantasy.

Several writers and scientists, such as Yuri Artsutanov, Jerome Pearson, and Arthur C. Clarke, have shown that a "super elevator" is technically possible. It would have to be built on the equator, so its centre of gravity could stay in geostationary orbit around the Earth. This elevator would soar 36 000 km into the sky. The speedy elevator cars would be powered by electromagnetism, just as high-speed trains in Japan are now.

So far, no one has built such an elevator, because there is no material strong enough to withstand the great stress it would face. However, in 1991, Japanese scientist Sumio Iijima discovered carbon nanotubes. These nanotubes are about one hundred times stronger than steel and are strong enough to be used in the elevator. At the moment, carbon nanotube material costs about $500 per gram, so the cost to make a space elevator is too great. But researchers hope to reduce the cost to $1 per gram. And then—away we go!

Chapter 7U Review

Investigating Loci and Conics

Check Your Understanding

1. Create a table that displays all of the standard forms of the equations of the conics. Include information about the foci, vertices, asymptotes, and so on.
2. The equation of any conic has the general form $ax^2 + by^2 + 2gx + 2fy + C = 0$. Create a table to show the restrictions on these values for each of the four conics. For example, for a circle, $a = b$.
3. Explain "asymptote" in your own words. Draw several graphs that have asymptotes.
4. Describe the procedure for finding the intersection of a line and a conic.
   (a) What things do you need to consider?
   (b) What different situations could arise?
   (c) Draw diagrams to show the different cases.
5. In your own words, explain the purpose of a locus definition.
6. Draw diagrams to show the reflective properties of the conics.

Review and Practice

7.1U Introducing Locus Definitions

1. Name several ways that you can define a mathematical "object."
2. State the locus definition of a circle.
3. Describe the shape defined by the locus of points that are equidistant from two fixed points.
4. Describe the shape defined by the locus of points that are equidistant from a fixed point and a fixed line.
5. Find the locus of the points that are equidistant from $(-6, 2)$ and $(4, 1)$.
6. Find the locus of points that are 2 units from the circle $x^2 + y^2 = 25$. Express this locus using geometry and as an equation, or equations.

7.2U–7.3U Revisiting the Circle

7. State the centre and radius of each circle.

(a) $4x^2 + 4y^2 = 1$

(b) $x^2 + y^2 + 16x - 6y + 72 = 0$

(c) $2x^2 + 2y^2 + 6x - 10y - 1 = 0$

8. Find the equation of the circle with centre (0, 0) and that passes through (8, −6).

9. Find the equation of the circle with centre (2, 1) and that passes through (5, 2).

10. Find the equation of the circle that is tangent to the *x*-axis and has centre (−3, 4).

11. Graph $y = \sqrt{16 - x^2}$ and describe the graph.

7.4U The Ellipse

12. State the locus definition of an ellipse.

13. Give the standard form for an ellipse with

(a) its major axis along the *x*-axis

(b) its major axis along the *y*-axis

14. For each ellipse in question 13, state the length of both the major and minor axes.

15. State the relationship between *a*, *b*, and *c*.

16. State the *x*- and *y*-intercepts of $\frac{x^2}{25} + \frac{y^2}{64} = 1$.

17. Graph $x^2 + 4y^2 = 100$, labelling the vertices, the foci, and the major and minor axes.

18. Find the equation of the ellipse with centre (0, 0), foci (5, 0) and (5,0), and *y*-intercepts ±6.

19. The ceiling in a hallway 10 m wide is in the shape of a semiellipse. The semiellipse is 9 m high in the centre. The walls of the hallway are 6 m high. Find the height of the ceiling 2 m from either wall.

7.5U–7.6U The Parabola

20. Draw a diagram showing a parabola, with its focus, its directrix, and its vertex.

21. State the locus definition of a parabola.

22. State the equation of the parabola

 (a) with a vertical axis of symmetry and the vertex at the origin

 (b) with a vertical axis of symmetry and the vertex (h, k)

 (c) with a horizontal axis of symmetry and the vertex at the origin

 (d) with a horizontal axis of symmetry and the vertex (h, k)

23. A point on a parabola is 8 units from the focus. How far is this point from the directrix? Use a diagram to show your answer.

24. Find the coordinates of the focus and the vertex and write the equation of the directrix for each parabola.

 (a) $y^2 = 12x$ (b) $(x - 3)^2 = 8(y + 2)$

25. Find the equation of the parabola.

 (a) with vertex (0, 0) and focus (0, 2)

 (b) with vertex (1, 2) and directrix $y = -2$

7.7U–7.9U The Hyperbola

26. State the locus definition of a hyperbola. Include a diagram.

27. State the standard form of a hyperbola with the transverse axis along

 (a) the x-axis (b) the y-axis

28. Draw a diagram of each hyperbola, clearly marking the transverse and the conjugate axes, the foci, the vertices, and the asymptotes.

 (a) centred at the origin and having x-intercepts

 (b) centred at the origin and having y-intercepts

29. Find the equation of the locus of the points such that the difference between the distance to $A(-14, 6)$ and the distance to $B(6, 6)$ is 6 units.

30. Graph $16x^2 - 9y^2 = 144$, labelling the transverse and the conjugate axes, the foci, the vertices, and the asymptotes.

31. Find the equation of the hyperbola with centre $(3, -5)$, vertex $(7, -5)$, and one focus at $(8, -5)$. Include a diagram with your solution.

7.10U The General Form of Conics

32. Describe the steps for graphing a conic in general form.

33. Describe how to determine the type of conic when the conic is in general form.

34. For each of the following,

i. identify the conic
ii. write the equation in standard form
iii. graph the conic

(a) $4x^2 + 9y^2 + 8x - 36y + 4 = 0$
(b) $3x^2 + 3y^2 - 6x - 9 = 0$
(c) $3x^2 - 6y^2 - 2y + 4 = 0$
(d) $x^2 + 2y^2 - 12y + 2 = 0$
(e) $4x^2 - y^2 + 56x + 2y + 199 = 0$

7.11U When Lines Meet Conics

35. Draw diagrams to show the different ways in which each of the four conics can intersect with a line.

36. Discuss why graphing a system of equations is not always the best solution.

37. Use both algebra and a graph to determine the intersection of $x - 2y = -8$ and $x^2 + 4y^2 = 32$.

38. The centre of a circle is on the y-axis and is on the line $x - 5y - 15 = 0$. If the circle passes through (4, 2), then find its equation.

39. Solve $x^2 + 4y^2 = 40$ and $x + 2y = 8$.

40. Find the intersection of $x^2 + y^2 = 5$ and $x + y - 1 = 0$.

Chapter 7U Summary

In this chapter, you studied locus definitions and conic sections.

You may define a geometric figure, a region, or an equation of a relation using a locus definition that sets specific conditions.

You also studied these conic sections: the circle, the ellipse, the parabola, and the hyperbola. You saw these conics in different ways: as locus definitions, standard and general forms of the equations, and graphs. You compared similar and different features of the conics. You also compared conics that were first centred at the origin and then translated.

The reflective properties of conic sections are very useful in automobile headlights, navigation systems, satellite dishes, and architectural structures. You explored these applications of conics.

You investigated the intersection of conics with lines and explored both graphical and geometric solutions.

Chapter 7U Review Test

Investigating Loci and Conics

1. Identify the conic and state the coordinates of the vertices and foci.

(a) $\frac{x^2}{16} + \frac{y^2}{9} = 1$

(b) $x^2 - y^2 = 1$

(c) $2x^2 + 2y^2 = 18$

(d) $y^2 = 8(x - 3)$

(e) $\frac{(x + 2)^2}{25} + \frac{(y + 1)^2}{9} = 1$

2. **Knowledge and Understanding:** Find the equation of each conic.

(a) a circle with radius 3 units and centre $(0, -2)$

(b) a hyperbola with vertices at $(-2, 0)$ and $(2, 0)$ and a conjugate axis 6 units long

(c) a parabola with vertex $(0, 0)$ and directrix $x = -6$

3. State the focus and directrix of $x^2 = -5y$.

4. **Communication:** Describe how you can determine whether the transverse axis of a hyperbola is horizontal or vertical.

5. For the conic $25x^2 - 9y^2 = -225$,

(a) state the vertices

(b) find the asymptotes

(c) graph the relation

6. For the conic $\frac{x^2}{25} + \frac{y^2}{64} = 1$,

(a) name the x- and y-intercepts

(b) state the coordinates of the foci

(c) state the length of the major axis

(d) name the vertices

(e) graph the conic

7. Graph each conic and then state the vertices and find the foci.

(a) $25x^2 + 9y^2 = 900$

(b) $4x^2 - y^2 = 100$

(c) $\frac{x^2}{4} + \frac{y^2}{12} = 1$

(d) $y^2 - 4y + 4x = 0$

(e) $\frac{x^2}{25} - \frac{y^2}{144} = 1$

8. Find the equation for the ellipse, centred at $(0, 0)$, with foci on the x-axis. The length of the major axis is four times the length of the minor axis, and the point $(-3, 2)$ is on the ellipse.

9. **Application:** A conical act came to town with the circus. The Bolic Twins performed the great feat of walking across an untight cable that happened to be so untight that it fell into a parabolic curve. (Assume the cable will stay in the parabolic shape, even as they walk across it.) The cable was attached to two 30 m high poles placed 20 m apart. The lowest point of the cable was 5 m above the ground. After the Bolic twins had taken two steps on the cable, they became quite nervous and reached out for the pole. They could just reach it. If the arms of each twin are 1 m long, then how high from the ground are they?

10. Determine the type of conic.

(a) $x^2 + y^2 - 6x + 8y - 9 = 0$

(b) $4x^2 - 8y^2 - 16y - 40 = 0$

(c) $x^2 + 9y^2 + 2x = 0$

(d) $y^2 + 4x - 12y + 4 = 0$

(e) $2x^2 - 3y^2 - 12x - 12y - 6 = 0$

11. Obtain the equation of the parabola with the vertex at the origin and the focus on the x-axis, that opens to the right, and with a focus on the line $4x - 7y - 12 = 0$.

12. Find the equation of the diameter of the circle $x^2 + y^2 - 4x + 6y - 1 = 0$ that passes through point $(0, -2)$.

13. **Thinking, Inquiry, Problem Solving** The base of a triangle lies on the x-axis with one vertex at the origin. The length of the base is 12 units. The product of the tangents to the base angles is $\frac{9}{16}$. Let $P(x, y)$ be the vertex of the triangle that is not on the x-axis. Find the equation for the locus of this vertex of the triangle.

14. Find the intersection of $5x - y - 20 = 0$ and $y^2 = 50x$. Use both a graphical solution and an algebraic solution.

Cumulative Review Test 4

Course Review: Chapters 1 to 7

1. For each sequence, find

i. the general term

ii. t_{25}

iii. S_{20}

(a) $-4, 5, 14, \ldots$

(b) $3, 3.3, 3.63, 3.993, \ldots$

2. Determine the number of terms in each sequence.

(a) 3, 12, 48, …, 201 326 592

(b) 18, 22, 26, …, 162

3. George has retired from teaching and will receive his first pension cheque next month. His pension will pay him \$55 000 annually, plus an additional percentage to cover inflation. If this additional percentage averages 2.5%/a, determine the total amount of money he will receive over the next fifteen years.

4. Determine

(a) the amount \$8500 will grow to if invested at 8%/a compounded quarterly for 10 years

(b) the principal that must be invested now at 6%/a compounded annually to be worth \$10 000 in 5 years

(c) the total accumulated amount of \$500 invested every 6 months, starting 6 months from now, at 7%/a compounded semiannually for 8 years.

(d) the principal that must be invested now to provide monthly payments of \$100, beginning next month, over a 10-year period, if interest is paid at 4.8%/a compounded monthly

5. Judy bought a stereo system for \$300 down and 24 monthly payments of \$120, beginning next month.

(a) If the store charges 18%/a compounded monthly, what was the cash price of the system?

(b) What was her cost for financing the stereo system?

6. Clarrisa has just graduated from medical school. She must repay her student loans that total \$23 000. She decides that she can afford to make monthly payments of \$420. The bank is charging 5.4%/a compounded monthly in interest charges. Determine how long it will take her to repay her student loan.

7. The Morrison family is about to buy a new home for \$245 000. They intend to make a 25% down payment to qualify for a conventional mortgage and finance the remainder over 25 years. They negotiate a fixed five-year term mortgage rate of 7.9%/a compounded semiannually.

(a) Determine the monthly payment required to repay the loan.

(b) Determine the outstanding balance on the mortgage at the end of each of the first 5 years.

(c) At the end of the five-year term, determine how much principal has been repaid and how much interest has been paid.

(d) Assume interest rates do not change. Find the total interest the Morrisons can expect to pay over 25 years and the total cost of their home.

8. Simplify.

(a) $\dfrac{16^{\frac{3}{4}} - 27^{-\frac{2}{3}}}{4^{-\frac{1}{2}}}$ (b) $\left(\dfrac{27x^2y^{-5}}{64x^{-1}y^4}\right)^{\frac{2}{3}}$

(c) $\left(\dfrac{4}{x}\right)^{n-m}(2x^2)^m$

9. Solve each equation. Round answers to two decimal places where necessary.

(a) $2x^2 - 4x + 5 = 0$

(b) $\dfrac{90\ 000}{x} = \dfrac{90\ 000}{x+6} + 2500$

(c) $4^{x-2} = \dfrac{1}{64}$

(d) $2^{x^2+20} = \left(\dfrac{1}{8}\right)^{3x}$

10. For each relation,

i. identify the domain and range

ii. tell whether it is a function or not. Justify your answer.

(a)

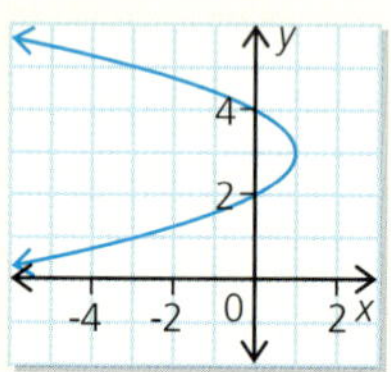

(b)

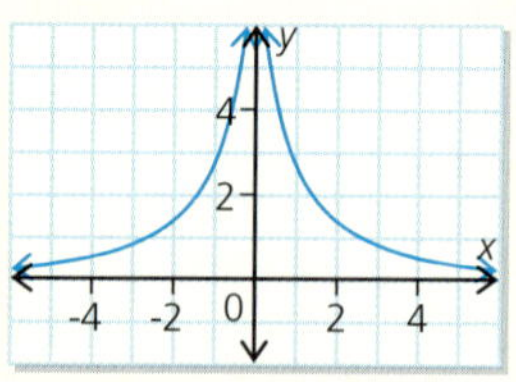

(c) $y = \sqrt{x-5}$

(d) $y = 2(x-3)^2 + 4$

11. For $g(x) = -3x^2 + 6x + 2$

(a) graph g and g^{-1} on the same set of axes

(b) determine the equation for g^{-1}

(c) state restrictions on the domain or range of g so that its inverse is a function

(d) assume the domain of g is $\{x \mid 0 \le x \le 5, x \in \mathbf{R}\}$. Would the inverse be a function? Justify your answer.

12. The graph of $f(x)$ is shown, and $g(x) = -2f(2x+6) + 3$. Sketch the graph of $g(x)$.

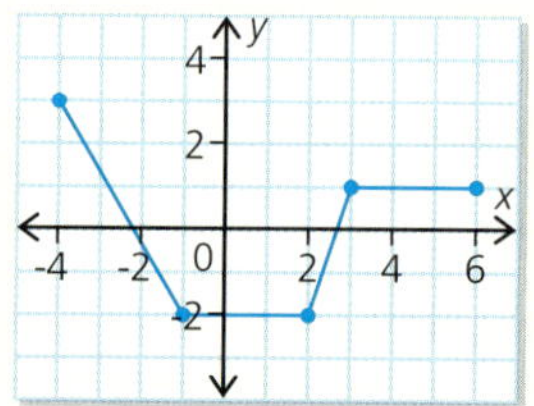

13. Solve each inequality and graph the solution set, $x \in \mathbf{R}$.

(a) $4(x-3) + x \le 6 - 2(x+2)$

(b) $\dfrac{x}{3} - \dfrac{2x-3}{4} > \dfrac{5}{6}$

14. (a) What transformations must you apply to the graph of $y = x^2$ to obtain the graph $y = \frac{2}{3}x^2 - \frac{3}{4}x + 1$? Show all your work and explain each step.

(b) Graph $y = x^2$ and $y = \frac{2}{3}x^2 - \frac{3}{4}x + 1$ on the same set of axes.

15. Find the value(s) of k so that the graph of each function has

i. two x-intercepts

ii. one x-intercept

iii. no x-intercepts

(a) $f(x) = kx^2 - 9x + 6$

(b) $f(x) = 3x^2 + kx + 12$

(c) $f(x) = 9x^2 + 3x + k$

16. In each case, draw the graph of $y = f(x)$ and use it to graph $y = \frac{1}{f(x)}$ on the same axes.

(a) $f(x) = x^2 + 2$

(b) $f(x) = (x + 4)^2 - 2$

(c) $f(x) = \sqrt{x + 5}$

17. For each function

i. state the zeros, asymptotes, and domain

ii. graph the function and estimate the range

(a) $f(x) = \frac{x}{x + 1}$

(b) $g(x) = \frac{1}{x^2 - x - 6}$

(c) $h(x) = \frac{x^2 - 4}{x}$

18. Simplify.

(a) $2x(3x - 1)(3x + 1) - (4x + 2)^3$

(b) $(6x - 2y)(x^2 + 4xy - 3y^2)$

19. Simplify. State any restrictions.

(a) $\frac{5x^2 - 5}{x^2 - 4x - 5}$

(b) $\frac{4x^4y}{3x^2y^4} \times \frac{-6x^3y^2}{10x^4}$

(c) $\frac{2m^2 - m - 15}{m + 2} \times \frac{m^2 - m - 6}{m^2 - m + 9}$

(d) $\frac{x^2 - y^2}{2x^2 - 8x} \times \frac{(x - y)^2}{2xy}$

(e) $\frac{1}{x} - \frac{3}{y} + \frac{3x - y}{xy}$

(f) $\frac{x + 2}{x^2 + 5x + 6} - \frac{x - 3}{x^2 - 3x - 10}$

20. Point $P(-6, -8)$ lies on the terminal arm of an angle, θ, in standard position. Determine the exact value of $\frac{\sin \theta + \cos \theta}{\tan \theta}$.

21. Express each angle in radians.

(a) 35° (b) 320°

(c) −180° (d) 225°

22. Express each angle in degrees.

(a) $\frac{7\pi}{8}$ (b) $-\frac{\pi}{12}$

(c) $\frac{8\pi}{3}$ (d) $\frac{5\pi}{16}$

23. Verify that $\sin^2\frac{\pi}{6} + \cos^2\frac{\pi}{6} = 1$.

24. Sketch the graph of each function.

(a) $f(x) = 3 \sin x - 2, 0 \leq x \leq 2\pi$

(b) $f(x) = -2 \cos (x - 30°) + 2,$
$0° \leq x \leq 360°$

25. Determine an equation that models each function.

(a)

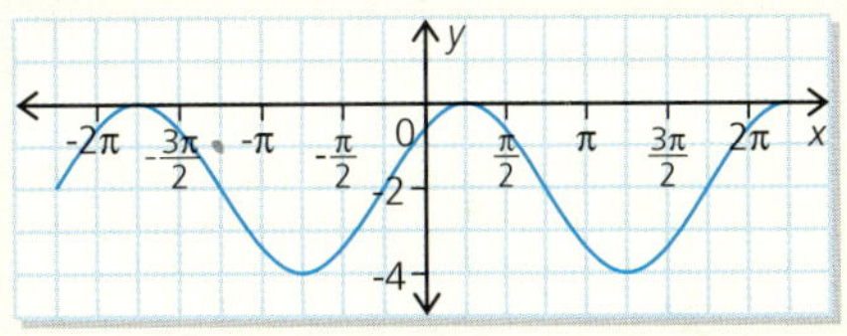

(b)

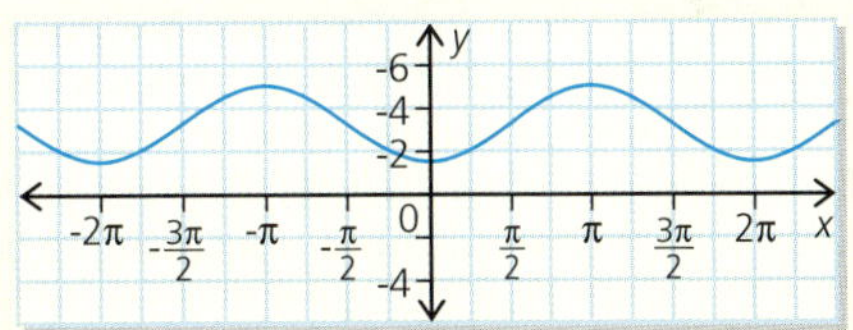

26. During high tide, at 12:06 a.m, the water in an inlet is 18 m deep. During low tide, which occurs 12 h later, it is 11.5 m deep.

(a) Determine an expression for the water depth in the inlet, *t* hours after high tide.

(b) Graph the function over a 24-h period.

(c) Determine the times on this day when the water is 15 m deep and 12 m deep.

27. Solve. Round to the nearest tenth where necessary.

(a) $2 \sin x = \sqrt{3}, 0 \leq x \leq 2\pi$

(b) $5 \cos x - 4 = 0, 0° \leq x \leq 360°$

(c) $\sin 2x(2 \cos x + 1) = 0, 0 \leq x \leq 2\pi$

(d) $3 \sin^2 x - 11 \sin x - 4 = 0,$
$0° \leq x \leq 360°$

28. Prove each identity.

(a) $\frac{2}{\sin^2 \theta} = \frac{1}{1 - \cos \theta} + \frac{1}{1 + \cos \theta}$

(b) $\tan^2 \theta + \cos^2 \theta + \sin^2 \theta = \frac{1}{\cos^2 \theta}$

29. Two bike trails diverge at an angle of 102°. Two riders leave the intersection at the sane time, with one rider heading northwest at 18 km/h and the other going northeast at 20 km/h. How far apart are they after 1.5 h?

30. Solve ΔLMN, given $\angle L = 38°$, $l = 30$ cm, and $n = 45$ cm.

31. A forest ranger at the top of a 95-m high observation tower sees a tent at an angle of depression of 12°. Turning in a different direction, the ranger sees a second tenty at an angle of depression of 17°. The angle between these two lines of sight is 40°. How far apart are the campsites?

Functions and Relations

32U. Determine the first six terms of the sequence in which $t_1 = 5$, $t_2 = 3$, and $t_n = 4t_{n-1} + 2t_{n-2}$.

33U. Evaluate.

(a) $(i + 3)^2$

(b) $3i^4$

(c) $(4 - 5i)(3 + 2i)$

(d) $(5 - 7i) + (6 - 4i) - (3 - 2i)$

(e) $\frac{5 + 2i}{4 + 6i}$

(f) $[2i + (1 - i)]^2$

(g) $\frac{(3 + 6i)}{(2 - 3i)(3 + 2i)}$

(h) $\frac{(5 + 8i) + (-3 + 5i)}{(6 + 7i) - (5 - 4i)}$

34U. Sketch the graph of
$x^2 - 6x + 4y + y^2 - 9 = 0$.

35U. Graph each conic. Then state the coordinates of the vertices and the foci.

(a) $9x^2 + 16y^2 = 144$

(b) $x^2 - 9y^2 = 9$

(c) $y^2 - 8y + 2x = 0$

(d) $4x^2 - y^2 = -16$

36U. Determine the equation of each conic.

(a)

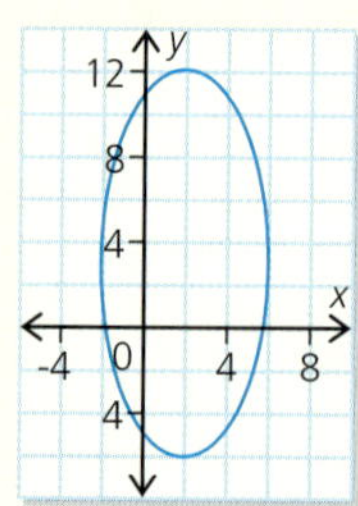

(b)

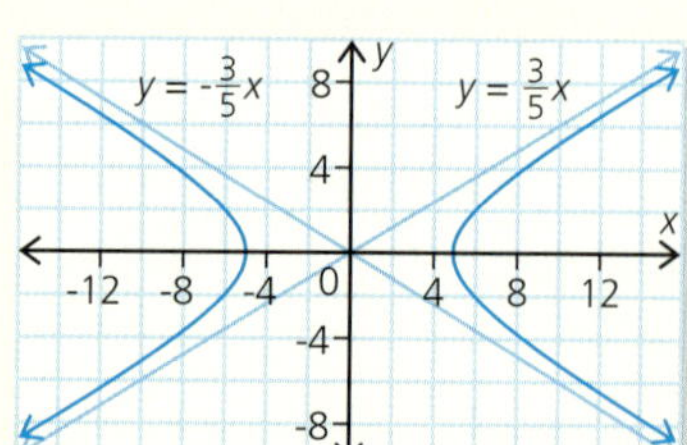

37U. For each equation

i. identify the type of conic that it represents

ii. graph the equation

(a) $9x^2 + 4y^2 + 18x - 16y = 11$

(b) $x^2 - 12x - 4y = 0$

(c) $4x^2 - y^2 - 16x - 6y + 3 = 0$

(d) $x^2 - 10x + y^2 - 10y = -49$

38U. Sketch the locus and determine the equation of each situation.

(a) The product of the coordinates of any point is 8.

(b) The set of points that are equidistant from (0, 4) and (2, 6)

39U. Determine the intersection points of $y = 2x - 4$ and $x^2 - 6x + y^2 + 8y + 16 = 0$.

Performance Tasks for Part 4

Loci and Conics

THE FOLLOWING ACTIVITIES SHOULD EACH TAKE LESS THAN A PERIOD TO COMPLETE.

1. Orbiting the Earth

Satellites normally orbit the Earth in an elliptical orbit, with the centre of the Earth being one focal point of the orbit. The point where the satellite is nearest the Earth is the **perigee** and the point at which it is farthest from the Earth is the **apogee**. Suppose a satellite is 620 km from the Earth's surface at its perigee and 1200 km from the Earth's surface at its apogee. Determine the equation for the orbit of the satellite. Include a diagram with your solution. (Note that the Earth has a radius of about 6.34×10^3 km.)

2. Conics and Foci

The ratio of the distance between the centre of a conic and one of its foci to the distance between the centre and one of the vertices is called the **eccentricity** of a conic.

(a) Create several equations of ellipses and several equations of hyperbolas and determine the eccentricity of each ellipse and hyperbola.

(b) Make a conjecture comparing the eccentricity of ellipses to the eccentricity of hyperbolas.

(c) State the equations of one other hyperbola and one other ellipse and determine their eccentricities. Does your conjecture prove true?

(d) Investigate the eccentricity of the other conics and create a summary of your findings.

(e) Submit a report showing all of your work that supports your summary.

3. What Are the Equations?

(a) Create equations of conics and lines so that the given diagram will result when graphed:

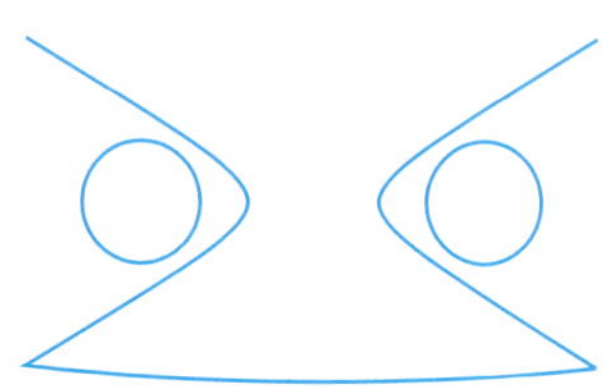

(b) State the equations and draw the graphs of your equations.

(c) Describe the process you went through to determine the equations. Include key words such as foci, vertices, radius, and centre.

(d) Add another feature to this diagram by using the equation of a line or a conic. This new line or conic must intersect one of the given graphs. Explain the relationship of this new equation and graphs to the others.

(e) Find at least one intersection point in your graph.

4. What Are the Solutions?

Create both graphical and algebraic solutions to these problems:

(a) Find an equation of the circle that passes through points (10, 9), (4, −5), and (0, 5).

(b) Find the distances from the foci of the ellipse $16x^2 + 25y^2 = 400$ to a point on the curve whose x-coordinate is 2.

(c) Find the equation of two parabolas in standard position that pass through $P(4, -2)$.

(d) Show that the hyperbola $9x^2 - 16y^2 = 144$ and the ellipse $3x^2 + 4y^2 = 300$ have the same focus.

THE FOLLOWING ACTIVITIES COULD EACH TAKE MORE THAN A PERIOD TO COMPLETE.

5. Blaise Pascal

Blaise Pascal (1623–1662) was a great French mathematician and philosopher. The computer language Pascal and the metric unit the pascal are both named for him. One of Pascal's theorems deals with circles, ellipses, hyperbolas, and parabolas. To investigate the theorem, try the following. You may find it useful to use *The Geometer's Sketchpad* for your exploration.

(a) Pick any six points on a conic and label them A through F, in order of position.

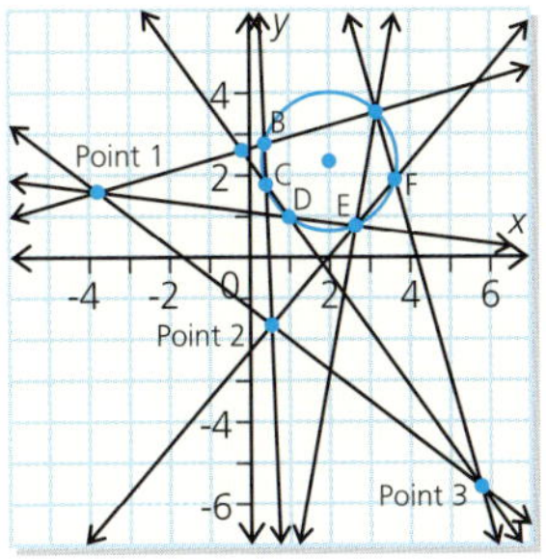

(b) Draw lines that connect consecutive points. In other words, draw lines *AB*, *BC*, *CD*, *DE*, *EF*, and *FA*.

(c) Mark the intersection of these sets of lines.

i. Mark the intersection of *AB* and *DE* as point 1.

ii. Mark the intersection of *BC* and *EF* as point 2.

iii. Mark the intersection of *CD* and *FA* as point 3.

(d) What do you notice about these three points?

(e) Test your conjecture with the other conics.

(f) Submit a report with the graphs and equations of several conics that you investigated. Summarise and justify your results.

6. Constructing an Ellipse

There are many different ways to construct an ellipse. One way is to use two concentric circles with two perpendicular lines drawn through the centre as in the diagram.

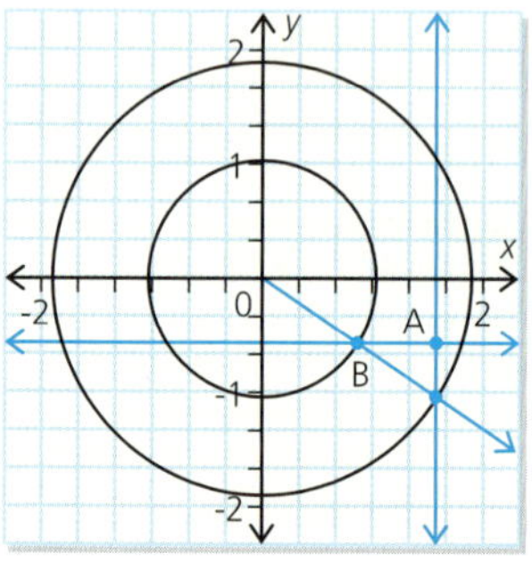

When *B* is dragged around the circle, point *A* traces an ellipse. Experiment with this construction and then prove that this construction produces an ellipse.

Answers

Review of Essential Skills—Part 1

Pattern Recognition, page 2

1. **(a)** 1, 3, 5, 7; 9 **(b)** 1, 4, 9, 16; 25 **(c)** 2, 4, 6, 8; 10
   (d) 1, 4, 9, 16; 25 **(e)** 2, 4, 6, 8; 10 **(f)** 8, 10, 12, 14; 16
2. **i.** **(a)** 4, 10, 16, 22 **(b)** 4, 12, 24, 49 **(c)** 7, 13, 19, 25
   (d) 3, 9, 18, 30 **(e)** 5, 9, 13, 17 **(f)** 24, 30, 36, 42
   ii. **(a)** 28 **(b)** 71 **(c)** 31 **(d)** 45 **(e)** 21 **(f)** 48
3. **(a)** linear, 17 **(b)** exponential, 0.0625
   (c) quadratic, −301 **(d)** exponential, 256
4. **(a)** linear **(b)** quadratic
5. exponential
6. linear
8. **(a)** 13 **(b)** 0.002 43 **(c)** −100 **(d)** $\frac{43}{24}$

Operations with Rational Numbers, page 4

1. **(a)** $1\frac{1}{6}$ **(b)** $-\frac{1}{15}$ **(c)** $-\frac{10}{33}$ **(d)** $-1\frac{1}{3}$ **(e)** $-3\frac{1}{2}$
   (f) $2\frac{13}{20}$ **(g)** $-4\frac{3}{4}$ **(h)** $2\frac{1}{20}$ **(i)** $-\frac{43}{60}$ **(j)** $\frac{19}{42}$
2. **(a)** $\frac{3}{5}$ **(b)** $\frac{1}{5}$ **(c)** $\frac{1}{9}$ **(d)** $-14\frac{1}{6}$ **(e)** $-\frac{2}{3}$
   (f) $-3\frac{2}{5}$ **(g)** -2 **(h)** $-\frac{13}{18}$ **(i)** $11\frac{11}{12}$ **(j)** $-\frac{7}{8}$
3. **(a)** $\frac{1}{2}$ **(b)** $\frac{9}{16}$ **(c)** $-\frac{2}{3}$ **(d)** $-1\frac{1}{2}$ **(e)** 14
   (f) $-1\frac{1}{2}$ **(g)** $\frac{4}{7}$ **(h)** $-1\frac{1}{2}$ **(i)** $1\frac{1}{2}$ **(j)** $-\frac{7}{11}$
4. **(a)** $\frac{1}{5}$ **(b)** $-1\frac{7}{30}$ **(c)** $-1\frac{32}{105}$ **(d)** $-\frac{7}{54}$ **(e)** $-\frac{83}{32}$
   (f) $2\frac{2}{5}$ **(g)** $-13\frac{61}{96}$ **(h)** $-\frac{27}{32}$ **(i)** $-\frac{5}{77}$ **(j)** $\frac{21}{88}$
5. **(a)** $-2\frac{5}{8}$ **(b)** $1\frac{3}{4}$ **(c)** $\frac{65}{231}$ **(d)** $\frac{476}{1245}$

Exponent Laws, page 6

1. **(a)** 16 **(b)** 1 **(c)** $\frac{1}{9}$ **(d)** −9
   (e) 9 **(f)** $\frac{1}{8}$ **(g)** $\frac{1}{8}$ **(h)** $\frac{9}{4}$
   (i) −1 **(j)** 1 **(k)** 0.25 **(l)** −125
   (m) 0.063 **(n)** 0.034 **(o)** −0.002 **(p)** 1861.594
2. **(a)** $3^0 + 5^0, 1$ **(b)** $\frac{1}{2} + \frac{1}{3}, \frac{5}{6}$ **(c)** $5 - \frac{1}{4}, \frac{19}{4}$
   (d) $\left(\frac{1}{2}\right)\left(\frac{3}{2}\right), \frac{3}{4}$ **(e)** $\frac{1}{2^2} + \frac{1}{2^3}, \frac{1}{8}$ **(f)** $2 + 3, 5$
   (g) $12\left(\frac{1}{2} - \frac{1}{3}\right), 2$ **(h)** $\dfrac{\frac{1}{2} + \frac{1}{3}}{\frac{1}{3}}, \frac{5}{2}$
3. **(a)** $\frac{1}{9}$ **(b)** -5^3 **(c)** $\frac{1}{8}$ **(d)** $\frac{1}{441}$
4. **(a)** x^8 **(b)** m^{-1} **(c)** y^{-3} **(d)** a^{bc}
   (e) x^{12} **(f)** c **(g)** t^7 **(h)** 1
   (i) n^5 **(j)** m^8n^{12} **(k)** m^{24} **(l)** $\frac{x^6}{y^{-9}}$
5. **(a)** $x^{-1}y^6$ **(b)** $108m^{12}$ **(c)** $5x^2$ **(d)** $-\frac{1}{128}v^2$
6. **(a)** −50 **(b)** 3^{17}

Expanding, Simplifying, and Factoring Algebraic Expressions, page 8

1. **(a)** $-2x - 5y$ **(b)** $-9m + 6n - 3p$ **(c)** $11x^2 - 4x^3$
   (d) $8 - 13x - 4y$ **(e)** $-9x - 10y$ **(f)** $11x^3 - 9y^2$
   (g) $4m^2n - p$ **(h)** $2x^3 + 3y^3$
2. **(a)** $6x + 15y - 6$ **(b)** $-5x + 5y + 10z$
   (c) $-2m^2 + 2mn$ **(d)** $5x^3 - 5x^2 + 5xy$
   (e) $-10a^2 + 8a^3 + 6a^4$ **(f)** $-14yx^2 + 21y^3$
   (g) $3m^4 - 2m^2n$ **(h)** $18uv^6 - 15u^7v^{-1}$
   (i) $4x^7y^7 - 2x^6y^8$
3. **(a)** $8x^2 - 4x$ **(b)** $-34h^2 - 27h$
   (c) $-13m^5n - 22m^2n^2$ **(d)** $-x^2y^3 - 12xy^4 - 7xy^3$
4. **(a)** $12x^2 + 7x - 10$ **(b)** $14 + 22y - 12y^2$
   (c) $20x^2 - 23xy - 7y^2$ **(d)** $15x^6 - 14x^3y^2 - 8y^4$
   (e) $15m^2n^4 + 2m^2n^2 - 8m^2$ **(f)** $12m^{10}n^6 + 11m^7n^4 - 15m^4n^2$
5. **(a)** $4(1 - 2x)$ **(b)** $3n(3m - 4)$ **(c)** $x(6x - 5)$
   (d) $3m^2n^3(1 - 3mn)$ **(e)** $14x(2x - y)$ **(f)** $mn(5 - 7n^2)$
6. **(a)** $(x - 3)(x + 2)$ **(b)** $(x + 5)(x + 2)$ **(c)** $(x - 5)(x - 4)$
   (d) $(x - 7)(x + 4)$ **(e)** $3(y + 4)(y + 2)$ **(f)** $2(t - 5)(t + 3)$
   (g) $(m - 3)(m + 3)$ **(h)** $(5n - 8p)(5n + 8p)$
7. **(a)** $(3y - 2)(2y + 1)$ **(b)** $(4x - 1)(3x + 1)$ **(c)** $(5a - 3)(a + 2)$
   (d) $(3m - 2)(2m - 1)$ **(e)** $(5x - 3)(2x + 3)$ **(f)** $(3x + 2)(x - 5)$
   (g) $(5n - 3)^2$ **(h)** $2(6x + 3)(x - 2)$ **(i)** $4(5x - 3)(x + 1)$

Solving Linear and Quadratic Equations Algebraically, page 10

1. **(a)** $y = \frac{2}{3}x + 3$ **(b)** $x = 0.8$ **(c)** $m = 3$ **(d)** $m = -4$
   (e) $m = -6$ **(f)** $y = 3$ **(g)** $r = \frac{23}{10}$ **(h)** $n = 9$
2. **(a)** $x = 100$ **(b)** $x = 20$ **(c)** $m = \frac{2}{3}$ **(d)** $y = \frac{75}{7}$
   (e) $y = \frac{7}{18}$ **(f)** $m = -\frac{6}{5}$ **(g)** $x = \frac{10}{7}$ **(h)** $x = 3$
   (i) $x = -3$ **(j)** $m = 7$
3. **(a)** $x = 3, x = -2$ **(b)** $x = -\frac{5}{2}, x = \frac{1}{3}$ **(c)** $m = -4, m = -3$
   (d) $x = \frac{3}{2}, x = -\frac{4}{3}$ **(e)** $y = -\frac{5}{2}, y = \frac{7}{3}$ **(f)** $n = -\frac{3}{5}, n = \frac{4}{3}$
4. **(a)** $x = 2, x = -1$ **(b)** $x = -5, x = 4$ **(c)** $m = -5, m = 3$
   (d) $x = \frac{2}{3}, x = -\frac{1}{2}$ **(e)** $x = -\frac{4}{3}, x = \frac{1}{2}$ **(f)** $x = -5, x = 3$
5. **(a)** $x = \frac{2 \pm \sqrt{3}}{2}$ **(b)** $x = \pm\frac{3}{2}$ **(c)** $x = -\frac{1}{3}, x = \frac{1}{2}$
   (d) $x = \frac{3}{5}, x = -2$ **(e)** $x = \frac{2}{3}, x = -\frac{1}{4}$ **(f)** $x = \frac{2 \pm \sqrt{2}}{2}$
   (g) $x = 3, x = -2$ **(h)** $x = 7, x = 2$
6. **(a)** 6 cm **(b)** 16 m
7. 6 s
8. 2010

Chapter 1

Getting Ready, page 14

1. **(a)** 15, 18, 21 **(b)** 15, 20, 26 **(c)** 25, 36, 49
   (d) 13, 20, 33 **(e)** −80, −160, −320
   (f) $\frac{10}{11}, \frac{12}{13}, \frac{14}{15}$

2. **(a)** 0.45 **(b)** 0.39 **(c)** 0.08 **(d)** 0.03 **(e)** 0.98 **(f)** 0.045 **(g)** 0.0525 **(h)** 0.005 **(i)** 1.25 **(j)** 1.10

3. **(a)** 1 **(b)** 43.2 **(c)** 1.8 **(d)** 0.756 **(e)** 96 **(f)** 202.5 **(g)** 278.64 **(h)** 45

4. **(a)** $-\frac{1}{2}$ **(b)** $1\frac{1}{6}$ **(c)** $-\frac{1}{2}$ **(d)** $-1\frac{7}{20}$ **(e)** $\frac{1}{5}$ **(f)** 2 **(g)** $-24\frac{5}{12}$ **(h)** $\frac{1}{2}$ **(i)** 2 **(j)** $-4\frac{3}{4}$ **(k)** $1\frac{7}{9}$ **(l)** $-4\frac{1}{2}$ **(m)** $1\frac{37}{128}$ **(n)** $7\frac{1}{5}$ **(o)** $-1\frac{7}{24}$

5. **(a)** 16 **(b)** 9 **(c)** −125 **(d)** $\frac{1}{36}$ **(e)** $\frac{1}{8}$ **(f)** $1\frac{7}{9}$ **(g)** 1 **(h)** $5\frac{1}{16}$ **(i)** $\frac{1}{49}$ **(j)** 256 **(k)** 72 **(l)** 2

6. **(a)** 11 **(b)** 23 **(c)** 250 **(d)** 320 **(e)** 1104.62 **(f)** 4528.65

7. **(a)** x^7 **(b)** x^2 **(c)** e^6 **(d)** d^4 **(e)** $10x^3y^5$ **(f)** $16x^{10}$ **(g)** $81a^8b^{12}$ **(h)** $\frac{4n^6}{m}$ **(i)** $\frac{-c^9}{8d^{15}}$ **(j)** $\frac{9x^4}{16y^6}$ **(k)** $-3x^5y^2$ **(l)** $3c^7d^2$

8. **(a)** $-3x$ **(b)** $-3x^2 + 2y^3$ **(c)** $-3x + 8$ **(d)** $10x + 15y$ **(e)** $18a - 22b$ **(f)** $6a + 15ab - 10ac - 4bc + 4c$ **(g)** $x^2 + 3x - 10$ **(h)** $4x^2 - 16x + 16$ **(i)** $24x^2 - 4xy - 8y^2$ **(j)** $4x^2 - 25$

9. **(a)** $3x(2x - 4y + 3)$ **(b)** $(a - 9)(a + 9)$ **(c)** $(x + 2)(x + 6)$ **(d)** $(a - 5)^2$ **(e)** $(2x + 3)(5x + 1)$ **(f)** $2(c + 2)(3c - 7)$

10. **(a)** $x = 10$ **(b)** $x = 2$ **(c)** $x = \pm 5$ **(d)** $x = -3, x = 5$ **(e)** $x = 4, x = -3$ **(f)** $x = -1.721, x \doteq 0.387$ **(g)** $x = 0, x = -1$ **(h)** no solution

11. **(a)** All 3; linear
(b) 13, 15, 17, 19, 21; nonlinear
(c) $\frac{1}{8}, \frac{1}{4}, \frac{1}{2}$, 1, 2; nonlinear
(d) All −2; linear

12. **(a)** straight line through (0, 6) and (−3, 0), $x = -3$
(b) upward parabola, vertex (0, −4), $x = \pm 2$
(c) upward parabola, vertex (−1.5, −20.25), $x = -6, x = 3$
(d) upward parabola, vertex (−2.5, 0.25)$x = -2, x = -3$

Practise, Apply, Solve 1.1, page 21

1. **(a)** 625, 3125, 15 625, 78 125 **(b)** 0, −4, −8, −12 **(c)** 32, 38, 44, 50 **(d)** $\frac{1}{25}, \frac{1}{36}, \frac{1}{49}, \frac{1}{64}$
(e) 98 765, 987 654, 9 876 543, 98 765 432
(f) −48, 96, −192, 384 **(g)** 35, 57, 92, 149
(h) 106, 156, 216, 286 **(i)** 32, 256, 8192, 2 097 152
(j) 125, 216, 343, 512 **(k)** 1.1, 1.3, 1.5, 1.7
(l) 0.75, 0.375, 0.1875, 0.093 75

2. **(a)** not predictable **(b)** 1032, 1034, 1036, 1038
(c) not predictable **(d)** 768, 1536, 3072, 6144
(e) \$49 134.06, \$51 099.42, \$53 143.40, \$55 269.14
(f) not predictable

3. **(a)** 5, 6, 7, 8, 9 **(b)** −1, 2, 7, 14, 23 **(c)** 2, 4, 8, 16, 32
(d) 3, 8, 13, 18, 23 **(e)** −3, 0, 5, 12, 21 **(f)** 5, $\frac{5}{2}, \frac{5}{3}, \frac{5}{4}$, 1
(g) 12, −24, 48, −96, 192 **(h)** −1, 1, −1, 1, −1
(i) 4, 1, −2, −5, −8

4. **(a)** 38 **(b)** 96 **(c)** $\frac{10}{11}$ **(d)** 0 **(e)** 7 **(f)** 2

5. **(a)** $t_n = 4n - 1$ **(b)** $t_n = 6n + 30$ **(c)** $t_n = 4(3)^{n-1}$
(d) $t_n = \frac{2}{3^n}$ **(e)** $t_n = 5(-1)^{n+1}$ **(f)** $t_n = \sqrt{n}$
(g) $t_n = -4n + 69$ **(h)** $t_n = \frac{n+1}{n+2}$ **(i)** $t_n = \frac{1}{n^2}$

6. 4, 9, 8, 1, 0, ..., $t_{10} = 9\ 765\ 625$, ...

7. **(a)** 2, 5, 8, 11, 14 **(b)** 81, 27, 9, 3, 1
(c) 2, 0, −2, −4, −6 **(d)** 2.4, 2.6, 2.8, 3. 3.2
(e) 1.5, 1, 0.75, 0.6, 0.5 **(f)** 3, 18, 45, 84, 135

8. **(a)** 7, 11, 16 **(b)** 56
(c) The difference between successive terms increases by 1.

9. **(a)** 1.414 213 562 4, 1.189 207 115, 1.090 507 732 7, 1.044 273 782 4, 1.021 897 148 7, 1.010 889 286 1, 1.005 429 901 1, 1.002 711 275 1, 1.001 354 719 9, 1.000 677 130 7
(b) The terms are approaching 1. **(c)** 1

10. The independent variable of a sequence uses only values from the set of natural numbers, so the points cannot be joined with a line or smooth curve.

11. **(a)** *Example*: {3, 6, 9, 12, 15, ...}, {3, 6, 3, 6, 3, ...}, {3, 6, 12, 24, 48, ...}, {3, 6, 10, 15, 21, ...}
(b) *Example*: increase by 3; add 3, subtract 3; double previous term; add one more than term
(c) *Example*: $t_n = t_{n-1} + 3$; $t_1 = 3$, $t_n = 9 - t_{n-1}$; $t_n = 2t_{n-1}$; $t_n = t_{n-1} + (n + 1)$

12. **(a)** $5n - 15$, −5, 10, 35 **(b)** n^4, 16, 625, 10 000
(c) $\frac{5}{n}$, 2.5, 1, 0.5 **(d)** $(3n + 4)^2$, 100, 361, 1156
(e) 2^{n+1}, 8, 64, 2048 **(f)** $(-1)^{n+3}$, −1, 1, −1
(g) $\frac{n-1}{2n+2}, \frac{1}{6}, \frac{1}{3}, \frac{9}{22}$ **(h)** $3n^2 + 2n - 1$, 15, 84, 319
(i) $(n - 1)^3$, 1, 64, 729

13. **(a)** finite **(b)** infinite **(c)** infinite
(d) infinite **(e)** finite

14. **(a)** \$1045, \$1090, \$1135 **(b)** $t_n = \$1000 + \$45n$
(c) \$1450

15. **(a)** {1, 8, 27, ...} **(b)** 64, 125, 216
(c) $t_n = n^3$ **(d)** 3375

16. **(a)** {10, 5, 2.5, 1.25, 0.625, ...} **(b)** $t_n = 20(0.5)^n$
(c) 0.0195 m
(d) The ball will stop bouncing eventually, so the sequence is finite. The sequence of numbers itself is infinite and the terms approach zero but will never reach it.

17. **(a)** {\$0.25, \$0.50, \$0.75, \$1.00, \$1.25, ...}
(b) $t_n = \$0.25n$ **(c)** \$13.00

18. **(a)** 98 **(b)** $t_n = 2n^2$

19. **(a)**, **(b)** (Time, Bacteria): (1, 20), (2, 40), (3, 80), (4, 160), (5, 320), (6, 640), (7, 1280), (8, 2560)
(c) $b_n = 10(2)^n$ **(d)** 10 240

20. 216, 492, 750

21. **(a)** {6, 16, 30, ...} **(b)** 48, 70, 96
(c) $t_n = 2n(n + 2)$ **(d)** 880

22. **(a)** {2, 8, 18, ...} **(b)** 32, 50, 72
(c) $t_n = 2n^2$ **(d)** 800

23. **(a)** 24, 40 **(c)** 220

Practice 1.2, page 26

(a) 6, 8, 10, 12, 14, 16, 18, 20, 22, 24
(b) 1, 8, 27, 64, 125, 216, 343, 512, 729, 1000
(c) 3, 2, $\frac{5}{3}, \frac{3}{2}, \frac{7}{5}, \frac{4}{3}, \frac{9}{7}, \frac{5}{4}, \frac{11}{9}, \frac{6}{5}$
(d) 1, 1.414 213 562 4, 1.732 050 807 6, 2, 2.236 067 977 5, 2.449 489 742 8, 2.645 751 311 1, 2.828 427 124 7, 3, 3.162 277 660 2
(e) −7, −12, −17, −22, −27, −32, −37, −42, −47, −52

(f) 0.5, 0.25, 0.125, 0.062 5, 0.031 25, 0.015 625, 0.007 812 5, 0.003 906 25, 0.001 953 125, 0.000 976 562 5
(g) 6, 18, 54, 162, 486, 1458, 4374, 13 122, 39 366, 118 098
(h) 1, 4, 27, 256, 3125, 46 656, 823 543, 16 777 216, 387 420 489, 10 000 000 000

Practise, Apply, Solve 1.3U, page 32

1. **(a)** 3, 12, 21, 30, 39 **(b)** 6, 24, 96, 384, 1536 **(c)** 36, 18, 9, 4.5, 2.25 **(d)** 22, 20, 18, 16, 14 **(e)** 3, 4, 12, 48, 576 **(f)** −5, 7, 2, 9, 11
2. **(a)** 4, 9, 14, 19, 24 **(b)** −3, −8, −18, −38, −78 **(c)** 8, 4, 2, 1, 0.5 **(d)** 4, 16, 256, 65 536, 4 294 967 296 **(e)** $5, \frac{5}{2}, \frac{5}{6}, \frac{5}{24}, \frac{1}{24}$ **(f)** 1, 2, 2, 4, 8 **(g)** 2, −1, 1, 0, 1 **(h)** 1, 1, −1, −5, −7
3. **(a)** $t_1 = 2, t_{n+1} = t_n + 5$ **(b)** $t_1 = -2, t_{n+1} = -2t_n$ **(c)** $t_1 = 10, t_{n+1} = 0.5\,t_n$ **(d)** $t_1 = 2, t_{n+1} = (t_n)^2$ **(e)** $t_1 = 243, t_{n+1} = \frac{t_n}{3}$ **(f)** $t_1 = 34, t_{n+1} = t_n - 9$
4. **(a)** $t_1 = 3, t_n = t_{n-1} + 9$ **(b)** $t_1 = 6, t_n = 4t_{n-1}$ **(c)** $t_1 = 36, t_n = \frac{1}{2}t_{n-1}$ **(d)** $t_1 = 22, t_n = t_{n-1} - 2$ **(e)** $t_1 = 3, t_2 = 4, t_n = (t_{n-1})(t_{n-2})$ **(f)** $t_1 = -5, t_2 = 7, t_n = (t_{n-1}) + (t_{n-2})$
5. **(a)** 85% **(b)** \$29 750, \$25 287.50, \$21 494.38, \$18 270.22, \$15 529.69 **(c)** $t_1 = \$35\ 000, t_n = 0.85(t_{n-1})$
6. **(a)** $t_1 = 4200, t_n = 0.8(t_{n-1}) + 850$ **(b)** Over time, the number of trees levels off to 4250.
7. 369 600
8. **(a)** 3, 5, 7, 9, 11 **(b)** −5, −10, −20, −40, −80 **(c)** 8, 4, 2, 1, 0.5 **(d)** 2, 8, 2, 8, 2
9. **(a)** $t_1 = \$40\ 000, t_n = t_{n-1} + 1250$ **(b)** \$40 000, \$41 250, \$42 500, \$43 750, \$45 000 **(c)** \$51 250, no
10. **(a)** stage 2: $s = 12, l = 6, p = 72$ cm; stage 3: $s = 48, l = 2, p = 96$ cm **(b)** $s_n = 4\,s_{n-1}, s_1 = 3; l_n = \frac{1}{3}l_{n-1}, l_1 = 18; p_n = \frac{4}{3}p_{n-1}, p_1 = 54$ **(c)** 3072 **(d)** 0.0247 cm **(e)** 404.5 cm
11. **(a)** $t_n = 0.8(t_{n-1}), t_1 = 50$ m **(b)** 50 m, 40 m, 32 m, 25.6 m, 20.48 m **(c)** 336.16 m
12. Answers will vary.
13. 357.14 mg
14. **(a)** 42 **(b)** $t_n = t_{n-1} + 2n, t_1 = 2$
15. 8
16. **(a)** $a_n = 1.05a_{n-1} - 50\ 000$ **(b)** $a_{19} = \$0.02$ **(c)** A prize of \$1 000 000 can be awarded even though only \$604 266.05 was invested.
17. **(a)** $t_n = 2t_{n-1}, t_1 = 3500$ **(b)** 112 000
18. **(a)** $t_n = 2t_{n-1}, t_1 = 2$ **(b)** 510
19. 12, 18, 36
20. 8 h
21. general formula
22. $t_n = t_{n-1} + n^2, t_1 = 5$
23. **(a)** $t_n = t_{n-1} + 2(n-1), t_1 = 20$ **(b)** 110 **(c)** 530
24. 35

Practice 1.4, page 38

Part 1

(a) $t_{10} = 63, t_{15} = 93, t_{20} = 123$
(b) $t_{10} = 100, t_{15} = 225, t_{20} = 400$
(c) $t_{10} = 0.1, t_{15} = 0.067, t_{20} = 0.05$
(d) $t_{10} \doteq 3.162, t_{15} \doteq 3.872, t_{20} \doteq 4.472$
(e) $t_{10} = 1990, t_{15} = 6735, t_{20} = 15\ 980$
(f) $t_{10} = -10, t_{15} = -15, t_{20} = -20$
(g) $t_{10} \doteq 25.937, t_{15} \doteq 41.772, t_{20} \doteq 67.274$
(h) $t_{10} \doteq 0.009, t_{15} \doteq 0.000\ 305, t_{20} \doteq 0.000\ 009\ 536$

Part 2

(a) $t_5 = 19, t_{10} = 39$ **(b)** $t_5 = 3750, t_{10} = 11\ 718\ 750$
(c) $t_5 = 65, t_{10} = -2047$ **(d)** $t_5 = 32, t_{10} = 1024$
(e) $t_5 = 6.25, t_{10} = 0.195\ 312\ 5$ **(f)** $t_5 = -7, t_{10} = -5$

Practise, Apply, Solve 1.6, page 47

1. **(a)** not arithmetic **(b)** arithmetic, $d = -9$ **(c)** not arithmetic **(d)** not arithmetic **(e)** arithmetic, $d = 11$ **(f)** arithmetic, $d = \frac{1}{4}$
2. **(a)** arithmetic, 3 **(b)** not arithmetic **(c)** arithmetic, −4 **(d)** not arithmetic **(e)** arithmetic, $\frac{1}{2}$ **(f)** not arithmetic
3. **(a)** $d = 5, t_n = 5n, t_{10} = 50$ **(b)** $d = 6, t_n = 6n - 36, t_{10} = 24$ **(c)** $d = -2, t_n = -2n + 15, t_{10} = -5$ **(d)** $d = \frac{1}{3}, t_n = \frac{1}{3}n, t_{10} = \frac{10}{3}$ **(e)** $d = 0.15, t_n = 0.15n + 0.05, t_{10} = 1.55$ **(f)** $d = 0, t_n = -3, t_{10} = -3$
4. **(a)** $t_n = t_{n-1} + 5, t_1 = 5$ **(b)** $t_n = t_{n-1} + 6, t_1 = -30$ **(c)** $t_n = t_{n-1} - 2, t_1 = 13$ **(e)** $t_n = t_{n-1} + \frac{1}{3}, t_1 = \frac{1}{3}$ **(e)** $t_n = t_{n-1} + 0.15, t_1 = 0.2$ **(f)** $t_n = -3, t_1 = -3$
5. **(a)** $t_n = 6n + 1$ **(b)** $t_n = -2n - 7$ **(c)** $t_n = -6n + 31$ **(d)** $t_n = 12n + 109$
6. **(a)** 31, 40, 49 **(b)** $t_n = 9n - 14$ **(c)** 1786
7. **(a)** $t_n = 2n, t_{24} = 48$ **(b)** $t_n = -3n + 2, t_{24} = -70$ **(c)** $t_n = 5n + 5, t_{24} = 125$ **(d)** $t_n = -10n - 20, t_{24} = -260$
8. **(a)** dots in straight line through (0, −6) and (1.5, 0) **(b)** dots in straight line through (0, 3) and (0.6, 0) **(c)** dots in straight line through (0, −1) and (−1, 0) **(d)** dots in straight line through (0, 4) and (−8, 0) **(e)** dots in straight line through (0, 0.5) and (−1, 0) **(f)** dots in straight line through (0, −2) and (1, 8) **(g)** dots in straight line through (1, 0) and (0, –3) **(h)** dots in straight line through (0, 4) and (2, 0)
9. **(a)** (1, −9), (2, −6), (3, −3), (4, 0), (5, 3), (6, 6) **(b)** t_{11} **(c)** t_{11} **(d)** general term
10. **(a)** \$40 **(b)** \$525 **(c)** \$807.50 **(d)** \$248.80 **(e)** \$11.84
11. **(a)** 22 **(b)** 33 **(c)** 40 **(d)** 15 **(e)** 14 **(f)** 19
12. **(a)** \$90 **(b)** \$2000, \$2090, \$2180, \$2270, \$2360 **(c)** $t_n = \$90n + \$1910, t_1 = \$2000$ **(e)** 16
13. 32 a
14. **(a)** 37 **(b)** 22
15. **(a)** $t_n = 1531 + 76n$ **(b)** 2063 **(c)** 23rd century (2215 and 2291) **(d)** No; comet may not return.
16. $t_n = t_{n-1} + d, t_1 = a$
17. **(a)** $a = 8, d = 3, t_n = 3n + 5$ **(b)** $a = -14, d = -5, t_n = -5n - 9$ **(c)** $a = -25, d = 7, t_n = 7n - 32$ **(d)** $a = 10.5, d = 0.5, t_n = 0.5n + 10$ **(e)** $a = 28, d = 6, t_n = 6n + 22$

(f) $a = 38$, $d = -7$, $t_n = -7n + 45$

18. \$116.25

19. **(a)** $t_n = 6n + 11$, $t_{25} = 161$
(b) common difference between terms, can be written as $t_n = a + (n - 1)d$

20. \$602.50

21. $\frac{c + d}{2} - c = \frac{d - c}{2}$ and $d - \frac{c + d}{2} = \frac{d - c}{2}$

22. $t_n = (-2x - 1)n + (7x - 2)$

23. 320

Practise, Apply, Solve 1.7, page 57

1. **(a)** geometric, $r = 3$ **(b)** geometric, $r = -3$
(c) not geometric **(d)** geometric, $r = 4$
(e) not geometric **(f)** geometric, $r = \frac{1}{2}$

2. **(a)** geometric, $r = 3$ **(b)** not geometric
(c) not geometric **(d)** geometric, $r = 6$
(e) not geometric **(f)** geometric, $r = -1$

3. **(a)** $r = 5$, $t_n = 3(5)^{n-1}$, $t_8 = 234\ 375$
(b) $r = 12$, $t_n = -12^n$, $t_8 = -429\ 981\ 696$
(c) $r = \frac{1}{2}$, $t_n = 4\left(\frac{1}{2}\right)^{n-1} = \frac{1}{2^{n-3}}$, $t_8 = 0.031\ 25$
(d) $r = -2$, $t_n = 6(-2)^{n-1}$, $t_8 = -768$
(e) $r = 0.1$, $t_n = 0.2(0.1)^{n-1}$, $t_8 = 2 \times 10^{-8}$
(f) $r = 1$, $t_n = 5$, $t_8 = 5$

4. **(a)** $t_1 = 3$, $t_n = 5\,t_{n-1}$ **(b)** $t_1 = -12$, $t_n = 12\,t_{n-1}$
(c) $t_1 = 4$, $t_n = \frac{1}{2}t_{n-1}$ **(d)** $t_1 = 6$, $t_n = -2\,t_{n-1}$
(e) $t_1 = 0.2$, $t_n = 0.1\,t_{n-1}$ **(f)** $t_1 = 5$, $t_n = t_{n-1}$

5. **(a)** $t_n = 3(7)^{n-1}$ **(b)** $t_n = -4\left(\frac{-1}{4}\right)^{n-1} = (-1)^n 4^{-n+2}$
(c) $t_n = 125(-0.2)^{n-1} = (-1)^{n-1}5^{-n+4}$
(d) $t_n = -2(3)^n$

6. **(a)** arithmetic, $t_n = 10n + 20$ **(b)** geometric, $t_n = 4^n$
(c) neither **(d)** geometric, $t_n = 30\left(\frac{1}{5}\right)^{n-1}$
(e) arithmetic, $t_n = -15n + 160$ **(f)** neither

7. **i.** $t_n = 2^{n-1}$, $t_{10} = 512$
ii. $t_n = -40\left(\frac{1}{2}\right)^{n-1} = -5(2^{-n+4})$, $t_{10} = -\frac{5}{64}$
iii. $t_n = 4(-1)^{n+1}$, $t_{10} = -4$
iv. $t_n = 8\left(\frac{1}{2}\right)^{n-1} = 2^{-n+4}$, $t_{10} = \frac{1}{64}$

8. **(a)** dots of right side of upward parabola
(b) dots of curve going upward to right through (0, 0.2)
(c) dots of curve in first quadrant through (1, 5) and (3, 1.25)
(d) dots alternating above and below x-axis in increasing magnitude to right (−1, 3), (0, −6), (2, 12), ...
(e) dots in fourth quadrant curving up to right through (−2, 4)
(f) dots above x-axis curving up to right through (0, 1)
(g) dots above x-axis curving up to right through (1, 0.125)
(h) dots in third quadrant curving down to right through (−1, −1)

9. **(a)** $t_n = \left(-\frac{2}{3}\right)^{n-1}$ **(b)** $t_8 = -\frac{128}{2187}$

10. **(a)** \$28 500, \$25 080, \$22 070.40, \$19 421.95, \$17 091.32, \$15 040.36
(b) $t_n = \$28\ 500\ (0.88)^{n-1}$ **(c)** \$10 249.58

11. **(a)** \$34 000, \$34 850, \$35 721.25, \$36 614.28, \$37 529.64
(b) $t_n = \$34\ 000\ (1.025)^{n-1}$ **(c)** \$42 461.34

12. \$1006.10

13. 1.776×10^{-12} g

14. 81 920

15. **(a)** $t_n = (1.65 \times 10^9)(1.0135)^{n-1900}$ **(b)** 7.21×10^9

16. The value is multiplied by a factor of 0.75 each year.

17. **(a)** 1, 3, 9, 27 **(b)** 2187
(c) $3, \frac{9}{2}, \frac{27}{4}, \frac{81}{8}$ **(d)** 34.17 units

18. $t_1 = a$, $t_n = rt_{n-1}$

19. 11 a

20. **(a)** $a = -0.001\ 28$, $r = 5$, $t_n = -0.00128(5)^{n-1}$
(b) $a = 4$, $r = 2$, $t_n = 2^{n+1}$; $a = -4$, $r = -2$, $t_n = (-1)^n(2)^{n+1}$
(c) $a = 2$, $r = 3$, $t_n = 2(3)^{n-1}$

21. **(a)** $t_n = 4(7)^{n-1}$, $t_{10} = 161\ 414\ 428$
(b) $t_1 = 108$, $t_2 = 36$, multiply by $\frac{1}{3}$ to get next term

22. *Example:* {5, 5, 5, ...}

23. 35.44 units^2

24. $(a, b) = (1, -6)$ or $(a, b) = (16, 24)$

25. $\frac{-b^8}{a^7}$

Practise, Apply, Solve 1.8, page 70

1. **(a)** $i = 0.06$, $n = 5$ **(b)** $i = 0.04$, $n = 18$
(c) $i = 0.011$, $n = 28$ **(d)** $i = 0.005$, $n = 36$
(e) $i = 0.05$, $n = 5$ **(f)** $i = 0.0205$, $n = 5\frac{1}{3}$
(g) $i = 0.0225$, $n = 7$ **(h)** $i = 0.001$, $n = 104$
(i) $i = 0.000\ 15$, $n = 1095$

2. **(a)** 3.1384 **(b)** 0.3769 **(c)** 2.4325
(d) 0.9140 **(e)** 512.6608 **(f)** 2837.1343
(g) 3405.3486 **(h)** 12 403.0161

3. **(a)** amount of investment **(b)** principle amount invested
(c) interest rate for each conversion period
(d) number of conversion periods

4. **(a)** $A = \$4502.04$, $i = \$502.04$
(b) $A = \$10\ 740.33$, $i = \$3240.33$
(c) $A = \$16\ 906.39$, $i = \$1906.39$
(d) $A = \$48\ 516.08$, $i = \$20\ 316.08$
(e) $A = \$881.60$, $i = \$31.60$ **(f)** $A = \$2332.02$, $i = \$107.02$

5. **(a)** $P = \$4444.98$, $i = \$555.02$
(b) $A = \$10\ 625.83$, $i = \$2874.17$
(c) $A = \$8999.01$, $i = \$2200.99$
(d) $A = \$77\ 030.40$, $i = \$51\ 469.60$
(e) $A = \$797.31$, $i = \$52.69$
(f) $A = \$4849.55$, $i = \$1375.45$

6. The amount is the future value of the principal amount after the principal amount earns interest. The present value is the principal amount that must be invested now to grow to a specific amount in the future.

7. Plan A

8. **(a)** \$1628.89 **(b)** \$2653.30 **(c)** \$4321.94

9. 14 a

10. \$4353.04

11. $A = \$13\ 431.36$, $P = \$7500$

12. \$1407.10

13. \$16 637.84

14. \$14 434.24

15. \$1348.05

16. \$5200

17. Each amount is multiplied by $(1 + i)$ each conversion period.

18. \$4514.38

19. \$4534.14

20. \$3427.09

21. **(a)** \$1226.32 **(b)** \$1178.31

22. Justin, with \$2.85 more

23. 10.4%

24. 9.75 a

25. no

Practise, Apply, Solve 1.9, page 79

1. (a) 64 (b) 36 (c) −9 (d) −729 (e) 1 (f) $\frac{1}{8}$ (g) $\frac{16}{81}$ (h) $\frac{-8}{27}$ (i) $1\frac{7}{9}$ (j) −64
2. (a) 11 (b) 2 (c) 2 (d) 5 (e) 4
3. (a) 2 (b) −2 (c) −3 (d) 3 (e) 5 (f) $\frac{1}{4}$ (g) $\frac{1}{6}$ (h) $\frac{1}{5}$ (i) $\frac{2}{3}$ (j) $\frac{1}{2}$
4. (a) 64 (b) 4 (c) −8 (d) 81 (e) 243 (f) $\frac{1}{4}$ (g) $\frac{1}{9}$ (h) $\frac{1}{625}$ (i) $\frac{8}{125}$ (j) $\frac{1}{8}$
5. (a) 3.32 (b) −2.88 (c) −3.16 (d) 3.68 (e) 2.78 (f) 0.76 (g) 0.98 (h) 0.17 (i) 1.53 (j) 0.49
6. (a) 125.00 (b) 14.46 (c) 1.18 (d) 2.77 (e) 46.46 (f) 0.94 (g) 0.01 (h) 0.01 (i) 0.51 (j) 0.17
7. (a) \$6059.41 (b) \$2626.88 (c) \$13 327.45 (d) \$13 795.99 (e) \$3899.86 (f) \$6325.42
8. (a) \$2882.08 (b) \$10 295.11 (c) \$6158.63 (d) \$85 677.09 (e) \$142.32 (f) \$2974.05
9. (a) \$25 000 (b) 15% (c) \$15 353.13 (d) \$12 362
10. (a) $V_t = 500(1.06)^t$ (b) \$669.11 (c) \$524.53
11. (a) $M_t = 700\left(\frac{1}{2}\right)^t$ (b) 1.367 mg (c) 588.627 mg
12. 12.1%
13. (a) $M_t = 40\left(\frac{1}{2}\right)^{\frac{t}{5}}$ (b) 5 mg (c) 30.3 mg
14. (a) $5x$ (b) $-3x$ (c) $2x$ (d) no solution (e) $3x$ (f) $x + 2$ (g) no solution (h) $2x + 5$
15. [(], [(-)], [1], [2], [5], [)], [^], [(], [(-)], [5], [÷], [3], [)], [=]
16. (a) $125x^6$ (b) $9a^2b^2$ (c) $\frac{4x^2}{25}$ (d) $\frac{9}{16y^2}$
17. (a) $\frac{1}{64x^3}$ (b) $\frac{1}{343c^9}$ (c) $-\frac{3}{x}$ (d) $\frac{27y^6}{8}$
18. \$750.00
19. (a) Yes, since the voltage will be 0.01 V. (b) 1.498 V
20. 493.28 cm
21. $\frac{1}{8}$
22. (a) \$3599.99 (b) 6.98%
23. (a) 93 min 29.7 s (b) 35 848.51 km

Practise, Apply, Solve 1.10, page 85

1. (a) x^7 (b) c^{20} (c) x^3 (d) a^3b^3 (e) d^3 (f) $\frac{1}{b^5}$ (g) $4x^6$ (h) $\frac{-8x^3}{27y^6}$
2. (a) 2^9 (b) 2^{n+m} (c) 2^{4x} (d) 2^6 (e) 2^{3n} (f) 2^8 (g) 2^{8-m} (h) 2^{12x-4}
3. (a) 243 (b) 1 (c) $\frac{1}{64}$ (d) 81 (e) $\frac{-1}{8}$ (f) 2 (g) 4 (h) 8 (i) $\frac{1}{5}$ (j) $\frac{1}{10}$ (k) −3 (l) 64 (m) 9 (n) $\frac{1}{8}$ (o) 16
4. (a) $\frac{1}{x^6}$ (b) $x^{\frac{1}{3}}$ (c) $c^{\frac{5}{4}}$ (d) $\frac{1}{a^{\frac{2}{3}}}$ (e) $\frac{1}{c^3}$
5. (a) x^3y^3 (b) $3b^4$ (c) $\frac{-a^6}{b}$ (d) c^6d^6 (e) a^6 (f) a^8b^2 (g) $-x^7y$ (h) $\frac{1}{y^{10}}$
6. (a) 9 (b) −18 (c) $15\frac{2}{3}$ (d) $\frac{-3}{32}$ (e) $\frac{253}{4}$ (f) 3 (g) $4\frac{3}{4}$ (h) $\frac{9}{10}$
7. (a) $\frac{1}{8}$ (b) $\frac{1}{12}$ (c) $2\frac{1}{4}$ (d) $4\frac{1}{4}$ (e) 6 (f) $\frac{1}{26}$ (g) $\frac{1}{6}$ (h) $1\frac{23}{34}$ (i) $\frac{-1}{9}$
8. (a) xy^{-2} (b) m^3n^{-2} (c) $2x^3y^{-5}z^{-2}$ (d) $5a^2bc^{-2}$ (e) $-5m^2n^4$ (f) x^2 (g) $m^{-5}n^4$ (h) $2x^3y^{-2}z^3$
9. (a) $\frac{a^4}{b^3}$ (b) $\frac{4b^3c^2}{a^2}$ (c) $\frac{5}{a^3b}$ (d) $\frac{2a^2c^4}{3b^4}$ (e) $\frac{3b}{16a^2}$
10. (a) 9 (b) 9 (c) $\frac{1}{9}$ (d) $\frac{2}{3}$ (e) 9 (f) $\frac{1}{81}$ (g) 9 (h) 9
11. (a) 4 (b) 8 (c) 5 (d) 3 (e) 12 (f) 10 (g) 5 (h) 14 (i) 24 (j) 1 (k) 3 (l) 15
12. (a) false (b) true (c) false (d) true (e) false (f) true
13. (a) x (b) c (c) z^3 (d) d^2 (e) $\frac{4}{9}$ (f) 2 (g) $\frac{4y^{\frac{3}{2}}}{x^{\frac{2}{3}}}$ (h) $\frac{9u^{\frac{6}{5}}}{v^{\frac{2}{5}}}$ (i) $\frac{3y^2}{4z^{\frac{4}{3}}}$ (j) $\frac{1}{a^{\frac{1}{4}}}$ (k) $\sqrt{c}$ (l) $\frac{1}{k^{\frac{1}{5}}}$
14. (a) $x^{\frac{11}{12}}$ (b) x (c) $\frac{1}{4y^2}$ (d) 1 (e) $\frac{x^2}{3}$ (f) 1
15. (a) x^{10-2r} (b) $\frac{1}{a^{r+1}}$ (c) b^{m+4n} (d) x^{-2r+21} (e) a^{10-2p} (f) $3^{(6-m)}x^{(24-5m)}$
16. (a) $9x^6$ (b) $\frac{y^8}{16x^4}$ (c) $4x^5y^2$ (d) $\frac{4}{27x^{16}}$ (e) $\frac{x^2}{8y^2}$ (f) $\frac{8y^4}{243x^7}$
17. $\frac{243x^{18}}{32y^{14}}$
18. (a) 3 (b) 25 (c) 512 (d) 32
19. (a) $\frac{-1}{6}$ (b) $\frac{27}{2}$
20. A

Practise, Apply, Solve 1.11, page 94

1. (a) 3^3 (b) 3^4 (c) 3^{-2} (d) 3^{4x} (e) 3^{-3x}
2. (a) 4 (b) 0 (c) −4 (d) $\frac{-3}{10}$
3. (a) 7 (b) 3 (c) 6 (d) 2 (e) 10 (f) 3 (g) 4 (h) 6
4. (a) 5 (b) 3 (c) 2 (d) 5 (e) 3 (f) −3 (g) $\frac{1}{3}$ (h) 4
5. (a) 4.32 (b) 2.21 (c) 4.19 (d) 2.90 (e) 2.82 (f) 0.86 (g) 2.08 (h) 0.43
6. (a) $\frac{7}{4}$ (b) $\frac{2}{5}$ (c) $\frac{5}{6}$ (d) $1\frac{4}{9}$
7. (a) −5
8. (a) 8 (b) −6 (c) −7 (d) 2 (e) 2 (f) 6
9. (a) 5, −1 (b) 3, −1 (c) −2 (d) −2, −4 (e) −5, −4 (f) $\frac{2}{3}$, −4 (g) 5, −1 (h) $\frac{1}{2}$, 2 (i) 1, 4
10. (a) 10 (b) 12 (c) 6 (d) 11 (e) 8 (f) 7
11. (a) 3.10 (b) 1.43 (c) 2.38 (d) 17.67 (e) −0.72 (f) 1.25 (g) 0.87 (h) 1.68
12. 195 min
13. 2
14. (a) 6.489 GW•h (b) 1570.590 GW•h (c) 1989 (d) End of June, 1989

15. 7.5 a
16. If the left and right sides cannot easily be expressed with a common base, then the graphical solution should be used.
17. 42.72 days
18. (a) 5730 a (b) 19 034.6 a
19. 7.73 a
20. 7.66 a
21. 3.45 h
22. 6
23. (a) 0, 5 (b) 1, 2
24. (a) $\frac{\pm\sqrt{3}+3}{2}$ (b) $\pm\sqrt{5}-3$
25. 41.1 a

Chapter 1, Review and Practice, page 98

1. A sequence is an ordered set of numbers. A term is a single element of a sequence. For example, {1, 3, 5, 7, ...} is a sequence, and 5 is the third term.
2. The general term is an expression or formula for all the terms in a sequence. It is a function of a natural number, and using numbers in this formula generates the terms of this sequence.
3. (a) *Example,* {1, 2, 3, ..., 100} (b) *Example,* {1, 4, 9, 16, ...}
4. (a) 5, 9, 13, 17, 21 (b) 0, 4, 12, 24, 40 (c) 1, 3, 9, 27, 81 (d) −1, −4, −7, −10, −13 (e) 3, 15, 35, 63, 99 (f) 10, 5, $\frac{10}{3}$, $\frac{5}{2}$, 2
6. (a) $t_n = 5n - 3$ (b) $t_n = -6n + 36$ (c) $t_n = 3^{n+1}$ (d) $t_n = \frac{5}{2^n}$ (e) $t_n = n^2 + 1$ (f) $t_n = \frac{n+1}{n+2}$
7. (a) $18 000, $13 500, $10 125, $7593.75 (b) $t_n = \$24\ 000\left(\frac{3}{4}\right)^n$ (c) $3203.61
8. A recursive formula defines each term as a function of one or more previous terms, whereas a general term defines each term as a function of a natural number.
9. A recursive formula defines each term as a function of previous terms, and initial conditions.
10. (a) 7, −3, −13, −23, −33 (b) −3, −9, −39, −189, −939 (c) −4, −8, −16, −32, −64 (d) 3, 34, 4622, 8.545×10^7, 2.9208×10^{16}
11. (a) $t_1 = 2, t_n = t_{n-1} + 3$ (b) $t_1 = 18, t_n = t_{n-1} - 7$ (c) $t_1 = 3, t_n = (t_{n-1})^2$ (d) $t_1 = 2, t_2 = 4, t_n = t_{n-1} + t_{n-2}$ (e) $t_1 = 1, t_n = \frac{2}{3}t_{n-1}$ (f) $t_1 = 4, t_n = (1 + 2^{n-3})t_{n-1}$
12. (a) 6, 9, 12, 15, 18 (b) −4, −12, −36, − 108, −324 (c) 8, 4, 2, 1, 0.5 (d) 2, 8, 2, 8, 2
13. (a) 333.3 mg (b) About 72 h
14. If the first differences between the terms of a sequence are constant, then the sequence is arithmetic.
15. (a) $t_n = a + (n-1)d$ (b) t_n − term, a − first term, n − term index, d − common difference
16. (a) 4, 7, 10, 13, 16 (b) 10, 8, 6, 4, 2
17. (a) $d = 6, t_n = 6n, t_{15} = 90$ (b) $d = 15, t_n = 15n - 55, t_{15} = 170$ (c) $d = -5, t_n = -5n + 41, t_{15} = -34$ (d) $d = \frac{1}{4}, t_n = \frac{1}{4}n, t_{15} = 3\frac{3}{4}$ (e) $d = 0.7, t_n = 0.7n + 0.5, t_{15} = 11$ (f) $d = 32, t_n = 32n - 28, t_{15} = 452$
18. (a) dots in straight line through (0, 5) and (5, 0) (b) dots in straight line through (0, −4) and $\left(\frac{4}{7}, 0\right)$ (c) dots in straight line through (0, 7) and $\left(\frac{7}{3}, 0\right)$ (d) dots in straight line through (0, 2) and (−4, 0)
19. (a) $162.50 (b) $5000, $5162.50, $5325, $5487.50, $5650 (c) $t_n = \$162.50n + \$4837.50$ (e) 7 a
20. (a) $a = 12, d = 3, t_n = 3n + 9$ (b) $a = -11, d = -6, t_n = -6n - 5$ (c) $a = 1, d = 9, t_n = 9n - 8$ (d) $a = 7, d = -15, t_n = -15n + 22$
21. If the ratio between any two successive terms is constant, then the sequence is geometric.
22. Answers will vary.
23. (a) $t_n = ar^{n-1}$ (b) t_n − term, a − first term, r − common ratio, n − term index
24. (a) $r = 7, t_n = 2(7)^{n-1}, t_{12} = 3\ 954\ 653\ 486$ (b) $r = 4, t_n = -3(4)^{n-1}, t_{12} = -12\ 582\ 912$ (c) $r = \frac{1}{2}, t_n = 160\left(\frac{1}{2}\right)^{n-1}, t_{12} = 0.078\ 125$ (d) $r = -3, t_n = 7(-3)^{n-1}, t_{12} = -1\ 240\ 029$ (e) $r = 0.2, t_n = 0.4(0.2)^{n-1}, t_{12} = 8.19 \times 10^{-9}$ (f) $r = \frac{1}{3}, t_n = \frac{1}{3^{n-9}}, t_{12} = \frac{1}{27}$
25. (a) $149 500, $127 075, $108 013.75, $91 811.69, $78 039.93, $66 333.94 (b) $t_n = \$149\ 500\ (0.85)^{n-1}$ (c) $47 926.27
26. In simple interest, only the principal amount earns interest, whereas in compound interest, in addition to the principal amount, the interest earns interest as well.
27. (a) $A = P(1+i)^n$ (b) A − the amount of the investment, P − the principal amount invested, i − interest rate, n − number of compounding periods
28. Solve for P in $A = P(1+i)^n$
29. (a) $A = \$7518.15, I = \$2518.15$ (b) $A = \$12\ 717.67, I = \$2217.67$
30. (a) $P = \$13\ 367.01, I = \$8132.99$ (b) $P = \$78\ 119.84, I = \$21\ 880.16$
31. $16 783.48
32. $15 745.09
33. (a) $x^{\frac{1}{n}} = \sqrt[n]{x}$ (b) $x^{\frac{m}{n}} = \sqrt[n]{x^m}$ (c) $x^{-\frac{m}{n}} = \frac{1}{(\sqrt[n]{x})^m} = \frac{1}{\sqrt[n]{x^m}}$
34. (a) 3 (b) −3 (c) −2 (d) 2 (e) 2 (f) $\frac{1}{16}$ (g) $\frac{1}{3}$ (h) $\frac{1}{16}$ (i) $\frac{8}{27}$ (j) $\frac{1}{16}$
35. (a) 5.10 (b) −2.71 (c) −3.06 (d) 3.27 (e) 2.89 (f) 0.91 (g) 0.01 (h) 0.01 (i) 1.57 (j) 0.27
36. (a) $5207.48 (b) $6470.94
37. (a) $1466.03 (b) $77 702.94
38. (a) $t_n = \$1200(1.05)^n$ (b) $1954.67 (c) $1344.69
39. multiplication: $a^m \times a^n = a^{m+n}$; division: $a^m \div a^n = a^{m-n}$; power of a power: $(a^m)^n = a^{mn}$; power of a product: $(xy)^m = x^m y^m$; power of a quotient: $\left(\frac{x}{y}\right)^m = \frac{x^m}{y^m}$; zero as an exponent: $a^0 = 1$; negative exponents: $a^{-m} = \frac{1}{a^m}$; rational exponents: $x^{\frac{m}{n}} = \sqrt[n]{x^m} = (\sqrt[n]{x})^m$
40. (a) 13 (b) −7 (c) $\frac{-19}{216}$
41. (a) $\frac{-2}{3}$ (b) $\frac{1}{19\ 683}$ (c) $\frac{1}{243}$ (d) $\frac{-4}{45}$
42. (a) $\frac{4b^2}{9a^4}$ (b) $\frac{16x^4z^8}{y^6}$ (c) $\frac{625x^7}{y^3}$
43. (a) a^{p+2} (b) $(2^{3-2m})x^{(6-6m)}$ (c) 1 (d) x^{n-4m}

44. *Example*: $21 = 3^x$

45. when both sides of an exponential equation are expressible as a power of common base

46. (1) Consider an exponential equation. (2) Graph y = L.S. and y = R. S. (3) Carefully determine the intersection point.

47. **(a)** 2 **(b)** 2 **(c)** -1 **(d)** $\frac{7}{4}$

48. **(a)** 2.43 **(b)** 1.39 **(c)** 5.03 **(d)** 8.31

49. **(a)** $-3, -4$ **(b)** -1 **(c)** $\frac{3}{2}, 1$ **(d)** $\frac{\pm\sqrt{17}-3}{2}$

50. **(a)** 8 **(b)** 10

51. 13.87 a

Chapter 1 Review Test, page 104

1. **(a)** 11, 17, 23, 29; arithmetic
   (b) $1, \frac{1}{3}, \frac{1}{6}, \frac{1}{10}$; neither
   (c) 3, 12, 48, 192; geometric
   (d) 5, 1, -7, -23; neither
2. **(a)** 31 **(b)** 6
3. $a = -137, d = \frac{10}{3}, t_n = -\frac{10}{3}n - \frac{401}{3}$
4. **(a)** $\frac{9}{4}$ **(b)** 60
5. **(a)** $8xy^2$ **(b)** a^n
6. In an arithmetic sequence, each term is the sum of the previous term plus a fixed amount In a geometric sequence, each term is the product of the previous term and a fixed ratio.
7. **(a)** 4 **(b)** -2
8. 0.36 m
9. $13 511.28
10. 2.24 a
11. 70
12. $9252.25

Chapter 2

Getting Ready, page 108

1. **(a)** $-4, -1, 2, 5, 8$ **(b)** $-4, 1, 6, 11, 16$
   (c) 3, 6, 12, 24, 48 **(d)** $11, 7, 3, -1, -5$
   (e) $8, 4, 2, 1, \frac{1}{2}$ **(f)** $\frac{1}{2}, -1, 2, -4, 8$
   (g) 55, 60.5, 66.55, 73.205, 80.5255
   (h) 1000, 1060, 1123.6, 1191.016,1262.477
   (i) $15, 7, -1, -9, -17$
2. **(a)** arithmetic **(b)** geometric **(c)** neither
   (d) geometric **(e)** neither **(f)** arithmetic
   (g) geometric **(h)** neither **(i)** neither
3. **(a)** $t_n = 11n - 6$ **(b)** $t_n = 3(-2)^{n-1}$ **(d)** $81\left(\frac{1}{3}\right)^{n-1}$
   (f) $t_n = -6n + 67$ **(g)** $t_n = 1000(1.1)^{n-1}$
4. **(a)** 8 **(b)** 32 **(c)** $\frac{1}{4}$ **(d)** $\frac{16}{9}$
5. **(a)** 3.4641 **(b)** -3.3019 **(c)** 0.6407 **(d)** 0.9839
   (e) 1.0344 **(f)** 0.0031 **(g)** 1.2842 **(h)** 0.1402
6. **(a)** $-\frac{19}{3}$ **(b)** 3 **(c)** 5 **(d)** 5
7. **(a)** 1210 **(b)** 1376.92 **(c)** 7724.89 **(d)** 666.02
   (e) 1754.87 **(f)** 53266.80
8. **(a)** $1560 **(b)** $210 **(c)** $108.49 **(d)** $5923.08
9. **(a)** 14 **(b)** 15
10. $13.83
11. $10 462.10
12. **(a)** A = $5979.62, i = $2379.62
    (b) A = $27 355.25, i = $9355.25
    (c) A =$9616.18, i = $1916.18
    (d) A = $15 621.92, i = $2121.92
13. **(a)** P = $2360.76, i = $1239.24
    (b) P = $550.96, i = $249.04
    (c) P = $16 429.72, i = $6270.28
    (d) P = $4003.46, i = $1296.54
14. $5354.46
15. $6480.74
16. about 265.75 min or 4.43 h
17. about 70 quarters or 210 months
18. **(a)** 9 **(b)** 12

Practise, Apply, Solve 2.1, page 114

1. **(a)** yes **(b)** no
   (c) yes **(d)** no
2. **(a)** $t_{10} = 74, S_{10} = 380$
   (b) $t_{10} = -35, S_{10} = 325$
   (c) $t_{10} = 45, S_{10} = 135$
   (d) $t_{10} = 3\frac{1}{6}$ or $\frac{19}{6}, S_{10} = \frac{50}{3}$
3. $\frac{200 \times 201}{2}$
4. **(a)** 465 **(b)** 1830 **(c)** 500 500 **(d)** 300
5. **(a)** 348 **(b)** 690 **(c)** 850 **(d)** 1245
6. **(a)** 465 **(b)** 2310 **(c)** -1647 **(d)** $\frac{147}{8}$
7. 142.8
8. **(a)** 1183 **(b)** -154 **(c)** 4200 **(d)** $\frac{55}{6}$
9. 3925
10. 1170
11. 410
12. $-7, -5, -3$
13. 875 seats
14. 20
15. 21
16. 303 seats
17. 514.5 m
18. It is better to use $S_n = \frac{n(t_1 + t_n)}{2}$ when n and the first and last term of the series are known. In both cases the values of a (the first term) and n must be known.
19. $12 850
20. **(a)** 26 rows **(b)** 13 560
21. 5 squares
23. -102
24. 101

Practise, Apply, Solve 2.3, page 123

1. **(a)** geometric, $r = \frac{1}{2}$ **(b)** geometric, $r = \frac{4}{5}$
   (c) neither **(d)** geometric, $r = -\frac{3}{2}$
   (e) geometric, $r = -\frac{1}{2}$
   (f) neither
2. **(a)** $t_n = 2(3)^{n-1}, S_n = 2(3^n - 1), S_8 = 13\,120$
   (b) $t_n = \left(-\frac{2}{3}\right)^{n-1}, S_n = -\frac{3}{5}\left[\left(-\frac{2}{3}\right)^n - 1\right], S_8 = 0.58$
   (c) $t_n = 6(-2)^{n-1}, S_n = 2[1 - (-2)^n], S_8 = -510$
   (d) $t_n = 81\left(\frac{1}{3}\right)^{n-1}, S_n = \frac{243}{2}\left[1 - \left(\frac{1}{3}\right)^n\right], S_8 = 121.48$
   (e) $t_n = 0.4(0.1)^{n-1}, S_n = \frac{4}{9}[1 - (0.1)^n], S_8 = 0.44$
   (f) $t_n = 8(-1)^{n-1}, S_n = 4[1 - (-1)^n], S_8 = 0$

3. **(a)** $S_7 = -107.5$ **(b)** $S_{10} = 81.00$
(c) $S_8 = 4.805 \times 10^{10}$ **(d)** $S_9 = 104.43$
(e) $S_n = \frac{1 - x^n}{1 - x}$ **(f)** $S_n = \frac{5w[1 - (2w)^n]}{1 - 2w}$
4. **(a)** −13 122 **(b)** −9840
5. **(a)** 7161 **(b)** −1533 **(c)** 406.234
(d) 64 125 **(e)** 18 882.137 67
6. 49 205
7. 8 rounds
8. Since his pay increases by 10% each month, his salary each month is 1.10 times the previous month. His monthly salary can be represented by the geometric sequence $t_n = 1200(1.10)^{n-1}$ for the nth month. To calculate his total pay for the last 6 months of his first year, we can: **1.** Find the geometric sum from $n = 1$ to $n = 12$ and then subtract the geometric sum from $n = 1$ to $n = 6$; or **2.** Find the geometric sum from $n = 7$ to $n = 12$.
9. **(a)** Original e-mail leads to 5 people, each of these leads to 5 people. (1, 5, 25)
(b) first e-mailing: 5; second e-mailing: 25; third e-mailing:125
(c) $S_n = \frac{a(r^n - 1)}{r - 1} = \frac{5(5^n - 1)}{5 - 1}$
(d) 488 280; This is unlikely since not all receivers of the e-mailing would forward it to 5 people. Also, it is likely that several people would receive the e-mailing more than once since many receivers will forward it to some of their common friends or relatives.
10. 794.7
11. **(a)** \$21 960.17 **(b)** \$213 519.56
12. **(a)** \$566 699.89 **(b)** \$4 974 410.97
13. 68.20 m
14. **(a)** \$7080.84 **(b)** \$45 400.55
16. **(a)** 12 tickets **(b)** \$14 200
18. **(a)** $t_2 = 3r$ $t_3 = 3r^2$
(b) −3 or 2; If $r = -3$ then $t_1 = 3$, $t_2 = -9$, $t_3 = 27$, and $S_3 = 21$; If $r = 2$ then $t_1 = 3$, $t_2 = 6$, $t_3 = 12$, and $S_3 = 21$.
20. **(a)** −50 **(b)** 3267
21. **(a)** 1 **(b)** no
(c) if the series converges; i.e. $-1 < r < 1$

Practice 2.4, page 128

(a) nonlinear with points (year, balance) at {(1, 2080), (2, 2163.20), (3, 2249.70), ... (10, 2960.50)}

	A	B	C	D
1	Period	Prev.	Int.	Year End
2		Bal.	4.0%/a	Balance
3	1	2000	=B3 * 0.04	=B3 + C3
4	=A3 + 1	=D3	=B4 * 0.04	=B4 + C4
			Total Interest after 8 years = \$737.14	**Balance after 8 years = \$2737.14**

(b) nonlinear with points (quarter, balance) at {(1, 8160), (2, 8323.30), (3, 8489.70), ... (40, 17664.32)}

	A	B	C	D
1	Period	Prev.	Int.	Year End
2		Bal.	4.0%/a	Balance
3	1	8000	=B3 * 0.02	=B3 + C3
4	=A3 + 1	=D3	=B4 * 0.02	=B4 + C4
			Total Interest after 8 years = \$7076.32	**Balance after 8 years = \$15 076.32**

(c) The total interest earned over the first 8 years for (a) is \$737.14 and for (b) is \$7076.32.
(d) nonlinear with points (month, balance) at {(1, 30 150), (2, 30 300.75), (3, 30 452.25), ... (120, 54 581.90)}

	A	B	C	D
1	Period	Prev.	Int.	Monthly
2		Bal.	6.0%/a	Balance
3	1	30000	=B3 * 0.05	=B3 + C3
4	=A3 + 1	=D3	=B4 * 0.05	=B4 + C4
				Balance After 10 years = \$54 581.90

(e) nonlinear with points (half-year, balance) at {(1, 5150), (2, 5304.50), (3, 5463.64), ... (20, 9030.56)}

	A	B	C	D
1	Period	Prev.	Int.	Semiannual
2		Bal.	6.0%/a	Balance
3	1	5000	=B3 * 0.03	=B3 + C3
4	=A3 + 1	=D3	=B4 * 0.03	=B4 + C4
				Balance After 10 years = \$9030.56

Practise, Apply, Solve 2.5, page 138

1. **(a)** \$600.00
(b) ordinary annuity: payments are made at the end of every 3 months
(c) Her periodic payment corresponds to the interest conversion period (both calculated quarterly).
(d) interest = \$131.40; new balance = \$7301.23
(e) Change cell B3 from 0 to 1500.
2. **(a)**

Period	Interest	New Balance
1	\$12	\$612
2	\$12.24	\$1224.24
3	\$24.48	\$1848.72
4	\$36.97	\$2485.69
5	\$49.71	\$3135.40
6	\$62.71	\$3798.11
7	\$75.96	\$4474.07
8	\$89.48	\$5163.55

(b) annuity due
(c) \$363.55
(d) The interest cell C3 should be changed to " = (B3 + D3) * 0.02" so interest is also earned on the payment.
3. **(a)** one month
(b) This number is used because the interest rate is compounded monthly and there are 36 months in 3 years, resulting in 36 pay periods.
(c) \$68.09
(d) If the payment were reduced by \$0.01 to \$298.27, then the balance would be less than \$12 000. In order to have a balance of \$12 000, the payment would have to be rounded to a fraction of a penny, which is not possible.
(e) Change cell C3 to = B3 * 0.005.
4. **(a)** The difference in balances is attributed to the increase in the payments and to the interest earned on the increased payments.
(b) \$7.27

5. A good first guess might be $\$6500 \div 16$ or \$406.25. This guess could be increased to allow for interest payments to a guess of about \$450 or \$470.

6. **(a)** 4 years or 48 months
(b) 3 months **(c)** 16 payments **(d)** 2.5%

7. **(a)**

Pay. #	Amount Paid	Int. Paid	Princ. Paid	Out. Bal.
0				\$3600
1	\$625	\$198	\$427	\$3173
2	\$625	\$174.51	\$450.49	\$2722.51
7	\$625	\$36.23	\$588.77	\$70.02
8	\$625	\$3.85	\$621.15	−\$551.13

(b) \$73.87
(c) \$695.02

8.

Pay. #	Pay.	Int. Paid	Princ. Paid	Bal.
0				\$3600.00
1	\$625.00	\$198.00	\$427.00	\$3173.00
2	\$625.00	\$174.52	\$450.49	\$2722.52
7	\$625.00	\$36.23	\$588.77	\$70.04
8	\$625.00	\$3.85	\$621.15	−\$551.11

9. **(a)**

Period	Prev. Bal.	Int. (5%/a)	Pay. Made	New Bal.
1	\$12 000.00	\$150.00	\$500	\$12 650.00
2	\$12 650.00	\$158.13	\$500	\$13 308.13
19	\$25 030.02	\$312.88	\$500	\$25 842.90
20	\$25 842.90	\$323.04	\$500	\$26 665.94

(b) \$1128.14 **(c)** \$476.18
(d) Answers will vary. **(e)** Answers will vary.

10. **(a)** \$669.18
(b) \$221.82
(c) ($\$221.82 \times 3 = \$665.46$) By making monthly payments the balance is reduced each month rather than every 3 months. This produces a slight reduction in interest charges and hence a reduction in payments. If payments are made more frequently the total interest paid is reduced.

11. **(a)** 1.5%
(b) and **(c)**

Pay. #	Pay.	Int. Paid	Princ. Paid	Bal.
0				\$1800.00
1	\$165.25	\$27.00	\$138.25	\$1661.75
2	\$165.25	\$24.93	\$140.32	\$1521.43
11	\$165.25	\$4.81	\$160.44	\$159.90
12	\$165.25	\$2.40	\$162.85	−\$2.95

(d) nonlinear with points (payment, balance) at {(0, 1800), (1, 1661.75), (2, 1521.43), … (12, −2.95)}

12. 22%

13. Bev always earns always greater interest than the interest and deposit Cindy makes, so Cindy will never catch up to Bev.

14. **(a)** \$27 046.45 **(b)** \$46 121.88

15. \$7211.82

16. Answers will vary.

17. **(a)** 14%/a compounded monthly
(b) \$732.68
(c) The advertised value is based on \$13 200 being borrowed because of the \$3000 down payment.
(d) His payments would be \$597.00 and he would save \$882.48.

18. **(a)**

Pay. #	Pay.	Int. Paid	Princ. Paid	Out. Bal.
0				\$48000.00
1	\$595.00	\$336.00	\$259.00	\$47741.00
2	\$595.00	\$334.19	\$260.81	\$47480.19
119	\$595.00	\$5.10	\$589.90	\$138.89
120	\$595.00	\$0.97	\$594.03	−\$455.14

(b) 120 months **(c)** \$139.86
(d) \$22 944.86
(f) in 102 months or 18 months sooner
(g) about \$5127.84

19. **(a)** \$1631.14
(b) \$1640.11. Interest is earned on the first payment and that interest in turn is compounded for 7 more months.

20. **(a)** By making monthly payments the principal is reduced each month, instead of every 3 months, thereby reducing the interest owed over each 3-month period. However, 12%/a compounded monthly is a greater interest charge than 12%/a compounded quarterly.
(b) Using a spreadsheet, it can be found that it will take 17 full quarterly payments of \$3000 and an additional payment of \$854.01. Total loan cost is \$51 854.01. It will take 51 full monthly payments of \$1000 and an additional payment of \$338.67. Total loan cost is \$51 338.67. She should make monthly payments, which will save her about \$515.34 in interest costs.

21. \$17 656.04

Practice 2.6, page 144

1. **(a)** 285 **(b)** 3025 **(c)** 3069 **(d)** −245
(e) 17 531.17 **(f)** 55 **(g)** 1320.68 **(h)** 430

2. **(a)** 6, 17, 33, 54, 80, 111, 147, 188, 234, 285
(b) 1, 9, 36, 100, 225, 441, 784, 1296, 2025, 3025
(c) 3, 9, 21, 45, 93, 189, 381, 765, 1533, 3069
(d) −2, −9, −21, −38, −60, −87, −119, −156, −198, −245
(e) 1100, 2310, 3641, 5105.1, 6715.61, 8487.17, 10 435.89, 12 579.48, 14 937.43, 17 531.17
(f) 1, 3, 6, 10, 15, 21, 28, 36, 45, 55
(g) 105, 212.25, 331.01, 452.56, 580.19, 714.2, 854.91, 1002.66, 1157.79, 1320.68
(h) 25, 54, 87, 124, 165, 210, 259, 312, 369, 430

Practise, Apply, Solve 2.7, page 151

1. **(a)** 2.158 925 **(b)** 1.973 823 **(c)** 2.032 794
(d) 1.348 850 **(e)** 4.247 851 **(f)** 10.401 270

2. **(a)** 53 175.25 **(b)** 11 433.50
(c) 47 898.65 **(d)** 1 247 260.00

3. **(a)** $i = 3\%, n = 12$ **(b)** $i = 6.5\%, n = 10$
(c) $i = 1.5\%, n = 84$ **(d)** $i = 0.25\%, n = 260$

4. **(a)** 2014.06 **(b)** 163 688.28 **(c)** 18 783.01

6. **(a)** \$13 416.80, \$12 308.99, \$11 292.65, \$10 360.23, \$9504.80, \$8720, \$8000, $A = 8000 + 8000(1.09) + 8000(1.09)^2 + \ldots + 8000(1.09)^6$, \$73 603.48
(b) \$379.60, \$365.00, \$350.96, \$337.46, \$324.48, \$312, \$300; $A = 300 + 300(1.04) + \ldots + 300(1.04)^6$; \$2369.49
(c) \$861.51, \$844.62, \$828.06, \$811.82, \$795.91, \$780.30, \$765, \$750; $A = 750 + 750(1.02) + \ldots + 750(1.02)^7$; \$6437.23

7. 4 years, each divided into 4 equal segments. Amount of each payment, proceeding from most recent to first: 1600, $1600(1.025)^1$, $1600(1.025)^2$, …, $1600(1.025)^{39}$

8. **(a)** 10 years with no divisions. Amount of each payment, proceeding from most recent to first: 5000, $5000(1.05)^1$, $5000(1.05)^2$, …, $5000(1.05)^9$
$A = 5000 + 5000(1.05) + ... + 5000(1.05)^8 + 5000(1.05)^9$; \$62 889.46
(b) 5 years, each divided into 4 equal segments. Amount of each payment, proceeding from most recent to first: 750, $750(1.02)^1$, $750(1.02)^2$, …, $750(1.02)^{19}$;
$A = 750 + 750(1.02) + ... + 750(1.02)^{19}$; \$18 223.03
(c) 2 years, each divided into 52 equal segments. Amount of each payment, proceeding from most recent to first: 50, $50(1.0025)^1$, $50(1.0025)^2$, … $50(1.0025)^{103}$;
$A = 50 + 50(1.0025) + ... + 50(1.0025)^{102} + 50(1.0025)^{103}$; \$5930.19
(d) 7 years, each divided into 2 equal segments. Amount of each payment, proceeding from most recent to first: 4300, $4300(1.0475)^1$, $4300(1.0475)^2$, …, $4300(1.0475)^{13}$;
$A = 4300 + 4300(1.045) + ... + 4300(1.045)^{13}$; \$81 408.07
9. For all time lines, shift all payments in the corresponding timelines from question 8 one conversion period to the left.
(a) $A = 5000(1.05)^1 + 5000(1.05)^2 + … + 5000(1.05)^{10}$
$= \$66\ 033.94$
(b) $A = 750(1.02)^1 + 750(1.02)^2 + … + 750(1.02)^{20}$
$= \$18\ 587.49$
(c) $A = 50(1.0025)^1 + 50(1.0025)^2 + … + 50(1.0025)^{104}$
$= \$5945.01$
(d) $A = 4300(1.0475)^1 + 4300(1.0475)^2 + … + 4300(1.0475)^{14}$
$= \$85\ 071.43$
10. **(a)** 3 years, each divided into 12 segments. Amount of each payment (R) proceeding from most recent to first: R, $R(1.005)^1$, $R(1.005)^2$, …, $R(1.005)^{35}$
(b) $S_{36} = R + R(1.005) + ... + R(1.005)^{35}$
(c) \$762.66
11. \$7599.64
12. \$36 724.36
13. yes
14. *Example*: Both formulas are based on being able to express the future value of the payments as a geometric series. This can only be accomplished if the payment and interest interval coincide.
15. **(a)** 3 years, each divided into 12 segments. Amount of each payment, proceeding from most recent to first: 75, $75(1.005)^1$, $75(1.005)^2$, …, $75(1.005)^{35}$
(b) $A = 75 + 75(1.005) + 75(1.005)^2 + ... + 75(1.005)^{35}$
(c) \$2950.21
(d) nonlinear with points (month, balance) at {(1, 75), (2, 150.38), (3, 226.13), … (36, 2950.21)}
(e) 60
16. **(a)** 20
(b) nonlinear with points (quarter, balance) at {(1, 2000), (2, 4030), (3, 6090.45), … (20, 46 247.33)}
17. **(a)** n years, each divided into 4 segments. Amount of each payment, proceeding from most recent to first: 450, $450(1.021)^1$, $450(1.021)^2$, …, $450(1.021)^{n-2}$, $450(1.021)^{n-1}$
(b) $S_n = 24\ 000 = 450 + 450(1.021) + ... + 450(1.021)^{n-1}$
(c) 16 years old
(d) 1 year or 4 quarters
18. \$2584.07
19. **(a)** 20 years, each divided into 12 segments. Amount of each payment (R) proceeding from most recent to first: R, $R(1.005\ 25)^1$, $R(1.005\ 25)^2$, …, $R(1.005\ 25)^{239}$
(b) $S_{240} = R + R(1.00525) + R(1.00525)^2 + ... + R(1.00525)^{238} + R(1.00525)^{239}$
(c) \$167.08 **(d)** \$268.12 **(e)** \$8162.40
20. \$24 317.34
21. Answers will vary. However, in most cases, it is more advantageous to double the interest.
22. **(a)** By starting her deposits earlier, her deposits would be reduced substantially for two reasons. She would be making an extra 60 payments and these 60 payments would accumulate interest over an extra five years.
(b) \$181.59
23. **(a)** 5 years, each divided into 2 segments. Amount of each payment, proceeding from most recent to first: 3000, $3000(1.04)^2$, $3000(1.04)^4$, $3000(1.04)^6$, $3000(1.04)^8$
(b) \$17 656.04
24. \$358.22

Practise, Apply, Solve 2.8, page 163

1. **(a)** 0.463 193 **(b)** 0.506 631 **(c)** 0.491 934
(d) 0.741 372 **(e)** 0.235 413 **(f)** 0.096 142
2. **(a)** 898.47 **(b)** 11 997.96
(c) 23 165.20 **(d)** 87 057.00
3. **(a)** 1098.30 **(b)** 159 958.35 **(c)** 12 474.91
4. **(a)** \$7339.45, \$6733.44, \$6177.47, \$5667.40, \$5199.45, \$4770.14, \$4376.27, $P = 8000(1.09)^{-7} + 8000(1.09)^{-6} + ... + 8000(1.09)^{-2} + 8000(1.09)^{-1}$, \$40 263.62
(b) \$288.46, \$277.37, \$266.70, \$256.44, \$246.58, \$237.09, \$227.98, $P = 300(1.04)^{-7} + 300(1.04)^{-6} + ... + 300(1.04)^{-2} + 300(1.04)^{-1}$, \$1800.62
(c) \$735.29, \$720.88, \$706.74, \$692.88, \$679.30, \$665.98, \$652.92, \$640.12, $P = 750(1.02)^{-8} + 750(1.02)^{-7} + ... + 750(1.02)^{-2} + 750(1.02)^{-1}$, \$5494.11
5. **(a)** 3 years, each divided into 4 segments. Present value of each payment, proceeding from most recent to first: $1200(1.0225)^{-11}$, $1200(1.0225)^{-10}$, $1200(1.0225)^{-9}$, …, 1200
(b) annuity due
(c) $P = 1200(1.0225)^{-11} + 1200(1.0225)^{-10} + ... + 200(1.0225)^{-1} + 1200$
(d) \$12 778.93
6. **(a)** 11 years, with no divisions. Present value of each payment, proceeding from most recent to first: $8000(1.07)^{-11}$, $8000(1.07)^{-10}$, $8000(1.07)^{-9}$, …, $8000(1.07)^{-1}$;
$P = 8000(1.07)^{-11} + 8000(1.07)^{-10} + ... + 8000(1.07)^{-1}$, \$59 989.39
(b) 6 years, each divided into 4 segments. Present value of each payment, proceeding from most recent to first: $650(1.02)^{-24}$, $650(1.02)^{-23}$, $650(1.02)^{-22}$, …, $650(1.02)^{-1}$;
$P = 650(1.02)^{-24} + 650(1.02)^{-23} + ... + 650(1.02)^{-1}$, \$12 294.05
(c) 3 years, each divided into 52 segments. Present value of each payment, proceeding from most recent to first: $60(1.25)^{-156}$, $60(1.25)^{-155}$, $60(1.25)^{-154}$, …, $60(1.25)^{-1}$
$P = 60(1.25)^{-156} + 60(1.25)^{-155} + ... + 60(1.25)^{-1}$, \$7742.72
(d) 8 years, each divided into 2 segments. Present value of each payment, proceeding from most recent to first: $3800(1.0325)^{-16}$, $3800(1.0325)^{-15}$, $3800(1.0325)^{-14}$, …, $3800(1.0325)^{-1}$
$P = 3800(1.0325)^{-16} + 3800(1.0325)^{-15} + ... + 3800(1.0325)^{-1}$, \$46 832.56
7. **(a)** \$13 728.16 **(b)** \$14 757.77
(c) \$11 050.63
8. **(a)** 4 years, each divided into 4 segments. Present value of each payment (R) proceeding from most recent to first: $R(1.025)^{-16}$, $R(1.025)^{-15}$, $R(1.025)^{-14}$, …, $R(1.025)^{-1}$
(b) $P = R(1.025)^{-16} + R(1.025)^{-15} + ... + R(1.025)^{-1}$

(c) $574.49

9. $8702.34
10. $14 877.47
11. (a) $418.89 (b) $31.11
12. (a) $389.47 (b) $23 368.36
    (c) monthly bank payment $386.68; he should choose the bank option
13. (a) $961.63 (b) $108.37
14. (a) 7-year term: a = $1029.70; 10-year term: a = $810.72
    (b) $10 791.60
    (c) *Example*: other expense, affordability, down payment, taxes
15. The payment using the dealer's special rate is $566.51, while using the bank loan is $552.60.
16. $4282.71
17. The variable i appears twice in the present value formulas, so it is not possible to isolate and solve for i.
18. (a) $3210.47 (b) $4987.47
19. (a) present value of $1000/week for 25 years is $627 136.80; take cash
    (b) 1502 weeks or 28.9 years
20. Answers will vary.
21. (a) $20 516.61 (b) Answers will vary.
22. 63 months
23. 31 months by increasing last payment slightly

Practice 2.9, page 171

(a) $14 774.55 (b) $6315.27
(c) $45 301.49 (d) $3305.57
(e) $37 936.57 (f) $58 874.59

Practise, Apply, Solve 2.10, page 178

1. (a) $1 + i$ (b) $1 + i$ (c) $1 + i$ (d) $1 + i$
2. (a) 1.1236 (b) 1.3605 (c) 1.0380 (d) 1.4233
3. (a) 0.1038 (b) 0.1268 (c) 0.0488 (d) 0.0012
   (e) 0.0296 (f) 0.0083 (g) 0.0023 (h) 0.1533
4. (a) 8.16% (b) 8.24% (c) 10.95%
   (d) 9.15% (e) 19.25% (f) 23.14%
5. (a) 19.25% (b) 18.40% (c) 17.77%
   (d) 17.64% (e) 17.61%
6. (a) 10 years, with no divisions. Amount of each payment, proceeding from most recent to first:
   5000, $5000(1.0816)^1$, $5000(1.0816)^2$, ..., $8000(1.0816)^9$
   $S_{10} = 5000 + 5000(1.0816) + 5000(1.0816)^2 + ... + 5000(1.0816)^9$, $72 985.49
   (b) 5 years, each divided into 4 segments. Amount of each payment, proceeding from most recent to first: 800, $800(1.019\,426\,547)^1$, $800(1.019\,426\,547)^2$, ..., $800(1.019\,426\,547)^{19}$; $S_{20} = 800 + 800(1.019\,426\,547) + 800(1.019\,426\,547)^2 + ... + 800(1.019\,426\,547)^{19}$, $19 327.29
   (c) 2 years, each divided into 52 segments. Amount of each payment, proceeding from most recent to first: 150, $150(1.001\,878\,304)^1$, $150(1.001\,878\,304)^2$, ..., $150(1.001\,878\,304)^{103}$
   $S_{104} = 150 + 150(1.001\,878\,304) + 150(1.001\,878\,304)^2 + ... + 150(1.001\,878\,304)^{103}$, $17 210.15
   (d) 7 years, each divided into 2 segments. Amount of each payment, proceeding from most recent to first: 3300, $3300(1.050\,625)^1$, $3300(1.050\,625)^2$, ..., $3300(1.050\,625)^{13}$
   $S_{14} = 3300 + 3300(1.050\,625) + 3300(1.050\,625)^2 + ... + 3300(1.050\,625)^{13}$, $64 956.71
   (e) 3 years, each divided into 12 segments. Amount of each payment, proceeding from most recent to first: 1000, $1000(1.007\,207\,323)^1$, $1000(1.007\,207\,323)^2$, ..., $1000(1.007\,207\,323)^{35}$
   $S_{36} = 1000 + 1000(1.007\,207\,323) + 1000(1.007\,207\,323)^2 + ... + 1000(1.007\,207\,323)^{35}$, $40 934.61
7. 18 months, each segment is one month. Present value of each payment (R) proceeding from most recent to first: $R(1.013\,888\,430\,3)^{-18}$, $R(1.013\,888\,430\,3)^{-17}$, $R(1.013\,888\,430\,3)^{-16}$, ..., $R(1.013\,888\,430\,3)^{-1}$; $221.10
8. (a) 3.5 years, each year divided into 52 segments. Amount of each payment (R) proceeding from most recent to first: R, $R(1.001\,381\,431)^1$, $R(1.001\,381\,431)^2$, ..., $R(1.001\,381\,431)^{181}$
   (b) $S_{182} = R + R(1.001\,381\,431) + ... + R(1.001\,381\,431)^{181}$
   (c) $120.91
9. (a) $8755.62
   (b) The 0.782 129%/month interest rate is very close to the 9.8%/a compounded monthly he was charged in section 2.8. Also, because the loan was for such a short period of time (3 years), the difference in the two rates has little effect on the present value.
10. (a) *Example*: Michael needs $2800 to go travelling in one year. How much must he deposit at the end of every three months into an account that pays 8%/a compounded quarterly?
    (b) *Example*: Alisha buys a new car by agreeing to mature equal monthly payments of $350 for 5 years at a rate of 6%/a compounded semiannually. What did she pay for the car?
11. $92.49
12. (a) $74 118.37, $74 402.62, $74 650.93, $74 690.11, $74 700.23
    (b) Considering they are saving for a fairly lengthy period of time (6 years), the compounding period does not have a significant effect on their total savings. However, compounding daily is preferred over compounding yearly if the annual rate is fixed.
13. (a) $71 779.39 (b) $73 048.96
    (c) $74 283.82 (d) $74 317.12
    (e) The greater the frequency of the payments, the greater the value of the savings. By going from yearly to daily deposits they can save an additional $2537.73.
14. (a) $75 443.35, $76 791.50, $71 536.58
    (b) A change from 6%/a to 7.8%/a would enable them to save an additional $3906.77.
15. (a) $81 530.21, $66 706.54, $71 267.67
    (b) A decrease in their deposits by $32 to $800 would result in a decrease in savings of about $2850.
16. (a) $74 549.05 (b) $59 523.36
    (c) $63 809.04 (d) $81 805.34
    (e) The sooner they begin to save, the sooner their savings can accumulate compound interest. The longer time period they save, the more they can accumulate.
17. Key features should include: start saving now, do not wait; make deposits as large and as often as possible; shop for best interest rate; save for as long as you can to accumulate a larger deposit; the compounding period is not as important but look for shortest compounding period if the interest rates are the same.
18. (a) 21% (b) $557.44
19. 12%/a compounded monthly will produce 1%/month compounded monthly. This means that for the second and third months, interest will be earned on the 1% interest earned in the previous month. After 3 months, the initial deposit will grow by (1.01)(1.01)(1.01), 1.030 301 times its value, or 3.0301% over 3 months while 12%/a compounded quarterly earns 3% over 3 months. Therefore, 12%/a compounded monthly is a greater rate than 12%/a compounded quarterly.

20. **(a)** 20.04% **(b)** 1%

21. **(a)** no **(b)** yes

Practice 2.11, page 186

(a) \$172.90 **(b)** \$462.18

(c) \$1208.33 **(d)** \$147.90

(e)

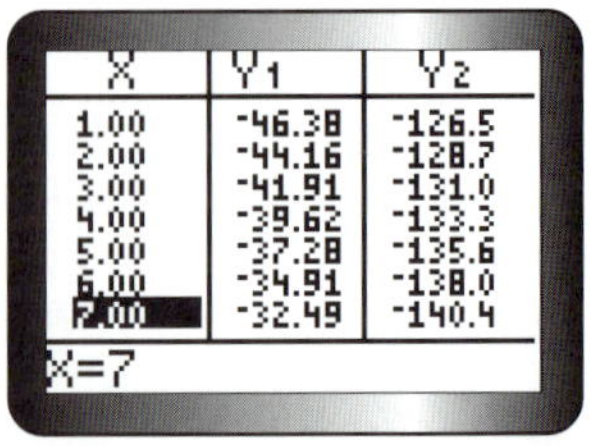

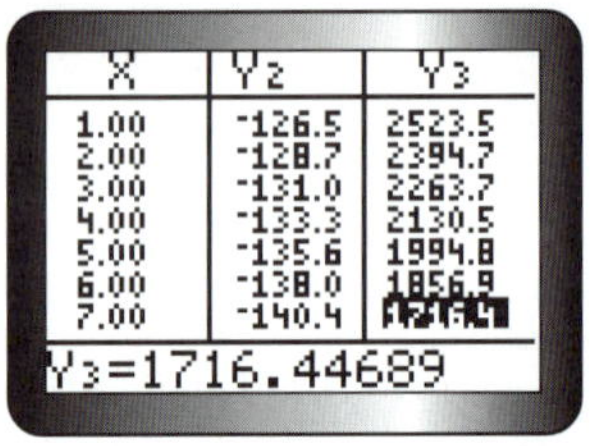

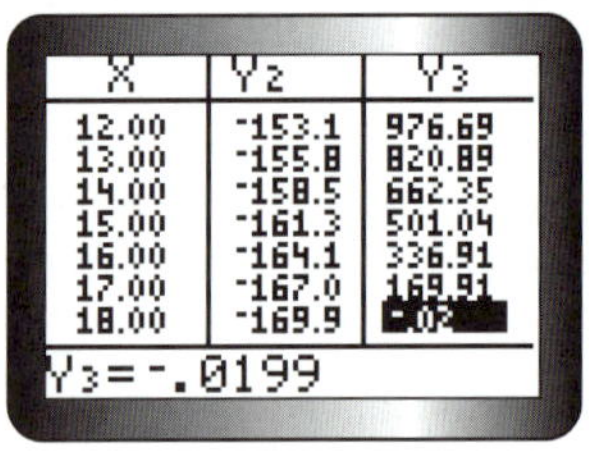

Practise, Apply, Solve 2.12, page 191

1. **(a)** 0.008 164 85 **(b)** 0.005 750 04
   (c) 0.003 273 74 **(d)** 0.002 243 63
   (e) 0.000 293 42 **(f)** 0.002 061 38
2. **(a)** 0.005 750 04 **(b)** 0.006 961 06
   (c) 0.008 084 82 **(d)** 0.009 758 79
3. Answers will vary.
4. **(a)** \$646.18/month is equivalent to 646.18 × 12 or \$7754.16 per year, while \$161.55/week is equivalent to 161.55 × 52 or \$8400 per year.
   (b) \$149.12
   (c) By making weekly payments of \$149.12, the loan is repaid in 1040.5 weeks. By making monthly payments of \$646.18, the loan is repaid in 20 years or 1040 weeks. Changing the payment frequency has little or no effect on the time needed to repay the loan.
   (d) Payment amount
5. *Example*: Interest on Canadian mortgages can be compounded at most semiannually. However, payments are generally made monthly, weekly, or biweekly, which does not coincide with the interest period.
6. **(a)** \$651.90, \$701.51 **(b)** \$27 207.60
   (c) Shorten the amortization period of your loan by increasing the payment amount.
7. **(a)** 152.35 months, 303.84 payment periods or 151.92 months, 657.34 payment periods or 151.69 months
   (b) very little effect
8. **(a)** 132.94 months
   (b) between \$4788.60 to \$4789.81 depending on method and accuracy used
9. **(a)** \$1282.96
   (b) end of year 1: \$158 049.86; end of year 2: \$155 928.38; end of year 3: \$153 620.55; end of year 4: \$151 109.99; end of year 5: \$148 378.88
   (c) principal paid \$11 621.12; interest paid \$65 356.48
   (d) total interest paid \$224 888.23; total cost of home \$427 888.23
10. **(a)** monthly payment: \$1200.78; save in total interest: \$24 651.48
    (b) About 49 months (over 4 years)
11. **(a)** \$1411.26; \$1552.38
    (b) end of year 1: \$158 049.86; end of year 2: \$154 327.75; end of year 3: \$148 518.07; end of year 4: \$142 198.01; end of year 5: \$135 322.74
    (c) 104 months
12. **(a)** \$735.50
    (b)

Pay. #	Pay.	Int. Paid (0.56%/a)	Princ. Paid	Out. Bal.
0				\$49200.00
1	\$735.50	\$275.52	\$459.98	\$48740.02
2	\$735.50	\$272.94	\$462.56	\$48277.46
83	\$735.50	\$8.37	\$727.13	\$767.94
84	\$735.50	\$4.30	\$731.20	\$36.74

    (c) principal: \$489.68; interest: \$245.82
    (d) principal: \$605.17; interest: \$130.33
    (e) \$74 081.98 **(f)** \$73 295.61
13. Answers will vary.
14. about 533 payments or 22 years and 2.5 months
15. 65 fewer months; \$49 851.14
16. **(a)** monthly payment: \$761.33; balance: \$75 495.39
    (b) \$1363.85 **(c)** 79.14%
    (d) Because interest rates increased so dramatically, when people came to renew their mortgages, the new payment required to maintain the mortgage was beyond what they could afford.
17. cash back option
18. Answers will vary.
19. Interest rate changed; amount borrowed; term (length) of the mortgage.

Chapter 2, Review and Practice, page 197

1. $t_n = a + (n - 1)d$; t_n: the nth term, n: number of terms in sequence, a: first term, d: common difference
2. A series is the sum of all of the terms in a sequence. To add the first n terms of an arithmetic series, use $S_n = \frac{n}{2}[2a + (n - 1)d]$ where n is the position of the term in the series, a is the first term, and d is the common difference between each term in the series.
3. **(a)** 1768 **(b)** −828 **(c)** −95 **(d)** $\frac{377}{6}$
4. 2198
5. −42, −39, −36, −33
6. \$1017
7. $t_n = r^{n-1}$; t_n : nth term, n: number of terms, a: first term, r: common ratio
8. $a + ar + ... + ar^{n-2} + ar^{n-1}$ The formula used to add the first n terms of a geometric series is $S_n = \frac{a(r^n - 1)}{r - 1}$ where n is the position of the term in the sequence, a is the first term, and r is the common ratio between each term.
9. **(a)** 1 953 124 **(b)** 51 889 **(c)** 127 500 **(d)** 6415.29
10. **(a)** \$28 474.08 **(b)** \$284 623.03
11. **(a)** 11 tickets **(b)** \$114 270

12. An annuity is an investment plan in which fixed amounts of money are deposited or paid out at regular intervals over a specified period of time. An ordinary annuity is an annuity in which periodic payments are made at the end of each time interval, whereas an annuity due is an annuity in which periodic payments are made at the beginning of each time interval.

13. The amortization period of a loan or mortgage is the length of time that it would take for the debt to be paid in full if all blended payments (payments used to pay both the interest and the principal) are made punctually. An amortization table is used to show the amount of the regular blended payment, how much of the payment is interest, how much is used to reduce the principal, and the outstanding balance after each payment. A spreadsheet is useful in creating amortization tables and for analyzing the effects of changing the parameters of a loan problem.

14. **(a)** 0.5%
(b) Ewen's savings plan is an example of an ordinary simple annuity because his payments are made at the end of each time interval and his periodic payments correspond to the interest conversion period (both calculated monthly).
(c) \$2797.52 **(d)** \$157.52 **(e)** \$3962.78

15. **(a)** \$1607.32
(b)

	A	B	C	D	E
1	Pay. #	Pay.	Int. Paid	Princ. Paid	Out. Bal.
2	0				\$2400
3	=A2 + 1	\$130	=E2 * 0.015	=B3 − C3	=E2 − D3

(c) about 21.78 months (about 1.81 years); \$101.27
(d) \$2831.40 **(e)** \$153.13

16. 20%/a

17. \$567.10

18. R: amount of periodic payment, i: interest rate for each period, n: number of periods

19. $S_n = \dfrac{a(r^n - 1)}{r - 1}$ and $FV = \dfrac{R \times (1 + i)^n - 1}{i}$.

20. **(a)** 17 years, each divided into 4 segments. Amount of each payment proceeding most recent to the first: 450, $450(1.02)^1$, $450(1.02)^2$, …, $450(1.02)^{67}$
(b) $S_{68} = 450 + 450(1.02) + \ldots + 450(1.02)^{66} + 450(1.02)^{67}$
(c) S_{68} = \$63 995.64, i = \$33 395.64

21. **(a)** 20 months each segment is one month. Amount of each payment (R) proceeding from most recent to first: $R, R(1.0075)^1, R(1.0075)^2, \ldots, R(1.0075)^{19}$
(b) $S_{20} = R + R(1.0075) + \ldots + R(1.0075)^{18} + R(1.0075)^{19}$
(c) \$148.90

22. **(a)** n years each divided into 12 segments. Amount of each payment, proceeding from most recent to first: 75, $475(1.005)^1$, $475(1.005)^2$, …$475(1.005)^{n-2}$, $475(1.005)^{n-1}$, $475(1.005)^n$
(b) $S_n = 475 + 475(1.005) + \ldots + 475(1.005)^{n-2} + 475(1.005)^{n-1}$
(c) 55 months (about 4.67 years)
(d) \$554.55

23. The present value is the sum of all the equivalent present values of each of the payments at the beginning of the term, whereas the future value is the sum of all the future values of each payment at the end of the term.

25. **(a)** 9 years, no divisions. Present value of each payment, proceeding from most recent to first: $3000(1.05)^{-9}, 3000(1.05)^{-8}, 3000(1.05)^{-7}, \ldots, 3000(1.05)^{-1}$
$PV = 3000(1.05)^{-9} + 3000(1.05)^{-8} + \ldots + 3000(1.05)^{-1}$, \$21 323.47
(b) 5 years, each divided into 4 segments. Present value of each payment, proceeding from most recent to first: $500(1.015)^{-20}$, $500(1.015)^{-19}, 500(1.015)^{-18}, \ldots, 500(1.015)^{-1}$
$PV = 500(1.015)^{-20} + 500(1.015)^{-19} + \ldots + 500(1.015)^{-2} + 500(1.015)^{-1}$, \$8584.32

26. **(a)** \$1499.51 **(b)** \$200.49

27. **(a)** 4 years, each divided into 4 segments. Present value of each payment (R) proceeding from most recent to first: $R(1.025)^{-16}, R(1.025)^{-15}, R(1.025)^{-14}, \ldots, R(1.025)^{-1}$
(b) $PV = R(1.025)^{-16} + R(1.025)^{-15} + \ldots + R(1.025)^{-2} + R(1.025)^{-1}$
(c) \$704.71

28. A simple annuity is an annuity where the periodic payment corresponds to the interest conversion period, whereas a general annuity is an annuity where the periodic payment does not correspond to the interest conversion period.

29. **(a)** 15.865% **(b)** 14.816% **(c)** 14.746%

30. **(a)** 3 years, each divided into 12 segments. Amount of each payment, proceeding from most recent to first: 270, $270(1.0041)^1, 270(1.0041)^2, \ldots, 270(1.0041)^{35}$
(b) $S_{36} = 270 + 270(1.0041) + \ldots + 270(1.0041)^{34} + 270(1.0041)^{35}$
(c) \$10 450.94 **(d)** \$167.82

31. **(a)** 4 years, each divided into 12 segments. Present value of each payment (R) proceeding from most recent to first: $R(1.014)^{-48}, R(1.014)^{-47}, R(1.014)^{-46}, \ldots, R(1.014)^{-1}$
(b) $PV = R(1.041)^{-48} + \ldots + R(1.014)^{-2} + R(1.041)^{-1}$
(c) \$249.54

32. **(a)** \$253.40 **(b)** 9 payments less **(c)** \$252.12

33. **(a)** \$723.09, \$788.43 **(b)** \$27 704.40 **(c)** choose shorter term

34. **(a)** \$625.92
(b)

Pay. #	Pay.	Int. Paid 0.688%/a	Princ. Paid	Bal.
0				\$43800.00
1	\$624.90	\$301.34	\$323.56	\$43476.44
2	\$624.90	\$299.12	\$325.78	\$43150.66
95	\$624.90	\$8.51	\$616.39	\$620.73
96	\$624.90	\$4.27	\$620.63	\$0.10

(c) \$16 191.90

35. **(a)** 1158 weeks (about 22.27 years)
(b) \$282 543.18 **(c)** \$40 154.77

36. **(a)** \$766.52
(b) year 1: \$176 290.35, year 2: \$170 468.67, year 3: \$164 532.76, year 4: \$158 480.39, year 5: \$152 309.25
(c) \$486.31, \$571.79 **(d)** \$659.16
(e) \$116 918.90

Chapter 2 Review Test, page 203

1. **(a)** 1026 **(b)** 29 526

2. **(a)** 30 rows **(b)** 15.7%

3. yes

4. **(a)**

Pay. #	Amount Paid	Int. Paid	Princ. Paid	Out. Bal.
0				\$1400
1	\$110	\$18.20	\$91.80	\$1308.20
2	\$110	\$17.01	\$92.99	\$1215.21
3	\$110	\$15.80	\$94.20	\$1121.01
4	\$110	\$14.57	\$95.43	\$1025.58
5	\$110	\$13.33	\$96.67	\$928.91
6	\$110	\$12.08	\$97.92	\$830.99

(b) \$95.43

5. (a) 2.5 years, each year divided into 12 segments. Present value of each payment (R) proceeding from most recent to first: $R(1.0135)^{-30}$, $R(1.0135)^{-29}$, $R(1.0135)^{-28}$, ..., $R(1.0135)^{-1}$
(b) $S_{30} = R(1.0135)^{-1} + R(1.0135)^{-2} + R(1.0135)^{-3} + \ldots + R(1.0135)^{-29} + R(1.0135)^{-30}$
(c) \$85.59

6. (a) \$387 566.74 (b) \$7575.56

7. (a) 20 years, each divided into 4 segments. Present value of each payment, proceeding from most recent to first: $1250(1.02)^{-80}$, $1250(1.02)^{-79}$, $1250(1.02)^{-78}$, ..., $1250(1.02)^{-1}$
(b) $S_{80} = 1250(1.02)^{-80} + 1250(1.02)^{-79} + 1250(1.02)^{-78} + \ldots + 1250(1.02)^{-1} = \$49\,680.\,64$
(c) Choose \$50 000 cash today.

8. (a) \$432.97 (b) \$108 344.40
(c) *Example*: negotiate a lower rate, make weekly payments, shorten term of mortgage, make extra payments, increase size of payment

Cumulative Review Test 1, page 205

1. (a) $t_1 = -2, t_2 = 0, t_3 = 6, t_4 = 16$
(b) $t_{15} = 390$
(c) nonlinear with points (term number, term value) at {(1, −2), (2, 0), (3, 6), (4, 16), (5, 30), (6, 48), (7, 70), (8, 96)}
(d) $t_{22} = 880$

2. (a) 50 000, 52 000, 54 000, 56 000, 58 000
(b) $t_n = a + (n - 1)d$ (c) 68 000
(d) \$1 380 000

3. (a) $t_n = (-18)3^{n-1}$, $t_{15} = -860\,934\,42$, $S_{25} = -7.626 \times 10^{12}$
(b) $t_n = 30 + (n - 1)(-4)$, $t_{15} = -26$, $S_{25} = -450$

4. (a) 62 (b) 11

5. (a) \$15 227.83 (b) \$6249.59

6. (a) 125 (b) 0.11
(c) 10.99 (d) 92.64

7. (a) $-15x^2$ (b) $\frac{9y^8}{14}$

8. (a) $x = \frac{-7}{3}$ (b) $x = -5$ or $x = 0.5$

9. 4.5 a

10. (a)

Pay. #	Pay.	Int.	Prin.	Bal.
0				4800.00
1	220	60.00	160.00	4640.00
2	220	58.00	162.00	4478.00
3	220	55.98	164.02	4313.98
4	220	53.92	166.08	4147.90
5	220	51.85	168.15	3979.75
6	220	49.75	170.25	3809.50

(c) 26 months; final payment: \$138.34
(d) \$5638.34 (e) \$427.89

11. (a) n years, each divided into 12 segments. Amount of each payment, proceeding from most recent to first: 450, $450(1.0067)^1$, $450(1.0067)^2$, ..., $450(1.0067)^{n-2}$, $450(1.0067)^{n-1}$
(b) $10\,000 = 450[(1.0067) + (1.0067)^2 + (1.0067)^3 + \ldots + (1.0067)^n]$
(c) 21 months

12. (a) 4 years, each divided into 12 segments. Amount of each payment (R) proceeding from most recent to first: R, $R(1.0125)^1$, $R(1.0125)^2$, ..., $R(1.0125)^{47}$
(b) $4600 = \frac{x}{1.15} + \frac{x}{1.15^2} + \frac{x}{1.15^3} + \ldots + \frac{x}{1.15^{48}}$
(c) \$125.84

13. (a) just over 13 years (b) \$250 297.14 (c) \$67 378.69

14U. $t_1 = -5, t_2 = 23, t_3 = -61, t_4 = 191, t_5 = -565, t_6 = 1703$

15U. (a) $a_n = 0.32(a_{n-1}) + 350$
(b) 514.7 mg (c) 54 h

Review of Essential Skills—Part 2

Using Properties of Relations to Sketch Their Graphs, page 211

1. (a) straight line through (0, −2) and (3, 0); $x = 3, y = -2$
(b) straight line through (0, 5) and (−3, 0); $x = -3, y = 5$
(c) straight line through (−8, 0) and (0, 3); $x = -8, y = 3$
(d) straight line through (0, −12) and (8, 0); $x = 18, y = -12$

2. (a) straight line through (0, 7) and $(\frac{7}{3}, 0)$; $m = -3, b = 7$
(b) straight line through $\left(-2\frac{2}{3}, 0\right)$ and (0, −2); $m = -\frac{3}{4}$, $b = -2$
(c) straight line through (0, 2) and (3, 0); $m = -\frac{2}{3}, b = 2$
(d) straight line through (0.5, 0) and (0, 1.5) $m = 9, b = \frac{3}{2}$

3. (a) parabola opening up, vertex (1.5, 0.5) through (1, 1) and (3, 1)
(b) parabola opening down, vertex (1.5, 4.75) through (1, 4) and (2, 4)
(c) parabola opening up, vertex (−0.5, 4.25) through (−1, −3) and (0, −3)
(d) parabola opening down, vertex (1, 5) through (0, 3) and (2, 3)

4. (a) parabola opening up, vertex (−2, −16) through (−6, 0) and (2, 0)
(b) parabola opening up, vertex (3.5, 2.25) through (2, 0) and (5, 0)
(c) parabola opening up, vertex $\left(1.25, -6\frac{1}{8}\right)$ through (−0.5, 0) and (3, 0)
(d) parabola opening up, vertex $\left(\frac{13}{12}, -\frac{289}{24}\right)$ through $\left(-\frac{1}{3}, 0\right)$ and (2.5, 0)

5. (a) parabola opening up, vertex (2, 3) through (1, 4) and (3, 4)
(b) parabola opening up, vertex (−4, −10) through (−7, −1) and (−1, −1)
(c) parabola opening up, vertex (1, 3) through (0, 5) and (2, 5)
(d) parabola opening down, vertex (−1, −4) and (−2, −7) and (0, −7)

6. 27.45 m

7. $\frac{525}{12}$ million dollars

Completing the Square to Convert to the Vertex Form of a Parabola, page 212

1. (a) $(x + 1)^2$ (b) $(x + 2)^2$ (c) $(x + 3)^2$ (d) $(x + 5)^2$
(e) $(x - 6)^2$ (f) $(x - 7)^2$ (g) $(x - 9)^2$ (h) $(x - 10)^2$

2. (a) $y = (x + 1)^2$ (b) $y = (x + 2)^2 + 2$
(c) $y = (x - 6)^2 + 4$ (d) $y = (x - 9)^2 - 1$

3. (a) $y = 2(x - 1)^2 + 5$ (b) $y = 5(x + 1)^2 + 1$
(c) $y = -3(x + 2)^2 + 14$ (d) $y = -\frac{1}{2}\left(x - \frac{5}{4}\right)^2 + \frac{89}{32}$
(e) $-0.1(x + 2.5)^2 + 1.025$ (f) $y = -\frac{3}{4}\left(x - \frac{10}{3}\right)^2 + \frac{19}{3}$

4. (a) $x = 9$ or $x = 1$ (b) $x = \frac{5}{3}$ or $x = -\frac{1}{3}$
(c) $x = \frac{5}{2}$ or $x = -4$

5. (a) 6.10 m (b) 1.02 s

6. 1977; 19 000

Solving Quadratic Equations: The Quadratic Formula, page 214

1. (a) two imaginary or non-real roots
   (b) two real roots (c) one real root
   (d) one real root (e) two real roots
   (f) two imaginary or non-real roots
2. (a) $x = \frac{1 \pm \sqrt{281}}{20}$ (b) $m = \frac{-27 \pm \sqrt{471}}{30}$
   (c) $p = \frac{9}{7}, p = \frac{5}{4}$ (d) $y = \frac{5}{6}, y = -\frac{6}{7}$
   (e) $x = \frac{8}{9}, x = \frac{4}{5}$ (f) $x = -\frac{7}{6}, x = \frac{5}{3}$
3. (a) 0.49 s, 4.6 s (b) 5.18 s
4. 2.9 m

Transformations of Quadratic Relations, page 216

1. (a) (2, 7) (b) (−2, −1) (c) (−5, 1)
   (d) (7, 1) (e) (3, −3) (f) (2, 8)
2. (a) (−4, 9) (b) (3, −3) (c) (−2, 1) (d) (−5, −4)
3. (a) $y = x^2 + 2$ (b) $y = 3x^2$
   (c) $y = (x - 4)^2$ (d) $y = -x^2 - 2$
4. (a) parabola opening up, vertex (0, 3) through (−1, 4) and (1, 4)
   (b) parabola opening up, vertex (0, −4) through (−2, 0) and (2, 0)
   (c) parabola opening up, vertex (3, 0) through (2, 1) and (4, 1)
   (d) parabola opening up, vertex (−4, 0) through (−5, 1) and (−3, 1)
   (e) parabola opening up, vertex (0, 0) through (−1, 2) and (1, 2)
   (f) parabola opening up, vertex (−2, 2) and (2, 2)
5. (a) parabola opening up, vertex (1, 3) through (−2, 5) and (2, 5)
   (b) parabola opening down, vertex (−1, 2) through (−2, −1) and (0, −1)
   (c) parabola opening up, vertex (2, −1) through (0, 1) and (4, 1)
   (d) parabola opening down, vertex (−2, −4) through $\left(-3, 4\frac{1}{3}\right)$ and $\left(-1, -4\frac{1}{3}\right)$

Chapter 3 Answers

Getting Ready, page 220

1. (a) 24 (b) 78 (c) 46 (d) −210
   (e) −9200 (f) 1 (g) 6 (h) 1
2. (a) straight line through (0, 2) and (1, 5)
   (b) straight line through (0, −4) and (2, 0)
   (c) parabola opening up, vertex (0, 2) through (−1, 3) and (1, 3)
   (d) parabola opening up, vertex (−3, −7) through (−5, −3) and (−1, −3)
   (e) parabola opening up, vertex (3, 1) through (2, 3) and (4, 3)
   (f) parabola opening down, vertex (1, 16) through (0, 15) and (2, 15)
3. (a) $x = 6$ (b) $x = 2$ (c) $d = -2$
   (d) $c = 2.5$ (e) $m = 1$ (f) $g = 4$
   (g) $x = 8$ (h) $c = 72$ (i) $y = 1$
4. (a) > (b) < (c) > (d) >
5. (a) cost; depends on distance
   (b) \$0.25/km (c) $c = 0.25d + 45$.
   (d) straight line starting at (0, 45) going up to right through (240, 105)
   (e) \$155 (f) 320 km
6. (a) $y = 2x + 5$ (b) $y = \frac{-3}{2}x + 5$
   (c) $y = \frac{-2}{3}x + \frac{5}{3}$ (d) $y = \frac{-2}{3}x + \frac{4}{3}$
   (e) $y = \frac{1}{10}x - \frac{1}{3}$ (f) $y = \frac{-5}{3}x - 5$
7. (a) 0.776 m (b) 29 m (c) 28.216 m
   (d) The ball hit the ground before 5 s have elapsed.
8. (a) $y = (x + 3)^2 - 9$ (b) $y = 2(x + 1)^2 - 2$
   (c) $y = 2(x - 1)^2 + 3$ (d) $y = -3(x - 1)^2 - 4$
   (e) $y = 2(x + 5)^2 - 7$ (f) $y = -5(x - 1)^2 - 6$
9. (a) (2, 4), $x = 2$, opens up
   (b) (−3, 5), $x = -3$, opens down
   (c) (−1, −9), $x = -1$, opens up
   (d) (2.5, 9.5), $x = 2.5$, opens down
10. (a) Reflect $y = x^2$ in the x-axis and then translate + 4 units vertically (4 units up).
    (b) Translate $y = x^2$ horizontally 5 units to the right.
    (c) Translate $y = x^2$ horizontally −3 units (3 units left) and then vertically −1 unit (1 unit down). The order does not matter.
    (d) Reflect $y = x^2$ in the x-axis, stretch vertically by factor 2 (these two could be reversed) and then translate 4 units right and 5 units down.
11. (a) parabola opening up, vertex (0, 2) through (−1, 3) and (1, 3)
    (b) parabola opening up, vertex (−3, 0) through (−4, 1) and (−2, 1)
    (c) parabola opening down, vertex (0, 0) through (−2, −4) and (2, −4)
    (d) parabola opening up, vertex (0, 0) through (2, 2) and (−2, 2)
    (e) parabola opening up, vertex (−1, 3) through (−3, 7) and (1, 7)
    (f) parabola opening up, vertex (2, 12) through (0, 0) and (4, 0)
12. Stretch $y = x^2$ vertically with factor 2 and then translate 3 units right and 11 units down.
13. (a) neither; line sloping downward to right
    (b) quadratic; $y = -4.9x^2 + 20x + 1$; parabola opening downward with vertex (2.04, 21.4)
14. (a) $x = \pm 6$ (b) $x = -7$ or $x = 3$
    (c) $x = \pm 7$ (d) $m = 3$

Practise, Apply, Solve 3.2, page 234

1. (a) D = {1, 3, 4, 5}, R = {3, 4, 5, 6, 7, 8}
   (b) 1 to 3, 1 to 6, 3 to 5, 4 to 7, 5 to 4, 5 to 8
   (c) not a function: 1 and 5 both map onto two different range values
2. (a) D = {1, 3, 4, 7}, R = {1, 2}; function: each domain value maps onto one range value
   (b) D = {1, 4, 6}, R = {1, 2, 3, 5}; not a function: 1 maps onto both 2 and 3
   (c) D = {0, 1, 2, 3}, R = {0, 1, 2, 3}; function: each domain value maps onto one range value
   (d) D = {1, 2, 3}, R = {4, 5, 6}; not a function: 1 maps onto both 4 and 5
   (e) D = {1, 2, 3}, R = {4}; function: each domain value maps onto one range value
   (f) D = {2}, R = {4, 5, 6}; not a function: 2 maps onto different values
3. (a) $\sqrt{25} = 5$ (b) no
   (c) When the square root button on the calculator is used, the output must be consistent. It must be a function.
   (d) negative number (e) $D = \{x \mid x \geq 0, x \in \mathbf{R}\}$
4. (a) 25 maps onto ±5. Both 5 and −5 are valid square roots of 25.
   (b) Every positive real number produces 2 different output values.
   (c) not a function: at least one input value with more than one output value.
   (d) No negative numbers can be used as input.

5. **i.** D = {−2, 0, 2, 3, 5, 6}, R = {1, 2, 3, 4, 5}
ii. 4, 2, 5, −2;
iii. They are not the same function because of order of operations.
iv. $f(2) = 5$ corresponds to (2, 5). 2 is x-coordinate of the point and $f(2)$ is y-coordinate of it.

6. **(a)** −3 **(b)** 3 **(c)** 7 **(d)** 2 **(e)** 4 **(f)** 13 **(g)** $3 - 2a$

7. **(a)** not a function: fails vertical line test
(b) function: passes vertical line test
(c) function: passes vertical line test
(d) not a function: fails vertical line test at end points
(e) not a function: fails vertical line test at right-hand part of curve
(f) not a function: fails vertical line test at most domain values
(g) function: passes vertical line test
(h) not a function: fails vertical line test at most domain values
(i) not a function: fails vertical line test (in a region, there are an infinite number of points above each other)

8. **i.** straight line through (0, 5) and $\left(-\frac{5}{3}, 0\right)$
ii. **(a)** 5 **(b)** 8 **(c)** 11 **(d)** 14 **(e)** 3 **(f)** 3 **(g)** 3 **(h)** 3 **(i)** 3 **(j)** 3
iii. first differences, part (j) is the slope of the straight line between (0, $g(0)$) and (4, $g(4)$). Since it is a linear relation, the slope is equal to the first differences.

9. **(a)** curve in first quadrant sloping down to right through (1, 1); curve in third quadrant through (−1, 1);
$D = \{x \mid x \neq 0, x \in \mathbf{R}\}$, $R = \{y \mid y \neq 0, y \in \mathbf{R}\}$; f is a function: graph passes vertical line test.
(b) straight line through (0, 6) and (3, 0); D = **R**, R = **R**; function: every x-value corresponds to one y-value.
(c) straight line through (0, 2) and (6, 0); D = **R**, R = **R**; function: passes vertical line test
(d) parabola opening upward with vertex (0, 3) through (−1, 4) and (1, 4): D = **R**, $R = \{y \mid y \geq 3, y \in \mathbf{R}\}$; function: passes vertical line test

10. There may be several brands of tires in the size requested, so different prices are possible for one tire size: therefore not a function. To be a function, the input needs to be more specific, so only one tire can be identified.

11. **i.** $y = 2x + 3$ **ii.** $g(x) = 2x + 3$ **iii.** 13, 7, 4, 13

12. **ii.** **(a)** 9 **(b)** 4 **(c)** 1 **(d)** 0 **(e)** 1 **(f)** −5 **(g)** −3 **(h)** −1 **(i)** 1 **(j)** 2 **(k)** 2 **(l)** 2 **(m)** 2
iii. first differences, second differences

13. **(a)** 49
(b) y-coordinate of the point on the graph with x-coordinate −2
(c) D = **R**, $R = \{y \mid y \geq -1, y \in \mathbf{R}\}$
(d) function: graph passes vertical line test
(e) The equation shows that every value of x yields only one possible value for $f(x)$.

14. **(a)** no
(b) This must be a function because of the answer to part (a). Its graph is a parabola that opens up, so it passes vertical line test.

15. **(a)** circle centred on origin, radius 5
(b) not a function: fails vertical line test for all values of x between −5 and 5.

16. **(a)** straight line through (0, −1) and (2, 5); D = **R**, R = **R**; function: passes vertical line test
(b) parabola opening downward with vertex (0, 10) through (−1.4, 0) and (1.4, 0); D = **R**, $R = \{y \mid y \leq 10, y \in \mathbf{R}\}$; function: passes vertical line test
(c) parabola opening upward with vertex ((2, −5) through (0, 7) and (4, 7); D = **R**, $R = \{y \mid y \geq -5, y \in \mathbf{R}\}$; function: passes vertical line test
(d) curve in first quadrant down to right through (1, 0), curve in fourth quadrant down to left through (−1, 1);
$D = \{x \mid x \neq 0, x \in \mathbf{R}\}$, $R = \{y \mid y > 0, y \in \mathbf{R}\}$; function: passes vertical line test
(e) parabola opening upward with vertex (1.5, −2.25) through (0, 0) and (3, 0); D = **R**, $R = \{y \mid y \geq -2.25, y \in \mathbf{R}\}$; function: passes vertical line test
(f) parabola opening upward with vertex (2, −4) through (0, 0) and (4, 0); D = **R**, $R = \{y \mid y \geq -4, y \in \mathbf{R}\}$; function: passes vertical line test
(g) line through (0, 5) and (3, 0); D = **R**, R = **R**; function: passes vertical line test

17. $D = \{x \mid x \geq 1\}$, $R = \{y \mid y \geq 2, y \in \mathbf{R}\}$

18. **(a)** If this relationship were not a function, customers would become upset if they found out that someone else received a better price for the same number of meals served.
(b) $D = \{x \mid x\ 0 \leq x \leq 200, x \in \mathbf{R}\}$,
$R = \{y \mid 1250 \leq y \leq 3700, y \in \mathbf{R}\}$
(c) The domain must have an upper limit because the room has a maximum seating capacity.
(d) Reasonable: the hall's owners would want to receive a minimum total payment. If fewer than 50 people attend, they will charge $1250 because they could rent the room to a larger group and make more money. They do not want to reserve a room, then discover only 10 people are coming − and only receive payment for those 10.

19. **(a)** parabola opening down, vertex (1.5, 20) through (0, 2) and (3, 0)
(b) $D = \{t \mid 0 \leq t \leq 3.1, t \in \mathbf{R}\}$, $R = \{h \mid 0 \leq h \leq 20, h \in \mathbf{R}\}$
(c) is a function: every value of t corresponds to a unique value of h.
(d) parabola opening to left with vertex (20, 1.5) through (0, 3) and (2, 0)
(e) not a function: each height between 1.6 m and 20 m corresponds to two different times; fails vertical line test

20. **(a)** Every quantity ordered must have a unique, reliable price.
(b) $D = \{x \mid x \geq 0, x \in \mathbf{R}\}$, $R = \{y \mid y \geq 0, y \in \mathbf{R}\}$
(c) straight line from (0, 0) to (100, 400) (open dot); straight line at same angle from (100, 350) up
(d) 99 kg could cost more than 400 kg. Sample change: charge $4/kg for the first 100 kg and then $3.50/kg for the part of the order over 100 kg.

21. **(a)** $D = \{s \mid 0 \leq s \leq 16\,000, s \in \mathbf{R}\}$,
$R = \{p \mid 300 \leq p \leq 1200, p \in \mathbf{R}\}$
(b) To ensure fairness: two employees with the same sales should receive the same pay.
(c) *Example*: weekly pay of $300 for sales under $2000; $200 plus 5% commission for sales from $2000 to $8000; 7.5% sales commission for sales over $8000.

22. **(a)** curved line up to right
(b) $D = \{i \mid 0 \leq i \leq 0.2, i \in \mathbf{R}\}$,
$R = \{A \mid 10\,000 \leq A \leq 25\,000, A \in \mathbf{R}\}$

23. **(a)** Age is the independent variable, so if two members of the family are the same age and have different foot lengths, the relationship will not be a function. If they are all different ages, the relationship will be a function.
(b) Some of Sarah's friends are likely to be her age and are likely to have feet of different lengths, so the relationship will not be a function.

(c) The line of best fit will be a function.

(d) no; a person's age cannot be determined from foot length

24. *Example*: function: (x, y): (0, 3), (1, 4), (2, 5) Each value of x corresponds to a unique value of y. non-function: (x, y): (0, 3), (0, 4), (2, 5) The 0 corresponds to both 3 and 4.

25. (a) 13

(b) function: each binary number is converted to a unique decimal number

(c) 21, 3, 8 (d) $R = \{y \mid y \le 15, y \in \mathbf{W}\}$ (e) 8 bits

26. (a) Answers will vary.

(b) rand does not appear to produce a unique output; for truly random numbers an unpredictable output is wanted.

(c) 0.943 597 402 5, 0.908 318 861, 0.146 687 829 2, 0.514 701 950 5, 0.405 809 641 8. These values are the same for everyone.

(d) This list is the same as before.

(e) For 0.4: 0.943 597 402 5, 0.908 318 861, 0.146 687 829 2
For 0.8: 0.943 597 402 5, 0.908 318 861, 0.146 687 829 2
For 1.2: 0.745 560 772 8, 0.855 900 597 1, 0.225 360 061 7
For 1.6: 0.745 560 772 8, 0.855 900 597 1, 0.225 360 061 7
For 2.0: 0.491 121 545 1, 0.711 801 117 9, 0.450 720 047 5
For 2.4: 0.491 121 545 1, 0.711 801 117 9, 0.450 720 047 5
For 2.8: 0.491 121 545 1, 0.711 801 117 9, 0.450 720 047 5

(f) The calculator truncates (eliminates any decimals) from the number stored to rand, then generates a list of numbers using that seed number. The random number obtained depends on the seed number and the number of times rand is chosen.

(g) Yes: rand is a function of the seed number and the number of times it is selected. For example, when 0 is stored in rand, and rand is selected 3 times, 0.146 687 829 2 is always produced. These are not random numbers. If an experiment is done using random numbers from the calculator, the result will not be random, but predictable.

Practise, Apply, Solve 3.3, page 245

1. (a) two closed dots on 4 and 5

(b) closed dot on −1, solid line to right

(c) open dot on −3, solid line to left

(d) solid line between open dots at 1 and 2

(e) solid line between closed dot at −3 and open dot at 1

(f) solid line between closed dots at 1 and 3

(g) solid line to left of open dot at −3, solid line to right of open dot at 2

(h) solid line between closed dot at 2 and open dot at 5

(i) solid line between open dots at −4 and 4

(j) solid line to left of open dot at −3, solid line to right of open dot at 3

2. (a) $\{x \mid -3 \le x \le 3, x \in \mathbf{I}\}$ or $\{x \mid x^2 < 16, x \in \mathbf{I}\}$

(b) $\{x \mid x > -2, x \in \mathbf{I}\}$ or $\{x \mid x \ge -1, x \in \mathbf{I}\}$

(c) $\{x \mid x \le -2, x \in \mathbf{R}\}$

(d) $\{x \mid x > -1, x \in \mathbf{R}\}$

(e) $\{x \mid -5 \le x < 3, x \in \mathbf{R}\}$

(f) $\{x \mid x > 1 \text{ or } x < -1, x \in \mathbf{R}\}$ or $\{x \mid x^2 > 1, x \in \mathbf{R}\}$

(g) $\{x \mid -3 \le x \le 3, x \in \mathbf{R}\}$ or $\{x \mid x^2 \le 9, x \in \mathbf{R}\}$

3. (a) solid line to left of closed dot at 3, $a \le 3$

(b) solid line to left of open dot at −2, $t < -2$

(c) solid line to left of open dot at 4, $x < 4$

(d) solid line to left of closed dot at 9, $s \le 9$

(e) solid line to left of open dot at −2, $x < -2$

(f) solid line to left of open dot at −1, solid line to right open dot at 1; $x > 1$ or $x < -1$

(g) solid line between closed dots at −5 and 5, $-5 \le r \le 5$

(h) solid line to right of open dot at 3, $t > 3$

4. (a) $-2 \le x < 1$ (b) $0 \le x < 9$

(c) $8 < b < 14$ (d) $-3 \le x \le 3$

5. (a) $b > -\frac{5}{2}$ (b) $\frac{9}{2} \le x \le 6$ (c) $x > \frac{-1}{8}$

6. (a) line passing through (0, 5) and (2.5, 0)

(b) $R = \{y \mid y \ge 3, y \in \mathbf{R}\}$

(d) $D = \{x \mid -6 \le x \le 0, x \in \mathbf{R}\}$

7. (a) $R = \{y \mid y > 6, y \in \mathbf{R}\}$

(b) $R = \{y \mid 4 \le y \le 22, y \in \mathbf{R}\}$

(c) $D = \{x \mid 1 \le x \le 5, x \in \mathbf{R}\}$

9. $D = \{x \mid -2 < x < 3, x \in \mathbf{R}\}$, $R = \{y \mid 3 \le y < 8, y \in \mathbf{R}\}$

10. $D = \{t \mid 0 \le t \le 5, t \in \mathbf{R}\}$

11. (a) no solution (b) $x > 2$ (c) $x < 2$

12. The coefficient of x^2 in the equation of the parabola must lie between $\frac{1}{2}$ and 2.

Practise, Apply, Solve 3.4, page 255

1. (a) relationship and inverse are both functions: each element of the domain corresponds to a unique value of the range

(b) relationship is a function: passes vertical line test; inverse not a function: 3 maps onto more than one value

(c) relationship not a function: 1 maps onto more than one value; inverse is a function: each x-coordinate corresponds to a unique y-coordinate.

2. (a) $4 \to 1, 4 \to 2, 5 \to 1, 6 \to 3$; not a function: 4 maps onto 1 and 2

(b) $4 \to 1, 4 \to 2, 4 \to 3$; not a function: 4 maps onto 1, 2, and 3

(c) $4 \to 2, 5 \to 2, 6 \to 2$; inverse is a function: each element of the domain corresponds to one value in the range.

3. (a) first differences are all −1

(b) first differences are all −2

(c) (−1, 7), (0, 5), (1, 3), (2, 1), (3, −1), (4, −3), (5, −5)

(d) $\frac{-1}{2}$ (e) −2

(f) $f(x) = -0.5x + 2.5, x \in \{-5, -3, -1, 1, 3, 5, 7\}$

(g) $f^{-1}(x) = -2x + 5, \{x \mid -1 \le x \le 5, x \in \mathbf{I}\}$

(h) The slope of the line through the points in f is the reciprocal of the slope of the line through the points in f^{-1}. Normally, the first differences would also be reciprocals of each other, but the x-coordinates in f increase by 2 each time.

4. (a) (5, 0), (3, −1), (2, −2), (2, −3), (3, −4), (5, −5)

(b) (−2, 6), (−1, 5), (0, 4), (1, 3), (2, 2), (3, 1), (4, 0), (5, −1), (6, −2)

(c) (5, 5), (2, 2), (0, 1), (−1, 0), (−1, −1), (0, −2), (2, −3), (5,−4)

(d) (−2, 2), (−1, 1), (0, 0), (1, −1), (2, −2), (3, −3), (4, −4), (5, −5)

(e) (−1, −2), (−1, −1), (−1, 0), (0, 1), (1, 2), (2, 2), (3, 2), (4, 3), (5, 4), (5, 5), (5, 6)

(f) straight line from (0, 6) to (5, −5)

(g) connected points: (1, 6) to (−1, 4) to (−1, 1) to (5, −2) to (5, −5)

(h) connected points: (4, 3) to (3, 0.5) to (2.5, 1.5) to (2, −1) to (1.5, −0.5) to (1, −3) to (−1, −1)

5. (a) no points common (b) all points common

(c) (−1, −1) and (2, 2)

(d) (−2, 2), (−1, 1), (0, 0), (1, −1), and (2, −2)

(e) (2, −1), (-1, 2), and $(\frac{1}{3}, 0)$ (f) $(\frac{15}{8}, \frac{15}{8})$

(g) no points common (h) (-1, -1)

6. **i.** (1, 6), (2, 5), (4, 3), (5, 2), (4, 0), (3, −2)
   ii. D = {1, 2, 3, 4, 5}, R = {−2, 0, 2, 3, 5, 6}
   iii. 4, −2, 5, 5, 2, 0 or 3
   iv. not a function: 4 maps onto 0 and 3.
   v. (1, 6); 1 is the x-coordinate of that point; $f^{-1}(1)$ is y-coordinate of that point.

7. **(a)** −2 **(b)** 0 **(c)** 13 **(d)** 5 **(e)** $\frac{t+2}{3}$
   (f) $\frac{2}{3}$ **(g)** $\frac{7}{3}$ **(h)** $\frac{a+2}{3}$ **(i)** $\frac{x}{3}$ **(j)** a
   (k) $t + 2$ **(l)** t **(m)** $\frac{1}{3}$ **(n)** $\frac{1}{3}$ **(o)** $\frac{1}{3}$
   (p) 3 **(q)** $\frac{1}{3}$

8. **(a)** −6 **(b)** 2 **(c)** 14 **(d)** $\frac{3}{2}x + 5$
   (e) $\frac{2}{3}(x - 5)$ **(f)** −6 **(g)** 9 **(h)** $\frac{3}{2}a + 5$
   (i) $\frac{3}{2}(a + 1) + 5$ **(j)** $\frac{3}{2}$ **(k)** t
   (l) $\frac{3}{2}$ **(m)** $\frac{2}{3}$
   (n) $\frac{3}{2}$ if $a \neq b$; undefined if $a = b$

9. f: straight line through (5, −1) and (−4, 5); f^{-1}: straight line through (5, −4) and (−1, 5)
   (a) $\frac{-2}{3}x + \frac{7}{3}$ **(b)** $\frac{-3}{2}x + \frac{7}{2}$ **(c)** −4
   (d) (−4, 5) **(e)** (5, −4) **(g)** −1
   (h) (5, −1) **(i)** (−1, 5) **(k)** 1.4
   (l) (1.4, 1.4) **(m)** (1.4, 1.4)

10. **(a)** Multiply by 10, then divide by 4.
    (b) *Example*: convert a person's height from feet and inches to centimetres
    (c) $\frac{4x}{10}$ **(d)** $\frac{10x}{4}$ **(e)** $f(15)$ **(f)** $f^{-1}(66)$

11. **(a)** −2 **(b)** −2 **(c)** $-x + 5$
    (d) g: straight line through (0, 5) and (5, 0); g^{-1}: straight line through (5, 0) and (0, 5) (They are the same.)
    (e) g and g^{-1} represent the same line because of symmetry in the line $y = x$

12. **i.** f: straight line through (1.5, 0) and (0, 3), f^{-1}: straight line through (0, 1.5) and (3, 0)
    ii. **(a)** $\frac{3}{2}$ **(b)** 3 **(c)** 1 **(d)** 1 **(e)** 1
    iii. **(a)** For $f(x) = 0$, y-coordinate = 0, so x-intercept = $\frac{3}{2}$ and y-intercept of f^{-1} is $\frac{3}{2}$ **(b)** For $f^{-1}(x) = 0$, y-coordinate = 0, so x-intercept = 3 and y-intercept of $f = 3$ **(c)** For $f(x) = x$, y-coordinate = x-coordinate, so (1, 1) is a point on f where x- and y-coordinates are equal, a point on graph of f^{-1} where x- and y-coordinates are equal, and the intersection point of each graph with graph of $y = x$. **(d)** For $f^{-1}(x)$, y-coordinate = x-coordinate on f^{-1}. **(e)** For $f^{-1}(x) = f(x)$, both y-coordinates are equal; so $x = 1$ at the point of intersection of f and f^{-1}.

13. **(a)** Multiply sales by 0.05, then add $100.
    (b) $20(s - 100)$
    (c) Subtract $100 from weekly pay, then multiply by 20.
    (d) employee could check that paycheque is correct
    (e) D = $\{s \mid 0 \le s \le 20\,000, s \in \mathbf{R}\}$, R = $\{p \mid 100 \le p \le 1100, p \in \mathbf{R}\}$

14. **(a)** series of vertical bars (graph in question rotated 90° counterclockwise)
    (b) not a function: price does not uniquely determine the mass of the letter
    (c) 50 g < mass < 100 g

15. $y \doteq 0.380x + 0.490$

16. **(a)** horizontal line from (0, 322) to (1000, 322), then slope upward to right through (1800, 362)
    (b) $f(s) = 272 + 0.05s$
    (c) vertical line from (322, 0) to (322, 1000), then slope upward through (362, 1800)
    (d) If $s > 322$, $f^{-1}(s) = 20s - 5440$; if $s = 322$, then $f^{-1}(s)$ can be any value between 0 and 1000.
    (e) $f^{-1}(420) = 20(420) - 5440 = 2960$

17. **(b)** $f(p) = -3040p + 14\,700$
    (c) (1000, 4.39), ((2500, 4.070, (700, 4.65), 800, 4.59), (2700, 3.94)
    (d) $f^{-1}(m) = -0.000\,314m + 4.81$
    (e) $f^{-1}(m) = -0.000\,329m + 4.84$
    (f) They are similar. The process for determining the line of best fit causes slight differences.
    (g) 260 kg **(h)** none **(i)** $3.55

18. **(a)** A postal code must be a function because each address in Canada must have a reliable, consistent postal code. One address cannot have more than one postal code.
    (b) The inverse converts the postal codes into address. Several neighbouring houses may have the same postal code, so one postal code produces several possible addresses. It is not a function.

19.

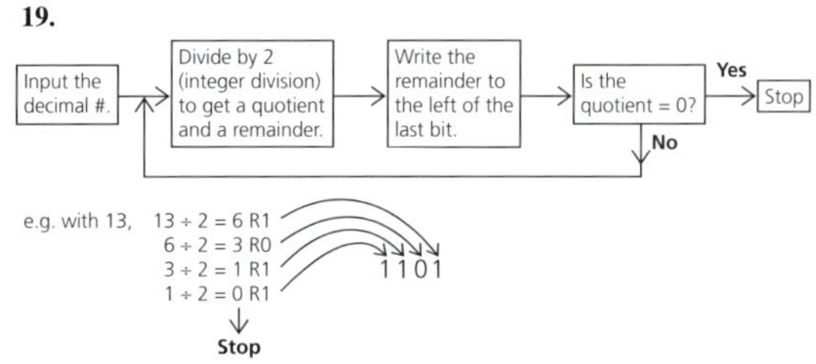

Divide by 2, giving a quotient and a remainder. Write the remainder as the next bit (moving left). Repeat using the quotient. Continue until the number is 0 after the remainder is subtracted.

20. **(a)** 5 667 821 743 **(b)** 792 543 872
    (c) $f(x) = 9 - x$, $\{x \mid x \le 9, x \in \mathbf{W}\}$
    (d) $f^{-1}(x) = 9 - x$, $\{x \mid x \le 9, x \in \mathbf{W}\}$
    (e) same graph: (0, 9), (1, 8), (2, 7), (3, 6), (4, 5), (5, 4), (6, 3), (7, 2), (8, 1), (9, 0)

21. **(a)** 21 525
    (b) function: each word can only be coded in one way.
    (c) BOTTOM or BOB_TOM or many other combinations that may not be English words.
    (d) inverse is not a function: knowing the encoded digits does not uniquely determine the message because we cannot be sure how the letters are grouped.

22. **(a)** soft drink received
    (b) combination of coins and a button selection
    (c) set of all the different drinks the machine produces
    (d) set of all possible combinations of coins and button selections that would yield a drink from the machine
    (e) no: type of coins entered does not uniquely determine the size and type of drink

Practice 3.5, page 264

1. **(a)** $f^{-1}(x) = \pm\sqrt{\frac{x-3}{-2}} - 1$
   D = **R**, R = $\{y \mid y \le 3, y \in \mathbf{R}\}$; D = $\{x \mid x \le 3, x \in \mathbf{R}\}$, R = **R**; no: fails vertical line test

(b) $f^{-1}g(x) = x^2, x \geq 0$

$D = \{x \mid x \geq 0, x \in \mathbf{R}\}, R = \{y \mid y \geq 0, y \in \mathbf{R}\}$;

$D = \{x \mid x \geq 0, x \in \mathbf{R}\}, R = \{y \mid y \geq 0, y \in \mathbf{R}\}$; function: passes vertical line test

(c) $f^{-1}(x) = x^2 + 2$

$D = \{x \mid x \geq 2, x \in \mathbf{R}\}, R = \{y \mid y \geq 0, y \in \mathbf{R}\}$;

$D = \{x \mid x \geq 0, x \in \mathbf{R}\}, R = \{y \mid y \geq 2, y \in \mathbf{R}\}$; function: passes vertical line test

(d) $y^{-1}(x) = x^{\frac{1}{3}}$

$D = \mathbf{R}, R = \mathbf{R}$; for inverse, $D = \mathbf{R}, R = \mathbf{R}$; function: passes vertical line test

(e) $g^{-1}(x) = \frac{1}{x}$

$D = \{x \mid x \neq 0, x \in \mathbf{R}\}, R = \{y \mid y \neq 0, y \in \mathbf{R}\}$;

$D = \{x \mid x \neq 0, x \in \mathbf{R}\}, R = \{y \mid y \neq 0, y \in \mathbf{R}\}$; function: every value of x corresponds to a unique value of y

(f) $f^{-1}(x) = 3 - \frac{1}{x}$

$D = \{x \mid x \neq 3, x \in \mathbf{R}\}, R = \{y \mid y \neq 0, y \in \mathbf{R}\}$;

$D = \{x \mid x \neq 0, x \in \mathbf{R}\}, R = \{y \mid y \neq 3, y \in \mathbf{R}\}$; function: passes vertical line test

(g) $y^{-1}(x) = \frac{1}{x^2} + 2$

$D = \{x \mid x > 2, x \in \mathbf{R}\}, R = \{y \mid y > 0, y \in \mathbf{R}\}$;

$D = \{x \mid x > 0, x \in \mathbf{R}\}, R = \{y \mid y > 2, y \in \mathbf{R}\}$; function: passes vertical line test

(h) $f^{-1}(x) = \sqrt{9 - x^2} + 2$

$D = \{x \mid -1 \leq x \leq 5, x \in \mathbf{R}\}$,

$R = \{y \mid 0 \leq y \leq 3, y \in \mathbf{R}\}$; $D = \{x \mid 0 \leq x \leq 3, x \in \mathbf{R}\}$,

$R = \{y \mid -1 \leq y \leq 5, y \in \mathbf{R}\}$; not a function: fails vertical line test

(i) $g^{-1}(x) = \frac{1}{3} \sin^{-1} x$

$D = \mathbf{R}, R = \{y \mid -1 \leq y \leq 1, y \in \mathbf{R}\}$;

$D = \{x \mid -1 \leq y \leq 1, x \in \mathbf{R}\}, R = \mathbf{R}$;

not a function: fails vertical line test

(j) $f^{-1}(x) = \frac{1}{3} \cos^{-1}(x - 1)$

$D = R, R = \{0 \leq y \leq 2, y \in \mathbf{R}\}$; $D = \{x \mid 0 \leq x \leq 2, x \in \mathbf{R}\}$,

$R = \mathbf{R}$; not a function: fails vertical line test

2. **ii.** $f^{-1}(x) = \sqrt{\frac{x + 2}{3}} + 1$

iii. for f: $D = \{x \mid -0.3 \leq x \leq 2, x \in \mathbf{R}\}$,

$R = \{y \mid -2 \leq y \leq 3.07, y \in \mathbf{R}\}$; for f^{-1}:

$D = \{x \mid -2 \leq x \leq 3.07, x \in \mathbf{R}\}$,

$R = \{y \mid -0.3 \leq y \leq 2, y \in \mathbf{R}\}$

iv. **(a)** $f^{-1}(x) = 3 - \frac{1}{x}$

for f: $D = \{x \mid -1 \leq x \leq 2, x \in \mathbf{R}\}$,

$R = \{y \mid 0.25 \leq y \leq 1, y \in \mathbf{R}\}$; for

f^{-1}: $\{x \mid 0.25 \leq x \leq 1, x \in \mathbf{R}\}, R = \{y \mid -1 \leq y \leq 2, y \in \mathbf{R}\}$

(b) $g^{-1}(x) = \sqrt{9 - x^2} + 2$

for g: $D = \{x \mid -1 \leq x \leq 2, x \in \mathbf{R}\}$,

$R = \{y \mid 0 \leq y \leq 3, y \in \mathbf{R}\}$; for g^{-1}:

$D = \{x \mid 0 \leq x \leq 3, x \in \mathbf{R}\}, R = \{y \mid -1 \leq y \leq 2, y \in \mathbf{R}\}$

(c)

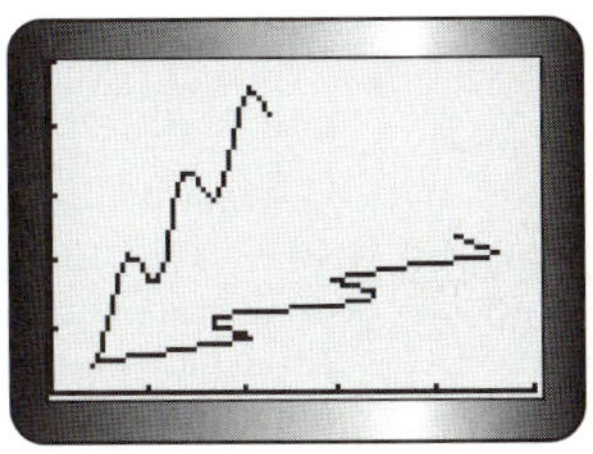

for y: $D = \{x \in \mathbf{R} \mid 0.4 \leq x \leq 2.3\}$,

$R = \{y \mid 0.4019 < y < 4.625, y \in \mathbf{R}\}$; for y^{-1}:

$D = \{x \mid 0.4019 < x < 4.625, x \in \mathbf{R}\}$,

$R = \{y \mid 0.4 \leq y \leq 2.3, y \in \mathbf{R}\}$

(d)

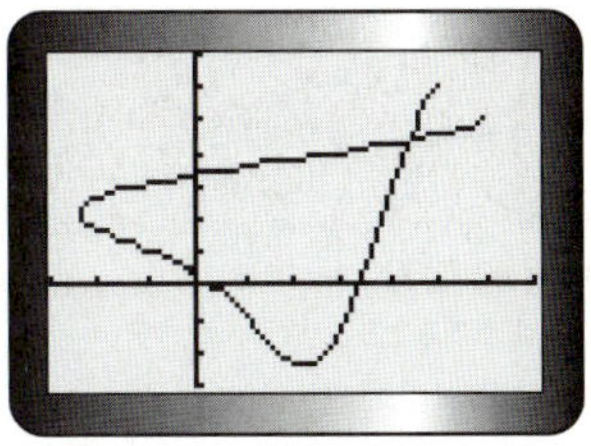

for f: $D = \{x \mid 0 \leq x \leq 5, x \in \mathbf{R}\}$,

$R = \{y \mid -2.4006 < y < 5.976\ 99, y \in \mathbf{R}\}$; for f^{-1}:

$D = \{x \mid -2.4006 < x < 5.976\ 99, x \in \mathbf{R}\}$,

$R = \{y \mid 0 \leq y \leq 5, y \in \mathbf{R}\}$

Practise, Apply, Solve 3.6, page 273

1. **(a)** (5, 0), (3, −1), (2, −2), (2, −3), (3, −4), (5, −5)

(b) *Example*: {(2, −3), (3, −4), (5, −5)}

2. **(a)** connected points: (1, 6), (−1, 4), (−1, 1), (5, −2), (5, −5)

(b) $D = \{x \mid -5 \leq x \leq 6, x \in \mathbf{R}\}, R = \{y \mid -1 \leq y \leq 5, y \in \mathbf{R}\}$

(c) $D = \{x \mid -1 \leq x \leq 5\ x \in \mathbf{R}\}, R = \{y \mid -5 \leq y \leq 6, y \in \mathbf{R}\}$

(d) when domain of g is $-2 \leq x \leq 1$, g^{-1} is a function and has same domain as g^{-1}

3. **(a)** no restrictions; parabola opening to left with vertex (1, −2) through (0, −1) and (0, −3); $D = x \geq -2$ or $x \leq -2$

(b) no restrictions; parabola opening to right with vertex (0, 3) through (2, 4) and (2, 2); $R = x \geq 3$ or $x \leq 3$

(c) $R = y \geq 3$ or $y \leq 3$; parabola opening upward with vertex (3, 0) through (2, 2) and (4, 2); no restrictions

(d) no restrictions; left half of downward opening parabola with vertex (2, 1) and passing through (0, −3); no restrictions

(e) $R = y \geq 4$ or $y \leq 4$; parabola opening downward with vertex (4, 1) through (2, −3) and (6, −3); no restrictions

(f) no restrictions; parabola opening to left with vertex (4, 3) through (−4, 1) and (−4, 5); $D = x \geq 3$ or $x \leq 3$

4. **(a)** $f(x) = -(x - 4)^2 + 1$; parabola opening to left with vertex (1, 4) through (0, 5) and (0, 3); when domain of relation is $x \geq 4$ or $x \leq 4$, inverse is a function;

f^{-1} is $y = \pm\sqrt{-x + 1} + 4$

(b) $f(x) = (x - 1)^2 - 3$; parabola opening to right with vertex (−3, 1) through (−2, 2) and (−2, 0); when domain of relation is $x \geq 1$ or $x \leq 1$, inverse is a function;

f^{-1} is $y = \pm\sqrt{x + 3} + 1$

(c) $f(x) = (x + 3)^2 - 2, x \leq -3$; bottom half of parabola opening to right with vertex (−2, −3) passing through (2, −5); no restrictions; f^{-1} is $y = -\sqrt{x + 2} - 3$

(d) $f(x) = 3 + \sqrt{-x + 2}$; right half of parabola opening downward with vertex (3, 2) and passing through (4, 1); no restrictions; f^{-1} is $y = -(x - 3)^2 + 2, x \geq 3$

5. **(a)** f: parabola opening downward with vertex (−1, 3) through (−3, −5) and (1, −5)

(b) f^{-1}: parabola opening to left with vertex (3, −1) through (−5, 1) and (−5, −3)

(c) $D = x \geq -1$ or $x \leq -1$

6. **(a)** g; bottom half of parabola opening to right with vertex (0, 0) through (1, −1)

(b) g^{-1}: left half of parabola opening upward with vertex (0, 0) through (−1, 1)

(c) $D = \{x \mid x \leq 0, x \in \mathbf{R}\}, R = \{y \mid y \geq 0, y \in \mathbf{R}\}$

(d) $g^{-1}(x) = x^2, x \leq 0$

7. **(a)** g: top half of parabola opening to right with vertex (0, 3) through (4, 5)
(b) g^{-1}: parabola opening up, vertex (3, 0) through (0, 9) and (6, 9)
(c) $g^{-1}(x) = (x - 3)^2, x \geq 3$
(e) $T_{min} = 3$ for correct graph

8. **(a)** f: top half of parabola opening right, vertex (2, 0) and through (6, 2)
(b) f^{-1}; parabola opening up, vertex (0, 2) through (2, 6) and (−2, 6)
(c) $f^{-1}(x) = x^2 + 2, x \geq 0$
(e) $T_{min} = 0$ for correct graph

9. f: right half of parabola opening downward with vertex (1, 7) through (2, 5), f^{-1}: top half of parabola opening to left with vertex (7, 1) through (−1, 3)
(a) −1 **(b)** $f^{-1}(x) = 1 + \sqrt{\dfrac{7 - x}{2}}$
(c) 2 **(d)** $1 + \sqrt{-a}$ **(e)** x

10. **(a)** (3, 14) **(b)** $D = x \geq 3$ **(c)** $f^{-1}(x) = 3 + \sqrt{-x + 14}$

11. **(a)** $D = \{x \mid -2 < x < 3, x \in \mathbf{R}\}, R = \{y \mid -3 \leq y < 24, y \in \mathbf{R}\}$
(b) f^{-1} is $y = 1 \pm \sqrt{\dfrac{x + 3}{3}}, -2 < y < 3$

12. bottom half of parabola opening right, vertex (0, 5) through (25, 0)
(a) $D = \{x \mid x \geq 0, x \in \mathbf{R}\}, R = \{y \mid y \leq 5, y \in \mathbf{R}\}$
(b) $f^{-1}(x) = (x - 5)^2, x \leq 5$

13. $y = \sqrt{x}$ is one branch of the inverse of $y = x^2$. The inverse of $y = \sqrt{x}$ is the right-hand branch of $y = x^2$ (i.e. $y = x^2, x \geq 0$.)

14. **(a)** first differences: 12.375, 10.125, 7.875, 5.625, 3.375, 1.125, −1.125, −3.375, −5.625, −7.875, −10.125; second differences: all −2.25
(b) $y = -4x^2 + 27x$, parabola opening down, vertex (3, 40.5)
(c) parabola opening left, vertex (40.5, 3) through (0, 0) and (0, 6)
(d) not a function: fails vertical line test

15. $y = -\sqrt{x + 2}$ defines the lower branch of a parabola that opens to the right. The inverse of this function is a single branch of the parabola opening up. The graph of $y = x^2 - 2$ is a parabola (both branches) with vertex at (0, −2), so it cannot be the inverse of $y = -\sqrt{x + 2}$.

16. No: $y = \sqrt{x + 2}$ is the upper branch of a parabola opening to the right with vertex at (−2, 0). Its inverse is a function already, without any restriction.

17. **(a)** $f(x) = x(x - 2), 0 \leq x \leq 9, x \in \mathbf{W}$
(b) f^{-1} is $y = 1 \pm \sqrt{x + 1}, 0 \leq y \leq 9, y \in \mathbf{W}$
(c) no: fails vertical line test
(d) $R = \{0, 3, 8, 15\}$ **(e)** 3, 4, or 5
(f) For f^{-1} to be a function, range of $f^{-1} = 1 \leq y \leq 9, y \in \mathbf{W}$; Then each input value corresponds to a unique output value.

18. Reflect the graph in $y = x$. If no two points of the function lie on the same horizontal line, then its inverse is a function; if not, then restrict its domain so that no two points are on a horizontal line.

19. **(a)** $P(x) = (x - 3.21)(14\,700 - 3040x)$
(b) P^{-1} is $y = 4.02 \pm \sqrt{\dfrac{-x + 2008}{3040}}$
(c) \$4.21/kg or \$3.83/kg **(d)** \$4.02/kg **(e)** \$2290
(f) *Example*: (supply cost in \$/kg, profit): (3.21, \$2008), (2.50, \$4146), (4.00, \$531), (4.80, \$0.94)
(g) *Example*: increased supply could mean lower prices, resulting in greater sales; decreased supply could mean higher prices, resulting in fewer sales.

20. $R = \{y \mid y > \dfrac{1}{3}$ or $y < -0.5, y \in \mathbf{R}\}$

Practise, Apply, Solve 3.7, page 285

1. The "Base Function" determines the shape that is preserved after the transformations. For example, if $f(x) = \sqrt{x}$, then the graph of $y = 3f(x - 2) + 7$ will be the same shape, but will be stretched and translated into a new position. Neither reflections, translations, nor stretches will change the graph's basic shape.

2. (−1, 5), (0, 3), and (1, 7)

3. **(a)** (1, 4), (2, 10), (3, 14), (4, 16)
(b) (1, 4), (2, 7), (3, 9), (4, 10)
(c) (−1, 2), (0, 5), (1, 7), (2, 8)
(d) (0.5, 2), (1, 5), (1.5, 7), (2, 8)

4. **(b)** Multiply x-coordinates of f by 5; subtract 3 from y-coordinates.
(c) x → [÷5] → (f) → [−3] → y
(÷5: must be the opposite operation)
(d) $g(x) = f\left(\dfrac{x}{5}\right) - 3$
(e) Divide x-coordinates of g by 5; add 3 to y-coordinates.
(f) x → [×5] → (g) → [+3] → y
(g) $f(x) = g(5x) + 3$

5. **(a)** no stretches or flips; translate left 2 units and up 3 units.
(b) x → [+2] → (f) → [+3] → y
(c) $g(x) = f(x + 2) + 3$

6. **(a)** x → [−3] → (f) → [×2] → y
(b) Stretch $y = f(x)$ vertically with factor 2, then translate 3 units right (order does not matter).
(c) f: (−2, 4), (2, 4), (1, 1), (1, −1), (0, 0); y: (5, 8), (4, 2), (1, 8), (3, 0), (2, 2), (5, 8)

7. **(a)** ii **(b)** iv **(c)** x
(d) viii **(e)** iii **(f)** i

8. **(a)** ix **(b)** xii **(c)** iii **(d)** xvii

9. **i.** curve in first quadrant down to right through (1, 1), curve in third quadrant down to right through (−1, 1)
ii. **(a)** f is translated 2 units to the right; **(b)** f is translated 1 unit left; **(c)** f is translated up 2 units; **(d)** f is translated down 6 units; **(e)** f is stretched vertically with factor 0.5; **(f)** f is stretched vertically with factor 2; **(g)** f is stretched horizontally with factor 2; **(h)** f is stretched horizontally with factor 0.5; **(i)** f is reflected in x-axis
iv. **(a)** $D = \{x \mid x \neq 2, x \in \mathbf{R}\}, R = \{y \mid y \neq 0, y \in \mathbf{R}\}$;
(b) $D = \{x \mid x \neq -1, x \in \mathbf{R}\}\ R = \{y \mid y \neq 0, y \in \mathbf{R}\}$;
(c) $D = \{x \mid x \neq 0, x \in \mathbf{R}\}, R = \{y \mid y \neq 2, y \in \mathbf{R}\}$;
(d) $D = \{x \mid x \neq 0, x \in \mathbf{R}\}, R = \{y \mid y \neq -6, y \in \mathbf{R}\}$;
(e) $D = \{x \mid x \neq 0, x \in \mathbf{R}\}, R = \{y \mid y \neq 0, y \in \mathbf{R}\}$;
(f) $D = \{x \mid x \neq 0, x \in \mathbf{R}\}, R = \{y \mid y \neq 0, y \in \mathbf{R}\}$;
(g) $D = \{x \mid x \neq 0\}, R = \{y \mid y \neq 0, y \in \mathbf{R}\}$;
(h) $D = \{x \mid x \neq 0, x \in \mathbf{R}\}, R = \{y \mid y \neq 0, y \in \mathbf{R}\}$;
(i) $D = \{x \mid x \neq 0, x \in \mathbf{R}\}, R = \{y \mid y \neq 0, y \in \mathbf{R}\}$
v. The equations are equivalent.

10. **(a)** x → [−2] → (g) → [x(−3)] → [+1] → y
(b) (6, −47)
(c) Add 2 to x-coordinates: horizontal translation 2 units right; multiply y-coordinates by −3: vertical stretch factor 3 and reflection in x-axis; add 1 y-coordinate: vertical translation, 1 unit up. The horizontal translation can take place at any time, but the vertical stretch and reflection must happen before the vertical translation.

(d) D = **R**; R = $\{y \mid y \geq 0, y \in \mathbf{R}\}$; Only horizontal transformations affect the domain, and vertical transformations affect the range. The horizontal translation does not change the domain since it is **R**. The new domain is **R**. The reflection in x-axis caused new range to be $\{y \mid y \leq 0, y \in \mathbf{R}\}$. The vertical stretch has no further effect. The vertical translation of $+1$ gives new R = $\{y \mid y \leq 1, y \in \mathbf{R}\}$.

11. **(a)** -2 **(b)** $(5, -4)$
(c) parabola opening up, vertex $(3, -4)$ through $(1, 4)$ and $(5, 4)$

12. **(a)** bottom half of parabola opening right, vertex $(5, -2)$ through $(9, 8)$
(b) $y = -3\sqrt{x - 5} - 2$

13. **(a)**

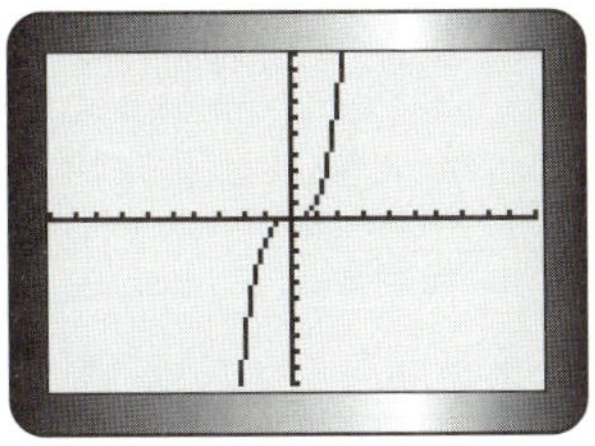

(b) $y = (x + 5)^3 + 3$

14. **(a)**

x ← [-1] ← [x(-1)] ← (f) → [×3] → [+2] → y

(b) $y = 3f(-x - 1) + 2$

15.

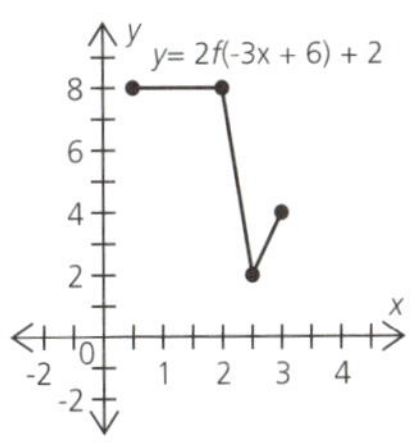

16. **(a)** D = $\{x \mid x \geq -4, x \in \mathbf{R}\}$, R = $\{y \mid y < -2, y \in \mathbf{R}\}$
(b) D = $\{x \mid x \leq 4, x \in \mathbf{R}\}$, R = $\{y \mid y < -1, y \in \mathbf{R}\}$
(c) D = $\{x \mid x \geq -5, x \in \mathbf{R}\}$, R = $\{y \mid y < 1, y \in \mathbf{R}\}$
(d) D = $\{x \mid x \leq 9, x \in \mathbf{R}\}$, R = $\{y \mid y > 3, y \in \mathbf{R}\}$

17. **(b)** $y = 0.55\sqrt{x}$
(c) points on left are above; points on right are below curve in (b). It appears that a translation is needed.
(d) $y = 0.46\sqrt{x} + 0.14$

18. **(a)** The order of the two vertical transformations does matter, but the "right 3" translation can be applied at any time, since it has no impact on y-coordinates. If $(0, 1)$ is stretched first to $(0, 2)$ and then translated down, the image is $(0, -2)$; if $(0, 1)$ translated first to $(0, -3)$ and then stretched, the image is $(0, -6)$.
(b) Yes, the horizontal translation could happen at any time.

19. **(a)** Stretch vertically by factor of 3, then stretch horizontally with factor $\frac{1}{2}$, then translate 2 units to right.
(b) Stretch horizontally by factor $\frac{1}{2}$, stretch vertically by factor 3, then translate 2 units right; horizontal stretch by $\frac{1}{2}$, translation right 2 units, vertical stretch by 3.

20. **(a)** Let H_1 represent the first horizontal transformation: a stretch factor $\frac{1}{2}$. Let H_2 represent the second horizontal transformation: translation 1 unit left. Let V_1 represent the first vertical transformation: reflect in x-axis. Let V_2 represent the second vertical transformation: translate 3 units up. Any sequence that keeps H_1 before H_2 and V_1 before V_2 will work.
All possible sequences are: H_1, H_2, V_1, V_2; H_1, V_1, H_2, V_2; H_1, V_1, V_2, H_2; V_1, H_1, H_2, V_2; V_1, H_1, V_2, H_2; V_1, V_2, H_1, H_2.
(b) Yes, translate horizontally 2 units left, stretch horizontally with factor $\frac{1}{2}$, translate vertically 3 units down, and then reflect in x-axis.

21. Use order of operations to draw a mapping diagram. Operations to the right of the base function correspond to vertical transformations. Multiplication/ division yields a stretch, and addition/ subtraction gives a translation. Multiplication by -1 is a reflection. The order of operations on the right matches the order the transformations are to be applied. Operations to the left of the base function correspond to horizontal transformations. Reverse the operations and their sequence to find the correct transformations to apply to the base function to graph the required function.

22. **(a)** 1. Reflect $y = x^2$ in x-axis; 2. Stretch vertically with factor $\frac{1}{4}$; 3. Translate 6 units left; 4. Translate 2 units up.
(b) $y = -\frac{1}{4}(x + 6)^2 + 2$

23. **(a)** $y = 5\sqrt{x - 3.1}$ **(b)** $y \doteq 4.34\sqrt{x - 3.11} + 0.87$
(c) The equations are similar. The second equation involves a vertical translation that made it closer to the points on the left of the scatter plot.

24. **(a)** A translation of 3 right and 1 down is needed after any necessary stretches and reflections. The required quadratic equation is $y = \frac{3}{4}\left(x - 3\right)^2 - 1$.
(b) (1) Stretch horizontally factor 2 (multiply x by 2). (2) Stretch vertically factor 3 (multiply y by 3). (3) Translate vertically down 1 (subtract 1 from y); (4) Translate horizontally right 3 (add 3 to x). The required quadratic equation is $y = 3[\frac{1}{2}(x - 3)]^2 - 1$.
(c) The equation in (b) is the same as in (a); any two parabolas with the same vertex can be stretched into each other using any two points (not the vertices) to find a correspondence.

Chapter 3, Review and Practice, page 293

1. **(a)** D = $\{1, 2, 3, 4\}$, R = $\{3, 5, 7, 9\}$
(b) $1 \to 9, 2 \to 7, 3 \to 5, 4 \to 3$
(d) $y = -2x + 11$, $\{x \mid x \leq 4, x \in \mathbf{N}\}$
(e) $x \to -2x + 11$, $\{x \mid x \leq 4, x \in \mathbf{N}\}$;
$f(x) = -2x + 11$, $\{x \mid x \leq 4, x \in \mathbf{N}\}$
(f) function: each domain element corresponds to a unique range element; passes vertical line test
(g) *Example*: $(1, 1)$

2. **(a)** D = $\{-3, -2, -1, 0, 1, 2\}$ or $\{x \mid -3 \leq x \leq 2, x \in \mathbf{I}\}$, R = $\{-1, 0, 1, 2, 3, 4, 5\}$ or $\{y \mid -1 \leq y \leq 5, y \in \mathbf{I}\}$, not a function: -2 maps onto 2 and 5
(b) D = $\{x \mid -3 \leq x \leq 4, x \in \mathbf{R}\}$, R = $\{y \mid -1 \leq y \leq 5, y \in \mathbf{R}\}$, not a function: 0 maps onto 5 and -1
(c) D = **R**, R = $\{y \mid y \geq -1, y \in \mathbf{R}\}$, function: passes vertical line test

3. **(a)** 20
(b) parabola opening upward with vertex $(1.5, -4.5)$ through $(0, 0)$ and $(3, 0)$
(c) function: passes vertical line test
(d) $f(5) = 20$ **(e)** $x = 0$ or $x = 3$

4. **(a)** top half of parabola opening to left with vertex $(9, 0)$ through $(0, 3)$
(b) D = $\{s \mid s \leq 9, s \in \mathbf{R}\}$, R = $\{y \mid y \geq 0, y \in \mathbf{R}\}$

5. **(a)** independent variable: weekly sales; dependent variable: weekly earnings. It should be a function because the same value for her sales should produce the same total earnings. It is important that the employee's pay be reliable and predictable.

(b) *Example*: D = $\{x \mid 0 \le x \le 20\,000, x \in \mathbf{R}\}$ and R = $\{y \mid 85 \le y \le 1035, y \in \mathbf{R}\}$

(c) 285

(d) horizontal line from (0, 85) to (1000, 85), then upward to right through (5000, 285)

6. **(a)** solid line between open dot at -2 and open dot at 4

(b) closed dots at 1, 2, and 3

(c) solid line to left of open dot at -1, solid line to right of open dot at 1

7. **(a)** $\{x \in \mathbf{I} \mid x \ge -2, x \in \mathbf{I}\}$ **(b)** $\{x \mid -5 < x \le 3, x \in \mathbf{R}\}$

8. **(a)** D = $\{x \mid x < -3, x \in \mathbf{R}\}$ **(b)** R = $\{y \mid 0 < y \le 4, y \in \mathbf{R}\}$

9. **(a)** parabola opening downward with vertex $(-1, 4)$ through $(-4, -5)$ and $(2, -5)$.

(b) D = $\{x \mid -3 \le x \le 1, x \in \mathbf{R}\}$

10. **(a)** D = $\{-5, -3, -2, -1, 0, 1, 2, 3, 4\}$; R = $\{-1, 0, 1, 2, 3, 4, 5\}$

(b) $f^{-1} = \{(-1, 0), (0, -1), (0, 1), (1, 2), (2, -2), (3, -3), (3, 3), (4, -5), (5, 4)\}$

(d) 0 **(e)** 2 **(f)** ±1 **(g)** undefined

11. connected points (1, 6) to (1, 3) to $(-2, 2)$ to $(-2, -1)$ to $(3, -4)$

12. $f^{-1}(x) = 2x - 3$

13. **(a)** $g(s) = 100 + 11.5s, s \in \mathbf{W}$

(b) $g^{-1}(x) = \dfrac{x - 100}{11.5}, g^{-1}(x) \in \mathbf{W}$

(c) Subtract \$100 from total charge, then divide by \$11.50.

(d) D = $\{x \mid x = 100 + 11.5s, s \in \mathbf{W}\}$

(e) *Example*: A school council ordered shirts from a printing company and received a bill for \$1000 (excluding tax). If the company charges \$100 plus \$11.50/shirt, determine the number of shirts ordered.

14. $y = x^2$ defines a parabola that opens up and has vertex at (0, 0). $y = \sqrt{x}$ defines the upper branch of a parabola that opens to the right and has vertex at (0, 0). The inverse of $y = x^2$ is a parabola that contains the branch defined by $y = \sqrt{x}$ and the branch defined by $y = -\sqrt{x}$. The inverse of $y = \sqrt{x}$ is the right branch of the parabola defined by $y = x^2$. When $y = x^2$ is reflected in $y = x$, the result is the parabola that contains the branch defined by $y = \sqrt{x}$. When $y = \sqrt{x}$ is reflected in $y = x$, the result is the right branch of the parabola defined by $y = x^2$.

15. *Example*: $f^{-1} = \{(-1, 0), (0, 1), (1, 2), (2, -2), (3, 3), (4, -5), (5, 5)\}$

16. **(a)** g: parabola opening upward with vertex (3, 1) through (2, 5) and (4, 5), g^{-1}: parabola opening to right with vertex (1, 3) through (5, 4) and (5, 2)

(b) about (2.2, 3.55), (2.4, 2,4), (3.55, 2.2), and (3.84, 3.84)

(c) $x = 4(y - 3)^2 + 1$ **(d)** g^{-1} is $y = 3 \pm \sqrt{\dfrac{x - 1}{4}}$

(e) $x \ge 3$ (or $x \le 3$) **(f)** no: $g^{-1}(5) = 2$ and $g^{-1}(5) = 4$

17. **(a)** f: top half of parabola opening to left with vertex (1.5, 0), f^{-1}: parabola opening downward with vertex (0, 1.5) through $(-3, -3)$ and $(3, -3)$

(b) $x = \sqrt{3 - 2y}$ **(c)** f^{-1} is $y = \dfrac{3 - x^2}{2}$

18.

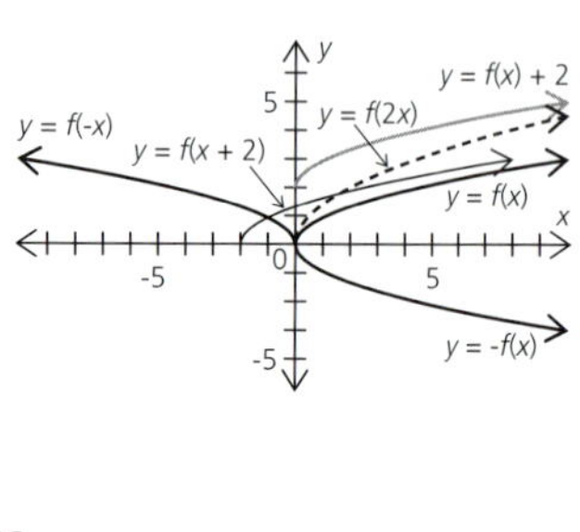

19. **(a)** 28 **(b)** 22 **(c)** undefined

(d) $g = \{(1, 22), (0, 19), (-1, 28), (-2, 49)\}$

20. **(a)**

(b) vertical stretch by factor of $\frac{1}{2}$, horizontal stretch by factor of $\frac{1}{3}$, 2 units left, 4 units down

(c) D = $\{x \mid \frac{-4}{3} \le x \le \frac{-1}{3}, x \in \mathbf{R}\}$, R = $\{y \mid y \ge -5, y \in \mathbf{R}\}$

21. **(a)**

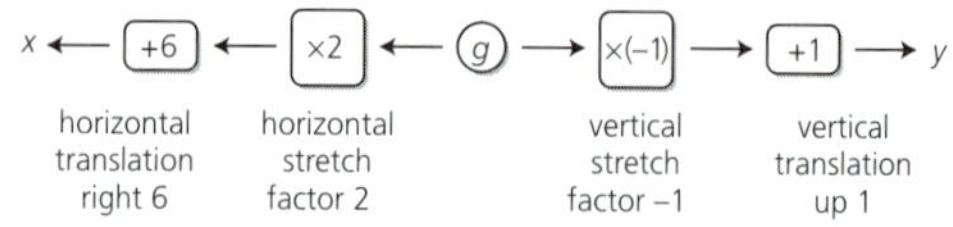

(b) D = $\{x \mid -2 \le x \le 18, x \in \mathbf{R}\}$, R = $\{y \mid -2 \le y \le 3, y \in \mathbf{R}\}$

(c) 3

(d)

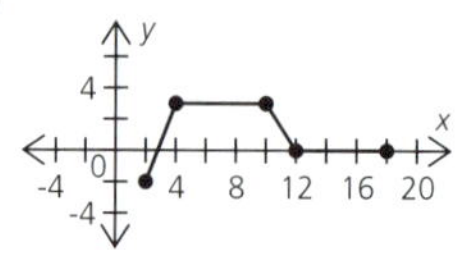

Chapter 3 Review Test, page 297

1. **(a)** 0, D = $\{x \mid -5 \le x \le 5, x \in \mathbf{R}\}$, R = $\{y \mid -5 \le y \le 5, y \in \mathbf{R}\}$, not a function: fails vertical line test

(b) 8, D = $\{1, 3, 5, 7, 9, 13\}$, R = $\{3, 6, 8, 9, 12\}$, function: each domain value has a unique range value

(c) -2, D = $\{1, 4, 5, 8\}$, R = $\{-2, 2, 5, 7, 10\}$, not a function: 1 maps to 2 and 5

(d) 8, D = $\{x \mid x \in \mathbf{R}\}$, R = $\{y \mid y \in \mathbf{R}\}$, function: passes vertical line test

(e) $\sqrt{2}$, D = $\{x \mid x \ge 3, x \in \mathbf{R}\}$, R = $\{y \mid y \ge 0, y \in \mathbf{R}\}$, function: passes vertical line test

(f) 59, D = $\{x \mid x \in \mathbf{R}\}$, R = $\{y \mid y \ge -5, y \in \mathbf{R}\}$, function: passes vertical line test

2. **(a)** $x \le 2$, a solid dot above $x = 2$ and a line extending infinitely to the left

(b) $x \le \frac{45}{7}$, a solid dot above $x = \frac{45}{7}$ and a line extending infinitely to the left

3. **(a)** $f^{-1}(x) = \dfrac{x - 6}{5}$ **(b)** $f^{-1}(x) = x^2 - 4$

(c) f^{-1} is $y = \pm\sqrt{x + 5}$

4. no; interchanging the domain and range values to find the inverse does not necessarily yield a function

5. easy to use: draw a vertical line and count the intersection points with the function

6. **(a)** parabola with vertex (3, 5), opening downward, passing through (2, 4) and (4, 4)

(b) D = $\{x \mid x \in \mathbf{R}\}$, R = $\{y \mid y \le 5, y \in \mathbf{R}\}$

(c) $g^{-1}(x) = -(y - 3)^2 + 5$

(d) parabola with vertex (5, 3), opening left, passing through (1, 5) and (1, 1)

(e) D = $\{x \mid x \le 5, x \in \mathbf{R}\}$, R = $\{y \mid y \in \mathbf{R}\}$

(f) $g(x)$ is a function; passes vertical line test

7. **(a)** $I(x) = \$50 + \$0.05x$, x is number of bags of peanuts sold

(b) $R(x) = \$2.50x$, x is number of bags of peanuts sold

(c) 21

8. **(a)** apply in this order: vertical stretch by factor of 2, reflection in x-axis, vertical translation up 3 units, horizontal stretch by factor of $\frac{1}{2}$, reflection in y-axis, horizontal translation left 1 unit

(b) straight line from $\left(-\frac{1}{2}, -7\right)$ to $\left(\frac{1}{2}, -7\right)$, diagonal line to $(-1, -1)$, diagonal line down to $(-2, -9)$, diagonal line down to $(-3, -13)$

9. **(a)** 0 or 1 point(s) of intersection
(b) 0, 1, 2 or 4 point(s) of intersection
(c) 0, 1, or 2 point(s) of intersection

Chapter 4

Getting Ready, page 302

1. **(a)** $\frac{-7}{20}$ **(b)** $\frac{-67}{18}$ **(c)** $\frac{9}{14}$ **(d)** $\frac{175}{8}$
(e) 6 **(f)** $\frac{5}{14}$ **(g)** 3 **(h)** $\frac{-1}{12}$
(i) $\frac{-217}{240}$ **(j)** $\frac{-1}{26}$ **(k)** $\frac{-27}{80}$ **(l)** $\frac{-185}{64}$

2. **(a)** $-24xyz$ **(b)** $30ab^2c^2$ **(c)** $9p$
(d) $\frac{2m^3}{n}$ **(e)** $30a^2bc^2d^2$ **(f)** $4bc^3$

3. **(a)** $-4x^3 + 8x^2 - 12xy$ **(b)** $15x^2y + 5x^2y^2 - 10xy^2$
(c) $-21a^4 + 12a^3 - 6a^2$ **(d)** $17x^2 - 13x$
(e) $-24y^2 + 33y$ **(f)** $-7y^2 + 3y$
(g) $2x^3 + x^2$ **(h)** $x^4 - x^2 - 6x$

4. **(a)** $-2a^2 - 3c^2$ **(b)** $3y^3 - 2z^2 + 5$
(c) $1 - z$ **(d)** $2r - 3p + 5k$

5. **(a)** $x^2 - 4x + 4$ **(b)** $x^2 - 3x - 4$
(c) $2x^2 + x - 6$ **(d)** $12x^2 - 7x - 10$
(e) $16a^2 - 9$ **(f)** $4x$
(g) $\frac{3}{2}x^2 + \frac{3}{4}x - \frac{1}{6}$ **(h)** $0.06x^2 + 0.03x + 0.3$

6. **(a)** 200 **(b)** 75.2997
(c) $\frac{-10\,003}{9999}, \frac{-9997}{10\,001}$ **(d)** 999, −1001
(e) −99.83, 100.17

7. **(a)** $x(5y - 2)$ **(b)** $x(2x - 3y)$
(c) $6m^2n^2(3m + 2n)$ **(d)** $3p^3q^2r(5pr + 7pqr)$
(e) $(x - 5)(x - 4)$ **(f)** $(y + 4)(y - 8)$
(g) $(t - 6)(t + 8)$ **(h)** $3(x + 3)(x + 5)$
(i) $21(x + 2)(x - 1)$ **(j)** $(x - 7)(x + 7)$
(k) $(5y + 8)(5y - 8)$ **(l)** $2(5x - 6)(5x + 6)$
(m) $7(y + 2z)(y - 2z)$ **(n)** $(3x - 1)^2$
(o) $(2a + 5)^2$ **(p)** $(2x - 3)(x + 2)$
(q) $(2y - 3)(y + 4)$ **(r)** $(2a - 1)(5a + 3)$

8. **(a)** line, x-intercept: $-\frac{4}{3}$, y-intercept: 1
(b) line, x-intercept: $-\frac{2}{3}$, y-intercept: −2
(c) vertical line, x-intercept: 7.5
(d) horizontal line, y-intercept: −1.2
(e) line, x-intercept: 5, y-intercept: 2

9. **(a)** $y = -1$ **(b)** $2x + 3y - 11 = 0$
(c) $5x + 2y - 10 = 0$

10. **(a)** parabola, opens up, zeros at 3, 5; vertex: (4, −1), y-intercept: 15
(b) parabola, opens down, zeros at −3, 2; vertex: (−0.5, 6.25), y-intercept: 6
(c) parabola, opens down, zeros at 3, 5; vertex: (4, 2), y-intercept: −30
(d) parabola, opens down, zeros at $\pm\sqrt{5}$, vertex: (0, 5), y-intercept: 5
(e) parabola, opens up, zeros at −7.16, −0.84; vertex: (−4, −5), y-intercept: 3
(f) parabola, opens down, zeros at 0, 4; vertex: (2, 12), y-intercept: 0
(g) parabola, opens down, no zeros; vertex: (2, 3), y-intercept: 7

11. **(a)** $x = -7, x = 3$ **(b)** $x = -2, x = -6$
(c) $x = \frac{1}{3}, x = -\frac{5}{2}$

12. **(a)** 6000 **(b)** 2061
(c) no, since $P = 0$ has no real roots

13. **(a)** $x = \pm\sqrt{10} - 3$ **(b)** $\pm\sqrt{11} + 4$
(c) $1 \pm \frac{3}{\sqrt{2}}$ **(d)** $\frac{3}{4} \pm \frac{\sqrt{3}i}{4}$

14. **(a)** $x = 1.50, x = -1.00$ **(b)** $x \doteq 0.42, x \doteq 3.58$
(c) $x \doteq -3.93, x \doteq 0.59$ **(d)** $x = 1.85, x = -1.20$

15. **(a)** 0 **(b)** 2 **(c)** 0 **(d)** 2

Practice 4.1, page 306

1. **(a)** $2(x^2 - 3x)$ **(b)** $3\left(x^2 + \frac{2}{3}x\right)$ **(c)** $-4\left(x^2 - \frac{1}{2}x\right)$
(d) $\frac{1}{2}(x^2 - 10x)$ **(e)** $-1.2(x^2 - 5.5x)$ **(f)** $\frac{2}{3}\left(x^2 + \frac{5}{4}x\right)$
(g) $-\frac{4}{3}\left(x^2 + \frac{3}{2}x\right)$ **(h)** $2.7\left(x^2 - \frac{1}{3}x\right)$ **(i)** $-6\left(x - \frac{1}{10}x\right)$

2. **(a)** $\frac{9}{4}$ **(b)** $\frac{49}{4}$ **(c)** $\frac{1}{9}$
(d) $\frac{9}{100}$ **(e)** 1.5625 **(f)** 0.050 625
(g) 125.44 **(h)** $\frac{25}{324}$ **(i)** $d = 2.5 \times 10^{-5}$

3. **(a)** $f(x) = \left(x - \frac{3}{2}\right)^2 - \frac{1}{4}$ **(b)** $f(x) = (x + 3)^2 - 17$
(c) $f(x) = 3\left(x - \frac{2}{3}\right)^2 - \frac{1}{3}$ **(d)** $f(x) = \left(x - \frac{1}{2}\right)^2 - \frac{1}{4}$
(e) $f(x) = \left(x + \frac{3}{2}\right)^2 + \frac{11}{4}$ **(f)** $f(x) = -\left(x - \frac{5}{2}\right)^2 + \frac{17}{4}$
(g) $f(x) = (x - 1.3)^2 - 4.39$ **(h)** $f(x) = (x + 2.7)^2 - 9.09$
(i) $f(x) = (x - 1.7)^2 - 5.69$

4. $g(x) = 2\left(x + \frac{5}{4}\right)^2 + \frac{7}{8}$

5. **(a)** $f(x) = \left(x - \frac{3}{2}\right)^2 - \frac{1}{4}$ **(b)** $f(x) = 2\left(x + \frac{5}{4}\right)^2 - \frac{57}{8}$
(c) $f(x) = 3\left(x - \frac{2}{3}\right)^2 - \frac{1}{3}$ **(d)** $f(x) = 5\left(x - \frac{1}{10}\right)^2 - \frac{101}{20}$
(e) $f(x) = -2\left(x - \frac{3}{4}\right)^2 + \frac{49}{8}$ **(f)** $f(x) = -4\left(x + \frac{7}{8}\right)^2 + \frac{17}{16}$
(g) $f(x) = 1.4(x - 1.75)^2 - 6.9875$
(h) $f(x) = -3.6(x - 0.75)^2 + 0.355$
(i) $f(x) = \frac{1}{2}(x - 4)^2 - 7$ **(j)** $f(x) = \frac{2}{3}\left(x - \frac{15}{4}\right)^2 - \frac{91}{8}$
(k) $f(x) = -\frac{3}{2}\left(x + \frac{7}{24}\right)^2 + \frac{241}{384}$
(l) $f(x) = -\frac{4}{5}\left(x - \frac{5}{12}\right)^2 - \frac{29}{180}$

6. **(a)** $f(x) = (x + 5)^2 - 1$; vertex: (−5, −1); $D = \{x \mid x \in \mathbf{R}\}$, $R = \{y \mid y \geq -1, y \in \mathbf{R}\}$; parabola, opens up, zeros at −6, −4
(b) $f(x) = 4(x + 1)^2 + 3$; vertex: (−1, 3); $D = \{x \mid x \in \mathbf{R}\}$, $R = \{y \mid y \geq 3, y \in \mathbf{R}\}$; parabola, opens up, no zeros; y-intercept 7
(c) $f(x) = -2\left(x - \frac{5}{4}\right)^2 + 3$; vertex: (5/4, 3); $D = \{x \mid x \in \mathbf{R}\}$, $R = \{y \mid y \leq 3, y \in \mathbf{R}\}$; parabola, opens down, zeros at 0.025, 2.47
(d) $f(x) = \frac{1}{2}(x - 3)^2 - \frac{1}{2}$; vertex: (3, −1/2); $D = \{x \mid x \in \mathbf{R}\}$, $R = \{y \mid y \geq -\frac{1}{2}, y \in \mathbf{R}\}$; parabola, opens up, zeros at 2, 4
(e) $f(x) = -2\left(x - \frac{7}{4}\right)^2 - \frac{47}{8}$; vertex: $\left(\frac{7}{4}, \frac{-47}{8}\right)$; $D = \{x \mid x \in \mathbf{R}\}$, $R = \{y \mid y \leq -\frac{47}{8}, y \in \mathbf{R}\}$; parabola, opens down, no zeros; y-intercept −12

(f) $f(x) = -2\left(x - \frac{7}{4}\right)^2 + \frac{49}{2}$; vertex: $\left(\frac{7}{4}, \frac{49}{2}\right)$; $D = \{x \mid x \in \mathbf{R}\}$, $R = \{y \mid y \le \frac{49}{2}, y \in \mathbf{R}\}$; parabola, opens down, zeros at 0, 3.5

7. (a) $d(x) = 5\left(x - \frac{3}{10}\right)^2 + \frac{11}{20}$ (b) $x = \frac{3}{10}$
(c) $\left(\frac{3}{10}, \frac{11}{20}\right)$ (d) minimum value: $d = \frac{11}{20}$
(e) $D = \mathbf{R}$ (f) $R = \{y \mid y \ge \frac{11}{20}, y \in \mathbf{R}\}$
(g) parabola, opens up, no zeros; y-intercept: 1

8. (a) 31.63 m (b) at 2.5 s

9. (a) $(\frac{5}{24}, \frac{-169}{288})$ (b) $(\frac{-1}{9}, \frac{85}{108})$
(c) $(-4, -16)$

10. Vertical compression, factor 2.5; Horizontal translation to the right 2.5 units; Vertical translation up 3.5 units

11. 3.75 m/ha

12. $2 < t < 10$

13. (a) $D = \mathbf{R}$, $R = \{y \mid y \le -\frac{25}{4}, y \in \mathbf{R}\}$
(b) $D = \mathbf{R}$, $R = \{y \mid y \le \frac{17}{8}, y \in \mathbf{R}\}$
(c) $D = \mathbf{R}$, $R = \{y \mid y \ge \frac{19}{36}, y \in \mathbf{R}\}$
(d) $D = \mathbf{R}$, $R = \{y \mid y \ge -0.325, y \in \mathbf{R}\}$

14. You should be able to write the equation of the same quadratic function in several different forms to obtain different information about the function, as long as the algebra performed does not change the question. (1) Factor the coefficient of x^2 from the first two terms. (2) Add and subtract the square of half the coefficient of x inside the brackets. (3) Group the three terms that form the perfect square. Multiply the fourth term by the factor in front of the brackets and move it outside the brackets. (4) Factor the perfect square.

Practise, Apply, Solve 4.2, page 314

1. (a) $\left(\frac{5}{2}, \frac{-57}{4}\right)$, minimum (b) (4, 15), maximum
(c) $\left(\frac{-3}{4}, \frac{-11}{4}\right)$, maximum (d) $(2, -7)$, maximum

2. (a) parabola, opens up, zeros at 3, 8; y-intercept: 24; $\left(\frac{11}{2}, \frac{-25}{4}\right)$
(b) parabola, opens down, zeros at -2, 1; y-intercept: 4; $\left(\frac{-1}{2}, \frac{9}{2}\right)$
(c) parabola, opens up, zeros at -3.2, 1.1; y-intercept: -2.464; $(-1.05, -3.24)$
(d) parabola, opens down, zeros at $\frac{-1}{6}, \frac{2}{3}$; y-intercept: $\frac{5}{54}$; $\left(\frac{1}{4}, \frac{125}{864}\right)$

3. (a) $\left(\frac{3}{2}, \frac{-9}{2}\right)$, minimum (b) $\left(\frac{3}{2}, \frac{45}{4}\right)$, maximum
(c) (2, 41.6), maximum (d) $(3, -46.5)$, minimum

4. (a) $R(x) = -x^2 + 7x$, \$12.25
(b) $R(x) = -3x^2 + 11x$, \$10.08
(c) $R(x) = -0.05x^2 + 12x$, \$720

5. (a) $P(x) = -x^2 + 12x - 28$, $x = 6$
(b) $P(x) = -2x^2 + 18x - 45$, $x = 4.5$
(c) $P(x) = -3x^2 + 18x - 18$, $x = 3$
(d) $P(x) = -2x^2 + 22x - 17$, $x = 5.5$

6. (a) $R(x) = -5x^2 + 21x$
(b) $P(x) = -5x^2 + 17x - 14$
(c) $x = 1.7$ (d) 1400 items, 2000 items
(e) parabola, opens down, vertex (1.7, 0.45); zeros at 1.4, 2; y-intercept: -14

7. 1250 items/h

8. Ball reaches max height at 0.61 s; max height is 2.44 m.

9. 25

12. (a) 37 or 38 trees (b) 37

14. (a) 44 200 kg/ha (b) $y(x) \doteq -343.9x^2 + 965.5x - 243.2$
(c) 1.404 ha•m

15. rectangle 6 m × 12 m

16. 52 days

18. (a) factored form, vertex form, standard form
(b) Answers will vary.
(c) Factored form identifies x-intercepts of parabola; vertex form identifies vertex of parabola and maximum or minimum value of function; standard form identifies y-intercept.
(d) Answers will vary.

19. $t = \frac{v_0}{9.8}$

20. rectangle 7.03 m × 4.46 m, triangle: 7.03 m × 7.03 m × 7.03 m

21. (a) 79.58 m
(b) Yes, the straight part of the track is 125 m long.

Practise, Apply, Solve 4.3, page 325

1. (a) 2 (b) 2 (c) 1 (d) 0
2. (a) 0 (b) 2 (c) 1 (d) 0
3. (a) 2 (b) 0 (c) 0 (d) 1
4. (a) 0 (b) 2 (c) 2 (d) 1
5. (a) 2 (b) 2 (c) 1 (d) does not meet
6. Machine B is better: maximum profit is greater than Machine A and Machine B, and it reaches this maximum profit before Machine A and B reach their respective maximum profits.
7. $k < -2$ or $k > 2$
8. $m = 1$
9. (a) $k > \frac{4}{3}$ (b) $k = \frac{4}{3}$ (c) $k < \frac{4}{3}$
10. $k = -4$ or $k = 8$
11. yes; $p = -6$ or $p = -8$
12. no
13. 1.5×10^8 items
14. 14 m/s
15. (a) $(4, 3), (-3, -4)$ (b) $k = \pm 5\sqrt{2}$
17. (a) no k (b) no k (c) $k \in \mathbf{R}$
18. 3.65 cm, 8.23 cm

Practise, Apply, Solve 4.4, page 331

1. (a) **R, I, C, Q** (b) **R, Q, C** (c) **C**
(d) **R, $\tilde{\text{Q}}$, C** (e) **R, Q, C** (f) **R, Q, C**
(g) **R, Q, C** (h) **R, I, N, W, C, Q**

2. (a) $4i$ (b) $11i$ (c) $-3i$
(d) $3\sqrt{2}i$ (e) $-2\sqrt{7}i$ (f) $\pm 5\sqrt{2}i$

3. (a) $1 - i$ (b) $2 + 3i$ (c) $-3 + 4i$
(d) $-7 - 5i$ (e) $11 + 11i$ (f) $2 - \sqrt{2}i$

4. (a) yes (b) no (c) yes (d) no

5. (a) $\pm 2i$ (b) $\pm 8i$ (c) $\pm 3i$
(d) $\pm 7i$ (e) $\pm 4\sqrt{2}i$ (f) $\pm 5\sqrt{3}i$

6. (a) $2 \pm i$ (b) $1 \pm 4i$ (c) $2 \pm 3i$
(d) $\frac{-1}{2} \pm \frac{1}{2}i$ (e) $\frac{1}{4} \pm \frac{\sqrt{7}}{4}i$ (f) $-1 \pm \sqrt{5}i$

7. (a) -16, two complex roots (b) 16, two real roots
(c) -24, two complex roots (d) 0, one real root

8. (a) $x = -1 \pm 2i$ (b) $x = -1, x = 3$
(c) $\frac{2}{5} \pm \frac{\sqrt{6}}{5}i$ (d) 4

9. (a) $x = 3, x = -8$ (b) $x = 2 \pm \sqrt{5}$
(c) $1 \pm \sqrt{\frac{2}{3}}$ (d) $-1 \pm 2i$

10. **(a)** $x = -2i, (x + 2i)(x - 2i) = 0$
(b) $x = 2 + i, (x - 2 - i)(x - 2 + i) = 0$
(c) $x = 1 - 3i, (x - 1 - 3i)(x - 1 + 3i) = 0$
(d) $x = -1 + i, (x + 1 + i)(x + 1 - i) = 0$
(e) $x = 3 + 4i, (x - 3 + 4i)(x - 3 - 4i) = 0$
(f) $x = -12 - 5i, (x + 12 + 5i)(x + 12 - 5i) = 0$

11. **(a)** $(x + 2 - i)(x + 2 - i)$ **(b)** $(x + 2 - 3i)(x + 2 + 3i)$
(c) $\left(x - \frac{1}{2} - \frac{\sqrt{3}}{2}i\right)\left(x - \frac{1}{2} + \frac{\sqrt{3}}{2}i\right)$
(d) $(x - 1 - 5i)(x - 1 + 5i)$

12. **(a)** $\frac{-1}{3} \pm \frac{\sqrt{2}}{3}i$ **(b)** $\frac{3}{4} \pm \frac{\sqrt{47}}{4}i$
(c) $\frac{1}{3} \pm \frac{\sqrt{29}}{3}i$ **(d)** $\frac{-1}{10} \pm \frac{\sqrt{139}}{10}i$

13. $2 + 3i, 2 - 3i$

14. $2.5 + 0.5^3i, 2.5 - 0.5\sqrt{3}i$

15. No, the graph of $n(t) = -0.75t^2 + 6t + 51$ has a maximum value of 63 when $x = 4$, the fifth month of sales. Thus, the company can sell at most 63 000 units according to this model.

16. A complex number can be written in the form $a + bi$, where a and b are real numbers and i is a non-real number such that $i^2 = -1$. The real number system includes all rational and irrational numbers, contains the set of natural numbers, whole numbers, and integers.

18. Complex numbers in form $a + bi$ are useful in solving quadratic equations because they can be used to show non-real roots.

19. $x = \pm 3, x = \pm 3i$

20. Complex numbers cannot be ordered.

21. $x = -1, x = \frac{1}{2} \pm \frac{\sqrt{3}}{2}i$

Practise, Apply, Solve 4.5U, page 336

1. **(a)** $7 + 5i$ **(b)** $5 - 2i$ **(c)** $-1 - 2i$
(d) $1 - 10i$ **(e)** $1 + 3i$ **(f)** $3 + 2\sqrt{2}i$

2. **(a)** $-3 + 7i$ **(b)** $3 - 4i$ **(c)** $7 + 16i$
(d) $-3 + 16i$ **(e)** $-1 + 7i$ **(f)** 3

3. **(a)** $1 + 13i$ **(b)** $38 - 16i$ **(c)** $-11 + 2i$
(d) $-1 + 5i$ **(e)** $3 + 4i$ **(f)** 13

4. **(a)** 2 **(b)** 13 **(c)** 20

5. **(a)** $5 + 7i$ **(b)** $2 + 3i$ **(c)** -4
(d) 1 **(e)** -1 **(f)** $\frac{1}{2}$
(g) $-3 + 4i$ **(h)** $40 - 9i$ **(i)** $7 - i$
(j) i **(k)** $28 - 37i$ **(l)** $7i, -3i, 3i$, or $-7i$

6. **(a)** $0 = x^2 + 4$ **(b)** $0 = x^2 - 2x + 10$
(c) $0 = x^2 - 6x + 25$ **(d)** $0 = x^2 + x + 1$

7. $3 + i, 0 = x^2 - 6x + 10$

9. $10 - 11i$

10. $19 + 80i$

12. $i = -\frac{a}{b} \in \mathbf{R}$, but i is not real

13. $a = 5, b = 7$

14. $z + w = 2 + 2i, z - w = -6 + 4i, zw = -5 + 14i,$
$w^2 = 15 - 8i, z\bar{z} = 13$

15. $\pm(3 + 2i)$

Practise, Apply, Solve 4.6, page 345

1. **(a)** Is inverse variation; x increases as y decreases; xy remains 48.
(b) Is inverse variation; x decreases as y increases; xy remains 3600.
(c) Not inverse variation; x and y both increase; xy does not remain constant.

2. **(a)** $y = \frac{48}{x}$ **(b)** $y = \frac{3600}{x}$ **(c)** $y = x^2$

3. **(a)** $y = \frac{1}{2x}, x = 0$ **(b)** $y = \frac{1}{x + 5}, x = -5$
(c) $y = \frac{1}{x - 4}, x = 4$ **(d)** $y = \frac{1}{2x + 5}, x = \frac{-5}{2}$
(e) $y = \frac{1}{-3x + 6}, x = 2$ **(f)** $y = \frac{1}{(x - 3)^2}, x = 3$
(g) $y = \frac{1}{x^2 - 3x - 10}, x = -2, x = 5$
(h) $y = \frac{1}{3x^2 - 4x - 4}, x = -\frac{2}{3}, x = 2$

4. **(a)** $f^{-1}(x)$: $\frac{1}{16}, \frac{1}{14}, \frac{1}{12}, \frac{1}{10}, \frac{1}{8}, \frac{1}{6}, \frac{1}{4}, \frac{1}{2}$, undefined, $-\frac{1}{2}, -\frac{1}{4}, -\frac{1}{6}$; $f(x)$: line, x-intercept -4; y-intercept 8; $\frac{1}{f(x)}$: hyperbola, vertical asymptote $x = 4$; horizontal asymptote $y = 0$
(b) $y = -2x + 8, y = \frac{1}{-2x + 8}$

5. **(a)** $\frac{1}{y} = \frac{1}{-x - 1}$
(b) $\frac{1}{y} = \frac{1}{\frac{3}{2}x - 2}$ and $\frac{1}{y} = -\frac{1}{\frac{3}{2}x - 2}$
(c) $\frac{1}{y} = \frac{1}{36 - x^2}$
(d) $\frac{1}{y} = \frac{1}{2}, -6 \le x \le -2, \frac{1}{y} = \frac{1}{-2x - 2}, -2 \le x \le -1,$
$\frac{1}{y} = \frac{1}{2x + 2}, -1 \le x \le 1,$

6. when $x = 4$, $y = 78.75$, not $y = 87.5$; $y = \frac{315}{x}$

7. 5 s, $a = \frac{60}{t}$

8. **(a)** 0.545 A **(b)** 1650 W **(c)** $\frac{I}{W} = \text{constant} = \frac{1}{V}$

9. **(a)** $f(x) = x + 2$: line, x-intercept: -2, y-intercept: 2; $f(x) = \frac{1}{x + 2}$: hyperbola, vertical asymptote $x = -2$, horizontal asymptote $y = 0$
(b) $D = \{x \mid x \neq -2, x \in \mathbf{R}\}, R = \{y \mid y \neq 0, y \in \mathbf{R}\}$;
$f^{-1}(x) = \frac{1}{x} + 2$

10. **(a)** $y = x - 1$: line, x-intercept: 1, y-intercept: -1; $y = \frac{1}{x - 1}$: hyperbola, vertical asymptote $x = 1$; horizontal asymptote $y = 0$; $\frac{1}{f(x)} = \frac{1}{x - 1}$ has $D = \{x \mid x \neq 1, x \in \mathbf{R}\}$,
$R = \{y \mid y \neq 0, y \in \mathbf{R}\}; f^{-1}(x) = 1 + \frac{1}{x}$
(b) $y = 5 - x$: line: x-intercept: 5, y-intercept: 5; $y = \frac{1}{5 - x}$: hyperbola, vertical asymptote $x = 5$; horizontal asymptote $y = 0$; $\frac{1}{f(x)} = \frac{1}{5 - x}$ has $D = \{x \mid x \neq 5, x \in \mathbf{R}\}$,
$R = \{y \mid y \neq 0, y \in \mathbf{R}\}; f^{-1}(x) = 5 - \frac{1}{x}$

11. **(a)** $y = 2x - 5$: line, x-intercept: 2.5, y-intercept: -5; $y = \frac{1}{2x - 5}$: hyperbola, vertical asymptote $x = 2.5$, horizontal asymptote $y = 0$; $f(x) = \frac{1}{2x - 5}$ has
$D = \{x \mid x \neq \frac{5}{2}, x \in \mathbf{R}\}, R = \{y \mid y \neq 0, y \in \mathbf{R}\}$
(b) $y = 3x + 4$: line, x-intercept $-\frac{4}{3}$, y-intercept 4; $y = \frac{1}{3x + 4}$: hyperbola, vertical asymptote $x = \frac{-4}{3}$, horizontal asymptote $y = 0$; $f(x) = \frac{1}{3x + 4}$ has $D = \{x \mid x \neq \frac{-4}{3}, x \in \mathbf{R}\}$,
$R = \{y \mid y \neq 0, y \in \mathbf{R}\}$
(c) $y = -x$: line, x-intercept 0, y-intercept 0; $y = \frac{1}{-x}$ hyperbola; vertical asymptote $x = 0$, horizontal asymptote $y = 0$;
$f(x) = \frac{1}{-x}$ has $D = \{x \mid x \neq 0, x \in \mathbf{R}\}, R = \{y \mid y \neq 0, y \in \mathbf{R}\}$

12.

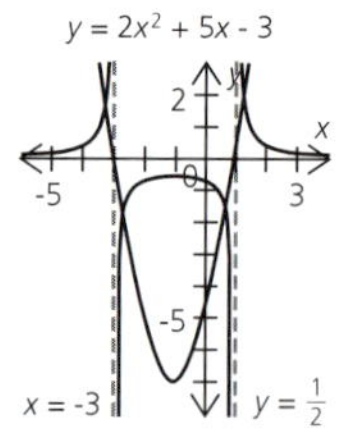

13. (a) $y = \frac{1}{x^2 - 4}$ (b) $y = \frac{1}{(x-2)^2 - 3}$
(c) $y = \frac{1}{x^2 - 3x + 4}$ (d) $y = \frac{1}{(x+3)^2}$
(e) $y = \frac{1}{x^2 + 2}$ (f) $y = \frac{1}{-(x+4)^2 + 1}$

14. The graph of $y = \frac{1}{x^2 - 3x - 10}$ will pass through points $(x, 1)$ and $(x, -1)$ from $y = x^2 - 3x - 10$.

15. (a) $\frac{1}{f(x)} = \frac{1}{2x+1}$, $f^{-1}(x) = \pm\sqrt{x+1}$
domain of $f = \mathbf{R}$, range of $f = \mathbf{R}$; domain of $\frac{1}{f} = \{x \mid x \neq \frac{1}{2}, x \in \mathbf{R}\}$, range of $\frac{1}{f} = \{y \mid y \neq 0, y \in \mathbf{R}\}$; domain of $f^{-1} = \mathbf{R}$, range of $f^{-1} = \mathbf{R}$
(b) $\frac{1}{f(x)} = \frac{1}{x^2 - 1}$, $f^{-1}(x) = \pm\sqrt{\frac{1}{x} + 1}$
domain of $f = \mathbf{R}$, range of $f = \{y \mid y \geq 1, y \in \mathbf{R}\}$;
domain of $\frac{1}{f} = \{x \mid x \neq \pm 1, x \in \mathbf{R}\}$, range of $\frac{1}{f} = \{y \mid y > 0 \text{ or } y < -1, y \in \mathbf{R}\}$; domain of $f^{-1} = \{x \mid x \geq -1, x \in \mathbf{R}\}$, range of $f^{-1} = \mathbf{R}$
(c) $\frac{1}{f(x)} = \frac{1}{\sqrt{x-4} - 3}$, $f^{-1}(x) = (x+3)^2 + 4$
domain of $f = \{x \mid x \geq 4, x \in \mathbf{R}\}$, range of $f = \{y \mid y \geq -3, y \in \mathbf{R}\}$; domain of $\frac{1}{f} = \{x \mid x \geq 4, x \neq 13, x \in \mathbf{R}\}$, range of $\frac{1}{f} = \{y \mid y \neq 0, y \in \mathbf{R}\}$; domain of $f^{-1} = \mathbf{R}$, range of $f^{-1} = \{y \mid y \geq 4, y \in \mathbf{R}\}$

16. Answers may vary. Key point: $f(x) = \frac{1}{x}$ is the reciprocal of $f(x) = x$.

17. (a) $\left(x, \frac{1}{x}\right) = (1, 1), (2, 0.5), (4, 0.25), (7, 0.14), (10, 0.10)$
(b) $\left(\frac{1}{x}, y\right) = (1, 5.5), (0.5, 4), (0.25, 3.3), (0.14, 2.9), (0.10, 2.8)$
(c) $k = 3, b = 2.5, y = 3\left(\frac{1}{x}\right) + 2.5$

18. $(x, A(x)) = (1, 0), (2, 0.69), (3, 1.1), (4, 1.38), (5, 1.61), (6, 1.79), (7, 1.94), (8, 2.08), (9, 2.20), (10, 2.30), (11, 2.40), (12, 2.48)$
(a) $A(3) + A(4) = A(12)$ (b) $A(2) + A(4) = A(8)$
(c) $A(10) - A(2) = A(5)$ (d) $A(9) = A(3) + A(3)$
i. 2.89 ii. 3.22 iii. 0.92 iv. 1.51

19. $y = \frac{1}{x+4} - 1$

Practice 4.7, page 350

(a) vertical asymptote $x = 4$, horizontal asymptote $y = 2$
(b) vertical asymptote $x = 2$, horizontal asymptote $y = -3$
(c) vertical asymptote $x = \pm\sqrt{5}$, horizontal asymptote $y = 1$
(d) vertical asymptote $x = -3$, horizontal asymptote $y = 1$
(e) vertical asymptote $x = \pm 1$, horizontal asymptote $y = 0$
(f) vertical asymptote $x = -3, x = -1$, horizontal asymptote $y = 0$
(g) vertical asymptote $x = 2$, horizontal asymptote $y = 1$
(h) vertical asymptote $x = 3, x = -2$, horizontal asymptote $y = 0$

Practise, Apply, Solve 4.8, page 353

1. (a) $x \neq 1$ (b) $y \neq \frac{1}{2}$ (c) $m, n \neq 0$
(d) $x \neq 0, 3$ (e) $p \neq -2, 4$ (f) $a \neq -b$
(g) $m \neq -3, 0$ (h) $x \neq \frac{3}{2}$ (i) $a \neq -\frac{4}{3}, 0$
(j) $k \neq \pm\frac{3}{2}$

2. (a) $4(x + 3)$ (b) $5(x + 3)$ (c) $\frac{4}{5}, x \neq -3$

3. (a), (c), (d)

4. (a) 1 (b) −1 (c) 1
(d) 1 (e) 1 (f) −1

5. (a) $\frac{1}{x+5}, x \neq -5, 2$ (b) $\frac{4y}{3y+4}, y \neq \pm\frac{4}{3}$
(c) $\frac{3x+5}{2x+1}, x \neq -\frac{1}{2}, x \neq 1$

6. (a) $(k + 2)(k - 2)$ (b) $(3k - 1)(k + 2)$
(c) $\frac{k-2}{3k-1}, x \neq -2, x \neq \frac{1}{3}$

7. (a) $6(p + 2)(p + 3)$ (b) $3(p + 2)(p - 3)$
(c) $\frac{2(p+3)}{p-3}, x \neq -2, 3$

8. (a) $\frac{2}{5}, b \neq -4$ (b) $\frac{3x-2}{3x-6}, x \neq 0, 2$
(c) $\frac{1}{3}, m \neq 0, 4$ (d) $-5, x \neq 0, 3$
(e) $\frac{x+2}{x-3}, x \neq 2, 3$ (f) $\frac{p+4}{3}, p \neq 5$
(g) $\frac{y-3}{y+3}, y \neq -3, y \neq 4$ (h) $\frac{a+5}{a-7}, a \neq 4, 7$

9. (a) $\frac{9x}{-4y}, x \neq 0, y \neq 0$ (b) $\frac{3}{2}, x \neq -4$
(c) $\frac{3m+2}{3m+1}, m \neq -\frac{1}{3}, \frac{2}{3}$ (d) $\frac{x-5y}{x+5y}, x \neq -5y$

10. (a) $\frac{3m+2}{2m+2}, m \neq \pm 1$ (b) $\frac{a+3}{a-3}, a \neq \frac{1}{2}, 3$
(c) $\frac{-2(3x+4)}{3x+2}, x \neq -\frac{2}{3}, \frac{5}{3}$ (d) $\frac{3x-1}{x(3x+1)}, x \neq -\frac{1}{3}, 0$

11. Restrictions express the values for which a rational expression is not defined.

12. (a) $x - y = -(y - x)$ (b) $\frac{-(x+2y)}{x+y}, x \neq \pm y$

13. (a) $-2a - b, b \neq 2a$ (b) $1 - x, x \neq 1$
(c) $\frac{5-k}{5+k}, k \neq \pm 5$

14. (a) 20.83 mg and 0.08 mg (b) 17.36 mg and 0.05 mg

15. $\frac{\text{Surface Area}}{\text{Volume}} = \frac{2(r+h)}{rh}$
By symmetry, a change in height or radius has equal effect on the ratio.

16. No, should be $\frac{a+5b}{2a+b}$.

17. all x except $-\frac{3}{4}, 0, \frac{1}{2}$, and 4

18. Drug B would need to be taken more.

Practise, Apply, Solve 4.9, page 359

1. (a) $\frac{xy}{12}$ (b) $\frac{10a}{b}$ (c) $9x$ (d) $\frac{4}{3}$ (e) $2y^2$

2. (a) $\frac{4a}{3b}$ (b) $\frac{3m}{2}$ (c) $\frac{21}{8a^2b}$ (d) $-\frac{9r}{4p^2q^2}$ (e) $\frac{a}{2b}$

3. (a) 2 (b) $\frac{5(y-5)}{4}$ (c) $\frac{1}{3}$
(d) 4 (e) $\frac{b(b+4)}{3(b-1)}$ (f) $\frac{3s+1}{3s(s+1)}$

4. (a) $\frac{8}{3y}$ (b) $\frac{4}{5}$ (c) $\frac{x+y}{x+4}$

5. (a) $\frac{1}{k}$ (b) $(x - 3)(x + 2)$ (c) $\frac{2q-1}{1+3q}$

6. There may be more than one variable factor in the denominator.
Example: $\frac{1}{(x+3)(x-3)}, x \neq 3, x \neq -3$

7. **(a)** $x + 1, x \neq \pm 1, x \neq 0$ **(b)** $\frac{1}{3(x - 1)}, x \neq \pm 1$
(c) $1, x \neq \pm 1, x \neq -2, x \neq \frac{3}{2}$ **(d)** $\frac{(x + 4)(x + 5)}{(x - 4)(x - 5)}, x \neq 4, x \neq 5$
(e) $1, x \neq \pm 2, x \neq -3, x \neq 4$
(f) $\frac{2x - 1}{x + 2}, x \neq \pm 3, x \neq -2, x \neq -\frac{1}{2}$

8. **(a)** $\frac{x - 3}{x - 7}, x \neq \pm 7, x \neq -3$ **(b)** $\frac{x - 1}{x + 1}, x \neq -1, -2, -\frac{1}{2}$
(c) $\frac{6}{x^2(x + 2)}, x \neq 0, -2, -3$ **(d)** $\frac{(x + 5)(x - 3)}{x(x + 1)}, x \neq \pm 1, \pm 3$
(e) $\frac{2(x - 5)}{4x + 3}, x \neq -3, -\frac{3}{4}$ **(f)** $\frac{1}{x(x - 1)}, x \neq 0, 1, 2$

9. **(a)** $\frac{x + 1}{x + 3}, x \neq \pm 3, 1$
(b) $\frac{m + 2}{-m(m + 6)}, m \neq -1, -6, 0, 3$
(c) $\frac{2(2x - 3y)}{x}, x \neq 0, x \neq -\frac{3}{2}y$ **(d)** $\frac{z^3(2z + 1)}{2z - 1}, z \neq 0, -\frac{1}{2}, \frac{1}{2}$
(e) $\frac{(a + 2)(a + 3)}{(a - 2)(a - 3)}, a \neq -5, 3, 2$
(f) $\frac{(21 - 3p)(14 - 9p + p^2)}{(16p + 4)(12 + 7p + p^2)}, p \neq 0, -\frac{1}{4}, -3, -4$

10. **(a)** $\frac{x}{2}$ **(b)** 1

11. **(a)** -5 **(b)** 3 **(c)** $-\frac{9}{5}$ **(d)** 1
(e) $-\frac{7}{3}$ **(f)** $\frac{1}{3}$ **(g)** $x \neq 0, x \neq 4$

12. **(a)** \$50 408 307.30 **(b)** \$50 494 900.50 **(c)** \$50 504 030.70

13. $x \neq 2.5$

14. **(a)** $\frac{a + b}{-a^2 - b^2}$ **(b)** x

15. **(a)** $\frac{1}{5}$ **(b)** 1

16. $f(x) = 3q(x)$

17. **(a)** $\frac{(x - 2)(3x + 2)}{(2x - 1)(x + 1)}, x \neq \frac{2}{3}, -\frac{1}{2}, \frac{1}{2}, -1, 1$
(b) $\frac{(3a + b)(1 - 2a)}{(a + 5b)(2a + 1)}, a \neq \frac{b}{4}, -5b, -\frac{3}{2}b, \frac{3}{2}b, -\frac{1}{2}$
(c) $\frac{m(m + 2n)}{(m + n)(4m + n)}, m \neq -\frac{3}{2}n, -\frac{1}{3}n, \pm n, 2n, -\frac{1}{4}n$

Practise, Apply, Solve 4.10U, page 362

1. **(a)** $1 + i$ **(b)** $-1 - 2i$ **(c)** $\sqrt{3} + i$
(d) $-2 - \sqrt{2}i$ **(e)** $-\frac{1}{2} + \frac{\sqrt{3}}{2}i$ **(f)** $x - yi$

2. **(a)** $\frac{1}{2} + \frac{1}{2}i$ **(b)** $-\frac{1}{5} - \frac{2}{5}i$ **(c)** $\frac{\sqrt{3}}{4} + \frac{1}{4}i$
(d) $-\frac{1}{3} - \frac{\sqrt{2}}{6}i$ **(e)** $-\frac{1}{2} + \frac{\sqrt{3}}{2}i$ **(f)** $\frac{x}{x^2 + y^2} - \frac{y}{x^2 + y^2}i$

3. **(a)** $9 - 3i$ **(b)** $1 - i$ **(c)** $-2 + 2i$
(d) $-4 + 2i$ **(e)** $-\frac{1}{2} + \frac{5}{2}i$ **(f)** $\frac{1}{5} - \frac{7}{5}i$
(g) $-\frac{1}{13} + \frac{18}{13}i$ **(h)** $1 - 4i$ **(i)** $-5 - 2i$
(j) $\frac{x^2 - y^2}{x^2 + y^2} + \frac{2xy}{x^2 + y^2}i$

4. $\frac{1}{2} + \frac{\sqrt{3}}{2}i$

5. $\frac{1}{10} - \frac{7}{10}i$

6. $-\frac{9}{25} - \frac{13}{25}i$

7. $\frac{7}{50} - \frac{i}{50}$

9. Only if a variable appears in the denominator; i is not a variable.

10. **(a)** 6 **(b)** $\left(a + \frac{a}{a^2 + b^2}\right) + \left(b - \frac{b}{a^2 + b^2}\right)i$

11. **(a)** $\frac{7}{2} + \frac{3}{2}i$ **(b)** $-2 + 3i$ **(c)** $-2 + i$
(d) $-\frac{13}{578} + \frac{42}{289}i$

12. **(a)** $\frac{9}{5} + \frac{4}{5}i$ **(b)** $\frac{-2bi}{a^2 + b^2}$

13. $a = 4, b = -5$

14. $-3 - i$

16. $w = -1 + i, z = 3 - 2i$

Practise, Apply, Solve 4.11, page 369

1. **(a)** xy **(b)** ab **(c)** $x(x - 1)$
(d) $(b + 2)(b + 1)$ **(e)** x^2y **(f)** $(2m + 3)(m - 3)$
(g) y^2z^2 **(h)** $(s - 1)(s + 1)$ **(i)** $(x + 2)(x - 2)$

2. **(a)** $\frac{2a + 7a}{ab}, a, b \neq 0$ **(b)** $\frac{3x + 2}{x^2}, x \neq 0$
(c) $\frac{4z + 5x}{xyz}, x, y, z \neq 0$ **(d)** $\frac{7y + 4x}{x^2y^2}, x, y \neq 0$
(e) $\frac{3(1 + 2xy)}{y^2}, y \neq 0$ **(f)** $\frac{2x^2 + 5x + 5}{x(x + 1)}, x \neq 0, -1$
(g) $\frac{13y + 6}{5y(y + 2)}, y \neq 0, -2$ **(h)** $\frac{5x + 11}{(x + 3)(x + 1)}, x \neq -3, -1$
(i) $\frac{3x^2 + x}{x^2 + 2x - 3}, x \neq 1, -3$

3. **(a)** $\frac{5}{12x}, x \neq 0$ **(b)** $\frac{3 - 2y}{y^2}, y \neq 0$ **(c)** $-\frac{10}{3x}, x \neq 0$
(d) $\frac{2(5y - 3x)}{x^2y^2}, x, y \neq 0$ **(e)** $\frac{27a - 10b}{12a^2b^2}, a \neq 0, b \neq 0$
(f) $\frac{3(y - 3)}{(y + 1)(y - 1)}, y \neq \pm 1$ **(g)** $\frac{x^2 - 19x}{(x + 5)(x - 3)}, x \neq -5, 3$
(h) $\frac{-t^2 + 6t + 3}{(t - 1)(t + 1)}, t \neq \pm 1$ **(i)** $\frac{-3x - 2}{x(x + 2)}, x \neq 0, -2$

4. **(a)** $\frac{-14x + 15}{3x^2}, x \neq 0$
(b) $\frac{-2(2p^2 - 3p + 4)}{p^2q}, p \neq 0, q \neq 0$
(c) $\frac{x(2y - 3yz - 9)}{y^2z}, y \neq 0, z \neq 0$
(d) $\frac{7a + 5}{(a + 1)(a + 3)}, a \neq -1, -3$
(e) $\frac{-3x - 5}{(x + 2)^2}, x \neq -2$ **(f)** $\frac{x^2 + 3x + 20}{2(x + 4)^2}, x \neq -4$

5. **(a)** $\frac{2x + 9}{6(x - 2)}, x \neq 2$ **(b)** $\frac{17x + 1}{5x(x + 3)}, x \neq 0, -3$
(c) $\frac{3(2y - 3)}{y(y - 2)}, y \neq 0, 2$ **(d)** $\frac{2}{p + 3}, p \neq 0, -3$
(e) $\frac{5x + 4}{(x - 2)(x + 1)}, x \neq 2, -1$ **(f)** $\frac{2}{a - 3}, a \neq \pm 3$
(g) $\frac{2}{(y + 4)(y - 1)}, y \neq -4, 1$
(h) $\frac{3(m^3 + m^2 - 10m - 3)}{(2m - 3)(m + 3)(m - 3)}, m \neq \pm 3, \frac{3}{2}$

6. **(a)** $\frac{1}{x + 1}, x \neq \pm 1$
(b) $\frac{2x - 11}{(x - 5)(x - 2)(x + 5)}, x \neq \pm 5, 2$
(c) $\frac{a(21a - 13)}{(2a + 1)(3a - 2)(5a - 3)}, a \neq -\frac{1}{2}, \frac{2}{3}, \frac{3}{5}$
(d) $-\frac{1}{3x(3x + h)}, x \neq 0, -\frac{h}{3}, h \neq 0$
(e) $\frac{7k - 5}{(2k - 3)(k - 2)(k + 1)}, k \neq \frac{3}{2}, 2, -1$
(f) $\frac{a^2 + 4a + 1}{(a - 3)(a + 3)(a + 1)}, a \neq \pm 3, -1$

7. If you find the LCD, then it is easier to put the final answer in lowest terms. Examples may vary.

8. **(a)** $\frac{6x^2 - 17xy - 14y^2}{24xy}, x, y \neq 0$ **(b)** $\frac{x^2 + 3x + 20}{2(x + 4)^2}, x \neq -4$

9. **(a)** $\frac{2x + 3}{(x - 5)(x + 1)}, x \neq -1, 2, 5$ **(b)** $\frac{1}{(x - 1)(x + 4)}, x \neq -4, 1, 3$
(c) $\frac{10k^2 + 21k + 5}{(3k - 1)(2k + 5)(2k + 3)}, k \neq \frac{1}{3}, -\frac{5}{2}, -\frac{3}{2}$
(d) $\frac{9q^2 - 4q - 4}{6(4q + 3)(3q - 2)(q - 2)}, q \neq -\frac{3}{4}, -\frac{2}{3}, 2$

(e) $\frac{(x+4)(x-2)}{(x-3)(2x-3)}$, $x \neq \frac{3}{2}, \pm 3, -\frac{1}{2}$

(f) $\frac{a^2-3a-14}{2(2a+1)(a+5)}$, $a \neq 0, \frac{5}{3}, -\frac{1}{2}, -5$

10. (a) $x = 0$ or $x = -\frac{2}{3}$ (b) $x = \frac{3}{2}$ or $x = -\frac{2}{3}$
11. (a) 1 (b) $-\frac{3}{2}$ (c) $\frac{1}{3}$
    (d) -2 or $\frac{2}{3}$ (e) 8 (f) 3 or $\frac{3}{2}$
12. Arshia's speed: 8.0 km/h; Sarah's speed: 8.4 km/h; Arshia's time: 5.5 h; Sarah's time: 5.25 h
13. 6.67 km/h
14. 3.74 km/h
15. 18 tickets
16. 12 days
17. 33 students
18. (1) Factor the numerators and denominators for both expressions. (2) Express the sum or difference of the expressions with a common denominator. (3) Simplify. Explanations of steps may vary.
19. $A = 3, B = -7$
20. $A = -\frac{2}{9}, B = \frac{2}{9}, C = \frac{1}{3}$
21. $x = \frac{bc \pm \sqrt{b^2c^2 + 4abc}}{2b}$

Practise, Apply, Solve 4.12, page 374

1. (a) $4x^2 - x + 1$ (b) 2
   (c) $-x^2 - 3x - 3$ (d) $x^3 - 5x^2 + 2x - 3$
   (e) $-x^4 + x^3 - 3x^2 - 3$
   (f) $x^5 + 2x^4 + 2x^3 - 4x^2 - 3x + 1$
   (g) $2x^2 + x + 2$
2. (a) $-x^2 - 10x$ (b) $x^2 - 7x$
   (c) $6x^3 + 2x^2$ (d) $-4x^3 + 11x^2 + 8x$
   (e) $-4x^4 + 15x^3 - 2x^2 - 8x$
   (f) $-2x^6 + 6x^5 - 2x^4 - 5x^3 + 4x^2$
3. (a) 2 (b) 2 (c) 3
   (d) 3 (e) 4 (f) 6
4. (a) $34x - 24$ (b) $-11x - 13$ (c) $10x^2$
   (d) $-6x^2 + 9x$ (e) $-16a^3 + 25a^2$ (f) $10a^3 + 5a^2$
5. (a) $x^3 + 2x^2 - 5x - 6$ (b) $-x^4 + 2x^3 - 4x^2 + 3x$
   (c) $x^4 - 3x^3 - x^2 - 3x - 2$ (d) $x^5 - x^4 - 2x^3 - x^2 + 6$
   (e) $x^5 - 3x^4 - x^3 + 8x^2 - 6x + 3$
   (f) $x^7 - 2x^6 + 6x^5 - 4x^4 - 6x^2 + 3x + 2$
6. (a) $9x - 13$ (b) $-2x^2 - 6x + 8$
   (c) $-23 + 16x - 2x^2$ (d) $10x^2 - 36x + 28$
   (e) $3x^4 + 4x^2 - 15$ (f) $47x^5 - 28x^3 - 4x$
7. (a) $x^3 + 5x^2 - 6x - 1$ (b) $x^3 + x^2 - 3x - 27$
   (c) $12a^3 + 26a^2 - 15a - 104$ (d) $5t^3 - 3t^2 - 2t$
   (e) $-9x^3 + 4x^2 - 8x - 53$ (f) $6x^3 + x^2 - 16x - 5$
8. (a) $-x^2 + 2 + 12$ (b) $4x^3 - 14x^2 + 17x$ (c) $-x^5 - 2x^4 + 1$
9. Jake did not distribute the negative sign to all of the terms from the expansion of $(x + 2)(x - 3)$. The calculation should be:
   $(x+1)^2 - (x+2)(x-3) = x^2 + 2x + 1 - (x^2 - 3x + 2x - 6)$
   $= x^2 + 2x + 1 - (x^2 - x - 6)$
   $= x^2 + 2x + 1 - x^2 + x + 6$
   $= 3x + 7$
10. (a) $2a^4 - 7a^3 + 8a^2 - 5a + 3$
    (b) $2y^4 - 5y^3 - 7y^2 + 23y - 30$
    (c) $x^4 - 2x^3 + 3x^2 - 2x + 1$ (d) $x^4 + 4x^3 - 2x^2 - 12x + 9$
11. *Example*:
    $(x+2)(x+3) - 3x(x^2 + x + 3)$
    $= (x^2 + 3x + 2x + 6) - (3x^3 + 3x^2 + 9x)$
    $= x^2 + 5x + 6 - 3x^3 - 3x^2 - 9x$
    $= -3x^3 - 2x^2 - 4x + 6$
    The degree is 3.
12. (a) $2a^4 + 8a^2 - 8a + 2$ (b) $2a^3b - 3a^2b^2 + 2ab^3$
14. -1
15. $a = 5, b = 6, c = 2; 2 \pm 2i$ or $-\frac{3}{5} \pm \frac{i}{5}$
16. $a = b = c = 1; 1, -\frac{1}{2} + i\frac{\sqrt{3}}{2}, -\frac{1}{2} - i\frac{\sqrt{3}}{2}$

Chapter 4, Review and Practice, page 378

1. Vertex form is $f(x) = a(x - h)^2 + k$, where (h, k) is the vertex. This form is found by transforming the equation in standard form by completing the square. A quadratic function may be in standard form: $f(x) = ax^2 + bx + c$, where $(0, c)$ is the y-intercept, or in factored form: $f(x) = a(x - p)(x - q)$, where $(p, 0)$ and $(q, 0)$ are the x-intercepts.
2. To complete the square: factor the coefficient of x^2 from the first two terms; add and subtract the square of half the coefficient of x inside the brackets; group the three terms that form the perfect square; multiply the fourth term by a, and move it outside the brackets; factor the perfect square and simplify.
3. (a) $f(x) = (x - 3)^2 - 2$ (b) $f(x) = \left(x - \frac{5}{2}\right)^2 - \frac{21}{4}$
   (c) $f(x) = 2\left(x + \frac{7}{4}\right)^2 - \frac{73}{8}$ (d) $f(x) = -4\left(x + \frac{3}{8}\right)^2 + \frac{41}{16}$
   (e) $f(x) = -1.6(x + 0.75)^2 - 0.1$
   (f) $f(x) = \frac{2}{3}\left(x - \frac{1}{3}\right)^2 + \frac{52}{27}$
4. (a) $y = (x + 4)^2 - 3$, vertex: $(-4, -3)$, D = **R**, R = $\{y \mid y \geq 3, y \in \mathbf{R}\}$; parabola, opens up, zeros at $-5.67, -2.27$; y-intercept: 7
   (b) $y = -2\left(x - \frac{5}{4}\right)^2 + \frac{25}{8}$, vertex: $\left(\frac{5}{4}, \frac{25}{8}\right)$, D = **R**, R = $\{y \mid y \leq \frac{25}{8}, y \in \mathbf{R}\}$; parabola, opens down, zeros at 0, 2.5; y-intercept: 0
   (c) $y = \frac{1}{2}(x - 5)^2 + \frac{5}{2}$, vertex: $\left(5, \frac{5}{2}\right)$, D = **R**, R = $\{y \mid y \geq \frac{5}{2}, y \in \mathbf{R}\}$; parabola, opens up, no zeros; y-intercept: 15
5. 0.8 m
6. (a) *Example*: y-intercept: for $f(x) = 2x^2 + 6x + 1$, $(0, 1)$ is y-intercept.
   (b) *Example*: x-intercepts: for $f(x) = (x - 5)(x - 2)$, $(5, 0)$ and $(2, 0)$ are x-intercepts.
   (c) *Example*: vertex: for $f(x) = (x - 2)^2 + 3$, vertex is $(2, 3)$.
7. The graph of $g(x)$ is graph of $f(x)$, translated c units down; therefore, to find the maximum and minimum points of $g(x)$, one can just add c to the maximum and minimum points of $f(x)$. To find the maximum or minimum points of $f(x)$, factor: $ax^2 + bx = x(ax + b)$. Therefore, the intercepts are $(0, 0)$ and $\left(-\frac{b}{a}, 0\right)$. The maximum and minimum points are halfway between these points, so $-\frac{b}{2a}$ is the x-coordinate of the vertex for both functions. To find the y-coordinate of the vertex for $g(x)$, substitute $x = -\frac{b}{2a}$ into the equation. This y-value is the maximum or minimum value of $g(x)$. To find the maximum or minimum value for $f(x)$, subtract c from the y-coordinate for the vertex for $g(x)$.

8. When the coefficient of the x^2 term is positive, the function has a minimum value; when negative, it has a maximum value.
(**a**) maximum, $x = 1, 6$ (**b**) minimum, $x = -2, -21$
(**c**) maximum, $t = 2, 0$ (**d**) minimum, $x = 0.55, -0.672$
(**e**) minimum, $x = 1.1, -4.5$
(**f**) minimum, $x = -225, -1827$

9. (**a**) Revenue $= -5x^2 + 22x$ (**b**) $P(x) = -5x^2 + 19x - 15$
(**c**) $x = 1.9$ (**d**) 1100 or 2700
(**e**) $P(x) = -5(x - 1.9)^2 + 3.05$; parabola, opens down, vertex (1.9, 3.05) zeros at 1.12 and 2.68; y-intercept: -15

10. 8 empty seats

11. *Examples*:
parabola opens up, with vertex above x-axis or parabola opens down, with vertex below x-axis; no zeros since graph does not cross x-axis.
(**a**) parabola opens up or down, vertex on x-axis; one zero since graph touches x-axis once.
(**b**) parabola opens up, vertex below x-axis or parabola opens down, vertex above x-axis; two zeros since graph crosses x-axis twice.

12. discriminant: $b^2 - 4ac$; if $b^2 - 4ac = 0$, function has 1 zero; if $b^2 - 4ac > 0$, it has 2 zeros; if $b^2 - 4ac < 0$, it has no zeros.
Examples:
(**a**) $4x^2 - 5x + 2$ (**b**) $x^2 - 2x + 1$
(**c**) $8x^2 + 9x + 1$

13. When the signs of a and k are opposite, function has 2 zeros; when they are the same, it has no zeros; when $k = 0$, it has 1 zero.
Examples:
(**a**) $y = 4(x - 3)^2 + 1$ (**b**) $y = 2(x - 1)^2$
(**c**) $y = -3(x - 1)^2 + 2$

14. (**a**) 2 zeros, 2 points (**b**) 2 zeros, 2 points
(**c**) one zero, one point (**d**) no zeros, no points
(**e**) 1 zero, 1 point (**f**) 2 zeros, 2 points

15. (**a**) $k < 8, k = 8, k > 8$
(**b**) $k > 20$ or $k < -20$, $k = \pm 20$, $-20 < k < 20$
(**c**) $k > 12$ or $k < -12$, $k = \pm 12$, $-12 < k < 12$
(**d**) $k > 1$ or $k < -3$, $k = -3$ or $k = 1$, $-3 < k < 1$

16. **N** = set of natural numbers, **W** = set of whole numbers, **I** = set of integers, **Q** = set of rational numbers, $\overline{\mathbf{Q}}$ = set of irrational numbers, **R** = set of real numbers, and **C** = set of complex numbers.

17. Complex numbers are expressed in the form $a + bi$, where a and b are real and $i^2 = -1$.

18. The quadratic equation $ax^2 + bx + c$ has no real roots when $b^2 - 4ac = < 0$. The two complex roots are $a + bi$ and $a - bi$, which are conjugates of one another.

19. (**a**) **Q, R, C** (**b**) **I, Q, R, C** (**c**) **C**
(**d**) $\overline{\mathbf{Q}}$**, R, C** (**e**) **C** (**f**) $\overline{\mathbf{Q}}$**, R, C**
(**g**) $\overline{\mathbf{Q}}$**, R, C** (**h**) $\overline{\mathbf{Q}}$**, R, C** (**i**) **W, R, C**
(**j**) **N, W, I, Q, R, C**

20. (**a**) $2 + i$ (**b**) $1 - 3i$ (**c**) $-4 + 5i$
(**d**) $-5 - 6i$ (**e**) $13 + 13i$ (**f**) $3 - \sqrt{3}i$

21. (**a**) $\pm 9i$ (**b**) $\pm 6i$ (**c**) $1 \pm \sqrt{2}i$
(**d**) $2 \pm 4i$ (**e**) $\frac{3 \pm \sqrt{7}i}{4}$ (**f**) $\frac{-6 \pm \sqrt{6}i}{3}$

22. The sum or difference of complex numbers consists of the sum or difference of the real numbers and the sum or difference of the imaginary numbers. For example, $(4 + 6i) + (5 - 2i) = 9 + 4i$. The sum of complex conjugates is a real number, with no imaginary part. For example, $(4 + 6i) + (4 - 6i) = 8$.

23. Use the distributive law to multiply complex numbers. For example, $(4 + 6i)(2 - i) = 8 - 4i + 12i - 6i^2 = 14 + 8i$. The product of two complex conjugates is a real number, with no imaginary part. For example, $(2 - i)(2 + i) = 5$.

24. (**a**) -9 (**b**) i (**c**) $12 - i$
(**d**) $-18 + i$ (**e**) 50 (**f**) $5 - 3i$
(**g**) $-15 - 8i$ (**h**) $\frac{1}{5}$ (**i**) $58 - 14i$
(**j**) $7 + 4i$

25. (**a**) 10 (**b**) 25 (**c**) 29

26. $-11 + 26i$

27. (**a**) $-3i, x^2 + 9 = 0$ (**b**) $1 + 2i, x^2 - 2x + 5 = 0$
(**c**) $-\frac{1}{2} + \frac{\sqrt{3}}{2}i, x^2 + x + 1$

28. It displays inverse variation because y decreases as x increases. Value of xy remains constant; reciprocal function graph; $D = \{x \mid x \neq 0, x \in \mathbf{R}\}$, $R = \{y \mid y \neq 0, y \in \mathbf{R}\}$.

29. The x-intercept(s) of $f(x)$ will give the equation(s) of the vertical asymptotes for $y = \frac{1}{f(x)}$. The y-intercept of $y = \frac{1}{f(x)}$ is $y = \frac{1}{y\text{-intercept of } f(x)}$. Find the points $(x, 1)$ and $(x, -1)$ of $f(x)$: graph of $y = \frac{1}{f(x)}$ will also go through these points.

30. (**a**) **i.** inverse variation **ii.** inverse variation **iii.** no inverse variation
(**b**) **i.** $y = \frac{60}{x}$ **ii.** $y = \frac{2880}{x}$ **iii.** $y = 2x^2 - 1$

31. 4 s, $a = \frac{60}{t}$, hyperbola in first and third quadrants; vertical asymptote $x = 0$; horizontal asymptote $y = 0$

32. (**a**)

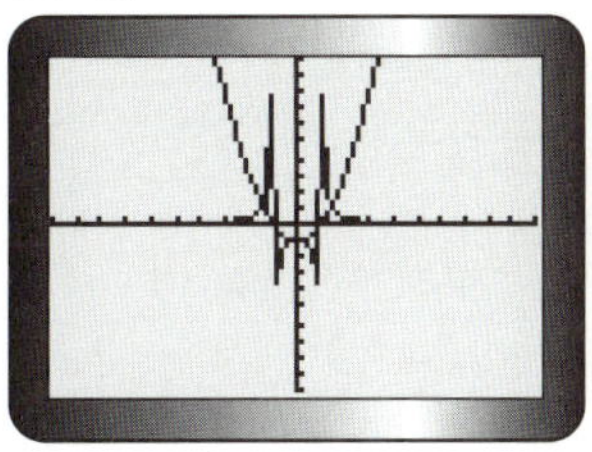

(**b**)

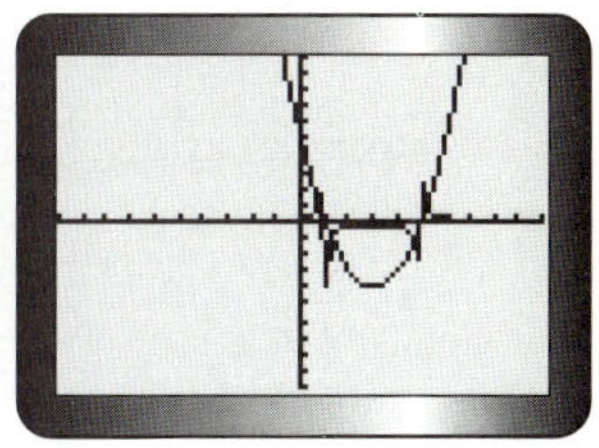

(**c**)

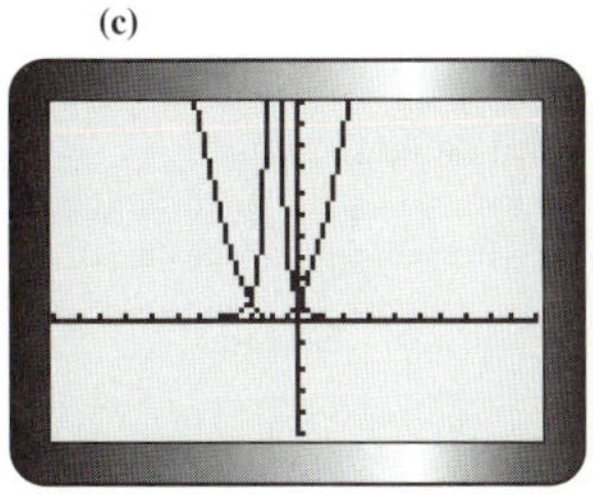

(**d**)

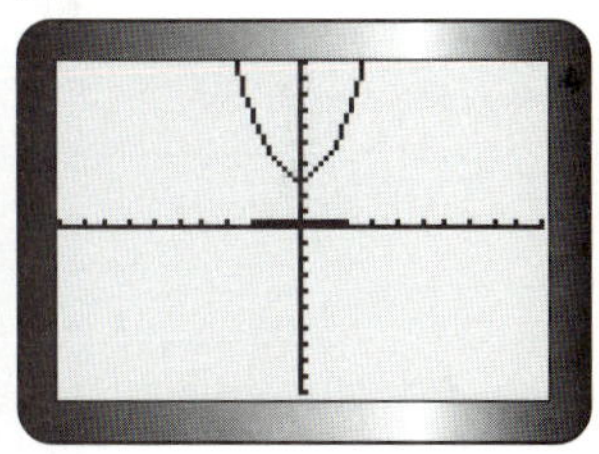

(**e**)

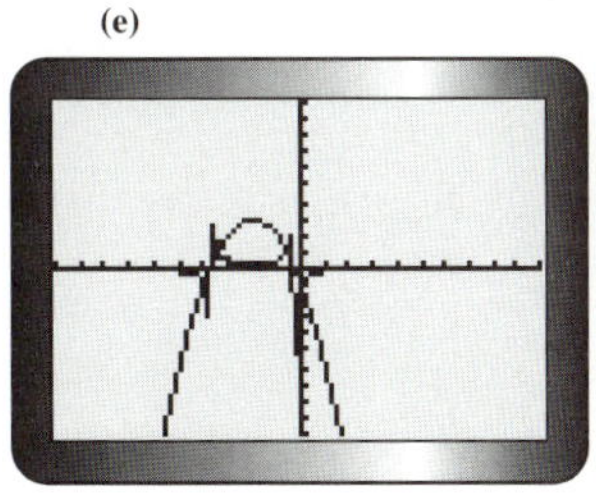

(**f**)

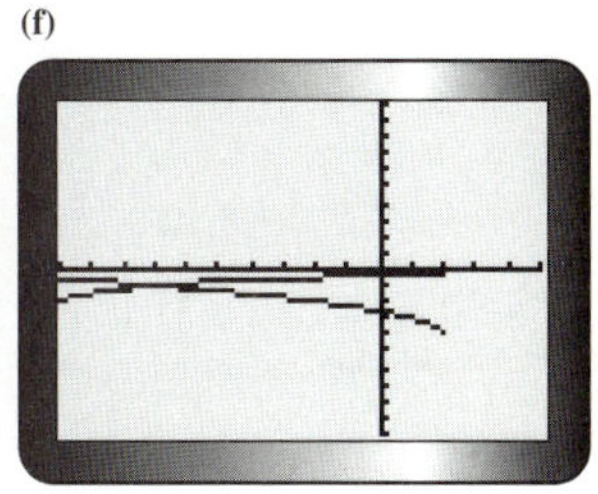

33. (**a**)

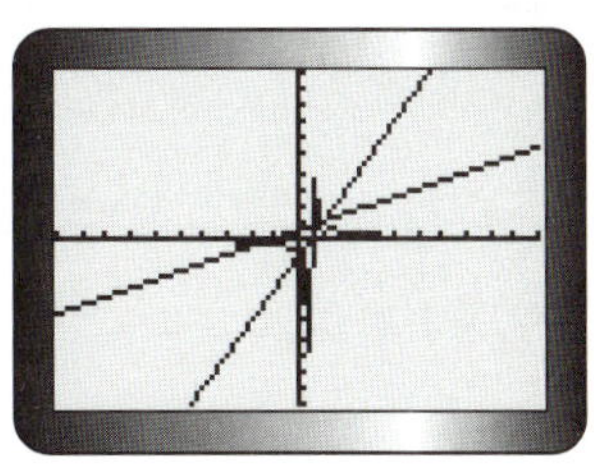

$f(x)$: D = **R**, R = **R**; $\frac{1}{f(x)}$: $D = \{x \mid x \neq \frac{1}{2}, x \in \mathbf{R}\}$, $R = \{y \mid y \neq 0, y \in \mathbf{R}\}$, $f^{-1}(x)$: D = **R**, R = **R**

(b)

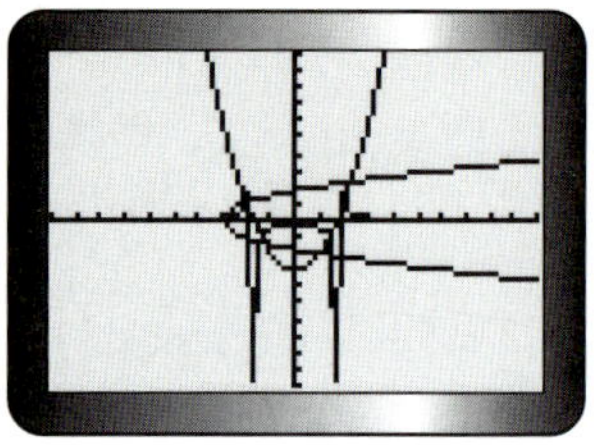

$f(x)$: D = **R**, R = **R**; $\frac{1}{f(x)}$: D = $\{x \mid x \neq \pm 3, x \in \mathbf{R}\}$, R = $\{y \mid y \neq 0, y \in \mathbf{R}\}$, $f^{-1}(x)$: D = $\{x \mid x \geq -3, x \in \mathbf{R}\}$, R = **R**

(c)

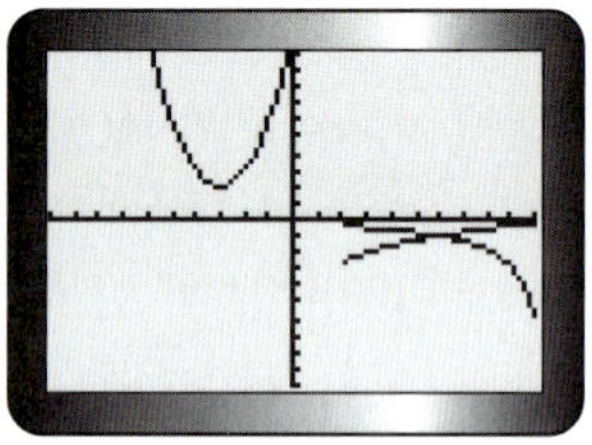

$f(x)$: D = $\{x \mid x \geq 2, x \in \mathbf{R}\}$, R = $\{y \mid y \geq -3, y \in \mathbf{R}\}$; $\frac{1}{f(x)}$: D = $\{x \mid x \geq 2, x \in \mathbf{R}\}$, R = $\{y \mid y \leq -\frac{1}{3}, y \in \mathbf{R}\}$, $f^{-1}(x)$: D = **R**, R = $\{y \mid y \geq 2, y \in \mathbf{R}\}$

34. sum, difference, product or quotient of two polynomial functions; to find common factors.

35. when the denominator is 0; must state restrictions on the variables

36. **(a)** $-\frac{3}{5}, x \neq -3$ **(b)** $-\frac{8p^2}{3q}, p, q \neq 0$
(c) $\frac{4x+3}{x+1}, x \neq -1, \frac{3}{4}$ **(d)** $\frac{a+2}{a+3}, a \neq -3, 4$
(e) $\frac{2x-3}{2x+3}, x \neq -\frac{2}{5}, -\frac{3}{2}$ **(f)** $\frac{x-3}{-(3+x)}, x \neq 3, -3$
(g) $\frac{x-2y}{-(y-x)}, x \neq \frac{y}{2}, y$

37. **(a)** 1.1, 1.7, 1.7 **(b)** $4.5h$

38. factor numerator and denominator, state restrictions, divide out common factors, multiply the numerators and multiply the denominators, then express as a single rational expression.

39. the reciprocal is used

40. **(a)** $\frac{y}{2}, x, y \neq 0$ **(b)** $m, m, n \neq 0$
(c) $\frac{2b}{3c^2}, a, b, c \neq 0$ **(d)** $\frac{5}{2p}, p, q \neq 0$

41. **(a)** $\frac{1}{(x+3)(x-2)}, x \neq 2, \pm 3$ **(b)** $\frac{2}{-a^2}, a \neq 0, 5$
(c) $\frac{1}{2(y-5)}, y \neq \pm 3, 5$
(d) $\frac{(x-3)^2(x-5)}{(x+2)^2(x-8)}, x \neq -7, -2, 8$

42. **(a)** -4 **(b)** 2 **(c)** $\frac{1}{5}$
(d) $\frac{5}{4}$ **(e)** undefined **(f)** 0
(g) $-\frac{2(x+3)}{(x-3)}, x \neq 0, \pm 3$
$f(x)$: $x \neq 0, 3$; $g(x)$: $x \neq 0, 2$

43. **(a)** $\frac{x}{36y}, x \neq 0, y \neq 0$
(b) $\frac{(x-3)(x+1)}{(x-1)}, x \neq \pm 1, \pm 2, 5$
(c) $\frac{x(1-x)}{-y(y+1)}, x \neq 0, -1, y \neq 0, \pm 1$
(d) $(x-y), y \neq \pm 2x, -x, -\frac{2}{3}x$
(e) $\frac{a+b}{a-b}, a \neq \pm 3b, \pm 2b, \pm b$

44. product is a real number

45. multiply numerator and denominator by the complex conjugate of the denominator

46. **(a)** $2+i, \frac{1}{2-i}, \frac{2}{5}+\frac{1}{5}i$ **(b)** $-1-i, \frac{1}{-1+i}, -\frac{1}{2}-\frac{1}{2}i$
(c) $\sqrt{2}+\sqrt{2}i, \frac{1}{\sqrt{2}-\sqrt{2}i}, \frac{1}{2\sqrt{2}}+\frac{1}{2\sqrt{2}}i$
(d) $-3-\sqrt{3}i, \frac{1}{-3+\sqrt{3}i}, -\frac{1}{4}-\frac{1}{4\sqrt{3}}i$
(e) $-\frac{1}{2}-\frac{\sqrt{3}}{2}, \frac{2}{-1+\sqrt{3}i}, -\frac{1}{2}-\frac{\sqrt{3}}{2}i$

47. **(a)** $2+2i$ **(b)** $2-i$ **(c)** $3+3i$
(d) $\frac{4}{5}+\frac{12}{5}i$ **(e)** $1-i$ **(f)** $\frac{11}{13}+\frac{16}{13}i$
(g) $-1-5i$ **(h)** $-4-3i$
(i) $\frac{a^2-b^2}{a^2+b^2}+\frac{2ab}{a^2+b^2}i$ **(j)** $2-3i$
(k) $-\frac{7}{25}+\frac{74}{25}i$

48. **(a)** $\frac{13\sqrt{3}}{4}-\frac{5}{4}i$
(b) real: $\frac{x^3+xy^2+x}{x^2+y^2}$, imaginary: $\frac{x^2y+y^3-y}{x^2+y^2}$

49. **(a)** $\frac{1}{2}-\frac{7}{2}i$ **(b)** $\frac{2}{5}+\frac{14}{5}i$

50. must have common factors;
Example: $\frac{9}{x^2+x-12}+\frac{5}{x^2-9}=\frac{14x+47}{(x+4)(x-3)(x+3)}$

51. must include all points where the function is undefined

52. **(a)** $\frac{2}{15x}, x \neq 0$ **(b)** $\frac{3a+5b}{a^2b^2}, a, b \neq 0$
(c) $\frac{3x-7}{(x+1)(x-1)}, x \neq 1$ **(d)** $\frac{x-9}{(x+3)^2}, x \neq -3$
(e) $\frac{2(x-2)}{(x+4)(x-1)(x-3)}, x \neq -4, 1\ 3$
(f) $\frac{5}{(x-2)(x-3)(x+3)}, x \neq \pm 3, 2$
(g) $\frac{x}{2y}, x \neq 0, -2y, y \neq 0$
(h) $\frac{6}{(x+3)(x-1)(x+1)}, x \neq \pm 1, -3$
(i) $\frac{3}{(x+1)(x-2)}, x \neq -1, 2, -3$
(j) $\frac{-6b}{(a+b)(a-b)}, a \neq 0, b, b \neq 0$

53. **(a)** $x = \frac{-3}{2}, \frac{5}{2}$ **(b)** $x = \frac{-5}{3}, \frac{1}{3}$

54. **(a)** $x = 4, 7$ **(b)** $x = \frac{-1+\sqrt{7}}{3}, \frac{-1-\sqrt{7}}{3}$
(c) $x = \pm\frac{1}{3}, 0$ **(d)** $x = \frac{5}{3}$

55. **(a)** Tom: 20.0 m/s, Genna: 25.0 m/s
(b) Tom: 32.5 s, Genna 26 s

56. *Example:* $p(x) = 5x^3 + x + 1$, $q(x) = 2x^2 + x + 3$, $r(x) = x + 6$, degree = 3, 2, 1; exponents are non-negative integers; degree is the highest exponent of the variable

57. *Example:* $p(x) + q(x) = 5x^3 + 2x^2 + 2x + 4$;
$p(x) - r(x) = 5x^3 - 5$; $q(x) * r(x) = 2x^3 + 13x^2 + 9x + 18$

58. **(a)** *Example:* $(x+1)(x^2-x+6)+x-(x+2)$, degree = 3
(b) *Example:* $(x+1)(x-1)(2x+2)+(x-3)-2$, degree = 3
(c) *Example:* $(x^2+x+1)^2+x-(x+2)$, degree = 4

59. **(a)** $4x^4+2x^3-4x^2+3$ **(b)** $-2x(x+1)$
(c) $x(-4x^2+9x+14)$
(d) $x(-3x^5+8x^4-5x^3-3x^2+12x)$
(e) $x(11x-8)$ **(f)** $5x(x-4)$

60. **(a)** $x^4-2x^3+7x^2-8x+12$ **(b)** $x(25x^4-14x^2+1)$
(c) $11t^3-20t^2+3t-14$ **(d)** $10x^2-20x-55$
(e) $3x^4+10x^3-14x^2+x+2$
(f) $3a^4+10a^3-13a^2+22a-12$
(g) $x^4-6x^3+13x^2-12x+4$
(h) $x^4-6x^3+x^2+24x+16$

Chapter 4 Review Test, page 387

1. (a) $-1 + i, -5 + 3i, 13, \frac{-3 + 2i}{4 - 2i}$ (b) $37 + 55i$
2. (a) $\frac{4x^2}{-3y}, x, y \neq 0$
   (b) $\frac{4x + 27}{(x + 2)(x - 2)(x + 3)}, x \neq \pm 2, -3$
   (c) $\frac{3b}{a}, a \neq 0, -b, -3b$ (d) $8x^3$
3. (a) i. $\left(\frac{4}{3}, \frac{16}{3}\right)$, maximum; ii. $(-2, -9)$, minimum
   iii. (2.5, 36.625), maximum
   (b) \$64.00
4. 12.5 m/s
5. (a) i. $k < 2$ ii. $k = 2$ iii. $k > 2$
6. Answers will vary. $time = \frac{16}{speed}$; as speed increases, time decreases; as speed decreases, time increases; inverse relation
7. $y = 3x - 4$: line, x-intercept: $\frac{4}{3}$, y-intercept: 4; $y = \frac{1}{3x - 4}$: hyperbola, vertical asymptote $x = \frac{4}{3}$; horizontal asymptote $y = 0$; $D = \{x \mid x \neq \frac{4}{3}, x \in \mathbf{R}\}, R = \{y \mid y \neq 0, y \in \mathbf{R}\}$
8. (a) 54.6 mg (b) undefined
9. Jovanna: 42.3 km/h, Marissa: 47.3 km/h

Cumulative Review Test 2, page 389

1. (a) $D = \mathbf{R}, R = \mathbf{R}$; is a function: each x-value corresponds to a unique y-value
   (b) $D = R, R = \{y \mid y > 0, y \in R\}$; is a function: graph passes vertical line test
   (c) D = (about) $\{x \mid 0.98 \leq x \leq 3.02, x \in \mathbf{R}\}$; $R = \{y \mid -1.8 \leq y \leq 4.8, y \in \mathbf{R}\}$; not a function: fails vertical line test
   (d) $D = \{1, 2, 3, 4\}, R = \{5, 12, 23, 31\}$, not a function: 3 maps onto 12 and 31
   (e) $D = \{-1, 0, 3, 4, 5\}, R = \{2, 4, 5, 6, 9\}$; not a function: 3 maps onto 5 and 6
   (f) $D = \{x \mid x \geq -\frac{5}{2}, x \in \mathbf{R}\}$, range $= \{y \mid y \geq 0, y \in \mathbf{R}\}$; is a function: each x-value corresponds to a unique y-value
   (g) $D = \{x \mid x \leq -3, x \in \mathbf{R}\}, R = \mathbf{R}$; not a function: fails vertical line test
   (h) $D = \{x \mid -3 \leq x \leq 3, x \in \mathbf{R}\}, R = \{y \mid -3 \leq y \leq 3, y \in \mathbf{R}\}$; not a function: fails vertical line test
2. (a) -4 (b) -2 (c) $\frac{2}{3}$ (d) 4
3. (a)
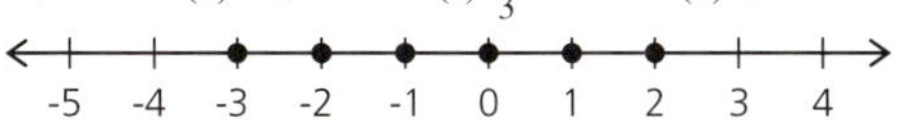

   (b)

   (c)
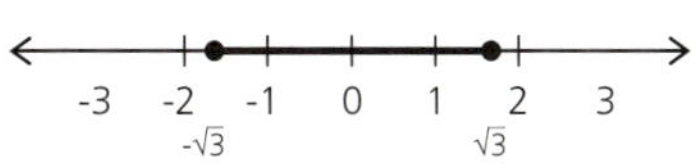

4. $\{x \mid -2 < x < 11, x \in R\}$
5. (a)
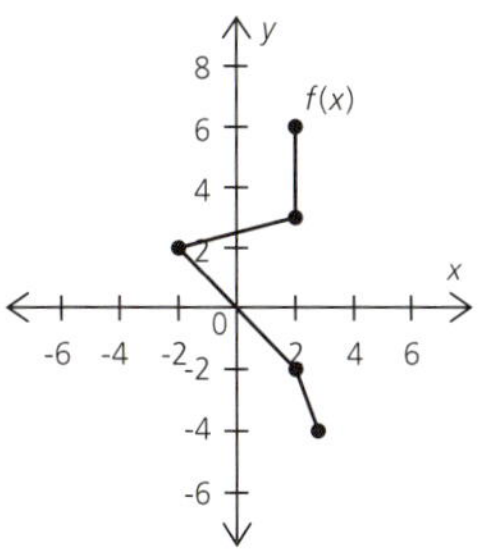

   (b) $f(x)$ not a function: fails vertical line test

6. (a) $(-5, -47)$, $D = \mathbf{R}, R = \{y \mid y \geq -47, y \in \mathbf{R}\}$, parabola opens up; vertex $(-5, -47)$; zeros at -11.8, 1.8; y-intercept: -22
   (b) $\left(-\frac{4}{3}, -\frac{16}{3}\right)$, $D = \mathbf{R}, R = \{y \mid y \geq -\frac{16}{3}, y \in \mathbf{R}\}$, parabola opens up; vertex $\left(-\frac{4}{3}, -\frac{16}{3}\right)$; zeros at -2.67, 0; y-intercept: 0
   (c) $(-3, -14)$, $D = R, R = \{y \mid y \geq -14, y \in \mathbf{R}\}$, parabola opens up; vertex $(-3, -14)$; zeros at -7.6, 1.53; y-intercept: -8
7. (a) g^{-1} is $y = \pm\sqrt{\frac{x + 14}{2} + 9} - 3$, $g(x)$: parabola opens up; vertex $(-3, -32)$; zeros at -7, 1; y-intercept: -14; g^{-1}: parabola opens right; vertex $(-32, -3)$; zeros at -14, 1; y-intercepts -7, 1, domain of $g(x) = \mathbf{R}$, range of $g(x) = \{y \mid y \geq -32, y \in R\}$; domain of g^{-1} is $y = \{x \mid x \geq -32, x \in \mathbf{R}\}$, range of $g^{-1} = \mathbf{R}$
   (b) $g^{-1}(x) = \frac{x^2 - 8}{4}$, $g(x)$: upper branch of parabola opens right, vertex $(-2, 0)$, y-intercept: 2.87; $g^{-1}(x)$: right branch of parabola opens up; vertex $(0, -2)$; zero at 2.87, domain of $g(x) = \{x \mid x \geq -2, x \in \mathbf{R}\}$, range of $g(x) = \{y \mid y \geq 0, y \in \mathbf{R}\}$, domain of $g^{-1}(x) = \mathbf{R}$, range of $g^{-1}(x) = \{y \mid y \geq -2, y \in \mathbf{R}\}$
8. (a) $f(x)$, narrower by $\frac{1}{3}$ (b) $f(x)$, wider by 2
   (c) $f(x)$, 2 units right (d) $f(x)$, 2 units up
   (e) $f(x)$, reflected in x-axis (f) $f(x)$, reflected in y-axis
9. (a)
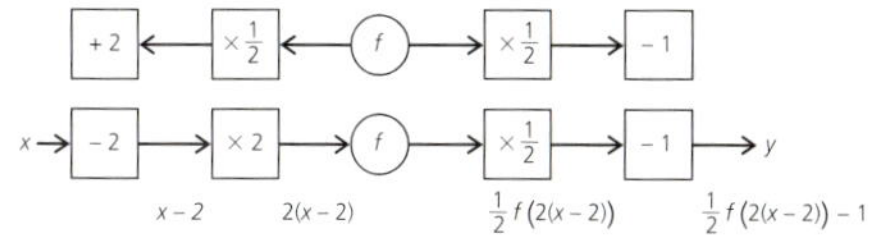

   (b) $D = \{x \mid -1 \leq x \leq 4, x \in \mathbf{R}\}, R = \{y \mid -0.5 \leq y \leq 0.5, y \in \mathbf{R}\}$
   (c) 0.25
   (d)
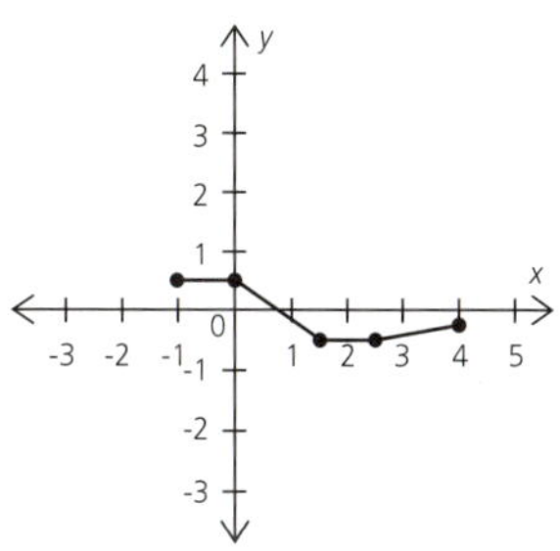

10. (a) $R(x) = -4x^2 + 28x$ (b) $P(x) = -4x^2 + 24x - 12$
    (c) -3 (d) 5.45 or 0.55
    (e) parabola opens down, vertex (3, 24), zeros at 0.6 and 5.47; y-intercept -12
11. 202 500
12. (a) 1 zero, touches x-axis at 1 point
    (b) 2 zeros, intersects x-axis at 2 points
    (c) 1 zero, touches x-axis at 1 point
13. (a) -3 or $\frac{1}{2}$ (b) $\pm 4i$
    (c) $\frac{1 \pm 2\sqrt{2}i}{3}$ (d) $\frac{2 \pm 4\sqrt{6}i}{5}$
14. (a)
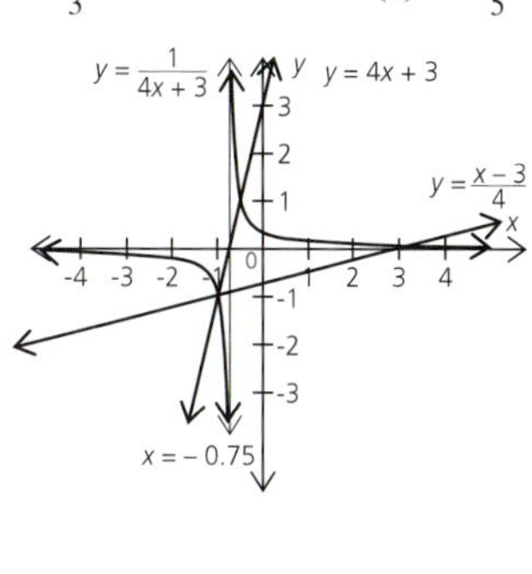

domain of $f(x) = \mathbf{R}$, range of $f(x) = \mathbf{R}$, domain of $\frac{1}{f(x)} = \{x \mid x \neq -\frac{3}{4}, x \in \mathbf{R}\}$, range of $\frac{1}{f(x)} = \{y \mid y \neq 0, y \in \mathbf{R}\}$, domain of $f^{-1}(x) = \mathbf{R}$, range of $f^{-1}(x) = \mathbf{R}$

(b)

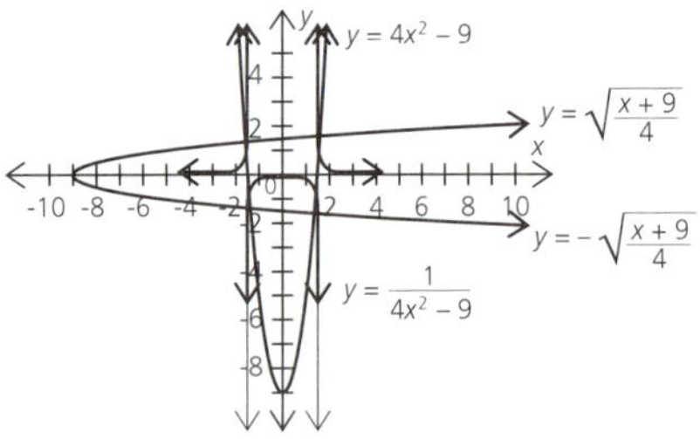

domain of $f(x) = \mathbf{R}$, range of $f(x) = \mathbf{R}$, domain of $\frac{1}{f(x)} = \{x \mid x \neq \pm 1.5, x \in \mathbf{R}\}$, range of $\frac{1}{f(x)} = \{y \mid y \neq 0, y \in \mathbf{R}\}$, domain of $f^{-1}(x) = \{x \mid x \geq -9, x \in \mathbf{R}\}$, range of $f^{-1}(x) = \mathbf{R}$

(c)

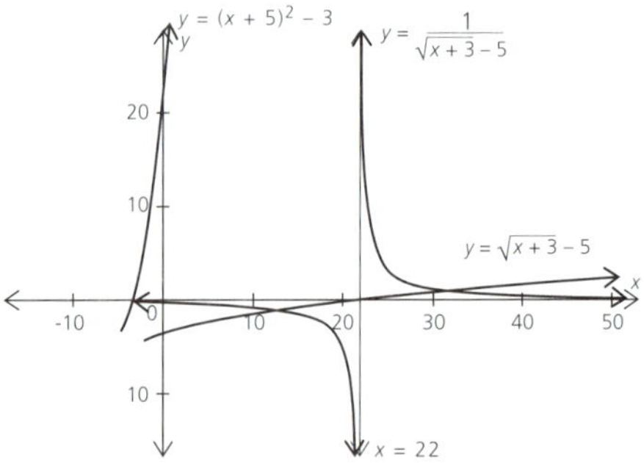

domain of $f(x) = \{x \mid x \geq -3, x \in \mathbf{R}\}$, range of $f(x) = \{y \mid y \geq -5, y \in \mathbf{R}\}$, domain of $\frac{1}{f(x)} = \{x \mid x \neq 22, x \in \mathbf{R}\}$, range of $f(x) = \{y \mid y \neq 0, y \in \mathbf{R}\}$, domain of $f^{-1}(x) = \{x \mid x \geq -5, x \in \mathbf{R}\}$, range of $f^{-1}(x) = \{y \mid y \geq -3, y \in \mathbf{R}\}$

15. **(a)** $x = -2, x = 1$, $D = \{x \mid x \neq 1, x \in \mathbf{R}\}$

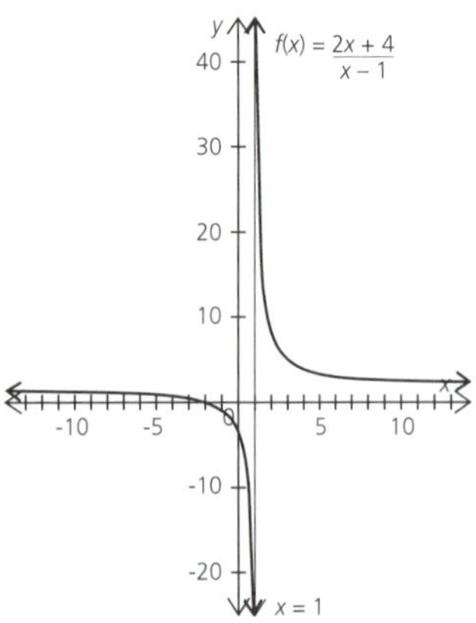

$R = \{y \mid y \neq 2, y \in \mathbf{R}\}$

(b) $x = 0, x = 3$, $D = \{x \mid x \neq 3, x \in \mathbf{R}\}$

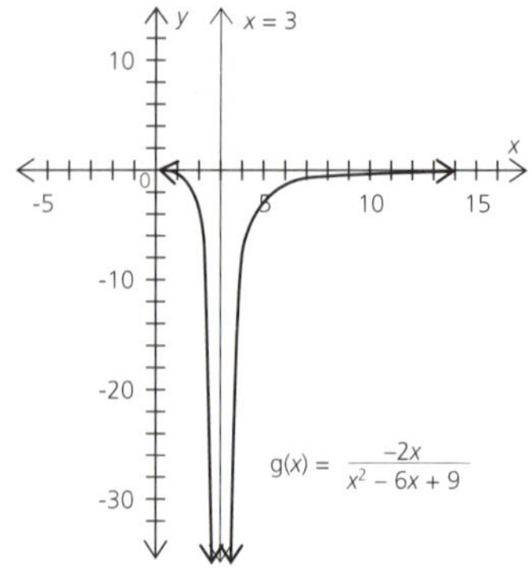

$R = \{y \mid y \neq 0, y \in \mathbf{R}\}$

(c) $x = 6$ or -5, $x = -2$, $D = \{x \mid x \neq -2, x \in \mathbf{R}\}$, $R = \mathbf{R}$

16. **(a)** $8x^4 - x^3 + x^2 - 1$
(b) $2x^4 + 5x^3 - 10x^2 - 20x + 8$
(c) $-13x^3 + 8x^2 - 11x$
(d) $-5x^6 - 6x^5 - 2x^4 + 22x^3 - 4x^2$
(e) $-20x$ **(f)** $2x^3 + 29x^2 - 4x - 252$
(g) $x^4 + 10x^3 + 19x^2 - 30x + 9$

17. **(a)** $\frac{2}{x - 2}, x \neq 2$ **(b)** $\frac{-3p^3}{q}$
(c) $\frac{2(5x - 3)}{(x + 1)^2}, x \neq -1$
(d) $\frac{(a - 5)(a + 2)(a + 4)}{(a - 4)(a^2 - 5a - 15)}, a \neq 4, -2.11, 7.11$
(e) $\frac{(a + 4b)(a - b)(a + 5b)}{(a^2 + 14ab + 20b^2)(a + 2b)}, a \neq -2b, -7 \pm b\sqrt{29};$ $b \neq -\frac{1}{2}a, -\frac{7}{20} \pm \frac{a\sqrt{29}}{20}$
(f) $\frac{29 - 3b}{(b + 7)(4 - 3b)}, b \neq -7, \frac{4}{3}$
(g) $\frac{x + 6}{(x + 4)(x + 3)(x + 4)}, x \neq 4, -3, -4$
(h) $\frac{b^3 + 2ab^2 - 3a^2 - 2ab}{ab(a + b)}, a \neq 0, -b; b \neq 0, -a$

18. **(a)** -16 **(b)** $2i$
(c) 53 **(d)** $-5 - 2i$
(e) $\frac{9}{55} - \frac{49}{55}i$ **(f)** $-297 + 54i$
(g) $-\frac{23}{10} + \frac{7}{10}i$ **(h)** $-\frac{7}{10} - \frac{9}{10}i$

Review of Essential Skills—Part 3

The Trigonometry of Right Triangles, page 399

1. 27 m

2. **(a)** $\sin A = \frac{12}{13}$, $\cos A = \frac{5}{13}$, $\tan A = \frac{12}{5}$
(b) $\sin A = \frac{12}{15}$, $\cos A = \frac{9}{15}$, $\tan A = \frac{12}{9}$
(c) $\sin A = \frac{8}{17}$, $\cos A = \frac{15}{17}$, $\tan A = \frac{8}{15}$
(d) $\sin A = \frac{3}{5}$, $\cos A = \frac{4}{5}$, $\tan A = \frac{3}{4}$

3. **(a)** 4.4 **(b)** 6.8 **(c)** 5.9 **(d)** 26.9

4. **(a)** 38.7° **(b)** 53.8° **(c)** 40.8° **(d)** 64.6°

5. **(a)** 8.7 cm **(b)** 20.3 cm **(c)** 19.7 cm **(d)** 24.3°

6. **(a)** 12.4 cm **(b)** 5.7 cm **(c)** 27.5° **(d)** 46.2°

7. 8.7 m

8. 84.2 m
9. 195.3 m

Trigonometry of Acute Triangles: the Sine Law and the Cosine Law, page 402

1. **(a)** $c = 10.3$ **(b)** $\angle B = 36.2°$ **(c)** $\angle A = 85.1°$
   (d) $c = 12.4$ **(e)** $\angle A = 47.3°$ **(f)** $b = 5.8$
2. **(a)** 16° **(b)** 42.3° **(c)** 23.4
   (d) 13.2 **(e)** 33.1° **(f)** 30.3
3. **(a)** $t = 6.1$ cm, $\angle A = 72.8°$, $\angle C = 48.2°$
   (b) $\angle A = 33.8°$, $\angle B = 42.1°$, $\angle C = 104.1°$
   (c) $\angle F = 31.5°$, $\angle E = 109.5°$, $e = 25.8$
4. 46.6
5. 1068.3 m
6. 12.2 m

Chapter 5

Getting Ready, page 406

1. **(a)** 6.9 cm **(b)** 18.4 cm **(c)** 32.7 cm
2. **(a)** 20.683 **(b)** 5.5481 **(c)** 10.442
   (d) 54.094 **(e)** 2.250 **(f)** 15.880
3. **(a)** 30° **(b)** 30° **(c)** 60°
   (d) 70° **(e)** 75° **(f)** 89°
4. **(a)** 39° **(b)** 56° **(c)** 60°
5. 39.1 m
6. 9.2
7. **(a)** $t_n = 2n - 1$ **(b)** $t_n = 4n - 11$
   (c) $t_n = 9n + 8$ **(d)** $t_n = 0.5n - 3.75$
   (e) $t_n = -\frac{3}{8}n + \frac{5}{4}$ **(f)** $t_n = 180°n - 180°$
   (g) $t_n = 180°n - 315°$ **(h)** $t_n = 60°n - 150°$
8. **(a)** parabola opening up, vertex (0, 2) through (1, 3) and (−1, 3)
   (b) parabola opening up, vertex (0, −3) through (1, −2) and (−1, −2)
   (c) parabola opening up, vertex (0, 0) through (1, 2) and (−1, 2)
   (d) parabola opening up, vertex (0, 0) through (2, 2) and (−2, 2)
   (e) parabola opening up, vertex (1, 0) through (2, 1) and (0, 1)
   (f) parabola opening up, vertex (−2, 0) through (−1, 1) and (−3, 1)
   (g) parabola opening down, vertex (0, 0) through (1, −1) and (−1, −1)
   (h) parabola opening up, vertex (0, 0) through (1, 4) and (−1, 4)
9.

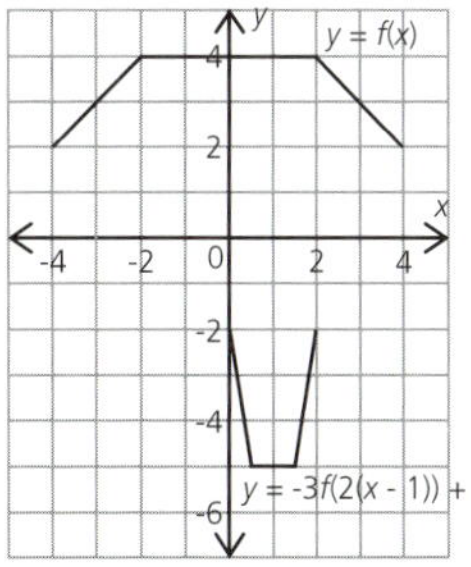

10. **(a)** maximum: (3, 4), minimum: none, zeros: 0, 6
    (b) maximum: none, minimum: $(-1, \frac{-5}{2})$, zeros: −3, 1
    (c) maximum: none, minimum: (3, 3), zeros: none
    (d) maximum: (5, 1), minimum: none, zeros: 3, 7
11. **(a)** $x = \frac{1}{4}$ **(b)** $x = \frac{-1}{3}$ **(c)** $m = \frac{3}{5}$
    (d) $n = \frac{1}{2}$ **(e)** $v = \frac{\sqrt{3}}{2}$ **(f)** $z = \frac{1}{2}$
    (g) $p = \frac{-1}{2}$ **(h)** $x = 12$

Practise, Apply, Solve 5.1, page 413

1. **(a)** iv, quadratic model **(b)** i, periodic function
   (c) v, periodic function **(d)** iii, linear model
   (e) ii, exponential model
2. **(a)** Average monthly temperature in Sudbury is periodic because it generally repeats itself on a monthly basis from year to year. For example, the average temperature in July should be about the same regardless of the year.
   (b) Rabbit and coyote populations depend on each other. As the rabbit population increases, the coyote population, which eats rabbits also increases to the point where the rabbit population starts to decrease. This in turn causes the coyote population to decrease, which then causes the rabbit population to increase.
   (c) The melting of winter snow and the run off of spring rain causes the lake level to rise. The heat of the summer sun increases evaporation and causes the lake level to decrease. This cycle generally repeats itself over a twelve-month period.
   (d) As the earth revolves around the sun, the position of the sun in the morning sky changes with the seasons. In winter, the sun is further south in the Ontario sky, appearing closer to the equator. As the months progress to summer, the sun is further north in the Ontario sky, appearing further from the equator. As the months continue towards winter, the sun moves south in the Ontario sky.
   (e) As a tuning fork vibrates, it moves back and forth from its rest position. The tines of the fork move a fixed distance in one direction, back to rest and a fixed distance in the other direction and back to rest a certain number of times per second. The motion repeats itself in a predictable pattern.
3. (b) and (c) are periodic.
4. **(a)** 3 s; Nolan is increasing his jump height with each jump.
   (b) 2 s; This is the time for one complete jump.
   (c) $H = 2.25$
   (d) 1.75 m, twice the amplitude of the curve added to the minimum height is Nolan's maximum height off of the ground
5. **(a)**

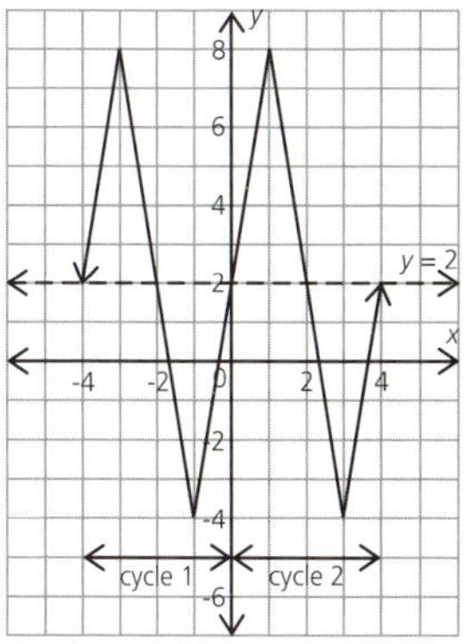

(b)

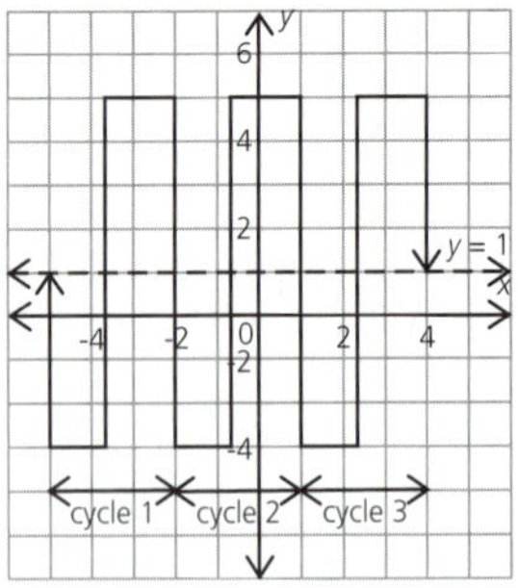

(c)

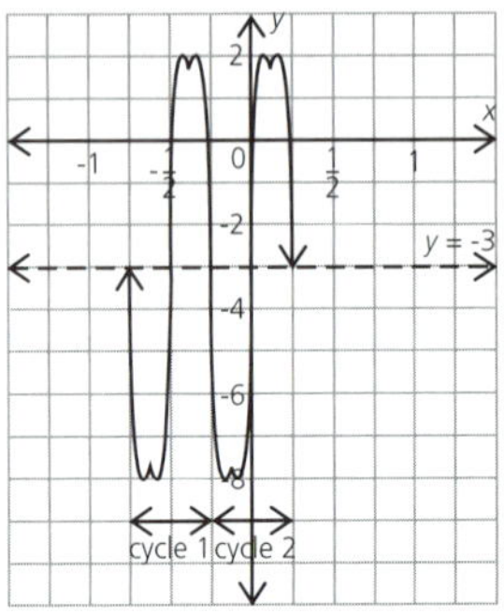

6. **(a)** period: 2, amplitude: 5.5, $y = -2.5$
   (b) period: 4, amplitude: 1, $y = 3$
   (c) period: 180°, amplitude: 3, $y = 9$
7. Answers will vary.
8. Answers will vary.
9. **(a)** The separate parts of the graph represent the wash, spray, rinse and spin cycles.
   (b) 4 min **(c)** 50 L, 10 L, 50 L
   (d) 110 L **(e)** $V = 25$ L **(f)** 25
10. **(a)** maximum: 30 m, minimum: 10 m
    (b) 20 s
    (c) 10 m, radius of the Ferris wheel
    (d) $H = 20$ m
11. The migration of the swallows follows the same pattern every year. The repeated pattern is periodic.
12. **(a)**

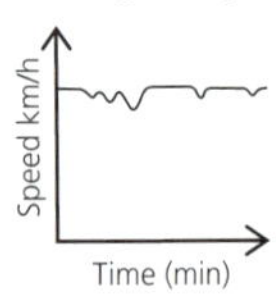

    (b) Add two cycles to the previous graph.
    (c) one lap around the track
13. **(a)** The traffic light goes from one colour to the next following the same pattern of colour and the same time interval for each colour.
    (b) a long green light changes to yellow for a short time and then turns red
    (c) 120 s
    (d) 140 s; shift given graph up two squares on the grid and right 20 s. The Advanced Green block will cover two squares along the y-axis and 20 s along the x-axis and be below the Green light section. Repeat the graph to show two cycles.
14. A specified interval of the independent variable produces specific values of the dependent variable. If the length of the interval of the independent variable is repeated, then the exact value of the dependent variable is also repeated.

Practise, Apply, Solve 5.2, page 422

1. **(a)** terminal arm in second quadrant; related acute angle 45°
   (b) terminal arm in third quadrant; related acute angle 30°
   (c) terminal arm in fourth quadrant; related acute angle 45°
   (d) terminal arm in fourth quadrant; related acute angle 30°
   (e) terminal arm in second quadrant; related acute angle 45°
   (f) terminal arm in first quadrant; related acute angle 30°
   (g) terminal arm in second quadrant; related acute angle 30°
   (h) terminal arm in third quadrant; related acute angle 60°
   (i) terminal arm in second quadrant; related acute angle 75°
   (j) terminal arm in third quadrant; related acute angle 17°
   (k) terminal arm in fourth quadrant; related acute angle 39°
   (l) terminal arm in first quadrant; related acute angle 80°
2. **(a)** 45° **(b)** 30° **(c)** 45° **(d)** 30°
   (e) 45° **(f)** 30° **(g)** 30° **(h)** 60°
   (i) 75° **(j)** 17° **(k)** 39° **(l)** 80°
3. **(a)** terminal arm in first quadrant; 360° counterclockwise + 19° related acute angle
   (b) terminal arm in second quadrant; 450° counterclockwise, + 41° related acute angle of 49°
   (c) terminal arm in second quadrant; 540° clockwise + 5° related acute angle
   (d) terminal arm in first quadrant; 630° clockwise + 10° related acute angle of 80°
   (e) terminal arm in third quadrant; 540° counterclockwise + 53° related acute angle
4. **(a)** yes **(b)** no **(c)** yes **(d)** yes **(e)** no
   (f) yes **(g)** no **(h)** yes **(i)** yes **(j)** no
5. **(a)** 492°, 852° **(b)** 635°, 995° **(c)** 665°, 1025°
   (d) 433°, 793° **(e)** 630°, 990°
6. **(a)** −413°, −773° **(b)** −498°, −858° **(c)** −659°, −1019°
   (d) −540°, −900° **(e)** −552°, −912°
7. **(a)** vi **(b)** i **(c)** ii **(d)** v
   (e) iii **(f)** iv **(g)** viii **(h)** vii
8. **(a)** 173° **(b)** 50° **(c)** 293° **(d)** 185°
   (e) 78° **(f)** 350° **(g)** 135° **(h)** 191°
9. **(a)** 156° **(b)** 215° **(c)** 341° **(d)** 63°
10. **(a)** 1491°, 1851°, 2211° **(b)** −431°, −71°, 289°, 649°
    (c) −843°, −483°, −123° **(d)** 1995°, 2355°, 2715°
11. **(a)** Plot point $(-9, 4)$ on coordinate grid: principal angle is angle between 0° and terminal arm of P
    (b) 24° **(c)** 156°
12. **(a)** Plot point $(7, -24)$ on coordinate grid: principal angle is angle between 0° and terminal arm of P.
    (b) 74° **(c)** 286°
13. **(a)** Plot point $(-5, -3)$ on coordinate grid: principal angle is angle between 0° and terminal arm of P.
    (b) 31° **(c)** 211° **(d)** −149°
14. The right triangle helps to determine what the related acute angle is. You can use the related acute angle as well as the knowledge about what quadrant the angle is situated in to determine the principal angle.
15. –482°, –122°, 238°,

Practise, Apply, Solve 5.3, page 433

1. **(a)** iii **(b)** i **(c)** iv **(d)** ii
2. **(a)** ii **(b)** iii **(c)** iv **(d)** i
3. **(a)** iii **(b)** iv **(c)** ii **(d)** i
4. **(a)** positive **(b)** positive **(c)** negative
   (d) negative **(e)** negative **(f)** negative
   (g) negative **(h)** negative

5. (a) $\sin\theta = \frac{-4}{5}$, $\cos\theta = \frac{-3}{5}$, $\tan\theta = \frac{4}{3}$
(b) $\sin\theta = \frac{4}{5}$, $\cos\theta = \frac{3}{5}$, $\tan\theta = \frac{4}{3}$
(c) $\sin\theta = \frac{12}{13}$, $\cos\theta = \frac{5}{13}$, $\tan\theta = \frac{12}{5}$
(d) $\sin\theta = \frac{5}{13}$, $\cos\theta = \frac{-12}{13}$, $\tan\theta = \frac{5}{-12}$
(e) $\sin\theta = \frac{-24}{25}$, $\cos\theta = \frac{7}{25}$, $\tan\theta = \frac{-24}{7}$
(f) $\sin\theta = \frac{24}{25}$, $\cos\theta = \frac{-7}{25}$, $\tan\theta = \frac{24}{-7}$
(g) $\sin\theta = -1$, $\cos\theta = 0$, $\tan\theta$ undefined
(h) $\sin\theta = 0$, $\cos\theta = -1$, $\tan\theta = 0$

6. (a) 66° (b) 347° (c) 240° (d) 119°

7. (a) (7.2 cos 56°, 7.2 sin 56°)
(b) (7.6 cos 113°, 7.6 sin 113°)
(c) (25.1 cos 293°, 25.1 sin 293°)

9. $\sin\theta = \frac{1}{\sqrt{5}} \doteq 0.447$

10. $\cos\alpha = \frac{-5}{\sqrt{61}} \doteq -0.640$

11. 118.07°, 241.93°

12. –298.07°, –241.93°, 61.93°, 118.07°

13. (a) Plot the points from the table. Refer to section 5.3 for the graph.

θ	–360°	–270°	–180°	–90°	0°
$f(\theta)$	1	0	–1	0	1

θ	90°	180°	270°	360°
$f(\theta)$	0	–1	0	1

(b) maximum:(–360°, 1), (0°, 1), (360°, 1),
minimum: (–180°, –1), (180°, –1)
(c) (–270°, 0), (–90°, 0), (90°, 0), (270°, 0)
(e) $f(\theta) = \cos\theta$ is symmetric about y-axis

14. (a) Plot the points from the table. Refer to section 5.3 for the graph

θ	0°	30°	60°	90°	120°
$f(\theta)$	0	0.6	1.7	—	–1.7

θ	150°	180°	210°	240°
$f(\theta)$	–0.6	0	0.6	1.7

θ	270°	300°	330°	360°
$f(\theta)$	—	–1.7	–0.6	0

(b) (0°, 0), (180°, 0), (360°, 0)
(c) $\tan\theta = \frac{\sin\theta}{\cos\theta}$, function undefined when $\cos\theta = 0$.
$\theta \neq -90° + 180°n, n \in \mathbf{I}$
(d) $\theta = 180°n, n \in \mathbf{I}$
(f) $f(\theta) = \tan\theta$ is symmetric about the origin

15. 134°, 226°, 494°

16. –17°, 197°, 343°

17. (a) $\frac{1}{2}$ (b) 3.6, 14.4

18. (a) –3.5 (b) 1.8, 4.2

19. (a) –4.0 m, 1.5 m, –5.0 m (b) 1.4 s, 7.2 s
(c) 26.7 s

20. Refer to section 5.3 for standard tangent graph; extend graph over given domain; asymptotes: $x = -90°, 90°, 270°, 450°, 630°$; zeros: (0°, 0), (180°, 0), (360°, 0), (540°, 0); –90°, 90°, 270°, 450°, 630°

21. (a) quadrant I: cos θ positive, sin θ positive, tan θ positive; quadrant II: cos θ negative, sin θ negative, tan θ negative; quadrant III: cos θ negative, sin θ negative, tan θ positive; quadrant IV: cos θ positive, sin θ negative, tan θ negative
(b) quadrant I: all positive; quadrant II: sin θ positive; quadrant III: tan θ positive; quadrant IV: cos θ positive
(c) $y = \cos\theta$: shade under curve between 0° and 90° and between 270° and 360°; $y = \sin\theta$: shade under curve between 0° and 180°; $y = \tan\theta$: shade under curve between 0° and 90° and between 180° and 270°.

23. (a) straight line from (0, 0) to (5, 5) to (15, 5) to (25, –5) to (35, –5) to (40, 0)
(b) 40 cm of string; period is 40 cm; perimeter of cross-section of cube and period of graph are both 40 cm
(c) 80 cm of string to go around cube twice; extend graph in (a) for one more cycle
(d) –5 cm, 25 cm

24. $\theta = -315°, -135°, 45°, 225°$

25. (a) $\csc\theta = \frac{1}{\sin\theta}$, $\sec\theta = \frac{1}{\cos\theta}$, $\cot\theta = \frac{1}{\tan\theta}$
(b) $\csc\theta = \frac{r}{y}, y \neq 0$, $\sec\theta = \frac{r}{x}, x \neq 0$, $\cot\theta = \frac{x}{y}, y \neq 0$
(c) (θ, csc θ) = (0°, –), (30°, 2), (60°, 1.2), (90°, 1), (120°, 1.2), (150°, 2), (180°, –), (210°, –2), (240°, –1.2), (270°, –1), (300°, –1.2), (330°, –2), (360°, –)
(θ, sec θ) = (0°, 1), (30°, 1.2), (60°, 2), (90°, –), (120°, –2), (150°, –1.2), (180°, –1), (210°, –1.2), (240°, –2), (270°, –), (300°, 2), (330°, 1.2), (360°, 1)
(θ, cot θ) = (0°, –), (30°, 1.7), (60°, 0.6), (90°, 0), (120°, –0.6), (150°, –1.7), (180°, –), (210°, 1.7), (240°, 0.6), (270°, 0), (300°, –0.6), (330°, –1.7), (360°, –)

$y = \csc\theta$

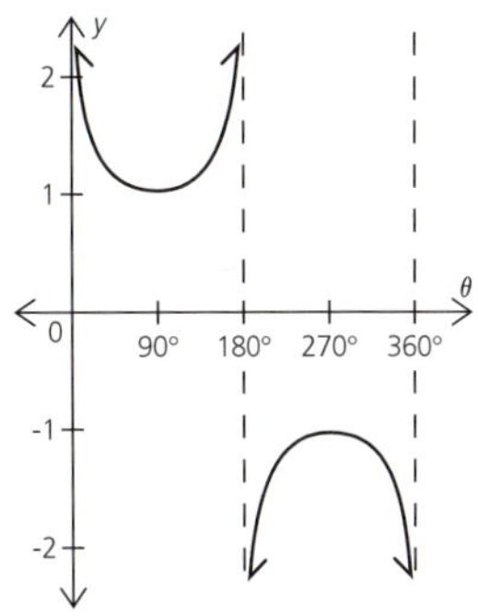

$y = \sec\theta$

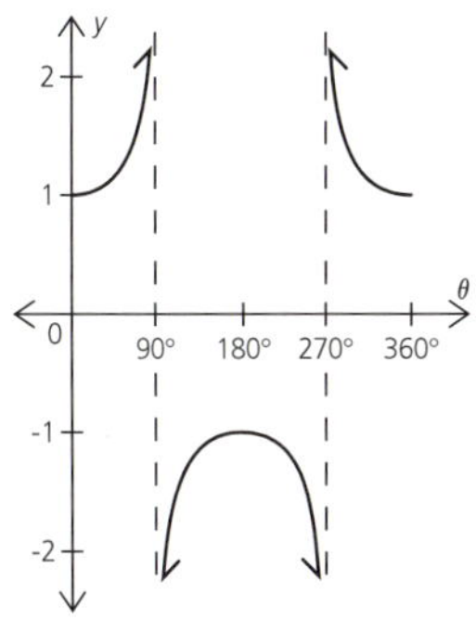

$y = \cot\theta$

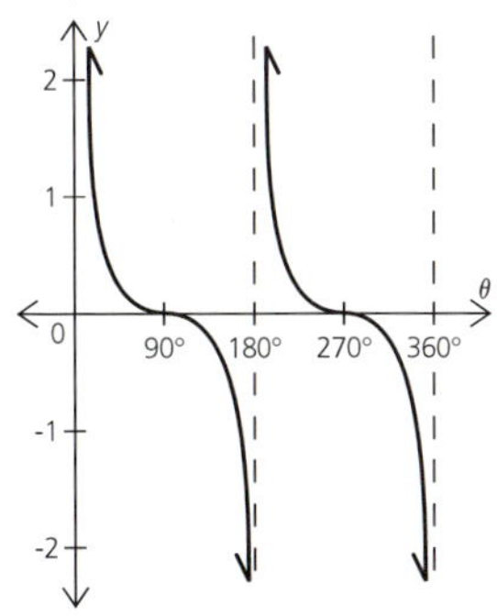

(d) The restrictions are shown as vertical asymptotes.
(e) $y = \csc\theta$: D = $\{\theta \mid \theta = m°, m \in \mathbf{R}, \theta \neq 180°n, n \in \mathbf{I}\}$,
R = $\{y \mid y \leq -1 \text{ or } y \geq 1, y \in \mathbf{R}\}$; $y = \sec\theta$:
D = $\{\theta \mid \theta = m°, \theta \neq 90° + 180°n, m \in \mathbf{R}, n \in \mathbf{I}\}$;
R = $\{y \mid y \leq -1 \text{ or } y \geq 1, y \in \mathbf{R}\}$; $y = \cot\theta$:
D = $\{\theta \mid \theta = m°, \theta \neq 180°n, m \in \mathbf{R}, n \in \mathbf{I}\}$; R = $\mathbf{R}$

Practise, Apply, Solve 5.4, page 442

1. (a) π, 180° (b) $\frac{\pi}{2}$, 90° (c) $-\pi$, $-180°$
   (d) $\frac{-3\pi}{2}$, $-270°$ (e) -2π, $-360°$ (f) $\frac{3\pi}{2}$, 270°
   (g) $\frac{-4\pi}{3}$, $-240°$ (h) $\frac{3\pi}{4}$, 135°
2. For each diagram, extend the terminal arm so that it intersects with the circle. Then, highlight the circle from 0 to this intersection point.
   (a) Highlight unit circle from 0 to π (180°).
   (b) terminal arm at 60° counterclockwise
   (c) terminal arm at 120° counterclockwise
   (d) terminal arm at 240° counterclockwise
   (e) terminal arm at 300° counterclockwise
   (f) terminal arm at 180° clockwise
   (g) terminal arm at 90° clockwise
   (h) terminal arm at 45° clockwise
3. (a) 120° (b) $-300°$ (c) 45°
   (d) $-135°$ (e) 210° (f) $-270°$
   (g) 330° (h) $-810°$
4. (a) rotate counterclockwise to 9 o'clock
   (b) rotate counterclockwise to 11 o'clock
   (c) rotate counterclockwise to 12 o'clock
   (d) rotate counterclockwise to 7 o'clock
   (e) rotate clockwise to between 1 and 2 o'clock
5. (a) $\frac{\pi}{2}$ (b) $\frac{3\pi}{2}$ (c) $-\pi$ (d) $\frac{\pi}{4}$
   (e) $\frac{-3\pi}{4}$ (f) $\frac{\pi}{3}$ (g) $\frac{4\pi}{3}$ (h) $\frac{-2\pi}{3}$
6. (a) terminal arm rotated counterclockwise in 1st quadrant, $\frac{\pi}{4}$
   (b) terminal arm rotated counterclockwise in 2nd quadrant, $\frac{\pi}{3}$
   (c) terminal arm rotated counterclockwise in 4th quadrant, $\frac{\pi}{6}$
   (d) terminal arm rotated clockwise to positive y-axis, no related acute angle
   (e) terminal arm rotated counterclockwise in 3rd quadrant, $\frac{\pi}{4}$
   (f) terminal arm rotated counterclockwise in 4th quadrant, $\frac{\pi}{3}$
7. (a) Graph points $(\theta, f(\theta)) = (-2\pi, 0), \left(\frac{-11\pi}{6}, 0.5\right), \left(\frac{-5\pi}{3}, 0.87\right), \left(\frac{-3\pi}{2}, 1\right), \left(\frac{-4\pi}{3}, 0.87\right), \left(\frac{-7\pi}{6}, 0.5\right), (-\pi, 0), \left(\frac{-5\pi}{6}, -0.5\right), \left(\frac{-2\pi}{3}, -0.87\right), \left(\frac{-\pi}{2}, -1\right), \left(\frac{-\pi}{3}, -0.87\right), \left(\frac{-\pi}{6}, -0.5\right), (0, 0), \left(\frac{\pi}{6}, 0.5\right), \left(\frac{\pi}{3}, 0.87\right), \left(\frac{\pi}{2}, 1\right), \left(\frac{2\pi}{3}, 0.87\right), \left(\frac{5\pi}{6}, 0.5\right), (\pi, 0), \left(\frac{7\pi}{6}, -0.5\right), \left(\frac{4\pi}{3}, -0.87\right), \left(\frac{3\pi}{2}, -1\right), \left(\frac{5\pi}{3}, -0.87\right), \left(\frac{11\pi}{6}, -0.5\right), (2\pi, 0)$
   (b) maximum: $\left(\frac{-3\pi}{2}, 1\right), \left(\frac{\pi}{2}, 1\right)$; minimum: $\left(\frac{-\pi}{2}, -1\right), \left(\frac{3\pi}{2}, -1\right)$
   (c) $\theta = -2\pi, -\pi, 0, \pi, 2\pi$
8. (a) Graph points $(\theta, f(\theta)) = (-2\pi, 0), \left(\frac{-11\pi}{6}, 0.6\right), \left(\frac{-5\pi}{3}, 1.7\right), \left(\frac{-3\pi}{2}, -\right), \left(\frac{-4\pi}{3}, -1.7\right), \left(\frac{-7\pi}{6}, -0.6\right), (-\pi, 0), \left(\frac{-5\pi}{6}, 0.6\right), \left(\frac{-2\pi}{3}, 1.7\right), \left(\frac{-\pi}{2}, -\right), \left(\frac{-\pi}{3}, -1.7\right), \left(\frac{-\pi}{6}, -0.6\right), (0, 0), \left(\frac{\pi}{6}, 0.6\right), \left(\frac{\pi}{3}, 1.7\right), \left(\frac{\pi}{2}, -\right), \left(\frac{2\pi}{3}, -1.7\right), \left(\frac{5\pi}{6}, -0.6\right), (\pi, 0), \left(\frac{7\pi}{6}, 0.6\right), \left(\frac{4\pi}{3}, 1.7\right), \left(\frac{3\pi}{2}, -\right), \left(\frac{5\pi}{3}, -1.7\right), \left(\frac{11\pi}{6}, -0.6\right), (2\pi, 0)$
   (b) maximum: $(-2\pi, 1), (0, 1), (2\pi, 1)$;. minimum: $(-\pi, -1), (\pi, -1)$
   (c) $\theta = \frac{-3\pi}{2}, \frac{-\pi}{2}, \frac{\pi}{2}, \frac{3\pi}{2}$
9. (a) Graph points $(\theta, f(\theta)) = (-2\pi, 0), \left(\frac{-11\pi}{6}, 0.6\right), \left(\frac{-5\pi}{3}, 1.7\right), \left(\frac{-3\pi}{2}, -\right), \left(\frac{-4\pi}{3}, -1.7\right), \left(\frac{-7\pi}{6}, -0.6\right), (-\pi, 0), \left(\frac{-5\pi}{6}, 0.6\right), \left(\frac{-2\pi}{3}, 1.7\right), \left(\frac{-\pi}{2}, -\right), \left(\frac{-\pi}{3}, -1.7\right), \left(\frac{-\pi}{6}, -0.6\right), (0, 0), \left(\frac{\pi}{6}, 0.6\right), \left(\frac{\pi}{3}, 1.7\right), \left(\frac{\pi}{2}, -\right), \left(\frac{2\pi}{3}, -1.7\right), \left(\frac{5\pi}{6}, -0.6\right), (\pi, 0), \left(\frac{7\pi}{6}, 0.6\right), \left(\frac{4\pi}{3}, 1.7\right), \left(\frac{3\pi}{2}, -\right), \left(\frac{5\pi}{3}, -1.7\right), \left(\frac{11\pi}{6}, -0.6\right), (2\pi, 0)$
   (b) $\frac{\pi}{2} + \pi n, -2 \le n \le 1, n \in \mathbf{I}$
   (c) $-2\pi, -\pi, 0, \pi, 2\pi$
10. (a) Refer to Key Ideas 5.3 for graph of standard sine curve; extend domain from -2π to 2π.
    (b) Extend domain of sine curve from $-180°$ to 540°.
11. (a) Refer to Key Ideas 5.3 for graph of standard cosine curve.
    (b) Extend domain of cosine curve from $-\pi$ to 3π.
12. (a) Refer to Key Ideas 5.3 for graph of standard tangent curve; extend domain from $-180°$ to 180°.
    (b) Extend domain of tangent curve from $-\pi$ to $\frac{3\pi}{2}$.
13. (a) $-150°, -30°, 210°, 330°$
    (b) $-34°, -326°, 34°, 326°$
    (c) $-94°, -274°, 86°, 266°$
14. (a) 1.1, 2.1, 8.4, 7.3
    (b) -2.1, 2.1, 4.2, 8.4
    (c) -1.3, 1.8, 4.9, 8.1
15. (a)

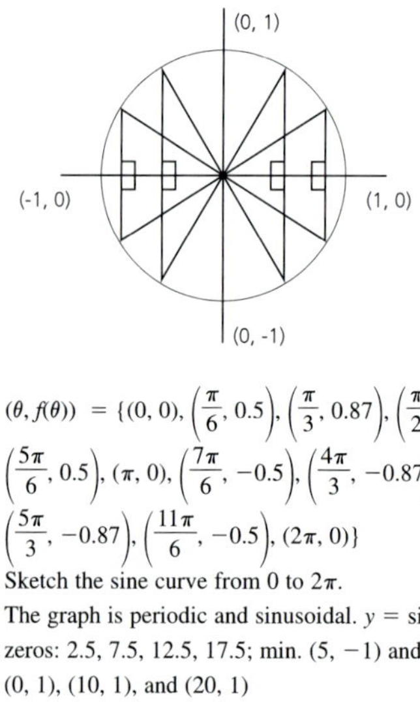

    (b) $(\theta, f(\theta)) = \{(0, 0), \left(\frac{\pi}{6}, 0.5\right), \left(\frac{\pi}{3}, 0.87\right), \left(\frac{\pi}{2}, 1\right), \left(\frac{2\pi}{3}, 0.87\right), \left(\frac{5\pi}{6}, 0.5\right), (\pi, 0), \left(\frac{7\pi}{6}, -0.5\right), \left(\frac{4\pi}{3}, -0.87\right), \left(\frac{3\pi}{2}, -1\right), \left(\frac{5\pi}{3}, -0.87\right), \left(\frac{11\pi}{6}, -0.5\right), (2\pi, 0)\}$
    (c) Sketch the sine curve from 0 to 2π.
    (d) The graph is periodic and sinusoidal. $y = \sin\theta$
16. (a) zeros: 2.5, 7.5, 12.5, 17.5; min. $(5, -1)$ and $(15, -1)$; max. (0, 1), (10, 1), and (20, 1)
    (b) 10 s (c) -1 m (d) 4 s
17. (a) $(T, D) = (0, 0.5), (1, -0.2), (2, -0.3), (3, 0.5), (4, -0.1), (5, -0.4), (6, 0.4), (7, 0.1), (8, -0.5), (9, 0.3)$
    (b) Plot the points in (a).
    (c) The function repeats itself about every 3.1 s.
    (d) The amplitude and the displacement from rest are the same.
18. The interval over which periodic phenomena repeat themselves can be the number of degrees of rotation of a point around a circle or it can be measured in terms of the actual circumference of the circle, which is a real number.

19. **(a)** clockwise **(b)** 6 s

(c) (time(s), small) = (0, 0), (0.5, 1), (1, 0), (1.5, −1), (2, 0), (2.5, 1), (3, 0), (3.5, −1), (4, 0), (4.5, 1), (5, 0), (5.5, −1), (6, 0), (6.5, 1), (7, 0), (7.5, −1), (8, 0), (8.5, 1), (9, 0), (9.5, −1), (10, 0), (10.5, 1), (11, 0), (11.5, 1), (12, 0)
(time(s), large) = (0, 0), (1.5, 3), (3, 0), (4.5, −3), (6, 0), (7.5, 3), (9, 0), (10.5, −3), (12, 0)

(d) 2.8 m **(e)** 0.8 m **(f)** 0 m

Practice 5.5, page 446

(a) Graph resembles diagram on page 428, with 45° intervals.
(b) Graph resembles cos diagram on page 429, with axis extended to 720°.
(c) See tan graph on page 429.
(d) Graph resembles diagram on page 428, with axis extended back to −360°.
(e) Graph resembles cos diagram on page 429, with intervals in radians.
(f) Graph resembles tan diagram on page 429, with $\frac{\pi}{4}$ intervals to 3π.
(g) Graph resembles diagram on page 428, with axis from -2π to 2π.
(h) Graph resembles diagram on page 428, with axis from -4π to 4π.

Practise, Apply, Solve 5.6, page 455

1. **(a)** shifted up two units
(b) two cycles of the graph where $y = \sin\theta$ has one
(c) vertically stretched by factor of 2
(d) vertically stretched by factor of 2, reflected in θ-axis

2. **(a)** vertical compression by factor of $\frac{1}{2}$
(b) horizontal expansion by factor of 2
(c) vertical shift upward by $\frac{1}{2}$
(d) vertical compression by factor of $\frac{1}{2}$ and reflection about θ-axis

3. **(a)** 120° **(b)** 1440° **(c)** 60°
(d) 72° **(e)** 240° **(f)** 1080°
(g) 90° **(h)** 360° **(i)** 540°

4. **(a)** $\frac{\pi}{2}$ **(b)** $\frac{\pi}{3}$ **(c)** $\frac{6\pi}{5}$
(d) 1 **(e)** 5π **(f)** 3π
(g) $\frac{\pi}{3}$ **(h)** $\frac{3\pi}{2}$

5. **(a)** ii **(b)** iii **(c)** i

6. **(a)** ii **(b)** iii **(c)** i

7. **(a)** 3, 180°, 30°, 1 **(b)** 5, 120°, −15°, −2
(c) 2, 1080°, −45°, 2 **(d)** $\frac{1}{2}$, 720°, 15°, −3
(e) $-4, \frac{\pi}{3}, -\frac{\pi}{18}, 1$ **(f)** $3, \frac{\pi}{2}, \frac{\pi}{2}, 2$

8. **(a)** zeros: none, min. at (90°, 1), max. at (270°, 3), axis of symmetry at $y = 2$
(b) zeros: none, min. at (270°, −2.5), max. at (90°, −1.5), axis of symmetry at $y = -2$
(c) zeros: 0 and 360°, min. at (180°, −2), axis of symmetry at $y = 0$

9. **(a)** zeros: none, min. at (0, 1) and $(2\pi, 1)$, max. at $(\pi, 3)$, axis of symmetry at $y = 2$
(b) zeros: none, min. at $(\pi, -2.5)$, max. at (0, −1.5) and $(2\pi, -1.5)$, axis of symmetry at $y = -2$
(c) zeros: π, min. at (0, −2), max. at (0, 2), axis of symmetry at $y = 0$

10. **(a)** zeros: 0, 180°, 360°, asymptotes at 90° and 270° (standard tangent curve reflected in x-axis)
(b) zeros: 0, 90°, 180°, 270°, 360°, asymptotes at 45°, 135°, 225°, and 315°
(c) zeros: 270°, y-intercept: 1, asymptotes: 180°

11. **(a)** −2.5 **(b)** −1.0 **(c)** 0.0 **(d)** −1.0

12. **(a)** −1.0 **(b)** −1.0 **(c)** −3.0 **(d)** −2.4

13. **(a)** −1.5 **(b)** −3.0 **(c)** 6.5 **(d)** 21.9

14. **(a)** alike: both sinusoidal, have 360° period, amplitude of 1, maximum value of 1, and minimum value of −1; the axis of each curve is $y = 0$. Different: they appear to start at different places.
(b) $\sin\theta = \cos\left(\theta - \frac{\pi}{2}\right)$ **(c)** $\cos\theta = \sin\left(\theta + \frac{\pi}{2}\right)$

15. zeros: $\frac{\pi}{4}, \frac{5\pi}{4}$, min. $\left(\frac{7\pi}{4}, -2\right)$, max. $\left(\frac{3\pi}{4}, 2\right)$, axis of symmetry $y = 0$, y-intercept −1

16. $y = 2\sin 3\left(\theta - \frac{\pi}{2}\right) - 2$

17. $y = -3\cos\frac{1}{2}\left(\theta + \frac{2\pi}{3}\right) + 1$

18. **(a)** axis of symmetry $y = 1$, min. (−195°, −2), (−15°, −2), (165°, −2), (345°, −2), max. (−285°, 4), (−105°, 4), (75°, 4), (255°, 4), passing through points $(x, 1)$ where x = 330°, −240°, −150°, −60°, 30°, 120°, 210°, 300°
(b) axis of symmetry $y = -2$, min. (−315°, −7), (−195°, −7), (−−75°, −7), (45°, −7), (165°, −7), (285°, −7), max. (−255°, 3), (−135°, 3), (−15°, 3), (105°, 3), (225°, 3), (345°, 3), passing through points $(x, -2)$ where x = −345°, −285°,−225°, −165, −105°, −45°, 15°, 75°, 135°, 195°, 255°, 315°
(c) axis of symmetry $y = 2$, min. (225°, 0), max. (−315°, 4), y-intercept 1.5
(d) axis of symmetry $y = -3$, min. (−345°, 0), max. (15°, −2.5), passing through (180°, −3) and (−180°, −3)

19. **(a)** axis of symmetry $y = 1$, min. $\left(\frac{5\pi}{18}, -3\right), \left(\frac{11\pi}{18}, -3\right), \left(\frac{17\pi}{18}, -3\right), \left(\frac{23\pi}{18}, -3\right), \left(\frac{29\pi}{18}, -3\right), \left(\frac{35\pi}{18}, -3\right)$, max. $\left(\frac{\pi}{9}, 5\right), \left(\frac{4\pi}{9}, 5\right), \left(\frac{7\pi}{9}, 5\right), \left(\frac{10\pi}{9}, 5\right), \left(\frac{13\pi}{9}, 5\right), \left(\frac{16\pi}{9}, 5\right)$
(b) axis of symmetry $y = 2$, min. $\left(\frac{3\pi}{8}, -1\right), \left(\frac{7\pi}{8}, -1\right), \left(\frac{11\pi}{8}, -1\right), \left(\frac{15\pi}{4}, -1\right)$, max. $\left(\frac{\pi}{8}, 5\right), \left(\frac{5\pi}{8}, 5\right), \left(\frac{9\pi}{8}, 5\right), \left(\frac{13\pi}{8}, 5\right)$

20. $\cos\theta$: stretched vertically by factor of 3, reflected in x-axis, moved up one unit on the y-axis, horizontally shifted $\frac{\pi}{8}$ units right, period: 180°; $\sin\theta$: vertically stretched by factor of 3, reflected in x-axis, moved up one unit on y-axis, period: 180°, horizontal phase shift of $\frac{\pi}{4}$ units right

21. **(a)** period: $\frac{6}{5}$, represents the time between one beat of a person's heart and the next beat
(b) 50 beats/min
(c) axis of symmetry $p(t)$ = 100 mm, min. (0, 80), $\left(\frac{6}{5}, 80\right), \left(\frac{12}{5}, 80\right), \left(\frac{18}{5}, 80\right), \left(\frac{24}{5}, 80\right)$, (6, 80), max. $\left(\frac{3}{5}, 120\right), \left(\frac{9}{5}, 120\right)$, (3, 120), $\left(\frac{21}{5}, 120\right), \left(\frac{27}{5}, 120\right)$
(d) range: $80 \leq P(t) \leq 120$; lowest blood pressure is 80 and the highest blood pressure is 120

22. **(a)** (t, T) = (0, 32), (1, 28.9), (2, 20.5), (3, 9), (4, −2.5), (5, −10.9), (6, −14), (7, −10.9), (8, −2.5), (9, 9), (10, 20.5), (11, 28.9), (12, 32), (13, 28.9)
(b) Plot the points in (a). Let x-axis represent time and y-axis represent temperature. axis of symmetry $T = 9$, min. (6, −14), max. (0, 32) and (12, 32)

(c) maximum = axis + amplitude, minimum = axis − amplitude
(d) 12
(e) stretch vertically by factor of 23, vertical shift: 9 units up, period: 12, maximum: 32°, minimum: −14°

23. **(a)** The number of hours of daylight increases to a maximum and decreases to a minimum in a regular cycle as the Earth revolves around the sun.
(b) Mar. 21: 12 h, Sept. 21: 12 h, spring and fall equinox
(c) The sine function is shifted right 80 days.
(d) June 21: 16 h, Dec. 21: 8 h, longest and shortest day of year
(e) 12 is the axis of the curve representing half the distance between the maximum and minimum hours of daylight.
(f) Let x-axis represent the day of the year and y-axis represent the number of hours of daylight. axis of symmetry $D(t) = 12$, min. (0, 8) and (360, 8), max. (182.5, 16)
(g) maximum: 16 h in late June, minimum: 8 h in late Dec. or early Jan.
(h) Mar. 21, Sept. 21

24. **(a)** Feb. 8: −10.5°, May 15: 22.3°
(b) Let the x-axis represent the day of the year and the y-axis represent the angle of the sunset. axis of symmetry $P(t) = 0°$, min. (0, −28°) and (365, −28°), max. (180, 28°)
(c) maximum: 28°, minimum: −28°
(d) 365; 365 days in a year
(e) horizontal shift to the right 81 days, representing the spring equinox around June 22

25. **(a)** a: vertical stretch by factor of a, b: horizontal phase shift by b units, shift left for $b < 0$, shift right for $b > 0$, k: horizontal stretch by factor of $\frac{1}{k}$, d: vertical translation of d units, shift up $d > 0$, shift down $d < 0$
(b) Use sketch of $y = \sin\theta$ as starting graph. Horizontally compress by factor of $\frac{1}{2}$, shift left 45°, vertically expand by factor of 3, and shift vertically up 1.
(c) axis of symmetry $y = 1$, min. (90°, −2) and (270°, −2), max. (0°, 4) and (180°, 4) and (360°, 4)

26. Use graphing calculator to graph both graphs. When the rabbit population is high, the fox population increases causing a decrease in the rabbit population. The decrease in rabbits causes a corresponding decrease in fox. As the number of fox decrease there is a corresponding increase in the number of rabbits. This starts the cycle over again.

Practise, Apply, Solve 5.7, page 463

For questions 1–4, plot the points from the table. The axis of symmetry is at y = 0.

1. **(a)** min. (−90°, −3) and (270°, −3), max. (90°, 3), zeros −180°, 0°, 180°, and 360°; $y = 3\sin\theta$
(b) min. $\left(\frac{\pi}{2}, -2\right)$, max. $\left(\frac{-\pi}{2}, 2\right), \left(\frac{3\pi}{2}, 2\right)$, zeros $-\pi, 0, \pi, 2\pi$; $y = -2\sin\theta$

2. **(a)** min. (90°, −1) and (90°, −1), max. (0°, 1) and (180°, 1), zeros −45°, 45°, 135°; $y = \cos 2\theta$
(b) min. $(-2\pi, -1)$ and $(2\pi, -1)$, max. (0, 1) and $(4\pi, 1)$, zeros $-\pi, \pi, 3\pi$; $y = \cos\frac{\theta}{2}$

3. **(a)** min. (300°, −1), max. (120°, 1), zeros 30°, 210°, 390°; $y = \sin(\theta - 30°)$
(b) min. (225°, −1), max. (45°, 1), zeros −45°, 135°, and 315°; $y = \sin(\theta + 45°)$

4. **(a)** min. $\left(\frac{4\pi}{3}, -1\right)$, max. $\left(\frac{\pi}{3}, 1\right), \left(\frac{7\pi}{3}, 1\right)$, zeros $\frac{5\pi}{6}, \frac{11\pi}{6}$; $y = \cos\left(\theta - \frac{\pi}{3}\right)$
(b) min. $\left(\frac{5\pi}{6}, -1\right)$, max. $\left(\frac{-\pi}{6}, 1\right)$ and $\left(\frac{11\pi}{6}, 1\right)$, zeros $\frac{\pi}{3}, \frac{4\pi}{3}$; $y = \cos\left(\theta + \frac{\pi}{6}\right)$

5. $y = \sin 2(\theta + 30°)$

6. $y = 5$

7. $y = -9$

8. **(a)** $y = 2\sin 2(\theta + 45°)$ **(b)** $y = 3\sin 2\theta + 2$
(c) $y = 2.5\sin\frac{1}{2}(\theta - 180°) + 2.5$
(d) $y = 2\sin 2(\theta + 90°) + 4$ **(e)** $y = 3\sin 4(\theta - 22.5°) - 2$

9. **(a)** $y = 2\cos 2\theta$ **(b)** $y = 3\cos 2(\theta - 45°) + 2$
(c) $y = -2.5\cos\frac{\theta}{2} + 2.5$ **(d)** $y = 2\cos 2(\theta + 45°) + 4$
(e) $y = -3\cos 4\theta - 2$

10. **(a)** $y = 3\sin\left(\theta - \frac{\pi}{4}\right) - 1$ **(b)** $y = \frac{1}{2}\sin 2\left(\theta + \frac{\pi}{3}\right) + 2$
(c) $y = 2\sin 4\left(\theta - \frac{\pi}{6}\right) + 3$ **(d)** $y = -2\sin\frac{1}{2}\left(\theta - \frac{\pi}{8}\right) - 3$
(e) $y = \frac{-3}{4}\sin\frac{2}{3}\left(\theta - \frac{\pi}{2}\right) - 2$

11. $y = \sin k\theta$ has the same graph as $y = \cos k\left(\theta - \frac{\pi}{2k}\right)$.

12. **(a)** $y = 3\cos\left(\theta - \frac{3\pi}{4}\right) - 1$ **(b)** $y = \frac{1}{2}\cos 2\left(\theta + \frac{\pi}{12}\right) + 2$
(c) $y = 2\cos 4\left(\theta - \frac{7\pi}{24}\right) + 3$ **(d)** $y = -2\cos\frac{1}{2}\left(\theta - \frac{9\pi}{8}\right) - 3$
(e) $y = \frac{-3}{4}\cos\frac{2}{3}\left(\theta - \frac{5\pi}{4}\right) - 2$

13. $d(t) = 55\cos\frac{\pi}{30}(t - 5)$ or $d(t) = 55\sin\frac{\pi}{30}(t + 10)$

14. **(a)** Plot the points given. Let x-axis represent time and y-axis represent elevation.
(b) sinusoidal model
(c) $e(t) = 19.91\cos\frac{\pi}{12}(t - 2) + 23.04$
(d) This equation cannot be used to evaluate the present day elevation of the sun because its domain is $0 \le t \le 24$.
(e) between 6 A.M. and 7 A.M. and between 10 P.M. and 11 P.M.

15. **(a)** Plot the points given. Let x-axis represent month and y-axis represent temperature.
(b) sinusoidal model
(c) $T(t) = -17.8\cos\frac{\pi}{6}t - 0.8$
(e) −16.22°C

16. **(a)** Plot the points given. Let x-axis represent time and y-axis represent depth; $D(t) = -6\cos\frac{\pi}{6}t + 11.5$
(c) 7.3 m
(d) 1:24 A.M., 10:36 A.M., 1:24 P.M., and 10:36 P.M.

17. **(a)** The respiratory cycle is an example of a periodic function because we inhale, rest, exhale, rest, inhale, and so on, in a cyclical pattern.
(b) Plot the points given. Let x-axis represent time and y-axis represent velocity.
(c) The equation is almost an exact fit on the scatter plot.
(d) 0 L/s
(e) $t = 0.6$ s and 2.4 s

18. Plot the points for each city, as given, on the same grid. Let x-axis represent time in months and y-axis represent temperature; Athens: $T(t) = -10.5\cos\frac{\pi}{6}t + 22.5$, Lisbon: $T(t) = -7\cos\frac{\pi}{6}t + 20$, Moscow: $T(t) = -16\cos\frac{\pi}{6}t + 7$

19. **(a)** $h(t) = -16.5\cos\frac{\pi}{60}t + 18.5$
(b) 30.2 m **(c)** 1 min, 3 min

20. **(a)** $a = \frac{\text{maximum} - \text{minimum}}{2}$
(b) period $= \frac{2\pi}{k}$ or $= \frac{360°}{k}$
(c) Determine the horizontal distance the typical starting point for

the graph is from the vertical axis. If to the right, $b < 0$; if to the left, $b > 0$.

(d) $d = \frac{\text{maximum} + \text{minimum}}{2}$

21. **(a)** $H(d) = -25 \cos \frac{1}{25}d + 25$
(b) 34.19 cm **(c)** 450 cm
(d) The driver moves in a continuous way meaning no spinning of the tires or skidding to a stop.

Practise, Apply, Solve 5.8, page 474

1. **(a)** $\frac{\pi}{2}$ **(b)** $\frac{3\pi}{2}$ **(c)** $\frac{\pi}{6}, \frac{5\pi}{6}$ **(d)** $\frac{7\pi}{6}, \frac{11\pi}{6}$

2. **(a)** $0, 2\pi$ **(b)** π **(c)** $\frac{\pi}{3}, \frac{5\pi}{3}$ **(d)** $\frac{2\pi}{3}, \frac{4\pi}{3}$

3. **(a)** two possible solutions
(b) quadrants I and II **(c)** 60° **(d)** 60°, 120°

4. **(a)** two possible solutions
(b) quadrants II and III **(c)** 30° **(d)** 150°, 210°

5. **(a)** two possible solutions
(b) quadrants I and III **(c)** 1.22 **(d)** 1.22, 4.36

6. **(a)** 40.5°, 139.5° **(b)** 36.9°, 323.1° **(c)** 56.3°, 236.3°
(d) 8.6°, 171.4° **(e)** 36.9°, 323.1° **(f)** 130.9°, 229.1°

7. **(a)** 0.44, 2.70 **(b)** 1.41, 4.87 **(c)** 1.17, 4.31
(d) 3.67, 5.76 **(e)** 2.58, 5.72 **(f)** 2.43, 3.85

8. **(a)** 45°, 225° **(b)** 45°, 135° **(c)** 30°, 330°
(d) 240°, 300° **(e)** 135°, 225° **(f)** 60°, 240°

9. **(a)** 210.0°, 330.0° **(b)** 132.8°, 228.2° **(c)** 56.3°, 236.3°
(d) 221.8°, 318.2° **(e)** 78.5°, 281.5° **(f)** 116.6°, 296.6°

10. **(a)** There are two solutions unless the solution is at a minimum.
(b) 53.1°, 306.9°

11. **(a)** 0.52, 2.62 **(b)** 0.52, 5.76
(c) 1.05, 5.24 **(d)** 3.67, 5.76

12. **(a)** 0.4, 1.2, 3.5, 4.3
(b) 0.13, 1.70, 3.27, 4.84, 0.65, 2.23, 3.80, 5.37
(c) 1.40, 3.49, 5.59, 1.75, 3.84, 5.93
(d) 0.59, 2.16, 3.73, 5.30, 0.98, 2.55, 4.12, 5.69
(e) 1.05, 2.09, 4.19, 5.23
(f) 1.05

13. min. $\left(\frac{3\pi}{4}, -1\right)$ and $\left(\frac{7\pi}{4}, -1\right)$, max. $\left(\frac{\pi}{4}, 1\right)$ and $\left(\frac{5\pi}{4}, 1\right)$, zeros $0, \frac{\pi}{2}, \pi, \frac{3\pi}{2}, 2\pi$, solutions are 1.96, 5.11, 2.75, 5.89

14. Answers will vary.

15. **(a)** 8 m **(b)** 15 m **(c)** 6 s
(d) 1 m **(e)** 18 s **(f)** 48 s

16. **(a)** 25 cm
(b) 10.6°, 61.4°, 82.6°, 133.4°, 154.6°, 205.4°, 226.6°, 277.4°, 298.6°, 349.4°
(c) 28.6°, 43.4°, 100.6°, 115.4°, 172.6°, 187.4°, 244.6°, 259.4°, 316.6°, 331.4°
(d) 15 s

17. **(a)** 194.5°, 345.5° **(b)** 78.5°, 281.5°
(c) 66.8°, 246.8°
(d) 105.0°, 165.0°, 285.0°, 345.0°
(e) 60.0°, 180.0°, 300.0° **(f)** 22.6°
(g) 60.0°, 300.0° **(h)** 60.0°

18. **(a)** 3.48, 5.94 **(b)** 6.28
(c) 0.23, 1.80, 3.37, 4.94,
(d) 1.22, 1.92, 3.32, 4.01, 5.41, 6.11
(e) 2.09, 4.19 **(f)** 1.77, 4.91
(g) 4.71 **(h)** 0.32, 3.97

19. **(a)** 37.3 m/s **(b)** 19.8°, 70.2°

20. **(a)** maximum: May, minimum: Nov. / Dec.
(b) Sept. and Dec. **(c)** Mar. and June

21. **(a)** Plot the points given.
(c) $T(t) = 13.5 \sin \frac{\pi}{6}(t - 4.5) + 6.8$
(d) May and Sept.

22. **(a)** Plot the points from the table. Let x-axis represent month and y-axis represent daily mean temperature.
(c) $H(t) = -102.7 \cos \frac{\pi}{6}t + 175.3$
(d) maximum: June, minimum: Dec.
(e) The model is reasonable but not exact. Individual results vary up to 10%.

23. **(a)** two possible solutions
(b) 1.05, 5.24

24. $\frac{\pi}{4}, \frac{5\pi}{4}$

25. 25°, 85°, 205°, 265°

Practice 5.9, page 480

1. $y \doteq 20 \sin (6.283x) + 100$

Chapter 5, Review and Practice, page 485

1. It has a repeating part.

2.

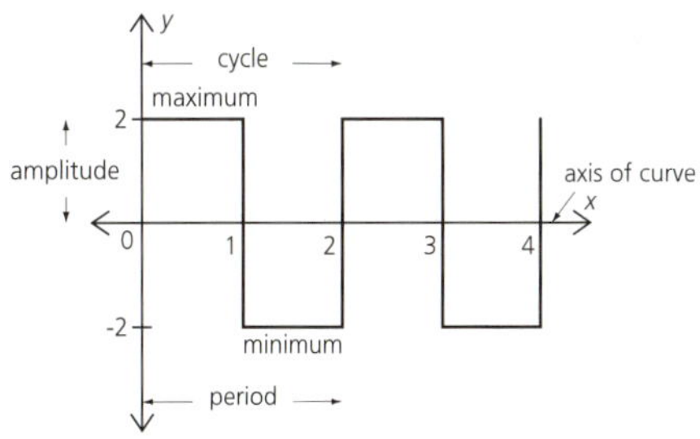

(a) cycle: exact portion of the curve that repeats
(b) period; length of one cycle
(c) amplitude: distance from axis of the curve to the maximum or minimum value
(d) axis of curve: horizontal line midway between maximum and minimum values of the curve
(e) maximum: uppermost point on the curve, minimum: lowest point on the curve

3. **(a)** Ice cream consumption follows a regular pattern as it increases from a low in the cooler months to a high in the warmer months and then decreases as the temperature cools. This cycle repeats each year.
(b) As temperatures cool, natural gases for heating purposes increase and as temperatures increase heating needs decrease. This cycle repeats each year.
(c) The pendulum swings from a point to the right of vertical, through the vertical position to a point on the left of vertical. It then swings back to its starting point.
(d) When the string is plucked it moves away from rest, then back through rest to the other side. This vibration, over a short period of time, could be considered as periodic although it will eventually stop.
(e) Temperatures rise and fall with the seasons in a predictable manner from one year to the next.
(f) The sound is repeated over and over again for the same length of time.

4. **(a)** The first cycle starts at $t = 0$ s and ends at $t = 10$ s. The minimum of the graph is V = 0 L and its maximum is V = 20 L. Repeat the given relation starting at $t = 10$ s.

(b) The first cycle starts at $t = 0$ S and ends at $t = 50$ s. The minimum of the graph is $h = 1$ m and its maximum is $h = 5$ m. Repeat the given relation starting at $t = 50$ s.

5. (a) maximum: 11 m, minimum: 1 m
(b) 60 s
(c) amplitude: 5 m, radius of the Ferris wheel
(d) $h = 6$ m

6. (a) vertex of angle is at origin and initial arm lies along positive x-axis
(b) angle is formed by a counterclockwise rotation of terminal arm
(c) angle is formed by a clockwise rotation of terminal arm
(d) angles that share the same terminal arm
(e) the angle θ between 0° and 360°
(f) the angle formed by terminal arm of an angle in standard position and x-axis

7. Quadrant I: 90° or $\frac{\pi}{2}$, Quadrant II: 180° or π, Quadrant III: 270° or $\frac{3\pi}{2}$, Quadrant IV: 360° or 2π

8. (a) rotate terminal arm clockwise to third quadrant, principal angle: 230°, related acute angle: 50°
(b) rotate terminal arm counterclockwise 360° + 140° to the second quadrant, principal angle: 140°, related acute angle: 40°
(c) rotate terminal arm clockwise 360° + 160° to the second quadrant, principal angle: 160°, related acute angle: 20°
(d) rotate terminal arm counterclockwise to the 4th quadrant, principal angle: 280°, related acute angle: 80°

9. (a) −658°, −298°, 62°, 422°, 782°, 1142°
(b) −497°, −137°, 223°, 583°

10. (a) −250°, 110°, 470°
(b) −530°, −170°, 190°, 550°

11. (a) Plot (−11, 14) on the coordinate grid. The principal angle is the angle between 0° and the terminal arm of the point P; Quadrant II
(b) 52° (c) 128°

12. (a) $\sin\theta = \frac{y}{r}$, $\cos\theta = \frac{x}{r}$, $\tan\theta = \frac{y}{x}$, $x \neq 0$
(b) $(x, y) = (r\cos\theta, r\sin\theta)$

13. (a) Refer to Key Ideas 5.3 for graph of standard sine curve; extend domain from −360° to 360°.
(b) period: 360°, amplitude: 1, range = $\{y \mid -1 \leq y \leq 1, y \in \mathbf{R}\}$, axis: $y = 0$
(c) maximum: (−270°, 1), (90°, 1), minimum: (−90°, −1), (270°, −1), zeros: −360°, −180°, 0°, 180°, 360°

14. (a) Refer to Key Ideas 5.3 for graph of standard cosine curve; extend domain from −360° to 360°
(b) period: 360°, amplitude: 1, range = $\{y \mid -1 \leq y \leq 1, y \in \mathbf{R}\}$ axis: $y = 0$
(c) maximum: (−360°, 1), (0°,1), (360°, 1), minimum: (−180°, −1), (180°, −1), zeros: −270°, −90°, 90°, 270°

15. (a) Refer to Key Ideas 5.3 for graph of standard tangent curve; extend domain from −360° to 360°.
(b) $\tan\theta = \frac{y}{x}$, so function is undefined when $x = 0$
(c) There is a vertical asymptote where the function is undefined.

16. (a) $\sin\theta = -\frac{20}{\sqrt{689}}$, $\cos\theta = -\frac{17}{\sqrt{689}}$, $\tan\theta = \frac{20}{17}$
(b) $\theta = 230°$

17. 37.0 m

18. Both degrees and radians are used to determine the measure of an angle. Degree measure is based on a 360° rotation of a point around a circle and does not depend on the radius of the circle. Radian measure is also based on rotation about a circle but is dependent on the radius of the circle. For the unit circle, $\pi = 180°$.

20. (a) $\frac{\pi}{9}$, 0.3 (b) $\frac{-5\pi}{18}$, −0.9 (c) $\frac{8\pi}{9}$, 2.8
(d) $\frac{7\pi}{3}$, 7.3 (e) $\frac{-14\pi}{9}$, −4.9

21. (a) 45° (b) −225° (c) 480° (d) −120° (e) 330°

22. (a) 183°, rotate counterclockwise to between 8 and 9 o'clock
(b) −80°, rotate clockwise to between 5 and 6 o'clock
(c) 476°, rotate counterclockwise 360° to 11 o'clock
(d) 86°, rotate counterclockwise to between 12 and 1 o'clock
(e) 126°, rotate counterclockwise to 10 o'clock

23. Refer to Key Ideas 5.3 for graph of standard sine curve; extend domain from $\frac{-3\pi}{2}$ to $\frac{5\pi}{2}$.

24. (a) −5.4, −3.9, 0.8, 2.3 (b) −4.4, −1.9, 1.9, 4.4
(c) −4.9, −1.7, 1.4, 4.6

25. (a) 0.95 m
(b) 10 s; the ship rises and falls with the waves each 10 s
(c) 6.8 s, 8.2 s, 16.8 s, 18.2 s, 26.8 s, 28.2 s, 36.8 s, 38.2 s, 46.8 s, 48.2 s, 56.8 s, 58.2 s

26. The transformations are applied to the base graph of $y = \sin\theta$. a corresponds to the vertical stretch; for $a < 0$, the graph is reflected about the x-axis; the graph undergoes a horizontal stretch by factor of $\frac{1}{k}$; b corresponds to the horizontal phase shift; $b > 0$ implies a phase shift of b units left, $b < 0$ implies a phase shift of b units right; d corresponds to a vertical translation; $d > 0$ indicates an upward shift of d units, $d < 0$ indicates a downward shift of d units.

27. (a) The period is 12, the number of months in a year.
(b) $y = \cos\theta$ has a maximum of 1 and a minimum of −1. Substitute −1 and 1 for $\cos\frac{\pi}{6}t$ to find the maximum and minimum temperatures.

28. (a) $\left(\frac{\pi}{2}, -3\right)$, $(\pi, 0)$ (b) $\left(\frac{\pi}{2}, 2\right)$, $(\pi, 1)$
(c) $\left(\frac{3\pi}{4}, 1\right)$, $\left(\frac{5\pi}{4}, 0\right)$ (d) $\left(\frac{\pi}{4}, 1\right)$, $\left(\frac{\pi}{2}, 0\right)$

29. (a) Apply the transformations as follows: horizontal stretch, phase shift, vertical stretch, vertical shift amplitude = 2, phase shift $= \frac{\pi}{6}$ right, period $= \frac{2\pi}{3}$, vertical shift = −4, min. (0, −6), $\left(\frac{2\pi}{3}, -6\right)$, $\left(\frac{4\pi}{3}, -6\right)$, $(2\pi, -6)$, max. $\left(\frac{\pi}{3}, -2\right)$, $(\pi, -2)$, $\left(\frac{5\pi}{3}, -2\right)$, axis of symmetry $y = -4$
(b) Apply the transformations as follows: horizontal stretch, phase shift, vertical stretch, vertical shift; amplitude = 3, reflection in the y-axis, phase shift $= \frac{\pi}{4}$ left, period $= \pi$, vertical shift = 2, min. $\left(\frac{3\pi}{4}, -1\right)$, $\left(\frac{7\pi}{4}, -1\right)$, max $\left(\frac{\pi}{4}, 5\right)$, $\left(\frac{5\pi}{4}, 5\right)$, axis of symmetry $y = 2$

30. (a) amplitude: 2, period: 720°, phase shift: 120° right, vertical shift: +1
(b) amplitude: 3, period: 180°, phase shift: 45° left, vertical shift: −1
(c) amplitude: 2, period: $\frac{2\pi}{3}$, phase shift: $\frac{\pi}{6}$ right, vertical shift: +1

31. (a) Graphing the data gives the general shape of the trigonometric model and whether or not it is sinusoidal. It shows the maximum and minimum value and a starting point for the typical sinusoidal curve. These are necessary when completing the equations $y = a\sin k(\theta + b) + d$ or $y = a\cos k(\theta + b) + d$.
(b) The four key pieces of information are amplitude, phase shift, period, and vertical shift (axis of the curve). amplitude $= \frac{\text{maximum} - \text{minimum}}{2}$, period $= \frac{2\pi}{k}$, vertical shift $= \frac{\text{maximum} + \text{minimum}}{2}$, phase shift: determine where the starting point of the graph has moved. If the starting point is right of 0, $b < 0$. If the starting point is left of 0, $b > 0$.

32. (a) $f(\theta) = 4 \sin 3\theta$ (b) $f(t) = \cos \frac{\pi}{6}t + 5$

33. (a) Ice cream production rises to a maximum with warmer weather and then falls to a minimum with cooler weather. It is cyclical.

(b) $p(t) = 54 \sin \frac{\pi}{6}(t - 3) + 222$ or $-54 \cos \frac{\pi}{6}t + 222$

(c) The scatter plot and the graph follow the same pattern with the graph touching over 70% of the data points.

34. (1) Sketch the graph and interpolate. (2) Find points of intersection between two corresponding functions that make up the original equation. (3) Determine the zeros of the single corresponding function.

35. (a) yes (b) no

36. (a) 41.8°, 138.2° (b) 128.7°, 231.3° (c) 70.3°, 250.3° (d) no solution (e) 132.8° (f) 133.6°

37. (a) 0.51, 5.78 (b) 3.42, 6.01 (c) 0.39, 1.96, 3.53, 5.10 (d) 4.71 (e) 0.39, 1.71, 2.48, 3.80, 4.58, 5.90 (f) 2.33

38. (a) 53.1°, 126.9° (b) 104.5°, 255.5° (c) 71.6°, 251.6° (d) 30.0°, 150.0°, 210.0°, 330.0°

39. (a) 0.46, 3.61 (b) 1.05, 3.14, 5.24 (c) 0.52, 2.62, 4.71 (d) 1.57, 4.71

40. (a) maximum: July, minimum: Jan. (b) Dec. and Jan (c) May and Aug.

Chapter 5 Review Test, page 491

1. (a) exponential (b) linear (c) quadratic (d) periodic, period: 4 s, maximum: 25 cm, minimum: −25 cm

2. Modify the amplitude, period, phase shift, and vertical shift of a sine curve or a cosine curve to match the data.

3. (a) −313°, 47°, 407° (b) $\frac{-4\pi}{3}, \frac{2\pi}{3}$ (c) 15°, 375°, 735°

4. (a) $\frac{13\pi}{9}$ (b) $\frac{-\pi}{12}$

5. (a) 450° (b) −630°

6. 0.47

7. (a) $\sin \theta = \frac{7}{\sqrt{58}}$, $\cos \theta = \frac{-3}{\sqrt{58}}$, $\tan \theta = \frac{7}{-3}$ (b) 113°

8. (a) period: 120°, amplitude: 2, phase shift: 30° right, vertical shift: +1

(b) Apply the transformations as follows: horizontal stretch, phase shift, vertical stretch, vertical shift; amplitude = 2; phase shift = 30° right; period = 120°; vertical shift = 1; min. (0°, −1), (120°, −1), (240°, −1), (360°, −1); max. (60°, 3), (180°, 3), (300°, 3); axis of symmetry $y = 1$

9. (a) 95°, 265° (b) 72°, 108°, 192°, 228° (c) 3.1 (d) 0.7, 5.5

10. (a) Plot the points given. Let x-axis represent the month and y-axis represent temperature; $T = -18.9 \cos \frac{\pi}{6}t + 5.8$

(b) On a yearly basis, the average temperature each month will be roughly the same.

(c) maximum: 24.7°C, minimum: −13.1°C

(d) period = 12; the curve repeats after 12 months, representing one year

(e) $T = 5.8$°C (f) no phase shift

(g) $T = -18.9 \cos \frac{\pi}{6}t + 5.8$

(h) −10.6°C. Month 38 is February and the table shows a temperature close to that value.

11. (a) The initial speed of the ball is 36.7 m/s.

(b) The fly ball is struck at an angle of 64°. The line drive is struck at an angle of 26.3°.

12. $2k$ solutions

Chapter 6

Getting Ready, page 496

1. (a) 0.7431 (b) 0.9781 (c) −0.8391 (d) −0.6428 (e) 0.9659 (f) 0.5000 (g) undefined (h) 0.9969

2. (a) 135.0° (b) 220.0° (c) 200.5° (d) 335.2°

3. (a) 0.7854 (b) 3.6652 (c) 2.4435 (d) 5.9341

4. All angles have a vertex of (0, 0), initial arm on the positive x-axis, and counterclockwise rotation.

(a) terminal arm rotated counterclockwise in first quadrant passing through (6, 8); $\sin \theta = \frac{4}{5}$, $\cos \theta = \frac{3}{5}$, $\tan \theta = \frac{4}{3}$, $\theta \doteq 53°$

(b) terminal arm rotated counterclockwise in second quadrant passing through (−2, 4); $\sin \theta = \frac{2}{\sqrt{5}}$, $\cos \theta = \frac{-1}{\sqrt{5}}$, $\tan \theta = -2$, $\theta \doteq 117°$

(c) terminal arm rotated counterclockwise in third quadrant passing through (−2, −5); $\sin \theta = \frac{-5}{\sqrt{29}}$, $\cos \theta = \frac{-2}{\sqrt{29}}$, $\tan \theta = \frac{5}{2}$, $\theta \doteq 248°$

(d) terminal arm rotated counterclockwise in fourth quadrant passing through (1, −2); $\sin \theta = \frac{-2}{\sqrt{5}}$, $\cos \theta = \frac{1}{\sqrt{5}}$, $\tan \theta = -2$, $\theta \doteq 297°$

5. (a) 90° (b) 180° (c) 45° (d) 90°, 270° (e) 60°, 300° (f) 210°, 330° (g) 0°, 180°, 360° (h) 135°, 315°

6. (a) 199.5°, 340.5° (b) 131.8°, 228.2° (c) 63.4°, 243.4° (d) 270.0°

7. (a) 1.3, 5.0 (b) 2.4, 5.5 (c) 3.3, 6.1 (d) 1.0, 5.2

8. (a) amplitude: 1, period: $\frac{2\pi}{3}$, phase shift: 0, vertical shift: 0

(b) amplitude: 3, period: 2π, phase shift: left $\frac{\pi}{2}$, vertical shift: 0

(c) amplitude: ∞, period: π, phase shift: 0, vertical shift: down 1

(d) amplitude: 2, period: 720°, phase shift: right 30°, vertical shift: up 2

(e) amplitude: ∞, period: $\frac{\pi}{3}$, phase shift: 0, vertical shift: 0

(f) amplitude: 1, period: π, phase shift: left $\frac{\pi}{4}$, vertical shift: 0

9. (a) zeros at 0, π, 2π; max. at $\left(\frac{\pi}{2}, 1\right)$, min. at $\left(\frac{3\pi}{2}, -1\right)$

(b) zeros at $\frac{\pi}{2}, \frac{3\pi}{2}$; max. at (0, 1) and ($2\pi$, 1), min. at ($\pi$, −1)

(c) vertical asymptotes $x = \frac{\pi}{2}$ and $x = \frac{3\pi}{2}$; zeros at 0, π, 2π

(d) zeros at $\frac{\pi}{4}, \frac{3\pi}{4}, \frac{5\pi}{4}, \frac{7\pi}{4}$; max. at (0, 1), ($\pi$, 1), ($2\pi$, 1): min. at $\left(\frac{\pi}{2}, -1\right), \left(\frac{3\pi}{2}, -1\right)$

(e) no zeros; y-intercept 2; max. at $\left(\frac{\pi}{2}, 3\right)$: min. at $\left(\frac{3\pi}{2}, 1\right)$

(f) zeros at $\frac{\pi}{4}, \frac{5\pi}{4}$; y-intercept 1.414; max. at $\left(\frac{7\pi}{4}, 2\right)$; min. at $\left(\frac{3\pi}{4}, -2\right)$

(g) vertical asymptotes $x = 0$, $x = \pi$ and $x = 2\pi$; zeros at $\frac{\pi}{2}, \frac{3\pi}{2}$

(h) zero at π; y-intercept −1; max. at (π, 0)

10. (a) $y = 2 \sin x$, $y = 2 \cos \left(x - \frac{\pi}{2}\right)$

(b) $y = \sin \left(x + \frac{\pi}{4}\right)$, $y = \cos \left(x - \frac{\pi}{4}\right)$

(c) $y = 2x + 1$, $y = \cos 2\left(x - \frac{\pi}{4}\right) + 1$

(d) $y = -\sin x - 1$, $y = -\cos \left(x - \frac{\pi}{2}\right) - 1$

11. (a) $x \doteq 6.4$ (b) $\theta \doteq 53.1°$

(c) $x \doteq 4.1$ cm (d) $\theta \doteq 39.8°$

12. (a) $x \doteq 12.1$ cm (b) $\theta \doteq 1.1°$
(c) $x \doteq 9.4$ cm (d) $\theta \doteq 48.8°$

13. (a) $x \doteq 4.6$ cm (b) $\theta \doteq 53.1°$
(c) $x \doteq 8.7$ (d) $x \doteq 6.2$ m

14. (a) $\angle A = 57°$, $AB \doteq 2.7$ cm, $BC \doteq 4.1$ cm
(b) $\angle D = 67°$, $DE \doteq 3.6$ cm, $EF \doteq 3.7$ cm
(c) $h \doteq 4.9$ cm, $\angle G \doteq 79.5°$, $\angle I \doteq 57.5°$

15. (a) $(x - 8)(x + 8)$ (b) $(x + 5)(x + 7)$
(c) $(2x - 5)(3x + 1)$ (d) $(2x - 5)^2$
(e) $2x(x^2 + 2)$ (f) $(4x - 1)(2x + 3)$
(g) $(x - 7)(x - 2)$ (h) $(x - 8)(x + 5)$

16. (a) $x = 3, -7$ (b) $x = 3, 8$ (c) $x = 0, \frac{8}{5}$ (d) $x = -9, 6$
(e) $x = -\frac{1}{2}, 5$ (f) $x = \frac{1}{2}, \frac{2}{3}$ (g) $x = \frac{2}{3}, \frac{1}{2}$

Practise, Apply, Solve 6.1, page 509

1. (a) 47° (b) does not exist
(c) 20° (d) 112°

2. (a) 12.4 cm (b) 12.1 or 11.7 cm
(c) 18.1 cm (d) 7.0 or 9.2 cm

3. (a) 92° (b) 55°
(c) 32° (d) 61°

4. (a) 25.5 cm (b) 35.9 cm
(c) 19.0 cm (d) 15.0 cm

5. (a) two solutions (b) one solution
(c) no solution (d) two solutions

6. (a) (i)
(ii) $b \sin A \doteq 1.5250$ cm
(iii) no solution (iv) no solution
(b) (i)
(ii) $b \sin A = 7.3$ cm,
(iii) one solution (iv) 12.6 cm
(c) (i)
(ii) $b \sin A \doteq 5.3343$ mm
(iii) two solutions
(iv) 12.5 mm, 2.8 mm
(d) (i)
(ii) $b \sin A \doteq 16.6139$ cm
(iii) one solution
(iv) 22.2 cm

7. (a) $m \doteq 15.0$ cm, $\angle L \doteq 46°$, $\angle N \doteq 29°$
(b) $t \doteq 13.9$ cm, $r \doteq 15.7$ cm, $\angle R = 32°$
(c) $\angle A \doteq 98°$, $\angle B \doteq 30°$, $\angle C \doteq 52°$
(d) $\angle X = 124°$, $z \doteq 12.9$ cm, $y \doteq 8.1$ cm
(e) $b \doteq 21.6$ cm, $c \doteq 14.3$ cm, $\angle B = 105°$
(f) $l \doteq 17.2$ cm, $\angle M \doteq 53°$, $\angle N \doteq 92°$
(g) $q \doteq 7.1$ cm, $r \doteq 13.2$ cm, $\angle S = 92°$
(h) $\angle D \doteq 46°$, $\angle E \doteq 58°$, $\angle F \doteq 76°$

8. (a) $\angle B \doteq 52°$, $c \doteq 11.1$, $\angle C \doteq 60°$
(b) no solution
(c) $(\angle I, f, \angle F) \doteq (50°, 16.2$ cm$, 95°), (130°, 4.3$ cm$, 15°)$
(d) $\angle D \doteq 129°$, $d \doteq 89.0$ cm, $\angle F \doteq 6°$
(e) $(\angle X, \angle Z, z) \doteq (56°, 86°, 18.3$ cm$), (124°, 18°, 5.6$ cm$)$

9. $(\angle E, \angle F, f) \doteq (50°, 89°, 18.3$ cm$), (130°, 9°, 5.7$ cm$)$

11. 4139 m

12. Yes, consider ΔABC, with $a = 430$ m, $\angle A = 35°$ and $b = 110$ m. Then, $\angle B \doteq 8.4°$, $\angle C \doteq 136.6°$, and $c \doteq 515.1$ m.

13. (a) 12.98 m (b) 25.87 m (c) 11.86 m

14. 11.7 cm

15. 4.92 cm

16. (a) $l < m \sin L$ (b) $l = m \sin L$ (c) $m \sin L < l < m$

17. (a) 16.2 m, 17.5 m (b) 11.3 m

18. 32 km

19. 24.6 m

20. 28.5 km

21. 57.6 cm

23. 35.33 cm

24. 5.5 cm

25. 59.5 cm^2

Practise, Apply, Solve 6.2, page 522

1. 80.2 m

2. 3.6 m

3. (a) 16.6 cm (b) 21.5 cm

4. 6.4 cm, 49.0 cm^2

5. 60 cm

6. 135°

7. (a) 15 cm (b) 38 cm (c) 20 cm (d) 65°

8. *Example*: solve ΔABC where $a = 10.4$, $b = 6$, $\angle B = 19°$, and $\angle C = 23°$: $C = 7.2$, $\angle A = 138°$

9. 5.1 m, 6.1 m

10. (a) 53.3 m (b) 53.1 m

11. (a) The *Argus* is 85.5 nautical miles from the lifeboat; the *Baffin* is 75.1 nautical miles.
(b) The *Baffin* will arrive first.

12. 540 m

13. Plane *Abel* will land first.

14. Tower *A* is 31.5 km from the fire; Tower *B* is 22.3 km from the fire.

15. 21.1 km

16. (a) 44.299° (b) 5.56 km (c) 1.51 km

17. 8.34 km

18. (a) 30.7° (b) 1258.875 cm^2 (c) 2707.5 cm^3

19. A diagram is essential; use primary trigonometric ratios if the triangle is a right triangle; use sine law if two angles and any side or if two sides and an angle are given; use cosine law if two sides and contained angle or the other side is known.

20. (a) 2.4 km
(b) The balloon on the left 209 m higher.

Practise, Apply, Solve 6.3, page 532

1. (a) See diagram in Key Ideas of this section.

2. (a) See diagram in Key Ideas of this section.

3. (a) $\frac{\sqrt{3}}{2}$ (b) $-\sqrt{3}$ (c) $\frac{-1}{\sqrt{2}}$

4. (a) $\frac{1}{\sqrt{3}}$ (b) $\frac{\sqrt{3}}{2}$ (c) $\frac{1}{\sqrt{2}}$

5. (a) $\frac{1}{\sqrt{2}}$ (b) $\sqrt{3}$ (c) $\frac{\sqrt{3}}{2}$ (d) $\frac{-1}{\sqrt{3}}$

6. (a) $\frac{1}{\sqrt{2}}$ (b) $\frac{-\sqrt{3}}{2}$ (c) $\frac{1}{\sqrt{3}}$ (d) $\frac{-1}{\sqrt{2}}$

7. (a) $\frac{-1}{\sqrt{2}}$ (b) $-\frac{\sqrt{3}}{2}$ (c) $\sqrt{3}$ (d) $\frac{\sqrt{3}}{2}$

12. (a) 135°, 315° (b) 45°, 135°
(c) 150°, 210° (d) 60°, 120°
(e) 45°, 315° (f) 120°, 300°
(g) 30°, 150° (h) 150°, 330°
(i) 22.5°, 67.5°, 202.5°, 247.5°
(j) 30°, 150°, 210°, 330°
(k) 30°, 330° (l) 120°, 240°

13. zeros at $-360°, -180°, 0°, 180°, 360°$; max. at $(-270°, 1)$, $(90°, 1)$; min. at $(-90°, -1)$, $(270°, -1)$

θ	$y = \sin\theta$
$-315°$	$\frac{1}{\sqrt{2}}$
$-225°$	$\frac{1}{\sqrt{2}}$
$-135°$	$\frac{-1}{\sqrt{2}}$
$-45°$	$\frac{-1}{\sqrt{2}}$
$45°$	$\frac{1}{\sqrt{2}}$
$135°$	$\frac{1}{\sqrt{2}}$
$225°$	$\frac{-1}{\sqrt{2}}$
$315°$	$\frac{-1}{\sqrt{2}}$

$y = \sin\theta$ is a function: passes vertical line test

14. zeros at $\frac{-3\pi}{2}, \frac{-\pi}{2}, \frac{\pi}{2}, \frac{3\pi}{2}$; max: $(-2\pi, 1), (0, 1), (2\pi, 1)$; min: $(-\pi, -1), (\pi, -1)$,

θ	$y = \cos\theta$
$\frac{-11\pi}{6}$	$\frac{\sqrt{3}}{2}$
$\frac{-7\pi}{6}$	$\frac{-\sqrt{3}}{2}$
$\frac{-5\pi}{6}$	$\frac{-\sqrt{3}}{2}$
$\frac{-\pi}{6}$	$\frac{\sqrt{3}}{2}$
$\frac{\pi}{6}$	$\frac{\sqrt{3}}{2}$
$\frac{5\pi}{6}$	$\frac{-\sqrt{3}}{2}$
$\frac{7\pi}{6}$	$\frac{-\sqrt{3}}{2}$
$\frac{11\pi}{6}$	$\frac{\sqrt{3}}{2}$

$y = \cos\theta$ is a function: passes vertical line test

15. **(a)** $AB = 6\sqrt{3}, AD = 12, BC = 6, CD = 6\sqrt{2}$
(b) $\sin A = \frac{1}{2}, \cos A = \frac{\sqrt{3}}{2}, \tan A = \frac{1}{\sqrt{3}}; \sin C = \frac{1}{\sqrt{2}}$, $\cos C = \frac{1}{\sqrt{2}}, \tan C = 1$

Practise, Apply, Solve 6.5, page 538

2. **(a)** $\tan x$ **(b)** $\sin x$ **(c)** $\sin^2 x$ **(d)** $\cos^2 x$ **(e)** 1 **(f)** $\cos^2 x$ **(g)** $\frac{1}{\cos x}$ **(h)** 1 **(i)** $\cos x$ **(j)** $\frac{1}{\sin^2 x}$ **(k)** $\tan x$ **(l)** $\tan x$ **(m)** $\frac{\cos x + \sin x}{\sin x \cos x}$ **(n)** $\frac{\sin x + 1}{\cos x}$ **(o)** $\frac{\cos x + \sin^2 x}{\sin x}$
3. **(a)** $(1 - \cos\theta)(1 + \cos\theta)$ **(b)** $(1 - \sin\theta)(1 + \sin\theta)$ **(c)** $(\sin\theta - \cos\theta)(\sin\theta + \cos\theta)$ **(d)** $\sin\theta(1 - \sin\theta)$ **(e)** $(\cos\theta + 1)^2$ **(f)** $(\sin\theta - 1)^2$
4. **(a)** $\frac{1 - \sin^2\alpha}{\sin\alpha}$
5. **(a)** $\frac{1 - \sin^2 x}{1 - \sin x}$ **(b)** $\frac{(1 - \sin x)(1 + \sin x)}{1 - \sin x}$
10. **(a)** identity **(b)** not identity **(c)** identity **(d)** identity

Practise, Apply, Solve 6.6, page 545

1. **(a)** $5x(x - 2)$ **(b)** $(x + 5)(x + 8)$ **(c)** $(5x + 2)(2x - 3)$ **(d)** $(x - 9)(x + 9)$
2. **(a)** $\sin\theta(\sin\theta - 1)$ **(b)** $(\cos\theta - 1)^2$ **(c)** $(\sin\theta - 1)(3\sin\theta + 2)$ **(d)** $(2\cos\theta - 1)(2\cos\theta + 1)$
4. **(a)** 0°, 90°, 180°, 270°, 360° **(b)** 0°, 180°, 360° **(c)** 90°, 270° **(d)** 90°, 60°, 120°, 270° **(e)** 45°, 135°, 225°, 315° **(f)** 90°, 180°
5. **(a)** $\frac{\pi}{6}, \frac{\pi}{2}, \frac{5\pi}{6}, \frac{3\pi}{2}$ **(b)** $\frac{3\pi}{2}$ **(c)** $0, \frac{5\pi}{6}, \pi, \frac{7\pi}{6}, 2\pi$ **(d)** $\frac{\pi}{3}, \frac{4\pi}{3}, \frac{5\pi}{3}$ **(e)** $\frac{\pi}{4}, \frac{3\pi}{4}, \frac{5\pi}{4}, \frac{7\pi}{4}$ **(f)** $0, \frac{3\pi}{2}, 2\pi$
6. **(a)** 90°, 270° **(b)** 0°, 180°, 360° **(c)** 45°, 135°, 225°, 315° **(d)** 60°, 120°, 240°, 300° **(e)** 30°, 150°, 210°, 330° **(f)** 45°, 135°, 225°, 315°
7. **(a)** $(2\sin x + 1)(\sin x - 1)$ **(b)** $\frac{\pi}{2}, \frac{7\pi}{6}, \frac{11\pi}{6}$
8. **(a)** $(2\cos x - 1)(\cos x + 1)$ **(b)** 60°, 180°, 300°
9. **(a)** 0°, 30°, 150°, 180°, 360° **(b)** 0°, 90°, 270°, 360° **(c)** 45°, 124°, 225°, 304° **(d)** 30°, 150°, 200°, 341° **(e)** 0°, 360° **(f)** 49°, 131°, 270°
10. **(a)** $\frac{\pi}{3}, \pi, \frac{5\pi}{3}$ **(b)** $\frac{\pi}{6}, \frac{5\pi}{6}, \frac{3\pi}{2}$ **(c)** π **(d)** $\frac{\pi}{6}, \frac{5\pi}{6}$ **(e)** $\frac{\pi}{4}$, 2.82, $\frac{5\pi}{4}$, 5.96 **(f)** 0.73, 2.41, 3.99, 5.44
11. **(a)** 45°, 90°, 135°, 225°, 315° **(b)** 90°, 270°
12. **(a)** $0, \pi, 2\pi$ **(b)** $\frac{\pi}{2}$ **(c)** $\frac{\pi}{2}$ **(d)** 1.23, 1.98, 4.30, 5.05
13. **(a)** 0°, 180°, 222°, 318°, 360° **(b)** 60°, 104°, 256°, 300° **(c)** 83°, 180° **(d)** 6°, 84°, 186°, 264°
14. **(a)** 1.57, 4.71 **(b)** 0.52, 2.62 **(c)** 1.82, 4.46 **(d)** 1.57, 3.48, 5.94
15. **(a)** *Example*: $2\cos^2 x = \cos x$
(b) no; some equations have irrational roots
(c) period and domain
16. **(a)** 15°, 75°, 105°, 165°, 195°, 255°, 285°, 345°
(b) 0.96

Chapter 6, Review and Practice, page 549

1. given AAS or ASA, can find side using sine law; given SAS, can find side using cosine law; given SSS, can find angle using cosine law; given SSA, can find angle using sine law
2. **(a)** $\frac{\sin L}{l} = \frac{\sin M}{m} = \frac{\sin N}{n}$ **(b)** $m^2 = l^2 + n^2 - 2ln\cos M$
3. **(a)** $8 < b < 9.06$
(b) $b = \frac{8}{\sin 62°} \doteq 9.06$ cm or $0 < b < 8$
(c) $b > \frac{8}{\sin 62°} \doteq 9.06$ cm
4. **(a)** 28.0 cm **(b)** 149.1° **(c)** 180° **(d)** 13.0 cm
5. **(a)** $b \doteq 19.4$ cm, $\angle A \doteq 34.1°$, $\angle C \doteq 30.9°$
(b) $r \doteq 53.5$ cm, $q \doteq 94.0$ cm, $\angle S = 107°$
6. two solutions: $(\angle B, \angle C, c) \doteq (49.7°, 92.3°, 21.7 \text{ cm})$ or $(130.3°, 11.7°, 4.41 \text{ cm})$
7. (1) Does the problem involve right, acute, or obtuse angle triangles? (2) Does it involve two or three dimensions? (3) Is the sine law or cosine law used? A diagram should be part of every solution.
8. 110 m
9. 148.4 km

10. 197.0 m
11. 13.1 km
12. 125°
13. See diagram in Key Ideas of section 6.3.
(a) $\frac{1}{\sqrt{2}}$ (b) $\frac{1}{\sqrt{2}}$ (c) $\frac{-1}{\sqrt{2}}$ (d) -1
14. See diagram in Key Ideas of section 6.3.
(a) $\frac{1}{2}$ (b) $\frac{\sqrt{3}}{2}$ (c) $\frac{-1}{\sqrt{3}}$ (d) $\frac{-\sqrt{3}}{2}$
15. (a) $\frac{3}{4}$ (b) $1\frac{1}{2}$ (c) $\frac{3+4\sqrt{3}}{8}$ (d) $\frac{3}{4}$
17. (a) 60°, 120° (b) 60°, 120°, 240°, 300° (c) 30°, 210°
18. *Example*: $\tan\theta\cos\theta = \sin\theta$
19. An identity has infinite solutions.
24. In a quadratic trigonometric equation, $\sin^2 x$, $\cos^2 x$, or $\tan^2 x$ will appear.
25. factoring
26. (a) 30°, 90°, 150°, 270° (b) 30°, 150°, 210°, 330°
(c) 60°, 180°, 300° (d) 42°, 138°
(e) 0°, 139°, 221°, 360°
(f) 39.23°, 140.77°, 219.23°, 320.77°
27. (a) $0, \frac{3\pi}{2}, 2\pi$ (b) $\frac{\pi}{3}, \frac{2\pi}{3}, \frac{4\pi}{3}, \frac{5\pi}{3}$
(c) $0, \frac{\pi}{4}, \frac{3\pi}{4}, \pi, \frac{5\pi}{4}, \frac{7\pi}{4}, 2\pi$ (d) $\frac{\pi}{6}, \frac{5\pi}{6}$
(e) $\frac{\pi}{3}, \frac{2\pi}{3}, \frac{4\pi}{3}, \frac{5\pi}{3}$ (f) no solution

Chapter 6 Review Test, page 552

1. (a) $l \doteq 125.4$ m, $\angle M \doteq 57.9°$, $\angle N \doteq 47.1°$
(b) $c \doteq 10.0$ cm, $\angle B \doteq 44.9°$, $\angle C \doteq 27.1°$
2. $c \doteq 34.0$ cm, $\angle B \doteq 47.1°$, $\angle C \doteq 94.9°$ and $c \doteq 5.4$ cm, $\angle B \doteq 132.9°$, $\angle C \doteq 9.1°$
3. (a) $\frac{1}{2}$ (b) $\frac{-1}{\sqrt{2}}$ (c) $\frac{1}{\sqrt{3}}$ (d) $\frac{-\sqrt{3}}{2}$
4. (a) 30°, 330° (b) 30°, 150°, 210°, 330°
6. 60°, 300°
7. $\frac{\pi}{3}, \pi, \frac{5\pi}{3}$
8. 10.8 m^2
9. 6.2 m

Cumulative Review Test 3, page 553

1. All angles have their vertex at (0, 0) and initial arm on the positive x-axis.
(a) principal angle: 260°, related acute angle: 80°, terminal arm rotated clockwise 100° stopping in 3rd quadrant
(b) principal angle: 125°, related acute angle: 55°, terminal arm rotated counterclockwise 845°, stopping in 2nd quadrant
(c) principal angle: $\frac{9\pi}{8}$, related acute angle: $\frac{\pi}{8}$, terminal arm rotated clockwise $\frac{7\pi}{8}$, stopping in 3rd quadrant
(d) principal angle: $\frac{5\pi}{6}$, related acute angle: $\frac{\pi}{6}$, terminal arm rotated counterclockwise $\frac{17\pi}{6}$ stopping in 2nd quadrant
2. (a) vertex at (0, 0) and initial arm on the positive x-axis, terminal arm rotated counterclockwise passing through (−3, 8) in 2nd quadrant
(b) $\sin\theta = \frac{8}{\sqrt{73}}$, $\cos\theta = \frac{-3}{\sqrt{73}}$, tan θ = -8\3
(c) $\theta = 69°$ or 110°
3. (a) $\frac{\pi}{12}$ (b) $\frac{2\pi}{3}$ (c) $\frac{-3\pi}{2}$ (d) $\frac{6\pi}{5}$
4. (a) 390° (b) 160° (c) −225° (d) 146°
5. (a) amplitude: 3, period: 2π, phase shift: none, vertical shift: down 1, zeros at 19.5°, 160.5°; y-intercept −1; max. (90°, 2), min. (270°, −4)
(b) period: 180°, phase shift: none, vertical shift: none, zeros at 0°, 180°, 360°; asymptotes $x = 90°$, $x = 270°$
(c) amplitude: 2, period: 360°, phase shift: 30° right, vertical shift: up 2, y-intercept 0.27; zero at 30° min. at (30°, 0); max. at (210°, 4)
(d) amplitude: 3, period: 180°, phase shift: 45° left, vertical shift: down 1, zeros at 35.3°, 144.7°, 215.3°, 324.7°; max. at (0°, 2), (180°, 2), (360°, 2); min. at (90°, −4), (270°, −4)
(e) amplitude: 0.5, period: $\frac{2\pi}{3}$, phase shift: $\frac{\pi}{6}$ right, vertical shift: up 4, y-intercept 4; max. at (0.524, 4.5), (2.618, 4.5), (4.712, 4.5); min. at (1.571, 3.5), (3.665, 3.5), (5.760, 3.5)
(f) amplitude: 5, period: 4π, phase shift: $\frac{4\pi}{3}$ right, vertical shift: up 1, y-intercept 5.33; zero at 4.592; max. at (1.047, 6)
6. (a) $h(t) = 10\sin 10(t-9) + 11$
(b) 12.74 m (c) 18 s, 21 m
7. (a) $\theta = \frac{\pi}{6}, \frac{5\pi}{6}$ (b) no solution
(c) $\theta = 37.86°, 82.14°$ (d) $x = 33.02°, 123.02°$
8. (a) $d(t) = 2.5\sin\left[\frac{\pi}{6}(t-1)\right] + 3.75$, y-intercept 2.6; max. at (4, 6.25), (16, 6.25); min. at (10, 1.25), (22, 1.25)
(b) 6.25 m
(c) Yes; the minimum amount of water is 1.25 m, which is greater than 1 m.
9. (a) $b = 31.6$ cm, $\angle A = 28.2°$, $\angle C = 22.8°$
(b) $a = 17.3$ cm, $\angle A = 52.1°$, $\angle C = 72.9°$
(c) $\angle D = 46.1°$, $\angle E = 60.1°$, $\angle F = 73.8°$
(d) $q = 36.5$ cm, $r = 28.2$, $\angle S = 117°$
10. 446.8 cm^2
11. 14.87 km
12. (a) 0 (b) $-\frac{\sqrt{3}}{2}$ (c) -1
(d) $-\frac{\sqrt{3}}{2}$ (e) $-\frac{1}{6}$ (f) $-\frac{\sqrt{3}}{2}$
14. (a) $0, \frac{\pi}{4}, \frac{3\pi}{4}, \pi, \frac{5\pi}{4}, \frac{7\pi}{4}, 2\pi$
(b) 41.8°, 138.2°, 191.5°, 348.5°
(c) $\frac{\pi}{4}, \frac{5\pi}{4}$ (d) 30°, 150°, 210°, 330°
15. high tide: 3:00 a.m. and 3:00 p.m., low tide: 9:00 a.m. and 9:00 p.m.

Review of Essential Skills—Part 4

Analytic Geometry: Lines and Line Segments, page 560

1. (a) $d = \sqrt{65}$ (b) $m = -7, d = \sqrt{50}$
(c) $m = -\frac{3}{2}, d = \frac{\sqrt{13}}{8}$ (d) $m = 2, d = \sqrt{80}$
2. (a) $y = -\frac{2}{3}x + \frac{4}{3}$ (b) $y = \frac{3}{5}x + 6$
(c) $y = \frac{5}{7}x - \frac{34}{7}$ (d) $y = \frac{8}{5}x - 8$
3. (a) $x^2 + y^2 = 25$ (b) $x^2 + y^2 = \frac{64}{9}$ (c) $x^2 + y^2 = 0.09$
4. y ±12
5. (a) parallel (b) perpendicular (c) perpendicular
(d) neither (e) parallel
6. (a) l_1, l_3 (b) l_1, l_2

7. **(a)** l_1, l_2 or l_1, l_3 **(b)** l_1, l_2
8. **(a)** (0, 24) **(b)** 10 **(c)** $x^2 + (y - 24)^2 = 100$
9. $y = \frac{7}{4}x - \frac{29}{8}$
10. $y = -x + 1$

Solving a System of Linear Equations, page 564

1. **(a)** (3, 2) **(b)** (5, −10) **(c)** (7, 3)
2. **(a)** two straight lines intersecting at (0, 3), one passing through (4, 0), the other through (4.5, 0)
   (b) two straight lines intersecting at (0, −4), one passing through (−4, 0), the other through (2, 0)
   (c) two straight lines intersecting at $\left(\frac{11}{7}, \frac{6}{7}\right)$, one passing through (2, 0), the other through (−1, 0)
   (d) two straight lines intersecting at (−1, 1), one passing through (−1.5, 0), the other through (1, 0)
3. **(a)** $x = 12 + 3y$ **(b)** $x = 15 + 4y$ **(c)** $y = 12 - 2x$
   (d) $y = 8x - 4$ **(e)** $x = y - 9$ **(f)** $y = 2x - \frac{4}{3}$
   (g) $x = \frac{12}{15}y - \frac{14}{15}$ **(h)** $y = -\frac{5}{2}x - 5$ **(i)** $y = 12 - \frac{3}{4}x$
4. **(a)** x **(b)** y **(c)** y **(d)** x
5. **(a)** (1, −1) **(b)** (6, 9) **(c)** (6, −6) **(d)** (2, 1)
6. **(a)** (4, 0) **(b)** (−2, 3) **(c)** (3, 4) **(d)** (2, 8)
7. **(a)** (1, 1) **(b)** (8, −1) **(c)** $\left(\frac{11}{7}, \frac{30}{7}\right)$ **(d)** (−5, −15)

Chapter 7U

Getting Ready, page 568

1. **(a)** $x^2 + 4x + 4$ **(b)** $x^2 - 6x + 9$ **(c)** $x^2 - 5x + \frac{25}{4}$
   (d) $x^2 - x + \frac{1}{4}$ **(e)** $x^2 + 3x + \frac{9}{4}$
2. **(a)** $(x + 1)^2$ **(b)** $(x + 2)^2$ **(c)** $(x - 4)^2$
   (d) $5(x - 3)^2$ **(e)** $2(x - 7)^2$
3. **(a)** vertex: (0, 0), axis of symmetry: $x = 0$
   (b) vertex: (0. −3), axis of symmetry: $x = 0$
   (c) vertex: (2, 6), axis of symmetry: $x = 2$
   (d) vertex: (−1, −1), axis of symmetry: $x = -1$
   (e) vertex: (4, 0), axis of symmetry: $x = 4$
4. **(a)** parabola, opens up, vertex (0, 0), through (2, 4) and (−2, 4)
   (b) parabola, opens up, vertex (0, −3), through (−1, −1) and (1, −1)
   (c) parabola, opens up, vertex (2, 6), through (0, 10) and (4, 10)
   (d) parabola, opens up, vertex (−1, −1), through (0, 2) and (−2, 2)
   (e) parabola, opens up, vertex (4, 0), through (2, 8) and (6, 8)
5. **(a)** $x^2 + y^2 = 25$ **(b)** $x^2 + y^2 = 64$ **(c)** $x^2 + y^2 = 2$
   (d) $x^2 + y^2 = 15$ **(e)** $x^2 + y^2 = 18$
6. **(a)** $AB = \sqrt{2}$ **(b)** $AB = \sqrt{2}$ **(c)** $AB = \sqrt{145}$
   (d) $AB = \sqrt{34}$ **(e)** $AB = \sqrt{2}$
7. **(a)** slope: $\frac{2}{3}$, x-int.: 3, y-int.: −2
   (b) slope: −1, x-int.: 8, y-int.: 8
   (c) slope: 0, x-int.: none, y-int.: −3
   (d) slope: 2, x-int.: $-\frac{1}{2}$, y-int.: 1
   (e) slope: −4, x-int.: −3, y-int.: −12
   (f) slope: 4, x-int.: 2, y-int.: −8
   (g) slope: undefined, x-int.: 2, y-int.: none
8. **(a)** $y = 4x + 2$ **(b)** $y = -\frac{4}{3}x + 4$ **(c)** $y = 2x + 2$
   (d) $y = 5$ **(e)** $y = -x + 4$
9. **(a)** (2, −2) **(b)** (−4, 6) **(c)** $y = -3$ **(d)** $x = 2$
10. **(a)** (3, 2) **(b)** (−1, 2) **(c)** (3, 5) **(d)** (1, 7)
11. **(a)** 3 **(b)** $2x$ **(c)** $x + 5$ **(d)** $4x - 3$
    (e) 7 **(f)** x **(g)** $(x - 5)$ **(h)** $3x + 9$
12. **(a)** $y = 2x - 5$ **(b)** $y = -\frac{1}{3}x - 2$
    (c) $y = \pm\sqrt{x - 5}$ **(d)** $y = \pm\sqrt{-3 - x} - 1$
    (e) $y = \pm\sqrt{\frac{x - 4}{2}} + 3$ **(f)** no solution
    (g) $y = \pm\sqrt{9 - x^2}$ or $y = \pm\sqrt{(3 - x)(3 + x)}$
13. **(a)** straight line through (0, 30 and (−1.5, 0); D = **R**, R = **R**
    (b) top half of parabola opening to right, vertex (−2, 0) through (2, 2); D = {x| $x \geq -2$, $x \in$ **R**}, R = {y| $y \geq 0$, $y \in$ **R**}
    (c) circle centred on origin, radius 5; D = {x| $-5 \leq x \leq 5$, $x \in$ **R** }, R = {y| $-5 \leq y \leq 5$, $y \in$ **R**}
    (d) straight line through (0, 3) and (2, 3); D = **R**, R = {y| $y = 3$, $y \in$ **R**}
    (e) parabola, opens down, vertex (0, 2) through (−2, −2) and (2, −2); D = **R**, R = {y| $y \leq 2$, $y \in$ **R**}
    (f) straight line through (0, −20 and (5, 0); D = **R**, R = **R**
    (g) circle centred on origin, radius 4; D = {x| $-4 \leq x \leq 4$, $x \in$ **R**}, R = {y| $-4 \leq y \leq 4$, $y \in$ **R**}
    (h) parabola, opens up, vertex (−1, −4) through (−3, 0) and (1, 0); D = **R**, R = {y| $y \geq -4$, $x \in$ **R**}
    (i) parabola, opens right, vertex (3, 2) through (7, 0) and (7, 4); D = {x| $x \geq 3$, $x \in$ **R**}, R = **R**
    (j) straight line through (−4, 0) and (−4, 2); D = {x| $x = -4$, $x \in$ **R**}, R = **R**
    (k) hyperbola, horizontal asymptote y = −2, vertical asymptote $x = 0$; D = {x| $x \neq -2$, $x \in$ **R**}, R = {y| $y \neq 0$, $y \in$ **R**}
    (l)

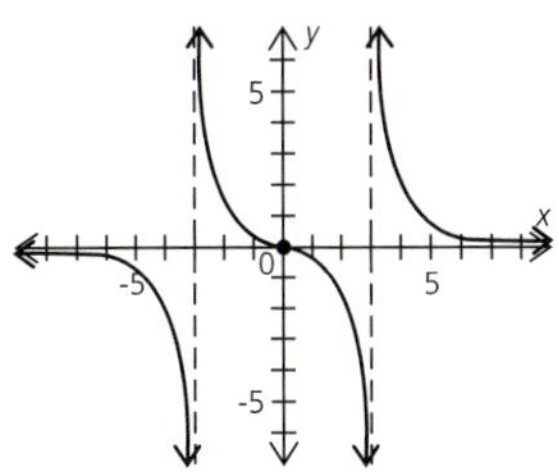

D = {x| $x \neq \pm 3$, $x \in$ **R**}, R = **R**

14. **(a)** $y = (x + 5)^2 - 33$ **(b)** $y = \left(x + \frac{7}{2}\right)^2 - \frac{41}{4}$
    (c) $y = 2(x + 2)^2 - 13$ **(d)** $y = -3\left(x - \frac{5}{6}\right)^2 + \frac{37}{12}$
    (e) $y = 4\left(x - \frac{9}{8}\right)^2 - \frac{177}{16}$ **(f)** $y = -5\left(x - \frac{1}{10}\right)^2 - \frac{201}{20}$

Practise, Apply, Solve 7.1U, page 574

1. **(a)** circle
   (b) vertical line pointing upward
   (c) diagonal line pointing downward
   (d) square with a diagonal line leading from one corner to opposite corner
2. **(a)** circle with radius 10 cm
   (b) line; two parallel lines 3 cm apart
   (c) two other parabolas—one inside the original parabola and one outside it
   (d) another sphere with a radius 1 cm greater than that of original sphere

3. (a) 2 horizontal lines, one below the line and one above it; algebraic expressions: $y = 7$ and $y = -3$.

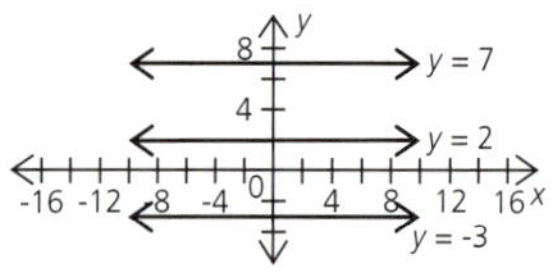

(b) 2 vertical lines, one to the right of $x = -2$ and one to the left of it; algebraic expressions for them are: $x = 1$ and $x = -5$.

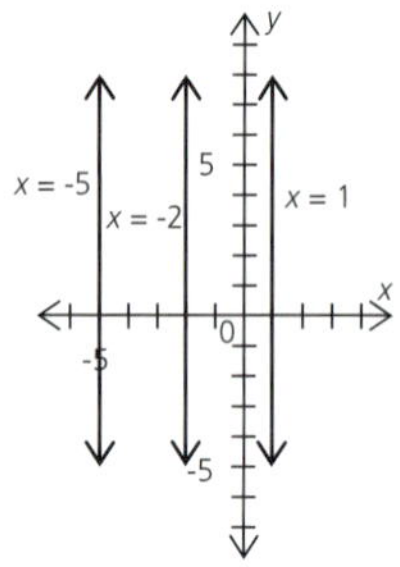

(c) 2 lines parallel to the original line, one above the original line and the other below it; algebraic expressions for them are: $y = 2x - 5$ and $y = 2x - 1$.

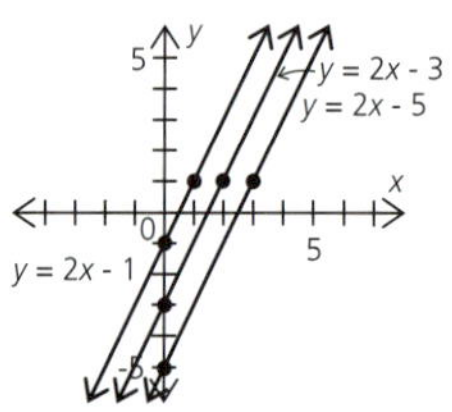

(d) 2 lines parallel to the original line; algebraic expressions for them are: $y = -3x + 6$ and $y = -3x - 2$.

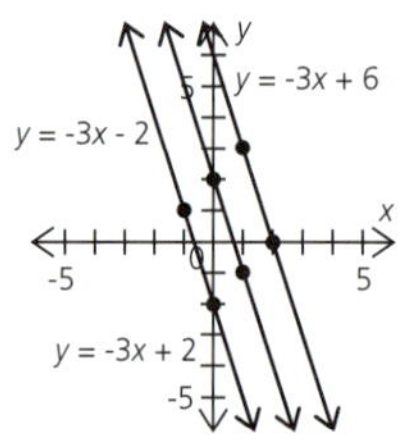

4. (a) circle with radius 5 and equation $x^2 + y^2 = 25$
   (b) $x^2 + y^2 = 100$
5. (a) circle with centre $(3, -1)$ and radius 6
   (b) circle with centre $(0, 3)$ and radius 3
   (c) circle with centre $(2, 3)$ and radius 4
6. (a) diagonal line with y-intercept at 10, x-intercept at $\frac{-10}{3}$, $y = 3x + 10$
   (b) diagonal line with y-intercept at -5, x-intercept at -10; $y = -\frac{1}{2}x - 5$
   (c) circle with radius of 7 units centred at the origin; $x^2 + y^2 = 49$
   (d) parabola opens up, vertex $(5, 0)$
7. (a) a line with equation $y = 4$
   (b) perpendicular bisector of line segment between given points, equation $y = -\frac{1}{2}x + \frac{5}{2}$
   (c) perpendicular bisector of line segment between given points, equation $y = -x$
   (d) perpendicular bisector of line segment between given points, equation $-3x + y - 7 = 0$
   (e) line $y = 2x + 3$
   (f) line $y = -\frac{1}{3}x$
8. (a) diagonal line with y-intercept at 8, x-intercept at 8; $x + y = 8$
   (b) $y - x = 3$: y-intercept at 3, x-intercept at -3; $x - y = 3$: y-intercept at -3, x-intercept at 3
   (c) diagonal line with y-intercept at 4, x-intercept at 4; $\frac{x + y}{2} = 2$ or $x + y = 4$
   (d) asymptotes at $y = 0$, $x = 0$; quadrant 1: x and y approach positive ∞; quadrant 2: x and y approach negative ∞; $xy = 20$
9. Multiple solutions are possible.
   (a) locus of points equidistant from the positive x and y-axes or from the negative x- and y-axes
   (b) locus of points $\sqrt{5}$ units from the origin
   (c) locus of points $P(x, y)$ whose coordinates have a sum of 5
   (d) locus of points 2 units to the left of y-axis
   (e) locus of points 2 units above line $y = 3$
   (f) locus of points above the x-axis 4 units from origin
10. The path of M will be a circle centred at R.

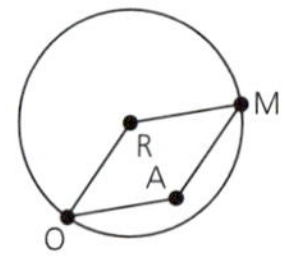

The path of Y is also a circle with the midpoint of RO as the centre.

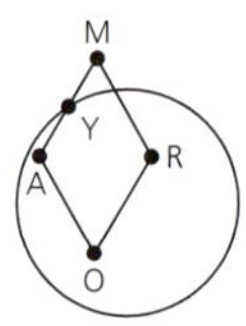

11. $y = \frac{3}{4}x - 1$
12. $y = x$, $y = -x$
13. $y = (x - 1)^2 - 2$
14. (a) circle centred at origin with radius 3
    (b) $x^2 + y^2 = 9$
15. Answers will vary.
16. (a) Neither Amy nor Sara can be seen from within the shaded region.

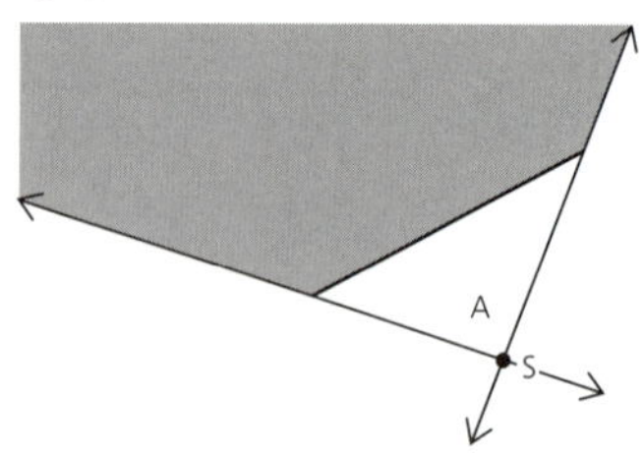

(b) From within the shaded regions, Sara can be seen but not Amy.

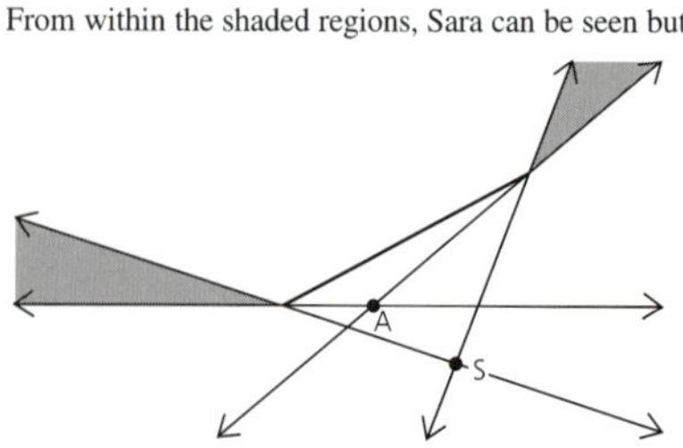

(c) They can both be seen from the unshaded area.

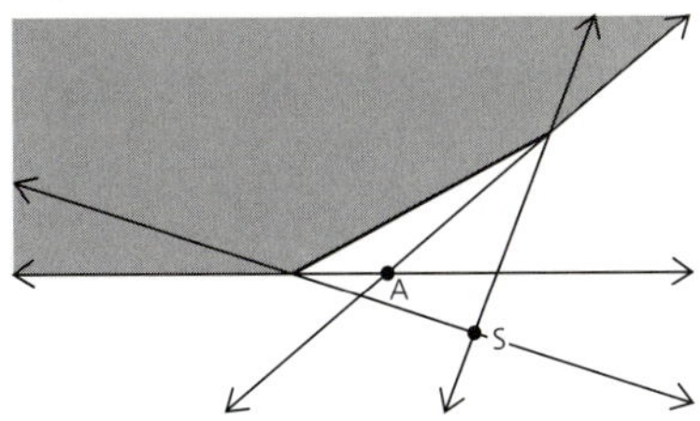

17. **(a)** the y-axis
(b) line perpendicular bisector of segment joining $(-2, 1)$ and $(6, 3)$, with equation $y = -4x + 10$
(c) line with equation $y = 1$
(d) line with equation $x + y - 11 = 0$

18. The path of the point will be a larger circle that has a diameter equal to the sum of the diameters of the other two circles.

19. circle

20. the diameter of the larger circle through point B and the centre

Practise, Apply, Solve 7.2U, page 581

1. **(a)** $x^2 + (y - 2)^2 = 16$ **(b)** $(x - 3)^2 + y^2 = 1$
(c) $(x - 1)^2 + (y - 5)^2 = 81$ **(d)** $(x + 2)^2 + (y - 4)^2 = 64$
(e) $(x + 2)^2 + (y + 5)^2 = 6$ **(f)** $(x - 4)^2 + (y + 6)^2 = 20$

2. **(a)** centre: (0, 0), radius: or $3\sqrt{2}$
(b) centre: (2, 0), radius: 3
(c) centre:(6, −8), radius: 9
(d) centre: (−4, 3), radius: or $4\sqrt{2}$
(e) centre: (5, 4), radius: or $3\sqrt{3}$
(f) centre: (1, −6), radius: or $2\sqrt{10}$

3. **(a)** $(x - 3)^2 + (y - 2)^2 = 9$, original: centre (0, 0), radius of 3; new: centre (3, 2), radius 3
(b) $(x + 4)^2 + (y + 3)^2 = 4$, original: centre (0, 0), radius of 2; new: centre (−4, −3), radius 2
(c) $(x - 4)^2 + (y + 4)^2 = 1$, original: centre (0, 0), radius of 1; new: centre (4, −4), radius 1
(d) $x^2 + y^2 = 9$, original: centre (2, 3), radius of 3; new: centre (0, 0), radius 3
(e) $(x - 2)^2 + (y - 2)^2 = 9$, original: centre (−4, 5), radius of 3; new: centre (2, 2), radius 3

4. **(a)** standard form: $x^2 + y^2 = 25$, general form: $x^2 + y^2 - 25 = 0$
(b) standard form: $(x - 1)^2 + (y - 4)^2 = 16$, general form: $x^2 + y^2 - 2x - 8y + 1 = 0$
(c) standard form: $(x + 4)^2 + (y - 5)^2 = 1$, general form: $x^2 + y^2 + 8x - 10y + 40 = 0$
(d) standard form: $(x + 2)^2 + (y - 3)^2 = 9$, general form: $x^2 + y^2 + 4x - 6y + 4 = 0$

5. **(a)** $(x + 4)^2 + (y + 3)^2 = 25$ **(b)** $(x - 2)^2 + (y + 1)^2 = 16$
(c) $(x - 1)^2 + (y + 5)^2 = 4$ **(d)** $(x - 6)^2 + (y + 3)^2 = 49$

6. **(a)** centre (0, 2), radius: 2 **(b)** centre (0, 0), radius: 2
(c) centre $\left(\frac{3}{2}, -1\right)$, radius: $\frac{\sqrt{11}}{2}$
(d) centre (3, −1), radius: 3 **(e)** centre (4, −3), radius: 6

7. **(a)** $x^2 + y^2 = 4$ **(b)** $(x + 1)^2 + (y - 2)^2 = 9$
(c) $x^2 + (y - 4)^2 = 5$ **(d)** $(x + 2)^2 + (y - 7)^2 = 24$

8. $(x + 3)^2 + (y - 4)^2 = 16$

9. The equations of the family of circles will all be of the form: $(x - a)^2 + (y - a)^2 = 64$. Graphically, the circles' centres will all be on the line $y = x$.

10. **(a)** $x^2 + (y - 6)^2 = 8$ **(b)** $(x - 2)^2 + (y + 2)^2 = 17$
(c) $x^2 + y^2 = 64$ **(d)** $x^2 + (y - 2)^2 = 16$
(e) $(x + 1)^2 + (y - 2)^2 = 20$

11. $x^2 + y^2 - 8x + 6y + 30 = 0$ is not a circle since the radius cannot be a negative number.

12. **(a)** semicircle above x-axis with centre at origin and radius 2
(b) semicircle above x-axis with centre at origin and radius 3
(c) semicircle below x-axis with centre at origin and radius 4
(d) semicircle to right of y-axis with centre at origin and radius 3
(e) semicircle above x-axis with centre (0, 2) and radius 3
(f) semicircle with centre at (0, 3), radius 5, x-intercepts at 4 and −4

13. **(a)** $x^2 + y^2 = 25$ **(b)** $(x - 2)^2 + (y - 3)^2 = 20$
(c) $x^2 + y^2 = 5$ **(d)** $(x + 1)^2 + y^2 = 17$
(e) $(x - 8)^2 + (y - 2)^2 = 53$

14. 6 units

15. **(a)** Answers will vary. **(b)** $(x - 4)^2 + (y + 3)^2 = 12$
(c) The standard form will give the centre and the radius of the circle.

16. **(a)** Yes, you can make a call using a cell phone because you are within reach of the second tower.
(b) about 222.75 km^2 **(c)** 20.01 km

17. $(x \pm 8\sqrt{2})^2 + y^2 = 64$ and $x^2 + (y \pm 8\sqrt{2})^2 = 64$

18. $(x - 1)^2 + y^2 = 4$; circle with centre (1, 0) and radius 2.

19. semicircle above x-axis with centre at origin and radius 5
(a) $A(-5, 0)$, $B(5, 0)$ **(b)** $C(0, 5)$

20. $(x, y) = (0.22, -1.66)$ and $(-2.22, 5.66)$

Practice 7.3U, page 584

1. **(a)** $y = \sqrt{25 - x^2}$ and $y = -\sqrt{25 - x^2}$

2. **(a)** graph moves 2 spaces to left
(b) graph moves 4 units up
(c) graph will be centred at origin with radius 4 units
(d) graph will be move 1 unit right and 5 units down

3. **(a)** centre (0, 0), radius 3 **(b)** centre (3, 0), radius 4
(c) centre (0, −2), radius 2 **(d)** centre (1, −2), radius 5

Practise, Apply, Solve 7.4U, page 591

1. **(a)** vertices: (0, 3) and (0, −3), major axis: 6, minor axis: 4
(b) vertices: (5, 0) and (−5, 0), major axis: 10, minor axis: 8
(c) vertices: (7, 0) and (−7, 0), major axis: 14, minor axis: 6
(d) vertices: (7, 0) and (−7, 0), major axis: 14, minor axis: 8
(e) vertices: (0, 10) and (0, −10), major axis: 20, minor axis: 10
(f) vertices: (9, 0) and (−9, 0), major axis: 18, minor axis: 16

2. **(a)** centre: (2, 0), major axis (horizontal): 6, minor axis: 4
(b) centre: (−1, 3), major axis (horizontal): 10, minor axis: 2
(c) centre: (3, −4), major axis (horizontal): 20, minor axis: 8
(d) centre: (1, −2), major axis (vertical): 4, minor axis: $2\sqrt{2}$
(e) centre: (−1, −1), major axis (vertical): 16, minor axis: 8
(f) centre: (−3, 4), major axis (horizontal): 6, minor axis: 4

3. **(a)** major axis: 12, minor axis: 8, foci: $(0, 2\sqrt{5})$ and $(0, -2\sqrt{5})$; centre: (0, 0), vertices: (0, 6) and (0, −6)
(b) major axis: 12, minor axis: $6\sqrt{2}$, foci: $(0, 3\sqrt{2})$ and $(0, -3\sqrt{2})$; centre: (0, 0), vertices: (0, 6) and (0, −6)
(c) major axis: $4\sqrt{3}$, minor axis: $4\sqrt{2}$, foci: (0, 2) and (0, −2); centre: (0, 0), vertices: $(0, 2\sqrt{3})$ and $(0, -2\sqrt{3})$
(d) major axis: $12\sqrt{2}$, minor axis: 6, foci: $(3\sqrt{7}, 0)$ and $(-3\sqrt{7}, 0)$, centre: (0, 0), vertices: $(\sqrt{72}, 0)$ and $(-\sqrt{72}, 0)$
(e) major axis:8, minor axis: 4, foci: $(2\sqrt{3}, 0)$ and , $(-2\sqrt{3}, 0)$; centre: (0, 0), vertices: (−4, 0) and (4, 0)
(f) major axis: 10, minor axis: 4, foci: $(0, \sqrt{21})$ and $(0, -\sqrt{21})$; centre: (0, 0), vertices: (0, 5) and (0, −5)

4. **(a)** $\frac{x^2}{9} + \frac{y^2}{20.25} = 1$ **(b)** $\frac{x^2}{25} + \frac{y^2}{9} = 1$

(c) $\frac{x^2}{100} + \frac{y^2}{36} = 1$ (d) $\frac{x^2}{16} + \frac{y^2}{12} = 1$

(e) $\frac{x^2}{28} + \frac{y^2}{64} = 1$

5. (a) centre: (1, 0), major axis (vertical): 6, minor axis: 4
(b) centre: (2, 0), major axis (horizontal): 6, minor axis: 4
(c) centre: (0, 0), major axis (vertical): 12, minor axis: $6\sqrt{2}$
(d) centre: (−3, 1), major axis (horizontal): 20, minor axis: 14
(e) centre: (0, 3), major axis (vertical): $4\sqrt{10}$, minor axis: 8
(f) centre: (1, 0), major axis (horizontal): 6, minor axis: 2

6. (a) vertices: (0, 4), (0, −4); major axis: 8, minor axis: 6; foci: $(0, \sqrt{7}), (0, -\sqrt{7})$; equation: $\frac{x^2}{9} + \frac{y^2}{16} = 1$,
$D = \{x| -3 \le x \le 3, x \in \mathbf{R}\}, R = \{y| -4 \le y \le 4, y \in \mathbf{R}\}$
(b) vertices: (6, 0), (−6, 0); major axis: 12, minor axis: 10; foci: $(\sqrt{11}, 0), (-\sqrt{11}, 0)$; equation: $\frac{x^2}{36} + \frac{y^2}{25} = 1$;
$D = \{x| -6 \le x \le 6, x \in \mathbf{R}\}, R = \{y| -5 \le y \le 5, y \in \mathbf{R}\}$
(c) vertices: (0, 8), (0, −8); major axis: 16, minor axis: 12; foci: $(0, 2\sqrt{7}), (0, -2\sqrt{7})$; equation: $\frac{x^2}{36} + \frac{y^2}{64} = 1$;
$D = \{x| -6 \le x \le 6, x \in \mathbf{R}\}, R = \{y| -8 \le y \le 8, y \in \mathbf{R}\}$
(d) vertices: (4, 0), (−4, 0); major axis: 8, minor axis: 4; foci: $(2\sqrt{3}, 0), (-2\sqrt{3}, 0)$; equation: $\frac{x^2}{16} + \frac{y^2}{4} = 1$;
$D = \{x| -4 \le x \le 4, x \in \mathbf{R}\}, R = \{y| -2 \le y \le 2, y \in \mathbf{R}\}$

7. The ellipse will be very wide and not very tall. The major axis is 100 units long and the minor axis is about 20 units long.

8. (a) centre: (2, −1), major axis: 8, minor axis: 4
(b) centre: (−1, −2), major axis: 8, minor axis: $2\sqrt{2}$
(c) centre: (−1, 2), major axis: 8, minor axis: $2\sqrt{3}$
(d) centre: (0, 3), major axis: $2\sqrt{40}$ or $4\sqrt{10}$, minor axis: 8

9. (a) $y = \pm\sqrt{32 - x^2}$ (b) $y = \pm 3\sqrt{1 - \frac{x^2}{5}}$
(c) $y = \pm\sqrt{-4x^2 + 8x + 12}$

10. $\frac{x^2}{169} + \frac{y^2}{144} = 1$

11. $\frac{x^2}{9} + \frac{y^2}{25} = 1$

12. (a) 2.996×10^8 km (b) $\frac{x^2}{2.2500 \times 10^{16}} + \frac{y^2}{2.2493 \times 10^{16}} = 1$

13. The equation is $\frac{x^2}{6} + \frac{y^2}{12} = 1$.

14. The running area is an ellipse 8 m wide and $4\sqrt{3}$ m high.

15. (a) $x^2 + \frac{(y-1)^2}{4} = 1$ (b) $\frac{(x-1)^2}{9} + \frac{(y+1)^2}{4} = 1$
(c) $\frac{(x-2)^2}{4} + \frac{(y+1)^2}{16} = 1$ (d) $\frac{x^2}{9} + \frac{(y+5)^2}{16} = 1$

16. (a) $D = \{x| -5 \le x \le 5, x \in \mathbf{R}\}, R = \{y| -3 \le y \le 3, y \in \mathbf{R}\}$
(b) $D = \{x| -4 \le x \le 4, x \in \mathbf{R}\}, R = \{y| -6 \le y \le 6, y \in \mathbf{R}\}$
(c) $D = \{x| -5 \le x \le 5, x \in \mathbf{R}\}, R = \{y| -2 \le y \le 2, y \in \mathbf{R}\}$
(d) $D = \{x| -3 \le x \le 3, x \in \mathbf{R}\}, R = \{y| -4 \le y \le 4, y \in \mathbf{R}\}$
(e) $D = \{x| -4 \le x \le 4, x \in \mathbf{R}\}, R = \{y| -2 \le y \le 2, y \in \mathbf{R}\}$
(f) $D = \{x| -7 \le x \le 5, x \in \mathbf{R}\}, R = \{y| -1 \le y \le 3, y \in \mathbf{R}\}$

17. $\frac{x^2}{90} + \frac{y^2}{10} = 1$

18. A circle is an ellipse with both foci at the centre. The length of the major and minor axes is the length of the diameter of the circle. The circle could also satisfy the locus definition of the ellipse.

19. The driver's truck will just fit under the arch.

20. Yes, points (40, 120) and (60, 80) both lie within the ellipse.

Practise, Apply, Solve 7.6U, page 602

1. (a) focus: (0, −4) directrix: $y = 4$
(b) focus: $\left(\frac{15}{4}, 0\right)$ directrix: $x = -\frac{15}{4}$
(c) focus: $\left(0, \frac{1}{4}\right)$ directrix: $y = -\frac{1}{4}$
(d) focus: $\left(0, \frac{1}{8}\right)$ directrix: $y = -\frac{1}{8}$
(e) focus: (2, 0) directrix: $x = -2$
(f) focus: $\left(0, \frac{1}{40}\right)$ directrix: $y = -\frac{1}{40}$

2. (a) vertex: (0, 4), opens upward
(b) vertex: (2, 0), opens to the right
(c) vertex: (0, −12), opens upward
(d) vertex: (3, 0), opens upward
(e) vertex: (3, 2), opens downward
(f) vertex: (−2, 1), opens to the right

3. (a) $(y-2)^2 = 4(x-1)$, vertex: (1, 2), opens to the right
(b) $x^2 = 4(y+2)$, vertex: (0, −2), opens upward
(c) $(x-1)^2 = 4(y-1)$, vertex: (1, 1), opens upward
(d) $(y-3)^2 = 2(x-1)$, vertex: (1, 3), opens to the right
(e) $(y-1)^2 = 8(x+2)$, vertex: (−2, 1), opens to the right
(f) $(x-2)^2 = 2(y+10)$, vertex: (2, −10), opens upward

4. *Refer to the vertex and direction of opening given in Question 3 when drawing the parabolas.*
(i) (a) through (2, 0) and (2, 4) (b) through $(2\sqrt{2}, 0)$ and $(-2\sqrt{2}, 0)$ (c) through (3, 2) and (−1, 2) (d) through (5.5, 0) and (5.5, 6) (e) through $(15, 1 + 2\sqrt{34})$ and $(15, 1 - 2\sqrt{34})$
(f) through $(2 + 2\sqrt{5}, 0)$ and $(2 - 2\sqrt{5}, 0)$
ii. (a) $D = \{x| x \ge 1, x \in \mathbf{R}\}, R = \mathbf{R}$ (b) $D = \mathbf{R}$, $R = \{y| y \ge -2, y \in \mathbf{R}\}$ (c) $D = \mathbf{R}, R = \{y| y \ge 1, y \in \mathbf{R}\}$
(d) $D = \{x| x \ge 1\}, R = \mathbf{R}$ (e) $D = \{x| x \ge -1, x \in \mathbf{R}\}$, $R = \mathbf{R}$ (f) $D = \mathbf{R}, R = \{y| y \ge -10, y \in \mathbf{R}\}$

5. Answers will vary.

6. $y^2 = 16x$

7. (a) $y^2 = 12x$ (b) $x^2 = 8y$
(c) $y^2 = -16x$ (d) $y^2 = -2x$

8. (a) $y^2 = -2x$ (b) $(-\frac{1}{2}, 0)$
(c) $x = \frac{1}{2}$

9. The bulb should be at the focus (8, 0).

10. (a) $f > 2.25$ m (b) $1.5 \text{ m} \le f \le 2.25$ m
(c) $f < 1.5$ m

11. 301.6 cm^2

12. 125 cm

13. $y = (x-2)^2 - 2$: parabola opens up, vertex (2, −2), y-intercept at (0, 2), x-intercepts at $(2 - \sqrt{2}, 0)$ and $(2 + \sqrt{2}, 0)$;
$y = 2 + \sqrt{x+2}, y = 2 - \sqrt{x+2}$: parabola opens right, vertex (−2, 2), through (2, 4) and (2, 0); take the square root of both sides, then add 2 to both sides.

14. (a) $y^2 = 12(x+1)$ (b) $x^2 = 6(y - 2.5)$
(c) $(x-1)^2 = 4(y-1)$

15. $\frac{(x-1)^2}{9} - \frac{(y-6)^2}{16} = 1$

16.

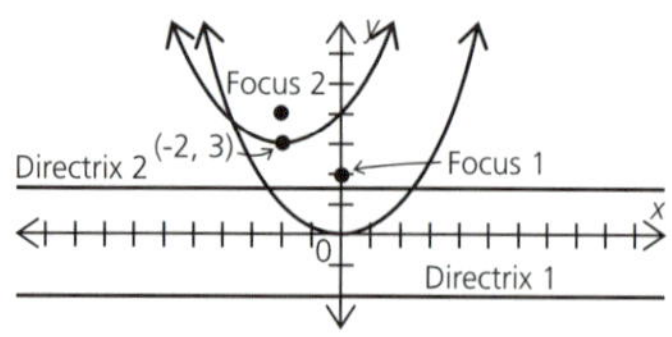

17. 10 m

18. $(x-4)^2 = -(y-3)$

19. (a) Similarities: both equations have hs and ks and an $(x-h)^2$. Differences: second equation has $4p$ and $(y-k)$ in brackets whereas k is on the other side of the first equation.

(b) Start with the second form: $(x - h)^2 = 4p(y - k)$;
$\frac{1}{4p}(x - h)^2 = y - k$; $\frac{1}{4p}(x - h)^2 + k = y$. If $a = \frac{1}{4p}$, then we have $a(x - h)^2 + k = y$, which is same as first equation.

20. Parabolas can intersect in four ways:

infinite points of intersection

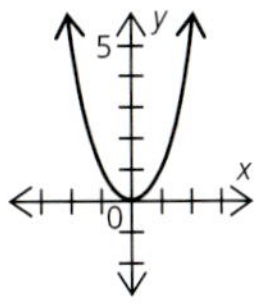

one point of intersection

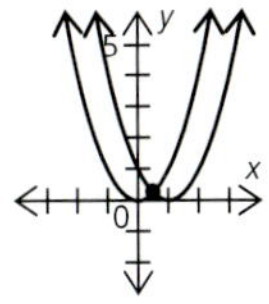

two points of intersection

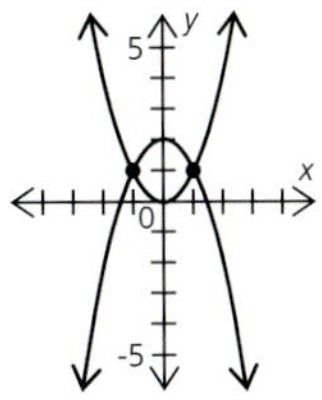

and four points of intersection.

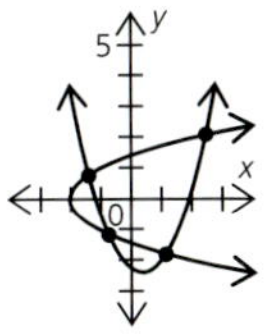

21. $\left(\frac{-1}{3}, \frac{-20}{9}\right)$ and $(3, -10)$

Practice 7.8U, page 608

1. **(a)** parabola; opens upward and is 4 units above x-axis; passing through $(-1, 5)$ and $(1, 5)$
(b) circle; centred at origin with radius 3 units
(c) ellipse; centred at origin, with major vertical axis of 16 units and minor axis of units 8
(d) ellipse; centred at $(2, -1)$ with major vertical axis of 8 units, and minor axis of 6 units
(e) circle; centred at $(-3, 0)$ with radius 2 units
(f) parabola; opens upward with a vertex of $(2, -1)$; y-intercept at $(0, 1)$, x-intercepts at $(2 - \sqrt{2}, 0)$ and $(2 + \sqrt{2}, 0)$

2. **(a)** $\frac{x^2}{9} + \frac{y^2}{4} = 1$
(b) ellipse centred at $(0, 0)$ with major (horizontal) axis: 6, minor axis: 4

3. **(a)** $(x + 3)^2 = 2(y - 2)$; parabola, opens up, vertex $(-3, 2)$, through $(-6, 6.5)$ and $(0, 6.5)$
(b) $(x - 1)^2 = 2(y + 1)$; parabola, opens up, vertex $(1, -1)$, x-intercepts at $(1 - \sqrt{2}, 0)$ and $(1 + \sqrt{2}, 0)$
(c) $(x - 2)^2 = 2(y - 3)$; parabola, opens up, vertex $(2, 3)$, through $(4, 5)$ and $(0, 5$
(d) $(x + 1)^2 = 2(y + 5)$; parabola, opens up, vertex $(-1, 5)$, through $(3, 3)$ and $(-5, 3)$

Practise, Apply, Solve 7.9U, page 615

1. **(a)** x-int.: ± 3 **(b)** y-int.: ± 2
(c) x-int.: $\pm\sqrt{18}$ or $\pm 3\sqrt{2}$ **(d)** y-int.: $\pm\sqrt{12}$, $\pm 2\sqrt{5}$
(e) x-int.: $\pm\sqrt{20}$ or $2\sqrt{5}$ **(f)** x-int.: $\pm\sqrt{10}$

2. **(a)** $a = \sqrt{5}, b = \sqrt{20}$ or $2\sqrt{5}, c = 5$
(b) $a = 6, b = 3, c = \sqrt{45}$ or $3\sqrt{5}$
(c) $a = \sqrt{20}$ or $2\sqrt{5}, b = \sqrt{5}, c = 5$
(d) $a = 2, b = 4, c = \sqrt{20}$ or $2\sqrt{5}$
(e) $a = \sqrt{12}$ or $3\sqrt{2}, b = \sqrt{8}$ or $2\sqrt{2}, c = \sqrt{20}$ or $2\sqrt{5}$
(f) $a = 12, b = 9, c = 15$

3. **(a)** asymptotes: $y = \frac{3}{2}x, y = -\frac{3}{2}x$; intercepts: $(2, 0), (-2, 0)$; foci: $(-\sqrt{13}, 0), (\sqrt{13}, 0)$
(b) asymptotes: $y = \frac{4}{\sqrt{5}}x, y = -\frac{4}{\sqrt{5}}x$; intercepts: $(-\sqrt{5}, 0)$ and $(\sqrt{5}, 0)$; foci: $(\sqrt{21}, 0), (-\sqrt{21}, 0)$
(c) asymptotes: $y = \frac{9}{5}x, y = -\frac{9}{5}x$; intercepts: intercepts: $(0, 9)$ and $(0, -9)$; foci: $(0, \sqrt{106}), (0, -\sqrt{106})$
(d) asymptotes: $y = \frac{2\sqrt{2}}{5}x, y = -\frac{2\sqrt{2}}{5}x$; intercepts: $(0, 2\sqrt{2})$, $(0, -2\sqrt{2})$; foci: $(0, -\sqrt{33}), (0, \sqrt{33})$
(e) asymptotes: asymptotes: $y = \frac{1}{\sqrt{2}}x, y = -\frac{1}{\sqrt{2}}x$; intercepts: $(0, 3), (0, -3)$; foci: $(0, \sqrt{27}), (0, -\sqrt{27})$
(f) asymptotes: $y = \frac{4}{3}x$ and $y = -\frac{4}{3}x$, intercepts: $(0, 4), (0, -4)$; foci: $(0, 5), (0, -5)$

4. **(a)** centre: $(0, 0)$, vertices: $(3, 0), (-3, 0)$; asymptotes: $y = \frac{4}{3}x$, $y = -\frac{4}{3}x$
(b) centre: $(0, 0)$, vertices: $(5, 0), (-5, 0)$; asymptotes: $y = \frac{2}{5}x$, $y = -\frac{2}{5}x$
(c) centre: $(0, 0)$, vertices: $(2, 0), (-2, 0)$; $y = \sqrt{2}x, y = -\sqrt{2}x$
(d) centre: $(0, 0)$, vertices: $(6, 0), (-6, 0)$; asymptotes: $y = \frac{3}{2}x$, $y = -\frac{3}{2}x$
(e) centre: $(2, 0)$, vertices: $(5, 0), (-1, 0)$; asymptotes: $y = \frac{5}{3}(x - 2), y = -\frac{5}{3}(x - 2)$
(f) centre: $(-6, 1)$, vertices: $(-7, 1), (-5, 1)$; asymptotes: $y = \frac{1}{2}x + 4, y = \frac{-1}{2}x + 4$

5. **(a)** $y = x, y = -x$ **(b)** $y = 2x, y = -2x$
(c) $y = \frac{5}{3}x, y = -\frac{5}{3}x$ **(d)** $y = 2x, y = -2x$

6. **(a)** $(-7, 0)$ and $(7, 0)$ **(b)** 14 units
(c) $(-\sqrt{65}, 0)$ and $(\sqrt{65}, 0)$ **(d)** $y = \frac{4}{7}x$ and $y = -\frac{4}{7}x$

7. **(a)** $\frac{x^2}{28} - \frac{y^2}{36} = -1$ **(b)** $\frac{x^2}{27} - \frac{y^2}{9} = -1$
(c) $\frac{x^2}{4} - \frac{y^2}{16} = -1$ **(d)** $\frac{x^2}{9} - \frac{y^2}{16} = 1$

8. **(a)** asymptotes: $y = \frac{1}{3}x, y = -\frac{1}{3}x$, intercepts: $(3, 0), (-3, 0)$
(b) asymptotes: $y = \frac{1}{3}x, y = -\frac{1}{3}x$, intercepts: $(0, 1), (0, -1)$
(c) asymptotes: $y = 3x, y = -3x$, intercepts: $(1, 0), (-1, 0)$
(d) asymptotes: $y = 3x, y = -3x$, intercepts: $(0, 3), (0, -3)$
The asymptotes of the first two graphs are the same but the graphs are oriented different ways. The asymptotes of the second two graphs are the same but the graphs are oriented different ways.

9. Asymptotes are $y = x$ and $y = -x$; conjugate and transverse axes are same length; $c = \sqrt{2}a$

10. $\frac{x^2}{5} - \frac{y^2}{4} = -1$; asymptotes: $y = \frac{2}{\sqrt{5}}x, y = -\frac{2}{\sqrt{5}}x$; intercepts: $(0, 2), (0, -2)$

11. centre $(2, -4)$, asymptotes: $y = x - 6, y = -x - 2$

12. **(a)** $\frac{(x + 3)^2}{9} - \frac{(y - 2)^2}{25} = 1$ **(b)** $\frac{(x - 4)^2}{9} - \frac{(y + 3)^2}{25} = 1$
(c) $\frac{(x - 2)^2}{9} - \frac{y^2}{25} = 1$ **(d)** $\frac{(x + 8)^2}{9} - \frac{(y + 4)^2}{25} = 1$

13.

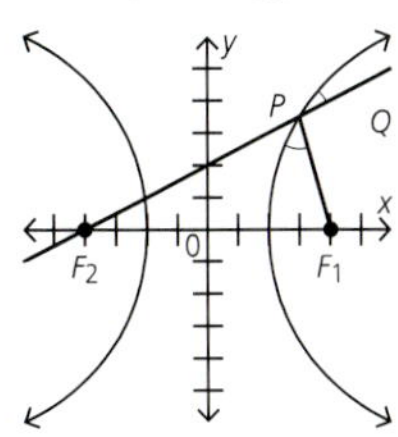

Answers will vary. According to this diagram: A ray originating at one focal point, F_1, will reflect at P and follow to Q. An exterior of PQ will pass through F_2.

14. 10.16 m

15. $\frac{(x-1)^2}{9} - \frac{(y-6)^2}{16} = 1$

16. $\frac{(x-1)^2}{4} - \frac{(y-4)^2}{5} = 1$

17. $\frac{x^2}{225} - \frac{y^2}{2275} = 1$

18.

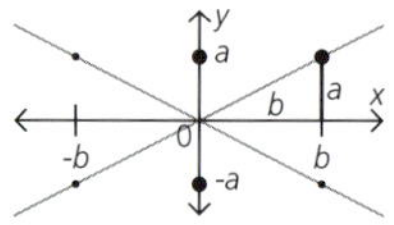

From the diagram, the slope of the asymptotes is $\frac{a}{b}$ and $-\frac{a}{b}$. The equations of the asymptotes are: $y = \frac{a}{b}x$ and $y = -\frac{a}{b}x$.

19. The asymptotes are $y = \frac{5}{3}(x-2)$ and $y = -\frac{5}{3}(x-2)$. The asymptotes for a hyperbola are $y - k = \frac{b}{a}(x-h)$ and $y - k = \frac{-b}{a}(x-h)$.

20. foci: $(-4, 0)$, $(4, 0)$

Practise, Apply, Solve 7.10U, page 620

1. **(a)** parabola, vertex $(-1, 2)$ **(b)** hyperbola, centre $(-1, 0)$ **(c)** ellipse, centre $(3, 8)$ **(d)** ellipse, centre $(0, -6)$ **(e)** parabola, vertex $(-1, 1)$ **(f)** hyperbola, centre $(2, -2)$

2. **(a)** hyperbola **(b)** ellipse **(c)** parabola **(d)** ellipse **(e)** circle **(f)** hyperbola **(g)** ellipse **(h)** parabola

3. **(a)** hyperbola, centre $(-4, 2)$, foci on horizontal axis
(b) ellipse, centre $(1, 0)$, foci on vertical axis
(c) hyperbola, centre $(-3, -4)$, foci on horizontal axis

4. **(a)** parabola
(b) $(x-1)^2 = \frac{1}{3}(y+2)$
(c) vertex: $(1, -2)$, passing through $(0, 1)$ and $(2, 1)$

5. **(a)** hyperbola
(b) $\frac{(x-2)^2}{\frac{1}{3}} - (y-2)^2 = 1$
(c) centre $(1, 2)$, asymptotes: $y = 3x - 1$, $y = -3x + 5$, x-axis is the transverse axis

6. **(a)** circle **(b)** $(x-2)^2 + (y+3)^2 = 1$
(c) centre $(2, -3)$, radius 1

7. **(a)** ellipse, $4x^2 + 9y^2 - 54y + 45 = 0$
(b) ellipse, $x^2 + y^2 + 6x - 2y + 1 = 0$
(c) hyperbola, $x^2 - 4y^2 + 8x + 24y - 4 = 0$
(d) parabola, $x^2 - 4x + 6y + 10 = 0$
(e) hyperbola, $5x^2 - 4y^2 - 10x - 16y - 31 = 0$
(f) parabola, $y^2 + 6y - 2x + 11 = 0$

8. **(a)** $\frac{(x-2)^2}{9} + \frac{(y+3)^2}{4} = 1$, ellipse, centre: $(2, -3)$, major axis (horizontal): 6, minor axis:
(b) $\frac{(x-3)^2}{9} + \frac{4\left(y+\frac{9}{2}\right)^2}{81} = 1$; hyperbola, centre: $\left(3, \frac{9}{2}\right)$, asymptotes: $y = \frac{3}{2}x - 9$, $y = -\frac{3}{2}x$, y-axis is transverse axis
(c) $\frac{(x-3)^2}{3} - \frac{(y+2)^2}{2} = 1$, ellipse, centre :$(3, -2)$, major axis (horizontal): $2\sqrt{3}$, minor axis: $2\sqrt{2}$
(d) $\frac{-4\left(x-\frac{3}{2}\right)^2}{17} + \frac{2(y-1)^2}{17} = 1$; hyperbola, centre: $\left(\frac{3}{2}, 1\right)$, asymptotes: $y = -\sqrt{2}x + \frac{3\sqrt{2}}{2} + 1$ and $\sqrt{2}x - \frac{3\sqrt{2}}{2} + 1$, y-axis is transverse axis
(e) $(y-4)^2 = 8(x+2)$; parabola, opens to right, vertex $(-2, 4)$, passing through $(0, 8)$ and $(0, 0)$

9. This equation appears to be of an ellipse since a and b do not equal 1. But, $a = b$; so this equation is of a circle.

10. **(a)** $(2, 0)$
(b) foci: $(2, 6)$, $(2, -6)$, vertices: $(2, \sqrt{30})$, $(2, -\sqrt{30})$
(c) transverse axis: $2\sqrt{30}$, conjugate axis: $2\sqrt{6}$
(d) $y = \pm\sqrt{5}(x-2)$

11. $y^2 - 4y + 12x - 44 = 0$

12. $x^2 + y^2 - 4x - 6y - 12 = 0$

13. **(a)** parabola, opens to right, vertex $(4, -3)$, passing through $(5, -1)$ and $(5, -5)$
(b) hyperbola, centre $(2, 3)$, asymptotes: $y = \frac{3}{4}x + \frac{3}{2}$, $y = \frac{-3}{4}x + \frac{9}{2}$, y-axis is transverse axis
(c) ellipse, centre: $(1, 0)$, major axis (vertical): 8, minor axis: 4
(d) parabola, opens up, vertex $(2, 8)$, passing through $(0, 12)$ and $(4, 12)$
(e) ellipse, centre: $(-2, 2)$, major axis (vertical): 10, minor axis: 4

14. $2x^2 - y^2 - 16x + 2y + 31 = 0$

15. $(x, y) \rightarrow (x+3, y+3)$

16. $11x^2 - 25y^2 - 275 = 0$

17. $x^2 + y^2 - 4x - 6y - 4 = 0$

18. Answers may vary.

19. $\frac{x^2}{4} - \frac{y^2}{7} = 1$

20. **(a)** $16x^2 + 25y^2 - 32x - 384 = 0$
(b) $7x^2 - 9y^2 + 14x - 56 = 0$
(c) $9x^2 + 25y^2 + 36x - 150y + 36 = 0$
(d) $11x^2 - 25y^2 + 22x + 200y - 664 = 0$

Practise, Apply, Solve 7.11U, page 626

1. **(a)** $(-3, 4)$ $(4, -3)$ **(b)** $(-2, 1)$ **(c)** $(-1, -2)$ $(1, -2)$

2. hyperbola, vertices $(-2, 0)$, $(2, 0)$; straight line through $(2, 0)$ and $(0, 4)$; intersect at $(2, 0)$

3. parabola, opens up, vertex $(0, 0)$; straight line through $(0, 5)$ and $\left(\frac{5}{3}, 0\right)$; intersect at $(1, 2)$ and $(-2.5, 12.5)$

4. circle centred on $(7, -4)$, radius $(7, 4)$; straight line through $(0, 5)$ and $(2.5, 0)$; intersect at $(5, -5)$

5. straight line through $(0, 0)$ and $(1, 1)$; ellipse, with centre $(1, 1)$, major axis (horizontal) $4\sqrt{5}$; minor axis $2\sqrt{5}$; intersect at $(-1, -1)$ and $(3, 3)$

6. **(a)** ellipse, vertices $(0, 2\sqrt{5})$ and $(0, -2\sqrt{5})$; straight line through $(0, 2)$ and $(1, 0)$
(b) $\left(-\frac{2}{3}, \frac{10}{3}\right)$, $(2, -2)$

7. **(a)** $(-8, -6)$, $(6, 8)$ **(b)** $(\sqrt{21}, 5)$, $(-\sqrt{21}, 5)$
(c) $(1, -1)$, $(-4, 14)$ **(d)** $\left(\frac{3}{2}, 2\right)$, $(-1, -3)$
(e) $(-2.4, 4.4)$, $(4.4, -2.4)$

8. $(1.08, -6.8)$, $(-6.8, 10.43)$

9. *Examples*:
(a) $y = -\frac{2}{3}x + 2$, intersect at $(3, 0)$ and $(0, 2)$
(b) $y = -2$, intersect at $(0, -2)$
(c) $y = -\frac{2}{3}x + 4$, no intersection

10. *Examples*:
(a) $x = 1$, intersect at $\left(0, 2\sqrt{\frac{5}{3}}\right)$ and $\left(0, -2\sqrt{\frac{5}{3}}\right)$

(b) $y = \sqrt{6}$, intersect at $(0, \sqrt{6})$

(c) $y = 1$; no intersection

11. $(-0.29, 0.71)$ and $(-1.71, -0.71)$

12. (a) parabola, opens right, vertex $(1, 0)$; straight line through $(0, -10)$ and $(5, 0)$; solution: $(9, 8)$ and $(3, -4)$

(b) hyperbola, centre $(2, -2)$; straight line through $(0, -0.5)$ and $(1, 0)$; solution: $(7.88, 3.44)$ and $(-0.54, -0.77)$

13. intersection points: $(5, -7)$ and $(-1, 1)$

14. Answers can vary. The lines $y = -2$ and $y = 2$ are possible solutions.

15. yes

16. Answers will vary. In each case, the algebraic solution for (i) one solution would have 1 real root; (ii) two solutions would have 2 real roots; and (iii) no solution would have no real roots; not factorable; negative under the root sign.

17.

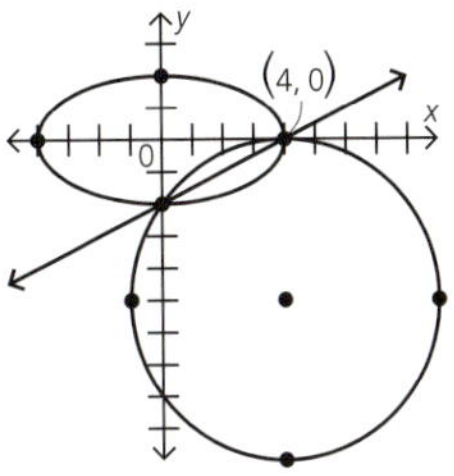

intersection points: $(4, 0)$ and $(0, -2)$

18. equation of perpendicular bisector: $y = \frac{1}{3}x + \frac{10}{3}$

19. (a) ellipse, vertices $(-7, 0)$ and $(7, 0)$; hyperbola, vertices $(0, 2)$ and $(0, -2)$

(b) solutions: $(3, \sqrt{10})$, $(-3, \sqrt{10})$, $(3, -\sqrt{10})$, $(-3, -\sqrt{10})$

20. circle centred on origin, radius 5, parabola, opens down, vertex $(0, -2)$: $(2.51, -4.32)$, $(-2.51, -4.32)$

Chapter 7, Review and Practice, page 629

1. A mathematical object can be a table of values, a curve, a line, a geometric figure, or a relation defined by an equation.

2. A circle is a locus of points equidistant from another point, the centre of the circle.

3. A straight line defined as the right bisector of the segment joining those points.

4. parabola

5. $20x - 2y + 23 = 0.$

6. two circles centred on origin, one with radius of 7 ($x^2 + y^2 = 49$) and the other with radius 3 ($x^2 + y^2 = 9$)

7. (a) centre $(0, 0)$, radius $\frac{1}{2}$ (b) centre $(-8, 3)$, radius 1

(c) centre $\left(-\frac{3}{2}, \frac{5}{2}\right)$, radius 3

8. $x^2 + y^2 = 100$

9. $(x - 2)^2 + (y - 1)^2 = 10$

10. $(x + 3)^2 + (y - 4)^2 = 16$

11. a semicircle above x-axis with centre $(0, 0)$ and radius 4

12. An ellipse is the set or locus of points in a plane such that the sum of the distances from two fixed points to any other point is constant.

13. (a) $\frac{x^2}{a^2} + \frac{y^2}{b^2} = 1$, where $a>b$

(b) $\frac{x^2}{b^2} + \frac{y^2}{a^2} = 1$ where $a>b$

14. (a) major axis $2a$ units, minor axis $2b$ units.

(b) major axis $2b$ units, minor axis $2a$ units

15. $a^2 = b^2 + c^2$

16. x-int.: $(-5, 0)$, $(5, 0)$, y-int.: $(-8, 0)$, $(8, 0)$

17. ellipse, vertices $(-10, 0)$ and $(10, 0)$, passing through $(0, 5)$, $(0, -5)$

18. $\frac{x^2}{61} + \frac{y^2}{36} = 1$

19. 13.2 m

20. Refer to Key Ideas 7.6.

21. A parabola is the locus of points in a plane the same distance from a fixed point, called the focus, and a fixed line, called the directrix.

22. (a) $x^2 = 4py$ (b) $(x - h)^2 = 4p(y - k)$

(c) $y^2 = 4pk$ (d) $(y - k)^2=4p(x - h)$

23. 8 units

24. (a) focus: $(3, 0)$, vertex: $(0, 0)$, directrix: $x = -3$

(b) focus: $(3, 0)$, vertex: $(3, -2)$, directrix: $y = -2$

25. (a) $x^2 = 8y$ (b) $(x - 1)^2 = 8(y - 2)$

26. A hyperbola is a set or locus of points, in a plane, whose distances from two fixed points have a constant difference. The two fixed points are called the foci.

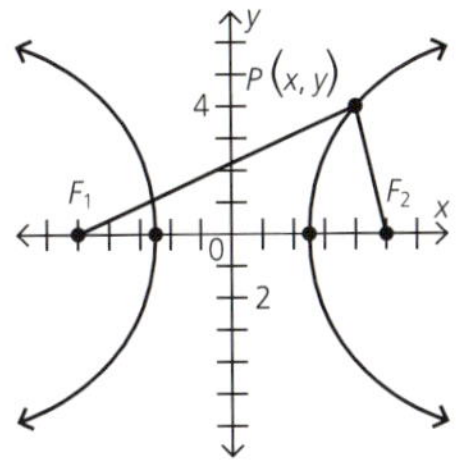

27. (a) $\frac{x^2}{a^2} - \frac{y^2}{b^2} = 1$ (b) $\frac{x^2}{b^2} - \frac{y^2}{a^2} = 1$

28. Refer to first and second diagrams in Key Ideas 7.9.

29. $\frac{(x + 4)^2}{9} - \frac{(y - 6)^2}{81} = 1$

30.

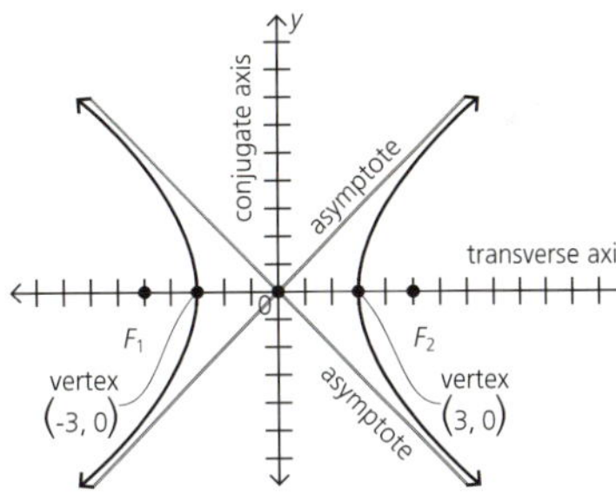

31. $\frac{(x - 3)^2}{16} - \frac{(y + 5)^2}{9} = 1$

32. First, identify the type of conic by inspecting the coefficients, a and b, of the first two terms. Then, complete the squares to identify the vertices, major/minor axes, foci, or radii of the equations. Finally, determine if there are any transformations.

33. You can write any conic in the general form: $ax^2 + by^2 + 2gx + 2fy + C = 0$. To determine the type of conic, look at the sign of ab. If $a = b$, then the conic is a circle; if $a < b$, it is an ellipse; if $a > b$, it is a hyperbola.

34. (a) ellipse, $\frac{(x + 1)^2}{9} - \frac{(y - 2)^2}{4} = 1$, vertices $(-4, 2)$, $(2, 2)$; goes through $(-1, 0)$, $(-1, 4)$

(b) circle, $\frac{(x - 1)^2}{4} - \frac{y^2}{4} = 1$, centre $(1, 0)$, radius 2

(c) hyperbola, $\frac{x^2}{\left(\frac{25}{18}\right)} - \frac{\left(y + \frac{1}{6}\right)^2}{\left(\frac{25}{26}\right)} = -1$, vertices $\left(0, \frac{2}{3}\right)$, $(0, -1)$

(d) ellipse, $\frac{(x - 6)^2}{34} - \frac{y^2}{17} = 1$, vertices $(-4, 3)$, $(4, 3)$

(e) hyperbola, $(x + 7)^2 - \frac{(y - 1)^2}{4} = 1$, vertices $(-7, 3)$, $(-7, -1)$

35.

Circle:

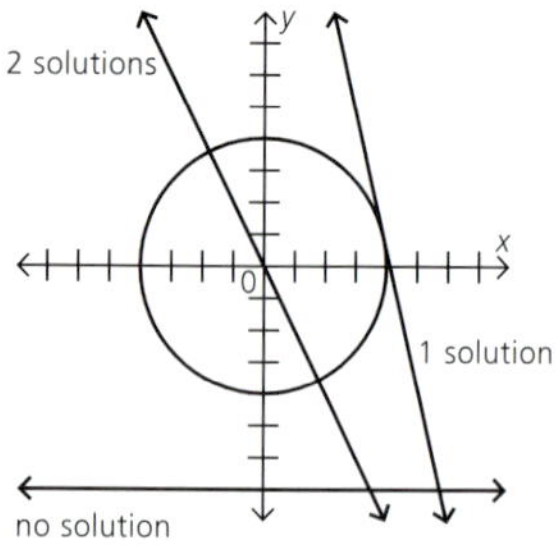

Ellipse:

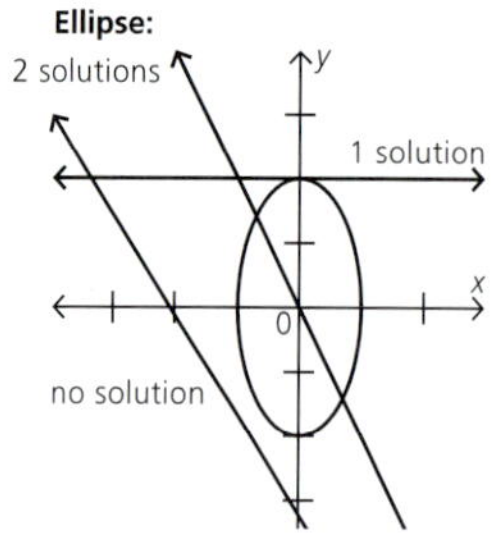

Hyperbola:

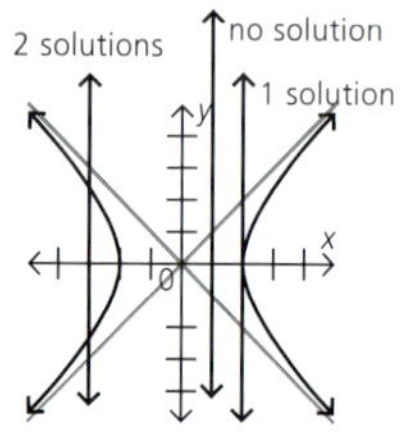

Parabola:

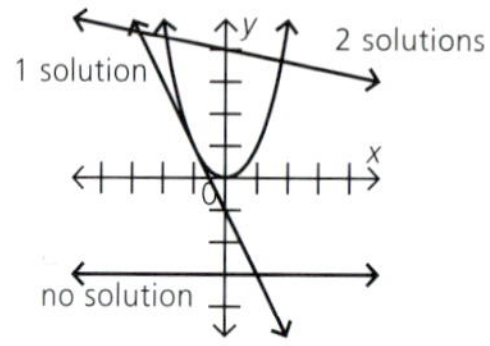

36. Graphing a system of equations is not always the best solution to finding intersection points because the solutions are not always easily read from the graph.

37. $(-4, 2)$

38. $x^2 + (y + 3)^2 = 41$

39. $(2, 3), (6, 1)$

40. $(2, -1), (-1, 2)$

Chapter 7U Review Test, page 633

1. (a) ellipse, vertices $(4, 0), (-4, 0)$, foci: $(\sqrt{7}, 0), (-\sqrt{7}, 0)$
(b) hyperbola, vertices: $(1, 0), (-1, 0)$, foci: $(\sqrt{2}, 0), (-\sqrt{2}, 0)$
(c) circle, vertices $(3, 0), (-3, 0), (0, 3), (0, -3)$, foci: $(0, 0)$
(d) parabola, vertex: $(3, 0)$, foci: $(2, 0), (-2, 0)$
(e) ellipse, vertices: $(-7, -1), (3, -1)$, foci: $(-6, 0), (2, 0)$

2. (a) $x^2 + (y + 2)^2 = 9$
(b) $\frac{x^2}{4} + \frac{y^2}{9} = -1$ (c) $x^2 = 24y$

3. focus: $\left(0, \frac{-5}{4}\right)$, directrix: $y = \frac{5}{4}$

4. In the equation: $\frac{x^2}{a^2} - \frac{y^2}{b^2} = 1$, the transverse axis is horizontal (along the x-axis). In the equation: $\frac{x^2}{b^2} - \frac{y^2}{a^2} = 1$, the transverse axis is vertical (along the y-axis).

5. (a) vertices: $(0, 5), (0, -5)$ (b) $y = \pm\frac{5}{3}x$
(c) hyperbola

6. (a) x-int.: $(5, 0), (-5, 0)$, y-int.: $(0, 8), (0, -8)$
(b) $(0, \sqrt{39}), (0, -\sqrt{39})$ (c) 16
(d) vertices: $(0, 8), (0, -8)$ (e) ellipse

7. (a) ellipse, vertices: $(0, 10), (0, -10)$, foci: $(0, 8), (0, -8)$
(b) hyperbola, vertices: $(5, 0), (-5, 0)$, foci: $(5\sqrt{5}, 0)$, $(-5\sqrt{5}, 0)$
(c) ellipse, vertices: $(0, \sqrt{12}), (0, -\sqrt{12})$, foci: $(0, 2\sqrt{2})$, $(0, -2\sqrt{2})$
(d) parabola, opens left, vertex: $(1, 2)$, focus: $(-1, 2)$
(e) hyperbola, vertices: $(5, 0), (-5, 0)$, foci: $(13, 0), (-13, 0)$

8. $\frac{x^2}{73} + \frac{16y^2}{73} = 0$

9. $\frac{101}{4}$ m

10. (a) circle (b) hyperbola (c) ellipse
(d) parabola (e) hyperbola

11. $y^2 - 12x = 0$

12. $y = -\frac{1}{2}x - 2$

13. $\frac{(x - 6)^2}{36} - \frac{y^2}{\left(\frac{81}{4}\right)} = 1$

14. $(8, 20), (2, -10)$

Cumulative Review Test 4, page 635

1. (a) $t_n = -13 + 9n$, 212, 1630
(b) $t_n = 3(1.1)^{n-1}$, 29.55, 171.82

2. (a) 14 (b) 37

3. \$986 255.97

4. (a) \$18 768.34 (b) \$7472.58 (c) \$10 485.51 (d) \$9515.60

5. (a) \$2703.65 (b) \$176.35

6. 64 months

7. (a) \$1391.05
(b) \$181 258.24, \$178 565.66, \$175 656.07, \$172 512.00, \$169 114.55
(c) principal: \$14 635.45, interest: \$68 827.55
(d) total interest: \$233 569.25, total cost: \$478 565.00

8. (a) $\frac{142}{9}$ (b) $\frac{9x^2}{16y^2}$ (c) $\frac{2^{2n}x^{3m}}{2^m x^n}$

9. (a) $x = 1 \pm \frac{\sqrt{6}}{2}i$ (b) $x = 12, x = -18$
(c) $x = -1$ (d) $x = -4, x = -5$

10. (a) $D = \{x \mid x \le 1.5, x \in \mathbf{R}\}$, $R = \{y \mid y \in \mathbf{R}\}$, not a function, fails the vertical line test
$D = \{x \mid x \in \mathbf{R}\}$, $R = \{y \mid y > 0, y \in \mathbf{R}\}$, function, passes the vertical line test
$D = \{x \mid x \ge 5, x \in \mathbf{R}\}$, $R = \{y \mid y \ge 0, y \in \mathbf{R}\}$, function, every x value corresponds to a unique y value
$D = \{x \mid x \in \mathbf{R}\}$, $R = \{y \mid y \ge 4, y \in \mathbf{R}\}$, function, every x value corresponds to a unique y value

11. (b) g^{-1} is $y = \pm\sqrt{\frac{2 - x}{3} + 1} + 1$
(c) $D(g(x)) = \{x \mid x \ge 1, x \in \mathbf{R}\}$ or $D(g(x)) = \{x \mid x \le 1, x \in \mathbf{R}\}$
(d) no, graph of g in that region fails the horizontal line test

13. (a) $x \le 2$ (b) $x < -\frac{1}{2}$

14. (a) horizontal shift $\frac{9}{16}$ units right, horizontal stretch by factor $\frac{2}{3}$, vertical translation $\frac{101}{128}$ units up

15. (a) $k < \frac{27}{8}, k = \frac{27}{8}, k > \frac{27}{8}$ (b) $|k| > 12, |k| \pm 12, |k| < 12$
(c) $k < \frac{1}{4}, k = \frac{1}{4}, k > \frac{1}{4}$

17. (a) zero: $x = 0$, asymptote: $x = -1$, $D = \{x \mid x \ne -1, x \in \mathbf{R}\}$, $R = \{y \mid y \ne 1, y \in \mathbf{R}\}$ no zeros, asymptotes: $x = -2$ and $x = 3$, $D = \{x \mid x \ne -2, x \ne 3, x \in \mathbf{R}\}$, $R = \{y \mid y \ne 0, y \in \mathbf{R}\}$
(c) zeros: $x \pm 2$, asymptote: $x = 0$, $D = \{x \mid x \ne 0\ x \in \mathbf{R}\}$
$R = \{y \mid y \in \mathbf{R}\}$

18. (a) $-46x^3 - 96x^2 - 50x - 8$ (b) $6x^3 + 22x^2y - 26xy^2 + 6y^3$

19. (a) $\frac{5x(x - 1)}{(x - 5)(x + 1)}, x \ne 5, -1$ (b) $-\frac{4x}{5y}, x \ne 0, y \ne 0$
(c) $\frac{(2m + 5)(m - 3)^2}{m^2 - m + 9}, m \ne -2, \frac{1 \pm \sqrt{35}i}{2}$
(d) $\frac{y(x + y)}{(x - 4)(x - y)}, x \ne 0, 4, y; y \ne 0$ (e) $0, x \ne 0, y \ne 0$
(f) $\frac{-3x - 1}{(x + 3)(x - 5)(x + 2)}, x \ne -3, 5, -2$

20. $\theta = 42.36°$

21. (a) $\frac{7\pi}{36}$ rad (b) $\frac{16\pi}{9}$ rad (c) $-\pi$ rad (d) $\frac{5\pi}{4}$ rad

22. (a) 157.5° (b) −15° (c) 480° (d) 56.25°

25. (a) $y = 2\cos\left(\theta - \frac{\pi}{4}\right) - 2$ or $y = 2\sin\left(\theta + \frac{\pi}{4}\right) - 2$

(b) $y = -1.75\cos\theta + 3.25$

26. (a) $d(t) = 3.25\cos\left(\frac{\pi}{12}\right)(t - 0.1) + 14.75$

(c) 5:48 a.m and 6:12 p.m; 10 a.m and 2 p.m

27. (a) $x = 0, \frac{\pi}{3}, \frac{2\pi}{3}$ (b) 36.9°, 323.1°

(c) $x = 0, \frac{\pi}{2}, \frac{2\pi}{3}, \pi, \frac{3\pi}{2}, \frac{4\pi}{3}, 2\pi$ (d) $x = 340.5°, 199.5°$

29. 44.34 km

30. $\angle N = 67°$, $\angle M = 75°$, $m = 47$ cm

31. 289.03 m

32. 5, 3, 22, 94, 464, 2044

33. (a) $8 + 6i$ (b) 3 (c) $22 - 7i$ (d) $8 - 9i$

(e) $-\frac{8}{5} + \frac{10}{11}i$ (f) $2i$ (g) $\frac{6}{169} + \frac{87}{169}i$ (h) $\frac{145}{22} - \frac{9}{122}i$

35. (a) vertices: (−4, 0) (4, 0); foci: (−2.65, 0) (2.65, 0)

(b) vertices: (−3, 0) (3, 0); foci: (−3.16, 0) (3.16, 0)

(c) vertex: (8, 4); focus:(7.5, 4)

(d) vertices:(0, −4) (0, 4); foci: (0, −4.5) (0, 4.5)

36. (a) $\frac{(x-2)^2}{16} + \frac{(y-3)^2}{81} = 1$ (b) $\frac{9}{25}x^2 - y^2 = 9$

37. (a) ellipse (b) parabola (c) hyperbola (d) circle

38. (a) $xy = 8$ (b) $y = -x + 6$

39. $(0, -4)$ and $\left(\frac{6}{5}, -\frac{8}{5}\right)$

Using the TI-83 Plus Graphing Calculator

Preparing the Calculator

Before you graph any relation, be sure to clear any information left on the calculator from the last time it was used. You should always do the following:

1. **Clear all data in the lists.**
   Press [2nd] [+] [4] [ENTER].

2. **Turn off all stat plots.**
   Press [2nd] [Y=] [4] [ENTER].

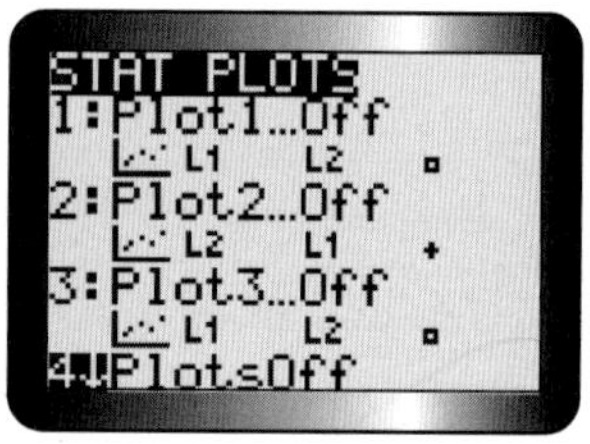

3. **Clear all equations in the equation editor.**
   Press [Y=], then press [CLEAR] for each equation.

4. **Set the window so that the axes range from –10 to 10.**
   Press [ZOOM] [6]. Press [WINDOW] to verify.

Entering and Graphing Relations

Enter the equation of the relation into the equation editor. The calculator will display the graph.

1. **Graph.**
   To graph $y = 2x + 8$, press [Y=] [2] [X,T,Θ,n] [+] [8] [GRAPH]. The graph will be displayed as shown.

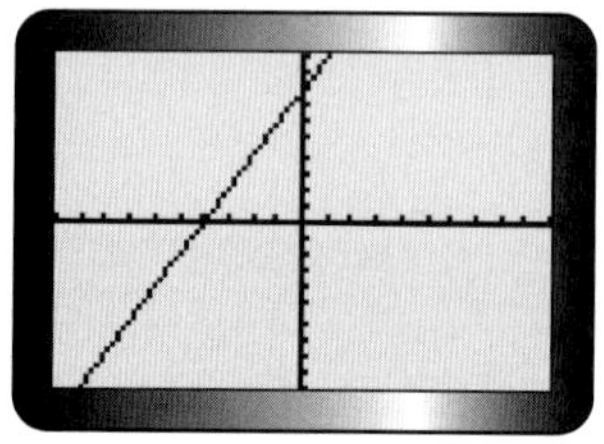

2. **Enter all linear equations in the form $y = mx + b$.**
   If m or b are fractions, enter them between brackets. For example, enter $2x + 3y = 7$ in the form $y = -\frac{2}{3}x + \frac{7}{3}$, as shown.

3. **Press [GRAPH] to view the graph.**

Tracing on the Graph

Press [TRACE] to find the coordinates of any point on a graph. Use the left and right arrow keys to cursor along the graph. Press [ZOOM] [8] [ENTER] [TRACE] to trace using integer intervals.

Viewing the Graph in Better Detail

To a closer view of a particular area of a graph, cursor over to that point, and press [ZOOM] [2] [ENTER]. To see a broader view of the graph, press [ZOOM] [3] [ENTER].

Sometimes when you enter an equation and press [GRAPH], the graph does not appear in the viewing window at all or appears, incorrectly, as a vertical or horizontal line. This happens when the viewing window is too small or too big. In this case, use **ZoomFit**. Press [ZOOM] [0]. You may still have to zoom in or out.

Using the Split Screen

To see a graph and the equation editor at the same time, press [MODE] and cursor to **Horiz.** Press [ENTER] to select this, then press [2nd] [MODE] to return to the home screen.

Enter $y = x^2$ in **Y1** of the equation editor, then press [GRAPH].

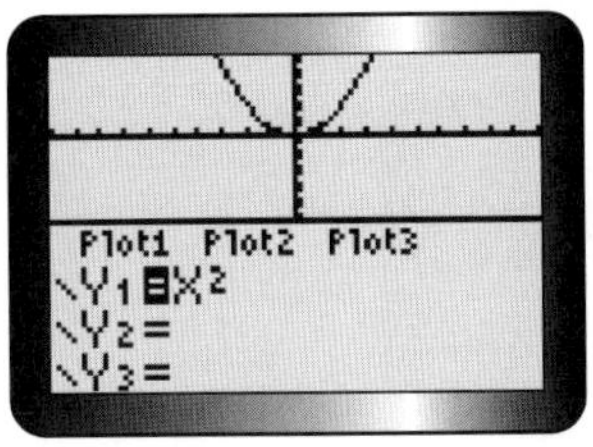

To see a graph and a table at the same time: press [MODE] and cursor to **G-T** (Graph-Table). Press [ENTER] to select this, then press [GRAPH].

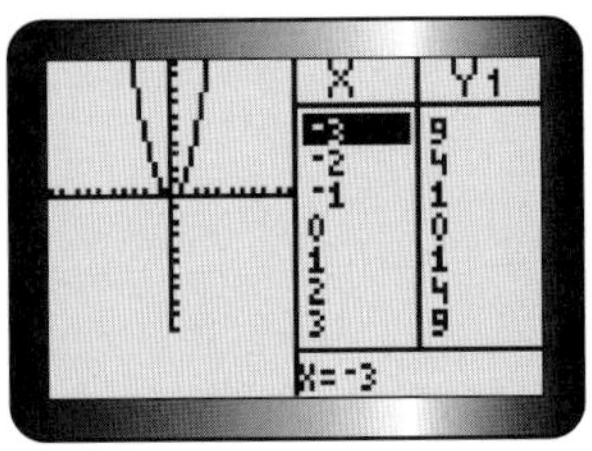

It is possible to view the table with different increments. For example, to see the table start at $x = 0$ and increase in increments of 0.5, press [2nd] [WINDOW] and adjust the settings as shown.

Press [GRAPH].

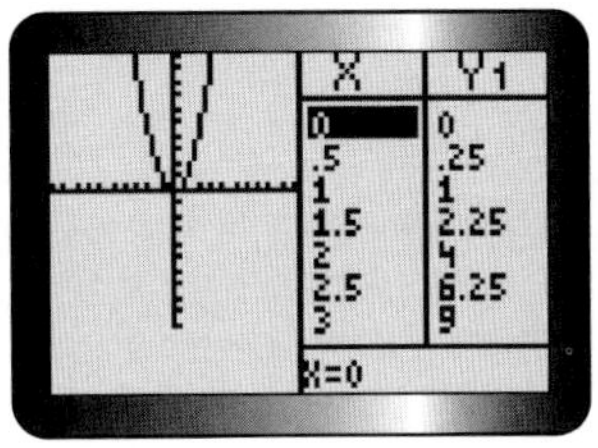

Finding the Point of Intersection

The TI-83 Plus can draw several graphs at the same time. This feature lets you graph simple linear equations and find their point of intersection. For example, find the point where $y = 5x + 4$ and $y = -2x + 18$ intersect as follows.

1. **Enter both equations into the equation editor.**
2. **Press [GRAPH].**
   The point of intersection is out of view.
3. **Use the intersect command.**
   Press [2nd] [TRACE] [5].

4. **The calculator will ask you to verify the two curves and enter a guess (optional) for the point of intersection.**
   Press [ENTER] after each screen appears.

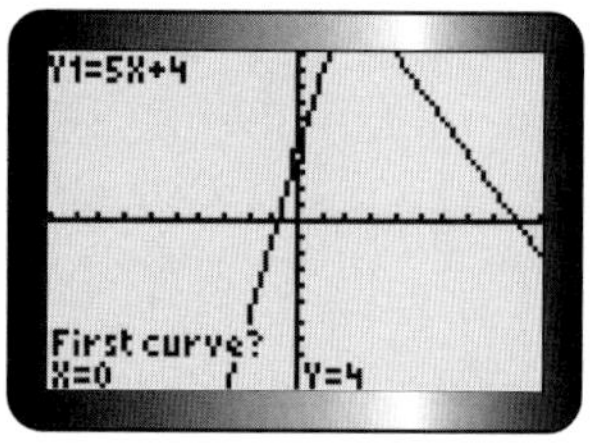

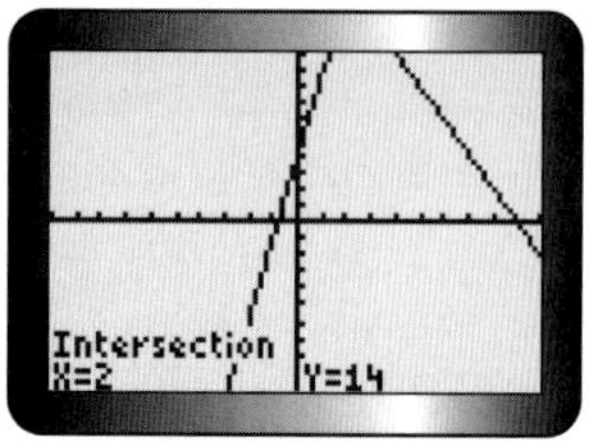

The point of intersection is exactly (2, 14).

Finding the Zeros of a Relation

To find the zeros of a relation, use the **zero** command.

1. **Start by entering $y = -(x + 3)(x - 5)$ in the equation editor, then press** [GRAPH] [ZOOM] [6].
2. **Access the zero command.**
   Press [2nd] [TRACE] [2].

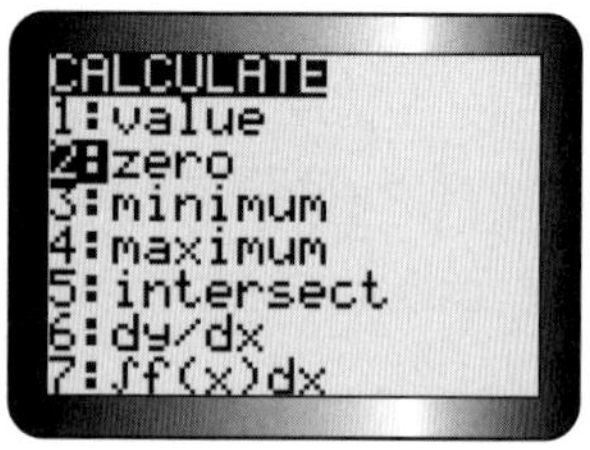

3. **Use the left and right arrow keys to cursor along the curve to any point to the left of the zero.**
   Press [ENTER] to set the left bound.

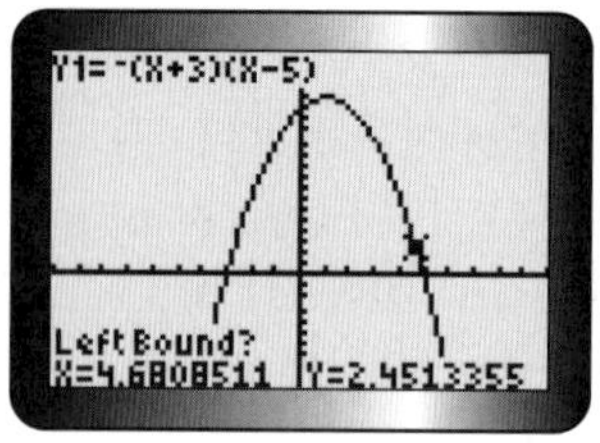

4. **Cursor along the curve to any point to the right of the zero.**
   Press [ENTER] to set the right bound.
5. **Press [ENTER] again to display the coordinates of the zero (the *x*-intercept).**

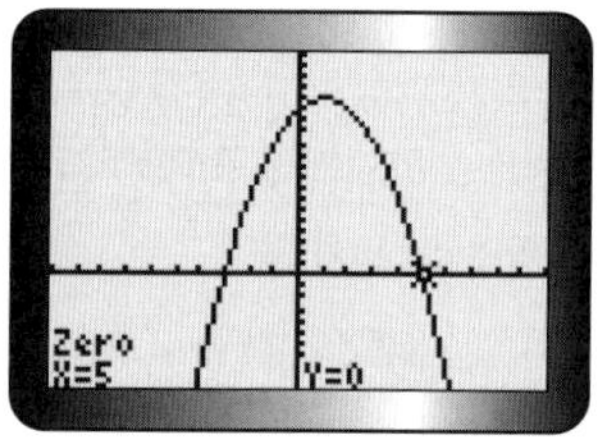

6. **Repeat to find the second zero.**

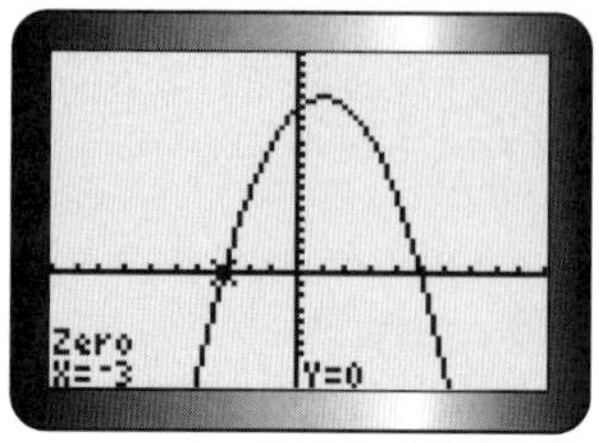

Finding the Maximum or Minimum Values of a Relation

The optimal value can be found using the **minimum** command or the **maximum** command.

1. **Enter $y = -2x^2 - 12x + 30$.**
   Graph it and adjust the window as shown. This graph opens downward, so it has a maximum.

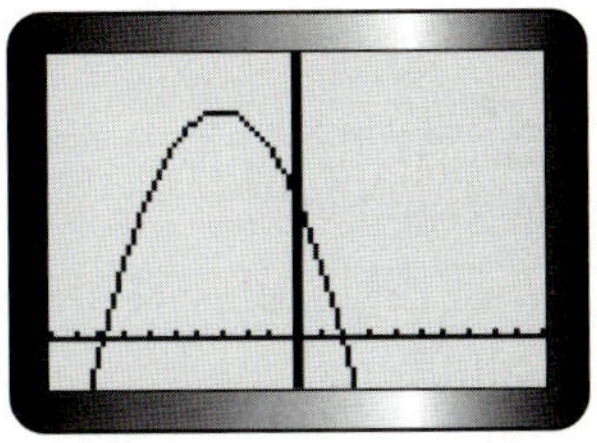

2. **Use the maximum command.**
   Press [2nd] [TRACE] [4]. For parabolas that open upward, press [2nd] [TRACE] [3] to use the **minimum** command.

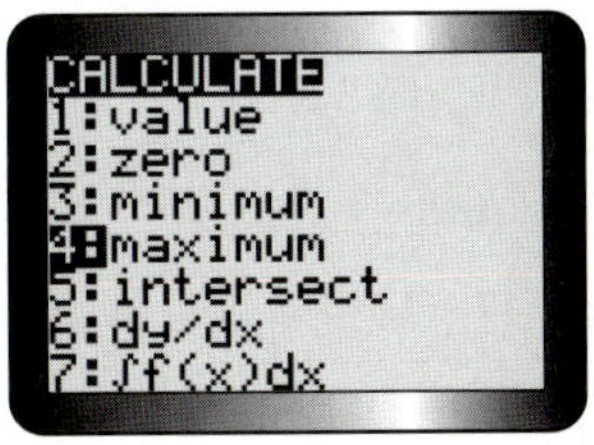

3. **Use the left and right arrow keys to cursor along the curve to any point to the left of the maximum value.**
   Press [ENTER] to set the left bound.

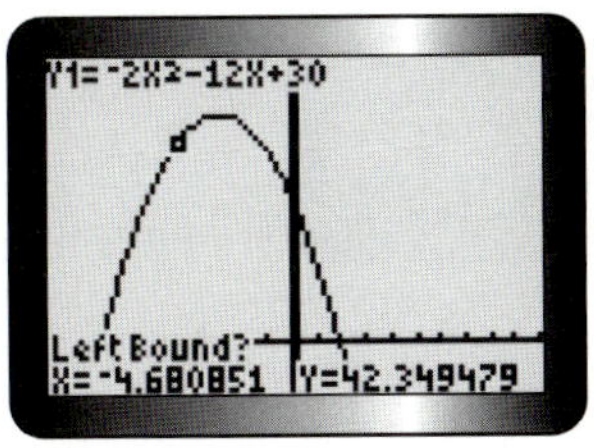

4. **Cursor along the curve to any point right of the maximum value.**
   Press [ENTER] to set the right bound.

5. **Press [ENTER] again to display the coordinates of the optimal value.**

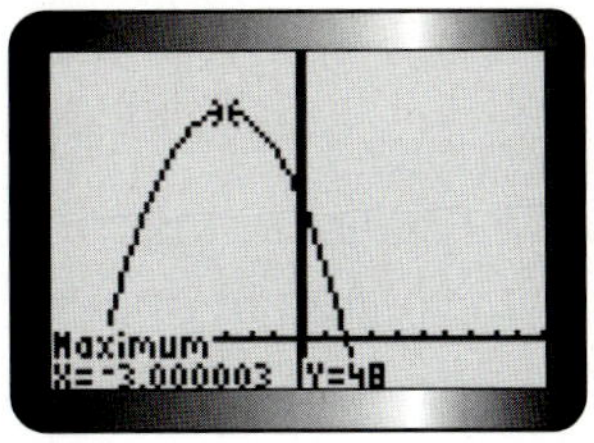

Scatter Plots and Lines and Curves of Best Fit

The coach of a soccer team wants to know if there is a relationship between the number of shots his team takes during a game and the number of goals they score. He collected this data from the last few games.

Shots	11	20	24	28	27	33	17	38
Goals	1	2	0	3	2	3	1	4

1. **Enter the data into lists.**
   Press [STAT] [ENTER]. Cursor over to the first position in **L1** and enter the values for shots. Press [ENTER] after each value. Enter the goals in **L2**.

2. **Turn on the stat plots.**
   To create a scatter plot, press [2nd] [Y=] [1] [ENTER]. Turn on Plot 1 by making sure the cursor is over **On**, the **Type** is set to the graph type you prefer, and **L1** and **L2** appear after **Xlist** and **Ylist**.

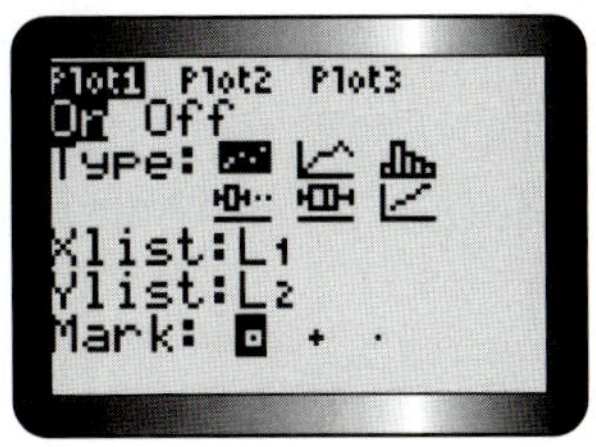

3. **Display the graph.**
   Press [ZOOM] [9] to activate **9:ZoomStat**.

Finding the Line of Best Fit Using Linear Regression

For linear data, a line of best fit can be determined.

4. Draw the linear regression line.
Superimpose a line of best fit on the scatter plot by pressing [STAT] and moving the cursor to **CALC** and pressing [4]. This activates the linear regression function.

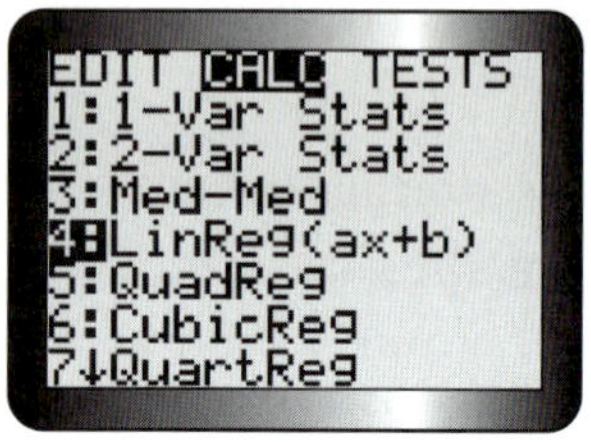

5. Enter the data to be analyzed.
Enter each list, separated by a comma. Press [2nd] [1] [,] [2nd] [2] [,] [VARS]. Scroll over to **Y-VARS** . Press [1] twice. This action stores the equation of the line of best fit into **Y1** of the equation editor.

6. Display the results of the analysis.
Press [ENTER].

7. Plot the line.
Press [GRAPH].

8. Analyze the results.
The letter a is the slope of the line and b is the y-intercept. The letter r is the correlation coefficient and is used to determine how well the model fits the data. The value r^2 is the percentage of data represented by the model.

In this case, the equation is about $y = 0.11x - 0.84$.

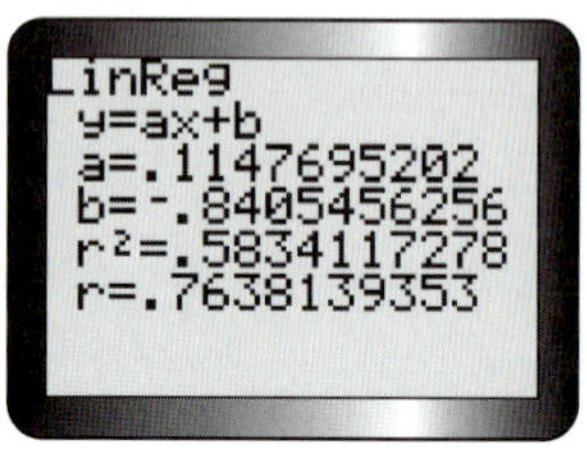

Note: If r is not displayed, turn on the diagnostics function. Press [2nd] [0] and scroll down to **DiagnosticOn**. Press [ENTER] twice. Repeat steps 4 to 6.

Finding the Curve of Best Fit Using Quadratic Regression

This table gives the height of a baseball above ground, from the time it was hit to the time it touched the ground.

Time (s)	0	1	2	3	4	5	6
Height (m)	2	27	42	48	43	29	5

Create a scatter plot of the data. (See steps 1 to 3 in the second column of the previous page.) The data is clearly nonlinear. Use a curve of best fit to model the data.

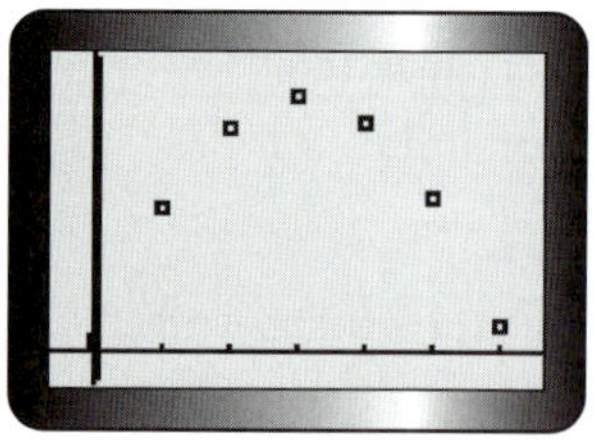

To find the equation of the curve of best fit use quadratic regression.

1. Press [STAT] and scroll over to CALC.
Press [5] to enable **QuadReg**.

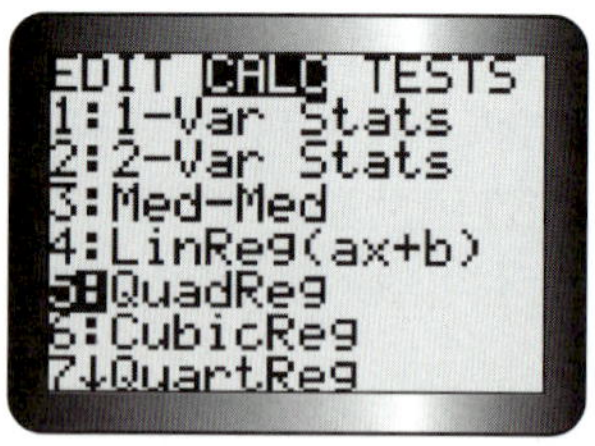

2. Enter the data to be analyzed.
Enter each list, separated by a comma. Press [2nd] [1] [,] [2nd] [2] [,] [VARS]. Scroll over to **Y-VARS**. Press [1] twice. This action stores the equation of the curve of best fit into **Y1** of the equation editor.

3. **Display the results of the analysis.**
Press [ENTER].

4. **Plot the curve.**
Press [GRAPH].

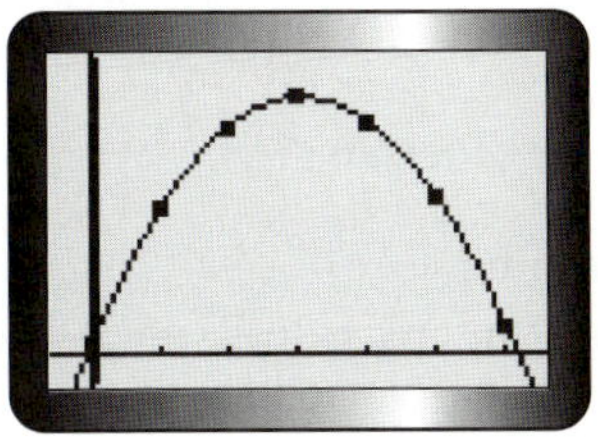

5. **Analyze the results.**
The letters *a*, *b*, and *c* are the coefficients of the general quadratic equation $y = ax^2 + bx + c$ for the curve of best fit. R^2 is the percentage of the data represented by the model. In this case, the equation is about $y = -4.90x^2 + 29.93x + 1.98$.

Using a Spreadsheet

What Is a Spreadsheet?

A spreadsheet is a computer program that can be used to create a table of values and then graph the values. It is made up of cells that are identified by column letter and row number, such as A2 or B5. A cell can hold a label, a number, or a formula.

Creating a Table

Use spreadsheets to solve problems like this: How long will it take to double your money if you invest $1000 at 5%/a compounded quarterly?

To create a spreadsheet, label cell A1 as Number of Quarters, Cell B1 as Time (years), and cell C1 as Amount ($). Enter the initial values of 0 in A2, 0 in B2, and 1000 in C2. Enter the formulas "=A2+1" in A3, "=A3/4" in B3, and "=1000*(1.0125^A3)" in C3 to generate the next values in the table.

	A	B	C
1	Number of Quarters	Time (years)	Amount ($)
2	0	0	1000
3	=A2+1	=A3/4	-1000*(1.0125^A3)
4			

Notice that an equal sign is in front of each formula, an asterisk (*) is used for multiplication, and a caret (^) is used for exponents. Next, use the cursor to select cell A3 to C3 and several rows of cells below them. Use the **Fill Down** command. This command inserts the appropriate formula into each selected cell.

	A	B	C
1	Number of Quarters	Time (years)	Amount ($)
2	0	0	1000
3	1	0.25	
4			

When the **Fill Down** command is used, the computer automatically calculates and enters the values in each cell, as shown.

	A	B	C
1	Number of Quarters	Time (years)	Amount ($)
2	0	0	1000
3	1	0.25	1012.50
4	2	0.5	1025.16
5	3	0.75	1037.97
6	4	1	1050.94

Continue to select the cells in the last row of the table and use the **Fill Down** command to generate more values until the solution appears.

	A	B	C
1	Number of Quarters	Time (years)	Amount ($)
2	0	0	1000
3	1	0.25	1012.50
4	2	0.5	1025.1563
⋮	⋮	⋮	⋮
56	54	13.5	1955.8328
57	55	13.75	1980.2807

Creating a Graph

Use the spreadsheet's graphing command to graph the results. Use the cursor to highlight the portion of the table you would like to graph. In this case, Time versus Amount.

	A	B	C
1	Number of Quarters	Time (years)	Amount ($)
2	0	0	1000
3	1	0.25	1012.50
4	2	0.5	1025.1563
⋮	⋮	⋮	⋮
56	54	13.5	1955.8328
57	55	13.75	1980.2807
58	56	14	2005.0342

Different spreadsheets have different graphing commands. Check your spreadsheet's instructions to find the proper command. This graph appears.

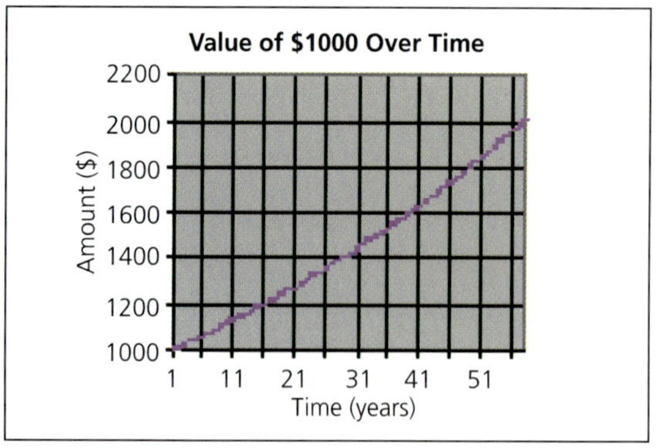

TECHNOLOGY APPENDIX

Glossary

accumulated value: see *amount.*

amplitude: the magnitude of the distance from the axis of the curve to either the maximum or minimum value of a periodic function.

amortization period: the term of a loan.

amortization table: a record of payments, interest and principal paid, and outstanding balances.

amortize: to reduce, or pay, a debt or loan through a series of regular blended payments.

amount: (annuity) the sum of all the future values of all payments at the end of the term. Also called accumulated value or future value.

angle: a geometric figure formed by one ray rotating about another at a common end point or vertex. In standard position, the initial arm of the angle lies along the positive x-axis, and the terminal arm rotates about the initial arm. When the terminal arm rotates counterclockwise, the angle is positive. When it rotates clockwise, the angle is negative. See also *coterminal angles, related acute angle.*

annuity: a series of payments, or deposits, at regular intervals. In a **simple** annuity, the payment interval coincides with the interest conversion period. In a **general** annuity, the payment interval does not coincide with the payment interval. In an annuity **due**, periodic payments are made at the *beginning* of each payment interval. In an **ordinary** annuity, periodic payments are made at the *end* of each payment interval.

The amount of a simple, ordinary annuity is

$S_n = \dfrac{a(r^n - 1)}{r - 1}$, where $a = R$, $r = 1 + i$, and n is the number of payments, or $FV = R \times \dfrac{(1 + i)^n - 1}{i}$.

arithmetic sequence: a linear sequence where the common difference, d, is constant. $t_n = a + (n - 1)d$, where a is the first term and n is the number of terms.

arithmetic series: the sum of the terms in an arithmetic sequence, $S_n = \dfrac{n}{2}[2a + (n - 1)d]$.

asymptote: a line that a function approaches but does not touch or intersect.

axis of the curve: the horizontal line that is halfway between the maximum and minimum values of a periodic curve. Also called axis of the shape.

blended payment: a payment that includes interest.

break-even points: the points at which profit equals zero, that is, where revenue equals costs.

CAST rule: **C** means quadrant IV, **A** means quadrant I, **S** means quadrant II, and **T** means quadrant III. $\cos\theta$ is positive in quadrant IV (**C**), all angles are positive in quadrant I (**A**), $\sin\theta$ is positive in quadrant II (**S**); and $\tan\theta$ is positive in quadrant III (**T**).

circle: a set of points equidistant from one other point, the centre.

common difference: the constant difference between two consecutive terms in an arithmetic sequence or series.

common ratio: the constant ratio between two consecutive terms in a geometric sequence or series. See *geometric sequence.*

completing the square: the method of changing a quadratic equation in standard form to vertex form.

complex number: any number, real or imaginary, in the form $a + bi$, where a and b are real numbers and $i^2 = -1$.

conjugate pair: the complex roots of a quadratic equation, $a + bi$ and $a = bi$, where a and b are real numbers and i is a non-real number such that $i^2 = -1$.

conversion period: the period for calculating interest.

cosine law: For acute triangle ABC, $a^2 = b^2 + c^2 - 2bc\cos A$, $b^2 = a^2 + c^2 - 2ac\cos B$, and $c^2 = a^2 + b^2 - 2ab\cos C$.

cost function, $C(x)$: the relation between the costs of making an item and the number of items, x.

coterminal angles: rotated angles having the same initial arm and the same terminal arm. The principal angle, between 0° and 360° is the smallest positive angle for all the angles in a group of coterminal angles. See *angle.*

curve of best fit: a model that best represents the relation between the variables for a set of points.

cycle: the portion of a graph is the smallest complete repeating pattern of the graph.

degree of a polynomial: the value of the highest exponent of any one variable in the polynomial. A polynomial of degree 0 is called a constant. A polynomial of degree 1 is linear. A polynomial of degree 2 is quadratic. A polynomial of degree 3 is cubic.

demand function, $p(x)$: the relation between the price of an item, p, and the number of items sold, x.

depreciation: the rate at which an asset's value decreases.

domain: the set of all possible values of the independent variable.

ellipse: the set of points such that the sum of the distances from two fixed points to any other point is constant. The longest horizontal and vertical line segments in the ellipse are the axes. The longer axis is the major axis; the other axis is the minor axis. The end points of the longer axis are the vertices. The foci lie on the major axis.

equivalent interest rates: different rates that produce the same amount at the end of the same period.

exponential equation: an equation in which at least one of the exponents is, or has, a variable.

factored form (of a quadratic function): a quadratic relation in the form $f(x) = a(x - p)(x - q)$.

Fibonacci sequence: the sequence of numbers 1, 1, 2, 3, 5, 8, 13, 21, … . Each number, after the first two numbers, is the sum of the previous two numbers.

first differences: the differences between consecutive y-coordinates.

focal points or foci: fixed points.

function: a relation in which each element of the domain corresponds to exactly one element of the range.

function notation: the function f at x is written as $f(x)$ which is read "f at x" or "f of x."

fundamental trigonometric identities: see *Pythagorean identity* and *quotient identity.*

future value: see *amount.*

general annuity: see *annuity.*

general form of a circle: $x^2 + y^2 + 2gx + 2fy + C = 0$

general form of a conic: $ax^2 + by^2 + 2gx + 2fy + C = 0$, where the centre is not at the origin. For $a = b$, the conic is a circle. For $ab > 0$, it is an ellipse. For $ab < 0$, it is a hyperbola. For $ab = 0$, it is a parabola.

general form of a parabola: $x^2 + 2gx + 2fy + C = 0$

general term: the rule or algebraic expression for generating the terms of a sequence or series.

geometric sequence: a sequence where the ratio of any term, except the first one, to the previous term is constant for all pairs of consecutive terms. The general term is $t_n = ar^{n-1}$, where a is the first term and r is the common ratio.

geometric series: the sum of the terms in a geometric sequence, $S_n = \frac{a(r^n - 1)}{r - 1}$, $r \neq 1$.

half-life: the time required for a radioactive material to decay to one-half its original mass.

hyperbola: a set of points whose distances from two fixed points have a constant difference. The points at which the hyperbola intersects the longest line of symmetry are the vertices. This line segment is the transverse axis. The other perpendicular line of symmetry is the conjugate axis. The two fixed points along the transverse axis are the foci. The point at which the axes intersect is the centre of the hyperbola. In a rectangular hyperbola, the asymptotes are perpendicular. See *standard form of a hyperbola.*

identity: a statement of equality that is true for all values of the variables. See *trigonometric identity.*

imaginary number: the number i, where $i^2 = -1$.

inequality: a statement that one quantity is less than, or greater than, another quantity.

initial arm: see *angle.*

interest: the cost of using money. The formula for **simple** interest is $I = Prt$, where I is the simple interest, P is the principal (the amount of money borrowed or invested), r is the annual interest rate, and t is the time in years. The formula for **compound** interest is $A = P(1 + i)^n$, where A is the amount, or the future value, of an investment, or loan, P is the original principal invested or borrowed, i is the interest rate per conversion period, and n is the number of conversion periods.

inverse: the inverse of a relation and a function maps each output of the original relation back onto the corresponding input value. The inverse, f^{-1}, is the reverse of the original relation or function, f.

inverse variation: in this relation, the value of one variable increases while the value of the other variable decreases. The products of corresponding x- and y-values are constant.

linear trigonometric equation: an equation with a trigonometric function, whose highest power is 1.

loan: the lending of property by a lender to a borrower who returns the property to the lender after a specific period for a fee, that is, interest.

locus: a set of points that satisfy a given condition(s).

mortgage: a type of loan by which the borrower, or the mortgagor, gives the lender, or the mortgagee, a lien on property as security for repayment of a loan. The term or interest rate may be renegotiated or changed during the life of the mortgage. In an open mortgage, the interest rate changes as prime lending rate changes.

nominal interest rate: the annual interest rate.

oblique triangle: a triangle with no right angle.

ordinary annuity: see *annuity.*

parabola: a set of points that are equidistant from a fixed point, the focus, and a fixed line, the directrix. See *standard form* and *general form of a parabola.*

payment interval: the time period of successive payments.

period (of a cycle): the length of one cycle.

periodic payment: see *annuity.*

perpetuity: an annuity that pays out a specified amount beginning on a specific date and continuing forever.

phase shift: horizontal translation.

polynomial: an algebraic expression in the form $a_0 + a_1x + a_2x^2 + a_3x^3 + \ldots + a_nx^n$, where a_0, a_1, a_2, a_3, …, a_n are real numbers and the exponents are non-negative integers. A polynomial with one term is a monomial, a polynomial with two terms is a binomial, and a polynomial with three terms is a trinomial.

positive angle: see *angle.*

present value: the amount that is invested now to yield a larger amount in the future. Also called discounted value. The present value of a simple, ordinary annuity is $S_n = \frac{a(r^n - 1)}{r - 1}$, where $a = R(1 + i)^{-n}$, $r = 1 + i$, and n is the number of payments, or $PV = R \times \frac{1 - (1 + i)^{-n}}{i}$.

principal: the amount borrowed by loan or the amount invested.

principal angle: see *coterminal angles.*

profit function, $P(x)$: the relation between profit and the number of items sold, x. $P(x) = R(x) - C(x)$

Pythagorean identity: $\sin^2 \theta + \cos^2 \theta = 1$ or $\sin^2 \theta = 1 - \cos^2 \theta$ or $\cos^2 \theta = 1 - \sin^2 \theta$

quadratic trigonometric equation: the equation for a trigonometric function, and the highest power is 2.

quadrant: see *x-y plane.*

radian measure: the real number measure of an angle. Use $\frac{\text{radians}}{\pi} = \frac{\text{degrees}}{180°}$ to convert between radian and degree measures.

radical: the indicated root of a quantity, for example, $\sqrt[4]{x}$.

range: the set of all possible values of the dependent variable.

rational exponent: an exponent that can be expressed in the form $\frac{a}{b}$, where $b \neq 0$.

real numbers: the set of real numbers has rational, irrational, integers, whole, and natural numbers.

reciprocal function: The reciprocal function of $f(x)$ is $[f(x)]^{-1}$ or $\frac{1}{f(x)}$.

recursive sequence: a sequence of numbers in which each number is defined according to the previous term(s).

recursive formula: a formula that defines each new term in a sequence according to the previous term or terms.

registered income fund: a type of annuity.

related acute angle: a positive angle between 0° and 90° that corresponds to an angle whose measure is more than 90°. For example, the acute angle related to 135° is 45° and the acute angle related to −45° is 45°.

restriction: a statement that tells which values make a relation or function untrue.

revenue function, $R(x)$: the relation between the price of an item and the number of items sold, x. $R(x) = x\,p(x)$

sequence: a function whose domain is a subset of the set of natural numbers. The values of the range of the function are called the terms of the sequence. A sequence can be finite or infinite. The general term, t_n, of a sequence is an algebraic expression that may be used to generate terms of the sequence. See *arithmetic sequence.*

series: the sum of the terms of a sequence.

simple annuity: see *annuity.*

standard form of a circle: $(x - h)^2 + (y - k)^2 = r^2$ with centre (h, k)

standard form of an ellipse: where the centre is at the origin, $\frac{x^2}{a^2} + \frac{y^2}{a^2} = 1$, $a > b$ and the major axis is along the x axis, or $\frac{x^2}{b^2} + \frac{y^2}{a^2} = 1$, $a > b$ and the major axis is along the y-axis. Where the centre is not at the origin, $\frac{(x - h)^2}{a^2} + \frac{(y - k)^2}{b^2} = 1$, $a > b$ and the major axis is horizontal, or $\frac{(x - h)^2}{b^2} + \frac{(y - k)^2}{a^2} = 1$, and $a > b$ and the major axis is vertical.

standard form of a hyperbola: Where the centre is at the origin and where the foci, intercepts, and transverse axis are on the x-axis, $\frac{x^2}{a^2} - \frac{y^2}{b^2} = 1$. The asymptotes are $y = \pm\frac{b}{a}x$. Where the centre is at the origin and where the foci, intercepts, and transverse axis are on the y-axis, $\frac{x^2}{b^2} - \frac{y^2}{a^2} = -1$ or $\frac{y^2}{a^2} - \frac{x^2}{b^2} = 1$. The asymptotes are $y = \pm\frac{a}{b}x$. Where the centre is not at the origin, $\frac{(x - h)^2}{a^2} - \frac{(y - k)^2}{b^2} = 1$, for a horizontal transverse axis, or $\frac{(x - h)^2}{b^2} - \frac{(y - k)^2}{a^2} = -1$, for a vertical transverse axis.

standard form of a parabola: $(x - h)^2 = 4p(y - k)$ or $(y - k)^2 = 4p(x - h)$.

standard form of a quadratic relation: $f(x) = ax^2 + bx + c$

tangent: a line that touches a circle at exactly one point.

term: see *sequence* or *amortization period.*

time line: a line divided into equal sections and each section is a conversion period.

trigonometric identity: an equation with trigonometric expression(s) that is true for all values of the variable. See *quotient identity* and *Pythagorean identity.*

vertex form (of a quadratic function): a quadratic relation in the form $f(x) = a(x - h)^2 + k$.

vertical line test: a test to determine whether the graph of a relation is a function or not. The relation is not a function if any vertical line drawn through the graph of the function passes through two or more points.

zeros of a relation: the x-intercepts of the graph of the relation.

Index

Technology Index

MATHEMATICS 11 PHOTO CREDITS

Cover Richard Cummins/CORBIS/Magna

Chapter 1 Page 11 Bruce Heinemann/PhotoDisc; Page 12 top: © Eric and David Hosking/CORBIS/Magma, bottom: Corel; Page 13 © Richard Hamilton Smith/CORBIS/Magma; Page 16 Siede Preis/PhotoDisc; Page 25 © Eric and David Hosking/CORBIS/Magma; Page 27 CP Picture Archive CNW; Page 32 Akira Kaede/PhotoDisc; Page 35 © Eric and David Hosking/CORBIS/Magma; Page 39 Michael Lamotte/Cole Group/PhotoDisc; Page 41 Javier Pierini/PhotoDisc; Page 42 www.comstock.ca; Page 50 © Eric and David Hosking/CORBIS/Magma; Page 51 © Roger Ressmeyer/CORBIS/Magma; Page 52 Norm Betts/CP Picture Archive; Page 59 © Jonathan Blair/CORBIS/Magma; Page 60 © Eric and David Hosking/CORBIS/Magma; Page 61 Ryan McVay/PhotoDisc; Page 73 PhotoDisc; Page 81 CORBIS/Magma; Page 82 © Eric and David Hosking/CORBIS/Magma; Page 88 Keith Brofsky/PhotoDisc; Page 95 Jim Linna/PhotoDisc; Page 96 © Eric and David Hosking/CORBIS/Magma

Chapter 2 Page 105 Superstock; Page 106 CORBIS/Magma; Page 110 © Layne Kennedy/CORBIS/Magma; Page 115 Brian Thompson/CP Picture Archive; Page 116 © Layne Kennedy/CORBIS/Magma; Page 116 © Bettman/CORBIS/Magma; Page 117 Dave Starrett; Page 119 CORBIS/Magma; Page 126 © Layne Kennedy/CORBIS/Magma; Page 129 © Robert Estall/CORBIS/Magma; Page 140 Siede Preis/PhotoDisc; Page 142 © Layne Kennedy/CORBIS/Magma; Page 145 © Robert Estall/CORBIS/Magma; Page 153 Corel; Page 155 © Layne Kennedy/CORBIS/Magma; Page 164 Viktor Pivovarov/CP Picture Archive; Page 167 © Layne Kennedy/CORBIS/Magma; Page 179 © Joseph Sohm/CORBIS/Magma; Page 182 © Layne Kennedy/CORBIS/Magma; Page 187 © Michael Freeman/CORBIS/Magma; Page 193 Rob Melnychuk/PhotoDisc; Page 195 © Layne Kennedy/CORBIS/Magma

Chapter 3 Page 217 Arthur S. Aubry/PhotoDisc; Page 218 top: © Archive Photos, bottom: Courtesy of Professor Alfred J. Menezes; Page 219 Anne Bradley/Nelson Thomson Learning; Page 225 © CORBIS/Magma; Page 237 Andrew Kolesnikow; Elizabeth Whiting & Associates/CORBIS/Magma; Page 240 © Archive Photos; Page 247 Jonathan Hayward/CP Picture Archive; Page 259 Joe Gibbons/CP Picture Archive; Page 260 © Archive Photos; Page 276 Eric Gay/CP Picture Archive; Page 277 © Archive Photos; Page 291 © Archive Photos

Chapter 4 Page 299 David Buffington/PhotoDisc; Page 300 Hans Deryk/CP Picture Archive; Page 308 © Alan Oddie/Photo Edit; Page 315 © Richard Hamilton Smith/CORBIS/Magma; Page 317 Hans Deryk/CP Picture Archive; Page 318 CORBIS/Magma; Page 326 Corel; Page 327 Hans Deryk/CP Picture Archive; Page 328 © Gianni Dagli/CORBIS/Magma; Page 33 top: © Robert Holmes/CORBIS/Magma, bottom: Hans Deryk/CP Picture Archive; Page 338 S.Meltzer/Photolink/PhotoDisc; Page 355 top: Buccina Studios/PhotoDisc, bottom: Hans Deryk/CP Picture Archive; Page 360 Corel; Page 364 Andrew Vaughan/CP Picture Archive; page 371 top: Doug Menuez/PhotoDisc, bottom Hans Deryk/CP Picture Archive

Chapter 5 Page 403 both: Barrett and MacKay Photography; Page 404 Superstock; Page 405 © Kelly-Mooney Photography/CORBIS/Magma; Page 408 © Roger Ressmeyer/CORBIS/Magma; Page 414 © Kevin Fleming/CORBIS/Magma; Page 417 Superstock; Page 424 © Island Images/CORBIS/Magma; Page 437 Superstock; Page 444 top Dave Starrett, bottom: Superstock; Page 447© Bettman/CORBIS/Magma; Page 459 Superstock; Page 467 Superstock; Page 478 Superstock; Page 482 Dave Starrett; Page 483 Dave Starrett

Chapter 6 Page 493 Corel; Page 494 Janis Christie/PhotoDisc; Page 499 CORBIS/Magma; Page 514 top: CORBIS/Magma, bottom: Janis Christie/PhotoDisc; Page 515 © Patrick Ward/CORBIS/Magma; Page 523 Photolink/PhotoDisc; Page 525 Janis Christie/PhotoDisc; Page 547 Janis Christie/PhotoDisc

Chapter 7 Page 566 Dick Hemingway; Page 567 © Danny Lehman/CORBIS/Magma; Page 574 Jules Frazier/PhotoDisc; Page 567 © Dave G. Houser/CORBIS/Magma; Page 583 top: Nancy R. Cohen/PhotoDisc, bottom: Dick Hemingway; Page 585 both © Bettman/CORBIS/Magma; page 593 © CORBIS/Magma; Page 594 Dick Hemingway; Page 604 top: CORBIS/Magma, bottom: Dick Hemingway; Page 606 © John Heseltine/CORBIS/Magma; Page 609 Corel; Page 617 © Bob Krist/CORBIS/Magma; Page 618 © Ric Ergenbright/CORBIS/Magma; Page 623 Dan Callis/CP Picture Archive; Page 627 Corel